Alan Simpson's
Windows Vista™ Bible

Alan Simpson's Windows Vista™ Bible

Alan Simpson
Todd Meister

BICENTENNIAL

1807
WILEY
2007

BICENTENNIAL

Wiley Publishing, Inc.

Alan Simpson's Windows Vista™ Bible

Published by
Wiley Publishing, Inc.
10475 Crosspoint Boulevard
Indianapolis, IN 46256
www.wiley.com

Copyright © 2007 by Wiley Publishing, Inc., Indianapolis, Indiana

Published simultaneously in Canada

ISBN: 978-0-470-04030-0

Manufactured in the United States of America

10 9 8 7 6 5 4 3 2 1

1B/RS/QR/QX/IN

About the Author

Alan Simpson is an award-winning computer book author with some 120 published books to his credit. His books are published in many languages throughout the world and have sold millions of copies. Alan is best known for his light, conversational writing style and clear jargon-free approach to dealing with technical topics. Prior to writing books full time, Alan taught introductory and advanced computer programming courses at San Diego State University and University of California, San Diego Extension. He also worked as a freelance programmer and computer consultant. He maintains the www.coolnerds.com Web site (when time permits) and can be reached via that Web site.

To Susan, Ashley, and Alec, as always.

Credits

Acquisitions Editor
Katie Mohr

Development Editor
Kelly Dobbs Henthorne

Technical Editors
Dan DiNicolo
Todd Meister

Production Editor
Angela Smith

Copy Editor
Kim Cofer

Editorial Manager
Mary Beth Wakefield

Production Manager
Tim Tate

**Vice President and Executive
Group Publisher**
Richard Swadley

Vice President and Executive Publisher
Joseph B. Wikert

Project Coordinator
Kristie Rees

Graphics and Production Specialists
Carrie Foster
Jennifer Mayberry
Alicia B. South
Ronald Terry

Quality Control Technicians
John Greenough
Brian H. Walls

Book Designer
Elizabeth Brooks

Proofreading
Laura L. Bowman

Indexing
Techbooks

Anniversary Logo Design
Richard Pacifico

Contents at a Glance

Contents

Contents

Contents

Contents

Contents

Contents

Contents

Contents

Contents

Part VI: Managing Files and Folders   **653**

Contents

Part VII: Printing, Faxing, and Scanning   827

Chapter 35: Installing and Managing Printers 829

Chapter 36: Printing Documents and Screenshots 837

Chapter 37: Managing Print Jobs 845

Contents

Contents

Acknowledgments

Writing a book is no small feat, and it takes a lot more people than you'd think. So I'd like to express my sincerest thanks to everyone who helped get this book from the idea stage to the finished product you now hold in your hands. Many thanks to Todd Meister, who acted both as technical editor and contributor, writing several of the chapters you'll read in this book.

At Wiley I'd like to thank Katie Mohr, acquisitions editor; Mary Beth Wakefield, managing editor; Kelly D. Henthorne, developmental editor; and Angela Smith, production editor.

Many thanks to Carole McClendon, Maureen Maloney, and everybody else at Waterside Productions (my literary agency) for making everything work out.

Many thanks to my students for reminding me that not everyone is a computer geek and that someone has to explain things in ways that make sense to non-nerds.

And, of course, all my love and thanks to Susan, Ashley, and Alec for tolerating months of neglect while Dad pounded furiously away at the keyboard through day and night.

Introduction

Welcome to *Alan Simpson's Windows Vista Bible*, a really big book about a really big operating system. Microsoft Windows has been around for nearly a couple of decades now. During that time, we've seen many versions. Sometimes the change from one version to another was minor. At other times, the change was more drastic.

Windows Vista is definitely one of the more drastic changes. Not so much on the outside. Virtually anything you already know about Windows still applies. The basic terminology is the same. The basic skills are the same. Most of the really big changes are in areas you don't see.

Windows Vista was designed and built with security as a key component from the ground up. It's a very forward-looking operating system, designed to take advantage of today's powerful hardware, and the ever more powerful hardware coming to us at the fastest pace ever.

Being secure and being future-oriented are definitely good things. The only downside is that the transition to Vista is likely to be a bit more painful than the transitions we've gone through in the past. Some old hardware may not work until you get Vista drivers. Some old programs won't work unless you upgrade to a version specifically designed for Vista. Not fun.

But every now and then you just need to give the current trend a kick in the pants to move things in a better direction. And Vista certainly does that. In the not-too-distant future, when computing is better, cheaper, faster, safer, and easier for everyone, I think people will look back on Windows Vista as a key turning point in making things play out that way. Simply stated, it's just a better way to do things.

But enough about Windows Vista. Hundreds of pages follow on that topic. The real purpose of an "Introduction" is to introduce the book starting with. . .

Who This Book Is For

As an educator, I get plenty of reminders that not everyone is a computer expert. In fact, in the overall scheme of things, hardly anyone is a computer expert. If you think of every person you know and rate their computer knowledge on a scale of 1 to 10, I'll bet the vast majority will rate somewhere between 0 and 2.

Furthermore, not everyone wants to be a computer expert. Most people just want to use a computer to get things done, or even just to have some fun. This should come as no surprise. After all, not everyone who drives a car wants to be a professional mechanic. Not everyone who uses a cell phone wants to be an electrical engineer. So why should everyone who uses a computer want, or need, to be a computer geek? They shouldn't. Some people need to just be computer *users*, people who use the computer without being total nerds about it.

This book is for the computer *users*. The people who just want to use their computers to have some fun and get some things done. It might seem like an awfully big book for such an audience. The only reason it's such a big book is because there are *so many* things you can do with Windows Vista. But nobody ever said you have to do them all. And you certainly don't have to read the whole darn book to have some fun and get things done with your computer.

Besides, nobody really wants to *read* about computers or *learn* about computers. Too boring. Most of us prefer to learn by discovery, by exploring and trying things out. It's a lot more fun that way. However, just a couple of problems are evident with that approach. For one, you can get yourself into a bind from time to time. For another, when you get to a place where you don't know what's going on, sometimes you need to fill in some gaps before you can move on and continue learning by discovery.

A book can help with that by covering all the stuff everyone else assumes you already know. Especially if that book is divided up into sections and chapters that deal with one topic at a time, so you can focus on just the thing you need to know, when you need to know it. Which brings us to. . .

How to Use This Book

A book that supports learning by discovery needs to have some elements of a tutorial and some elements of a reference book. I guess you could say it has to be a reference book divided into multiple mini-tutorials, so you can learn what you need to know about one topic, when you need to know it. To that extent, this book is divided into 10 major parts, each of which covers a large topic.

Each part, in turn, is divided into multiple chapters, each chapter covering a smaller topic. Chapters are divided into sections and subsections, all designed to help you find the information you need, when you need it. The Table of Contents up front covers all the specifics. The index at the back of the book helps you find things based on a keyword or topic. The only thing missing is a high-level view of just the parts. So that's what I'll provide here.

Part I: Getting Started, Getting Secure: How you get started with Windows Vista depends on where you're coming from. Part I tries to cover all fronts. If you're an experienced Windows user, then you probably want to know what's new. Chapter 1 covers that turf. If you're relatively new to PCs, you'll likely be interested in learning the most important basic skills for using a computer. Chapter 2 covers that ground. Chapters 3–6 cover important getting started topics for everyone. Chapter 6 provides solutions to common problems with getting started.

Part II: Batten Down the Security Hatches: There is no such thing as a 100-percent secure computer. Even with all of its advanced built-in security, there are certain things that you, the user, need to contribute to make sure that your computer is safe and stays up-to-date with ever-changing security threats. The chapters in Part II cover that ground.

Part III: Personalizing Windows Vista: We all like to tweak things to suit our personal needs, taste, and style. That's what Part III is all about. But it's not just about changing the look and feel of things. It's about really making the computer a useful tool for whatever your work (or play) requires.

Part IV: Power Using the Internet: Just about everyone who uses a computer also uses the Internet. And Windows Vista has many tools to make that possible. Chapter 17 covers Microsoft Internet Explorer, the program for using Web sites like eBay, Google, and millions of others. Chapter 18 covers Windows Mail, a great new program for e-mail and newsgroups. Other chapters get into lesser-known, but still useful, aspects of the Internet and techniques for troubleshooting common Internet problems.

Part V: Pictures, Music, and Movies: The Internet isn't the only place to have fun with a computer. You can have a lot of fun offline with pictures, music, and movies. The chapters in Part V tell you how.

Part VI: Managing Files and Folders: Boring as it is, we all have to make some effort to get our stuff organized and keep it organized. Otherwise, we spend more time looking for stuff than actually doing things. Part VI covers all the necessary housekeeping kinds of chores to help you spend less time looking for things and more time doing things.

Part VII: Printing, Faxing, and Scanning: Sometimes, you just have to get a thing off the screen and onto paper. That's what printing is all about. Sometimes, you need to get a thing off of paper and into the computer. That's what scanning is about. And sometimes you have to use a fax machine rather than e-mail to get a printed page to someone. Such are the topics of VII.

Part VIII: Installing and Removing Programs: Hot topics here include downloading programs, installing programs from CDs and floppies, getting older programs to run, controlling access to programs, getting rid of unwanted programs, and dealing with problem programs and processes. After all, what good is a computer without some programs to run on it?

Part IX: Hardware and Performance Tuning: Hardware is the computer buzzword for physical gadgets you can hold in your hand. As the years roll by hardware just keeps getting smaller, better, faster, cheaper, and, well, cooler. This part covers everything you need to know about adding and removing hardware and troubleshooting hardware problems.

Part X: Networking and Sharing: Whether you have two PCs or 20, eventually you'll want to link them all together into a single private network so they can share a single Internet account and printer, or perhaps several printers. And if you've been wasting time transferring files via floppies, CDs, or some other removable disk, you'll want to replace all that with simple drag-and-drop operations on your screen. Part X tells you how to make all of that happen.

That's a lot of topics and a lot to think about. But there's no hurry. If you're new to Windows, or your experience is limited to things like e-mail and the Web, Chapter 2 is probably your best first stop. Those of you with more extensive Windows experience might want to hop over to Chapter 1 for a quick look at things that are new in Windows Vista.

Part I

Getting Started, Getting Secure

Windows users range in experience from people who are just getting started with their first PC, to folks with years of Windows experience under their belts. Part I attempts to address both audiences by tackling topics that everyone needs to know in order to get started.

Chapter 1 highlights the new features of Vista and is geared toward folks with many years of experience. The idea there is to point out the main Vista features that make it different from earlier Windows versions.

Of course, if you have little or no Windows experience, you don't really care about what's new versus what's not. All you care about is learning how to work the darn thing. If you're in that category, you can skip Chapter 1 and go straight to Chapter 2.

Chapter 3 then covers user accounts and the new User Account Control (UAC) features of Windows Vista. Chapter 4 moves on to Parental Controls, something that many parents have wanted in their computers for a long time. Beginners and experienced users alike will find much that's new and useful in those chapters.

In today's enormous and ever-changing high-tech landscape, no one resource of information is ever enough. You need to learn to be resourceful and use all of the resources available to you. Chapter 5 takes you through that journey. Chapter 6 tackles some common problems you might encounter in getting things to work throughout the first five chapters.

Chapter 1

What's New in Windows Vista

Welcome to Vista! This chapter is for people who have experience with Windows XP or other versions of Windows and just want to know what's new. If you're new to PCs, this chapter won't help much because everything will be new to you. So feel free to skip this chapter and head over to Chapter 2 if you're not a long-time Windows user.

For the folks who do stick around here, the first thing you need to understand is that Windows Vista is more than just a new "version" of Windows. It's not just Windows XP with eye candy. It's a whole new operating system, inside and out.

But that doesn't mean you have to throw away all your existing hard-earned knowledge. In fact, you don't have to throw away any of that, because the old familiar ways of doing things still apply. You just have to be ready to expand your horizons to bigger and better things.

If you're like most people (myself included), your first inclination might be to get out of Vista as quickly as possible and return to a more familiar environment, like Windows XP. But if you do that, you'll be missing out on many new features and improvements. If you invest a little time in learning what's new and different, you'll find that you really *can* get things done more quickly and easily in Vista. This chapter provides a quick overview of what's new, so you can decide for yourself which features are most relevant to how you use your computer.

W FEATURE The new Aero Glass interface provides a more intuitive interface that better reflects how things are stacked up on your desktop.

A New Look and Feel

The most obvious (though certainly not the most important) new feature is the Aero Glass interface. Windows users have been using a 3D interface for years. You can open as many programs as you want, and they stack up like sheets of paper on a desktop. It just wasn't very obvious that you were using a 3D interface with items stacked up on your desktop.

Aero Glass changes that by making the borders around program windows semitransparent, so you can see when there's something behind whatever you're looking at. Aero also adds a little drop-shadow around the window border to make it look more raised. Figure 1.1 shows a small example. But it's much more noticeable on the actual screen.

FIGURE 1.1

Sample Aero Glass windows.

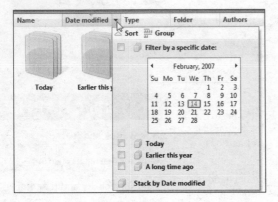

Flip 3D

Along with the 3D appearance of Aero Glass comes a new way to take a quick look at all your open program windows. The old ways of doing things still work. For example, you can click the Show Desktop button in the Quick Launch toolbar to minimize all open program windows. You can still use the Alt+Tab shortcut key to switch between open programs. For the new alternative method, press ⊞+Tab or click the Switch Between Windows button in the Quick Launch toolbar. Either way, all your open windows arrange themselves as in Figure 1.2.

When displayed in 3D, you can cycle through the open windows by spinning your mouse wheel or by pressing the ↑ and ↓ keys. Click any visible portion of a window to bring it to the top of the stack.

 If your prior experience with Windows doesn't include a concept or term from this chapter, you can fill in the gap by reading Chapter 2.

Of course, you can still use the taskbar to bring any open program window to the top of the stack. Vista's taskbar is better than the old ones. As you point to each button, you see a thumbnail of the program window it represents (see Figure 1.3). That makes it really easy to find exactly the program for which you're looking. Pressing Alt+Tab displays thumbnails, which is a lot better than seeing only icons! And that works even if you don't have Aero Glass.

FIGURE 1.2

Flip 3D in action.

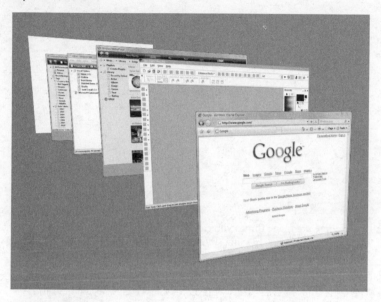

FIGURE 1.3

Point to a taskbar button for thumbnail.

Why don't I have Aero Glass?

Aero Glass isn't available on all computers because it requires some heavy-duty graphics processing. More specifically, you need a graphics card that supports the Windows Display Driver Modem (WDDM). If your computer doesn't have the necessary graphics hardware, you won't get the semitransparent look, the drop-shadows, or the Flip 3D option. But other than that, the rest will look and act roughly the same. For example, the window in Figure 1.4 is displayed with Aero Glass turned off.

FIGURE 1.4

Program window without Aero Glass.

What if I don't like Aero Glass?

If you have Aero Glass but don't like it, there are many things you can do to change its appearance. If you have Aero Glass, you can turn it on or off by pressing Ctrl+Shift+F9. Or, if you just want to tweak colors and transparency in Aero Glass, click the Window Color and Appearance in the Personalize window.

If you want an even more classic view of things, click Theme in the Personalize window. Then choose Windows Classic and click OK. (The Ctrl+Shift+F9 trick won't work in the Classic view. You'll have to choose the Windows Vista theme in the Theme dialog box and click OK before pressing Shift+Ctrl+F9 will work again.)

NOTE   For more information on personalizing Windows Vista, see Part III.

NEW FEATURE   Sidebar sets aside a portion of your desktop for live Internet data and other tools you might use often.

Windows Sidebar

Windows Sidebar lets you place *gadgets* on your desktop. Many gadgets hook into Internet services to keep you informed in real time. For example, there are gadgets for watching the weather, watching stock prices, and keeping up with headlines from your subscribed RSS feeds. Figure 1.5 shows the sidebar at the right side of the screen with a clock up top. The window in the middle is the Gadget Gallery from which you can choose the gadgets you want to use. You might have different gadgets. Not to worry. There are plenty of gadgets online that you can download for free.

If the sidebar gets in your way, you can put it into hiding until you need it. Or, you can turn it off completely and forget it even exists — whatever works for you. See Chapter 11 for the full lowdown on Windows Sidebar.

NEW FEATURE   Vista's Windows Explorer provides many new ways of viewing and navigating through folders.

FIGURE 1.5

Windows Sidebar and Gadget Gallery.

Quicker, Easier Navigation

Hard disk space is cheap these days, so everyone has a ton of it. Many people have thousands of files stored in all the space, organized into many folders and subfolders. Navigating up and down through folders all the time gets old. Vista has quite a few new tricks up its sleeve to help with that.

Probably the most important trick is the breadcrumb trail (also called an eyebrow menu) in the Address bar at the top of every folder. Some of you may recognize the concept from Web sites that offer similar navigation. In Vista's eyebrow menu, you can click the name of any folder you see in the trail to go to that folder. But there's much more to it than that. You can also click the arrow that appears next to any item in the trail to see other items at that same level in the folder hierarchy, like in Figure 1.6.

The eyebrow menu is worth its weight in gold. But it's not the only improvement. There's an optional navigation pane at the left side of every folder that contains quick links to common places. The links you see under Favorite Links are just examples. You can put links to any folders you like in there, and remove them just as easily. So you can constantly customize to reflect the folder you're using most.

The trusty Folders list is still available, too. You might not see it at first. To bring it up, just click the arrow next to Folders at the bottom of the navigation pane.

FIGURE 1.6

Breadcrumb trail and navigation pane.

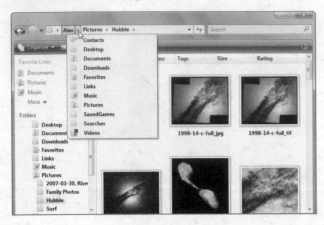

Sizing icons

You're not limited to discrete views of icons anymore either. In any folder, clicking the arrow next to Views in the toolbar takes you to a slider where you can choose a view and also adjust the size of icons. If your mouse has a wheel, hold down the Ctrl key while spinning the mouse wheel to adjust the icon size to your liking.

Vista gives you more control over the size of desktop icons too. Right-click an empty portion of the desktop and choose View, then an icon size. Or, if your mouse has a wheel, click an empty portion of the desktop. Then hold down the Ctrl key as you spin your mouse wheel.

Sorting, grouping, and stacking

Across the top of every folder you'll see column headings. You can sort, group, search, filter, or stack items by any column heading. Just point to any column heading and click the arrow like the example in Figure 1.7.

If you want to sort, group, filter, or stack icons by something that's not in the column headings, no problem. Just right-click any column heading and add whatever column headings you need.

So what's a stack, you ask? Well, it's kind of like a stack of paper and kind of like a folder. It looks like a stack of paper, like the icons in Figure 1.7, but opens like a folder. When you open the stack, you see everything inside the stack. See Chapters 28 and 29 for the full story on all the cool things you can do in folders.

Previous versions and undelete

Have you ever made a mess of a file while editing it? Then you close the file, and out of habit choose Yes when asked if you want to save your changes? Thereby replacing your good copy with the one you just ruined! If that happens in Vista, it may not be a problem. Right-click the file's icon and choose Restore previous versions. The file's Properties sheet opens to the Previous Versions tab as in Figure 1.8. Then click the version you want to restore.

FIGURE 1.7

Sort, group, filter, or stack.

FIGURE 1.8

Previous Versions tab.

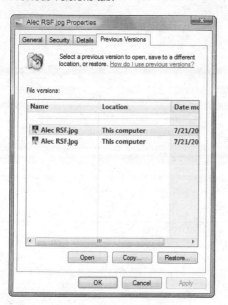

Have you ever accidentally deleted a file *and* emptied the Recycle Bin, making it impossible to recover the file? You can get those back in Vista, too. The trick is in knowing how. See "Using System Protection" in Chapter 33 for all the secrets.

NEW FEATURE   If you have thousands of files and messages to manage, the new Search feature will greatly reduce the amount of time you spend finding and getting to things you use most often.

Search and Virtual Folders

The new navigation tools really help make it quicker and easier to get around. But when it comes to getting around quickly and easily, no navigation is better than improved navigation. That's what Search and Virtual Folders (saved searches) are all about. To understand these features, you first have to erase from your mind any thought of "looking for lost items" or the Windows XP Search Companion. That's not what Search is about in Vista.

In its simplest form, Search starts right at the bottom of the Start menu. If you know the name of a program or Control Panel applet you want to open, or some keyword associated with a document, person in your Contacts folder, or Windows Mail message, you don't have to navigate at all to get to the item. Instead, open the Start menu by clicking the Start button or by pressing ▣ or Ctrl+Esc. Then just start typing your search word. As you type, the Start menu shows items that contain the characters you are typing (see Figure 1.9). When you see the item you want, just click it.

FIGURE 1.9

Start menu search.

Search for tags (keywords)

The Start menu search is handy. But there's much more. Searching in Vista goes way beyond looking for lost files. You can search all your documents for "relevance" or "meaning" rather than just by filename. The searches are much quicker than in earlier versions because Vista's search doesn't slog through the whole file system every time you search. Instead it searches an internal index of filenames, file properties (tags and metadata), and document contents.

If you've used Media Player, you've already had a sense of how that works. In Media Player you can click a genre like Classical, and see all your Classical songs, no matter who the artist or what folder the songs are stored in. Likewise, you could click Artist and see all songs by a given artist, regardless of what folder each song is in. Windows Vista extends that capability from Media Player to all the files on your hard disk. And any external hard disks you have, too.

Searches in Vista don't slog through the whole file system looking at tens of thousands of irrelevant files along the way. That's too slow and tedious. Instead, Windows Vista searches through a *search index*. The index contains filenames, tags (keywords), and even the contents of messages and files. So when you search for something like "catwalk" you get all files that have that in the filename, tag, or even inside the document. And you get it much more quickly than you would in XP.

> **TIP** If you're familiar with online search engines like Google, then the best way to think of the new search feature is as a search engine for files and folders on your own computer. Because that's what it *really* is.

You can launch a search the old-fashioned way, by clicking the Start button and choosing Search. Use the Advanced Search options shown in Figure 1.10. Use the Location option to choose where you want to search. Use the other boxes to search by date, size, filename, tags, or other file properties.

FIGURE 1.10

Advanced Search.

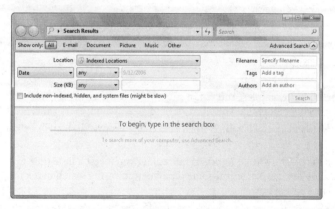

You can also launch a search from the Search box at the top-right corner of any folder. But you have to be aware that those searches include only the current folder and its subfolders. Nonetheless, it's very powerful and useful because you're not limited to searching for filenames and wildcards. You can include specific file properties in your search criteria. For example, a search for `genre: rock` finds all files that have Rock in the genre property. A search for `to:hobart` finds all Windows Mail messages addressed to Hobart. A search for `subject:vista` finds all files that have Vista in the Subject property. The possibilities are endless.

To take full advantage of the new search capabilities, you have to invest a little time in learning how searches really work. If you just try a few searches and give up, you'll never truly appreciate all that the new search index has to offer.

Saved searches (virtual folders)

You can save the results of any search you perform as a *virtual folder*. A virtual folder acts like a real folder. When you open it, you see the files it contains as icons. To see examples of virtual folders, click the Start button, click your user name on the Start menu, and open your Searches folder. Figure 1.11 shows icons for some sample saved searches (virtual folders).

FIGURE 1.11

Saved searches.

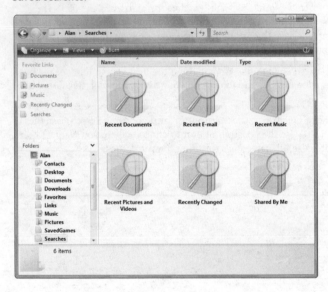

The virtual folders in your Searches folder are just examples. You're not stuck with just using those. You can create all the virtual folders you want. The beauty of it is that you don't have to go searching every time, because the virtual folder always reflects what's on your hard drive right now, not what was on it when you last performed the search.

Getting the most from searches, the search index, and virtual folders requires that you invest a little time in learning and understand how it all works. For best results, spend some time fine-tuning the search index to work the way you need it to. Chapters 30 and 31 tell how.

NEW FEATURE Windows Vista was designed and built from the ground up with security in mind, making your system much less vulnerable to security threats.

Security

Security is a huge issue these days. The basic problem is that the PC and early operating systems were conceived and built before there was an Internet. The idea was that a PC would be a *personal* computer, and people didn't need a whole lot of security. After all, who would write a malicious program to wreak havoc on their own computer?

The Internet changed all that. The Internet allowed the bad guys who could write malicious software to harm other people's computers. Personal computers were sitting ducks for such attacks because nobody was thinking about such things when personal computers were initially conceived.

All of the solutions to the security problems so far are like afterthoughts, held in place with spit and paper clips. You have to purchase and install third-party programs, learn to use them, and keep them up to date. It's just a pain.

Ask any security professional what the *real* solution to the security problem is, and you'll get this answer: "Security has to be designed and built into a program from the ground up." And that's just what the people at Microsoft did with Vista. It's not just Windows XP with a pretty face. It's an entirely new operating system built from the ground up with security in mind at every step in the process.

Still, there's no such thing as a 100 percent secure computer or network. (Any security professional will tell you that, too.) The computer is a programmable machine. And as such, it can be programmed to do good things or bad things. It all depends on who wrote the program and for what purpose.

Designing security into Vista from the ground up makes it a lot tougher for the bad guys to write programs that do bad things to your PC. But where there's a will, there's usually a way, so you still need some security programs.

Well, actually, you just need one security program. You need an antivirus program because that's the only security that's not built into Vista. But you don't need a third-party firewall or anti-spyware software. The new Windows Firewall keeps out hackers and worms from the minute you start your computer. Windows Defender keeps away the spyware. For more information on Vista security, see Part II.

User Account Control

Surely one of the most *unpopular* security features of Windows Vista is called *User Account Control* (UAC). Here's how it works. Any time you run a program that makes some change to your important system files, you get a little message on the screen, like in Figure 1.12.

FIGURE 1.12

User Account Control.

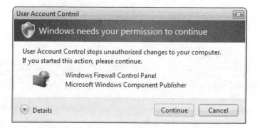

Ninety-nine times out of a hundred, you'll just be irritated by this because you know what program you're running so of course you want to continue. So why show the message and make you click the button? Because if ever a malicious program does sneak past your defenses, you have the opportunity to stop and think "Whoa, where did that come from?" And you also have the opportunity to just say no and stop the malicious program in its tracks, before it can do any harm.

The fact that User Account Control is there for everyone's safety isn't going to make it any more popular. You can turn it off, if you like, and do things the old-fashioned way where every program runs with the permissions of your current user account without warning. See Chapter 3 for the full story.

Parental controls

Parental controls, shown in Figure 1.13, are another security feature for which many parents will be very thankful. As you can see in the figure, Parental Controls lets you control how and when your child can use the computer and access the Internet. You don't need to be a computer genius to set up parental controls. Chapter 4 provides all the details.

FIGURE 1.13

Parental Controls.

NEW FEATURE If you use your computer to manage digital photos, you'll appreciate Photo Gallery's ability to help you fix and organize your pictures.

Windows Photo Gallery

Windows Photo Gallery offers a single place in which you can view, change, and manage all your photos and videos. You can tag pictures and videos with keywords. That makes them easy to bring together into a single view, regardless of their actual location on your disk. It has a Fix feature (see Figure 1.14) that makes it easy to adjust brightness and contrast, crop pictures, and fix the common "red eye" problem.

FIGURE 1.14

Photo Gallery Fix feature.

Photo Gallery makes it easy to create slide shows. You can even burn them to DVDs to watch on TV and to share with family and friends. If you're into photos, be sure to check out Chapter 22 for the full scoop.

 **NEW FEATURE** Windows Mail and Internet Explorer offer a plethora of new features. Better yet, they tie into the Search index, making it easy to find messages and favorite Web sites.

Windows Mail and Internet Explorer

In Vista, Windows Mail replaces Outlook Express as the built-in e-mail client. And it's a major improvement! It has a built-in junk mail filter that works like a charm (if you configure it wisely). It has a phishing filter to alert you to fake e-mail messages that attempt to steal your passwords by looking official. And it ties into your Contacts folder where you can store all your names and addresses, and even pictures of people!

Internet Explorer in Vista supports tabbed browsing, meaning that you can have multiple home pages and also switch among open pages more easily. Internet Explorer also makes it extremely easy to subscribe to RSS feeds. Be sure to check out Part IV for the full scoop on all the Internet-related enhancements in Vista.

NEW FEATURE Gone are the days where you had to rely on third-party programs for CD and DVD burning. All of that is built right into most editions of Windows Vista.

Built-in CD and DVD Burning

Vista has built-in support for using CDs and DVDs for all their many uses. As always, you can use Windows Media Player (see Chapter 23) to create your own music CDs. Now you can also create your own DVD movies using Windows DVD Maker. You can even transfer movies straight from digital video tape to DVDs that you can watch on TV (see Chapter 32).

Just want to copy some files to a CD or DVD to send through the mail? No problem. Just drag-and-drop files like you would to a floppy disk (see Chapter 32). Want to back up your files to CDs or DVDs? That's easy, too. Use the new Backup and Restore Center (see Chapter 33).

NEW FEATURE Although Speech Recognition isn't entirely new, Vista extends the capability to more programs and even your desktop.

Speech Recognition

Speech Recognition in Windows Vista is a big improvement over Windows XP's speech recognition. You can use it to dictate Windows Mail messages and other documents. You can bark commands at Windows and other programs with your voice. It takes a good headset microphone and some training, but it sure can come in handy if you're suffering from aching "mouse shoulder," or just can't type worth beans. See "Using Speech Recognition" in Chapter 12 for the full story.

NEW FEATURE System Protection and the new Backup and Restore Center make it easier to protect your important files from damage and loss.

Better, Easier Backups

The new Backup and Restore Center in Windows Vista replaces the old NT Backup that has eluded most users for years. You can back up to CDs, DVDs, or an external hard disk. In the Premium and Ultimate editions of Vista, you can even automate backups. Furthermore, System Protection keeps *shadow copies* of many document files right on the hard disk, which means you can often recover a lost or damaged file without even using the external backup media. See Chapter 33 for the full story.

NEW FEATURE ReadyBoost uses modern flash memory to provide a quicker, smoother, overall computing experience.

Windows ReadyBoost

Readers who know computer hardware know that for years we've been doing everything with two types of memory. RAM (random access memory) holds the stuff you're using right now. The hard disk is more like a filing cabinet in that it holds everything you *can* use. RAM is much faster than disk storage, which is why you use it to hold stuff you're working with at the moment.

Historically, we've also used a *paging file* as a kind of intermediary between fast RAM and slow disk access. Although this conserves and extends RAM, it does so at a cost of little time delays each time the processor needs to get something out of the paging file. It's not a long delay, just a half a second to a couple of seconds. But over the course of a day, those little delays add up.

ReadyBoost gets rid of the delays by letting you use flash memory to store the paging file. Flash memory is a much better choice because on average it's about 10 times faster than the hard drive. Many new hard drives and motherboards will come with ReadyBoost flash memory built right in. As an alternative to using built-in hardware, you can use an external flash drive that plugs into a USB 2.0 port for ReadyBoost.

There are some restrictions on the jump drives you can use, because it only makes sense to use flash memory that's large enough and fast enough to produce results. But once you have the right hardware, Vista takes care of all the details. The result is a smoother, more fluid computing experience without the usual delays when the OS needs to get data from the paging file.

Wrap Up

When people ask me what's new in Vista, what I really want to say is *Everything*. It's really a whole new way of using a computer. Long gone are the days when people managed a few files and folders on external disks without an Internet connection. In today's connected world, we deal with massive amounts of digital information in many forms, and from many sources. Vista was designed and built from the ground up with that new reality in mind.

This chapter has been a sort of view from 30,000 feet of what's new in Vista. Here I've focused on the main things that most users will want to explore. But really there's much more than can be covered in a single chapter. Here's a quick recap of what's hot:

- Aero Glass brings a three-dimensional quality to the basic user interface to better reflect what's really happening on your desktop.
- Although it doesn't look like much, the little breadcrumb trail at the top of every folder greatly reduces the amount of time and effort you'll spend navigating through folders.
- Previous versions of files let you easily recover accidentally messed up and deleted files, even if you haven't backed them up.
- Searching in Windows Vista is nothing like the old Search Companion. And it's not about finding lost files. Instead, it provides a new layer of organization that transcends location and filename, bringing things together based on meaning and relevance.
- Security isn't tacked onto Windows Vista as an afterthought through countless extra security programs and patches. Most of the security is hidden deep inside where you'll never see it, keeping malicious software from doing its desired dirty work.
- Parental controls finally give parents the ability to control their children's computer and Internet use.
- Windows Photo Gallery is a great tool for managing, tagging, and fixing your photos.
- Windows Mail and Internet Explorer bring new ways to manage your mail, surf the Internet, and keep your computer, and yourself, more secure.
- Use Windows Vista's built-in support for CD and DVD burning to create music CDs, DVD movies, and backups of all your files.
- Speech Recognition is greatly improved and works virtually everywhere.
- The Backup and Restore Center makes it easy to back up and protect your important files.
- Windows ReadyBoost can use modern flash memory to dispense with the short delays caused by fetching data from the paging file, providing a smoother, more fluid computing experience.

Chapter 2

Getting Around

In today's busy world, few people have the time to sit down and really learn to use a computer. Many books and online tutorials don't really help because they assume you already know all the basic concepts and terminology. That's a big assumption because the truth is, most people don't already know those things. Most people don't know a file from a folder from a megabyte from a golf ball. These just aren't the kinds of things we learned about in school or from our day-to-day experiences.

This chapter is mostly about the kinds of things everyone else assumes you already know. It's for the kind of person who bought their first computer and discovered it has this thing called Windows Vista on it. Or the kind of person who could get by with an older computer, and now has a new Windows Vista computer and really wants to know more about how to use it.

I often refer to the skills in this chapter as "everyday skills" because they're the kinds of things you'll likely do every time you sit down at the computer. I point out the name and purpose of many things you'll see on your screen. All of these things combine into a kind of basic knowledge about how you use a computer, in general, to get things done. And it all starts with logging in.

Terminology for Things You Do

If you're new to computers, the first step is to learn a little terminology about things you do to operate the computer. I assume you know what the *mouse* is. When you move the mouse, the *mouse pointer* on the screen moves in whatever direction you move the mouse. Most mice have two buttons. The one on the left is called the *primary* or *left* mouse button. It's called the primary button because it always takes an immediate action. When you rest your hand comfortably on the mouse, the left mouse button should be under your index finger. You don't want to hold the button down though. Just rest your index finger on it lightly.

The button on the right is called the *secondary* or *right* mouse button. Unlike the primary mouse button, the secondary mouse button doesn't take an immediate action. Instead, it shows you options for different things you can do with whatever you're pointing to at the moment.

Mouse terminology

There are some specific terms everyone uses to refer to things you do with the mouse. You need to know these terms in order to understand instructions that tell you how to do things. The mouse terms include *point*, *click*, *double-click*, *right-click*, and *drag*.

Point

The term *point*, when used as a verb, means to touch the mouse pointer to an item. For example "point to the Start button" means to move the mouse pointer so it's on the Start button in the lower-left corner of the screen. If the item you want to point to is smaller than the mouse pointer, make sure you get the tip of the mouse pointer arrow on the item. Whatever the tip of the mouse pointer is on is the thing to which you're pointing.

The term *hover* means the same thing as *point*. For example, the phrase "*hover the mouse pointer over the Start button*" means the same thing as *point to the Start button*.

When you point to an item, the item's name typically appears in a *tooltip*. For example, if you point to the Start button (the large round button near the lower-left corner of your screen that shows the Windows logo) the word Start appears in a tooltip near the mouse pointer. The tooltip tells you that the thing you're pointing to is named Start. Figure 2.1 shows an example of pointing to the Start button. The word "Start" is the tooltip.

FIGURE 2.1

Pointing to the Start button.

Tooltip

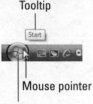

Mouse pointer

Start button

> **TIP** You can learn the name and purpose of many things on your screen just by pointing to the item and reading the tooltip that appears near the mouse pointer.

Click

The term *click* means to point to an item, then tap the left mouse button. Don't hold down the left mouse button. Just tap it. It makes a slight clicking sound when you do. For example, the term "click the Start button" means "put the mouse pointer on the Start button and tap the left mouse button. When you do, the Start menu appears. Click the Start button a second time and the Start menu goes away.

Double-click

The term *double-click* means to point to an item, then tap the left mouse button twice as fast as you can. Don't hold down the button, and don't pause between clicks. Just tap the left mouse button twice as quickly as you can. You'll use double-clicking to *open* items that icons on your screen represent.

Right-click

The term *right-click* means to point to an item, then tap the right mouse button. Again, don't hold down the mouse button. And don't use the left mouse button. Whereas clicking an item usually takes an immediate action, right-clicking presents a shortcut menu of things you can do with the item. You'll see many examples throughout this book.

Drag

The term *drag* means to point to an item and hold down the left mouse button while you're moving the mouse. You typically use dragging to move and size things on the screen. You'll see examples a little later in this chapter.

 **TIP** As you'll discover in Chapter 29, you can also use dragging to move and copy files from one location to another.

Keyboard terminology

The keyboard is the thing that looks like a typewriter keyboard. The keys labeled F1, F2, and so forth across the top are called *function keys*. The keys that show arrows and names like Home, End, PgUp (Page Up), and PgDn (Page Down) are *navigation keys*.

Tab, Enter, and Spacebar

The Tab key shows two opposing arrows pointing left and right. That key is usually to the left of the letter Q. The Enter key (also called the Carriage Return or Return key) is located where the carriage return key is on a standard typewriter. It may be labeled Enter, Return, or just show a bent left-pointing arrow. The Spacebar is the wide key centered at the bottom of the keyboard. When you're typing text, it types a blank space.

If in doubt, Escape key out

The Esc or Escape key is the one labeled Esc or Escape (or maybe even Cancel). It's usually at the upper-left corner of the keyboard. It's a good one to know because it often allows you to escape from unfamiliar territory.

The Help key (F1)

The Help key is the F1 function key. That's a good one to know because it's the key you press for help. Not the kind of help where someone appears and helps you along. Unfortunately, it's not possible to get that kind of help from a computer. Instead, pressing Help opens a help window. You'll learn more about getting help in Chapter 5.

The ⊞ Key

If you have a Windows keyboard, you'll also have a *Windows key*, which shows the Windows logo. In text, that's often referred to as ⊞. That one is usually near the lower-left corner of the keyboard. That key might also show the word Start, because you can tap it to show and hide the Start menu.

Shift, Ctrl, and Alt

The keys labeled Shift, Ctrl (control), and Alt (alternate) are *modifier* keys. There are usually two of each of those keys on a keyboard, near the lower left and lower right of the main typing keys. The Shift key may just show a large up-pointing arrow. One is to the left of the letter Z, the other to the right of the ? key. They're called modifier keys because they don't do anything by themselves. Instead, you hold down a modifier key while pressing some other key. For example, when you hold down the Shift key and press the A key you get an uppercase *A* rather then a lowercase *a*.

Shortcut keys

The term *press* always refers to a key on the keyboard rather than something you do with the mouse. For example, the term *press Enter* means to press the Enter key. When you see an instruction to press two keys with a + in between (*key+key*), that means "hold down the first key, tap the second key, release the first key." For example, an instruction to

```
Press Ctrl+Esc
```

means "hold down the Ctrl key, tap the Esc key, release the Ctrl key."

You'll often see the term *shortcut key* used to refer to *key+key* combinations. The "shortcut" part comes from the fact that the keystroke is an alternative way of doing something with the mouse. (Though it may not seem like much of a "shortcut" if you can't type worth beans!)

Much as we all hate to learn terminology, knowing the terms and keyboard keys I just described is critical to learning how to use a computer. All written and spoken instructions assume you know what those terms mean. If you don't, then the instructions won't do you any good.

Okay, let's move onto to using the computer, and the names of things you'll do, see, and use often.

Logging In

Obviously, the first step to using a computer is to turn it on. Shortly after you first start your computer you're taken to the Windows Vista Login screen. Exactly how that screen looks depends on what user accounts exist on your computer. By default, Windows Vista comes with a built-in user account named Administrator. But it's unlikely that you'll ever see that user account because it's not for day-to-day computer use. If you've never used your computer or Vista before, you'll likely be taken through a process where it asks you to create a user account. Just follow the onscreen instructions if faced with that question.

If your computer already has user accounts, you'll likely be taken to a *login page* where you see icons (little pictures) and names for one or more *user accounts*. You learn about user accounts in Chapter 3. But for now all you need to know is that if you see user account icons shortly after you first start your computer, you have to click one in order to move on.

> **TIP** The blue circle near the lower-left corner of the screen provides Ease of Access options for the visually impaired. The red button at the lower-right corner lets you turn off the computer rather than log in.

If the user account isn't password-protected, you'll be taken straight to the Windows desktop. If the user account you clicked is password-protected, a rectangular box appears instead. You have to type the correct password for the account to get to the Windows desktop. The letters you type won't show in the box.

Instead you'll see a dot for each letter you type as in the example shown in Figure 2.2. This is to prevent people from learning your password by looking over your shoulder as you type it on the screen. After you type the password, press Enter or click the arrow to the right of the password box.

Typing a password.

After you've successfully logged in, you're taken to the Windows desktop.

What's on the Desktop

The interface that Windows Vista provides is called the *Windows desktop*. The name "desktop" comes from the fact that it plays the same role as a real, wooden desktop. You work with programs on the Windows desktop in much the same way that you work with paper on a wooden desktop.

The desktop is on the screen from the moment you log in to the moment you turn off your computer. The desktop may get covered by program windows and other items, but the desktop is still under there no matter how much you clutter up the screen. It's the same as a real desk in that sense. Although your real desktop may be completely covered by random junk, like mine is right now, your desktop is still under there somewhere. You just have to dig through the mess to get to it.

The two main components of the Windows desktop are the desktop itself and the taskbar. The desktop is where everything that you open piles up. The taskbar's main role is to make it easy to switch from one open item to another. Everything you'll ever see on your screen has a name and a purpose. Virtually nothing on the screen is there purely for decoration. Figure 2.3 shows the main components of the Windows desktop and other items. Your desktop might not look exactly like the picture, and might not show all of the components. But don't worry about that. Right now you want to focus on learning the names of things so you know what people are talking about when they refer to these things.

FIGURE 2.3

The desktop, taskbar, and other items.

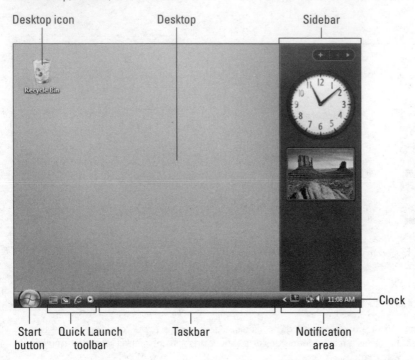

Here's a quick overview of what each component represents. The sections that follow the list look at each component in detail.

TIP You learn to personalize your desktop in Chapter 11. But here's a quick hint. Virtually everything you'll ever see on your screen, including the desktop, is an *object* that has *properties*. To customize any object, right-click that object and choose Properties.

■ **Desktop:** The desktop itself is everything above the taskbar. Every program you open appears in a window on the desktop.

■ **Desktop icons:** Icons on the desktop provide quick access to frequently used programs, folders, and documents. You can add and remove desktop icons as you see fit.

■ **Sidebar:** An optional component for showing *gadgets* that you might want to use often.

■ **Start button:** Click the Start button to display the Start menu. The Start menu provides access to programs installed on your computer, as well as commonly used folders such as Documents, Pictures, and Music.

■ **Quick Launch toolbar:** Provides easy one-click access to frequently used programs.

■ **Taskbar:** A task is an open program. The taskbar makes it easy to switch among all your open programs.

■ **Notification area:** Displays icons for programs running in the background, often referred to as *processes* and *services*. Messages coming from those programs appear in speech balloons just above the Notification area.

■ **Clock:** Shows the current time. Right-clicking the clock provides easy access to options for customizing the taskbar and organizing open program windows.

That's the quick tour of items on and around the Windows Vista desktop. The sections that follow look at each major item. But first, I should point out that your desktop might be partially covered by the Welcome Center. If so, and it gets in your way while you're trying things out in this chapter, you can close the Welcome Center so it's out of your way. See "The Welcome Center" near the end of this chapter for more information.

Using the Start Menu

Clicking the Start button displays the Start menu. The left side of the Start menu shows icons for some (but not all) of the programs on your computer. The right side of the menu offers links to commonly used folders and other features. Figure 2.4 shows an example.

FIGURE 2.4

Start menu.

The icons on your Start menu won't necessarily match those shown in the figure, so don't worry if yours looks different. The figure is just an example. You will notice, however, that some of the program names on the left side of the Start menu are boldface and some are not. There's a horizontal line separating the two types of names.

Items above the horizontal line (shown in boldface) are *pinned* to the Start menu and never change. Items below the horizontal line are *dynamic*, meaning they change automatically based on programs you use most frequently. As the weeks and months roll by, the left side of your Start menu will eventually list just the programs you use most often.

To see all the programs available on your system, click All Programs near the bottom of the Start menu. In the All Programs menu, some icons look like folders, others like logos. Any icon that looks like a logo represents a program. To start (open) a program, you click its name or logo.

Icons that look like folders represent program groups. To see the names of programs in a group, click the folder icon or name. For example, in Figure 2.5 I clicked the Accessories folder. So now the left side of the Start menu includes programs and program groups from the Windows Vista Accessories program group.

You can choose from many more programs than can fit on the left side of the Start menu. Use the vertical scroll bar just to the right of the program name to scroll up and down through the complete list. If you want to leave the All Programs menu and return to the dynamic menu, click <Back at the bottom of the list.

FIGURE 2.5

All Programs menu and Accessories group.

The right side of the Start menu

The right side of the Start menu shows icons for frequently used folders and features. The name at the top of the list (Alan in the previous examples) is the name of the user account into which you're currently logged. Clicking the user name opens a folder containing icons for other folders that represent things like documents, pictures, music, and other information saved and stored by this user.

Items labeled Documents, Pictures, and Music open folders in which you can store things like documents, photographs, and songs. The Games link opens a folder of games you can play on your computer.

> **TIP** A folder in Windows Vista is like a manila file folder in a filing cabinet. It's a container in which you can store documents. You use folders in Windows to organize things, just as you use folders to organize things in a filing cabinet.

The Computer link opens a folder that shows icons representing disk drives, memory card slots, and other connected hardware devices like cameras and scanners. Chapter 28 tells the whole story on that folder.

> **TIP** Like everything else in Vista, you can customize many aspects of the Start menu. For instance, you can choose which options you do/don't want to appear on the right side of the Start menu. Right-click the Start button and choose Properties to get to its Properties dialog box. See Chapter 11 for a description of its options.

We'll have plenty of time to get into the various folders and document types described previously. For now we'll stay focused on the Start menu.

The Start menu Search box

> **NEW FEATURE** Down near the bottom of the Start menu, you'll see a Search box. As its name implies, it allows you to search for things based on a word or phrase. For example, say you click the Start button (or press ▦ or Ctrl+Esc on your keyboard) to open the Start menu, then type the letters *cal*. The Start menu will list all programs that contain the letters "cal." For example, in Figure 2.6, Windows Calendar and Calculator are both listed under Programs.

Below the list of programs that contain the search letters, you may see files, contacts, and e-mail messages that also contain those letters. As you type more letters, the list shrinks to show only the items that contain all the letters you've typed so far. When you see the item you want to open, just click its name in the Start menu.

To cancel a search without making a selection, press Escape (Esc).

> **TIP** For experienced users, the instant searches from the Start menu are one of Vista's best new features. It can save you a lot of time you'd otherwise spend opening programs and folders to find something.

FIGURE 2.6

Start menu search for cal.

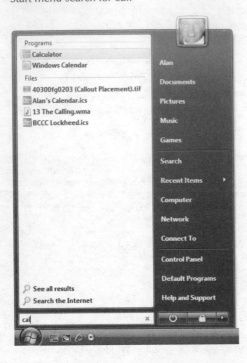

Shut Down and Lock buttons

The buttons at the lower-right side of the Start menu play several roles. The one with the circle puts your computer in a low power state without shutting it all the way down. When you restart the computer and log in, you're taken back to wherever you left off before clicking that button.

The lock button hides your desktop and shows the login screen. To get back to where you were, just click your user account picture on the screen that appears. If your account is password-protected, you'll need to enter your password. In a work environment, this hides your desktop from passersby and prevents them from using the computer while you're away.

Clicking the arrow on the Lock button displays several options, as shown in Figure 2.7 and summarized in the following list.

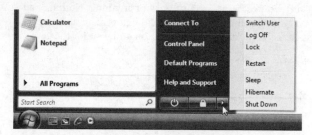

FIGURE 2.7

Lock and Shut Down buttons.

- **Switch User:** Switches to another user account without logging out of the current account.

CAUTION Using Switch User all of the time to switch between user accounts can slow down or even crash a computer. Use Switch User only to temporarily visit another user account. Otherwise, users should always log out of their accounts when done using the computer.

- **Log Off:** Closes all open items, logs out of the current user account, and returns to the login screen.

- **Lock:** Hides the desktop behind a login screen. Regaining access requires entering the user account password.

- **Shut Down:** Closes all open items and shuts down the computer.

- **Restart:** Closes all open items and restarts the computer (also called a *reboot* or *warm boot*).

- **Sleep:** Puts the computer in a state where it consumes little power, without losing your place on the screen.

- **Hibernate:** Saves what's on your desktop, then shuts down the computer all the way so it's consuming no power at all. When you restart the computer and log in, your desktop is returned to wherever you left things.

- **Shut Down:** Clears off the desktop and shuts down the computer. When you restart the computer and log in, you're taken to a clean desktop.

Different types of computers offer different options for sleeping, hibernating, and shutting down. How you restart the computer also varies. For example, when you put the computer to sleep, you can often wake it up just by tapping a key on the keyboard or by moving the mouse. Or, on a notebook computer, simply opening the lid to view the screen may wake the computer up.

When you hibernate or shut down, you have to use the main On/Off switch to turn the computer back on. But because these do vary from one computer to the next, I can't say exactly which options your computer offers or how they'll work. If you have any trouble with those options, refer to the instruction manual that came with your computer for specifics.

At times, the button for powering down the computer might show a shield and exclamation point as in Figure 2.8. When you point to that button, the tooltip shows information like that shown in the figure. The button and tooltip are telling you that your computer has automatically received an update that requires you to click that button. Go ahead and do so. Don't worry, it's not a security risk or anything. Nothing bad will happen, it won't cost you any money, and everything will work the way it did before. The update is just a security patch or minor fix. Go ahead and click the exclamation point button and wait for the computer to shut down on its own.

FIGURE 2.8

Shut Down button and tooltip.

Installs updates and then shuts down your computer.

   Chapter 9 talks about automatic updates in depth.

Using the Windows Desktop

As mentioned, the Windows desktop is the electronic equivalent of a real, wooden desktop. It's the place where you keep stuff you're working on right now. Every program that's currently open will be contained within some program window. When no programs are open, the desktop and all your desktop icons are plainly visible on the screen.

About desktop icons

Desktop icons are just like the icons on the Start menu. Each icon represents a *closed* object that you can *open* by double-clicking the icon. Most desktop icons are shortcuts to files and folders. They're shortcuts in the sense that they duplicate icons available elsewhere. They just save you the extra clicks required to get to the same icon through the Start menu or All Programs menu.

There's always an exception to the rule. When it comes to desktop icons, the Recycle Bin is the exception. The Recycle Bin icon exists only on the desktop, and you won't find it anywhere else. The role of the Recycle Bin is that of a safety net. Whenever you delete a file or folder from your hard drive, the item is actually just moved to the Recycle Bin. You can restore an accidentally deleted icon from the Recycle Bin back to its original location.

In addition to the Recycle Bin, you have five other built-in desktop icons from which to choose. There's no hurry on that. But if you want to take a shot at it, you have to get to the Personalization page and make some selections. You can use either of the following techniques to get to the Personalization page:

- Click the Start button, type `pers`, and click Personalization.
- Right-click the desktop and choose Personalize.

NOTE   If you don't see Personalize when you right-click the desktop, that means you didn't right-click the desktop. You right-clicked something that's covering the desktop. You learn to close and hide things that are covering the desktop a little later in this chapter.

The Personalization control panel opens. In its left column click Change desktop icons. You see a *dialog box* like the one in Figure 2.9. It's called a dialog box because you carry on a sort of dialog with it. It shows you options from which you can pick and choose. You make your choices and click OK. You'll see menu dialog boxes throughout this book.

FIGURE 2.9

The Desktop Icon dialog box.

To make an icon visible on your desktop, select (check) the checkbox next to the icon's name. To prevent an icon from appearing on the desktop, click the checkbox to the left of its name. In the figure, I've opted to see all icons except the Network and Control Panel icons.

You can choose a different picture for any icon you've opted to show on the desktop. Click the icon's picture in the middle of the dialog box. Then click the Change Icon button. Click the icon you want to show, then click OK. If you change your mind after the fact, click Restore Default.

Click OK after making your selections. The dialog box closes and the icons you choose appear on the desktop. However, you might not see them if that part of the desktop is covered by something that's open. Don't worry about that. You learn about how you open, close, move, and size things on the desktop a little later in this chapter.

If nothing is covering the desktop, but you still don't see any desktop icons, they might just be switched off. We'll talk about that next.

Arranging desktop icons

As you'll discover in Chapter 11, you have many ways to customize the Vista desktop. But if you just want to make some quick minor changes to your desktop icons, right-click the desktop to view its shortcut menu. Items on the menu that have a little arrow to the right show submenus. For example, if you right-click the desktop and point to View on the menu, you see the View menu as in Figure 2.10.

FIGURE 2.10

Right-click the desktop.

The last item on the View menu, Show Desktop Icons, needs to be selected (checked) for the icons to show at all. If there is no checkmark next to that item, click that item. The menu closes and the icons appear on the desktop. When you need to see the menu again, just right-click the desktop again.

The top three items on the menu, Large Icons, Medium Icons, and Classic Icons, control the size of the icons. Click any option to see its effect. If you don't like the result, right-click the desktop again, choose View, and choose a different size.

NEW FEATURE   **If your mouse has a wheel, you can also size icons by holding down the Ctrl key as you spin the mouse wheel.**

The Sort By option on the desktop shortcut menu lets you arrange desktop icons alphabetically by Name, by Size, by Type, or by Date Modified. However, no matter how you choose to sort icons, the built-in icons are always listed first. Custom shortcut icons you create yourself are listed after the built-in icons. So if you sort by name, the built-in icons will be listed alphabetically first. Then any shortcut icons you created will be alphabetized after those.

TIP   **To create a custom desktop shortcut icon to a favorite program, right-click the program's icon on the All Programs menu and choose Send To ⇨ Desktop (create shortcut).**

You learn more about personalizing your desktop in Chapter 11. For now, let's stay focused on basic skills like clicking and right-clicking, and the names of things you see on your screen.

Running Programs

You can start any program that's installed on your computer by getting to the program's icon on the All Programs menu and then clicking that icon. There are other ways to start programs as well. For example, if there's an icon on the left side of the Start menu to start the program, just click that instead. If there's an icon for the program in the Quick Launch toolbar, you can click that. If there's a shortcut icon to the program on the desktop, you can click (or double-click) that icon to start the program.

NOTE   **Whether you need to single-click or double-click a desktop icon to open it is up to you. See "To Click or Double-Click" in Chapter 28 for details.**

Every time you start a program, an *instance* of that program opens in a program window. There's no rule that says you can have only one program open at a time. And there's no rule that says you can have only one copy of any given program open at a time. You can have as many programs as you can cram into your available memory (RAM) open all at the same time. And most programs will allow you to run multiple instances. The more memory your system has, the more stuff you can have open without any slowdown in performance.

NOTE   When it comes to using programs, the terms *start, run, launch,* and *open* all mean the same thing — to load a copy of the program into memory (RAM) so it's visible on your screen. You can't use a program until it's open and visible.

Any item you open on the desktop will show its own name somewhere near the top of the program window. Figure 2.11 shows an example where I have the Welcome Center open on the desktop. You see its name in the Address bar near the top of the window.

Most items that you open will also have a taskbar button. The name in the taskbar button matches the name of the item. For example, the taskbar button for the open Welcome Center also shows the words Welcome Center. You can click the Welcome Center taskbar button to make the open window appear and disappear. That's a good thing to know, because sometimes you want to get something off the screen temporarily so you can see something else that's on the screen.

When you have multiple program windows open, they stack up on the desktop just like multiple sheets of paper on your real desktop stack up. When you have multiple sheets of paper in a pile, you can't see what's on every page. You can only see what's on the top page, because all the other pages are covered by that page.

FIGURE 2.11

Sample title bar and taskbar button.

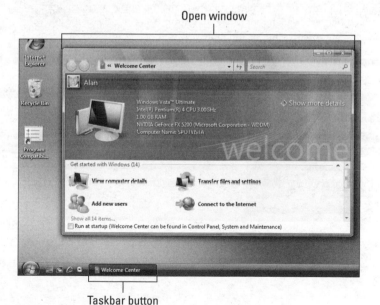

It works the same way with program windows. When you have multiple program windows open, you can only see the one that's on the top of the stack. We call the program that's on the top of the stack the *active window*.

The active window

When two or more program windows are open on the desktop window, only one of them can be the active window. The active window has some unique characteristics:

- The active window is always on the top of the stack. Any other open windows will be under the active window so they don't cover any of its content.
- The taskbar button for the active window has a pushed-in appearance, and the taskbar buttons for all the inactive windows have a pushed-out appearance.
- Anything you do at the keyboard applies to the active window only. You cannot type in an inactive window.

Switching among open programs

Whenever you have two or more programs open at the same time, you want to be able to easily switch among them. There are several ways to switch among open programs, as discussed in the sections to follow.

NEW FEATURE   Pointing to a taskbar button shows a miniature version of the window that the button represents.

Switching with taskbar buttons

As mentioned, every open program has a button on the taskbar. When you have multiple open programs, you have multiple taskbar buttons. To bring any one particular program to the top of the stack, click its taskbar button. If you're not sure which button is which, point to each button. You'll see the name and a miniature copy of the program that the button represents, as in Figure 2.12.

FIGURE 2.12
_____

Pointing to a taskbar button.

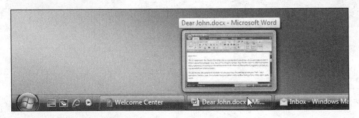

TIP   If any portion of the window you want to bring to the top of the stack is visible on the screen, you can just click that visible portion of the window to bring it to the top of the stack.

Switching with the keyboard

If you prefer the keyboard to the mouse, you can use Alt+Tab to switch among open windows. Hold down the Alt key and then press the Tab key. You'll see an icon for each open program window as in the example shown in Figure 2.13. Keep the Alt key pressed down and keep pressing Tab until the name of the program you want to switch to appears above the icons. Then release the Alt key.

 The Tab key shows two opposing arrows and is usually just to the left of the letter Q on the keyboard.

FIGURE 2.13

Alt+Tab window.

The last (rightmost) item in the Alt+Tab window represents the desktop rather than an open program. If you release the Alt key with that selected, you'll end up at a clear desktop. But you can still bring up any open program by clicking its taskbar button.

Switching with Flip 3D

If you're using the Aero Glass interface in Windows Vista, you can use Flip 3D to switch among windows. Hold down the 🏁 key and press Tab. Or click the Switch between windows button shown near the mouse pointer in Figure 2.14 to switch among open program windows. The desktop darkens and any program windows you have open appear in the three-dimensional view as in Figure 2.15.

 Flip 3D is a new Vista feature. But it only works if you use the Aero Glass interface. See Chapter 1 for more information.

FIGURE 2.14

Quick launch button for Flip 3D.

When you see the three-dimensional stack, you can click any window to bring that window to the top of the stack on your desktop. If your mouse has a wheel, you can cycle through windows by spinning the mouse wheel. If you use the keyboard, keep the 🏁 key held down and press the Tab key until the window you want is at the front of the stack. When you release 🏁, that same window will be on the top of the stack on the desktop.

FIGURE 2.15

Flip 3D stack of open windows.

Switching among multiple instances

You can have multiple copies of the same program at the same time. For example, say you're browsing the Web with Microsoft Internet Explorer. You're about to click a link to go to another page, but you don't want to lose your place in the current page. Rather than click the link, you can right-click it and choose Open In New Window. A second copy of Internet Explorer opens to show the new page. The original page remains open on the desktop so you can still see that page as well.

Initially, each instance of the program will have its own taskbar button. But if you open many instances, and the taskbar buttons are becoming too small to see, the instances will collapse into a single taskbar button. That button will show a number indicating how many instances are currently open.

To switch to a particular instance of that program, use any of the three techniques I just described. Optionally, you can click the single taskbar button that represents all the open instances of the program. The titles of all the documents (or Web pages in this case) that are open in that program will appear in a menu, like in Figure 2.16. To bring a particular instance to the top of the stack, just click its name in that menu.

FIGURE 2.16

Multiple instances of Internet Explorer are open.

Here are some other handy things to know about a single taskbar button that represents multiple open instances of a program window. You can right-click the taskbar button that sports the number of open instances and then choose any of the following from the context menu that opens:

- **Cascade:** Stacks all the opens instances like sheets of paper, with just their title bars visible.
- **Show Windows Stacked:** Stacks open windows like horizontal bars, one atop the other, on the desktop, or like tiles if there are too many open windows to stack one atop the other.
- **Show Windows Side by Side:** Same as above, but each window spans the height of the desktop. Also as above, displays them as tiles if there are too many to show side by side.
- **Minimize Group:** Temporarily removes all open instances from the desktop. Use any option previously given to bring them back to the desktop.
- **Close Group:** Closes all the open instances in one click.

The main point to keep in mind here is that program windows on the desktop stack up just like sheets of paper on a desk. It doesn't matter whether you're talking about a single instance of multiple programs, multiple instances of a single program, or multiple instances of multiple programs—they're all just program windows.

Arranging program windows

You can use options on the taskbar shortcut menu to arrange all currently open program windows. To get to that menu, right-click an empty portion of the taskbar, or right-click the clock in the lower-right corner of the screen. Figure 2.17 shows the options on the menu.

FIGURE 2.17

Taskbar shortcut menu.

The four options that apply to program windows on the desktop are similar to the options you get when you right-click a taskbar button that represents multiple instances of one program:

- **Cascade Windows:** Stacks all the open windows like sheets of paper, fanned out so all of their title bars are visible, as in Figure 2.18.
- **Show Windows Stacked:** Arranges the windows in rows across the screen, or as equal-sized tiles.
- **Show Windows Side by Side:** Arranges the windows side by side. As above, if there are too many open windows to show that way, they'll be displayed in equal-sized tiles.

■ **Show the Desktop:** Minimizes all open windows so only their taskbar buttons are visible. You can see the entire desktop at that point. To bring any window back onto the screen, click its taskbar button. To bring them all back, right-click the clock or taskbar again and choose Show Open Windows.

FIGURE 2.18

Cascaded program windows.

The only way to really appreciate these options is to try them out for yourself. Open two or more programs. Then try each of the options described to see their effects on your open program windows.

Sizing program windows

Most program windows can be any size you want them to be, but there are a few exceptions to the rule. For example, the tiny Calculator program can't be sized much. Some programs like Movie Maker, Media Player, and Solitaire will shrink down only so far. But in general, most open program windows can be three sizes:

■ Maximized, in which the program fills the entire screen above the taskbar, covering the desktop.

■ Minimized, in which only the program's taskbar button is visible, and the program window takes up no space on the desktop.

■ Any size in between those two extremes.

Often you'll want to work with two or more program windows at a time. Knowing how to size program windows is a critical skill for doing that, because it's often difficult to work with multiple program windows if you can't see at least some portion of each one.

Maximize a program window

A maximized program window will fill all the space above the taskbar. This makes it easy to see everything inside the program window. If a program window isn't already maximized, you can maximize it in several ways:

- Click the Maximize button in the program's title bar (see Figure 2.19).
- Double-click the program's title bar.
- Click the upper-left corner of the window you want to maximize and choose Maximize. Optionally, right-click anywhere near the center top of the window and choose Maximize.
- Right-click the program's taskbar button and choose Maximize.

FIGURE 2.19

Maximize button in a title bar.

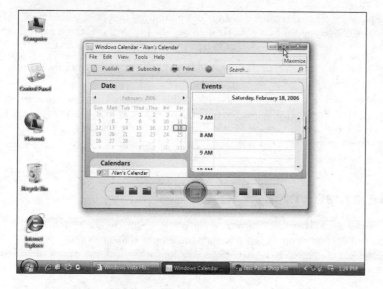

 Remember, few buttons on the screen show their name. But you can find out a button's name just by touching the button with the tip of the mouse pointer.

Minimize a program window

If you want to get a program window off the screen temporarily without losing your place, minimize the program window. When you minimize the program window, the program remains open. However, it takes up no space on the screen, and, therefore, can't cover anything else on the screen. When minimized, only the window's taskbar button remains visible. You can minimize a window in several ways:

- Click the Minimize button in the program's title bar (see Figure 2.20).
- Click the upper-left corner of the window you want to minimize (or right-click anywhere near the center top of the window) and choose Minimize.

- Click the program's taskbar button once or twice. (If the program isn't in the active window, the first click will just make it the active window. The second click will then minimize the active window.)
- Right-click the program's taskbar button and choose Minimize.

FIGURE 2.20

Minimize button in a title bar.

Size at will

Between the two extremes of maximized (hog up the entire desktop) and minimized (not even visible on the desktop), most program windows can be any size you want them to be. The first step to sizing a program window is to get it to an in-between size, so that it's neither maximized nor minimized. To do that:

- If the program window is currently minimized, click its taskbar button to make it visible on the screen.
- If the program window is currently maximized, double-click its title bar or click its Restore Down button to shrink it down a little. Figure 2.21 shows the tooltip that appears when you point to the Restore Down button. Optionally, use the Cascade Windows option described earlier to get all open program windows down to an in-between size.

Minimize versus Close

Everything that's "in your computer," so to speak, is actually a file on your hard disk. The stuff on your hard disk is always there, whether the computer is on or off. When you open an item, two things happen. The most obvious is that the item becomes visible on the screen. What's not so obvious is the fact that a copy of the program is also loaded in the computer's memory (RAM).

When you minimize an open window, the program is still in memory. The only way you can tell that is by the fact that the program's taskbar button is still on the taskbar. When you want to view that program window, you just click its taskbar to make it visible on the screen again. It shows up looking exactly as it did before you minimized it.

When you close a program, its window and taskbar button both disappear, and the program is also removed from RAM (making room for other things you might want to work with). The only way to get back to the program is to restart it from its icon. However, this new program window will be an entirely new instance of the program, unrelated to how things looked before you closed the program.

FIGURE 2.21

The Restore Down button in a maximized program window.

After the program window is visible but not hogging up the entire screen, you can size it to your liking by dragging any edge or corner. You have to get the tip of the mouse pointer right on the border of the window you want to size, so that the pointer turns to a two-headed arrow, as in Figure 2.22.

FIGURE 2.22

Mouse pointer positioned for sizing a window.

When you see the two-headed arrow, gently hold down the left mouse button without moving the mouse. Once the mouse button is down, drag in the direction you want to size the window. Release the mouse button when the window is the size you want.

You can also size a program window using the keyboard. Again, the program window has to be at some in-between size to start with. And you'll always begin the process from the program window's taskbar button. Here are the steps:

1. If the window is minimized or maximized, right-click its taskbar button and choose Restore. Otherwise, you can skip this step.

2. Right-click the program window's taskbar button and choose Size.

3. Press the navigation keys (←, →, ↑, ↓) until the window (or the border around the window) is the size you want.

4. Press the Enter key.

Moving a program window

You can easily move a program window about the screen just by dragging its title bar. However, you can't start with a maximized or minimized window. You have to get the program window to an in-between size before you even get started. Then just get the mouse pointer somewhere near the top center of the window you want to move, hold down the left mouse button, and drag the window around. Release the mouse button when the window is where you want it on the desktop.

Dialog boxes work the same way. You can't size or minimize a dialog box, and dialog boxes don't have taskbar buttons. But you can easily drag a dialog box around the screen by its title bar.

Moving and sizing from the keyboard

As you've seen, most of the techniques for moving and sizing program windows rely on the mouse. There are some keyboard alternatives, but they're not available in all program windows. The only way to find out if these will work in the window you're using at the moment is to press Alt+Spacebar and see if a system menu drops down from the upper-left corner, as in Figure 2.23.

FIGURE 2.23

System menu from a program window.

If you see the menu, you just have to press the underlined letter from the menu option you want to select. For example, press the letter x to Ma<u>x</u>imize or n to Mi<u>n</u>imize. If you press m to <u>M</u>ove or s to <u>S</u>ize, you can then use the ←, →, ↑, ↓ keys to move or size the window. Then press Enter when the window is positioned or sized to your liking.

Closing a Program

When you've finished using a program for the time being, that's the time to close it. Every open program and document consumes some resources, mostly in the form of using memory (RAM). When RAM is full, the computer has to start using *virtual memory*, which is basically space on the hard disk configured to look like RAM to the computer.

RAM has no moving parts and, thus, can feed stuff to the processor (where all the work takes place) at amazing speeds. A hard disk has moving parts and is much, much slower. As soon as Windows has to start using virtual memory, everything slows down. So, you really don't want to have a bunch of stuff you're not using anymore open and consuming resources.

There are lots of ways to close a program. Use whichever of the following techniques is most convenient for you because they all produce the same result — the program is removed from memory, and both its program window and taskbar button are removed from the screen:

- Click the Close (X) button in the program window's upper-right corner.
- Right-click the title bar across the top of the program window and choose Close.
- Choose File ➪ Exit from the program's menu bar.
- Right-click the program's taskbar button and choose Close.
- If the program is in the active window, press Alt+F4.

If you were working on a document in the program and have made changes to that document since you last saved it, the program will (hopefully) ask whether you want to save those changes in a message box like the example in Figure 2.24.

FIGURE 2.24

Last chance to save a document.

Never take that dialog box lightly, because whichever option you choose is final, and there's no going back and changing your mind. Your options are as follows:

- **Yes:** The document will be saved in its current state; both the document and the program will close.
- **No:** Any and all changes you made to the document since you last saved it will be lost forever. Both the document and the program will close.
- **Cancel:** The program and document will both remain open and on the screen. You can then continue work on the document and save it from the program's menu bar (choose File ➪ Save).

Using the Quick Launch Toolbar

The Quick Launch toolbar is an optional component that provides one-click access to frequently used programs. Exactly which programs you can start from there is entirely up to you. Chapter 11 talks about how you add and remove Quick Launch buttons. For now, let's just talk about how you use the Quick Launch toolbar.

NEW FEATURE Here's a simple way to add a program from the left side of the Start menu, or the All Programs menu, to the Quick Launch toolbar: Right-click the program's startup icon and choose Add To Quick Launch.

If your taskbar doesn't show the Quick Launch toolbar, right-click the clock and choose Toolbars ➪ Quick Launch. (Use the same steps to hide the Quick Launch toolbar if you don't want it on your taskbar.) If there are more buttons on the toolbar than can fit, you'll see a >> symbol at the right side of the toolbar. Click that to see additional Quick Launch icons, like the example in Figure 2.25.

FIGURE 2.25

Quick Launch toolbar.

Each icon on the Quick Launch toolbar represents a program you can run. When you click the icon, the program starts. If you're not sure what an icon represents, just point to the icon for more information.

Using the Notification Area

Over on the right side of the taskbar is the Notification area (also called the *system tray* or *tray*). Each icon in the Notification area represents a program or service that's running in the background. For example, antivirus and anti-spyware programs often show icons in the Notification area so you know they're running.

To conserve space on the taskbar, Windows Vista gives you the option of hiding inactive icons. When inactive icons are hidden, you'll see a button with a < symbol on it at the left side of the Notification area. Click the button to see icons that are currently hidden.

As with any icon or button, you can point to an icon in the Notification area to see the name of that icon. Right-clicking an icon usually provides a context menu of options for using the item. Clicking or double-clicking the icon usually opens a program window that's associated with the running background service.

For example, the Volume icon provides a simple service: it lets you control the volume of your speakers when sound is playing. To change the volume, you click the icon and then drag the slider (shown in Figure 2.26) up or down. Optionally, you can mute the speakers by choosing the button at the bottom of the slider. Click it again to un-mute. The Mixer option opens a window where you can control the volume of different kinds of sounds independently.

FIGURE 2.26

Volume control slider.

Unlike the Quick Launch toolbar, the icons in the Notification area don't represent programs that you *can* run. They represent programs that *are* running. The icon simply serves as a notification that the program is running, although in most cases, the icon will also provide options for closing the program or changing how it runs. Different computers will have different Notification area icons. But some common examples include the following:

- **Network Connections:** When you're online or connected to some other network, you might see an icon that lets you disconnect from the network.

- **Instant Messaging Programs:** If you use Windows Messenger, AOL Instant Messenger, or a similar program, the icon will be visible while you're online.

- **Security programs:** Programs that protect your system from malware (like viruses and spyware) often display icons in the Notification area.

- **Updates:** Notifies when updates are available for downloading or installing.

- **Safely Remove Hardware:** If you have a USB device connected to your computer, the Safely Remove Hardware icon lets you disable the device before removing it, to make sure that it doesn't disconnect while the device is in use.

Showing/hiding notification icons

You can choose for yourself which Notification area icons you do and don't want to see at any time. There's rarely any need to see them all, so you can hide some from yourself just to conserve the taskbar space they would otherwise take up. To make choices about those icons, right-click the clock and choose Customize Notifications. The Customize Notifications dialog box shown in Figure 2.27 opens.

FIGURE 2.27

Customize Notifications dialog box.

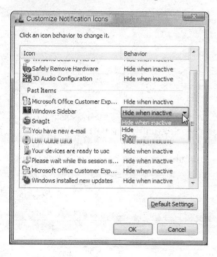

The Customize Notifications dialog box lists items that are currently active, as well as inactive items that were active in the past. You can choose if and how you want to display an icon by clicking the Behavior icon to the right of the item's name. Your options are

- **Hide when inactive:** The icon will be visible only when it's active and serving some purpose.

- **Hide:** The item will always be hidden.

- **Show:** The item will always be visible in the Notification area.

As always, what you choose to show or hide is entirely up to you. Just make your selections and click OK in each of the open dialog boxes.

If you always want all notification area icons to be visible, follow these steps:

1. Right-click the current time in the lower right of the screen and choose Properties.
2. In the Taskbar and Start Menu Properties dialog box that opens, click the Hide Inactive Icons checkbox.
3. Click OK.

Chapter 11 discusses additional techniques for customizing the desktop, taskbar, Quick Launch toolbar, and Notification area.

Responding to notification messages

Icons in the Notification area may occasionally display messages in a speech balloon. Many messages just provide some feedback and don't require any response from you. For example, the message in Figure 2.28 contains a circled letter *I*, indicating that the message is for information only. That kind of message generally fades away on its own after a few seconds. But you could also close the message by clicking the Close (X) button in its upper-right corner.

FIGURE 2.28

An informational notification message.

Messages that show a shield icon, like the one in Figure 2.29, are security related. That message is a fairly common one. Notice that you can click the balloon to "fix the problem." (Actually, that part of the message is a bit misleading. Clicking the balloon doesn't fix anything. It just opens the Security Center where you can get more information.) Optionally, you can right-click the icon and choose Open Security Center to find out more.

FIGURE 2.29

A security warning from the Notification area.

Chapters 7 through 9 discuss security in some depth. For now it's sufficient to note that the message in Figure 2.29 says you *might* not have virus protection. In truth, the message just means that Windows hasn't detected any known virus protection yet. So don't be too alarmed if you see that message and know for a fact that you do have virus protection.

Using scroll bars

Scroll bars appear in program windows whenever there's more information in the window than you can fit. You may not see any on your screen right now. But don't worry about that. The trick is to recognize them when you do see them, to know what they mean, and to know how to work them. Figure 2.30 shows an example of a vertical scroll bar and a horizontal scroll bar.

FIGURE 2.30

Examples of scroll bars.

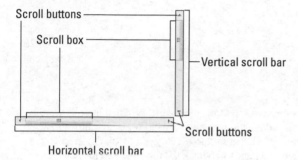

When you see a scroll bar, that means that there's more to see than what's currently visible in the window. The size of the scroll box relative to the size of the scroll bar tells you roughly how much more there is to see. For example, if the scroll bar is about 10% the size of the bar, that means you're only seeing about 10% of all there is to see.

To see the rest, you use the scroll bar to scroll through the information. There are basically three ways to use scroll bars:

- Click a button at the end of the scroll bar to move a little bit in the direction of the arrow on the button.

- Click an empty space on the scroll bar to move the scroll box along the bar toward the place where you clicked. That moves you farther than clicking the buttons would.

- Drag the scroll box in the direction you want to scroll. To drag, place the mouse pointer on the button, and hold down the left mouse button while moving the mouse in the direction you want to scroll.

If your mouse has a wheel, you can use that to scroll as well. If the window shows a vertical scroll bar, spinning the mouse wheel scrolls up and down. If the window shows only a horizontal scroll bar, spinning the mouse wheel scrolls left and right.

You can also use the keyboard to scroll up and down. But understand that they only work in the active window (the window that's on the top of the stack). If necessary, first click the window to bring it to the top of the stack. Then you can use the ↑ and ↓ keys to scroll up and down slightly. Use the Page Up (PgUp) and Page Down (PgDn) keys to scroll up and down in larger increments. Press the Home key to scroll all the way to the top (or all the way to the left). Press the End key to scroll all the way to the end.

Using Back and Forward buttons

Back and Forward buttons help you navigate through multiple pages of items. Like scroll bars, they only appear when useful. So don't expect to see them on your screen right now, or all the time. At times they may be *disabled* (dimmed), as at the top of Figure 2.31. At other times they will be enabled (not dimmed), as at the bottom half of that same figure.

FIGURE 2.31
_____

Back and Forward buttons.

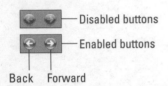

A disabled button isn't broken. You don't have to buy anything to make it work. When an item is disabled, it's just not appropriate at the moment. For example, when you first open a window, both buttons may be disabled because there's no page to switch to. When you click a link that takes you to another page, the Back button will then be enabled, because now there is a page to go back to (the page you just left). Once you go back to the previous page, the Forward button will be enabled because now there is a page to go forward to — the page from which you just backed out.

When a button is enabled, you just click it to go back or forward. When a button is disabled, clicking it has no effect, because there is no page back or forward to go to!

The Welcome Center

The Welcome Center is a program window that might, or might not, appear automatically when you first log in to Windows. It shows information about your computer and provides some links to a few Windows features and some online resources. Figure 2.32 shows an example. Yours might look a little different.

When you click an icon in the lower half of the window, the upper half changes to show you more information. Click the Show more... or See More... link message in the upper half of the window to see more information. To leave the "more information" page and return to where you were, click the Back button in the upper-left corner, or press the Backspace key on your keyboard.

If you don't want the Welcome Center to open automatically each time you log in, clear the checkmark next to Run at startup in the lower-left corner of the window. (Click the checkmark to clear the checkbox.)

If you don't see the Welcome Center, but want to, click the Start button, type `wel`, and then click Welcome Center on the Start menu. If you want it to open automatically each time you start your computer, click the empty checkbox next to Run at startup to select that option.

You can maximize, minimize, restore, move, size, and close the Welcome Center window as you can any open window. See the sections on sizing, arranging, moving, and closing program windows earlier in this chapter for more information.

FIGURE 2.32

The Welcome Center.

Quick Help for Getting Started

If you're new to computers, the Windows Basics item in the Welcome Center provides a quick overview of basic skills and concepts. If you don't see the Windows Basics icon, click Show all 14 items in the top half of the window. Then click the Windows Basics icon and click Open Windows Basics in the top half of the program window. Optionally, on most systems you can click the Start button and choose Help and Support. Click the box that shows *Search Help*, type basics, and press Enter. Then click Windows Basics: All Topics. Either way you should end up in a window that looks like the example shown in Figure 2.33.

Each short chunk of blue text is a link that takes you to a help topic. Click any link to see that topic. You'll need to use the scroll bar in many pages to scroll up and down through all the text. You can use the Back and Forward buttons, when enabled, to scroll through pages you've already visited. Using the help in this manner will give you some practice with skills you've learned in this chapter. And at the same time, it will help you reinforce what you already know, and teach you some new things you haven't learned yet.

To leave the Help window, just close it (click the Close [X] button in its upper-right corner). See Chapter 5 for more information on using the Help system.

TIP You'll often see a little blue button with a white question mark in program windows. That's the Help button. You can click it for information. You can also press the Help key (F1) on your keyboard at any time for help.

FIGURE 2.33

Windows Basics help.

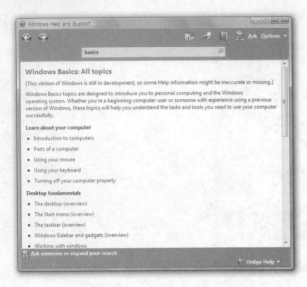

Logging Off, Shutting Down

Here's a question a lot of people ask: "Should I shut down my computer if I won't be using it for a while, or should I just leave it on?" Everybody has an opinion about this. So here's mine: It doesn't matter. Personally, about the only time I ever shut down my computers is when I need to, such as when installing certain types of hardware. Aside from that, all my computers are on, and online, 24 hours a day, 7 days a week.

I've built, worked the daylights out of, and then thrown away dozens of computers after they've served their purpose and better technology came along. Not a one ever broke down before it had served its purpose. So, I'd have to say that not one ever suffered from being left on too long, or shut down too often.

The Lock and Shut Down buttons on the Start menu are shown back in Figures 2.7 and 2.8. Understand that turning off a PC isn't quite the same as turning off a TV or radio. You don't want to just hit the main power switch to shut down while you have things open on the desktop. You want to close everything first. Then click the Start button and do one of the following:

- Click the right side of the Lock button and choose Shut Down from the menu that appears.
- Click the Off button to the left of the lock button (Figure 2.8) to power down the computer.

Don't expect the computer to turn off immediately. It takes a few seconds for Windows to get everything closed up and ready to shut down. On most computers, you don't have to do anything else. The computer will eventually shut itself down completely. Some older computers may show a message stating "It is now safe to shut down your computer." If you see that message, you need to hold in the main power button on your computer for a few seconds to finish shutting down the system.

Stuff You Can Do with a Computer

There's so much you can do with Windows Vista and your computer, I hardly know where to start. So I'll just throw some ideas out there, and point you to the chapter where that topic is discussed. Of course, you can get much more detailed information about the contents of this book from the Table of Contents up front. And you can look things up in the Index at the back of the book. For the folks who are just getting started and don't know quite what to do next, here are some quick suggestions:

- Set up parental controls: Chapters 3 and 4
- Get help: Chapter 5
- Personalize the screen to your own style: Chapter 11
- Dictate text: Chapter 12
- Do some basic math with Windows Calculator: Chapter 15
- Type letters and other text with WordPad: Chapter 15
- Create and share appointments with Windows Calendar: Chapter 15
- Use Web sites like eBay and Google: Chapter 17
- Do e-mail: Chapter 19
- Manage names and addresses: Chapter 20
- Organize, fix, and print photos: Chapter 22
- Collect music and make your own CDs: Chapter 23
- Make your own movies from home videos: Chapter 25

The terms and skills you've learned in this chapter should be enough to get you started on whichever topic looks most interesting. You will need an Internet connection for e-mail and the Web. But you should be able to do everything else using just Windows Vista. You don't need to buy extra programs to do those things.

Wrap Up

So that about wraps it up for the main terminology and basic skills. Much of what you've learned in this chapter is the kind of stuff most people assume you already know. You may have to read the chapter a few times, and practice things, before it all sinks in. Use the Windows Basics help I mentioned for more information and for hands-on practice.

Here's a quick summary of the most important points covered in this chapter:

- The Windows desktop is where you'll do all your work.
- You'll use your mouse and keyboard to operate the computer.
- Most of your work will involve opening and using programs.
- You can start any program that's installed on your computer from the All Programs menu.
- Each open program will appear in its own program window on the desktop. Program windows stack up like sheets of paper.
- Each open program window has a corresponding taskbar button. The taskbar buttons help you switch from one open program window to another.

- You can move and size program windows to see exactly what you need to see, when you need to see it.

- When you've finished using your computer and want to shut it down, don't go straight for the main power switch. Instead, click the Start button and then click the Shut Down button on the Start menu.

That's enough for now about the desktop and programs. These days, with just about everyone using their computers to access the Internet, security is a major issue. So that topic is addressed starting in Chapter 3 with a discussion of user accounts and how they relate to computer security.

Chapter 3

Sharing and Securing with User Accounts

Every person who uses your computer is called a *user*. When two or more people share a single computer, you can set up a *user account* for each person. Giving each person a user account is a lot like giving each person their own separate PC, but a lot cheaper. Each user can personalize the desktop and other settings to their liking. Each person can have his or her own separate collection of pictures, music, videos, and other documents. Each user can also set up his or her own separate e-mail account.

User accounts allow parents to create and enforce parental controls in Windows Vista. This is a great boon to parents who can't always monitor when and how children use the computer. Parental controls allow you to control and monitor children's computer use 24 hours a day, 365 days a year, even when you're not around to do it yourself.

User accounts also add a level of security to your computer. Many security breaches occur not because of a problem with the computer or Windows. Rather, they occur because the user is in an account that grants malware (bad software) *permission* to do its evil deeds. Of course people don't realize they're granting permission, because the program doesn't ask for permission. It gets its permission, automatically, from the type of user account into which you're currently logged.

Creating and managing user accounts is easy. But before getting into the specifics of all that, let's take a look at how you, as a user, experience user accounts.

Logging In and Out of User Accounts

If you already have multiple user accounts on your computer, you see an icon for each one shortly after you first start your computer. Figure 3.1 shows an example of some icons that represent user accounts.

FIGURE 3.1

Sample user account icons.

To log in to an account, click its picture. If the user account is password-protected, you must also enter the password that protects that account from unauthorized entry.

Where am I now?

To see the name of the user account into which you're currently logged, click the Start button. The name at the top-right side of the Start menu is the name of the user account into which you're currently logged. In Figure 3.2, that user account name is Alan. But it could be anything on your computer. If Windows Vista came pre-installed on your computer, it might be a generic name like Owner or User.

FIGURE 3.2

User name on the Start menu.

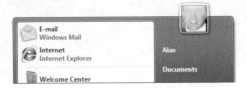

Logging out of an account

There are a few different ways to switch from the account into which you're currently logged to another account (assuming there is more than one user account on your computer already). The first step is to click the Start button, then click the arrow next to the lock, as in Figure 3.3. The first three items have to do with the user account into which you're currently logged:

Why Switch User Can Be Bad

When you use Switch User, rather than Log Off, to leave your account, all the programs and documents on your desktop remain open and in memory. This leaves less working memory for other users in their accounts.

If multiple users consistently use Switch User to leave their accounts, you end up with lots of people's stuff in memory all the time. The likely result is that the entire computer will run much slower for everyone. Furthermore, the whole system is more likely to crash, especially if you use older programs that were created before the advent of user accounts in Windows.

Ideally, every user should log off from their account when they've finished using the computer. If you find that other users won't stay with that plan, and the computer is often running slower than molasses in Antarctica, you can disable the Switch User option.

FIGURE 3.3

Logging out options.

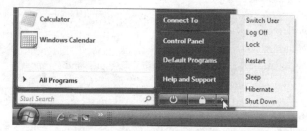

- **Switch User:** Lets you go to another user account without losing your place in the current user account. This is fine for temporarily using another account to perform a simple task (like checking e-mail).

- **Log Off:** This option closes all open programs and gives you the opportunity to save any unsaved work. Use this option when you plan to be away from the computer for a while.

- **Lock:** If your user account is password-protected, use this option to hide what's on your screen and keep other people from using the computer under your user account. When you log back in, you'll be right back where you left the computer.

If your user account isn't password-protected, then other people aren't really locked out of your account. Anyone can come along, click your user account name, and be at your desktop.

Creating Strong Passwords

I'll talk about techniques for creating, managing, and password-protecting user accounts in a moment. But before I get into the details, I think it might be worthwhile to talk about passwords in general. Not just passwords for user accounts, but for all types of accounts you create, including online accounts.

A password that's easily guessed is a weak password. A strong password is one that's not easily guessed, and is also immune to *password-guessing attacks*. The two most common forms of password-guessing attacks are the *dictionary attack* and the *brute force attack*. Both types of attacks rely on special programs that are specifically designed to try to crack people's passwords and gain unauthorized entry to their user accounts.

The dictionary attack tries many thousands of passwords from a dictionary of English terms and commonly used passwords. The brute force attack tries thousands of combinations of characters until it finds the right combination of characters needed to get into the account.

Admittedly, both types of attacks are rare in a home PC environment. They're also easily frustrated by common techniques like forcing the user to wait several minutes before trying again after three failed password attempts. But nonetheless, the general guidelines used to protect top-secret data from password-guessing attacks can be applied to any password you create. A strong password is one that meets at least some of the following criteria:

- It is at least eight characters long.
- It does not contain your real name, user account name, pet names, or any name that's easily guessed by other family members or work cohorts.
- It does not contain a word that can be found in a dictionary.
- It contains some combination of uppercase letters, lowercase letters, numeric digits, and symbols (like !, &, ?, @, or #).

Again, I realize that few of us need Fort Knox security on our personal PCs. You don't want to come up with a password that's difficult to remember and a pain to type. But any steps you take to make the password less susceptible to guessing are well worth some effort. Some Web sites offer password checkers, programs that analyze a password and tell you how strong it is. See `www.microsoft.com/athome/security/privacy/password_checker.mspx` for an example. Or go to any search engine, like `www.google.com`, and search for *password checker*.

Remembering passwords

The most common problem with passwords is forgetting them after the fact. When you set up a password for a Web site, you can usually find out what it is just by clicking an "I forgot my password" link at the sign-in page. But there is no such link for passwords that protect your Windows user accounts. Therefore, it's extremely important that you *not* forget your Windows passwords!

Before you even think about password-protecting a user account, you should write the password down on a sheet of paper. Make sure you use exactly the same uppercase and lowercase letters that you'll be typing. All passwords are always case-sensitive, which means uppercase and lowercase letters count big time!

For example, let's say you jot down your password as `tee4me!0` (where that last digit is a zero). But later you type it in as `Tee4Me!o` (with the last digit being the letter "o"). Still later you forget the password and dig out the sheet of paper. The `tee4me!0` you wrote down won't work, because the password is actually `Tee4Me!o`.

> **CAUTION** On a typewriter, the number 0 is basically the same as an uppercase letter "O." The number 1 is basically the same as a lowercase letter "l." But that is *not* true of computers. You must use the 1 and 0 keys near the top of the keyboard or on the numeric keypad to type 1 (one) and 0 (zero).

Devising a password hint

With Windows passwords, you can also specify a password hint to help you remember a forgotten password. But still, it's tricky. Anyone who uses your computer can see the password hint. So the hint can't be so obvious that it tells a potential intruder what the password is.

By the same token, the hint might trigger your basic memory of the password. But perhaps not the exact uppercase and lowercase letters you used. So you need to have that written-down password handy in case of an emergency. Of course, that written-down password won't do you any good if you can't find it when you need it. And it won't offer much protection is it's in plain sight where anyone can see it either.

So the bottom line on remembering and jotting down passwords is simple: There is no margin for error. A password that's "sorta like" the one you specified is not good enough. It must be *exactly* like the one you specified. You must treat passwords as though they are valuable diamonds. Keep them safe, keep them secure. But don't keep them so safe that even *you* can't find them!

Okay, that's enough general advice about passwords. Next we need to talk about types of user accounts.

Types of User Accounts

Windows Vista offers four basic types of user accounts, the built-in Administrator account, user accounts with administrative privileges, standard accounts, and a Guest account. They vary in how much privilege they grant to the person using the account.

The built-in Administrator account

There is a single user account named Administrator built into Windows Vista. This is not the same as an administrative account you create yourself or see on the login screen. This account is hidden from normal view. It doesn't show up on the usual login screen.

The built-in Administrator account has unlimited computer privileges. So while you're logged in to that account you can do anything and everything you want with the computer. Any programs you run while you are in that account can also do anything they want. That makes the account risky from a security standpoint, and very unwise to use unless absolutely necessary.

In high-security professional settings, a new computer usually goes straight to a highly trained and certified network or security administrator who logs in to the Administrator account to set up the computer for other users. There the administrator configures accounts on the *principle of least privilege*, where each account is given only as much privilege as necessary to perform a specific job.

The administrator also sets up a user account for himself. That account also has just enough privilege to do day-to-day computer tasks. Once the administrator is finished, he typically renames the built-in Administrator account, and password-protects it, to keep everyone else out. The account is always hidden from view, except from other administrators who know how to find it. All of this is standard operating procedure in secure computing environments, though hardly the norm in home computing.

In Windows Vista, there's really no need for you to find, log in to, and use the built-in Administrator account unless you're an advanced user with a specific need, in which case you can get to it through Safe Mode. As a regular home user, you can do everything you need to do from a regular user account that has administrative privileges.

NOTE Experienced users who need access to the built-in Administrator account can get to it through Safe Mode. I talk about that in Chapter 14. But if you're not a professional, I suggest you stay away from that and use an administrative account, discussed next.

Administrative user accounts

Most of the time when you hear reference to an administrator account in Windows Vista, they're talking about a regular user account that has administrative privileges. This is an account that has virtually all the power and privilege of the built-in Administrator account. But it also has a lot of security built in to help thwart security threats that might otherwise abuse its privileges to do harm to your computer.

Ideally, you want to create one user account with administrative privileges on your computer. If you intend to implement parental controls, you'll need to password-protect that account to keep children from disabling or changing parental controls.

Standard accounts

A standard user account is the kind of account everyone should use for day-to-day computer use. It has enough privilege to do day-to-day things like run programs, work with documents, do e-mail, and browse the Web. It doesn't have enough privilege to make changes to the system that would affect other people's user accounts. It doesn't have enough privilege to allow children to override parental controls. And most importantly, it doesn't have enough privilege to let malware like viruses and worms make harmful changes to your system.

If you use a standard account all of the time, and use a built-in administrative account only when absolutely necessary, you'll go a long way toward keeping your computer safe from Internet security threats.

Guest account

The optional Guest account is there to allow people who don't regularly use your computer to use it temporarily. Basically it will let them check their e-mail, browse the Web, maybe play some games. But it definitely won't let them make changes to your user account or anyone else's. And its limited privileges also help protect your system from any malicious software they might pick up while online.

Creating and Managing User Accounts

The best way to handle user accounts is for one person to play the role of administrator, even if that person isn't a professional. In a home environment, it would most likely be a parent who needs to define parental controls. It's best to log in to a user account that already has administrative privileges to get started. If you only have one user account, or are taken straight to the desktop at startup, then that account probably has administrative privileges.

Like most configuration tasks, you create and manage user accounts through the Control Panel. And like most tasks, there are several pages you can use, and several ways to get to them. As always, there is no right way or wrong way. No good way or bad way. You just use whatever is easiest and most convenient for you at the moment. Here are a couple of ways to get to options for managing the user account you're logged in to at the moment:

- Press ⊞, type `user` in the search box, and click User Accounts.
- Click the Start button, choose Control Panel, click User Accounts and Family Safety, and then click User Accounts.

You are taken to a page that lets you make changes to the account into which you're currently logged, as in the example shown in Figure 3.4. Options marked with shield icons require administrative privileges. (Not from the built-in user account, but from a regular user account with administrative privileges.)

FIGURE 3.4

The User Accounts control panel.

To create a new user account, click Manage another account. If you're in an administrative account, you'll have to click the Continue button to proceed. If you're in a standard account on a computer that already has a password-protected administrative account, you'll have to enter the password for the Administrator account. Or, if the administrative account doesn't have a password, press Enter to leave the password box empty. You end up in the Manage Accounts page. There you see an icon for every user account on your system. You can also tell the type of each account. Figure 3.5 shows an example where I've already created one password-protected administrative account named Admin. The rest are standard user accounts. You'll use that page to create and manage user accounts on your own computer.

FIGURE 3.5

Manage Accounts page.

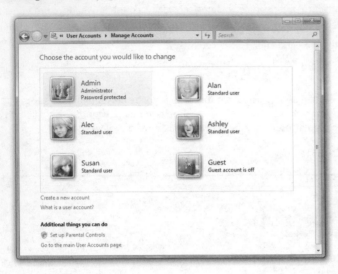

Creating a user account

Creating a new user account is easy. Ideally, you want one password-protected user account. Then you want one standard account for your day-to-day computing, plus one standard account for every other person who will use your computer.

Keep in mind that each user account has its own collection of files. If you've been using your administrative account for a while, you may not want to create a new standard account from scratch. Better to create a new administrative account from scratch, then change your current account from an administrative account to a standard account. That way you won't have to move files from your current account to the new account.

To create a new user account, click Create a new account to get to the page shown in Figure 3.6.

Type in a name for the user account. If you're creating a new administrative account, consider naming it Admin or something like that. You can't use the name Administrator because that name is already taken by the built-in administrative account. If you're creating a new standard account for yourself or a family member, use the person's first name as the account name.

After you've typed the account name, choose Standard user to create a standard user account. Or choose Administrator to create a user account that has administrative privileges. Then click Create Account to create the user account. You're returned to the previous Manage User Accounts page where you see that the new user account has been added to the system.

You can repeat the process to create as many user accounts as you wish.

FIGURE 3.6

Create a new user account.

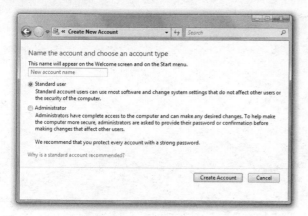

Changing user accounts

When you create a user account, you're just giving it a name and choosing a type. After you've created a user account, you can change it to better suit your needs. Use the Manage User Accounts page shown back in Figure 3.5 to make changes to accounts.

CAUTION When you delete a user account, you might also delete all the files in that account if you're not careful. Deleting is serious business. Read the section titled "Deleting User Accounts" later in this chapter before you delete an account.

Changing a user account type

You can change an Administrator account to a standard account, or vice versa, from the main user accounts page. For example, if you've been using an administrative account for your day-to-day computing since buying your computer, you might want to change it to a standard account for the added security a standard account provides. At least one user account must have administrative privileges, so you can only do this if there is at least one other user account on the system that has administrative privileges.

To change an account's type, click the account icon or name in the Manage Accounts page. First you're taken to the Change an Account page. As you can see in Figure 3.7, that page lets you change the account in a number of ways, or even delete the account.

Click Change the account type to change the account from an administrative account to a standard account, or vice versa. To change the account type, click Change the account type. You're taken to the Change Account Type page. Click the type of account you want this user account to be, and then click Change Account Type.

FIGURE 3.7

Change an Account page.

Password-protecting an account

If you share your computer with other people, chances are you'll want to keep some people out of the Administrator account. Likewise, you'll want to keep some users from having administrative privileges. This is especially important with parental controls. If the administrative account isn't password-protected, then it won't take long for the kids to figure out how to bypass any controls you impose.

Password-protecting an account is easy enough. Just remember, you do *not* want to forget the password you impose. Otherwise, nobody will have administrative privileges, and that will cause a world of headaches. So think up a good password and password hint. And write the password down on a piece of paper *before* you password-protect the account.

To password-protect a user account, get to the main page for the user account. For instance, if you're in the Manage Accounts page, click the user account you want to password-protect. Then click Create a password. You're taken to a page like the one in Figure 3.8. If you've been using the account for a while without a password, heed the warnings. If it's a brand-new account, then you don't have anything to worry about.

To password-protect the account, type your password in the New Password box. Then press Tab or click the second box and type the same password again. You won't see the characters you type, just a placeholder for each character. Typing passwords always works that way to prevent *shoulder surfing*. Shoulder surfing is a simple technique for discovering someone's password just by watching over their shoulder as they type it on the screen.

Then type in your password hint. The hint should be something that reminds you of the forgotten password, but not a dead giveaway to someone trying to break into the account. Click Create Password after you've filled in all the blanks.

If you see a message indicating that your passwords don't match, you'll have to retype both passwords. Make sure you type the password exactly as you wrote it down in both boxes. Then click the Change Password button again. You'll be taken back to the main page for the user account when you've successfully entered the password in both boxes and provided a password hint.

FIGURE 3.8

Password-protecting an account.

You can repeat the process to password-protect as many accounts as you wish. If you're creating user accounts for people other than yourself, it's best not to password-protect their accounts. Let those other users decide for themselves whether or not they want to password-protect their accounts. And let them create and manage their own passwords.

Changing the account picture

Every user account has an associated picture. The picture is like an icon, giving you a quick visual reference without having to read the name. The picture you choose can be any one of several built-in pictures, or it can be a picture of your own choosing.

If you decide to use your own picture, try to avoid using one that comes straight from a digital camera. The file size on such pictures is really too large for a user account picture. You want the picture you choose to be perfectly square so it doesn't get distorted. Your best bet would be to crop out a perfect square from a photo, and size it to about 100 x 100 pixels. The picture you choose must be the JPEG, BMP, PNG, GIF, or PNG file type.

TIP If you don't know enough about pictures to meet all the requirements, you can use built-in pictures. Then after you've acquired some of the skills covered in Chapter 22, you can create a suitable user account picture and apply it to any user account.

To change the picture for a user account, get to the main page for that user account and click Change the picture (or Change my picture, depending on how you got there). Then:

- To use a built-in picture, click the picture you want and click the Change Picture button.
- To use a custom picture, click Browse for more pictures and navigate to the folder that contains your custom user account pictures as in the example shown in Figure 3.9. Then click (or double-click) the picture you want to use.

FIGURE 3.9

Changing a user account picture.

The picture you selected replaces the original picture.

Changing the account name

The account name is the name that appears on the login screen and at the top of the Start menu when you're logged in to an account. If you inadvertently misspelled the name when you first created the account, you may want to change the name to correct that misspelling. Or, if an account has a generic name like Owner, you might want to change it to a more personal name. But other than that, there wouldn't really be any need to change an account.

To change an account name, just get to the main page for the user account. Click the Change name link, type the new name, and click the Change Name button.

Enabling or disabling the Guest account

The Guest account is for anybody who might need to use your computer on a temporary basis. For example, with a home computer, you might set up a Guest account for a temporary house guest. Then let that person use the Guest account to check their e-mail, browse the Web, and such. The Guest account has very limited privileges, so you don't have to worry about them messing things up while using your computer.

The Guest account is turned off by default. You can keep it that way until there's actually a need for it. To activate the Guest account, go to the Manage Accounts page and click the Guest account icon. Then choose Turn On. Likewise, should you ever need to disable the Guest account in the future, click its icon on the Manage Accounts page, then click Turn off the guest account.

Navigating through user account pages

As you can see, it's pretty easy to create and manage user accounts. It's largely just a matter of choosing options and reading text that's right on the screen. Remember, any blue text you see is a link, meaning you can click it. You can use the Back and Forward buttons to get around from page to page. On most pages you can click the Manage another account link to get to the Manage Accounts page. You can also use the Address bar at the top of the window to get around. Click any name in the Address bar to jump to that page. Or click the arrow between any two page names, or to the left of the page names (like in Figure 3.10) to get to other pages.

FIGURE 3.10

Use the Address bar to get around.

Creating a Password Reset Disk

A password reset disk is an important part of any password-protected PC. It's the only method of password recovery that allows you to retain all data in an account in the event of a forgotten password. Advanced features like EFS encryption, personal certificates, and stored network passwords can only be recovered using a password reset disk.

The main trick is to create the password reset disk *before* you forget the password. You can't do it after you've forgotten the password. Keep that disk in a safe place where you can find it when you need it, but where others can't find it to gain unauthorized access to the administrative account.

Jump Drive? Memory Card? Huh?

A *jump drive* (also called a *USB flash drive*) is a small device that plugs into a USB port on your computer, and looks and acts like a disk drive. A memory card is a storage device commonly used to store pictures in digital cameras. If your computer has slots for such cards, you can slide a card into the slot and treat the card just as you would a floppy disk. See Chapter 28 for more information.

To see examples and get an idea of costs, check out some online retailers. For example, you might go to www.tigerdirect.com, www.cdw.com, www.froogle.com, www.newgg.com, www.staples.com, or www.walmart.com. Then search the site for jump drive or memory card reader to view available products. If you're looking at memory card readers, the kind that plugs into a USB will be the easiest to install.

Your best bet would be to use a floppy disk for the password disk. If your computer doesn't have a floppy disk drive, you can use a jump drive or memory card instead. However, a memory card will only work if your computer has slots for inserting a memory card.

To create a password reset disk, log in to the password-protected administrative account you created. Then insert a blank floppy disk in the floppy drive. Or connect a jump drive to a USB port, or put a spare memory card in a memory card slot. Then get to the main User Accounts page. If you've already closed the user account window, press ⊞, type user, and click User Accounts on the Start menu. Or go through the Control Panel (click the **Start** button, and choose Control Panel ➪ User Accounts and Family Safety ➪ User Accounts). Then follow these steps:

1. In the left column click Create a password reset disk.
2. Read the first page of the wizard that opens and click Next.
3. Choose the drive into which you inserted the floppy, or the drive letter that represents the jump drive or memory card, then click Next.
4. Type the password for the administrative account into which you're currently logged and click Next.
5. When the progress indicator is finished, click Next, then Finish.

Keep the disk (or drive, or card) in a safe place. If you use a jump drive that you also use for other purposes, make sure you don't erase the userkey.psw file. That's the file needed for password recovery.

Using the password reset disk

If you ever need to use the disk (or drive, or card) to get into the administrative account, first start the computer and click the administrative account for which you created the password reset disk. Take a best guess at the password and press Enter.

If the password is rejected, insert the floppy disk, jump drive, or memory card you created as a password reset disk. Wait a few seconds for Windows to recognize and register the item. Then click Reset password under the password hint on the login screen.

Follow the instructions presented by the wizard that opens. You won't be required to remember the original password. Instead you'll create an entirely new password and hint for the account. Use that new password whenever you log in to the account from that point on.

Cracking into standard user accounts

If a standard user forgets their password, you can use an account that has administrative privileges to get the standard user back into their account. If you're an administrator and just want to see what a standard user is up to, you can use this same technique to remove the password from the account and have full access to its folders.

 **CAUTION** This approach will cause the standard user to lose access to encrypted files and e-mail messages. If the standard user is advanced enough to use those things, better to use a password reset disk to gain access to the account.

To remove the password from a standard user account:

1. Log in to a user account that has administrative privileges.

2. Get to the Manage Accounts page (click the Start button and choose Control Panel ⇨ Add or Remove User Accounts).

3. Click the password-protected account for which the user has forgotten the password.

4. Click Remove password, then click the Remove Password button.

The standard user account will no longer be password-protected. Anybody can log in to that account from the login page just by clicking the user's account icon.

Deleting User Accounts

An administrator can easily delete user accounts. If nobody has ever used a user account, then deleting the account is no big deal. But if anybody has used the account, there is much to consider before deleting it because when you delete the user account, you also delete all e-mail messages, the e-mail account, and Internet favorites. You could also delete all of that user's saved files if you're not careful. Doing this by accident would be a disaster, because there's no way to undo the deletion. So just to make sure nobody misses this important point, here's a caution:

CAUTION Deleting a user account can have very serious consequences. Don't do it unless you fully understand the ramifications.

If you want to save the user's e-mail messages and Internet favorites, export them to that user's Documents folder first. How you export depends on the programs you use for e-mail and Web browsing. If those programs are Windows Mail and Internet Explorer, you can use the techniques described in Chapters 17 and 18 to export.

So let's assume you understand the consequences and have no intention of deleting an account just for the heck of it. Only administrators can delete user accounts. So if you're in a standard account, you at least need to know the administrative password to delete a user account. You'll also need to log in to any account except the one you intend to delete. Then:

1. Click the Start button, choose Control Panel, and click Add or remove user accounts.

2. If prompted, enter an administrative password.

3. Click the account you want to delete.

4. Click Delete the account and read what the message is telling. Then click one of the following buttons:

   - Delete files: Click this button only if you intend to delete *everything* associated with the account, including all files that the user has created and saved.

   - Keep files: Click this option to save the user's files. You will still lose the user's saved e-mail messages, Internet favorites, and user account.

5. Read the next page to make sure you understand the consequences of your choice. Then click Cancel if you change your mind, or click Delete Account if you're sure you know what you're doing.

If you choose Delete Account, the user's account will no longer exist. If you choose Keep Files, the user's saved files will be in a folder on the desktop. That folder will have the same name as the user account you just deleted. Otherwise, nothing of the user's account, not even his saved files, will remain. (If you choose Cancel in step 5, the entire account remains intact and unchanged.)

If you create a new user account with the same name as the one you just deleted, the new account is still an entirely new account. It will not inherit any files or settings from the account you previously deleted.

Using User Accounts

As mentioned at the start of this chapter, each user account is like its own separate PC. Every user has his or her private Documents, Pictures, Music, and Video folders for storing files. Each user account can have its own e-mail account and Internet favorites. Each user can customize the desktop, Start menu, and other settings to their own liking.

When you first start your computer, or log out of your user account, you see a name and icon for each available user account. If you click a user account that isn't password-protected, you're taken straight into the account. But if you click the icon for a password-protected account, a password prompt appears as in Figure 3.11.

FIGURE 3.11

Log in to a password-protected account.

To get into the account, you need to enter the appropriate password. Entering the wrong password just displays the password hint and gives you another shot at entering the correct password. You can't get into the user account until you've entered the correct password for the account.

The first time you (or someone else) log in to a new user account, it's just like starting Windows Vista on a brand-new PC. The desktop has the default appearance. All of the document folders in the account are empty. There is no e-mail account, no Internet favorites. To use e-mail, the user (or administrator) needs to set up the account with an e-mail account, preferably an account used only by that user.

The user does have access to all the programs installed on the computer. (Except for rare cases where someone installed a program for personal use only.) The user will likely have Internet connectivity through the same modem or network as all other user accounts.

If the user account is a standard account, there are some limitations to what the user can do. Basically, the user cannot make any changes to the system that would affect other users. That's where Vista's User Account Control (UAC) security comes into play.

NEW FEATURE   Vista is the first Windows version to employ User Account Control (UAC) as a security measure.

Understanding User Account Control (UAC)

User Account Control (UAC) is the general term for the way administrative and standard user accounts work in Windows Vista. As you browse around through various pages in the Control Panel, you'll notice that many links have a shield next to them. For example, if you click the Start button, choose Control Panel, and click User Accounts and Family Safety, you'll see the options shown in Figure 3.12.

FIGURE 3.12

User accounts and family safety.

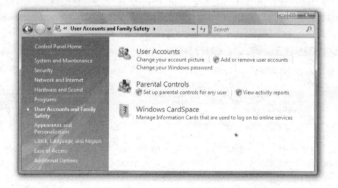

Items that have a shield next to them require administrative approval. Items without a shield don't. For example, any user can change their Windows password, with or without administrative approval. You can tell just by the fact that there's no shield next to the Change your Windows password link.

Options that do have a shield next to them require administrative approval. But you don't necessarily need to be logged in to an administrative account to use those options. You just have to prove that you have administrative privileges. You do that by entering the password for an administrative account. When you click a shielded option, you see a dialog box similar to the one in Figure 3.13. To prove you have administrative privileges on this computer, just enter the password for the administrative user account and click Submit (or OK in some dialog boxes).

FIGURE 3.13

User Account Control dialog box.

Of course, when someone who doesn't know the administrative account password encounters the User Account Control dialog box, they're stuck. They can't go any further because they don't know the appropriate password. This prevents the standard user from doing things that might affect the overall system and other people's user accounts. It also prevents children from overriding parental controls. You'll learn how to set up parental controls in Chapter 4.

Privilege escalation in administrative accounts

If you happen to be logged in to an administrative account when you click a shielded option, you don't need to enter an administrative password. After all, if you're in an administrative account, you must already know the password required to get into that account. There's no need to prove you know that password again. But, you'll still see a prompt telling you that the program you're about to run makes changes to the system, like the example in Figure 3.14. You have to click Continue to proceed.

It might seem odd (and irritating) that you still have to click something to get to the item you clicked. But it works that way for a reason. The dialog box lets you know that the program you're about to run makes changes to the overall system. You expect to see that dialog box after you click a shielded option. And with time and experience you'll learn to expect it when you do other things that affect the system as a whole, like when you install new programs.

There are times when you don't expect to see it. For example, when opening an e-mail attachment, you wouldn't normally expect to see that message. After all, opening an e-mail attachment should just show you the contents of the attachment, not make a change to the system as a whole. Seeing the warning in that context lets you know something fishy is going on, most likely something bad in the e-mail attachment. You can click Cancel to *not* open the attachment, thereby protecting your system from whatever virus or other bad thing lies hidden within the e-mail attachment.

FIGURE 3.14

Status-checking prompt.

 See Chapter 8 for the full story on protecting your system from viruses and other malicious software.

On a more technical note, UAC operates on a principle of least privilege, whereby all users run with a limited set of privileges. When you're in an administrative account, you actually run with the same privileges as a standard user. This is done to protect your system from malware that would otherwise exploit the privileges of your administrative account to make malicious changes to your system.

When you enter a password or click Continue in response to a UAC prompt, you temporarily *elevate* your privileges to allow that one change to be made. Once that change is made, you're back to your more secure standard user privileges. Even though this is definitely something new in Vista, it's nothing new in the larger scheme of things. This is how things have been done in high-security settings for years, and is considered a security *best practice*. If at all possible, you should follow suit and keep UAC active on your own computer. But if it proves to be impractical, you can turn off UAC.

Turning UAC on and off

User Account Control (UAC) is not going to be a particularly popular Vista feature. After all, nobody wants a feature that makes them do more work, even when the extra work is nothing more than an occasional extra mouse click. Furthermore, there are times when UAC is just impractical. For example, if you give your kids standard user accounts, they can't install their own programs. But if you give them administrative accounts, you can't institute parental controls. In such situations, turning off UAC might be your best and safest bet.

Before you turn off UAC, I recommend that you first ensure that all of the other security measures discussed in Part II of this book are installed and working on your PC. UAC is just one component of an overall security strategy. The more components you have on and working, the better.

Turning off UAC is a simple process. Get to the main User Accounts control panel. From the desktop, press ⊞, type user, and click User Accounts. Or click the Start button and choose Control Panel ➪ User Accounts and Family Safety ➪ User Accounts. You'll see a shielded option titled Turn User Account Control on or off. Click that and then click Continue or enter an administrative password to get to the page shown in Figure 3.15.

To turn User Account Control off, clear the checkbox. Or, if it was already off and you want better security, select (check) the checkbox. Then click OK. You'll be prompted to restart the computer. You can click Restart Now to activate the change on reboot. Or, click Restart Later to if you need to save any work before proceeding.

FIGURE 3.15

Turn User Account Control on or off.

When the computer restarts, things will still look the same. But when you click a shielded option there will be no prompting for credentials or status checking. Things will basically be like they were in Windows XP and other earlier versions of Windows.

You can still institute parental controls, provided you have one password-protected administrative account and each child has a standard account. (Assuming, too, that the kids don't know the password to the administrative account.) When a child tries to change or deactivate parental controls, a message box will appear telling them they don't have sufficient privileges. To change parental controls, you'll need to log in to the password-protected administrative account.

One other side effect will be little reminder messages, like the example shown in Figure 3.16, popping up from the Notification area. It's just a reminder for people who may have turned off UAC by mistake. You don't have to do what the prompt says to "fix" the problem. You can click the Close (X) box in the message to make it go away.

FIGURE 3.16

Reminder when UAC is turned off.

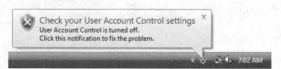

 **For more advanced information and other ways to control UAC, go to** www.live.com **or** http://search.microsoft.com **and search for** Vista UAC.

Running Programs as Administrator

Most newer programs work with UAC's privilege escalation on-the-fly. But there will be times when that won't work, especially with older programs. You can run any program with administrative privileges by right-clicking its startup icon and choosing Run as administrator as in the example shown in Figure 3.17.

FIGURE 3.17

Run a program as administrator.

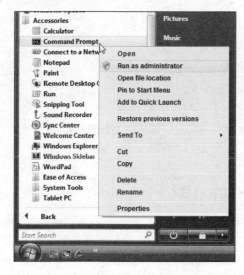

The same method works for programs that you can't launch from the Start menu. Use Windows Explorer to get to the folder that contains the executable file for the program. Then right-click the filename and choose Run as administrator.

You can make older programs that aren't part of Windows Vista run with elevated privileges automatically by changing program compatibility settings. Right-click the startup icon for the program, or the executable file's icon, and choose Properties. In the Properties dialog box, click the Compatibility tab. Then under Privilege Level, select Run this program as an administrator and click OK.

If the option to run the program as an administrator is disabled, then either the program doesn't require administrative privileges to run, you are not logged in to an administrative account, or the program is blocked from always running elevated.

Add the Built-in Administrator Account to the Login Screen

The built-in Administrator account is intentionally hidden to keep out users who don't have sufficient knowledge to understand the risks involved in using such an account. Typically the only way to get to it is by starting the computer in Safe Mode. If you're an advanced user, and want to be able to get to that account from the login page, you just have to enable the account. Here's how:

1. Log in to an account that has administrative privileges.
2. Click the Start button, right-click Computer, and choose Manage.
3. In the left column of the Computer Management tool that opens, click Local Users and Groups.
4. In the center column, double-click the Users folder.
5. Right-click the Administrator account and choose Properties.
6. Clear the checkmark next to Account is disabled and click OK.
7. Close the Computer Management window.

When you log out of your current account, you'll see the Administrator account on the login page. It will also appear there each time you start the computer.

Stop Entering Password on Lockout

If you leave the computer for a few minutes without logging out, you're taken to a *lockout* screen that shows your user account information. If your user account is password-protected, you need to enter your password to get back to the desktop. This is to prevent other people from using your computer while you're away. But it only makes sense in a work environment. In a home environment, it may be overkill. You can reconfigure Vista so that you don't have to re-enter your password to get back to your desktop. Here are the steps:

1. Click the Start button, type pow, and click Power Options.
2. In the left column, click Require a password on wakeup.
3. If the options under Password protection on wakeup are disabled, click Change settings that are currently unavailable. Then elevate your privileges by clicking Continue or by entering the password for an administrative account.
4. Choose Don't require a password.
5. Click Save Changes.

For more information on power options settings, see Chapter 50.

Advanced Security Tools

IT professionals and highly experienced users can continue to use Local Users and Groups and Local Security Policy consoles for more advanced security configuration. Options in those tools are beyond the scope of this book, and not the kinds of things the average home user wants to mess with. To get to Local Users and Groups, click the Start button, right-click Computer, and choose Manage. Or press ⊞, type comp, and click Computer Management. Then click Local Users and Groups in the left column.

To get to Local Security Policy, press ⊞, type loc, and click Local Security Policy. To find the new settings related to UAC, expand Local Policies in the left column, then click Security Options. The new UAC settings are at the bottom of the list in the content pane.

 **Windows CardSpace lets you set up relationships with online services that require logging in.**

About Windows CardSpace

Windows CardSpace lets you store user account information for online services that support the CardSpace feature. It's a means of creating a digital identity that can be used instead of a username and password to log in to online accounts that support the CardSpace feature.

NOTE **Some of you might be more familiar with the term *InfoCard*. CardSpace is basically a new name for InfoCard.**

CardSpace adds security to Web relationships by encrypting data in your card before sending the information to a Web site. You can also review cards from Web sites that use them to get more information about a site before signing up for an account.

As I write this section, CardSpace is entirely new and not many Web sites support it. Whether or not it catches on as a technology remains to be seen. But the idea is fairly simple. You can create one or more digital cards, each with whatever information you want to provide to Web sites with whom you do business. For example, you might want cards that include only your name and no further identifying information. Other cards might include your street address and phone number.

When you set up an account with an online site that supports CardSpace, you can send your card rather than filling in blanks on their user form. Once you've established an account, you can submit your card whenever you need to log in to the site.

There are two kinds of cards you can use:

- **Personal cards:** These you create yourself, and provide to online Web services as you see fit.
- **Managed cards:** These are like membership cards provided to you by organizations and businesses that support the CardSpace identity system.

Because there are currently no Web sites that support the CardSpace feature, there's nothing I can demonstrate here. About the only thing I can do is tell you how to get to the program for managing your cards. Use whichever method is easiest for you:

- Click the Start button and choose Control Panel ⟿ User Accounts and Family Safety ⟿ Windows CardSpace.
- Tap ⊞, type card, and click Windows CardSpace.

If you're taken to a welcome page, click OK to proceed. To create a personal card, click Add a card in the right column. Click Personal Card and fill in whatever blanks you're comfortable with. You might want to start by creating a basic card that contains your name, e-mail address, and perhaps a picture or logo. You can create other cards with more information, if necessary, for sites that you trust with that information.

You don't create managed cards yourself. Instead, you set up an account with a service that uses managed cards. When you receive such a card, you'll likely get instructions on its use. But the basic procedure is to go into CardSpace, click Add a Card, click Install a Managed Card, and then import the card that the online service has sent you.

If the CardSpace technology catches on, you'll be able to access your cards right from your Web browser. When you go to log in to a site, you'll see an option to log in the traditional way through a user account and password, or by using CardSpace (or an InfoCard). Click the option to use CardSpace, click the card you want to use, and you're logged in.

Wrap Up

When two or more people share a computer, user accounts let each person treat the computer as if it was their own. Each user can personalize settings to their liking, and keep their files separate from other users.

User accounts also work in conjunction with parental controls. A parent can set up a password-protected administrative account, and then use that account to set up parental controls. Create standard accounts for children, and allow them to log in to their own accounts only. Parental controls are covered in Chapter 4.

User accounts also add security to your system by making all users run with limited privileges. The general term for security through user accounts is User Account Control (UAC). Some key points to keep in mind:

- At least one person should play the role of administrator for the computer. That person should create a password-protected user account with administrative privileges.

- The administrator should also create a standard account for himself, and one for each person who shares the computer.

- All users (including the administrator) should use their standard accounts for day-to-day computing.

- All the tools for creating and managing user accounts are accessible from User Accounts and Family Safety in the Control Panel.

Chapter 4

Parental Controls and Family Safety

IN THIS CHAPTER

Setting up parental controls

Setting time limits

Controlling Web browsing

Viewing and printing activity reports

Keeping kids safe online isn't always easy for parents. Especially for the parent who hasn't exactly been riding the crest of the tech wave in recent years. Parental controls are a great first step to keeping children safe online. Better yet, you don't need to be a computer guru to set parental controls. After you've set up standard user accounts for children (as discussed in Chapter 3), the rest is fairly easy. In this chapter, you see just how easy it is to set up parental controls in Windows Vista.

Before You Get Started

For parental controls to work, your computer must be set up with at least one password-protected administrator user account. If you set up multiple user accounts with administrative privileges, make sure that they're all password-protected. And make sure the kids don't know the password. Otherwise, the kids can easily go in and change any parental controls you import.

Furthermore, each child should have his or her own standard user account. If you have no idea what I'm talking about here, see Chapter 3. There you'll learn everything you need to know about setting up user accounts.

NEW FEATURE Parents can easily set up computer parental controls without buying and installing third-party programs.

Getting to the Parental Controls Page

Fortunately, you don't need to be a computer guru to set up parental controls. After you've set up appropriate user accounts, the rest is easy. Here are the steps:

1. Log in to a user account that has administrative privileges.

2. Do whichever of the following is most convenient for you at the moment:
   - Tap ⊞, type par in the search box, and click Parental Controls.
   - Click the Start button, choose Control Panel, and click Set up parental controls for any user.

3. You come to a page that shows the name and picture for each user account you've created, like the example in Figure 4.1. Click the user account for which you want to set up parental controls.

FIGURE 4.1

Click a standard account to create parental controls.

Now you're in the parental controls page shown in Figure 4.2. Any options you choose are applied to the account shown in the page. For example, in Figure 4.2, I'm setting up parental controls for a user named Alec.

To activate parental controls for the account, choose On, enforce current settings under the Parental Controls heading. You can also monitor your child's computer usage by choosing On, collect information about computer usage under the Activity Reporting heading.

Next, you want to specify exactly what the child can and can't do with the computer. Your options are described in the sections to follow.

Defining Web restrictions

The World Wide Web contains millions of Web sites and billions of Web pages. No one person or company has control over what goes on the Web. It's very much a public place where anyone can post any content they wish. Obviously, not all of that content is suitable for children. (Much of it isn't particularly appropriate for normal adults either.)

To define Web restrictions, click Windows Vista Web Filter. You're taken to the page shown in Figure 4.3.

FIGURE 4.2

Creating parental controls for user Alec.

FIGURE 4.3

Web restrictions.

There are many ways to block Web content. The first step is to choose the first option, Block some websites or content. From there, the approach you take depends on the age of the child and what you as a parent feel is appropriate for your child. For example, a very young child should probably be limited to viewing only specific Web sites. After all, there are likely millions of Web sites the child shouldn't visit. And there's no way you can type all their addresses!

To define specific Web sites that the child can view, select (check) Only allow websites which are on the allow list. Then click Edit the Allow and block list. Under the Website address heading, type or paste the URL of a single site that the child can visit. Then click Allow to place that site's URL in the list of allowed sites. Make sure you also check the Only Allow websites which are on the allow list option. That way you won't have to worry about your child accidentally (or intentionally) browsing to any other Web sites.

Figure 4.4 shows an example where I've listed the URLs for a few kid-friendly Web sites. If you have another child with another user account for which the same list of Web sites would apply, click Export to export your current list. Then when setting up restrictions for your other child, you can click Import to import that exported list.

FIGURE 4.4

Allowed Web sites list.

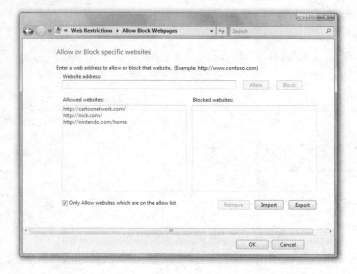

If you only want to prevent the child from viewing certain Web sites, you can add URLs to the Blocked web-sites list. But do keep in mind that, depending on the age of the child and what you feel is appropriate, there are potentially millions of unacceptable sites. Far more than you could possibly place in the Blocked websites list. But if that's the approach you want to take, go ahead and place URLs in the Blocked websites list. And *don't* select the Only Allow websites which are on the allow list option. The child will be prevented from viewing only the sites you put in that Blocked websites list. Click OK after completing your list.

If you ever need to change the list, just click Edit the Allow and block list again to return to the page of allowed or blocked Web sites.

How Do I Paste a URL?

Every Web site has a unique address called a URL (Uniform Resource Locator). To allow the child to visit a Web site, you either have the type or paste the URL of that site into the box under the Website address heading. To paste, rather than type, browse to a Web site (or have the child browse to the site) in Internet Explorer or another Web browser. When you're at the Web site, you know that the URL in the Web browser's Address bar is the correct URL for that site.

To paste that URL, you first have to copy it. First select the URL by clicking the icon just to the left of the http:// in the browser's Address bar. If that doesn't work, drag the mouse pointer through the whole URL. When all the letters in the URL are highlighted (show as white text against a blue background), press Ctrl+C to copy. (You won't see anything happen on the screen.) Then go to the Allow Block Webpages page (by clicking its button in the taskbar). Click in the box under Website address where you would have typed the URL, and press Ctrl+V to paste. Then click the Allow button to add the URL to the list of Allowed sites.

Copy-and-paste is a valuable basic skill, because any place you can type text, you can also paste text. So there's rarely any need to paste text that you can just copy from some other place on the screen. For more information on working with text, including copy-and-paste, see "Typing with WordPad" in Chapter 15.

For older children, you might want to take a more lenient approach and have Internet Explorer block sites automatically based on content. If you want to take that approach, don't select Only allow websites which are on the allow list. When you clear that checkbox, the options under "Block web content automatically" are enabled (no longer dimmed and disabled). Click each option under "Choose a web restriction level" to see what it means. For example, when you click High you see a box that explains the kinds of sites that are blocked.

To block specific types of content automatically, choose Custom. Then select (check) the kind of content you want to block (for example, Mature content, Weapons, Drugs).

If you do not want the child to download files, select (check) the Block file downloads checkbox. Click OK after making your selections. You're returned to the page where you can define other parental controls.

Setting time limits

To specify times when the child is allowed to use the computer, click Time Limits. You'll see a grid of days and times. Initially all squares are white, meaning there are no restrictions. You can click any time slot for which the child isn't allowed to use the computer to turn it blue. Or, drag the mouse pointer through a longer stretch of time to block more time.

Optionally, you can place the mouse pointer in the upper-left corner of the grid and drag down to the lower-right corner to block all times. Then drag the mouse pointer through the times that the child is allowed to use the computer. For example, in Figure 4.5 the child is allowed to use the computer from 10:00 AM to 7:00 PM on Sunday, 3:00 to 7:00 on Monday, Tuesday, Wednesday, and Thursday, 3:00 to 9:00 on Friday, and 10:00 AM to 9:00 PM on Saturday.

Click OK after setting allowable times. You can change those settings at any time by clicking Time Limits again when appropriate. For example, if the child needs a "time out" from the computer, you can block out all of the times, so that the child can't use the computer at all!

FIGURE 4.5

White squares indicate when your child is allowed to use the computer.

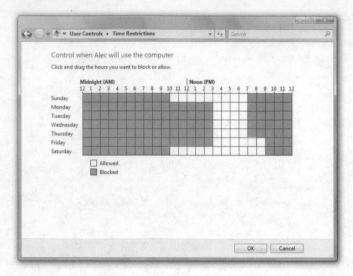

Controlling game play

To control the child's game play, click Games. You'll come to the page shown in Figure 4.6. If you don't want the child to use the computer for game play at all, choose No. Otherwise, choose Yes.

FIGURE 4.6

Controlling children's game play.

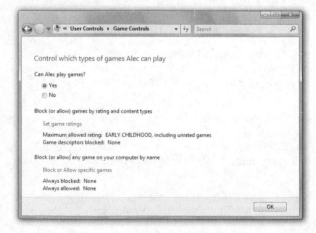

If you choose Yes, you can block games based on content. Click Set game ratings. Your first options will be based on ESRB ratings. ESRB stands for Entertainment Software Rating Board, an independent third party that rates games for age appropriateness and specific content. The ratings are similar to movie ratings (G, PG, R, and so forth), but specific to computer games.

TIP To use a rating system other than ESRB, click the Back button until you get to the first parental controls page that shows user accounts. Then click *Select a games rating system* in the left column.

To prevent the child from playing games that have no ESRB rating, choose Block games with no rating. Then read each rating and click whichever rating is the most appropriate for your child. The child will be able to play games up to, and including, the rating you choose.

Then you can scroll down the page and block more games based on content type. To block games based on content, select (check) the type of content you want to block. When you get to the bottom of the list and have blocked all the content that you feel is inappropriate, click OK.

Finally, you can click Block or Allow specific games to allow or block games installed on your computer. For each listed game, you can choose User Rating Setting to block based on the ESRB rating. Or you can choose Always Allow to let the child play the game. Or choose Always Block to prevent the child from playing that game. Click OK after making your selections. Then click OK again to return to the main parental controls page for your child.

Blocking and allowing programs

Clicking Allow and Block Specific Programs takes you to a page that lists all of the programs installed on your computer. There you can opt to allow the child to use all programs. Or choose <child> can only use the programs I allow. If you choose the second option, you need to select (check) the checkbox next to each program that the child is allowed to use. Click OK after making your selections.

When you've finished setting up parental controls for the child, the account name and picture summarize your settings. You can click OK to return to the list of user accounts. From there you can click another account to which you want to assign parental controls. Or close the window if you're finished setting up parental controls.

Of course you can add or change parental controls at any time. Just use any technique described under "Getting to the Parental Controls Page" to get to the main page. Then click the account for which you want to add or change parental controls.

Get Web sites working

If you've set restrictions on Web sites, you might need to do a little tweaking to get the sites working. Log out of your administrative account (click the Start button, click the arrow next to the lock, and then click Log Off). Then log in to the child's account. Browse to an allowed Web site. If some content from the site is blocked, you'll see a warning in the information bar. You can click that to review portions of the site that are blocked. Typically it's perfectly safe to allow the child to see the blocked content, because it's still age-appropriate. But you'll need to choose Always Allow when prompted to make sure the child can visit the site when you're away.

You can also use one of the child's allowed sites as the default home page that appears when the child first opens the Web browser. In Internet Explorer, browse to whatever Web page you want to make the default. Then click the Home button in the toolbar (or press Alt+M) and click Add or Change Home Page. Choose

Use this webpage as your only home page and click Yes. You might also want to add all the allowed sites to the child's Favorites. For more information on Internet Explorer, Favorites, and default home pages, see Chapter 17.

When you want to get back to performing parental (administrative) tasks, log out of the child's account. Then log back into your administrative account.

Viewing User Activity Reports

User activity reports provide a summary of user activity. As an administrator, you can view the report for any user at any time. You may see occasional reminders about activity reports in the Notification area. When you see such a message, you can click it if you want to review activity right then and there. But the message isn't your only opportunity. You can review the child's computer activity at any time by following these steps:

1. Log in to a user account that has administrative privileges.
2. Get to Parental Controls using either of the following methods:
   - Tap ⊞, type par, and click Parental Controls under Programs on the Start menu.
   - Click the Start button, choose Control Panel, and click Set up Parental Controls for any user.
3. Click the user account name or picture for which you want to view activity.
4. Click View activity reports.

The report shows the top 10 visited Web sites overall, the last 10 visited sites, file downloads, login times, programs used, games played, instant messaging information, e-mails sent and received, and more. Basically you get to see everything the child has done.

For a more detailed printable copy of the report, click Generate Report in the toolbar. In the Save As dialog box that opens, enter a filename for the report. To place it in the Documents folder for the current administrative account, click Browse Folders. Then click Documents in the links at the left side of the Save As dialog box. Then click Save.

To view the saved report, open the folder in which you placed it, and double-click the icon with whatever filename you provided. After you can see the page, you can choose File ⇨ Print to print a copy.

Reviewing system activity

You aren't limited to reviewing activity for children. You can view activity for the system in general. Starting from the desktop, click the Start button and choose Control Panel ⇨ User Accounts and Family Safety ⇨ View Activity Reports. The Activity Viewer shown in Figure 4.7 opens. Click any user account name to review that user's activity. Or click the + sign next to General System and any option that appears beneath that heading. The main pane to the right shows activity related to whichever item you click. Be sure to use the vertical and horizontal scroll bars to see all entries.

You can also enable activity reports even for standard user accounts that have no parental controls. Just get to the main parental controls page shown back in Figure 4.1 near the start of this chapter. Click a user account and turn on parental controls and activity reports. If you only want to view activity reports, set the Web restrictions to allow all Web sites, and leave the other options turned off. The user account won't have any parental restrictions, but the activity reports will keep track of that user's activity.

FIGURE 4.7

Activity Viewer.

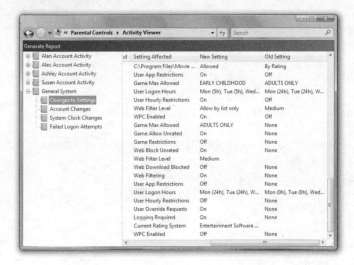

Family Safety Resources for Parents

Technical approaches to online safety, like parental controls, are a good thing. But they cannot cover all possible risks. Kids like to get involved with instant messaging and chats where people aren't always who they claim to be.

Children should be taught some basic ground rules. For example, children should never give out personal information like where they live or go to school. If anything makes them feel uncomfortable, they should report it to their parents. They should never agree to meet with anyone.

As a parent, you have many online resources for sharing your concerns with others and getting advice. You don't need to be a technical whiz to take advantage of these sites. Here are some you might want to add to your Favorites:

- **Safe Kids:** www.safekids.com
- **Child Safety:** www.microsoft.com/athome/security/children
- **CyberAngels:** www.cyberangels.org/
- **GetNetWise:** www.getnetwise.org/
- **Yahooligans Parent's Guide:** yahooligans.yahoo.com/parents

Wrap Up

The Internet is here to stay. Today's children will likely use it as their main source of information and communication throughout their lives. The Internet is also very much a public place, a direct reflection of the world at large. Although most of the people online are perfectly normal, the Internet has its share of whackos and other undesirables, just like the real world.

Knowledge is a parent's best defense against Internet dangers. A parent who has been "out of the loop" in terms of technical advances over recent years will feel some helplessness and insecurity about keeping kids safe online. Setting up user accounts and parental controls is a great way to get started in taking control of kids' computer use. Monitoring their activity is another. Here's a quick wrap-up of the main points covered in this chapter:

- A parent should set up at least one password-protected administrative user account to take control of the computer.
- Each person who uses the computer can also have a standard account, which offers greater security than an administrative account.
- The person with the administrative account can use parental controls to set limits on Internet and computer usage for people using standard accounts.
- The administrator can also use activity reports to monitor standard users' activities.
- Parents can find support and stay up-to-date through many Web sites dedicated to online safety.

Chapter 5

Help, Support, and Troubleshooting

Ever heard the saying "If all else fails, read the instructions"? It's sarcastic, of course. But it's also somewhat profound, because it touches on our natural desire for immediate gratification. Believe me, when it comes to wanting and expecting immediate gratification, I'm as guilty as the next person.

Unfortunately, there really are no instructions for using a computer. If there were, they would be bigger than the *Encyclopedia Britannica*—probably big enough to fill a decent-sized public library. Truth is, there are so many things you can do with a computer and such a huge volume of information is available, there really is no single source of information to which you can turn.

To survive in the digital world these days, you have to be resourceful. And being resourceful means having enough skills to find the information you need, when you need it, wherever that information might be. But being resourceful isn't a skill anyone is born with. You have to *learn* to be resourceful. And that's what this chapter is all about.

IN THIS CHAPTER

Learning about Help and Support

Help from people

Troubleshooting

Introducing Help and Support

By far, the most important resource for getting the information you need, when you need it, is the Help and Support built into Windows Vista. It doesn't cover everything in great depth. But it does cover all the main features with a focus on things most people want to do with their computers.

There are a couple of ways to get to Vista's Help. When you're in a specific Vista program like Photo Gallery, Media Player, or whatever, click the Help button (if any) in its upper-right corner (see Figure 5.1). Or if the program has a menu bar, click Help in that menu bar to see options for getting help. Or press the Help key (F1).

FIGURE 5.1

A sample Help button in a Vista program.

 **CAUTION**   If your keyboard has a Function Lock (or F Lock) key, the function keys (F1 through F12) only work if that key is on.

When you access help from a particular program, you get *context-sensitive* help. In other words, you get help that's relevant to the program or component from which you requested the help.

To get more general help with Windows Vista, open the Help and Support Center from the Start menu (see Figure 5.2) or press Help (F1) at the desktop.

FIGURE 5.2

Help and Support on the Start menu.

If you don't see a Help and Support option on your Start menu, don't panic. Some computer manufacturers replace that with their own Help or Support option. Clicking that option will take you to a help page that's similar to the Vista help page. It's just rearranged to promote your computer manufacturer.

If you don't see Help and Support on your Start menu, it might also just be turned off. You can probably turn it back on. Right-click the Start button and choose Properties. In the dialog box that opens, click the Customize button. Then scroll down through the list of options and check Help. Click OK in each open dialog box.

TIP   See "Personalizing the Start Menu" in Chapter 11 for the full scoop on Start menu options.

The Help and Support Center (see Figure 5.3) provides access to all help features. Right off the bat you can see that it's divided into six main categories, each represented by an icon in the top half of the window. Click any one of those items to see what's available. You can also click any blue text for help with that specific topic.

For beginners and casual users, Windows Basics is the best place to start, especially when you need reminders of key terms and concepts that the rest of Help assumes that you already know. That includes terms like hardware, software, point, click, double-click, right-click, drag, function keys, navigation keys, keyboard shortcuts, menu, command, desktop, icon, taskbar, Quick Launch, Sidebar, program, window, document, minimize, maximize, restore, scroll bar, open, save, close, undo, file, folder, move, copy, delete, and print.

For folks who already have all those terms and concepts down pat, the What's New? icon might be the better place to start.

FIGURE 5.3

The Help and Support Center home page.

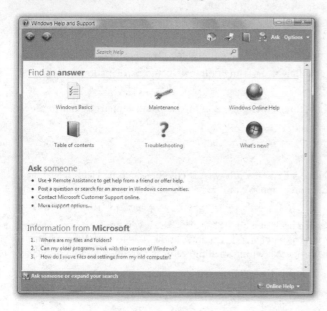

Navigating Help

Across the top of the Help and Support Center, you see the buttons shown in Figure 5.4. (On your own screen, you can point to any button to see its name.) Here's what each button offers:

FIGURE 5.4

The Help and Support Center toolbar.

- **Back:** Takes you back to the help page you just left (if any). Disabled (dimmed) when there's no page to go back to.
- **Forward:** Returns to the page you just backed out of. Disabled if you didn't just back out of a page.
- **Help and Support Home:** Takes you to the same page that opens when you first open Help and Support.
- **Print:** Lets you print whatever help information you're currently viewing.
- **Browse Help:** Takes you to the Table of Contents.
- **Ask:** Takes you to options for getting online help from humans. (But there isn't anyone just sitting there waiting to answer your questions. It's more complicated than that.)

■ **Options:** Provides the following options:

   ■ **Print:** Same as clicking the Print button.

   ■ **Browse Help:** Same as clicking the Browse Help button.

   ■ **Text Size:** Changes the size of the text in the help window. (A life saver if the text is too small to read!)

   ■ **Find (on this page):** Searches the current help page (only) for a word or phrase you specify.

   ■ **Settings:** Provides options for enabling or disabling online help and participation in Help Experience Improvement program.

 **TIP** As always, you can point to any button across the top of the Help and Support Center to see its name.

Using the Search box

The Search box at the top of the Help and Support Center window is strictly for searching Help. It searches both the help that's in your computer and the more extensive online help (if you're online when you use the Search box).

Use the Search box as you would the index at the back of a book. It works best if you know the exact term you're looking for and know how to spell that term. But even if you don't know how to spell it exactly, it works pretty well. For example, a search for "desk top" (wrong spelling) returns roughly the same results as "desktop" (correct spelling).

You can also phrase your search as a question. For example, "What is a user account?" or "How do I create a user account?"

Press Enter or click the Magnifying glass button after typing your search term or question. The results will be a series of links to pages in Help that are relevant to your search phrase or question.

Online Help and Offline Help

There are really two types of help in Windows Vista. There's *offline Help*, which you can access at any time. There's also *online Help,* which you can access only when you're connected to the Internet. The online help is more extensive than the offline help.

In the Help window's lower-right corner, you'll see an indicator that tells you which help you're currently accessing (see Figure 5.5). Click that to choose to use Offline Help (only), or Online Help (which includes both offline help and online help). To automatically include online Help in your searches, choose Settings and then choose Include Windows Online Help and Support when you search for help.

FIGURE 5.5

Online/Offline options.

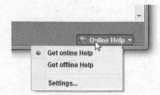

Vista's Help Is Only About Vista

It's important to understand that the Help and Support in Vista is *only* for Vista and the programs that come with Windows Vista. There are at least 100,000 other programs you can purchase separately. Vista's Help and Support doesn't cover any of those programs.

When you want help with some program other than Vista, you have to look in the Help for *that* program, not Vista's help. Typically, you do so by choosing Help from that program's menu bar or by pressing F1 while that program is open and in the active window.

E-mail is the same way. E-mail isn't really a component of Windows Vista. E-mail is a service provided by your ISP (Internet service provider) or a third party like Google for Google Mail or Yahoo! for Yahoo! Mail. Your ISP or mail service provider are your best resource for questions about e-mail.

Help from People

When we can't figure something out by guessing, usually our next thought is to call someone on the phone. Whether or not that works depends on whom you call. Many of the larger companies charge for telephone support, and it can be quite expensive, especially if you don't know all the terminology. When you don't know the terminology, it's hard to ask the question and even harder to understand the answer.

There are some online alternatives to using the phone where you can get help from an actual living, breathing person without spending a fortune. Clicking the Ask button in the Help and Support Center shows what they are (see Figure 5.6). The sections to follow describe what each option is about.

FIGURE 5.6

Resources for live help.

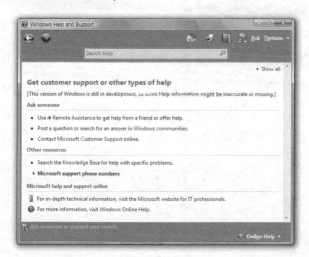

Remote Assistance

Remote Assistance is a technology that allows another person to see what's on your computer screen and operate your computer with their mouse and keyboard. The idea here is to turn control of your computer over to a trusted expert to resolve your problem.

Unfortunately, you have to provide your own trusted expert. There aren't any companies (that I know of) that have trusted experts willing to hook into your computer and fix things for free. For more information, see "Using Remote Assistance" in Chapter 19.

Windows Communities

Windows Communities are *newsgroups* in which other users hang out, ask questions, and answer questions. Nobody gets paid to work on newsgroups. It's all done voluntarily. So there's no charge to access the newsgroups.

Newsgroups aren't an immediate gratification type of help. There isn't anyone there waiting for your questions and ready to answer on the spot. It's more like group e-mail where people post messages and other people reply as convenient. This is another resource you can add to your list of resources for information.

To get to the newsgroups, first make sure that your computer is online. Then click the Ask button in Help and Support and click Windows Communities. Your Web browser opens to the home page for the communities. I can't say exactly how it will look because it's a Web page, and Web pages change all the time. But you should see a Search For box and some basic instructions as in Figure 5.7.

FIGURE 5.7

Home page for online communities.

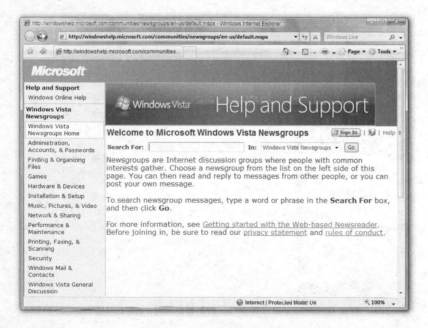

It's important to understand that when you type something in the Search For box, you're not sending your question to an expert to read and answer. There is no live person on the other end to read and respond to your question. Instead, what you get is a list of all the previous newsgroup posts that contain the word or phrase for which you searched, something like the example in Figure 5.8.

Results of search for Aero Glass.

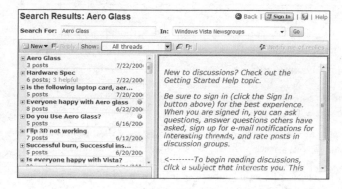

The idea is to scroll through all the messages to see whether one looks like it might help. Then click its message header (the text in bold) to expand the *thread*. A thread consists of the original message and all the replies to that message. To read any message in the thread, click its header in the left pane. The message text appears in the right pane.

To post your own question to a group, you'll need to set up an account. Don't worry, it's not the kind of thing where you have to give up any personal information. Nor will there ever be a charge. You need to set up the account only once, not every time you use the newsgroups.

Posting a question starts with clicking the word New in the toolbar and choosing Question (see Figure 5.9). If you haven't set up an account yet, you'll be given the opportunity to on the next page that opens. Otherwise, if you already have set up an account, you can sign in by entering your user name and password.

Post a question.

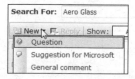

When you've set up an account, you might find it easier to use an NNTP client rather than your Web browser to access the newsgroups. You can use Windows Mail as that NNTP client (even if you don't use Windows Mail for e-mail). For more information on doing newsgroups with Windows Mail, see Chapter 19.

Microsoft Customer Support

Clicking the Microsoft Customer Support link takes you to a Web page that provides still more support options. There, you'll find a ton of links to different kinds of support for different kinds of questions. Take a look at all of your options and decide what's best for you.

Troubleshooting

Troubleshooting isn't easy with computers. It's a skill that takes a lot of time, education, and experience. But you can use some resources to troubleshoot some of the more common problems without being a total computer geek.

First, it's important to understand that troubleshooting only comes into play when you already know how to do something, but things don't work as they should. It's not the same as not knowing how to do something or not being able to figure out how to do something by guessing. It's an important distinction to make because if you can't do something because you don't know how, troubleshooting won't help.

As to nongeek troubleshooting, there are many resources for that. The first is Vista's automated troubleshooting. Vista can often recognize when something's gone wrong. When it does, it may pop up a message asking whether it's okay to send information about the problem to Microsoft. You should always choose Yes. No human will receive the message. Nobody will call or pop up on your screen to solve the problem. Instead, another computer will check to see whether it's a known problem that's already been solved.

If there is an available solution, you'll (eventually) see a message in your Notification area offering to solve the problem. Just click that message and follow any additional instructions that appear on the screen. Hopefully, the problem will go away without having to call in the pricey computer nerds.

There's also the Troubleshooting link in the Help and Support Center shown back in Figure 5.3. Click that to find solutions to common problems.

I've also included a troubleshooting chapter at the end of each part of this book. Like the Troubleshooting icon in Help and Support, it only covers some of the more common problems. There isn't a book in the world that's large enough to cover every possibility.

Finally, the communities mentioned in the previous section can be a great resource. Just make sure that you explain exactly what the problem is so people reading your post can determine what's happening. Chances are someone who reads your message has already encountered that problem and will offer a solution. Hey, it's free. So it's certainly worth a try.

Wrap Up

Finding the information you need, when you need it, is a big part of using a computer these days. A single resource, like a book, computer course, the built-in Help, communities, the Web, and so on, isn't really enough. The field is much too big now. To survive in the digital world, you need access to many resources. This chapter has been about the different resources available to you. To summarize:

- Windows Help and Support is one of your best resources for information about Windows Vista.
- There are three ways to get to help, which you surely want to memorize: Press the Help key (F1) on your keyboard. Or click a Help button (blue circle with question mark). Or click the Start button and choose Help and Support.

- Most programs that aren't built into Windows Vista have their own help. To get to that help, you typically press the Help key (F1) or choose Help from that program's menu bar.

- If pressing the F1 key has no effect, tap the F Lock (or Function Lock) key on your keyboard, and then press the F1 key again.

- Windows Communities are a resource for free help from live human beings.

- You need to invest a little time in learning to use the communities. They're not an instant gratification thing. But the time you spend will be well worth it.

Chapter 6

Troubleshooting Startup Problems

Each major part in this book ends with a troubleshooting chapter like this. The troubleshooting chapters provide quick solutions to common problems. That's about it. You won't catch me yammering on for paragraph after paragraph in these troubleshooting chapters!

The Computer Won't Start

If the computer does absolutely nothing when you first turn it on, first check all cable connections. Make sure the power plug on every device that plugs into the wall is firmly plugged in. Also, make sure the mouse, keyboard, and all other devices are firmly plugged into their slots.

If it's a desktop computer, look for a 0/1 power switch on the back of the computer and make sure it's on (flipped to the 1 position).

Turn on the computer again and as it's powering up, push the button on the floppy disk drive (if the computer has one) and the CD or DVD drive. If there is a disk in either drive, remove it.

If the computer sounds like it's starting up, but you don't see anything on the screen, make sure all plugs to the monitor are firmly seated. If it's a desktop computer, make sure the monitor's power cable is firmly attached to the monitor and wall socket, and that the cable connecting the computer to the monitor is firmly attached at both ends of the cable. Make sure the monitor is turned on. Then restart the computer.

Non System Disk or Disk Error

This message appears when the computer attempts to boot from a disk on which Windows is not installed. If there's a floppy disk in the floppy drive, remove it. Likewise for any disk in the CD drive or DVD drive, or any drive that's connected to the computer through a USB port. Press any key to continue startup. If that doesn't work, press Ctrl+Alt+Del or restart the computer with the main on/off switch.

Computer starts but mouse and keyboard don't work

If the computer starts, but doesn't respond to the mouse and keyboard, turn off the computer. Unplug both the mouse and keyboard from the computer. If the mouse connects to a round PS/2 port, make sure you plug it in firmly. If the plug is round, make sure you plug in into the PS/2 port for the mouse (usually colored green). Make sure nothing is resting on the keyboard and holding down a key. Then firmly plug in the keyboard. If the plug is round, plug it into the PS/2 port for keyboard (usually purple in color). Check *all* cable connections to the computer one more time. Then restart the computer.

Computer keeps trying to start, but never gets there

Get to Safe Mode and choose the option to disable automatic restart. If that doesn't help, get to the Safe Mode options again and try the Last Known Good Configuration option. See "Troubleshooting Startup" in Chapter 14.

Screen turns blue during startup, then stops

This is commonly referred to as a Blue Screen of Death (BSOD). It doesn't mean your computer is permanently broken. The most likely cause of this problem is a device driver that doesn't work with Windows Vista.

If you recently connected or installed a new hardware device, disconnect or uninstall it. Then start the computer again. That's your best bet.

If you still get the Blue Screen of Death, you'll likely have to boot to Safe Mode and disable the device through Device Manager. This is not the sort of thing the average user normally performs. This is more the kind of thing that a professional would handle. But if you want to take a shot at fixing it yourself, see "Troubleshooting Startup" in Chapter 14 and "Dealing with Devices that Prevent Vista from Starting" in Chapter 47.

If the error persists, look for an error number on the Blue Screen of Death page. It will most likely start with the characters 0x. Jot that number down on a sheet of paper. Then, if you can get online through another Web site, go to Microsoft's site (http://search.microsoft.com) and search for that number. You might find a page that offers an exact solution to that problem.

If you can get online through another computer, you might also consider posting a question at the Windows Communities site. Be sure to include the error number in your post. You might find someone who has already experienced and solved that very problem.

Computer Takes Too Long to Start

When the computer takes much longer to start than it used to, the problem is usually caused by too many programs trying to auto-start. Consider uninstalling any programs you don't really use as discussed in Chapter 43. For the remaining programs, use Windows Defender to prevent unnecessary programs from starting automatically. See "Conquering Spyware with Windows Defender" in Chapter 8 for more information. See Chapter 14 for additional information on controlling auto-start programs.

Many things that prevent a computer from starting have nothing to do with Windows Vista. It often takes even seasoned pros many hours to diagnose and repair startup problems. But before you resort to the repair shop, here are some other things you can try.

Restore system files to an earlier time

If you can get the computer to start in Safe Mode, try restoring your files to an earlier time. In Safe Mode, click the Start button, type Restore, then click System Restore on the Start menu. Follow the onscreen instructions to restore system files from a date prior to when the problem began. Choose the most recent date. For example, if the problem started today, restore files from yesterday or the day before.

Repair Install Windows Vista

If you have a CD or DVD with Windows Vista on it, you can boot from that disc and do a repair installation. Put that disc in the CD or DVD drive and start the computer. Watch the screen for a message that shows "Press any key to boot from CD or DVD" (or a similar message), then tap the Enter key or Spacebar.

If the option to boot from the CD or DVD never appears, and the computer won't boot from that disc, you need to change your BIOS options to start from the CD drive. How you do that varies from one computer to the next. Typically, start the computer, then immediately start pressing the F1, F2, or Del key (perhaps all three, if you don't know which is required) repeatedly as the computer is starting. This should take you to the BIOS Setup options. There you can configure the computer to try starting from the CD before it tries starting from the hard drive. Close and save the new settings. The computer will restart, and this time you should be able to boot from the CD or DVD.

If you're able to boot from the CD, the first screen you see will likely ask about your language and locale. Make any necessary changes and click Next. On the next page, click Repair your computer (not the Install Now option). Then just follow the onscreen instructions to do a repair install of Windows Vista.

The instruction manual that came with your computer

Most computer manufacturers provide some means of helping you troubleshoot and repair startup problems. Be sure to look through whatever documentation you have for your computer manufacturer's recommendations. That could be your best bet, because all computers are unique in some ways. The manual that came with your computer provides information that's specific to your exact make and model of computer.

Resources in this book

I've thrown a lot of technical terms and concepts at you in this chapter. But when it comes to solving startup problems, there's no way around that. Here are some additional resources within this book that might help you solve a startup problem:

- **Using Safe Mode:** The "Troubleshooting Startup" section in Chapter 14 provides information on starting your computer from Safe Mode. If you can get to Safe Mode, techniques described in the chapters referenced in this list might help you solve the problems.

- **Restore from a CompletePC image:** If you've backed up your entire hard disk using Backup and Restore, see "Using the Backup and Restore Center" in Chapter 33 for information on restoring from that backup.

- **Restore to an earlier time:** For information on restoring your computer to an earlier time, see "Using System Protection" in Chapter 33.

- **Removing programs:** If you think a faulty program might be preventing your computer from starting, you can uninstall the program using techniques described in Chapter 43 (assuming you can get to Safe Mode so you have access to that program).

- **Removing Hardware:** When faulty hardware or drivers are preventing Windows Vista from starting, techniques described under "Removing Hardware" in Chapter 47 might help.

- **Troubleshooting Hardware:** Startup problems are often hardware problems. See Chapter 51 for more information on troubleshooting hardware.

Resources in Windows Help

If you can start the computer in Safe Mode, you can get to Windows Help too. In fact, the Help window should open automatically as soon as you enter Safe Mode. If it doesn't, click the Start button and choose Help and Support. Then search for `Safe Mode` for additional information on using Safe Mode to troubleshoot startup options.

Online resources

If you can start in Safe Mode with Networking, you can access online resources. You might try searching Windows Communities (which you can get to from Windows Help) for words related to the startup problem you're having. Or post a question describing the problem in as much detail as possible.

You can also search Microsoft's Web site for words that describe the problem you're having. Be sure to include the word `Vista` in your search. Otherwise the search result will likely include other irrelevant Microsoft products. Starting your search from `http://search.microsoft.com` will help limit the search to Microsoft, rather than the entire Web. If that doesn't help, you can try searching the entire Web from `www.live.com`, `www.google.com`, or whatever search engine you prefer.

If you're not a technical person, don't expect it to be easy. Like I said, startup problems can be difficult to troubleshoot, even for the pros. If all else fails, you may have to take the system to a repair shop to get the problem resolved. Or call a mobile service that will send a computer geek to your home or office.

Programs Won't Start

If a favorite old program won't start, it's most likely an incompatibility issue. Try right-clicking the startup icon for the program and choosing Run as administrator. If that doesn't help, try the program compatibility features. See Chapter 42 for more information on getting older programs to run with Windows Vista.

Part II

Batten Down the Security Hatches

In the early years of personal computers, nobody gave much thought to computer security. After all, why would someone need high security on a computer that they alone use? The Internet changed all of that. Suddenly personal computers were connected to an enormous public network fraught with all forms of malicious software. And people have suffered many security breaches ever since, ranging from minor annoyances to true data disasters.

Windows Vista was designed, built, and tested from the ground up to be the most secure Windows ever created. But ask any security professional whether there is anything such thing as a 100-percent secure computer, and you'll surely get "No" as your answer. You simply cannot create a machine that's totally programmable and also 100-percent secure. The best you can do is to minimize the likelihood of security breaches.

Virtually everyone today uses their computers to access the Internet. You want to make your computer as secure as possible as soon as possible. Part II takes you through the "big three" elements of doing that. Chapter 7 covers the built-in Windows Firewall. Chapter 8 covers tools and techniques for warding off malicious software, including Windows Defender, which comes free with Windows Vista. Chapter 9 covers automatic updates, an important component for keeping your computer secure against the latest security threats. Chapter 10 covers techniques for troubleshooting common security problems.

Chapter 7

Blocking Hackers with Windows Firewall

If you use the Internet, a firewall is a must-have security tool. It's not the only tool you need, but it's an important one. It protects your computer from hackers and worms. Hackers are people and programs that would attempt to access your computer through the Internet without you knowing it. Worms are bad programs, like viruses, that are usually written to do intentional harm.

Windows Vista comes with its own built-in firewall. If you didn't know about it before going online, relax. It's enabled by default. So most likely it's been protecting you since the very first moment you went online. In this chapter, you learn how the firewall works and how to configure it for maximum protection.

IN THIS CHAPTER

How firewalls protect your computer

Using Security Center

Using Windows Firewall

Configuring Windows Firewall

How Firewalls Work

To understand what a firewall is, you need to first understand what a network connection is. Even though you have only one skinny wire connecting your computer to the Internet (through a phone line or cable outlet), that connection actually consists of 65,535 *ports*. Each port can simultaneously carry on its own conversation with the outside world. So, theoretically, you could have 65,535 things going on at a time. But of course, nobody ever has that much going on all at once. One, or maybe a few, ports is more like it.

The ports are divided into two categories: TCP (Transmission Control Protocol) and UDP (User Datagram Protocol). TCP is generally used to send text and pictures (Web pages and e-mail), and includes some error checking to make sure all the information that's received by a computer matches what the sending computer sent. UDP works more like broadcast TV or radio, where the information is just sent out and there is no error checking. UDP is generally used for real-time communications, such as voice conversations and radio broadcasts sent over the Net.

Each port has two directions: incoming (or *ingress*) and outgoing (or *egress*). The direction is in relation to stuff coming into your computer from the outside: namely the Internet. It's the stuff coming into your computer that you have to watch out for. But you can't close all ports to all incoming traffic. If you did, there'd be no way to get the good stuff in. But you don't want to let everything in either. You need a way to separate the wheat from the chaff so to speak — a way to let in the good stuff while keeping out the bad stuff.

Anti-spyware and antivirus software are good tools for keeping out viruses and other bad things that are attached to files coming into your computer. But hackers can actually sneak worms and other bad things in through unprotected ports without there even being a file involved in the process. That's where the firewall comes into play. A *stateful* firewall, like the one that comes with Windows Vista, keeps track of everything you request. When traffic from the Internet wants to come in through a port, the firewall checks to make sure the traffic is something you requested. If it isn't, the firewall assumes this is a hacker trying to sneak something in without your knowing it, and therefore prevents the traffic from entering your computer. Figure 7.1 illustrates how it works.

FIGURE 7.1

How a stateful firewall works.

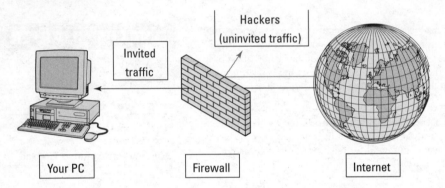

So, there's really more to it than just having a port open or closed. It's also about *filtering*. About making sure that data coming into an open port is something you requested and not some rogue uninvited traffic sent by some hacker. Many of the worms that infected so many computers in the 1990s did so by sneaking in undetected through unfiltered ports. These days, you really want to make sure you have a firewall up whenever you go online to prevent such things.

What a firewall doesn't protect against

It's important to understand that a firewall alone is not sufficient protection against all Internet threats. A firewall is just one component in a larger defense system. Specifically:

- A firewall *doesn't* protect you from spyware and viruses. See Chapter 8 for more information on that protection.
- A firewall *doesn't* protect you from attacks based on exploits. Automatic updates (Chapter 9) provide that protection.
- A firewall *doesn't* protect you from pop-up ads. See Chapter 17 for information on pop-up blocking with Internet Explorer.

■ A firewall *doesn't* protect you from phishing scams. See Chapters 17 and 18 for that protection.

■ A firewall *doesn't* protect you from spam (junk e-mail). See Chapter 18 for tools and techniques on managing spam with Windows Mail.

So a firewall isn't a complete solution. Rather, it's an important component of a larger security strategy.

Introducing Security Center

Before you get into Windows Firewall, take a look at the Security Center. As its name implies, this is a single point of administration for most of your PC's security. You can open the Security Center in several ways. Use whichever is most convenient for you:

■ Double-click the Windows Security Alerts (shield) icon in the Notification area.

■ If you see a Security Center alert above the Notification area (see Figure 7.2), click that alert.

FIGURE 7.2

Security Center alert.

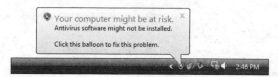

■ Press ⊞, type sec, and click Security Center.

■ Click the Start button, choose Control Panel, click Security, and then click Security Center.

■ In the Welcome Center, click Show More Details, and click Security Center in the left column.

Whichever method you use, the Security Center opens. Figure 7.3 shows an example. I clicked the arrow button to the right of each heading so you can see the descriptive text under each heading. You can click that button to show or hide the same descriptive text.

By default, Windows Firewall is turned on and working at all times, so your Security Center should show "On" in the Firewall box like in Figure 7.3. If yours shows "Off" or "Not Monitored," it might be because you have a third-party firewall program running in place of Windows Firewall. There are many such programs available, such as McAfee, Symantec (Norton), Gibson Research, and other companies. If your firewall is turned off, and you don't know why, it would be good to find out — perhaps from your computer manufacturer or someone who knows. If you don't have any firewall up, you should definitely turn on Windows Firewall.

NOTE There is no advantage to having two or more firewalls running simultaneously. In fact, more than one firewall is likely to cause unnecessary problems.

Turning Windows Firewall on or off

To turn Windows Firewall on or off, you must have administrative privileges. In the left column of the Security Center, click Windows Firewall. You see options for controlling the firewall. Click Change Settings or Turn Windows Firewall On or Off in that window to see the options shown in the foreground of Figure 7.4.

FIGURE 7.3

Security Center.

FIGURE 7.4

General tab of the Windows Firewall dialog box.

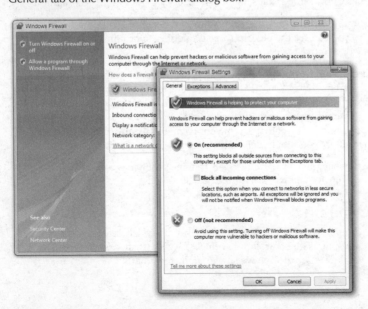

 Use the Block All Programs checkbox only to temporarily disable exceptions when connecting to public Wi-Fi networks. There's more on that topic in the sections to follow.

If you have a third-party firewall that you feel is more secure than the Windows Firewall, you can choose the Off option to turn off Windows Firewall. Just make sure you have a firewall up when you go online. Otherwise you won't have anything to stop uninvited traffic on your network connection.

Making Exceptions to Firewall Protection

When Windows Firewall is turned on and running, you don't really have to do anything special to use it. It will be on constant vigil, automatically protecting your computer from hackers and worms trying to sneak in through unprotected ports. Ports for common Internet tasks like e-mail and the Web will be open and monitored so you can easily use those programs safely.

Internet programs that don't use standard e-mail and Web ports may require that you create an *exception* to the default firewall rules. Examples include instant messaging programs and some online games. When you try to use such a program, Windows Firewall will display a security alert like the one in Figure 7.5.

FIGURE 7.5

Windows Firewall security alert.

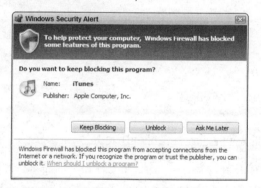

The message doesn't mean the program is "bad." It just means that to use the program, the Firewall has to open a port. If you want to use the program, go ahead and click Unblock. If you don't recognize the program name and publisher shown, choose Keep Blocking. If you're not sure what you want to do and want to look into the program some more, click Ask Me Later.

Unblocking a port doesn't leave it wide open. It just creates a new rule that allows that one program to use the port. You're still protected because the port is closed when you're not using that specific program. The port is also closed to programs other than the one for which you unblocked the port. Should you change your mind in the future, you can always reblock the port as described in the next section.

Manually configuring firewall exceptions

Normally when you try to use a program that needs to work through the firewall, you get a message like the example shown in Figure 7.5. Occasionally you might need, or want, to manually block or unblock a port.

If you have administrative privileges, you can do that via the Exceptions tab in the Windows Firewall dialog box. To open that dialog box, click Windows Firewall in the Security Center. Then click the Exceptions tab to see options like those in Figure 7.6.

FIGURE 7.6

Windows Firewall exceptions.

Items listed on the Exceptions tab represent Windows Vista features that work through the firewall. You'll also see any exceptions you created in response to a security alert. For example, iTunes isn't a Windows Vista feature, so you might not see that one. It shows in Figure 7.6 because I chose Unblock in response to the security alert shown back in Figure 7.5.

Of course, nobody was born already knowing what those things listed on the Exceptions tab are about. So there's no way to know whether you should check or uncheck a box just by guessing. But there's no need to guess either. If you just leave things as they are, everything will be fine. If you later decide to use one of the listed features, you'll be prompted at that point to unblock the port if it's necessary to do so.

Adding a program exception

Buttons at the bottom of the Exceptions tab let you unblock ports for programs that aren't listed under Programs and Services. You would only do this if specifically instructed to do so by a program manufacturer you know and trust.

If the program for which you want to create an exception isn't listed under Programs and Services, click the Add program button to add a specific program to the list. When you click Add program, you'll see a list of installed programs that might require Internet access, as in Figure 7.7. Click the program that you want to add to the list, then click OK. Optionally, if the program isn't listed, but you know where it's installed, you can use the Browse button to get to the main executable for that program (typically the `.exe` file). If you also need to change the scope of the exception, click Change scope. (More on that in a moment.)

FIGURE 7.7

Choose a firewall exception.

As an alternative to adding a program, you can click Add port to add a specific port to the list. The Add a Port dialog box shown in Figure 7.8 opens. Type a name of your own choosing for the port. Then specify the required port number and protocol. You should be able to get that information from whatever documentation you're using to get the program to work on your system.

FIGURE 7.8

Add a port exception.

After you've filled in the name, port number, and protocol, you can click Change Scope to change the scope of the exception, as described next.

Choosing a scope

Clicking the Change Scope button lets you define the addresses from which any unsolicited traffic is expected to originate. For example, if you're using a program that provides communications among programs within your local network only, you wouldn't want to accept unsolicited traffic coming to that port from the Internet. You'd only want to accept unsolicited traffic coming from computers within your own network. When you click the Change Scope button, you see the options shown in Figure 7.9. Your options are as follows:

FIGURE 7.9

The Change Scope dialog box.

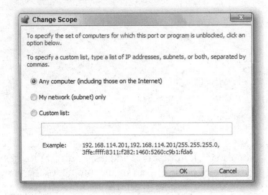

- **Any computer (including those on the Internet):** If you want to use the Internet program normally (so your computer has access to the Internet), choose this option.

- **My network (subnet) only:** If the program in question has nothing to do with the Internet, and is for your home or small business network only, choose this option to block Internet access but allow programs within your own network to communicate with each other through the program.

 The term *subnet* is another term for a home or small-office network.

- **Custom list:** If you want only certain computers in your local network, as opposed to all programs in that network, to use the program, you can specify their IP addresses individually.

If you choose the Custom list option, you need to type all the IP addresses that can use the program. Separate each IP address by a comma. Follow the last IP address with a slash and the subnet mask for the entire network. For example, the following allows hosts 1, 2, and 160 in a local network to communicate with one another through a firewall via whichever program you chose in the list of exceptions:

```
192.168.0.1,192.168.0.2,192.168.0.160/255.255.255.0
```

IP Addresses on Home/Office Networks

When you set up a network using the Network Setup Wizard described in Part X of this book, each computer is automatically assigned a 192.168.0.x IP address, where x is unique to each computer. For example, if the computers are sharing a single Internet connection, the first computer will be 192.168.0.1, the second computer you add will be 192.168.0.2, and so forth (although that last number could vary).

All computers will have the same subnet mask of 255.255.255.0. The subnet mask just tells the computer that the first three numbers are part of the *network address* (the address of your network as a whole), and the last number refers to a specific *host* (computer) on that network. The 192.168 . . . addresses are called *private addresses* because they cannot be accessed directly from the Internet.

To see the IP address of a computer on your local network, go to that computer, click the Start button, and choose All Programs ⇨ Accessories ⇨ Command Prompt. At the command prompt, type `ipconfig /all`, and press Enter. You'll see the computer's IP address and subnet mask listed along with other Internet Protocol data.

After you've defined a program, port, or scope, click OK as necessary to work your way back to the Exceptions tab. The item you specified appears in the list of Programs and Services. Its checkbox will be checked, indicating that the port is open so the program works through the firewall.

Disabling, changing, and deleting exceptions

The checkboxes in the Exceptions list indicate whether the exception is enabled or disabled. When you clear a checkbox, the exception is disabled and traffic through the port is rejected. This makes it relatively easy to enable and disable the port on an as-needed basis, because the program name always remains in the list of exceptions.

To change the scope of an exception in your exceptions list, click the exception name and click the Edit button. Then, click the Change Scope button and choose your new scope. To remove a program from the exceptions list, and stop accepting unsolicited traffic through its port, click the exception name, and then click the Delete button.

Advanced firewall settings

The Advanced tab of the Windows Firewall dialog box, shown in Figure 7.10, lets you choose the network cards you want the firewall to protect. If you have multiple network interface cards, you should select them all, unless you have some good reason for leaving one unprotected. The Restore Defaults button lets you change the firewall back to its original settings. That'll come in handy if you ever mess things up while manually configuring options and just want to get back to square one.

FIGURE 7.10

Advanced tab of the Windows Firewall dialog box.

Advanced Firewall Configuration

NEW FEATURE The firewall in Windows Vista includes some new advanced features for network and security professionals.

The rest of this chapter goes way beyond anything that would concern the average home computer user. It's for more advanced network and security administrators who might need to configure Windows Firewall to comply with an organization's security policy. All of these options require administrative privileges (of course). I won't go into great detail on what the various options mean, because I'll assume you are working to comply with an existing policy.

CAUTION If you're not a professional administrator, it's best to stay out of this area altogether. You certainly don't want to guess and hack your way through things just to see what happens. Doing so could lead to a real can of worms that makes it impossible or extremely difficult to access the Internet.

Open the Windows Firewall with Advanced Security icon

To get to the advanced configuration options for Windows Firewall, first open Administrative Tools in the Control Panel. Then click the Windows Firewall with Advanced Security icon. Or press ⊞, type fire, and click Windows Firewall with Advanced Security. The Firewall console opens as in Figure 7.11.

FIGURE 7.11

Windows Firewall with Advanced Security console.

As you can see in the figure, you have three independently configurable profiles to work with. The Domain Profile is active when the computer is logged in to a domain. The Private Profile applies to computers within a local, private network. The Public Profile protects your computer from the public Internet.

Changing Firewall Profile Properties

Clicking the Windows Firewall Properties link near the bottom of the console takes you to the dialog box shown in Figure 7.12. Notice that you can use tabs at the top of the dialog box to configure the Domain, Private, and Public settings. The fourth option applies to IPsec (IP Security), commonly used with VPNs (Virtual Private Networks) described a little later in this section. By default, Inbound connections are set to Block. Outbound ports are set to Allow by default. You can change either setting by clicking the appropriate button.

Firewall alerts, unicast response, local administrator control

Each profile tab has a Customize button in its Settings section. Clicking that button provides an option to turn off firewall notifications for that profile. Administrators can also use options on that tab to allow or prevent unicast responses to multicast and broadcast traffic. There's also an option to merge local administrator rules with rules defined through group policy.

FIGURE 7.12

Windows Firewall advanced properties.

Security Logging

Each profile tab also offers a Logging section with a Customize button. Click the Customize button to set a name and location for the log file, a maximum size, and to choose whether you want to log dropped packets, successful connections, or both. You can use that log file to review firewall activity and to troubleshoot connection problems caused by the firewall configuration.

Why Outbound Connections Are Set to Allow

Contrary to some common marketing hype and urban myths, having outbound connections set to Allow by default does not make your computer more susceptible to security threats. Firewalls are really about controlling traffic between trusted and untrusted networks. The Internet is always considered untrusted because it's open to the public and anything goes. It's necessary to block inbound connections by default so that you can control exactly what does, and doesn't, come in from the Internet.

Things that are already inside your computer (or local network) are generally considered "trusted." That's because, unlike the Internet, you do have control over what's inside your own PC or network. Your firewall and anti-malware programs also help to keep bad stuff out. Therefore, there shouldn't be any need to block outbound connections by default.

There are exceptions of course. In a secure setting where highly sensitive data is confined to secure workstations in a subnet, it certainly makes sense to block outgoing connections by default. That way you can limit outbound connections to specific hosts, programs, security groups, and so forth. You can also enforce encryption on outbound connections.

Customizing IPsec settings

The IPsec Settings tab in the firewall properties provides a way to configure IPsec (IP Security). Clicking the Customize button under IPsec Defaults reveals the options shown in Figure 7.13. The Default settings in each case cause settings to be inherited from a higher level GPO (Group Policy Object). To override the GPO, choose whichever options you want to apply to the current Windows Firewall instance. When you override the default, you can choose key exchange and data integrity algorithms. You can also fine-tune Kerberos V5 authentication through those settings.

Clicking OK or Cancel in the Customize IPsec Settings dialog box takes you back to the IPsec Settings tab. There you can use the IPsec Exemptions section to exempt ICMP from IPsec, which may help with connection problems caused by ICMP rules.

NOTE   IPsec is a set of cryptographic protocols for securing communications across untrusted networks. It is commonly associated with tunneling and virtual private networks (VPNs).

That covers the main firewall properties. There's plenty more you can configure outside of the properties dialog box. Again, most of these go far beyond anything the average home user needs to be concerned with, so I'll be brief here. Advanced users needing more information will find plenty of information in the Help for the firewall.

FIGURE 7.13

IPsec Settings dialog box.

Inbound and Outbound Rules

In the left column of the main Windows Firewall with Advanced Security window shown back in Figure 7.11, you see Inbound Rules and Outbound Rules links. These provide very granular control over Windows Firewall rules for incoming and outgoing connections. Figure 7.14 shows a small portion of the possibilities there. Use scroll bars to see them all.

FIGURE 7.14

Advanced outbound exceptions control.

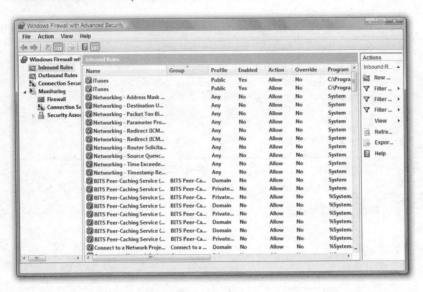

Here we're getting into security matters that go beyond the scope of this book. But I think it will be easy for any professional administrator to figure out what's going on there. Options (and the Help link) in the Actions column on the right tell all. You can also change any exception in the center column by right-clicking and choosing Properties.

Wrap Up

A firewall is an important component of a larger overall security strategy. Windows Vista comes with a built-in firewall that's turned on and working from the moment you first start your computer. The firewall is automatically configured to prevent unsolicited Internet traffic from getting into your computer, thereby protecting you from worms and other hack attempts. The Vista firewall also provides advanced options for professional network and security administrators who need more granular control over its behavior. In summary:

- A firewall protects your computer from unsolicited network traffic, which is a major cause of worms and other hack attempts.

- A firewall will not protect your computer from viruses, pop-up ads, or junk e-mail.

- You don't need to configure the firewall to use standard Internet services like the Web and e-mail. Those will work through the firewall automatically.

- When you start an Internet program that needs access to the Internet through a closed port, you'll be given a security alert with options to Unblock, or Keep Blocking, the port. You must choose Unblock to use that program.

- Windows Firewall is one of the programs in the Security Center. To open Security Center, click the Start button and choose Control Panel ⇨ Security ⇨ Security Center.

- From the Start menu, you can search for `fire` to get to Windows Firewall configuration options.

- Exceptions in Windows Firewall are programs that are allowed to work through the firewall.

- Professional network and security administrators can configure Windows Firewall through the Windows Firewall with Advanced Security console in Administrative Tools.

Chapter 8

Conquering Malicious Software

Malicious software (also called *malware*) is any software program that's intentionally designed to cause your computer harm or invade your privacy. These are not programs you purchase, or programs from reputable software manufacturers like Microsoft, Adobe, Corel, and others. They generally don't have icons, and you don't have to run them yourself. Rather, they're tiny programs that are hidden inside your system and do their dirty work without you knowing it.

As you'll learn in this chapter, several forms of malware exist including viruses, worms, spyware, and adware. As you'll also discover in this chapter, you can do things to prevent your computer from getting malware. And when it's too late for that, there are things you can do to get rid of malware. This chapter starts with a discussion of the most prevalent form of malware today, spyware.

Types of Malware

Malicious software comes in many forms. All forms have certain things in common though. For one, they're invisible in that you don't even know they're there. For another, they all do something that's bad, something you don't really want happening on your computer. Thirdly, they're all written by human programmers to intentionally do these bad things. The differences have to do with how they spread and what they do once they're on your computer. We'll look at the differences in the sections to follow.

Viruses and worms

Viruses and worms are self-replicating programs that spread from one computer to the next, usually via the Internet. A virus needs a *host file* to spread from one computer to the next. The host file can be anything, though they're typically hidden in e-mail attachments and programs you download.

119

A worm is similar to a virus in that it can replicate itself and spread. However, unlike a virus, a worm doesn't need a host file to travel around. It can go from one computer to the next right though your Internet connection. That's one reason why it's important to always have a firewall up when you're online — to keep out worms that travel through Internet connections.

The harm caused by viruses and worms ranges from minor pranks to serious damage. A minor prank might be something like a small message that appears somewhere on your screen where you don't want it. A more serious virus might erase important files, or even try to erase all your files, rendering your computer useless.

Spyware and adware

Spyware and adware is malware that's not designed to specifically harm your computer. Rather, it's designed to help people sell you stuff. A common spyware tactic is to send information about the Web sites you visit to computers that send out advertisements on the Internet. That computer analyzes the Web sites you visit to figure out what types of products you're most likely to buy. That computer then sends ads about such products to your computer.

Adware is the mechanism that allows ads to appear on your computer screen. When you get advertisements on your screen, seemingly out of the clear blue sky, there's usually some form of adware behind it. Spyware and adware often work in conjunction with one another. The adware provides the means to display ads. The spyware helps the ad server (the computer sending the ads) choose ads for products you're most likely to buy.

Trojan horses and rootkits

You may have heard the term "Trojan horse" in relation to early mythology. The story goes like this. After 10 years of war with the city of Troy, the Greeks decided to call it quits. As a peace offering, they gave to the people of Troy a huge horse statue named the Trojan horse.

While the people of Troy were busy celebrating the end of the war, Greek soldiers hidden inside the horse snuck out and opened the gates to the city from inside. This allowed other Greek soldiers, lying in wait hidden outside the city, to storm into the town and conquer it. (This is definitely a case where it would have been wise to look a gift horse in the mouth.)

A Trojan horse is a program that works in a similar manner. Unlike other forms of malware, a Trojan horse is a program you can actually see on your screen and use. And on the surface, it does do something useful. However, hidden inside the program is some smaller program that does bad things, usually without your knowledge.

A Trojan horse can also be a program that hides nothing, but could be used in bad ways. Take, for example, a program that can recover lost passwords. On the one hand, it can be a good thing if you use it to recover forgotten passwords from files you created yourself. But it can be a bad thing when used to break into other people's password-protected files.

A *rootkit* is a program that is capable of hiding itself, and the malicious intent of other programs, from the user and even from the system. Like Trojan horses, not all rootkits are inherently malicious. However, they can certainly be used in malicious ways. Windows Vista protects your system from rootkits on many fronts, including Windows Defender.

Conquering Spyware with Windows Defender

NEW FEATURE Windows Defender was a popular download for Windows XP. It comes free with Windows Vista, so there's nothing to download.

Spyware (and its close cousin adware) isn't specifically designed to cause your computer harm. But even without the direct intent to do harm, spyware can have serious consequences. Too much spyware can bog your system down, causing everything to run slower than it should. Spyware can make unwanted changes to your Internet settings, causing your Web browser to act in unexpected ways. Spyware can lead to many annoying pop-up ads. And in the worst cases, it can send personally identifiable information about you to identity thieves.

Most spyware comes from software that you can download for free, such as screen savers, custom toolbars, and file-sharing programs. However, it can also be installed automatically from scripts and programs embedded in Web pages.

There are many programs on the market designed to prevent and eliminate spyware (and adware). But you don't have to spend any money or download any third-party programs to protect your system from these threats. You can use Windows Defender, which comes with Windows Vista for free. Despite its focus on spyware, Defender actually protects your computer from any potentially unwanted programs. That includes many types of adware, Trojan horses, and rootkits.

When Windows Defender is running and protecting your computer, you might see its icon in the Notification area, shown near the mouse pointer in Figure 8.1. But don't be alarmed if you don't see that icon. It's optional and may be hidden even when Defender is protecting your system.

FIGURE 8.1

Windows Defender Notification area icon.

The Security Center is the best and most accurate way to find out if Defender is protecting your computer. You can get to the Security Center through Search or the Control Panel. Press ⊞, type sec, and click Security Center. Or click the Start button and choose Control Panel ➪ Security ➪ Security Center. In Security Center, the Malware Protection bar will be green and show On if you have adequate protection from malware. Click that bar to expand it. If Windows Defender is on and protecting your system, you'll see an entry like the one under "Spyware and other malware protection" in Figure 8.2.

FIGURE 8.2

Windows Defender listed in Security Center.

Opening Windows Defender

Windows Defender doesn't need to be open to protect your computer. Its Security Center entry or notification icon is enough to let you know it's protecting your computer. But you can do other things with Defender that do require opening the program. Like most programs, there are many ways to open Defender. Use whichever is most convenient for you at the moment:

- Click Windows Defender in the left column of Security Center.
- Double-click the Windows Defender Notification area icon.
- Click the Start button and choose All Programs ⇨ Windows Defender.
- Press ⊞, type def in the Search box, and then click Windows Defender.

When Windows Defender opens, it will look something like Figure 8.3.

FIGURE 8.3

Windows Defender open on the desktop.

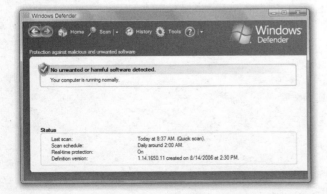

Removing spyware from your computer

Windows Defender offers many tools for fighting spyware. One of them is the ability to scan your system for any spyware that you might have already acquired. You can do a Full Scan, which takes a while, but gives you the peace of mind of knowing that your system is free of malicious spyware. Or you can do a Quick Scan. As its name implies, the Quick Scan takes less time because it focuses on areas where spyware is most likely hiding. You can also opt for a Custom Scan where you can choose which drives you want to scan. To perform a scan, click the arrow next to the Scan button as in Figure 8.4.

FIGURE 8.4

Scan for sypware.

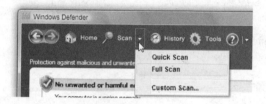

> **NOTE**   If you're unable to scan for spyware from a standard account, an administrator may need to enable scanning for you. See "Advanced and administrator configuration options" later in this chapter.

A full scan takes several minutes. So you'll need to be patient. When the scan is complete, you should see a clean bill of health. If not, suspicious items will be *quarantined* (disabled). You should be taken to the quarantined list automatically, though you can get there any time by choosing Tools ⇨ Quarantined Items.

Each item in the quarantined list has an alert level associated with it. Here's what each alert level means:

- **Severe:** This item is known to compromise the security of your computer. It should be removed immediately.

- **High:** This item may be too new to be well known. But all indications point to malicious intent, so the item should be removed immediately.

- **Medium:** This item appears to collect personal information or change Internet settings. Review the item details. If you do not recognize or trust the publisher, block or remove the item.

- **Low:** This is a potentially unwanted item that should be removed if you did not intentionally install it yourself.

- **Not yet classified:** This item is unrecognized, but is potentially something you don't want on your computer. You may want to check with the Windows Defender newsgroups described later in this chapter for further advice.

To remove an item, click its name and click Remove. You can usually click Remove All, because valid, useful programs are rarely detected as spyware or other potentially unwanted items. If in doubt, you can leave the item quarantined for a while. Use your computer normally to see if some useful program no longer works. After you've determined that everything is okay, you can go back into Quarantined Items and remove anything you left behind.

Should you ever encounter a false positive (where an innocent program is quarantined), don't remove it. Instead, click its name and then click Restore.

Doing a quick scan

A full scan takes some time because it scans every file on your hard disk. You can save some time by doing a quick scan. A quick scan checks only new files and the kinds of files commonly used by spyware. Once you've done a single full scan, quick scans are sufficient.

Doing a custom scan

A custom scan lets you scan a specific drive or folder. For example, if someone sends you a CD or DVD, you might want to check that disk before copying or opening any files from it.

For downloads, you might consider creating a subfolder within your Documents folder, perhaps named Unscanned or something similar. Whenever you download a file or save an e-mail attachment that you don't trust 100 percent, save it to that Unscanned folder. Then scan just the folder to make sure all is well. If the files check out okay, you can then move them to any folder you like. Or, in the case of a downloaded program, click the icon to start the program installation.

To do a custom scan, click Scan in Windows Defender and choose Custom Scan. Then click the Select button and select (check) the drive you want to scan. Or, expand any drive icon and select the specific folder you want to scan. Then click OK to start the scan.

Automatic scanning

You can also set up Defender to automatically scan your system daily, weekly, or however often you wish. You must be logged in to an account with administrative privileges to set up automatic scanning. From the Administrator account, start Windows Defender normally. Then click Tools and Options. Automatic scanning options appear as in Figure 8.5.

FIGURE 8.5

Automatic scanning options.

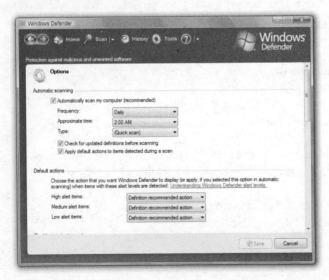

To enable automatic scanning, make sure the Automatically scan my computer (recommended) checkbox is selected (checked). Then you can set a schedule for scanning. For example, if you use a desktop computer that you leave on 24 hours a day, choose Daily and a time during which you're unlikely to be using the computer. If the computer isn't turned on when the scheduled time arrives, the scan will take place the next time you start the computer. Choose the type of scan you want to perform on the schedule.

If your computer is on and online 24 hours a day, you can also choose Check for updated definitions before scanning. Doing so ensures that Defender is up-to-date with all known spyware when it scans. Choose Apply actions on detected items after scanning if you want Defender to automatically delete severe items, or other items you specify under the Default Actions heading.

Under the Default Actions heading, you can choose how you want an automatic scan to treat High, Medium, and Low alert items, as follows:

- **Definition recommended action:** Choose this option to take the action that's recommended in the item's definition.
- **Remove:** Choose this option if you want the item removed automatically when found.
- **Ignore:** Have Defender ignore the item.

If in doubt about what to choose, your best bet is to choose the Definition recommend action. Each malware item that Defender identifies has a *definition* that specifies its intent, severity, and recommended actions. The definitions are created by human experts who have previously found and analyzed the item. Unless you're an expert yourself, your best bet is to allow those expert definitions to choose a course of action.

Preventing spyware

You've probably heard the saying "An ounce of prevention is worth a pound of cure." That's certainly true of spyware. Getting rid of spyware that has already infected your computer is a good thing. But preventing it from getting there in the first place is even better. That's where *real-time protection* comes into play. The term "real time" means "as it's happening."

The Windows Defender real-time protection analyzes files as they approach your computer from the Internet. Any spyware or suspicious-looking files are blocked to keep your computer from being infected.

Real-time protection is turned on, by default. You can control whether it's on or off, and optionally tweak what it monitors by clicking Tools in Defender and choosing Options. Scroll down from the first set of options to see the real-time options shown in Figure 8.6.

FIGURE 8.6

Defender real-time protection options.

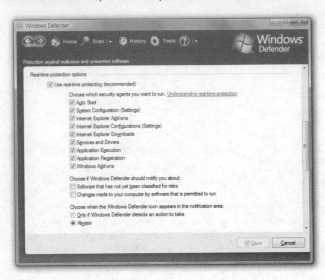

Most people will want to check all the boxes that are checked in Figure 8.6. The first option is especially important. If you clear that checkbox you have no real-time spyware protection. The remaining items represent real-time *agents*, small programs that offer a specific type of protection. Here's a quick summary of what each agent does:

- **Auto Start:** Monitors programs that start automatically when you start your computer.
- **System Configuration:** Monitors security-related programs to prevent spyware from lowering your system's defenses.
- **Internet Explorer Add-ons:** Monitors programs that start automatically whenever you open Internet Explorer.
- **Internet Explorer Configurations (Settings):** Monitors security settings in Internet Explorer to prevent spyware from compromising your Internet security.
- **Internet Explorer Downloads:** Monitors downloadable programs and files that are designed to work with Internet Explorer, including ActiveX controls.
- **Services and Drivers:** Monitors Windows Vista services and device drivers to prevent spyware from gaining access to critical systems and components.
- **Application Execution:** Monitors application programs when first starting, and while running.
- **Application Registration:** Prevents spyware from changing registry settings that would allow the spyware program to run automatically at startup.
- **Windows Add-ons:** Monitors add-on programs designed to enhance communications, browsing, and multimedia.

The two remaining checkboxes let you control when Windows Defender notifies you of changes. These are entirely optional. You can select them to be notified whenever a change is made. If anything suspicious happens, you may want to run a Quick Scan to see if the change generates an alert. The main drawback to choosing those options is that you get a whole lot of warnings about software that's perfectly safe. This can be very annoying, and puts the onus of choosing what to do in every case on you. If you leave those checkboxes empty, you'll still get the kind of protection you really need without the constant warnings and decision making.

Below those two checkboxes are options for configuring the Windows Defender Notification area icon. You can choose to have that icon appear only when Defender detects a problem and needs to take action. Or you can choose to have that icon displayed at all times while Defender is protecting your system.

NOTE Options in the Customize Notifications dialog box still apply to Defender's icon. To get to that dialog box, right-click the current time in the lower-right corner of the screen and choose Customize Notification Icons.

Advanced and Administrator configuration options

If you scroll down a little more from the options shown in Figure 8.6, you'll see the Advanced options shown in Figure 8.7.

FIGURE 8.7

Advanced Defender configuration options.

Choosing the Scan the contents of archived files... option tells Defender to scan within archived file groups created by Windows Backup and other archiving products. Choosing Use heuristics... tells Defender to check for potentially unwanted programs using logic rather than just known definitions. Defender is more likely to detect new unknown threats if you select this option, though there's a slight chance you'll get more false positives, where Defender incorrectly flags an innocent program as suspicious.

The Create a restore point before taking action... option tells Defender to create a System Protection Restore Point before deleting detected items. This provides a means of rolling back changes made by Defender should a scan ever inadvertently delete items that you need to use all of your programs. Use the technique described under "Returning to a Previous Restore Point" in Chapter 33 to restore everything to its previous state.

If, for whatever reason, you don't want Defender to scan specific drives or folders, you can use the Add button to add those locations to the Do not scan the following paths list.

The options under Administrator options allow an administrator to fully disable Windows Defender. The only reason to do this would be if Defender has serious conflicts with some other program that makes your system or favorite programs unusable. An administrator can also choose whether or not to allow all users, even those with standard user accounts, to use Windows Defender.

Using Software Explorer to control startup programs

The Software Explorer component of Windows Defender provides detailed information about programs that are currently running on your system. You can also use it to control programs that start automatically when you start your computer.

To get to Software Explorer, click Tools in Defender. Then click Software Explorer. Initially you'll see a list of startup programs, with just one of those programs selected in the left pane. The pane on the right shows detailed information about the selected program, as in the example shown in Figure 8.8.

FIGURE 8.8

Software Explorer.

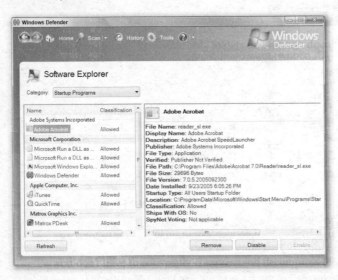

Why Defender Monitors Startup Programs

Many spyware and other malicious programs have to load automatically at startup to do their malicious deeds. Computers infected with a lot of malware took a really long time to start up, because Windows had to spend so much time loading malware programs before it could display the desktop. The record at my local PC repair shop was over 100,000 spyware items on one PC!

Getting rid of these things was virtually impossible for the average computer user, because there are several ways to get programs to auto-start without making it obvious on the screen. Windows Defender protects from such maladies in several ways. First, it keeps spyware from getting on your system in the first place. Second, you can do an occasional spyware scan to remove any items that might have snuck through your defenses in the past. And third, you can use Software Explorer to see exactly what programs are auto-starting.

Just remember that you can't remove Startup programs in a willy-nilly manner and expect things to work out okay. You should first click an item and check its Spyware Voting entry. If there's nothing there to indicate the item is bad, don't remove the item!

The programs that show up in Software Explorer usually aren't bad. In fact, they're probably useful programs that are totally harmless. The idea behind Software Explorer is just to monitor and review certain types of programs. For starters, you can use the Category drop-down list to choose among different types of programs to review:

- **Startup Programs:** These are programs that start automatically when you first start your computer.
- **Currently Running Programs:** Programs that are currently running onscreen or in the background. Onscreen programs have a program window and taskbar button. Background programs have no onscreen presence. Some may be represented by an icon in the Notification area.
- **Network Connected Programs:** Programs that provide network connectivity. The connection could be to the Internet or to a local network.
- **Winsock Service Providers:** Programs that perform low-level networking and communication services for Windows and other programs.

Within any category of programs, you can click any name in the left pane to see detailed information about that item in the right pane. For the average computer user, the most important entry in the right pane is SpyNet Voting. In most cases, that will show Not applicable, and that's a good thing. It means that there's no doubt as to the program's necessity and safety, so voting is unnecessary.

Depending on the category you're viewing, you may see buttons that allow you to remove, disable, or block the currently selected program. You don't want to use any of those options unless you're 100 percent certain that the program doesn't belong on your system and serves no useful purpose.

Disallowing allowed programs

There may be times when you allow a program that you know and trust to run without any warnings from Windows Defender. Later, you might change your mind about that. If you do, you can click Tools in Defender to get to its page or options. Then click Allowed Items. From there you can click any item and choose Remove from List to have Windows Defender start monitoring the program again.

Joining the SpyNet community

The SpyNet community is a huge group of Windows Defender users who keep a watchful eye on potential spyware. Joining the community allows you to see how others are treating suspicious software that hasn't yet been classified by experts. Seeing how others deal with a suspicious file can help you make decisions about suspicious files on your computer. When Defender finds a suspicious file, the community's rating appears as a graph indicating the number of members who have allowed the item.

To join the Microsoft SpyNet community, open Windows Defender, click Tools, and choose Microsoft SpyNet. Then choose the basic membership, advanced membership, or no membership option as described on the page that opens.

Windows Defender Web site

The Windows Defender Web site is a great resource for staying up-to-date with spyware threats and tools. The Community link on that page offers further resources for live interaction with others grappling with spyware decisions, and experts to help you make those decisions. You can get to the Web site by clicking the Windows Defender Web site link on Defender's Tools page.

Using Antivirus Software

Windows Defender helps to protect your computer from spyware and other malicious software. But it doesn't protect against all viruses. For virus protection, you'll need a *third-party program* (a program that doesn't come free with Windows Vista). The Windows Security Center can detect some (but not all) antivirus programs.

If you don't have antivirus software, or Windows can't recognize the product you're using, you'll see a security warning stating that Antivirus software *might* not be installed, as in Figure 8.9.

FIGURE 8.9

Antivirus might not be installed.

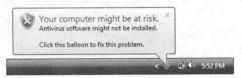

> **NOTE** You might see the message from Figure 8.9 briefly even if you do have virus protection, only because the message sometimes appears before your antivirus solution is fully loaded. If your malware protection is On in Security Center, you can ignore the alert.

Your ISP (Internet service provider) might provide virus protection. Or your computer manufacturer might have pre-installed antivirus on your system. If you don't know what your situation is, it might be wise to check with your ISP and computer manufacturer before you go out and purchase another product.

Virus protection

There are basically two ways to deal with viruses. One is to *prevent* them in the first place. The other is to detect and remove them after your computer has already been infected. Of course, an ounce of prevention is worth a pound of cure. But it's also worth some money because you can scan your system and remove viruses at any time for free. But programs that prevent viruses generally cost some money.

That's not to say they *do* cost money. As mentioned, your ISP might have virus protection built right in. That means viruses are detected and removed by your ISP before they ever get to your computer, as illustrated in Figure 8.10. There is no extra charge for that. You pay for it when you pay the monthly bill for your Internet connection. Furthermore, you don't really have to do anything to keep your virus protection up-to-date. Your ISP takes care of that too.

FIGURE 8.10

ISP blocks viruses before they get to your PC.

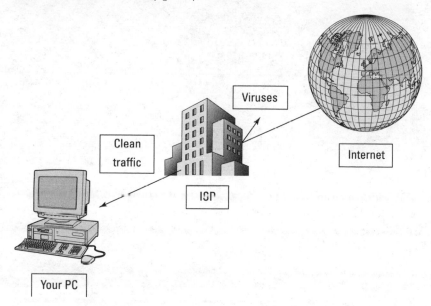

A second approach to virus protection is to have the antivirus program right on your own computer, as illustrated in Figure 8.11. Some popular brands include Norton Antivirus, McAfee VirusScan, and Trend PC-cillin. Some ISPs will actually pay for such a service on your computer. But you still have to take some steps to install the program and keep it up-to-date.

Viruses Mutate

Computer security is always a moving target. The good guys come up with ways to thwart existing malware (including viruses). The bad guys keep inventing new ways to create viruses and other bad programs. To keep up-to-date with current threats, most antivirus programs need to download current *signatures* on a regular basis. Each signature basically tells the antivirus program what to block in order to keep your computer free of viruses.

FIGURE 8.11

Antivirus software on your own PC.

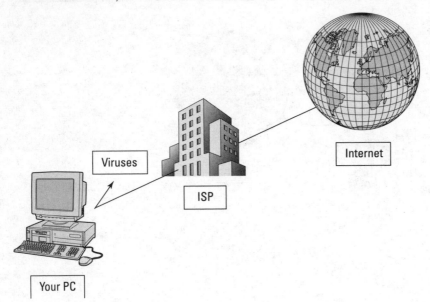

If neither your ISP nor computer manufacturer has provided an antivirus program, then you may have to purchase and install one yourself. It's not absolutely necessary to do so. I know many people who don't use antivirus programs. But they're all pros who can spot suspicious software a mile away, and never download anything that looks even remotely suspicious. Nor do they open suspicious-looking e-mail attachments (the means by which many viruses are spread from computer to computer). If you're not a pro, you should seriously consider installing antivirus software. You can click the Find a Program button (visible in Figure 8.13 later in this chapter) to browse through available products.

Finally, you might also consider looking into Windows Live OneCare, which combines virus protection with a host of other useful services. See www.WindowsOneCare.com for more information.

Virus protection and removal

Whether or not you're a pro, you should scan your computer for viruses at least once a month. Scanning doesn't prevent viruses from infecting your computer. Rather, it analyzes all the files on your hard disk seeking out viruses hiding there. If it finds any, it alerts you to the problem and lets you remove the virus. In other words, it works just like spyware scanning in Windows Defender.

You can scan your computer for viruses at any time, free of charge. You don't have to buy or own antivirus software at all. Just browse to the Windows Live Safety Center (`http://safety.live.com`) and click the link to scan for and remove viruses. It takes quite a bit of time, though, so you may want to start the process just before going to bed at night so you can leave the computer running without using it.

Antivirus and Security Center

Let's get back to that "Antivirus software might not be installed" message shown back in Figure 8.9. If you have antivirus software installed and protecting your computer already, you won't see that message. That message only appears if 1) Windows can't detect your antivirus strategy or 2) You really don't have an antivirus strategy.

 Some options in Security Center will require that you know the administrative password.

If you know for a fact (or learn from your ISP) that you do have an antivirus strategy in place, you can make that message stop appearing. You just have to change the Malware Protection setting in the Windows Security Center to Not Monitored. To open the Security Center, you have several options:

- Click the Start button, choose Control Panel ➪ Security ➪ Security Center.
- Press ⊞, type sec, and click Security Center under Programs.
- Click the "Your computer might be at risk" message the next time it appears.
- Double-click the Security Center icon in the Notification area (see Figure 8.12).

FIGURE 8.12

Double-click the shield to open Security Center.

In Security Center, the Malware Protection bar (see Figure 8.13) informs you of virus protection. If that shows as "On," then you know you have virus protection. All is well and you probably don't need to do anything else, unless you see a message saying you should update your virus definitions or signatures. In that case, you should do as the message instructs.

If the Malware Protection bar shows Not found, then you have a decision to make. If you know for a fact that your ISP provides virus protection, or you have an antivirus program installed, click Show me other available options. Then click I have an antivirus solution program that I'll monitor myself. That will change the bar's color to Yellow and its status to Not Monitored.

If you're sure you don't have any virus protection, and would like to explore your options, click the Find a program button.

FIGURE 8.13

Malware Protection is Not Found in this example.

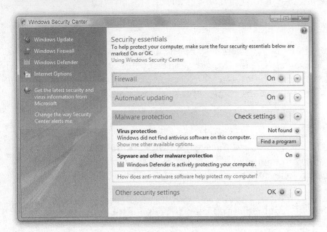

User Account Control and Malware

User Account Control (UAC) is yet another form of malware protection. Unlike the anti-malware programs described in this chapter, designed to keep malware out of your PC, UAC prevents malicious programs that have already infiltrated your system from doing their evil deeds. It will be tempting to turn off UAC, to get rid of that occasional extra mouse click for approval it requires. But do keep in mind that in doing so, you're lowering your computer's resistance to malware. For more information on User Account Control, see Chapter 3.

The Malicious Software Removal Tool

There is one last malware protection tool you'll want to know about before we put this topic to rest. It's called the Malicious Software Removal Tool (MSRT). Its primary focus is on worm and rootkit removal. It's an online tool. The page has been at this address for a while:

```
www.microsoft.com/security/malwareremove/
```

Microsoft is notorious for changing URLs frequently, so I can't guarantee that address will work by the time you read this book. If you can't find the page, click Get the latest security and virus information from Microsoft in Security Center's left column. When the page opens, you should have no problem finding a link to the Malicious Software Removal Tool.

Wrap Up

Malicious software (called malware for short) is computer software that's intentionally written to invade your privacy or cause harm. This is not the kind of thing you purchase or download from legitimate software vendors. Nor does it announce its presence to you on the screen. Rather, it sneaks into your computer through tainted programs and e-mail attachments without your knowledge. This chapter has covered the main types of malware and defenses to take against them:

- Spyware is a form of malware designed to invade your privacy, and it is the largest and most common Internet threat today.

- Windows Defender is a program that comes free with Windows Vista to protect your computer from spyware and similar forms of malicious software.

- Windows Defender can scan your system for unwanted software and remove it.

- Defender's real-time protection prevents spyware from getting on your computer in the first place.

- Viruses and worms are harmful programs that can spread from one computer to the next via the Internet (or any network connection for that matter).

- Most viruses are spread through e-mail attachments or tainted programs from non-legitimate Web sites.

- Windows Vista offers no built-in virus protection. Typically you acquire this from your ISP, your computer manufacturer, or by purchasing it yourself.

- The Windows Security Center alerts you if it cannot find antivirus software on your computer.

- The Malicious Software Removal Tool (MSRT) is an online tool specializing in worm removal. Run it once a month or so to ensure your computer is free of worms.

Chapter 9

Automatic Updates as Security

Internet security is a never-ending cat-and-mouse game between the security experts and the hackers who seem to have endless amounts of time to search for new ways to exploit the basic programmability of PCs. It seems that every time the good guys find a way to patch some security hole the bad guys have learned to exploit, the bad guys find two more holes to exploit.

Windows Vista is certainly the most secure Windows ever, by a long shot. But there is no such thing as a 100-percent secure computer, because people can always find a way to take something good and turn it into something bad. So in addition to the security features discussed in the preceding chapters, you need to keep your computer up-to-date with security patches as they become available. That's what Windows Update and this chapter are all about.

IN THIS CHAPTER

Why you want automatic updates

Enabling automatic updates

Managing updates

Thwarting exploits with DEP

Understanding Automatic Updates

Many people are afraid of Windows Update. They're afraid that the changes to their system that the updates make will break something that they can't fix. It's certainly true that any change to your system could create a problem. But it's unlikely that keeping up with updates will cause any significant problems — certainly nowhere near as many problems to which you expose yourself by *not* keeping up with updates.

Others fear that Microsoft will somehow exploit them through automatic updates. That's not the way it works. Microsoft has tens of millions of customers, and tens of billions of dollars. It doesn't need to exploit anybody to be successful. Desperate people (and companies) do desperate, exploitive things. Microsoft is as far from desperate as you can get.

Microsoft is also a publicly held company on the stock exchange, which means it is subject to constant scrutiny. Such companies are not the ones that distribute malware. Most malware comes from e-mail attachments and free programs from

Some Hacking Lingo

The hacking world is replete with its own terminology. A *zero day exploit* is one that becomes available before a software product is even released to the public. A *blackhat* is a bad guy who has sufficient technical knowledge to find and publish exploits. A *script kiddie* is an inexperienced programmer who doesn't have enough skill to create or discover his own exploits, but does have enough expertise to create malware based on known exploits. A *whitehat* is one of the good guys — the security experts who find ways to thwart the efforts of blackhats and script kiddies.

unknown sources. When it comes to knowing who to trust and not to trust, large publicly held companies are by far the most trustworthy, if for no other reason than they can't afford to be untrustworthy.

A third common fear of automatic updates centers around the question "What's this going to cost me?" The answer to that is simple: Absolutely nothing. Which brings us to the difference between *updates* and *upgrades*.

Updates versus upgrades

People often assume that the terms *update* and *upgrade* are synonymous. We certainly use the terms interchangeably in common parlance. But in the computer world, there is a big difference. Upgrades usually cost money, and involve a fair amount of work. For example, upgrading from Windows XP to Windows Vista will cost you some money, and will take some time. You might even need to hire someone to verify that the upgrade will work, and do the upgrade for you.

Updates are much different. Updates are small, simple, and free of charge. Some people turn of automatic updates because they're afraid they'll get some mysterious bill for something they downloaded automatically without realizing it. That will never happen. Turning on and using automatic updates will never cost you a penny.

Why updates are important

Automatic updates are an important part of your overall security. Many forms of malware, especially viruses and worms, operate by exploiting previously unnoticed flaws in programs. The term *exploit*, when used as a noun in computer science, refers to any piece of software that can take advantage of some vulnerability in a program in order to gain unauthorized access to a computer.

Some hackers actually publish, on the Internet, exploits they discover, which is both a good thing and a bad thing. The bad thing is that other hackers can use the exploit to conjure up their own malware, causing a whole slew of new security threats. The good thing is that the good guys can quickly create security patches to prevent the exploits from doing their nefarious deeds. Automatic updates keep your system current with *security patches* that fix the flaws that malware programs attempt to exploit.

Enabling Automatic Updates

Automatic updates are the best way to keep up with security patches. In fact, chances are they are already enabled on your system. To find out, just open Security Center. In case you skipped the preceding chapters, or forgot how, you can use any technique that follows to open Security Center:

- Click the Start button and choose Control Panel ⇨ Security ⇨ Security Center.
- Tap ⊞, type sec, and click Security Center under Programs.
- Double-click the shield icon in the Notification area.

If the Automatic updating bar is green and shows "On," as in Figure 9.1, there's no need to change anything. Your computer has been getting automatic updates all along. It will continue to do so provided you don't turn automatic updates off.

FIGURE 9.1

Security Center, all systems Go!

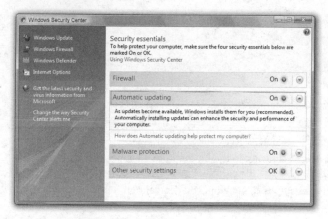

If automatic updates are turned off, seriously consider turning them on. To do so, just click the Turn on Now button in Security Center.

Managing Updates

Automatic updates related to security require little or no effort on your part. But there may be times where you're faced with optional updates. These updates aren't security related. Rather they're new versions of drivers, fixes for minor bugs, and so forth. They're optional because your computer is secure whether you install the update or not.

Managing optional updates

To manage optional updates, and tweak some settings, use the Windows Update page in Control Panel. To get to that page:

- Click the Start button and choose Control Panel ⇨ Security ⇨ Check for Updates.
- Or press ⊞, type win, and choose Windows <version> Extras.

A window like the one in Figure 9.2 opens. Yours probably won't look exactly like the figure, because there are multiple versions of Windows Vista. But whatever you see will likely offer the same kinds of options as shown in the figure.

FIGURE 9.2

Windows Update status and options.

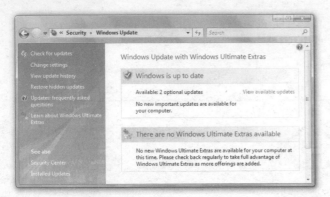

If there are any optional updates, click View available updates to see what they are. The name of each will be listed next to an empty checkbox. You have three options for dealing with each one:

- If you want to download and install the update, select (check) its checkbox.

- If you want to hide the item so it doesn't show up in the future, right-click it and choose Hide update. (It won't go into hiding until you leave the current window.)

- If you want to get more information about the item before you decide, right-click its name as in Figure 9.3 and choose View details.

FIGURE 9.3

Optional update.

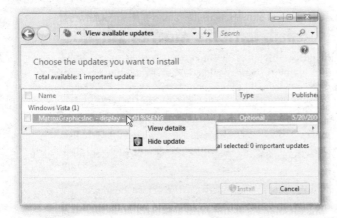

If you opted to install any optional updates, click the Install button and follow the onscreen instructions to proceed. If you don't want to install any optional updates, click Cancel.

Change how updates work

In the left column of the Windows Update page, you can click Change settings to change how automatic updating works. You'll come to the options shown in Figure 9.4. The preferred (and most secure) setting is the one shown, where Windows checks for critical updates daily at 3:00 A.M.

So, what if your computer isn't turned on and online at 3:00 in the morning? Will you miss out on something important? Not at all. For one thing, there is no time limit on updates. After an update is posted, it stays posted forever. So you can download and install it at any time.

If your computer isn't on and online at 3:00 A.M., it will check for updates and download them in the background as soon as you do go online. ("In the background" means "without interfering with whatever you want to do yourself.") Also, if you shut down the computer before the scheduled time, Windows will offer to check for updates before you shut down. So any way you slice it, you don't have to worry about missing out on anything important.

FIGURE 9.4

Change update settings.

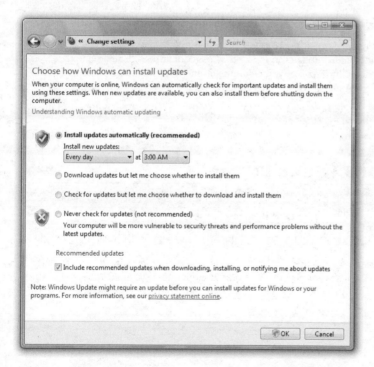

Of course, you're free to choose a different schedule if you prefer, such as weekly at noon or whatever. But daily at 3:00 A.M. is fine.

As an alternative to fully automatic updates, you can choose one of the other options shown on the page. For example, you can have Windows download the updates, but ask your permission before actually installing them. Or, you can just be alerted to available updates, then choose whether or not you want to download or install them.

Finally, you can choose to turn off automatic updating altogether. If you choose that option, the only way to get updates is to click Check for updates at the left side of the Windows Update page.

By default, only critical updates are downloaded and installed. A critical update is one that's needed to protect your computer against current Internet threats. Choosing Include recommended updates... extends that to less-critical updates that aren't directly related to security. Recommended updates are usually things like minor bug fixes or improvements to Windows and other Microsoft products.

Click OK after making any changes to your settings, or click Cancel to leave all settings in their original state.

Reviewing and removing updates

The fact that there are well over 200,000 hardware and software products available for Windows means that once in a while, an update could cause problems with a particular device or program. Typically you fix that problem by going to the product manufacturer's Web site and finding out what they recommend. If the manufacturer hasn't fixed the problem yet, and you need immediate access to the device or program, you might want to temporarily remove the conflicting update, especially if it isn't a critical security update.

To review your history of installed updates, click View update history in the left column. If you need to remove any installed updates, click Installed updates in the history page that opens. Click the update you want to remove and then click Remove. If necessary, you can reinstall the update later by clicking Check for updates in the left column of the Windows Update page.

 For more information and general troubleshooting, click the Updates: frequently asked questions link at the left side of the Windows Updates page.

Thwarting Exploits with DEP

Thwarting malware attacks that exploit software vulnerabilities is the most important element of automatic updates. But Windows Vista offers a second way of thwarting such attacks. It's called Data Execution Prevention or DEP for short. You don't want to use DEP as an alternative to other techniques described in this part of the book. Rather, you want to use it as an addition to all the other techniques described in this book.

For a little background, many malware attacks use a technique called *buffer overflow* (or *buffer overrun*) to sneak code (program instructions) into areas of memory that only the operating system (Windows) should be using. Those areas of memory have direct access to everything on your computer. So any bad code that sneaks into that area can do great damage.

More Security Tricks up Its Sleeve

Some malware techniques rely on well-known memory locations to exploit system vulnerabilities. Vista has a surprise for those programs too. It no longer loads essential programs to well-known predictable locations. Instead it uses Address Space Layout Randomization (ASLR) to load things in a random location each time you start your computer. So malware writers can't really know in advance where a particular exploit resides in memory, making it much more difficult to exploit those memory addresses.

Data Execution Prevention is a security antidote to such attacks. It monitors programs to make sure they use only safe and appropriate memory locations. If DEP notices a program trying to do anything sneaky, it shuts that program down before it can do any harm.

By default, DEP is enabled for essential Windows programs and services only. When coupled with antivirus protection, that setting is usually adequate. You can crank it up to monitor all programs and services. But if you do, you might also have to individually choose programs that are allowed to bypass DEP. Knowing when that's okay may require technical expertise that goes beyond the scope of this book.

To get to options for DEP, first open the System window using whichever technique is most convenient:

- Click the Start button, right-click Computer, and choose Properties.
- Click the Start button and choose Control Panel ⇨ System and Maintenance ⇨ System.
- Tap ▓, type sys, and click System under the Programs heading.
- In the Welcome Center, click More Details.

Regardless of the method used, you end up in the System window. In the left column, click Advanced System Settings. That takes you to the System Properties dialog box. In System Properties, click the Advanced tab, click the Settings button on the Performance heading, and then click the Data Execution Prevention tab. At last you see the options shown in Figure 9.5.

By default, the option to apply DEP to essential Windows programs and services only is selected. For stronger protection, you can turn on DEP for all programs and services. If you choose that option, there may be times where DEP shuts down a program to prevent it from running.

NOTE　Many modern processors offer *NX technologies*, which prevent buffer overflows at the hardware level. When that's the case, Windows supports that hardware-based DEP. For processors that don't have hardware DEP, Windows uses DEP software to achieve the same result.

If DEP does shut down a program you need, you have a couple of choices. One is to contact the program manufacturer to find out if there's a version of the program that runs under DEP. Otherwise, if you trust the program, you can add it to the list of programs that are allowed to bypass DEP. To accomplish that, you'll need to click the Add button, then navigate to and double-click the executable (typically .exe) file that DEP is shutting down.

FIGURE 9.5

Data Execution Prevention options.

Wrap Up

When it comes to general computer security, the "big three" items are 1) a firewall, 2) malware protection, and 3) automatic updates. Chapters 7, 8, and 9 have covered those bases. But don't forget that running under a standard user account (Chapter 3) counts, too. Furthermore, there are less technical "social" threats to consider, like phishing scams and pop-up ads. Those are covered in Chapters 17 and 18.

As far as this chapter goes, the main points are as follows:

- Automatic updates provide a quick and simple way to protect your computer against current software exploitation malware.
- Unless you have some compelling reason to do otherwise, you should allow Windows Vista to automatically download and install updates daily.
- Data Execution Prevention (DEP) offers yet another layer of protection against threats that work by sneaking errant code into sensitive parts of system memory.

Chapter 10

Troubleshooting Security

Troubleshooting Firewall Problems

The Windows Firewall that comes with Windows Vista really battens down the hatches on ports. So, you may experience a few problems when you first make the switch to Windows Firewall. Here are some common problems and solutions to those problems.

Some Internet programs do not work when installed on Windows Vista

The tighter security imposed by Windows Firewall may prevent some online games and other Internet programs from working correctly. Microsoft maintains a list of such programs and ways to correct the problem in Knowledge Base article 842242. To get to that page, browse to http://support.microsoft.com and search for 842242. Optionally, you can browse directly to http://support.microsoft.com/default.aspx?scid=kb;en-us;842242&Product=windowsxpsp2.

Although the preceding article is based around Windows XP Service Pack 2, the list of applications and configurations for the applications are still applicable with Vista.

Error message "Windows Firewall has blocked this program from accepting connections"

The message is actually just an alert. Assuming that you're familiar with the FTP site and trust its owners, you can choose Unblock and proceed with uploading the file(s).

Can't adjust Windows Firewall for AOL dial-up connection

AOL doesn't follow the same standard that other ISPs do, so you may have to disable the firewall to access America Online. (That's risky business, and you may want to consider contacting AOL about a better workaround, or consider switching to a different ISP.) If you need to disable Windows Firewall to get online, follow these steps:

1. If you're currently online, disconnect from the Internet.
2. Press ⊞, type sec, and click Security Center. Or click the Start button and choose Control Panel ⇨ Security ⇨ Security Center.
3. In the Windows Security Center window, choose Windows Firewall from the left column.
4. Click Change Settings. Elevate your privileges by clicking Continue or by entering the password from an administrative account.
5. Click Off (not recommended).
6. Click OK.
7. Close all open windows.

You should be able to get online. It would be best to search AOL's site for an alternative solution that allows you to get online without disabling Windows Firewall. Hopefully there will be a better solution by the time you read this, because going online without a firewall up poses a significant security risk to your system.

Phone dialer does not work after installing Windows Vista

Windows Firewall blocks TCP port 1720, which is used by many phone-dialing programs. It does so to prevent unauthorized dialing programs from connecting to a network without your knowledge. To get your phone dialer to work, you'll need to open that port as follows:

1. Click the Start button and choose Control Panel ⇨ Security Center. Or press ⊞, type sec, and click Security Center.
2. In the Windows Security Center window, choose Windows Firewall from the left column.
3. In the left column, click Allow a program through Windows Firewall and then elevate your privileges by clicking OK or by entering the password for an administrative user account.
4. In the Windows Firewall Settings dialog box that opens, click the Exceptions tab.
5. Click the Add port button.
6. Type any name you like in the Name box, such as Dialup Port 1720.
7. Type 1720 as the port number and choose TCP.
8. Click OK in each open dialog box.
9. Close the Windows Firewall and Security Center windows.

CAUTION   Opening port 1720 allows all dialers to dial out through that connection, even unauthorized programs you might pick up accidentally from the Internet. To block that port, return to the Exceptions tab of the dialog box and clear the checkmark to the left of the name you provided in step 6 of the preceding set of steps.

Troubleshooting Antivirus Programs

If you have trouble installing an antivirus program, make sure you're installing the version for Windows Vista. Security programs written for Windows XP or some other version of Windows probably won't work with Vista, because Vista is a much different operating system. Check the antivirus program publisher's Web site for updates and additional information about products for Windows Vista.

Troubleshooting Automatic Updates

Automatic updates have changed many times over the years and continue to evolve to this day. Your best bet for troubleshooting problems with automatic updates is to go straight to the source for the most current information. Click the Start button and choose All Programs ⇨ Windows Update.

In the left column of the Windows Update page that opens, click Updates: frequently asked questions. Scroll to the bottom of the Help window that opens and click Troubleshoot problems with installing updates.

Troubleshooting Windows Defender

Your best resource for Windows Defender will be the Defender Web site, which you'll find at www.microsoft.com/defender.

Troubleshooting ActiveX Control Downloads

The Windows Firewall will block ActiveX control downloads. If clicking a link doesn't provide the results you expected, look to Internet Explorer's Information bar for more information. Assuming that you consider the ActiveX control safe, click the bar and choose Run ActiveX control or Install ActiveX control as in Figure 10.1.

 Accept ActiveX controls only from legitimate companies with which you've done business in the past and can trust.

FIGURE 10.1

Sample blocked ActiveX control and menu options.

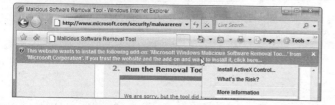

Part III

Personalizing Windows Vista

Everybody likes to have a choice. Most of the chapters in this section are about tweaking Vista to look and act the way you want it to. Chapter 11 starts off with the main *look-and-feel* issues, and the ways in which you can customize them to your liking. Chapter 12 moves on to things you can do to adapt Vista to specific sensory and motor impairments, as well as spoken and written languages. You'll also discover the new and improved Speech Recognition in Vista through Chapter 12.

Chapter 13 moves on to the topic of getting files from an old computer onto a new Windows Vista computer. Chapter 14 covers customization from the standpoint of how Vista, and other programs, start when you first fire up your computer.

Chapter 15 covers the handy accessory programs that come free with Windows Vista. Chapter 16 looks at common customization problems and their solutions.

Chapter 11

Personalizing Your Work Environment

The Windows desktop is your main workplace. Or maybe *play place*, depending on how you use your computer. But the point is, your Windows desktop is similar to a real, wooden desktop. It's where you keep all the stuff you're using right now — the stuff that's *open*. Your hard disk and its folders, by comparison, are more like your filing cabinet. Where you keep stuff you might need in the future.

We all like to set up our own desktop and work environment in unique ways. What works best for one person isn't necessarily great for someone else. The way things look and work on your Windows Vista desktop aren't set in stone. You can personalize things in many ways to make them look and work the way you like. That's what this chapter is all about — having things your way.

Most of the options described in this chapter apply only to the user account you're currently logged in to. So any changes you make to your own desktop apply only to you (assuming you're logged in to your own user account). This means everyone can have things just the way they want without stepping on each others' toes.

IN THIS CHAPTER

Personalizing your screen, mouse, and keyboard

Customizing your Start menu

Personalizing your taskbar

Using Windows Sidebar and gadgets

Showing/Hiding the Welcome Center

On most computers, the Welcome Center shown in Figure 11.1 appears automatically when you first log in to your user account. By the way, I've also labeled some other things on the screen that you'll learn to customize in this chapter. The desktop is actually everything above the taskbar — the big picture you see underneath the desktop icons, Welcome Center, and Sidebar.

FIGURE 11.1

A sample Windows Vista desktop.

If you don't want it to do that anymore, clear the checkbox next to Run at startup (Welcome Center can be found in the Control Panel). Then close the Welcome Center by clicking the Close (X) button in its upper-right corner. When the Welcome Center is closed, you can open it at any time using either of the following methods:

- Press ▦, type wel, and click Welcome Center under Programs.
- Click the Start button and choose Control Panel ➪ System and Maintenance ➪ Welcome Center.

When the Welcome Center is open, the top pane shows some basic information about your computer. Clicking Show More Details in that top pane takes you a page where you can find more information about your system. You'll discover what those things are about in Chapter 50. For now they're not directly relevant to using your computer.

You can click any icon below the top pane to see more information about what the icon offers. Then click the Open or Go To or Start link that appears in the top pane if you want to go to that page. Optionally, click Show all 12 items to see even more icons. If you're new to computers, you might want to click the Windows Basics item that appears when you show all 12 items. Then click Open Windows Basics. A help window opens with links to brief tutorials on basic computer terms and concepts.

You can move, size, and close Welcome Center as you would any other program window. (See "Sizing program windows" in Chapter 2 for details.) Other than that, all you need to know about Welcome Center right now is that you can use the Run at startup... checkbox to choose whether or not Welcome Center opens automatically each time you log in.

Let's focus next on things you can do to tweak Windows Vista's look and feel to better suit your own work habits and tastes.

Using the Personalization Page

Many options for personalizing the look and feel of Windows Vista are on the Personalization page shown in Figure 11.2. As with most things in Vista, there are many ways to get to the Personalization page. Use whichever is most convenient for you at the moment.

FIGURE 11.2

Personalization page.

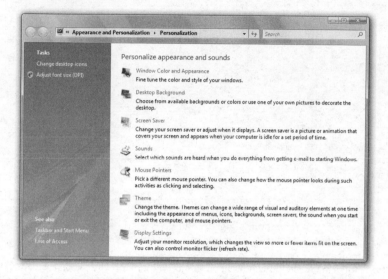

- Right-click the desktop and choose Personalize.
- Press ⊞, type pers, and click Personalization.
- In Welcome Center, double-click Personalize Windows.
- Click the Start button and click Control Panel ⇨ Appearance and Personalization ⇨ Personalization.

The sections to follow look at how you can use the various options on the page to fine-tune the look and feel of Windows Vista on your screen.

Choosing a screen resolution

One of the first things you might want to adjust is your screen resolution, because it determines how much stuff can fit on your screen. Resolution is measured in *pixels*, where each pixel represents a tiny lighted dot on the screen. The pixels are too small to see individually. But suffice it to say the higher the resolution, the smaller everything looks, and the more stuff you can get on the screen. Click Display Settings in the Personalization page to open the Display Settings dialog box shown in Figure 11.3.

FIGURE 11.3

Display Settings dialog box.

There is no right or wrong setting for the screen resolution. A high resolution is good because you can see more stuff on your screen. But a high resolution isn't good if things are so small on your screen that you can't see them. As you move the slider from one resolution to the next, you can see the general shape to the *aspect ratio* of the current selection. You can't really judge how small things will look on your screen as you move the slider, so it may take a little trial and error to get things just right. But let's stop a second to talk about that *aspect ratio* term here.

Understanding aspect ratio

There was a time when all computer monitors had a 4:3 aspect ratio. This means that for every 4 pixels of width, you get 3 pixels of height. These days you'll come across other aspect ratios including 5:4 and the 16:9 ratio found on widescreen TVs. There are some others. You can check the manual that came with your monitor or notebook computer for your screen's exact aspect ratio. Or, just choose a resolution that looks good on your screen. Table 11.1 lists some common aspect ratios and resolutions that fit them.

TABLE 11.1

Common Aspect Ratios and Resolutions

Aspect Ratio	Shape	Resolutions that Fit
4:3	1	800 x 600, 1024 x 768, 1152 x 864, 1600 x 1200
5:4	1	1280 x 1024, 1600 x 1280
16:9	1	1088 x 612, 1280 x 720, 1600 x 900

So, the trick here is to move the slider to a resolution (for instance 1024 x 768) and then click the Apply button. The new resolution is applied to your screen. If the screen went blank, don't panic. It means that you chose a setting that won't work. The setting will be undone automatically in about 15 seconds and everything will be okay again. To try a different resolution, move the slider to another setting and click Apply again. If you find a setting you like, you can click OK and be done with it. If you need to do some further tweaking, read on.

Filling the screen

The first time you choose a new resolution, the image on your screen might not fill all the available space on the screen. It might be too small with black space all around it, as on the left in Figure 11.4. Or it might be too large, so that icons, the Start button, or other components are cut off, like the middle of Figure 11.4. Or it might be off-center, leaving much empty black space around one or two edges, as on the right in Figure 11.4.

FIGURE 11.4

New resolution doesn't fit screen.

that are right on the monitor itself. The trick is to reduce the width and height of the whole desktop until you can see it all on the screen. Then gradually adjust the width, height, vertical centering, and horizontal centering until the desktop fills the screen exactly. It takes some trial and error. But, fortunately, you need only do it once.

CAUTION When adjusting monitor settings, avoid options like pincushion, trapezoid, and tilt. You should-n't have to change those. If you do, it may be difficult to get them right again. For more information on adjusting your monitor, refer to the manual that came with your computer or monitor.

Other Ways to Size Things

The resolution you choose really only sets a basic default size for things on the screen. There are countless other ways to adjust the size of text, icons, and pictures on your screen, and they work no matter what resolution you choose. For example, holding down the Ctrl button while spinning your mouse wheel affects icon size. In Internet Explorer, you can click the Page button and choose Zoom or Text size to change the size of pictures and text on your screen.

Many programs have a View option in their menus that let you zoom in and out of things to make them larger or smaller. DPI scaling and the Accessibility Settings described later in this chapter offer many options for making things larger and easier to see on the screen.

If things look squished or stretched after you've adjusted things to fit nicely on your screen, you probably chose a resolution that doesn't match the aspect ratio of your monitor. Choose a resolution that does fit your screen's aspect ratio, and then use monitor buttons to adjust from there.

Adjusting color depth

The Colors button allows you to choose a *color depth* for the monitor. The rule here is simple: The higher the color depth, the more colors your monitor shows. And the more colors your monitor shows, the better things look—especially photos and video. So all you have to do is click the button and choose the highest available setting. Typically that will be either 32-bit or 24-bit.

Using multiple monitors

Windows Vista supports the use of multiple monitors in a variety of configurations. In many cases, adding a second monitor is a simple matter of connecting to the external monitor and turning it on. If the device supports Extended Display Identification Data (EDID), Windows will detect the device and adjust the resolution automatically.

If the external monitor is a television set, you may need to connect, turn on the TV, and then use the Input Select or TV/Video button on the TV or remote control to select the external input (often shown as AV1 or Component on the TV screen). You can also add multiple video cards to the PC and connect a monitor to each one.

After you connect to an external monitor and configure it to show input from the plug to which you connected the computer, the New Display Detected dialog box might appear on your primary display automatically. If it doesn't appear automatically, try restarting your computer. Log in to an administrative account and wait a few seconds to see if it starts automatically. If it does start, it will look something like Figure 11.5.

> **TIP** If you can't get the New Display Detected dialog box to open, don't worry. As discussed in a moment, you should be able to activate and configure the second screen through the Display Settings dialog box.

FIGURE 11.5

New Display Detected dialog box.

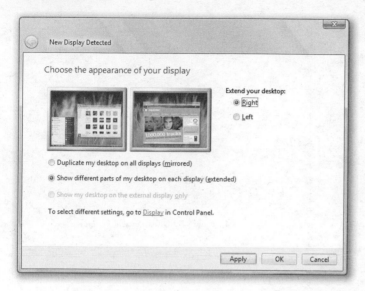

The options available to you depend on the type of device to which you're connecting. Options that don't apply to your connection are dimmed and cannot be selected. Basically, you have two choices:

- **Mirrored:** Choose this option when using the second display to teach a course or give a presentation. The external display shows what's on the primary display.

- **Extended:** Choose this option to use the second monitor as an extension of your desktop. You can use standard techniques for moving and sizing program windows to move a window from one screen to the other, or to extend a program across two screens to double its width. Choose Left or Right depending on whether the extended display is to the left or right of the original primary display.

 Extending Microsoft Excel across two monitors lets you see twice as many columns!

You can also display content on the second monitor only, leaving the first monitor black. If you're using a mobile computer on batteries, this option will conserve battery power.

Regardless of how you set things in the New Display Detected window (or even if it doesn't appear at all), you can use the Display Settings dialog box to configure the second monitor. Open Display Settings as described at the top of this section. Then click the second monitor's box (with the number 2 in it). If that second monitor is grayed out, choose Extend my desktop onto this monitor as in Figure 11.6. If the second monitor still doesn't light up, click Apply.

FIGURE 11.6

Display settings with two monitors working.

> **NOTE** If you can't get the second monitor to work, make sure it's properly connected and turned on. If the second monitor is a TV, make sure you choose the right input setting using Input Select or TV/Video on the TV or its remote control.

When both monitors are working, you can set the color depth and resolution of each one independently. Click the monitor box (1 or 2) that you want to change. Then use the Resolution slider and Colors button to adjust, within the limits of each monitor.

If you're not sure which square in the dialog box represents which monitor, click Identify Monitors. Each monitor will display a large number that corresponds to the square in the dialog box that represents that monitor.

You can arrange the squares in the dialog box to match the arrangement of the monitors. For example, if monitor 2 is to the left of monitor 1, drag the 2 square to the left of the 1 square. If the monitors are stacked with 1 on top of 2, drag the 1 square so it's above the 2 square.

Reducing monitor flicker

If a monitor seems to flicker, adjusting its refresh rate can help. You shouldn't change the refresh rate just for the heck of it though. Do so only to reduce flicker. First click the Advanced Settings... button. Then click the Monitor tab in the dialog box that opens. Use the button under Screen Refresh Rate to try a higher setting.

> **CAUTION** Don't clear the checkmark from Hide modes that this monitor cannot display checkbox. Doing so will allow you to choose settings that could damage the monitor!

After you choose a new refresh rate, click Apply. The monitor might go blank for a few seconds. When it comes back on, see if the situation has improved. If not, you can try another refresh rate (followed by a click on the Apply button) until you find an optimal setting. When you find the best setting, click OK to close the Advanced Settings dialog box.

More Stuff You Can Do with Monitors

Your monitor attaches to a graphics card or onboard graphics chip inside your computer. That card or chip defines the full range of your visual display. Windows Vista might not give you access to the full range of settings available to you, even after you click the Advanced Settings button.

To take full advantage of your graphics card (or chip) capabilities, you may want to use the program that came with that device. There are hundreds of such devices on the market. And there is no rule that applies to them all. To fully understand the capabilities of your graphics card and the programs for using it, refer to the manual that came with the card, or with your computer.

Don't forget to click OK after adjusting settings in the Display Settings dialog box. Remember, the settings you choose aren't set in concrete. You can re-open that dialog box and change things any time you like.

Choosing a theme

A theme is a collection of appearance settings that determine how things look on your screen. For example, Figure 11.7 shows how Windows Vista looks with the Windows Vista theme selected. Figure 11.8 shows how it looks with the Windows Classic theme selected to make the screen look more like Windows 98 or XP.

FIGURE 11.7

Windows Vista theme.

To choose a theme, starting from the Personalization window shown back in Figure 11.2, click Theme. The Theme Settings dialog box shown in Figure 11.9 opens. A good way to personalize your screen is to choose a theme that looks most like how you'd like your screen to look. You can certainly create your own custom themes. But going with a theme that has things you like is a good way to get started.

FIGURE 11.8

Windows Classic theme.

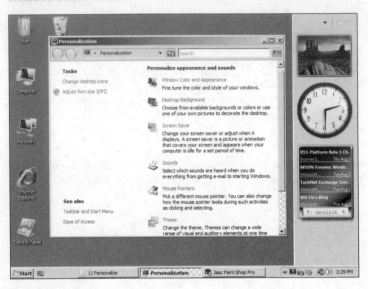

FIGURE 11.9

Theme Settings dialog box.

To try a theme, click the button under the Theme: heading. The preview area below the button gives you a sneak peek at how things will look if you apply the theme. If you can tell, right off the bat, that you hate a theme, just choose a different one. If you'd like to take a closer look, click the Apply button. The theme is applied to your desktop.

Feel free to try out as many themes as you like. When you find one you want to use, select its name and click Apply. If you plan to further customize things to your own liking, click Save As. Then enter a name for the theme. The suggested name will be My Favorite Theme. But you can replace that with any name you like. Of course, you can create as many custom themes as you like. Just remember to give each one a unique name after you click Save As.

When you're done in the Themes dialog box, click OK as usual. The remaining sections describe other ways to personalize your work environment. Any changes you make will be applied to whatever theme is currently selected.

Personalizing your color scheme

NEW FEATURE Aero Glass and the ways in which you can tweak it to your liking are new to Windows Vista.

To choose a basic color scheme for your screen and selected theme, click Window Color and Appearance in the Personalization window. If you're using Aero Glass and a theme that uses it, you'll see the options shown in Figure 11.10.

FIGURE 11.10

Change your color scheme.

I trust that most of the options are self-explanatory. Click any example under the Pick a color heading. Use the Enable Transparency checkbox to enable or disable the transparency effect on window borders. If you opt to enable transparency, you can control how transparent the borders are using the slider. The farther right you drag the slider the less intense the transparency. If you don't enable transparency, the slider affects only the intensity of the color you choose under Pick a color.

Transparency and Computer Performance

When choosing a color scheme, you might see a warning about transparency affecting your computer's performance. Applying transparency on a computer screen takes a significant amount of mathematical calculations. If your computer doesn't have the hardware horsepower to do the task instantly, you might experience a general slowdown in computer performance when you enable transparency. It shouldn't be an issue with newer computers that are specifically designed to run Windows Vista.

If you want to create your own colors, click Show color mixer to see the additional sliders shown in Figure 11.11. You can use those to create your own color.

FIGURE 11.11

Color mixer sliders.

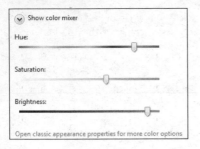

Before you start creating a color, you might find it useful to drag the Intensity slider to the middle or far right end of the bar, and clear the Enable transparency checkbox. Also, drag the Saturation and Brightness sliders to the middle. That will make it easier to see your color selection on the window's border.

Drag the Color slider along the rainbow bar until you find a color you like. Move the Saturation slider to adjust, deepen, or fade your selected color. Use the Brightness slider to brighten or darken the color. You can also enable transparency and adjust the intensity as you go. Just keep playing around with things until you get a color you like.

If you're not using Aero Glass, clicking Visual Appearance in the Personalization window takes you to the dialog box shown in Figure 11.12. You can also get to that dialog box by clicking in the window shown back in Figure 11.10.

Aero Glass Requirements in Depth

To use Aero Glass, you need a Direct X 9 class graphics processor that supports WDDM, 32 bits per pixel, and Pixel Shader 2.0 in hardware. The graphics card needs at least 64 MB of graphics memory. But 256 MB of graphics memory (or better) is preferred, especially for higher-resolution displays.

Many newer graphics cards meet all those requirements. But onboard graphics chips rarely do. If you're thinking of adding a graphics card to your system to get all the visual bells and whistles, look for a card that's Windows Vista compatible. You'll also need to get a card that fits in an available slot on your motherboard. These days, PCI Express X16 is the preferred graphics slot, followed by PCI Express (PCIe), AGP, and PCI (in that order).

If you don't know what slots are available on your motherboard, or aren't comfortable installing hardware, your best bet would be to take the system into a professional. Tell them you're looking to upgrade your graphics display to full Windows Vista graphics capabilities. They can advise you on cards you can purchase and estimates for installation.

FIGURE 11.12

Classic appearance settings.

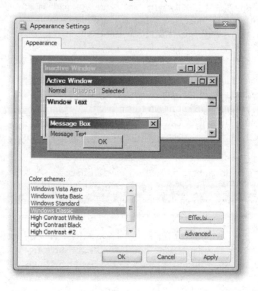

Click any Color scheme name in the list. The preview area above the list shows an example of how things will look on the screen if you apply that scheme. The High Contrast options are mostly for people with visual impairments that make it difficult to see the screen. The other color schemes are more traditional.

Making text sharper

Clicking the Effects button takes you to the options shown in Figure 11.13. The first two options are the most important because they affect the clarity of text on your screen. Choose the first option to enable text sharpening (even though that's worded as "smooth edges of screen fonts"). On an LCD display, you'll almost certainly want to choose ClearType from the second box as in the figure; however, ClearType could clear up fuzzy-looking text on any monitor. It's certainly worth a try. If you don't like the results, you can return to the dialog box at any time and use the Standard setting instead.

FIGURE 11.13

Effects dialog box.

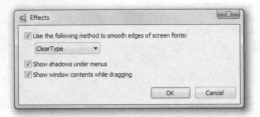

The other two options enable or disable shadows under menus and specify whether or not you can see an entire program window when dragging. On an older computer that just barely has enough hardware horsepower to run Vista, clearing those two checkboxes might help speed things up on your screen.

Coloring individual screen elements

Clicking the Advanced button in Classic appearance settings takes you to the Advanced Appearance dialog box shown in Figure 11.14. As always, the word Advanced is a good way of knowing that these settings are not for beginners or the technologically faint of heart. People have been known to do crazy things in this dialog box, like set everything to the same color, then wonder why they can't see anything on their screen. (They can't see anything because when everything is exactly the same color, the screen is basically one big blob of whatever color they choose.)

If you're savvy enough to tackle the Advanced Appearance options, here's how they work. First you choose an item to color from the Item drop-down button. Controls that apply to that item are instantly enabled. Controls that don't apply are disabled. From the enabled options, you can choose colors and fonts, as applicable. Your choices are reflected in the preview above the buttons.

CAUTION You definitely don't want to experiment or try things out for the heck of it in Advanced Appearance options. If you plan to use it to solve some problem, don't. It will not solve any problems. If it's too late for that and you've already made a mess of things, go back to the Theme Settings dialog box described earlier and choose a different theme.

Personalizing your desktop background

You can *wallpaper* your desktop with any picture or color you like. In the Personalization window, click Desktop Background to open the Desktop Background page shown in Figure 11.15.

FIGURE 11.14

Advanced Appearance dialog box.

FIGURE 11.15

Choose a desktop background.

Click the drop-down button and choose a category of pictures, like Vistas, Textures, or Painting. Or choose Pictures to view pictures from your own Pictures folder, or Public Pictures from the shared Pictures folder. (Of course, if either folder is empty or doesn't contain any compatible picture types, you won't see any pictures after making your selection.) After you choose a category, point to or click any picture to see it applied as your desktop background.

If you have pictures in some folder other than the Pictures folder for your user account or the Public Pictures folder, click Browse. Navigate to the folder that contains those pictures. Then click (or double-click) the picture you want to use as your desktop background. All pictures from that folder will appear in the Desktop Background window. Click whatever picture you want to use.

If the desktop is covered, click the Show Desktop Quick Launch button or right-click the time in the lower-right corner of the screen and choose Show the Desktop. Then to get back to where you were, click the Show Desktop button again, or right-click the time and choose Show Open Windows. Try out different pictures until you find one you like.

Try the options under How should the picture be positioned? to view it in different ways. The options will have little or no effect on large pictures. But if you choose a small picture of your own, the center option will show it repeatedly, like tiles. The third option will show it centered on the screen. If you choose that third option, you can click Change background color to color the border surrounding the picture.

If you don't want a picture on your desktop, choose Solid Colors from the drop-down list. Then click whatever color you like. Or click More for a wider selection of colors. When you've found and chosen a picture or color you like, click OK.

Personalizing desktop icons

In the left column of the Personalization window, you'll see a link titled Change desktop icons. Click that to see the dialog box shown in Figure 11.16. Select (check) any icons you want to see on your desktop. Clear the checkbox of any icon you don't want to see. As always, choosing icons is purely a matter of personal taste. And you can change the icons you see on your desktop at any time. Click OK after choosing the icons you want to see.

Creating your own desktop icons

The Desktop Icons Settings dialog box shows only the few icons built into Windows Vista. Many programs you install create other desktop icons. And you're free to create your own desktop icons. The desktop isn't a good place to store things though. So most desktop icons are actually just *shortcuts* to other places or programs.

Shortcut icons are unique in a couple of ways. For one, they show a little curved arrow like the examples in Figure 11.17. For another, deleting a shortcut icon has no effect on the item that the shortcut opens. Instead, deleting a shortcut icon only deletes the icon. The program or folder to which the icon referred still exists. You can still open that item through a non-shortcut method.

FIGURE 11.16

Desktop icon settings.

FIGURE 11.17

Sample shortcut icons.

If you often go through a series of clicks or steps to open some item, creating a desktop shortcut will make it quicker and easier. Get to the icon you normally click (or double-click) to open a program, folder, or document. Then right-click that icon and choose Send To ➪ Desktop (create shortcut).

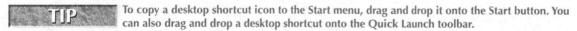

TIP   To copy a desktop shortcut icon to the Start menu, drag and drop it onto the Start button. You can also drag and drop a desktop shortcut onto the Quick Launch toolbar.

Sizing, arranging, showing, and hiding desktop icons

You can size and arrange desktop icons as you see fit. First, minimize or close all open program windows so you can see the entire desktop. Then right-click any empty area on the desktop to see the shortcut menu shown in Figure 11.18.

FIGURE 11.18

Right-click the desktop to see this menu.

The View submenu, shown in Figure 11.19, contains several options for arranging icons. An item on that menu that has a checkmark is currently selected and active. An item without a checkmark is deselected and inactive. Clicking an item selects it if it's not already selected, or deselects it if it is selected. Here's what each option does:

FIGURE 11.19

View submenu.

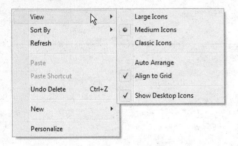

- **Large Icons:** Shows desktop icons at a large size.
- **Medium Icons:** Shows desktop icons at a medium size.
- **Classic Icons:** Shows desktop icons at a smaller size similar to earlier Windows versions.

 If your mouse has a wheel, you can make desktop icons almost any size by holding down the Ctrl key as you spin the mouse wheel.

- **Auto Arrange:** Choosing this option keeps icons neatly arranged near the left side of the desktop. If you clear this option, you can put desktop icons wherever you like. Just drag any icon to wherever you want to put it on the desktop.
- **Align to Grid:** Choosing this option keeps icons aligned to an invisible grid, to make the spacing between them equal.
- **Show Desktop Icons:** If this option is selected (checked), desktop icons are visible. Clearing this option makes the desktop icons invisible. But it doesn't delete them. They'll come back into view when you choose this option again in the future.

The Sort By option on the desktop shortcut menu lets you quickly sort icons by name, size, file extension, or date modified. Regardless of which option you choose, built-in icons are always listed first, followed by your own custom icons in whatever order you specified.

The remaining options are similar to their counterparts in folders. The Refresh option ensures that icons on the desktop are up-to-date with changes you may have made elsewhere in the system. If you accidentally delete a shortcut icon, you can choose Undo Delete (or press Ctrl+Z) to bring it back. The New option lets you create a new folder or document on the desktop. And Personalize opens the Personalization page shown near the start of this section.

Customizing icons

To change a built-in icon, open the Desktop Icon Settings dialog box shown in Figure 11.16. Then click the icon you want to customize and click Change icon. To change the appearance of a shortcut icon, right-click it and choose Properties ➪ Change icon. A dialog box named Change Icon opens, showing possible alternative icons. Figure 11.20 shows a general example.

FIGURE 11.20

Change Icon dialog box.

NOTE   Not all programs offer optional icons. If the Change Icon button is disabled, that means you can't change that particular icon.

If you have your own .ico files and would prefer to use one of those, click the Browse button in the Change Icon dialog box. Navigate to the folder that contains the .ico file and choose the icon you want to use.

TIP   To explore programs that let you create your own icon pictures, search the Web for `icon maker`. To find pre-made icons you can download, search the Web for `download Windows icons`.

Adjust the font size (DPI)

In the left column of the Personalization window, you'll notice a shielded item titled Adjust font size (DPI). The shield indicates that only administrators are allowed to use that option, and for good reason. It's the kind of option that can really get you into a pickle if not handled correctly. Basically it lets you increase the size of text (and just about everything else) by adjusting the *dots per inch* (DPI) on the screen. The problem is that if you make things too large for your current screen resolution, you won't be able to get to the options you need to change the settings back to what they were before.

Adjusting the font size DPI isn't the only way to enlarge text on the screen. Many programs offer a Zoom option on their View menus to enlarge things. The Accessibility options described later in this chapter also offer some safer alternatives. But if nothing else really works for you, using the Adjust font size (DPI) setting might be your best bet.

The setting requires a restart after you've made a new selection, so here's the best way to go about using it. In some of the following steps, I'll have you use the keyboard rather than the mouse, because if you make things so large that the mouse can't get to options, the keyboard method provided in the steps should work. And (hopefully) get you out of any jam you might get yourself into:

1. Close all open programs and log in to a user account that has administrative privileges.
2. Open the Personalization window (right-click the desktop and choose Personalize).
3. Click Adjust font size (DPI) to open the DPI Scaling dialog box shown in Figure 11.21.

FIGURE 11.21

DPI Scaling dialog box.

4. To make text larger, choose the next highest setting (for example, 120 DPI). Or, to get out of a jam, click a smaller size or the Default scale option.

5. Press the Tab key twice to get to the OK button and press Enter.

NOTE You can click the Custom DPI button and choose a percentage increase. But be careful to increase the current percentage value only slightly. Otherwise, you might make things so huge that hardly anything fits on the screen.

6. Click Restart or press Enter.

The new setting will be applied after the computer restarts. If the things are too large on your screen, repeat the preceding steps, choosing a smaller size in step 4.

Personalizing your screen saver

A screen saver is a moving picture or pattern that fills the screen after a period of inactivity. The name screen saver harkens back to the olden days where leaving a fixed image on the screen for too long a time could cause permanent damage to the screen. But that problem has been solved for a long time. So a screen saver is completely optional nowadays. Still, it's a nice way to have your screen do something entertaining when the computer is on but nobody is using it.

In the Personalization window, click Screen Saver to choose a screen saver. The Screen Saver Settings dialog box shown in Figure 11.22 opens. Click the drop-down button to see a list of screen savers from which you can choose. Click any name in that list to get a sneak peek at how it will look if you apply it.

FIGURE 11.22

Screen Saver Settings dialog box.

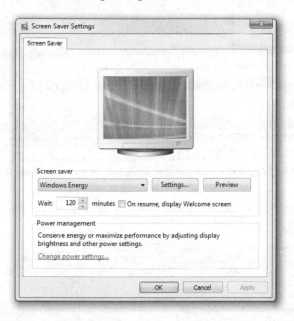

Some screen savers are customizable. Click the Settings button to see if the screen saver you selected has optional settings you can change. If it does, you'll see those options in a dialog box. Choose whatever options look interesting.

If you have pictures in Photo Gallery, choose Photos from the drop-down button. The screen saver will be a slide show of pictures from your gallery. If you choose Photos from the drop-down list, you can also click the Settings button to see the options shown in Figure 11.23.

FIGURE 11.23

Photo slide show options.

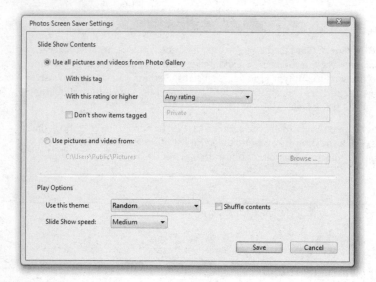

 For the goods on photos and Photo Gallery, drop by Chapter 22.

As you can see in Figure 11.23, the default setting is for the screen saver to show all pictures and videos from your Photo Gallery. You can narrow that down by choosing to show only photos that have a specific tag or rating. Optionally, you can hide pictures that have a specific tag.

As an alternative to showing pictures from your Photo Gallery, you can choose Use pictures and video from and then specify any folder you like.

Options under the Play Options heading let you choose a theme, shuffle the order in which pictures are displayed, and choose a speed. Click Save after making your choices.

Regardless of which screen saver and settings you choose, the small preview window in the dialog box shows you how it will look. For a larger view, click the Preview button. Your selected screen saver will play full screen. To make it stop, just move your mouse.

After you've chosen your screen saver, specify how many minutes of inactivity are required before the screen saver starts playing. A period of inactivity means that nobody has touched the mouse or keyboard. So if you set the Wait option to 5 minutes, the screen saver will kick in after the computer has been sitting there unused for five minutes. The screen saver plays until someone moves the mouse or presses a key on the keyboard.

Choosing On resume, display welcome screen causes the screen saver to show the login page rather than your desktop when someone moves the mouse. If you're using a password-protected user account, this will prevent that other person from accessing your desktop. It also means that when *you* end the screen saver, you have to log back in to your own account.

The screen saver won't kick in at all if your power options are set to turn off the monitor before the screen saver kicks in. The Change power settings link in the dialog box lets you check, and optionally change, when the monitor goes off.

For example, the Power Save plan turns off the monitor after 20 minutes. If you set the screen saver to kick in after 21 or more minutes, you'll never see the screen saver, because the monitor will be off. If you prefer the screen saver to an empty screen, you should choose High Performance plan in Power Options. Or use a different plan but change the plan settings so that the screen (display) never goes off, or only goes off after a long period of inactivity.

 See "The Power Settings" in Chapter 50 for more information on using Power Options.

When you're happy with your screen saver selections, click OK. Remember, the screen saver won't actually play until you've left the computer alone and untouched for the number of minutes you specified in the Wait box.

Personalizing sound effects

You might have noticed some little beeps and whistles as you do things in Windows Vista. Those are called *sound effects* and you can customize those from the Personalize window. Just click Sounds to open the Windows Sounds dialog box shown in Figure 11.24.

FIGURE 11.24

Windows Sounds dialog box.

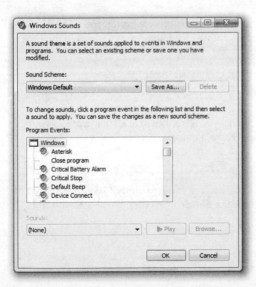

If you don't want to assign sound effects one at a time, you can choose a predefined sound effects scheme from the Sound Scheme drop-down list. Or choose No Sounds if you don't want any sound effects.

The Program Events list shows different events to which you can assign sounds. Items that have a speaker icon to the left already have a sound effect associated with them. To hear one, click any program event that shows a speaker icon. The Sounds drop-down menu below the list shows the filename in which the sound effect is stored. Click the Play button to the right of the sound effect name to hear that sound effect.

Sound effects only play when your computer has a sound card with speakers plugged into the correct jack. If the speakers have their own power switch, they must be turned on. Likewise, if the speakers have their own volume control, the volume must be turned up loud enough to hear. And if the speakers have a Mute button, it must be turned off. Likewise, the volume control in the Notification area must have its volume set to a level you can hear and must not be muted, as in Figure 11.25.

FIGURE 11.25

Windows volume control.

Getting back to the Windows Sounds dialog box, you can assign any sound effect you like to any program event. First click the program event to which you would like to assign or change a sound effect. Then click the drop-down button under Sounds to see a list of built-in sound effects. Click the sound effect you'd like to assign. Then click the Play button to hear that sound effect.

If you have your own sound effect to assign to a program event, click the Browse button and navigate to the folder that contains your sound effects. Then double-click the sound effect you want to assign to the program event.

> **TIP**   Some good Web sites for downloading sound effects include www.ilovewavs.com, www.frogstar.com/wav/effects.asp, and www.partnersinrhyme.com/pir/PIRsfx.html.

If you change the sound effects associated with program events, you'll want to save all that work as your own sound scheme. Click the Save As button and give the scheme a name.

Personalizing your mouse

If you grow tired of the same old mouse pointer, or need to make your mouse pointer easier to see, click the Mouse Pointers link in the Personalization window. You'll see the Mouse Properties dialog box with the Pointers tab selected as in Figure 11.26.

FIGURE 11.26

Pointers tab in Mouse Properties.

To change your mouse pointers, choose a Scheme from the drop-down button. The list under the Customize heading shows you how the pointers in that scheme look. You can keep all the mouse pointers in the scheme just by clicking OK. Or you can assign a mouse pointer of your own choosing to any item. Double-click the pointer you want to change, or click it and click the Browse button. Clicking Browse takes you to a folder named Cursors, which contains all of the built-in Windows Vista mouse pointers.

> **TIP** After you click Browse, you can enlarge the mouse pointer icons in the Browse dialog box for a better look. Hold down the Ctrl key and spin your mouse wheel. Or click the Views button and choose Medium icons or a larger size.

If you do assign mouse pointers on a case-by-case basis, click the Save As button to save your selections as a theme with any name you like.

> **TIP** Don't forget, most dialog box options aren't actually applied until you click the Apply or OK button.

Mice for lefties

If you're left-handed and you want the main mouse button to be below your left index finger, you need to reverse the normal functioning of the buttons. Generally, the left mouse button is the primary button, and the right mouse button is the secondary button. To reverse that, first click the Buttons tab in the Mouse Properties dialog box so you see the options shown in Figure 11.27. Then check the Switch primary and secondary mouse buttons checkbox.

FIGURE 11.27

Buttons tab in Mouse Properties.

If you do reverse your mouse buttons, you'll have to adjust all the standard mouse terminology accordingly. Table 11-2 shows how the various mouse terms apply to right-handed mouse settings and to left-handed settings.

TABLE 11-2

Mouse Terminology for Righties and Lefties

Standard Terminology	Righties	Lefties
Primary button	Left	Right
Secondary button	Right	Left
Click	Left button	Right button
Double-click	Left button	Right button
Drag	Left button	Right button
Right-click	Right button	Left button
Right-drag	Right button	Left button

Adjusting the double-click speed

To double-click an icon, you have to tap the primary mouse button twice very quickly. Otherwise, it counts as two single clicks. If it's difficult to tap the button quickly enough, or if you're so fast that two single clicks are being interpreted as a double-click, adjust the Double-click speed slider on the Buttons tab of the Mouse Properties dialog box.

TIP To do away with the need to double-click anything, switch to single-clicking in the Folder Options dialog box. Tap ▦, type `fol`, and choose Folder Options for that dialog box. Or see "To click or double-click" in Chapter 28 for details.

To test your current setting, double-click the folder icon. If the closed folder doesn't change to an open one (or vice versa), you didn't double-click fast enough. Move the slider box toward the Slow end of the scale and try again. When the slider is at a place where it's easy to open/close the little folder next to the slider, that's a good setting for you.

Using ClickLock

If you find it difficult to select multiple items by dragging the mouse pointer through them, you may want to try activating the ClickLock feature. Enabling that feature lets you select multiple items without holding down the mouse button. First you need to choose Turn on ClickLock on the Buttons tab of the Mouse Properties dialog box. Then, use the Settings button to specify how long you need to hold down the primary mouse button before the key is "locked."

For example, let's say that you turn on ClickLock and set the required delay to about one second. To drag the mouse pointer through some items, you position the mouse pointer to where you plan to start selecting and hold down the mouse pointer for one second. Then, you can release the mouse button and move the mouse pointer through the items you want to select. Those items will be selected as though you were actually holding down the left mouse button.

When you've finished selecting, just click some area outside the selection. The mouse pointer returns to its normal function, and the items you selected remain selected.

Speed up or slow down the mouse pointer

Clicking the Pointer Options tab in the Mouse Properties dialog box reveals the options shown in Figure 11.28. The first option, Select a pointer speed, controls how far the mouse pointer on the screen moves relative to how far you move the mouse with your hand. If you find it difficult to zero in on small things on your screen, drag the slider to the Slow end of the scale. If you feel you have to move the mouse too much to get from one place to another on the screen, move the slider toward the Fast end of the scale.

FIGURE 11.28

Pointer Options tab in Mouse Properties.

Selecting Enhance pointer precision makes it easier to move the mouse pointer short distances. It's especially useful if you move the pointer speed slider to the Fast side of the scale.

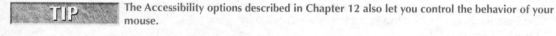

TIP   The Accessibility options described in Chapter 12 also let you control the behavior of your mouse.

Making the mouse pointer more visible

If you keep losing sight of the mouse pointer on your screen, the remaining pointer options can make it easier to find, as follows:

- **Snap To:** If selected, this causes the mouse pointer to jump to the default button (typically okay) automatically as soon as the dialog box opens.

- **Display pointer trails:** If selected, this causes the mouse pointer to leave a brief trail when you move it, making it easier to see the pointer.

- **Show location of pointer when I press the CTRL key:** If you select this option, you can easily locate the mouse pointer on your screen by holding down the Ctrl key.

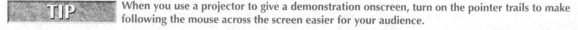

TIP   When you use a projector to give a demonstration onscreen, turn on the pointer trails to make following the mouse across the screen easier for your audience.

Yet another way to make your mouse pointer more visible is to use a large or animated mouse pointer.

Changing mouse wheel behavior

The Wheel tab in the Mouse Properties dialog box lets you control how far you scroll when spinning the mouse wheel. The default is usually 3 lines per notch. But you can change that to any value from 1 to 100 lines. Optionally you can configure the wheel to move an entire page with each notch.

NOTE The Hardware tab in Mouse Properties shows information about your mouse, and provides a means of manually updating the mouse driver, should the need ever arise.

Don't forget to click OK after making your selection in the Mouse Properties dialog box.

That wraps it up for options in Control Panel's Personalization page. But as you'll see in the sections to follow, there are many more things you can do to tweak Windows Vista to better suit your needs and tastes.

Personalizing the Keyboard

There are a few things you can do to change how the keyboard works. Some are in the Keyboard Properties dialog box, which I cover here. Others come under the heading of accessibility, a topic I address in Chapter 12. To get to the Keyboard Properties dialog box, use whichever of the following methods is easiest for you:

- Press ⊞, type key, and click Keyboard under Programs.
- Click the Start button and choose Control Panel ⇨ Hardware and Sound ⇨ Keyboard.

The Keyboard Properties dialog box shown in Figure 11.29 opens.

FIGURE 11.29

Keyboard Properties dialog box.

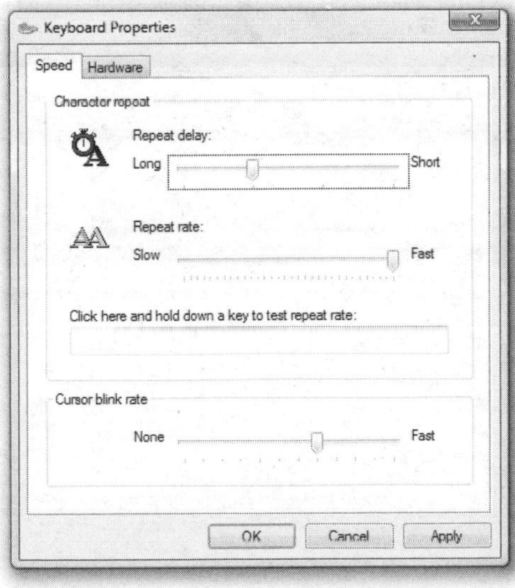

The options in Keyboard Properties are as follows. As always, there is no right or wrong setting. It's all a matter of choosing settings that suit your typing style:

- **Repeat delay:** Determines how long you have to hold down a key before it starts autotyping (repeating itself automatically).
- **Repeat rate:** Determines how fast the key types automatically while you're holding it down.
- **Cursor blink rate:** Determines how quickly the cursor blinks in a document.

If your keyboard offers programmable buttons, there may not be any options in the Keyboard Properties dialog box for defining those keys. More likely, you'll need to install and use the program that came with the keyboard to do that. There is no "one rule fits all" for that sort of thing. The only places to get the information you need will be from the instructions that came with the keyboard and the keyboard manufacturer's Web site.

 See "Creating Custom Shortcut Keys" later in this chapter for tips on launching favorite programs from your keyboard.

Personalizing the Start Menu

The Start button is the gateway to every program currently installed on your computer. The Start menu also provides easy access to commonly used folders such as Documents, Computer, Control Panel, and any others you care to add. As a rule, you want the Start menu to contain items you use frequently, so you can get to those items without navigating through too many submenus.

The Windows Vista menu is split into two columns with icons for programs on the left and icons for folders and other places on the right. The left side of the menu is split into two groups. Icons above the horizontal line are *pinned* to the menu, meaning that they never change unless you change them. Beneath the horizontal line are icons that represent programs you use frequently. Those latter icons change frequently to reflect programs you use frequently. Figure 11.30 shows a sample Start menu.

FIGURE 11.30

Windows Vista Start menu.

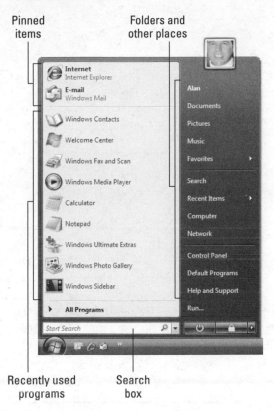

Pinned items

Folders and other places

Recently used programs

Search box

Opening Taskbar and Start Menu Properties

Use the Start Menu tab of the Taskbar and Start Menu Properties dialog box to personalize the appearance of your Start menu and some of the options it displays. As always, there are many ways to open that dialog box. Use whichever is most convenient for you:

- Right-click the Start button and choose Properties.
- Click the Start menu, type sta, and click Taskbar and Start Menu.
- Click the Start button and choose Control Panel ⇨ Appearance and Personalization ⇨ Customize the Start menu.

When the dialog box opens, click the Start Menu tab to see the options shown in Figure 11.31.

FIGURE 11.31

Start Menu tab in Taskbar and Start Menu Properties dialog box.

Your first choice is between Start menu and Classic Start menu. The first option displays a two-column Start menu like the one shown in Figure 11.30. If you choose the second option, your Start menu will look more like the one shown in Figure 11.32. It's called the "classic" menu because it looks and works like the Start menu from older versions of Windows.

FIGURE 11.32

Classic Start menu.

Under the Privacy heading, you can choose or clear the following items. But note that if your user account is password-protected, then privacy isn't really an issue, because no other users can see your Start menu.

- **Store and display a list of recently opened files:** If selected, displays the Recent Items option on the right side of the Start menu. Clicking that option lists all recently opened files. That makes it really easy to re-open a file you've worked with recently.

- **Store and display a list of recently opened programs:** If you clear this option, the left side of the Start menu will not show icons for recently used programs.

Personalize the right side of the Start menu

To choose other options for your Start menu, click the Settings button next to Start menu or Classic Start menu. Figure 11.33 shows how that tab looks if you're using the Vista style Start menu. You'll have fewer options if you go with the Classic Start menu. For the newer style Start menu, items in the Customize Start Menu dialog box let you choose what appears on the right side of the menu.

FIGURE 11.33

Customize Start Menu dialog box.

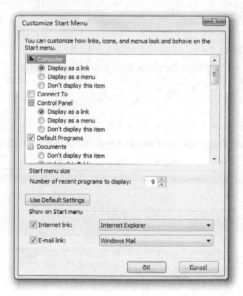

Start menu folders

The list box contains options that control the appearance and behavior of your Start menu. Items on the menu that open folders give you these three options:

- **Display as a link:** Choosing this option tells Windows to open the corresponding folder when you click the menu option. This is the most natural method, once you're familiar with working in folders.

- **Display as a menu:** Choosing this option tells Windows to show items within the folder as options on a menu, without opening the folder. This option is a reasonable alternative for folders that contain few icons but is unwieldy for folders that contain many icons.

- **Don't display this item:** As it says, choosing this option will prevent the option from being displayed at all on the right side of the Start menu.

Folders you can open directly from the Start menu are summarized in the following list. If you're new to all of this and don't know what might be useful, set them all to Display as a link. If after a few months you discover you don't need one, set it to Don't display this item.

- **Computer:** Contains icons for all of your computer's disk drives. Useful for copying files to and from external disks and memory cards.

- **Control Panel:** Contains all the pages and dialog boxes for personalizing your system and for managing hardware and software.

- **Documents:** Stores all of your private documents excluding digital media (pictures, music, video).

- **Games:** A folder of saved games and scores. If you don't play computer games, set this one to **Don't display this item**.

- **Local User Storage:** Shows at the top right of the Start menu as your user name. Opening it reveals icons for all of your private folders including your Favorites, Contacts, and Saved Searches.

- **Music:** Contains songs in your Windows Media Player media library.

- **Pictures:** Contains photos and video clips from your digital camera, Photo Gallery, and any other resources you choose.

Start menu places

Some checkbox items in the list box let you access other resources. Of course, all of them are optional. You should choose only those options you'll actually use. Here's a brief description of each and some suggestions:

- **Connect to:** Select this option only if you need to manually connect to a wireless, dial-up, or VBP connection often.

- **Default Programs:** It's unlikely you'd need to get to this often enough to warrant putting it in the Start menu. You can get to Default Programs through Control Panel or by clicking Start and typing def.

- **Favorites menu:** Choose this option only if you keep track of favorites in Internet Explorer and your Links folder. If you don't use Favorites, this option won't get you much.

- **Help:** If selected, displays a Help and Support option on the right side of the Start menu. Because this is an important resource for information that everyone should learn to use, and use often, it's a good idea to select this option.

- **Network:** Choose this option if your computer is connected to a local network and you need access to shared resources often.

- **Printers:** Choose this option only if you need to get to your printer icons often to manage print jobs. If you don't put this on the Start menu, you can still open the Printers folder through Control Panel. Or click the Start button, type pri, and click Printers.

- **Run command:** Shows a Run option for more advanced users who run programs that don't have icons. If you don't choose this option, you can type the program name in the Search box and then click its name on the Start menu. Or type run in the Search box and click Run on the menu.

- **System Administrative Tools:** If selected, provides quick access to advanced tools often used by system and network administrators. You can choose to display on the All Programs menu only, or both the Start menu and All Programs menu. If you choose Don't display this item, you can still open Administrative Tools from Control Panel, or by clicking the Start button and typing adm.

Start menu searching

NEW FEATURE Searches in Windows Vista are a huge improvement over searches in earlier versions of Windows. But you need to understand how it works to take full advantage. See Chapters 30 and 31 for the whole story.

Several options in the Customize Start Menu dialog box center around searching. They're all selected by default. Here's what each one means:

- **Search:** If selected, shows a Search option on the right side of the Start menu. Clicking that option opens the main search box for searching your computer.

- **Search Box:** If selected, shows the Search box at the bottom left of the Start menu (the one that contains the words Start Search).

- **Search Communications:** If selected, searches launched from the Search box will include Windows Mail e-mail messages for people in Windows Contacts.

- **Search Favorites and History:** If selected, searches launched from the Search box will include Internet Explorer favorites and its history of visited Web sites.

- **Search Files:** If you choose Don't search for files, searches launched from the Search box won't include document files. If you choose Search entire index, those searches will include all indexed files. The default setting, Search the user's files, searches documents in the user's document folders (Documents, Pictures, Music, and such).

- **Search Programs:** If selected, searches launched from the Search box include programs and Control Panel items.

Start menu behavior

Some items in the Customize Start Menu list are about how the menu behaves rather than what you see on the menu. Those options are as follows:

- **Enable dragging and dropping:** If selected, this allows you to rearrange icons on the All Programs menu by dragging them with the right mouse button. But if you choose the Sort All Programs menu by name, this won't do you much good because that option will put them right back into alphabetical order!

- **Highlight newly installed programs:** If you select this option, the All Programs menu won't fan out across the screen when you open it. Instead, you'll have to scroll through the menu using buttons at the top and bottom. I would recommend that you clear (not select) this option.

- **Sort All Programs menu by name:** Choosing this option keeps items on the Start menu in alphabetical order. Programs are listed first, followed by program groups (folders). If you don't choose this option, you can alphabetize those items by right-clicking any item on All Programs and choosing Sort by name.

- **Use large icons:** Choosing this option displays the large icons on the Start menu. Clearing this option displays smaller icons, which makes room for more items on the menu.

The Number of recent programs to display option dictates how many program icons can appear at the left side of the Start menu. If you set this number too high for your current screen resolution and icon size, you might see the "Some items cannot be shown" message when you click the Start button.

Clicking the Use default settings button resets the Start menu options and number of recent programs to display options back to their original settings.

The checkboxes below the list let you decide whether or not you want to keep options for Internet access pinned to the top left of the Start menu.

Customizing the left side of the Start menu

If you use the modern two-column Start menu, there are many ways you can customize it. Recall that items above the horizontal line are pinned to the menu and never change. Items below that line reflect programs you use often. So those items are likely to change over time.

Of course, you're never stuck with whatever happens to be on the left side of the Start menu. You can right-click any item, as in the example shown in Figure 11.34. Choose Remove from this list to remove an item. If an item isn't already pinned to the Start button, choose Pin to Start Menu to pin it.

There are also easy ways to control items on the Start menu. One is to right-click an item that's already on the left side of the menu, as in Figure 11.34. To remove an item, right-click and choose Remove from this list. To pin an item to the top of the Start menu, right-click it and choose Pin to Start Menu.

FIGURE 11.34

Right-click a Start menu item.

All Start Menu Items Are Shortcuts

Start menu icons are shortcuts, even though they don't show a shortcut arrow. That means when you remove or unpin a Start menu item, you don't lose the program, folder, or file that the item opens. In other words, deleting an icon from the Start menu doesn't delete the program, folder, or file that the item opens.

Therefore, you don't need to be shy about sticking things on the menu as convenient, and removing them as convenient. You can even change the name of an item on the Start menu without changing the actual item's name. Just right-click the item, choose Rename, and give it any name you like. The program, folder, or file that the item opens will retain its original name.

On the All Programs menu, you can right-click any program's icon and choose Pin to Start Menu. That's a quick and easy way to put the icon for a program you use often near the top of the Start menu.

If you use a folder often, you can pin its icon to the Start menu too. For that matter, if you use a single document often, you can pin its icon to the Start menu as well. Just drag the file or folder icon and drop it right on the Start button. Similarly, you can pin a copy of any desktop shortcut icon to your Start menu. Again, just drag the desktop icon and drop it right on the Start button. To unpin an item from the top-left side of the Start menu, right-click its icon and choose Unpin from Start menu.

Reorganizing the All Programs menu

The All Programs menu provides access to virtually all application programs installed on your system. Items at the top of the All Programs menu represent individual programs. Items marked with folder icons represent groups of programs. When you click a folder icon, it expands to show programs within that group.

Any program group can contain still more groups, each group identified by a folder icon. Figure 11.35 shows an example where I've opened a program group named Microsoft Office. Within that program group, I found, and opened, another group named Microsoft Office Tools.

NOTE Microsoft Office doesn't come free with Windows Vista. It's a program you have to purchase separately. So don't be alarmed if you have no Microsoft Office group on your All Programs menu. I'm just using that as a general example.

If you enable dragging and dropping, you can move things around on the All Programs menu using the right mouse button. But doing so can be awkward. As an alternative, you can work in a more typical folder window. Right-click the Start button and choose one of the following options, depending on what you want to accomplish:

- **Open:** Opens a folder containing icons from the current user's Start menu.
- **Explore:** Same as above but also opens the Navigation pane automatically.
- **Open All Users:** Opens a folder containing icons that appear in all users' Start menus.
- **Explore All Users:** Same as above but the folder opens with the Navigation pane already open.

NOTE As always, you need administrative privileges to make any changes that affect all user accounts.

A folder named Start Menu opens. Its icons represent items that are on the Start menu. Within that Start Menu folder is a folder named Programs. When you open the Programs folder, you see icons that represent items on the All Programs menu. Any changes you make in that Programs folder are reflected in the All Programs menu.

FIGURE 11.35

Microsoft Office and Tools program groups.

For example, suppose you have half a dozen conversion programs on your All Programs menu. You'd like to group them into a single program group, perhaps named Converters, on the All Programs menu. In the Programs folder, click the Organize button and choose New Folders. Name the folder Converts. Then move the icons for the conversion programs into that folder.

Suppose you want to go the other way. Take all or some of the programs out of the Microsoft Office group and put them right on the All Programs menu. Open the Microsoft Office folder in Programs and select the icons you want to move. Then press Ctrl+X to cut them. Click Programs in the breadcrumb menu to go back up to the Programs folder and press Ctrl+V to paste them. The pasted programs will be on the All Programs menu rather than in the Microsoft Office group.

When you've finished making changes, close the Programs or Start Menu folder (whichever is open). Then click the Start button and choose All Programs. Any organizational changes you made in the Programs folder show up in the All Programs menu.

Creating Custom Shortcut Keys

Windows Vista offers many shortcut keys that you can use as an alternative to the mouse. They're summarized in Appendix C at the back of this book. Most programs also offer shortcut keys. Those you can discover by looking at pull-down menus or by searching that program's Help for "shortcut keys."

You can create your own custom shortcut keys for launching favorite programs or opening folders. By default, these custom keys will be a Ctrl+Alt+*key* combination to avoid conflicts with built-in shortcut keys.

Also, they'll only work when you're at the desktop. That's because keystrokes only apply to the active window. So if there's any program window open at all on the desktop, your keystrokes will apply only to that window.

TIP You can minimize all open windows to get to the desktop without losing your place in open program windows. Right-click an empty area of the taskbar or the clock and choose Show the Desktop. Or click Show Desktop in the Quick Launch toolbar, if available.

Before you create a custom shortcut key, make sure it's not already assigned to something else. Get to the desktop and press the Ctrl+Alt+*key* combination you intend to use. If nothing opens, you know the shortcut is available. If something does open, you need to come up with a different shortcut key, or remove the shortcut key from the item to which it's currently assigned.

You can assign a shortcut key to any item that offers a Shortcut Key option in its Properties dialog box. But the easiest way is to first create a desktop shortcut to the item. Then define the key in the desktop shortcut icon. So the first step is to get to the icon that opens the program or folder of interest. Then right-click that icon and choose Send To ➪ Desktop (create shortcut).

NOTE If all of your desktop icons are hidden, right-click an empty portion of the desktop and choose View ➪ Show Desktop Icons.

Next, get to the desktop and locate the shortcut icon you just created. Right-click that icon and choose Properties. Click the Shortcut tab in the Properties sheet. Then click in the Shortcut Key box and type the letter you want to use as the shortcut. For example, in Figure 11.36 I typed the letter *C* in the Shortcut Key box for a Windows Calendar shortcut's properties. Windows automatically added the Ctrl+Alt+ in front of that letter *C* I typed.

FIGURE 11.36

Ctrl+Alt+C shortcut assigned to Windows Calendar.

Click OK to close the dialog box. To test the shortcut, make sure you're at a clean desktop and press the shortcut key combination. For example, pressing Ctrl+Alt+C after doing the preceding example opens Windows Calendar.

There is one slight disadvantage to assigning the shortcut key in a shortcut icon. If you delete the shortcut icon from your desktop, you also delete the shortcut key. If that's a problem, you can hide, rather than delete, the desktop icon. Just right-click that icon and choose Properties. Click the General tab in the Properties dialog box and select (check) the Hidden checkbox. Then click OK. The icon will disappear (or go dim), but the shortcut key will still work.

Whether hidden icons are dim or invisible depends on a setting in Folder Options. To get to that dialog box, click the Start button, type `fol`, and click Folder Options on the Start menu. Click the View tab in the dialog box. To make hidden icons invisible, choose Do not show hidden files and folders. To make them visible but dim, choose Show hidden files and folders. Click OK after making your selection.

Customizing the Taskbar

The taskbar at the bottom of your screen is one of the most useful tools in Windows. It contains the Start button, a button for each open program window, and the Notification area. It can also contain some tool-bars, such as the Quick Launch toolbar, which provides easy one-click access to a few programs. You can customize the taskbar in many ways, so don't worry about what you see on yours right at this moment.

Some options for customizing the taskbar are in the Taskbar and Start Menu Properties dialog box. To open that dialog box, use whichever of the following techniques is easiest for you:

- Right-click the Start button, current time, or any empty spot on the taskbar and choose Properties.
- Tap ⊞, type `task`, and click Taskbar and Start Menu.
- Click Start and choose Control Panel ➪ Appearance and Personalization ➪ Taskbar and Start Menu.

In the dialog box, click the Taskbar tab to see the options shown in Figure 11.37. The options on that tab are summarized as follows:

FIGURE 11.37

Taskbar tab in Taskbar and Start Menu Properties dialog box.

- **Lock the taskbar:** If you select this option, you'll lock the taskbar, which will prevent you from accidentally moving or resizing it. If you want to move or resize the taskbar, you first need to clear this option to unlock the taskbar.

- **Auto-hide the taskbar:** If you select this icon, the taskbar will automatically slide out of view when you're not using it, to free up the little bit of screen space it takes up. After the taskbar hides itself, you can rest the tip of the mouse button on the thin line at the bottom of the screen to bring the taskbar out of hiding.

- **Keep the taskbar on top of other windows:** Selecting this option ensures that the taskbar is always visible and can't be covered up by open program windows. To ensure that the taskbar is always visible, select (check) this option, and clear the *Auto-hide the taskbar* checkbox.

- **Group similar taskbar buttons:** Choosing this option allows the taskbar to combine multiple open documents or pages for a program into a single taskbar button. Taskbar buttons that represent multiple documents will display a number next to the program name on the button. You can open any document by clicking the taskbar button and clicking a document name. To close all open documents or pages in one fell swoop, right-click the button and choose Close Group.

- **Show Quick Launch:** Select this option to make the Quick Launch toolbar visible on the taskbar. Clear this option to hide the Quick Launch toolbar. (More on the Quick Launch toolbar later.)

- **Show window previews (thumbnails):** Choose this option to make mini-versions of open program windows available from taskbar buttons. To see the mini-version of any open program window, point to its taskbar button, as in the example shown in Figure 11.38.

FIGURE 11.38

Thumbnail when pointing to a taskbar button.

Click OK after making your selections from the dialog box. There are some other things you can do to customize the taskbar, outside that dialog box, as described next.

Locking and unlocking the taskbar

The taskbar doesn't have to be at the bottom of the screen. And it doesn't need to be a specific height either. When the taskbar is unlocked, you can move and size it at will. If the taskbar is unlocked, putting the tip of the mouse pointer at the top of the taskbar changes the pointer to a two-headed arrow. Also, if you have any toolbars on the taskbar, you'll see a *dragging handle* (columns of dots) next to each toolbar. Also, when you right-click and empty area of the taskbar or the current time, the Lock the Taskbar option on the menu is unchecked (see Figure 11.39).

FIGURE 11.39

Unlocked taskbar.

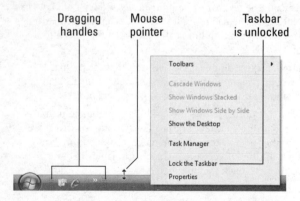

If the taskbar is locked, just right-click an empty portion of the taskbar or the current time and click Lock the Taskbar to unlock. The option is a toggle, so you can use the same procedure to lock the taskbar when it's unlocked.

Moving and sizing the taskbar

When the taskbar is unlocked, you can dock it to any edge of the screen as follows:

1. Place the tip of the mouse pointer on an empty portion of the taskbar (not in a toolbar or on a button).

2. Hold down the left mouse button, drag the taskbar to any screen edge, and release the mouse button.

To change the height of the taskbar, put the tip of the mouse pointer on the top of the taskbar so it changes to a two-headed arrow. Then hold down the left mouse button and drag up or down until the bar is at a height you like. The minimum height is one row tall. The maximum is about a third of the screen.

TIP If you have any problem getting the taskbar back to the original one-row tall size, close all open toolbars. Then size the taskbar to the height you want. Then choose which toolbars you want to view.

If you want to hide the taskbar altogether, select the Auto-hide the taskbar option in the Taskbar and Start Menu Properties dialog box described earlier in this chapter. The taskbar will stay hidden until you move the mouse pointer to the edge of the screen where you placed the taskbar.

Showing toolbars on the taskbar

Windows Vista comes with some optional toolbars you can add to the taskbar or allow to float freely on the desktop. To show or hide a toolbar, right-click the clock in the lower-right corner of your screen and choose Toolbars. You see the names of toolbars shown in Figure 11.40 and summarized here.

FIGURE 11.40

Show or hide optional toolbars.

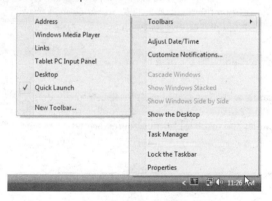

- **Address:** Displays an Address bar like the one in your Web browser. Typing a URL into the bar will open your Web browser and the page at the URL.

- **Windows Media Player:** Adds a set of Play Controls to the taskbar. This toolbar will be visible only if you open, then minimize, Windows Media Player. Unlike the others, this one can't be dragged off the taskbar onto the desktop.

- **Links:** Displays the contents of Internet Explorer's Links folder as a toolbar. See "Customizing the Links toolbar" later in this chapter for more information.
- **Tablet PC Input Panel:** Displays the handwriting recognition window used with tablet PCs. This one will likely appear jutting out from the side of your screen rather than in the taskbar.
- **Desktop:** Shows all the icons from your desktop in a condensed toolbar format.
- **Quick Launch:** Shows icons for frequently used programs, providing quick, one-click access to those programs.

 You might also see a Language Bar toolbar option. That one applies to multi-language keyboards as discussed under "Working with multiple languages" in Chapter 12.

- **New Toolbar:** Create a custom toolbar containing icons from any folder you wish. For example, after choosing this option, click your User Account name in the New Toolbar dialog box and click OK. The new toolbar that appears will provide quick access to all your folders.

On the Toolbars menu, any toolbar that has a checkmark next to its name is "on" and visible in the taskbar. Any toolbar whose name isn't checked is hidden. Click a name to hide, or show, the toolbar.

When you first choose a custom toolbar, there may not be room for it on the taskbar. Especially if the taskbar is already loaded up with buttons or other toolbars. The next section explains ways to deal with that.

Sizing and positioning taskbar toolbars

There isn't a lot of room on the taskbar, so things will get crowded if you add too many things to it. If you want a lot of optional toolbars on your taskbar, consider making it taller so it can show more things. Try moving it to the side of the monitor to see if that helps.

 **Unfortunately, there's no way to stretch the taskbar across two or more monitors to widen it.**

When there are more items on a toolbar than there is space, you see a >> symbol at the right side of the toolbar. Clicking that shows the items that don't fit on the toolbar. If there are more open program windows than space for taskbar buttons, use the up and down arrows to the right of the visible taskbar buttons to see additional buttons.

TIP **You can also switch from one open program window to the next by pressing Alt+Tab or ⊞+Tab.**

When the taskbar is unlocked, you'll see a dragging handle at the left side of each toolbar. You can drag those handles left and right to move and size toolbars. You can also show or hide the toolbar titles and text. Figure 11.41 shows an example of the text, titles, a handle, and taskbar button scrolling arrows.

FIGURE 11.41

Taskbar and toolbar handles, titles, text, and buttons.

Toolbar title

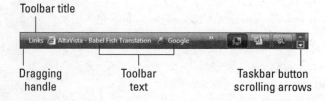

Dragging handle   Toolbar text   Taskbar button scrolling arrows

To show or hide the title or text, right-click the toolbar's title or dragging handle. Then choose Show Title to show or hide the toolbar's title. Click Show Text to show or hide text for icons on the toolbar.

NOTE Text always appears next to icons when you click >> on a toolbar. The Show Text option has no effect on that. To change the text that appears next to an icon, right-click that text, choose Rename, type the new name (or edit the existing name), and press Enter.

Customizing the Quick Launch toolbar

The Quick Launch toolbar provides easy one-click access to programs. Initially yours will likely contain just a few icons. Maybe even for programs you don't use very often! But the default icons are just examples. You can put any icons for any program you like on the Quick Launch toolbar. Likewise, you can remove any you don't need.

First, you want to make sure the Quick Launch toolbar is visible. If it's on it will appear just next to the toolbar (unless you move it somewhere else). Like any toolbar, you can show or hide the Quick Launch toolbar by right-clicking the current time or an empty portion of the taskbar and choosing Toolbars ➪ Quick Launch.

You can add new icons to the Quick Launch toolbar in several ways. Perhaps the easiest is to click the Start button, then right-click a program icon at the left side of the Start menu and choose Add to Quick Launch. If the program you want to add isn't on the left side of the Start menu, click All Programs, right-click the program's icon on the All Programs menu or a submenu, as in Figure 11.42, and choose Add to Quick Launch.

FIGURE 11.42

Right-click a program's icon.

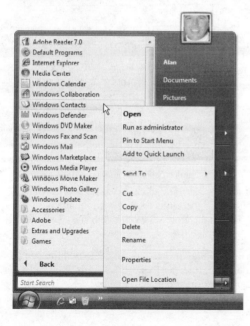

If the Quick Launch toolbar isn't wide enough to show all of its icons, the new icon won't be visible until you click the >> button on the right side of that toolbar.

The Quick Launch toolbar isn't just for programs. You can also add icons for frequently used folders or even files. You don't want to get too carried away. A Quick Launch toolbar that contains a zillion icons isn't going to feel very "quick." But here's how it's done:

1. Navigate to the folder icon (or document icon) for the item to which you want to create a Quick Launch icon.

2. Right-click that folder or file icon and choose Send To ⇨ Desktop (create shortcut).

3. Get to the desktop so you can see the shortcut icon you just put there.

4. Drag that shortcut icon and drop it between any two icons that are already on the Quick Launch toolbar.

You can delete the desktop shortcut icon if you don't want it. You just used that as an intermediate step here to create the Quick Launch icon.

Contrary to popular belief, icons in the Quick Launch toolbar don't consume computer resources or slow down your PC. So don't delete useful icons on the assumption that doing so will fix a problem or make your computer faster. It won't. But if you want to get rid of some Quick Launch icons that you never use, the process is simple. To remove an icon from the Quick Launch toolbar, right-click it and choose Delete. Click Yes when asked for verification.

If you delete a Quick Launch icon by accident, you can restore it from the Recycle Bin. When placed back on the Quick Launch toolbar, it will be added to the end of the list of icons. So you might need to click >> to see it.

 Items in the Quick Launch toolbar are shortcuts. So deleting a Quick Launch icon will never delete the actual item to which the icon refers.

To rearrange Quick Launch icons, just drag the icon to a new location between existing icons. Make sure you get the tip of the mouse pointer between two existing Quick Launch icons before you release the mouse button to drop.

If there are more icons than space on your Quick Launch toolbar, you'll see a >> symbol at the right side of the toolbar. To alphabetize Quick Launch icons by name, click that >> symbol. Then right-click any icon on the menu and choose Sort by Name.

 You can also use the sidebar Launcher gadget to store shortcuts to frequently used programs. See "Using Windows Sidebar" later in this chapter for more information on gadgets.

Customizing the Links toolbar

The links toolbar is similar to the Quick Launch toolbar, but it offers easy one-click access to favorite Web sites. As with the Quick Launch toolbar, you don't want to clutter up the Links toolbar with too many icons. Better to use Favorites in Internet Explorer for a really large collection of favorite Web sites. Use the Links toolbar only for sites you visit very often.

You can make the Links toolbar visible in Internet Explorer, the taskbar, or both. It's easiest to add links to the toolbar from Internet Explorer. So if you don't see that toolbar in Internet Explorer, click its Tools button and choose Toolbars ⇨ Link. Normally it shows up under the Address bar as in Figure 11.43. The rest is easy:

FIGURE 11.43

Links toolbar in Internet Explorer (bottom).

- To create an icon for the page you're currently viewing, drag the icon to the left of the URL in the Address bar to the far right edge of the Links toolbar (so the mouse pointer turns to an I-beam). Then release the mouse button.

 **As with any toolbar, when there are more links than space, you see >> at the end of the toolbar. Click that to see hidden links.**

- To create an icon for a link on the current page, drag the link from the page onto the Links toolbar.
- To remove an icon from the Links toolbar, right-click the item and choose Delete.
- To rearrange items on the Links toolbar, drag the item's icon to a new location on the toolbar.

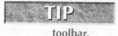 **To manage Links toolbar shortcuts as a folder, click the Start button and click your User Account name. Then open the Links folder. Each icon in that folder is an icon on your Links toolbar.**

Any changes that you make to the Links toolbar in Internet Explorer will automatically be reflected in the Links toolbar on the taskbar.

Customizing the Notification Area

The Notification area appears at the right side of the taskbar. It contains icons for programs and services that are running in the *background*, which means it's a program that doesn't have a specific program window or taskbar button associated with it. Icons in the Notification area represent things like your antivirus software, volume control, network connection, Windows Sidebar, and other things. Pointing to an item displays its name or other information.

To conserve space on the taskbar, non-essential or inactive icons can be hidden. When there are hidden items, you see a < symbol at the left side of the Notification area as in Figure 11.44. Click the < symbol to see the hidden items.

FIGURE 11.44

Notification area.

There are a couple different dialog boxes you can use to customize the Notification area. The first is Taskbar and Start Menu Properties, which you've seen in previous sections. To open that, right-click the Start button and choose Properties. Then click the Notification Area tab to see the options shown in Figure 11.45.

FIGURE 11.45

Notification Area tab.

The main options are self-explanatory. Choose Hide inactive icons to keep the Notification area down to a reasonable size that conserves space on the taskbar. Then use the checkboxes to show or hide the clock, Volume control, Network Connection, and Power icons. Any items that are disabled (dimmed) aren't relevant to your system. So don't worry about those.

NOTE As always, the items you checked or unchecked will have no effect until you click Apply or OK.

For more detailed control over the Notification area, click the Customize button. Or right-click the current time in the lower-right corner of the screen and choose Customize Notification Icons. Either way, the Customize Icons dialog box opens. Figure 11.46 shows an example. But yours will list programs on your system that can run in the background on your system.

NOTE The Customize button and the Customize Notification Icons option on the shortcut menu are disabled (dimmed) if you don't opt to hide inactive icons. That's because if you don't choose to hide inactive icons, there's no reason to choose which icons should always show, never show, or show only when active.

The Customize Notification Icons dialog box lists items that are currently in the Notification area, and others that have shown up in the past. To change the behavior of any item, click its name. Then use the drop-down list in the Behavior column to decide how you want it to behave:

- **Hide when inactive:** The item will be hidden except when it is active or needs your attention.
- **Hide:** The item will always be hidden, no matter what.
- **Show:** The item will always be visible.

FIGURE 11.46

Customize Icons dialog box.

If you're not sure how you want to display items, click Default Settings to go with the factory default settings. This will mostly likely be "Hide when inactive" because icons really only need to be visible when they're active.

Getting rid of Notification area icons

You cannot delete a Notification area icon by right-clicking and choosing Delete. That's because unlike toolbars, its icons are not shortcuts for opening programs. Icons in the Notification area represent things that are already running—albeit in the background where there's nothing showing on the screen.

There is no single, simple step you can perform to get rid of a Notification area icon. There are hundreds of programs on the market that can run in the background. To keep such a program from showing up in your Notification area, you might need to prevent that program from auto-starting with your computer. Or you might need to remove the program from your system altogether. Then again, you might only need to get to the program's Options dialog box and clear the checkbox that makes it show a Notification area icon.

One thing's for sure, you don't want to delete anything from the Notification area unless you know exactly what you're deleting and why. For example, an icon could represent your virus or spyware protection. You wouldn't necessarily want to delete such programs, or prevent them from auto-starting, because they need to be running in the background to keep your computer secure.

To see what options are available for a Notification area icon, right-click the icon. Some Notification area icons can show up on the screen in a program window. If so, double-clicking the Notification area icon will usually open that program. From there you can learn more about the program that the icon represents. If it has a menu bar, choosing Tools ➪ Options might take you to a dialog box where you can prevent the program from auto-starting, or prevent it from showing up in the Notification area.

If the Notification area icon represents a program you don't want on your system at all, you can remove the program through Control Panel. Just make sure you don't remove a program you actually need and cannot replace. See Chapter 43 for the goods on removing programs.

If you want to keep a program, but just want to prevent it from auto-starting and can't find a way to do that from within the program, there are still a couple of other ways to do that. If the program has an icon in your Startup folder, you can just remove that icon from that folder. Or, you can click Change startup programs in Control Panel to disable auto-starting. See "Using Software Explorer to control startup programs" in Chapter 8 for more information.

Tweaking the clock

The clock in the lower-right corner of the screen doesn't look like much. But there are quite a few things you can do with it. If you point to it, you see the current date. If you click it, you see the current date marked on a calendar, and the time on a clock. If you right-click the time and choose Adjust Date/Time, you come to the dialog box shown in Figure 11.47. There you can do several things with the clock.

FIGURE 11.47

Date and time properties.

NOTE   You need administrative privileges to change some aspects of the date and time. That might sound silly, but in a home environment, it keeps the kids from getting around parental controls that limit when they can use the computer.

First, you want to make sure your clock is set to the time zone you're in. Click Change time zone and choose your time zone. If you're in an area that honors daylight savings time, check the option that allows that to be handled automatically.

If the date or time is wrong on your clock, you can click Change Date and Time to manually enter the correct information. Or click the Internet Time tab and click Change Settings. Then click Update Now to synchronize your calendar and clock with the "official time" on the Internet.

NEW FEATURE You can show clocks for up to three different time zones.

You can also make the clock show the current time for up to three time zones. Click Additional Clocks. Then just follow the onscreen instructions to add one or two more times to your clock. Click OK after adjusting all your time settings.

Back on the desktop, the current time in the Notification area will be accurate. Likewise when you point to the time to see more information. If you set up multiple time zones, you'll see them all when you point to the current time. Clicking the time shows times for all time zones as clocks, like in Figure 11.48.

FIGURE 11.48

Clocks for multiple time zones.

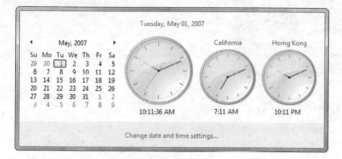

Using Windows Sidebar

NEW FEATURE Sidebar is a handy way to keep things you need often visible on your desktop at all times.

Windows Sidebar is an optional desktop item for showing *gadgets*. If the sidebar is open, it's hard to miss. It's at the right side of the desktop as in Figure 11.49. Each item on the sidebar is a gadget. When your computer is new, you'll see a few sample gadgets. But there are many more to choose from. Some are in the Gadget Gallery (also shown in Figure 11.49). Others you can download from the Internet. If you don't see the sidebar at all, don't worry.

FIGURE 11.49

Sidebar at the right side of the desktop.

Showing/hiding the sidebar

Use the Windows Sidebar Notification area icon to show or hide the sidebar. If you're not sure which icon that is, just point to each one until you find the one named Windows Sidebar. If it's not among the visible icons, click the < symbol at the left side of the Notification area to locate the icon. To keep that icon from going into hiding, set its Behavior property to Show, as described in the preceding section "Customizing the Notification Area."

If you can't find the sidebar or the Notification area icon, click the Start button and choose All Programs ➪ Accessories ➪ Windows Sidebar. That will open both the sidebar and its Notification area icon.

Once you see the Windows Sidebar icon, right-click it as in Figure 11.50. If the sidebar is hidden, click Show Sidebar to make it visible. Likewise, you can hide the sidebar at any time by choosing Hide Sidebar from that same menu.

 **You can also just double-click the Windows Sidebar Notification area icon to show/hide the sidebar.**

To personalize the sidebar, right-click the sidebar or its Notification area icon and choose Properties. The Windows Sidebar Properties dialog box opens as in Figure 11.51. The options in the dialog box are mostly self-explanatory. But here's a quick summary:

FIGURE 11.50

Windows Sidebar Notification area icon.

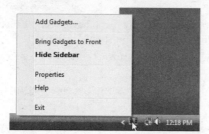

FIGURE 11.51

Windows Sidebar Properties dialog box.

- **Start sidebar when Windows starts:** Choose this option to have the sidebar and its Notification area within easy reach when you first start the computer.

- **Sidebar is always on top of other windows:** Choose this option to make the sidebar opaque and prevent program windows from covering it. Clear this checkbox to allow program windows to cover the sidebar.

TIP Even when a program window covers the sidebar, it's easy to get to your gadgets. Right-click any visible portion of the sidebar, or the Windows Sidebar Notification area icon, and choose **Bring gadgets to front**.

- **Display Sidebar on this side of screen:** Choose the side of the screen on which you want to place the sidebar. If you choose Left and also choose to keep the sidebar on top, you won't be able to click desktop icons that are under the sidebar. So think twice before using the left side of the screen.

- **Display Sidebar on monitor:** This option applies only if you have multiple monitors connected to and enabled on your computer. Otherwise this option should be set to 1.

- **View a list of running gadgets:** Shows the names of gadgets currently on your sidebar. You can remove any listed gadget.

- **Restore gadgets installed with Windows:** Resets gadgets to the ones that appeared the first time you used Windows Vista.

Click OK after viewing or changing any settings. When the sidebar is open, you can right-click it or the Windows Sidebar Notification area icon and choose Show sidebar or Hide sidebar to show or hide the sidebar.

To close the sidebar and remove its Notification area icon, right-click the sidebar or icon and choose Exit. To re-open the sidebar in the future, click the Start button and choose All Programs ➪ Accessories ➪ Windows Sidebar.

Adding and removing gadgets

Each item in the sidebar is a gadget. There are no required gadgets. Nor are there right, wrong, good, or bad gadgets. The idea is to simply look around through available gadgets and pick ones you like. To add gadgets to the sidebar:

- Click the + sign near the top of the sidebar.
- Or right-click an empty area on the sidebar and choose Add Gadgets.
- Or right-click the Windows Sidebar Notification area icon and choose Add Gadgets.

It doesn't matter which method you use because the result is the same: The Gadget Gallery opens. When the gallery first opens, you'll see a few sample gadgets. If you see numbers like 1/2 or 1/3 near the upper-right corner of the gallery, they mean you're viewing page one of multiple pages. Click the Up or Down button above those numbers to scroll through other pages of gadgets.

When you click a gadget, a description appears near the bottom of the gallery. If you don't see a description, click the v button near the bottom of the gallery to enlarge it.

After you've checked out gadgets you already have, click Get more gadgets online to see more. You're taken to a Web page where you can scroll through many more available gadgets. Just read and follow the instructions on that page to shop around and download any gadgets that look interesting. Downloaded gadgets are placed in your gallery, which makes them easy to get to and put on your sidebar.

To add a gadget to the sidebar, just double-click it. Or right-click it and choose Add, or just drag it from the gallery onto the sidebar. If there isn't enough room for all your gadgets, some will be placed on additional pages. Use the < and > buttons at the top of the sidebar to scroll through all the gadgets on your sidebar.

To remove a gadget from your sidebar, right-click it and choose Remove. Or point to the gadget and click the Close (X) button at its upper-right corner. A copy of the gadget remains in your gallery, in case you want to add it back on later. To remove a gadget from the gallery and your computer, right-click the gadget in the gallery and choose uninstall.

Using and manipulating gadgets

Different gadgets do different things and work in different ways. But most are easy to figure out. If the gadget has options or settings you can change, you'll see a checkmark near its upper-right corner. Click that checkmark to see what it has to offer. Or right-click the gadget and choose Settings. When the Settings dialog box opens, the options will be self-explanatory.

Some gadgets have options like Opacity to control transparency, Detach from sidebar to make the gadget free-floating, and Attach to sidebar to put a detached gadget back on the sidebar. Right-click a gadget and choose Move to turn the mouse pointer to a four-headed "move" arrow, then drag the mouse to put it wherever you want.

Gadgets are meant to be simple, useful, and fun. So feel free to try things out and play around with them. Because there is no set of rules that apply to all gadgets, you'll need to experiment with any gadget you choose to figure out how it works. Remember, once a gadget is on the sidebar, you can right-click it to see options for using and customizing the gadget.

Using Windows SideShow

Windows SideShow is similar to Windows Sidebar, except that it doesn't show gadgets on your desktop. Rather, it shows them on alternative display devices found on some notebooks, cell phones, and other portable devices. It only works with devices that sport the Windows SideShow logo. Furthermore, you have to install the device to work with Windows SideShow. I can't help you with that step because there are many such devices and no one-rule-fits-all. Refer to the instructions that came with the device for specifics.

On the computer side of things, you'll use the SideShow control panel to tweak settings on the alternative screen and to choose gadgets. Use either of the following methods to get to that control panel:

- Press ⊞, type side, and click Windows SideShow.
- Click the Start button and choose Control Panel ➪ Hardware and Sound ➪ Windows SideShow.

What you see in the SideShow control panel depends on the device you've installed. But the options should be self-explanatory enough that you can figure it out on your own. Basically you choose the gadgets you want to display from the list of available gadgets. Click the Get more gadgets online link to find other SideShow gadgets. Use the Help links in the control panel for more information about SideShow and configuring it to best work with your hardware.

Wrap Up

This chapter has been all about the many ways you can customize the Windows desktop, Start menu, and taskbar to set up your screen in a way that works for you. You have many options. The important thing to keep in mind is that they *are* options, and there is no right or wrong way to do things. It's all about making choices that work for you. Here's a quick recap of the essentials:

- The Windows desktop is basically your entire screen — the place where you do all of your work.
- Most tools for personalizing your system are in the Control Panel Personalization page. To get there quickly, right-click the desktop and choose Personalize.
- To personalize your Start menu, taskbar, or Notification area, right-click the Start button and choose Properties.
- To create a custom shortcut key for launching a program, right-click the program's icon and choose Properties. Then click the Shortcut tab and fill in the Keyboard Shortcut box.
- To add or remove taskbar toolbars, right-click the clock and choose Toolbars.
- To add a program to the Quick Launch toolbar, right-click the program's icon and choose Add to Quick Launch.
- To show or hide Notification area icons, right-click the clock or an empty taskbar area and choose Customize Notifications.
- To show or hide the sidebar, right-click the Windows Sidebar Notification area icon and choose Show sidebar or Hide sidebar. Or, click the Start button and choose All Programs ⇨ Accessories ⇨ Windows Sidebar.
- Windows SideShow is like a sidebar for alternative display devices. It only works with devices that sport the Windows SideShow logo.

Chapter 12

Ease of Access, Speech, and Language

This chapter is all about Vista's Ease of Access, Speech Recognition, Text-to-Speech, Handwriting Recognition, and Language options. Although somewhat separate features, all offer alternatives to standard read, type, and click interaction with the computer.

Some features are designed for people with specific sensory, motor, cognitive, or seizure-related disabilities. Others aren't for any specific disability, but rather just an alternative way of doing things.

For example, if you just can't type worth beans, speech recognition lets you work your computer by talking. The Text-to-Speech option reads text aloud from the screen, which is good for any preschooler or any over-40 adult whose eyesight isn't what it used to be. In short, this isn't just a chapter for people with impairments or disabilities. There's something for just about everyone here.

If several people share your computer, and different people have different needs, you should set up a user account for each person first. That way you can tailor settings for each user. If you haven't gotten around to setting up user accounts yet, take a look at Chapter 3.

IN THIS CHAPTER

Ease of Access for sensory and motor impairments

Making Windows talk with Narrator

Using speech recognition

Working in multiple languages

Introducing Ease of Access Center

Accessibility features for sensory and motor impairments are in the Ease of Access Center. If you have multiple user accounts, you can get to its options right from the login page after you start your computer or log out of your account. Just click the blue and white Ease of Access button in the lower-left corner of the screen. The window shown in Figure 12.1 opens.

FIGURE 12.1

Ease of Access from login page.

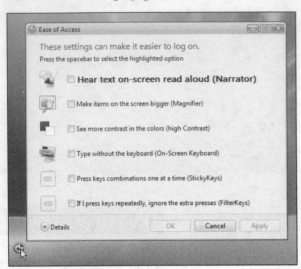

When the dialog box opens, a voice reads each option aloud and makes the currently selected option larger. To activate an accessibility feature, press the Spacebar to check its checkbox. After you've selected the features you need, a dialog box appears so you can tweak settings for that feature. I'll get into the specifics as we look at each feature in more detail. But I think most are self-explanatory, so feel free to adjust whatever you want, or just click OK to accept the default settings.

When you've finished choosing Ease of Access options, click the name or picture of your user account. Don't worry if you miss the opportunity to choose Ease of Access options at the login page. You can choose and configure things right from you user account as described next.

After you've logged in to a user account, you can use the Ease of Access Center to enable, disable, or tweak accessibility options. Use whichever of the following techniques is easiest for you to get to the Ease of Access Center:

- Press ⊞, type ea, and click Ease of Access.
- Hold down ⊞ and tap U.
- Click the Start button and choose Control Panel ➪ Ease of Access ➪ Ease of Access Center.
- Right-click the desktop and choose Personalize, then click Ease of Access in the lower-left corner of the Personalization page.
- Click the Start button and choose All Programs ➪ Accessories ➪ Ease of Access ➪ Ease of Access Center.

Regardless of how you get there, the Ease of Access Center opens as in Figure 12.2.

FIGURE 12.2

Ease of Access Center.

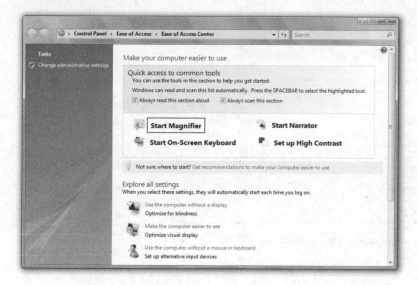

If the Always read this section aloud and Always scan this section checkboxes are selected, each option will be read aloud and magnified to help with visual impairments. After an option is read aloud, you have a few seconds to press the Spacebar and select that feature. If you don't want to turn on a feature, don't press the Spacebar. To disable the spoken instructions, clear those checkboxes.

If the preceding approach doesn't work for you, click Get recommendations to make your computer easier to use. Just follow the instructions on each page, selecting (checking) only items that apply to you personally and click Next. Continue on that way until you get to the last page and answer its questions. Then click Done.

After answering questions on the last page, you'll see a list of recommended settings. None are selected (checked). You need to select all the options yourself, or at least the options that seem most likely to apply to your impairments. Click Save to save the suggested settings and close the window.

Yet a third approach to choosing Ease of Access options is to click an option in the lower half of the Ease of Access Center (see Figure 12.3). Use the scroll bar at the right side of the Ease of Access Center program window to reach the additional options. Again, this is just another way of approaching accessibility options. Like the other approaches, these are self-explanatory. Just click any blue text that applies to you under the Explore all settings heading. The next page to open provides options, instructions, and information.

FIGURE 12.3

More Ease of Access Center options.

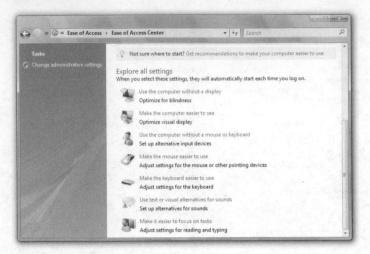

Regardless of which approach you use to choose your basic Ease of Access options, you end up with one or more specific Windows Features turned on to help you out. Each of those features has a name like Magnifier, Narrator, On-Screen Keyboard, and others. Some have additional settings you can tweak to better suit your own needs. The rest of this chapter is about those individual tools to improve accessibility.

Help for visual impairments

Visual impairments range from poor eyesight to near or total blindness. The Ease of Access Center provides some helpers for visual impairments. However, total blindness usually requires alternative input devices that go beyond the kinds of things you can do by changing settings in Windows. For more information on such devices, see the assistive technologies Web page at www.microsoft.com/enable.

For visual impairments that don't require special hardware devices, Windows Vista offers the built-in tools described in this section.

Using Microsoft Screen Magnifier

Microsoft Screen Magnifier is an assistive tool for those with visual impairments who require magnification of items on the screen. When activated, a portion of the screen shows the area around the mouse pointer magnified along the top of the screen. For example, in Figure 12.4 the top portion of the screen is a magnified version of the area near the mouse pointer. As you move the cursor around on the main screen, the magnifier follows, showing an enlarged version of whatever you're pointing to with the mouse pointer.

FIGURE 12.4

Microsoft Magnifier.

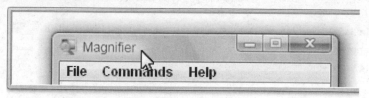

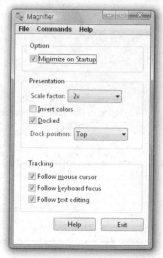

The dialog box shown in Figure 12.4 provides options for tweaking Magnifier settings. That dialog box appears automatically when you opt to use Microsoft Magnifier. If you didn't turn on Magnifier from the Ease of Access Center, you can do so from the Start menu. Click the Start button and choose All Programs ➪ Accessories ➪ Ease of Access ➪ Magnifier. Or tap 🎗, type mag, and click Magnifier.

The options in the dialog box let you tweak things as follows:

- **Minimize on Startup:** Displays the Microsoft Magnifier dialog box as a taskbar button when first opened, so it's not on the screen. Click the taskbar button when you need to open the dialog box.

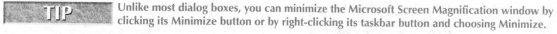

TIP Unlike most dialog boxes, you can minimize the Microsoft Screen Magnification window by clicking its Minimize button or by right-clicking its taskbar button and choosing Minimize.

- **Scale factor:** Specify how big you want things to look in the magnifier window.
- **Invert colors:** Makes the content inside the magnifier look like a negative of the original.
- **Docked:** If selected, this option keeps the magnifier anchored to the top of the screen. Clear this option to convert the magnifier so that you can size and position at will.
- **Dock position:** If you choose the Docked option, you can choose this option to specify where you want the magnifier to appear on the screen.

- **Follow mouse cursor:** If selected, tells the magnification window to always reflect content near the mouse pointer.

- **Follow keyboard focus:** If selected, ensures that any text you type is visible in the magnifier as you're typing.

- **Follow text editing:** Similar to above but ensures that any text you're editing is magnified.

- **Help:** Opens a help window for Magnifier.

- **Exit:** Closes the magnification window and dialog box.

To close the dialog box without closing the magnification window, click the Minimize button in the dialog box or right-click its taskbar button or title bar and choose Minimize.

TIP   To create desktop or Quick Launch shortcuts to some Ease of Access tools, click the Start button and choose All Programs ⇨ Accessories ⇨ Ease of Access. Then right-click any item that shows and choose Add to Quick Launch or Send To ⇨ Desktop (create shortcut).

Using Microsoft Narrator

Microsoft Narrator is an assistive technology that reads aloud text on the screen for visual impairments. It announces events and things that happen on the screen. If you didn't enable Narrator in the Ease of Access Center, you can start it at any time. Click the Start button and choose All Programs ⇨ Accessories ⇨ Ease of Access ⇨ Narrator. (Or press ⊞, type nar, and click Narrator).

When Narrator opens, you'll see the dialog box shown in Figure 12.5 (or a taskbar button for it). You'll hear the talking voice immediately, or as soon as you start doing things. The dialog box helps you tweak Narrator settings as follows:

FIGURE 12.5

Microsoft Narrator options.

- **Echo User's Keystrokes:** If selected, the narrator speaks every key you press at the keyboard.

- **Announce System Messages:** If selected, Narrator reads aloud any system message that appears on the screen.

- **Announce Scroll Notifications:** If selected, keeps you informed of how far down you've scrolled in a window.

- **Start Narrator Minimized:** If selected, starts Narrator with its dialog box minimized rather than open. Clicking the Microsoft Narrator taskbar button opens the dialog box.

- **Quick Help:** Starts spoken help for Narrator.

- **Voice Settings:** Lets you change the voice, speed, volume, and pitch of the speaking voice.

- **Exit:** Closes Narrator and its dialog box. You won't hear any more spoken narration until you restart Narrator. If you want to keep the narration but lose the dialog box, minimize (rather than close) the dialog box.

 Microsoft Narrator is weak compared to more sophisticated assistive technologies for the blind. To explore better Vista-compatible devices, browse to www.microsoft.com/enable.

Narrator is specifically designed to aid with visual impairments. As such, it reads everything on the screen. If you're looking for a more casual program to have e-books read aloud, consider Adobe Reader and Microsoft Reader. You can download both free from www.adobe.com/reader and www.microsoft.com/reader.

TextAloud is a popular text-to-speech tool designed to read e-mail, Web pages, and similar documents aloud. It's not free, but it's not expensive either. You can learn more and download a free trial version from www.textaloud.com.

Using High Contrast

High Contrast is a Windows feature that shows items in highly contrasting colors to help with visual impairments that make things on the screen look blurry. Click Set up High Contrast in the Ease of Access Center to get to options for controlling high contrast. Choose the first checkbox, Turn on High Contrast, then click Apply to activate the high contrast colors.

If you don't like the default high contrast color scheme, click the button under Select the color scheme you see when High Contrast is turned on, then choose another scheme and click Apply. Try each of the available schemes until you find the one that works best for you.

By default, you can turn High Contrast on and off by pressing Alt + Left Shift + Print Screen (hold down the Alt key, hold down the Shift key next to the letter Z, tap the Print Screen [PrtScrn] key, then release all keys). You can also turn off High Contrast by clicking the Turn on High Contrast checkbox in the window for setting up High Contrast.

 If your keyboard has a Function Lock or F Lock key, you might need to turn that off for Alt + Left Shift + Print Screen to work.

Using the computer without a display

Down in the "Explore all settings" section of Ease of Access you'll see a Use the computer without a display link. Clicking that link presents the options shown in Figure 12.6.

FIGURE 12.6

Use computer without display.

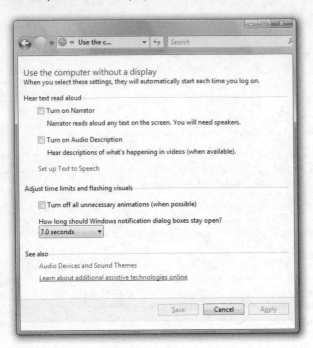

The first option turns on Microsoft Narrator, described in the preceding section. Turn on Audio Description, if selected, uses speech to describe what's happening in videos. Not all videos support that capability. So even if you choose that option you won't get voice descriptions with every video that plays. Videos that do support audio description will use your current text-to-speech settings, described later in this chapter, for voice. The Set up Text to Speech link takes you to the dialog box for configuring text-to-speech.

Choosing Turn off all unnecessary animations (when possible) turns off special animation effects that aren't relevant to alternative display devices, and also allows them to work faster. You can also control how long Notification area messages stay on the screen. If they tend to disappear before you get a chance to click on them, adjust the slider to make them stay on the screen longer.

If you made any changes in the window, click Apply to apply them without closing the window. Or click Save to apply them and close the window. To return to Ease of Access without saving changes, click Cancel or the Back button.

Optimize visual display

Ease of Access also provides a Make the computer easier to see link for visual impairments. Click that link for options related to your visual display. The first few options control High Contrast, Narrator, Audio Description, and Magnifier as described earlier. Scroll down to the options shown in Figure 12.7 for some other options, described next.

FIGURE 12.7

Make computer easier to see.

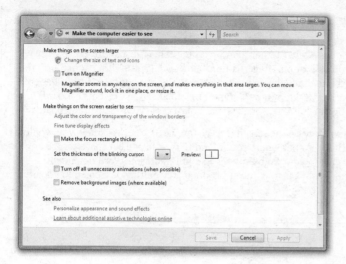

- **Change the size of text and icons:** Choosing this option takes you to the dialog box for changing the DPI (dots per inch) scaling. The default is 96dpi. Choosing a higher number makes items look larger. However you don't want to make this so large that they no longer fit on the screen. See "Adjust the font size (DPI)" in Chapter 11 for more information.

- **Make the focus rectangle thicker:** As you press the Tab key to move from one option to the next in a dialog box, a focus rectangle appears around the currently selected option. Choose this option to make that rectangle easier to see.

- **Set the thickness of the blinking cursor:** When you're typing text, a blinking vertical cursor appears at the place where the next character to type will appear. If it's difficult to see that cursor, use the drop-down button to increase its thickness. The line to the right of the Preview setting shows how wide that cursor will be.

- **Turn off all unnecessary animations (when possible):** Some animation effects on the screen serve no practical purpose. They're just there for amusement. They might be an unnecessary distraction or annoyance for some visual impairments. Choose this option to get rid of them.

- **Remove background images (where available):** Background pictures on the desktop, in folders, and in other locations can make it difficult to see text and other content on a page. Choose this option to get rid of those images.

As always, your choices won't be activated until you click Save or Apply (the only difference being that Save closes the window and Apply leaves it open).

Help for motor impairments

The Ease of Access Center offers several options for helping with motor impairments that make it difficult to use the mouse and keyboard. These include the On-Screen Keyboard, Sticky Keys, Filter Keys, and others. You can get to these options through the Ease of Access Center and other methods described in the sections that follow.

> **TIP** Speech recognition is the ultimate tool for motor impairments, because it lets you control the computer and dictate text with your voice. Speech recognition is covered a little later in this chapter.

Using the On-Screen Keyboard

The On-Screen Keyboard is just what its name implies — it's a keyboard that appears on the screen, so you can type by clicking on keys with the mouse pointer rather than by typing. This is useful for those with a variety of motor impairments, but not too bad for one-fingered hunt-and-peck typists either. You'll find the option for enabling On-Screen Keyboard under Use the computer without a mouse or keyboard in Ease of Access Center. You can also get to it from the desktop (tap ⊞, type on, and click On-Screen Keyboard). Or click the Start button and choose All Programs ➪ Accessories ➪ Ease of Access ➪ On-Screen Keyboard.

The keyboard appears in a free-floating window on the screen (see Figure 12.8). You work it as you would a normal keyboard. First, on the screen, click the spot where you intend to type text. That space can be anyplace that accepts text, from the Address bar in your Web browser to a full Microsoft Word document. Then, just start typing one character at a time by clicking the appropriate key on the On-Screen Keyboard.

FIGURE 12.8

The On-Screen Keyboard.

Use the Backspace (bksp) and Delete (del) keys to delete text. To type an uppercase letter, click the Shift key, then type the letter you want to type in uppercase. To press a *key+key* combination, such as Ctrl+Esc, click the first key, then the second key.

When you've finished with the On-Screen Keyboard, click the Close (X) button in its upper-right corner. To see a more complete set of keyboard helpers, use whichever method is easy and works for you:

- In the Ease of Access Center, click Make the keyboard easier to use.
- Or from the desktop click the Start button and choose Control Panel ➪ Ease of Access ➪ Change how your keyboard works.

You're taken to the options shown in Figure 12.9. We'll look at each in the sections to follow.

FIGURE 12.9

Make the keyboard easier to use.

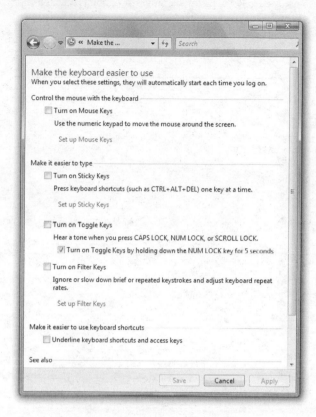

Some of the options show Notification area icons when they're turned on, as in Figure 12.10. That makes it easy to see, at a glance, which features are currently running. When Filter Keys and Sticky Keys are showing their icons, you can double-click either one to change its settings.

FIGURE 12.10

Notification area icons for keyboard helpers.

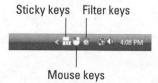

Sticky keys   Filter keys

Mouse keys

Using Mouse Keys

Mouse Keys lets you use your keyboard to move the mouse pointer around on the screen using arrow keys on the numeric keypad instead of the mouse. To use Mouse Keys, first make sure that option is selected (checked) in "Make the keyboard easier to use" (Figure 12.9). To configure Mouse Keys, click Set up mouse keys. You'll see the options shown in Figure 12.11.

FIGURE 12.11

Set up Mouse Keys.

Each option is briefly explained within the window and in the following list:

- **Turn on Mouse Keys:** Select the checkbox to enable Mouse Keys. Clear the checkbox to disable Mouse Keys.

- **Turn on Mouse Keys with ALT+left SHIFT + NUM LOCK:** Choose this option if you want to be able to turn Mouse Keys on and off using the shortcut key (hold down the Alt key, hold down the Shift key to the left of the letter Z, then tap the Num Lock key).

- **Display a warning message when turning a setting on:** Choose this option if you want some visual feedback on the screen so you know when you've turned on Mouse Keys.

- **Make a sound when turning a setting on or off:** Choose this option if you want to hear some auditory feedback when turning a feature off.

- **Top speed:** Use this slider to determine how fast the mouse pointer can go when you hold down an arrow key.

- **Acceleration:** The longer you hold down an arrow key, the faster the mouse pointer moves. Use this slider to determine how quickly that acceleration occurs.

■ **Hold down CTRL to speed up and SHIFT to slow down:** Choose this option if you want to control mouse pointer speed by holding down Ctrl or Shift while moving the mouse pointer with the arrow keys.

■ **Use Mouse Keys when Num Lock is:** Choose when Mouse Keys is operable, either when the Num Lock key is on or when it is off.

■ **Display the Mouse Keys icon on the taskbar:** Clearing this option will prevent Mouse Keys from displaying a Notification area icon.

For Mouse Keys to work, several things have to happen. First, you should see the Mouse Keys icon in the Notification area. If you don't, press left Alt+left Shift+Num Lock or turn it on. Click Yes in the dialog box that opens. Optionally, you can click Make the keyboard easier to use in the Ease of Access Center. Then check the Turn on Mouse Keys checkbox and click Apply.

If you see a red "No" symbol on the Mouse Keys Notification area icon, that means the Num Lock key isn't set for moving the mouse pointer. Tap the Num Lock key once to make the "No" symbol go away. Now you can move the mouse pointer using navigation keys on the numeric keypad as summarized next.

CAUTION   Navigation keys that aren't on the numeric keypad probably won't move the mouse pointer at all, whether Num Lock is on or off. So make sure you use the navigation keys on the numeric keypad.

To move the mouse pointer while Mouse Keys is active:

■ Use the ↑ and ↓ keys on the numeric keypad to move the mouse pointer vertically.

■ Use the ← and → keys to move the mouse pointer horizontally.

■ Use the Home, PgDn, PgUp, and End keys to move the mouse pointer diagonally.

■ To click the item under the mouse pointer, press the 5 key on the numeric keypad.

■ To double-click, press the + key on the numeric keypad.

■ To right-click, press the − key on the numeric keypad or press Shift+F10.

■ To rename, press F2.

■ To drag, press the Insert (Ins) key on the numeric keypad, and then move the mouse pointer with the keys previously described.

■ To drop, press the Delete (Del) key on the numeric keypad.

To disable Mouse Keys and hide its Notification area icon, press the same shortcut key used to show it: Alt+Left Shift+Num Lock.

You can also customize the appearance of the mouse pointer. In the Ease of Access Center, click Make the mouse easier to use to get to the options shown in Figure 12.12.

From the top of the dialog box, choose a size and color scheme for the mouse from the nine options provided. If you want to be able to bring a partially covered program window to the top of the stack just by pointing to it, choose Activate a window by hovering over it with the mouse. Clicking Mouse Settings takes you to the general mouse personalization dialog box described under "Personalizing your mouse" in Chapter 11.

FIGURE 12.12

More Mouse Keys options.

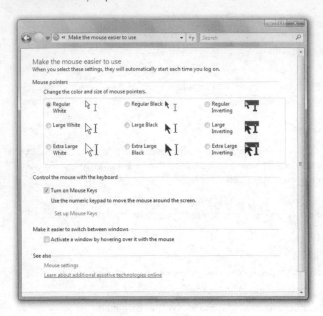

Using Sticky Keys

Sticky Keys eliminates the need to hold down two keys simultaneously to press shortcut keys, such as Ctrl+Esc. When Sticky Keys is active, you need only tap the *modifier key* (the first key in the *key + key* sequence) once, then tap the second key separately. For example, to press Ctrl+Esc with Sticky Keys active, tap the Ctrl key and then tap the Esc key.

When Sticky Keys is active, you see its icon in the Notification area (Figure 12.10). If it's not on, you may be able to activate it by pressing the Shift key five times and clicking Yes. If that method doesn't work, click Make the keyboard easier to use in the Ease of Access Center and then check the Turn on Sticky Keys checkbox in the Ease of Access Center.

Each modifier key that you can make stick is indicated by a little square in the Notification area icon. The square turns blank when the key is in the "on" position. To try it out, just pick a key (Ctrl, Alt, Shift, or the Windows Logo key) and tap it a few times. You'll see the little square turn black when the key is locked down. You'll see that same square turn white when the key is unlocked.

You can tweak Sticky Keys behavior to work best for you. To get to its settings, double-click the Sticky Keys Notification area icon and click Set up Sticky Keys. Or click Make the keyboard easier to use in Ease of Access Center, then click Set up Sticky Keys. The options shown in Figure 12.13 open.

FIGURE 12.13

Configure Sticky Keys.

Most of the options in the dialog box are self-explanatory, so I won't belabor them. The first one lets you turn Sticky Keys on or off. The second option controls the Sticky Keys shortcut key behavior. But the following two options deserve some mention:

- **Lock modifier keys when pressed twice in a row:** Choose this option if you want to have the ability to lock down a modifier key for more than one subsequent use. For example, if you choose the option, you can press the Shift key twice to keep that key locked down. Each single key you press after that will be typed as though you were holding down the Shift key. The key stays in that locked down position until you tap it a third time.

- **Turn off Sticky Keys if two keys are pressed at once:** Selecting this option lets you disable Sticky Keys by pressing any two keys simultaneously. (If you clear this option, you can turn off Sticky Keys by pressing the Shift key five times.)

The Notifications options control audio and Notification area icons. Make your selections, then click Save or Apply, as always, to activate your selections.

Using Toggle Keys

Toggle Keys is a simple keyboard helper that emits a sound whenever you press a toggle key (Caps Lock, Num Lock, or Scroll Lock). To activate Toggle Keys, choose its checkbox near the center of the keyboard helpers shown back in Figure 12.9. So long as you don't disable its shortcut key, you can turn Toggle Keys on or off by holding down the Num Lock key for five seconds.

TIP They're called *toggle keys* because each has two possible settings, either "on" or "off." When you tap the key, you go to the opposite setting. Many keyboards have little light indicators that go on when the key is in the "on" position.

If you turn Toggle Keys on and want to hear the sound, tap the Caps Lock key a few times. You'll hear a high-pitched tone when the key comes on and a low-pitched tone when the key goes off. There is no Notification area icon for Toggle Keys. The only way to know it's on is if you hear a sound when you tap one of those toggle keys, like Caps Lock.

Using Filter Keys

The Filter Keys option disables autotyping (repeated typing of the character) when a key is held down too long or when multiple rapid keystrokes occur. This helps to avoid unwanted keystrokes caused by shakiness and involuntary muscle movements associated with Parkinson's and similar motor impairments.

To activate Filter Keys, check Turn on Filter Keys in the "Make the keyboard easier to use" window. When Filter Keys is active, you should see its icon in the Notification area, as pointed out back in Figure 12.10. You can also turn Filter Keys on or off by holding down the right Shift key for eight seconds and clicking Yes.

To personalize Filter Keys so it works best for you, get to its settings shown in Figure 12.14. You can do so by double-clicking the Filter Keys Notification area icon. Or open the Ease of Access Center, click Make the keyboard easier to use, and then click Set up Filter Keys.

The first two sections, and Other Settings near the bottom of the window, are similar to those for other keyboard helpers — you can enable or disable Filter Keys and configure the keyboard shortcut. The rest are unique:

- **Turn on Bounce Keys:** If your fingers unintentionally press a key repeatedly when you mean to press it once, choose this option to ignore repeated keystrokes. Then specify how long you want Windows to wait before considering the next keypress an intentional one.

- **Turn on Repeat Keys and Slow Keys:** Choose this option if you inadvertently hold down a key too long causing it to repeat, or if you inadvertently brush keys due to involuntary muscle movements. Then click Set up Repeat Keys and Slow Keys to turn off, or tone down, repeat keys, and to put a minimum duration on how long you have to press a key before it counts as a valid keystroke.

You can test your current settings in the textboxes provided in the window. The last two options allow you to assign audible feedback to accepted keystrokes, and show the Filter Keys icon in the Notification area. As always, click Save or Apply to activate your selections.

Don't expect to get all the settings for keyboard helpers right on your first attempt. The best you can do, for starters, is guess what might work. Then use the settings until you get the hang of the feature. Once you get a feel for how the keyboard helper works, it will be easier to go back and fine-tune your settings until you find what works best for you.

FIGURE 12.14

Set up Filter Keys.

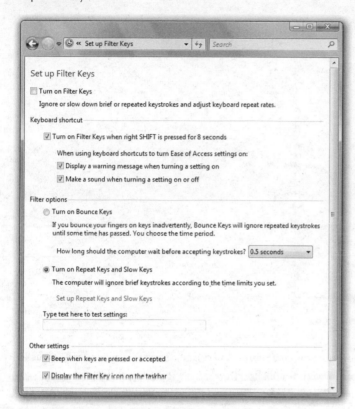

NOTE   See "Personalizing your mouse" and "Personalizing the Keyboard" in Chapter 11 for other options on configuring your mouse and keyboard.

Help for hearing impairments

Clicking the Use text or visual alternatives for sounds link near the bottom of the Ease of Access Center presents the options shown in Figure 12.15. These help with hearing impairments by replacing little sound effects and other auditory alerts with visual ones.

FIGURE 12.15

Use text or visual alternatives for sounds.

Your options in Sounds are as follows:

- **Turn on visual notifications for sounds (Sound Sentry):** Choosing this option replaces the little beeps and other sounds that alert hearing people to events with visual alerts.

- **Choose visual warning:** Lets you choose how large you want the warning to be, ranging from none at all to flashing the entire desktop.

- **Turn on text captions for spoken dialog (when available):** Choosing this option is similar to turning on closed captions on a TV. Spoken text is displayed onscreen as written text whenever possible.

As always, you need to click Save or Apply to activate any options you've selected or cleared.

Make it easier to focus on tasks

Down at the bottom of Ease of Access Center there's a link titled Make it easier to focus on tasks. Clicking that takes you to the options shown in Figure 12.16. All of the options turn on (or off) features described earlier in this chapter.

FIGURE 12.16

Reasoning Tasks options.

As always, if you do select or clear any options, you need to click Save or Apply to activate those selections.

Ease of Access administrative settings

The Change administrative settings option at the left side of Ease of Access Center allows an administrator to apply the selected Ease of Access options to the login page that all users see when first starting the computer. You need administrative privileges to set that one because it's the only setting that affects all users. You can also set a Restore point from that page as a backup to all the Ease of Access settings in play.

Accessibility keyboard shortcuts

For future reference, Table 12-1 lists shortcut keys used to turn Ease of Access features on or off from the keyboard. But keep in mind that these only work if you didn't disable shortcut access while configuring the feature.

How Do I Turn These Things Off?

Ease of Access options are no different from options you choose in dialog boxes. When you activate a feature, Vista assumes you mean it. Any features you activate will remain activated through the current session and into all future sessions. There isn't a "just experimenting" or "just kidding" mode where they turn themselves off automatically after a while.

To further complicate things, there are lots of ways to turn these things on or off. And if you don't remember where you turned a feature on, turning it off could be tricky. If you have trouble turning off some features, first clear all the checkmarks at the top of the Ease of Access Center. Then open the first item under "Explore all settings." Clear the checkboxes for features you don't want, then click Save. Then do the same for all the remaining links under the "Explore all settings" section until you've turned off everything you don't need.

TABLE 12-1

Shortcut Keys for Ease of Access

Open Ease of Access Center	Windows logo key +U
Turn High Contrast on/off	Press left Alt +left Shift +PRINT SCREEN (PrtScrn)
Turn Filter Keys on/off	Hold down right Shift for eight seconds
Turn Mouse Keys on/off	Press Left Alt +left Shift +Num Lock
Turn Sticky Keys on/off	Press Shift five times
Turn Toggle Keys on/off	Hold down Num Lock for five seconds

Using Speech Recognition

NEW FEATURE   **I know that XP has some speech recognition capabilities. But the Vista version is so much better than the XP version, it practically is a new feature.**

Speech recognition is a Vista feature that lets you perform many tasks by talking rather than by typing or clicking. It's a great solution to problems caused by motor impairments that make it difficult to use the mouse and keyboard. But it can also be useful if you just can't type worth beans. You can use speech recognition to open programs, folders, and files, make selections in dialog boxes, dictate text that you'd normally type by hand, and more.

To use speech recognition, you need a microphone. A USB headset microphone with *noise cancellation* to filter out background sound is best. If you don't have one, you can purchase one at any place that sells geek gear. To see examples or purchase online, go to an online retailer (www.cdw.com, www.newegg.com, www.tigerdirect.com, www.walmart.com, www.amazon.com, or whomever you like) and search for USB headset microphone.

NOTE As I write this chapter, speech recognition is available only for English (United States and Great Britain), traditional Chinese, simplified Chinese, Japanese, German, French, and Spanish. Others may be available by the time you read this book. Search the Web or Microsoft's site for `vista speech recognition engine` **for current information resources.**

After you have a microphone, learn enough about it to plug it into the computer, make sure it's not muted, and control its volume (if it has Mute and volume controls). Plug it into the computer and wait a few seconds for Vista to see it and show you a notification that it's ready to use. Then try to set aside about an hour where you can have some peace and quiet without interruptions so you can learn how to use speech recognition. If you provide the microphone and time, Vista will provide the training, as discussed in the next section.

Getting started with speech recognition

The first step to using speech recognition is to connect your microphone to the computer as per the manufacturer's instructions. The second step is to open the Speech Recognition control panel using whichever technique is easiest for you.

NOTE If the Speech Recognition control panel is already open and running, right-click its microphone or Notification area icon and choose **Configuration ⇨ Open Speech Recognition Control Panel.**

- Click the Start button and choose Control Panel ⇨ Ease of Access ⇨ Speech Recognition Options.
- Tap ⊞, type spe, and click Speech Recognition Options.
- If you're already in Ease of Access Center, click the arrow next to Ease of Access in the breadcrumb trail and choose Speech Recognition Options.

The Speech Recognition Options open as in Figure 12.17.

FIGURE 12.17

Speech Recognition control panel.

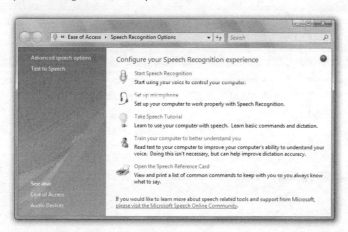

Your first hour of learning to use speech recognition begins when you click Start Speech Recognition. You'll be taken through the entire process of setting things up and learning how to do things. (Assuming you haven't already been through that process.) I won't repeat everything in the tutorial here because you're better off just doing what the onscreen tutorial tells you to do. If you pay attention and try the things it tells you to, you'll be up-to-speed on the basics of using speech recognition.

If you can't make it through the whole tutorial, click Set-up microphone or Take Speech Tutorial when you can resume. As in all things related to using a computer, the hour you invest in learning will save you hours of hair-pulling frustration later.

When you've finished setting things up and taking the tutorial, you should see a round Notification area icon whose tooltip shows the words Speech Recognition when you point to it. Clicking that icon opens the menu shown in Figure 12.18. Double-clicking that icon displays the Speech Recognition microphone shown near the top of that same figure.

FIGURE 12.18

Speech Recognition microphone and Notification area icon.

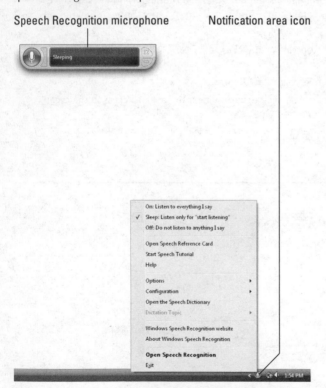

The rest of this section assumes you've completed the Speech tutorial and learned the basics. You should be able to open the menu and Speech Recognition microphone at the top of Figure 12.18 on your own. Most of what follows is for reminders of specific things you can say.

Control speech recognition by voice

When the Speech Recognition Notification area icon is visible, you can speak any phrase at the left side of Table 12-2 to perform the action shown in the right column. (Don't forget to don your headset or activate your microphone first.)

TABLE 12-2

Controlling Speech Recognition by Voice

To do this	Say this
Wake up sleeping speech recognition	`Start listening`
Move the Speech Recognition icon to top or bottom of screen	`Move speech recognition`
Hide Speech Recognition microphone	`Minimize speech recognition`
Show Speech Recognition microphone	`Open speech recognition`
See special words you can say	`What can I say?`
Put speech recognition to sleep	`Stop listening`

Commanding Windows by voice

Table 12-3 lists things you can do by voice to control Windows at that desktop, as well as program windows that are already open. Speak only the text shown in monospace font. Other text is for clarification. Replace italicized text with an actual name. For example in `Open` *programName*, say the name of the program in place of *programName*. So to open WordPad, you'd say `Open WordPad`.

But be aware that if the cursor is in a word processing or text editing program (WordPad or Word, for example), your speech might be taken as dictation and typed into your document. You can say *minimize Word* or *minimize WordPad* to minimize either program to prevent that. Plain text in parentheses is for clarification and not to be spoken. Text shown in italics isn't to be spoken literally. Rather, replace it with a spoken name. For example, `Open` *ProgramName* means you say "Open" then say the name of the program you want to open. For example, to open WordPad you say `Open WordPad`.

TIP   If you have Folder Options set to single-clicking, it may be difficult to select icons by voice. Consider switching to double-clicking so you can say `Click` and `ShiftClick` to select icons.

TABLE 12-3

Spoken Words for Windows and Program Windows

To do this	Say this
Open the Start menu	`Click Start`
Choose Start menu items	*OptionName*
Click an item	`Click` *ItemName*
Double-click an item	`DoubleClick` *ItemName*
Right-click an item	`RightClick` *ItemName*
Shift+Click an item	`ShiftClick` *ItemName*
Open a program	`Open` *ProgramName*
Choose menu commands	*CommandName* (for example `File Open`)
Go to a field or control	`Go to` *fieldName* or *controlName*
Go to next field or control	`Tab` or `Press tab`
Undo last action	`Undo that` or `scratch that`
Redo last action	`Redo`
Scroll one line	`Scroll up` or `Scroll down`
Scroll multiple lines	`Scroll direction lines`
Scroll by page	`Scroll` *direction number* `pages`
Switch to an open program	`Switch to` *programName*
Maximize open window	`Maximize that` (for active window) or `Maximize` *programName*
Restore maximized window	`Restore that` or `Restore` *programName*
Minimize open window	`Minimize that` (for active window) or `Minimize` *programName*
Minimize all windows	`Show Desktop`
Close a program	`Close that` (for active window) or `Close` *programName*
Show numbers for items	`Show numbers`
Click numbered item	`Click` *number*
Double-click numbered item	`Double Click` *number*
Right-click numbered item	`Right Click` *number*
Hide numbers	`Hide numbers`
Cut	`Cut that` or `Cut`
Copy	`Copy that` or `Copy`
Paste	`Paste`
Delete	`Delete that` or `Delete`
Undo	`Undo that` or `Scratch that` or `Undo`

Work anywhere by voice

When it's difficult to refer to things by name, you can use numbers or a mousegrid to click areas by number. Say `show numbers` to show numbers, say `mousegrid` to see the mousegrid. Then look to the Speech Recognition microphone for guidance on other things you can say. Table 12-4 shows words you can say while in click anywhere mode. If you get stuck in either display and just want to bail out, say `hide numbers` to get rid of numbers, or `cancel` to end the mousegrid.

TABLE 12-4

Spoken Words for Clicking Anywhere

To do this	Say this
Number *clickable* items	`Show numbers`
Click a numbered item	`Click` *number*
Show the mousegrid	`Mousegrid`
Zoom in a grid	*Number*
Move the mouse pointer to mousegrid square	*Number* or *numbers*
Click any mousegrid square	`Click` *number* or `Click` *numbers*
Select an item to drag with the mousegrid	*Number* `mark` or *numbers* `mark`
Drag selected item in mousegrid square	*Number* or *numbers* `click`
Hide the mousegrid	`Cancel`

TIP In Microsoft Internet Explorer, you can say `Press tab` and `Tab` to move from one link to the next on a page. When the link you want to click has the focus, say `Click that` or `Click` to click that link. Say `Click back` to return to the previous page.

Dictating text

You can dictate text just about anywhere you can type text. Speak one sentence at a time and follow each by saying `period` (or `exclamation point` or `question mark`). To start a new paragraph, say `new paragraph`. Use the words shown in the right column of Table 12-5 to insert other punctuation marks.

TABLE 12-5

Spoken Words for Punctuation

To type this	Say this
,	`Comma`
;	`Semicolon`
.	`Period` or `Dot` or `Full stop`
:	`Colon`

continued

TABLE 15.2   *(continued)*

To type this	Say this
"	Double quote
'	Single quote or apostrophe
>	Greater than
<	Less than
/	Forward slash
\	Backslash
~	Tilde
@	At sign
&	Ampersand
!	Exclamation mark or Exclamation point
?	Question mark
...	Ellipses
#	Number sign
$	Dollar sign
%	Percent or Percent sign
^	Caret or Caret sign
(	Open parenthesis
)	Close parenthesis
_	Underscore
-	Hyphen or Minus sign or Dash
=	Equal sign
+	Plus sign
{	Open brace
}	Close brace
[	Left bracket or Open bracket
]	Right bracket or Close bracket
|	Pipe sign
:-)	Smiley face or Happy face
:-(	Frown face or Unhappy face
;-)	Wink face
(tm)	Trademark sign
3/4	Three quarter symbol
1/4	One quarter symbol
1/2	One half symbol

Table 12-6 shows spoken commands for formatting and editing text. Don't forget that you can also choose menu commands just by saying the names of things on the menu bar and drop-down menus. You can also press special keys like Home, End, Page Up, Page Down, Backspace, Spacebar, and Tab just by saying their names. You can press any key by saying the word press followed by the letter, number, or name. For example, Press Up, Press Down, Press Left, Press Right, Press Tab, Press Escape. Any time you goof and make matters worse, say Undo that.

TABLE 12-6

Spoken Words Formatting and Editing

To do this	Say this
Start a new line	New line
Start a new paragraph	New paragraph
Put cursor before a specific word	Go to *word*
Put cursor after a specific word	Go after *word*
Go to start of current sentence	Go to start of sentence
Go to start of current paragraph	Go to start of paragraph
Go to start of document	Go to start of document
Go to end of current sentence	Go to end of sentence
Go to end of current paragraph	Go to end of paragraph
Go to end of document	Go to end of document
Select a word	Select *word*
Select all text from one word to another word	Select *word* through *word*
Select all text in document	Select all
Select previous *x* words (up to 20)	Select previous *number* words
Select next *x* words (up to 20)	Select next *number* words
Select the last text you dictated	Select that
Boldface selected text	Bold
Italicize selected text	Italic
Delete selected text	Delete that
Undo last change	Undo that or Undo
Re-do last undo	Redo that or Redo
Un-select selected text	Clear selection
Center text	Center
Change next *x* of words to uppercase	Change next *number* to uppercase
Change next *x* words to lowercase	Change next *number* to lowercase
Delete previous sentence	Delete previous sentence
Delete next sentence	Delete next sentence
Delete previous paragraph	Delete previous paragraph
Delete next paragraph	Delete next paragraph

233

Dictate an E-mail Message

Dictating e-mail messages in Windows Mail is fairly easy. The only tricky part is typing the e-mail address, because it contains words not found in the dictionary. If the person is in your Contacts, you can say their name instead. But even names can be tricky. You have to spell them, by saying `press` followed by each letter to type. Optionally, you can add names and domain names to the speech dictionary.

Here's an example of opening Windows Mail and sending a message to a hypothetical recipient at `alan@coolnerds.com`. The dashes indicate pauses in speech — you don't say "dash" or anything else where you see a dash.

```
Show desktop – Open Windows Mail – Create Mail – Press a-l-a-n atsign Press c-o-o-l-
n-e-r-d-s period Press c-o-m Go to subject Sample dictated message Press Tab I'm
practicing my voice dictation period. It takes some practice but I think I'll get
the hang of it Period New paragraph See ya exclamation point Send.
```

Making dictation better

Voice dictation isn't always easy. It's certainly not like *Star Trek* where they just say whatever they want and the computer "understands." Real computers don't "understand" anything to say or type. They're just mindless, brainless machines. When you use speech recognition and dictation, you're not really "talking to" or "conversing with" the computer as you would another person. You're trying to control a dumb machine with your voice. Because yours is the only brain in the "conversation," the onus of getting it to work falls on you.

Speech recognition often fails when there are homonyms involved — words that sound alike such as wood/would, to/too/two, and I am/IM (try saying `I'm` instead on that last one). Names and slang terms that aren't in the dictionary are often mistaken for similar-sounding words from the dictionary. There are things you can do to improve matters, as discussed in the next three sections.

Correct that

When speech recognition gets a spoken word wrong, correcting it by voice helps it to learn your unique speaking style. To correct a wrong word, say `Correct` *word* (where *word* is the word you want to correct). If that word appears in several places, each will show a number. Say the number of the word you want to correct, then say `OK`. The Alternatives Panel opens. As instructed in the panel, say the number of the corrected word then say `OK`. Or say `I'll spell it myself` and follow the onscreen instructions.

Improve voice recognition

Speech recognition offers little five-minute training sessions to help it better recognize your voice. To ensure it doesn't think you're dictating, close or minimize any open windows (say `show desktop` or right-click the clock and choose Show the Desktop). Then say `stop listening`. Right-click the Speech Recognition microphone or Notification area icon and choose Configuration ➪ Improve Voice Recognition. Then follow the onscreen instructions in the Voice Recognition Wizard that opens.

 You can say `Next`, rather than click Next, after reading each line in the Voice Training Wizard.

There are several different training sessions available from that same set of commands, so don't feel that you can choose Configuration ⇨ Improve Voice Recognition only once. You can choose it whenever you have a spare five minutes to improve speech recognition.

Add words to the speech dictionary

Speech recognition operates by comparing sound waves of words you say to words in its dictionary. You can add your own words to the dictionary, remove words, or change words. Adding words is especially useful for things like people's names, domain names, e-mail addresses, and slang terms.

To open the speech dictionary, right-click the Speech Recognition microphone or Notification area icon and choose Open speech dictionary. You'll see the options shown in Figure 12.19. Just click whichever action you want to do and follow the onscreen instructions.

FIGURE 12.19

Speech dictionary.

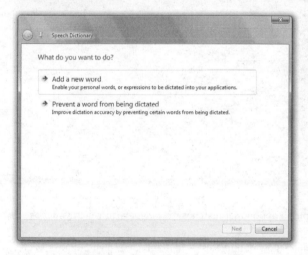

Advanced speech recognition configuration

Advanced Speech Recognition options let you choose a speech recognition engine (language), control automatic startup, and more. To get to those options, open the Speech Recognition Control Panel. Right-click the Speech Recognition microphone or Notification area icon (if available) and choose Configuration ⇨ Open Speech Recognition Control Panel. Otherwise use any method described under "Getting started with speech recognition" earlier in this chapter. Then click Advanced speech options to see the dialog box shown in Figure 12.20.

FIGURE 12.20

Text to Speech Properties dialog box.

The advanced options are as follows:

- **Language:** Choose the speech recognition option that matches the language in which you'll be speaking.

- **Recognition Profiles:** Use this option to allow multiple users to define their own unique speech profiles. Each user can then train speech recognition independently for the best accuracy.

- **Run Speech Recognition at startup:** If you clear this checkbox, you can still start speech recognition manually by clicking Start and choosing All Programs ➪ Accessories ➪ Ease of Access ➪ Speech Recognition.

 **TIP**   As with any program, you can create desktop or Quick Launch shortcuts to Speech Recognition. See "Customizing the Quick Launch toolbar" in Chapter 11.

- **Allow computer to review your documents and mail:** Clear this option only if you think the review is slowing down your computer.

- **Number of spaces to insert after punctuation:** Sets the number of spaces to type after end-of-sentence punctuation. The standard is 2 in English.

- **Microphone:** Use this option to make sure your microphone hears you or to adjust its settings.

As always, click OK after changing anything in the dialog box.

More speech recognition help

To get the most from speech recognition, you want to have easy access to all of your resources. You'll find lots of information in Windows Help and Support. Click the Start button, choose Help and Support, type Speech Recognition, and press Enter. Or say the following. But don't say anything where you see a hyphen. The hyphen means to just pause briefly until the computer responds to what you just said: Click Start - Help and Support - Search - 1 - OK - Speech Recognition - Press Enter.

Be sure to check out the Speech Recognition Web site. There you'll find news, tips, tricks, and a Community where you can ask questions. To get there, right-click the Speech Recognition microphone or Notification area icon and choose Windows Speech Recognition Website. Once you get there, add the site to your Favorites and name it Speech. In the future you can get there by voice: Say Open Internet Explorer - Go to Address - Favorites - 1 - OK - Speech.

Regional and Language Settings

Different regions and languages show numbers, dollar amounts, dates, and times in different ways. For example, in the United States, dollar amounts are shown in $1,234.56 format. The United Kingdom uses a £1,234.56 format. French Canada would show that as 1 234,56 $. If your computer isn't showing numbers, dollar amounts, times, or dates correctly for your region, you can fix that. First you need to open the Regional and Language Settings dialog box using whichever method is easiest for you:

- Press ⊞, type lang, and click Regional and Language Options.
- Click the Start button and choose Control Panel ➪ Clock, Language, and Region ➪ Regional and Language Options.

The dialog box opens looking something like Figure 12.21. Click the Formats tab shown in the figure to change your regional settings.

FIGURE 12.21

Formats tab of Regional and Language Options.

Change how numbers, dates, and times look

The Formats tab of Regional and Language Options shows how numbers, currency values, dates, and times are displayed on your screen. But you're not stuck with those formats. To change them, click the drop-down button under the Current format heading and choose whichever option best describes your region. The formats beneath your selection will change to reflect how things are shown in that region.

If you need to change one or more of the formats shown under your selected language, click Customize this format. In the dialog box that opens, specify exactly how you want Vista to show Number, Currency, Time, and Date formats on your screen. When you're happy with the examples shown in your Formats tab, click Apply. You might want to take a look at the next section before you close the dialog box.

Let them know your correct location

Some programs and online services tailor their content to match the location in which your computer is located. If that information seems incorrect, click the Location tab in the Regional and Language Options dialog box. Choose your actual location from the drop-down button, then click Apply.

Working with multiple languages

For people who work in multiple languages, Windows Vista offers some handy options for adjusting your keyboard to work in a specific language. These features are especially useful for translators who need to switch from one language to another. There are two different types of languages you can work with:

- **Input Language:** The language you use to type, edit, and read documents is called the input language. Input languages come pre-installed. There's nothing to download or buy. When you install an input language for reading and typing, you can also choose to use that language for speech recognition.

- **User Interface Language:** The user interface language determines the language displayed on menus, in dialog boxes and wizards, and elsewhere on the screen. A few of these are installed by default, others have to be installed separately. There are two different types of user interface languages you can install:

  - **Language interface packs (LIPs):** These user interface languages translate about 80% of the user interface. These are preferred if your goal is to change the language that's on your screen for everyone who uses the computer. These work with all versions of Windows, are free, and are easy to install.

  - **Multilingual user interface (MUI) packs:** These user interface languages translate the entire user interface. They can be applied to individual user accounts. So if some users need an English version of Windows, while others need a Spanish version, these are the way to go. But MUI packs work only with Vista Ultimate and Windows Vista Enterprise editions. They can be installed from your original Microsoft Windows DVD or downloaded from Microsoft's Web site.

Tools for adding input languages and user interface languages are on the Keyboard and Languages tab of the Regional and Language Options dialog box. As you can see in Figure 12.22, the top box is strictly for input languages (how your type, read, and edit documents). The bottom half is for user interface languages (text that appears in menus, dialog boxes, and wizards).

We'll look at techniques for working with all the different types of languages and files in the sections to follow.

 You don't need anything described in this chapter to type special characters. Those you can insert with Character Map. See "Typing Special Characters with Character Map" in Chapter 15.

Using input languages

If you're a translator or need to type, edit, and read documents in multiple languages, input languages described here are for you. To install an input language, click the Change keyboards button. The Text Services and Input Languages dialog box shown in Figure 12.23 opens.

FIGURE 12.22

Keyboards and Languages tab.

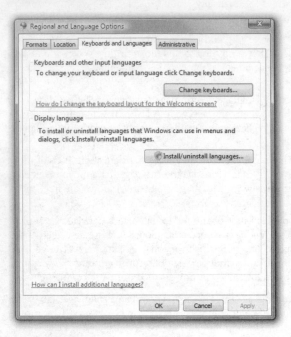

FIGURE 12.23

Text Services and Input Languages dialog box.

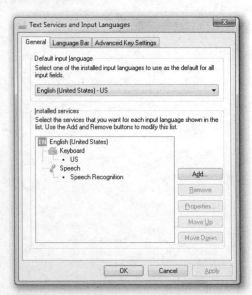

To install an input language, click the Add button. A dialog box containing a long list of languages appears. Scroll through that list until you find the language you need. Then click the + sign next to that language. Then you can choose which keyboard style you want to use with that language. Click the Preview button to see the layout of whichever keyboard you choose.

> **TIP** You can translate text electronically without using input languages. Copy-and-paste text from any language to a translator like `http://babelfish.altavista.com/`. Then copy-and-paste the translated text to any document.

For languages that use complex characters, you can also choose an Input Method Editor (IME). These allow you to use alternatives to the keyboard, such as a pad, for typing.

You can select (check) the Speech checkbox for most languages. However, speech recognition engines are available for a limited number of languages. To see which speech recognition engines are currently available, go to the Windows Vista Web site (`www.microsoft.com/vista`) and search for `vista speech recognition engines`. Click OK after making your selection.

You can install as many languages and keyboards as you wish. You don't have to do them all in one fell swoop either. You can add them on an as-needed basis. Each language you add appears in the Installed Services list. Figure 12.24 shows an example where I've added Chinese with an IME, and Spanish with a Latin keyboard. I still have English installed, it's just scrolled out of view.

FIGURE 12.24

Added Chinese and Spanish as input languages.

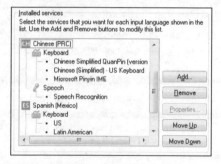

Note the two-letter acronym next to each language in Figure 12.24. That's important because that's how you'll know, later, which language is currently selected. As always, you can click OK after adding input languages.

Switching languages and keyboards

When you have two or more input languages installed, only one is active at any given time. You need to be in a program that can use alternative languages, like WordPad, Word, or the On-Screen Keyboard, for the language bar to be relevant at all. When that program is in the active window, you see which language is currently in use for that program. If the language bar is open, you see the language in the bar as at the top of Figure 12.25. If the language bar is minimized, you see the two-letter language abbreviation in the taskbar, as at the bottom of that same figure. Click either one to choose a different language for that program.

FIGURE 12.25

Language bar and taskbar icon.

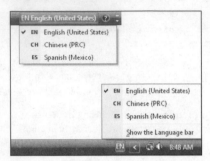

Here are some basic good-to-know facts about the language bar:

- When the language bar is minimized, click its taskbar button and choose Show the Language bar to make it visible.

- If you've selected multiple keyboards for a language, you can choose both a language and a keyboard for whatever program is in the active window.

- When the language bar is visible, click the Settings button in the lower-right corner to set default behavior and appearance options.

- When the language bar is visible, click the Minimize symbol in its upper-right corner to minimize it.

Keep in mind that you can choose different languages and keyboards for different programs. So if you have multiple programs open, make sure you first click the title bar of the one you want to configure, so you can see the language and keyboard currently assigned to that program.

When you choose a different language and keyboard from the language bar, the symbols on your keyboard's keys (obviously) don't change to show the keyboard you've selected. Ideally, you would want to plug in a keyboard that already has the keys in the right layout. Or at least use some kind of template that shows how keys are laid out. In a pinch, you can use the On-Screen Keyboard or an onscreen layout to see the keyboard layout. You can find small layouts for the screen by browsing to `www.microsoft.com/vista` with Internet Explorer and searching for `windows keyboard layouts`.

Figure 12.26 shows an example where I selected (clicked on) the On-Screen Keyboard, then chose Spanish as the language and Latin America as the keyboard. That figure also shows a small floating keyboard layout from Microsoft's Web site. In both cases, the keyboard looks almost the same as the English keyboard, but there are some differences. For example, there is an upside down question mark to the left of the Backspace (bksp) key, which doesn't exist on English keyboards. Pressing the Shift key turns that to an upside down exclamation point.

FIGURE 12.26

Language bar and menu.

There is also a *dead key* to the right of the letter P. It's gray on the On-Screen Keyboard, yellow on the floating keyboard layout. A dead key is one that does nothing when first pressed, but rather is applied to the next character you type. The dead key next to P is an accent mark. Tap the dead key then a letter to type the accented letter, like á. Pressing the Shift key changes the dead key to a tilde. Hold down the Shift key and tap the dead key, then type the letter n for ñ.

Languages that don't use standard keyboard layouts will offer an IME as an alternative. For example, in Figure 12.27 I've chosen Chinese as the language and IME Pad from the language bar. The IME pad below the On-Screen Keyboard lets you compose Chinese characters on the screen.

Removing input languages

Removing an input language is much like adding one. Get back to the Keyboards and Languages tab or Regional and Language Options and click the Settings button. Click the language or keyboard you want to remove and then click the Remove button. Then click OK.

FIGURE 12.27

Chinese language bar and IME pad.

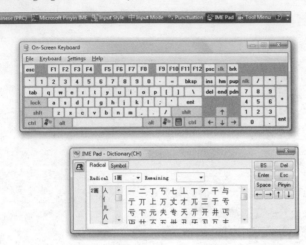

Installing user interface languages

Unlike input languages, user interface languages change the language used in menus, dialog boxes, and wizards. You need administrative privileges to install these languages because they affect all user accounts. As mentioned earlier, language interface packs work in all versions of Vista. To download, go to http://download.microsoft.com and search for Vista Language Interface Pack. Download according to instructions at the site. Once you have the file, just double-click its icon and follow the onscreen instructions to install.

Multilingual user interface language packs work only in Ultimate and Enterprise editions of Vista. These come with the product on the DVD. Or you can search http://download.microsoft.com for multilingual user interface to see what's available online.

After you have an MUI file and know its location on your system, follow these steps to install:

1. Open the Regional and Language Options dialog box as described earlier in this section.

2. Click the Keyboards and Languages tab, then click Install/Uninstall Languages (available only in the editions that support MUI).

3. Follow the onscreen instructions to install the MUI of your choice.

After you change the user interface language, check the Formats tab of Regional and Language Options. If necessary, you can choose a different format as described under "Change how numbers, dates, and times look" previously in this section.

Wrap Up

Windows Vista's Ease of Access options provide many alternatives to traditional mouse-and-keyboard computer interaction. Speech Recognition lets you control your computer and dictate text by voice. Regional and Language Options provide a means of internationalizing your copy of Windows Vista. Here is a quick rundown of the most important things to know:

- To open Ease of Access from the login screen, click the blue Ease of Access button near its lower-left corner.

- To open the Ease of Access Center from the desktop, hold down the Windows logo key and press U. Or click the Start button and choose Control Panel ➪ Ease of Access ➪ Ease of Access Center.

- Microsoft Magnifier, Narrator, and High Contrast help with visual impairments.

- The On-Screen Keyboard, Mouse Keys, Sticky Keys, Toggle Keys, Filter Keys, and speech recognition can help with motor impairments.

- Speech recognition takes some time and practice on your part, but can be used both to control Windows and to dictate text.

- Regional and Language Option input languages let you choose languages and keyboards for reading and editing text.

- User interface languages control the language of text displayed in menus, dialog boxes, and wizards.

Chapter 13

Transferring Files from Another Computer

If you bought a new computer with Windows Vista pre-installed, you may want to bring some files from an older computer into the new one. If both computers are on the same network, this is a simple matter of using drag-and-drop across folders. But if the two computers are not on the same network, it's a little trickier.

You could copy files from the old computer to a jump drive or other external disk. Then copy files from that drive or disk into corresponding folders on the new computer. But that could take some time, especially if you have hundreds or thousands of files to copy.

Windows Easy Transfer provides a better way to get files from an old computer to a new one. You connect the two computers using a special cable. Then you run the program, tell it what you want to copy, and go to lunch. (Or possibly to bed, as it could take several hours.) This chapter explores all the possibilities. But first, let's talk about what you can and can't transfer, so you come into the whole thing with realistic expectations.

IN THIS CHAPTER

Knowing what you can and can't transfer

Choosing a transfer method

Using Windows Easy Transfer

Transferring files from older computers

What You Can Transfer

You can't transfer everything from your old computer to the new one. But you can transfer just about everything you created or downloaded yourself. Specifically, you can transfer the following:

- **Files and folders:** Everything within the My Documents, Shared Documents, and their subfolders to corresponding folders on the new computer.

- **Media Files:** Music, playlists, album art, pictures, and videos — most of which are likely stored in your My Music, My Pictures, My Videos (or their Shared . . .) folder equivalents.

- **E-mail settings and messages:** The settings you need to access your e-mail, and all saved e-mail messages.

- **Contacts:** If you stored names and address in Windows Address Book (WAB) or Microsoft Outlook on your old computer, you can transfer those to the new computer.

- **Internet settings and favorites:** Settings required for your Internet connection to work as well as Favorites you've collected. You can also transfer cookies, which retain information that allows you to gain access to certain Web sites that might otherwise require logging in.

- **Personal settings:** Windows personalization settings like desktop backgrounds, screen savers, Start menu and taskbar options, fonts, network connections, color schemes, accessibility options, and so forth. However, Vista is a completely different operating system. So don't expect everything to look and work exactly like it did on your old computer.

- **User accounts:** If you have multiple user accounts on your old computer, you can transfer those as well. Each user account will retain its documents and settings.

- **Program settings:** Settings you chose within programs to personalize things can be transferred. However, it's important to keep in mind that the programs themselves are not transferred.

What you can't transfer

About the only things you can't transfer are the old version of Windows and programs on the old computer. That's because all programs (including Windows) need to be *installed* on the computer on which they'll run. Copying an installed program from one computer to another just flat-out won't work.

Getting programs onto the new computer

Even though you can't transfer installed programs from one computer to another, you can install those same programs on the new computer. For programs you purchased on CD, just insert the CD into the new computer's CD drive and install as you normally would.

CAUTION Do not install old utility programs (virus scanners, file managers, firewalls, and such) on your Windows Vista computer. See "What not to install" later in this chapter for more information. Stick with *application* programs like word processors, spreadsheets, graphics programs, and such — the types of programs used to create and edit documents.

For programs you downloaded, the rules are a little different. If you chose the Save option when downloading and kept that file, you can transfer the saved file to the new computer. Then open that file to start the installation process again. Otherwise, you have to go back to the Web site from which you originally downloaded the program and download again.

As far as Windows goes, you first have to understand that a computer can only run one operating system at a time. It makes no sense to try to "transfer" Windows XP, Windows 2000, Windows 98, or any other version of Windows to the new Vista computer.

What not to install

Utility programs are specifically designed for security or to enhance features of the operating system. Each is generally designed to work with a specific operating system or family of operating systems. You should never install a utility program that wasn't specifically designed for Windows Vista on your Vista computer. If in doubt, you should contact the program manufacturer to find out whether it's okay.

One Computer, Multiple Operating Systems

You can install and use multiple operating systems on a single PC in a couple of ways. One method, called *dual booting*, involves installing each operating system on its own hard disk *partition*. You can use the Disk Management tool described in Chapter 47, or a third-party program like Partition Magic to create the partitions. But either way, you risk losing everything on your hard disk, so you must make backups first. If you're not a hard disk or computer expert, you might seriously consider having multiple operating systems installed professionally rather than trying to do it yourself.

Virtual machine software provides another approach to using multiple operating systems on a single computer. You can download and use Microsoft Virtual PC for free from `www.microsoft.com/windows/virtualPC`. Or browse to `search.microsoft.com` and search for `Vista Virtual PC` for more specific information. You can also use a third-party product like VMware described at `www.vmware.com/products/`.

Also, before you even bother installing such programs, learn what's available in Vista and how to use it. Chances are you won't even need those old utility programs. For example, Windows Vista has extensive security built right into the very core of the operating system, plus lots of extras to protect your computer from many kinds of security threats. You can learn what those are and how to use them from Part II of this book.

Choosing a Transfer Method

To make transferring files as safe and painless as possible, Windows Vista comes with a program named Windows Easy Transfer. The program takes you step-by-step through the process of getting usable files and settings from your old computer to your new Windows Vista computer. Windows Easy Transfer works only with Windows XP, Windows 2000, and Windows Vista. If the computer from which you're transferring files is running one of those operating systems, you'll have to use an alternative method described later in this chapter.

Easy Transfer provides several methods of transferring files. You need to choose a method that both of your computers can support. The sections to follow describe the three methods: Easy Transfer cable, home network, and external disks.

NOTE If you upgraded your operating system from Windows 2000 or XP, there's no need to transfer files. Your old files are still on your computer and should be available in Windows Vista automatically.

Using a USB Easy Transfer cable

If at all possible, you should use the USB Easy Transfer cable method to transfer files from your old computer to your new computer. You'll need a USB Easy Transfer cable. If your new computer came with Windows Vista pre-installed, it might also have come with a USB Easy Transfer cable. Check the documentation that came with your computer if you're not sure, or contact your computer manufacturer.

If you don't have a USB Easy Transfer cable, you can purchase one online or at any retailer that sells computers or electronics equipment. Online, go to any computer retailer's site (www.cdw.com, www.newegg.com, www.tigerdirect.com, www.amazon.com) and search specifically for USB Easy Transfer Cable. Or ask for it by name at your local retailer. It should come with a CD that includes the programs you need to make it work. Insert that CD in the old computer's CD drive and follow the onscreen instructions to install the drives and connect the cable.

CAUTION Don't use the Easy Transfer CD in your new Windows Vista computer. That computer already has everything you need.

If the transfer cable isn't long enough to connect the two computers, and there's no way to re-situate one computer, you might consider using a USB extension cable with the Easy Transfer cable. You can find these at many electronics stores. Or search the Web or an online retailer for USB extension cable.

Using a home network

If you already have a home network and your new Windows Vista computer is on that network, you can run Windows Easy Transfer on the new Vista computer without connecting any more cables. However, this only works if the Windows Vista computer is already part of your home network. See Part X for more information on creating and using a home network.

Using external disks

If you have no way to connect the new Vista computer to the old computer, you can use external disks. First you need to choose which type of disk you can use.

Using a jump drive or external hard disk

You can use a *jump drive* (also called a Flash drive) or an external hard disk that connects via USB. An external hard disk would be the quickest and easiest. If you use a jump drive, you'll need one with enough storage capacity for the largest file. It doesn't need capacity for *all* of the files, because you can make the transfer in several steps. If the jump drive contains backups of many important files, consider moving those to another location temporarily during the transfer. The more room you have on the jump drive the better.

Using CDs or DVDs

You can use CD-RW, DVD-RW, or DVD+RW discs to transfer files. Both computers must have a drive that can read and write to the type of disc you choose. For example, if one computer can read and write CD-RW discs only, then you have to use CD-RW discs.

What About Floppy Disks?

By the way, you may have noticed I didn't mention floppy disks. That's because you can't use floppies with Windows Easy Transfer. The floppy disk's extremely small capacity (1.4 MB) makes it an unrealistic medium for this sort of thing. In fact, most people would call it an unrealistic medium for much of anything, which is why many computer manufacturers don't even bother to put floppy drives in many systems they sell. Floppies are basically in the "obsolete" category of computer media — except for making backups of small files like digital licenses and certificates.

How Long Does It Take?

How long it takes to transfer files from your old computer to the new one depends on how much stuff you're transferring and the method you use. But it could be several hours. So you should definitely start the process when you can concentrate on it for a while without interruptions.

If you have a lot of old junk on your old computer that you've been ignoring, a little spring cleaning may be in order. Delete anything you know for sure you will never need again for the rest of your life. No sense transferring trash. If you do, you'll eventually have to clean it off of both computers!

Make sure that you have at least one empty CD-RW or DVD-RW disc on hand before you begin the transfer. Put it in the appropriate drive on the new Vista computer. If AutoPlay or a program opens after you insert the disc, just close that item by clicking the Close (X) button in its upper-right corner.

NOTE A DVD holds much more information than a CD. So if you can use DVDs, you'll use fewer discs. You can use dual-layer (8.5 GB) DVDs only if the DVD drives in both computers support that format.

If the old computer is *really* old (Windows 98 or earlier), none of the preceding options will work for you. See "Transferring without Windows Easy Transfer" near the end of this chapter for alternatives.

Doing the Transfer

After you've decided on a transfer method, Windows Easy Transfer will take you through the steps required to complete your transfer. To get started, sit at your new Windows Vista PC and use whichever of the following techniques works and is easiest for you:

- Click the Start button and click Windows Easy Transfer.
- Press ⊞, type `trans`, and click Windows Easy Transfer on the Start menu.
- Click the Start button and choose All Programs ⇨ Accessories ⇨ System Tools ⇨ Windows Easy Transfer.

Windows Easy Transfer opens looking like Figure 13.1.

The program will take you step-by-step through the rest of the process. Make sure you read all the text on a page, and accurately answer any questions, before you click Next (or any other button) at the bottom of a page. A couple of things you might notice along the way:

- If you left any other programs open before you started Easy Transfer, you'll be prompted to close them. Click Close all and, if prompted, save any unsaved work you left behind.
- If asked for permission to work through your firewall, click Yes or OK. Don't worry, you're not making your computer vulnerable to hackers or malware. You're just giving Easy Transfer the right to do what it needs to do, and nothing more.
- If you'll be using discs to make the transfer, you'll need to follow instructions to copy Easy Transfer to a disc. Then you'll need to insert that disc in the other computer, choose the option to run Easy Install on that computer, and continue the transfer from that computer.

FIGURE 13.1

First page of Windows Easy Transfer.

Regardless of which method you use, you'll eventually come to a page like the one in Figure 13.2. Your choices are as follows:

FIGURE 13.2

Decide what to transfer.

- **Everything:** Copies all files and settings from every user account on the old computer to the new computer. This makes the new computer as much like your old computer as possible.

- **Only my user account, files, and settings:** Copies all files and settings from your user account on the old computer to the new computer. Other user accounts are ignored. You might want to choose this option if you won't be sharing the new computer with the other users.

- **Custom:** This option lets you choose specific settings and files to transfer. Be forewarned — there may be thousands of items to choose from, which is both tedious and confusing. You might be better off using one of the other previously mentioned options and then getting rid of things you don't want on the new computer after the transfer is done.

After you've made your selection, you're back to just reading and following instructions on the screen. Those instructions will be tailored to the method you're using and the files you're transferring.

When the Transfer Is Finished

When Easy Transfer has completed its task, your new computer will contain whatever you opted to transfer. Keep in mind that some folder names are different in Windows Vista. The "My" folders don't have "My" in their names anymore (My Documents is named Documents in Vista, My Pictures is named Pictures, and so forth). The "Shared" folders are now "Public" folders (Public Documents, Public Pictures, and so forth).

 The `Documents and Settings` folder from Windows XP is named `Users` in Vista. The `All Users` subfolder is named `Public` in Vista.

Remember, programs from your old computer are never transferred and cannot be transferred. All programs must be installed to the computer on which they'll run. You need to start that installation from the original program CD or a download.

Documents for which there is no program on the new computer will not open on the new computer. When you attempt to open such a document, you'll see an error message like the one in Figure 13.3.

FIGURE 13.3

No program on this computer can open this document.

To open the document, you'll need to install whatever program you used on the older computer to the new computer. Note that choosing "Use the Web service" from the message box does not make the required program install automatically. The service simply provides information about the program needed to open that type of file, and links to more information. If the program is one you can download and install for free, then the service might take you to the appropriate page for performing the download. But not all programs are free, and not all programs are available for download.

> **NOTE**   When downloading a program, you need to choose Run to install the program while downloading. If you choose Save, the program won't install. You'll need to open (double-click) the icon of the file you downloaded to install the program. See Chapter 40 for more information on downloading programs.

Transferring without Windows Easy Transfer

No built-in program enables you to transfer files from Windows 98 and earlier versions. So you'll need to use some other method, of which you have many to choose from. One possibility is to purchase a PC-to-PC file transfer program that works with Vista and your old computer's operating system. I can't give any specific product recommendations here. But if you search an online retailer or a search engine like Google for PC to PC File Transfer, you should find some products. Just make sure you get one that works with both of your computers.

Another choice is to copy any files you need on the new computer to some external medium. A jump drive or external hard disk would be best. You can use CDs or DVDs if both computers have appropriate burners. After you've copied all the necessary files to that external disk, put that disk in your Vista computer and copy files from it to appropriate folders on your hard disk (for example, Documents, Pictures, Music, Videos).

Copying files won't help with Internet favorites, e-mail messages, contacts, and such. But you can usually *export* those items to files. Then copy those files to your external medium. Then *import* those files to corresponding programs on your Vista computer. Options to import and export are usually on a program's File menu. If in doubt, you can search that program's Help for Export or Import, depending on which you need to do.

The sections to follow offer a few handy tips and techniques. But first a couple of cautions for people who skipped or didn't understand the preceding sections of this chapter.

> **CAUTION**   You don't need to do anything from the following sections if you're copying from a Windows XP or Windows 2000 computer. Windows Easy Transfer will take care of all those items. The sections to follow apply only to Windows 98 and earlier versions.

> **CAUTION**   The techniques assume you know how to navigate folders, use your My Computer folder (or Computer folder in Vista), and how to copy files. Most of the concepts and skills presented in Part VI of this book apply to all versions of Windows. But if you never learned to do those things in your previous version of Windows, it might be difficult to learn how to do things on your old computer from a book like this, which is about Windows Vista.

Manually transfer Internet Explorer Favorites

To export Internet Export Favorites on the old computer choose File ➪ Import and Export ➪ Export Favorites. Put that file on your external disk. Or put it in your Documents folder (or someplace else that's easy to get to) and copy it to the external disk. The Favorites are stored in a file named bookmark.htm.

> **TIP**   It's really not necessary to do this with importing and exporting cookies. Those files are created and deleted on-the-fly by Web sites you visit, and are rarely "necessary" for accessing a Web site. But if you really want to, you can choose to export and import cookies.

On the Windows Vista computer, open Internet Explorer. Tap the Alt key to see the classic menus. Choose File ⇨ Import and Export. In the wizard, choose to Import Favorites. Browse to your external disk and double-click the bookmark.htm file. Continue on through the wizard clicking Next, OK, and Finish where appropriate. When you're done, click the Favorites Center star at the left side of the toolbar. You should see all your imported favorites.

Manually transfer contacts

If you use Outlook Express or Microsoft Outlook on the old computer to manage contacts, you can export them to a .csv file on an external disk. Then put that disk in the Windows Vista computer and import them to your Contacts folder.

To export Windows Address Book contacts from Outlook Express, open Outlook Express and click Address Book. Or open Windows Address Book from the Start menu. Once you're in Windows Address Book, choose File ⇨ Export ⇨ Other Address Book ⇨ Text File (Comma Separated Values). Then browse to your external disk and enter a filename. When you get to the "Select fields" page, you can select (check) every checkbox. Then click Finish.

To export Contacts from Microsoft Outlook, open Outlook and click Contacts so you're viewing you contacts. Choose File ⇨ Import and Export from the menu. In the wizard that opens, choose Export to a File, Comma Separated Values (Windows), and Contacts. Use the Browse button to navigate to your external disk, give the file a name, and click Next and Finish until the copy is complete.

In Windows Vista you'll use your Contacts folder to manage names and address. Chapter 20 provides all the details. But in terms of importing contacts from that .csv file, the process goes like this. First insert the disk or connect the drive that contains the exported contacts. Then open your Contacts folder. (Log in to your user account, click the Start button, click your user name, and open the Contacts icon.)

In your open Contacts folder, click Import in the toolbar. If you don't see Import in the toolbar, click >> at the end of that toolbar then click Import. Click CSV (Comma Separated Values) and click Import. On the next page, click the Browse button and navigate to the disk or drive that contains those contacts you exported. Click the filename that contains the contacts and click Open. Then click Next and Finish. Each imported contact is represented by an icon in your Contacts folder.

Manually transfer Outlook Express e-mail messages

There isn't really any sure-fire simple way of transferring e-mail messages from all older versions of Outlook Express to Vista. But this seems to work with many versions. The idea is to open Outlook Express normally. Drag the message headers of any messages you want to transfer to a folder window for your external disk. You can select multiple headers using the standard Ctrl+Click and Shift+Click methods, then drag any one of them. Each e-mail message them becomes an .eml file on the external disk.

Now comes the strange-but-true part of the transfer. Insert the disk that contains the .eml files in the Vista computer. Open Windows Mail and click your Inbox (or any folder under your Inbox). Or maybe better still, create a folder under your Inbox and name it something like Imported (in case this doesn't work with *all* versions of Outlook Express). Select all the icons for the .eml files on the external disk and drag them to the main pane in Windows Mail where you normally see message headers. They should just fall right into place, no problem (although they'll be at the bottom of the list of message headers that are already in that folder).

As an alternative to transferring by disk, you can forward any saved messages to yourself so they end up back on your ISP's mail sever. Just make sure you don't download the messages to your old computer again. When you check your e-mail on the your new Windows Vista computer, the forwarded messages will download to your Inbox there.

> **NOTE** E-mail is an Internet service provided by your ISP. Not all ISPs provide the same service. If you have questions about, or problems with, your e-mail, contact your ISP. They're really the only people who can help you with the service they provide.

Transferring fonts

If you purchased or downloaded any TrueType or OpenType fonts and want to copy them over, open the Fonts folder on the old computer. This is typically C:\Windows\Fonts. Open that folder and copy any fonts you want to transfer to your external disk. Stick with TrueType and OpenType fonts (with `.ttf` extensions) that you acquired on your own. Don't try to copy all fonts. Windows Vista already has many fonts built into it, and you don't want to replace those fonts with older versions of similar fonts.

After you've copied fonts to an external disk, put that disk into the Windows Vista computer. Log in to an administrative user account. Open the Fonts folder on the Windows Vista computer (click the Start button, type `fonts`, and click Fonts under the Programs heading). If you don't see a menu bar in your Fonts folder, tap the Alt key. Then choose File ⇨ Install New Font.

In the Add Fonts dialog box, choose the drive that contains the fonts. Then click Select All, then click Install. If you get a message saying a font is already installed, you'd do well *not* to replace it with the one you're importing. The new fonts that you do transfer will be available in every program that allows you to apply fonts to text.

Wrap Up

Transferring files and settings from an old Windows 2000 or Windows XP computer is fairly easy. Use the USB Easy Transfer cable that came with your new computer. Or purchase one from any computer retailer. If the old computer isn't running Windows 2000 or XP, you can't use the Easy Transfer program and cable. But there are still ways to get files to the new computer, providing you have sufficient basic skills to locate and copy files. To summarize:

- Windows Easy Transfer is the quickest and easiest way to transfer user accounts, folders, files, and settings from an old Windows 2000 or XP computer to your new Vista computer.

- You cannot transfer programs from an old computer to a new one through any means. That's because every program must be *installed* — not transferred or copied to the computer.

- Do not install older utility programs (virus scanners, firewalls, file managers, and such) on Windows Vista. Such programs are designed to work with a specific version or family of Windows, and may cause problems if installed on Windows Vista.

- Windows Easy Transfer, which comes free with Windows Vista, provides the quickest and easiest method of transferring user accounts, files, and settings from a Windows 2000 or XP computer to a new Windows Vista computer.

- To start Windows Easy Transfer, click the Start button, type `trans`, and click Windows Easy Transfer. To transfer files, just read its instructions and choose options that make sense for your equipment.

- To transfer files from earlier versions of Windows, copy those files to an external disk. Then copy from that same disk on the Windows Vista computer.

- To transfer contacts from an older computer, export them to a CSV file on an external disk. Then import them from that disk into your Contacts folder on the Windows Vista computer.

Chapter 14

Customizing Startup Options

A computer is basically a machine that's designed to do one thing: run programs. There are more than 100,000 different programs that can run on your computer. Nobody owns them all or needs them all. But there are certainly many to choose from.

Your computer already has many programs installed on it. Many are programs that you can start at will from icons on the Start menu and All Programs menu. Some programs start automatically as soon as you start your computer. These are referred to as *autostart* programs. Many of those programs run in the background, which means they don't have program windows on your desktop or taskbar buttons. However, many of them do show icons in the Notification area. These kinds of programs are often referred to as *services*.

This chapter is about controlling exactly which programs and services do, and don't, start automatically when you first start your computer and Windows.

IN THIS CHAPTER

Understanding applications and services

Starting programs automatically

Preventing programs from autostarting

Managing services

Bypassing the login page

First Things First

First we need to make a distinction between application programs and services. For our purposes we'll refer to such a program as an application program (or *application*, or *app* for short). These are programs that, when open, have a program window on your desktop and a rectangular button in the taskbar. Typically you open and use such a program to perform some specific task, like check your e-mail or browse the Web. Then you close the program when you've finished that task. To close such a program, you can typically click the Close (X) button in its upper-right corner or right-click its taskbar button and choose Close. You can re-open the program at any time by clicking its icon on the Start or All Programs menu.

We'll use the general term *service* to refer to any programs that don't show program windows or taskbar buttons. Most of these programs show a little icon in the Notification area. Typically when you rest the mouse pointer on such an icon, a tooltip appears showing the name of the program or service that the icon represents. Clicking or double-clicking such an icon often opens a dialog box or similar window. Right-clicking such an icon often displays a list of things you can do with the icons. Figure 14.1 illustrates this distinction between applications and services.

FIGURE 14.1

Examples of application programs and services.

Taskbar buttons   Services

As mentioned, each little icon in the Notification area represents some small program or service that's running in the background. To prevent Notification area icons from taking up too much space on your taskbar, you can opt to hide some of them.

You can also choose whether or not you want certain icons to appear at all. These include the current time in the lower-right corner of your screen, volume control, network option, and battery power. Right-click the clock or any empty portion of the taskbar and choose Properties. Then click the Notification tab in the Taskbar and Start Menu Properties dialog box that opens. See "Customizing the Notification Area" in Chapter 11 for more information.

Starting Application Programs Automatically

If you always use a certain application program when you start your computer, you can configure Windows to start that program automatically. The same is true for folders. For example, you could have Windows automatically open the main folder for your user account at startup, so you can quickly get to other folders like Documents, Pictures, or Music.

The first step to making an application program autostart is to open the Startup folder for your user account. Assuming you're already logged in to that user account, the steps are easy:

1. Click the Start button and choose All Programs.
2. If necessary, scroll down until you see the Startup folder icon on the menu.
3. Right-click that Startup icon and choose Open. It opens as a folder on the desktop.

Optionally, to give yourself some elbow room, size and position the window like in Figure 14.2. You don't need the navigation pane here, so you can close that if it's open (click the Organize button and choose Organize ➪ Layout ➪ Navigation Pane).

FIGURE 14.2

Startup folder on the desktop.

To make an application program autostart, drag its icon from the All Programs menu into the main pane of the Startup folder and drop it there. Keep in mind that the more programs you add to the folder, the longer it will take for your computer to start. So don't get carried away and put all your favorite programs in there. One or two should be sufficient.

CAUTION   If you see a message about moving the icon, that wasn't your intent. So you should click Cancel to cancel that operation. Then drag using the right mouse button. After you drop, choose **Create shortcut here**. If it's too late to cancel the move, right-click some empty space in the Startup folder and choose **Undo Move**.

When you've finished, close the Startup folder. Windows Defender may show a message alerting you to the fact that your startup options have changed. No cause for alarm. In this case the message is superfluous because you intentionally changed your startup programs. But Defender doesn't know that. It's just doing one of its many jobs. In this case, keeping you informed of changes to your startup options.

Stopping autostart applications

Should you ever change your mind about autostart applications, you just need to re-open that Startup folder for your user account. Then delete the shortcut icon for any program you don't want to autostart. However, not all programs that autostart will be in the Startup folder for your user account. Some may be in the Startup folder for all users. (Still others will be in other locations. We'll get to those in the section on Windows Defender later in this chapter.)

To view, and optionally remove, programs that start automatically in all user accounts, you need to get to the All Users Startup folder. You may need administrative privileges to make changes to that folder. So be prepared to enter an administrative password if you're working from a standard account. But the basic procedure is easy. Click the Start button and choose All Programs. Right-click the Startup folder again, but this time choose Open All Users (see Figure 14.3).

FIGURE 14.3

Open the Startup folder for all user accounts.

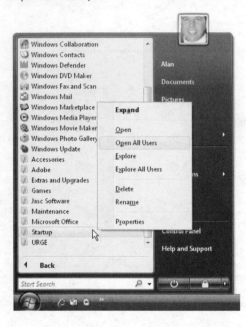

The All Users Startup folder works just like the Startup folder for a single user account. If you want a program to autostart in all user accounts, drag that program's icon into the folder. If you want to stop a program from autostarting in all user accounts, delete its icon from that Startup folder. But again, stick with programs you know. Removing programs from the All Users Startup folder at random could have unpleasant consequences that you weren't expecting.

Controlling Autostart Programs from Windows Defender

Windows Defender is a security program for protecting your computer from spyware and other Internet security threats. It comes free with Windows Vista, so you already have it. Chapter 8 covered the Defender program in some depth. This chapter focuses on using it to control autostart programs that you can't find in the Startup folder for all users or a user account.

When Defender alerts you to autostart programs

Whenever you choose to autostart on your computer, Defender shows a message like the one in Figure 14.4. It also shows that same message when you download or install a program that configures itself to autostart — even if that program is a service that appears only in the Notification area. The message is nothing to be alarmed about. It's just an informational message and not an indication of an attack on your computer or a security threat.

FIGURE 14.4

Windows Defender notification about new startup programs.

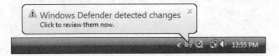

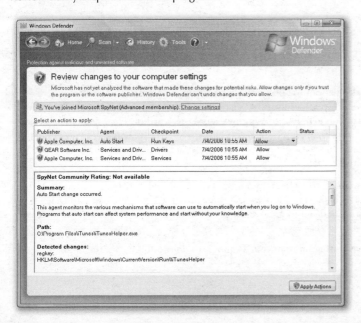

| NOTE | Some services don't even autostart in the Notification area. For example, Adobe Reader autostarts a little subcomponent of itself called Speed Launch that just allows it to start more quickly when you open it. |

You can click that message to open Windows Defender and review programs that have recently been configured to autostart. If you miss that opportunity, the Defender icon will remain in the Notification area with a little question mark icon. Double-click that icon. Either way, you're taken to a page where you can review changes made to your computer, as in Figure 14.5.

FIGURE 14.5

Review newly acquired autostart programs.

The idea here is to review the new items and decide what you want to do about each. By default, each will be set to "Allow" in the Action column. This is because you most likely already granted permission for the item to autostart, either directly or indirectly. For example, when you drag an icon into your Startup folder, you are granting permission for that program to autostart. When you download certain kinds of programs, you may be inherently allowing that program to autostart because it works best if it's autostarted. When you install a new hardware device, you are inherently allowing that device's driver to install automatically, because the device won't work if you don't allow that to happen.

You can get more detailed information about any item by clicking its name and scrolling through the large text box below it. Basically what you're looking for is anything that seems to have been installed out of the clear blue sky. Look to the Spyware community ratings for any hints of malicious software. If all looks well, click Apply Actions. (Don't worry, you're not making any big commitment. You can disable any autostart program at any time, as discussed next.)

Reviewing and disabling autostart programs

The Software Explorer component of Windows Defender lets an administrator review and change autostart programs at will. It's not limited to programs you put in the Startup folder. It covers everything. To get to Software Explorer, first start Windows Defender using any of these techniques:

- Click the Start button, choose Control Panel, and click Change startup programs under the Programs heading.
- Click the Start button and choose All Programs ⇨ Windows Defender.
- Press ⊞, type defend, and click Windows Defender.

Windows Defender opens. If you used one of the latter two options, click Tools up top, then click Software Explorer. If you're in a standard user account, you'll need to enter an administrative password. Finally, choose Startup Programs from the Category button. The left side of the main pane below lists all programs that autostart. The main pane to the right shows detailed information about whichever item you click in the left pane. Figure 14.6 shows an example.

CAUTION Remember, don't remove or disable an autostart program just because you don't know what it is. Click the item's name and look at the SpyNet Voting entry in the main pane first. If it's marked Not Yet Classified, better to leave it alone. It might be something that's critical to proper functioning of your system!

The right pane shows much information about the program. The Startup Type entry shows from where the program is autostarting, such as the Startup folder for All Users, or the Registry. The Ships with Operating System entry lets you know if the program is built into Windows Vista (Yes) or not (No). The Classification entry lets you know if the program has been analyzed for risks. The SpyNet Voting entry lets you know if the item is a risk. Note that widely used programs by trusted software manufacturers are marked as Not Yet Classified and can generally be regarded as safe.

If you're thinking about removing an autostart program, your best bet would be to disable it first. Restart your computer and use it for a while to make sure all is well. If there are problems, go back into Defender and re-enable the program. It would be best not to remove the program until you know exactly what it is and whether or not it's safe to remove.

TIP The best way to remove a program from your system is to uninstall it as per the method described in Chapter 43.

FIGURE 14.6

Software Explorer showing Startup programs.

Autostarting from the Services Snap-In

Windows Vista includes an advanced system configuration tool called the Microsoft Management Console (MMC). The MMC provides access to various *snap-ins*, where each snap-in provides options for different types of configuration options. One of those snap-ins is named Services.msc. It's not a user-friendly program. It's really designed for professionals. Beginners and casual users are better off sticking with the Startup folders and Software Explorer in Windows Defender as a means of working with autostart programs.

NOTE If you want to make any changes in the Services snap-in, log out of any standard accounts and into an account that has administrative privileges.

To start the Services snap-in, click the Start button, type `serv`, and click Services under the Program heading on the Start menu. Once the Services snap-in is open, use the View menu options to choose how you want to view icons. Figure 14.7 shows how things are displayed in the Details view. The toolbar contains a couple of buttons for showing and hiding optional Console Tree and Action panes. (Both are hidden in Figure 14.7.) Extended and Standard tabs are near the bottom of the window. The figure shows how things look in the Standard tab.

FIGURE 14.7

Services snap-in.

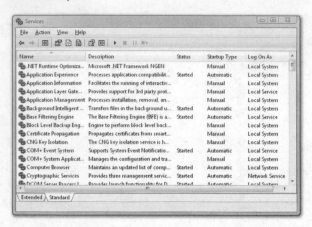

Clicking the Extended tab opens a new pane at the left side of the program window that shows detailed information about any service name you click on. It also provides options to start a service that's not running, or to stop or restart the service if it's not running.

 Due to enhanced security in Vista, you do not have as much leeway in starting and stopping services as you did in earlier Windows versions. Some services cannot be stopped at all!

If you scroll through the list of Services, you'll probably see there are quite a few. Exactly which services are listed will vary from one computer to the next. Few, if any, of the services will have any meaning to the average computer user. These things are really only of use to professional programmers, network administrators, or other experienced professionals. What follows is really for those folks. I won't bother to summarize what each service does, because doing so would eat up several pages and only repeat the information that's already in the Description column.

The Status column shows "Started" for those services that are currently running. It shows nothing for services that aren't running. The Startup Type column shows whether or not the service is configured to run automatically, if at all. Common settings are

- **Automatic:** The service starts automatically when the computer starts or when a user logs in.
- **Manual:** The service doesn't start automatically. You can start the service, however, by right-clicking the service name and choosing Start or by choosing Start from the Action menu.
- **Disabled:** The service is disabled and must be enabled from the Properties dialog box before it can be started.

To get more information about a service, or change its Startup Type, right-click the service name and choose Properties. You'll see a dialog box like the one in Figure 14.8.

FIGURE 14.8

Properties for the DNS client service.

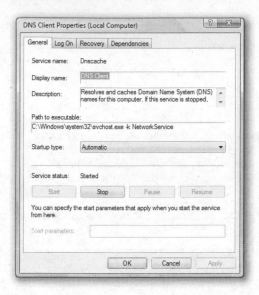

The DNS client service is critical for networking because it converts textual names to IP addresses such as 68.32.232.6. When you type a URL into your Web browser and press Enter, the DNS service changes that name to the numeric address, because the name has no meaning to the Internet. Only the number has meaning to the Internet. Of course, you can browse the Web for the rest of your life without knowing anything about DNS or IP addresses. But, you couldn't browse the Web without a DNS service running. So, again, the Services snap-in is not a place to play around.

Anyway, the options you see in Figure 14.8 are typical of the items listed in the Services snap-in. The Description textbox provides a description of the services and also tells what will happen if you disable or stop the service. The Path to executable textbox shows the location and name of the program that provides the service. The Startup type option provides the Automatic, Manual, and Disabled options.

The buttons let you stop, pause, resume, or start the service. Some programs will accept parameters, which you can add to the Start parameters textbox.

The Log On tab provides options for granting rights to services that need permissions to run. The Recovery tab provides options for dealing with problems when a service fails to start.

The Dependencies tab is one of the most important of the bunch, because it specifies which services the current service depends on (if any), and which services depend on the current service. For example, DNS is a TCP/IP thing (which is the protocol used by the Internet and most modern local networks). If a service isn't starting and you can't figure out why, seeing what services the current one depends on might provide a clue. Because if that service isn't running, the one you're looking at can't start. So you need to go to that service and make sure it's autostarting.

If you're interested in learning more about TCP/IP and how the Internet works, a Windows book isn't really the place to look. But any book on TCP/IP, or any book or course that prepares you for MCSA (Microsoft Certified Systems Administrator) or MCSE (Microsoft Certified Systems Engineer) certification, would explain all that in depth. For broader technical coverage of services, consult a technical reference such as *Microsoft Windows Vista Resource Kit,* Second Edition.

 **For more information on Microsoft certifications, see** www.microsoft.com/learning/mcp.

Bypassing the Login Page

This is one of those little Vista secrets everyone likes to know about, but should be cautious about using. It lets you bypass the login screen and start up Windows Vista in a specific user account automatically. Though it does save you one click at startup, it means anyone who sits at your computer can just turn on the power switch and have full access to everything in your user account. So don't do this if you want to keep other people out of your user account.

Doing this trick requires administrative privileges. So know the password or log in to an administrative account first. Here are the steps:

1. Click the Start button, type netplwiz, and then click netplwiz in the Start menu.
2. Grant permission or enter an administrative password if prompted.
3. Clear the checkbox for Users must enter a username and password to use this computer.
4. Click Apply.
5. In the dialog box that opens, type the name of the user account to which you want to log in automatically.
6. If that user account requires a password, type the password once in the Password box, then again in the second box for confirmation. If the user account isn't password-protected, leave both boxes empty.
7. Click OK in each open dialog box.

That's it. The next time you restart your computer there will be no logon page. You'll be taken straight into your user account. If there are other user accounts on the computer, and you want to let another use log in, log out of your account (click the Start button, the arrow next to the lock symbol, and choose Log Off). You're taken to the login page, which works normally. For example, if you want to get into a password-protected administrative account, you'll still click that account's icon and have to enter the correct password.

If you ever change your mind about doing this, just repeat steps 1 and 2 in the preceding list. But this time check the Users must enter a username and password to use this computer checkbox and click OK.

Troubleshooting Startup

Many things can prevent Windows from starting properly. There is no simple solution to the problem. There are just too many things that might be wrong. Typically, you need a professional to fix such problems. But I can tell you a few things that even the average user might try to get things going again.

Getting rid of disabled devices

If your computer contains a hardware device that Windows Vista can't use, you should still be able to get to the desktop. But each time you do, you'll see a notification message about a device being disabled. That can get tiresome. If you manually disable the device through Device Manager, you won't see that message anymore. And, it should take a little less time for Vista to start.

CAUTION **Don't take wild guesses here. If you disable a hardware device you really need, you might not be able to start Vista at all! If in doubt, better to take the computer into a repair shop and let the pros figure it out.**

To make this happen, you need to first log in to a user account that has administrative privileges. Then press ⊞, type dev, and click Device Manager on the Start menu. Expand the category to which the device belongs. If you're not sure which category to look in, try the Other Devices category. You'll be looking for a device whose icon shows an exclamation point in a tiny yellow circle. After you find the device, right-click its name and choose Disable.

When you've disabled the device, the yellow icon changes to a white down-arrow. That means the device is disabled and Windows Vista won't try to reinstall it on future bootups, which should mean a slightly quicker boot-up time and no irritating message about the disabled device.

When Windows won't start at all

If Windows won't start at all, try to start Vista in Safe Mode. This is a special mode in which Vista loads only the minimum services, drivers, and programs it needs to get going. Getting to Safe Mode isn't always easy. You have to restart the computer and then press the F8 key after the POST (Power on Self Test), but before Windows starts to load. If your keyboard has a Function Lock (F Lock) key, you have to make sure that it's on before you press F8. In a pinch, you can restart the computer, and press F8 repeatedly for the first few seconds. But again, keep an eye on the Function Lock key because it might go off once or twice during the restart.

When you've hit the F8 key at just the right time, you'll come to a screen that shows several options for starting Windows as summarized here:

- **Safe mode:** Starts Windows with a minimal set of drivers and services so you can use other tools like System Restore, Device Manager, Installed Programs, and such to try to fix the problems. For example, you could uninstall known faulty programs and devices. Then return to an earlier restore point.

- **Safe mode with networking:** Same as previous, but provides access to the Internet and a private network.

- **Safe mode with command prompt:** Starts windows without the GUI (graphical user interface).

- **Enable boot logging:** Creates a log file named ntbtlog.txt that lists all drivers that were loaded during startup.

- **Enable VGA mode:** Starts with low resolution and refresh rates to reset display settings.

- **Last known good configuration:** Starts Windows with the last successful configuration (an easy fix for many problems!).

- **Directory services restore mode:** Starts a domain control running Active Directory so directory services can be restored.

- **Debugging mode:** Starts in an advanced troubleshooting mode for professionals.

- **Disable automatic restart on system failure:** Prevents Windows from automatically restarting during a failed startup. This gets you out of the endless loop of crashing and restarting.

- **Start Windows normally:** Starts normally with all drivers and services.

- **Disable Driver Signature Enforcement:** Allows improperly signed drivers to be loaded at startup.

- **View system recovery options:** Available only if Startup Repair is installed on the computer. If not available from the hard disk, you may be able to get to it by booting from a Vista CD or DVD.

Often, choosing the Last Known Good Configuration option will get you back to the desktop. Or you can go into Safe Mode to get to a minimal desktop. Either way, once you're at the desktop, you may be able to fix the problem. For example, if the problem started right after you installed new hardware, use Device Manager to uninstall the device driver. Then shut down the computer, physically remove the device, then restart. See Chapter 47 for more information.

If a program is causing the problem, uninstall that program through Control Panel. See Chapter 43 for the details on uninstalling programs.

You can also use System Restore to restore to a previous restore point. For more information, see "Using System Protection" in Chapter 33.

If you're not sure what's causing the problem, you can use System Configuration as a diagnostic tool for finding out. This is similar to MSConfig in earlier Windows versions. To start System Configuration, click the Start button, type sys, and click System Configuration. If you start it from Safe Mode, it will have a Windows 95 look as in Figure 14.9.

FIGURE 14.9

System Configuration.

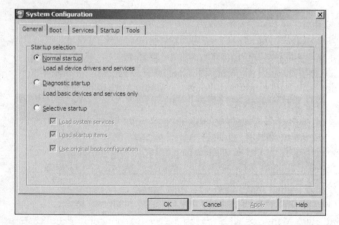

You can start by choosing Diagnostic startup and closing System Configuration. Then restart the computer but don't go into Safe Mode. The computer will start with a minimal set of drivers and programs, and System Configuration will open. Then you can use options on the Boot, Services, Startup, and Tools tabs to choose other options. For example, you might want to try enabling a few services or programs on the Services and Startup tabs and then restart the computer again to see whether it will boot. Repeat the process until you find the specific program or service that won't allow normal startup. When you've diagnosed the problem that way, you can prevent the service or program from autostarting. Or uninstall the problem program.

When everything is back in shape, you should be able to choose Normal startup from System Configuration and have the computer start normally.

Of course, the tools I've described here are really for pros. This is a book for users, and there really isn't room to go into great depth on these more technical topics. But you can find plenty more information in Help and online. For example, you can click Start and choose Help and Support to use Windows Help. Then search for terms like *safe mode*, *system configuration*, or *startup repair* for more information. Or go to Windows Live Search or `http://search.microsoft.com` and search for any of those terms preceded by *Vista*. For example, search for *Vista safe mode* or *Vista system configuration*.

Wrap Up

This chapter has covered all the different ways you can control which programs do, and don't, automatically start when Windows first starts up or when you first log in to your Windows user account.

- Icons that automatically appear in the Notification area represent programs and services that start automatically when you log in to Windows.
- The clock and Volume Control, Network, and Power icons in the Notification area can be turned on or off via the Taskbar and Start Menu Properties dialog box.
- Some programs have their own built-in options for choosing whether or not the program starts automatically and appears in the Notification area.
- You can start any application program automatically, or even open a folder automatically, by adding a shortcut for the program to the Startup folder.
- The full set of services that can be started and stopped automatically are listed in the Services.msc snap-in.
- The Services.msc snap-in is an advanced tool designed for professional programmers and network engineers. As such, it contains very little information that would be useful to the average computer user.
- You can use netplwiz to bypass the login page and go straight to any user account you wish.
- Safe Mode provides a means of starting Vista with the fewest drivers and services. It helps you get the system started so you can diagnose and repair whatever is preventing normal startup.

Chapter 15

Using Vista Programs and Accessories

Windows Vista is your computer's operating system (often abbreviated OS). As such, it's mainly responsible for getting your computer started, and making sure all the programs in, and devices attached to, your system work together. It's also responsible for defining how you operate the computer. In that regard, it's by far the most important program on your system. Without an operating system, a computer won't even start. It's little more than a very expensive boat anchor.

Windows Vista also comes with many application programs that aren't really part of the system. Rather they're extra goodies you can use to view and create things. Many of those programs are so large and sophisticated that they get entire chapters of their own in this book. Internet Explorer (Chapter 17), Windows Mail (Chapter 18), Windows Contacts (Chapter 20), Windows Media Player (Chapter 23), and Movie Maker (Chapter 25) are just a few examples of such programs.

This chapter looks at some of the smaller, easier programs that come with Windows Vista. Many of these are referred to as *accessories*. In fact, you'll find many of them in the Accessories program group on your Start menu. Before we get started with specific programs, let's take a look at some general topics that apply to virtually every program you'll ever use.

IN THIS CHAPTER

Using Calculator and Calculator Plus

Working with text, special characters, and fonts

Zipping and unzipping files

Taking and annotating screenshots

Using Windows Calendar

Important Stuff About Programs

There are more than 100,000 different programs that you can run on your computer. Nobody owns them all or needs them all. But everyone has some programs on their computer already. For example, you have Windows Vista and all the programs that came with Windows Vista. If you bought your computer with Windows Vista pre-installed, your computer manufacturer may have pre-installed some other programs as well.

Most of the programs at your disposal have icons on the All Programs menu (or in one of the folders on the All Programs menu). To start a program, you click its icon on that menu. When you start a program, it opens in a program window on your desktop. You can move and size that window, switch among multiple open program windows, and close a program (and its window) when you've finished using it.

 **See Chapter 2 for more information on the Start menu and working with program windows.**

Of all the general things there are to know about programs, the most important is this: Every program has its own built-in Help. There is really no need to try to "figure out" a program by guessing. Once you understand that every program has its own built-in help, you can *find out* how to use that program or one of its features without all the hair-pulling frustration and ensuing problems of trial-and-error guesswork.

Many people make the mistake of looking in the wrong place for help with a program. For example, the Help described in Chapter 5 of this book is help for Windows Vista. That's not really the place to look for help with any other programs. Many people search the Web for help. But there you're searching through billions of pages of text, most having nothing to do with the program you're seeking help on. When you need help with a specific program, the first place to look is the Help for that program. It's as simple as that.

There are two ways to get to a program's Help. First, the program must be open. Then, do the following:

- Choose Help from that program's menu bar, and click the first option on the Help menu. Figure 15.1 shows an example.

FIGURE 15.1

Sample Help menu in a program.

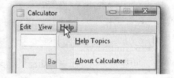

- Or, if you see a Help button, click that. Often that button will just show a question mark, as in the example shown in Figure 15.2.

FIGURE 15.2

Sample Help button near the mouse pointer.

- Or, make sure that the program is in the active window and press the Help key (F1) on your keyboard.

Once the Help opens, it should be easy to find your way around. It's largely a matter of reading what you see, and clicking on the topic you need help with.

The rest of this chapter looks at most of the programs and accessories that come with Windows Vista. There isn't enough room in this book to cover each one in great depth. So if you find a program that's useful for you, keep in mind that you can use its Help (not Windows Help) for more information about that program.

Using Windows Calculator

The easiest (and sometimes the handiest) little program in Vista is Calculator. It looks and acts just like a pocket calculator. To open it, click the Start button and choose All Programs ➪ Accessories ➪ Calculator. Or tap ⊞, type **cal**, and choose Calculator. Once it's open on the screen, you can use the standard view shown at the top of Figure 15.3. Or you can use the more advanced Scientific view shown at the bottom of that same figure.

FIGURE 15.3

Two ways to view Windows Calculator.

NOTE You can move Calculator around by dragging its title bar. And you can minimize it to a taskbar button. But you can't maximize it or size it by dragging a corner or edge.

If you know how to work a pocket calculator, you know how to work the one on your screen. The only difference is that you click the buttons with your mouse rather than with your finger. For example, to multiply 123.45 by 678.9 you click the following buttons:

```
123.45*678.9=
```

To clear the current entry and start a new calculation, click the button with the large red C. For help with Calculator, choose Help ➪ Help Topics from its menu. Or press F1 when Calculator is in the active program window.

If you need to do conversions, like feet to meters, Fahrenheit to Celsius, even currencies, the built-in Calculator won't help. There's a better one you can download for free. It's called Microsoft Calculator Plus. Browse to http://download.microsoft.com and search for Calculator Plus. When you find the download link, click it and follow the onscreen instructions. Make sure you choose Run or Install whenever given the option.

Once the program is installed, click the Start button and choose Start ➪ All Programs ➪ Microsoft Calculator Plus ➪ Microsoft Calculator Plus. (It will also show up when you do a Start menu search for cal.) If you don't see the options shown at the left side of Figure 15.4, click the View button and choose Conversion.

FIGURE 15.4

Calculator Plus.

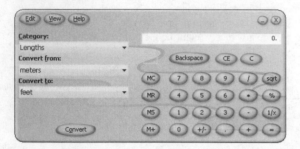

The rest is easy. From the first option at left, choose the type of conversion you want to make. Choose what you want to Convert from, and what you want to Convert to from the other two drop-downs. Use the calculator buttons to punch in the value to convert. Then click the Convert button.

Most of the conversions are easy. Currency conversion is a little awkward though. Exchange rates change all the time. You either have to manually enter the current conversion rates (Choose Edit ➪ Currencies), or you can download current exchange rates from the European Central Bank (ECB). (Click the Edit button and choose Import ECB Exchange Rates.) But the imported ECB rates work only if you convert from euros to some other currency. Click the Help button in Calculator Plus for more information.

 **TIP**   The Currency Conversion gadget you can add to Windows Sidebar provides live exchange rates. See "Using Windows Sidebar" in Chapter 11 for information on using Sidebar gadgets.

If you're not converting from euros, you may want to do your conversion online. Try www.xe.com or finance.yahoo.com/currency. Or if you don't like those, use a search engine like Google to search for Free real time currency conversion to see what else turns up.

Typing with WordPad

As most readers probably know, *word processing* is all about using a computer as sort of a high-tech typewriter. Windows Vista comes with its own built-in word processor named WordPad. It's not as fancy as Microsoft Word or WordPerfect. But it is free, and it's sufficient for typing basic letters and reports. To open WordPad, click the Start button and choose All Programs ➪ > Accessories ➪ WordPad. Or tap ⊞, type wor, and choose WordPad from the Start menu.

NOTE   If you can't find WordPad on your Accessories menu, your computer manufacturer may have left it off because you already have a better word processor, like Microsoft Word or WordPerfect. If you have one of those, better to use it than WordPad.

WordPad, Word, WordPerfect — What's the Diff?

Just as there are many brands of toothpaste, shampoo, and cars, there are many brands of word processing programs. WordPad, Microsoft Word, and WordPerfect are basically different "brands" of word processing programs. WordPad is a simple word processor that comes free with every copy of Windows Vista. You don't have to buy or install anything to use it. It's just there.

Microsoft Word is Microsoft's professional-grade word processing program. WordPerfect is Corel's professional-grade word processing program. Neither Word nor WordPerfect come free with Windows Vista. If you have one or the other, but don't know why, it's because your computer manufacturer bundled it with your system.

When WordPad opens, you'll see a title bar, menu bar, and toolbar up top. The large document area beneath that is basically a blank sheet of paper on which you'll type your document. Typing on a computer screen is different than typing on paper. So for those of you who are new to all of this, the following sections explain some things you really need to know about typing with computers in general.

Typing and navigating text

Typing in a document, e-mail message, or anywhere else on a computer screen is similar to typing with a typewriter. The main difference is that when you type on a computer screen, you don't press Enter at the end of each line. You only press Enter after typing the entire paragraph. Pressing Enter a second time adds a blank like above the next paragraph you type.

Figure 15.5 shows an example where a bent arrow (↵) shows where I pressed the Enter key to end a line or paragraph, or to insert a blank line. (When typing your own document, you won't see any bent arrows. They're just for illustration in the figure.)

FIGURE 15.5

The bent arrows show where I pressed the Enter key.

```
June 15, 2007↵
↵
Frankly Dubious↵
123 Oak Tree Lane↵
Pine Valley, PA  12345↵
↵
To Whom It May Concern: ↵
↵
The main difference between typing on a computer
screen and using a typewriter is this: On a typewriter
you press the Carriage Return at the end of every line.
On a computer screen you press Enter only to end a
short line of text, to end an entire paragraph, or to
insert a blank line. ↵
↵
The bent arrow symbols you see in this document are
not part of the document. They don't show on the
screen, they don't appear on printed version of the
document. The bent arrows just show you where you
press the Enter key to type a letter like this. ↵
↵
Sincerely, ↵
↵
↵
Your Name Here↵
```

When typing your own document, don't worry about making, or leaving, space for margins. Don't even presume that the margins you see on the screen match how margins will look on the printed page. Most likely, they won't.

To see how your document will look when you print it, choose File ⇨ Print Preview from WordPad's menu bar. The margins outside the dotted lines surrounding your text are the margins that you'll see when you print the document. To return to your document for more editing, click the Close button at the top of the Print Preview window.

> **TIP** Most programs have a Print Preview option. You can use it to get a sneak peek at how your document will look before you print it.

If you make a mistake while typing, use the Backspace key to back up and erase what you just typed. If it's too late for that, because you've typed a whole lot of text since the mistake, use the basic editing techniques described in the next section to make corrections.

Basic text editing

To insert or delete text, first get the *cursor* to where you want to make the change. Note that the cursor is not the same as the mouse pointer. The cursor is usually a blinking vertical bar that shows where the next character you type will appear. One way to get the cursor where you want it is to get the tip of the mouse pointer right where you want to put the cursor, then click (tap the left mouse button).

You can also move the cursor around using the keys listed in Table 15-1. I titled it "*Almost* Universal" because you never know where there will be some exception to the rule. Note, however, that you cannot use those keys to move the cursor *outside* of text. If the cursor is at the bottom of your document and you need to move down, press the Enter key to insert blank lines. If you need to move the cursor to the right in an empty line, press the Tab key or Spacebar.

TABLE 15-1

(Almost) Universal Keys for Moving the Cursor through Text

Key	Where it moves the cursor
→	One character to the right
←	One character to the left
↑	Up one line
↓	Down one line
Home	Beginning of the line
End	End of line
Ctrl+Home	Top of document
Ctrl+End	End of document
Page Up (PgUp)	Up a page (or screenful)
Page Down (PgDn)	Down a page (or screenful)
Ctrl+←	One word to the left
Ctrl+→	One word to the right
Ctrl+↑	Up one paragraph

Key	Where it moves the cursor
Ctrl+↓	Down one paragraph
Ctrl+Page Up (PgUp)	To top of previous page
Ctrl+Page Down (PgDn)	To top of next page
Alt+Ctrl+Page Up (PgUp)	To top of visible text
Alt+Ctrl+Page Down (PgDn)	To bottom of visible text

To delete text near the cursor, do one of the following:

- Press Backspace to delete the character to the left of the cursor.
- Press Delete (Del) to delete the character to the right of the cursor.

To insert text at the cursor position, just start typing. If you're in Insert mode, the new text will be inserted without replacing any existing text. If you're in Overwrite mode, the new text will replace (overwrite) existing text. To switch from Insert to Overwrite mode, or vice versa, press the Insert (Ins) key once.

 If pressing the Insert key doesn't switch from Insert to Overwrite mode, and your keyboard has a Function Lock (or F Lock) key, press that key first. Then try the Insert key again.

Selecting text

If you want to work with larger chunks of text (as opposed to working with one character at a time), you first need to *select* the text with which you want to work. Selected text is highlighted. For example, in Figure 15.6, I selected the highlighted paragraph by dragging the mouse pointer through it.

 To drag, hold down the left mouse button while moving the mouse.

FIGURE 15.6

One paragraph of text selected.

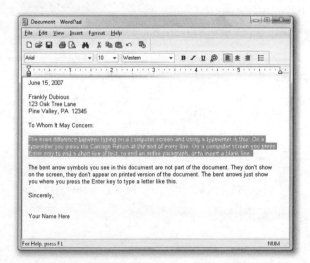

You can select text using either the mouse or the keyboard. With the mouse, you can just drag the mouse pointer through any chunk of text you select. There are some optional mouse *shortcuts* you can use in most programs for selecting specific chunks of text as follows:

- **Select one word:** Double-click the word.
- **Select one sentence:** Hold down the Ctrl key and click the sentence.
- **Select one line:** Move the cursor into the white space to the left of the line, and then click.
- **Select one paragraph:** Triple-click the paragraph (works in WordPad, Word, and Internet Explorer, and maybe some other programs). If triple-clicking doesn't work, drag the mouse pointer through the paragraph.
- **Select multiple paragraphs:** Drag through all of them, or click where you want to start the selection. Then, hold down the Shift key and click the location you want to extend the selection to.
- **Select all text in the document:** Choose Edit ⇨ Select All from the menu bar, or press Ctrl+A.

If one of the preceding methods doesn't work in the program you're using, dragging the mouse pointer through the text you want to select should work.

If you make a mistake while selecting and want to start over, just unselect the text. Clicking just outside the selected text will usually do the trick. Or press the ↑, ↓, ←, or → key by itself (without holding down the Shift key).

NOTE In Adobe Acrobat Reader, you need to click the Select Text or Select Tool button in the toolbar before you select. Otherwise, dragging will cause the entire document to scroll. Remember, you can see the name of any toolbar button in any program by pointing to the button (rest the tip of the mouse pointer on the button).

To select text using the keyboard rather than the mouse, just hold down the Shift key as you press any of the navigation keys listed in Table 15-1.

Formatting text

Many forms of text formatting are based on a *select, then do* principle. First you select the text to which you want to apply formatting (using any selection technique previously mentioned). Then you *do* the necessary command, either by making selections from the program's menu bar or by clicking buttons in its toolbar. For example, in WordPad you can apply a font (print style) to any text you've typed.

As an example, Figure 15.7 shows where I've selected a chunk of text I typed into a WordPad document.

FIGURE 15.7

Some text selected for formatting.

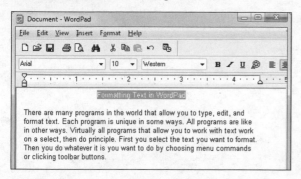

Next choose Format ➪ Font from WordPad's menu bar. In the Font dialog box that opens, choose the font, size, and color you want as in the example shown in Figure 15.8.

FIGURE 15.8

Choose a font, size, and color.

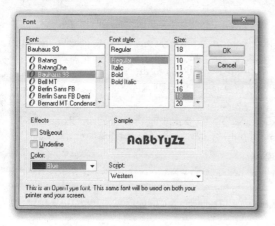

Click OK in the dialog box. Your selections are applied to the selected text, as in the example shown in Figure 15.9.

FIGURE 15.9

Font selections applied to the (previously) selected text.

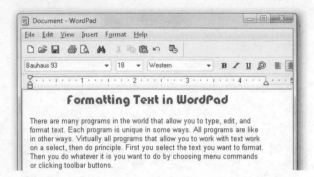

The *select, then do* approach also works for deleting, replacing, copying, and moving text.

Deleting and replacing chunks of text

To delete a large chunk of text, select the text you want to delete, and then press the Delete key. Optionally, you can select the text, and then just start typing new text. The selected text will disappear the moment you start typing, and only the new text you type will remain.

Using copy-and-paste and cut-and-paste

Anyplace you can select text, you can copy text. Anyplace you can type text, you can paste text. So there is never any need to re-type text you already see on your screen. You can just copy-and-paste it instead. For example, if there's some text in a Web page you want to add to a WordPad or other document you're creating, there's no need to re-type the text that's already in that page. Just copy-and-paste it.

For this to work, you need to know how to have multiple program windows on the screen and how to switch between them. These kinds of basic skills are described under "Running Programs" in Chapter 2. After you've mastered those basic skills, copy-and-paste should be fairly easy. First understand that there are two documents involved:

- **Source:** The document or page that already has the text you want to copy. In other words, the place you're copying *from*.
- **Destination:** The place where you would have typed the text yourself, if you had to. In other words, the place you're copying *to*.

So assuming you can see the text you want to copy, and get to the place where you want to paste it, here are the steps:

1. At the source, select the text you want to copy using any method cited earlier.
2. Copy the selected text using whichever of the following methods is most convenient at the moment:
   - Press Ctrl+C.
   - Right-click the selected text and choose Copy.
   - Click the Copy button in that program's toolbar.
   - Choose Edit ➪ Copy from that program's menu bar.

Figure 15.10 shows an example where I've selected a chunk of text in a Web page, right-clicked that text, and am about to click Copy.

FIGURE 15.10

Text selected in a Web page.

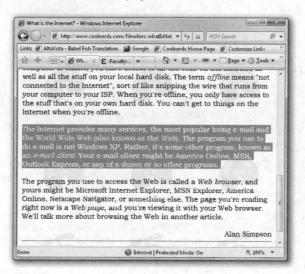

3. Get to the destination and click where you want to paste the text. The cursor should be where it would be if you were going to type that text yourself.

4. Use whichever method is most convenient to paste the text you copied:
   - Press Ctrl+V.
   - Right-click near the cursor and choose Paste.
   - Click the Paste button in the destination program's toolbar.
   - Choose Edit ➪ Paste from the destination program's menu bar.

The text you copied will be placed right where you pasted it.

Moving text within a document

If you want to move a chunk of text within a document, the technique is similar to copy-and-paste. Except you use cut-and-paste. As the name implies, when you *cut* text, you remove it from its present location. This only works in documents that you *can* edit. For example, you can't cut-and-paste from a Web page because you don't own the Web page and aren't allowed to change it. You can only copy from a Web page.

But when you create a document yourself, you can do anything you want to it, including cut-and-paste. The steps are the same, it's just a matter of cutting rather than copying:

1. Select the text you want to move using any selection technique you like.

2. Cut the text using whichever method here is most convenient at the moment:
   - Press Ctrl+X.
   - Right-click the selected text and choose Cut.

■ Click the Cut button in the program's toolbar.

■ Choose Edit ⇨ Cut from that program's menu bar.

3. Move the cursor to wherever you want to put the cut text.

4. Paste the text (press Ctrl+V, or right-click and choose Paste, or click the Paste toolbar button, or choose Edit ⇨ Paste from the program's menu bar).

The methods given here work the same in small textboxes, not just word processing documents. You could, for example, copy a URL (Web site address) from any page and then paste it into the Address bar of your Web browser to get to that page.

Copy-and-paste a picture

You can copy-and-paste a picture from an open document into a WordPad document. The picture needs to be open for this to work. By "open" I mean already visible in some other open document (like a Web page), or open in a graphics program. Right-click the picture and choose Copy. Then click at about where you want to put the picture in your WordPad document and paste (press Ctrl+V or right-click near the cursor and choose Paste).

Once the picture is in your document, clicking the picture will display sizing handles (little black squares around the border of the picture). You can drag any one of those handles to make the picture larger or smaller.

> **NOTE** WordPad isn't a great program for creating complex documents with pictures. You can do some basic things with pictures in a WordPad document. But if you're serious about creating complex documents with many pictures, you need a serious word processor like Microsoft Word or WordPerfect.

Saving a WordPad document

Any typed document you create with WordPad (or Microsoft Word, or WordPerfect, or any other program) exists on your screen (so you can see it) and in your computer's *memory* (RAM). There is nothing permanent about it. If you shut off your computer without saving the document, that document simply ceases to exist. There is no way to "get it back" because it is gone forever and there is no record of it anywhere in the known universe.

About the Windows Clipboard

When you cut or copy text using any of the preceding techniques, whatever you cut or copied is placed in an area of your computer's memory called the Windows Clipboard. The formal name often confuses people because they figure they should be able to see something named Clipboard on the screen, in their menus, or someplace. But there is no such thing to be concerned about.

The Clipboard is nothing more than a place in your computer's memory where Windows temporarily stores the last thing you copied or cut. When you shut off the computer, the Clipboard is emptied. So you should make no attempt to use the Clipboard for any form of long-term storage. The Clipboard is not for documents and files or for long-term storage.

Every time you do a copy-and-paste or cut-and-paste you should do so in one smooth motion. Select the text you want, copy or cut it, and paste it where you want to put it.

When you do save something, you have to think about where you're going to put it, and what you're going to name it. Otherwise, if you just save it "someplace," you may not be able to find it again when you need it. This topic is covered under "Saving Things in Folders" in Chapter 28. Here we'll just talk about saving documents you create in WordPad or similar programs like Microsoft Word and WordPerfect. Here's how saving works:

1. Choose File ➪ Save from the menu bar. The first time you save a new document, the Save As dialog box opens.

2. Tell Windows *where* you want to put the document by navigating to that folder.

   If you don't know and don't have a preference, use your Documents folder. Most likely it will already be selected for you (you see the name Documents at the right side of the breadcrumb trail). If you see some other name there, click the arrow next to your user name and choose Documents. Or click Documents in the navigation pane at the left.

3. In the File Name box, enter a brief filename that will make it easy to identify the file later (when all you can see is the name).

Figure 15.11 shows an example where I've opted to put the new document in the Documents folder for my user account (Alan). I've named the document My First Document.

FIGURE 15.11

Ready to save My First Document in my Documents folder.

4. Near the lower-right corner of the dialog box, click the Save button.

Everything that's currently in the document is now saved in a file in the folder you specified. Note, however, that any additional changes you make are *not* saved. If you make more changes and want to save those, do any of the following to save:

- Press Ctrl+S.
- Click the Save toolbar button.
- Choose File ➪ Save from the menu.

You won't get any feedback on the screen. Nor will Windows ask you where to put the file or what to name it. You already gave Windows that information. Subsequent saves just ensure that all changes you've made since that last save are added to that file.

CAUTION   Never turn off your computer without first closing all open programs and saving all unsaved work! Always shut down properly by clicking the Start button, clicking the arrow next to the lock symbol, and choosing Shut Down.

To print your document, choose File ➪ Print from WordPad's menu bar. Then click the Print button in the Print dialog box that opens. For the complete lowdown on printing, see Chapter 36.

When you've finished using WordPad and working on your document, close them both. (Actually, you just need to close WordPad because in so doing you'll also close the document.) To close WordPad, click the Close (X) button in its upper-right corner. Or choose File ➪ Exit from its menu. If you've left any unsaved work behind in your document, you'll see a message like the one in Figure 15.12.

FIGURE 15.12

Warning and last chance to save unsaved work.

This is your last chance to save your work, and any changes you've made since the last time you saved. If you choose No, you lose everything you accomplished since your last save. So you should choose Yes unless you're certain you don't want to save that work.

Both WordPad and your document close (meaning they are no longer visible on your screen).

Opening a WordPad document

Anytime you want to start WordPad again in the future, just click the Start button and choose All Programs ➪ Accessories ➪ WordPad again. But don't expect that last document you worked on to appear automatically. Documents are separate from programs. You can create all the documents you want in any program. Programs never presume that you want to reopen the last document you worked on. They presume you want to create a new document, and so open with a new blank sheet of paper.

You can, of course, open any document you created and saved in WordPad. If it's a document you created recently, just click File in the menu bar, then click the document's name at the bottom of the File menu, as in Figure 15.13.

Opening a recently saved document.

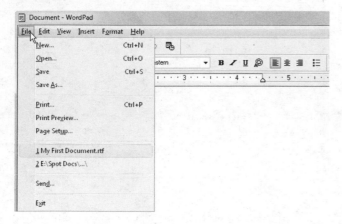

If the document is one you haven't worked on recently, its name might not be at the bottom of the File menu. In that case, choose File ➪ Open from the menu. That brings up an Open dialog box where you can navigate to the folder in which you placed the document, then double-click its icon. Once the document opens, it will appear in WordPad looking exactly as it did the last time you saved it.

It's not necessary to open the program first. The Recent Items option on the right side of the Start menu lists documents you've worked with recently. Often you just have to click the Start button, click Recent Items, and then click the name of the document you want to open. No need to open the program first.

Similarly, you can navigate to any folder and double-click the icon of the document you want to open. There's no need to open the program first. When you double-click the document's icon, the default program for that file type opens to display the document. See Chapter 28 for the full story on folders and files.

NOTE   If you double-click the icon for a saved WordPad document, Microsoft Word (if installed on your system) will open the document. That's because once installed, Microsoft Word becomes the default program for many kinds of text documents. If you have Microsoft Word, there's really no compelling reason to use WordPad.

Typing Special Characters with Character Map

There are many characters you can type right from your keyboard. There are many you can't, like ® © ™ ∑ ≠ ÷ to name a few. Any character you can't type, you can insert from Windows Character Map. First get the cursor to where you want to type the character. Then click the Start button and choose All Programs ➪ Accessories ➪ System Tools ➪ Character Map. Or tap ⊞, type char, and click Character Map. The Character Map opens as in Figure 15.14.

FIGURE 15.14

Character Map.

You have thousands of characters to choose from in Character Map. Finding just the one you want isn't always easy. But a good starting place is the Symbols font, which you can view by choosing Symbol from the Font drop-down list. Then use the scroll bar at the right side of the map to look through all the available symbols. To see a larger version of any character, click it.

When you find the character you want to insert, click it and then click the Select button. You can select a bunch of characters if you want. They line up in the Characters to copy box. When all the characters you want are in the box, click the Copy button. Then switch back to the document you're typing and paste (press Ctrl+V). The characters are pasted at the cursor position.

If you don't find the character you want in the Symbol set, try a different font. The Wingdings and Webdings fonts contain many special characters. If you're looking for non-English characters, like ñ é ¿ ¡¡ , select the same font in which you're typing (Arial or Times New Roman) from the Font drop-down list. Then scroll through the list of available characters.

To search for a character by name, choose the Advanced view checkbox. Type the name of the character you want and click Search. For more information on using Character Map, click its Help button.

Installing Fonts

Windows Vista comes with a large selection of fonts. You'll see just how many there are when you apply a font to selected text. Each font that you can apply to text is stored as a file in your Fonts folders. You can use either of the following techniques to open that folder:

- Press ⊞, type font, and click the Fonts folder icon under Programs on the Start menu.
- Click the Start button and choose Control Panel ➪ Appearance and Personalization ➪ Fonts.

Figure 15.15 shows an example of how things might look in that folder. Because it's a folder, you can use the Views button to control the size of icons.

FIGURE 15.15

The Fonts folder.

> **NOTE** The Fonts folder has nothing to do with *applying* fonts to text. You apply fonts in programs where you can type and format text, like WordPad. The Fonts folder is just a repository where all of your available fonts are stored.

To see what a font looks like, double-click its icon. A window opens showing a sample. Close that window after viewing the font.

If the fonts you already have aren't enough, you can certainly add more. First you have to acquire those fonts. There are many places where you can purchase fonts, and a few places where you can download fonts for free without being overwhelmed by ads. For example, www.webpagepublicity.com/free-fonts-v2.html has more than 6,000 free fonts to choose from. (At least, it did last time I checked.) If that doesn't work, browse to a search engine like www.google.com and search for download free Windows fonts or purchase Windows fonts, or something like that.

When you do find some fonts, try to download TrueType or OpenType .ttf files because those are the easiest to work with. You'll have to keep track of where you put them, because you'll need to know their location later to install them. So consider putting them all in the Downloads folder for your user account, or perhaps your own subfolder within that folder.

If the fonts you download are in a compressed folder (Zip file), you'll need to extract the .ttf file before you can install the font. See "Zipping and Unzipping Files" later in this chapter for more info.

Anyway, once you've acquired some fonts and have a .ttf file for each, the rest is easy. The fonts you install will be available to all user accounts. Which means you're about to make a change that affects all users, and therefore you need administrative privileges. So you may want to log in to an administrative user account before you begin.

If you haven't already done so, open the Fonts folder as described previously. If you don't see a menu bar in that folder, tap the Alt key to open it. Then choose File ⇨ Install New Font from the menu. Use the Drives and Folders list near the bottom of the dialog box to navigate to the folder in which you've placed the .ttf files. Then select the fonts you want to install (or click Select All to select them all). I suggest you also select (check) the "Copy fonts to Fonts folder" so that all of your fonts are together in that folder. Figure 15.16 shows an example where I've selected a bunch of fonts I downloaded to a subfolder within my Downloads folder.

FIGURE 15.16

Ready to install new fonts.

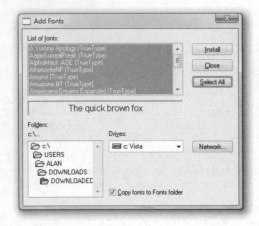

Click the Install button. You'll get some brief feedback as the fonts install. When that's done, each new font will be represented by an icon in your Fonts folder. Close the Fonts folder. You apply the new fonts just as you do the fonts you already had.

 Since Fonts is a folder and not a program, it doesn't have its own built-in help. For more information on Fonts, search Windows Help (click the Start button and choose Help and Support).

To remove a font, just delete its icon from the Fonts folder (right-click its icon and choose Delete).

Using Notepad

Notepad is similar to WordPad in that it's mainly about typing text. The basic typing and editing skills, and techniques for saving and opening files, apply as well. The main difference is that Notepad is about creating *plain text documents*. These are typically files that contain computer code or HTML tags for the computer to process, not for humans to read directly. There's no need to use fonts, pictures, and such in a plain text document because a computer can't "see" the document. It just does whatever the code in the text document tells it to do.

So for non-programmers and casual users, it all works something like this. If you have Microsoft Word or WordPerfect, use that for typing text documents. Each has its own Help so you can learn more. There are also entire books about those products. If you don't have Word or WordPerfect, you can get by with WordPad. You just won't have some of the more advanced features like spell-checking.

Don't use Notepad at all unless you specifically need to create a text file that contains code written in a computer language. If you do want to use Notepad, you can start it in the usual manner. Tap ⊞, type note, and choose Notepad. Or click the Start button and choose All Programs ➪ Accessories ➪ Notepad.

Zipping and Unzipping Files

Zipping is a way of combing multiple files and folders into a single *compressed folder*. This is often done to make it easier to e-mail a large number of files as a single attachment. For example, when I write a book, each chapter contains many files—one file containing all the text and a separate file for each picture. Before I submit a chapter to the publisher, I combine all the files into a single compressed file named Chapter *x* (where *x* is the chapter number). Then I send in that file.

When the editor receives the file, it's easy for her to pass on a copy to each editor who needs to see it. Well, certainly a lot easier than if I'd sent 20 or 30 separate little files for that one chapter.

In Windows Vista, the terms *compressed folder* and *Zip file* mean the same thing—a single file with a .zip extension that contains still more files and/or folders. The icon for a Zip file looks like a manila file folder with a Zip file on it. If filename extensions aren't hidden, the extension is .zip, as in the example shown in Figure 15.17.

Sample compressed folder (Zip file).

A side benefit to using compressed folders is that Windows will attempt to make the files smaller by compressing them. This means that the compressed folder will consume less disk space, and transfer more quickly over a wire, than the individual uncompressed files will. Exactly how much compression you get, though, depends on what kinds of files you put into the Zip file. Many file formats, like JPEG, PNG, WMV, MPEG, WMA, and MP3, are already compressed, so they don't shrink much (if at all) when you zip them. But many other kinds of files will shrink when placed in a Zip file.

NOTE The compression affects only the amount of disk space the files consume. It doesn't make the files visually smaller on the screen, or remove any content from the files.

Zipping files

To place two or more files into a Zip file, you first need to select their icons. If you don't know how to do that yet, see in Chapter 29. Then, right-click any selected icon and choose Send To ➪ Compressed (zipped) Folder as in Figure 15.18.

You get some brief feedback, then see the compressed folder icon. The original files remain intact and unaffected. This is because the assumption is that you created the Zip file to send to someone by e-mail, and want to keep the original files to yourself in the uncompressed form.

FIGURE 15.18

About to zip selected files.

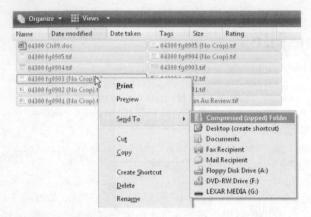

 **TIP** To add more files to a Zip file, drag icons for those files to the Zip file's icon and drop them right on that icon.

Assuming you do want to e-mail the Zip file to someone, and you're using Windows Mail or some other compatible POP3 or MAPI e-mail client, you can right-click the Zip file's icon, choose Send To ➪ Mail Recipient, and you're on your way. If that approach doesn't work for you, because you use some incompatible e-mail system, you can still attach the file to an e-mail message using the standard method for your e-mail account.

NOTE See Chapter 18 for more information on Windows Mail. If you don't use Windows Mail, and don't know how to attach files or save attachments, check the Help page for your e-mail service or contact your ISP.

Unzipping files

If someone sends you a Zip file, the first thing you need to do is save the attachment as a file. In Windows Mail, this is a simple matter of clicking the message header, clicking the paper clip icon in the preview area as in Figure 15.19, and then clicking Save Attachments. In many e-mail clients, it's a matter of right-clicking the attachment icon and choosing Save As.

FIGURE 15.19

Saving an e-mail attachment with Windows Mail.

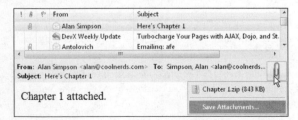

Regardless of how you save the attachment, it's important to know where you saved it because you need to get to the saved file to extract its contents. If in doubt, save the file to your Documents folder.

Next, you need to navigate to the folder in which you saved the Zip file. Then right-click its icon and choose Extract All as in Figure 15.20.

FIGURE 15.20

About to extract files from a compressed folder (Zip file).

The Extract Compressed (Zipped) Folders Wizard opens. You can specify where you want to put the extracted files if you like. Or do the easy thing and just accept the suggested location and click Extract. If you use that method, you end up with a new, regular folder with the same name as the compressed folder, as in the example in Figure 15.21. You can delete the Zip file, because you really don't need it anymore. Use the files in the uncompressed folder for whatever you intend to do with them.

FIGURE 15.21

Regular folder (right) extracted from compressed folder (left).

Zipping and unzipping are built into Windows. There is no program window or menu bar from which to get Help. But there is information in Windows general help. Click the Start button, choose Help and Support, and search for `compressed folder` or `zip file`.

Annotating Screenshots with Snipping Tool

The Snipping Tool makes it easy to take screenshots and annotate them with text.

Snipping Tool is a program that makes it easy to take a snapshot of part of the screen. You can annotate that picture with text and highlights. Here's how it works. First, set up the screen so that you can see whatever it is you want to capture to a picture. Then use either of the following techniques to open the Snipping Tool:

- Click the Start button and choose All Programs ➪ Accessories ➪ Snipping Tool.
- Tap ⊞, type `snip`, and choose Snipping Tool.

A small window with some instructional text appears as in Figure 15.22. Everything behind that window may be dimmed.

FIGURE 15.22

Snipping Tool with no picture.

The first time the Snipping Tool opens, you'll be given the option to add an icon for it to your Quick Launch toolbar. Choose Yes if you think you'll use the tool often. But don't worry if you miss that opportunity. You can add the Snipping Tool to your Quick Launch toolbar at any time. Just right-click its name on the All Programs menu and choose Add to Quick Launch.

When the Snipping Tool is open, follow these steps to capture a screenshot:

1. Click the arrow on the New button and choose how you want to take your screenshot:
   - **Free Form Snip:** Take a snapshot of any area you like in any shape you like.
   - **Rectangular Snip:** Take a snapshot of any rectangular portion of the screen.
   - **Window Snip:** Take a snapshot of any open program window.
   - **Full-screen Snip:** Take a snapshot of the entire screen.
2. Specify what area of the screen you want to snip, as follows:
   - If you chose the Free Form or Rectangular Snip, drag a circle or rectangle around the area you want to snip.
   - If you chose Window Snip, click anywhere within the window you want to snip.
   - If you chose Full-Screen Snip, do nothing. The entire screen is snipped automatically.

A larger version of the Snipping Tool opens showing whatever you snipped. For example, in Figure 15.23, I snipped Windows Media Player as it was playing a song.

FIGURE 15.23

Snipping Tool with snapshot of Media Player.

With the snapshot in place, you can use the Pen to draw on the picture. Choose Tools ⇨ Pen and a pen color. Or choose Tools ⇨ Pen ⇨ Customize to define your own pen color, thickness, and tip. Choose Tools ⇨ Pen ⇨ Custom Pen to use your custom pen. Then just draw on your screenshot by dragging. If you make a mess of things, click the Eraser and click the thing you messed up.

To highlight an area in yellow, click the Highlighter tool and drag the mouse pointer through the item you wish to highlight. Again, if you mess up, click the Erase tool and click the bad highlight.

Saving a snip

To save the screenshot, click the Save Snip button or choose File ⇨ Save As from the menu. Navigate to the folder in which you want to place the saved picture. Name the snapshot as you would any other file. From the Save As type drop down list, choose a picture format (JPEG, PNG, or GIF). If you don't have a preference, JPEG would likely be your best bet because it conserves all colors and is compatible with most graphics programs.

Optionally, you can save the snip as an HTML file with an .MHT extension. However, it won't be a standard graphics image if you choose that option. You'll be limited to opening the picture in Internet Explorer and Microsoft Word. And you won't be able to do further editing in a graphics program.

Copy-and-paste a snip

To copy-and-paste the snip into an open document, click the Copy toolbar button or choose Edit ⇨ Copy. Then navigate to where you want to insert the picture and paste as usual (press Ctrl+V or right-click and choose Paste).

E-mail a snip

If you use Windows Mail or a similar compatible e-mail client, you can e-mail the snip to someone directly from the program. Click the arrow on the Send Snip button or choose File ⇨ Send To. Then choose one of the following options:

- **E-mail Recipient:** Opens a new e-mail message with the snip embedded in the body of the message.
- **E-mail Recipient (as attachment):** Allows you to specify a size for the picture, then attaches to a new empty e-mail message as a JPEG image.

When the e-mail message opens, fill in the recipient address (or addresses) and Subject line as usual. You can also type in the body of the message, as usual. Then click Send.

 If you can't e-mail directly from the Snipping Tool, save the image as a file. Then attach that saved file to an e-mail message using whatever method your e-mail client or service provides.

Change Snipping Tool options

To change how the Snipping Tool works, click its Options button or choose Tools ⇨ Options from the menu. Make your selections as summarized here:

- **Hide instruction text:** Choose this to hide the small instructions that appear at the bottom of the empty Snipping Tool.
- **Always copy snips to Clipboard:** Choosing this option copies every snip straight to the Clipboard, which means you can paste the snip into an open document without first clicking the Copy toolbar button.
- **Include URL below snips (HTML only):** If you use the Snipping Tool to capture screenshots of Web pages, choose this option to automatically annotate each snip with a link to the page from which it was taken. When saving the snip, you must choose HTML as the Save As Type.
- **Prompt to save snips before exiting:** If you clear this option, you won't be asked if you want to save the latest unsaved snip when you close the Snipping Tool.
- **Display icon in Quick Launch toolbar:** Selecting this adds a Snipping Tool option to the Quick Launch toolbar. So you can just click that option to open the tool without going to the Start menu.
- **Show screen overlay when Snipping Tool is active:** If you clear this option, the screen won't go dim when waiting for you to take your snapshot.
- **Ink Color:** Specify a color for the border that surrounds each snipped image.
- **Show selection ink after capturing snips:** If you clear this option, the border that normally surrounds each snip won't appear inside the Snipping Tool.

To activate your selections, click OK in the Options dialog box. Some changes might also require you to exit the Snipping Tool and reopen it.

Screenshots the old-fashioned way

The old method of capturing screens with the Print Screen key still works. It may be a better choice in cases where you need to hold down the mouse button to show something, because the Snipping Tool doesn't provide a means for doing that. For more information on taking screenshots with the Print Screen key, see "Taking Screenshots" in Chapter 22.

Using Paint

Paint is a simple drawing and graphics editing tool that comes free with Windows Vista. The truth be told, it's little more than a toy for doodling on the screen. Just about any graphics editing program on the market can do everything Paint can do and more. In fact, if your computer manufacturer bundled a graphics editing program with your system, they might not have even installed Paint. Because whatever program they gave you is probably much better than Paint.

 **If you want to crop or edit photos, use the Fix feature in Windows Photo Gallery (Chapter 22).**

One thing that Paint is still good for is resizing large photos. For example, your digital camera might shoot enormous 5 megapixel pictures that look great on the screen and in print. But those huge dimensions and potentially large file size can be a pain when trying to e-mail photos or post them on a Web site.

If you use Windows Mail to e-mail photos, solving that problem is simple. When you send the pictures, you'll see a prompt asking what size you want them to be. Just choose 640 x 480 (or whatever). The e-mailed copies of the pictures will be reduced in size without compromising the size or quality of the originals.

If you don't use an e-mail client that automatically reduces picture sizes, or if you need to shrink some pictures for Web publication, you can use Paint to reduce their sizes. Unfortunately, it doesn't let you reduce to specific dimensions. So you're better off using a "real" graphics program if you can. But in a pinch, you can pull it off with Paint.

First you'll need to know the dimensions of the original picture. One way to do that is to open the folder in which the picture is contained. Use the Details view. If there is no Dimensions column, right-click a column heading and add a Dimensions column. In Figure 15.24, I added the column and dragged it over so it's next to the Name column.

FIGURE 15.24

Viewing picture icons in Details view.

If you just want to see the dimensions of a single picture, you don't need to use the Details view. Instead you can right-click the picture's icon and choose Properties. Then click the Details tab in the Properties sheet. Scroll through all the details if necessary to see if you can find the picture's dimensions.

 Not all file types store or can display picture dimensions. I'm using JPEGs in this example. Those do contain dimension information.

Now you need to do a little math to figure out how much you need to reduce the picture to get it to the size you want. In this case, I'd probably just shrink a picture to about 25 percent of its current size, which gets it down to about the 640 x 480 range (give or take a few pixels).

The next step is to make a copy of the picture. You never want to shrink or reduce the quality of your original picture. You always want to keep that one because it's the best one for printing and editing. A simple way to do that would be to right-click the picture's icon and choose Copy. Then press Ctrl+V to paste. The copy has the same name as the original picture followed by – Copy. You can rename that to something more meaningful. For example, change – Copy to (Small).

Next, right-click the copied picture's icon and choose Open With ⇨ Paint. (This only works if Paint is installed and if the picture you're working with is compatible with Paint.) Once in Paint, choose Image ⇨ Resize/Skew. Then set the Horizontal and Vertical Size options to the percent value you want. For example, in Figure 15.25 I set those each to 25%.

FIGURE 15.25

Reducing a picture to 25 percent its current size.

Click OK in the Resize and Skew dialog box, close Paint, and choose Yes when asked about saving your changes. You're done.

Using Sound Recorder

Sound Recorder is a simple program for recording sounds from a connected microphone. To use it, first make sure your microphone is properly connected to your sound card or computer. To avoid potential problems, you might want to make sure the microphone you're using is properly configured.

TIP Use Windows Media Player to copy songs from CDs (Chapter 23). To copy music from vinyl LPs or cassette tapes, consider using the Analog Recorder from Microsoft Plus or SuperPack (www.micosoft.com/Plus). To narrate a movie, use Windows Movie Maker (Chapter 25). To dictate text, use Speech Recognition (Chapter 12).

To check and configure your microphone, double-click the speaker icon in the Notification area. If there is no such icon, click the Start button, type audio, and click Audio Devices and Sound Themes. In the dialog box that opens, click the Recording tab to view all of your recording devices as in Figure 15.26.

FIGURE 15.26

Audio Devices.

First make sure that the microphone you intend to use is set as the default (shows a checkmark in a green circle). If it's not, right-click the icon for that microphone and choose Set As Default for. Then choose All Uses if that's your only microphone. Or choose Console if you want to use that microphone only for Sound Recorder, and some other microphone for other purposes.

Next, speak into the microphone to make sure it hears you. You should see some activity on the meter that's on the icon. If there is little or no activity:

- Make sure the microphone is plugged into the correct port on your computer.
- If the microphone has any switches or controls, make sure it's on, not muted, and doesn't have its volume turned down too low.
- Right-click the microphone's icon and choose Properties. Click the Levels tab in the dialog box that opens and drag the slider to the right. Then click OK.

When you can see activity on the default microphone's icon, you know you're ready to go. Click OK in the Audio Devices window.

To start Sound Recorder, do either of the following:

- Tap ⊞, type sou, and click Sound Recorder.
- Click the Start button and choose All Programs ➪ Accessories ➪ Sound Recorder.

Sound Recorder opens as in Figure 15.27.

FIGURE 15.27

Sound Recorder.

When you speak into your microphone, you should see a green indicator moving with your voice. This lets you know Sound Recorder is hearing you. To start recording, click the Start Recording button and say whatever it is you want to record.

When you've finished saying what you want to record, click Stop Recording. A Save As dialog box opens so you can save what you spoke. Navigate to the folder in which you want to save the recording, name the file, and click OK. (Or, if you don't want to save the recording, click Cancel.)

For help with Sound Recorder, click its Help button (the blue one with the question mark).

When you've finished recording, you can close Sound Recorder. To play the file you recorded, navigate to the folder in which you saved the recording and double-click its icon.

Using Windows Calendar

NEW FEATURE Windows Calendar is a handy tool for keeping track of things to do, sharing schedules, and keeping abreast of local or online events.

Windows Calendar is a great way to keep track of, and share, appointments. Each computer user can have any number of calendars. You can have a calendar you keep to yourself, and others that you share with other people. Many sports teams, TV shows, and other institutions publish their own event calendars online. You can subscribe to these calendars so you're always on top of upcoming events and can plan your time accordingly.

To open Windows Calendar, use whichever method is easiest for you:

- Click the Start button and choose All Programs ➪ Windows Calendar.
- Tap ⊞, type cal, and choose Windows Calendar.

TIP If you use Calendar often, consider adding an icon for it to your Quick Launch toolbar, Start menu, or desktop. Just right-click Windows Calendar on the All Programs menu and choose Pin to Start Menu, Add to Quick Launch, or Send To ➪ Desktop (Create Shortcut). You can do all three if you want lots of icons for starting Calendar.

When Windows Calendar first opens, it will likely look something like Figure 15.28.

FIGURE 15.28

Windows Calendar.

Title bar   Menu bar   Toolbar   Search box

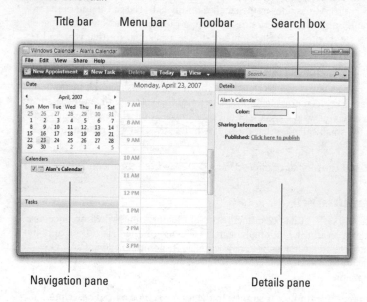

Navigation pane   Details pane

Regardless of how Calendar looks when you first open it, you can change its appearance at any time using the View menu on the menu bar (see Figure 15.29). Optionally, use the shortcut keys shown on that same menu. Or use the arrow on the toolbar View button to choose a view. You can change the view at any time, so feel free to try some out.

FIGURE 15.29

View menu.

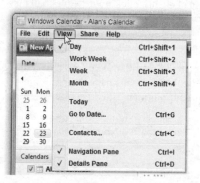

Navigating the Calendar

The Calendar usually opens to the current date. But you can easily scroll through future and past dates. To move month by month, use the left and right triangles in the small monthly calendar at the top of the Navigation pane. Optionally, you can double-click the month and year at the top of the Navigation pane calendar to see years. Click a year to see months, and click a month to see a calendar for that year and month. When you get to the month and year you want to see, click any day on the small calendar to bring that day to the main calendar in the center pane.

You can also get to any date by choosing View ➪ Go To Date from the menu bar, or from the menu that appears when you right-click the top of the center pane. Optionally, press Ctrl+G to go to another date. In the dialog box that opens, type the date you want to go to, or click the arrow at the right side of that Date box and navigate to the date using the small calendar that drops down. Use the Show In option to choose how you want to view the date and click OK.

To return to today's date, click Today in the toolbar or choose View ➪ Today from the menu bar.

Entering a task or appointment

Use Windows Calendar to keep track of tasks and appointments. Use Tasks for things you'll do once; use Appointments for recurring events and meetings. Optionally, start by clicking on the date task or appointment date. Click the New Task button to create a new task, or click New Appointment to create a new appointment. Then fill in the blanks in the Detail pane. (If the Details pane is closed, press Ctrl+D or choose Details Pane from the View menu.)

Filling in information about the appointment or task is simple. In the top box, type a brief description of the appointment or task, like you might write on a paper calendar. Everything else is optional. But as you'll see, you can enter information about the location, the URL (if it's an online event at a Web site), start time, end time, reminders, attendees (for a meeting), and so forth. If you've already set up multiple calendars, you can choose the specific calendar on which you want to place the appointment.

If you're setting up an appointment, you can list attendees and send out e-mail invitations. This is easiest to do if you use Windows Contacts (Chapter 20) to manage all your names and addresses. Click Attendees and then use the dialog box that opens and click the To>> button to add people to the Attendees list. Click OK and all those people's names will be added to the Participants list. If you want to send an e-mail to all attendees (and you're using Windows Mail or another compatible e-mail client), click Invite. An e-mail message pre-addressed to all recipients opens. It also contains an attachment that recipients that have Windows Vista can open to add the appointment to their own calendars. Just type the main body of the message and click Send.

After you've filled in the blanks, the task or appointment title appears in the calendar. If you need to change or review an appointment, click the appointment entry on the calendar. If the Details pane is closed, press Ctrl+D or use the View menu to open it. Figure 15.30 shows a sample appointment titled Faculty Meeting.

 **Appointments aren't just for meetings. If you have to pay a bill each month, you can set it up like a recurring appointment, so you see the due date in each month of your calendar.**

FIGURE 15.30

Faculty Meeting appointment.

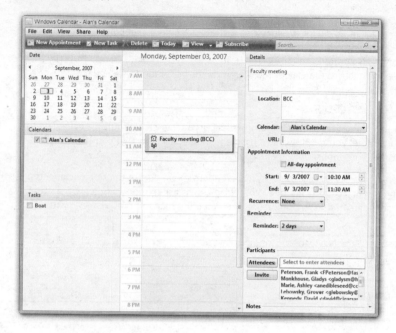

Adding a received invitation to your Calendar

If someone sends you an appointment invitation from Windows Calendar, the message subject will start with INVITE in uppercase letters. When you click the message header, you'll see the text of the message and a large paper clip icon representing the attachment, as in Figure 15.31.

FIGURE 15.31

Received calendar appointment by e-mail.

CAUTION It would be fairly easy for someone to make an attachment look like an appointment when in fact the attachment contains malware. Always exercise judgment when opening any kind of e-mail attachment. If the message is from someone you don't know, don't open the attachment. Just delete the entire message.

To add the appointment to your calendar, click the paper-clip icon, then click its name in the drop-down menu. In the dialog box that opens, choose Open. In the dialog box that opens, choose your main calendar (or another calendar of your own choosing) from the Destination button. Then click Import. To verify that the appointment was imported, navigate to the date of the appointment in Windows Calendar.

Creating multiple calendars

You can use a single calendar for all your tasks and appointments. Or you can create multiple calendars for different types of events. For example, you might want to have a personal calendar that you keep to yourself. Create a second calendar that you publish for other people to see.

To create a new calendar, choose File ➪ New Calendar from Calendar's menu bar. In the Details pane, type a name for the calendar. Then choose a color from the Colors drop-down list. Windows Calendar shows appointments from different calendars in different colors, so you can tell which appointments go with which calendar.

To use multiple calendars, first open the Navigation pane (if it isn't already open). You'll see a list of calendars in the left column as in Figure 15.32.

FIGURE 15.32

Two calendars in the Navigation pane.

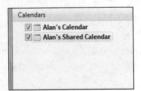

To show appointments from a calendar, select (check) that calendar's checkbox. For example, to see everything from all calendars, check all the checkboxes. To hide appointments from a calendar, click the checkmark next to the calendar's name. For instance, you might want to hide all but your shared calendar just before sharing your calendar for others to see.

Sharing calendars

Calendar sharing is a great way for people to see each other's schedules and plan accordingly. For example, imagine a family where everyone shares a single PC. Each family member has a user account and uses Windows Calendar to manage their schedule. Family members can share calendars so everyone knows what events are planned. To share a calendar, first select its name in the list of calendars you've created in the Navigation pane. Then choose Share ➪ Publish from the menu bar. You see options like those in Figure 15.33.

FIGURE 15.33

Sharing a calendar.

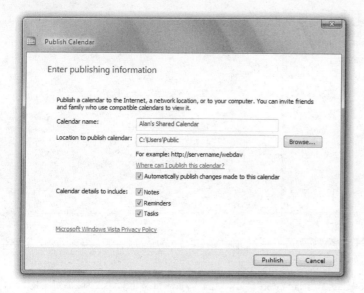

If you just want to share the calendar with other people who use the same computer, or are on the same network, you can click Browse and choose Public to put the calendar in the Public folder. Otherwise, if you have access to a server that allows you to publish your calendar to the Internet, you can type the appropriate URL into the "Location to publish calendar" box. Click the "Where can I publish this calendar?" link for more information on places you can publish a calendar.

The rest is easy. To ensure that your shared copy of the calendar is always up-to-date with changes you make, choose the Automatically publish changes made to this calendar checkbox. Then choose the items you want to share from the calendar using the checkboxes.

Click Publish after making your selections. On the next page, you can click the Announce button to create a Windows Mail e-mail message that contains information about your shared calendar. Fill in the To: line with the e-mail address of each person to whom you want to announce your calendar. Be sure to put a semicolon (;) between each address. Then send the e-mail. Click Finish when you're done.

Viewing shared calendars

To view a calendar that someone else has shared, you subscribe to that calendar. You need to know where that calendar is located. Hopefully the person who published the calendar has sent you an e-mail, which contains the address of the calendar. If so, you can drag the mouse pointer through the calendar's location in the e-mail message, then press Ctrl+C to copy that location. Once you know the location, click Subscribe in Calendar's toolbar, or choose Share ⇨ Subscribe from the menu bar. Then type (or paste) the calendar's location into the Subscribe window that opens. For example, in Figure 15.34, I'm about to subscribe to a calendar in the C:\Users\Public folder.

FIGURE 15.34

Subscribing to a calendar.

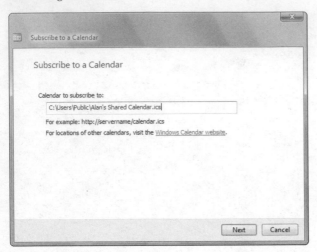

Click Next after entering the shared calendar's location and filename. On the next page, you can specify a different name for the calendar, if you like. You can choose how often you want Windows Vista to check the shared calendar for changes. And you can choose to include or remove reminders and tasks. Then click Finish.

The shared calendar shows up in your list of calendars in the Navigation pane in the left column. When its name is selected (checked), appointments from that calendar show up in your main calendar in the center pane. To hide those appointments, clear the checkmark next to the shared calendar's name.

Subscribing to online .iCalendars

Many companies that stage events, as well as TV and radio shows, publish their schedules online using the popular .iCalendar format. Windows Calendar fully supports that format. So you can subscribe to any calendar you find online. Often you'll find the link for subscribing to a calendar near any links for subscribing to RSS feeds. The link for the calendar will show ICAL or something to that effect. Click that link and follow the onscreen instructions to subscribe.

The calendar to which you've subscribed is listed along with others in your Navigation pane. Select or clear its checkbox to show or hide events from the calendar.

Searching the Calendar

You can search the Calendar from the Search box in its upper-right corner. Type as many characters as necessary to make the item you're searching for show up under Search Results. Then double-click the item to move to it in your Calendar.

If Windows Calendar isn't open, you don't have to open it first. Press ⊞ and type some characters from the appointment or task title or description. Calendar items that match what you've typed appear on the Start menu as the calendar's name. Click an item to open Windows Calendar with the appointment showing in the Details pane.

Managing and printing calendars

You can manage calendars in much the same way you do files. For example, to rename a calendar, right-click its name in the Navigation pane, choose Rename, and press Enter. To delete a calendar, right-click its name and choose Delete. To e-mail a calendar to someone using Windows Mail, right-click the calendar name and choose Send Via E-mail. To bring a subscribed calendar up-to-date, right-click its name and choose Sync. Or choose Sync All to bring all your subscribed calendars up-to-date.

To change the color coding used for a calendar, click the calendar's name in the Navigation pane. Then open the Details pane if it isn't already open (press Ctrl+D). Then choose a color from the Color drop-down list.

To print a calendar, click Print in the toolbar or choose File ➪ Print from the menu bar. Choose the style of calendar you want to print (Day, Work Week, Week, Month). Then specify starting and ending dates under Print Range and click OK.

To import a calendar that someone sent you as a standalone .ics file, choose File ➪ Import from Calendar's menu bar. Use the Browse button to navigate to the folder in which you've stored the calendar. Then under Destination, choose whether you want to create a new calendar, or merge the calendar's appointments into one of your existing calendars. Then click Import.

NOTE Importing a calendar is a one-shot deal. The calendar is updated to reflect changes or new appointments. This is different from subscribing, where your copy of the calendar can be automatically updated to reflect the most recent version of the calendar.

To export a calendar, choose File ➪ Export and specify a location and name for the calendar. You can then e-mail that, as an attachment, to other folks if you wish. Note, however, that this is not the same as publishing or sharing a calendar. Exporting, like importing, is a one-shot deal. The exported calendar is not automatically updated to reflect new appointments or changes you make after exporting.

Like all programs, Windows Calendar has its own Help system that you can refer to for more information. Choose Help ➪ Windows Calendar Help, or press F1 while Calendar is in the active window. But most of all, you'll just want to spend some time using it and exploring the different views. Like anything, it's real easy to use once you get the hang of it.

Wrap Up

This chapter has covered some of Windows Vista's relatively small and simple accessory programs. The bigger programs get entire chapters elsewhere in the book. Here's a quick review of what we covered here:

- Most programs have their own built-in help. You should always refer to the Help for information that's specific to that program.

- Use Calculator as you would a simple pocket calculator or a more advanced scientific calculator.

- WordPad is a freebie watered-down version of Microsoft Word that comes free with Vista. You can use it to type letters and other relatively simple documents.

- The basic skills for typing and editing text in WordPad apply to virtually all programs that allow you to work with text. Most even work in small textboxes found on forms.

- Copy-and-paste, which works in WordPad, is really a universal Windows Vista basic skill that every computer user needs to learn.

- To type special characters into a document, use Character Map.

- To add new fonts to your system, use the Fonts folder.
- To combine multiple files and folders into a single compressed folder (Zip file), select their icons. Then right-click any selected icon and choose Send To ➪ Compressed (zipped) Folder.
- To extract files and folders from a Zip file, right-click its icon and choose Extract All.
- To take and annotate screenshots, use the Snipping Tool.
- To resize pictures, use Paint (unless you have a better graphics program installed).
- To record your spoken voice, use Sound Recorder.
- Windows Calendar is a great way to keep track of, and share, appointments.

Chapter 16

Troubleshooting Customization Problems

Desktop Problems

The desktop is where you'll spend most of your time. To keep it looking the way you want, here are some tips to common problems you might run into while configuring your desktop.

My screen is too large/small; my screen colors look awful

For the best view of your desktop, your screen resolution should be set to at least 800x600 and color depth to at least 16 bits. To do so, follow these steps:

1. Right-click the Vista desktop and choose Personalize. Or tap ⊞, type pers, and click Personalization.
2. Click the Display Settings link.
3. Set the Resolution option to 800x600 or greater.
4. Set the Colors setting to at least 16 bit, as in Figure 16.1.
5. Click OK.

If you're not happy with the results, you can repeat the steps to try other resolutions and color depths. If the desktop doesn't fit right on the screen after you change the resolution, see the next troubleshooting section.

If you can't get your screen to show anything better than the absolute minimum, the driver for your card probably isn't compatible with Windows Vista. See "Updating your Display Driver" later in this chapter.

FIGURE 16.1

Screen Resolution and Color quality settings.

When I right-click the Vista desktop, I don't get a Personalize option

You're most likely right-clicking something that's covering the desktop, such as an icon or program window. Right-click the clock in the lower-right corner of the screen and choose Show the Desktop. Then you'll see, and can right-click, the actual Vista desktop.

As an alternative, click the Start button, type `pers`, and click Personalization to get to the Personalization options.

Parts of my screen are cut off or blank

When the desktop doesn't fill the screen correctly, you need to adjust settings on the monitor. You use knobs or buttons on the monitor to do that, not your mouse or keyboard. Exactly how you do it varies from one monitor to the next. But the typical scenario is to use the monitor's OSD (onscreen display) options. In particular, you need to adjust the Height, Vertical Centering, Width, and Horizontal Centering settings.

If you can't figure out how to use the monitor buttons, your only other recourse is to check the documentation that came with the monitor or notebook computer. Or, search the manufacturer's Web site for information on that specific model of monitor or notebook computer.

My desktop picture doesn't fit right

You can use any picture that's on your computer as the background (also called a *wallpaper*) for your desktop. Any picture that's as large as, or larger than, your screen (as defined by the Resolution setting in Display Settings) will automatically fill the screen. Smaller pictures can be centered, tiled, or stretched to fill the screen. To choose a picture and how you want it displayed, follow these steps:

1. Right-click the Windows desktop and choose Personalize.
2. In the Personalization window that opens, click the Desktop Background link.
3. Clicking the drop-down box lists different categories of backgrounds. Selecting one of the options in the drop-down list will display all of the available backgrounds for that category. After you've selected a category, you can select the background or click the Browse button to find a different picture.
4. If the picture does not fit the desktop, choose one of the following options from the How should the picture be positioned? section, as in Figure 16.2:
   - **Fit to screen:** The picture is stretched to fill the screen.
   - **Tile:** The picture is shown at actual size, but tiled to fill the screen.
   - **Center:** The picture is shown at actual size centered on the screen.
5. Click OK.

FIGURE 16.2

Available options for setting the appearance of the desktop background.

If you choose the Tile option but the picture doesn't repeat, it's because the picture is as large, or larger, than the desktop. The Tile option only works with pictures that are smaller than the desktop.

Everything is huge; can't see all of dialog boxes

If you get carried away with setting a larger DPI (dots per inch), you could end up in a situation where everything is so large, you can't even get to the buttons needed to change things back to the way they were. Follow the steps under the heading "Adjust the font size (DPI)" in Chapter 11. Step 5 in that procedure uses the keyboard rather than the mouse to make sure you can get to the OK button, even if it isn't visible on your screen.

Icon names are too big or too small

In Chapter 11 you learn how to get your screen looking just the way you want. For now, if you just want to increase the size of the text on your screen, follow these steps:

1. Right-click the desktop and choose Personalize.
2. Click the Windows Color and Appearance link.
3. Click the Open classic appearance properties for more color options link.
4. Click the Advanced button.
5. In the Advanced Appearance window that opens, select Icon from the Item drop-down list.
6. From the Size drop-down list associated with the Font, choose the size of the font desired, as shown in Figure 16.3. Optionally, you can choose a different Size and Color, and set the Bold and Italics settings for your Icon font.
7. Click OK twice to return to the Personalization screen.

That should be enough to make the text large enough to read.

 To make the icons larger or smaller, click any empty area on the desktop. Then hold down the Ctrl key as you spin your mouse wheel.

FIGURE 16.3

Adjust the icon desktop font.

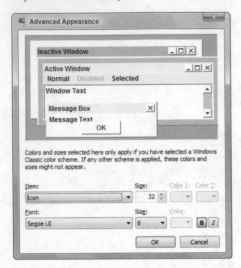

I don't have any desktop icons (or don't like their size)

If you don't have any desktop icons, they're probably turned off. Right-click the desktop and choose View ⇨ Show Desktop Icons. To change their size, right-click the desktop and choose View. Then click one of the icon sizes to the right (Large, Medium, Classic). If your mouse has a wheel, hold down the Ctrl key while spinning the wheel for other sizes.

I can't put my desktop icons where I want them

If you drag an icon to a new location on the desktop, and it moves right back to where it was, right-click the desktop and choose View ⇨ Auto Arrange to turn off that feature.

To sort desktop icons, right-click the desktop, choose Sort By, and try different options on the submenu to see different sort orders.

My screen saver never kicks in

If your monitor is set to power down before your screen saver starts, you'll never see the screen saver. You either have to make your screen saver start sooner or make your monitor turn off later. To make the monitor turn off later, press ⊞ or click the Start button, type pow, and click Power Options. In the left column, click "Choose when to turn off the display" and set a time limit that's longer than the screen saver delay. Similarly, if the computer goes to sleep before the screen saver kicks in, you'll never see the screen saver.

See Chapter 50 for more information on power options.

Missing Aero Glass, Flip 3D, or Switch between Windows button

Aero Glass is an optional interface that's available only with certain kinds of video cards. For more information, see "A New Look and Feel" in Chapter 1.

To use Aero Glass, you must have a compatible video card and also choose an Aero Glass theme. To ensure that you're using an Aero Glass theme, follow these steps:

1. Click the Start button, type `pers`, and click Personalize. Or right-click the desktop and choose Personalize.
2. In the Personalization window, click Theme.
3. Click the Theme button and choose Windows Vista.
4. Click OK.

If your video card supports Aero Glass, you should see the transparency effect. If you hold down ⊞ and press Tab, you should see the Flip 3D effect.

If you can get Aero Glass, and also the Flip 3D effect from the ⊞+Tab keys, you should already have a Switch between Windows button on your Quick Launch toolbar. Point to each button to see its name. If there's a >> symbol at the right side of the Quick Launch toolbar, click that to see other buttons that don't fit.

If your video card is supposed to support Aero Glass but doesn't, you might need to update its driver. See "Updating your Display Driver" near the end of this chapter.

Start Menu Problems

Most applications will install an icon on the Start menu. When your Start menu stops looking the way it should, it can really slow you down. Here are some tips to keep your Start menu looking the way you want.

My Start menu shows one column, not two

1. Right-click the Start button and choose Properties.
2. Choose the Start menu option (not the Classic Start menu option).
3. Click OK.

Some Start items can't be displayed

If clicking the Start button displays *Some Start items can't be displayed*, you'll need to reduce the number of items on the Start menu or use small icons. Try reducing the number of items first by following these steps:

1. Right-click the Start button and choose Properties.
2. Click the enabled Customize button next to Start menu.
3. In the Customize Start Menu window, deselect the Use large icons checkbox that appears at the bottom of the list box. Then:
   - If you want to use smaller icons, scroll down the list of options and clear the checkmark next to "Use large icons."
   - If you want to keep using large icons, reduce the number next to Start menu size to a smaller number like 6.
4. Click OK in each open dialog box.

Eventually you'll get a sense of how many icons can fit in the lower-left side of the menu. If you set the Start menu size number to the number of icons that can fit in that space, you'll get just the right amount of icons in that space without seeing the "Some Start menu items can't be displayed" message.

The right side of my Start menu is missing some options

Chapter 11 explains how to customize your Start menu. If you're just looking for a quick fix right now, follow these steps:

1. Right-click the Start button and choose Properties.

2. Click the Customize button.

3. In the list box that appears on the Customize Start Menu window, choose (check) any items you want on the menu and clear the checkmark next to any items you don't want.

4. Click OK in each of the open dialog boxes.

Taskbar Problems

The taskbar provides quick access to all of your open applications, assuming it's working correctly. The taskbar includes the Quick Launch toolbar, which enables you to run applications that have shortcuts created in this area. Here are some tips for managing your taskbar problems.

My taskbar is missing

It's probably just hidden. Touch the mouse pointer to the very bottom of the screen and it should scroll up into view. To make it stop going into hiding:

1. Press ⊞ or Ctrl+Esc to open the Start menu, type `task`, and click Taskbar and Start Menu on the Start menu.

2. Click the Taskbar tab and click the checkmark next to Auto-Hide the taskbar. Select (check) all other options.

3. Click OK.

My taskbar is too tall (or messed up)

First make sure the taskbar is unlocked and close all optional toolbars so you can better see what's going on. Here's how:

1. Press ⊞ or Ctrl+Esc to open the Start menu, type `task`, and click Taskbar and Start Menu on the Start menu.

2. Click the Taskbar tab and click the checkmark next to Lock the taskbar. Select (check) all other options.

3. Click the Toolbars tab and clear all checkmarks.

4. Click OK or press Enter.

5. Put the tip of the mouse pointer on the top of the taskbar until the mouse pointer turns into a two-headed arrow, and then hold down the left mouse button while moving the mouse toward you to shrink the taskbar to one row tall.

6. Right-click the current time in the lower-right corner of the screen and choose Lock the taskbar to lock the taskbar to that height.

See "Customizing the Taskbar" in Chapter 11 for more information.

I don't have a Quick Launch toolbar

Right-click the current time in the lower-right corner of the screen and choose Toolbars ➪ Quick Launch from the menu that appears.

I don't have a Show Desktop button on my Quick Launch toolbar

First make sure the Quick Launch toolbar is visible. Right-click the current time in the lower-right corner of the screen and choose Toolbars. If Quick Launch doesn't have a checkmark next to it, click that option to open the Quick Launch toolbar. If Quick Launch is already checked, press Esc to close the menu without making a selection.

If you see a >> symbol at the right side of the Quick Launch toolbar, click it. The button may just be hidden because it doesn't fit on the Quick Launch toolbar. You can move any button by dragging it to a new location on the Quick Launch toolbar. Widen the Quick Launch toolbar to see more buttons. See the section "Customizing the Taskbar" in Chapter 11 for more information.

If the Show Desktop button is nowhere to be found on your Quick Launch toolbar, it may be in the Recycle Bin. Open the Recycle Bin and look for an icon named Shows Desktop. If you find it, right-click it and choose Restore. The button will either be on the Quick Launch toolbar or the menu that appears when you click >> on the Quick Launch toolbar.

If all else fails, you may be able to find another instance of the icon by following these steps:

1. Click the Start button and choose Search.
2. In the Search folder, click Advanced Search.
3. Click the Location button and choose Local Hard Drives.
4. In the Filename box, type Show Desktop and click Search. Wait a few seconds for the search to complete.
5. If Search finds an icon named Show desktop of the type Shortcut, right-click that icon and choose Send To ➪ Desktop (Create Shortcut).
6. Close the Search window.
7. Drag the Show Desktop icon from the desktop onto the Quick Launch toolbar.

To remove the icon that's still on the desktop, right-click it and choose Delete ➪ Yes.

Updating your Display Driver

Problems that prevent you from setting a reasonable desktop size and color depth are often caused by the device driver for the video card. Similarly, if a video card meets all of the requirements for Aero Glass, and you still can't get Aero Glass to work, you might need to update your display driver. Follow these steps:

1. If you're in a standard user account, log in to an account that has administrative privileges.
2. Connect to the Internet so Windows can look for a new driver online.
3. Open Device Manager (press 🎛 or click the Start button, type dev, and click Device Manager).
4. Click the + sign (if any) next to Display Adapters.
5. Right-click the icon that represents your video card and choose Update Driver Software. Figure 16.4 shows an example.

 The name that shows under Display Adapters will likely be different on your computer. Also, only one name will likely be listed.

FIGURE 16.4

Updating the device driver for a video card.

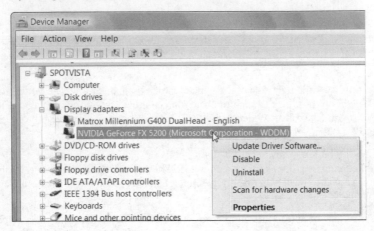

6. Follow the onscreen instructions.

If the search doesn't find an updated driver, you might already have the latest driver for your video card. The only way to know for sure is to visit the card manufacturer's Web site and look up the latest driver for your specific video card.

Part IV

Power Using the Internet

The Internet has become so interwoven into our daily lives it's nearly impossible to get things done without it. Without a doubt, most people use their PCs to access the Internet more than anything else. This part of the book is all about the tools that come with Vista to do just that—use the Internet.

Chapter 17 starts off with an in-depth look at Microsoft Internet Explorer, the Web browser that comes free with Windows Vista. You need a Web browser to access Web sites like eBay, Google, Windows Live, and others.

Chapter 18 covers Windows Mail, the built-in program for doing e-mail and accessing newsgroups like the Windows Communities. Windows Mail is a big improvement over its predecessor Outlook Express and is well worth a look. It ties in with Vista's new search features, which makes it easy to find e-mail messages right from the Start menu, without opening the program first and digging around through folders.

Chapter 19 moves on to other Internet-related topics like newsgroups, FTP, and Remote Assistance. Chapter 20 covers Windows Contacts, a handy feature for managing names and addresses and a big improvement over the Windows Address Book (WAB) of yesteryear. Chapter 21 then covers some solutions to common Internet problems.

Chapter 17

Browsing and Blogging with Internet Explorer

Next to e-mail, the World Wide Web is one of biggest reasons many people buy and own computers. The Web consists of billions of pages of information as well as pictures, music, and video. The Web is also home to Windows Live, which brings Web content to your computer in fun and novel ways.

To use the Web, you need an Internet connection and a *Web browser*. A Web browser is a program that lets you browse (explore) the Web and find whatever you're looking for. The Web browser that comes with Windows Vista is named Internet Explorer 7. And that's what this chapter is mainly about. It starts with a brief look at how the Web works.

How the Web Works

The Internet consists of tens of millions of computers throughout the world connected by cables. A few million of those computers are *Web servers*, computers that store, and dish out, copies of Web pages to anyone who asks for a copy. The program you use to access and view Web pages is called a *Web browser*. Many brands of Web browsers are on the market, including AOL Explorer, Netscape Navigator, Firefox, and Windows Internet Explorer. This chapter is about Windows Internet Explorer Version 7, the Web browser that comes free with Windows Vista.

All Web pages use the Hypertext Transfer Protocol (HTTP). For that reason, the URL (Uniform Resource Locator) for every Web page starts with `http://`. After the `http://` comes the host name, the name of a particular computer at some location. The host name is often www (for World Wide Web), but can be any combination of letters.

A Web site can consist of any number of pages. The first or main page for a Web site is called its *home page*. The home page for a Web site is just the protocol, host name, and domain name. For example, Microsoft's home page is at `http://www.microsoft.com`. Google's home page is at `http://www.google.com`. eBay's home page is at `http://www.ebay.com`.

Notice how all the URLs I just showed you end in `.com`. That last part of the URL is called the top-level domain (TLD). The examples I just showed you all end in `.com` because they're *com*mercial (business) Web sites. The most common top-level domains, their meaning, and examples are shown in Table 17.1.

TABLE 17.1

Examples of Top-Level Domains and URLs of Web Sites

Top-Level Domain (TLD)	Type	Example URL
.com	Commercial	`www.amazon.com`
.edu	Education	`www.ucla.edu`
.gov	Government	`www.fbi.gov`
.org	Nonprofit organization	`www.redcross.org`
.net	Network	`www.comcast.net`
.mil	Military	`www.army.mil`

Notice that I didn't put the http:// in front of the example URLs in Table 17.1. You rarely see the http:// used at the front of a URL. Typically you just see them expressed as `www.microsoft.com` or `www.ebay.com`. That's because virtually all Web pages use http:// as the protocol. In fact, when you type a URL into your Web browser's Address bar and leave off the http:// part, the browser just fills it in for you and makes the connection.

All Web browsers work the same way. You type a URL into the Address bar and press Enter or click Go. That sends a packet of information off to your ISP (Internet service provider) who in turns hands if off the Internet. When on the Internet, the packet arrives at the Web server as a request that means "Hey, send me your Web page." The Web browser dutifully responds by sending out the requested page, which makes its way back to your ISP and then to your PC. You see the results as a Web page in your Web browser. Figure 17.1 illustrates the basic idea.

Remember, there are billions of Web pages out on the Web. You can access any one of them with any Web browser and any type of Internet connection. It doesn't matter who your ISP is or what Web browser you're using. Everyone has access to all Web pages.

The time it takes from when you first make the request for a page and when you actually see the page, depends on the speed of your Internet connection. It's usually only a matter of seconds. With really fast Internet connections, it might seem like no time at all.

FIGURE 17.1

Requesting and viewing a Web page.

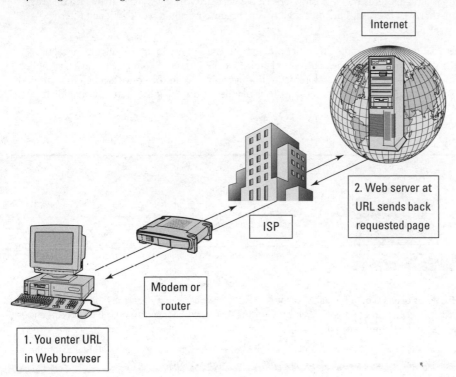

Internet

2. Web server at
URL sends back
requested page

ISP

Modem or
router

1. You enter URL
in Web browser

Windows Explorer versus Internet Explorer

People often confuse Windows Explorer and Internet Explorer because of their similar names. But there is a big difference. Windows Explorer (often called Explorer for short) is a program for exploring things *inside* your computer. Things like disk drives, folders, and files that you can use without being online. If your computer is part of a local network, you use Windows Explorer to access shared resources on those nearby computers as well.

Internet Explorer is for exploring stuff *outside* your computer. Mainly World Wide Web pages on the Internet. You have to be online (connected to the Internet) to explore those outside resources. The items outside your computer are mostly Web pages, rather than drives, folders, and files. Web pages have longer names, usually in the form of www.something.com. Not short, simple names like Computer, Documents, Pictures, and such.

Using Internet Explorer

As mentioned, Internet Explorer is the Web browser that comes with Windows Vista. There's no rule that says you must use that Web browser. But you certainly can, because it should work with any Internet account with any ISP.

You start Internet Explorer as you would any other program. If Internet Explorer is configured as your *default* (preferred) Web browser, click the Start button and click the Internet Explorer icon near the top left of the Start menu. Or, click the Internet Explorer icon (lowercase blue e) in the Quick Launch toolbar. Both are pointed out in Figure 17.2. If neither of those icons is plainly visible, click the Start button and choose All Programs ➪ Internet Explorer.

FIGURE 17.2

Starting Internet Explorer.

When Internet Explorer opens, you'll be taken to your *default home page*. That's just the fancy name for the first Web page you see when you open your Web browser. As discussed later in this chapter, you can choose any page you like as your default home page.

 **TIP** You can minimize, maximize, move, and size Internet Explorer's program window using the basic skills described under "Arranging program windows" in Chapter 2.

Browsing to a Web site

To browse to a Web site for the first time, click inside Internet Explorer's Address bar and type the URL. You don't need to type the http:// part. But you do need to type everything that comes after that part. Don't type any blank spaces, and be sure to use forward slashes (/), not backslashes (\). After you've typed the URL, press Enter or click the Go button to the right. Figure 17.3 shows an example of the URL for the Google search site typed into Internet Explorer's Address bar.

FIGURE 17.3

Typing a URL.

After you press Enter or click Go, Internet Explorer adds the leading http:// part for you. The page at that URL shows up on your screen shortly thereafter. If it seems to be taking forever for the page to appear and you don't want to wait any longer, click the Stop button. Then click the Back button, if necessary, to return to the previous page.

 URLs aren't case-sensitive, so it's okay to type them in all lowercase letters.

It's not entirely necessary to type the entire URL. If the URL that's currently in the Address bar is similar to the one you're about to type, you can select just the part you want to change. Then type in the new part. For example, Figure 17.4 shows the `google` portion of a URL selected by dragging the mouse pointer in it. Type another name, like `ebay` at that point, replacing `google` with `ebay` so the URL becomes `www.ebay.com`. Press Enter or click Go to browse.

FIGURE 17.4

Editing an URL.

Using AutoComplete

Internet Explorer remembers URLs you've typed in the past. When the URL you're typing matches ones you've typed in the past, a *history menu* will drop down, showing those previous URLs. For example, you can select (drag the mouse pointer through) all of the text after the `http://www.` to select it. Start typing the replacement text, and the drop-down menu will show previously visited pages that start with the same letters.

For example, the top of Figure 17.5 shows all the text to the right of the `www.` selected after browsing to eBay. Typing the letter g then shows all previously visited URLs that start with `http://www.g` as in the bottom of that figure. Rather than continue typing the URL, just click the full URL in the drop-down menu.

FIGURE 17.5

Drop-down menu of previous URLs.

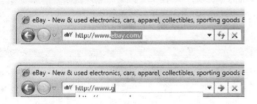

 Although convenient, the drop-down menu of visited sites isn't the best way to organize and revisit favorite Web sites. Better to use the Favorites Center described under "Managing Favorite Sites" later in this chapter. To clear out or disable the drop-down menu, see "Deleting the Browser History" later in this chapter.

Using hyperlinks

When you're at a Web site, you may not have to do much more typing of URLs. After you're at a page, you can click any *hyperlink* (also called a *link*) to go to whatever page the link represents. A hyperlink can be text, a picture, or a button. A text hyperlink is usually blue, underlined text. However, if you've already visited the page that a text hyperlink points to, the hyperlink is magenta.

A picture hyperlink might not look like anything special. But you can tell if a picture is a hyperlink by putting the mouse pointer on it. If the mouse pointer changes to a small pointing hand, then you can click the picture to go to the page or item that's linked to the picture.

Using Back, Forward, and History buttons

The Back and Forward buttons maintain a history of your current Web-browsing session. A session starts when you first open your Web browser. The session ends when you close your Web browser. For this reason, the Back button is always disabled (dimmed) when you first open your browser. That's because there's no page to go back to when you first open your browser. But as soon as you go to another page, the Back button is enabled so you can click it to return to the previous page.

 **TIP**   You can also press the Backspace key to go back to the previous page.

The Forward button is disabled until you've clicked Back at least once. When the Forward button is enabled, you can click it to return to the page where you clicked the Back button.

Clicking the little arrow to the right of the Forward button (see Figure 17.6) displays a menu of pages you've visited recently. Click any page in that list to return to it. Or click History at the bottom of the menu to see the History pane. The History pane shows a more extensive list of recently visited Web sites. Click any one to expand it to see pages within the site you've been to lately. Click any page under the heading to go to the page.

FIGURE 17.6

Back, Forward, and History buttons.

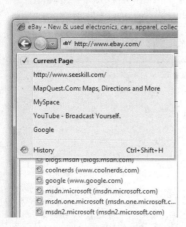

To delete a link from the History pane, right-click it and choose Delete. To close the History pane so it's out of your way, click the X button near its upper-right corner.

 **TIP**   To clear out the entire History, click the Tools button and choose **Delete Browsing History**.

Magnifying a page

Now you can increase just the text size, or the entire page — including pictures.

If it's difficult to read the small text on a Web page, you can zoom in for a closer look. There are actually two ways to do this. You can enlarge only the text and keep pictures at their current size. Or you can zoom in on pictures and text.

■ To change the text size only, click the Page button (see Figure 17.7), click Text Size, and then click a text size.

FIGURE 17.7

Page button and menu.

■ To change the size of text and pictures, click the Page button, click Zoom, and choose a magnification.

 For quick zooming from the keyboard, hold down the Ctrl key and tap the + key repeatedly to zoom in. Hold down the Ctrl key and press the – (hyphen) key to zoom out.

Panes and toolbars

Like many programs, Internet Explorer has optional panes and toolbars. These are all accessible from the View menu on the menu bar. If you don't see the menu bar, press the Alt key or click Tools and choose Menu bar.

■ To show or hide an optional pane, choose View ➪ Explorer Bar and click a pane name.

■ To show or hide a toolbar, choose View ➪ Toolbars from the menu bar.

■ You can widen or narrow a pane by dragging its inner border left or right.

■ To customize the Command Bar (the one with the Page and Tools buttons), right-click an empty area at the right side of the menu bar or links bar and choose Customize Command Bar.

Full screen viewing

When you're viewing a large Web page that's partially cut off, you can switch to full screen view. That will get Internet Explorer's program window out of the way temporarily so you can see more of the page. To go to full screen view, choose View ⇨ Full Screen from the menu, or press F11.

While you're in full screen view, you can bring down just the Address bar and toolbar so you can go to another page, print the current page, or whatever. Just move the mouse pointer to the top of the screen and those items will drop down into view. They'll slide out of view again when you move the mouse pointer back to the page.

To leave full screen view and get back to the regular program window, press F11.

Change your default home page

The page that first appears when you open your Web browser is called your *default home page*. Initially it's whatever Microsoft or your computer manufacturer wanted it to be. But you can change that at any time. It's a simple process:

1. Browse to the page that you want to make your new default home page.

2. Click the arrow on the Home button, shown near the mouse pointer in Figure 17.8, and choose Add or Change Home Page.

FIGURE 17.8

Home button.

3. If you haven't yet used multiple tabs (discussed next), choose Use this webpage as your only home page and click Yes.

No matter where you are on the Internet, you can always get back to your default home page just by clicking the Home button in Internet Explorer.

If you have two or more Web sites you visit regularly, you can set up multiple home pages using tabs.

Using Tabs

NEW FEATURE   Use tabs to keep multiple Web pages open. Or use them to set up multiple home pages so all your favorite sites are in easy reach as soon as you open Internet Explorer.

Tabbed browsing is a new feature of Internet Explorer. Tabs appear under the menu bar. They let you keep multiple pages going in a session. When you use multiple tabs, each tab shows the title of the page that's currently open in that tab. To open a new tab and display a page in it, click the empty tab to the right of the open tabs, or press Ctrl+T. Then enter the URL of the page you want to visit in the Address bar.

 If tabs aren't available in your Internet Explorer, see "Personalizing tabbed browsing" later in this section.

You can switch from one tabbed page to the next just by clicking any tab. To switch from tab to tab using the keyboard, press Ctrl+Tab to go to the next tab. Press Shift+Ctrl+Tab to go to the previous tab.

You can also open tabs in the background. When you do, the new tab opens to display a page. But you're not taken directly to that page. You stay where you are so you can open additional tabs from the current page. To open a tab in the background:

- Hold down the Ctrl key while you click any hyperlink.
- Or right-click any hyperlink and choose Open in New Tab.
- Or, if your mouse has a wheel, click the hyperlink with the mouse wheel.

The new page will open in a separate tab, but you'll only see the tab, not the page. When you're ready to view the page, just click its tab.

When you close Internet Explorer with multiple tabs open, you'll see a prompt asking if you want to close all tabs. Click Cancel if your intent was to close only one tab. Otherwise, click Close Tabs to close all open tabs and Internet Explorer. To stop seeing that message, check the Do not warn me when closing multiple tabs checkbox.

Here are some other good things to know about tabs:

- To open a page in a new tab and bring it to the foreground, hold down the Ctrl and Shift keys when you click a hyperlink.
- To open a new page in the foreground from the Address bar, type the URL in the Address bar and press Alt+Enter.
- To close a tab, click it with your mouse wheel. Or click it and then click the Close (X) button on that tab or press Ctrl+W.
- To close all tabs except one, right-click the tab you want to keep and choose Close Other Tabs (see Figure 17.9).

FIGURE 17.9

Right-click a tab.

 You can also save tab groups as favorites. See "Managing Favorite Sites" later in this chapter.

Using Quick Tabs

You can click the Quick Tabs button, or choose View ⇨ Quick Tabs or press Ctrl+Q to see a miniature version of each open page. Click any miniature page to open and view its tab. Figure 17.10 shows an example with four pages open in four tabs and the Quick view open. Click any miniature page to bring the full page to the foreground.

FIGURE 17.10

Quick Tabs.

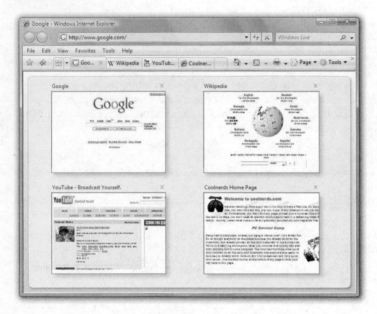

Creating multiple home page tabs

You can create multiple default home pages that all open automatically as soon as you start your Web browser. They're called *home page tabs* and are easy to set up. First click the empty tab. You see a blank page. Use the Address bar to browse to the page that you want to use as the default home page for that tab. Then click the Home button and choose Add or Change Home Page ⇨ Add this webpage to your home page tabs ⇨ Yes.

You can have as many home page tabs as you wish. But keep in mind that the more you have, the longer it will take for your Web browser to start. You don't want to use home page tabs as a substitute for Favorites. Limit them to perhaps the three or four Web sites you visit most often. If you get carried away, you can always remove a home page tab. Click the Home button, choose Remove, click the page you want to remove, and click Yes.

When you have all the default home pages you want open, each in its own tab, click the Home button, choose Add or Change Home Page, click Use the current tab set as your home page, and click Yes.

To test your multiple home pages, close Internet Explorer. Then re-open it. All of the home pages should open, each in its own tab. No matter where you happen to be in Internet Explorer, you can always get back to any one of your default home pages. Just click the arrow on the Page button and click the page you want to jump to.

 To browse without changing the contents of any tab, click the new, empty tab before entering an address. Or right-click a link in an existing tabbed page and choose Open in New Tab.

Rearranging and removing home page tabs

When you open Internet Explorer with multiple home page tabs. only the page in the first tab is visible. You may decide you want to rearrange those pages after you've been using them for a while. To rearrange home page tabs:

1. Click the Tools button and choose Internet Options or choose Tools ➪ Internet Option from Internet Explorer's menu bar.
2. On the General tab, select (drag the mouse pointer through) the URL you want to move. For example, in Figure 17.11, www.google.com is selected.

FIGURE 17.11

Home pages in Internet Options.

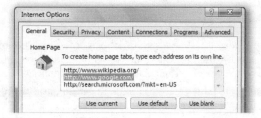

3. Press Ctrl+X to cut the line.
4. Press Delete (Del) to delete the blank line.
5. Move the cursor to the start of the line where you want to place the URL.
6. Press Ctrl+V to paste, and press Enter.
7. Make sure each URL appears on its own line and click OK.

To test the new arrangement, close and re-open Internet Explorer.

To remove a page from your home page tabs, remove its URL from the list on the General tab. To do that, select the line and press Delete (Del) twice; once to remove the text and a second time to delete the blank line left behind. Then click OK.

Personalizing tabbed browsing

You can enable or disable tabbed browsing, or tweak how tabs work. Click Tools and choose Internet Options or choose Tools ➪ Internet Options from Internet Explorer's menu. Then click the Settings button under the Tab heading. You'll see the options shown in Figure 17.12.

Tabbed browsing settings.

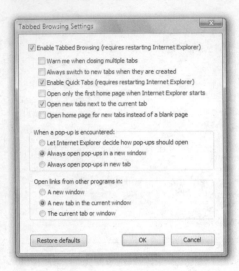

Here's what each option offers:

- **Enable Tabbed Browsing:** If you clear this checkbox, tabbed browsing is disabled and all options that apply to tabbed browsing are disabled. Check this option to allow tabbed browsing. If you change this setting, you need to click OK. Then close and re-open Internet Explorer.

- **Warn me when closing multiple tabs:** Clear this option to get rid of the warning that appears when closing Internet Explorer. Select this checkbox to bring the warning back.

- **Always switch to new tabs when they are created:** If you check this option, new tabs won't open in the background. So when you hold down the Ctrl+Click a link or click it with your mouse wheel, the linked page will still open in a new tab. But that tab will come to the foreground automatically.

- **Enable Quick Tabs:** Clearing this option removes the Quick Tabs button. The Quick Tabs button won't be visible to the left of the tabs. The Quick Tabs option on the View menu is disabled, and pressing Ctrl+Q has no effect. Select (check) this option to enable Quick Tabs. After you change this option, click OK, close Internet Explorer, and then re-open Internet Explorer.

- **Open only the first home page when Internet Explorer starts:** Select this option to allow for quicker startup. Only the first tabbed home page will open when you open Internet Explorer. To bring up other tabbed home pages, right-click the first tab and choose Restore Last Tab Group.

- **Open new tabs next to the current tab:** Choose this option to have each new tab open next to the current tab. Clear this option to make each new tab open at the end of current tabs.

- **Open home page for new tabs instead of blank page:** Choose this option to make new tabs open to the default home page. Clear this option to have new tabs open to a blank page with tabbing instructions.

- **When a pop-up is encountered:** A pop-up is any Web page that tries to open in a new Web browser. You'll learn more about pop-ups later in this chapter. But in the Tabbed Browsing Settings dialog box, your options are

    - **Let Internet Explorer decide:** Choose this option to let Internet Explorer decide how to open pop-ups based on your pop-up blocker settings and the URL of the pop-up.
    - **Always open pop-ups in a new window:** Choose this option to have acceptable pop-ups open in a new, separate instance of Internet Explorer.
    - **Always open pop-ups in a new tab:** Choose this option to have acceptable pop-ups open in a new tab rather than in a new instance of Internet Explorer.

- **Open link from other programs in:** These settings apply to other programs that can open Web pages, such as Window Mail. They only apply if Internet Explorer is already open when you click a link in that other program:

    - **A new window:** Pages you open from outside Internet Explorer open in a separate program window.
    - **A new tab in the current window:** Keeps current tabs intact by opening the new page in a new, separate tab.
    - **The current tab or window:** The new page opens in the current Internet Explorer window, replacing what was showing before. Clicking Internet Explorer's Back button takes you back to the page that was showing before.

- **Restore defaults:** Click this button to restore all Tabbed Browsing Settings.

Don't forget to click OK after making your choices. If you chose an option that requires restart, close Internet Explorer and restart it.

Shortcut keys for tabs

I mentioned several shortcut keys for using tabs in the preceding sections. For easy reference, Table 17.2 lists them all.

TABLE 17.2

Shortcut Keys for Tabs

Action	Shortcut
Open linked page in background tab	Ctrl+click the link or click with mouse wheel
Open linked page in foreground tab	Shift+Ctrl+Click the link
Open new page in foreground from the Address bar	Type the URL and press Alt+Enter
Open a new empty tab in the foreground	Ctrl+T
Open Quick Tabs	Ctrl+Q
Switch from tab to tab	Ctrl+Tab, Shift+Ctrl+Tab
Go to a specific tab	Ctrl+n where n is a number from 1 to 8
Go to the last tab	Ctrl+9
Close the current tab	Ctrl+W or click with mouse wheel
Close all tabs except the one in the foreground	Ctrl+Alt+F4

RSS Feeds: Blogging with Internet Explorer

NEW FEATURE You don't have to browse all your sites to see what's new. Use RSS feeds to have your favorite Web content delivered straight to your door.

The term *blog* is short for Web log. Blogs are also referred to as *XML feeds*, *RSS feeds*, or *syndicated content*. RSS stands for Really Simple Syndication, and that's basically what a blog is. It's informal content usually created and maintained by a single author.

The main difference between a blog and a Web page is that blogs are delivered to you automatically. Unlike a Web page, you don't have to browse to a blog to see what's new. When you subscribe to a blog, new blogs come to you automatically as soon as they're published. For this reason you're likely to find feeds at news sites, such as your local newspaper or TV station's Web sites. But any site can host RSS feeds.

When you browse to a Web page, take a look at the Feeds button in the Command Bar (see Figure 17.13). If it's orange and enabled, that means there are one or more feeds available from that page. Click the Feeds button to learn more about the available feeds. You might see several feeds when you click the Feeds button.

FIGURE 17.13

Feeds button at mouse pointer.

If you see a feed that looks interesting, click it in the drop-down menu under the Feeds button. You'll come to a new page that shows current feeds. If it looks interesting, you can subscribe to the feed. Most subscriptions are free. And you can unsubscribe at any time, so you're not making any big commitment when you subscribe to a feed. To subscribe, click + Subscribe to this feed on the feeds page. You'll see a dialog box like the one in Figure 17.14. To subscribe to a feed, just click the Subscribe button.

FIGURE 17.14

Subscribe to a feed.

Finding Feeds

The sample feeds in Figure 17.15 are just examples. You'll discover many on your own in your day-to-day Web browsing. As you browse from page to page, just glance up at the Feeds button to see if it's enabled. Here are some sites you might want to check out to get started:

www.mtv.com/rss

www.rss.cnn.com

news.google.com

www.microsoft.com/ie

www.ieaddons.com

weather.msn.com

www.nytimes.com

www.microsoft.com/vista

www.microsoft.com/athome/community

www.si.com

abclocal.go.com

online.wsj.com

www.reuters.com

www.microsoftgadgets.com

You can subscribe to as many feeds as you like. Internet Explorer automatically checks all feeds in the background for fresh content. To view feeds, click the Favorites Center button and then click Feeds (see Figure 17.15). You'll see a link to each subscribed feed. Click any feed's link to see current content.

FIGURE 17.15

Feeds in Favorites Center.

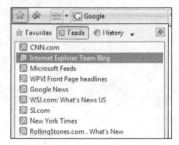

Optional settings for RSS feeds

There are a couple of settings you can tweak to change how RSS feeds behave. To get to them:

1. Click Tools on the Command Bar and choose Internet Options or choose Tools ⇨ Internet Options form Internet Explorer's menu.
2. Click the Content tab in the dialog box that opens.
3. Under the Feeds heading, click the Settings button.

The options in the dialog box that opens are largely self-explanatory. You can control if, and how often, feeds update automatically. The Automatically mark feed as read when reading a feed option automatically colors feeds you've read different from unread feeds to help you keep track. That option is only available if you also choose Turn on feed reading view. If you disable the feed reading view, your feeds will be difficult to read because they're displayed in the native XML format. Choosing Play a sound when a feed is found for a webpage is a good way to get an extra "heads up" beep when you land on a page that offers feeds.

As always, click OK in all open dialog boxes after making your selections.

Using the RSS Feeds gadget

If you use the Windows Sidebar, you can use the RSS Feeds gadget to keep an eye on feeds. Click the Add Gagdet (+) button at the bottom of the sidebar. Then drag the RSS Feeds gadget onto the sidebar. Once on the sidebar, touch the mouse pointer to the gadget. You'll see a white checkmark near the upper-right corner. Click that checkmark to open the dialog box shown in Figure 17.16. From there you can choose to have All Feeds displayed in the gadget. Or use the drop-down list to choose a specific feed.

FIGURE 17.16

RSS Feeds gadget dialog box.

> **NOTE**   For the full lowdown on Windows Sidebar and gadgets, see "Using Windows Sidebar" in Chapter 11.

You can have multiple RSS Feed gadgets on the sidebar. For instance, you might use one gadget to show content from a favorite feed and use a second gadget to show content from all feeds.

Managing Favorite Sites

Getting back to favorite Web sites by re-typing the URL each time gets tiresome. Fortunately it's also unnecessary because you get to any favorite site with a simple mouse click. You just have to remember to add the site to your Favorites while you're there. That's easy to do:

1. If you're not already at a favorite Web site or page, browse to it.
2. Do any of the following to add the page to your Favorites:
   - Click the Add to Favorites button (next to the Favorites start) and choose Add to Favorites.
   - Right-click some empty white space on the page and choose Add to Favorites.
   - Choose Favorites ➪ Add to Favorites from Internet Explorer's menu.

 You can create folders, rename folders, change page titles, and organize favorites into folders at any time. So feel free to skip all of the optional steps to follow.

   3. Optionally, if you want to type your own descriptive title for the page, replace the text shown in the Name box with your own name.

   4. Optionally, if you've already set up custom Favorites folders, click the Create In button and choose the folder in which you want to place the favorite.

   5. Optionally, to create a new Favorites folder, click New Folder, type the new folder name, and click Create.

   6. Click Add.

The Web site's title is added to your Favorites menu and the Favorites Center. To return to the site at any time in the future, choose Favorites from the menu and click the Web site's title. Or click the Favorites Center button (star) and click the site's title there.

TIP To create a desktop shortcut to the page you're currently viewing, choose File ⇨ Send ⇨ Shortcut to Desktop from Internet Explorer's menu. To e-mail a link or Web Page to someone, click Tools or choose File Í Page by E-mail or Link by E-mail.

Adding tab groups to Favorites

You can add a whole group of pages organized into tabs to your Favorites. For example, you might open several favorite shopping sites, music sites, sports sites, or whatever, each in its own tab. To save the whole tab group to your Favorites:

   1. Choose Favorites ⇨ Add Tab Group to Favorites from the menu. Or click the Add to Favorites button (+) and choose Add Tab Group to Favorites.

   2. Type in a folder name that describes the pages in the tab group (for example, Shopping Sites) and click Add.

The tab group is added to the Favorites Center and Favorites menu. To re-open the tab group and all its pages in the future, click the Favorites Center button (the one with the star in Figure 17.17). Then point to the name of the tab group and click the blue arrow that appears to the right. Or right-click the tab group name and choose Open in Tab Group.

FIGURE 17.17

Tab group in Favorites Center.

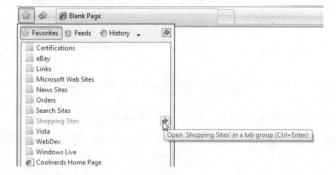

Starting Your Favorites Collection

If you're new to the Web and want to visit some useful Web sites that you might want to add to your Favorites, here are a few to help you get started. Not everyone will want to add all of these to his or her Favorites, of course. But you're likely to find some sites you'll want to revisit:

- `www.dictionary.com`: Look up a word in a dictionary or thesaurus, or translate text from one language to another.

- `www.wikipedia.org`: An online encyclopedia covering a multitude of topics in many languages.

- `www.ebay.com`: The ever-popular buy-and-sell-anything-and-everything site.

- `www.fandango.com`: Find out what movies are playing in your local theaters, their start times, and so forth.

- `www.google.com`: A popular site for searching the World Wide Web.

- `www.mapquest.com`: A great resource for maps and driving directions.

- `search.microsoft.com`: Search Microsoft's Web site for technical support. Other useful Microsoft pages include `www.microsoft.com/vista`, `download.microsoft.com`, and `www.windowsmarketplace.com`.

- `www.tucows.com`: A great resource for hard-to-find programs that you can download and try for free. Also try `www.download.com`.

- `www.usps.gov`: The United States Postal Service site, including a Calculate Postage option to figure out the cost of shipping an item.

Organizing Favorites

As your collection of favorite Web sites and RSS feeds grows, you might find it useful to organize them into folders. That way, you won't be faced with a huge list of favorites each time you open your Favorites bar. To organize your favorites, click the Add to Favorites button (+) and choose Organize Favorites. Or choose Favorites ⇨ Organize Favorites from Internet Explorer's menu bar. Either way, you'll be taken to the Organize Favorites window shown in Figure 17.18.

To create a new folder, click the New Folder button, type a folder name, and press Enter. To create a subfolder within an existing folder, first open the parent folder. Then click New Folder and enter the subfolder name.

To move a page or tab group into a folder, choose the item you want to move and then click Move. Click the folder into which you want to move the item and click OK. Or, just drag the item onto the folder into which you want to move it.

To rename a link or folder, choose the item you want to rename, click Rename, type the new name, and press Enter.

CAUTION   Deleting a folder deletes all items in that folder. If the folder contains any items you want to keep, move them to another folder before you delete.

To delete an item or folder, choose the item you want to delete, click Delete, and click OK.

FIGURE 17.18

Organize Favorites.

To put items into alphabetical order, right-click a folder name or some empty space and choose Sort by Name.

Click Done when you've finished organizing your Favorites. To view your reorganized favorites, click the Favorites Center button.

Importing and exporting Favorites

If you've been using another Web browser for a while, and want to start using Internet Explorer, you can import your Favorites and other items from your other browser. That way Internet Explorer will have all the favorite Web sites you're accustomed to from your previous browser.

Similarly, if you want to use some browser other than Internet Explorer, you can export Favorites and other items from Internet Explorer to your other browser. Either way, the steps are as follows:

1. Choose File ⇨ Import and Export from Internet Explorer's menu.
2. Click Next on the first page of the wizard that appears.
3. On the next wizard page, choose whichever option describes what you want to do and click Next.
    - To import directly from another program on your computer, choose Import from an application and the name of the program from which you want to import. Or choose Export to an application and the name of the program to which you want to export.
    - To import a file that you exported from some other program, or to export directly to a file, choose Import from a file or Export to a file. Then specify the file.
4. Follow any additional instructions and click Finish.

Why Would I Import/Export a File?

If the program you want to import from or export to isn't on the same computer, you can use a file as a go-between. Let's say you have two computers, which we'll call OldComputer and NewComputer. To get Favorites from OldComputer to NewComputer, you would go to OldComputer. There you would export Favorites to a file named `bookmark.htm` on a floppy disk or jump drive. Then go to NewComputer and import them from `bookmark.htm` on the floppy disk or jump drive.

You can also export your favorites to the Web. The advantage here being that you can access them from any computer. For more information on exporting favorites to the Web, browse to `http://favorites .live.com`.

Blocking Pop-Ups

A pop-up is any Web page that opens in its own separate browser window. Some pop-ups are OK. For example, a pop-up might open to display a larger copy of a small picture. Or it might open so you can still see the page that contains the link that opened the page. Other pop-ups, like advertisements, aren't so great. These are often referred to as automatic pop-ups because they appear on their own, without your clicking a link.

Microsoft Internet Explorer has a built-in pop-up blocker to help you deal with pop-ups. To activate or deactivate the pop-up blocker:

1. Click Tools and choose Internet Options or choose Tools ➪ Internet Options from Internet Explorer's menu.
2. Click the Privacy tab.
3. To block pop-ups, select (check) Block pop-up windows. To allow all pop-ups through, clear that checkbox.

If you opt to use the pop-up blocker, you can click the Settings button to configure it to your own tastes. When you click the Settings button, the dialog box shown in Figure 17.19 opens.

First you can choose how aggressively you want to block pop-ups (remember, they're not all ads). Use the Filter Level drop-down list at the bottom of the dialog box to choose one of the following filter levels:

- **High:** Blocks all pop-ups, even when you click a link to open the pop-up. If you choose this setting, you'll have to hold down the Ctrl and Alt keys while clicking a link to allow a legitimate pop-up page to open.
- **Medium:** Blocks most automatic pop-ups, but not pop-ups that open when you click a link.
- **Low:** Blocks relatively few pop-ups. Always allows pop-ups from secure and trusted Web sites.

The Notification options let you hear a sound and display the Information bar when a pop-up is blocked. It's a good idea to select (check) both those options so you know when a page has been blocked. That way you can decide whether or not you want to allow a Web site to show pop-ups. (Remember, not all pop-ups are bad.)

FIGURE 17.19

Pop-up blocker settings.

If you already know that you want to allow pop-ups from a specific site, you can type the site's URL under Address of website to allow, then click the Add button. But it's not really necessary to do so. Because if you choose the Show Information Bar when a pop-up is blocked option, you can allow sites as you go. Click the Close button at the bottom of the Pop-up Settings dialog box after making your selections. Then click OK to close the Internet Options dialog box.

Using the Information bar

The Internet Explorer Information bar appears whenever the pop-up blocker prevents a page from opening. It also appears when you're about to download certain kinds of programs, like ActiveX controls. Typically you'll hear a beep when the Information bar opens. And you may see the message shown in Figure 17.20.

FIGURE 17.20

Information bar.

The Information bar is the one below the tabs. To use it you'll need to click the Close button in the information box. When you get accustomed to recognizing the Information bar, you can choose Don't show this message again to keep the message box from alerting you to the Information bar. After closing the message, click the Information bar and choose what you want to do:

- **Temporarily Allow Pop-ups:** Choose this option to take a look at the pop-up to see if it's something useful. If it is okay, you can close the pop-up window, click the Information bar again, and choose the option described next.

- **Always Allow Pop-ups from This Site:** Choose this option if you trust the current Web site enough to always allow pop-ups. Choose Yes when asked for confirmation.

If you later regret choosing to always allow pop-ups, go back to the Pop-up Blocker Settings dialog box shown in Figure 17.19. Click the Web site's URL and click Remove.

When pop-ups still get through

If you've enabled Internet Explorer's pop-up blocker, but still get pop-up ads when you use it, your computer may be infected with spyware or adware. Consider using Windows Defender, discussed in Chapter 8, to scan your entire system for spyware. Remove any spyware it finds. You might also consider downloading and running LavaSoft Ad-Aware. You can download the Personal edition of Ad-Aware from www.lavasoft.com or from a shareware site like www.tucows.com or www.download.com.

Internet Explorer never blocks pop-ups from Web sites in your Local Intranet or Trusted site zones. See "Using Internet Security Zones" later in this chapter for more information.

Using the Phishing Filter

NEW FEATURE   Thwart identity thieves with the new Phishing Filter.

Phishing is a technique used by thieves to get passwords and PINs. It usually works something like this. You get an e-mail message that appears to be from a legitimate bank or business. PayPal, eBay, and banks are favorite targets because people have accounts and deal in money at those sites. The message tells you that you need to respond to some message or check your account.

When you click a link in the e-mail message, your browser opens and appears to take you to the normal sign-in page for your account. However, it only looks like the real sign-in page. It's really a page at some other Web site. You type in your user name and password, and then they send you to the real site. In the meantime, the thieves have stored your user name and password in their own database. And now they can get into your account, and get all the personal information in that account, which can be used for identity theft. Depending on the type of site, they may even be able to transfer money out of your account and into their own.

The scam works because everything looks legitimate, both in the e-mail message and on the sign-in page. In the past, the only way you would know it was a scam would be if you took a close look at where the links are really sending you. Or if you happened to notice that the URL in the Address bar at the account sign-in page wasn't really the business's URL.

> **TIP** In Windows Mail, point to any link in any e-mail message. The status bar at the bottom of the program window shows where the link really takes you. In Internet Explorer, you just have to look at the Address bar at the sign-in page to see where you really are.

The Phishing filters in Windows Mail and Internet Explorer keep an eye out for you. In Internet Explorer, the Address bar turns a reddish color and shows a red shield with a white X. You'll also see the words "Suspicious Website" if the site looks suspicious but hasn't been verified as a scam yet. You'll see "Phishing Website" and a large warning page if the site has been reported and verified as a scam. Figure 17.21 shows an example where I was supposed to be at the sign-in page for my PayPal account. PayPal's URL is not www.nubbtech.com.

FIGURE 17.21

Phishing Web site.

Another dead giveaway is when the Address bar shows an IP address in front of a legitimate site name. For example, http://206.83.210.40/chase-online.com looks like it has something to do with Chase bank. However, the IP address (206.83.210.40) is the actual Web server address. The part after the IP address, chase-online.com, is just a folder on that server and can be any name the crooks want it to be. It's unlikely that a legitimate business would show an IP address instead of its registered domain name.

How the Phishing Filter works

Internet Explorer's Phishing Filter takes a three-pronged approach to detecting phishing scams. First, it compares the addresses of Web sites that you visit against a list of known, legitimate sites stored in your computer. Secondly, it analyzes sites you visit for tactics commonly used by phishing sites. Thirdly, it can send URLs of sites you visit to a Microsoft database of reported phishing sites to catch them before you get there. But it will only do so with your permission.

The approach appears to be effective. All of the sites that I, personally, have reported are on the list of known phishing sites. And I've reported dozens, because I get phishing scam e-mail all the time. They always end up in my Junk Mail folder. But I always check them out anyway because I enjoy busting crooks.

Most of the time when the Phishing Filter reports a suspicious Web site, it's correct. Occasionally I see a *false positive*, where a legitimate site is marked as suspicious. But as Web masters around the world learn how to prove the legitimacy of their Web sites, those false positives should decrease.

Getting the most from the Phishing Filter

By default, Internet Explorer only uses the first two approaches of identifying phishing sites. It won't use the third approach unless you give it permission to send URLs you visit to Microsoft. The first time the filter detects a suspicious Web site, you'll see a message asking if you want to check Web sites automatically. If you choose Yes, then your URLs will be sent to Microsoft for further verification.

If you choose No, you can manually check the page you're currently viewing by clicking Tools ⇨ Phishing Filter ⇨ Check this Website.

 **CAUTION**   Of course the next tactic will be that fraudulent Web sites will tell you to ignore Phishing Filters. Don't believe it. The URL in the Address bar tells all.

If you initially chose No when asked about automatic checking of Web sites and have just changed your mind, you can easily turn it back on. Click the Tools button or choose Tools from the menu bar. Then click Phishing Filter and choose the option to turn on Automatic Website Checking.

If the Phishing Filter doesn't appear to be working at all, make sure it's not disabled. Here are the steps:

1. Choose Tools ⇨ Internet Options from Internet Explorer's menu.
2. In the dialog box that opens, click the Advanced tab.
3. Scroll down to the Phishing Filter and make sure Disable Phishing Filter is *not* selected, as in Figure 17.22.
4. Click OK.

FIGURE 17.22

Disable Phishing Filter *not* selected.

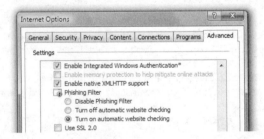

What if I've already been tricked?

If you think you may have given away your password to a phishing scam already, change your password or PIN as soon as possible. Log in to your account through your Web browser, not from a link in any e-mail message. Then use whatever means that Web site provides to change your password.

How do I protect myself in the future?

When you get an e-mail concerning any online account you have, don't click links in the e-mail message. Go to the Web site directly with your browser, using the same URL you always do. Also, never give out a password or PIN in an instant message, e-mail message, or over the phone.

Remember, when it comes to protecting your online assets, knowledge is power. Ignorance is vulnerability. To keep abreast of current scams and ways to stay safe online, visit `www.microsoft.com/athome/security`. Also, consider subscribing to the Security At Home RSS Feed at `www.microsoft.com/athome/security/rss/rssfeed.aspx`.

 **TIP**   Parental controls, discussed in Chapter 4, provide tools and techniques for keeping children safe online.

Deleting the Browser History

The term *browser history* covers the many different things that Internet Explorer tracks automatically. This includes Web site addresses, things you type into forms, cookies, and even entire pages. Here we'll look at ways you can clear those things out, and disable them entirely where appropriate.

Clearing out AutoComplete entries

AutoComplete is a feature of Internet Explorer that remembers passwords and other data you've entered in the past. When you go to a Web site with a remembered password, it types in the password for you automatically. When you start filling in the Name, Address, or a similar item on a form, it displays text that matches what you've typed into similar form fields in the past.

AutoComplete also keeps track of URLs you've typed in the past. Whenever you type a new address into your Web browser's Address bar, it displays past URLs that match what you've typed so far.

 **TIP**   To remove a single item from a drop-down menu, rather than all items, point to the item you want to delete and press Enter. It doesn't work on all drop-down menus, but it works on many of them.

If you're using a public computer, you certainly don't want to leave that behind. Even on your own personal computer, you might want to delete those things if you've made a lot of mistakes in the past. Or if you share your user account with many people, you may want to clear out those items for your own basic privacy. Whatever the reason, it's easy to empty those things out and start with a clean slate. For precise control of what gets deleted, follow these steps:

1. Click the Toolbar button and choose Internet Options, or choose Tools ➪ Internet Options from the menu bar.

2. On the General tab, click Delete... to see the Delete Browsing History dialog box shown in Figure 17.23.

3. The rest is self-explanatory:

   ▪ To delete the list of sites you've visited recently and the menu that appears under the Address bar when you type, click Delete history and then click OK.

   ▪ To delete remembered text you've typed into forms, click Delete forms... and then click OK.

   ▪ To delete remembered passwords, click Delete passwords... and then click OK.

4. If you're finished, click Close and then click OK.

FIGURE 17.23

Delete Browsing History dialog box.

Preventing AutoComplete

If you don't want AutoComplete to keep track of things you type, you can turn it off. Here's how:

1. Click Tools and choose Internet Options or choose Tools ⇨ Internet Options from the menu bar.
2. Click the Content tab.
3. Under the AutoComplete heading, click Settings. You see the options shown in Figure 17.24.

FIGURE 17.24

AutoComplete settings.

4. Clear checkmarks for any type of AutoComplete you want to disable.

5. Click OK.

The Delete Browsing History dialog box shown earlier lets you delete your temporary Internet files and cookies. It seems almost everyone who browses the Web has heard of those things. But there's a lot of confusion about what they are. So in the sections that follow, I'll take a crack at explaining them, hopefully without boring you to tears in the process.

Understanding cookies

A cookie is a tiny file placed on your computer by a Web site. The vast majority of cookies are perfectly harmless, and necessary for using certain types of sites. Most often, cookies are used to keep you signed into a Web site that requires logging in. When you log in, the Web server puts a cookie on your computer that contains information about your current session. Typically this is just some randomly assigned number that contains no information about you or your computer.

As you browse from one page to the next within the site, the Web server checks the cookie to see if you're already logged in. If you are logged in, it doesn't ask you to log in again. If it weren't for cookies, you'd have to log in every time you switched from one page to the next within the Web site. And that would be a major pain.

Of course, just about any tool can be exploited and used in bad ways. Cookies are no exception. Any cookie that contains account information or personal information is considered an *unacceptable cookie* or *unsatisfactory cookie*. Yes, those are the actual technical terms, despite the pictures those terms put into your mind. I picture a bunch of stale cookies on a platter left over from a party the night before. Or something much more gross.

Cookies can also be used to keep track of Web sites you visit. Advertisers use those cookies to target ads to your computer based on your apparent Web browsing interests. Such cookies also fall into the unacceptable and unsatisfactory categories.

Deleting cookies

You can easily wipe your computer clean of all cookies at any time. There's no such thing as a "required" cookie, so you don't have to worry about eliminating some important, necessary cookie. The worst that can happen is that you have to log into a secure Web site that might otherwise be able to log you in automatically. No big deal, as long as you know your username and password. To wipe your computer clean of all cookies:

1. Click Tools and choose Internet Options or choose Tools ➪ Internet Options from Internet Explorer's menu.

2. Under the Browsing History heading, click Delete….

3. Click Delete cookies and click OK.

4. Click Close and click OK.

Adjusting cookie privacy settings

You can easily protect your computer from unacceptable cookies by setting a security level for privacy. If your Internet Options dialog box isn't already open, choose Tools ➪ Internet Options from Internet Explorer's menu. Then click the Privacy tab. You see the slider shown in Figure 17.25.

Drag the slider to Medium (if it isn't already there). You could set it higher for even better protection. But you might find it difficult to use some legitimate Web sites if you do.

FIGURE 17.25

Privacy settings for cookies.

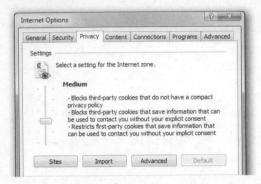

Looking at cookies and privacy policies

The main threat posed by cookies is invasion of privacy. As mentioned, unacceptable cookies might contain personal information that could be exploited. They might track your Web browser habits to help advertisers target ads to you.

Many Web sites that use cookies these days will back them up with a compact privacy policy. Sites that don't probably will soon. The privacy policy specifies how the site will protect your privacy. You can check to see what cookies, if any, a Web page has put on your system:

1. If you're not already at the Web page in question, browse to it normally.
2. Choose View ⇨ Web page privacy policy from Internet Explorer's menu.

A list of files downloaded from that page appears in a dialog box. If the page loaded a cookie, you'll see Accepted or Blocked in the Cookies column. To see if the cookie has a compact privacy policy, click the address to the left of Accepted or Blocked, and then click Summary.

If your current privacy settings blocked a cookie that you need for the page, you can choose Always allow this site to use cookies to loosen the restrictions on that site. Similarly, if a cookie was accepted, you can choose to block future cookies from that site. If trying to manage cookies on a case-by-case basis gets to be too much trouble, click the Settings button to get to the Privacy slider. Then you can drag the slider down a notch or two to loosen your restrictions.

 Third-party cookies, which come from a site other than the one you're visiting, are the greatest offenders. That's why most of the privacy settings focus on third-party cookie handling.

Understanding temporary Internet files

To understand temporary Internet files, you have to understand a little about how the Web works. When you type a URL into your browser's Address bar and press Enter, your computer sends a little *packet* of information to the Web server at that address. You don't actually "connect" to the server, you just send a message that says "Hey server, send your page to me at <*your IP address*>." The *your IP address* part is a number that uniquely identifies your computer on the Internet. Much the same as your phone number uniquely identifies your telephone among all the phones in the world.

TIP If you have a standard home Internet connection, your IP address probably changes each time you log on. If you want to see what it is right now, go to a search engine like www.google.com. Search for "what is my IP address?". You'll be given a list of Web sites that will display your current IP address.

When the Web server gets the packet, it sends out the Web page, addressed to your computer. Again, there's no actual connection being made. Furthermore, the page isn't sent as one big file, per se. It's sent as hundreds or thousands of tiny little packets. These packets don't even take the same path to your computer. They travel more like water dripping down a net, each following its own path, but eventually ending up in the same place.

The packets don't even arrive at your computer in the proper order. They have to be reassembled into the proper order. The reassembled packets are stored in your temporary Internet files folder as a single file. (Well, actually, it might be several files: One for the text of the page, another for each picture on the page, and perhaps even others. But that's not important here.)

As all the pieces come together in your temporary Internet files folder, your Web browser displays the page. With a fast Internet connection, this all happens so quickly, some of you probably think I'm clueless or lying. But that really is the way it works. I'm not guessing or making it up.

But anyway, the bottom line is that when you're looking at a Web page in your Web browser, you're not really looking at some far away document on another computer. You're actually looking at a copy of that document that's on your own computer, in your temporary Internet files folder.

When you've finished viewing the page and move onto the next page, Internet Explorer doesn't erase the copied page. It keeps it. That way, if you click Back to go back to that page, it doesn't have to go through the whole process of getting the page from the Web server again. It just shows the copy of the page that's already in your temporary Internet files folder.

So what's to keep these temporary Internet files from filling up your entire hard disk? Easy. There's a limit to how much stuff that temporary Internet files folder can hold. When it starts to get full, old pages you haven't viewed in a long time are automatically deleted to make room for new pages you're viewing. Hence the name *temporary* Internet files. They don't last forever.

Why It's So Fast

The reason it's all so fast is because the electrons carrying the packets of information are moving at near the speed of light, 186,000 miles per second. That's fast enough to circle the Earth at the equator seven times a second. The distances the electrons have to travel across the Web and inside your computer are so tiny, it takes virtually no time at all.

The only reason a dial-up connection seems slow is because the telephone lines put a stranglehold on the information, like water running through a very skinny tube rather than a big fat drainage pipe. It takes longer to drain a pool with a tiny tube than with a wide drainage pipe. Likewise, it takes longer to get Internet data from your ISP to your computer with a "skinny" dial-up connection than it does with a "wide" broadband connection.

DSL uses telephone lines too, just like dial-up connections do. But DSL is faster because the information is transmitted over the telephone line digitally. With a dial-up connection, the information is transmitted in analog format. It's really the combination of telephone lines and analog format that makes dial-up connections so slow.

Clearing out temporary Internet files

You can clean out those temporary Internet files any time you wish. It's never necessary to do so. Though it's useful to do so just before performing some task that operates on all files in your system; for example, a virus scan or disk defragmentation. Also, there's no such things as a "necessary" or "required" temporary Internet file. So there's never any harm in wiping them off of your computer.

Deleting temporary Internet files is much like deleting cookies. The steps are as follows:

1. Click Tools and choose Internet Options or choose Tools ⇨ Internet Options from Internet Explorer's menu bar.
2. Under the Browsing History heading click Delete....
3. Click Delete files.
4. Click OK.
5. Click Close and OK.

If you have a slow Internet connection, it might seem to take a little longer to view pages you've viewed in the past. That's because Internet Explorer has to download everything from scratch again. There are no temporary Internet files left that Internet Explorer can use as an alternative. If you have a fast Internet connection, you might not notice any difference at all.

Temporary Internet files settings

You can change some settings that apply to temporary Internet files. Once again, click Tools and choose Internet Options or choose Tools ⇨ Internet Options from Internet Explorer's menu bar. But this time click the Settings button under Browser History. The Temporary Files and History Settings dialog box shown in Figure 17.26 opens.

FIGURE 17.26

Temporary Internet Files and History Settings dialog box.

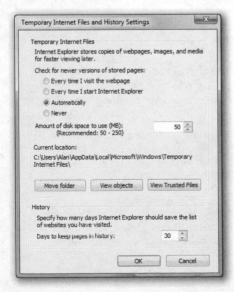

The first set of options determines how and when Internet Explorer checks for new versions of files that are in your temporary Internet files folder. Automatic is the preferred setting. This allows Internet Explorer to use its own built-in programming logic to make a best guess about whether or not it's worth taking the time to check for newer versions of files. The guess is usually right. But you can always click the Refresh button, or choose View ➪ Refresh to download the page to be sure.

The first two options force Internet Explorer to check every time you visit the page or every time you start Internet Explorer. Theoretically, either of these options would ensure that you always have the most up-to-date content. But, both will also likely force Internet Explorer to check more than is necessary, and perhaps slow down your whole Web-browsing experience, especially if you have a slow Internet connection.

The Never option is risky because you really have no way of knowing if the page you're viewing in your browser is in sync with what's currently on the Web server. You would have to use the Refresh button every time you visit a page to make sure you have the most current content.

The "Amount of disk space to use" option lets you decide how much hard disk space you're willing to sacrifice for storing temporary Internet files. Keep in mind that hard disk space is measured in gigabytes (GB), and the setting is measured in megabytes (MB). A gigabyte is 1,024 MB. So even the highest recommended setting, 250 MB, is only about one fourth of a gigabyte.

The Current location shows where your Temporary Internet Files folder is located on your hard disk. Offhand, I can't think of any particularly good reason for changing that. But if you come up with a good reason, you can click the Move button to change it.

NOTE The Temporary Internet Files folder is hidden and protected. If you try to get to it with Explorer, you may not have any luck. You'll have to choose Show hidden files and folders and clear the Hide protected operating system files checkbox in the Folder Options dialog box o see the folder.

The View objects button shows icons for Web objects in the Temporary Internet Files folder. Objects are different from pages and pictures. They're small programs that allow you to use more advanced Web features. For example, you'd likely find things like the Shockwave Flash Player and Windows Genuine Advantage tool in there, if you've downloaded those items.

Objects aren't deleted when you clear out your Temporary Internet Files folder. If they were, you would have to manually download and install them again. But if you ever needed to delete some object, on the advice of a professional, you could do so in that folder.

The View Trusted Files button shows files from trusted Web sites. Some of these may be retained when you clear out your temporary Internet files, because the convenience of keeping them outweighs the benefits of clearing them out. But if there was some problem with the site and the Web master recommended clearing out the file, you could do so from the folder.

The "Days to keep pages in history" setting relates to the History pane at the left side of Internet Explorer's program window. To see that pane, press Ctrl+H or click the Favorites Center button, and then click History. Or choose View ➪ Explorer Bar ➪ History. The number you enter specifies how bar back your History keeps track of visited Web sites. For example, if you set it to 7, your History list will never show addresses of sites you visited more than a week ago.

A note on certificates

As you're going through all the optional settings in the Internet Options dialog box, you'll eventually notice the Certificates section on the Content tab. First, let me just say there's really nothing you need to do, or should do, with those options unless you're specifically instructed to do so by a trusted Web site or certificate authority. Otherwise, it's all handled beautifully and automatically without any intervention on your part.

But since we're getting into some of the more obscure aspects of secure Web browsing here, it might be worth learning what certificates are about and how they provide secure Web browsing. After all, when it comes to Internet security, knowledge is your best defense.

Here's the basic problem. Virtually all Web traffic takes place in *plaintext*, meaning there's no effort made to disguise or hide the content being transmitted between a Web server and a Web browser. There's no need to disguise it. Most information on the Web is there for public consumption. And there's no need to disguise information that anybody and everybody can access from their own computer.

It's a different story when you make an online purchase and need to send your credit card information to the online store. That kind of information is most definitely not for public consumption. To make sure it doesn't fall into the wrong hands, credit card information (and some other types of personal information) is *encrypted* before it's put on the Internet.

Encryption means that the information is encoded in such a way that if someone did manage to intercept it, it would do them no good. When they open the intercepted file, all they will see is a bunch of meaningless gobbledygook. And there is no way they can decipher it back to meaningful text because they don't have the appropriate "secret decoder ring." Or, in correct terminology, they don't have the appropriate *private key* to decode the message. Only the company to whom you're sending the sensitive information has that private key.

A certificate is a means of making sure that the whole encryption process stays legitimate and safe. A site that wants to offer secure Web browsing to its customers applies to a company called a Certificate Authority (CA) for a certificate. They have to prove their legitimacy as a business, have a stable place of business, and have people who will be held criminally responsible for any shenanigans.

When they get the certificate, they also get a *public key* for encrypting files, and a *private key* for decrypting files. (It's not an actual physical key. It's a computer file.) They then set up a secure Web server that has an https:// address. The "s" stands for secure.

When you browse to a secure Web site (one that starts with https://), some things happen behind the scenes to protect you. First the server has to prove it's the actual Web site to your computer by sending its certificate. Your computer then checks the certificate holder's status with the CA to verify that the server is not an imposter, and that the business hasn't had its certificate revoked for doing bad things with it.

 **If a certificate holder uses the certificate to commit a crime (such as ripping off customers), the certificate is revoked. You'll see a warning message not to do business with the site.**

That certificate the server sends you also contains the site's public encryption key. So let's say you fill in your credit card information on a form on your screen. Then you click Submit to send it. Before that information leaves your computer, it's encrypted with the site's public key. It remains encrypted until it gets to the already-proven-safe Web server.

Once it gets to that safe server, it can be decrypted with their private key to complete the transaction. Overall, the whole process is probably much safer than handing your credit card over to an unknown waiter, waitress, gas station attendant, or store clerk.

The trick is knowing when you're on a secure site. The easy way to tell is by looking at the Address bar when you're on the page where you'll conduct the transaction. If its address starts with https://, then it's okay. You might also see the message shown in Figure 17.27 when you first enter the page. (If you previously chose the option not to see that message anymore, then you won't see that message.)

FIGURE 17.27

Message about entering a secure site.

Assuming you haven't already turned off that message, you'll also see a message when you leave the secure connection, as in Figure 17.28. And the address of the page you go to will start with http:// rather than https://.

FIGURE 17.28

Message about leaving a secure site.

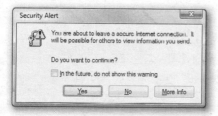

Both of the preceding messages are just there to keep you informed of when it is, and isn't, safe to send sensitive data across the Internet. If you did turn off those messages and want to see them again in the future, follow these steps:

1. Click Tools and choose Internet Options or choose Tools ➪ Internet Options from Internet Explorer's menu bar.

2. In the Internet Options dialog box, click the Advanced tab.

3. Scroll to the bottom of the list.

4. Select (check) the Warn if changing between secure and not secure mode and click OK.

Using Internet Security Zones

Internet Security Zones offer a means of separating Web sites you do trust from those you don't. There are four different security zones to choose from:

- **Internet:** Every Internet Web site you visit automatically falls into the Internet security zone unless you move it to another zone.

- **Local Intranet:** In large networks that have their own non-Internet Web sites, every Web site within that network automatically falls into the Intranet zone.

- **Trusted sites:** Initially, no sites fall into this category. But you can move any trusted site into this category so that you don't get a security warning every time you visit.

- **Untrusted sites:** Initially, no sites fall into this category either. But you can move any Web site that you use but don't fully trust into this zone to enforce maximum security.

To get to the Security Zones dialog box, choose Tools ⇨ Internet Options from Internet Explorer's menu. Then click the Security tab. You see the options in Figure 17.29.

FIGURE 17.29

Security Zones in Internet Options.

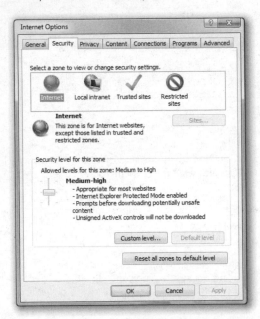

Each zone has its own security settings. Click one of the security zone icons near the top of the dialog box. The slider under "Security level for this zone" changes to show that zone's security level. For example, the security level for the Internet zone is Medium-high. This is the default setting and is appropriate for the vast majority of Web sites you're likely to visit. Characteristics of the security level include

- **Internet Explorer Protected Mode enabled:** In Protected Mode, Internet Explorer protects your computer from malware (malicious software) that could harm your computer. It also allows you to install safe downloaded software from a standard user account.

- **Prompts before downloading potentially unsafe content:** Displays a warning whenever you're about to download *potentially* unsafe software. If you trust the software you're about to download, it won't prevent you from doing so. But it will prevent bad Web sites from sneaking malware onto your computer without your knowledge.

- **Unsigned ActiveX controls will not be downloaded:** An ActiveX control is like a tiny program that can make your computer do things. (Web pages and pictures can't make your computer do things.) A signed ActiveX control is one in which the author of the control can be identified and held accountable for any harm it causes.

There probably is no reason to change the Security level for the Internet zone. If you have an account at a trusted Web site that won't work properly with these settings, it's really not necessary to lower the security level for all sites just to accommodate that one site. Instead you can put that site in your Trusted Sites zone and lower the security settings there. (More on the Trusted Sites zone in a moment.)

Rather than settle for one of the security levels along the slider, you can click Custom level and define your own security restrictions for the zone. However, many of the options provided require advanced professional knowledge that goes beyond the scope of this book.

The Trusted Sites zone is where you can put Web sites you trust that don't work properly in the Internet zone. To put a site in that zone, click the Trusted Sites icon and click Sites. Type the site's URL (if it isn't already in the box) and click Add. By default, you'll be limited to adding secure sites to that zone. A secure site is one whose address starts with https:// rather than http://. But you can eliminate that restriction by clearing the "Require server (https://) for all sites in this zone" checkbox. The security level for Trusted sites is Medium. You can reduce that to Medium-low or Low.

Use the Restricted Sites zone for sites you visit regularly but don't really trust. The security level for Restricted sites is High, which will make it extremely difficult for the Web site to sneak anything past you.

How Does a Beginner Know Whom to Trust?

It's hard to know whom to trust when you're just getting started with computers. But a key issue is whether or not you can find and hold responsible the party that owns the site. Large businesses that have physical stores and shopping malls and such are generally trustworthy. After all, their online business wouldn't last too long if word got out that they were downloading bad software to their customers.

The same is true with software companies. Software giants like Microsoft, Adobe, and Corel simply cannot afford to allow anything bad to leave their Web servers and harm customers' computers. So you can trust them. Any site that has a large customer base can also be considered trustworthy. After all, if they were doing something dishonest, word would get out and they wouldn't have many customers.

Sites that publish unsavory content, make promises that seem too good to be true, and have no real presence off the Internet are the most dubious. If you know an Internet-savvy computer geek, you can ask them what they think.

Keep in mind that the Medium-high security level applied to all Web sites will make it tough for a malicious site to sneak anything past you. The security measures discussed in Part II make it all the more difficult for the bad guys to do any harm. So you're never really flying blind with no security at all.

Printing Web Pages

Printing a Web page is basically the same as printing any other document. If you haven't fully mastered the art of printing, you might want to read Chapter 36 to discover all the possibilities. Here I'll focus on tools and techniques that are unique to printing Web pages. Some things to consider before you print are listed here:

- Look around the page for a *printer-friendly* or *printable page* link. If you find such a link, click it for a version of the page that's likely to work better with your printer.

- If the Web site consists of multiple individually scrollable frames, and you want to print only one frame, click some plain text or white space in the frame you want to print.

- If you only want to print a portion of the Web page, select (drag the mouse pointer through) the content you want to print.

- Consider using Print Preview, discussed next, to see how the printed document will look before you actually print. That way you won't waste paper on disappointing results.

To print the page, click the Print button and choose Print (see Figure 17.30). Or choose File ➪ Print from the menu, or press Ctrl+P.

FIGURE 17.30

Print button and menu.

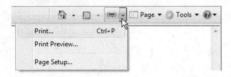

The Print dialog box opens as in Figure 17.31. First, click the printer you want to use. If you want to create an XPS document rather than go straight to paper, choose Microsoft XPS.

 **CAUTION**   **Don't choose Print to file unless you specifically want to create a** .prn **file. It's not necessary to choose that option when using the Microsoft Office or Microsoft XPS printers.**

Before you click the Print button, consider the following:

- If the page has multiple frames and you only want to print the one you previously clicked, click the Options tab, choose Only the selected frame, and click the General tab again.

- If you only want to print the content you previously selected, choose Selection.

- If you only want to print a portion of a multipage document, choose any option other than All. For example, click Current Page to print only the page you're viewing. Or choose Pages and enter a page range.

- To conserve color ink, consider clicking Preferences ➪ Paper/Quality ➪ Black and White ➪ OK. (Not available on all printers.)

- To preview how things will look before you print, click Apply then click Cancel. Then use Print Preview as described next to take a close look. Otherwise, click Print to start printing.

FIGURE 17.31

FIGURE 17.31

Print dialog box.

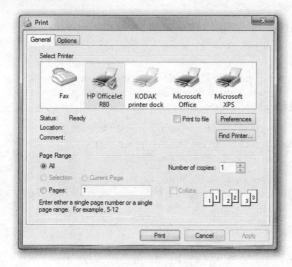

Using Print Preview

Print Preview is a great way to get a quick peek at how your printed pages will look. As when printing directly to paper, you'll want to start by clicking the frame you want to print (if the page has multiple frames). If you want to print a portion of the page, select that content that you want to print. Then click the Print button and choose Print Preview. Or press Alt+F+V or choose File ➪ Print Preview from the menu. The page opens in Print Preview. Figure 17.32 shows an example of a page in Print Preview.

FIGURE 17.32

Sample page in Print Preview.

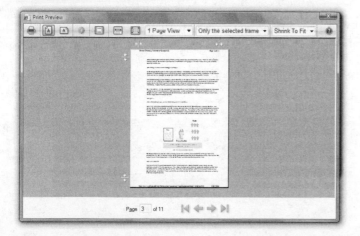

Across the top of the Print Preview window are several buttons and other controls. As always, you can point to any one of them to see its name. If the page has multiple frames, and you only want to print the frame in which you clicked, press Alt+F or choose Only the selected frame from the Select Content drop-down menu. If you selected specific content to print first, choose As selected on screen to see only that content.

To get a close-up view of how the printed page will look, click the View Full Width button or press Alt+W. If it looks like you're likely to have problems with text being cut off at the right margin, choose Shrink to Fit from the Choose Print Size drop-down list.

To adjust margins, first click the View Full Page button or press Alt+1. You'll see little lines and arrows around the corners of the page. Drag those in the directions indicated by the arrows to adjust the margins. Or, click the Page Setup button and Left, Top, Right, and Bottom margins in inches. Then click OK.

At the bottom left of the Print Preview window, use the arrows to scroll through pages. Depending on how many pages there are, use the Show Multiple Pages button to zoom out and see how multiple pages will look when printed.

When you're happy with the way things look in Print Preview, click the Print button near the upper-left corner. The Print dialog box opens. There you can still choose a page range, Paper/Quality, or other printing features before clicking the Print button to print.

Important printing tip

Don't expect the printer to start printing immediately. There's always a delay. If you keep clicking the Print button to hurry things along, you'll end up printing the same document over and over again. For more information on printing (and stopping the printer), see Chapters 36 and 37.

Saving Web Pages

Web pages don't generally go away, so there's rarely any need to save an entire Web page to your own computer. But there are exceptions. For example, if it's a lengthy document that you want to be able to refer to offline, saving a copy would make sense. If you want to be able to work with the material in a program like Microsoft Word, then it would definitely make sense to save a copy of the page to your own computer first. To save a copy of the Web page you're currently viewing:

1. Choose File ⇨ Save As from Internet Explorer's menu. The Save Webpage dialog box opens as in Figure 17.33.

2. Use the Favorite Links, Folders List, or Address bar to navigate to the folder in which you want to save the page. If you don't have a preference, just choose Documents from the Favorite Links pane to put it in your Documents folder.

3. Optionally, change the page's name using the File name option. To improve searching later, consider naming the file so it contains words you'd likely search for.

FIGURE 17.33

Save Webpage dialog box.

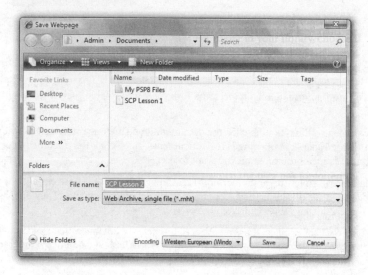

4. Optionally, choose a Save as type from one of these options:

- **Web Archive, single file (*.mht):** Stores the entire page, with pictures, in a single file with a single icon.

- **Web Page, complete (*.htm,*.html):** The entire Web page with all pictures is downloaded. You'll end up with two icons, one for the HTML page and the other for a folder containing pictures and perhaps other miscellaneous code files.

- **Web Page, HTML only (*.htm,*.html):** Saves all the text and HTML of the page, but no pictures.

- **Text File (*.txt):** Saves only the text of the page, no pictures or HTML tags.

5. Optionally, change the Encoding option, but only if you have a good reason, such as when saving non-English pages.

6. Click the Save button.

The page is saved to whatever folder you specified in Step 2. When you open that folder, you'll see one or two documents for the page. If you chose the Web page, complete option, you'll see two icons. One will be a document icon with whatever filename you entered in Step 3. The other icon will be a folder that has the same filename followed by _files. Figure 17.34 shows an example with the icons shown in Tiles view.

FIGURE 17.34

Webpage saved using the **Web page complete** option.

NOTE For more information on folders, the Tiles view, and related topics, see Chapter 28.

To view the saved page offline, double-click the document icon (the one on the left). Or if you have multiple programs that are capable of opening HTML documents, right-click the document icon, choose Open With, and click the name of the program you want to use.

The _files folder contains pictures and other non-HTML page elements. Those extra items are required because the document file doesn't actually contain pictures or other elements. They only appear to be in the page when you open the page with your Web browser.

NOTE To see what's *really* in the Web page, right-click the document icon and choose Open With ⇨ Notepad. If you're not familiar with HTML, it will look like a bunch of nonsense. But you will notice that there no pictures when you view the document in Notepad.

In a sense, the document file and folder are joined at the hip. If you delete one, you automatically delete the other. But the reverse isn't true. If you decide to fish them out of the Recycle Bin, you'll need to restore each one individually.

If you chose the Web Page, HTML only you'll get a document icon similar to the one on the left in Figure 17.34. But you won't get the folder icon. When you open that document, you'll see all the formatted text, but no pictures.

If you chose the Web Archive, single file, the icon will look more like the top example in Figure 17.35. That one contains text and pictures. You can double-click it to open it in your Web browser. Or right-click it, choose Open With, then choose the program you want to use.

FIGURE 17.35

Web page saved as archive (top) and text (bottom).

If you saved the page as a text document, it will have an icon like the bottom example in Figure 17.35. Because that's a plain text document, it will contain only unformatted text, no pictures. When double-clicked, it will likely open in a simple text editor like Notepad. Optionally, you could right-click its icon, choose Open With, then choose a word processing program like Microsoft Word. Then format the document using the features and capabilities of that word processing program.

Copying content from Web pages

As an alternative to saving a whole Web page as a file, you can copy-and-paste it (or any portion of it) to a word processing document. While you're viewing the Web page, press Ctrl+A to select everything in the document. Or drag the mouse pointer through the content you want to copy. Then press Ctrl+C to copy the selection to the Clipboard.

Next, open the document into which you want to paste the content. Then click where you want to put the copied content. Or, open Microsoft Word or WordPad so you start with a new, empty document. Then press Ctrl+V or right-click at about where you want to paste and choose Paste.

To copy just a single picture from a Web page, right-click the picture and choose Copy. Then open a graphics program and press Ctrl+V to paste. Or open a word processing document that can accept pictures, and click where you want to put the picture to position the cursor. Then press Ctrl+V or right-click that same spot and choose Paste.

Downloading pictures and videos

You can often (though not always) download multimedia items from Web pages as independent files on your own computer:

- To copy a picture you see on a Web page, right-click the picture and choose Save Picture As.
- To download a video or sound, you'll first need to get to the link that leads to that object. Right-click that link, and choose Save Target As.

The Save As dialog box will open, as usual, so you can choose a folder and specify a filename for the item you're copying. If you don't have a preference, put pictures in your Pictures folder and videos in your Videos folder.

> **TIP** If you're unable to copy a picture by right-clicking and choosing Copy, you can also take a picture of the entire screen with the picture visible. Then, paste the screenshot into a graphics program and crop out whatever you don't want. See "Taking screenshots" in Chapter 22.

Making Internet Explorer Your Default Browser

Your default Web browser is the one that opens automatically when you double-click (or click) an HTML file. It's also the one that usually appears at the top of the Start menu. If Internet Explorer isn't your default Web browser, but you'd like it to be, follow these steps:

1. Open Internet Explorer. Then click the Tools button and choose Internet Options, or choose Tools ➪ Internet Options from its menu.
2. In the Internet Options dialog box, click the Programs tab.
3. Click the Make Default button if it's enabled. If it's dimmed, that means Internet Explorer already is your default browser.

4. Optionally, to have Internet Explorer prompt you to be your default browser, in case it loses that status to another browser, select (check) the When Internet Explorer starts, prompt me if it's not the default browser.

5. Click OK.

If Internet Explorer is not the option at the top-left side of your Start menu, but you'd like it to be, follow these steps:

1. Right-click the Start button and choose Properties.

2. In the dialog box that opens, choose Start Menu and then click the Customize button (this technique won't work if you use the old-style Classic menus).

3. Make sure the Internet link checkbox is selected (checked).

4. Choose Internet Explorer from the drop-down button to the right of the Internet link label.

5. Click OK in each open dialog box.

Searching the Web

The World Wide Web contains more than 15 billion pages of information. You can find anything on the Web; you just need to know where to look and how to look for it. You can use the standard method of browsing to a search engine like www.google.com, www.yahoo.com, or whatever. Or you can configure Internet Explorer to make it all a bit more automatic. First, click the arrow next to the Search box as in Figure 17.36 to get your bearings. That's where you'll do most tasks related to searching.

FIGURE 17.36

Search box drop-down menu.

Choosing search providers

If you already have a favorite search engine, you can use it as your default search provider. If you have several favorites, you can add them all and make any one the default provider. If you're new to all of this, I can give you some advice on search providers to try. Here are the steps to follow to choose search providers:

1. Click the arrow on the Search box and choose Find More Providers. A Web page opens showing names of several search engines and searchable Web sites.

2. Click a provider name (like Google) and click Add Provider.

3. Repeat Step 2 for each provider you want to use. If you don't have any preferences, here are some examples:

- AOL, Ask.com, Google, Lycos.com, MSN, and Yahoo! are all general-purposes searches that cover most of the World Wide Web.
- About.com, www.cnet.com, and Microsoft.com are good resources for computer information.
- Wikipedia.org is a great online encyclopedia for information about virtually any topic.
- Amazon, BestBuy.com, eBay, Overstock.com, Shopzilla, Target, and Wal-Mart are all shopping-related sites.
- Monster is for job searching, ESPN for sports, USA Today for news.

When you've finished making selections, click the arrow on the Search box again. This time, all the search providers you've chosen will appear.

Choosing a default provider

Searching all your providers would probably be a bit extreme. You could end up with links to more Web pages than you could explore in a lifetime. So you need to pick one to be the default provider. The default provider is just the one that's used unless you specify otherwise. To choose a default provider:

1. Click the button on the Search box again and click Change Search Defaults.
2. Click the provider you want to use as your default and click Set Default.
3. Optionally, you can remove any provider by clicking its name and clicking Remove.
4. Click OK.

The text inside the Search box changes to reflect your default provider.

Searching from the Search box

Click the Search box and type the word or phrase you want to hunt for. This need not be in the form of a question. In fact, words like how, do, I, what, is, why, the, a, an, and other words that appear in virtually all pages are largely ignored. You're not asking a person (or the Internet) a question here. You're asking it to show you pages that contain a particular word or phrase. The more specific you make that word or phrase, the better the results will be.

After you type the word or phrase, press Enter or click the magnifying glass. The search results from your default search provider appear in the main document area where all Web pages appear.

To try the same search on a different search provider, click the arrow next to the Search box and choose the search provider you want to try. It's simple. Try your search on a few search providers. Try out several searches. You'll get the hang of it in no time.

Just remember that if you get far too many search results, your best bet is to try to be more specific in your search. For example, if you're looking for parts for a 1966 Ford Mustang convertible, don't search for *cars* or *Ford* or *Mustang* or *Mustang parts*. Search for *1966 Ford Mustang convertible parts*. If you're looking for Swarovski Crystal rhinestone wholesalers, don't search for one or two of those words. Search for *Swarovski Crystal rhinestone wholesalers*. Remember, the more specific the search, the fewer and better the search results.

Searching from the Address bar

Normally you use the Address bar to type the URL (address) of the page you want to visit. If you type regular text in the Address bar, it's treated like text you enter in the Search box. A page from your default provider opens showing links to pages that contain the word or phrase you typed.

If you're trying to access a local intranet resource, that default search bar behavior will cause problems. To disable that, click Tools, choose Internet Options, and click the Advanced tab. Choose Do not search from the Address bar. When you subsequently enter text in the Address bar, the Information bar may appear. Click it to see your options for enabling intranet settings.

Searching the Current Page

Some Web pages are large. There may be times where you just want to search the page you're currently viewing for a word or phrase. To do that, click the arrow on the Search box and choose Find on this Page. A Find box opens. Type the word or phrase you're looking for and click Next. The first occurrence of that word is highlighted. From there you can use the Next and Previous buttons to search down, and up, the page for your word. When you've found what you're looking for, close the Find box by clicking the X in its upper-right corner.

Getting More with Add-ons

Add-ons are programs used to extend the functionality of Internet Explorer. Some examples with which many readers will be familiar include Apple's QuickTime, Adobe Acrobat Reader, and Macromedia Flash Player. QuickTime and Adobe Reader are full stand-alone programs. But each also has an Internet Explorer add-on component that installed automatically with the application.

Shopping for add-ons

There are many add-ons for Internet Explorer, beyond the free and popular examples mentioned. They range in price from free to hundreds of dollars. They are entirely optional. So you're never required to download such add-ons.

You should wait until you've fully mastered all the capabilities of Internet Explorer before you consider using add-ons. Many older add-ons duplicate capabilities already available in Internet Explorer and Windows Vista. (Parental controls and pop-up blockers are good examples.) You're much better off using what you already have, if possible, than using an old program designed for older systems.

 See Chapter 4 for more information on using Windows Vista parental controls.

You should only use add-ons that are specifically designed for Internet Explorer Version 7 and Windows Vista. Using add-ons designed for older versions of Windows or Internet Explorer can cause Internet Explorer to freeze up or crash often.

All those caveats aside, to see what add-ons are currently available, click the Tools button and choose Manage Add-ons ➪ Find More Add ons. You're taken to the Internet Explorer Add-ons page (`www.ieaddons.com`) where you can shop around at your leisure.

Managing add-ons

To view add-ons already in Internet Explorer, choose Tools ➪ Manage Add-ons. The Manage Add-ons dialog box opens (see Figure 17.37). Use the Show drop-down button to view add-ons as follows:

Manage add-ons.

- **Add-ons that have been used by Internet Explorer:** Shows all add-ons in your computer.
- **Add-ons currently loaded in Internet Explorer:** Lists add-ons that were needed or used by the current Web page or recently visited pages.
- **Add-ons that run without requiring permission:** Shows add-ons that were pre-approved as safe by your ISP, computer manufacturer, or Microsoft. These are required for normal use of Internet Explorer.
- **Downloaded ActiveX Controls (32-bit):** Lists installed 32-bit ActiveX controls.

If you think an add-on is causing problems, disable it. Just click its name and choose Disable under Settings. If that doesn't resolve the problem, or causes new problems with another site, re-enable the add-on. As before, click its name and choose Enable.

To remove an ActiveX control add-on, click its name and then click the Delete ActiveX button. Most Browser Extensions and Helper objects can't be removed in that manner, because they're components of some larger program. If you're confident that one is causing a problem, remove the larger application program through Add or Remove Programs in Control Panel.

Internet Explorer Help and Troubleshooting

Like most programs, Internet Explorer has its own built-in help. To get to it, click the Help button on the Command Bar. Or, click >> at the end of the bar and choose Help as shown in Figure 17.38. Or choose Help from its menu bar.

FIGURE 17.38

Internet Explorer Help and Support.

If you're having difficulty getting online, try choosing Tools ⇨ Diagnose connection problems from Internet Explorer's menu. If that doesn't help, contact your ISP's tech support by phone. Be sure to tell them you've having difficulties connecting with Internet Explorer 7 in Windows Vista.

Wrap Up

In this chapter you've learned about the World Wide Web and Internet Explorer. The Web is the most comprehensive and widely used resource ever. The program you use to access the Web is called a Web browser. Internet Explorer is the Web browser that comes with Windows XP. Here's a quick summary of the key points made in this chapter about Internet Explorer 7:

- Internet Explorer tabs let you browse with multiple pages open simultaneously.

- RSS feeds are Web content that's delivered to you automatically. Blogs are a type of RSS feed.

- Favorites let you organize links to favorite Web sites for easy one-click return visits.

- Internet Explorer's pop-up blocker helps to keep annoying pop-up ads to a minimum.

- Internet Explorer's Phishing Filter alerts you to potentially fraudulent Web sites designed to steal your password, and possibly your identity.

- The Search box lets you search any number of search engines and Web sites for any word or phrase.

Chapter 18

Doing E-Mail with Windows Mail

It seems that just about everyone knows what e-mail is. The *e* stands for *electronic*. With e-mail, you type a letter or message on your computer, you send it to the recipient's e-mail address, and it ends up in the recipient's e-mail Inbox a few seconds later. You can attach things like pictures and other files to the message so that the recipient gets those too. It's a lot faster than the postal service (called *snail mail* by computer jocks), and it doesn't cost a cent.

To use e-mail, you need an Internet connection, an e-mail address, and an e-mail client. All e-mail addresses follow the format *someone@somewhere.tld*, where *someone* is your user name and *somewhere.tld* is your ISP's *domain name*. The e-mail client is the program you use to send and receive e-mail. This chapter is about Windows Mail, the optional e-mail client that comes with Windows Vista.

IN THIS CHAPTER

Sending and receiving e-mail

Sending and using attachments

Dealing with junk e-mail

Automatic organizing and responding

Personalizing Windows Mail

Security and protection from identity theft

How E-Mail Works

Every person who has Internet access has an account with an Internet service provider (ISP). That ISP provides the connection between your computer and the Internet. There are thousands of ISPs in the world. But there is only one Internet. The Internet is basically a system of cables covering the entire earth, like a giant net, connecting tens of millions of computers together through their ISPs.

When you send an e-mail message to someone, it goes from your computer to an *outgoing mail server* (a computer) at your ISP. That server then hands your message off to the Internet. The Internet moves the message to an *incoming mail server* at the recipient's ISP. That incoming mail server then gets the message to the recipient.

Figure 18.1 shows the basic idea using two computers. There are, of course, millions of PCs connected to the Internet. But they can all send e-mail messages back and forth because they're all connected to the one-and-only Internet. Pretty simple, really!

FIGURE 18.1

PCs connected to the Internet through their ISPs.

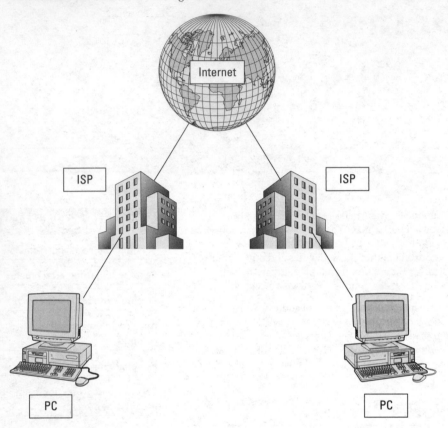

NEW FEATURE   Windows Mail is the replacement for Outlook Express and a major improvement.

Introducing Windows Mail

Windows Vista comes with an e-mail client named Windows Mail. If Windows Mail is your default e-mail client (the main program you use for sending and receiving e-mail), you can start Windows Mail by clicking the Start button and choosing E-mail Windows Mail. Figure 18.2 shows its icon (at the mouse pointer).

The first time you open Windows Mail, you might be taken to a wizard for setting up your e-mail account. If you have all the factual information you need about your account, you can proceed through the wizard to set up the account. Otherwise, you can click the Cancel button and open Windows Mail. Then set up your account later. Figure 18.3 shows how the Windows Mail program looks, and points out some of its main components. Don't be alarmed if you're missing some components. Many are optional and easily turned on and off with a mouse click or two.

FIGURE 18.2

Windows Mail icon on the Start menu.

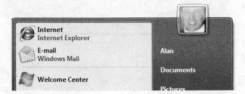

FIGURE 18.3

Windows Mail program window.

If Windows Mail isn't an option on your Start menu, you can still open it. Click the Start button, then click All Programs ➪ Microsoft Windows Mail. Whether or not you can *use* Windows Mail is an altogether different matter, which we'll tackle in a moment. The title bar, menu bar, and toolbar appear near the top of the program window and work the same as in other programs. The other components are as follows:

- **Folder bar:** Shows the name of the folder whose contents you're viewing in the contents pane.
- **Folder list:** Shows folders into which you can organize e-mail messages.
- **Contents pane:** Shows a message header for each e-mail message in the currently selected folder.
- **Sample message header:** Every e-mail message shows a header showing who sent the message, the Subject of the message, and the date you received it.
- **Preview pane header:** Shows the message header information in a large and more detailed format.
- **Preview pane:** Shows a portion of the e-mail message whose message header is selected in the contents pane.
- **Views bar:** Lets you choose what e-mail messages you want to see.
- **Status bar:** Tells you the status of various program facts and operations.

As with most programs, you can customize the appearance of Windows Mail to your liking. Choose View ⇨ Layout from its menu bar to get to the dialog box shown in Figure 18.4. Items that have checkmarks are currently "on" and visible in the program window. Items without checkmarks are "off."

Windows Layout Properties dialog box.

To change an option, click its checkbox and then click Apply. If you don't like the results, click that same checkbox again and click Apply again. When you're happy with how things look, click OK to save your current settings and close the dialog box.

Before you can use Windows Mail to send and receive e-mail, you have to configure it to work with your e-mail account. Your ISP (Internet service provider) supplies your e-mail account. Windows Mail is just the e-mail client (program) that lets you send and receive messages through the e-mail account that your ISP provides.

What you need to know to get started

Before you attempt to use Windows Mail as your e-mail client, you'll need to acquire some basic facts about your e-mail account. Only your Internet service provider, or e-mail provider, can give you that information. Here's a quick overview of the information you need:

- You need to find out if you can use Windows Mail with your Internet account. Only your Internet service provider (ISP) can give you that information.

- **E-mail address:** You must know your own e-mail address, the one that people use to send you e-mail messages. You get your e-mail address from your ISP or e-mail service.

- **Account type:** Typically this would be either POP or HTTP (Hypertext Transfer Protocol).

- **User account name:** The name you use to sign into your ISP's service.

- **E-mail password:** You should be able to define your own password. But if your ISP has set up a temporary password, you'll need to know what that is to set up your account.

- **Outgoing (SMTP) mail server:** You will need to know the exact name of your ISP's outgoing mail server.

- **Incoming (POP3) mail server:** You will need to know the exact name of your ISP's incoming mail server.

Feel free to use Table 18-1 to jot down the facts about your account. If you're tempted to fill in your own information by guessing, don't. Windows Mail won't work until you get exactly the right information in place. Guessing won't work.

TABLE 18-1

Information You Need to Set Up Windows Mail

Line	Information Needed	Example	Write Your Information Here
1	ISP allows Windows Mail as e-mail client?	Yes or No	
2	Your e-mail address	somebody@ somewhere.com	
3	E-mail account type	POP3, IMAP, HTTP, Web mail, or some other protocol	
4	Incoming (POP3) mail server	`mail.somewhere.com`	
5	Outgoing (SMTP) mail server	`smtp.somewhere.com`	
6	Server requires authentication	Yes or No	
7	Your e-mail user name	Somebody	
8	Your e-mail password	********	

Keep in mind that if you're dealing with multiple e-mail addresses and accounts, you'll need to fill in the blanks in Table 18-1 for each e-mail address. You'll need to set up a separate Windows Mail account for each e-mail address.

After you've filled in the Table 18-1 blanks for an e-mail account, you're ready of configure Windows Mail to use that account. Remember, Windows Mail doesn't work with all e-mail systems. So . . .

- If your answer to Line 1 is No, ignore this entire chapter. Use whatever e-mail client and methods your ISP provides.

- If your information for Line 3 is *not* POP3, or IMAP, check with your ISP for specific instructions on setting up Windows Mail as your e-mail client.

Assuming you know Windows Mail will work with your e-mail account, and you've accurately filled in the blanks in Table 18-1, you're ready to configure your e-mail account.

Setting up your e-mail account

If several people share a single computer, each user should have his or her own user account and e-mail address. (See Chapter 3 if you need to set up user accounts.) Before you configure Windows Mail, make sure you log in to the user account for the e-mail address you're about to configure. Then configure Windows Mail for that user's e-mail address only. Start Windows Mail as described earlier in this chapter and follow these steps:

1. From the Windows Mail menu bar, choose Tools ➪ Accounts and click Add.

2. In the Select Account Type box that opens, click E-mail Account and click Next.

3. On the page titled Your Name, type your name as you want it to appear in your e-mail messages. Typically this would be your first and last names. But you can enter your name or a nickname however you wish. Click Next.

 **When typing information in the remaining steps, be aware that even the tiniest typographical error, misspelling, or a blank space will prevent your account from working.**

4. On the Internet E-mail Address page, type your e-mail address exactly as provided by your ISP and in Line 2 in Table 18-1. Click Next.

5. On the Set up e-mail servers page (see Figure 18.5), choose options and fill in the blanks according to what you entered in Lines 3–6 in Table 18-1. Choose *Outgoing server requires authentication* only if your ISP requires it. Click Next.

FIGURE 18.5

The E-Mail Server Names page of the Internet Connection Wizard.

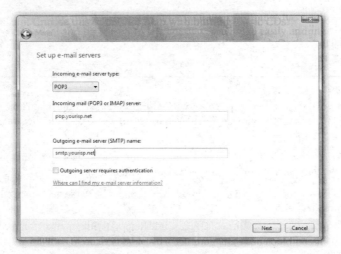

 **Copying the information from the example in Figure 18.5 won't work. You have to provide the information for your own e-mail account as provided by your ISP or mail service provider.**

6. On the Set up Internet Mail Logon page, type your e-mail account name and password as provided by your ISP (Lines 7 and 8). You won't be able to see the password as you type it. You must use the same uppercase/lowercase letters given by your ISP. So type carefully.

7. If you don't want to enter your password every time you check your e-mail, choose (check) Remember password. However, don't choose that option on a public computer, because it will allow anyone to use your e-mail account. Click Next.

8. If you see a page asking about customer improvement, you'll need to decide for yourself if you want to participate. There is no risk or penalty either way. Click Next after making your selection.

9. On the Congratulations page, click the Finish button.

The new account will be added to the Internet Accounts dialog box under the Main heading. The sample account shown in Figure 18.6 is just an example. Yours will likely be different.

FIGURE 18.6

Sample e-mail account, mail.comcast.net.

To test your account, click the Send/Receive button. If you get an error message, you made a mistake or entered wrong information somewhere in steps 1–9. To review, and optionally change, any information you entered, choose Tools ⇨ Accounts from the menu bar. Then click the name of the account you just created and choose Properties. In the Properties dialog box that opens, review what you entered and make any necessary corrections. Remember, only your ISP (or e-mail account provider) can help you troubleshoot any problems you might have.

TIP To give the account a more meaningful name of your own choosing, click its name in the Internet Accounts dialog box and click Properties. In the first text box on the General tab, replace the current name with a name of your own choosing. Then click OK. Click Close to close the Internet Accounts dialog box.

Writing E-Mail with Windows Mail

Once your e-mail account is properly configured, you're ready to send and receive e-mail. You can send an e-mail message to anyone who has an e-mail address. You can even send messages to yourself. That might be worthwhile if you're new to all of this and just want to test things out for starters. To write an e-mail message:

1. Click Create Mail in the toolbar (or press Ctrl+N or choose File ➪ New ➪ Mail Message from the menu bar). An empty message opens in a window titled New Message.

TIP To add a fancy background to your message, click the arrow on the Create Mail button, and then click a stationery name.

2. Type the recipient's e-mail address next to To:. If you want to send the message to several people, you can type several addresses separated by semicolons (;).

   ■ Optionally, to send carbon copies of the message to other recipients, put their e-mail addresses in the Cc: box. Again, you can separate multiple e-mail addresses with semicolons.

   ■ Optionally, to send blind carbon copies of the message to other recipients, type their e-mail addresses into the Bcc: box, again separating multiple addresses with semicolons.

TIP A blind carbon copy sends the e-mail message to the recipient with all other recipients' names hidden. This protects the privacy of other recipients and makes the e-mail look as though it was sent to the recipient directly. If you have multiple e-mail accounts and want to change the account from which you're sending, use the From: drop-down menu. If you don't see From: and Bcc: boxes, choose View ➪ All Headers from the New Message menu bar.

3. In the Subject: box, type a brief description of the subject of the message. This part of the message appears in the recipient's Inbox and is visible prior to the recipient's opening the message.

4. Type your message in the large editing window below the address portion of the e-mail. Figure 18.7 shows an example of a simple test message typed in the New Message window.

FIGURE 18.7

A simple test message.

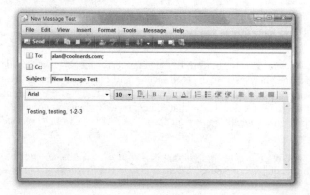

■ Optionally, use the basic editing techniques and spell checker described later to clean up your message before sending.

■ Optionally, set the message priority or request a read receipt using techniques described in the sections to follow.

5. Click the Send button in the toolbar.

Depending on how Windows Mail is configured, the message will either go to your Outbox or be sent immediately. If it goes to your Outbox, you'll see a 1 next to that folder name (see Figure 18.8). To send the message, click Send/Receive in the toolbar.

FIGURE 18.8

Message waiting in the Outbox.

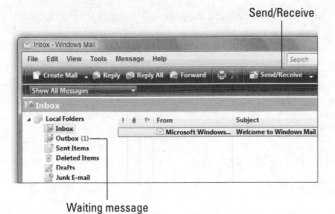

Send/Receive

Waiting message

If you sent the message to yourself, it might not appear right away. You'll have to wait a few seconds — maybe longer. Then click Send/Receive to get your messages from your ISP's incoming mail server.

Typing and editing tips

Here are some basic things to keep in mind when typing an e-mail message (or just about anything else on a computer screen):

■ When typing a paragraph, don't press Enter at the end of each line. Only press Enter at the end of the paragraph.

■ To insert a blank line, press Enter (for example, press Enter twice at the end of a paragraph).

■ The blinking cursor on the screen shows where the text you type next will appear. To change text, click where you want to make your change to get the blinking cursor to that spot. Then type your new text.

■ To delete a few characters, click where you want to delete. Press Delete (Del) to delete characters to the right of the cursor or a blank line. Press Backspace to delete characters to the left of the cursor.

■ To delete a larger chunk of text, select (drag the mouse pointer through) the text you want to delete. Then press Delete (Del).

- To undo a recent change to your text, press Ctrl+Z or click the Undo button in the toolbar, or choose Edit ⇨ Undo from the menu bar.
- Use standard copy-and-paste techniques to paste text into an e-mail message, and to move or copy text out of a message. See "Using copy-and-paste and cut-and-paste" in Chapter 15.

 There's rarely any need to re-type text you can already see on your screen. Just copy-and-paste the text instead. Anyplace you can type text, you can also paste text.

Check your spelling

To check your spelling in an e-mail message, choose Tools ⇨ Spelling from the New Message menu bar, or press F7, or click the Spelling (abc) toolbar button. The spell checker will compare each word in your message to an internal dictionary. When it finds a word that doesn't exist in its dictionary, the Spelling dialog box opens. From there you can do any of the following:

- If the Spelling box offers suggested words, click the word that's spelled correctly, then click Change.
- If the word is already spelled correctly (because it's a person's name or some other word not normally found in the dictionary), click Ignore.

TIP If you already know how to use a word processing program like Microsoft Word or WordPerfect, you can type, edit, and spell-check your message in that program. Press Ctrl+A then Ctrl+C in the word processing program to select and copy all text. Then click in the body of your e-mail message and press Ctrl+V to paste that copied text into the e-mail message.

Add a background color, picture, or sound

When you're in the New Message window writing your e-mail message, you can add a background color or picture, or even a sound to your message. First, choose Format ⇨ Background and then click whichever item you want to add. Then:

- If you chose Color, just click whatever color you want to use.
- If you chose Picture, click the Browse button and navigate to the picture you want to add. Then click OK.
- If you chose Sound, click the Browse button and navigate to the folder that contains the sound file you want to add. Click the sound file's icon and click Open.

If you chose a sound, the sound will play when the recipient clicks the message header to read the e-mail message.

CAUTION Don't use an entire song as a message background. Stick with small sound effect files. To send a song or other large audio file, attach it to the e-mail message.

Setting message priority

The Priority column at the left of the contents pane has an exclamation point (!) as its column heading. This column shows nothing for normal-priority messages. It shows a red exclamation point for high-priority messages. It shows a blue arrow for low-priority messages.

Every e-mail message you type will automatically be set to normal priority. To change that, click the Set Priority button in the New Message toolbar, or choose Message ➪ Set Priority from the menu bar. Then choose a priority. The appropriate symbol will show up in the Priority column of the recipient's Inbox.

 To see how priorities and read receipts work, apply those features to some test messages sent to your own e-mail address.

Requesting a read receipt

If you want to verify that a recipient has received and read your e-mail message, choose Tools ➪ Request Read Receipt from the New Message window's menu bar. Then send your message normally.

When the recipient receives and reads the message, she will see a box indicating that you've requested a read receipt. If she chooses Yes to send a read receipt, you will receive an e-mail message with the word Read in the Subject line. That message tells you the date and time that the recipient read the message.

 There's no guarantee that you'll always get a read receipt, because the recipient can opt not to send you one.

Getting Your E-Mail

To get e-mail messages addressed to you, you have do download them from your ISP's incoming mail server. Depending on how Windows Mail is configured, that might happen automatically as soon as you open Windows Mail. It might even happen automatically every few seconds. It all depends on how you configure Windows Mail. But regardless of how Windows Mail is configured at the moment, you can always download waiting messages by clicking Send/Receive in the toolbar.

New messages you receive may go straight to your Junk Mail folder, or to your Inbox. It all depends on (you guessed it) how you've configured Windows Mail. I'll talk about junk mail a little later in the chapter. Every folder shows a little number indicating how may unread messages it contains. To see unread messages, click the folder in the Folder list (either Inbox or Junk Mail). The contents pane shows message headers for every message currently in the folder. Headers for unread messages are boldface.

To preview what's in the message, click its message header. The Preview pane shows the message (or at least, part of it). In Figure 18.9 I've received the e-mail message I sent to myself. It ended up in my Inbox. So I clicked the Inbox folder, then clicked the message header. The body of that simple message appears in the Preview pane.

An unread message turns to a read message within a few seconds of clicking its message header. So its message header won't stay boldfaced for long. And the number next to the folder name will also go away once you've read all the messages in that folder.

The preview window may not be tall enough to show the entire message. But you have a couple choices there. You can use the scroll bar at the right side of the message to scroll up and down. Or you can adjust the height of the preview pane by dragging its upper border up or down. Or you can double-click the message header to *open* the message. An open message appears in its own window. You can position and size that window to your liking using the techniques described in Chapter 2.

Replying to a message

If you want to reply to the e-mail message you're currently reading, click one of the following:

- **Reply:** Click this button to reply to the original sender only.
- **Reply All:** Click this button to reply to the original sender plus everyone else to whom that sender sent the same message.

FIGURE 18.9

Viewing a received message.

Selected message header

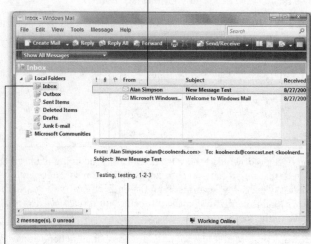

Selected folder (Inbox)   Content of selected message

The message opens in a new window with some empty space up top for you to type your reply. No need to delete the original message below that space. In fact, it's better to leave it there because that way the person to whom you're replying can review, if necessary, the original message to which you're responding. When you've finished typing your reply, click the Send button in the toolbar.

Forwarding a message

To pass on the message you're reading to a friend or colleague, click the Forward button. Type in the new recipient's e-mail address. Optionally, you can type multiple e-mail addresses separated by semicolons (;). Then click Send. Just remember that if your outgoing messages end up in your Outbox, they won't actually be sent until you click Send/Receive in the toolbar.

Other stuff you can do with a message

To see other things you can do with a message, right-click the message header. You'll see a menu like the one in Figure 18.10. The first few options let you do things we already discussed (open, print, reply, forward). The rest are summarized in the following list.

Here, in a nutshell, is what the rest of the options offer. Some options are covered in more detail later in this chapter:

- **Open:** Opens the e-mail message in a separate window. You can move, size, and position that window to your liking using the techniques described in Chapter 2.

- **Print:** Prints a copy of the message (on paper). See Chapter 36 if you need help with printing.

- **Reply to Sender**, **Reply to All**, **Forward:** As described under the "Replying to a message" and "Forwarding a message" sections, previously in this chapter.

FIGURE 18.10

Right-click a message header.

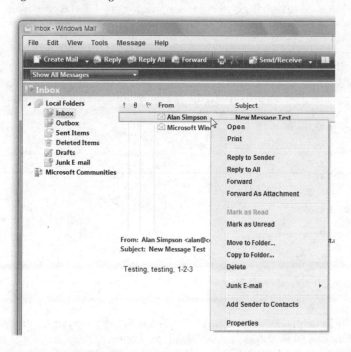

- **Forward As Attachment:** Forwards the message to senders of your choosing as an attached file rather than as a message. See "Using E-Mail Attachments" in this chapter for more information on attachments.

- **Mark as Read:** Removes the boldface from the message header.

- **Mark as Unread:** Makes the message header boldfaced.

- **Move to Folder:** Moves the message to any folder in the Folder list. (Optionally, you can drag any message header to any folder in the list.)

- **Copy to Folder:** Puts a copy of the message in a folder you specify, without removing it from its current folder.

- **Delete:** Sends the message to the Deleted Items folder.

- **Junk E-mail:** Offers numerous options for deciding how to treat future messages from the message sender.

- **Add Sender to Contacts:** Adds the message to your contacts (similar to a personal address book).
- **Properties:** Shows some detailed information about the message.

Magnifying e-mail text

To change the text size of an e-mail message, choose View ➪ Text Size from the menu bar, then click a text size. To return to the normal text size at any time, choose View ➪ Text Size ➪ Normal.

Sorting message headers

As in any columnar display of data, you can sort message headers however you see fit. Just click the column heading by which you want to sort. For example, to sort messages by Date Received, with the most recent messages at the top of the list, click the Received column until the little triangle in that heading points down.

Sizing and positioning columns

As in most columnar displays of data, you can choose, arrange, and size columns in the contents pane. To widen or narrow a column, get the tip of the mouse pointer right on the line at the right side of the column title so the mouse pointer changes to a two-headed arrow like in Figure 18.11. Then slowly drag left or right to widen or narrow the column.

FIGURE 18.11

Size a column.

Mouse pointer

From	Subject	↔ Received
Alan Simpson	Sample PlainText Message	4/17/200
Alan Simpson	Test message 1	4/17/200
Alan Simpson	Test Message 2	4/17/200
Microsoft Windows ...	Welcome to Windows Mail	4/13/200

 **TIP**   The term *drag* means "hold down the left mouse button while moving the mouse." It's the general method you use to move and size things on your screen.

To move a column left or right, get the tip of the mouse pointer right on the column name. Then drag the column name left or right.

 **NOTE**   To deal with blocked content and warning messages, see "E-Mail security options" later in this chapter.

Sizing the Preview pane

The Preview pane shows the contents of whatever message header you click. You can size it as you would most other panes: Get the tip of the mouse pointer on the upper border of the Preview pane so the mouse pointer changes to a two-headed arrow. Then slowly drag up or down until the pane is the size you like.

Don't forget that the Preview pane is just a sneak peek at what's in an e-mail message. You can double-click any message header to open the full message in its own window. You can size, position, and close that window using the standard methods described in Chapter 2.

Using E-Mail Attachments

Attachments provide a means of sending regular documents (the kind discussed in Chapter 11) through e-mail. For example, to send a picture, song, video, spreadsheet, or Microsoft Word or other document from a folder to someone, you *attach* that document to an e-mail message.

Every ISP puts a limit on how large a file you can attach. The number varies from one ISP to the next. With dial-up accounts the limit is usually 1–3 MB. With broadband accounts it's more like 10MB. To find out what your attachment size limit is, browse around your ISP's help documentation for e-mail. Or contact them by phone if need be.

You can attach multiple files to an e-mail message. But their combined sizes must be within the limit imposed by your ISP. Optionally, you can combine multiple files into a single compressed folder (Zip file) first. That allows both you and the recipient to handle multiple files as one, and can also reduce the overall file size. See "Zipping and Unzipping Files" in Chapter 15 for more information on using Zip files.

You can attach files to e-mail messages in Windows Mail in several ways. There isn't a right way or wrong way. And the end result is the same no matter which method you use — the e-mail recipient gets your e-mail message with the files you attached. So choosing one method or another is just a matter of deciding what's easiest for you based on what you're sending and how much you know about files and folders. We'll start with the basic method of writing an e-mail message then attaching one or more files.

Attaching a file to a message

You can write an e-mail message in Windows Mail first. Then attach one or more files to it. The file (or files) can be anything; word processing documents, spreadsheets, pictures, music, video — whatever. You just need to know what folder the file(s) are in, and how to navigate to the folder that the files are in. Here are the steps:

1. In Windows Mail, click Create Mail, fill in the To and Subject lines, and type the body of the message as you would with any other e-mail message. But don't send the message yet.

2. From the menu bar above the new message, choose Insert ➪ File Attachment. An Open dialog box opens as in Figure 18.12.

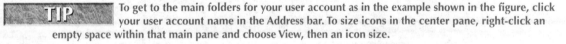 **TIP** To get to the main folders for your user account as in the example shown in the figure, click your user account name in the Address bar. To size icons in the center pane, right-click an empty space within that main pane and choose View, then an icon size.

3. Navigate to the folder that contains the files you want to attach to your message.

4. Click the icon for the file you want to attach, or select icons for all the files you want to attach. Then click Open. The file(s) you selected appear in the Attach box. Figure 18.13 shows an example where I've attached two files named SampleDoc.doc (a Microsoft Word document) and Scores.xls (an Excel spreadsheet).

5. Optionally, to attach files from other folders, repeat steps 2–4.

6. Click Send in the New Message window toolbar.

The message will be sent immediately or placed in your Outbox, depending on how you've configured Windows Mail. If the message goes to your Outbox, click Send/Receive to send the message.

FIGURE 18.12

Insert Attachment dialog box.

FIGURE 18.13

Icons for attached files.

Attached files

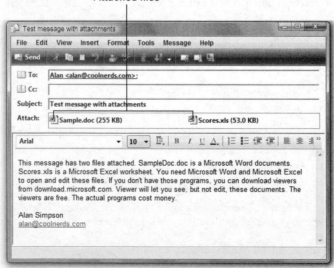

E-mailing documents from folders

The preceding steps assume you want to create your e-mail message first and then attach files to it. But there's another way to do it. If you happen to be in the folder that contains the file(s) you want to e-mail, there's no reason to open Windows Mail first. Instead you can follow these steps:

1. If you haven't already done so, open the folder that contains the file(s) you want to send.

2. Optionally, to send multiple files from the same folder, select their icons.

> **TIP** See "How to Select Icons" in Chapter 29 if you haven't yet learned how to select multiple icons.

3. Right-click the icon of the file that you want to e-mail (or any selected icon) and choose Send To ⇨ Mail Recipient (see Figure 18.14).

FIGURE 18.14

E-mailing from a folder.

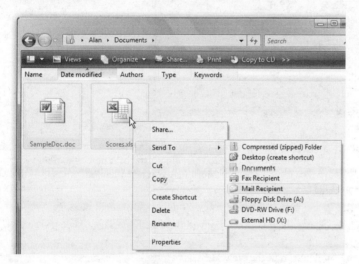

4. If you're sending pictures, the Attach Files dialog box opens. Choose whatever size you want the pictures to be. Just make sure the resulting Total Estimated Size is within the attachment size limit imposed by your ISP. Then click Attach. Try a smaller picture size if you go over the limit.

5. A new, empty e-mail message opens in the New Message window with the files already attached. Fill in the To and Subject lines as you would with any other e-mail message.

6. Optionally, change the text of the message to whatever you want to write in your e-mail message.

7. Click the Send button in the New Message toolbar.

The message and attached files will be sent immediately or placed in your Outbox. If placed in your Outbox, open Windows Mail and click the Send/Receive button in its toolbar to send the message and its attached files.

> **NOTE** If the preceding steps don't work for you, it's most likely because you're not using Windows Mail as your e-mail client. This chapter is strictly about Windows Mail.

E-mailing pictures from Windows Photo Gallery

If you've already learned how to use Windows Photo Gallery (Chapter 22), you can e-mail photos and video clips straight from the gallery. Here are the steps:

1. Open Windows Photo Gallery.

2. Choose options in the navigation pane so that you can see the photos and/or video clip icons of the items you want to send.

3. Select the icons of the items you want to send using the standard selection methods for Windows Photo Gallery (see "Selecting thumbnails in the gallery" in Chapter 22 to learn how).

4. Click E-mail in the toolbar. The Attach Files dialog box shown in Figure 18.15 opens.

FIGURE 18.15

Attach Files dialog box.

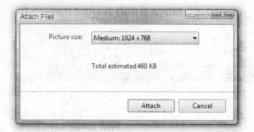

5. Choose a size for your pictures, making sure that the Total Estimated Size is within the attachment size limit imposed by your ISP. Then click Attach. A new e-mail message opens in the New Message window with the files already attached. Their filenames appear in the Attach box under the Subject line.

6. Fill in the To and Subject lines as you would with any e-mail message.

7. Optionally, change the text in the body of the e-mail message to whatever message you want to write.

8. Click the Send button in the New Message window.

As always, the message is either sent immediately or placed in your Windows Mail Outbox. If it ends up in your Outbox, open Windows Mail and click Send/Receive to send the message.

You can use the same technique to send pictures from your Pictures folder, or any folder that contains pictures. Open the folder, select the pictures you want to send, right-click any selected icon, and choose Send To ➪ Mail Recipient.

Opening received attachments

When somebody sends you an e-mail message with files attached, the header for that message shows a paper clip icon. For example, the first two messages in Figure 18.16 both have attachments. When you click the message header of such a message the Preview pane also shows a paper clip. Clicking the large paper clip icon in the Preview pane shows the filenames of the attachments and a Save Attachments option.

Most malware (viruses and such) is spread by e-mail attachments. Never open any e-mail attachment unless you know who it's from and what it contains. Do not trust e-mail messages that claim to be returning failed messages from your account. Most of the time they're fake. Their attached files contain things you do not want on your computer!

To open an attachment, first click the message header, then click the large paper clip icon in the Preview pane header. The name of each attached file appears in a menu like in Figure 18.16. To view the contents of an attachment, click its filename in the menu. You will probably get a security warning. If you're confident that the attachment is safe, click Open to open it.

FIGURE 18.16

E-mail message attachments.

Disabled (dimmed) items on the paper clip menu can't be opened or saved, due to your current security settings. See "E-mail security options" later in this chapter for more information.

The attachment will open in whatever program is currently configured for that file type on your system. (Assuming there is a program for that file type on your system.) If it opens, you can view it, save it to a regular file, print it, or do whatever you like with it in that program. (Again, assuming you know how to use that program to do all of those things.) Close that program when you're done viewing the attachment.

Now let's look at why you might not be able to open every attachment you receive.

There are thousands of different file types, and thousands of different programs. You can only open files (attachments) for a file type if you have a program that *can* open that file type. If you don't have an appropriate program installed on your system, you'll see an error message, perhaps like the one in Figure 18.17, when you try to open an attachment.

As an example, suppose someone sends you a Microsoft PowerPoint file with a .ppt extension. If you don't have the PowerPoint program (or a PowerPoint viewer), you won't be able to open that attachment. At least, not until you get a PowerPoint viewer.

It would probably take as many pages as there are in this entire book for me to list all the different filename extensions and the programs that can open them. So I won't even attempt that. But I can tell you some of the more common file types, and the programs you need to open them. I'll stick with free *viewers* here. The difference between a viewer and program is that the viewer will let you see the file, but not change it. Also, the viewer is free. The full program for the file type usually costs money.

Error message for attachment.

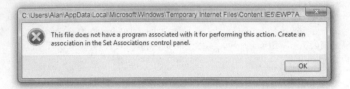

Table 18-2 lists some common file types, the name of the freebie you need to open that type of file, the Web site from which you can download the viewer, and the word(s) to search for (if needed) when you get to the suggested page in order to find the download. When downloading a program, be sure to choose Run or Open (rather than Save) to both download and install the program.

 See Chapter 40 for more information on downloading programs.

TABLE 18-2

Some Common File Types and Available Viewers

Extension	Program Needed	Web Site	Search for
.doc	Microsoft Word	`http://download.microsoft.com`	Word viewer
.kmz	Google Earth	`http://earth.google.com/ download-earth.html`	
.mov	QuickTime	`www.quicktime.com`	
.pdf	Adobe Reader	`http://www.adobe.com/products/ acrobat/readermain.html`	
.ppt	Microsoft PowerPoint	`http://download.microsoft.com`	PowerPoint viewer
.snp	Snapshot Viewer	`http://download.microsoft.com`	Snapshot viewer
.vsd	Microsoft Visio	`http://download.microsoft.com`	Visio Viewer
.xls	Microsoft Excel	`http://download.microsoft.com`	Excel viewer

If you can't find a viewer for an attachment, but you know the sender, you may be able to get them to re-send the file in a format you can open. For example, a WordPerfect user might be able to save a document in Rich Text Format (`.rtf`) or as a Word document (`.doc`). Then send that copy of the file as an e-mail attachment.

 Digitally licensed files, such as music you purchase online, will only play on the computer to which you downloaded the file. That's true even if you already have the correct player for the file.

Saving attachments as files

Files attached to e-mail messages don't automatically go to a regular document folder like the Documents, Pictures, and Music folders in your user account. To convert an attached file to a "normal" document in a "normal" folder like that, you need to *save* the attachment to the appropriate folder. Here's how:

1. Click the message header of the message that contains the attachments that you want to save as files.

2. Click the large paper clip icon in the Preview pane header, then click the Save Attachments option at the bottom of that menu (see Figure 18.18).

FIGURE 18.18

Paper clip icon for a message with attached files.

If Save Attachments at the bottom of the menu is disabled (dimmed), the next steps won't work. You have to clear the *Do not allow attachments to be saved or opened that could potentially be a virus* checkbox on the Security tab of the Options dialog box, then close and reopen Windows Mail. See "Personalizing Windows Mail" later in this chapter for details.

3. The Save Attachments dialog box opens. Initially all the filenames will be selected, like in Figure 18.19. You can hold down the Ctrl key and click the names of any files you do or don't want to save. Only selected files will be saved.

FIGURE 18.19

Save Attachments dialog box.

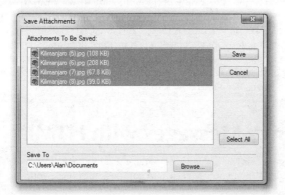

4. Click the Browse button and navigate to the folder in which you want to put the saved files. For example, if you're saving a picture, choose your Pictures folder. For a text document or work-sheet, choose your Documents folder. Click OK.

5. Click Save.

The Save Attachments dialog box closes and you're returned to Windows Mail. The original files will still be attached to the message. But you'll also find copies of those same attached files in whatever folder you specified in step 4. Use those saved copies of the attachments for day-to-day editing of files, printing, and so forth.

Once you've verified that the files are in the folder to which you saved them, feel free to delete the e-mail message. You won't need the message or the files attached to it anymore. Or you could keep the message and its attached files as a backup to the files in your document folder.

Saving embedded pictures as files

If you get an e-mail message that contains an embedded picture, you might want to keep a copy of the picture as a regular file in Windows Photo Gallery. That way the picture is just like any picture you get from a camera or other source, and not hidden away in some old e-mail message.

Saving a picture that's embedded in an e-mail message is the same as copying a picture from a Web page in Internet Explorer. Right-click the picture and choose Save Picture As. Choose a folder — your Pictures folder if you don't have a preference — and give the picture a filename of your own choosing. Then click Save.

The saved picture will be a normal document file in whatever folder you specified. If you chose a folder that Windows Photo Gallery monitors, the picture will show up in your gallery as well, most likely as an untagged picture. But you can tag it, open it, edit it, fix it, print it, and do anything else you can do with other pictures in your gallery.

Converting e-mail messages to files

Each e-mail message you receive is a file with a .eml filename extension stored in the Windows Mail folder for your user account. But you can save a copy of any message to a regular folder, like the Documents folder for your user account. Click the header of the message you want to save. Then choose File ⇨ Save As from the Windows Mail menu bar. Specify a document folder in which to store the message. Optionally, give the file a name of your own choosing, and click Save. The message will be saved as a file with the .eml file-name extension. You can't edit that file. All you can do is open and view it.

If you have (and know how to use) a word processing program like Microsoft Word or WordPerfect, you can copy-and-paste any e-mail message to a document in that program. Open the e-mail message by double-clicking its message header. Then press Ctrl+A (Select All) and Ctrl+C (Copy) to copy the message content to the clipboard. Then open your word processor, click inside a document, and press Ctrl+V to paste in the message. Save the document in your Documents folder, or some other Windows folder that makes sense for you. That copy of the message will be a normal, editable document. You can then delete the original e-mail message, or perhaps keep it as a backup.

Composing Fancy Messages with HTML

HTML (Hypertext Markup Language) is the formatting language used to create Web pages. You can also use it to compose e-mail messages. When you use HTML to compose messages, your message can contain much more than plain text. You can use fonts, hyperlinks, pictures, and other fancier formatting features in your messages.

HTML, default font, and stationery

The first step to creating fancy messages with HTML is to configure Windows Mail to use that setting automatically. Here are the steps:

1. In Windows Mail, choose Tools ⇨ Options from the menu bar.
2. In the Options dialog box that opens, click the Send tab.
3. Under Mail Sending Format, choose HTML as in Figure 18.20.

FIGURE 18.20

Send messages as HTML.

4. If you want to also set a default font and stationery, continue with the following steps. Otherwise you can click OK now and skip the remaining steps.
5. Click the Compose tab.
6. To set a default font, click Font Settings next to Mail. Choose your font name, size, and color, and then click OK.
7. Optionally, to choose a stationery (background picture), select (check) the checkbox next to Mail under the Stationery heading. Then click the Select button to the right.
8. In the Select Stationery dialog box that opens, point to each icon to see what it looks like in the Preview pane to the right. (Make sure Show Preview is selected if you don't see previews.) Take a look at each one. If you find one you like, click it, and then click OK.

> **TIP** If you want to try your hand at creating your own custom stationery, click Create New in the Select Stationery dialog box.

9. Click OK to save your settings and return to Windows Mail.

To compose a new e-mail message, click the Create New button. If you chose a stationery in the preceding steps, the new message will have that stationery automatically. Fill in the To and Subject lines as you normally would. Then type your message. If you chose a default font, text you type in the body of the message will be in that font.

> **TIP** To choose or change the stationery for an e-mail message that you're currently typing, choose Format ⇨ Apply Stationery from the New Message window's menu bar.

You don't have to worry about applying any fancy formatting while typing your message. You might find it easiest to just type the text of your message. Then go back and apply formatting using the *select, then do* method. Which means you *select* (drag the mouse pointer through) the text you want to format. Then *do* by clicking a button in the formatting toolbar just above the text. You'll see examples as we go here.

> **TIP** The *select, then do* approach described here works in virtually all word processors and Web page editors. Once you learn to do it in one program, you know how to do it in all programs. Also, pressing Undo (Ctrl+Z) to undo your last formatting change applies to virtually all formatting in all programs.

Using fonts, sizes, boldface, underline, italics, colors

The first few buttons in the New Message formatting toolbar let you apply a font, size, paragraph style, boldface, italics, underline, and a color to selected text. To apply formatting to a chunk of text, first *select* the text by dragging the mouse pointer through it. The selected text will be highlighted. If you select too much or too little, just click on any text and try again.

> **TIP** When typing a paragraph, don't press Enter at the end of each line. Just keep typing as though right off the edge. The text will automatically wrap down to the next line as you go. Press Enter only to end a short line of text or an entire paragraph. Press Enter again to insert a blank line.

For example, in Figure 18.21 I selected the first line of text by dragging the mouse pointer through it. Notice how the selected text is highlighted (white against a black background). Once you've selected a chunk of text, you can click any button in the Formatting toolbar. The formatting is applied only to the selected text. If you're not sure what a button is for, just point to it (rest the tip of the mouse pointer on it). The name of the button appears in a tooltip at the mouse pointer. For example, in Figure 18.21 the mouse pointer is touching the Font Color button in the Formatting toolbar.

FIGURE 18.21

Selected text, Formatting toolbar.

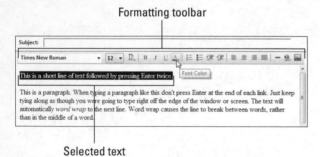

Figure 18.22 shows some text with different formats applied. The best way to get the hang of all this is to just try things out and practice in a fake e-mail that you don't intend to send anyone. Type a bunch of text. Then select any chunk of text and choose an option from the Font, Font Size, Paragraph Style, or Font Color button in the Formatting toolbar. Or just click the Bold, Italic, or Underline button. If you don't like what you see, press Ctrl+Z to undo that change.

Try combining things too. For example, you might want to apply a font, size, bold face, italic, and a font color to a chunk of text. You can't do any harm by trying things out. Especially if you practice in a message you don't intend to send to anyone.

FIGURE 18.22

Examples of formatted text.

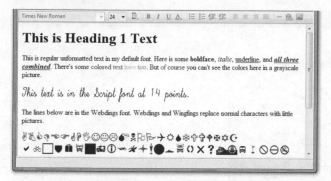

Typing a list

Numbered and bulleted lists are useful ways of organizing text. For example, you might want to show some numbered steps or a list of points or options in your text. To do so, type each item in the list, pressing Enter once at the end of each line. Do not type a number or symbol at the start of each line. Those will be added when you apply formatting later.

Next, select all the items in the list by dragging the mouse pointer through them. Figure 18.23 shows an example where I've selected multiple lines in a list. Next, click the Formatting Numbers or Formatting Bullets button in the Formatting toolbar (also shown in Figure 18.23).

FIGURE 18.23

Example of selected list.

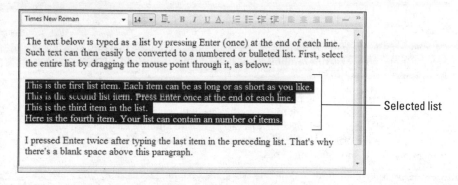

Selected list

Indenting and aligning text

Use the various alignment and indentation buttons in the toolbar (see Figure 18.24) to align or indent text. As always, you can start by typing a line or paragraph of text. Then select the text you want to align or indent, and click the appropriate buttons to apply formatting. That same figure shows examples of text to which indentation and alignment have been applied.

FIGURE 18.24

Alignment and indentation examples.

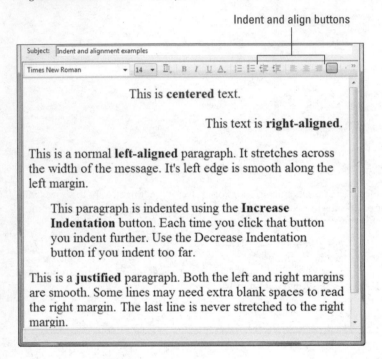

Inserting pictures

You can insert a small photo or picture into the body of your e-mail message. Unlike a picture attachment, your picture appears right in the body of your e-mail message. If the picture is small enough, you can even wrap text around the picture.

There is one catch to inserting pictures in e-mail messages. You can only insert BMP, JPEG, PNG, WMF, ART, and ICO picture types. If the picture you want to insert isn't one of those types, you can still attach it to an e-mail message as described under "Attaching a file to a message" earlier in this chapter. Or, if you have sufficient skill, you can open the picture in a graphics program. Then use that program to save a separate copy of the picture as one of the supported file types.

> **TIP** For more information on pictures and picture types, see Chapter 22. The more you know about pictures in general, the easier it will be to use them with e-mail messages.

If you're still with me, the rest is easy. Use the Create Message button to create a new e-mail message. Fill in the To and Subject lines, and type your message in the large pane — just as you would when sending any other e-mail message. Then follow these steps:

1. In your message, click where you want to put the upper-left corner of the picture.
2. Choose Insert ⇨ Picture form the menu bar, or click the Insert Picture toolbar button.
3. Click Browse, navigate to the folder that contains the picture, click the picture's icon, and then click Open. A Properties dialog box for the picture opens.
4. To place text to the left of neighboring text, set the Alignment property to Left. To put the picture to the right of the text, set the Alignment property to Right.

> **TIP**   Other Alignment options let you position a very tiny picture in line with text of the message.

5. To keep neighboring text from touching the picture, set the Horizontal spacing to 10 (or some other number of your own choosing).
6. Click OK.

Once the picture is in the message, you can make adjustments to its size. Click the picture so it shows sizing handles (little squares around its border). Then drag any handle to increase or decrease the height or width of the picture. To move the picture, just drag it to some new location within the message.

To change the alignment, spacing, or other feature of the picture, right-click the picture, choose Properties, choose your settings, and click OK. Figure 18.25 shows an example where I've placed a 150-pixel-wide photo in an e-mail message. That picture's Alignment property is set to left. Its Horizontal spacing is set to 10. The text wraps around the picture with a 10-pixel margin between the picture and the text.

FIGURE 18.25

Sample embedded picture.

It may take a little practice, especially if you're just getting started with computers and skipped straight to this chapter. If it proves too challenging, you can just attach pictures to messages without embedding. The recipient will still get the pictures, which is the main goal when e-mailing pictures to people.

Inserting a line

Did you notice that gray line under the second paragraph in Figure 18.25? If you want to insert a line like that in your own e-mail message, first click where you want the line to appear. Then choose Insert ⇨ Horizontal Line from the menu bar.

Writing and Editing HTML Tags

If you know HTML and want to work directly with tags, choose View ➪ Source Edit from the New Message menu bar. You'll see three new buttons at the bottom of the editing window:

- **Edit:** Same as the standard window for editing a message.
- **Source:** Shows all the HTML tags. You can add or change tags as you see fit (following the current specification for HTML 4.0 [also known as XHTML Transitional]).
- **Preview:** Similar to Edit view, but you can't make any changes.

In the Source view, place your custom HTML between the <body> and </body> tags. To return to the normal editing window without the extra buttons, choose View ➪ Source Edit from the menu bar again.

Adding hyperlinks to e-mail messages

A hyperlink is text you can click in a message to browse to a Web page or create a new e-mail message. You can add hyperlinks to e-mail messages in several ways. Here I'll assume you're already in the New Message window and have started typing your message.

Type a link

One way to insert a link to a Web page is to simply types the page's URL (address). For example, you could type a URL like www.coolnerds.com right into an e-mail message. As you move on to continue typing, that text automatically turns to a clickable hyperlink (it turns blue and gains an underline).

Copy and paste a link

If you want to send the address of a page you're currently viewing to someone, you can copy-and-paste that page's URL rather than re-type it. For example, let's say you're viewing the page in Internet Explorer. Click just to the right of the page's URL in the Address bar. Or drag the mouse pointer through the URL in the Address bar to select it. You'll know the address is selected when the text turns white against a blue background. Then press Ctrl+C to copy that selected URL.

Next, click in your e-mail message where you want the address to appear. Then press Ctrl+V to paste in the URL. If necessary you can press the Spacebar to insert a blank space. The URL will automatically become a hyperlink, as indicated by its color and underlining.

Custom links

The links you put in an e-mail message don't have to exactly match the link. For example, you could use the words Click here as the visible part of the link. There's a big drawback to this approach though. The recipient's e-mail client might flag your message as a potential phishing scam, because those scams use the same technique to hide actual URLs. You don't want people thinking your e-mail message is a scam. So I suggest you avoid using this technique in e-mail messages.

Nonetheless, Windows Mail lets you create such links. So if you want to give it a try, here are the steps:

1. Type the text you plan to use as a URL (for example, the words Click here).
2. Select the text that will act as a hyperlink.

3. Click the Create a Hyperlink button in the New Message toolbar, or choose Insert ➪ Hyperlink from the New Message menu bar.

4. In the Hyperlink dialog box that opens, type (or paste) the URL of the Web site into the URL textbox.

5. Click OK in the Hyperlink dialog box.

The text you selected in step 1 will be colored and underlined as a hyperlink. The recipient of your e-mail message need only click that link to visit the site.

Automatic e-mail signing

You can automatically add a signature to the bottom of every e-mail message you send. The signature could be as simple as your name. Or it can be you name, e-mail address, and any other text you want. For example, if you have your own Web site, you can include its URL in your signature. Creating a signature is easy:

1. From the menu bar in Windows Mail, choose Tools ➪ Options.

2. In the Options dialog box, click the Signatures tab.

3. Click the New button.

4. Click Text under Edit Signature.

5. To the right of the Text option, type the text of your signature. You can type as many lines as you wish.

6. Choose (check) Add signatures to all outgoing messages.

7. Optionally, select or clear Don't add signatures to Replies and Forwards depending on whether or not you want to sign replies and forwards. Figure 18.26 shows an example.

8. Click OK.

To test it out, click the New Message button. A new empty e-mail message opens with your signature already added to the bottom. As you type text above the signature in your message, the signature will move down so it stays at the bottom of the message.

If you manage multiple accounts with Windows Mail, you can create different signatures for different accounts. Follow the basic steps described earlier to create each signature. To assign a signature to an account, click its name under Signatures. Then click the Advanced button. Select (check) the accounts for which you want to use that signature, and click OK.

Advanced users who know HTML can create a fancier signature in Notepad or an HTML editor. Leave out the <head>, <body>, and <meta> tags used in Web pages. Following is an example of a three-column table with a picture in one of the columns:

```
<html>
<hr>
<table border="0" style="width: 100%;">
<tr>
  <td>
    <img src="C:\users\alan\pictures\PublicityPhoto.png" />
  </td>
  <td style="text-align: center">
    <span style="font-size: 14pt; font-family: Comic Sans MS">
      <a href="http://www.coolnerds.com">www.coolnerds.com</a>
```

```
        </span>
      </td>
      <td style="text-align: right">
        <span style="font-size: 14pt; color: #191970; font-family: Arial">
          Alan Simpson<br>
        </span>
        <a href="mailto:alan@coolnerds.com">alan@coolnerds.com</a>
      </td>
    </tr>
    </table>
    </html>
```

FIGURE 18.26

Sample signature.

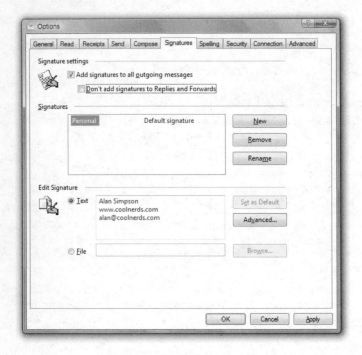

Save that file as an `.html` or `.htm` file. On the Signatures tab of the Options dialog box, click New to create a new signature. Then click File under "Edit Signature." Click the Browse button and navigate to the folder in which you stored the file. Next to the File Name, change `Text Files (*.txt)` to `HTML Files (*.htm, *.html)`. Then double-click the name of your html file and click OK. The signature will be applied to new messages you create from that point on.

NEW FEATURE Junk Mail filtering in Windows Mail is much better than in Outlook Express. The Safe Senders only option provides a simple yet effective means for filtering out the junk without all the effort of defining countless rules.

Dealing with Spam (Junk E-Mail)

Spam, the electronic equivalent of junk paper mail, is an unpleasant fact of life. Windows Mail offers some tools and strategies for dealing with it. But before we get into the specifics, it's important to understand that Windows Mail can't really tell a junk mail from a valid mail. No computer program can do that. That's because junk mail messages don't carry any special information that identifies them as junk.

Nonetheless, there are many ways to configure Windows Mail to minimize your exposure to junk mail. To see them, choose Tools ➪ Junk E-Mail Options from the Windows Mail menu bar. The dialog box shown in Figure 18.27 opens. Your first step is to choose the level of junk e-mail protection from the options given.

FIGURE 18.27

Junk E-Mail Options dialog box.

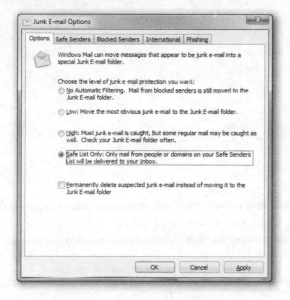

Personally, I think the easiest and most effective way to deal with junk e-mail is to choose the Safe Senders Only option. This lets you accept e-mail from specific people and domains only. If you accidentally forget to include someone as a safe sender, you can easily make them one later. But you can read all the options and choose whichever one best describes the strategy you want to try or use.

CAUTION Don't choose the Permanently delete suspected junk e-mail... option until you're confident that your strategy will never accidentally identify a valid e-mail message as junk.

Identifying safe senders

A safe sender is any person or company from whom you're willing to accept e-mail. To specify safe senders, click the Safe Senders tab. Use the Add button to add safe senders to your list. To accept e-mail from any-one at a company with which you do business, you can enter just the domain name of the safe sender (the part of the e-mail address that comes after the @ symbol).

For example, in Figure 18.28 I've listed the domain names of companies with which I regularly do business. Listing only the domain name ensures that I get e-mail sent by anyone who works for the company. In other words, it means I trust e-mail sent by anyone within that company.

Safe Senders tab.

You wouldn't want to list ISP domains like aol.com, comcast.net, or yahoo.com as safe senders. That's not because those companies are bad. But rather because they have millions of customers, most of whom you don't even know. But you might want to receive e-mail from people you *do* know from those domains. So in that case you'd enter the exact e-mail address of the person from whom you're willing to accept e-mail. For example, I have `koolnerds@comcast.com` listed to accept messages with that exact e-mail address.

You can choose Always trust e-mail from my Windows Contacts to always trust e-mail from people who you know well enough to put in your personal address book. Likewise, you can choose Automatically add people I e-mail to safe senders. There you're assuming that if you know or trust someone enough to send them an e-mail, you're also willing to accept e-mail from them.

As in all dialog boxes, you're not making any lifelong commitments in the Safe Senders list. You can add more safe senders at any time. Remove one at any time by clicking on it and then clicking Remove.

Blocking specific senders

The Blocked Senders tab is the opposite of Safe Senders. There you can list specific domains or addresses that should be blocked. Of course, there are millions of addresses from which you don't want to accept e-mail, and it wouldn't make sense to try to list them all. Furthermore, if you chose Safe Senders Only on the first page of the dialog box, you don't need to list any domains or addresses in Blocked Senders, because everyone except your safe senders will be blocked automatically.

Blocking by country and language

Most of us get junk e-mail messages written in languages we don't understand, often from countries we never even heard of. The International tab in Junk E-Mail Options lets you block messages from entire countries. For example, you can click the Blocked Top Level Domain List button to see a list of all countries that have a specific abbreviation in their international domain (US for United States, AU for Australia, and so forth).

You can really minimize your foreign junk mail by clicking Block Top Level Domain List. When the list opens, click Select All. Then scroll down through the list and clear the checkmark next to any country from which you are willing to accept e-mail.

Different languages require different *encoding* (characters). The Blocked Encoding List lets you block and accept messages based on that encoding. So again, you could click that option. Then select (check) encodings that support languages you can't read. But be careful there. Just because you don't know what an encoding means doesn't mean you can't read text written in that language. You should only block an encoding if you're sure it's for a language you can't read.

Blocking phishing scams

Phishing is perhaps the most prevalent threat on the Internet today. This is where people send out e-mail messages that appear to be from legitimate banks and businesses where people have accounts. They tell people there's a problem with their account and instruct them to log in to their accounts. Unaware users dutifully follow the instructions, not realizing that the place where they're signing in and divulging their user name, password, and other personal information is *not* the company the message and Web page purport to be. It's an imposter posing as a legitimate business to steal information.

Phishing scams like that are prevalent because they work. People see a name and logo they recognize, so they assume the e-mail and page are legitimate. Unfortunately, names and logos mean nothing in e-mail messages and Web pages. Anyone with even rudimentary computer skills can copy them off of legitimate Web sites and paste them into their own fraudulent e-mails. And they do it all the time. This is how they lure innocent folk into divulging information that leads to identity theft and unauthorized withdrawals from bank accounts.

On the Phishing tab of the Junk E-Mail Options dialog box, I *strongly* advise choosing both options, Protect my Inbox from messages with potential Phishing links and Move phishing E-mail to the Junk Mail folder as in Figure 18.29.

FIGURE 18.29

Protection from phishing scams.

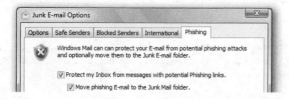

Click OK after choosing your Junk E-mail Options. Next we'll look at ways of dealing with junk e-mail.

Managing junk mail and good mail

Whatever settings you chose in the Junk E-mail Options dialog box will be active from that point forward. So when you click Send/Receive to check your mail, some messages will go straight to your Junk Mail folder, others to your Inbox. For example, if you chose the Safe Senders Only option, then only "safe" e-mail messages land in your Inbox. Everything else goes to the Junk Mail folder.

Regardless of how you set up your Junk Mail Options, you should occasionally click on Junk E-mail in the Folders list and take a quick look through your junk mail. Remember, Windows Mail doesn't really know if a message is really junk or not. It's just acting in accordance with options you chose in the dialog box. So some perfectly legitimate e-mail messages might occasionally land in your Junk Mail folder.

If you find a valid e-mail message in your Junk Mail folder, right-click its message header and choose Junk E-mail. You'll see the options shown in Figure 18.30. Choose whichever option best describes what you want to do. For example, you can choose Add Sender to Safe Senders List so no future messages from that sender end up in your Junk Mail folder.

FIGURE 18.30

Junk E-mail Options for a message.

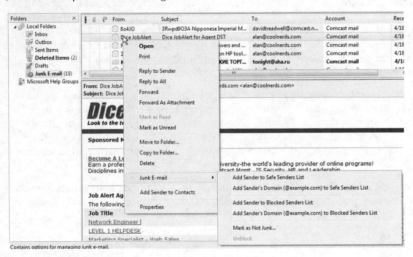

Phishing scams are a favorite form of identity theft, largely because they work. The new
NEW FEATURE Phishing Filter alerts you to potentially fraudulent messages.

Phishing scam e-mails

If you've enabled phishing scam protection, e-mail messages that could be phishing scams are marked by a red shield with the message header shown in red. You'll also see options to Delete or Unblock the message. There's no way for Windows Mail to know for sure if an e-mail is really a phishing scam. It's just looking for deceptive links in the message.

For example, the message in Figure 18.31 has been marked as a potential phishing scam due to the link that reads *Click here to active your account*. An obvious grammatical error like this is usually a pretty good indication of a scam in itself. Legitimate companies tend to be more careful about such things. But that's not the reason why Windows Mail marked it as a phishing scam.

FIGURE 18.31

Status bar shows true destination of a link.

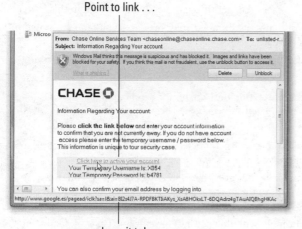

The real reason shows in the status bar at the bottom of the window. The message is supposedly from Chase bank. But when I point to the link, the status bar shows that the link target isn't Chase's Web site. Rather it's some Web site in Spain, as indicated by the .es in the link target URL. That's the main reason why this message is marked as a potential phishing scam. The message appears to be from a legitimate bank. But a link in the message actually sends you to some other Web site outside the Untied States altogether.

> **TIP** You can point to any hyperlink in any e-mail message to see the link target in the status bar. You can use this simple technique to bust any phishing scam, with or without phishing protection in your e-mail client.

PayPal and eBay PayPal are favorite targets of phishing scams. Banks are also favorite targets, because that's where the money is. That's why you'll often get messages about your account at banks where you don't even have an account. The scammers don't know who has bank accounts where. They just send the scam message to virtually everyone, to see who takes the bait. Hence the name "phishing."

Once in a while you'll get an e-mail message that's flagged as a potential phishing scam when, in fact, it's not. If you're certain that a message isn't a scam, you can click the Unblock button to unblock the message. If the message is in your Junk Mail folder, it will disappear into your Inbox where you can treat it as any other normal e-mail message. But if you're not absolutely sure, your best bet would be to delete the message. Or forward it to the company that the scammers are impersonating.

> **TIP** The Microsoft Safety home page at http://www.microsoft.com/mscorp/safety/ is a good resource for keeping abreast of trends in online safety.

Managing Mail Folders and Messages

All of your e-mail messages are organized into *mail folders*. Those mail folders are different from the document folders discussed in Chapter 28 because you get to them through the Windows Mail program, not from Explorer. Windows Mail comes with several pre-defined folders for storing messages. Those folders are represented by little folder icons in the Folders list at the left side of the Windows Mail program. They include

- **Inbox:** If you don't use junk mail filtering, every e-mail message you receive is stored in this folder. With junk mail filtering, only messages that get through the filter are stored in this folder.

- **Outbox:** If you disable the option to send messages immediately, messages you send are stored in this folder until you click the Send/Receive button.

- **Sent Items:** Stores a copy of every e-mail message you send, providing Windows Mail is configured to store copies of sent messages.

 **NOTE** Options for using the Outbox and Sent Items folders are on the Send tab of the Options dialog box. See "Personalizing Windows Mail" later in this chapter for the full suite of options available to you.

- **Deleted Items:** Acts like a wastebasket for messages you delete. Deleted messages are not permanently removed from your computer until you delete them from this folder.

- **Drafts:** If you start writing an e-mail message, but don't have time to complete it, you can store the message in this folder. Then come back to the message, finish writing the message, and then send it.

- **Junk E-mail:** Stores messages that your junk mail filter settings have deemed as junk mail. You should check the contents of this folder to make sure nothing important got in there before deleting them.

The names of mail folders that contain unread e-mail messages are boldfaced and have a number to the right. The number indicates how may unread messages are in that folder. To view the contents of any e-mail folder, click its name in the Folder list. The contents pane to the right shows a message header for each message in the folder. The message headers for unread messages are boldfaced.

TIP When you click a mail folder name, the status bar at the bottom of the program window shows how many messages are in that folder, and how many of them are unread.

Choosing columns for the contents pane

The contents pane shows a message header for each message in a mail folder. You can customize that contents pane to show information that's relevant to how you use Windows Mail. For starters, you can choose columns for display in that pane as follows:

1. Choose View ⇨ Columns from the Windows Mail menu bar. The Columns dialog box shown in Figure 18.32 opens.

2. Select (check) the columns you want to see. Clear checkmarks from columns you don't want to see. Your choices are

   - **Priority:** This column shows an exclamation point for messages marked high-priority by the sender; it shows a blue down-arrow for messages marked low priority; and it shows nothing for normal priority messages.

   - **Attachment:** Shows a paper clip for messages that have attached files.

FIGURE 18.32

The Columns dialog box.

- **Flag:** Provides an easy way for you to mark messages that require more attention later.
- **From:** Shows the sender's name.
- **Subject:** Shows the subject of the message.
- **Received:** Shows the date and time received.
- **To:** Shows to whom each message is addressed. Especially handy if you use Windows Mail to manage multiple e-mail accounts.
- **Account:** Shows the name of the e-mail account from which each message was downloaded. Handy if you use Windows Mail to manage multiple accounts.
- **Size:** Shows the file size of the message and its attachments (if any).
- **Sent:** Shows the date and time that each message was sent.
- **Watch/Ignore:** Used mainly with newsgroups (Chapter 19) to color-code ongoing conversations you're watching or ignoring.

3. Optionally, click any selected column name and use the Move Up or Move Down button to change its position in the list. (You can also rearrange columns after you exit the Columns dialog box.)

4. Optionally, click any selected column name and set its width in pixels.

> **TIP** You may find it easier to move and size columns after you exit the Columns dialog box. See "Sizing and positioning columns" earlier in this chapter.

5. Optionally, click the Reset button if all you want to do is get back to the columns that Windows Mail displays by default.

6. Click OK.

The column names appear across the top of the contents pane. If there are more than will fit in the available space, use the horizontal scroll bar below the message headers to scroll left and right. You can also rearrange columns, and change their widths, using techniques described under "Sizing and positioning columns" earlier in this chapter.

You can sort message headers based on information in any column. Just click the column heading on which you want to base the sort.

- An up-pointing arrow in the column heading means the headers are in ascending order (A to Z, or newest to oldest, or smallest to largest).
- A down-pointing arrow indicates descending order (Z to A, or largest to smallest, or oldest to newest).

Click the heading to switch between ascending and descending order. For example, to put the newest messages at the top of the list, click the Received column heading until that column heading shows a down-pointing triangle.

Flagging messages that need more attention

The Flag column is wonderfully simple to use and worth its weight in gold. Let's say you read a mail message and know it needs more attention. But you can't really give it the time right now. Click the Flag column for that message header. A little red flag appears, which acts as a perfect visual reminder. Of course, you can click the Flag column heading (once or twice) to quickly move all flagged message to the top of the list.

When you've finally given the message the attention it needs, click the little flag next to its header. The flag disappears.

Grouping conversation messages

Sometimes you'll get into an e-mail situation where someone writes you a message, and you send a reply. They reply to your reply. Then you in turn reply back. This kind of back-and-forth communication is often referred to as a *conversation*, because it is like a spoken conversation.

The message headers for these conversations don't usually look special in Windows Mail, other than the fact that messages to which you've already replied have a reply arrow in their icon, as at the top of Figure 18.33.

You can get better organized and save some space by grouping those conversational messages together. Just choose View ➪ Current View ➪ Group Messages by Conversation from the menu bar.

Once the messages are grouped, there are two ways you can view them. In the *collapsed* view, only one of the message headers is visible, as in the center of Figure 18.33. Reducing all the messages in the conversation to a single header like that can save a lot of space, and also make it easier to treat the whole conversation as a unit.

When you need to see messages within the conversation, just click the + sign. The conversation expands to show all the original message headers, as at the bottom of Figure 18.33. In that view you can click any message header to review its contents. When you're done with that, just click the – sign next to the first header to collapse all the messages into a single unit again.

Of course, these are all just different ways you can organize and view messages in a conversation. If you decide you want to go back to the old way, like at the top of Figure 18.33, just choose View ➪ Current View ➪ Group Messages by Conversation from the menu again to turn that option back off.

Filtering messages

Normally Windows Mail makes all messages in a folder visible. Often, that's more messages than you really want or need to see. There are many ways to put some messages into hiding, temporarily, so you don't have to go digging through them to find what you need. Here we'll look at different ways you can put some messages into hiding temporarily so they're out of your way.

Ways to manage conversations.

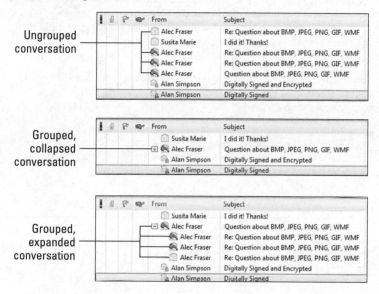

Ungrouped conversation

Grouped, collapsed conversation

Grouped, expanded conversation

The Views bar is the quick and easy way to put messages into hiding, and take them back out. If the Views bar isn't visible in Windows Mail, choose View ➪ Layout from the menu bar. Make sure Views bar is selected (checked), then click OK. Right off the bat you can click the Show All Messages button, shown near the mouse pointer in Figure 18.34, to put messages you've read or marked as ignored into hiding.

Views bar.

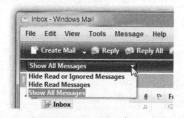

NOTE   Ignored messages are more relevant to newsgroups than e-mail. So they're covered in Chapter 19.

Each of those options on the drop-down menu in Figure 18.34 is called a *view*. You can define your own custom views to gain more control over exactly which messages you want to put into hiding. To create a view, choose Views ⇨ Current View ⇨ Define Views. The Define Views dialog box opens. It lists all of your current views. Click the New button to open the New View dialog box and define a new view.

The first list in the New View dialog box contains options that let you specify conditions for your view. Scroll through the list in box 1 to see all the different ways you can specify a condition for your view. Click the checkbox of whichever one helps you define a condition, then click the blue underlined text in box 2 and type what you're looking for. For example, choose Where the From line contains people. In box 2, click the contains people prompt and type something from the sender's e-mail address that will identify their messages. Then click Add and OK.

You can repeat the process to define multiple conditions. Then at the bottom of box 2, click the Show/Hide prompt and choose whether you want to show or hide messages that meet the conditions. When you're done, give the view a meaningful name of your own choosing.

For example, suppose you sell things on Amazon.com's Web site. For each item sold, Amazon sends an e-mail message with the words "Ship It Now" in the Subject line. Figure 18.35 shows a view, named Amazon Sales, that hides all messages except the e-mail messages from Amazon that have "Ship It Now" in the Subject line.

FIGURE 18.35

Sample view named Amazon Sales.

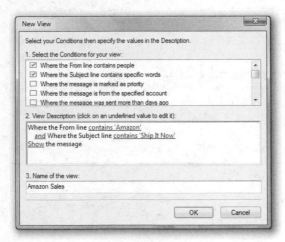

It's all pretty simple so I won't belabor the issue. But just as a second example, Figure 18.36 shows a second custom view named This Week. That one hides all messages received more than seven days ago.

As your collection of e-mail messages grows, you'll probably come up with ideas for new views. No problem because you can create a new view at any time. You can have as many views as you like. And of course you can change or delete any view at any time. Just choose View ⇨ Current View ⇨ Define Views from the Windows Mail menu bar and the rest is easy.

FIGURE 18.36

Sample view named This Week.

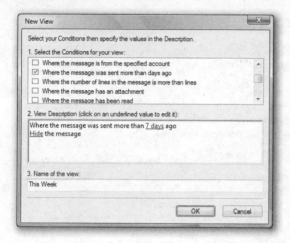

All of your custom views are listed on the Views bar button. For example, you can see my new Amazon Sales and This Week views on its drop-down menu in Figure 18.37. To apply a view, just click that button and click the view's name. To remove the view, click that same button and choose Show All Messages. It's the quick-and-easy way to view only those messages you want to see at any given moment in time.

FIGURE 18.37

Custom views on the drop-down menu.

Filtering is a great way to quickly narrow down visible messages to those you wish to see. But still, you may not want to keep all your e-mail messages in your Inbox. Especially when you have hundreds or thousands of them saved up. You might want to organize your e-mail messages into folders and subfolders, like you do with documents. No problem, because you can always...

Create your own mail folders

If you keep many of the e-mail messages that you receive, you might find it easiest to organize them into folders you've created yourself. That way you don't have to go digging through every message in your Inbox each time you want to find a specific message.

As you'll discover later in this chapter, any searches you conduct will look at your Inbox and its subfolders by default. So to keep life simple, you should make any new folders subfolders of Inbox. Or, subfolders of some other folder you already put under Inbox. Either way, here's how you create a new folder:

1. Right-click the Inbox folder, or a custom folder that will act as parent to the new folder, and choose New Folder.

2. Type a name of your own choosing for your new folder.

3. If you didn't right-click the appropriate parent folder in step 1, you can do so at the bottom of the New Folder dialog box that opens.

4. Click OK.

You can create as many folders as you wish. Figure 18.38 shows an example where I've created folders for messages from companies with which I do business and for personal messages.

FIGURE 18.38

Custom mail folders.

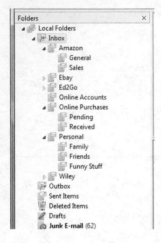

Moving, renaming, and deleting mail folders

If you goof or change your mind after creating folders, it's no big deal. Use the following techniques to change things:

■ To change the name of a folder, right-click its name and choose Rename. Edit the existing name or type the new name, then click OK.

■ To move a folder (so some other folder becomes its parent), drag the folder to the parent folder's name. Or right-click the folder, choose Move to Folder, then

CAUTION   Deleting a folder also deletes all the messages in that folder. If the folder already contains messages you want to keep, make sure you move those messages to a different folder before you delete the folder.

■ To delete a folder, right-click its name and choose Delete. Click Yes (if you're sure) when asked for confirmation.

 To undelete a deleted folder, click the triangle next to the Deleted Items folder. If the deleted folder's name appears, drag it to some other folder to get it out of Deleted Items.

Showing/hiding mail folders

Mail folders form a collapsible tree, meaning you can show and hide things at will. If a folder contains subfolders, it will have either a black triangle or a white triangle to its left. A white triangle indicates that subfolders are hidden. Click that triangle to bring subfolders out of hiding. A black triangle means subfolders are visible. Click that black triangle to put subfolders into hiding.

 Don't forget that you can widen or narrow the Folder list by dragging its inner border left or right.

Managing messages

Once you have some custom folders in place, you can start organizing your existing messages into those folders. If you already have many messages to deal with, you may not want to work with one message at a time. If you want to move (or delete) multiple messages, you first have to select their message headers.

Selecting multiple e-mail messages

You can select multiple messages and then move (or delete) them all in one fell swoop. Selected message headers are highlighted to look different from unselected headers. Figure 18.39 shows an example.

FIGURE 18.39

Selected message headers.

Selected message headers

Before you select multiple headers, you might find it easiest to sort the messages in some order that clumps together the ones you want to select. Or, if you've already created a view that isolates messages, choose that view name from the Views bar to filter out messages you don't want to select. It's not necessary to sort or filter first — just an option worth considering.

You can use any of the following techniques to select multiple message headers. You'll know which headers are selected because they're highlighted, usually as white text against a black background:

- To select one message header, click anywhere on that header.
- To select message headers above that one, hold down the Shift key while pressing ↑ or Page Up. Or to select messages below that one, hold down the Shift key while pressing ↓ or Page Down.

- Press Shift+End to select all messages to the end of the list. Or press Shift+Home to select to the top of the list.
- To extend the selection range to another message header, Shift+click the header to which you want to extend the selection.
- To select (or deselect) a single message without deselecting all selected messages, Ctrl+Click the message header you want to select or de-select.

 **Shift+Click means "hold down the Shift key on the keyboard while you click." Ctrl+Click means "hold down the Ctrl key on the keyboard while you click."**

- To select all message headers, press Ctrl+A.
- To deselect multiple selected headers, click any message header.

You can right-click any selected header to open, print, forward, or delete all of the selected messages. Or to mark them all as read or unread. If you use the Flag column, choose Message ➪ Flag Message to flag them all. You can also click any active toolbar button to perform a task on all the selected messages. You can also move all of the selected messages to another folder, as described next.

Moving messages to a folder

The simple way to move a message to a folder is to just drag it from the contents pane to whatever folder you want to put it in. To move a bunch of messages, select their headers first. Then drag any selected header to the target folder.

Alternatively, if you don't like dragging, you can use this method:

1. Click the message header of the message you want to move. Or select the message headers you want to move.
2. Right-click the message header (or any selected header) and choose Move to Folder.
3. Click the name of the folder to which you want to move the message(s) and click OK.

Whichever method you use, the result is the same. The message headers disappear from the contents pane. To see them again, click whichever folder you put them in.

You can use steps 1–3 to copy, rather than move, messages to a folder. You just have to choose Copy to Folder rather than Move to Folder in step 2. Of course, with that approach you end up with two copies of each message, one still in the original folder and another in the folder to which you copied.

Deleting messages

Most e-mail messages aren't worth keeping for long. Those you'll want to delete. That's easy to do. Click the message header for the message you want to delete, or select headers of multiple messages to delete. Then do one of the following:

- Right-click the header (or any selected header) and choose Delete.
- Press the Delete key (Del).
- Drag the header or any selected header to the Deleted Items folder.

Regardless of which method you use, the messages are moved into your Deleted Items folder. That folder is like a wastepaper basket in that you can still fish things back out if you goof or change your mind. Just click the Deleted Items folder and drag any message you intended to keep to some other folder.

Permanently deleting messages

The messages aren't really deleted until you empty the Deleted Items folder. In that regard, they're still taking up space on your hard disk. To really get rid of the unwanted messages, you need to *empty* the Deleted Items folder. But keep in mind that doing so is a lot like putting all the stuff from your wastepaper basket in a dumpster or incinerator. There's no changing your mind after that point and getting messages back. So before you empty your Deleted Items folder, you may want to review the messages that are in there, and move out any that you intended to keep.

To empty your Deleted Items folder, right-click its name in the Folder list and choose Empty Deleted Items folder (see Figure 18.40). Or choose Edit ➪ Empty 'Deleted Items' Folder from the menu bar.

FIGURE 18.40

Empty the Deleted Items folder.

You'll see a message warning that the messages will be permanently deleted. That means they'll be sent to software heaven and there will be no changing your mind if you proceed. You should have already verified that your Deleted Items folder doesn't contain anything you intended to keep before you go this far. If you didn't, you should choose No because that's your last chance to change your mind. But if you're certain that there's nothing in your Deleted Items folder worth keeping, click Yes. The folder is emptied, and the space they occupied on your hard disk is freed up.

Auto-organizing messages through rules

If you're looking for the ultimate in organization, consider have Windows Mail organize your messages into your custom folders for you, as soon as they arrive. That'll save you from having to move them after the fact. To pull off the high-tech feat, you have to define some *message rules* that put messages into folders based on certain conditions. The conditions can be just about anything, the sender's e-mail address or domain, a word or phrase in the Subject line, or a word or phrase in the body of the message.

There are a couple of ways to create a message rule. You can start from scratch. Or you can use an existing message as sort of a template for defining message rules. So you can do either of the following to get started:

- To start from scratch, choose Tools ➪ Messages Rules ➪ Mail.
- To use an existing message as a template, click that message's header and choose Create Rule from Message.

Either way, the New Message Rule dialog box opens. In the first box you define your conditions. You can define one condition or several. First, select the checkbox that best describes what part of the message contains the condition. For example, choose When the subject line contains specific words if you want the rule to be based on text in the Subject of the message.

Then, down in box 3, click the link and type exactly what you're looking for. A new dialog box opens so you can specify what you're looking for. Type in the word, phrase, or address you're looking for. Click the Add button. You can specify multiple terms, clicking Add after each one. Then click the Options button to specify the logic of the condition, such as the item does or does not contain the specified word, phrase, or address. Click OK.

Then go to box 2 and tell what you want to do with messages the meet your condition. For example, choose Move to folder, then navigate to the folder in which you want the message placed. Finally, give your rule a name you'll recognize down in box 4.

Figure 18.41 shows an example. There I've created a message rule that says When you get a message that has "Your order with Amazon.com," put it into my "Pending" folder (which is a subfolder under my Online Purchases folder). I named that rule New Amazon Purchases down in box 4.

FIGURE 18.41

A sample mail rule.

Click OK, and you'll be taken to yet another dialog box named Message Rules where Windows Mail keeps all your rules. You can create as many rules as you like to move different kinds of messages to different folders. And you can create rules that automatically delete certain messages, automatically forward certain messages, even automatically reply to certain types of messages with a canned response. (More on that in a moment.)

Of course you don't have to define all your rules in one sitting. You can create, change, and delete message rules at any time. Most people create rules slowly over time. The trick is mainly to remember that you *can* create message rules. When you find yourself doing the same thing every time you get a certain type of message, think to yourself "Hey, I could create a message rule to do this automatically." Then go in and create your new rule. Likewise, if you find an existing rule isn't quite working out as planned, you can change the rule. Or delete it and come up with a better rule.

> **TIP** On the General tab of the Options dialog box, you should enable the Automatically display messages with unread message options to ensure that you always see folders that contain new, unread messages in the Folder list. See "Personalizing Windows Mail" later in this chapter if you need help with that.

Auto-responding to messages

You can create a message rule that automatically responds to certain incoming messages (or all incoming messages). But before you go to the trouble, think about this: If the idea is to send an auto-response while you're away on vacation, the auto-responder will only work if you leave your computer on and online the whole time you're away, and you configure Windows Mail to automatically check your messages occasionally.

If that's not realistic, you'd have to set up your auto-responder at the e-mail server, not in Windows Mail. Whether you can do that, and how, depends entirely on your ISP or mail service provider. You'll need to search their Web site, or contact them, to find out if auto-responders are even an option, and how to set one up.

But, getting back to Windows Mail, you can certainly auto-respond to certain messages every time you check your mail. The first step is to define your canned response. Here's how:

1. Open Windows Mail and click the Create Mail button.
2. Leave the To: and CC: lines empty. Fill in the Subject line and type your canned response in the body of the message.
3. Choose File ➪ Save As from the menu bar above the message you just typed.
4. Navigate to the document folder in which you want to store the message (your Documents folder will do just fine), type in a filename of your own choosing, and click Save.
5. Close the window in which you wrote the message.

Now you have a canned response stored as an `.eml` file. To verify that, open the document folder in which you placed the message. Its icon will look like an envelope. The file named Auto-Responder.eml in Figure 18.42 shows an example. I'll use it as the example in the steps to follow.

Next, you need to set up a message rule that defines which messages get an auto-response. In Windows Mail, choose Tools ➪ Message Rules ➪ Mail to create a new mail message rule. In box 1, specify conditions that define messages that will get an auto-response. You could use All messages, but that might be overkill, especially because many messages you get are someone else's auto response. So you could define the rule more specifically, such as where the body of the message does not contain the words *Do not reply to this message*.

In box 2, choose Reply with message. Then click the message link in Line 3, navigate to the folder that contains your auto-response message, and double-click its icon. Figure 18.43 shows the basic design of my sample rule.

Unfortunately, you can't test the auto-responder by sending an e-mail message from your own account. If you try, you'll see a message indicating that no reply was sent because the incoming message was from your own account. But if you have access to some other account with a different e-mail address, you can test it from there.

FIGURE 18.42

Icon for a saved e-mail message (.eml file).

FIGURE 18.43

A sample message rule to auto-respond to some messages.

Searching for Messages

As your collection of e-mail messages grows, it will become increasingly difficult to find specific messages, especially old messages you haven't looked at in months. Fortunately Windows Mail has many of its own Search tools to help you find things.

To do a quick search for a word or phrase in a message header, use the Search box near the upper-right corner of Windows Mail. In Figure 18.44 it contains the word Search. As you type a word or phrase to search for, message headers that don't contain that word or phrase disappear. If no message headers contain the word or phrase, all of the headers disappear. Press Esc to cancel that search and bring back all of the message headers.

FIGURE 18.44

Search box and Find button.

To do a more thorough search, click the Find button in the toolbar. The mouse pointer is touching that button in Figure 18.44. Clicking that button opens the Find Message dialog box shown in Figure 18.45.

FIGURE 18.45

Find Message dialog box.

Most likely you'll want to search your Inbox and its subfolders. In that case leave Inbox and Include Subfolders selected as in the figure. If you want to search some other folder, click Browse and choose the folder you want to search. For example, to search all your mail folders, choose Local Folder from the Browse options.

Now just fill in the blanks to describe what you're searching for. You can fill in any number of boxes. For example, to search for messages that have a specific word or phrase in the subject line, type that word or phrase in the Subject box. To look for messages that have a certain word or phrase in the body of the message, type that word or phrase in the Message box.

You can also limit the search to messages sent before or after some date, to flagged messages, or to messages that have attachments. When you've finished filling in the blanks, click the Find Now button. Headers for messages that match your search criteria (if any) appear at the bottom of the Find Message window. If necessary, use the scroll bar to the right of the message headers to scroll through them. Optionally, you can enlarge the window to see more message headers.

If no messages match your search criteria, maybe you spelled a word wrong. Or maybe you used too many criteria. Click the New Search button and try again.

To open a found message, double-click its header in the lower pane. Optionally, you can right-click any message header to perform some task on that message. Or use commands from the menu bar at the top of the Find Message dialog box to do things with the message. As in the main Windows Mail program, you can select multiple found messages to perform some task on all of them in one fell swoop.

When you've finished with the Find Message dialog box, click its Close (X) button. Or choose File ➪ Exit from its menu bar.

NEW FEATURE You don't really need to open Windows Mail to search for messages. You can launch your search right from the Start menu or the Search window.

Searching from the Start menu

One of the beauties of Windows Mail is that all your messages are included in Vista's search index. This means you can search for any word or phrase in the body of any mail message right from the Start menu. For example, you can press ⊞, type a word, and see all files (including e-mail messages) that contain that word.

When typing in the Search box, you can also use To: or From: to limit the search to messages that are to or from a specific person or domain. For example, a search for `from:susan` finds only messages that have Susan in the "From" address. A search for `to:susan` finds only messages you sent to Susan. Use the keyword about: to search contents. For example, a search for `about:deadline` finds all messages that contain the word "deadline." To limit the search to the message subject line, use the subject: keyword. For example, a search for `subject:vista` finds only messages that have "vista" in the Subject line.

You can use AND and OR (uppercase letters) to specify multiple criteria. For example, a search for

`from:alan AND about:excel`

displays only messages from Alan that have the word "Excel" in the message body. A search for

`to:susan OR from:susan`

finds all messages that you sent to, or received from, Susan.

TIP If you have lots of files and messages to deal with, Vista's new search index is worth its weight in diamonds. But it takes a little time and knowledge to take advantage of all that it has to offer. See Chapters 30 and 31 for the whole story.

Searching from the Search window

Searches from the Start menu can be handy. But sometimes you need more control over your search, and a little more room for the search results. For those, you can use the Search window. Click the Start button and choose Search. To limit the search to messages, click E-mail in the Search window. Then type a word or phrase from the body of the message into the Search box. Or click the Advanced Search button to search by Subject, From, or To address.

Personalizing Windows Mail

There are many options for personalizing Windows Mail. Most are in its Options dialog box. You can open that dialog box at any time, and change any settings you like, by choosing Tools ⇨ Options from the Windows Mail menu bar. The sections to follow look at settings on each tab of the Options dialog box. Some are more relevant to newsgroups than e-mail. Newsgroups are covered in Chapter 19.

General options

The General tab displays the options shown in Figure 18.46. Here's a quick rundown of what they offer:

FIGURE 18.46

General tab.

- **Notify me if there are any new newsgroups:** If you use Windows Mail to participate in newsgroups, choosing this option will ensure that you'll be notified when new newsgroups become available.

- **Automatically display folders with unread messages:** If you use message rules to automatically route messages to folders, you should choose this option. Otherwise, if a message gets routed to a subfolder that's currently hidden in the Folders list, you might not be aware of the new message.

- **Use newsgroups Communities support feature:** Choose this option to participate in newsgroups that offer technical support for Windows and other products.

Under the Send/Receive heading, you'll find the following optional settings:

- **Play sound when new messages arrive:** Choose this option to get a small sound alert when new e-mail messages are downloaded to your Inbox.

- **Send and receive messages at startup:** Choose this option if you want Windows Mail to automatically send and receive messages as soon as you open Windows Mail. If you don't choose this option, you must manually send and receive messages. Choose Tools ➪ Send/Receive from the menu bar, or click the Send/Receive button in the toolbar to manually send and/or receive messages.

- **Check for new messages every *x* minutes:** Choose this option if you want Windows Mail to automatically check for new e-mail messages. If you choose this option, you can also set the number of minutes between checks.

- **If my computer is not connected at this time:** If you've opted to let Windows Mail automatically check for new messages, use the drop-down button to choose whether or not you also want Windows Mail to connect automatically if it's offline. You can also specify whether or not this option overrides the Work Offline option described in the following sidebar.

Under the Default Messaging Programs, you'll find options for making Windows Mail your default message handler. If you use multiple e-mail clients and messaging programs, only one can be the *default*. The default program is the one that appears at the top of the start menu. It's also the one that appears when you perform a messaging-related task from outside your messaging program.

If either Make Default button is dimmed, that just means that Windows Mail is already the default messaging program. So you don't need to do anything else there. But if some other program becomes the default messaging program, and you want to switch back to Windows Mail, the Make Default button(s) will be enabled so you can go back to using Windows Mail as your default program.

Working Offline

Working offline is a means of using Windows Mail to manage messages without being online. This allows you to read and reply to e-mail messages without being online. You might want to use this feature to minimize your connection time if you use your regular voice telephone line to connect to the Internet, or if your ISP charges by the hour.

To work offline, choose File ➪ Work Offline from the Windows Mail menu bar. You'll see a Working Offline indicator in the status bar. You can read and reply to e-mail messages, but your replies will be stored in your Outbox. To get back online and send your replies, choose File ➪ Work Offline to clear the checkmark from that option and go back online. Then click Send/Receive to send out your pending messages.

Read options

The Read tab in the Options dialog box, shown in Figure 18.47, offers options for personalizing how Windows Mail displays and handles messages you receive. Most options are fairly simple and don't have any big effect on how you handle messages. The sections to follow relate to options on that tab.

FIGURE 18.47

Read tab.

Mark message read after displaying for *x* seconds

When you first get a new batch of messages, their message headers are boldfaced to distinguish them from older messages. The boldface signifies an unread message. When you click on an unread message header to read the message, the header stays boldfaced for a few seconds. Exactly how many seconds depends on the number you specify for this setting. So if you feel your messages are being switched from Unread to Read too quickly, you could change the default of 5 seconds to 10 or 15 seconds.

Then again, you could clear the checkmark from this setting to disable it. If you do, unread messages will never be changed to read messages automatically. Every message will remain boldfaced until you right-click the message head and choose "Mark as unread."

Automatically expand grouped messages

If you use the Group Messages by Conversation feature, choosing this option will cause messages to appear in the expanded view, rather than in the collapsed view. In newsgroups, it means that you'll see every message header rather than just the initial post for a thread. You can still expand or collapse any conversation by clicking the + /– sign in the message header.

Automatically download message when viewing in the Preview Pane

The option that sports this section's title is a newsgroup thing. Some newsgroup messages are quite large, and you don't necessarily want to download and install copies of them on your own computer. Normally it's not even necessary to download newsgroup messages because you can always view them on the newsgroup server.

But if want to access the newsgroup messages offline, you can choose the "Automatically download…" option so that each newsgroup message is downloaded as soon as you display it in your Preview pane.

Read all messages in plain text

Choosing this option will remove fancy HTML and graphics from e-mail messages you receive. So every message contains plain text. There's no technical advantage to this. Some people just prefer plain text to fancy formatting.

Show ToolTips in the message list for clipped items

Here's another simple option for message headers. If selected, this option lets you see information that's clipped off in a column. For example, let's say the Subject line for a message is too wide for the Subject column in the contents pane. When this feature is selected, you just have to touch the tip of the mouse pointer to that subject line. The entire line will appear in a tooltip near the mouse pointer.

Highlight watched messages

This setting relates to the optional Watch/Ignore column in the contents pane. When you click in that pane to watch a conversation, the text of that header usually turns red. Use this option to make the message turn to some color other than red.

News settings

Options under the News heading control how many message headers get downloaded each time you connect to the group, and whether or not they're marked as Read. These settings only apply to newsgroups. I'll talk about these options in the next chapter where they're more relevant.

Fonts settings

The Fonts settings on the Read tab set default fonts and encodings for reading (not writing) e-mail messages. The default encoding should be Western European for English and similar languages. Use other encodings for Chinese, Arabic, and other languages that require special characters. But the fonts you choose and their size is entirely up to you.

Receipt options

The Receipts tab of the Options dialog box lets you configure both sending and receiving read receipts. A read receipt is a message like the one in Figure 18.48 that pops up as soon as you read a message that has a read receipt. If you click Yes, the sender gets an e-mail message verifying that you read the message. Options on the Receipts tab are mostly self-explanatory:

FIGURE 18.48

Read receipt.

If you choose the Request a read receipt for all sent messages option, every e-mail message you send will automatically request a read receipt. If you don't choose this option, you can still request a read receipt for any message you write. Just choose Tools ➪ Request Read Receipt before you click the Send button in the New Message window.

The options under Returning Read Receipts apply to how you respond when someone sends you a read receipt. Those are self-explanatory:

- Never send a read receipt.
- Notify me for each read receipt request (this is the default setting that displays the receipt box shown in Figure 18.48).
- Always send a read receipt.

 For security reasons, choosing "Always send a read receipt" is a bad idea. Spammers and identity thieves can use read receipts to verify e-mail messages.

Clicking the Secure Receipts button displays the options shown in Figure 18.49.

FIGURE 18.49

Secure Receipt Options dialog box.

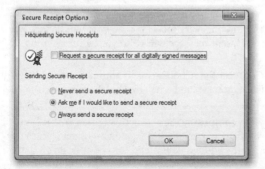

Those options only apply if you already have a digital signature. (I'll talk about those later in this chapter.) The options are the same as for regular receipts, but apply only to e-mail messages that you digitally sign.

Send options

The Send tab (see Figure 18.50) offers options that control how and when the messages that you write are sent. Here's what each option means:

The Send tab of the Options dialog box.

- **Save copy of sent messages in the 'Sent Items' folder:** Select (check) this option to keep a record of all sent e-mail messages in your Sent Items folder. It's a great way to keep track of what you've sent.

- **Send messages immediately:** If you choose this option, every message you write will be sent as soon as you click the Send button. Otherwise, each sent message will go to your Outbox, and won't be sent until you click Send/Receive.

- **Automatically put people I reply to in my Contacts list:** Choose this to automatically add people to whom you send e-mail to your Contacts list. You can add, change, or remove contacts at any time.

- **Automatically complete e-mail addresses when composing:** Selecting this option enables auto-complete for e-mail addresses. When you start typing an e-mail address, a menu of matching addresses appears under the one you're typing. If the address you intend to type appears on that menu, you can click it rather than type the rest of the address yourself.

■ **Include message in reply:** Choosing this option just ensures that when you reply to an e-mail message, a copy of the message to which you're replying appears below your reply. This is a good thing because it allows the original sender to review the message to which you're responding.

■ **Reply to messages using the format in which they were sent:** Choosing this option keeps your replies in sync with messages received. For example, if someone sends you a plain text message, your reply will also be in plain text, even if you chose HTML as your Mail Sending Format.

■ **Mail Sending Format:** Choose HTML or Plain Text as the default for new messages you compose. See "Composing Fancy Messages with HTML" earlier in this chapter for more information.

■ **News Sending Format:** Same idea as above but applies only to newsgroup messages. See Chapter 19 for more information on newsgroups.

Compose options

The Compose tab in the Windows Mail Options dialog box, shown in Figure 18.51, lets you define default settings for the e-mail messages you write.

FIGURE 18.51

The Compose tab of the Windows Mail Options dialog box.

Compose font

Use the Font Settings button next to the Mail heading to choose a default font for the e-mail messages you type. You can choose a different default font for newsgroup messages.

Stationery

A stationery is a background color, picture, or pattern for electronic messages. If you want to use a stationery on all (or most) of the e-mail messages you send, select (check) the Mail checkbox. Then click Select and pick whichever stationery you like best. You can do the same for newsgroups. But you might not want to because newsgroup folk tend to prefer to keep things plain and simple.

If you define a default stationery, it will appear as the background every time you click Create Mail to create a new e-mail message. If, for whatever reason, you don't want to use the stationery in the message you're about to write, choose Format ➪ Apply Stationery ➪ No Stationery to remove the stationery from that one message.

 Click the Download More button to explore additional stationeries online. Click Create New to create your own custom stationery.

Business cards

In the online world, the goal is generally to *never* expose personally identifiable information such as your home address and phone number, unless you're setting up an account through a secure Web site with a business you know and trust. People who expose personally identifiable information online expose themselves to identity theft and other bad things.

However, if you have a Web site, an eBay store, or your own business, chances are you do want to promote it online. One way to do that is by creating a signature that shows relevant information at the bottom of e-mail messages you send. Another way is to attach a virtual business card to your e-mail messages. A virtual business card is like a real business card, except that there's no paper involved. A virtual business card makes it easy for people to add your business or site to their Windows Contacts.

The first step to creating a virtual business card is to create a Windows Contact. Include only the information you would put on a real business card. Not your home address or phone number, but rather the business URL, e-mail address, or whatever else seems appropriate. If you're in the Windows Mail Options dialog box, you'll need to click OK to close it. Then choose Tools ➪ Contacts to open your Contacts folder. Then use the New Contact button to create a contact for your business. Include only the information needed to promote your business. Click OK and close the Contacts folder.

 See Chapter 20 for more information on creating and using Windows Contacts.

To add the business card to your e-mail messages, get back to the Compose tab of the Windows Mail Options dialog box and select (check) Mail under "Include my business card when creating new messages." Click the button to the right of Mail, then choose your business card contact from the drop-down list. Optionally, click the Edit button to review or edit the contact information.

After you've activated the card and clicked OK to leave the Options dialog box, every message you send will include your business card. When a recipient receives your message, the card appears as an icon in the Preview pane header as in Figure 18.52. The recipient can click the card icon to open and view the card, and then click Add to Contacts to add the card to their Windows Contacts.

FIGURE 18.52

Business card icon.

Business card

Signature options

The Signature tab of the Options dialog box allows you to create one or more signatures for your e-mail messages. The signature appears at the bottom of every e-mail message you compose. For more information on signatures, see "Automatic e-mail signing" earlier in this chapter.

Spelling options

The Spelling tab in the Options dialog box lets you configure spell-checking in e-mail messages. I'll assume most options are self-explanatory. The main option to consider is the one named Always check spelling before sending. Selecting (checking) that option will cause the spell checker to check your spelling as soon as you click Send after writing a message.

If you don't select the "Always check spelling before sending" option, spell-checking will never kick in automatically. You'll have to click the Spelling button, or press F7, or choose Tools ⇨ Spelling from the New Message menu bar to start the spell-checker manually.

E-mail security options

The Security tab in Windows Mail's Options dialog box (see Figure 18.53) provides some options for protecting yourself from e-mail security threats. These are no substitute for the full set of security tools discussed in Part II of this book. Rather, they're extra touches provided by Windows Mail for making e-mail safer. The options on the tab are divided into three categories, as described next.

Virus Protection

In the Virus Protection section, your first option is to choose between Internet Zone and Protected Zone. The Internet Zone uses settings defined in Internet Explorer. This setting allows certain scripts and add-ons to work in Windows Mail. However, this setting is best used only by professionals who need scripts and add-ons and are able to distinguish between those that are safe and those that aren't.

For everyone else, Protected Zone is the preferred choice. Although slightly more restrictive, it's also a lot safer. Most likely, the things the Protected Zone prevents you from using are things you don't want on your computer in the first place.

FIGURE 18.53

Security tab.

Most viruses spread through e-mail attachments. Once your computer is infected, the virus sends copies of itself to people in your Contacts. You won't be aware this is happening unless you choose Warn me when other applications try to send mail as me. With that option selected, you'll see a warning message when the virus attempts to spread itself to one of your e-mail contacts. At that point you'll know you picked up a virus and your first task should be to get rid of that virus.

The Do not allow attachments to be saved or opened that could potentially be a virus option blocks e-mail attachments that *could* be a virus. It does not detect actual viruses. Unfortunately, there are many file types that *could* contain a virus. So choosing this option will prevent you from opening or saving many attachments that are virus-free and perfectly safe. If you have virus protection through your ISP or on your system that's blocking infected attachments, then it's okay to clear this option. You don't need to worry about files that could contain a virus if your antivirus software is already preventing such attachments from reaching your Inbox.

Downloaded images

The Block images and other external content in HTML e-mail option is designed to protect you from certain types of spyware attacks associated with pictures and other external content in e-mail messages. Choosing this option also has the fringe benefit of speeding up your message downloads, especially if you're using a slow dial-up connection.

Blocked images in e-mail messages appear as a box with a red X and some alternate text in place of the picture. Above such messages you'll see a bar telling you that pictures have been blocked along with an instruction to click that bar to download the images, like in Figure 18.54.

Blocked images example.

What you do from here depends on whom the e-mail message is from:

- If the message is from someone you know and trust, and you want to see the images, just click the bar as instructed. The images will be downloaded and placed right where they belong.

- If the message is not from someone you know and trust, your safest bet would be to *not* download the images. Just move onto the next message. Or take a look at the text of the message without the images in place, then decide whether or not you really want to see the missing pictures.

Secure Mail

The Secure Mail options all concern the use of digital IDs. These options are relevant only if you already have a digital ID, or if you acquire one by clicking Get Digital ID. Digital IDs are a fairly large topic that I address later in this chapter under "Securing E-mail with Digital IDs."

Connection options

The Connection tab of the Windows Mail Options dialog box lets you configure Windows Mail for a dial-up Internet connection. The first option, "Ask before switching dial-up connections" just displays a prompt if Windows Mail has to switch to a separate dial-up account to access e-mail.

The second option, "Hang up after sending and receiving" is self-explanatory. It's designed to minimize connection time.

By default, Windows Mail will use the same dial-up connection Internet Explorer uses to access the Web. If you need to use a different account for Web mail, click the Change button and specify the account you want to use for e-mail.

Advanced options

The Advanced tab in the Windows Mail Options dialog box, shown in Figure 18.55, offers a mish-mash of options, mostly of interest to more advanced users. Options in the Settings list are described in the following sections.

FIGURE 18.55

Advanced tab in Windows Mail Options.

Contact Attachment Conversion

The Contact Attachment Conversion options let you convert Windows Vista Contacts to the vCard format used in Windows XP, Outlook Express, and many other earlier programs. Each option dictates what happens when you save contact information that's attached to a received e-mail message:

- **Always convert Contacts attachments to vCard:** If you choose this option, every Contact you save from that point forward will automatically be saved as a vCard.

- **Ask me each time:** If you want to have control over which Contacts get converted to vCards, choose this option. Each time you save a Contact, a dialog box will appear asking which format you want to use.

- **Leave contact attachments in Contacts format:** This is the default behavior where contract information is always stored in Windows Vista Contacts format.

None of these settings affect Contacts you already have. To make vCards of all your existing Contacts, you export them. First, create a new folder in which to store the vCards. Then from the menu bar in Windows Mail, choose File ➪ Export ➪ Contacts ➪ vCards (folder of .vcf files). Click Export, navigate to the folder in which you want to put the vCards, and click OK. Then click Close.

IMAP

IMAP (Internet Message Access Protocol) is often used in larger business settings that have their own mail server. Most ISPs use POP3 (Post Office Protocol, Version 3) for e-mail. But if you happen to be configuring an IMAP account, know that when you delete a message from an IMAP folder, Windows Mail marks the message as deleted. But it leaves the message in your message list until that message has been deleted from the IMAP server.

If you want to remove messages from the IMAP message list when you delete them in Windows Mail, choose the Move deleted IMAP e-mail to Deleted Items folder checkbox. That way, when you delete an IMAP message in Windows Mail, you also delete it from the message list.

Message Threads

A message thread is an e-mail or newsgroup conversation. In Windows Mail, you can mark conversations as "Watch" or "Ignore" by clicking in the Watch/Ignore column. Message headers in watched conversations are colored to draw attention. If you choose (check) the Mark message threads I start as "Watched" option, any new conversation you start will automatically be marked as watched.

Reply/Forward

The Reply/Forward options on the Advanced tab control where things appear in messages you reply to and forward. Normally, any text you type in a reply or forward appears above the original message. Similarly, if you use a custom signature, that signature appears above the original message (below the text you type in your message). The options under Reply/Forward change that positioning as follows:

- **Insert signature on the bottom of a reply:** Choosing this option causes customer signatures to appear at the very bottom of a message to which you reply.

- **Reply on the bottom of a message:** Choosing this option causes any text you type in a reply to appear below, rather than above, the original message to which you're replying.

Outside the Settings list are a couple of buttons, described next.

Restore Defaults

Clicking the Restore Defaults button changes the options listed under Settings back to their original default settings.

Maintenance

Clicking the Maintenance button on the Advanced tab opens the Maintenance dialog box for Windows Mail, shown in Figure 18.56.

The Maintenance tab in the Windows Mail Options dialog box provides a few options for automatically managing e-mail messages. The first option, Empty messages from the 'Deleted Items' folder on exit, permanently deletes all messages in the Deleted Items folder when you close Windows Mail. The advantage is that you free up that disk space immediately. The disadvantage is that you lose the safety net of being able to restore accidentally deleted items before you permanently delete them.

The second option, Purge deleted messages when leaving IMAP folders, only applies to IMAP e-mail accounts. If selected, this option permanently deletes any messages you marked for deletion as soon as you leave the folder.

FIGURE 18.56

Windows Mail Maintenance Options dialog box.

The Purge newsgroup messages in the background option is for newsgroups only. Purging has no effect on e-mail. The Delete read message bodies in newsgroups option deletes the body of any newsgroup message after you've read the message. The Delete new messages *x* days after being downloaded automatically deletes messages after *x* number of days.

All Windows Mail messages are stored in a database. As your collection of messages grows, so does that database. Compacting the database helps keep it to a reasonable size. The Compact the database on shutdown every *x* runs option, if selected, automatically displays a little message that reminds you to compact that database occasionally. The default is to display it after every 100 runs, which is fine. But you could change that number to compact more or less frequently. If you clear the checkbox, Windows Mail will never remind you to compact the database.

TIP You can choose File ➪ Folder ➪ Compact All Folders to manually compact the database at any time. Compacting is not a critical operation. Things will work even if you never compact message folders.

The Clean Up Now button lets you delete message bodies, or headers and bodies, from subscribed newsgroups. It has no effect on e-mail messages. Optionally, you can reset all the newsgroup folders so that newsgroup headers will be downloaded the next time you connect.

The Store Folder button shows you where messages are stored. By default, this will be `C:\Users\UserAcct\AppData\Local\Microsoft\Windows Mail` where UserAcct is the user name for the user account into which you're currently logged.

You can change the message store folder to some other location. That might be handy if you use Windows Mail in several different operating systems on one computer. For example, create a shared folder that all operating systems can access. Then configure Windows Mail in each OS to use that same folder as its message store.

The Troubleshooting options create log files of activity for advanced troubleshooting. The log files are stored in the message store folder. The log files contain copies of commands sent to and from servers. There is no "user friendly" information in the log files. These log files are strictly for advanced network and server administrators who are familiar with the commands sent to and from servers.

Managing E-Mail Accounts

The Options dialog box in Windows Mail contains options for the Windows Mail program as a whole. You can manage as many accounts as you wish within any user account. Each mail account that you create has its own settings, separate from the Windows Mail settings and separate from other mail accounts. To get to account settings:

1. From the menu bar in Windows Mail, choose Tools ⇨ Accounts.
2. Under Mail, click the icon for the mail account you want to change and click Properties.

The Properties dialog box to the account opens, like the example shown in Figure 18.57. Here's what each option provides:

FIGURE 18.57

Properties for an e-mail account.

- **Mail Account:** The name of the account. This can be any name you like.
- **Name:** Your name, a business name, or a nickname of your choosing. The name you type appears in the From column of recipient message headers.
- **Organization:** Can be any name you like. Does not appear in Windows Mail message headers.

- **E-mail address:** Your e-mail address. This address appears next to From: when someone opens an e-mail message you sent.

- **Reply address:** When a user replies to your message, this e-mail address is placed in the To: line and the reply is sent to that address. It can be any e-mail address you own, and need not be the same as the mail account you're configuring.

- **Include this account when receiving mail or synchronizing:** Clearing this option prevents the Send/Receive button from downloading messages from this account.

The Servers tab contains information needed by your ISP, as listed in Table 18-1 near the start of this chapter. Change this information only if the account isn't working. Do not attempt to fix a broken account by guessing. The information you put on this tab must be exactly as provided by your ISP.

The Connection tab allows you to configure a specific network connection for the account. There is no need to change anything there if you only have a single Internet account.

The Security tab lets you specify a digital ID for digital signatures and encryption. This only works after you've purchased and installed a digital ID. See "Securing E-mail with Digital IDs" later in this chapter for specifics.

The Advanced tab (see Figure 18.58) lets you change server port numbers and timeouts. You should change these only if your ISP or network administrator tells you to. Defaults are Port 25 for outgoing (SMTP) mail, and 110 for incoming (POP3) mail. The secure connection checkboxes should be left empty unless instructed by your ISP to select them. The default server timeout is 1 minute.

FIGURE 18.58

Advanced tab of e-mail account properties.

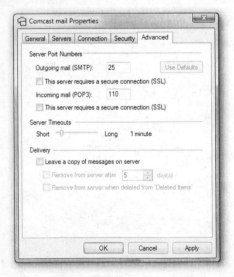

Options under the Delivery setting define the relationship between the e-mail client (Windows Mail) and your ISP's mail server. Normally when you check your mail, you *move* messages from the ISP's server to your computer, which means the messages don't exist on the server anymore. They exist only in your mail folders in Windows Mail.

Choosing Leave a copy of messages on server copies messages from the server to your PC, so they exist in both places. But you still need some way of getting rid of those messages on the server. Otherwise you'll just keep downloading the same messages over and over, and that's sure to get old.

There are basically three ways to get messages off the server. One is to choose the Remove from server after *x* day(s) option, and specify the number of days. Or you could choose Remove from server when deleted from 'Deleted Items'. That will remove messages from the server every time you empty your Deleted Items folder.

The third way to get messages off the mail server doesn't have anything to do with dialog boxes or settings. Rather, you just have a different computer move messages off the mail server when it downloads. That works well when you have two or more computers access the same e-mail account, as discussed in the next section.

Managing Messages with Multiple Computers

If you use two or more computers to access the same e-mail account, you can end up with some messages on one computer, and other messages on the other computer. This can really drive you batty if you have a "main" computer where you do most of your work. You'll probably want that main computer to have copies of all e-mail messages. To make that happen, you configure your other computers (not the main one) to leave a copy of messages on the server. Figure 18.59 shows the basic idea.

FIGURE 18.59

Main computer gets all e-mail messages.

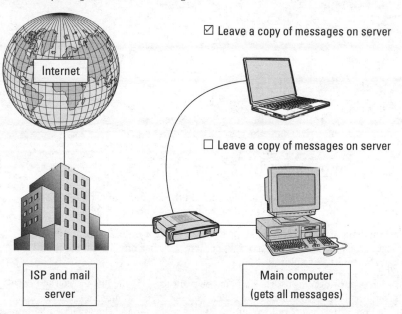

☑ Leave a copy of messages on server

☐ Leave a copy of messages on server

Internet

ISP and mail
server

Main computer
(gets all messages)

The option to leave a copy of messages on the server is in the Advanced e-mail account Properties dialog box. (See "Managing E-Mail Accounts" earlier in the chapter). Do not configure any computers to delete messages after x days or when you empty the Deleted Items folder. Just select that one "Leave a copy of messages on server" checkbox on all computers *except* the main computer.

That way the main computer will always get all messages. It will delete messages from the mail server so you don't end up downloading the same messages over and over again.

If you ever need to send a message from the main computer to another computer, just forward it back to yourself. Just make sure you retrieve messages on the other computer before you retrieve them on the main computer. Optionally, if the other computer is in a local area network, you can just drag the message header to a folder to which both computers have access.

Customizing the Toolbar

Like most programs, Windows Mail has a toolbar that provides one-click access to commonly used menu commands. But its buttons aren't set in stone. You can add and remove buttons at any time. To get started, right-click the Windows Mail toolbar and choose Customize. The Customize Toolbar dialog box shown in Figure 18.60 opens.

FIGURE 18.60

Customize the Windows Mail toolbar.

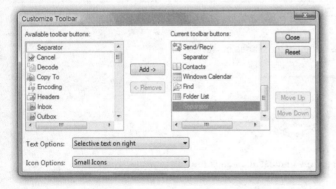

The rest is pretty easy. To add a button to the toolbar, click its name in the left column and click Add → . To remove a button from the toolbar, click its name in the right column and choose ← Remove.

The top-to-bottom order of items in the right column reflects their left-to-right order on the toolbar. You can arrange buttons by dragging them up and down that right column. Or click any button name and use the Move Up and Move Down buttons to position the button.

To add a separator line between groups of buttons, click where you want to place the line in the right column. At the top of the left column click Separator and then click Add → . You can move a separator up and down the right column, if need be, just as you would a button. Click a separator and then click ← Remove to remove it from the right column.

Down near the bottom of the Customize Toolbar dialog box are some options that apply to all buttons. For Text Options, you have the following choices:

- **Selective text on right:** Names of some (but not all) buttons appear to the right of the button icon.

- **Show text labels:** Every button's name appears under the button, as in Figure 18.61.

FIGURE 18.61

Customized toolbar with text labels.

- **No text labels:** No buttons show names (unless you rest the tip of the mouse pointer on a button, in which case its name appears in a tooltip at the mouse pointer).

For Icon Options, your choices are

- **Small Icons:** This is the default size I've been seeing all along.

- **Large Icons:** Button icons are slightly larger than usual, like in Figure 18.61.

When you're finished, click Close in the Customize Toolbar dialog box. Here are a few additional tips to keep in mind with toolbars:

- If there are more buttons than can fit, click >> at the right end of the toolbar to see more.

- Some items will appear only when viewing e-mail, others only while viewing newsgroups.

- To get back to the original buttons, right-click the toolbar and choose Customize. Then click Reset and click Close.

You can also customize the toolbar in the New Message window. Click Create Mail to open that window. Then right-click its toolbar and choose Customize. In fact, you can customize the toolbar in most programs and windows that way. If in doubt, right-click the toolbar to find out.

Securing E-Mail with Digital IDs

Digital IDs are a form of security that brings confidentiality, integrity, and authentication to e-mail. The authentication part refers to the fact that when someone gets a digitally signed message from you, they know for a fact that it's from you and not some imposter posing as you. This is accomplished by digitally signing your e-mail message with your digital ID. You can digitally sign any and all messages if you like.

The confidentiality and integrity parts mean that both you and the sender are assured that nobody has seen or tampered with the message in transit. This is accomplished through *encryption*. When you send the message, it gets encrypted into a secret code before it leaves your computer. If someone manages to grab hold of the message before it reaches the intended recipient, it won't do them any good. The message will look like meaningless gobbledygook and there's no way they can decrypt it back to the original text.

But, when the intended recipient gets the message, it's automatically decrypted back to its original form. So that person sees exactly what you sent. To use encryption, both sender and recipient must have digital IDs.

Getting a digital ID

If you work for an organization that requires secure e-mail, your security administrator will likely acquire and install a digital ID for you. So you can skip this section if someone has already taken care of that for you. Otherwise, you'll have to get your own digital ID. The steps involved depend on the type of ID you get and who you get it from, so I can't really help you there. I should warn you, however, that this requires some technical expertise beyond the basic day-to-day stuff and beyond the scope of this book. You may need some help from a person who has a background in computer security.

The first step is to choose Tools ➪ Options from the Windows Mail menu bar. Click the Security tab in the Options dialog box, then click Get Digital ID. You'll see the options described previously in this chapter (Figure 18.53). You won't be handed one. Instead you'll be presented with links to various *certificate authorities* (CAs) that sell (or maybe even give away) digital IDs. You need to find one that's specifically for e-mail. Then follow their instructions to download and install the ID.

When you've completed all the steps required by your certificate authority, click the Digital IDs button on the Security tab of the Options dialog box. The Certificates window shown in Figure 18.62 opens. You should see your certificate listed there. If not, you may have to Import it. But again, it all depends on who you get your certificate from. There's really nothing I can say here that applies to all certificate authorities.

FIGURE 18.62

Certificates window.

In the Certificates window, click your certificate and then click the Advanced button. Scroll through the list of certificate purposes. If Secure E-mail is listed but not checked, make sure you select (check) that option. Click OK and Close, as necessary, to get back to the Windows Mail Options dialog box. If you have any problems, you'll need to consult your certificate authority for help.

At the bottom of the Security tab you'll see two options related to digital IDs:

- **Encrypt contents and attachments for all outgoing messages:** Do *not* select this option unless you only send e-mail to people who can decrypt your messages. Better to leave this option un-selected and encrypt messages on a case-by-case basis as described later in this chapter.

- **Digitally sign all outgoing messages:** You can choose this option to digitally sign all messages. Recipients don't need anything special to read digitally signed messages. Optionally, you can leave that option un-selected and sign messages on a case-by-case basis.

Click OK to leave the Options dialog box. You'll use your digital ID when composing messages to send to people.

Using your digital ID

To secure an e-mail message with your digital ID, compose your e-mail message as you normally would. But before you click Send, decide if you want to digitally sign and/or encrypt the message. You can also opt to request a digital receipt. (Only people who have their own digital ID will be able to send a secure receipt.) Use the Digitally Sign Message and Encrypt toolbar buttons to sign and/or encrypt the message. Or choose Tools from the menu bar and choose whichever options you want.

Remember, you can send encrypted messages only to other people who have digital IDs. Furthermore, you must have a copy of that person's public encryption key. If you have trouble encrypting a message to such a person, have them send you a digitally signed e-message. When you get the message, open it. If you haven't already done so, add that person to your Contacts (right-click the message header and choose Add to Contacts). The sender's public encryption key will be added to Windows Mail so you can send encrypted messages to that person from that point on.

If you're still unable to send an encrypted message to the person, open the digitally signed message they sent you by double-clicking its message header. In the open message, choose File ⇨ Properties from the menu bar. Click the Security tab, click View Certificates, and then click Add to Contacts. Click OK in all open dialog boxes, close the message, and try again.

NOTE A public encryption key is a file that allows you to send encrypted messages to a digital ID holder. When the recipient gets the message, their private key decrypts it. That's what keeps the messages confidential and tamper-proof. The holder of the digital ID is the only person who has the private key required to decrypt the message.

Figure 18.63 shows an example where I've opted to digitally sign and encrypt a message to myself (for testing purposes). I've also requested a secure receipt. Checkmarks on the Tools menu show which options I've selected. The icons pointed out in the figure also show the message is digitally signed and encrypted.

TIP Use the Receipts tab of the Windows Mail Options dialog box (see Figure 18.48 earlier in this chapter) to configure secure receipt defaults.

When you receive digitally signed messages, the only difference you'll notice is a small ribbon symbol to the left of the Subject in the message headers. When you click the message header, the Preview pane header will show a similar ribbon (see Figure 18.64). That symbol is your guarantee that the message is from the person who digitally signed the message and not from an imposter.

FIGURE 18.63

Tools menu in the New Message window.

FIGURE 18.64

Received message in Preview pane.

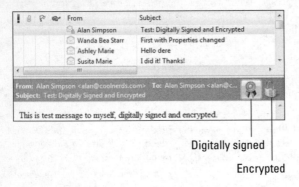

Digitally signed

Encrypted

NOTE The first time you receive an encrypted message, you might see a help page rather than the actual e-mail message in the Preview pane. Don't worry. You'll see a checkbox that lets you turn that feature off for future messages. Click the Continue button in the Preview pane to see the actual e-mail message.

If the message was digitally encrypted, you'll see a lock symbol in the Preview pane header. The message will be perfectly readable on your screen, because Windows Mail will have already decrypted the message. The lock symbol is your guarantee that the message was encrypted during transit. Thus, nobody else has seen or tampered with the message since it left the sender's computer.

It's Not a Toy

My quick overview of digital IDs here might make it seem that all of this is just some kind of toy. Nothing could be further from the truth. Governments use this stuff to protect information vital to national security. Businesses use it to protect trade secrets and financial information.

Unfortunately, there's not enough room in a general book on Windows Vista to get into all the details in any depth. If you're interested in computer security as a career, obtaining Comptia's Security+ credential is a good starting point (www.comptia.org). You'll learn the details of how digital IDs and encryption work while preparing for the exam.

Importing Messages from Other Programs

If you were already using some other e-mail program prior to using Windows Mail, you may want to bring its messages into Windows Mail. This is called *importing messages*. You can also import account information if you haven't already set up Windows Mail to use an account.

There are limits to the types of message you can import. For example, it may not be possible to import messages from Web mail accounts that you manage through your Web browser. But it all depends on your ISP and e-mail client. So I can't tell you how to do this in a step-by-step manner. You may need to contact your ISP or e-mail service provider for help. All I can really show you is how to get the ball rolling:

1. Open Windows Mail (if you haven't done so already).

   - To import e-mail messages from another program, choose File ⇨ Import Messages.
   - Or, to import e-mail account information from another program, choose File ⇨ Import ⇨ Mail Account Settings.

2. A wizard opens. Follow the instructions presented by the wizard to import messages.

How you proceed through the wizard depends on what you're importing. As with any wizard, it's simply a matter of reading and responding to whatever appears on the wizard page and clicking Next. Do so until you get to the last page, and click Finish.

Exporting Messages to Other Programs

To copy messages from Windows Mail to another program, you *export* them. There's a limit to which programs you can export to, and no single set of rules applies to all. I can't take you step-by-step through the process for every e-mail client on the planet. There's just too many of them and not enough pages in this book to cover all the possibilities. If you have any problems with this, you might need to get some support from the manufacturer or Web site of the program to which you're exporting. But the basic idea is

1. Open Windows Mail (if it isn't already open).
2. Choose File ⇨ Export ⇨ Messages.
3. Follow the instructions in the wizard that opens.

Where and How Messages Are Stored

By default, all of the Windows Mail e-mail messages for a user account are usually in the folder `C:\Users\username\AppData\Local\Microsoft\Windows Mail` (where username matches the account name). You can find the exact location by clicking the Store Folder button in the Maintenance dialog box shown back in Figure 18.56.

CAUTION This section is for experienced users with in-depth understanding of drives, folders, files, user accounts, and file types who need to move or copy messages from one message store to another. Nothing in this section is required for normal sending and receiving of e-mail.

Once you know the location, you can navigate to that folder through Explorer. (Or just copy the path from the Store Location dialog box and paste it into the breadcrumb trail in any Explorer window and press Enter.) E-mail folders and messages are in the Local Folders folder. When you open that folder, you'll see folders that correspond to folders in the Navigation pane (Deleted Items, Drafts, Inbox, and so forth).

Within any folder, subfolders and e-mail messages are represented by icons. Subfolders are usually listed first and indicated by the standard manila file folder icon. Each message is a file with a numeric name and an `.eml` filename extension. Figure 18.65 shows an example where I've opened the Local Folders Inbox folder for a mail account. The folders you see there are custom subfolders within the Inbox. The files with numeric names are e-mail messages within the current folder.

FIGURE 18.65

Windows Mail Inbox when viewed through Explorer.

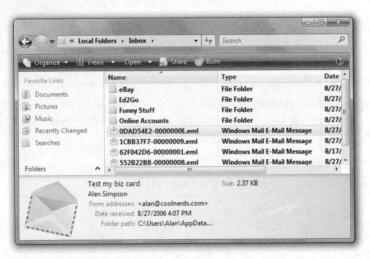

In Explorer, you can treat the mail folders and files as you would document folders and files. For example, if you want to copy the entire Inbox to an external disk or a separate folder, choose Select All from the Organize button, or press Ctrl+A to select everything in the folder. Then click Copy to CD to copy them to a CD, or right-click and choose Send To ➪ Floppy Disk Drive A: to copy to a floppy (if they'll fit on a floppy). Or just right-drag them to some other folder or drive and choose Copy Here after you release the mouse button.

 You *don't* want to move the files to another location. Otherwise, they won't exist in Windows Mail anymore. At least, not until you move or copy them back!

To copy the messages and subfolders to another user account, you'll first need to set up Windows Mail in that user account. Then navigate to its data store and copy messages and subfolders to the corresponding folder in the new user's message store.

More on Windows Mail

I've covered a lot of ground here in this chapter. But e-mail is one of those infinitely long topics where it's impossible to cover every nook and cranny. When it comes to e-mail, Windows Vista and even Windows Mail are relatively minor players. The real meat of how your e-mail works depends on your ISP, or your mail provider if you have an account with Hotmail, Yahoo!, Google, or some other e-mail provider.

Any time you have problems with e-mail, the first place to go is your ISP's tech support site. They're the ones who provide the service. They're the ones who know their service. Guys like me can only tell you general stuff. Keep in mind Windows Mail has its own built-in help, just like any other program. Just choose Help ⇨ View Help from its menu bar, or press F1 while Windows Mail is in the active window.

Microsoft Communities are another great resource for help. There are too many different e-mail services out there for any one person to know them all. But when you ask a question through the communities, there's a pretty good chance you'll find someone who is familiar with that service. You'll learn to use Microsoft Communities in Chapter 19.

Wrap Up

E-mail is a major application these days. In fact, many people use their computers strictly for e-mail and the Web, so I've given Windows Mail some substantial coverage in this chapter. Too much coverage for some readers, and not enough for others, I'm sure. Here's a quick recap of the main points:

- Windows Mail is an optional e-mail client for POP2 and IMAP e-mail accounts.
- Before you can use Windows Mail, you must configure it to work with your e-mail account.
- To write an e-mail message in Windows Mail, click the Create Mail button in its toolbar.
- To add an attachment to a message, choose Insert ⇨ File Attachment from the New Message menu bar.
- To download messages from your ISP's mail server, click Send/Receive.
- To save received attachments as regular document files, click the large paper clip icon and choose Save Attachments.
- To control junk mail, choose Tools ⇨ Junk E-mail options.
- To call attention to potential phishing scams, choose Tools ⇨ Junk E-mail Options and choose settings on the Phishing tab.
- To block or unblock risky pictures and attachments, choose Tools ⇨ Options from the menu bar and click the Security tab.
- To manage one or more e-mail accounts, choose Tools ⇨ Accounts from the menu bar.

Chapter 19

Beyond E-Mail and the Web

Newsgroups are online communities where people exchange information. When you have a question but don't know who to ask, newsgroups may be your best bet. You post your question so that everyone in the group can read it. Then come back a little later and see what kind of answers you've gotten.

File Transfer Protocol (FTP) is an Internet service used for transferring files from one computer to another across the Internet. Unlike sending files as e-mail attachments, FTP puts no limitations on file size and doesn't require an e-mail message, attaching, or anything else. You just drag and drop, or use any method you like, really, to move or copy any number of files and folders from one computer to another.

Remote Assistance lets you turn control of your computer over to a trusted expert for advice, troubleshooting, or general support. Remote Desktop allows you to control a distant computer from whatever computer you happen to be using. All of these topics are covered in this chapter.

About Newsgroups

Millions of people on the Internet communicate through newsgroups every day. You can find newsgroups that discuss just about any subject imaginable. The newsgroup game is replete with jargon. The buzzwords you're likely to encounter as you enter this realm are defined here:

- Each message in a newsgroup is officially called an *article*. But people are more likely to call each one a *post* (short for *posted message*). From the standpoint of Windows Vista, each item is a *message*, just as every e-mail you send and receive is a message.

- A series of messages that originate from a single post is called a *conversation* or *thread*. For example, if I post a question, and nine people respond, those ten messages constitute a conversation or thread.

- Many newsgroups are *moderated* by people who screen messages for suitability to the newsgroup. Others are *unmoderated*, and messages pass through to the newsgroup unscreened and uncensored.

- *Lurking* is hanging around a newsgroup to see what's being said without actually contributing anything. When you're new to a newsgroup, lurking for a while is a good idea, just to get an idea of what subject matter the group thinks is appropriate.

- *Spamming* is sending blatant advertisements or sneaky ads disguised as newsgroup messages to a newsgroup. Highly unacceptable, and sure to get you flamed!

- *Flaming* is sending nasty messages to people in the group. If you post irrelevant messages to a group, you might get flamed!

- *Ranting* is yelling, whining, and complaining about things you don't like. Even if you feel like ranting, never type in all caps. IT LOOKS LIKE YOU'RE SHOUTING and gets on people's nerves.

- *Netiquette* is observing proper newsgroup etiquette by not sending irrelevant comments and not spamming the group. A good *netizen* (network citizen) follows proper netiquette.

 For information on netiquette (newsgroup etiquette) see `http://www.microsoft.com/athome/security/online/netiquette.mspx`.

Newsgroups reside on *news servers* (also called *NNTP servers*, where NNTP stands for Network News Transport Protocol). Most news servers have a three-part name like Web sites. For example, the Microsoft news server I'll be showing here is at `msnews.microsoft.com`. Each newsgroup has its own name specifying the topic of the group. For example, `microsoft.public.windows.vista.general` is a public newsgroup where people ask general questions about Windows Vista.

 You can also access newsgroups and other kinds of support communities from your Web browser. See `www.microsoft.com/communities` for Microsoft's support options.

You participate in newsgroups by posting questions, comments, or replies to the group. Your post is basically an e-mail message sent to anyone in the group who cares to look at it. In fact, newsgroups share so many similarities to e-mail, you can use Windows Mail to manage your newsgroup messages along with your e-mail messages.

Creating a newsgroup account

You don't have to create a newsgroup account to use the Microsoft Communities. That account already exists. That's why you can see its name in the navigation pane at the left side of the Windows Mail program window. As mentioned, that's a great pace to get answers to your questions about Windows Vista and other Microsoft products. The only thing you'll need is a Windows Live ID. The ID is just a user name and password that provides access to many of Microsoft's online services. If you don't already have a Live ID, you can pick one up for free at `http://signup.live.com`. If that address changes, you should be able to pick up an ID just by clicking the appropriate link when prompted for a Live ID.

 Creating a Windows Live ID doesn't cost anything. It won't change the way you access the Internet. It won't change the way you do e-mail. So don't worry about any of that.

The first step to getting to any newsgroup is to open Windows Mail using any of the following methods:

- Click the Start button and click Windows Mail on the Start menu.
- Press ⊞, type `mail`, and click Windows Mail.
- Click the Start button and choose All Programs ➪ Windows Mail.

If you just want to use Windows Communities, you can click that name in the navigation pane at the left side of Windows Mail. If prompted, sign in with your Windows Live ID. Or set up a Live ID by following the prompts on the screen. Then you can skip to the section "Downloading newsgroup names."

If you're trying to set up an account at another news server, you'll need to read on here. First make sure you know the address of that server. Many ISPs provide NNTP servers as part of their service. Check your ISP's Web site, or give them a call to find out if they offer this feature. You'll need to know the name of the server, which will be in the format *name.yourdomain.xxx* where *name* is the name of the server and *yourdomain.xxx* is your ISP's domain name. Also find out if the news server requires logging on. Once you've gathered that information, follow these steps to set up an account:

> **CAUTION** Parents be aware that many public newsgroups contain content that's inappropriate for children. I'm not talking about Microsoft Communities here. But rather the public UseNet newsgroups you might be able to access through your ISP or a third-party service.

1. Choose Tools ➪ Accounts from the Windows Mail menu bar. The Internet Accounts dialog box shown in Figure 19.1 opens.

> **FIGURE 19.1**

Internet Accounts dialog box.

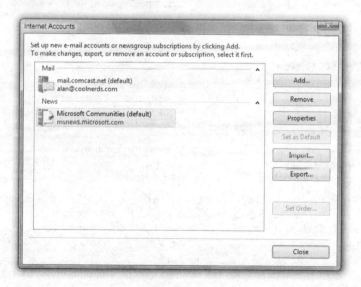

2. To add a newsgroup other than Microsoft Communities, click the Add button.

3. Click Newsgroup Account and click Next.

4. Enter a Display Name. This is the name others in the group will see and how they'll identify you. The name can be anything you like. Click Next.

5. Enter your e-mail address and click Next.

6. Enter the name of your news server. If the news server requires that you log on, check the My news server requires me to log on checkbox. Then click Next.

7. If your newsgroup requires logon, fill in your account name and password, as instructed by your ISP or the newsgroup on the next page. Click Next.

8. Click Finish when you get to the last wizard page.

The news server is added to your list of Internet Accounts. For future reference, any time you need to change or delete an account, you'll do so from that Internet Accounts dialog box. Just click the name of the account you want to change or delete. Then click Properties to change the account, or Delete to remove it.

TIP   To give an account a more user-friendly name, click the account and choose Properties. Change the name in the first textbox and click OK.

Downloading newsgroup names

Once you've set up an account for a news server, you can *download* newsgroups. The term "download" is a little misleading here because you don't actually download all the newsgroup messages to your computer. Basically you just download a list of newsgroup names. From there you can decide which groups you want to *subscribe* to.

If you just set up a new newsgroup account, you'll be prompted to download newsgroups as soon as you click Close in the Internet Accounts dialog box. If you miss that opportunity, no big deal. You can download newsgroups at any time. You'll see how in the next section.

Subscribing to newsgroups

After you've added a newsgroup server to your Internet accounts, its name appears under e-mail folder names in the left column. If you didn't download newsgroup names right after setting up your account, you can right-click that name and choose Download to view a list of newsgroups on that server. Figure 19.2 shows an example using newsgroups from Microsoft Communities.

Most news servers are home to hundreds of newsgroups. Far more than you'll want to participate in. To narrow the field to newsgroups that cover your topics of interest, type a word in the box under "Display newsgroups that contain." For example, you might type `vista` to see newsgroups about Windows Vista.

After you've narrowed the field, you can *subscribe* to any newsgroups that look interesting. Don't worry, subscribing won't cost you a cent. And you can unsubscribe from any newsgroup at any time. You're not making any commitments when you subscribe to a newsgroup. To subscribe to a newsgroup, just click its name and then click the Subscribe button. You can subscribe to as many newsgroups as you like.

NOTE   At Microsoft Communities, the public.de newsgroups are in German, Spanish (.es), French (.fr), Italian (.it), and Japanese (.jp). Newsgroups in English don't have a two-letter abbreviation after microsoft.public.

The names of any newsgroups to which you've subscribed appear under the newsgroup server name in the left column.

FIGURE 19.2

FIGURE 19.2

Newsgroups on a news server.

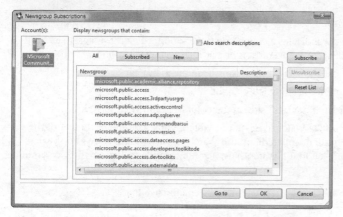

Viewing newsgroup messages

To see what's happening in a newsgroup, just click its name in the Folders list. Any new messages since your last visit will be downloaded to your computer and displayed in the pane on the right. That may take a couple of minutes, depending on the speed of your connection.

As with e-mail, the top-right pane in Windows Mail shows *message headers*. Unread messages are boldfaced. By default, replies to a message are collapsed beneath the message that started the conversation. Click the + sign next to any collapsed message to see replies. Click any message header to see the content of the message in the Preview pane below the headers, as shown in Figure 19.3.

FIGURE 19.3

Newsgroups in Windows Mail.

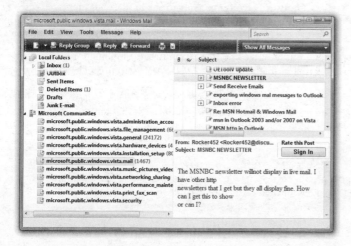

Also like e-mail, the following visual cues, tools, and techniques apply to newsgroup messages:

- **Boldface** indicates an unread message or a newsgroup that contains messages you haven't read.

- The number in parentheses to the right of a boldface newsgroup name indicates the number of unread messages in that newsgroup.

- A + sign next to a message header indicates a collapsed conversation. Click the + sign to expand the conversation. Click – to collapse a conversation or portion of a conversation.

- To choose columns to display, choose View ⇨ Columns from the menu bar.

- To move a column, drag the column heading left or right.

- To size a column, drag the border at the right side of the column heading left or right.

- To mark a conversation of interest as Watched, click the Watch/Ignore column to the left of the message header. The message header turns red and the Watch/Ignore column shows an eyeglass icon. To ignore a conversation, click in the Watch/Ignore column a second time so the No symbol appears.

 The Watch/Ignore column has an eyeglass symbol in its column heading.

- Right-click any newsgroup name or message header for quick access to commonly used commands.

- To mark an entire conversation as read, right-click the message header and choose Mark Conversation as Read.

- To mark all the messages in a newsgroup as read, right-click the newsgroup name in the left column and choose Catch Up.

 To automatically mark all newsgroup messages as read when you leave a newsgroup, choose Tools ⇨ Options, click the Read tab, select (check) **Mark all messages as read when exiting a newsgroup**, and click OK.

- To mark a conversation as Useful or Not Useful, right-click the message header and choose Rate. Or click the Rate button in the Preview pane header. You'll need to sign into your Windows Live account. If you don't see an option to rate messages, choose Tools ⇨ Options from the menu bar, check the Use newsgroup rating features checkbox, and click OK.

 Choose View ⇨ **Current View** ⇨ **Show only useful conversations** to filter out messages you haven't marked as Useful. Repeat that menu sequence to bring non-useful messages back out of hiding.

- Choose View ⇨ Current View to filter out message you don't want to see. Optionally, select a view form the Views bar. If the Views bar isn't visible, choose View ⇨ Layout, select (check) Views Bar, and click OK.

 If you skipped Chapter 18, you may want to take a quick read through that for a more thorough description of things you can do in the Windows Mail program.

Posting a newsgroup message

To post a question or comment to the newsgroup, create a new message. Before you do, there's an important little setting you might want to change to make your own posts more visible. Here are the steps:

Hide your Real E-Mail Address

When you post or reply to messages in a newsgroup, your e-mail address is posted along with it. Spammers are known to scout newsgroups for valid e-mail addresses. Therefore it's a good idea not to post your real e-mail address in newsgroups.

To hide your real e-mail address, choose Tools ➡ Accounts from the Windows Mail menu bar. Click the name of the newsgroup and click the Properties button. Set the Name to whatever name you want to use within the newsgroup. This can be any name you like, it doesn't have to be your real name. Set the E-mail address to something fake, like `noreply@nospam.com`. Leave the Organization and Reply Address fields empty. Click OK, then click Close.

1. Choose Tools ➡ Options from the Windows Mail menu bar.
2. Click the Advanced tab.
3. Select (check) Mark message threads I start as "Watched" (if it isn't already checked).
4. Click the Read tab.
5. Next to Highlighted Watched Messages choose a color for displaying watched messages (or keep the default Red).
6. Click OK.

You need only do these steps once, not each time you post a message. Choosing those options will highlight questions that you've posted so they're easier to find later.

Before you post a message, click the subscribed newsgroup that you think best covers the topic of your question. Some people get cranky when you post messages that aren't relevant to the newsgroup. Then click the Write Message button at the left side of the toolbar. Or choose File ➡ New ➡ New Message from the menu bar. A New Message window opens, like the one in Figure 19.4.

FIGURE 19.4

New Message window for newsgroups.

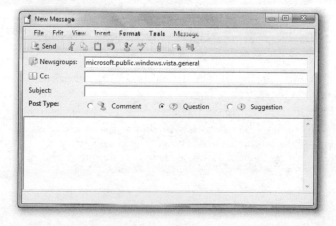

You don't need to change the To: portion of the message. It's already addressed to whatever newsgroup name you clicked in the Folders pane. When typing your Subject, be as brief and specific as you can be. Many newsgroup members ignore messages with vague subject lines like "Bug?", "Help!!!!!!!", or "What am I doing wrong?" Under the Subject line choose Comment, Question, or Suggestion to identify the type of message you're posting.

When typing the body of your message, don't bother trying to do any fancy formatting. Most message boards are plain text anyway, so all of your formatting will likely be for naught. Just try to phrase your comment in a way that's specific and easy for someone to answer. Consider clicking the Spelling toolbar button before you send to clean up any spelling errors.

When you've finished typing your message, click Send in the New Message toolbar. If Windows Mail isn't configured to send messages immediately, the message will be added to your Outbox. Click Send/Receive to send the message to the newsgroup.

Don't expect new messages to appear immediately. (And don't keep sending the same message over and over again!) In a moderated newsgroup, it could take days for your message to be approved and posted. But even in an unmoderated group, it may take a little time for your post to find its way to the group, then back to your downloaded messages.

The smart thing might be to close Windows Mail and attend to something else for a little while. Then re-open Windows Mail and click the name of the newsgroup to which you posted a message. When your message does show up, any replies may be collapsed beneath it. So if you see a + sign to the left of your message header, just click it to see replies. Again, be patient. It may take a little time for the right person to find and reply to your message.

Replying to newsgroup messages

If you read a message and decide to post a reply, you can do so in a couple of ways:

- **Reply to Group:** Your message is sent to the news server, and all newsgroup members can see it.
- **Reply:** Your message is sent to the poster's e-mail address, where only he or she will see your response.

To choose a reply option, click the Reply to Group or Reply button on the toolbar. Alternatively, right-click the message header to which you want to reply and choose Reply to Group or Reply to Sender. Then just type your reply and click Send.

Getting the latest messages

Most of the time the messages you see in any newsgroup will be reasonably up-to-date with what's actually on the news server. But you can manually get up-to-date at any time by synchronizing messages. Here's how:

1. Click a news account name (like Microsoft Communities) in the Folders list. The contents pane shows your subscribed newsgroups, like the example in Figure 19.5.
2. Select the checkbox for each account that you want to synchronize.
3. By default, each account is configured to download new messages only. If you want to change that, right-click New Messages Only in the Synchronization Settings column, choose Synchronization Settings, and then select the kinds of messages you want to download.

FIGURE 19.5

Click a news account name in the Folders list.

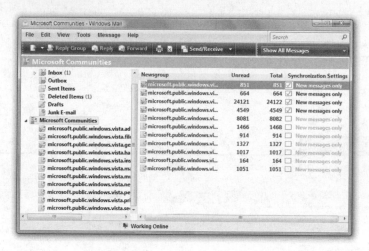

4. Choose Tools ⇨ Synchronize Account to synchronize messages in the current newsgroup only. If you have accounts on multiple news servers, you can choose Tools ⇨ Synchronize All to update all of the accounts.

You shouldn't have to repeat these steps often. The way things are set up by default, simply clicking a newsgroup name in the navigation pane downloads all new messages right on the spot.

Newsgroup Slang

When you get into a newsgroup, you may come across some unfamiliar acronyms. Here's what they mean:

- AFAIK: As far as I know.
- BTW: By the way
- FWIW: For what it's worth
- GMTA: Great minds think alike
- IMHO: In my humble opinion
- IMO: In my opinion
- LOL: Laughing out loud
- NG: Newsgroup
- OIC: Oh, I see
- OTOH: On the other hand
- ROFL: Rolling on the floor laughing
- TIA: Thanks in advance

Searching newsgroup messages

You can quickly search for newsgroup messages that contain a specific word or phrase. Here's how:

1. In the Windows Mail folder list, click the server or newsgroup you want to search. (For example, click Microsoft Communities to search all of your subscribed newsgroups.)

2. Click the Find toolbar button, or press Ctrl+Shift+F or choose Edit ➪ Find ➪ Message from the menu bar. The Find Message window opens.

3. Fill in the blanks to define your search. For example, if you want to see all posts about Movie Maker, type that name in the Message box as in Figure 19.6.

4. Click Find Now.

FIGURE 19.6

Find Message dialog box.

Message headers for posts that match your search criteria appear at the bottom of the Find New Message window. Double-click any message header to read the message.

NEW FEATURE Vista's indexed searches include newsgroup messages from Windows Mail. So you can get instant search results, even without opening Windows Mail first.

Quick Searches from the Search box

The Search box in the upper-right corner provides a quick way to search just the selected newsgroup. In the navigation pane, click the name of the newsgroup you want to search. (You can't search the whole server or account. It has to be one of the newsgroups under the account name.) Then type a word or phrase into the Search box. As you type, headers for messages that *don't* contain the word or phrase disappear.

To clear out the Search box and see all headers again, press Escape (Esc).

Searching from the Start menu

Newsgroup messages are included in Vista's search index, which means you can search for messages right from the Start menu. You don't even have to open Windows Mail first. Just press ⊞ or click the Start button. Then type a word or phrase into the Search box. Newsgroup messages that contain the word or phrase appear under Communications on the Start menu.

You can also search from the Search window. Click the Start button and choose Search to get there. Use the Search box in the upper-right corner for instant searches. Or click E-mail in the Find What bar. Then click Advanced search and search by date, subject, or sender (from). For more information on Vista searching, see Chapters 30 and 31.

Saving useful messages

You can copy newsgroup messages to custom mail folders you create in Windows Mail. In fact, you could create a folder (or several folders) just for special newsgroup messages you want to easily find in the future. Right-click Local Folders at the top of the Folders list and choose New Folder. Give your new folder a meaningful name like Newsgroup Keepers (or whatever).

Any time you come across an especially useful news conversation, just drag its message header to that new folder's icon. Or right-click the message header, choose Copy to Folder, and choose the folder into which you want to place the post.

 Copying favorite newsgroup messages to a mail folder is a great way to build up a reference library of useful information gleaned from the groups.

Hiding irrelevant messages

As with e-mail messages, you can apply a view to any newsgroup to hide irrelevant message headers. Choose View ➪ Custom View, then click the name of any view you want to apply. Or, if the Views Bar is open, choose a view name from its drop-down button.

You can create custom views for newsgroup messages, much like you can for e-mail. Here's how:

1. In the Folders list, click the name of any subscribed newsgroup.
2. Choose View ➪ Current View ➪ Define Views from the menu.
3. Click New to define a new view.
4. Specify conditions and criteria for the view and give it a name. For example, Figure 19.7 shows a view named Hide Ignored Messages, which hides all messages marked as Ignored.

FIGURE 19.7

Custom view to hide ignored messages.

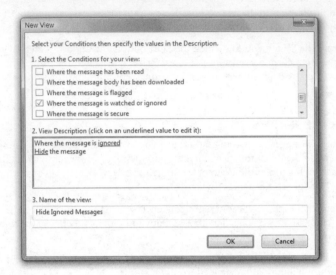

5. Click OK in each open dialog box to get back to Windows Mail.

 See "Introducing Windows Mail" in Chapter 18 for the basics of using the Windows Mail pro-gramming window. See "Filtering Messages" in Chapter 18 for more information on views.

Creating newsgroup message rules

As with e-mail messages, you can automate newsgroup message management using rules. From the Windows Mail menu bar, choose Tools ➪ Message Rules ➪ News. You'll be taken to the New Message Rule window automatically if you're creating your first rule. Otherwise, click New in the Message Rules window that opens to create a new rule.

In the New Message Rule window, choose the Conditions and Actions for your rule, and give the rule a name. Figure 19.8 shows an example of a rule named Watch TV, movie, video posts, which automatically highlights any message header that contains the word TV, Video, or Movie.

After creating a new rule, click OK to return to the Message Rules dialog box. From there you can create new rules, change existing rules, or delete rules.

FIGURE 19.8

Sample newsgroup message rule.

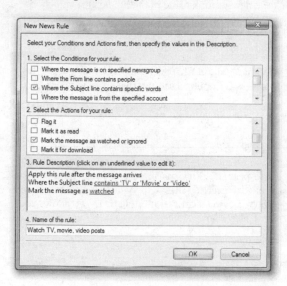

Rules are only applied to new message headers that you download after you've defined a new rule. But you can apply any rules to messages you already have by following these steps:

1. If you already closed the Message Rules window, choose Tools ⇨ Message Rules ⇨ News from the Windows Mail menu bar.

2. Click Apply Now.

3. Select (click) the name of the rule you want to apply, or click Select All to apply all rules.

4. Specify the newsgroup or server to which you want to apply the rule. For example, to apply the rule to all messages from Microsoft Communities, click Browse, click Microsoft Communities, and then click OK.

5. Click Apply Now. Then click OK after the rule is applied.

6. Click the Close and OK buttons to get back to Windows Mail.

Messages in whatever newsgroup(s) you specified in step 4 will be marked according to the rules you specified in step 3.

Unscrambling messages

Some newsgroups allow members to scramble messages that contain sensitive or offensive text. These are typically identified by the characters ROT13 in the message body. To read such a message, double-click its message header. From the menu bar of the message window that opens, choose Message ⇨ Unscramble (ROT13).

Unsubscribing from a group

If you find there are newsgroups that you're not using much and want to stop downloading their messages, just unsubscribe from the group. To do so, right-click the newsgroup's name in the Folders list and choose Unsubscribe.

Personalizing newsgroups

Many of the features described under "Personalizing Windows Mail" in Chapter 18 apply to newsgroups. If you skipped that chapter, take a look through that section now for optional settings that apply to newsgroups.

Using FTP

FTP stands for File Transfer Protocol and is a standardized method of transferring files from one computer to another on the Internet. FTP is not the same as peer-to-peer (P2P) file sharing where you can download files from any computer that's in the network. Nor is it like transferring files with Windows Messenger, where you can send and receive files with whomever you're having a conversation. Rather, FTP allows you to copy files from, and perhaps to, a computer called an FTP server.

In FTP, the words "upload" and "download" have very specific meanings:

- **Download:** To copy files from the FTP server to your own computer
- **Upload:** To copy files from your computer to the FTP server

Every Web server has a URL (address) that takes the general form:

ftp://host.domain.tld

where *host* is a specific computer's name, *domain* is the name of the company or site that owns the server, and *tld* is one of the common top-level domain names such as .com or .net.

Anonymous FTP versus FTP accounts

There are two basic ways to do FTP. *Anonymous FTP* allows you to download files from the FTP server without having an account name and password. Often, you can download files using anonymous FTP. However, the ability to upload to an FTP server using anonymous FTP is rare, because the owner of the FTP site doesn't want millions of people uploading files at random.

To upload files to an FTP server, you generally need an account that includes a user name and password. As an example, let's say that your ISP provides some empty space on a Web server on which you're allowed to publish your own Web pages. Or, maybe you've rented space on a Web server somewhere to publish your Web pages. Either way, the service provider may give you the URL of the Web server, a user account name, and a password that allows you to upload Web pages from your computer to the Web server. Once the pages are on the Web server, anyone with an Internet account and Web browser can view those pages.

To upload and download files with FTP, you may need an *FTP client*. As the name implies, the FTP client is a program that lets you transfer files between your computer and the FTP server to which you have access. However, like so many Internet things these days, many FTP sites will allow you to use Microsoft Internet Explorer, and perhaps other Web browsers, to upload and download files.

Using Explorer as an FTP client

You can use either Internet Explorer or Explorer (the one you use to browse local resources) to access FTP sites. In Internet Explorer, type or paste the FTP site's address into the Address bar and press Enter. If you see a message saying the site or page can't be opened, choose File ⇨ Log On As from the menu bar to open the Log On As dialog box shown in Figure 19.9.

 **If you don't see a menu bar in Internet Explorer, tap the Alt key, or click the Tools toolbar button and choose Toolbars ⇨ Classic Menus.**

FIGURE 19.9

Log On As dialog box.

It's the same basic idea using Explorer. Open any folder (Documents will do). Then type or paste the FTP site's address into the Breadcrumb menu box and press Enter. Typically, the Log On As dialog box shown in Figure 19.9 opens automatically. Fill in the Log On As dialog box as follows:

- If the FTP site allows anonymous access, choose Log on anonymously and then click Log On.

- Otherwise enter your user name and password. Optionally, choose Save Password so you don't have to log on each time. Then click Log On.

Either way, the FTP site opens looking much like any folder on your local computer.

To copy files to or from the FTP site, first open a local folder without disturbing the folder that's showing the FTP site. For example, click Start and then click your user name. Then navigate to a local folder to which you want to copy files, or to the local folder that contains files you want to copy to the FTP site. Then size and position the two folder windows so you can see at least a portion of each, like the example in Figure 19.10.

Once you have the two windows open like that, you can just drag items from the FTP folder to the local folder to download them. To upload, drag items from the local folder to the FTP folder.

 **See "Moving and copying by dragging" in Chapter 29 for info on moving and copying files between folders.**

FIGURE 19.10

Local folder and FTP site.

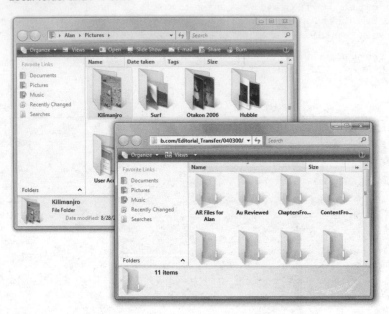

Using Remote Assistance

Remote Assistance is a way to give control of your computer to a trusted expert. A trusted expert is any computer expert you know well enough to trust not to damage your computer or steal any personal information. It might be someone from Desktop Support at your place of business. It may be a friend or relative who just happens to be a computer geek. Whoever it is, you'll have to find him/her yourself. Remote Assistance provides only the ability for a trusted expert to operate your computer from afar. It doesn't provide the trusted expert.

NOTE　　If you have any trouble using Remote Assistance, make sure that it's listed as an exception in Windows Firewall. To do so, click the **Start** button and choose **Control Panel**. In the Search box, type `file` and then click **Allow a program through Windows Firewall**. Select (check) **Remote Assistance** and click **OK**.

Setting up Remote Assistance

Before you try to use Remote Assistance, you'll want to make sure it's enabled in your user account. This requires administrative privileges. You'll find options for enabling and disabling it in the System Properties dialog box. Here's a quick and easy way to get to those options:

1. Click the Start button and choose Control Panel.
2. Type `remote` in Control Panel's search box, then click Allow Remote Access to your computer.
3. If prompted, enter an administrative password. The Remote tab of the System Properties dialog box opens as in Figure 19.11.

FIGURE 19.11

System Properties Remote tab.

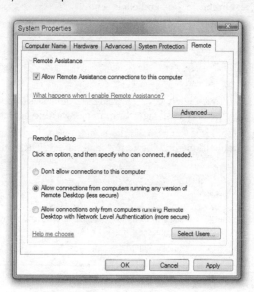

4. If you want to allow the computer to be used in Remote Assistance sessions, select the first check-box. Otherwise the computer cannot be used for Remote Assistance.

5. Optionally, click the Advanced button. Then, to allow trusted experts to control the computer remotely, select (check) the Allow this computer to be controlled remotely option.

6. Optionally, set a time limit on how long remote assistance invitations remain open. Also you can limit remote assistance to other computers running Windows Vista and future versions of Windows.

7. Click OK. You can also close Control Panel.

The next section assumes you've allowed Remote Assistance in the preceding steps.

Requesting remote assistance

Before you allow a trusted expert to take over your computer online, you'll need to agree on a time and a password. For security reasons, it would be best to agree on a password over the phone or in person.

If you know the e-mail address of an expert that you can trust to help with your computer, follow these steps to send a remote assistance request:

■ Tap ⊞, type remote, and click Windows Remote Assistance.

■ Or click the Start button, choose Help and Support, and click Remote Assistance (under Ask Someone).

How you proceed from there depends on how you do e-mail. If you use Windows Mail or another e-mail client that's compatible with Vista, follow these steps:

- Click Use e-mail to send an invitation.
- Type the password you previously agreed upon (twice) and click Next.
- Type the expert's e-mail address in the To: box and click Send.
- If your e-mail client isn't configured to send mail immediately, open that program and click Send/Receive.

If you use Web mail, follow these steps instead:

- Click Save this invitation as a file.
- Note where the file will be saved (most likely C:\Users*yourUserName*\Desktop, which is the desktop for your user account). Type the previously agreed upon password (twice) and click Finish.
- Compose an e-mail message to the expert and attach the Invitation (or Invitation.msrcincident) file to that message using the standard method for your e-mail service. Then send the message normally.

 If you don't know how to attach files to messages, search your e-mail service's support for Attach, or ask your trusted expert.

The e-mail message is sent to the trusted expert. You see the Remote Assistance window shown in Figure 19.12.

FIGURE 19.12

Remote Assistance window.

 If you close the Remote Assistance window, your invitation will expire and the expert won't be able to connect.

The trusted expert needs to receive your e-mail, open the attached file, and enter the agreed upon password. After your expert has done all that, you'll see a new message on the screen asking if you're willing to allow your helper to connect to your computer. Choose Yes.

When connected, the trusted expert sees your screen and options similar to those in the Remote Assistance window. To operate your computer from afar, the expert needs to take control of your computer. (She does so by clicking Request Control at her end.) You see another message asking if you're willing to share control. Again, you have to choose Yes.

You'll be able to see everything the expert is doing. Icons in the Remote Assistance window offer some things you can do while the expert is connected:

- **Disconnect:** Terminates the connection. The expert loses all access to your computer.
- **Stop sharing:** Keeps the expert connected visually. But the expert can't operate your computer.
- **Pause:** Temporarily breaks the expert's connection to your computer. Click Continue to re-establish the connection.
- **Settings:** Takes you to a Settings dialog box where you can control some optional remote assistance settings (click "What do these settings do?" in that dialog box for details).

- **Help:** Opens Windows Help and Support.
- **Chat:** Opens a chat window so that you and the expert can communicate during the session.
- **Send file:** Lets you send one or more files to the expert.

When you've finished with your Remote Assistance session, click the Disconnect button and close the Remote Assistance window.

Using Remote Desktop

Remote Desktop is a feature that allows you to control a computer from a remote location. It's often used to access computers on a corporate network from a home PC. A network administrator on the corporate side needs to set up that capability. She will also need to give you a fully qualified domain name or IP address, a user name, and a password that allows you to connect.

 A fully qualified domain name (FQDN) is a name in the common *host.domain.tld* format.

When you have the information you need, making the connection should be easy. You have to be online, of course. If the company requires connecting through a modem or VPN (Virtual Private Network), make that connection as specified by your company's network administrator.

Then open Remote Desktop Connection from the Start menu. As always, you can use the Search box at the bottom of the Start menu to find it. Or click All Programs ➪ Accessories ➪ Remote Desktop Connection. The Remote Desktop Connection window opens. Clicking its Options<< button expands it to look like Figure 19.13.

FIGURE 19.13

Remote Desktop Connection.

Before you connect to a remote computer, you might want to click the Options<< button and take a look at the options on the various tabs. The only required option is the name or IP address of the computer to which you're connecting.

Allowing remote connections on a home network

You can also use Remote Desktop to control your Vista PC from any other PC within your home network. For example, I have a notebook computer at home that doesn't have the hardware horsepower to run Windows Vista at a decent speed with all the bells and whistles. So it still has Windows XP installed. But I can use it to control the bigger, more powerful Vista computers in my home office. I'm seeing and using my Vista computer through the screen, mouse, and keyboard on my notebook.

 **Remote Desktop is not required for normal home networking tasks like sharing folders, files, and printers. Nor is it required to access those shared resources. You only use Remote Desktop if you want to operate the remote computer from the screen, keyboard, and mouse on another computer in the network.**

Because the notebook computer has a wireless connection to my home network, I can use Vista and my more powerful PCs from anywhere in the house. Even outside on the deck when the weather is nice. Everything even runs at the speed of the faster, more powerful, computers.

To set up this type of remote connection, you first need a home network of course. The computer you want to control remotely needs Windows Vista Ultimate or some other edition that offers Remote Desktop. Finally, you can only log in to password-protected accounts on the Vista computer. It can be a standard account, but it has to be password-protected.

The remote computer also needs to have a version of Windows that supports Remote Desktop. (I use Windows XP Professional on my notebook.)

Assuming you have all the hardware and software to meet the requirements, the first step is to set up the Vista computer to allow remote connections. This requires administrative privileges and the following steps:

1. On the Vista computer, log in to an account that has administrative privileges.
2. Open System Properties (click the Start button, right-click Computer, and choose Properties, or go through Control Panel).
3. Click Remote Settings in the left pane.
4. Under the Remote Desktop heading, choose one of the Allow connections... options.

NOTE **NLA (Network Level Authentication) provides more secure remote desktop connections, but isn't available in older Windows versions. For more information, click the Help me choose link.**

5. Click the Select Remote Users button.
6. Use the Add button to add user names of people who are allowed to connect remotely. The administrator is added to the list automatically. In Figure 19.14, I've added the user named Alan as the second person who can connect remotely. This lets me connect to my standard user account on the Vista computer from my XP notebook computer.

FIGURE 19.14

Added user Alan as Remote Desktop user.

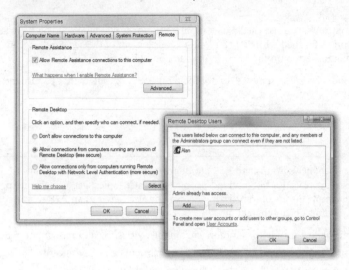

7. Click OK in each open dialog box.

Make sure you know the computer name of the Vista computer. You'll see that to the right of the Computer Name label on the main page of System Properties. For the sake of example, we'll say the Vista computer's name is Bowser. You can close System Properties and Control Panel. And you can log out of the administrative account, and log in to a standard account.

Connecting from a remote home network PC

To connect remotely to the Vista PC from another network in your LAN, open Remote Desktop Connection on that remote computer. For example, on my Windows XP Professional notebook, I click the Start button and choose All Programs ➪ Accessories ➪ Remote Desktop Connection.

In the dialog box that opens, enter the remote computer's name (Bowser in our example) and click Connect. If the user account name of the computer at which you're sitting is different from the user account on the Vista computer, click Log on as another user. Type in the user name and password for the user account on the Vista computer and press Enter.

What About Accessing my Home PC from the Internet?

There's no simple way to set up Remote Desktop as a server to let you connect to your home PC remotely. The main problem being that most home PCs don't have a fully qualified domain name or a static IP address to which you can connect. However, there are products and services that will let you make such connections, even to a home PC and Internet connection. Check with your ISP. Or take a look at products like GoToMyPC (www.gotomypc.com) and No-IP (www.no-ip.com).

The entire screen at which you're sitting will change to look exactly like the screen on the Vista machine. The only difference is a little tab that slides down from the top of the screen when you put the mouse pointer on the very top of the screen. You can use that to minimize, maximize, and restore the Vista screen on the remote computer.

From the remote computer, you use the Vista computer exactly as you would if you were sitting at that computer. When you've finished with your remote session, log out of the Vista user account. That is, click the Windows Vista Start button on the remote computer and choose Log Off.

For more information, check the Remote Desktop help on both computers that you intend to use in your own local network.

Wrap Up

Like e-mail and the Web, newsgroups and FTP are Internet services that everyone can use. Newsgroups provide a virtual meeting place for like-minded people to discuss topics, get and give help, or to just hang out. FTP provides a simple means of transferring files of any size between an FTP server computer and your local computer. Key points of this chapter are

- Newsgroups allow people to communicate online by posting and replying to messages.
- You can use Windows Mail to subscribe to and participate in newsgroups.
- FTP (File Transfer Protocol) is a technology for transferring files from one computer to another over the Internet.
- The easiest way to do FTP is with Microsoft Internet Explorer, because it allows you to manage files using the same techniques you use on your own computer.
- If you know a trusted computer nerd who can help with your computer, use Remote Assistance to get live help online.
- Some corporations allow employees to connect to a corporate network from home using Remote Desktop Connection.
- If you have a home network and suitable versions of Windows, you can use Remote Desktop to control one PC on the network from another PC in the same network.

Chapter 20

Managing Names and Addresses

In Windows Vista, the Contacts folder is your electronic address book. Each file in that folder is a *contact*, someone with whom you communicate. It doesn't have to be only people you contact online. You can store anybody's contact information in your Contacts folder. Like pictures, songs, videos, and other documents, each user account has their own Contacts folder. So each person who has a user account can have their own collection of names and addresses.

NEW FEATURE Even though storing names and addresses is nothing new, Windows Contacts makes it quicker and easier than ever.

Opening Contacts

To create or manage contacts, open your Contacts folder using whichever of the following methods is most convenient for you:

- Click the Start button, click your user name, and then click (or double-click) the Contacts folder.
- Tap ⊞, type con, and click Windows Contacts.
- Click the Start button and choose All Programs ➪ Windows Contacts.
- If you're in Windows Mail, click the Contacts toolbar button, press Ctrl+Shift+C, or choose Tools ➪ Contacts from the menu.
- If you're already in a folder, click your user name in the breadcrumb trail, and then click (or double-click) the Contacts folder icon.

If you've never used your Contacts folder before, it may be empty. Then again, it might already contain some icons. For example, if you use Windows Mail, and it's configured to add people to whom you reply, you'll see an icon for each of those people. If you upgraded from Windows XP and were using Outlook

Express, you'll see contacts from your Windows Address Book. Figure 20.1 shows a sample Contacts folder with some hypothetical contacts already in place.

FIGURE 20.1

Sample Contacts folder.

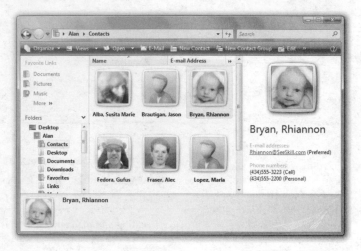

Changing how you view Contacts

Because Contacts is a folder, you can control how things look using the standard techniques described in Chapter 28. For example:

- To show or hide the Preview pane, click Organize and choose Layout ➪ Preview Pane.
- To show or hide the Navigation pane, click Organize and choose Layout ➪ Navigation Pane.
- To show or hide the menu bar, tap the Alt key or click Organize and choose Layout ➪ Menu Bar.
- To size icons, click the arrow next to Views and choose an icon size. Or, hold down the Ctrl key while spinning your mouse wheel.
- To sort or group contacts, point to any column heading and click the arrow that appears.

Making shortcuts to Contacts

Before we go any further with Contacts, let me point out some easy ways to create shortcuts to your Contacts folder. These will make it easier to open the folder in the future. You don't have to create any of these shortcuts, of course. They're entirely optional. But if you use your Contacts folder often, you'll probably find them handy.

First, if you've already opened your Contacts folder, click your user name in the breadcrumb menu so that you're in the main folder for your user account. Or click the Start button and choose All Programs. You should see a Windows Contacts icon on the menu bar. Right-click that icon as in Figure 20.2. Then choose any of the following options to create a shortcut icon that's easy to get to:

- Choose Pin to Start Menu to put a Windows Contacts icon near the top of your Start menu.
- Choose Add to Quick Launch to add an icon for opening Contacts from your Quick Launch toolbar.
- Choose Send To ⇨ Desktop (Create Shortcut) to create a desktop shortcut to your Contacts.

Right-click Windows Contacts.

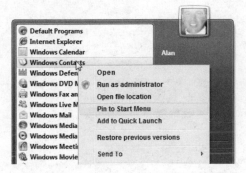

You can do any or all of the above to create as many shortcuts as you wish. In fact, you can do those things with any program you use often.

To add a shortcut to the Favorite Links pane in the navigation bar, click the Start button and then click your User Name. Then drag the Contacts folder into the Favorite Links box and drop it there.

Creating a contact

Creating a contact is simple. First open your Contacts folder if you haven't already. Then click the New Contact toolbar button. Or right-click some empty space in your Contacts folder (not on an icon) and choose New ⇨ Contact.

An empty fill-in the-blanks form opens. It's divided into multiple tabs. You don't have to fill in everything for a contact. Only fill in as much information as you need or want for the contact. Here are some tips for filling in a contact:

- After filling in a blank, press the Tab key to move to the next one. Or click the next blank you want to fill.
- After filling in the first and last names, click the Full Name drop-down button to choose how you want the name displayed for alphabetizing.
- To add an e-mail address, type it into the E-mail box and click Add. If the contact has several e-mail addresses, repeat the process to add each one. Then click the e-mail address you use most often for that person and click Set as Default.
- To add a picture, click the picture box and choose Change Picture. Then navigate to the folder that contains the picture you want to add and click (or double-click) the desired picture. The picture becomes the contact's icon in the Contacts folder.
- If this is a personal contact, use the Home tab to fill in the person's home address. If you mainly contact this person at home, check the Default checkbox on that tab.

- Use the Work tab to fill in the work address and other information. If you mainly contact this person at work, click the Default checkbox on the Work tab.

- Use the Personal tab to fill in personal information like birthday, anniversary, spouse, children, and so forth.

- Use the Notes tab to fill in any miscellaneous information you desire.

- The IDs tab shouldn't require any intervention on your part. It gets filled in automatically when you receive a digitally signed message from the person.

- When you've finished entering the contact, click OK.

> **TIP** You can have Windows Mail automatically create a contact for each person you reply to via e-mail. Open Windows Mail and choose Tools ⇨ Options from its menu. Click the Send tab, select (check) **Automatically put people I reply to in my Contacts list**, and click OK.

Opening and editing contacts

To open a contact, double-click its icon (unless you're using single-clicks, in which case you just have to click it). You'll see a Summary tab that contains e-mail, phone, and other basic information, like the example in Figure 20.3.

FIGURE 20.3

Summary tab of a sample contact.

While viewing a contact's information, you can do any of the following:

- To send the person an e-mail, click the e-mail address.
- To visit their Web site (if any), click the URL.

Tips for Contacts Pictures

For best results, you'll want to create copies of pictures specifically designed for contacts. You might want to create a subfolder, perhaps named Contact Pix, in your Pictures folder just for those pictures. That will make them easy to find.

If you want to use a photo you took with a digital camera, start with a copy of the photo so you don't compromise the original. Try to crop out a perfect square around the person's face. Then size that cropped image to about 250 x 250 pixels. Save it in BMP, JPEG, TIFF, or PNG format. If you're using a logo or icon rather than a photo, you can use the GIF or ICO extension. For picture editing tools and techniques, see Chapter 22.

- To add, remove, or change the picture, click the picture.
- To see or change any other information, click the appropriate tab.

NOTE Each contact you create in your Contacts file is stored as a `.contact` file. But the extension is visible only if you clear the "Hide extensions for known file types" checkbox on the View tab in the Folder Options dialog box.

Create a "me" contact

Don't forget to create a contact for yourself. You can e-mail that to folks so they don't have to type your contact information themselves. After you create a contact for yourself, right-click its icon and choose Set as My Contact.

If you want to e-mail your contact information to others who aren't using Windows Vista, attach a `.vcf` file to an e-mail message. To do that, right-click your Contact icon and choose Send Contact. A new message window opens with the card already attached. Fill in the To and Subject lines. Fill in the body of the message informing the recipient that your contact information is attached.

To make your contact information into a Windows Mail business card, open Windows Mail. Choose Tools ⇨ Options from Mail's menu bar and click the Compose tab. Under Business Card, select the Mail checkbox. Then choose your contact name from the drop-down list to the right of the checkbox. Your business card will automatically be included with every e-mail message you send. If you want to exclude your card from a message, you need to remember to choose Insert ⇨ My Business Card from the menu in the message before you send. Doing so clears the checkmark from My Business Card on the menu and removes the business card. See "Compose Options" in Chapter 18 for more information

 Contact Groups are easy to create and a fun way to send and forward messages to multiple recipients.

Creating Contact Groups

A contact group is any collection of contacts that have something in common. It could be people who go to the same church as you, members of the same club, work colleagues, or just pals to whom you forward funny messages. You might also think of a contact group as a mailing list. The beauty of a contact group is that you can send or forward an e-mail message to everyone in the group in one fell swoop.

Visually, a contact group is just a collection of contact names. For example, Figure 20.4 shows a contact group named Fun Pals.

FIGURE 20.4

Sample contact group.

To create a contact group in your Contacts folder:

1. Click the New Contact Group toolbar button.

2. In the Group Name box, enter any name that describes the group.

3. Add members using any of the following methods:

   ■ To add existing contacts, click Add to Contact Group. Click the first person who should be in the group. Then hold down the Ctrl key as you click everyone else who belongs in the group. Then click Add.

   ■ To add a new person to the group and also create a contact for that person, click New Contact. Fill in contact information for that person and click OK.

   ■ To add a person's name and e-mail address without creating a contact icon for that person, fill in the Contact Name and E-mail boxes near the bottom of the window and click Create for Group Only.

4. Optionally, click the Contact Group Details button and fill in details about the group. For example, if you're all members of the same club or church, you can add address and phone information for the building where you meet.

5. Click OK.

The group window closes and appears as an icon in the Contacts folder. You can use and treat the group in much the same way you do an individual contact:

- To send an e-mail to the group, right-click the group icon and choose Action ➪ Send E-mail. Or in a new mail message you just created, click the To: label, click the group name, click To ➪ , and then click OK. Then click Send.

- To forward a Windows Mail message to everyone in the group, click the message header and click Forward. Then click the To: heading, click the group name, and click To ➪ , and then click OK. Then click Send.

- To change the group, double-click the group's icon in Contacts.

- To delete the group, right-click its icon and choose Delete. Contacts within the group will remain. Only the group icon and non-contacts are deleted.

Don't forget that you have much leeway in how you view the contents of folders. For example, to view and organize your contacts as a list or table, choose Details from the Views menu. To choose columns to display, right-click any column heading as in Figure 20.5. If the drop-down menu doesn't show a column you want to include, click More. . . for a more complete list.

FIGURE 20.5

Choose columns to display.

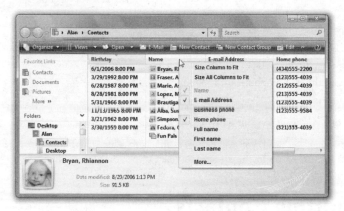

After you've selected the columns you want to view, you can arrange them however you like. Just drag any column heading left or right to place it where it's easy to see. You can sort, group, and filter contacts as you would files in any folder. For more information on how that works, see Chapters 28–31 for the full story.

Printing Contacts

Printing contact information is easy. If you only want to print certain contacts, select their icons using any of the standard techniques, such as Ctrl+Click. Then click the Print toolbar button. If that button isn't visible, click >> at the end of the toolbar and then click Print. The Print dialog box opens looking something like the example in Figure 20.6.

FIGURE 20.6

Print options for contacts.

To print all contacts, choose All Contacts under Print range. To print only selected contacts, choose Selected Contracts. Then choose a print format:

- **Memo:** Prints most business and address contact information.
- **Business Card:** Prints business address and phone information.
- **Phone List:** Prints phone numbers.

If you have multiple printers, click the one you want to print with. Then click the Print button.

If none of the available print formats fits what you need, you can export contacts to a file. Then import those contacts into some other program that gives you the flexibility you need to print as you see fit.

Importing and Exporting Contacts

Importing allows you to copy contacts from external programs into your Contacts folder. Exporting lets you copy contacts to another program or a format that's compatible with an outside program. Let's start with importing.

Importing people to your Contacts folder

You can import names and addresses from the following formats into your Windows Contacts folder:

- **CSV (Comma Separated Values):** This is a generic format to which many programs can export data. You start in the other program by exporting names and addresses to a CSV file. Then you open your Contacts folder and import the CSV file you created from the original program.

- **LDIF (LDAP server):** Use this format to import contacts from a directory server that uses Lightweight Directory Access Protocol (LDAP).

- **vCard (VCF file):** This format is used by many programs to store virtual business card data. Unlike other options described here, you might use this format to import a single contact whose data is stored in a `.VCF` file.

- **WAB (Windows Address Book):** This format imports contacts from the `.wab` file used by Windows Address Book and Outlook Express in earlier versions of Windows. Typically you'll find that file in the `x:\Documents and Settings\UserName\Application Data\Microsoft\Address Book` folder where `x` is the disk drive and `UserName` is the name of the user account.

If the data you wish to import isn't already in one of these formats, open the program you normally use to manage those contacts. Then search its Help for `export` to see if you can export to CSV or another compatible format.

When the data you wish to import are in an appropriate format and you know the location of the file, follow these steps to import the data to your Contacts folder:

1. Open Windows Contacts.

> **TIP** If you plan to import from Application Data or another hidden folder, click the **Organize** button and choose **Folder Options**. Click the **View** tab, then click **Show Hidden Files and Folders** ⇨ **OK**. That will ensure all folders and files are visible in the steps to follow.

2. Click the Import toolbar button.

3. Click the format in which the data to be imported are stored, and then click Import.

4. Navigate to the drive and folder in which the data to be imported are stored, and then click (or double-click) the file to import.

5. When the import is complete, click OK.

You should see an icon for each imported contact.

Exporting contacts to vCards

Many programs store contact information in virtual business cards, where each contact is a file with a `.vcf` extension. Before you get started, you might want to create a folder to store the exported data. That way all the exported contacts will be together in a single folder.

To export contacts in vCard format:

1. Open Windows Contacts.

2. Click the Export toolbar button.

3. Click vCards (folder of .vcf files).

4. Click Export.

5. Navigate to the folder in which you want to place the exported vCards.

6. Click OK.

7. When the export is complete, click OK.

To verify the export, open the folder to which you exported. You should see an icon for each exported contact. They won't show any pictures, because the vCard format doesn't support the use of pictures.

Exporting to a CSV file

You can export contacts to a single comma-separated values (CSV) file for later import to another program. For example, after exporting contacts to a CSV file, you can open them in Excel, import them to a Microsoft Access table, or use them for a Microsoft Word mail merge. With Word and Access, you can print form letters, mailing labels, and envelopes from the CSV file.

To export contacts to a CSV file, open Windows Contacts as you normally would. Then:

1. Click the Export toolbar button.
2. Click CSV (Comma Separated Values) ⇨ Export.
3. Type a name for the exported file. Or click the Browse button, navigate to the folder in which you want to store the file, enter a filename, and click Save.
4. Click Next.
5. Select (check) the fields you want to export and click Finish.
6. Click OK when the export is complete.

To verify that export, open the folder to which you exported the file. To view the contents of the file using Notepad, right-click its icon and choose Open With ⇨ Notepad. That will show you the file in its raw form. But in actual practice you'll likely import it into whatever program you want to use.

NEW FEATURE Finally — a way to quickly grab some contact information without opening programs and files!

Searching for Contacts

You don't need to open Windows Contacts to find a person's contact information. Just click the Start button or press ▦. Type a few characters from the person's first or last name — until you see that name on the Start menu. Then click the person's name on the Start menu. When the contact opens, click the Summary tab, and then click their e-mail address to send them an e-mail. Very quick and easy.

You can do the same kind of thing using the Search box in the upper-right corner of the Contacts window. Type a few characters from the person's name. The contact list shrinks to contain only the people whose names contain those letters. When you see the person you want, double-click the name to open. To un-filter and see all contacts again, click the x at the right side of the Search box.

Sharing Contacts on a Network

If your computer is part of a network, you can share a contact with other Windows Vista computers in that network. The process is the same as for sharing any other file. Right-click the contact and choose Share. Choose the people with whom you want to share, and set permission levels. For more information, see Chapters 53 and 54.

Wrap Up

Names and addresses are easy to manage in Windows Vista, thanks to the Contacts folder. Here's a summary of all the things you can do:

- To view contacts, open your Contacts folder. From the desktop, you can click Start and choose All Programs ⇨ Windows Contacts.

- To create shortcuts to your Contacts folder, click the Start button and choose your user name. Then drag the Contacts folder to the navigation pane, Quick Launch toolbar, or Start button depending on where you want to place shortcuts.

- To create a new contact, click the New Contact toolbar button in your Contacts folder.

- To open or change a contact's information, open the contact icon.

- To identify a contact as yourself, right-click your own contact icon and choose Set as My Contact.

- To create a mailing list, click Create Contact Group in the toolbar.

- To send an e-mail to a contact group, right-click the group icon and choose Action ⇨ Send E-mail. Or from a new message or forwarded message, click To: in the address field and choose the group as the recipient.

- To print contacts, click the Print toolbar button.

- Click Import or Export on the toolbar to import contacts form an external source, or copy contacts to an external file.

- To quickly find a contact without opening your Contacts folder, press ⊞ and type a few characters from the person's first or last name. When you see the name on the Start menu, click it.

Chapter 21

Troubleshooting Internet Problems

Troubleshooting Internet Explorer

Internet problems can be caused by your connection, a problem with the page you're viewing, or a problem with your Web browser. Here, we'll focus on problems that are related to Microsoft Internet Explorer.

Clicking a hyperlink has no effect

The link you clicked may open in a new window, which is being blocked as a pop-up. Click the Information bar to allow pop-ups, or click the No symbol in the status bar (see Figure 21.1) and choose an option to allow pop-ups.

> **NOTE** Everything described in Chapter 17 applies to Web pages that open in new browser windows as well.

Can't download program or ActiveX control

Windows Vista adds extra security, preventing downloads from occurring without your permission. When you click a link to start a download, you might see the window shown in Figure 21.2. Click either Run or Save to continue.

FIGURE 21.1

Choose an option to allow pop-ups.

FIGURE 21.2

Specify whether you want to download or run the application.

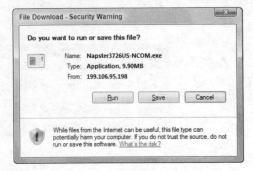

 Do not accept unsolicited downloads. Download only programs from sites you know and trust.

Security alert about leaving a secure Internet connection

Many sites on the Internet require personal information. Ordering products from Amazon or setting up your account on eBay require that you provide information about yourself. Reputable sites require that you enter this type of information in a secure manner. After entering information and submitting it, you may be prompted with the dialog box shown in Figure 21.3.

FIGURE 21.3

Internet Explorer warning that you are leaving a secure site.

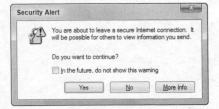

This warning is indicating that you were previously at a page that was passing information to the server encrypted, and you are now being redirected to a page that does not require encryption. In most cases this is not a problem because your information has already been sent to the server in a secure manner. Clicking the More Info button will provide additional details; if you are comfortable, you can check the box In the future, do not show this warning.

Error message "This page cannot be displayed"

The two most common causes of this problem are trying to browse to a Web page when you're offline, and mistyping a URL. If you have a dial-up account, first make sure that you're online. (If you can check your e-mail, then you know you're online.)

Keep in mind that there is no margin for typographical errors when typing a URL. Even a minor mis-spelling, such as typing `www.windowscatalogue.com` rather than `www.windowscatalog.com` will cause this error. Putting a blank space in a URL will almost always cause the same problem. (The blank space is changed to %20 after you press Enter.)

For additional causes of frequent Page not found errors and solutions, go to `http://support.microsoft.com` and search for `Page Cannot Be Displayed`.

Can't change the default home page

Normally, you can change your default home page (the page that opens automatically when you first open Internet Explorer) at any time. You just browse to whatever Web page you want to make your home page, choose Tools ⇨ Internet Options from Internet Explorer's menu bar, and then click Use current and click OK. You can add several home pages if you would like, and each will open in their own tab when you start Internet Explorer.

> **NOTE** In a corporate environment, an administrator can also control your home page by using the Internet Explorer Administration Kit. In that case, you can't override the change without the administrator's consent.

If you find that your default home page keeps being reset to something else, look in Add or Remove Programs for programs that know how to do this, such as SecondPower Multimedia Speedbar, GoHip! Browser Enhancement, and Xupiter toolbar, and uninstall those products. Similarly, you can choose Tools ⇨ Manage Add-ons ⇨ Enable or Disable Add-ons and disable any add-ons that include those names.

If the options to change your default home page are disabled (dimmed), your computer has probably been infected with a virus or worm such as the IRC.Becky.A worm or the Trojan.JS.Clid.gen virus. Use your antivirus software to scan your entire system for viruses, and delete everything that the scan finds. In addition to your antivirus software, you can use Microsoft's Windows Defender discussed in detail in Chapter 8. Defender is designed to remove unwanted applications.

Saved pictures stored as bitmaps (.bmp files)

When you right-click a picture on a Web page, it normally saves as a JPEG or GIF file with whatever file-name you provide. If all of your images are saved as bitmaps instead, follow these steps:

1. Choose Tools ⇨ Internet Options from Internet Explorer's menu bar.
2. Click the Delete button, then the Delete files button. When prompted to confirm the deletion, click Yes and wait for all the temporary Internet files to be deleted (don't worry; you won't lose any programs, documents, or anything else worth keeping).

3. When the deletion is complete, click Close in the Delete Browsing History dialog box, and when the mouse pointer works normally, click the Advanced tab in the Internet Options dialog box.

4. Scroll down to the Security heading in the advanced Settings list and clear the checkmark (if any) next to Do not save encrypted pages to disk.

5. Click OK to close the dialog box.

6. Click the Refresh button in Internet Explorer's toolbar or press F5.

Content Advisor dialog box or message opens

Content Advisor is an optional feature of Internet Explorer designed to allow parents to limit kids' access to Web sites. To use Content Advisor, the parent must think up a password. As always, *do not forget the password*! To activate or deactivate Content Advisor, choose Tools ➪ Internet Options from Internet Explorer's menu bar and click the Content tab. The rest is self-explanatory.

If you get an error messages relating to Content Advisor, go to http://support.microsoft.com and choose **Select a Product** from the top of the page. Then click Internet Explorer 7.0 and type content advisor as the Search Support (KB) text; then click the arrow.

All other Internet Explorer problems/features

Internet Explorer is a large program that has more to do with the Internet than Windows Vista per se. So, it's not something I can cover in depth in a general Windows book like this. But there's plenty of information available to you. I suggest that you start with the Help that's built into Internet Explorer, as follows:

1. Choose Help ➪ Contents and Index from Internet Explorer's menu bar (press the Alt key if you don't see the menu bar).

2. In the Help window that opens, click the Browse Help button, which looks like a small book in the toolbar. Then

   ▪ Click any item that sports a book icon to see topics within that category.

   ▪ Click any icon that shows a page with a question mark to open the information for that topic.

At any point, you can type text in the box labeled Search online Help for additional information not included on your local system. You're also able to post questions to the online community by clicking the Ask icon in the toolbar and then clicking the Windows communities link.

For current news, downloads, and more information about Microsoft Internet Explorer, visit the IE home page at www.microsoft.com/ie.

Troubleshooting Windows Mail

If you're having problems with e-mail, and use Windows Mail as your e-mail client, the troubleshooting tips that follow may help solve the problem. Microsoft occasionally adds more security to Windows Mail through automatic updates.

Error message "The host *name* could not be found . . ."

This error message occurs when the host name for your ISP or e-mail server is specified incorrectly for your service. To use Windows Mail as an e-mail client you must (1) make sure that your e-mail provider supports the use of Windows Mail, and (2) use the name, e-mail address, password, incoming mail server name, and outgoing mail server name specified by your ISP. If you have the correct information from your e-mail provider, here's how you can correct the entries for your account:

1. Click Start and E-mail.

2. Choose Tools ⇨ Accounts from the Windows Mail menu bar.

3. In the Internet Accounts dialog box that opens, click the name of the account you wish to correct and then click the Properties button.

4. In the Account Properties dialog box, click the Servers tab to get to the options shown in Figure 21.4.

FIGURE 21.4

The Servers tab of an e-mail account's Properties sheet.

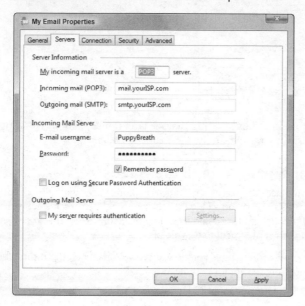

5. Fill in the blanks using exactly the information provided by your ISP or e-mail service provider.

CAUTION   Attempting to "figure out" appropriate entries on the Servers tab by guessing is like trying to guess a total stranger's phone number — futile. (The sample data shown in the figure is hypothetical, and also won't work.)

6. Follow any other instructions provided by your ISP to fill in information on other tabs.

7. When you've finished entering all of your account information, click OK in the Properties dialog box.

8. Click the Close button in the Internet Accounts dialog box.

Click the Send/Receive button in the Windows Mail toolbar to test the new settings.

Some of my mail is not showing up in my Inbox

Windows Mail includes a Junk Mail filter. If you receive a notification that you just received mail, either a sound or the small message icon that shows up in Notification bar, but you're unable to locate it, check in your Junk Mail folder. When you receive a message that looks questionable, you might see the dialog box shown in Figure 21.5.

FIGURE 21.5

Windows Mail notifying you that there may be something suspect about the message.

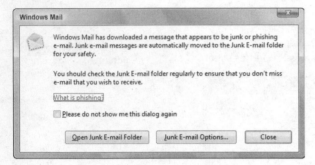

You can alter the settings for junk mail by selecting Tools ➪ Junk E-mail Options. To learn more about Junk Mail, see the section titled "Dealing with Spam (Junk E-mail)" in Chapter 18.

Pictures are missing from e-mail messages

Windows Mail intentionally replaces the pictures in some e-mail messages with a box containing a red X. Doing this protects you from *Web beacon* software, which alerts an online server when you click the picture, and also protects you from JPEG images that could be hiding malicious code. It also saves you from having to wait for all the pictures in your junk e-mail to download.

When you get a legitimate e-mail with pictures you do want to see, just click the Information bar (see Figure 21.6) to download and view images for that message only.

FIGURE 21.6

Information bar and a blocked image.

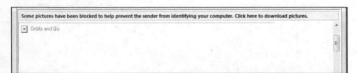

Can't open or save e-mail attachment

Windows Mail blocks access to potentially unsafe e-mail attachments. When it blocks such an attachment, you should see a message like *Windows Mail removed access to the following unsafe attachments in your mail* in the Information bar. See "Using E-mail Attachments" in Chapter 18 for details.

> **CAUTION** Don't trust the extension you see on an e-mail attachment, because there may be another hidden behind the one you see. For example, the ILOVEYOU virus was spread in an e-mail attachment named `Love-letter-for-you.txt.vbs`, and *a lot* of people fell for it. Never open any attachment unless you know exactly what it is and who it's from.

Message "Your current security settings prohibit running ActiveX controls . . ."

This is usually a good thing because an ActiveX control in an e-mail message is likely to be spyware or some other malicious code that you don't want. Click OK and delete the message.

All other Windows Mail problems/features

Windows Vista provides Windows Mail as an optional e-mail and newsgroup client for people who use ISPs that support that program. As such, it's not directly relevant to Windows Vista, the operating system, which is the main topic of this book. I don't have room in this book to cover Internet programs in great depth. But you can get plenty of information from the Help in the program. To do so:

1. Open Windows Mail in the usual manner.
2. Choose Help ➪ View Help from the Windows Mail menu bar.
3. In the Help window that opens, click the Browse Help button, which looks like a small book in the toolbar. Then

   ▪ Click any book icon to see a list of topics within that category.

   ▪ Click any icon that shows a page with a question mark to open the information for that topic.

At any point, you can type text in the box labeled Search online Help for additional information not included on your local system. You're also able to post questions to the online community by clicking the Ask icon in the toolbar and then clicking the Windows communities link.

But keep in mind that when it comes to e-mail, the only people who can really help with your account are the people who have provided you with that account — either your ISP or the e-mail service with whom you created the account.

More Internet Troubleshooting

Vista's built-in help offers many helpful suggestions for troubleshooting Internet connections, Web browsing, Windows Mail, FTP, and some other Internet resources. Click the Start button and choose Help and Support. Then click the Troubleshooting link. You should see some links for Internet-related troubleshooting right on the first page. The *Troubleshooting network and Internet connection problems* and *Connect to the Internet* links are good for general troubleshooting. The Help screens are subject to change, because computer manufacturers are allowed to customize, and because some help comes from the Internet. If you can't find those links, use the Search Help box to find specific information. For example, you might try one of the following, if it's relevant to the problem you're experiencing:

- `troubleshoot internet`
- `troubleshoot mail`
- `troubleshoot ftp`
- `troubleshoot messages`

- troubleshoot newsgroups
- troubleshoot internet explorer
- troubleshoot remote desktop
- troubleshoot remote assistance
- troubleshoot contacts

If you can get online and get into Microsoft Communities, `Microsoft.public.windows.vista.mail` and `Microsoft.public.internetexplorer` are good resources for asking questions about Internet Explorer and Windows Mail.

Part V

Pictures, Music, and Movies

Part V gets into the fun and creative things you can do with pictures, music, and video. Chapter 22 starts off with pictures and all the cool new things you can do with Windows Photo Gallery.

Chapter 23 covers Windows Media Player 11, a great tool for creating and organizing a music collection and creating your own custom music CDs.

Chapter 24 moves on to video files and DVD movies, mostly centering on using Windows Media Player. Chapter 25 covers Windows Movie Maker, the program that lets you take raw footage from your home videos and create truly entertaining movies with titles, special effects, custom sound, and more.

If you have the Premium or Ultimate edition of Windows Vista, you also have Windows Media Center. Media Center lets you access your entire media collection through a computer screen or TV screen. If you have the right equipment, you can work it all with a remote control like the one you use to operate your TV.

Despite all the potential fun, multimedia can pose some real technical challenges. Chapter 27 provides solutions to the most common problems faced when working with digital media.

Chapter 22

Playing with Pictures

In the computer world, the terms *picture*, *photo*, *image*, *graphic image*, and *digital image* all refer to the same thing—a still picture. Windows Vista offers lots of great tools for organizing, editing, printing, and e-mailing pictures.

Today's hard disks have room to store thousands of photos. The new Windows Photo Gallery provides an easy way to organize and find photos based on keywords called *tags*. The Fix pane in Photo Gallery makes common tasks like cropping and red-eye removal a breeze.

Getting Pictures into Your Computer

There are several ways you can acquire pictures to use in your computer. You can store pictures in any folder you like. If you don't have a preference, use the Pictures folder for your user account. You can always move or copy the pictures to another location later, should the need arise.

Getting pictures from a digital camera

Before I tell you how to get pictures from a digital camera, let me say that I'm talking about the digital cameras that connect through a USB cable and appear as a USB mass storage device. If the method described doesn't work for your camera, see the manual that came with that camera for details. You may have to install and use the software that came with your camera to get pictures from it. But the following steps will work with most modern digital cameras:

1. Use a USB cable to connect your camera to your computer and turn the camera on.

2. Wait a few seconds, then:
   - If you see an AutoPlay dialog box like the one in Figure 22.1, click Import. Then skip to step 4.

FIGURE 22.1

AutoPlay options for a digital camera.

- If nothing happens within a minute or so of connecting and turning on your camera, open Windows Photo Gallery (click the Start button and choose All Programs ⇨ Windows Photo Gallery). Then click File in its toolbar and choose Import from Camera or Scanner. Then click the icon for your camera and click Import.

3. In the dialog box shown in Figure 22.2, enter a *tag* (keyword) that will later help you identify pictures. For example, enter the event, location, or subject of the photos.

> **TIP** Entering a tag is optional, but very useful. Try to think of a single word that describes the pictures you're importing. You can add, change, or delete tags at any time. So don't knock yourself out trying to find a word that applies to every picture.

FIGURE 22.2

Add a tag to pictures.

4. Click Import.

5. The next dialog box keeps you apprised of progress. If you want to delete pictures from the camera after copying, select the Erase after importing checkbox.

> **TIP** If you miss the opportunity to erase pictures after importing, you can still erase them using buttons on your camera. Or, open the camera from your Computer folder and delete the pictures using standard techniques described in Chapter 29.

6. When copying is finished, turn off and disconnect the camera.

Depending on your camera and the types of pictures (and videos) you imported, Windows Photo Gallery might open and display thumbnails of your pictures. However, the pictures aren't actually stored in Photo Gallery, so don't worry if you don't see them in Photo Gallery. The pictures are actually in your Pictures folder described under "Using Your Pictures Folder" later in this chapter.

Getting pictures from a memory card

If you have pictures on a memory card, and your computer has slots for those cards, you can copy pictures directly from the card. Once you've inserted a memory card into a slot, the card is basically the same as any external disk drive. So you can use all the standard techniques discussed in Chapter 29 to move, copy, and delete files as you see fit.

Exactly what happens on your screen after you insert a memory card depends on your AutoPlay settings for cards. See "Change Autoplay Settings" in Chapter 44 for more information on AutoPlay. Regardless of what happens after you first insert a card, you can always get to its contents through your Computer folder. Here's how:

1. Click the Start button and choose Computer.

2. If necessary, scroll down through your removable drives. If you have multiple card slots, look for the one that shows a specific name. For example, in Figure 22.3, drive K is a slot that contains a memory card from a Kodak camera.

FIGURE 22.3

Drive K contains a Kodak memory card.

3. Open the card's icon. Then navigate through folders on the card until you find the icons that represent pictures.

4. Select the icons for the pictures you want to copy, or click Organize ➪ Select All (or press Ctrl+A) to select them all.

5. Drag or copy-and-paste the selected icons to your Pictures folder and ignore the following steps. Optionally, use the following steps to copy without dragging or copy-and-paste.

6. If the menu bar isn't visible, tap the Alt key. Choose Edit ➪ Copy to Folder from the menu (or Move to Folder if you want to delete the pictures from the memory card).

7. In the Copy Items dialog box that opens, click the Pictures folder under your user name (unless you prefer to put the pictures in some other folder).

8. Click Copy.

The pictures are copied to your Pictures folder. You can close the folder that's open and remove the memory card. Open your Pictures folder to see the copied pictures.

No Memory Card Slots?

If your computer doesn't have slots for memory cards, you can easily add those slots by purchasing and connecting a card reader. Go to any online site that sells computer stuff. Try www.tigerdirect.com or www.newegg.com if you don't have a preference. Then search for memory card reader. If you're not into installing hardware inside your computer, choose a product that connects through a USB port. Make sure you know what size card you need to read and get an appropriate reader. Or choose a reader that works with all types of memory cards.

 **After** (not before) you've verified that pictures have been copied, you can delete them from the memory card. Select all the icons in the card as in step 4. Then press Delete (Del) or right-click any selected icon and choose Delete.

Getting pictures from a CD or DVD

There are many ways to store pictures on CDs and DVDs, and many ways to copy them. If someone sends you a CD or DVD that contains only pictures, you will likely see a prompt on the screen shortly after you put the disk into your drive. A simple way to import the pictures from that prompt is to click Import Using Windows Picture and Video Import. Then just follow the instructions that appear on the screen. If you're prompted to enter a tag, just type in any word or short phrase that describes the pictures. All the pictures will be copied (imported) to your Pictures folder, where you can access them at any time without using the CD or DVD. But you should keep that disk as a backup.

TIP You can also copy pictures from a CD using the standard techniques described in Chapter 29.

Some commercial CDs might automatically launch some program when inserted. That might leave you wondering how in the heck you're going to copy pictures from the disk to your computer. The trick is to simply close that program and get to the CD's contents directly. So the process goes something like this:

1. Insert the disk into your CD/DVD drive and wait a few seconds. Then:

    - If an AutoPlay dialog box asks what you want to do with the disk, click Open Folder to View Files and go to step 3.

    - If some program opens automatically to show the pictures, close that program and go to step 2.

    - If nothing at all happens within a minute or so of inserting the disk, continue with step 2.

2. Click the Start button and choose Computer. Right-click the icon that represents your CD/DVD drive and choose Open.

3. Now you're viewing the contents of the CD. If necessary, navigate through any folders you find until you find icons for the pictures. Figure 22.4 shows an example where I've found some photos in the PICTURES folder of a Kodak Picture CD.

FIGURE 22.4

Copying pictures from a Kodak Photo CD.

4. Select the icons for the pictures you want to copy. Click Organize ⇨ Select All or press Ctrl+A to select them all.

5. Drag or copy-and-paste any selected icon to the Pictures folder in the Navigation pane. Make sure you get the mouse pointer right on that Pictures folder icon so that you see Copy to Pictures near the mouse pointer as in Figure 22.4. Then release the mouse button.

6. Wait for all of the pictures to copy and then remove the CD from the drive.

You won't need the CD to access those pictures anymore. You'll be able to access them directly from your Pictures folder. But keep the CD as a backup, in case you accidentally delete or destroy any of the copied pictures.

Getting pictures from a scanner

To get photographs on paper into your computer, you use a scanner. Optionally you can use a film scanner or slide scanner to get pictures from film or slides. But those are a bit more expensive than traditional paper scanners.

The first step is, of course, to install the scanner and any required software as per the instructions that came with the scanner. The second step is to read the instructions on how to work your scanner. There are differences among products. The steps I'm about to give you work with most, but not all scanners. And there may be differences among different products. So if all else fails here, read the instructions that came with *your* scanner to best understand the product you own.

The standard operating procedure for more modern scanners goes like this:

1. Turn the scanner on and put in the picture you want to copy.
2. Click the Start button and choose All Programs ➪ Windows Photo Gallery.
3. Click the File toolbar button and choose Import from Scanner or Camera.
4. In the Device Selection window that opens, click the scanner's icon and then click Import.
5. Select the scan settings from the options provided as summarized in the following list:

TIP   **If you previously saved settings in a scan profile, click Select Profile and then click the profile you want to use.**

- **Paper source:** Select the type of scanner you have (flatbed, feeder, or film scanner).
- **Paper size:** If you're using an automatic document feeder to scan multiple items, select the size of the paper you're scanning. Otherwise leave this empty.
- **Color format:** Choose Color, Grayscale, or Black and White.

NOTE   **For a black and white photo, choose Grayscale. The Black and White option provides only black and white with no shades of gray. Black and White, in this context, is best used only for typewritten documents (blank ink on white paper).**

- **File Type:** Choose a file format. Bitmap Image offers the highest quality at the cost of a large file size. Also, bitmap is an older format that doesn't support tagging and metadata as well as newer formats. Better to use JPEG or PNG for a photo. Use Microsoft Document Imaging File only for typewritten documents, not photos.
- **Resolution (DPI):** Select your resolution dots per inch (DPI). The larger the DPI the better the quality of the scanned image, but the larger the file will be. Your best bet for color photos is 300 DPI. Use 75 DPI only for black-and-white text documents. The 150 DPI setting is okay for photos you don't intend to print.
- **Brightness and Contrast:** Use these, if necessary, to enhance the picture's brightness and contrast. You'll need to do a Preview scan to see the effects of any changes you make.
- Optionally, if you plan to scan more pictures at the current settings, click Save Profile and give your profile a name.

6. Click Scan.

When the scan is complete, the picture will appear in the Photo Gallery. The actual picture file is in your Pictures folder.

 **For information on Windows Fax and Scan, see Chapter 38.**

Using pictures you get by e-mail

Pictures that are embedded in, or attached to, e-mail messages you receive won't show up in Photo Gallery at first. You need to save the picture(s) to your Pictures folder if you want to access and edit them using techniques described in this chapter.

Exactly how you save attachments and embedded pictures depends on how you do e-mail. If you use Windows Mail, see "Saving attachments as files" and "Saving embedded pictures as files" in Chapter 18.

For most other e-mail clients, it's usually a simple matter of right-clicking the attachment's icon and choosing Save As. Or in the case of a picture that's visible in the body of the message, right-click the picture and choose Save Picture As. However, do keep in mind that all e-mail clients and systems are different. If you can't figure out how to save attachments or pictures in your e-mail, search your ISP or e-mail provider's e-mail support for `attachment`, or contact their technical support.

Copying pictures from Web sites

Needless to say, there are billions of pictures on the Internet. You can often find just the picture you're looking for by going to a site like images.google.com and searching for an appropriate word or phrase.

If you find a picture you can use (and you're not infringing on anyone's copyright in the process), you can store a copy of the picture in any folder of your choosing. If the picture you see on the screen is a link to a larger copy of the image, click to get to the larger copy of the picture. Then use whatever options your Web browser provides to save a copy of the picture. Here are the steps for Internet Explorer, the Web browser that comes with Windows Vista:

1. In Internet Explorer, right-click anywhere on the picture you want and choose Save Picture As.
2. Click Pictures in the navigation pane (see Figure 22.5). Of course, you can choose some other folder if you prefer. For example, double-click any subfolder icon in the main pane to store the picture in that subfolder.

FIGURE 22.5

Save Picture.

- Optionally, to put the picture in a subfolder of the folder you just opened, double-click that subfolder's icon.
- Optionally, change the File name of the picture to a filename of your own choosing.
- Optionally, click to the right of the Save as type label and choose a format. (JPEG works best if you plan to use Windows Photo Gallery.)
3. Click Save.

A copy of the picture is saved in whatever folder you specified in step 2.

Form more information on saving files, see "Saving Things in Folders" in Chapter 28.

Copy and paste pictures

You can copy an open picture from just about any document to any document that accepts pictures. For example, you can copy and paste a picture from a Web page to a Microsoft Word document. You just have to make sure the picture is open (not just an icon or thumbnail). To copy-and-paste an open picture:

1. Right-click the picture and choose Copy.
2. Right-click where you want to put the picture and choose Paste.

You can use the same technique to make a copy of a picture within a folder or Windows Photo Gallery. Right-click the icon or thumbnail of the picture you want to copy and choose Copy. Then right-click some empty place within the folder (perhaps after the last icon) and choose Paste. The copy will have the same filename as the original followed by –Copy.

Taking screenshots

NEW FEATURE The new Snipping Tool lets you take a screenshot and also annotate it with your own text. Be sure to check that out under "Annotating Screenshots with Snipping Tool" in Chapter 15.

A screenshot is like a photo of something you see on your screen. Most of the pictures in this book are screenshots. There are two ways to create screenshots in Windows Vista. One is to use the new Snipping Tool. The other is to use the Print Screen key.

Using the Snipping Tool

To use the Snipping Tool, first get the screen looking the way you want the screenshot to look. Then use either of the following techniques to open the Snipping Tool:

- Click the Start button and choose All Programs ➪ Accessories ➪ Snipping Tool.
- Press ⊞, type sni, and choose Snipping Tool.

The first time you do these steps you'll be given the option to add the Snipping Tool to your Quick Launch toolbar. If you plan on using it often, choose Yes to make it easily accessible from your desktop.

TIP Whether or not you add the Snipping Tool to your Quick Launch toolbar when first prompted isn't important. As with any program, you can add or remove it at any time. For total Quick Launch mastery, see "Customizing the Quick Launch toolbar" in Chapter 11.

In the small Snipping Tool window that opens, click the arrow on the New button and choose what you want to capture:

- **Free-Form Snip:** If you choose this option, the screen goes dim. Lasso the area you want to capture by dragging a circle or any other shape around it.
- **Rectangle Snip:** If you choose this option, the screen goes dim. Drag a rectangle around the portion of the screen you want to capture.
- **Window Snip:** If you choose this option, you can then click anywhere in the window you want to capture.
- **Full Screen Snip:** Choosing this option captures the whole screen without further intervention on your part.

The Snipping Tool enlarges to full screen and displays your screenshot. Now you have two choices. If you're not happy with your capture, click the New button and try again. If you are happy with your screen capture, you can save it as a file in your Pictures folder. Click the Save Snip toolbar button (the one that looks like a floppy disk). Navigate to the folder in which you want to put the picture. If you don't have a preference, use your Pictures folder. Then give the snip a filename, and choose a type from the Save As Type button. If you don't have a preference, choose PNG or JPEG because either will give you good quality and excellent compatibility with other programs.

Optionally, you can copy-and-paste the snip into another open document or program. Click the Copy toolbar button (two sheets of paper button). Then open the program into which you want to paste the picture and paste (press Ctrl+V).

That's the Snipping Tool in a nutshell. See Chapter 11 for the whole story.

Using the Print Screen key

The Print Screen key gets its name from the olden days of computers where pressing it actually printed whatever was on your screen at the moment to paper. It hasn't worked that way in a long time. Nowadays the Print Screen key takes a snapshot of the screen and puts it in the Windows Clipboard where it just sits until you paste the Clipboard contents. There are two ways to use the Print Screen key:

- **Print Screen:** Takes a snapshot of the entire screen.
- **Alt+Print Screen:** Takes a snapshot of the active window only.

NOTE The Print Screen key may be labeled Prnt Scrn, PrtScn, or something like that on your keyboard.

To make a screenshot, get the screen looking the way you want. Then follow these steps:

1. Press Print Screen or Alt+Print Screen.
2. Open your favorite graphics program. If you don't have one, click the Start button and choose All Programs ➪ Accessories ➪ Paint to open Paint (which comes with Windows Vista).

NOTE You can paste the snapshot into a document (like a Microsoft Word document). But if you do, you won't be able to treat it like a normal editable picture. Better to paste it into Paint or some other graphics program and save it as a JPEG or PNG file. You cannot paste the snapshot into a folder or Windows Photo Gallery.

3. Choose Edit ➪ Paste from the menu, or press Ctrl+V. The screenshot is pasted into the program.
4. Exit Paint or your graphics program by clicking its Close (X) button.
5. When you see a message asking if you want to save your changes, click Yes. The Save As dialog box opens.
6. In the Save As dialog box, type a File name of your own choosing.
7. The Save in location should already be your Pictures folder (e.g., C:\Users\Your User Name\Pictures). If it's not, navigate to your Pictures folder (or the folder in which you want to store screenshots).
8. Set the Save as type option to PNG or JPEG unless you have a good reason for using a different format.
9. Click the Save button.

My Print Screen Key Doesn't Work

If the Paste option on Paint's Edit menu is disabled (dimmed), that means there is nothing in the Clipboard. There are a couple reasons why that might happen. You might have forgotten to press Print Screen or Alt+PrintScreen. Or perhaps you copied something else to the Clipboard after pressing Print Screen. And that "something else" isn't a picture.

The second possible problem is that your keyboard works differently. For example, on some keyboards you have to press Shift+Print Screen or Shift+Alt+PrintScreen. On one of my laptop computers, I have to click Fn+PrintScreen. On another keyboard, I have to make sure the F Lock key is turned off before pressing the Print Screen key.

If you can't find the right combination of keystrokes for your system, see if you can find the information in the manual that came with your computer. Or contact your computer manufacturer and see if they can help.

You won't see anything on your screen. But rest assured, the screenshot is saved as a file in whatever folder you specified in step 7, with whatever filename you specified in step 6. If you chose your Pictures folder in step 7, you'll find the file when you open your Pictures folder, described next.

Using Your Pictures Folder

As its name implies, the Pictures folder is the place to store pictures. Many of the techniques described in the preceding section will put pictures in that folder automatically. To view pictures, just open your Pictures folder using whichever technique is most convenient at the moment:

- Click the Start button and click Pictures (see Figure 22.6).

FIGURE 22.6

Pictures link on the Start menu.

- Click Pictures in Explorer's Navigation pane (see Figure 22.7).

FIGURE 22.7

FIGURE 22.7

Pictures link in Navigation pane.

■ Click your user name in a breadcrumb menu and choose Pictures (see Figure 22.8).

FIGURE 22.8

Pictures link from breadcrumb menu.

Your Pictures folder opens in Explorer. Your Pictures folder is no different from any other folder. You can use all the tools and techniques described under "Using Windows Explorer" in Chapter 28 to size and arrange icons, hide and show panes, and so forth.

Pictures that you copied from a camera or scanner will likely be stored in subfolders. The name of the subfolder will be the same as the date on which you acquired the pictures, followed by any tag word you added. Figure 22.9 shows an example. The folders whose names start with 2007 contain pictures I copied from a digital camera. The rest of folders I created and named myself.

FIGURE 22.9

Sample Pictures folder.

When you open a subfolder that contains pictures, you'll see a thumbnail icon for each one. The size of that thumbnail and the amount of textual information shown with each depends on where you place the Views slider in the toolbar. If the Preview pane is open, pointing to a thumbnail displays an enlarged copy of the thumbnail. Figure 22.10 shows an example. To choose which panes you want to show or hide, click the Organize toolbar button and make your selections on the Layout submenu.

FIGURE 22.10

Folder of pictures.

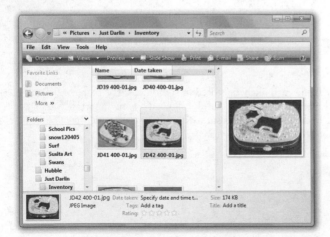

Pictures folder quick tips

NEW FEATURE Icons in folders are different from the way they were in earlier Windows versions. There is no Filmstrip view in Vista, but you can make icons large enough to get a good preview of any picture without opening it.

Here are some quick tips that apply to most folders, with a few things that are unique to your Pictures folder:

- If your mouse has a wheel, hold down the Ctrl key while spinning the wheel to size thumbnails and change views.
- Drag the inner border of the Navigation or Preview pane to widen or narrow the pane.
- To open a subfolder, click (or double-click) its icon. To leave a subfolder, click the Back button or press Backspace.

TIP Whether you need to click or double-click depends on settings in Folder Options. Click the Organize toolbar button and choose Folder and Search Options. Make your selection under "Click items as follows" and click OK.

- To rotate a picture, right-click its thumbnail and choose Rotate Clockwise or Rotate Counter Clockwise.

NOTE If the Rotate options are disabled or missing, the picture's file type can't be rotated in Windows. But you can open and rotate it in many graphics programs.

- To preview a larger version of a picture, click (or double-click) its thumbnail. See "Using the Photo Gallery Viewer" later in this chapter for things you can do there. After viewing, close the Photo Gallery Viewer to return to your Pictures folder.
- To view all the pictures in the folder as a slide show, click the Slide Show toolbar button.
- Right-click any thumbnail icon for a shortcut of things you can do with that item.
- Use standard techniques described under "How to Select Icons" in Chapter 29 to select multiple icons that you want to print, copy, burn to CD, and so forth. To select all icons, click Organize ➪ Select All or press Ctrl+A.
- To e-mail pictures using Windows Mail, select their thumbnail icons. Then click the E-mail toolbar button as in Figure 22.11.

FIGURE 22.11

E-mail button.

NOTE The E-mail button isn't visible until you select one or more icons in the folder. Also, it doesn't work with all e-mail accounts. See Chapter 18 for more information.

495

- Click Burn to copy all pictures in a folder to a writeable CD or DVD. To copy only specific items, select their icons and click Burn.

 **Copying to CD and DVD isn't like copying to other media. Chapter 32 provides the full story.**

- Right-click any column heading to choose which columns you want to show or hide.

NOTE **The columnar data is visible only in the Details view. But you can still use column headings in other views to sort and arrange icons.**

- Click any column heading to sort thumbnails into ascending or descending order by Name, Date Taken, Rating, or any other heading.

- Click the arrow next to any column heading as in Figure 22.12, or right-click empty space between icons, to sort, stack, group, or filter by Name, Date Taken, Tags, or Rating.

TIP **See "Using Windows Photo Gallery" later in this chapter for more information on tags. See "Using Windows Explorer" in Chapter 28 for more info on grouping, stacking, and filtering.**

FIGURE 22.12

Sorting, stacking, grouping options.

- When the Details pane is open, you can use it to add a tag or title to any selected pictures or multiple selected pictures.

- If you have multiple programs that can open a picture type, right-click the thumbnail and choose Open With to open the picture in whatever program you like. Or choose a program name from the Preview toolbar button.

- To show or hide the menu bar, tap the Alt key or click the Organize button and choose Layout ➪ Menu Bar (see Figure 22.13).

- To show or hide filename extensions, choose Folder Options from the Explorer Layout menu. Select or clear the Show extensions for known file types checkbox on the View tab, then click OK.

FIGURE 22.13

Layout options on Organize menu.

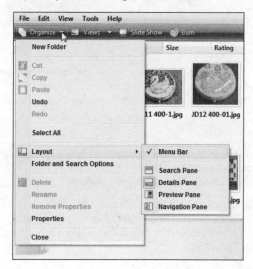

Why some pictures show icons

Not all file types show as pictures in your Pictures folder. Some, such as videos you import from a camera in MP4, MOV, or some other format, show only icons. For example, in Figure 22.14 the icon on the left is a video stored in the Windows Media Video format (a .wmv file). The icon on the right is a video stored in Apple's QuickTime format (.mov format).

FIGURE 22.14

Icon showing Q is a QuickTime movie.

If you have an appropriate player for a file type, you can still open it by double-clicking. For example, if you have the QuickTime player (available for free from www.QuickTime.com), you can double-click any QuickTime movie's icon to watch it.

CAUTION Changing the filename extension using Rename will not work. In fact, if you do that, you may not be able to open the file at all until you rename it back to the original filename extension!

If it's important to be able to see the thumbnail of a picture or icon, you have to convert the image or video to a compatible format like JPEG (for a picture) or WMV (for a video). For a single picture, you can often achieve this just by opening the picture in a graphics program. If you don't have a favorite graphics program, you can use Paint (right-click any picture and choose Open With ⇨ Paint). From the menu bar in your graphics program, choose File ⇨ Save As. Use the Save As Type option in the Save dialog box to save the picture as a JPEG or some other compatible format and click Save.

Some graphics programs, like Corel's Paint Shop Pro, will let you convert a whole slew of pictures from one format to another without doing them one at a time. You can also go to any online shareware service like www.tucows.com or www.download.com and search for convert picture to find programs that specifically offer batch conversions. Search for convert video for programs that can convert videos.

Videos in your Pictures folder

If your digital camera lets you shoot video clips, those will be imported along with your still pictures. If the video is in a compatible format, its thumbnail will show the first frame of the video. It will also show a film-like border and the icon of the default program for playing that type of video.

When you select a video thumbnail, the Preview pane turns to a small video screen with controls that work like a VCR or DVD player. Figure 22.15 shows an example where I've selected a video (the mouse pointer is touching it). The video preview pane to the right shows the first frame of the video. To watch the video in that preview, click the Play button under the video.

FIGURE 22.15

Video thumbnail icon selected.

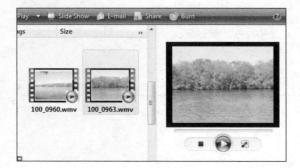

Once the video gets playing you can click the Full Screen button under the preview window to watch it full-screen. Click anywhere on that full-screen video to return to the desktop and your Pictures folder.

There's much more to pictures and videos than looking at them in your Pictures folder. Next we'll take a look at Windows Photo Gallery, a handy tool that comes with Windows Vista.

Renaming pictures and videos

Pictures and videos from cameras often have obscure meaningless filenames like 100_9630 or DCM1234. You can change the name of any file by right-clicking its thumbnail and choosing Rename. Or, select multiple thumbnails, right-click any one of them, and choose Rename. The current filename is highlighted.

Type the new name. (Never change the extension that comes after the period.) Then press Enter. If you renamed one file, only that file's name will be changed. If you renamed several files, they'll all have the same name followed by a number; for example, Swans (2), Swans (3), Swans (4), and so forth.

If you change your mind after renaming, press Undo (Ctrl+Z). But you have to do it right after pressing Enter. If you move on to other tasks, you may not be able to undo the rename.

TIP When you rename multiple files, the first renamed file won't have a number after its name. If that inconsistency bugs you, rename just that one file, adding a blank space and (1) after its current filename.

Using Windows Photo Gallery

NEW FEATURE Windows Photo Gallery is a great tool for managing a large photo collection.

Windows Photo Gallery is a program that helps you bring together pictures and videos from all the subfolders in your Pictures folder. Photo Gallery isn't a folder where you store files. Rather, it's a way of organizing and accessing files without having to navigate around through multiple folders. For example, you can view all your photos at once, regardless of what folders they're in. Or better yet, you can locate and work with pictures that have certain things in common, such as all the pictures of your child (if you're a parent).

The only disadvantage of Windows Photo Gallery is that it doesn't show icons for all pictures and videos. Anything that doesn't show a thumbnail in your Pictures folder doesn't show up at all in Photo Gallery! Photo Gallery shows thumbnails for BMP, JFIF, JPEG, PNG, TIFF, and WDP photos and WMV, AVI, ASF, and MPEG movies.

The easiest way to understand what Windows Photo Gallery is all about is to fire it up and take a look for yourself. Use whichever method shown here is easiest for you:

- Click (or double-click) any picture thumbnail in your Pictures folder to preview it, then click Gallery in the lower-right corner of the preview window that opens.
- Click the Start button and choose Windows Photo Gallery.
- Click Start and choose All Programs ➪ Windows Photo Gallery.
- Tap ⊞, type gal, and click Windows Photo Gallery.

What about RAW Pictures?

Some cameras store pictures as RAW files. The filename extension for this file type varies. For example, Canon uses .CRW and .CR2. Nikon uses .NEF. It's possible to view some of these files in Photo Gallery, but most require downloading special software.

When you open Windows Photo Gallery, it will check to see if any online updates are available to display your pictures. If it finds an appropriate update, you'll be given the opportunity to download and install it automatically.

Figure 22.16 shows an example of how Photo Gallery might look when you first open it. Of course the pictures you see will be your own (if you have any). The names of things in the program window are also pointed out in that figure.

FIGURE 22.16

Windows Photo Gallery

Like any program window, you can minimize, maximize, move, and size Photo Gallery to your liking. (Though there is a limit to how small you can make it.) Photo Gallery has its own Help. Click the blue Get Help button at the right side of its toolbar to open Help (or press F1 if Photo Gallery is the active window).

Choosing what to view and how

The Photo Gallery can show you all the photos and videos on your hard drive (or multiple hard drives). Or it can show only certain ones. To get started, you'll want to see everything that's in the Photo Gallery right now. To do that, click All Pictures and Videos at the top of the Navigation pane. If you just want to see pictures, click Pictures under the All Pictures and Videos heading. If you just want to see Videos, click Videos under that same heading.

The gallery to the right of the Navigation pane shows a thumbnail for each photo and video currently in the gallery.

Use the Thumbnail View and Thumbnail Size buttons to choose how you want those thumbnails to look. Clicking the Thumbnail View button offers Thumbnails, Thumbnails with Text, and Tiles views. Try each one to see how it looks. Then use the Thumbnail Size button to make the thumbnails whatever size you like. Or, if your mouse has a wheel, hold down the Ctrl key while spinning the wheel. To get back to the original sizes, click the Set Default Thumbnail Size button to the right of the Thumbnail Size button.

To group or arrange pictures in the gallery, click the Thumbnail View button, choose Arrange By or Group By and whatever option best describes how you want things organized.

Also in the Thumbnail View button is a Table of Contents option. Clicking that opens a Table of Contents pane to the left of the Thumbnails. The Table of Contents works in conjunction with the current Group By option on the Thumbnail View button. For example, if you group by Month, the Table of Contents lets you jump to all pictures taken in a specific month and year. If you group by Image Size, the Table of Contents provides links to large, medium, and small pictures, and so forth.

Go ahead and play around with those buttons and options for a while. You can't do any harm. But some of the grouping and arranging options won't have any real effect until you've built up a sizable collection of pictures. Remember, anything you choose right now you can change at any time in the future. You're not making any long-term commitments here while experimenting with views and arrangements.

Photo Gallery quick tips

Following are some other good things to know. If any item listed doesn't work for you, see "Choosing Photo Gallery options" later in this chapter.

- Rest the mouse pointer on any thumbnail to see a larger view of the picture.
- To rotate a picture, right-click it and choose a Rotate option. Or click the thumbnail and click a Rotate button in the picture controls.
- Click any picture to see it in the Info pane where you can rate it, add, change, or remove tags, or change its caption. Click the Info toolbar button to show/hide the Info pane.
- Double-click any picture to preview it at a larger size. Click Back to Gallery to leave the preview.
- Click Play Slide Show (center of the picture controls) or press F11 to watch a slide show.
- To open a picture or video in a program, click its thumbnail and then click the Open toolbar button and choose a program.
- Click the File button and choose Import from Camera or Scanner to import pictures from a digital camera or scanner.
- To print selected pictures, click the Print toolbar button. (See "Printing Pictures" later in this chapter for details and options.)
- To open the folder in which a picture is contained, right-click its thumbnail and choose Open File Location.

Selecting thumbnails in the gallery

As in folders, you can select multiple thumbnails in Photo Gallery. This can be handy when you want to apply a similar rating, tag, or caption to pictures. Or when you want to create a slide show from several pictures, print several pictures, and so forth. You can use the same techniques you use in folders to select thumbnails in the gallery.

In addition to the standard methods of selecting thumbnails (and icons), you can select multiple thumbnails just by clicking their checkboxes. Any thumbnail that has a checkmark is selected. Any thumbnail that doesn't have a checkmark is unselected.

To select all the pictures in the gallery, click any single picture and press Ctrl+A. Or right-click some empty space just outside the thumbnails and choose Select All. If you want to select most (but not all) of the pictures, select them all first. Then Ctrl+Click the pictures you want to un-select, or clear their checkboxes.

Dating, rating, tagging, and captioning

Tagging is one of the biggest advantages to having all of your pictures in Windows Photo Gallery. A tag is simply some keyword or phrase that you make up to identify pictures; for example, the location where the picture was shot, the subject of the picture, or the names of people in the picture. You can apply as many tags as you wish to a picture. And you can add, change, or delete tags at any time.

Rating allows you to rate photos on a scale of 1 to 5 stars based on how much you like the picture. Captions allow you to title pictures with words of your own choosing. Use the Info pane to rate, tag, and caption pictures.

First, click the thumbnail picture that you want to rate. Or, if you want to apply the same rating, tags, or caption to multiple pictures, select all of their icons. Then:

■ To rate the selected picture(s), click any star near the top of the Info pane (see Figure 22.17). To give a zero rating, right-click a star and choose Clear Rating.

FIGURE 22.17

Info pane.

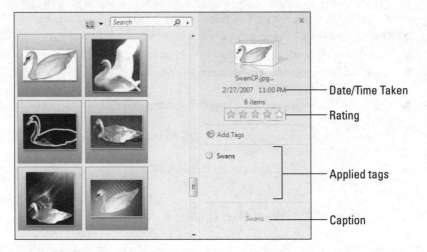

■ To tag the selected picture(s), click Add tags. Type one tag (preferably a single word or two) and press Enter. Optionally, type more tags in the same manner, pressing Enter after each tag.

> **TIP** If the picture contains people you know, consider typing each person's name as a separate tag. That way you can later search for pictures of that person, or pictures that contain several specific people. Don't use commas or semicolons in an attempt to apply multiple tags to a picture. Always press Enter after typing a single tag.

■ To caption, type a caption in the Add a caption box, or replace the text that already appears there with a caption of your own.

■ Optionally, if you want to change the date or time that the picture was taken, click the current date and time shown above the Ratings stars.

Filtering pictures

The coolest thing about tagging pictures is that it makes specific pictures very easy to find in the future. This is especially useful after you've accumulated hundreds or thousands of pictures, and don't want to go digging through folders to find specific pictures.

To see all pictures to which you've applied a tag, just click the tag in the Navigation pane. If you don't see those tags, click the triangle next to Tags to expand that list. When you click a tag, the gallery shows all pictures to which you've applied that tag. Figure 22.18 shows an example where I clicked the tag Ashley. The gallery to the right shows all pictures to which I've applied that tag.

FIGURE 22.18

Viewing all pictures tagged Ashley.

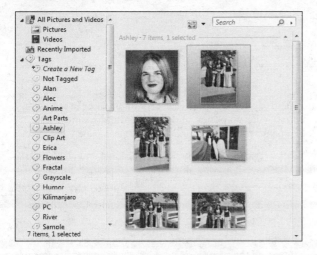

To see pictures that contain multiple tags, use the Search box. For example, suppose you entered each person's name as a separate tag in your photos. First click All Pictures and Videos in the Navigation pane so you're viewing all pictures. Then in the Search box type the names separated by a space. For example, a search for `Ashley Alec` shows only pictures that contain both Ashley and Alec.

To see all pictures to which you haven't yet applied any tags, click Not Tagged near the top of the tag list. From there you can start adding tags to any pictures that appear in the gallery.

Near the bottom of the Navigation pane you'll see the headings Date Taken, Ratings, and Folders (see Figure 22.19). Click the triangle next to any heading to expand or collapse its contents. Use them in the same way you use tags. For example, to see all pictures taken in a given year, click a year number. To see all pictures taken on a given day, expand the appropriate year and month, then click the appropriate date.

FIGURE 22.19

Other options in the Navigation pane.

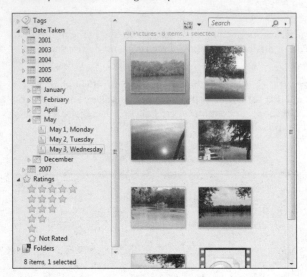

To see all the pictures you took in a certain year, month, or day, click the year, month, or date. To see all the pictures to which you've applied a rating (or no rating), click an option under the Ratings heading. To see all the pictures in a particular folder, click the folder name at the bottom of the Navigation pane.

To see all the pictures to which you applied a particular rating, expand the Ratings heading and click a rating. To see all the pictures you haven't yet rated, click Unrated. Having all your unrated pictures in the gallery is a good place to start rating from.

 **TIP**   To clear ratings, right-click a thumbnail (or any selected thumbnail) and choose Clear Ratings. This sets each selected thumbnail back to Not Rated.

At the bottom of the Navigation pane you'll see the Folders heading. Expand that heading to see the names of all folders currently displayed in Photo Gallery. To see all the pictures in a folder, click the folder name.

To search for pictures or videos by name, tag, or other keyword, first click All Photos and Videos at the top of the Navigation pane. Then type a word in the Search box. You can also narrow the search by first clicking Pictures, Videos, a tag, a year, or whatever to reduce the number of items in the gallery. Your next search will search only within items currently in the gallery.

Changing tags

Tags are flexible. You can add, rename, and change them at will. To change the spelling of a tag, just right-click it in the Navigation pane and choose Rename. Type in the corrected name and press Enter. The spelling will automatically be corrected in every picture that contains that tag.

To delete a tag from a single picture, without removing the tag from any other pictures, first select the picture's thumbnail. Or if you want to delete the tag from a few pictures, select their thumbnails. Then right-click the tag you want to remove and choose Delete. Note that deleting a tag will not delete any pictures. It simply removes the tag from any pictures to which you previously applied the tag.

Use a picture as your desktop background

If you have a favorite photo you'd like to use as a desktop background, right-click its thumbnail and choose Set as Desktop Background.

If you can't see the desktop, right-click the clock and choose Show the Desktop. Then click the Windows Photo Gallery taskbar button to bring Photo Gallery back onto the desktop.

 See "Using the Personalization Page" in Chapter 11 for more ways to personalize your Windows desktop.

Adding pictures to Photo Gallery

Photo Gallery doesn't scan your entire hard disk for photos. By default in includes only pictures from the Pictures folder in your user account. If you have pictures in other folders, there are several ways to add them to Photo Gallery. If the pictures are in some arbitrary location where they just happened to end up, consider moving them to your Pictures folder. Use any technique described in Chapter 29 to move and copy files.

If the pictures are in some other folder for good reason, you can add that folder to Windows Photo Gallery. This has no effect on the pictures or the folder. So you won't mess up your existing organization. To add a folder to the Photo Gallery:

1. Click the Files toolbar button and choose Add Folder to Gallery.
2. Navigate to any folder that contains pictures and videos you'd like to include in your gallery and click OK.

Repeat steps 1 and 2 for each folder you want to add. As you add new pictures to those folders in the future, they'll show up automatically in Photo Gallery.

If you want to add a single picture to the gallery, rather than a whole folder, you can do so from the Photo Gallery Viewer described next.

Using the Photo Gallery Viewer

The Photo Gallery Viewer is a relatively simple tool for viewing one picture at a time. There are many ways to get to the viewer. Typically just opening an appropriate file type by double-clicking its icon or thumbnail will do the trick. If some other program is set as the default for that file type, then you can right-click the icon or thumbnail and choose Open With ➪ Photo Gallery Viewer.

 If Open With or Photo Gallery Viewer aren't available when you right-click, that just means that the item you right-clicked isn't appropriate for the viewer.

The Photo Gallery Viewer looks much like Photo Gallery and offers the same basic tools and capabilities. The main difference is that it only shows one picture at a time, like the example in Figure 22.20.

 The Delete button deletes the picture from your computer. Do not use it to view a different picture. Use the Previous and Next buttons to look at different pictures in the folder.

FIGURE 22.20

Photo Gallery Viewer.

Zooming and panning

The Zoom tool (magnifying glass) lets you zoom in for a close-up look at any portion of the picture. As an alternative, you can click the picture and spin your mouse wheel to zoom in and out.

Once you're zoomed in, the mouse pointer changes to a small hand (when it's on the picture). When the pointer looks like a hand, hold down the left mouse button and drag to pan through the zoomed-in picture. Click the Fit to Window button to size the photo back to where it fits within the viewer.

 **Right-click the photo you're viewing in the Photo Gallery for a shortcut menu of things you can do with that picture.**

Back to the Gallery

The Photo Gallery Viewer offers most of the same tools as Photo Gallery. The main difference is that the Viewer only shows one picture at a time. To return to thumbnails of all your pictures, click Go To Gallery in the upper-left corner.

Making a duplicate photo

Sometimes you may want several copies of the same photo. For example, the original as it came from your camera. A smaller copy to e-mail to friends. Perhaps a cropped version to put in a small frame. You don't want to mess up your original photo in the process. So it's always a good idea to work with a copy of the original photo. Making a copy is easy in Photo Gallery:

1. Click the Thumbnail of the picture you want to duplicate.
2. Click the File toolbar button and choose Duplicate.

The duplicate will have the same filename as the original followed by –copy. It will be the last thumbnail in the gallery. If you click the Name column heading once or twice to bring them into alphabetical order, the copy will be close to the original.

Use your Photo Gallery as a screen saver

To use photos in your Photo Gallery as a screen saver, click the File toolbar button and choose Screen Saver Settings. Set the Screen Saver name to Photos. Then click the Settings button and choose Show all pictures and photos from Photo Gallery. If you like, you can narrow things down to only pictures that have a certain tag or rating. You can also set the general speed of the screen saver slide show. Click Save after making your selections. Click Preview for a preview of how the screen saver will look. Click OK when you're happy with your selections to return to Photo Gallery.

Fixing photos

NEW FEATURE   The Fix pane makes it easy to touch up your photos. It's a far cry from a "real" graphics editor like PhotoShop or Paint Shop Pro. But it can fix the most common photo problems.

Windows Photo Gallery comes complete with a simple graphics editor specifically designed to work with photos. It's called the Fix pane and you can get to it in a couple of ways:

- If you're in Windows Photo Gallery, click the thumbnail of the photo you want to edit and click Fix in the toolbar.
- If you're already viewing a single photo in the Photo Gallery viewer, just click Fix in the toolbar.

The Fix pane replaces the Info pane on the right as in Figure 22.21. Before you try anything, notice the Undo button at the bottom. If you don't like the results of a change, click that to undo the change. If you change your mind after Undo, click Redo to bring the change back. When you point to Undo and Redo after making changes to a picture, you'll see a little arrow on the button that you can click to Undo only one change, or all changes. The buttons are disabled (dimmed) when there's nothing to undo or redo.

The sections to follow describe each tool on the Fix pane.

FIGURE 22.21

The Fix pane at right.

Why Can't I Fix My Photo?

Sometimes clicking the Fix button won't work. There are several reasons for this. First, you cannot make changes to a read-only file. Every file on a CD or DVD is read-only. If the picture you're trying to fix is on such a disk, you need to copy it to your Pictures folder first. Then edit the copy that's in your Picture folder. The picture might also be in some remote location rather than on your own hard disk. You need to get a copy of that picture onto your own hard disk before you can edit it. If the picture is on your hard drive already, it may be marked read-only in its properties sheet. Right-click the picture's icon, choose Properties, clear the Read-only checkbox, and click OK.

The type of file you're editing plays a role as well. Windows Photo Gallery only supports modern file formats commonly used for digital photos, such as JPEG and TIFF. You cannot edit .GIF, .BMP, .WMF, and other older or non-photographic file types with Windows Photo Gallery. If you try, you'll see the message "Photo Gallery can't edit this picture in its current format." Click the Help link, or see "Changing a picture type or size" later in this chapter for information on how you can change a picture from an incompatible format (like BMP) to a compatible format (like TIFF or JPEG).

Auto Adjust

Click Auto Adjust to let Photo Gallery take a shot at cleaning up the brightness, contrast, and such. Don't expect miracles though. Sometimes Auto Adjust might make things worse. If so, just click Undo.

Adjust Exposure

Click this option to adjust the brightness and contrast of the picture. The Brightness slider is especially useful for pictures that are poorly lit. You may need to adjust the contrast as well to bring some depth to the picture. Just move the sliders around until you find a combination you like. If you can't seem to make an improvement, drag the slider boxes back to the middle of each bar. Or click Undo until the picture is back to its original form.

Adjust Color

Click Adjust color to change the Color Temperature, Tint, and Saturation. Adjust each by dragging the slider left or right. Each item has a different effect on the photo as follows:

- **Color Temperature:** The overall tone of your picture. Dragging to the left tends toward cool (bluish tint). Dragging to the right moves toward warm (reddish tint). Best used for pictures taken outdoors.

- **Tint:** Changes the color cast in a picture by adding or removing green from your picture.

- **Saturation:** Drag the slider left and right to change the intensity of all colors. Dragging all the way to the left converts the pictures to grayscale (black and white).

Cropping

Cropping a picture lets you get rid of any unnecessary background. This is useful when the main subject of the photo looks too small or far away. Figure 22.22 shows an example. If the idea is to show a picture of the boat, the original photo on the left isn't so great because the boat is too far away. The cropped photo on the right brings the boat more into the foreground by eliminating much of the background.

FIGURE 22.22

Original photo (left) and cropped (right).

Original (uncropped)   Cropped

> **TIP**   Figure 22.22 is also a good example of why you might want to make a duplicate of the original before cropping. The photo on the left isn't so bad as a photo, and is probably worth keeping. The cropped copy on the right is good for showing the boat as the main subject of the photo.

To crop a photo, first click Crop in the Fix pane. A white box with sizing handles (little squares) appears on the picture. The idea is to get exactly what you want the finished photo to look like inside that box. Anything you want to crop out of the picture should be outside the box.

If you plan on printing the finished photo on pre-sized photographic paper, click the Proportion button and choose your print size. Doing so will keep the proportions of the cropping box at the proper aspect ratio for that goal. Click Rotate Frame to switch between landscape (wide) and portrait (tall) orientations.

> **NOTE**   The aspect ratio is the ratio of the width of the photo to its height. Different print sizes have slightly different aspect ratios.

If you want to retain the original aspect ratio, click Original. If you're not concerned about printing on pre-sized photo paper, choose Custom. With that setting you can make the cropped picture any shape you like.

Here's how you use the cropping box that's on the picture:

■ To make the box larger or smaller, drag any sizing handle (little square) around the box border.

■ To re-center the box around the main subject of the photo, put the mouse pointer inside the box and drag it to a better location on the picture.

■ To zoom in and out while cropping, spin the mouse wheel or use the Zoom (magnifying glass) button.

When the inside of the box looks the way you want your photo to look, click the Apply button. The picture is cropped. (If you change your mind, click Undo.)

Fixing red eye

Red eye is a common problem caused by the retina at the back of the eye reflecting the flash back to the camera. Fixing it isn't too tough. First, if the eyes are very small in the photo, spin the mouse wheel or use the Zoom button to zoom in on the eyes. You may need to zoom a little, pan a little, zoom a little. The idea is to make the eyes as large as possible in the viewing area. Next, click Fix Red Eye in the Fix pane and follow the instructions that appear there. Drag a rectangle around the pupil of the eyeball, not the entire eye. Figure 22.23 shows an example where I've dragged a rectangle around a dog's eye. (Fortunately I don't know any people with eyes like that.)

FIGURE 22.23

Fixing red eye.

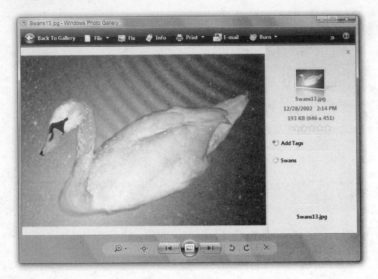

If dragging a rectangle around the eye once doesn't fix the red eye, drag another rectangle around the same eye. Keep doing so until all of the red is gone. Then, pan over to the other eye, if necessary, and drag a square around that eye. If you don't like the results, click Undo. Then try again.

Saving Fix pane changes

When you've finished touching up your photo in the Fix pane, click Back to Gallery. Your changes are saved automatically.

If you made a mess of things in the Fix pane and were hoping Back to Gallery *wouldn't* save your changes, don't panic. Click the Fix button again to open that same picture with the Fix pane. Then click Revert at the bottom of the Fix pane to undo your previous changes.

 You can recover previous versions of many different kinds of files, not just photos. If you're interested in that sort of thing, see "Using System Protection" in Chapter 33 for the whole story.

Choosing Photo Gallery options

Like most programs, Windows Photo Gallery has an Options dialog box that lets you tweak certain program features to your own work style. To open Photo Gallery's Options dialog box, click the File toolbar button and choose Options. Figure 22.24 shows the two tabs in that dialog box, General and Import.

FIGURE 22.24

Photo Gallery options.

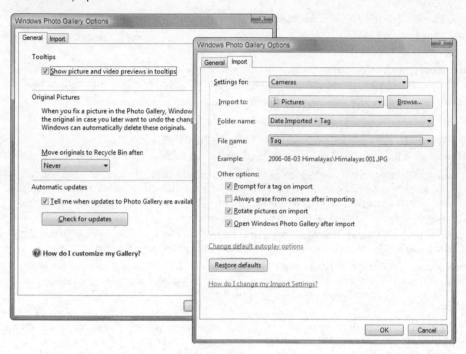

Selecting the first option, "Show picture and video previews in tooltips," ensures that when you point to a thumbnail in Photo Gallery, you see a larger version of the thumbnail or video. Clearing that checkbox prevents the tooltips from showing.

The Original Pictures section has to do with the Revert button in Fix. By default, previous versions of photos stay on the hard disk permanently, even though you don't see them. After a few years, or even months, the storage space they require could be significant. Choosing Move original files to Recycle Bin after lets you put a time on those saved originals. You can choose from among several timeframes ranging from one day to never.

NOTE The Recycle Bin is much like a wastepaper basket. It holds your trash (deleted files) until you empty it. See "Deleting Files" in Chapter 29 for more information.

Keep in mind that you will not be able to revert a modified picture to its original form, or find a previous version of a file after the time limit expires. If you consistently work with duplicates of pictures rather than originals, this isn't a big deal because you always have the original in plain sight in its folder.

The Import tab lets you customize how pictures that you import to Photo Gallery are handled. You can import pictures into Photo Gallery by clicking File in its toolbar and choosing Import from Camera or Scanner.

- **Settings for:** Specify the device or medium for which you want to define settings.
- **Import to:** Choose the folder to which pictures and videos will be imported. The default is the Pictures folder for your user account.
- **Folder name:** Imported pictures are automatically placed in a folder. Use this option to specify how you want that folder named. Items in square brackets are placeholders as summarized here:
  - **[Date Imported]:** Today's date (the date on which you're performing the import).
  - **[Tag]:** The tag you type when prompted to enter a tag.
  - **[Date Taken]:** The date in the first picture's Date Taken property.
  - **[Date Taken Range]:** The Date Taken property of the first and last pictures being imported.
- **File name:** Each imported picture is automatically assigned a filename. To use the tag you entered as a filename, choose Tag. To use the original filename as assigned by the camera, choose Original File Name. Some digital cameras organize photos into folders. To preserve both the camera folder and filenames, choose Original File Name (Preserve Folders).
- **Prompt for a tag on import:** If you opted to name folders and files based on tags, you'll definitely want to select (check) this option so you can tag pictures before they're imported.
- **Always erase from camera after import:** If selected, pictures and videos will be erased from the camera automatically after importing. If you clear this option, you either have to choose the Erase pictures during the import option or manually erase the pictures from the camera after the import.
- **Rotate pictures on import:** Some digital cameras can sense when you're holding the camera vertically and mark each such picture accordingly. Choosing this option causes those pictures to be rotated to the correct upright position automatically when imported.
- **Open Windows Photo Gallery after Import:** When selected ensures that Windows Photo Gallery opens automatically as soon as you've finished importing pictures.
- **Restore Defaults:** Sets options back to the original factory settings.

Click OK after making your selections. Your choices on the Import tab will be applied only to pictures you import in the future. They have no effect on pictures you've already imported. Of course, you can rename, rotate, tag, and move pictures at any time, regardless of settings in the Options dialog box.

Making movies from Photo Gallery

The Make A Movie button in Photo Gallery is really just a shortcut to Windows Movie Maker. The idea is to get all the pictures and videos you want to put in a movie into the gallery, perhaps by giving all those items a tag, then clicking the tag name in Photo Gallery's Navigation pane. Then you select all those items and click Make Movie. Movie Maker opens with all the selected items in its Storyboard/Timeline. If you don't care about editing, special effects, titles and credits, custom background music, and such, you can just create your movie from there. Click AutoMovie in Movie Maker, choose a style, and click Create AutoMovie.

If you *really* want to create cool movies, you really need to invest a little time and effort in learning what Movie Maker is about and how it works. Chapter 25 tells that story.

Printing Pictures

You can print pictures on a standard inkjet or laser printer that prints on 8.5-x-11-inch paper. If you have a photo printer, you can use that as well. However, you'll need to refer to the instructions that came with that printer for specifics on connecting the printer. You might even need to install or download a special driver from the printer manufacturer. If in doubt, refer to the manual that came with the photo printer, or the manufacturer's Web site.

Most modern inkjet and laser printers let you print on either plain paper or photographic paper. Photographic paper is considerably more expensive. So you might want to stick with plain paper for drafts and informal prints. Use photographic paper for more formal prints of your best photos.

Printing from Windows Photo Gallery

If the pictures you want to print are in Windows Photo Gallery, you can print from there. Use the Navigation pane to display the pictures you want to print. Then select (check) the picture (or pictures) you want to print. If you want to print all the pictures showing in the gallery, you can click the group heading to select all the icons. Or click any one picture in the gallery and press Ctrl+A. If you only want to print some pictures, select their icons. You can do so by pointing to any image and clicking its checkbox. Or you can use the universal techniques for selecting icons discussed in Chapter 29.

After you've selected the pictures you want to print, click the Print toolbar button and choose Print. The Print Pictures window shown in Figure 22.25 opens.

FIGURE 22.25

Print Pictures window.

 Don't worry about sideways pictures in the Print Pictures window. You don't need to rotate them. The printed pictures will look fine even if they're sideways in the Print Pictures window.

Now you get to make a whole bunch of choices as to how you want to print your picture (or pictures). The choices available to you depend on what kind of printer you're using. If you have multiple printers attached to your computer, the first step is to click the Choose a printer button (see Figure 22.26) and click the printer you want to use.

FIGURE 22.26

Choose a printer.

If your printer supports multiple paper sizes, click the Paper size button and choose the size paper you want to print to. Depending on your printer, you might also be able to click the Print quality button and choose between 330dpi (dots per inch), 600dpi, and other settings. The higher the dpi, the better the quality of the print, and the longer it takes to print.

If your selected printer supports multiple paper types, click Choose a paper type (see Figure 22.27) and choose the paper you're using.

FIGURE 22.27

Choose a paper type.

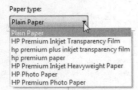

If you're printing multiple pictures on large paper, choose a layout from the right column. Use the scroll bar at the right side of the window to view all your options. Typically, you can choose any size from 8.5 x 11 down to tiny wallet-sized prints. After you scroll, be sure to click on the layout you want to use. The preview area shows you how things will look on each printed page. You can use the Next Page and Previous Page buttons under the page preview (see Figure 22.28) to navigate through the pages you'll be printing.

 **If you change your mind about the pictures you selected to print, click Cancel to return to Photo Gallery.**

To print more than one copy of each picture, specify how many you want to print next to Copies of each picture. Choose Fill each frame to ensure that any small pictures are expanded to fill the page on which they're printed.

FIGURE 22.28

FIGURE 22.28

Preview printed pages.

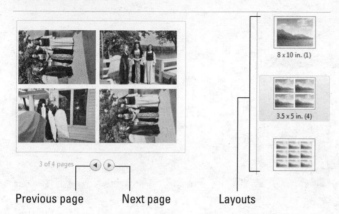

3 of 4 pages

Previous page   Next page   Layouts

Optionally, click the Open properties for selected printer icon (see Figure 22.29) to look at any remaining options that are unique to your printer. Exactly what appears there varies greatly from one printer to the next. But you might be able to refine or go beyond your current selections. For example, you might be able to choose a high-quality print with plain paper.

FIGURE 22.29

Preview printed pages.

With all the choices made, just click Print and wait. Don't expect the printer to start right away. It takes some time for the computer to get everything together before sending it to the printer. Be patient. When your pictures are finished printing, click Finish in the window that appears.

Printing pictures from a folder

If you have pictures that don't show in Windows Photo Gallery, you can print them straight from the folder in which they're stored. Open the folder that contains the pictures. Then select the icons of the pictures you want to print. Be careful you don't select any icons for non-picture files, or this technique won't work.

Once you've selected the picture icons, click the Print button in the toolbar, shown near the mouse pointer in Figure 22.30. If the Printer button isn't visible, first click >> at the end of the toolbar to see if it's just off the edge. If you still don't see a Print option, chances are one or more of your selected icons isn't a picture. When you do see the Print button, click it. You'll be taken to the Print Pictures window. Choose your settings, as described in the previous section, then click Print.

FIGURE 22.30

Print button near the mouse pointer.

Using the Slide Show Gadget

 You can use the Slide Show gadget to keep a slide show of all your favorite pictures playing.

The Slide Show gadget is a fun way to keep a slide show of all your favorite pictures playing in the sidebar. By default, it will display all pictures in your Pictures folder, although you can change that to have it show any folder you like.

If you want precise control over the pictures in the slide show, create a subfolder in your Pictures folder. Name it Slide Show Gadget or something like that. Then copy into that folder all of the pictures you want the slide show to show.

NOTE   For details on activating the Sidebar and Gadgets, see "Using Windows Sidebar" in Chapter 11.

To add the Slide Show gadget, first make sure the Sidebar is open on your desktop. Then click the Add Gadget (+) button at the bottom of the bar. In the Add Gadgets window that opens, find the Slide Show gadget and drag it to the Sidebar. It will show pictures from your Pictures folder in a slide show.

When you point to the Slide Show gadget, you'll see the tools pointed out in Figure 22.31. In addition to the tools shown, you can right-click the gadget to detach it from the sidebar, remove it, or get to its settings.

FIGURE 22.31

Slide Show gadget.

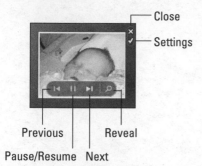

Close

Settings

Previous

Reveal

Pause/Resume   Next

To customize the gadget, click the Settings button, or right-click and choose Settings. The Settings box opens as in Figure 22.32. To have the gadget show pictures from a particular folder, click the ... button to the right of the Directory option. Then navigate to the folder that contains the pictures and click OK. The other two options let you determine the duration of the fade effect between pictures, and how long each picture shows.

FIGURE 22.32

Slide Show gadget settings.

Pixels and Megapixels

Every picture you see on your screen is actually a bunch of little lighted dots on the screen called pixels. You don't see the individual pixels because they're too small. But if you take a small original picture and zoom way in, each pixel reveals itself as a small colored square. Figure 22.33 shows an example. The small inset picture is the original. The larger picture is an extreme zoom in on the face. There you can see how the picture is actually lots of pixels — little colored squares.

FIGURE 22.33

Zoomed-in to see pixels.

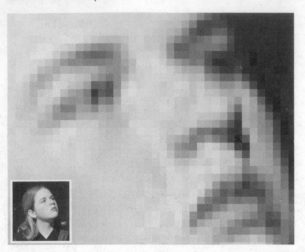

When shopping for digital cameras, *megapixels* is a key pricing factor. A megapixel isn't one humongous pixel. It's a million regular-sized pixels. The basic rule of thumb is, the more pixels, the better the quality of the pictures. The term "quality" in this context really means how big you can make it (or print it) without the picture looking *pixelated*. A pixilated picture looks, at best, blotchy. At worst, it looks like a bunch of pixels rather than a coherent picture.

Table 22.1 provides some general guidelines on how the number of megapixels translates to print quality. You can always print any picture at any size, of course. But you start to lose quality if you go above the recommended maximum size shown in the second column. All numbers are approximate, of course, because many other factors come into play in determining overall print quality.

TABLE 22.1

Megapixels and Print Size

Megapixels	Recommended maximum print size
1–2	3×5
2–3	5×7
3–4	8×10
4–5	11×14
>5	18×24

File extension, size, and dimensions

Every picture has a type, indicated by its filename extension. It also has a size measured in kilobytes (KB) or megabytes (MB). And it has dimensions. You see that information when you point to a picture's thumbnail in a folder (see Figure 22.34). The Details view in a folder can show the Dimension, Size, and Type of every picture in the folder. Right-click any column heading and choose the name of the column you want to see.

FIGURE 22.34

Pointing to a picture in a folder.

In Windows Photo Gallery, the file extension, size, and dimensions of a photo show when you point to a thumbnail or use the Tiles view.

A picture's dimensions are its width and height measured in pixels. As a rule, the bigger the dimensions the better, because it means you can print the picture at a very large size with no loss of quality. You can also zoom in quite far, and crop out quite a bit and still end up with a picture that has significant detail.

Recall that the term megapixels refers to the number of pixels in a picture, where one megapixel equals a million pixels. A 5-megapixel camera will create pictures with dimensions of around 2,576 × 1,932. Multiplying those two numbers gives you the total number of pixels in the picture, 4,976,832. That's just abut 5 million pixels, hence the 5-megapixel rating.

The file size is the amount of disk space required to store the picture. Bigger is better in terms of picture quality because a large file size indicates that there's lots of information in the file. Which means you can print it at large sizes and zoom in on any portion of the picture without losing much clarity.

The filename extension is the picture's file type. There are many types of picture files. Table 22-2 lists some examples. Some file types are so old or so rare you may never see one. The most commonly used picture types are TIFF, JPEG, PNG, BMP, and GIF, described next.

TABLE 22-2

Examples of File Formats for Pictures

Filename Extension	Format
.art	AOL Art file
.bmp	Windows Bitmap
.cdr	CorelDraw Drawing

continued

TABLE 22.2   *(continued)*

Filename Extension	Format
.cgm	Computer Graphics Metafile
.clp	Windows Clipboard
.cmx	Corel Clipart
.cut	Dr. Halo
.dcx	Zsoft Multipage Paintbrush
.dib	Windows Device Independent Bitmap
.drw	Micrografx Draw
.dxf	Autodesk Drawing Interchange
.emf	Windows Enhanced Metafile
.eps, .ai, .ps	Encapsulated PostScript
.fpx	FlashPix
.gem	Ventura/GEM Drawing
.gif	CompuServe Graphics Interchange
.hgl	HP Graphics Language
.iff	Amiga
.img	GEM Paint
.jpg, .jif, .jpeg	Joint Photographic Experts Group
.kdc	Kodak Digital Camera
.lbm	Deluxe Paint
.mac	MacPaint
.msp	Microsoft Paint
.pbm	Portable Bitmap
.pcd	Kodak Photo CD
.pct	Macintosh PICT
.pcx	Zsoft Paintbrush
.pgm	Portable Greymap
.pic	Lotus PIC
.pic	PC Paint
.png	Portable Network Graphics
.ppm	Portable Pixelmap
.psd	Photoshop
.psp	Paint Shop Pro
.ras	Sun RasterImage
.raw	Raw File Format

Filename Extension	Format
`.rle`	Windows or CompuServe RLE
`.sct, .ct`	SciTex Continuous Tone
`.tga`	Truevision Targa
`.tif, .tiff`	Tagged Image File Format
`.wdp`	Windows Digital Photo
`.wmf`	Windows Meta File
`.wpg`	WordPerfect Bitmap or Vector

TIFF pictures

TIFF (Tagging Information File Format) is the preferred method of storing high-quality photos for printing. In fact, TIFF is widely used by the publishing industry for that very reason. TIFF files tend to be large, because they contain much detailed information and generally use little or no compression to reduce file size.

JPEG pictures

JPEG (Joint Photographic Experts Group) is the most widely used photo format for photos displayed in Web pages. JPEG uses compression to reduce file size while maintaining large dimensions. The compression results in some small loss of picture quality. That loss usually isn't noticeable until you zoom in very tightly on some small area within the picture.

The amount of compression applied to a JPEG can vary. In fact many high-end graphics programs allow you to choose exactly how much compression you want when saving a picture as a JPEG. Many digital cameras save pictures as JPEGs with minimal compression to conserve picture quality while at the same time conserving storage space on memory cards.

GIF pictures

The GIF (Graphics Interchange Format) is commonly used in Web pages for illustrations and animations. It's limited to 256 colors, which makes it unsuitable for photos. Photos need millions of colors and tend to look blotchy when saved in GIF format. GIF also allows for transparency and simple animations.

PNG pictures

PNG (Portable Network Graphics) format is a compressed format that's gaining popularity as a format for Web pictures. Like JPEG, it supports millions of colors, and is therefore suitable for photos. Like GIF, it allows for transparency, and is therefore useful for creating images with a transparent background.

BMP pictures

BMP (Windows Bitmap) is an older uncompressed format that conserves picture quality at the cost of a large file size. Though once widely used in Windows, BMP is quickly becoming obsolete in favor of the more widely used TIFF and JPEG formats.

Changing a picture type or size

There are times when you'll need to change a picture's type, perhaps so you can edit it in Photo Gallery or publish it on a Web site. There may also be times when you want to reduce the file size and/or dimensions of a picture to send it by e-mail or, again, to post it on a Web site.

If you use Windows Mail to e-mail photos, you'll automatically be given the option to reduce the dimensions of large pictures. (See "Using E-mail Attachments" in Chapter 18.) Note that only the copies of images sent through e-mail will be reduced in size. Your original photo on your computer's hard disk remains unchanged.

If you don't use Windows Mail, you can manually create a smaller image for e-mailing, without losing your original picture. This also works if you want to post a picture on a Web site. Just about any graphics program on the market will allow you to resize a picture and save it in a different format. If you don't have a graphics program, you can use the Paint program that comes with Windows Vista.

1. Right-click the icon or thumbnail of the picture you want to reduce and choose Open With ⇨ Paint. Don't be alarmed if you see only a small portion of a large picture. Paint doesn't automatically scale the picture to fit in the program window.

2. Choose File ⇨ Save As and type a new name for this copy of the picture. For example, use the existing filename followed by TIFF if you're just changing the file type, or the word Small if you're also reducing the picture's dimensions.

3. If the picture isn't already a TIFF, JPEG, or PNG, click the current file type next to Save as type and choose JPEG or PNG.

4. Click Save.

NOTE   TIFF is best for pictures you intend to print, but don't intend to e-mail or post on a Web site. JPEG and PNG are best for pictures you do intend to e-mail or post on a Web site.for editing and printing purposes.

5. If your goal is simply to change the picture's type (like from BMP to another format), skip to step 10. Otherwise continue with the following steps.

6. To reduce the pictures size, choose Image ⇨ Resize/Skew from Paint's menu bar.

7. Under Resize, enter a percent value for both Horizontal and Vertical. Make sure to use equal numbers so as not to skew or stretch the pictures. For example, to resize a 2576 x 1932 picture down to near 644 x 483, enter 25% for both Horizontal and Vertical.

8. To see the picture as it will appear on a Web page or to an e-mail recipient, choose View ⇨ Zoom ⇨ Custom ⇨ 100%. (If Paint's program window is small, double-click its title bar to maximize it to full screen.)

9. If the picture it too large or too small, choose Edit ⇨ Undo and repeat steps 6–7 until you find a size you like.

10. Close Paint (click its Close button or choose File ⇨ Exit from its menu bar). If asked about saving your changes, choose Yes.

If you started from Photo Gallery, the new copy of the picture may not show up right away. You might have to close Photo Gallery and re-open it. Also, the new picture may not contain the tags that the original picture had. So you might find it in the Not Tagged category in Photo Gallery.

Pictures, Tags, and Virtual Folders

NEW FEATURE Photos Gallery's tagging capabilities are just the tip of the proverbial iceberg in Vista. Tagging applies to many file types, and is a key component in Vista's search capabilities.

You can use the Search box in Photo Gallery to find pictures that contain some tag or tags. But that's about it. Outside of Photo Gallery you can do much more with tags. And you can find and organize pictures in ways that transcend tags.

For starters, you can click the Search button or tap 🎴, type in a tag name, and see icons for all pictures that contain that tag. Then, on the Start menu, just click any picture to open it. Or right-click the picture's icon and choose Open File Location to, or right-click it and choose Open With, Preview, Send To, or whatever it is you want to do with that item. That's pretty cool. But the Start menu doesn't give you a whole lot of elbow room.

If you prefer, you can open your Pictures folder and use the Search box in its upper-right corner to search for a tag. That will limit the search to pictures in your Pictures folder and its subfolders. If you need to search more broadly than that, click the Start button and launch your search from the Search window.

When you search from the Search window, you can opt to search for all files or just pictures. If you click Advanced Search, you can search by date taken, file size, filename, tags, title, or any combination thereof (see Figure 22.35).

FIGURE 22.35

Advanced Search options.

If you want to find pictures that contain two tags, separate the tags with a space. For example, a search for

```
Ashley Alec
```

searches for pictures that contain both Ashley and Alec. Use OR to broaden the search to find pictures that contain either Ashley or Alec as here:

```
Ashley OR Alec
```

If you need to specify your search condition more stringently, use the Search box in the upper-right corner of the Search window. For example, here's a search that finds only TIF files that contain either Ashley or Alec:

```
type:tif AND tag:(ashley OR alec)
```

Here's a search that finds all JPEG images that have Hawaii as a tag:

```
type:jpeg AND tag:Hawaii
```

You can still use DOS and Windows wildcard characters to search for filenames. For example, you could type

```
haw*
```

into the Filename box and click Search, or type

```
filename:haw*
```

into the Search box to find all pictures whose filenames start with haw.

You can save the results of any search as a virtual folder. When you open that folder, it shows all pictures that currently meet the search condition. For people who have a lot of pictures to deal with, these kinds of searches can be an extremely valuable tool. For more information on searching and virtual folders, see Chapters 30 and 31.

Wrap Up

You can do lots of things with pictures and photos in Windows Vista. You don't get the kind of power and flexibility you would with a dedicated graphics program like Adobe PhotoShop or Corel Paint Shop Pro. But nonetheless, you can perform the most basic operations like cropping, red-eye removal, and some file type conversions with just the built-in Vista tools and programs.

- To get pictures from a digital camera, connect the camera to the computer, turn it on, and choose Import.
- To get pictures from a CD or memory card, insert the card or disk and choose Import. Or open the disk or card and copy files using standard methods.
- To copy-and-paste a picture, right-click the picture and choose Copy. Then right-click at the destination and choose Paste.
- Your Pictures folder is the best place to store pictures.
- Windows Photo Gallery lets you organize and find photos as though they were all stored in a single folder.
- Use the Fix button in Photo Gallery to crop and improve pictures.
- Use the Print button in your Pictures folder or Photo Gallery to print pictures.
- Large photos are good for printing and editing. Smaller, compressed photos are best for e-mail and Web publishing.

Chapter 23

Making Music with Media Player 11

U sing your computer to collect, manage, and play music is a lot of fun. You can build up a collection of all your favorite songs, make custom CDs from those songs, or copy them to a portable MP3 player. You can use your computer as a stereo to play any songs you like in any order you like. If your computer is part of a network, you can share songs and play them on any computer that's in the network.

Windows Vista comes with two programs for collecting and playing music. One is Windows Media Player, which we'll discuss in this chapter. The other is Media Center. If you prefer to use Media Center (or don't have Windows Media Player), see Chapter 26.

Controlling Sound Volume

Before we get into Windows Media Player, you need to know a few things up front about music and video. In particular, you want to get your sound working and under control, so you can listen to whatever you like, without blasting your eardrums out!

Before you get started, make sure that you can control the volume of your speakers. At any given time, you're likely to have at least three volume controls available to you. Whichever control is set the lowest wins, in the sense that it puts an upper limit on the other volume controls.

If you have powered speakers, you need to make sure that the speakers are plugged in and turned on and connected to the Speaker output jack on your computer. If the speakers have a Mute button, make sure that it's turned off. If the speakers have a volume control button, that needs to be turned up.

You can control the volume of sound coming from your computer's speakers using the Volume Control icon in the Notification area. It looks like a little speaker with sound waves coming out. Pointing to that icon shows the name of your sound card and current volume setting as in the left side of Figure 23.1. Clicking that icon displays a volume control slider and a Mute button, as in the right side of Figure 23.1.

FIGURE 23.1

Volume control icon (left) and slider (right).

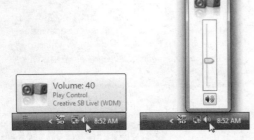

To adjust the volume, just drag the slider handle up or down the bar. To mute the sound, click the Mute button at the bottom of the slider. When the sound is muted, the icon shows a little red X and no sound comes from your computer. To get the sound back, click the Mute button a second time.

> **TIP**   In case you're wondering, Volume: 40 in the left side of Figure 23.1 means I have my speakers set to 40 percent of the maximum volume. If you don't see a speaker icon in your Notification area, chances are it's just hidden. To bring it out of hiding:
>
> 1. Right-click the Start button and choose **Properties**.
> 2. In the dialog box that opens, click the **Notification Area** tab.
> 3. Under System Icons, select (check) the **Volume** checkbox.
> 4. Click **OK**.
>
> Now you should have a speaker icon in your Notification area. Click it to see the volume control slider and Mute button. To ensure that you can hear any music you play, make sure the sound isn't muted and that the volume isn't turned down too low to hear.

With your speakers and volume control slider under control, you're ready to start using Media Player for Music.

> **TIP**   If you have multiple sound cards and can't get any sound, make sure the default sound card is the one that's connected to the speakers. Click the Start button, type sou, and click Audio Devices and Sound theme. Right-click the icon of the sound card you're using and choose Set As Default For ➪ All Uses. If both sound cards have speakers attached, you can configure each to act as the default for different types of audio using that same Set As Default For... option.

Starting Windows Media Player

To start Windows Media Player, use whichever method is easiest for you:

- Click the Start button and choose All Programs ➪ Windows Media Player.
- Click the Windows Media Player button in the Quick Launch toolbar.
- Press ⊞, type med, and choose Windows Media Player.
- Open any music file for which Windows Media Player is the default program.

The first time you open Windows Media Player, it will take you through a series of steps asking for your preferences. Don't worry if you don't know how to answer some questions. You can change your answer at any time. So if you see a window titled "Welcome to Windows Media Player 11!" and don't know what to do, just click "Accept default Windows Media Player configuration." You can change settings at any time, so you're not making any big commitment by accepting the suggested defaults.

Media Player program window

Like most programs, Windows Media Player opens in its own program window and has a taskbar button. The player can have many different appearances. Exactly how it looks at any time is up to you. We'll look at different ways to display things in a moment. For now, we need to cover the names of things so you know what I'm talking about in the sections to follow.

Figure 23.2 points out the major components of Media Player's program window. Items marked "optional" can be turned on or off at any time, so don't be alarmed if you don't see one of those items right away. You'll see how to turn those on and off as you progress through the chapter.

FIGURE 23.2

Major Media Player components.

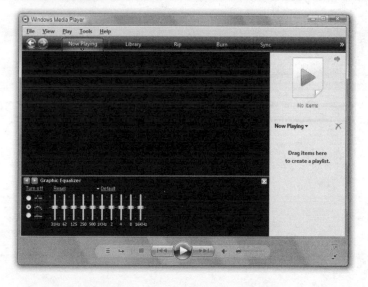

The features taskbar across the top of the program window represents different areas of Media Player, each of which helps you perform a specific task. In Figure 23.2, the Now Playing tab is selected. Here's a quick summary of what each tab in the features taskbar offers:

- **Now Playing:** Shows the movie or video you're currently watching, or a visualization of dancing colors when you're playing music.
- **Library:** Takes you to your collection of songs and other media files.
- **Rip:** Click this tab when you want to copy songs from a music CD to your Media Player library.
- **Burn:** This tab lets you create custom CDs from songs in your media library.
- **Sync:** Use this tab to copy songs and other media files to a portable media player.
- **Urge:** Some other name might appear here on your screen. It all depends on who you choose as your default online service for purchasing music online.

Media Player menus

Media Player has lots of menus. They're hidden from view most of the time. But they're also easy to get to. Each tab in the features taskbar also has its own menu. To see such a menu, first point to a tab in the features taskbar. You'll see a little down-pointing triangle at the bottom of the tab. Get the tip of the mouse pointer right on that little triangle and click the left mouse button to see the menu for that taskbar button. The bottom of Figure 23.3 shows an example in which I'm viewing the hidden menu on the Now Playing tab.

To see the main menu, right-click an empty area near the play controls, as at the bottom of Figure 23.3. Optionally, you can right-click an empty spot on the left or right side of the features taskbar to get to the same menu. To make those same options visible in a menu bar, choose Show Classic Menus from the bottom of that main menu.

FIGURE 23.3

Sample Media Player menus.

Play controls

The play controls (also called the *playback controls*) are at the bottom of Media Player's program window (see Figure 23.4). They work only when you're playing a song or video or have selected something to play. They work much like the controls on a VCR, stereo, or DVD player. The exact role of each button varies slightly with the type of content you're viewing. Here's what each of the play controls offers:

FIGURE 23.4

Media Player play controls.

- **Seek bar:** When content is playing, a green indicator moves along the seek bar. You can click anywhere along the seek bar to jump forward or backward in the playing item. When you point to the end of the green indicator, a button appears. You can drag that button left or right to move back or forward within the item that's playing.

- **Shuffle:** When selected, multiple songs from the current playlist are played in random order. When turned off, songs from the playlist are played in the same order as in the playlist.

- **Repeat:** When turned on, the same song or playlist plays repeatedly. When turned off, the song or playlist plays only once.

- **Stop:** Stops whatever is playing and rewinds to the beginning.

- **Previous:** Skips back to the previous song in the playlist or DVD chapter. Or, if you point to the button and hold down the left mouse button, plays the current item backwards in fast motion.

- **Play/Pause:** When content is playing, you can click this button to pause playback. Click again to resume playback.

- **Next:** Skips to the next song in the playlist or next chapter on a DVD. Point to this button and hold down the left mouse button to fast forward through the content that's playing.

- **Mute:** Click to mute playback sound. Click a second time to hear the sound again.

- **Volume:** Drag the handle left or right to increase or decrease the volume.

- **Full Screen:** Switches to full-screen mode. Useful when you want to see a video or DVD played at full-screen size. Once in the full-screen mode, right-click anywhere on the screen and choose Exit Full Screen to return to the program window.

- **Skin:** Use this button to switch to a different skin.

We'll talk about skins and other items in the features taskbar later in this chapter. For now, let's stick with some of the basics of using Media Player's program window.

Closing/minimizing Windows Media Player

You can close Windows Media Player as you would any other program:

- Click the Close (X) button in the upper-right corner of Media Player's program window.
- Or, choose File ⇨ Exit from Media Player's menu.
- Or, right-click Media Player's taskbar button and choose Close.
- Or, if Media Player is in the active window, press Alt+F4.

When you close Media Player, it stops playing whatever it was playing.

If you want to continue to listen to music, but want Media Player off the screen, minimize Media Player's program window. Use any of the following techniques to minimize Media Player's program window:

- Click the Minimize button in Media Player's title bar.
- Right-click Media Player's title bar and choose Minimize.
- Right-click Media Player's taskbar button and choose Minimize.

Depending on how you have your desktop toolbars configured, you'll either see a traditional taskbar button for Media Player or you'll see the mini-mode player. The latter consists of the play controls. You can control playback using controls on the mini-mode player. When you point to the mini-mode player, you see info about the song that's currently playing as in Figure 23.5.

FIGURE 23.5

Mini-mode player.

When the mini-mode player is visible, you can click the tiny Restore button in its lower-right corner (shown near the tip of the mouse pointer in Figure 23.5) to return the player to its normal size.

If you want to use the mini-mode player, you have to turn on its taskbar toolbar. Likewise, if you don't want to use it, you have to turn off that toolbar. To check, and optionally change, that setting, right-click the clock (or an empty portion of the taskbar) and choose Toolbars.

On the Toolbars submenu that appears, one of the options will be Windows Media Player. If that option is selected (checked), that means the mini-mode is enabled. If that option isn't checked, mini-mode isn't enabled. Clicking the option switches from on to off or off to on. Clicking outside the menu closes the menu without changing the current setting.

That should be enough to get you started using Media Player. Next we'll look at various ways in which you can use Media Player to listen to music or watch videos.

Listening to a CD

A *music CD* (also called an *audio CD*) is the kind of CD you normally play in a stereo or CD player. Typically you buy these at a music store. As you'll learn later in this chapter, you can also create your own custom music CDs.

To listen to a music CD, just put it in your CD drive, label side up, and close the drive door. Then wait a few seconds. Windows Media Player might open and start playing the CD automatically. However, other things could happen:

■ **A dialog box asks what you want to do:** If you see a dialog box like the example in Figure 23.6, click the Play audio CD using Windows Media Player, then click OK.

FIGURE 23.6

Dialog box asking about a music CD.

TIP To choose how your computer reacts when you insert a music CD, see Chapter 44.

■ **A program other than Media Player opens and plays the CD:** If a program other than Windows Media Player opens to play the CD, close that program. Then, do as indicated under the next item.

■ **Nothing happens:** If absolutely nothing happens after you insert an audio CD, or if some other program opened and you closed it, start Windows Media Player. From Windows Media Player's menu, choose Play ➪ DVD, VCD, or CD Audio.

■ **Windows Media Player opens:** If Windows Media Player opens and starts playing the song, you don't have to do anything else. Just continue reading on.

After the CD starts playing, you should be able to hear it (assuming your speakers are properly connected and not turned down too far). Use the Volume slider in the play controls to adjust the volume of the music.

Now Playing, Visualizations, and Enhancements

When music is playing, click the Now Playing tab to watch a *visualization* of the music. The visualization is a pattern of colors and shapes that change in rhythm to the music. You have many visualizations from which to choose.

To try a different visualization, first make sure that you're on the Now Playing tab. Then do whichever is easiest or most convenient for you:

■ Click the arrow under the Now Playing tab button and choose Visualizations.

■ Or, from Media Player's menu, choose View ⇨ Visualizations.

■ Or, right-click on the visualization (or album art) that's currently visible and choose Visualizations as in Figure 23.7.

FIGURE 23.7

Choosing a visualization.

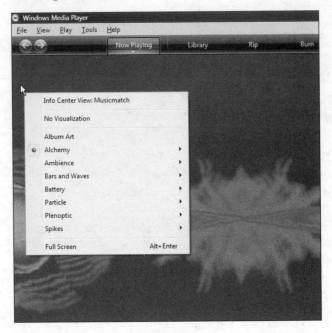

Regardless of which method you use, you'll see a menu of visualization names. Clicking a name will display a submenu of still more visualizations. Just pick any one to see how it looks. Go ahead and try a bunch while a song is playing to find one you like.

> **TIP** The Alchemy Random and Battery Chemicalnova visualizations are both worth checking out. Don't be alarmed if your menu lacks some of the visualizations shown in Figure 23.7. There are plenty of visualizations you can download for free. Click the arrow under Now Playing and choose Visualizations ⇨ Download ⇨ Visualizations.

Using the playlist

When you're playing a music CD, the playlist pane to the right of the visualization (see Figure 23.8) shows songs from the CD. That pane is optional. To show or hide that pane, click the arrow under Now Playing and choose Show List Pane.

FIGURE 23.8

Playlist pane on right side of window.

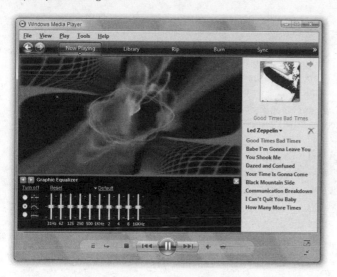

In the playlist pane, you might see the song titles, as in Figure 23.8. Or you might just see more generic names like Track1, Track2, and so forth. Most CDs don't have song titles stored on CD. So the song titles have to be downloaded from the Internet. So you'll only see song titles if you're online and the CD you're playing has song titles stored on the Internet.

 Song titles are a form of media information. We'll discuss how all of that works under "Options for ripping CDs" later in this chapter.

If you want to listen to a specific song on the CD, just double-click its title in the playlist pane. Or use the Previous and Next buttons in the play controls to highlight the song you want to listen to.

To change the width of the playlist pane, get the tip of the mouse pointer right on the left border of the pane, so the mouse pointer turns to a two-headed arrow. Then drag left or right.

Using Enhancements

While you're listening to music and are in the Now Playing area, you can also use Enhancements to adjust the sound and perform other tasks. Back in Figure 23.8, the Enhancements pane is shown under the visualization. In that example I'm showing the graphic equalizer.

To show or hide the Enhancements pane, choose View ➪ Now Playing Layout ➪ Show Enhancements from Media Player's menu. When the Enhancements pane is open, you can choose which type of enhancement you want to see. To cycle through the available options, click the Previous or Next button in the upper-left corner of the pane. To choose a specific enhancement, right-click an empty area in the Enhancements pane and click the enhancement you want to view. Your options are summarized here:

- **Color Chooser:** Change the color of the playlist pane.
- **Crossfading and Auto Volume Leveling:** When Crossfading is turned on, one song gradually fades out while the next song fades in. Auto Volume Leveling keeps songs at roughly equal volumes.

- **Graphic Equalizer:** Adjust the relative strengths of low, middle, and high tones. Optionally, click Default and choose a music type such as Rock or Classical. Click Reset to return to the default settings.

- **Media Link for E-Mail:** Allows you to e-mail a portion of online media to a friend. This does not work with songs stored on your local PC, nor does it send an actual file to the recipient. It simply sends a link to the online content.

- **Play Speed Settings:** Use this to adjust the play speed of content. This option only works when playing `.wma`, `.wmv`, `.wm`, `.mpe`, and `.asf` files. Careful with this one. You don't want all your albums sounding like The Chipmunks!

- **Quiet Mode:** Adjusts the audio dynamic range of music (the difference between the loudest and softest sounds). You'd most likely use this option when listening to headphones or watching a movie in Media Player.

- **SRS WOW Effects:** When activated, SRS WOW effects add depth to your music. This one is definitely worth turning on and trying out if you have good speakers attached to your system.

- **Video Settings:** Adjust the brightness, contrast, hue, saturation, and size of video when viewing a movie or video in Media Player.

 Like most panes, you can change the height of the Enhancements pane by dragging its upper border up or down.

Stopping a CD

When you've finished listening to a CD, click the Stop button in the play controls. To eject the CD, choose Play ⇨ Eject from Media Player's menu, press Ctrl+J, or push the Eject button on your CD drive.

Play CDs automatically with Media Player

If you want to ensure that Media Player opens and plays music CDs automatically, you need to make Media Player the default player for CDs. Here's how:

1. Click the Start button and choose Control Panel.

2. Click Hardware and Sound.

3. Click AutoPlay.

4. Next to Audio CD, choose Play audio CD using Windows Media Player.

5. If you also want Media Player to play DVDs automatically, choose Play DVD Video using Windows Media Player.

6. Click the Save button.

7. Close Control Panel.

From that point on, whenever you put a music CD in your CD drive, Windows Media Player should open and play the CD automatically.

 Here's a shortcut to the AutoPlay options: Click the Start button or tap ⊞. Type `auto` and choose AutoPlay from the Start menu.

534

Ripping (Copying) Music CDs

Media Player isn't just about playing CDs. The real idea is to build up a library of digital media on your hard drive, from which you can create custom playlists and music CDs. If you already own some music CDs, ripping a few CDs will be a great way to start creating your personal media library. Though the term "rip" might sound like something bad, it's not. It simply means to "copy," and no harm will come to the CD when you rip songs from it to your media library.

When you rip a CD, you store a copy of each song from the CD on your hard drive. That song is in a format that's more suitable for computers than the song that's on the CD. You can put the original CD back in its case, and leave it there so it doesn't get scratched up. Play the songs straight from your PC, or make your own CDs to play the songs in a stereo. Keep the original CD as a backup in case you accidentally delete some songs you've copied.

Ripping CDs is easy, as you'll see. But there are a few decisions you need to make up front, like where you want to put the songs, how you want them titled, what format you want them stored in, and so forth. We'll look at all of your options in the sections to follow.

Options for ripping CDs

To choose options for how you want to copy CDs to your hard disk, use the Rip Music tab in Media Player's Options dialog box. To get to those options:

1. Open Windows Media Player (if it isn't already open).
2. Click the arrow under Rip and choose More Options.

You're taken to the Rip Music tab in Media Player's Options dialog box, shown in Figure 23.9.

FIGURE 23.9

Rip Music tab in Media Player's Options dialog box.

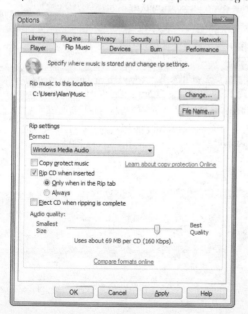

The sections that follow describe what each option offers. Note that you don't need to make selections from the dialog box for every CD you copy. Rather, you choose your options once. All CDs that you copy from that point forward will use whatever settings you chose.

Choosing where to put songs

By default, all songs you copy from CD will be placed in your Music folder. That's a perfectly fine place to put them. But there's no rule that says you have to put them there. You can store them in any folder you want. For example, you might put them in the Public Music folder if you want everyone who uses the PC to access the songs. Or, if you have multiple hard disks, you can put them in a folder on some drive other than C:.

> **NOTE** If you're not so sure what all this talk of disks and folders is about, don't worry about it. Just leave the "Rip music to this location" setting alone. Your songs will end up in your personal Music folder. Note that whatever folder you choose is referred to as the *rip music folder* in Media Player options.

To choose a drive and folder for storing CDs, click the Change. . . button in the dialog box. Then navigate to the drive and folder in which you want to store the songs. For example, if you want to put the songs in your Public Music folder, expand the Computer, Local Disk (C:), Users, and Public folders, and click Public Music. Then click OK.

The path in the dialog box shows where the songs will be stored. For example, in Figure 23.9, C:\Users\Alan\Music tells me that the songs will be stored in the personal Music folder for the user account named Alan. (C: is the hard disk and Users is the name of the folder in which all user accounts are stored.)

Choosing how to name files

Each song you copy from a CD is stored as a file. Like all files, each song will have a filename. Windows Media Player names the files automatically, based on the track number, song title, and other media information.

You're free to choose how you want song files named. How you name the songs is entirely up to you, and won't affect how they play. I like to have each song's filename start with the song title. You may want to have each file start with the track number from the CD. To make your selections, click the File Name . . . button on the Rip Music tab of the dialog box. The File Name Options dialog box shown in Figure 23.10 opens.

Choose the elements you want to use in each song's filename. At the very least you should choose Song Title and Artist, because those are certainly useful pieces of information. Use the Separator drop-down list to choose which character will separate each portion of the name.

To change the order of items in the filename, click any selected item and use the Move Up or Move Down button to change its position in the filename. As you choose components and change their order, the generic filename under Preview gives you a sense of how each song title will look with your current settings.

Click OK after deciding how you want your filenames to look. The options you choose here are referred to as *rip music settings* in some Media Player options, which you'll learn about later in this chapter.

FIGURE 23.10

The File Name Options dialog box.

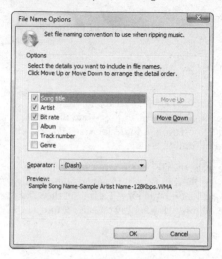

Choosing a file format and quality

Under Rip Settings on the Rip Music tab, the Format drop-down list lets you choose a format and quality in which to store songs you copy. Basically this all boils down to a trade-off between file size and music quality. File size has to do with how much hard disk space each song consumes. Quality has to do with the depth, clarity, and richness of the music when you listen to it. We measure music quality in kilobits per second, abbreviated Kbps. The higher the Kbps number, the better the music quality, but the more disk space each song consumes.

Options for choosing are under the Rip Settings heading in the Options dialog box. First, use the Format: drop-down list to choose one of the following formats:

- **Windows Media Audio:** Songs are copied to Windows Media Audio (.wma) format files and compressed to conserve disk space. You can choose the amount of compression using the Audio Quality slider in the same dialog box. This is a good general-purpose format that plays on all Windows computers and many portable media devices.

- **Windows Media Audio Pro.** Similar to the preceding format, but includes features that make the music sound better on high-end multi-channel sound systems.

- **Windows Media Audio (Variable Bit Rate):** Same as the preceding format, but the amount of compression varies with the complexity of the information being stored. As a rule, you get better quality with smaller file sizes using a variable bit rate. But this format is not compatible with all portable music players.

- **Windows Media Audio Lossless:** Same as the preceding format, but files are not compressed at all. The sound quality is excellent, but the files are huge. Still, if you're a true audiophile, or are interested in creating HighMAT CDs (High-Performance Media Access Technology), this is an excellent choice.

- **MP3:** MP3 is the most widely used format for digital music. It's been around the longest. Unlike the .wma formats, you're not limited to playing the songs on Windows-based computers. You can play MP3 songs on any MP3-compatible player.
- **WAV (Lossless):** Stores each song as a Wave file. These offer high quality, but create enormous files. So you probably want to stay away from this format unless you have some good reason to use it.

If you're new to all of this, and at a complete loss as to what to choose, go with WMA or MP3. Those are common formats that almost any device can play.

If you choose anything but a lossless format, you can then use the Audio Quality slider to choose what quality setting you want. Again, the basic rule of better quality creating larger files applies. Hard disk space is cheap and plentiful, so there's no need to settle for the lowest-quality setting. If in doubt, don't go below 128 Kbps or your music may all end up sounding shallow or kind of "tinny."

As you move the Audio Quality slider to different settings, text beneath the slider tells you roughly how much disk space an entire CD will consume at that setting. To better illustrate how format and audio quality relate to disk space consumption, I ripped a 3-minute song at various sound qualities. Then I put their sizes in Table 23.1. The last column, "Songs per GB," gives you a sense of how many songs you can get into a single gigabyte of hard disk space at various quality settings.

TABLE 23.1

A Three-Minute Song at Formats and Bit Rates

Format/Quality	Bit Rate	Size	Songs per GB
Windows Media Audio	192 Kbps	4.17 MB	246
Windows Media Audio Pro	192 Kbps	4.18 MB	245
WMA Variable Bit Rate	103 Kbps	2.22 MB	461
Window Media Audio Lossless	480 Kbps	14.20 MB	72
MP3	192 Kbps	4.12 MB	249
WAV (Lossless)	320 Kbps	30.30 MB	34

TIP See "Understanding Disks and Drives" in Chapter 28 for more information on disk drives, capacities, and discovering how much space you have. You might want to take a peek at your available space each time you copy a CD, so you can get a sense of how much free space each copied CD consumes.

After you've chosen a format and audio quality, there are a few more options on the Rip Music tab to choose from.

Copy protecting music

The Copy Protect Music option on the Rip Music tab lets you decide whether or not you want to put copyright protection on the songs you copy. I think a lot of people choose that option thinking it will somehow protect them from messing up the songs. But that's not how it works. The protection that the option offers is for the copyright holder, not for you.

If you choose the Copy Protect option, the songs you copy will play only on the computer at which you're sitting. You'll also put other restrictions on the songs. For example, you won't be able to import them into Movie Maker or other programs that normally let you edit music. If you want to keep things simple and make sure you can use your copied songs freely, I suggest you leave the Copy Protect Music checkbox empty.

Rip CD when inserted

If selected, this option tells Windows Media Player to copy all the songs from a CD as soon as you insert the audio CD. Choosing this option, along with the Eject CD option, described next, makes it easy to rip a whole collection of CDs in assembly-line fashion. For example, if you have a few dozen CDs you want to rip, you can just insert a CD, wait for it to be copied and ejected, and then insert the next CD.

If you choose to rip CDs automatically, you can limit that action to when you're actually in the Rip tab of Media Player, or always. If you're not copying CDs in an assembly-line fashion, it probably makes sense to choose the first option, "Only when in the Rip tab," because there will likely be many times when you insert a music CD with no intension of ripping that CD.

When you've finished ripping your CD collection, you can then clear this option so that you have more flexibility in deciding what you want to do with each CD you insert into your hard drive.

Eject CD when ripping is completed

If selected, this option just tells Media Player to eject the CD from the drive when it's finished copying the CD. As mentioned, choosing this option along with the *Rip CD when inserted* option is a great way to copy multiple CDs in a quick, assembly-line manner.

Still more rip options

Media Player's Options dialog box contains some additional options that affect what happens when you rip CDs. While you still have the Options dialog box open, click the Privacy tab. Then choose your options as summarized next. But remember, not all CDs have media information posted on the Internet. Therefore, even if you do select options as indicated, you may need to manually update media information for a song or album.

- **Display media information from the Internet:** Choose (check) this option to have media information, such as song titles, appear automatically when you play or copy a CD.
- **Update music files by retrieving media information from the Internet:** Choose this option to have Media Player automatically fill in information from songs you've already copied to your computer.

When you've finished making all of your selections, click OK in the Options dialog box. Now you're ready to start ripping CDs. Remember, you need not change the preceding settings every time you copy a CD. The settings you choose apply to all CDs that you copy.

Copying songs

With all the details of choosing how you want to copy CDs out of the way, you're ready to start copying. Here are the steps:

1. If your Internet account requires logging in, get online so that you're connected to the Internet and Media Player can download media information (song titles).
2. Insert the music CD you want to rip (copy) into your CD drive and close the drive door.

3. If Windows Media Player doesn't open automatically, open it yourself. (If some other program opened when you inserted the CD, close that program, then open Media Player.)

4. If you chose the "Copy CD when inserted" option described earlier in this chapter, skip down to step 10 now.

5. If the CD starts playing, click the Stop button down in the play controls.

6. Click the Rip taskbar button and wait for song titles to appear. If song titles don't appear within 30 seconds or so, the CD might not be in the CDDB. In that case, you can go ahead and rip the CD, and then fill in the details later in your media library.

 CDDB stands for Compact Disk Database. It's an online database that contains song titles for most (but not all) commercially sold CDs.

7. Optionally, clear the checkmark to the left of any songs that you don't want to copy. Media Player will only copy songs that have a checkmark.

8. Click the Start Rip button down near the lower-right corner of the program window.

9. Wait until the Rip Status column shows *Ripped to Library* for all songs you've opted to copy, as in Figure 23.11. If the CD doesn't eject automatically, go ahead and eject it.

FIGURE 23.11

All songs have been ripped to Media Player's media library.

10. Put the CD back to wherever you normally keep your CDs. You won't need it any more to play songs from your computer, or to copy files to custom audio CDs or an MP3 player.

That's it for ripping one CD. To rip more CDs, just repeat steps 4 to 11 for each CD. If at any time you want to check your available hard disk space, open your Computer folder. If you don't see any indication of available disk space for your hard disk (typically Local Disk C:), choose Tiles from the Views menu in that folder.

Copying songs from CDs you already own is one way to build up your Media Player music library. Any songs you don't already own, but would like to, you can purchase online and download to your Media Player library. We'll discuss how that works in the next section.

Getting Music Online

In addition to ripping CDs you already own, you can download music from online stores. The exact procedure varies from one online store to the next. Some are membership sites. Some let you purchase and download songs without joining or paying a membership fee. New stores and services come online all the time. So there's little that I can tell you specifically that applies to all of the available vendors, other than you should shop around and not necessarily sign up with the first vendor to pop up on your screen. As I write this chapter, MTV's URGE is getting top billing in the features taskbar. Click the arrow under that button and choose Browse Online Stores to see other options.

Using the Media Player Library

The whole point of a program like Windows Media Player is to build and manage a library of digital media. That includes music, pictures, video, and recorded TV (even though we're focusing on music in this chapter).

To see and manage your Media Player library, click the Library tab in the Media Player's features taskbar. There are many ways to view things in the Library. The Select a Category, View Options, and Layout Options buttons, pointed out in Figure 23.12, let you decide how you want to view things.

Navigating the library

There is no limit to the ways in which you can view, organize, and change things on the Library tab in Media Player's features taskbar. Use the navigational tools shown in Figure 23.12 to explore your library from different angles.

FIGURE 23.12

Tools for navigating your library.

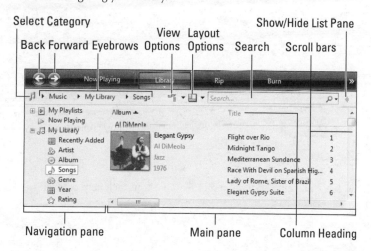

If your Media Player library doesn't show songs, but instead shows pictures or other kinds of media, click the Select a Category button and then click Music from the menu that drops down.

You'll find it easiest to get around if the Navigation pane on the left side of the program window is open. If you don't see that on your own screen, click the Layout Options button and choose Show Navigation Pane.

In the Navigation pane, you can click the + sign (if any) next to My Library to see the different ways you can view items in your media library. Then click any category name below My Library to see items organized as follows:

- **Recently Added:** Shows icons for items you've recently added to your library.
- **Artist:** Shows artist names in alphabetical order.
- **Album:** Shows album titles in alphabetical order.
- **Songs:** Shows song titles categorized by artist name.
- **Genre:** Shows names of music genres (like Classical, Rock, Jazz).
- **Year:** Shows albums organized by publication year.
- **Ratings:** Shows songs organized by rating (one to five stars). If you don't rate your songs, this view won't show Unrated (for songs you haven't rated yet) and three stars (which is an average rating applied to songs that you haven't rated yourself).

You'll be better able to appreciate the library if you have at least 30 or 40 songs in your library before reading this section. Or better yet, several hundred songs. As you explore your library, keep in mind that you can right-click any icon, stack, category name, or whatever to view, edit, or play items.

Use the View Options button to choose how you want to view things. Depending on where you are at the moment, some View options will be disabled (dimmed) because they're not applicable to the current way of looking at things. But in general, you can choose from the following views:

- **Icon:** Each item is represented by a single icon or stack of icons, as in the example shown in Figure 23.13.

FIGURE 23.13

Sample Icon view.

- **Tile:** Similar to the icon view, but with some additional information about each item or stack to the right. Figure 23.14 shows an example.

FIGURE 23.14

Sample Tile view.

- **Expanded tile:** Shows the album cover and a list of songs on each album. Available in the Recently Added and Songs categories only. Figure 23.15 shows an example.

FIGURE 23.15

Sample Expanded Tile view.

- **Details:** Shows detailed textual information about each item in a tabular format. Figure 23.16 shows an example.

FIGURE 23.16

Sample Details view.

Of course, there's no right way or wrong way to view icons. Just choose whichever view works best at the moment. Feel free to try things out. You can't do any harm by checking out different ways to view things. And nothing you choose is set in stone. You can change your view at any time.

How you use a view depends on what you're viewing. For example, if you're viewing Genres, you'll see an icon or stack for each genre in your library. Double-clicking an icon or stack shows you all the songs in that genre. Double-clicking an icon that represents a single album displays songs on that album. To play all the items that an icon represents, right-click the icon and choose Play. Again, doing some exploring on your own is your best bet. You're not permanently changing anything as you explore, so there's no need to be worried.

Choosing columns for Media Library

In addition to choosing how you want media information to look, you can choose exactly which information you do and don't want to see. The exact options available to you depend on what you're viewing and how you're viewing it at the moment. To see the full set of options, click Songs in the Navigation pane, then choose Details from the View Options button. You'll see detailed information about each song organized into rows and columns.

To choose which columns you want to view, right-click a column heading, like Title or Length, and click Choose Columns on the menu. The Choose Columns dialog box shown in Figure 23.17 opens.

FIGURE 23.17

The Choose Columns dialog box.

In the Choose Columns dialog box, select (check) the columns you want to see. Clear (uncheck) columns you don't want to see. You can also control the order of columns, either in the dialog box, or after you exit the dialog box. To control the order of columns while you're in the dialog box, click any selected column name, and then click the Move Up or Move Down button to move it up or down. The higher a column name is in the dialog box, the farther to the left it is in the Details view.

After you've chosen the columns you want to view, click OK. Most likely you won't be able to see all the columns at the same time. But you can use the horizontal scroll bar under the columns to scroll left and right through columns.

Sizing columns

To adjust the width of any column, get the mouse pointer to the right side of the column heading. You'll know the mouse pointer is in the right place when it turns to a two-headed arrow, like the example shown in Figure 23.18. When you see the two-headed arrow, hold down the left mouse button and drag left or right to adjust the column width. Release the mouse button when the column is the width you want.

What's with the Songs Category?

Intuitively, it seems as though clicking Songs in the Navigation pane should list song titles in alphabetical order without regard to artist or album. But for reasons I have yet to figure out, it doesn't work that way in Media Player 11.

To see song titles in alphabetical order, click Songs in the Navigation pane, then choose Details from the View Options button. Click the Title column heading to put songs in alphabetical order. You can also drag the Title column to the left to make it the first column.

FIGURE 23.18

Drag column head dividers to change widths.

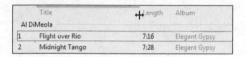

Moving columns

To move a column left or right, first put the mouse pointer right on the column heading, for example, the word Title, Length, Album, or Album Artist. Then hold down the left mouse button and drag the column left or right. Release the mouse pointer when the column is where you want it to be.

Sorting songs

When you're in a Details view you can also sort items by any column. For example, you can sort them by Title, Length, Album, Album Artist, or any other column heading. The first time you click, items will be sorted into ascending order (alphabetically, or smallest to largest). The second time you click, items will be sorted into descending order (reverse alphabetical, or largest to smallest).

 The techniques for sizing, moving, and sorting by columns apply to most columnar views of data in most programs. This feature is not unique to Media Player.

Getting missing media information automatically

Recall that media information refers to things like song titles, artist name, and so forth. That information might be missing from some of your songs for a couple of reasons. One reason might be that the information isn't available from the Internet. In that case, you may have to fill in the missing information manually, using techniques described later in this chapter.

A second reason why you might be missing media information is that you weren't online when you copied some CDs. If that's the case, it's not too late to retrieve that information. It's quicker and easier to retrieve the information automatically. So before you start manually changing media information, use the technique described in this section to see how much of that information you can get automatically.

First you need to check your options for updating media information automatically. Click the button under Library and choose More Options. You're taken to the Library tab in Media Player's Options dialog box, shown in Figure 23.19.

FIGURE 23.19

The Library tab in the Options dialog box.

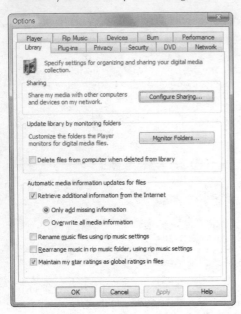

Under the "Automatic media information updates for files" heading, choose (check) Retrieve additional information from the Internet.

- If you've already added some media information manually and don't want the new information to replace that, choose Only add missing information.

- Otherwise, choose Overwrite media information if you want information you've added yourself to be replaced with information from the Internet.

When you've finished making your selection, click OK in the dialog box. Then click the button under Library and choose Apply Media Information Changes.

There's no guarantee that all missing information will be filled in. You may have songs for which there is no online media information. You'll still have to edit those manually. To change the title of a single song, right-click the current title (Track1, Track2, or whatever), choose Edit, and then type the correct song title.

Information other than the title is likely to be the same for all the songs on a given album. It's not necessary to change that information one song at a time. You can select multiple songs to which you want to make a change. The change you make is then applied to all the selected songs. We'll get to that in a moment. First let's look at how you can add songs that you have elsewhere on your computer to your Media Player library.

Choosing what files to include in your library

If you set up multiple user accounts on your computer, each user gets to have his or her own media library. Parents don't have to dig through the kids' songs and vice versa. But you're not stuck with only those songs.

Each user also has the option to share songs, and each user has the option to choose or reject songs shared by others. To choose which songs display in your own media library:

1. Choose the arrow under Library in the features taskbar and choose More Options.

2. Click the Monitor Folders button. The Add To Library dialog box opens.

   ■ If you only want songs from your Music folder in your library, choose the first option, My personal files.

   ■ If you want both your own songs and shared songs from other users in your library, choose the second option, My folders and those of others that I can access.

3. To add songs from additional drives and folders to your library, click Advanced Options to see the full set of options shown in Figure 23.20.

FIGURE 23.20

The Add To Library dialog box.

 **Even though we're focusing on music here, Media Player can also display pictures, videos, and recorded TV. You can add folders for those types of files while you're in the Add To Library dialog box.**

4. To add a new folder to the list of monitored folders, so the songs show up in your library, click the Add button. Then browse to the drive and folder that you want to include and click OK. You can repeat this step to monitor as many folders as you wish.

5. To prevent songs from a folder from being added to your library, click the folder you want to exclude and then click the Remove button.

6. If new folders you added contain songs you previously deleted from your library and you want those songs back in your library, choose Add files previously deleted from library.

7. If you want to add volume-leveling to any newly selected folders, choose Add volume-leveling values for all files (slow). This will make the search take longer.

8. To prevent small sound effects files from being added to your music library, consider cranking the Skip files smaller than option for Audio Files up to 100 KB or so. Likewise, you can crank the Video Files option up to about 500 KB to prevent small video clips from being added to your library.

 The 100 KB and 500 KB settings are approximate. You may have to experiment with those to gain precise control over what does and doesn't get added to your library.

9. Click OK after making your selections to have Media Player search any newly added folders.

10. When the search is complete, click Close and then click OK in the Options dialog box.

Media Player will update your library according to the selections you made in the Add A Folder dialog box.

Sharing your media library

 Now you can share all your songs with other users on the same computer or with other Vista computers on your network.

Each user can opt to share all songs, or some songs with other user accounts on the same computer. Likewise, if your computer is part of a private network, each user can choose to share songs with other Windows Vista computers or Vista-compatible devices (like the Xbox 360).

Click the Configure Sharing button shown in Figure 23.20. To share your music, select the "Share my music to:" checkbox. Use the Settings button to share only certain types of media, only files with certain ratings, and so forth. Use icons and the Allow and Deny buttons to choose with whom you want to share your library. For example, to share songs with other users on the same computer, click that icon and then click Allow. Click OK after making your selections.

See Part X for more information on private networks and sharing.

Automatically renaming songs

Earlier in this chapter you learned how you could control filenames of songs you rip (copy) from CDs. Those filenames don't have a big impact on how information shows up in your library. The media information from each song actually comes from Properties in the file rather than the filename. Nonetheless, it never hurts to have some consistency in your filenames.

For example, suppose you ripped a bunch of CDs before you realized you could control how the filenames of those songs are formatted. You change the rip settings to something you like better. That change won't affect songs you've already ripped. It will only affect songs that you rip after changing the setting. You can, however, get Media Player to rename previously named songs according to your new settings. Here's how:

1. Click the arrow under Library and choose More Options.

2. Choose Rename music files using rip music settings.

3. Optionally, if you also want to have the songs rearranged in your rip music folder (typically the Music folder in your user account), choose Rearrange music in rip music folder using rip music settings.

4. Click OK after making your selections.

5. To apply changes, click the arrow under Library and choose Apply media information changes from Media Player's menu.

It may take a while to update and rearrange all the songs in your rip music folder. When the change is complete, click the Close button that appears in the progress indicator. You may not notice any changes in Media Player's library. But you likely will notice changes when you open your rip music folder outside of Media Player.

Most of the options and settings discussed so far have to do with groups of songs and things the Media Player does on its own. No matter what settings you choose, there may be times when you need to manually edit (or remove) items in your library.

In some cases, you may need to change a single song title. For example, suppose you have songs named Track1, Track2, Track3, and so forth. You've already tried updating that information through techniques described earlier, but the song titles still don't appear because the song titles aren't available online. When that happens, you'll need to manually change the media information.

When changing a song title, you'll want to work with one song at a time. In other cases, such as when changing a genre or artist name, you may want to make the same change to several songs at once. To make the same change to multiple songs in your library, you first have to select the songs you want to change. So before we talk about manually editing songs, let's look at techniques for selecting the songs you want to change.

Selecting in Media Library

Your media library isn't set in stone. You can change the information you see at any time. Typically you just right-click the thing you want to change and choose Edit to change it or Delete to remove it. I'll get to the specifics in a moment. But first let's talk about *selecting* items in the library. Selecting two or more items allows you to make the same change to all those selected items in one fell swoop.

Selecting items in Media Library is much like selecting icons in folders. So if you already know how to do that you're ahead of the game. You can select items in any view. But you might find it easiest to work in the Details view. For example, click Songs in the Navigation pane at the left side of the window. Then choose Details from the View Options button. And finally click whatever column heading arranges the songs in a way that groups them in whatever way is easiest for you to work with at the moment.

One way to select all the items in a group is to click the heading that precedes the group. For example, in Figure 23.21, I clicked the artist name Dick Dale and his Dell Tones to select all the songs under that category. The selected songs are highlighted. Any change you make to one of the selected songs is applied to all the selected songs.

Another way to select multiple adjacent songs is to click the first one you want to select. Then hold down the Shift key and click the last one you want to select. The two songs you clicked and all the songs in between are selected.

To select multiple songs that aren't adjacent to one another, click the first one that you want to select. Then hold down the Ctrl key while clicking other songs you want to select. That same technique lets you unselect one selected song without unselecting any other songs.

You can also use the keyboard to select songs, as follows:

- To select every song in the library, click Songs in the Navigation pane, click a song title, then press Ctrl+A.
- To select all the songs from the current song to the bottom of the list, click the first song you want to select and then press Shift+End.
- To select all the songs to the top of the list, click the first song and then press Shift+Home.

FIGURE 23.21

Selected songs under Dick Dale heading.

To deselect songs, click a neutral area in the program window, such as the empty space to the left of the play controls.

Selecting songs doesn't have any effect on them, other than to highlight them. However, any action you take while the songs are selected is applied to all of the selected songs. Next we'll look at things you can do with any one song or any number of selected songs.

Changing a song title

Every song on a CD is likely to have its own unique title. So you generally have to change titles one at a time. To change just one song title, first make sure you don't have multiple songs selected. (Click the song you want to change so that only that song it selected.) Then right-click the title you want to change and choose Edit. Type the new title and press Enter.

Changing genre, artist, and such

You can change the genre, artist, album title, or any other media information for a song by right-clicking and choosing Edit. But because all the songs on a CD may have that same artist, or belong to the same genre, you might want to make the change to several songs. So first select all the songs to which you want to apply the change. Then click the word or name you want to change in any one of the selected songs and choose Edit. Type in the new name or word and press Enter. The change will occur in all the selected songs.

Changing incorrect media information

Sometimes Media Player will get media information from the Internet, but it's the wrong information. This is especially true when working with multiple CD sets. Rather than manually typing all the information for the CD, you can take a shot at finding the correct information online. To do so, click Album in the Navigation pane. Then scroll to the album that has the incorrect icon, right-click its icon, and choose Update Album Info. Then double-click the album's icon to see whether the situation has improved at all.

If updating the album info didn't help, you can try right-clicking the album title just above its song titles and choosing Find Album Info. Most likely you'll get the same faulty information you got the first time. But you can click the Search button in the lower-left corner of the Album Info window that opens and try searching by the artist's name or album title. You may get lucky and find the exact album you're looking for. The Album Info window acts like a wizard, so you can just follow the instructions on the screen and use the buttons along the bottom of the window to aid in your search.

If you do find the exact album you're looking for, click the Finish button in the Album Info window and Media Player will copy the media information to the album in your media library. If you don't have any such luck, you can still manually enter the correct information for each song on the album using the techniques described in the previous sections.

Rating songs

You've probably noticed the star ratings that Media Player adds to each song. By default, the ratings are all the same (three stars) because the idea is for you to rate each song according to your own likes and dislikes. Give five stars to your favorite songs, one star to songs you don't like, and something in between for all the rest.

To change the rating of a single song, right-click the title of the song you want to rate, choose Rate, then enter the number of stars you want to give it. To rate multiple songs, first decide what rating you want to apply (like five stars). Then select all the songs to which you want to apply that rating. (You can use the Ctrl+Click method to select multiple non-adjacent songs.) After you've selected all the songs to which you want to apply a rating, right-click any selected song, choose Rate, and choose your Rating.

Any time you want to view all the songs to which you've applied a rating, click Rating at the bottom of the Navigation pane. The contents pane in the center of the program window will show rating categories; one category for ratings you've applied and another for songs you haven't rated yet but were given ratings automatically, like the example in Figure 23.22.

To play all the songs to which you've given a certain rating, right-click the rating icon and choose Play. To see all the songs to which you've applied a given rating, double-click the rating icon.

FIGURE 23.22

Icons representing ratings.

Using the Advanced Tag Editor

For the true audiophile who wants to keep track of detailed information about every song, there's the Advanced Tag Editor. To use it, right-click the title of the song you want to change and choose Advanced Tag Editor. There are so many tags you can fill or change, they're divided into tabs, as you can see in Figure 23.23.

FIGURE 23.23

The Advanced Tag Editor.

NOTE If you select multiple songs before opening the Advanced Tag Editor, the fields will be protected against accidental change. You'll need to click the checkbox to the left of a field before you can change the contents of that field. But be careful—anything you change will be applied to all the selected songs!

I think the fields on the tabs in the Advanced Tag Editor are self-explanatory, so I won't belabor the issue by describing them all in detail. Just click each tab to see what your options are for storing detailed information about each song.

Adding lyrics

The Lyrics tab lets you fill in the lyrics for the currently selected song. You have to click the tab first, and then click the Add button on that tab. Then type or paste in the song lyrics.

It shouldn't be difficult to find the song lyrics online. Go to www.lyrics.com and search for the lyrics by artist name. Or, if that doesn't pan out, go to any search engine, like www.google.com, and search for the song title followed by the word *lyrics*. For example, a search for Macarena lyrics would probably get you to a page that contains the song lyrics for the song titled *Macarena* (after a few false leads that take you to ads trying to sell you something you don't need or want).

To see the lyrics as you're playing the song, double-click the song title in the Library to get the song playing. After you add the lyrics, click OK to close the Advanced Tab Editor. Then double-click the song title to get it playing and click Now Playing in Media Player's features taskbar. Choose Play ➪ Lyrics, Captions, Subtitles ➪ Style1 (or some other style if available). The lyrics show below the visualization pane as the music is playing. The lyrics won't move with the music. But you can use the scroll bar to the right of the lyrics to scroll through them.

If you have lots of spare time and patience, you can even make the lyrics scroll with the music. You need to get back to the Lyrics tab in the Advanced Tag Editor for the song. Then click Synchronized Lyrics. A new dialog box opens with the lyrics and a timeline. Click a line of lyrics and then click Play to see how well the lyric start time jibes with the actual time in the song. If the lyric starts too late or too early, click Edit, adjust the start time, and test that line again. It may take some trial and error to get it just right. Then click OK.

As an alternative to struggling with the Advanced Tag Editor's approach to lyrics, check out some of the optional plug-ins you can download and install from www.wmplugins.com. When you get to the page, search for *lyrics* to focus on plug-ins related to lyrics and Karaoke.

Finding missing album art

If an album you copy has no cover art, you get a generic picture like the example at the right in Figure 23.24. As the generic icon implies, you can paste any picture you like onto the generic icon. Of course, you'll need to find a picture and copy it to the Clipboard before you can paste a picture onto the icon.

You can go looking for the album cover art in a few ways:

- Right-click the generic icon and choose Find Album Art. If necessary, use the Search button to try to find a suitable picture for the album cover.
- Go to www.lyrics.com, search for the album's artist, and see whether you can find an appropriate picture to use as the album cover.
- Go to http://images.google.com and search for the album title. Maybe you'll be able to find a suitable picture that way.

FIGURE 23.24

Generic icon for an album.

When you find a picture you like, right-click it and choose Copy. Then right-click the generic icon in Media Player and choose Paste Album Art. The picture you copied replaces the generic icon.

Making Custom Playlists

A playlist is a group of songs. In Media Player's library, every icon, stack, and Navigation pane category is a playlist in its own right, which you can play by right-clicking and choosing Play. So every time you open Windows Media Player and click the Library button in the features taskbar, you have many playlists from which to choose.

A custom playlist is one you create yourself. A custom playlist can contain any songs you like, in any order you like. For example, you can create a Party playlist of songs to play during a party. You can create a Favorites playlist of just your favorite songs. You can also create custom playlists of songs you want to copy to your own custom CDs, DVDs, or portable music player.

To get started on creating a custom playlist, follow these steps:

1. If you haven't already done so, open Windows Media Player.
2. Click the Library button in the features taskbar.
3. If you don't see the Playlist pane at the right side of the program window, do any of the following to make it visible:
   - Click the button under Now Playing and choose Show List Pane.
   - Click the Layout Options button and choose Show List Pane.
   - Click the Show List Pane arrow to the right of the Search box.
   - Choose Tools ➪ Now Playing Layout ➪ Show List Pane from Media Player's menu.

To create your own custom playlist, you'll need to start with an empty one, like the example at the right side of Figure 23.25. If your list pane isn't empty, click the Clear List Pane icon pointed out in that figure.

FIGURE 23.25

Empty List pane.

To create your custom playlist, drag any song titles you want from the contents pane to the left of the playlist into the playlist. As an alternative to dragging one song title at a time, you can select multiple songs and drag them all at once. As an alternative to dragging, you can right-click any song title and choose Add to Untitled Playlist. Or select multiple songs, right-click any selected song, and choose Add to Untitled Playlist.

NOTE If you skipped the earlier section, "Using the Media Player Library," you'll need to go back and learn some basic library navigation skills before you can find songs to add to your playlist.

To add all the songs from an album to the playlist, right-click the album's icon and choose Add to Untitled Playlist. Likewise, you can right-click any icon or stack that represents a category of songs—like a genre, artist name, or rating—and choose Add to Untitled Playlist. All the songs within that category are added to the playlist.

Don't worry about adding too much stuff to the playlist. There's no limit to how large a playlist can be. And you can also remove any song from the playlist at any time.

Managing songs in a playlist

After you have some songs in a playlist, you can arrange them as you see fit. Use any of the following techniques to do so:

- Drag any song title up or down to change its position in the list.
- Right-click any song title and choose Move Up or Move Down.
- Click the playlist name (or Untitled Playlist), choose Sort, and then choose whichever option best describes how you want them sorted (see Figure 23.26).
- To put the songs in random order, choose Shuffle Now from the menu shown in Figure 23.26.

FIGURE 23.26

Sorting songs in a playlist.

 To widen or narrow the List pane, drag its inner border left or right.

To remove a song from the playlist, right-click the song title and choose Remove From List. Optionally you can select multiple songs using the Ctrl+Click or Shift+Click method. Then press Delete (Del) or right-click any selected item and choose Remove from this List.

Saving a playlist

To save a playlist, click the Save Playlist button near the bottom of the list pane. Type a name of your own choosing to the list and press Enter or click outside the name you just typed. The name you enter replaces Untitled Playlist as the playlist's name. If you make a mistake, click the new name, choose Rename Playlist, and change the name or enter a new name.

By default, the playlist will be saved in the My Playlists folder of your Music folder. If you prefer to save the playlist in another location, click the playlist name and choose Save Playlist As. Then navigate to the folder in which you want to save the playlist.

Viewing, playing, and changing playlists

To play all the songs in a playlist, or change a playlist, first click the Library tab button. If the Navigation pane isn't open, use the Layout Options button to open it. Finally, click My Playlists at the top of the Navigation pane. You'll see all of your saved playlists (and some Auto Playlists you didn't create yourself) in the contents pane. Recent playlists will be listed first, followed by all playlists, as in Figure 23.27. In that example I chose Tile from the View Options to show the playlists.

FIGURE 23.27

Playlists.

To use a playlist, right-click its icon or name and choose an option, depending on what you want to do:

- **Open:** Shows the contents of the playlist in the contents pane.
- **Play:** Plays all the songs in the playlist.
- **Add To. . . :** Adds the songs from the playlist to whatever playlist is currently in the List pane.
- **Edit in List Pane:** Shows the contents of the playlist in the List pane so you can change its contents.
- **Rename:** Lets you change the name of the playlist.
- **Delete:** Deletes the playlist.
- **Open File Location:** Opens the folder in which the playlist is stored.

Using and creating Auto Playlists

An Auto Playlist is one that gets its content automatically. Media Player comes with several built-in Auto Playlists based on ratings and when you last listened to a song. You can also create your own Auto Playlists based on any criteria you like. To create an Auto Playlist, right-click My Playlists at the top of the Navigation pane and choose New Auto Playlist. Or click the arrow under the Library tab button and the New Auto Playlist dialog box opens as shown in Figure 23.28.

FIGURE 23.28

New Auto Playlist dialog box.

To specify a criterion for the Auto Playlist, click the + sign under Music in My Library. Then specify criteria by clicking options that appear next to the funnel. For example, if you wanted to create an Auto Playlist for songs in which Carlos Santana is a contributing artist, you'd specify the criterion:

`Contributing Artist Contains Santana`

You could create an Auto Playlist, perhaps named "Today's Tunes" by specifying this criterion:

`Date added To Library Is After Yesterday`

Suppose you have many different types of files in your library and you want to be able to quickly view just the MP3 files. You could create an Auto Playlist named MP3s (or whatever) and give it this criterion:

`File Type Is MP3`

You can specify multiple criteria if you like. Multiple criteria are always treated as "and" logic, which means each new criterion will narrow, rather than expand, the Auto Playlist's contents. For example, if you specify the following two criteria under Music in My Library:

`File Type Is MP3`

`Bit rate (in Kbps) Is At Least 256`

the Auto Playlist will contain only MP3 songs with a quality of 256 Kbps or better. It will be empty if no songs meet those criteria.

To include pictures, video, or TV shows in the Auto Playlist, choose an option under the And Also Include heading. Or, to place additional restrictions on the content, choose options under "And apply the following restrictions to the auto playlist."

When you've finished specifying criteria for your Auto Playlist, click OK. The Auto Playlist will be listed in the contents pane along with all others. To play the Auto Playlist, and see its current contents, double-click its name or icon. To change the criteria that define the Auto Playlist's contents, right-click its icon and choose Edit. Or, if the Auto Playlist is already open, click the Edit button below the playlist contents.

Creating Your Own Music CDs

Creating your own custom music CDs is a lot of fun. It's also a great way to protect any new CDs you purchase from getting scratched and ruined. When you buy a new CD, rip it to your Media Library, then put it back in its case for safe-keeping. Burn a copy of the CD (or just your favorite songs from the CD along with some other favorite songs), and use the copy in your home or car stereo. You can also copy songs you purchased online to CDs.

If you buy blank CDs in spindles of 50 or more, you can get them pretty cheap. You won't get the little plastic jewel case. But you can buy paper sleeves instead. Or keep all the CDs in a CD binder.

Types of music CDs

Before I get into the specifics of burning CDs, it's important to understand that there are two different types of music CDs you can create:

- **Audio CD:** This type of CD will play in any home stereo, car stereo, or portable CD player, as well as on computers. You must burn songs to a CD-R disk (preferably an Audio CD-R) to create this type of CD because most non-computer players can't play CD-RW disks or DVD disks.

- **Data CD:** This type of music CD will play in computers, or in any stereo that's capable of playing this type of CD. You can use CD-R or CD-RW disks. However, you must choose a disk type that is compatible with both your computer's CD/ DVD burner and the device on which you want to play the disk.

> **TIP** CDs and DVDs are examples of *optical media*, so named because they use a laser rather than magnetism to read and write data. All the different types of disks (CD-R, CD-RW, DVD-R, DVD+R, DVD-RW, DVD+RW, and so forth) make things woefully confusing. Chapter 32 untangles the mysteries of the different types of optical media.

If you don't know what type of disks your stereo can play, refer to the instructions that came with that device. Optionally, create an RW (Read/Write) disk and try it out. There's no loss if the disk doesn't play, because you can always erase the disk and use it for something else. Once burned, R (Recordable) disks cannot be erased or changed.

Choosing music disk options

The first step to creating a music CD is to specify which type of disk you want to create, and perhaps some other options. In Media Player, click the arrow under the Burn button to see the menu shown in Figure 23.29. Choose options as summarized in the following list.

FIGURE 23.29

Burn options.

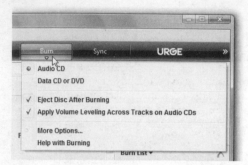

- **Audio CD:** Choose this option to create the type of CD that all stereos and players can play. For best results use an 80-minute Audio CD-R disk.

- **Data CD:** Choose this option if you want to create a music CD or DVD that plays only on computers and devices that are capable of playing non-traditional music CDs.

- **Eject CD after burning:** Choose this option to have the CD be ejected automatically when it's ready for use. This is especially useful when burning multiple CDs from a single Burn list.

- **Apply volume leveling. . .:** Choose this option to ensure that the volume of each song is the same when listening to the finished CD.

- **More options:** Choose this option to choose additional options described below this list.

- **Help:** Choose this option for help with burning music CDs.

Choosing More options takes you to the Burn tab of Media Player's Options dialog box, shown in Figure 23.30. Most of the options duplicate options on the menu. The ones that are unique are summarized in the following list.

FIGURE 23.30

Burn tab of the Options dialog box.

- **Burn Speed:** The default setting is Fastest. But if you have problems burning disks, or the sound quality isn't up to par on the disks you burn, consider reducing this to a slower speed.

 **NOTE** Items that follow this point in the list apply only to Data Discs. They have no effect on Audio Discs.

- **Add a list of burned files. . .:** Choose WPL if your player can read Windows playlists. Choose M3U if your player can only read MP3-style playlists.

- **Use media information to arrange files. . .:** If selected, items on the CD will be organized into folders. If you are unsure about whether or not your player can handle folders, clear the checkbox for this option.

- **Do not convert:** Choose this option to maintain the music quality you chose when ripping CDs, or the original quality of songs you purchased online.

- **Convert to. . .:** Choose this option to squeeze more songs onto a Data Disk than your current quality setting will allow. Then move the slider to the quality you desire. At the smallest size (32 Kbps) you can get about 47 hours of music on one CD, but the music won't sound too good. At the other extreme, 192 Kbps, you can get about 7 hours of music on one CD, but the music will sound great.

NOTE The average for music CDs is 128 Kbps, which provides for about 11 hours worth of music per CD. The Convert To option has no effect when burning an Audio CD, and the limit is always a little under 80 minutes on an 80-minute Audio CD-R.

Click OK in the Options dialog box to save any settings you changed. With your options selected and squared away, you're ready to choose which songs you want to copy to your custom CD.

Choosing songs to put on the CD

The skills needed to choose songs to put on a CD are the same as those for creating a custom playlist. You can drag songs individually, or you can drag an entire album or other category. But you have to make sure you're dragging to the Burn list, not just any playlist. So let's go through the basic process:

- If the Navigation pane (shown in Figure 23.31) isn't visible, choose Show Navigation Pane from the Layout Options button or the button under Now Playing.

- Click a playlist name under My Playlists or a category name under My Library. If you want to see all of your songs, click Songs under My Playlists. Use the View Options to choose how you want items in the contents pane to look.

- Click the Burn button in the features taskbar to make sure you're viewing the Burn list.

- If your Burn list contains songs from a previously burned CD, and you want to create a new one, click the Clear List Pane button (red X) in the Burn list, or click Burn List and choose Clear List.

- Click the button under Burn and choose Audio CD if you're burning a music CD for stereos. Otherwise you can choose Data CD or DVD if you're creating a music disk for computers and appropriate players.

- Use a felt-tip pen or disk labeler to write the name of your custom CD on a blank CD. Then put that CD in your CD drive.

At this point, your Media Player window should look something like Figure 23.31. The songs that appear in the center contents pane will, of course, be songs you have in your own library. How your icons look depends on what category you're viewing and what option you've selected from the View Options button.

At this point, just drag the songs you want to burn to your custom CD to the Burn list. Or right-click any song title and choose Add to Burn List. As you add songs, the indicator at the top of the Burn list keeps you informed of how much space is still available on the CD. You can keep adding songs until the disk capacity is exhausted and you see Next Disk in the Burn list. When you see Next Disk, only songs above that line will fit on a single CD.

 **Clicking the Length column heading sorts songs from longest-to-shortest or vice versa. When you have little time left on a CD, that order can make it easy to find a song that will fit.**

Options that apply to custom playlists also apply to the Burn list. For example, to remove a song from the Burn list, right-click its title and choose Remove from List. To change the order of songs, click Burn List, choose Sort, and choose a sort option. Or, drag any song title up or down within the list.

When you're happy with the songs you've selected and their order, you're ready to burn the CD.

FIGURE 23.31

Ready to copy songs to a Burn list.

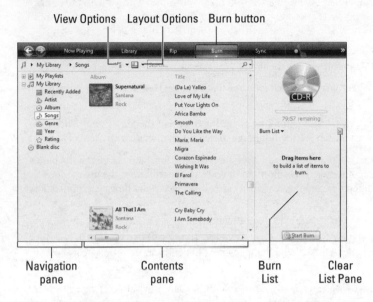

View Options   Layout Options   Burn button

Navigation pane   Contents pane   Burn List   Clear List Pane

Creating the disk

When the Burn list contains all the songs you want to copy to the CD, click the Start Burn button at the bottom of the Burn list. Then wait. How long it takes depends on the type of CD you're creating, the speed of your drive, and other factors. The status column in the contents pane and an indicator below the Burn list will keep you apprised of progress.

When the CD is finished, remove it from the CD drive. If you created a standard Audio Disk, you can insert and play it in a stereo as you would any other disk. If you created a Data Disk, you can play it in any device that supports the type of disk you created.

Saving a Burn List

It's a good idea to save each Burn list you create. That way, if you ever want to create another copy of the same CD, you can just open the saved Burn list. To save a Burn list, click the Burn list name and choose Save Playlist As. Change the name to something that describes the Burn list and click Save. Then to create a new Burn list, click the Clear List Pane button.

Copying Music to Portable Devices

A portable device is an MP3 player or similar device that lets you take your music with you. To put songs (or other media) on your portable device, you *sync* songs from Media Player's library to the device. You can put any songs you wish onto your player. The only limit is the storage capacity of the device.

Windows Media Player works with any device that meets Microsoft's PlaysForSure standards. It does not work with the Apple iPod (you use iTunes to sync to the iPod). Nor does it work with some older devices.

> **TIP** See "Converting File Types" later in this chapter for tips on using iTunes files with Windows Media Player.

If you don't already have a portable device, but are thinking of getting one, visit the PlaysForSure network at www.PlaysForSure.com. There you can see the full range of devices that work with Media Player 11.

Different devices work a little differently. So if you already have a device, the first step is to learn the basics of using it and connecting it to your computer. That information you can get only from the instructions that came with the device. Despite the differences among devices, I can tell you generally how synchronization works with Media Player 11.

The first step is to open Windows Media Player and click the Sync button in the features taskbar. Then connect your device to the computer and turn it on. If a dialog box opens asking you to name the device, type in a name of your own choosing and click Finish. What happens next depends on the storage capacity of the device:

- If the device capacity is 4 GB or greater, and your media library can fit within that capacity, Media Player automatically copies your entire library to the device. Each time you connect the device in the future, Media Player will copy any new songs you've acquired since the last connection, so that the device stays in sync with your library.

- If the device capacity is less than 4 GB, or your library is too large to fit in the device, nothing is copied automatically. But you can manually copy any songs you like to the device.

You can change what happens when you connect your device. We'll get to that in a moment. First, let's look at how you manually choose songs to put on your device.

Manual syncing

When your device is connected to your computer and you want to choose songs to copy to the device, click the Sync button in the features taskbar. The List pane at the right side of the program window shows the storage capacity of the device, and the amount of space that's currently on the device. Beneath that is an empty playlist, called the Sync list.

To add songs to the device, you need to drag them from the contents pane to the Sync list, just as you would when burning a CD or creating a custom playlist. As always you can select multiple songs and drag them all at once. You can also right-click any song, album, icon, or category name and choose Add To "Sync List."

As you add songs, an indicator near the top of the Sync list shows you how much space you have remaining. If the indicator turns red and shows "Filled," you've gone over the limit. To remove a song from the Sync list, right-click its title and choose Remove From List. Do so until the indicator turns green again. Figure 23.32 shows an example where I've chosen many songs already, and have about 15 MB of space left on my portable player.

FIGURE 23.32

Songs added to the Sync list.

As always, you can arrange songs in the Sync list by dragging them up or down. Optionally, click Sync List, choose Sort, and choose a sort order. When you're happy with the songs you've selected and their order, click the Start Sync button at the bottom of the Sync list.

The contents pane of Media Player will show the synchronization progress as songs are copied to the device. When the Status column shows "Synchronized to Device" for every song, you're done. You can disconnect the device from the computer, plug in your headphones, and take your music with you.

Managing songs on a device

Portable media players are much more flexible than CDs. For example, you can delete individual songs from a portable device, and replace them with other songs. When your device is connected, it shows up as it own set of categories in the Navigation pane. When you click a category name under the device name, the contents pane to the right shows the contents of the device only, not the contents of your entire library.

Figure 23.33 shows an example. If you look closely you can see I've clicked the Sync button in the features taskbar up top. In the Navigation pane at left I've clicked the Songs category name under Creative MuVo. So the contents pane to the right is showing songs that are currently on the MuVo player. When viewing songs in that manner with your own device, you can right-click any song title and choose Delete to remove it from the device.

Manual syncing is easy (once you've played around with it a bit). Most people like to choose exactly what's on their portable player. So manual syncing is also the most commonly used method. To use auto syncing, you need to enable automatic syncing, and specify what syncs automatically. Let's look at that next.

FIGURE 23.33

Songs on my portable MuVo player.

Auto-syncing devices

Auto-sync is a method of keeping a portable player up-to-date with whatever content is currently available in your Media Player library. If your device doesn't have enough capacity to store your entire library, exactly what you end up with can be somewhat arbitrary. The first step is to connect the device to the computer, and make sure it's turned on.

Next, click the arrow under the Sync button, point to your device name, and choose Set Up Sync. The Setup Device dialog box opens. The left column shows available playlists. The right column shows playlists that are currently used to sync songs to the device. To remove a playlist from the right column, click its name and choose Remove.

To add a playlist to the right column, click its name in the left column and click Add. To see Auto Playlists specifically designed for syncing, click the My Playlists button under Available Playlists and choose Sync Playlists.

If no playlist defines the kinds of songs you want to sync automatically, you can create your own. Click New Auto Playlist and give your playlist a name. For example, to make an Auto Playlist that copies new songs added to your library in the last week, create a criterion that specifies:

`Date added To Library is After Last 7 Days`

Give the new playlist a name, perhaps New This Week, and save it. Then click the Add button to copy it from Available Playlists to Playlists to Sync. If that's the only playlist you put in the right column, then each time you connect your device, Media Player will copy only songs that you've added to your library within the last week.

Optionally, choose Shuffle what syncs. If you do, each time you connect the device, files that are currently on the device will be removed automatically and replaced with songs that match the criteria of your selected Auto Playlists. So each time you connect the device, you automatically get however many songs your Playlist provides added to the device.

Click Finish when you're done, and Media Player will sync based on your selections. Remove the device when the syncing is finished. Any time you want to change the contents of your player, just connect it to the PC and click the Finish button.

Choose between manual and auto sync

You can choose whether you want to use manual sync or auto sync at any time. Just connect your device, click the arrow under Sync, click the device name, and choose Set Up Sync. To use manual syncing, clear the checkmark next to "Sync this device automatically." To enable auto syncing, select (check) that same checkbox. Then click Finish.

Setting player options

To see other options that your player supports, connect the player, right-click its name in the Navigation pane, and choose Advanced Options. A Properties dialog box for the device opens. The options available to you will depend on the capabilities of your player. If you're not sure what an option in the dialog box means, check the manual that came with your device. Or click the Help button in the dialog box for more information.

> **NOTE** Most portable players are USB mass storage devices. Once connected, these show up as a disk drive in your Computer folder. You can see the current contents of your device by opening its icon in your Computer folder. You can also erase any songs from the device using the same techniques you use to erase files from folders and drives.

Fun with Skins

Whenever you're using a program, the part that you see on the screen is just one snowflake on the tip of the proverbial iceberg The real "guts" are in memory, and invisible. That part you see on the screen is called the *user interface*, abbreviated UI, and often referred to as simply the *interface* or *skin*. Some programs, including Windows Media Player, allow you to change the interface without changing the functionality of the program.

Windows Media Player comes with several skins for you to try out. To see them, choose View ➪ Skin Chooser from Media Player's menu. Click each skin name in the left column to get a preview of how Media Player will look if you apply the skin. To download additional free skins, click the More Skins button above the left column. When you find a skin you like, click the Apply Skin button.

Figure 23.34 shows an example where I'm using a skin named Melvin. Once you're in a skin, you'll need to point to various symbols and buttons on it to figure out what's up. You'll see the name of the control in a tooltip. For example, in Figure 23.34 I'm pointing to Return to Full Mode control. Clicking that removes the skin and puts Media Player back to its default view.

FIGURE 23.34

Media Player in the Melvin skin.

When you're in the normal Full mode, you can click the Switch to Skin Mode button in the lower-left corner of Media Player's program window to switch to a skin. From the keyboard, press Ctrl+2 to switch to Skin mode. Press Ctrl+1 to switch back to Full mode. To get out of the Skin Chooser in Full mode, click Now Playing (or any other button) in the features taskbar.

Extending Media Player with Plug-ins

Plug-ins are optional add-on capabilities that you can purchase or, in some cases, download for free. A plug-in might be as simple as a new visualization or skin. Or it could be an audio or DVD driver or enhancer that extends the capabilities of Media Player. Some plug-ins add capabilities to Media Player. It all depends on what you download and install. To see your options, click the arrow under Now Playing and choose Plug-Ins ➪ Download Plug-Ins.

Some plug-ins are free, some aren't. Once you're at the site for downloading plug-ins, you'll need to review what's available and decide for yourself what's of value to you. If you don't see anything you like on the first page, click the link to get to the wmplugins.com site. Or, just browse to `www.wmplugins.com` with your Web browser. There you're more likely to find some freebies that you can try without paying for them.

To manage any plug-ins you acquire, click the button under Now Playing and choose Plug-ins ➪ Options.

Converting File Types

Suppose you've ripped a bunch of CDs to WMA format, and then acquire a portable media device that only plays MP3s. Do you need to rip all those same CDs again? The answer is No, provided you're willing to fork out a little money for a program that will do the conversions for you. Though there are several products on the market, you might want to take a look at Microsoft Plus Digital Media Edition or the SuperPack. In addition to being able to convert from WMA to MP3 (and vice versa), it offers many useful add-ons for Media Player and Movie Maker. To learn more about those products, browse to `www.microsoft.com/plus`.

For other types of conversion, consider searching any download site for the type of conversion you need to perform. For example, you might go to `www.tucows.com` or `www.download.com`. Or, you could use a more generic search engine like Google. Type in the words that best define the type of conversion you need to perform, like `Convert WMA MP4`.

Combining Multiple Tracks into One

This is a fairly common question from classical music lovers, though not directly related to Media Player. Classical music CDs are often broken into multiple tracks, even when the CD contains a single work. This leaves gaps between movements in a symphony. Media Player has no built-in capability for joining the tracks together. But you can use Windows Movie Maker, which comes with Windows Vista, to join the multiple tracks into Media Player. You should have some experience with Windows Movie Maker before attempting this (see Chapter 25).

The first step is to import the tracks into Movie Maker by choosing File ⇨ Import Media Items from its menu bar. Navigate to the folder that contains the tracks and import them. Then drag the tracks down to the Audio/Music track of the Timeline. Figure 23.35 shows an example where I have four music tracks in the Audio/Music track of Movie Maker's timeline.

FIGURE 23.35

Music tracks in Movie Maker's Audio/Music timeline.

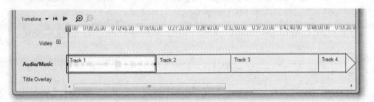

Listen to parts of the track where two clips meet to see whether there's still a gap. If necessary, you can drag the rightmost clip to the left so it overlaps slightly with the clip that precedes it. How far you have to drag depends on the gap. You may have to find the right amount to overlap through trial and error.

When you're happy with how the combined tracks play in Movie Maker, you can save it as a single WMA file. Choose File ⇨ Publish Movie from Movie Maker's menu. Choose My Computer as the location and click Next. Enter a filename and choose a folder in your Music folder as the folder to save to and click Next. When choosing a quality, choose Other Settings and a quality setting, preferably of 128 Kbps or better. Click Publish and wait for the file to be created. Then you can close Movie Maker without saving the project.

Music, Metadata, and Searches

NEW FEATURE   Whether or not you are in Windows Media Player, you can now search for and group things based on metadata, media information, in any file.

Earlier in this chapter you discovered how you can store media information like artist, album title, genre, and so forth with songs. That media information is a form of *metadata*. Metadata, in turn, is information *about* a file, and it doesn't apply only to music. Pictures, videos, Microsoft Office documents, and many other file types support metadata.

You don't have to be in Windows Media Player to take advantage of metadata. The new Search features in Windows Vista allow you to search and group things based on metadata in any file. For example, if you click the Start button and type an artist's name into the Search box, songs by that artist show up in the Start menu.

Of course, there isn't a whole lot of room on the Start menu. So you could instead click Start, choose Search, and type `jazz` in the Search box, and you'll get all the files that have the word Jazz in their metadata or content. You could narrow that down to only files whose Genre property contains the word jazz by searching for:

```
genre:jazz
```

You're also not limited to search one thing. You can specify multiple criteria separated by the words AND or OR (uppercase letters). For example, here's a search that finds all tracks in which the composer is either Beethoven or Mozart:

```
composer:beethoven OR composer:mozart
```

TIP   You might think that it should be `composer:Beethoven AND composer:Mozart`. **But it doesn't work that way. A song can't have both Beethoven *and* Mozart as the composer. You're looking for tracks that have either Beethoven *or* Mozart as the composer.**

If you want to locate all MP3 songs that have Clapton as an artist and a year greater than 2003, the following search would do the trick:

```
type:mp3 AND artists:clapton AND year:>2005
```

For experienced users, this is a far cry from the old days of searching for filenames. But it's not the kind of thing you master in a minute. Searches are only successful when you know how to construct them correctly. See Chapters 30 and 31 for the full story.

Wrap Up

In this chapter, we've looked at the Windows Media Player 11 main music capabilities. We haven't covered all of its capabilities yet. In the next chapter you'll learn about using Media Player with DVDs and videos. If you have the Premium or Ultimate edition of Windows Vista, you can also use Media Center to play songs from your media library. See Chapter 26 for the goods on Media Center. The main points from this chapter include the following:

- Controlling sound volume on your computer is a necessary first step to playing music.
- The features taskbar along the top of Media Player's program window provides easy access to all of its main components.
- The Now Playing tab shows a visualization of music that's playing or the visual content of the playing video or DVD.
- The Library button on the features taskbar gives you access to all songs and other media you've downloaded or copied from CDs.
- The Rip button in the features taskbar lets you copy songs from music CDs to your media library.
- The Burn button in the features taskbar lets you burn your own custom music CDs.
- The Sync button in the features taskbar lets you copy music to portable media devices.

Chapter 24

DVD, Video, and More

There's more to Windows Media Player than ripping and burning CDs. Media Player can play digital media stored on DVD, Enhanced DVD, VCD, and SVCD disks. It can play video files you acquire online or create yourself in Movie Maker. And you can even use it to manage pictures and copy them to portable devices.

If you have Media Center with your version of Windows Vista, you can use Media Player to manage and watch Recorded TV.

Watching DVD, VCD, and Such

If your computer has a DVD drive, you can use it to watch DVD movies — including movies you buy or rent at a movie store, as well as DVDs you create yourself using Windows DVD Maker. You can use the techniques described here to watch VCD and SVCD disks. You don't need a DVD drive for those kinds of disks; a CD drive will do.

First things first

Before you get started watching video, you should be aware that there are many different kinds of *codecs* associated with video. A codec is a *compressor/decompressor*, a file that needs to be installed on your system to see (and hear) certain types of videos.

Windows Vista comes with a built-in DVD decoder, which allows you to watch the vast majority of DVDs without any fuss. But occasionally you'll come across a situation where you get video but no sound, or sound but no video in a movie. That's because the movie uses a codec that isn't built into Vista. In many cases, Media Player will be able to download the codec automatically. But only if you allow it to. Follow these steps to allow Media Player to download codecs on an as-needed basis:

1. If you're in a Standard user account, log in to an account with administrative privileges.

2. Open Media Player (press ▦, type med, and click Windows Media Player).

3. Click the arrow under Now Playing and choose More Options.

4. Click the Player tab in the dialog box and make sure that Download codecs automatically is selected (checked).

5. Click OK.

Nothing will happen on your screen. All you've done here is ensure that *if* a codec you need is available as a free download from the Internet, Media Player will go get it for you when you need it. Of course, your computer must be online when the codec is needed.

TIP The www.free-codecs.com Web site offers many codecs that you can download for free. The K-Lite Codec pack is an especially popular one that solves many problems with missing audio and video in movies. But Media Player can't download that one automatically. You have to download and install it yourself from the Web site.

NEW FEATURE The new AutoPlay feature lets you set defaults for all kinds of CDs, DVDs, and many devices.

Setting defaults for DVDs

You can choose a default program for playing DVDs. The default program is the one that opens automatically and plays a DVD when you put a DVD disk in your DVD drive. Here's how to set your default player:

1. Insert a commercial DVD disk into your DVD drive.

2. If the program you want to use as your default player starts playing the DVD, skip the remaining steps. Otherwise, close the program that opened and continue with these steps.

3. Open your Computer folder (click the Start button and choose Computer).

4. Right-click the icon that represents your DVD drive and choose Open Autoplay. You should see a dialog box similar to the one in Figure 24.1, but the options available to you depend on the programs currently installed on your computer.

FIGURE 24.1

Autoplay defaults for DVD movies.

5. If you want all DVD movies to start with the program you select, choose (check) Always do this for DVD movies.

6. Click the name of the program you want to use as your default player (in this chapter I'll assume you chose Windows Media Player).

TIP   You can also choose a default DVD player through the AutoPlay page of Control Panel. Click the Start button, choose Control Panel, click Hardware and Sound, and then click AutoPlay. Then use the DVD and Enhanced DVD options to choose default programs.

Playing a DVD or VCD

To play a DVD (or VCD), put the disk into the drive and wait a few seconds. Assuming that you chose Windows Media Player as the default player, the movie should start playing within a few seconds. If it plays full screen, right-click the screen and choose Exit Full Screen to get to the Windows Media Player program window.

If a movie loads but doesn't start playing, click the arrow under Now Playing, and choose the first option, Play. . . .

When the movie is playing in Windows Media Player, you'll see the controls pointed out in Figure 24.2.

FIGURE 24.2

Watching a DVD in Media Player.

The controls in the window are similar to controls on a DVD player, with a few extras. Here's how they work:

- **Now Playing:** Click this button to watch your DVD. Other buttons will show other information relevant to music in your library, as discussed in Chapter 23. If the DVD isn't playing, click the arrow under this button and choose the Play option.

- **List Pane:** Shows the contents of the CD. Double-click a title or scene to play it. Use the arrow under Now Playing to show or hide the List pane.

- **Stop:** Stops playback and rewinds to the beginning of the movie.

- **Previous/Rewind:** Click to go to the previous scene. Hold down the left mouse button to rewind.

- **Play/Pause:** Click to pause or resume playback.

- **Next/Fast Forward:** Click to skip to the next scene. Hold down the left mouse button to fast forward.

- **Mute:** Turn sound off. Click again to turn the sound back on.

- **Volume:** Adjust the sound volume.

- **View Full Screen:** Switch to full screen mode. In full screen, right-click for playback controls or to exit full screen back to the Media Player program menu.

- **DVD Menu:** Offers options similar to those on a TV DVD player for watching the movie, as summarized here:

  - **Audio and Language Tracks:** Choose the spoken language of the movie.

  - **Lyrics, Captions, and Subtitles:** Show or hide closed captions.

  - **Root menu:** Takes you to the opening menu for the DVD. Typically offers options like Play Movie, Scene Selection, Language, and so forth. Click any item on the main menu to select it.

  - **Title menu:** Takes you to a menu of titles, if available, on the current DVD. If the Root menu option does nothing, try this one instead.

  - **Close menu (resume):** If you clicked Root menu during playback, you can then click this button to resume playback where you left off.

  - **Back:** If the movie you're watching contains Internet links and you're navigating through Internet pages, it works like the Back button in a Web browser, taking you back to the previous page.

  - **Camera Angle:** Lets you choose a camera angle on DVDs that offer multiple camera angles.

  - **Capture Image:** Takes a snapshot of the screen and puts it in the Windows Clipboard. To see the image or save it as a file, open a graphics program and choose Paste from its menu or press Ctrl+V.

  - **Update DVD Information:** If the DVD you're viewing has media information on the Internet, choosing this option will download media information.

Choosing the screen size

As your movie is playing or paused, right-click on the movie. Or right-click an empty area to the left of the play controls and choose View ➪ Video Size. Then choose options as summarized:

- **Fit Video to Player on Resize:** If selected, this option prevents Media Player from cropping the movie when the size of the video is larger than the program window. When you resize the program window to smaller than the dimensions of the video, the movie is resized as well.

- **Fit Player to Video on Start:** If selected, Windows Media Player automatically resizes its own program window to avoid cropping out a portion of the movie when you first start playing a DVD movie or video.

The recommended setting for the preceding options is to leave both on (checked). Options lower on the menu size the visible video image as a percentage of the movie's actual dimensions:

- **50%:** Plays the movie at half its actual size (same as pressing Alt+1).
- **100%:** Plays the movie at actual size (same as pressing Alt+2).
- **200%:** Doubles the size of the movie (same as pressing Alt+3). You'd more likely use this option for small video clips than a DVD movie.
- **Full Screen:** Expands the movie to full-screen size.

To quickly switch between full screen mode and the player window, press Alt+Enter. In full screen mode, you can right-click the screen for additional options.

Preventing screen savers during playback

If Windows is configured to play a screen saver after a period of inactivity, you probably don't want that kicking in while you're trying to watch a movie. To prevent your screen saver from disrupting your movie, follow these steps:

1. In Media Player, click the arrow under Now Playing and choose More Options.
2. Clear the checkmark next to Allow screen saver during playback.
3. Click OK.

Setting parental controls and language defaults

You can set parental controls to prevent children from watching DVDs above a specific rating. You can also choose a default language for DVDs that support multiple languages. Here's how:

1. In Media Player, click the arrow under Now Playing and choose More Options.
2. In the Options dialog box that opens, click the DVD tab.
3. Under DVD Playback Restrictions, click the Change... button. Then use the button in the Change Rating Restriction box to choose a maximum rating (like G or PG-13) and click OK.
4. Optionally, to choose a default language for DVDs, click Defaults.
5. Choose a language for audio, caption, and DVD menu languages, and then click OK.
6. Click OK to save your settings and close the dialog box.

Playing Video Files

A video file is a file on your hard disk that contains video and audio. These include videos you capture from video cameras, digital cameras, recorded TV shows, and videos you download from the Web. Video files come in many formats. Windows Media Player can't play them all. But it can play video files stored in the formats listed in Table 24.1.

TABLE 24.1

Video File Formats Supported by Media Player 11

File Format	Extensions
Audio-Video Interleave	.avi
Microsoft Recorded TV	.dvr-ms
MPEG (Moving Picture Experts Group)	.mpa, .mpe, .mpeg, .mpg, .m1v, .mp2, .mpv2, .mp2v
Windows Media File and Advanced Streaming Format	.asf, .asx, .wm, .wmd, .wmx, .wmz, .wpl
Windows Media Video	.wmv, .wmx

Using your Videos folder

NEW FEATURE You can store video files in any folder you want. But to stay organized, you may want to put video files that are private to your user account in your Videos folder. Video files that you want to share with all users should go into the Public Videos folder. Both folders offer similar features. So before we get to playing videos, take a moment to look at your Videos folder.

To open your Videos folder, click the Start button and click your user name near the top of the Start menu. Or, if you're already in a folder and the Navigation pane is open, click Folders near the bottom of the pane, then click Videos. Figure 24.3 shows an example where I already have some videos and other items in my Videos folder. Only the icons that look like thumbnails are actual videos. When you click one of those, it shows in the Preview pane (if the Preview pane is open).

FIGURE 24.3

Videos folder example.

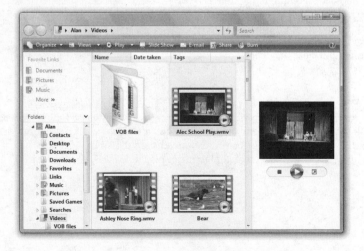

TIP   To open and close optional panes, click the Organize button and choose Layout. See Chapter 28 for the full story on folders and panes.

If you want to see filename extensions of video files, but they're not currently visible, click the Organize button and choose Folder and Search Options. Then click the View tab, clear the checkmark next to "Hide extensions for known file types," and click OK.

Recorded TV

Recorded TV shows are video files stored in the .dvr-ms (Digital Video Recording — Microsoft) format. You use Media Center (Chapter 26) to define times and channels to record, as on a VCR or DVD recorder. You can also decide where you want to store recorded TV shows in Media Center. And of course you can watch recorded TV shows in Media Center.

You can also watch recorded TV shows in Windows Media Player. When you open Media Player, you see a small icon at the left side of the toolbar, just under the Back button. When you point to it, the tooltip reads Select a Category. Click that and choose Recorded TV to see recorded TV shows that Media Player can find. Or, click the arrow under the Library button and choose Recorded TV for the same result.

If some of your recorded TV shows don't show up, Media Player may not be monitoring their folders. In Media Player's features taskbar, click the arrow on the Library button and choose Add to Library. If you don't see the list of monitored folders, click Advanced Options. Then use the Add button to add folders that contain recorded TV to the list of monitored folders.

Making Media Player the default video player

To watch a video file in Media Player, just open its icon (by clicking or double-clicking, depending on your click settings). If the video is stored in one of the formats listed back in Table 24.1, it should open in Media Player. If it opens in some other program, close that program. Then follow these steps to watch it in Media Player:

1. Right-click the video icon and choose Open With.
2. Click Windows Media Player (or whatever program you want to set as the default).
3. To ensure that files of that type open in Media Player by default, choose Always use the selected program to open this kind of file.
4. Click OK.

Adding videos to your media library

You can store information about your video files in Media Player's library. Depending on how Media Player is configured, video files from your Videos folder, and perhaps Public folders, might already be in Media Player. To find out, click Library to view your media library. Then click the arrow under the Library button and choose Video.

To add video files to your media library, monitor the folders in which they're stored. Here's how:

1. If you're not already in Windows Media Player, open that program.
2. Click the Library button in Media Player to view your library. Then click the arrow under Library and choose Video.
3. To add more videos to your library, click the arrow under Library again and choose Add to Library.

4. Choose whether you want to view video files from your personal Video folder (only), or from shared locations as well.

5. If you have video folders on other drives or in other folders, click Advanced Options >> (if necessary) to view more options.

6. Click the Add button and navigate to the drive and folder that contains other videos you want to include. Then click OK. Repeat this step for each folder you want to add.

7. Click OK in each open dialog box to save all of your changes.

Media files from the folders you specified are added to your library. As when working with music, you can use the View Options button to display icons in Tile, Icon, or Details view. You can also add your own media information to better organize your videos by genre, director, actor, or whatever. See "Using the Media Player Library" in Chapter 23 for details. Figure 24.4 shows an example where I've already categorized video files by Genre. I clicked the Genre icon in the Navigation pane at left to see video files stacked by categories.

FIGURE 24.4

Video files organized by Genre.

Recorded TV shows are stored in the Public Recorded TV folder by default. If you've been recording TV, click the arrow under Library and choose Recorded TV. If shows you've recorded don't appear, repeat the preceding steps to add the Recorded TV folder to your list of monitored folders.

Playing videos from your library

Playing videos in Media Player is no different from playing songs. In the library, just double-click the video's title or icon. Or right-click an icon, stack, or category name and choose Play. Make sure that you click the Now Playing tab so you can see the video content.

Internet Video

There are two ways to watch video on the Internet. There are *streaming* videos, which you can watch but not download. And there are video files, which you can watch or download. When you download a video, it becomes a file on your own hard disk, which you can then add to your media library. It's not always easy to tell the difference. But making Windows Media Player the default player for videos that it can play helps. I'll talk about that more in a moment.

Video files on the Internet also come in many formats. Some, like Apple QuickTime, won't play in Media Player at all. But as I'll also discuss in a moment, there are ways you can convert videos from incompatible formats to compatible formats. First let's talk about making Media Player the default player for Internet videos.

Downloading video files

There are a couple of ways to download video files from the Internet. In some cases it's easy to tell that the file is available for download, because the site tells you how to download the video. The usual procedure starts with the link that, if clicked, would play the video. Instead of clicking that link, you can right-click and choose Save Target As, like the example in Figure 24.5.

FIGURE 24.5

Right-click and choose Save Target As.

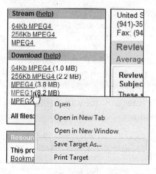

Figure 24.5 is an example where I'm using Internet Explorer 7 to download a video file from the Moving Images collection at www.archive.org. Other Web browsers and Web sites will show different options. If you're into outer space, black holes, and such, you can find some free videos at the Hubble Space telescope site at www.hubblesite.org. When you get there, click Newscenter. Then click the Video icon. To search for other video files, try using http://video.google.com or a similar option from another search engine.

If your browser doesn't support right-clicking and choosing Save Target As, click the link to the video to watch it play in Windows Media Player (assuming it's a video that can be viewed in Media Player). After watching the video, right-click some empty space next to the play controls in Media Player and choose File ➪ Save As. (This won't be possible with streaming media, because those files can't be saved.)

Whether you use Save Target As or File ⇨ Save As to save the video, you'll be taken to the usual Save As dialog box. There you can navigate to the folder in which you want to save the file. For example, to put it in your Videos folder, click your user name in the breadcrumb menu and choose Videos to open your Videos folder. Optionally, change the filename (but not the extension) and click the Save button. If all went well, you can play the video at any time by opening its icon in your Videos folder.

Playing downloaded video files

After you've downloaded a video file, there won't be any need to go online to view it. (That was the whole point in downloading it in the first place!) Just open the folder to which you downloaded the file and open the video file's icon.

If you downloaded to a folder that's monitored by Media Player, you can also play the movie from your Media Player library.

Ripping DVDs

DVD-Video disks contain folders and files specifically designed to work with DVD players rather than computers. When you view the contents of such a disk on a computer, you typically see a folder named Video_TS. You might also see a folder named Audio_TS. But that folder is mainly used for DVDs that contain audio only, no video.

When you open the Video_TS folder to view its contents, you'll likely find folders with .VOB, .IF, and .BUP filename extensions. The VOB files are actually mpeg files, and are the only ones that contain video content. The IFO file contains information about scenes and timing. The BUP files are backups of the IFO file. These aren't relevant to computers, so you can ignore them.

If you double-click a .VOB file, it may not play. However, there is a trick that often works to get them to play. It won't work on copy-protected commercial movies. But it might work with other kinds of DVD-Video disks. The trick is to copy the .VOB files to a folder on your hard disk. Then rename each .VOB file so its filename extension is .mpg. Make sure you can see filename extensions before you do. Otherwise you'll just add .mpg to the filename without changing the .VOB filename extension.

 **For help on copying files, renaming files, and seeing filename extensions, see Chapters 28 and 29.**

Even if you can copy .VOB files and rename them to .mpg, there's no guarantee that all of them will play when you double-click the icon. There are codec issues that might prevent some of them from playing properly until you acquire the correct codec.

When the copy-and-rename trick fails, DVD ripping software might succeed. These are programs that copy the .VOB files and convert them to a more computer-compatible format at the same time. Again, they won't work with copyright-protected content. (You don't want to copy those anyway, because it's illegal.) Most DVD-ripping programs will let you copy to AVI, MPEG, or WMV, all of which are compatible with Windows Media Player and Windows Movie Maker.

 **Deskshare's Digital Media Converter** (www.deskshare.com) **and AVS Video Tools** (www.avsmedia.com) **are inexpensive programs that provide both DVD ripping and file type conversion.**

If you have a DVD recorder or a video camera that records to DVD, ripping can be even trickier. You'll need to study the documentation that came with your recorder for the specifics. There's not much I can say in a Windows book that would apply to every make and model of digital video recorder and camera on the market. But I can tell you how it works on my own DVD recorder, and that might give you some clues.

On my own DVD recorder I have to initialize the disk for Video Mode (rather than Video Record [VR] mode). And after recording a TV show, I have to finalize (close) the disk. I imagine the same basic idea applies to many other DVD recorders as well. You'll still have to copy and rename .VOB files to .mpg, or use DVD-ripping software to rip content from the finalized DVD to your hard disk.

Converting Video Files

Windows has no built-in capabilities for converting video files from one format to another. But there are third-party programs that can do such conversions. You can try the AVS or DeskShare program mentioned in the preceding Tip. Or search a download site like www.tucows.com or www.download.com, or even Google, for such programs. To narrow your search, first know the file extensions of the files you want to convert, and use those in your search. For example, if you want to convert MOV files to WMV files, search for Convert MOV WMV.

The two DVD-ripping programs I mentioned in the previous section, Digital Media Converter and AVS Video Tools, both offer many options for converting video files. In fact, that's their main purpose. Of course, products change and evolve over time. So if you're thinking about buying such a program, you should research both products, and perhaps others, to make sure the product can do what you need it to do.

TIP If you want to convert from AVI, MPEG, or WMV to AVI or WMV, there's no need to purchase anything. Instead you can import the video file to Windows Movie Maker. Then publish it to an AVI or WMV file from Movie Maker.

Managing Pictures with Media Player

In Chapter 22 you discovered ways to acquire and manage pictures with Windows Photo Gallery. There's no need to bring that information into Media Player. But you can if you want to. For example, if you have a portable media device that displays pictures, you might want to bring the pictures into Media Player so you can sync music and video files.

To view pictures in Media Player, the pictures need to be in a folder that's monitored by Media Player. Or, you'll need to add that folder to your list of monitored folders by clicking the arrow under Library and choosing Add to Library.

To view pictures in Media Player, click the arrow under Library and choose Pictures. In the Navigation pane, you can view All Pictures, pictures by keyword, by date, and so forth. Figure 24.6 shows an example where I'm viewing pictures by keyword. Each stack represents a group of pictures.

FIGURE 24.6

Viewing pictures by keyword in Media Player.

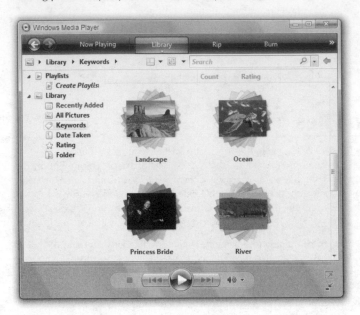

NEW FEATURE   Windows Media Player 11 includes some new features for managing your playlists.

More on Playlists

In Media Player, you include videos and pictures in any music playlists you create. This is mostly useful for creating Auto Playlists for syncing to devices that support music, pictures, and video. (When you play the playlist in Media Player, they play in sequence, not simultaneously. So you'll still see only a visualization when music is playing.)

TIP   If you want to create a movie that contains video, pictures, and music, use Windows Movie Maker, described in the next chapter. If you want to copy Media Player content to a DVD as a data disk, use the Burn tab in Media Player. See Chapter 32 for details on burning files to DVD.

To create an Auto Playlist that includes music, pictures, and/or videos, click the arrow under Library and choose Auto Playlist. Or, right-click the name of an existing Auto Playlist and choose Edit. Name the playlist however you like. Under Music in My Library, add your criteria for music. Then, under And Also Include, set criteria for Pictures, TV, and Video as you see fit. Figure 24.7 shows an Auto Playlist named Todays Music Pix TV Vids that automatically displays all four types of files for media items added today.

FIGURE 24.7

Auto Playlist for Music, Pictures, TV, and Video.

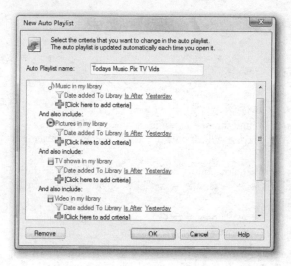

You can use that Auto Playlist to keep your portable media player up-to-date with media content on your computer on a daily basis. To update manually, connect your device and click Sync in the features taskbar. Drag the playlist name from the Navigation pane into the List pane. Then click the Start Sync button.

To use the daily Auto Playlist for automatic syncing, first connect your device. Then click the arrow under Sync, click the device name (or Removable Disk), and choose Set Up Sync. Choose "Sync this device automatically." Then add the Auto Playlist to the Device To Sync column. Remove any other playlists that are in that Devices to Sync column.

TIP If you want to copy music (only) daily to your portable player, remove the "And also include" criteria for pictures, recorded TV, and video. Just click whichever criterion you want to remove, and then click the Remove button at the bottom of the window.

Limiting playlist size

If you discover that your Auto Playlists are too large, containing more content than you can fit on your portable player, there are things you can do to limit the amount of content the playlist contains. At the bottom of the Auto Playlist, click the + sign under "And apply the following restrictions to the auto playlist." You'll see the options shown in Figure 24.8. Your options are as follows:

FIGURE 24.8

Options for restricting an Auto Playlist.

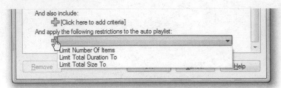

- **Limit number of items:** Choose this option to limit the number of items the playlist may contain. For example, if you choose 10, the Auto Playlist will list only the first 10 items that meet the criterion.

- **Limit total duration to:** Choose this option to set a maximum time limit to match the time duration of the disk to which you'll be copying items. For example, if you'll be copying playlist items to an Audio CD, the time limit is 80 minutes.

- **Limit total size to:** When syncing to portable devices, choose this option to limit the playlist items to the storage capacity of your device in megabytes (MB) or gigabytes (GB).

Click OK when you've finished setting criteria. To see which items the Auto Playlist includes, double-click its name under My Playlists in the Navigation pane. Or click My Playlists in the Navigation pane, and then double-click the playlist name in the Details pane. Or right-click the playlist name and choose Add To Now Playing to see items in the List pane.

To use your new playlist for auto syncing, connect your portable device to the computer. Then click the arrow under Sync, choose the device name (or Removable Disk option), and click Set Up Sync. Choose the "Sync this device automatically" checkbox and remove any items listed in the "Playlists to sync" column. Then add your new playlist to that same column.

Limiting playlists to favorite items

When you manually create playlists by dragging items to the List pane, criteria you set in an Auto Playlist have no effect. But you can limit manual playlists to favorite items, providing you rate your items before dragging them over.

First, before you drag an album or category to the List pane, open the album or group and rate the songs. To rate a song, right-click its title in the contents pane and choose Rate. Or select several songs to which you want to apply the same rating, right-click any one selected song, and choose Rate. Give a four- or five-star rating to any songs you do want copied to playlists. Give a three-star or lower rating to songs you don't want copied.

To copy only favorites from the category to the playlist, right-click the album's icon or category name and choose "<*playlist name*> (Favorites Only)." Only the 4- and 5-star rated items appear in the List pane. Optionally, click the button under Library and choose Add Favorites to List When Dragging. Then drag the album icon or category name to the List pane. Only 4- and 5-star rated songs from the album or category appear in the List pane.

The "Add Favorites to List When Dragging" option applies every time you drag to the List pane. So if songs appear to be missing when you drag, chances are you enabled the Add Favorites... option and then forgot about it. To turn that feature off, click the arrow under Library and choose Add Favorites to List When Dragging again to clear its checkmark and disable that feature.

Skipping playlist items

When you're playing items in a playlist, you can skip over any item by clicking the Next button in the play controls. Media Player can remember which items you skipped, then skip them automatically the next time you play the list. It can also automatically omit skipped items when you save the playlist.

To choose how Media Player treats skipped items, right-click the playlist name (or Untitled Playlist) and choose Skipped Items, as in Figure 24.9. A checked option is active, an unchecked option is inactive. You can click the option to activate or deactivate it. The next sections describe how those options work.

FIGURE 24.9

Options for restricting an Auto Playlist.

Prompt me to Remove upon Save

Choosing (activating) the "Prompt me to Remove upon Save" option causes the message shown in Figure 24.10 to appear whenever you save a playlist that contains skipped (dimmed) items. You can choose whether you want to leave the skipped items in the saved playlist or omit them. If you choose to keep the items in the playlist, you can choose "Do not play skipped items and display them as dimmed" to have the skipped songs show up as dimmed, and be skipped over, the next time you open the playlist. Clearing that option saves the playlist with no items dimmed or skipped.

FIGURE 24.10

Skipping options.

If you don't choose the "Prompt me..." option, Media Player automatically saves the playlist exactly as it looks in the List pane. So that when you reopen the playlist item in the future, skipped songs are still dimmed and will be skipped over on playback.

Skip During Playback

Choosing this option is what makes items go dim when you skip over them. If the dimming and skipping over isn't your cup of tea, clear the checkmark from this option. Songs in the playlist won't go dim when you skip them. Nor will they be skipped over automatically when you play the playlist again in the future.

Saving playlists in M3U format

Each playlist that you create is a file in the My Playlists subfolder in your Music folder. By default, each has a .WPL filename extension indicating a Windows playlist. You can also save playlists in M3U format, which is required on some MP3 players. To save a playlist in M3U format:

1. Click the playlist name in the List pane and choose Save Playlist As.
2. In the File name: box, type a name for the playlist.
3. Click next to Save as type: and choose (M3U Playlist *.m3u).
4. Click the Save button.

When you burn a data CD or DVD from a playlist, you can choose whether you want the playlist in that disk to be WPL or M3U. Click the button under Burn and choose More Options. Next to the "Add a list of burned files to the disk in this format," choose WPL or M3U. Then click OK.

What About iTunes Playlists?

As I write this chapter, I see nothing in the current version of iTunes that allows export to M3U playlists. But you may be able to get around that by using a third-party program. I found an easy two-step process. First use iTunes to export the playlist to XML format. Then use the Web site at `http://chimpen.com/itunes2m3u/convert.php` to convert the xml file to M3U format. You may want to search the Web for `convert iTunes playlist` for other solutions.

Media Player Help and Troubleshooting

Media Player has many features and supports many kinds of media files. I could probably write a book as large as this one just on Windows Media Player alone.

There are also lots of things that can go wrong when using Media Player, especially if you're new to all of this, or are not yet familiar with all of your computer hardware. But fear not, because there are plenty of places where you can get the information you need, when you need it.

- For general help with Media Player or to ask a question, click the arrow under the features taskbar button and choose Help.

- For troubleshooting, right-click an empty area to the left of the play controls and choose Help ⇨ Troubleshooting.

- For a world of information on Media Player, portable devices, media files, and such, right-click an empty area of Media Player's program window and choose Help ⇨ Windows Media Player Online.

You can also keep up with the latest in music, video, and radio for Windows Media Player by browsing to www.WindowsMedia.com.

Wrap Up

Windows Media Player 11 is the latest and greatest version of that program and comes free with most versions of Windows Vista. Here's a quick summary of key points made in this chapter about using Media Player to watch DVD, videos, and pictures:

- To watch a DVD movie in Media Player, insert the DVD disk into your drive and wait for Media Player to play.

- To download a nonstreaming video from the Internet, right-click the link to the video file and choose Save Target As.

- To open your Videos folder, click the Start button, click your user name, and open the Videos icon. (In the breadcrumb menu, click you user name and choose Videos.)

- To view video files you've imported to Media Player, click the arrow under Library and choose Video.

- For help, troubleshooting, and more information, right-click an empty spot in Media Player, choose Help, and click whichever option you want.

Chapter 25

Making Movies with Movie Maker

Every movie or TV show you've ever seen is a collection of *scenes* organized into a story. Windows Movie Maker is a program that lets you create professional-grade videos in a similar manner — by combining your favorite scenes from home videos, Internet videos, and personal photos.

You can embellish your movie with custom titles and credits, sound effects, voice narration, and special effects. In short, you get to be cameraman, director, and producer all wrapped into one. Anyone with a PC can watch your movie on a computer. And you can copy your movies to DVD to watch on TV and to share with family and friends.

Getting Started with Movie Maker

Movie Maker is a lot of fun. But it's not the kind of program you can figure out by guessing and hacking away at it. You may need to know some things about video files in general. Chapter 24 can help with that. If you want to edit video from your video camera, you'll need to know some things about your camera. The section titled "Import from Videotape" later in this chapter can help with some of that. But there's only one place where you can really learn about your video camera — the instructions that came with that camera.

Professional movie makers create their movies by going through a procedure. You'll want to follow a similar procedure when creating your movies. The basic steps to that procedure are

- Import video, pictures, and music for your movie into Movie Maker.
- Optionally, edit out any bad video you don't want to use in your movie.
- Organize the remaining good material (edited footage) into a story.
- Optionally, add embellishments like still photos, titles and credits, special effects, background music, voice narration, and sound effects.
- Publish the finished movie to a file or DVD.

591

The first step, of course, is to open Windows Movie Maker. Use whichever technique is easiest for you:

- Click the Start button and choose All Programs ➪ Windows Movie Maker.
- Press ▦, type mov, and click Windows Movie Maker under Programs.

If you see a message about using 800 x 600 resolution, don't worry. It's not an error — just a suggestion. Click OK.

> **TIP**   It's okay to use 800 x 600 resolution in Movie Maker. It won't have any effect on your movies. Things may just feel a bit cramped in the program window. To try a 1024 x 768 or higher resolution, see "Choosing a screen resolution" in Chapter 11.

Movie Maker opens in a program window. Like many programs, it has several different optional panes pointed out in Figure 25.1. Most panes you can show, hide, or size to your liking.

FIGURE 25.1

Windows Movie Maker.

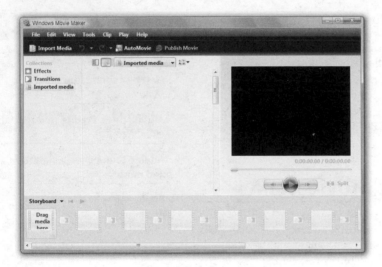

Each pane serves a purpose. You'll see that as you go through the chapter. The left pane can show either Tasks (steps involved in creating a movie) or Collections (video, pictures, and music you can use in your movie). To switch between the Tasks and Collections panes, use the buttons pointed out in Figure 25.2.

You can size all panes except the Tasks pane. Get the tip of the mouse pointer in the inner border of the pane you want to size so that the mouse pointer turns to the two-headed sizing arrow. Then drag left or right to size a side pane. Or drag up and down to size the Storyboard/Timeline pane.

FIGURE 25.2

FIGURE 25.2

View Tasks or Collections in the left pane.

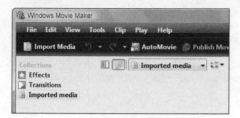

Choosing program options

Before you start working with video, take a minute to check your current settings. Follow these steps:

1. Choose Tools ⇨ Options from Movie Maker's menu bar.
2. In the Options dialog box that opens, click the Advanced tab to see the options shown in Figure 25.3.

FIGURE 25.3

Windows Movie Maker advanced options.

3. For Video Settings, choose NTSC if you live in the United States. Choose PAL if you live in Europe or another country that uses PAL format.

4. For Aspect Ratio, choose 4:3 for standard TV screen size. Choose 16:9 if you'll be working with widescreen DVD video.

5. If you plan to e-mail movies to friends, set the maximum e-mail attachment size as specified by your ISP.

NOTE The maximum size for an e-mail attachment is usually 1–3 MB for dial-up accounts, and 10 MB for broadband accounts. If you don't know the maximum attachment size for your account, ask your ISP or check their Web site.

6. Click OK.

With those basic options out of the way, it's time to bring some video into Movie Maker to work with.

Things you can use in movies

The movies you create can contain video, pictures, and music. The content must already be in a file on your hard disk. If you want to use content that's not already in a file on your hard disk, you need to get it onto your hard disk first. If you haven't gotten that far yet, here are some places you can look in this book for getting content from external disks and devices into files on your hard disk:

- **Video from a videotape:** "Import from Videotape" in this chapter.
- **Video from the Internet:** "Internet Video" in Chapter 24.
- **Video from a DVD Video disk:** "Ripping DVDs" in Chapter 24.
- **Pictures or video from a digital camera, the Web, or e-mail:** "Getting Pictures into Your Computer" in Chapter 22.
- **Music from CDs:** "Ripping (Copying) Music CDs" in Chapter 23.

NOTE You cannot import protected content into Movie Maker. That includes music you purchased online using Windows Media Player or iTunes. You cannot unprotect protected content.

There are also limits to the types of files you can import into Movie Maker, as summarized here:

- **Video files:** .asf, .avi, .m1v, .mp2, .mp2v, .mpe, .mpeg, .mpg, .mpv2, .wm, .wmv, and .dvr-ms
- **Picture files:** .bmp, .dib, .emf, .gif, .jfif, .jpe, .jpeg, .jpg, .png, .tif, .tiff, and .wmf
- **Audio files:** .aif, .aifc, .aiff .asf, .au, .mp2, .mp3, .mpa, .snd, .wav, and .wma (excluding licensed content, which cannot be imported).

If you have video or audio files that you want to use, but they're not one of the file types listed previously, you may be able to convert from the current format to a supported format. There are many different conversion programs on the market. A good one for converting video and audio files, as well as for ripping content from DVDs, is DeskShare Digital Media Converter (www.DeskShare.com). See "Ripping DVDs" and "Converting Video Files" in Chapter 24 for other suggestions.

NOTE It's also important to understand basic skills for navigating folders, especially if you want to use content from a variety of sources. Those tools and techniques are covered in Chapters 28 and 29.

Using collection folders

No rule says a movie can contain content from one videotape, or one folder, or one *anything*. Every movie you create can contain content from any combination of media files. To help keep things organized, you can create *collection folders* in Movie Maker. A collection folder is the same as a regular folder — it's jut a container in which you can store things. How you organize things into folders is entirely up to you.

The collection folders you create in Movie Maker will be in its Collections pane. To create a new collection folder:

1. If the Tasks pane is showing, click the Show Collections button.
2. In the Collections pane, right-click the Imported Media folder (or whatever folder you want to make the new folder's parent) and choose New Collection Folder.
3. Type a name for the new folder and press Enter.

Figure 25.4 shows an example. The Princess Bride folder is where I'll be importing some video from a school play. The Photos subfolder under it is where I'll be importing some still photos from that same play in upcoming examples.

FIGURE 25.4

New folders in Collections pane.

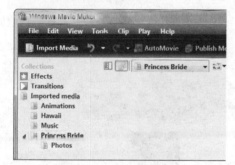

NEW FEATURE Windows Movie Maker in Vista offers several new tools and techniques for importing content.

Importing Content to Movie Maker

The first step to using content in your movie is to *import* a copy from its current folder on your hard disk into a collection folder in Movie Maker. You can do that in several ways. For example, you can drag pictures and video from Photo Gallery into a collection folder.

Import pictures and video from Photo Gallery

You can import any pictures or videos that are already in Windows Photo Gallery to a Movie Maker collections folder:

1. Open Windows Movie Maker (if it isn't already open). Then click Show Collections to open the Collections pane.

2. Optionally, create a collection folder for the content you're about to import.

3. Click the name of the folder into which you want to store the content you're about to import.

4. Open Windows Photo Gallery (click the Start button and choose All Programs ➪ Windows Photo Gallery).

5. Size and position the two programs so you can see the Photo Gallery and at least the Collections pane from Movie Maker, as in Figure 25.5. Use techniques described under "Running Programs" in Chapter 2 to move and size the program windows.

NOTE   You cannot important incompatible file formats like .MOV files. You'll need to use video conversion software to convert the files to a compatible format first. See "Converting Video Files" in Chapter 24 for more information.

FIGURE 25.5

Photo Gallery (left) and Movie Maker (right).

6. In Photo Gallery navigate to the icon(s) of a video or picture that you want to use in a movie.

7. Drag the icon for the video or folder to Movie Maker's contents pane. Optionally, select multiple items and drag them all.

TIP   You can select multiple items by dragging through them, by pressing Ctrl+A to select all items, or by using the Shift+Click or Ctrl+Click method. If you haven't learned how to do that yet, see "How to Select Icons" in Chapter 29.

8. Repeat steps 6 and 7 for as many items as you wish to import.

9. Close Photo Gallery.

To import music to movies, or import items that aren't in your Photo Gallery, use the next technique.

Import pictures, video, and music from folders

As an alternative to dragging items from Photo Gallery, you can follow these steps to import video, pictures, or music files from any folder on your hard drive:

1. In Movie Maker's Collections pane click the collection folder into which you want to import media items.

2. Click the Import Media button in the toolbar, or choose File ⇨ Import Media Items from Movie Maker's menu bar.

3. Navigate to the folder that contains music, pictures, or videos you want to use in your movies.

4. Click the item you want to import, or select multiple items to import.

5. Click the Import button.

6. Repeat these steps to import as many items as you wish.

The items you import are placed in whatever collection folder you clicked in step 1.

 The contents pane shows only the contents of the collection folder that's selected in the contents pane. So if you don't see an item you need, click its collection folder.

Import video from tape and DVD

When you click File in the menu bar you'll see the Import from Digital Video Camera option. That option works only if you have a digital video camera connected to the IEEE 1394 port or a USB 2.0 port of your computer. The camera must contain a tape and be turned on. If all those conditions are met, the Import Video program opens. Follow the instructions that appear on the screen to import video. See "Import from Videotape" later in this chapter for more information on importing video from tape.

To import from a DVD-Video disk, you'll need to first copy the .VOB files from the DVD to a folder on your hard disk. (This only works with non-copyright-protected DVDs.) In many cases you can then simply change the filename extension from .VOB to .mpg, then import the .mpg file. Unfortunately, it only works if you have the right codecs installed. Yet another alternative is to use DVD-ripping software to copy content from the DVD to a compatible AVI, MPEG, or WMV format. Then import that file. See "Ripping DVDs" in Chapter 24 for more information.

Working with Clips

At this stage of the game, you have some content with which to work. If you just want to copy from the tape directly to a movie or DVD, you can drag the one video clip to the Storyboard. Then publish it as described under "Publishing Your Movie" near the end of this chapter. But if you want to do a more creative, professional job, edit out junk you don't want, and use special effects, you'll need to spend a little time reviewing and organizing what you have. That means learning how to use clips in the contents pane.

The videos, pictures, and music files you import into Movie Maker are presented as icons called *clips*. Each collection folder has its own unique collection of clips. So to see the clips in a collection, you first need to click the collection's name in the Collections pane.

Thumbnails and Details views

You can view clips as Thumbnails or Details, as shown in Figure 25.6. In Thumbnails view, clips that represent video show the first *frame* of the clip. A video is actually a series of still pictures, called frames, presented in fast motion to give the appearance of motion. In Details view, you see only the clip name along with information like its duration.

FIGURE 25.6

Thumbnails (left) and Details (right) views.

Use the Views button or View menu to choose one view or the other. The Views button is above the contents pane, to the right of the button that shows the current collection's name (Princess Bride in the figure). You can also use the Arrange Icons By option in the View menu or the Views button to choose how you want clips ordered.

Watching video clips

To watch a video clip, double-click its icon in the Collections pane. The video clip plays in the monitor. Use the playback controls shown in Figure 25.7 to play, pause, and split a clip as summarized next.

I See a Red X!

Movie Maker doesn't contain video files, pictures, or songs. Each clip in Movie Maker *represents* a picture, music file, or video file in a folder on your hard disk. If you delete the item to which the clip refers, the clip can no longer show or play the file's content. So instead, it shows a red X in the Thumbnails view.

If you delete an underlying file without realizing that, all is not lost. If the file is still in the Recycle Bin, you can restore it from there. Once the item is back in its folder, the red X goes away and the clip is back to normal. If it's too late to restore the item from the Recycle Bin, you might be able to restore it from a backup or a shadow copy (previous version) of the file. See Chapter 33 for information on backups and previous versions.

FIGURE 25.7

FIGURE 25.7

Playback controls.

- **Seek:** Drag the button left or right to move quickly through the clip. Click anywhere along the bar to jump to a section of the clip.

- **Play/Pause:** Click to pause a playing clip. Click again to resume a pause clipped. Pressing the Spacebar has the same effect.

- **Previous Frame:** In a paused clip, moves back to the previous frame. Holding down the mouse button plays the frames backwards. On the keyboard, use Alt+left arrow or the letter J.

- **Next Frame:** In a paused clip, moves to the next frame. Holding down the mouse button plays the frames in forward motion. On the keyboard, press Alt+right arrow or the letter L.

- **Split:** Splits a single clip into two clips at the current frame. See "Splitting clips" later in this chapter for details.

> **TIP** While a clip is playing, press Alt+Enter or right-click the monitor and choose Full Screen to watch in full-screen mode. Click anywhere on the full screen view to return to Movie Maker.

Break a long video into smaller clips

If you're working with a long video clip, you might find it easier to have Movie Maker divide it into smaller, more manageable clips. That way you can get rid of the junk you don't want and organize the stuff you do want. To break a long video into shorter clips:

1. In the contents pane, click the icon of the video clip you want to make into smaller clips.
2. From Movie Maker's menu bar, choose Tools ➪ Create Clips.

Each clip represents a portion of the underlying video file. The video file itself isn't divided into multiple video files. In the Details view, the Start Time column shows where the clip starts within that larger video file. The End Time column shows where the clip ends within that larger file.

Creating a movie involves dragging the clips you want to use in the movie into the Storyboard/Timeline. This is easier to do if you familiarize yourself with what's in each clip, and get rid of any clips that you feel are useless. So let's take some time to look at how you can manage clips.

Organizing clips

As you watch each clip in a collection, you can decide whether or not you want to use it in your movie. You can also rename clips to give them names that better identify their actual content. That might help you remember what's in each clip when the first frame in the icon doesn't provide much of a clue. If you have a lot of clips, you can organize them into separate folders.

To rename the clip, right-click its name or icon in the contents pane, choose Rename, and type the new name. To keep clips in their original order, consider starting each with a number. For example, you might name them 01Clip, 02Clip, and so forth.

To delete a clip that's so bad you'd probably never use it in any movie, right-click the clip's icon and choose Remove. Optionally, you can rename the clip to something that indicates its dubious value. Or create a collection folder named Junk Clips and move all the dubious clips into that collection.

To move a clip to a different collection, drag its icon from the contents pane to the collection folder in which you want to store it.

Splitting clips

Some clips you watch may contain content you want to use, and content you don't want to use. When that happens, you can split the clip into two. Keep the good clip and delete, rename, or move the bad clip. To split a clip:

1. Double-click the clip to play it in the monitor, and pause playback near the place where you want to split the clip.
2. Use the Next and Previous buttons to get to the exact frame where you want to split. The frame that's visible in the monitor will be the first frame in the new clip.
3. Click the Split button in the playback controls.

Now you can rename the two clips to your liking. Or get rid of the bad chunk that was in the original clip.

 You can use the same technique to break a long audio clip into smaller chunks. Of course, you won't see anything in the monitor when you play an audio clip. But you can hear it.

Combining clips

When you use Create Clips to split a long movie into shorter clips, you might not agree with the way Movie Maker made the splits. For example, you might end up with a clip that's only a couple seconds long. The next clip in the collection continues the same scene, and it too is only a couple of seconds long. You might want to re-join those into a single, longer clip. To do that:

1. Select (click) the first clip.
2. Hold down the Ctrl key and click the next clip in sequence so both clips are selected.
3. Choose Clip ⇨ Combine from the menu bar to combine the two clips into one.

If you try to combine two clips that don't represent adjacent frames in the underlying video, the Combine option will be disabled. That's because you can only combine contiguous clips. But don't worry, that won't prevent you from showing the clips side-by-side in your movie. You can show the clips in any order you like just by dragging them to the Storyboard/Timeline. That's when you actually create your movie, as discussed next.

Making an AutoMovie

Once you have some clips in your collection, you can create an AutoMovie. This approach doesn't give you much control over the order of clips, special effects, or titles. But it is a quick and easy way to create a basic movie. Here's how it works:

1. In the contents pane, select the clips you want to include in the AutoMovie. Or press Ctrl+A or choose Edit ➪ Select All to select all the clips.

2. Click the AutoMovie button or choose Tools ➪ AutoMovie from the menu.

3. Choose an editing style from the list of options provided.

4. To add a title to the movie, click Enter a title for the movie and type a title.

5. Optionally, if you selected a sound clip in the contents pane, click Select audio or background music, then choose an audio clip from the drop-down button.

6. Click Create AutoMovie and wait a few seconds.

The title, selected clips, and some special effects appear in the Storyboard. To watch the AutoMovie, choose Play ➪ Play Storyboard from the menu. If you like the AutoMovie, you can save it by choosing File ➪ Publish Movie from the menu bar. See "Publishing Your Movie" later in the chapter for more information on ways that you can publish your movie.

If you're not too crazy about the AutoMovie and want to try a different style for it, choose Edit ➪ Clear Storyboard. Then repeat steps 1–6 in the preceding list using different settings in the AutoMovie options.

Although the AutoMovie feature is okay for creating a quick-and-easy movie from clips in a collection, most people will want more control over the content of their movies. That's what the rest of this chapter is about. To get off to a clean start, choose Edit ➪ Clear Storyboard from the menu so the Storyboard/Timeline is empty and you have a clean start from which to create your movie.

Creating Your Movie

Like every movie you see in a theater or on TV, the movie you create will be a series of scenes. To make the movie interesting, you want to avoid having the scenes played out in some random order. Rather, you want to try to organize scenes to give the movie a sense of having a beginning, middle, and end, like a story. You organize your scenes into a movie by adding them to the Storyboard/Timeline (also called the *workspace*). The Storyboard/Timeline determines exactly which clips will be part of the movie, as well as the order in which they'll be played.

There are three ways to view the contents of the Storyboard/Timeline. From the menu bar, choose View ➪ Storyboard or View ➪ Timeline. Or click the workspace button (see Figure 25.8) and choose Storyboard or Timeline. Or if you prefer the keyboard, press Ctrl+T.

FIGURE 25.8

Choose Storyboard or Timeline.

- ■ **Storyboard:** Shows only the first frame of each clip. Good for setting up the basic order in which you want clips to play.
- ■ **Timeline:** Shows much more information about the movie. Use to add music, titles and credits, and other advanced features.

> **TIP**   To change the height of the Storyboard/Timeline, drag its upper border up or down.

The movie you create will come entirely from the Storyboard/Timeline. Other content in the Collections pane isn't part of the movie. That's just stuff you *can* use in a movie. To create a movie, you drag clips from the contents pane into the Storyboard/Timeline. The left-to-right order of the clips in the Storyboard/Timeline represents the order that the clips will appear in the finished movie.

Adding video clips to the Storyboard/Timeline

The first step is usually to get all the video clips that you want your movie to show into the Storyboard. You can use any clips from any collection—they don't all have to come from the same collection. To add a clip to the Storyboard, do whichever is most convenient for you:

- ■ Drag any one clip from the contents pane to the Storyboard.
- ■ Or right-click any one clip and choose Add To Storyboard.
- ■ Or select multiple clips and drag any one of them to the Storyboard, or right-click any one of them and choose Add to Storyboard, or press Ctrl+D.

Figure 25.9 shows an example in which I've added many clips to the Storyboard.

FIGURE 25.9

Video clips in the Storyboard.

Previewing your movie

To see how your movie is shaping up, play the Storyboard/Timeline using whichever technique you like:

- Click the Rewind Storyboard button, then the Play Storyboard button near the top of the Storyboard (to the right of the Storyboard button).
- Or choose Play ⇨ Rewind Storyboard then Play ⇨ Play Storyboard from the menu bar.
- To stop playback, choose Play ⇨ Stop from the menu bar or press Ctrl+K.
- Or press Ctrl+Q to rewind to the beginning and then Ctrl+W to play the Storyboard.

The entire movie plays in the monitor. You can use the playback controls under the monitor to pause, rewind, and so forth.

Editing the Storyboard

If there's anything you don't like about your movie, you can change the contents of the Storyboard to change the movie. Here's how:

- To remove a clip from the Storyboard, right-click it and choose Remove. Doing so only removes it from the Storyboard, not its collection.
- To move a clip in the Storyboard, drag it left or right.
- To add more video clips to the Storyboard, use any technique described under "Adding video clips to the Storyboard/Timeline."
- To clear the Storyboard and start over, choose Edit ⇨ Clear Storyboard from the menu bar.
- To undo your most recent action, click Undo in the toolbar, or press Ctrl+Z, or choose Edit ⇨ Undo from Movie Maker's menu bar.

There's no hurry on getting things just right in the Storyboard. Your movie won't even exist until you publish it, as discussed later in this chapter.

Create media information for your movie

To give your movie an author name, rating, and description:

1. Choose File ⇨ Project Properties from the menu bar.
2. Type a title, author name, copyright name, rating (like G or PG), and description.
3. Click OK.

The media information will be visible in folders, Media Player, and Photo Gallery after you publish the movie.

Saving your work

The clips in the Storyboard are called a *project*, because they represent a work in progress. Depending on how complex and fancy your movie is, you may not be able to complete it in one sitting. You can save your project and resume work on it at any time in the future. To save your project:

1. Choose File ⇨ Save Project from Movie Maker's menu bar.
2. If this is the first time you've saved the project, a Save As dialog box will open so you can decide where you want to put the project and what you want to name it.

3. Navigate to the folder in which you want to put the project (the default is your Documents folder).

4. Type a brief descriptive name for the project in the File Name box.

5. Click the Save button.

The project is saved to the folder you specified. Note that the project is not a movie that you can play or copy to DVD. It's simply information about the contents of the Storyboard/Timeline at the moment you saved. This allows you to create and start a project, then resume work on it at any time without actually creating a movie. That's very handy because in large movies it might not be possible to do everything you want in one sitting.

When you close Movie Maker, be sure to choose Yes when asked whether you want to save your changes. Otherwise changes you made since the last save won't be saved.

Resuming work on a project

Once your work is saved, you can close Movie Maker. To resume work on a project at any time in the future, navigate to the folder in which you saved the project and open the icon that represents the project. The icon will look like the example in Figure 25.10. The .MSWMM filename extension will only be visible if your Folder Options are set such that extensions are visible.

FIGURE 25.10

Icon for a saved Movie Maker project.

Princess Bride
Project.MSWMM

As an alternative to opening the project icon, open Windows Movie Maker. Then click File on the menu bar and click the project's name at the bottom of the File menu. Or choose File ➪ Open Project and use the Open dialog box to open the project.

> **TIP** To have Movie Maker open your last-saved project automatically at startup, choose Tools ➪ Options from Movie Maker's menu bar. Then select (check) **Open last project on startup and click OK.**

Using Photos in Movies

Your movie can contain any photos or still pictures that you import to Movie Maker. Each photo appears for a specified amount of time. If you add several pictures in a row, they appear like a slide show within the movie. Before you add any pictures to your movie, you can choose how long you want each picture to appear, and a duration for any transition effects between the pictures. (We'll talk about transition effects a little later in the chapter.) To set default picture and transition durations:

1. Choose Tools ➪ Options from Movie Maker's menu.

2. In the Options dialog box that opens, click the Advanced tab.

3. Set a Picture duration for each picture (the default is 5 seconds).

4. Set a Transition duration for transitions between pictures (the default it 1.25 seconds).

5. Click OK.

The setting you specified will be applied to any pictures you add to the Storyboard/Timeline. Before we get to that, let's look at how you can take any single frame from a video and turn it into a still photograph.

Making photos from video

If you've ever wished you could take just one frame from a video and make it into a still photograph, you can stop wishing. That's easy to do in Movie Maker. Here's how it works:

1. In the contents pane, double-click the video that contains the frame you want to turn into a photo.

2. As the video plays in the monitor, click the Pause button when you get to where you want to make a photo. Use the Seek bar and Previous and Next buttons, as necessary, to get to the exact frame you want to make into a photo.

3. From the menu bar, choose Tools ⇨ Take picture from preview.

4. Enter a filename for the photo and click Save.

You can repeat these steps to make as many photos from as many video clips as you like. Each photo will be placed in your Pictures folder. Each photo is also added to the contents pane, so you can easily add it to your movie. In Thumbnails view, you can tell which icons represent photos by the missing film holes. For example, in Figure 25.11, the icon on the left is a still photo. The icon on the right is a video clip.

FIGURE 25.11

Photo (left) and video clip (right).

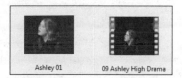

Ashley 01   09 Ashley High Drama

TIP If you need to crop or touch up the photo, find it in Photo Gallery, click Fix, make your changes, return to Photo Gallery, and then close Photo Gallery. The changes will carry over to the copy of the picture that's in Movie Maker.

Adding photos to the Storyboard

To add a still photo from the contents pane to your movie, just drag its icon onto the Storyboard at the place where you want it to appear during the movie. If you like, you can add several still photos to the beginning or end of the movie to act as a backdrop slide show for titles and credits. You can also place photos anywhere within the Storyboard to act as breaks between scenes, and perhaps for titles within the movie.

To see how your photos will look in the final movie, play the Storyboard. If you don't want to watch the whole movie, click the first photo clip in the Storyboard (or the clip to the left of the Storyboard), and then click the Play Storyboard button in Storyboard to play the movie from that clip forward.

Adding Titles and Credits

Titles and credits make for a nice addition to a movie. They're easy to add too. You can add an opening title to the start of the movie. You can add scrolling credits to the end of a movie. You can also add titles at any point within the movie. You can have the title play with a solid color background. Or have it play on top of a clip or photo in the Storyboard. To get started:

- If you want to add a title to the beginning of the movie, just click anywhere in the Storyboard.
- If you want the title to appear before, or on, a Storyboard clip, click the clip on which (or before which) the title should appear.

The rest of the process goes like this:

1. Choose Tools ➪ Titles and Credits from the menu bar.
2. Choose where you want the clip to appear by clicking the appropriate option under "Where do you want to add a title?"
3. Click Change the title animation. You'll see a list of possible options. Some are for a one-line title, some are for a two-line title, and some are for credits at the end of the movie. Click each one to see an example of it in the monitor.
4. When you find an animation you like, click its name. Then click Edit the title text.
5. Type the text of the title in the space provided.
6. Optionally, click Change the text font and color to get to the options shown in Figure 25.12.

FIGURE 25.12

Choose title font, color, size, and such.

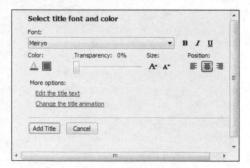

---

7. Use the controls provided to choose the font, text color, background color, transparency, size, and alignment of the title text. Each time you change a setting, the title plays in the monitor.
8. When you're happy with your title, click Add Title.

If you didn't overlay the title onto a clip, it appears as a new clip in the Storyboard. If you did overlay the title, you'll automatically be switched over to the Timeline view. But you can press Ctrl+T or click the Timeline button and choose Storyboard to get back to the Storyboard view.

To see how the title will look in your finished movie, right-click it or the Storyboard clip to its left, and choose Play Storyboard.

To change a title clip, right-click it and choose Edit Title. To remove a title clip, right-click it and choose Delete. If the title is an overlay, you'll need to switch to the Timeline view to change or remove the title. You'll discover how that works in a moment. First, some more cool things you can do in the Storyboard.

 **TIP**   To make an overlay title play longer, widen its clip in the Title Overlay track of the Timeline view. To make it play for less time, narrow the clip.

Adding Transition Effects

A transition effect is a special effect that plays between two clips. Windows Movie Maker comes with several transition effects. To see their names, click Transitions in the Collections pane. Or choose Transitions from the Location button in the toolbar. Each icon in the contents pane represents a transition effect you can use between any two clips in the Storyboard.

To preview how a transition will look, double-click its name or icon in the contents pane. The transition will play out against a couple of sample photos in the monitor.

When you find a transition you like, drag it to the small square between any two clips in the Storyboard. The square will change to show the transition's icon. Figure 25.13 shows an example in which I've already added one transition effect between two clips in the Storyboard.

FIGURE 25.13

Transition effects.

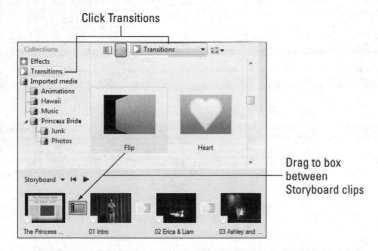

Click Transitions

Drag to box between Storyboard clips

To see how a transition will look in your movie, right-click the clip to the left of the transition box in the Storyboard and choose Play Storyboard. The effect will play between the end of the current clip and the start of the next clip.

To change a transition effect, just drag another effect icon onto the same box in the Storyboard. To remove a transition effect, right-click its box in the Storyboard and choose Remove. It's easy, fun, and worth playing around with for a while. You can't do any harm, and you can change or remove any effect you don't like.

Adding Video Effects

Video effects are special effects applied to video clips, photos, or titles in the Storyboard. To see the effects available to you, click Effects in the Collections pane, or choose Effects from the Location button in the toolbar. Each effect is represented by an icon and name in the contents pane.

To see an example of how an effect looks when applied to a clip, double-click its name or icon. The effect is played against a photo in the monitor. To apply a special effect to a video or photo clip in the Storyboard, drag its icon from the contents pane onto the clip in the Storyboard as illustrated in Figure 25.14.

FIGURE 25.14

Video effects.

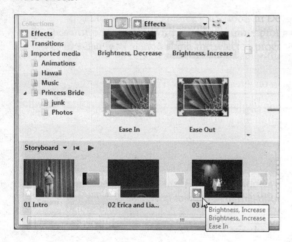

When you apply a video effect, the star in the clip's lower-left corner brightens. You can add up to six effects per clip. To see what effects you've added to a clip, point to the star on the clip. Near the bottom of Figure 25.14 you see an example where I'm pointing to a clip to which I've added Brightness, Increase effects, and an Ease In Effect.

To see how applied effects will look in the movie, right-click the Storyboard clip to which you've applied effects and choose Play Storyboard. The clip will play in the Monitor with the effects applied.

To add, change, or remove effects, right-click the Storyboard clip and choose Effects. The Effects dialog box for that clip opens, like the example in Figure 25.15. To add an effect to the clip, click its name in the left column and click Add. To remove an effect, click its name in the right column and choose Remove.

FIGURE 25.15

Effects box for a Storyboard clip.

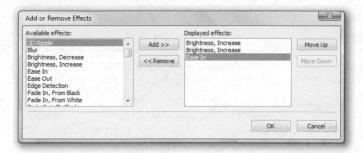

Brighten/darken clips

The Brightness, Increase and Brightness, Decrease effects are additive. For example, if a clip is too dark, you can add one Brightness, Increase effect to it to brighten it a little. Play the clip to see how it looks. If it's still too dark, you can add a second Brightness, Increase effect to brighten even more. You can apply a maximum of six effects to any one clip.

 Brightness, Increase and Brightness, Decrease cancel each other out. So don't bother adding both effects to a single Storyboard clip!

Slow motion/fast motion

To show a clip in slow motion, drag a Slow Down, Half effect to it. Multiple effects are additive. So if you drag two Slow Down, Half effects to a Storyboard clip, it will play at 1/4th its normal speed. Add a third, and it will play at 1/8th its normal speed, and so forth.

To make a clip play in fast motion, drag one or more Speed Up, Half effects to it. As with Brightness clips, a Slow Down, Half and Speed Up, Half effect applied to the same clip will have no effect, because the two effects cancel each other out.

Feel free to experiment with different effects and combinations of effects. Have fun, explore, and don't be afraid. You can't do any harm just by trying things out. And you're never committed to using the clips you've applied. If you don't like an effect, just remove it from the Storyboard clip.

 To remove all effects from a Storyboard clip, right-click the star in the clip and choose Remove Effects.

Instant Slow-Motion Replay

To make an instant replay of a Storyboard clip, right-click the clip and choose Copy. Then right-click the same clip and choose Paste. You end up with two copies of the same clip side-by-side. You can then apply Slow Down, Half effects to the second clip to make it play in slow motion. Feel free to add a title (and perhaps a sound effect) between the two clips to announce the upcoming instant replay clip!

So far you've been able to add all kinds of embellishments to your movie using the Storyboard. Some of the more advanced techniques, and fine-tuning, will require using the Timeline. So we'll take a moment to discuss that next.

Using the Timeline

The Timeline view of a project gives you more refined control over your movie. To switch from the Storyboard to the Timeline, click the Storyboard button and choose Timeline, or press Ctrl+T, or choose View ➪ Timeline.

Initially you'll see three tracks named Video, Audio/Music, and Title Overlay. If you click the + sign next to Video, that will expand to five tracks, as shown in Figure 25.16. The figure also points out tools you'll use in the Timeline to further enhance your cinematic masterpiece.

FIGURE 25.16

The Timeline.

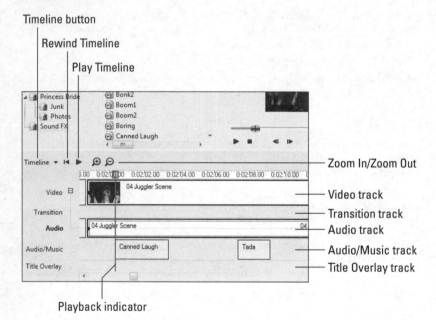

Here's a quick overview of what each tool and track provides:

- **Timeline button:** Switch between Storyboard and Timeline view.
- **Rewind Timeline:** Rewind to start of timeline.
- **Play Timeline:** Play timeline from play indicator forward.
- **Zoom In:** Magnify the timeline to see more detail. You can keep clicking until the icon is disabled (dimmed), meaning the clips are at their largest possible size.
- **Zoom Out:** Compress timeline to see more clips, fewer details. You can keep clicking until the icon is disabled (dimmed), at which point the clips are at their smallest possible size.

- **Playback indicator:** Indicates where playback is occurring, or will occur when you click Play Timeline. Use the handle at the top of the indicator to drag through the movie.

- **Video track:** Contains the video and photo clips in the order they're played. The size of each clip represents the amount of time it takes in the movie. (Long-playing clips are wider than short-playing clips.)

- **Transition track:** Contains clips representing transition effects added to the movie.

- **Audio track:** Each clip represents the sound that accompanies the video clip above it. You can control the volume of a video clip's sound by right-clicking its audio clip and choosing Volume.

- **Audio/Music track:** Shows custom music or audio that plays in addition to the audio from the original videotape.

- **Title Overlay track:** Each clip represents an overlay title that plays on top of content in the Video track.

The ruler above the Video track measures time. So the width of a clip matches its duration in the movie. In other words, the wider the clip, the longer it plays in the movie. So you get a visual representation of how long each clip plays as you look through clips in the Timeline.

Adding Audio to Movies

Any video you capture from a video camera, VCR, or TV will already have a sound track associated with it. You can replace the sound entirely with your own sound. Or you can keep that sound and add additional sound of your own, like background music. You can also add sound effects and voice narration.

If you have music and sound effects that you'd like to use in multiple movies, you might want to consider creating separate collection folders for those items. Just to keep things organized. See "Using collection folders" and "Import pictures, video, and music from folders" near the start of this chapter for details on creating folders and importing audio files.

Finding Sound Effects Online

You can find free sound effects files online. But it isn't always easy because many sites will make you wade through countless ads, sign-ups, false leads, and so forth. Here are three sites I've used that are free of the obnoxious hoopla:

- www.Frogstar.com/wav/effects.asp
- www.PartnersInRhyme.com
- www.IloveWavs.com

When you find a link to a sound file, click it to listen. Then click the Back button in your browser. If you want to download the file, right-click the same link and choose Save Target As. Navigate to the folder in which you want to store the file and click Save. Do that for as many files as you like. That will get the file into folders on your hard drive. Before you can use them in a movie, you'll need to import them to Movie Maker.

Adding sound effects

To add a sound effect or other audio file to your movie, first play your movie up to about the point where you want to insert the sound file. That way the playback indicator will be near the place where you want the sound to play, giving you a sense of where to place the clip. Then drag the audio clip from the contents pane to the Audio/Music pane at about where you want it to play.

You can add sound effect clips wherever you think they're appropriate (or funny). Figure 25.17 shows an example where I've added a couple of sound effect audio clips to the Audio/Music track.

FIGURE 25.17

Sound effect clips in the Audio/Music track.

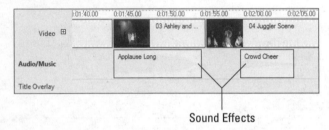

Sound Effects

 **TIP**   If a short audio clip is too narrow to work with in the Audio/Music track, click the Zoom In button until the clip is wide enough to see.

To test the effect, drag the playback indicator a little to the left and then play the movie from there. If the effect starts too early, drag it a little to the right. If it starts too late, drag it a little to the left. It may take a little trial-and-error to get it placed just right.

Adding narration to a movie

If you have a microphone or headset that works with your computer, you can record your own voice narration and add it to your movie. Plug in your microphone or headset as per the manufacturer's instructions. If necessary, adjust the volume and mute controls on the microphone to make sure that it can pick up your spoken voice.

Narration Tips

Narrating is more difficult than most people think. Not difficult in a technical sense, but difficult in that you may find yourself stumbling over your words as you try to speak into the microphone while watching your movie. It often helps to write a script to read from while doing your narration.

Also, rather than trying to narrate the entire movie in a single clip, consider creating multiple short clips. If you mess up a short clip, at least you only have to re-record that clip rather than the whole thing!

To start narration, choose Tools ⇨ Narrate Timeline from the menu. You'll see the options shown in Figure 25.18. Before you record, talk into the microphone and adjust the Input Level slider so that at your loudest spoken voice the indicator is bright green but not quite going into red. The red color indicates that the sound is so loud (to the microphone) it may be distorted on playback.

FIGURE 25.18

Narration options.

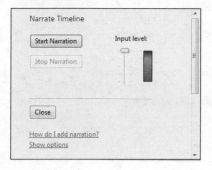

Next, drag the playback indictor or play the movie up to the point where you want to begin your narration. Then click the Start Narration button and speak your lines. Click Stop Narration when you've finished speaking your lines. Each clip of narration is saved as an audio file in the Narration folder for the movie. If you plan to create multiple narration clips, you can name them in sequence (for example, Narration 01, Narration 02, and so forth).

Each spoken narration clip also appears as a clip in the Audio/Music track. Figure 25.19 shows an example where I've recorded one short bit of voice narration.

FIGURE 25.19

Narration clip in the Audio/Music track.

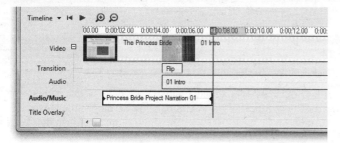

Adding background music

Imported music files are audio files that you add to the Audio/Music track like sound effects and voice narration. As always, you need to import a song to Movie Maker before you can add it to a movie. Remember, you can't import protected content or files that aren't compatible with Movie Maker. See "Things you can use in movies" and "Import pictures, video, and music from folders" at the start of this chapter for specifics.

If you intend to play background music throughout the entire movie, you cannot use sound effects or voice narration in the same Audio/Music track. But you can get around that problem by doing everything in your movie except the background music, and saving the completed movie without the background music. Then, import the finished movie as a new video and drag it to the Storyboard. Switch to the Timeline view. The entire Audio/Music track will be available because sound effects and voice narration are part of the video's Audio track in the imported movie.

With the Audio/Music track free, drag any song from the contents pane to the Audio/Music track of the Timeline. If the song runs longer than the movie, put the mouse pointer on the right edge of the clip until the two-headed arrow appears. Then drag to the left so that the music clip is the same length as the movie. Figure 25.20 shows an example.

FIGURE 25.20

Music in the Audio/Music track.

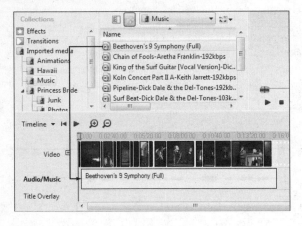

Fading music in and out

You can make any audio clip fade in and/or fade out. This is especially useful when you're working with portions of music clips, because it prevents the music from starting or ending abruptly during the movie. To add fading, right-click the audio clip in the Audio/Music track. You'll see the shortcut menu shown in Figure 25.21.

FIGURE 25.21

Music in the Audio/Music track.

Choose Fade In from the shortcut menu to have the music fade in. Choose Fade Out to have the music fade out. To do both, right-click and choose one option. Then right-click again and choose the other option. To clear a setting, repeat the process to remove the checkmark from the selected option.

Adjusting relative volume

When you add background music to a movie, it will play along with audio from the video's Audio track. You can adjust their relative volumes so that neither is too overpowering. For example, background music should be toned down when you don't want it to overpower people's voices and such from the video.

To adjust the relative volume of the tracks, play the movie from the start. While the movie is playing, choose Tools ➪ Audio Levels from the menu bar. The Audio Levels dialog box shown in Figure 25.22 opens.

FIGURE 25.22

Audio Levels dialog box.

Drag the slider left or right to adjust the relative volume of the two Audio tracks. When things sound good, just close the Audio Levels box. Save the project to save the setting you chose.

More Timeline Refinements

There's really no limit to how you can present content in your movie. After you've practiced and mastered the basics, you can use features of the Timeline to further control the exact timing and placement of content in your movie. By "basics" I mean topics discussed earlier in this chapter, such as:

- Importing content to Movie Maker
- Splitting clips (so you can make shorter clips from long ones)
- Adjusting the height of the Timeline

- Using the +/- button to the right of the Video label to show/hide the Audio and Transition tracks
- Using Zoom In, Zoom Out, and the horizontal scroll bar under the Timeline (Choose View ⇨ Zoom to Fit or press F9 to size the Timeline clips to fit within the program window.)
- Dragging and right-clicking clips
- Playing the movie from the playback indicator position to review the change you just made

Never presume that a change you just made is exactly what you want. Always review that portion of the movie to verify that you achieved the expected effect. Save the project when you're happy with the results of the change.

Trimming and extending clips

Changing the width of a clip in the storyboard changes how long it plays in a movie. To change the width of a clip, get the mouse pointer to its right edge (in the Timeline) so you see the two-headed arrow as in Figure 25.23. Then drag left to shorten the clip, or right to lengthen it (if possible).

FIGURE 25.23

Trim or extend a Timeline clip.

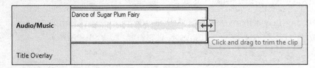

With video and music clips, you can only shorten the clip. You cannot extend its play time. When you shorten such a clip, the content plays up to the point where the clip ends.

 To split a clip in the Timeline, click the clip so it's selected. Then move the playback indicator to where you want to split and click the Split button in the monitor.

With Timeline clips that represent photos, transition effects, or titles, you can either shorten or extend the clip. The full content of the clip plays within the time that the clip's width specifies.

Overlapping clips

You can overlap clips in the Video, Audio/Music, or Title Overlay tracks. Doing so creates a *fade transition* between them. During that transition, the first scene in the pair fades out as the second scene fades in. The duration of the transition matches the width of the overlapping scenes. You cannot place one clip on top of another within a track. But you can overlap them to some extent.

To overlay, just click the clip that's on the right side of the two you want to overlap. Then drag the clip to the left. A sloping blue line shows the amount of overlay, as in Figure 25.24.

FIGURE 25.24

Overlap Timeline clips.

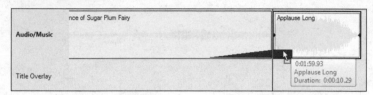

If you try to overlap more than is allowed, the overlap line will disappear and the second clip may jump back to its original position. So you may have to use a little trial-and-error to find exactly how far you can go with the overlap.

> **NOTE** Video clips with transition effects applied are already overlapped. The transition effect plays during the overlap.

When you want to move a clip only slightly, and the mouse isn't giving you enough control, you can nudge the selected clip. Press Ctrl+Shift+B (or choose Clip ➪ Nudge Left) to move the clip slightly to the left. Press Ctrl+Shift+N or choose Clip ➪ Nudge Right to move the clip slightly to the right.

Setting trim points

As a rule, the easiest way to control the duration of video scenes is by splitting and combining clips before you start adding them to the Storyboard/Timeline. But that's not the only way to do it. You might have a clip that you intend to use in several movies. But in the current movie you only want to use a portion of that clip. You can still add the whole clip to the current project. Then set trim points to indicate which portion of that clip should play.

For any Timeline clip, you can set a Start or End (or both) trim point. The difference is as follows:

- **Trim Beginning:** Determines where the clip will start to play. Content to the left of the start trim point, within the clip, won't play in the final movie.
- **Trim End:** Determines where the clip will stop playing. Content to the right of the end trim point won't play in the final movie.

To set a trim point in the Timeline, click the clip you want to trim. Play the clip to where you want to set a trim point and pause. Then choose Clip ➪ Trim Beginning or Clip ➪ Trim End to set the trim point. Everything to the left of a Start trim point disappears from the Timeline. Everything to the right of an End trim point disappears. If you change your mind, click the trimmed Timeline clip and choose Clip ➪ Clear Trim Points.

Replacing a video's audio content

You can totally replace the audio portion of any video clip with audio content of your own choosing. You need to get your custom audio clip directly under the video clip in the Video track. Click the + sign if necessary so you can see both the Audio and the Audio/Music tracks.

Next, right-click the audio for the video clip (in the Audio track) and choose Mute, as in Figure 25.25. Then right-click the corresponding clip in the Audio/Music track, choose Volume, and set it to whatever volume you like.

FIGURE 25.25

Mute an audio clip.

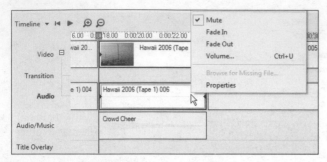

> **TIP** If you drag a video clip from the contents pane to the Audio/Music track, only that clip's audio will play. No video from that clip will appear in the movie.

Changing tiles and credits to overlays

Titles that you add to the start of the movie, and credits you add to the end, play against a colored background. You can get a more interesting effect by having them play against some other content — perhaps a slide show of still photos from the video. The first step, of course, is to add the photos to the start or end of the movie. Then, just drag the title or credit clip from the Video track down into the Title Overlay track. Figure 25.26 shows the difference.

FIGURE 25.26

Credits at end (top) and as overlay (bottom).

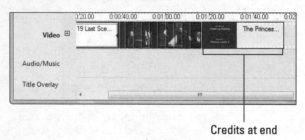

Credits at end

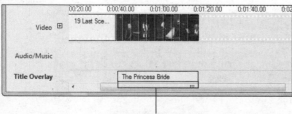

Credits as overlay

Once the title or credits clip is in the Title Overlay track, drag it left or right to determine where you want it to play. Widen or narrow the clip to determine its duration.

Publishing Your Movie

The clips in Movie Maker's Storyboard/Timeline are just a project — a work in progress. When you're happy with how the Storyboard/Timeline plays from beginning to end, you'll use the project to create your movie. (But don't forget to save the project first, in case you want to make changes or more movies from it in the future.)

The act of going from clips in the Storyboard/Timeline to an actual movie file you can share with others and watch on TV is called *publishing* the movie. You end up with a file on the hard disk you can share with other people through e-mail or on disk. You can also burn the movie straight to DVD if you have a DVD burner, a DVD Decoder, and the Ultimate or Premium Home Edition of Windows Vista.

TIP   If you can watch DVD movies on your computer, you already have the necessary DVD Decoder software. Otherwise, you can purchase and download one from the Windows Media Web site at www.WMPlugins.com.

If you don't have the Ultimate or Home edition, but do have DVD-burning software, you can publish your movie to one or more files. Then use your third-party DVD-burning software to burn the movie file to DVD. If you have a CD burner, you can also copy the finished movie to a CD for others to watch from the CD drive in their own computer.

The published movie will be an exact duplicate of what plays on Movie Maker when you play your Storyboard/Timeline. So step 1, of course, is to make sure you're happy with that movie before you publish.

Things to consider

When you publish a movie, you'll be given several options on how you want the resulting file to be formatted. These are basically trade-offs between movie quality and file size. The term *quality* in this context has to do with the size of the video onscreen, and how crisp and clear the video looks and the audio sounds. The standard rule of thumb applies: The higher the quality the larger the file.

Of course, you're not limited to making only one movie from your project. You can make as many as you want, all at different qualities if you like, so you're not making any lifelong commitments here or anything. But here are all the things to consider when choosing a quality.

File type

Your two basic options here are Windows Media Video (WMV) and DV-AVI (uncompressed digital video). DV-AVI produces better quality at the cost of a potentially enormous file. For DV-AVI you can also choose between NTSC (American television format) and PAL (European television format).

Bit rate

This setting defines the basic visual and audio quality in terms of clarity and crispness. The higher the bit rate, the better the quality, and the larger the file. Bit rate is measured in Mbps (megabits per second) and Kbps (kilobits per second). One Mbps equals roughly 1,000 Kbps.

If you choose a DV-AVI format, the bit rate will be equal to that of commercial DVD videos, 28.6 Mbps. Any other choice will produce a lower bit rate in the range of 120 Kbps (low quality) to 8.2 Mbps (very good quality).

Display size

This setting determines the dimensions on the screen. For standard TV choose at least 720 x 480 pixels. For widescreen TV choose 1,440 x 1,080 pixels. For playback on a computer monitor you can choose 640 x 480 (large) or 320 x 240 (small).

Aspect ratio

The aspect ratio is the basic shape of the video. For standard TVs and computer monitors use a 4:3 aspect ratio. For widescreen use 16:9.

Frames per second

The Frames per Second (fps) setting determines how many frames per second play while watching the video, where each frame is like one still picture on a movie film reel. The standard is 30fps for American TVs (NTSC) and 24fps for European (PAL). You can go to a lower rate to reduce the file size, but the video won't play quite as smoothly.

You'll make your quality decisions when you go through the steps to publish the movie. So let's do that next.

Publishing to a file

You'll probably want to publish a copy of your movie to a folder on your hard disk, even if you intend to publish to other media later. That will be your own personal copy to watch or to share with others through methods that Movie Maker doesn't provide. So let's start with that type of publishing:

1. Click the Publish button in Movie Maker's toolbar or choose File ➪ Publish Movie from the menu bar.

2. In the Publish Movie page that opens, choose My Computer and click Next.

3. Enter a filename for your movie and choose the folder in which you want to place it. Then click Next.

4. On the next page (see Figure 25.27), specify your movie quality. Choose an option and look to the Movie Settings and File Size boxes for details about the option you've selected. Try different options until you find one you like, then click Next.

5. Click the Publish button and wait.

FIGURE 25.27

Movie Settings page.

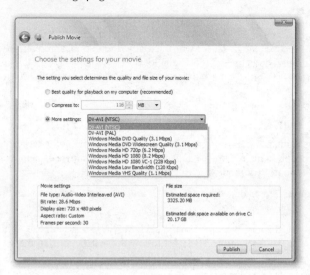

When the publishing is done, you can close Movie Maker (don't forget to save any changes to your project, if prompted). If you published to a folder that Photo Gallery watches, you'll find the movie there. Otherwise you can open the folder to which you published. The icon for the movie will show Media Player's logo (or whatever program is the default for the file type). Open that icon to watch the movie.

Icons for movies and projects

Don't confuse the icon for a finished movie with icons that represent Movie Maker projects. Opening a project opens Movie Maker with the clips in the Storyboard/Timeline. Sending that project file to someone else won't do them any good. The movie icon, shown at left in Figure 25.28, is the one that represents the finished movie that you can share with others.

FIGURE 25.28

Icons for a movie (left) and project (right).

Feel free to save the movie with different settings so you can see how these things play out in real life. Just be sure to give each movie a different filename so you don't keep overwriting the same movie and end up with only one.

 The Premium and Ultimate editions of Vista come with a free DVD-authoring program named DVD Maker.

Publishing to DVD

You can publish your movie straight to DVD, providing you have all the right hardware and software as described at the start of this section. Movie Maker won't actually do the publishing directly though. Instead, after you click the Publish button and choose DVD as the location, Windows DVD Maker opens and you'll use that program to burn the DVD. See "Using Windows DVD Maker" in Chapter 32 for the full story on that program.

Publishing to CD or tape

Publishing to CD or tape is similar to publishing to a file. To publish to CD, put a writeable CD into your CD drive. To publish to tape, put a blank Mini DV tape into your digital movie camera, connect the camera to the computer, and turn it on in VCR mode (not camera mode).

 You cannot publish to analog videotape (VHS, Video 8, or Hi-8).

When the CD is in the drive or the tape is in the camera, click Movie Maker's Publish button or choose File ➪ Publish Movie. Choose the destination. Then just follow the instructions on the screen.

Publishing movies for e-mail

Before you try to e-mail a movie to friends, you should be aware of your e-mail attachment size limits and set that accordingly, as described under "Choosing program options" near the start of this chapter.

The technique described here won't work with all e-mail clients. If you use Web mail rather than an e-mail client, this approach won't work. But you can save a copy of the movie to your computer as you go through the steps. Then attach that copy to an e-mail message using the standard method provided by your ISP.

NOTE   If you don't use Outlook Express or Outlook (or don't know what you use), and need help with e-mail attachments, contact your ISP for more information. They're the only people who know the details of the e-mail service they provide.

To publish a movie to an e-mail attachment from the project that's in your Storyboard/Timeline:

1. Click Movie Maker's Publish button or choose File ➪ Publish Movie.

2. Choose E-mail and click Next.

3. Wait while Movie Maker creates the movie. Then on the next page you'll be given two options you can choose or ignore (they have no effect on e-mailing the movie):

   ▪ **Watch the movie:** Choose this option to preview the movie so you know what your recipients will see.

   ▪ **Save a copy of the movie on my computer:** Choose this option to save a copy of the generated movie to your own computer.

4. Click Attach Movie.

5. An empty e-mail message with the movie already attached opens. Fill in the recipient e-mail address (or multiple addresses separated by semicolons).

6. Optionally, change the Subject line to words of your own choosing.

7. Fill in the body of the message. Figure 25.29 shows an example with all the pieces in place.

FIGURE 25.29

E-mail message with movie attached.

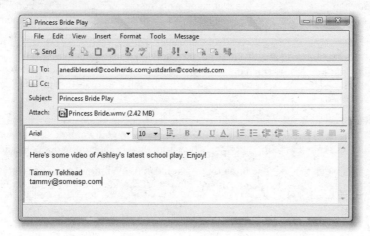

8. Click Send.

If your e-mail client isn't configured to send messages immediately, open it and click its Send/Receive button to send the message from your Outbox.

If you need to create a small movie to attach to e-mail messages with an incompatible e-mail program, go through the steps to publish a movie to a file. On the Movie Settings page, choose the Compress To: option and set the size to the maximum attachment size your ISP allows, and publish the movie. You can then attach the resulting file to an e-mail message using whatever method your ISP provides.

If you have any problems, or don't know how to attach files to e-mail messages, contact your ISP. They're the only ones who can tell you how to use the e-mail service they provide.

Import from Videotape

You may be wondering why I'm talking about importing video from tape at the end of this chapter, after I've already been through the whole process of creating a movie in Movie Maker. It's simply because you don't use Windows Movie Maker to import from tape. Rather, you use the new Import Video Wizard program. You can launch that program from Windows Movie Maker. But it's not entirely necessary to do so. When you connect your digital video camera to the computer, and turn the camera on in VCR mode, the Import Video Wizard might start automatically.

The process described here works only with digital video cameras that use tape (usually Mini DV tape). If you want to get video from an older analog camera, a VCR, VHS tape, Video 8, or Hi 8 tape, see the sidebar "Capturing Analog Video." If your digital video camera records to disk or Mini DV, refer to the instructions that came with that camera for information on transferring video to the computer.

Capturing Analog Video

Analog video needs to be converted to digital video before it will work on a computer. The easiest way to make the conversion is through an *analog capture device*. This allows you to connect an analog video camera or VCR to your computer. Use software that came with the device to capture analog video to AVI or WMV format for best compatibility with Windows Vista. MPEG format will also work but sometimes requires special codecs.

There are many products for capturing analog video on the market. Some require adding a new video capture card inside your computer. If you're not the type of person who likes to mess around inside your computer, you can use a bridge. Pinnacle Systems (`www.PinnacleSys.com`) and ADS Tech (`www.adstech.com`) are two companies that make such products.

If you have a digital video camera, you may be able to copy video from an analog video camera or VCR to DV tape in your digital video camera. Check the instructions that came with your camera. If you can do that, then you can use the method described here to import the video from the DV tape into your computer.

Once you capture analog video to files on your hard drive, you can use Windows Movie Maker to create your own custom movies from those files. Or, you can use Windows DVD Maker to copy the imported tape straight to DVD without editing in Movie Maker first.

Your camera needs an IEEE 1394 port (sometimes marked DV or iLink) or a USB 2.0 port for this to work. If you don't know what your camera has, refer to the manual that came with the camera.

Your computer needs to have the same kind of port that you'll be using on the camera: either IEEE 1394 or USB 2.0. If you don't know what kinds of ports your computer has, refer to the manual that came with your computer, or contact your computer manufacturer.

NOTE If your computer doesn't have an IEEE 1394 port and you need one, don't worry. They're fairly inexpensive and easy to install. You can probably find everything you need, including cables, at any Radio Shack or computer store.

Make sure the battery in your video camera is fully charged. Or better yet, plug it into a power source, if possible, so you don't have to worry about running out of battery power during the import process.

Once you understand your equipment and can connect the camera to the computer, the rest is easy:

1. Put the tape you want to copy into your video camera, and turn the camera off.
2. Connect the camera to the computer using an IEEE 1394 or USB 2.0 cable.
3. Turn the camera on in VCR mode (not in camera or record mode). Then:
   - If the Import Video Wizard starts automatically, go to step 4.
   - If an AutoPlay dialog box appears, click Import video using Windows Video Import.
   - If nothing happens, open Windows Movie Maker and choose Import from Digital Video Camera.

4. In the Name: box, type a brief but descriptive name for the video. This will be the filename of the video file you create.

5. Leave the Import To: option set to Videos unless you have another preference. (You can use any folder on any hard drive.)

6. Click the Format: button as in Figure 25.30 and choose one of the following:

FIGURE 25.30

First page of Windows Video Import.

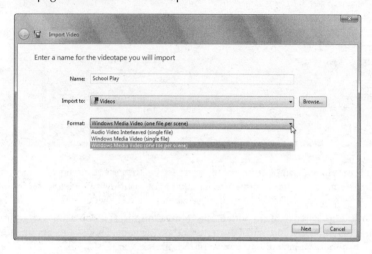

- **Audio Video Interleaved (one single file):** Creates a very high-quality uncompressed video file. But the file will be huge in terms of the hard disk space it uses. The enormous size of these files might limit the number of videotapes that you can copy to your hard disk.

- **Windows Media Video (single file):** Choose this option to create a single .wmv file from the tape. This allows you to manage the video as a single file and might be your best bet if you're not well versed in video and computers. In Movie Maker, you can split the lengthy video into smaller clips without breaking up the video file.

- **Windows Media Video (one file per scene):** Choose this option if you're creating a DVD and want to have a scene selection menu. You cannot control where scenes start and end. The program will decide for you.

7. Click the Next button.

8. On the second wizard page, shown in Figure 25.31, choose how to import:

FIGURE 25.31

Choose how you want to capture from videotape.

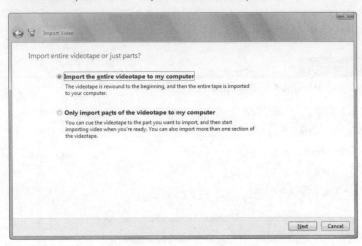

- **Import the videotape to my computer:** This is the easiest method if you want the entire tape's contents to use as raw material in creating your own movies with Movie Maker. You can always edit out the junk later, after you've imported the video into Movie Maker.

- **Only import parts of the videotape to my computer:** If you want to conserve disk space, and only intend to use small portions of the videotape, choose this option. You'll need to manually choose which content you want to import.

9. Click Next.

A page similar to one in Figure 25.32 opens. If you chose an "Import entire videotape. . ." option that captures the whole tape from beginning to end, you're done. You won't see controls for operating the camera, except a Stop button, in case you want to stop recording before capturing the entire tape.

If you choose the option to import only parts of the videotape, you'll see controls like those shown in Figure 25.32. Use those buttons as you would on a VCR to wind the tape to where you want to start copying video and pause (click the || button). While the tape is paused, you can use the Previous Frame and Next Frame buttons to get to the exact frame where you want to start copying. Then click Start Video Import to start recording. When you get to a part that you don't want to copy, click Stop Video Import. You can repeat the process to record as many or as few chunks of tape as you wish. Click Finish when you're done.

 Don't worry about getting every imported chunk exactly right. But it's better to capture too much than too little, because you can always trim off extra content in Movie Maker.

After you click Finish in the Import Video Wizard, you might have to wait a few minutes for Vista to create the file. Then you can disconnect the camera from the computer and store the tape in a safe place.

If you started the import from within Windows Movie Maker, the videotape will appear in your Imported Media collection folder. Click that folder name in the Collections pane to find the video. Most likely it will be divided into smaller clips, all of which start with the same name as the video file.

FIGURE 25.32

Getting content from videotape.

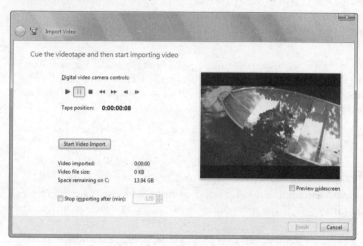

If you didn't start the import from Movie Maker, you won't see a new collection or the video clip. But don't worry. You don't have to import the whole tape again. Just import the video using the method described under "Importing Content to Movie Maker" at the start of this chapter.

Whether or not you imported straight to Movie Maker, the video file is in your Videos folder (or whatever folder you specified before importing). You can open that folder and double-click the file's icon to play the video at any time.

Movie Maker Help and Troubleshooting

In this chapter you've learned enough to create movies of almost any size and complexity. But any time you're working with digital media, there are things that can go wrong. This is especially true of video, which is a complex medium. So you'll want to get to know your other resources for information.

- For general help, choose Help ➪ Help Topics from Movie Maker's menu bar, or press the Help key (F1) while Movie Maker is in the active window.
- For online support and troubleshooting, choose Help ➪ Windows Movie Maker on the Web from Movie Maker's menu bar.

If you have problems getting video from your video camera, your best bet is to refer to the instructions that came with the camera. Optionally, you could go to the camera manufacturer's Web site, search for your camera's model number, and see what you can find out there.

You might also try the Windows Movie Maker community Web site. Use Windows Mail (Chapter 18) to connect. Then search for newsgroups that contain *moviemaker*. When posting a question, make sure to include the make and model of your video camera. Someone in the group might have that same camera, and an easy solution to whatever problem you're experiencing.

Wrap Up

Movie Maker is a lot of fun, once you get the hang of it. When creating movies, you want to do things in the order presented in this chapter. Get your content into Movie Maker. Clean up your clips and get rid of any junk you don't want. Add the good clips to the Storyboard/Timeline. Then you can add titles and credits and special effects if you like.

For more advanced features, like sound effects, narration, and music, you'll need to use the Timeline. You can also use the Timeline for more refined editing of your content. When you're happy with your project (the clips in your Storyboard/Timeline) you can publish them to a file, DVD, or other medium to share with family and friends. Here are the key things to know:

- You can import any compatible video, pictures, and audio files into Movie Maker, and use them to create your own movies.

- The imported content is arranged into collection folders. When you click a collection folder's icon, its contents appear in the contents pane.

- Clips in Movie Maker do not contain actual video, music, or pictures. Each clip is a reference to a larger file in a folder on your hard disk. If you move, delete, or rename that folder, each clip shows a red X.

- To define what you want your movie to show, and the order to show it, drag clips from the contents pane to the Storyboard.

- Choose Tools ⇨ Titles and Credits if you want to add titles and credits to your movie.

- You can also add transition effects between clips, and special effects to clips in the Storyboard/Timeline.

- The Timeline lets you add your own audio files to the movie, and also provides editing capabilities beyond the Storyboard's.

- The clips in your Storyboard/Timeline represent a project, which you can save and reopen at any time in the future.

- To create an actual movie from your project, click the Publish button in the toolbar and follow the instructions on the screen.

Chapter 26

Fun with Media Center

Windows Media Center is an optional program that comes with the Home Premium and Ultimate Editions of Windows Vista. It brings all your media (pictures, music, video) together in one easy-to-use center. If you connect your computer to a TV, you can use Media Center to enjoy them on a TV screen. If the graphics card that lets you connect to a TV screen came with a Windows Media Center remote control, you can control Media Center with that. No need to use a mouse and keyboard.

A second advantage of Media Center is that it allows you to watch and record live TV. But this requires special hardware in the form of a TV Tuner card or PVR (Personal Video Recorder) card.

In this chapter, I'll first focus on those aspects of Media Center that work with any computer. That way, if you have Media Center, you can try out the things that will work for you. I'll hold off on things that require special equipment until later in the chapter.

NEW FEATURE   Media Center isn't a separate product anymore. Instead it's built right into the Premium and Ultimate Editions of Vista.

IN THIS CHAPTER

Playing music with Media Center

Enjoying slide shows and movies

Watching and recording TV

Personalizing Media Center

Starting Media Center

If you have an edition of Windows Vista that includes Media Center, use any of the following methods to start it:

- Click the Start button and choose All Programs ⇨ Media Center.
- Press ⊞, type med, and click Windows Media Center.
- If you happen to have a Media Center remote control, click the button that shows the Windows Media Center logo.

If this is the first time you've used the program, it will take you through some questions and show you some examples of its use. If you're not a technical person, the trickiest part will be answering questions about your main monitor. If you don't know the answer to a question and guess wrong, your screen will go completely black. But don't panic, it will come back to life in 15 or 20 seconds. Try again (but not with the same incorrect answer).

 **TIP** If you missed the initial setup options or need to make a change, choose Tasks on the home page and then click Settings ➪ General ➪ Windows Media Center Setup.

After you've completed all the steps, you'll be taken to Media Center's "home page." (I put that in quotation marks because it's not an Internet home page like on the Web. You don't have to be online to start and use Media Center on your PC.) Figure 26.1 shows what that home page looks like. Well, sort of. Items in the corners only appear when you're using a mouse to control Media Center and only after you move the mouse.

FIGURE 26.1

Windows Media Center home page.

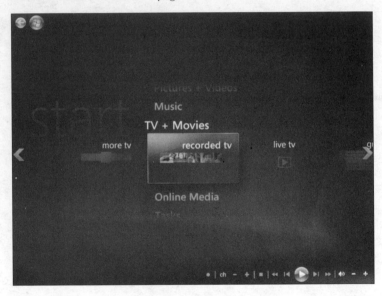

Windows Media Center is the kind of program you can learn by discovery without messing anything up, unless you go in and start changing settings just to see what happens. But most options don't let you change any significant settings. So you're safe there.

The interface on Media Center is much different from the desktop. That's because it's designed to work on a TV screen and through a remote control. But like I said, you don't have to hook up to a TV to use Media Center. You can use it on your computer with your mouse and keyboard.

Working Media Center with a mouse

Working Media Center with a mouse is relatively easy, although not intuitively obvious. Point above or below the names down the center of the screen or to the left or right of a horizontal row of names to see a white arrow. Then point to that to scroll through items. If your mouse has a wheel, you can use that to scroll up and down. Click any item to select it. Click the Back button in the upper-right corner to back out of a selected area. Click the Media Center logo near the Back button to get to Media Center's home page.

As on your desktop, you can often find extra options by right-clicking on the page. Often you'll find an option to change settings that apply to a page or to burn a CD/DVD from the content you're viewing.

Working Media Center with a keyboard

On a keyboard use the ↑, ↓, →, and ← keys to move around. If you use keys on the numeric keypad, make sure that the Num Lock key is turned off. When the item you want is highlighted, press Enter to select it. Press the Backspace key to back out of a selected area. Press Escape (Esc) to return to the home page.

Using a Media Center remote control

If you're using a Media Center remote control, use the arrow keys around the OK button to get around (see Figure 26.2). Press the OK button to select the currently highlighted option. Use the Back button to back out of any area. Press the button that shows the Media Center logo to return to Media Center's home page.

The More button on a remote works like right-clicking. Often you'll find options to change settings, burn a CD or DVD from the current item, and more.

Plenty of other buttons on your remote control can be used for getting around in Media Center. Because there are different brands of remotes, I can't say exactly what's in yours. But you can usually tell what a button does just by looking at its label. Or, check the manual that came with your remote control for more information.

FIGURE 26.2

Windows Media Center remote control buttons.

Moving and Sizing Media Center

Media Center usually opens full screen. But you don't need to leave it that way on a computer monitor. When you move the mouse, you'll see the standard Minimize, Restore, and Close buttons in the upper-right corner. Click the Restore button to shrink it down. Then drag any corner or edge to make it exactly the size you want. Figure 26.3 shows an example in which I have it down near the lower-right corner of the screen.

FIGURE 26.3

Media Center in the lower-right corner of the desktop.

If you have multiple monitors, you can also drag the Media Center window, by its title bar, over to another monitor. After it's on the other monitor, you can maximize it there to fill that screen.

For the next few sections, I'll talk about things you can do in Media Center on regular computers with regular monitors. I'll leave the optional TV things out of the picture until later.

Media Center Playback Controls

Media Center can play picture slide shows, videos, music, movies, and TV shows. When you get something playing, there are two ways to control playback. If you're using a mouse, move the mouse a little to reveal the playback controls shown in Figure 26.4. Depending on what you're playing, some controls may be disabled (dimmed). Don't bother clicking on those because they won't do anything.

FIGURE 26.4

Playback controls for a mouse.

If you're using a remote control, those buttons won't appear on the screen. Use the corresponding buttons on the remote to control playback.

Things You Can Do without TV

You can do many things in Media Center that don't require a TV Tuner card or TV. You can do these things with Media Center showing full screen or in a smaller window on the desktop.

Playing music in Media Center

The Music portion of Media Center gets albums and songs from Windows Media Player. You can also listen to online radio stations from Media Center. Choose Music from the home page. Options that appear across the horizontal row are summarized here:

- **Music Library:** Lets you choose songs from Windows Media Player categories and playlists to play. You can create a queue of songs to play and more.

> **NOTE** If there is no music in your media library yet, you'll be prompted to add some. You can choose Yes if you have put songs in your media library. If you don't have a media library, you can learn to create one in Chapter 23.

- **Play all music:** Plays all songs in your Media Player media library. Choose a visualization or play a slide show with your music. Click Buy Music to connect to an online music store to purchase and download music.
- **Play all:** Plays all the songs in your media library, or just selected songs.
- **Radio:** Lets you locate and play music from online radio stations. The first time you use this option, click Stations and then click the Music & Radio link.
- **Search:** Helps you find songs in your media library.
- **More music:** Takes you to online services for purchasing and downloading music online.

While music is playing, you'll see buttons as in Figure 26.5. Use them to view or change the queue (playlist), watch a music visualization, play a photo slide show with the music, and so forth. Use the playback controls to control volume, pause, stop, skip songs, and so forth. If you navigate away from the page shown in the figure, go to Media Center's home page and choose Now Playing to return.

FIGURE 26.5

Playing music in Media Center.

Viewing pictures and videos in Media Center

You can use Media Center to view and play pictures and videos in your Windows Photo Gallery and Pictures folder. Click Pictures + Videos on the home page (see Figure 26.6) to see pictures and videos from your Windows Media Player library. Click Picture Library to view your still pictures, or Video Library to view your video library. Use Play All to play picture slide shows and videos.

FIGURE 26.6

Pictures + Video in Media Center.

Online Media

The Online Media option takes you to online services to explore in Media Center. Online media includes TV, movies, music, radio, news, sports, games, and lifestyle as shown in Figure 26.7. Online content changes frequently, so what you see on any given day will likely be different (certainly different from Figure 26.7!).

FIGURE 26.7

Online media.

Playing movies in Media Center

The TV+Movies option on the home page is about commercial movies, TV shows, playing DVD movies, and TV. You can also use it to rent movies online and watch movies you've purchased. As always, your best bet is to simply explore your options.

When the movie is playing, use the playback controls as you would on a VCR to pause, resume, fast forward, rewind, and so forth.

Watching and Recording TV

If your computer has a TV Tuner or Personal Video Recorder card, you can use Media Center to watch and record TV. If your computer doesn't already have one, you can purchase and install one or have one professionally installed. Ideally, you want a card that's specifically designed to work with Media Center. One that comes with a Media Center remote control is ideal if you think there's a chance you might want to connect your computer to a TV.

The TV Tuner card you purchase will provide a connection for cable TV or an antenna. You'll need to connect that to get TV reception. You don't need to connect to a TV screen, though. You can watch and record TV from any standard computer monitor.

To use the TV features, choose TV on Media Center's home page. You'll see four options: Recorded TV, Live TV, Guide, and Search. The Guide option takes you to your online program guide of upcoming TV shows shown in Figure 26.8.

FIGURE 26.8

Media Center Guide.

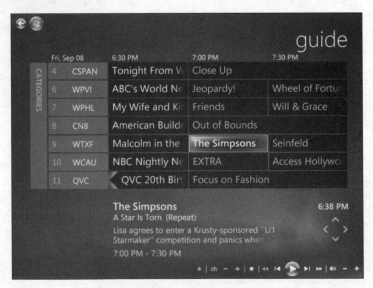

If you're using a remote control, you can scroll through times and channels using the navigation buttons. To watch or record a show that's currently airing, highlight its title and click the OK button. If you're using a mouse, move the mouse pointer onto the guide. You'll see some arrows just below the guide. Click those to scroll through times and channels. To watch or record a show that's currently airing, click its title.

TIP Click Categories at the left side of the guide to see shows organized into categories like Most View, Movies, Sports, Kids, and so forth.

When a TV show is playing, you can use the playback controls for just about anything except fast forwarding "into the future." For example, you can pause playback and then resume later. Or you can rewind. But you can't fast forward live TV beyond what's been aired so far.

You don't want to pause live TV for too long, though. Pausing for a few minutes is fine. Pausing for hours won't work because there's a limit to how much live TV your hard drive will store during a pause. The exact limit depends on the storage capacity and free space on the drive. But it's always a matter of minutes, not hours.

Recording TV

There are two ways to record TV. One is to just hit the Record button in the playback controls while you're watching the show. Then Media Center will record from that point to the end of the show.

As an alternative to manual recording, choose shows to record on a regular basis. The easiest method is to open the guide and navigate to the show you want to record. Double click it (with the mouse) or press the OK button on the remote control. You see options like those in Figure 26.9.

FIGURE 26.9

Options for recording an upcoming show.

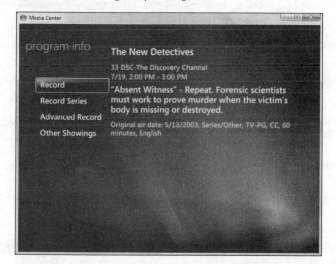

Click the Record button if you want to record only the selected show when it airs. Click Record Series to record all future airings. Or click Advanced Record to choose exactly what you want to record and how you want to record it.

To stop a recording in progress, right-click the red Record button in the play control of the Windows Notification area and choose Stop Recording. Or press the Stop button on your remote control.

It's important to keep in mind that recorded TV shows take up a lot of disk space. The higher the quality of settings chosen, the more disk space a recorded TV show requires. The numbers here are approximate:

- Best quality: 3 GB per hour
- Better quality: 2.5 GB per hour
- Good quality: 2 GB per hour
- Fair quality: 1 GB per hour

To decide on a quality, you need to think in terms of available disk space and how long you intend to keep each show on the disk. Open your Computer folder to see available disk space on your hard drive. If the available space on a drive doesn't show in a meter, choose the Details view or right-click the drive's icon and choose Properties.

TIP   See Chapter 28 for information on drives, your Computer folder, and storage capacities.

You can choose recording settings on a case-by-case basis. The Advanced Record option that appears when you choose a show to record is one way. Or you can choose TV on the home page, open Recorded TV, and then choose View Scheduled to see scheduled recording. Then click Record Settings. But the easiest thing would probably be to choose default settings that apply to all recordings. I'll talk about how that works under "Personalizing Media Center" later in this chapter.

You don't really have to keep a TV show on your hard disk forever. If you have a DVD burner, and the show isn't copy-protected, you can burn the show to a DVD and then delete the original from your hard disk. I'll talk about CD and DVD burning from Media Center a little later in this chapter.

Watching recorded TV

To watch a recorded TV show, starting from Media Center's home page, choose TV, and then Recorded TV. Scroll through the shows and choose any one by clicking or by pressing OK on the remote control. You'll see options like those in Figure 26.10.

I assume the buttons are self-explanatory. They let you play or delete the show. Set a time limit on how long you'll keep it on your hard drive. You can also choose to record the series or view other times.

FIGURE 26.10

Options for a recorded TV show.

Recorded TV files

Each recorded TV show is stored as a file with a .dvr-ms filename extension. (The extension stands for digital video recording—Microsoft.) Unless you choose another location, they'll likely be placed in the Recorded TV subfolder in your Public folder. You can use the Folders list to navigate to that folder as in Figure 26.11.

FIGURE 26.11

Icon for recorded TV show in Recorded TV folder.

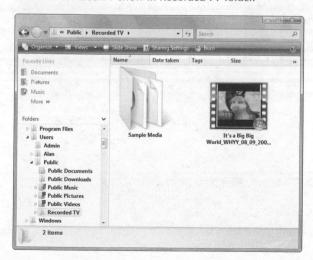

As with any file, you can right-click an icon to see different things you can do with it. For example, you can play a TV show in Windows Media Player rather than Media Center. You can also import a TV show into Windows Movie Maker. There, you could edit out the commercials and save it as a smaller .wmv file. If the file was too big to burn to a DVD before you edited out the commercials, it might fit after you take out the commercials.

Personalizing Media Center

Like most programs, Media Center has options that you can adjust to your own needs and preferences. To get to those settings, select Tasks on Media Center's home page and click Settings. You see buttons for changing General, TV, Pictures, Music, DVD, and Extender as shown in Figure 26.12. I'll cover each in the sections to follow.

FIGURE 26.12

Media Center Settings page.

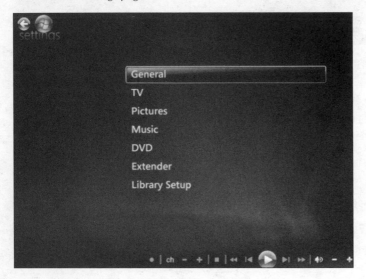

General Settings

Clicking General Settings takes you to still more options for personalizing Media Center. Under Startup and Window Behavior, you'll find the following.

Startup and Window Behavior

The Startup and Window Behavior button takes you to general options for controlling how Media Center behaves, as follows:

■ **Windows Media Center window always on top:** Choosing this option prevents other program windows on a computer monitor from covering Media Center's program window. It will also prevent you from switching to another program when Media Center is maximized to full-screen size!

■ **Show "Not designed for Windows Media Center" dialog:** Some of the online services and other Web content you can get to in Media Center can't be operated through a remote control or the normal Media Center interface. Choosing this option ensures that you see a warning when you encounter such content, so you can cancel out if you want. That way, you won't get stuck on some page that you can't operate with a remote control.

■ **Start Windows Media Center when Windows Starts:** Choosing this option makes Media Center open onto the desktop automatically each time you start Windows.

■ **Show taskbar notifications:** Choose this option to ensure that you see Notification area messages telling you when Media Center is up to something, such as recording a scheduled TV show.

■ **Show TV Tips in Guide:** Select this option to show optional tips in the program guide. Clear this option to hide those tips.

If your cable TV provider also provides your telephone service, and they support this feature, you can choose options under Show notifications to specify how you want to handle incoming calls. If you can't get it to work, check with your telephone service provider to see if they support Media Center.

Visual and Sound Effects

The Visual and Sound Effects options let you enable, or disable, the transition animations between pictures in a slide show. Here you can also enable or disable the audio feedback you hear when navigating in Media Center, choose a color scheme for your Media Center display, and choose a background color for videos that don't fill the entire screen.

Program Library Options

Choosing Program Library Options takes you to options that allow you to control the media experience (meaning some might temporarily override your personal settings outside of Media Center). You can choose to access media information (metadata) from your media files in Media Center. You can hide Internet security warnings that may pop up, if they're not really protecting you from anything and just getting in your way. Click Edit Program Library to remove unwanted options and programs.

Windows Media Center Setup

The Media Center Setup options allow you to set up your Internet connection, TV signal (if you have a TV Tuner), speakers, and TV/monitor. If you want to run through the initial setup process again, click Run Setup Again. That will take you through the entire process, step by step.

Parental Controls

Media Center setup has parental controls that are separate from those in Windows Vista. Think up a four-digit access code that you won't forget. (If you forget the code, you'll lock yourself out of blocked content.) Then click Parental Controls and enter that code as instructed onscreen.

After you entered the code (twice), you're taken to a page where you can activate TV blocking and DVD blocking, change your access code, or turn off parental controls.

Automatic Download options

The Automatic Download options allow you to enable or disable automatic downloading of media information and program guide data. If you disable downloading of media information, you'll see "Unknown" in place of many artist and album names, "Track" instead of song titles, and other generic information. Turn automatic downloading back on to replace the unknown and generic information with actual names and titles.

If you disable automatic program guide downloads, you'll need to update the program guide manually from time to time. To do that, go into the program guide, right-click a channel in the left column, and choose Get Latest Guide. If you're using a remote control, go into the guide, highlight a channel number, press the More button on the remote control, and choose Get Latest Guide.

Optimization

The Optimization option takes you to a page where you can schedule optimization tasks to run on a regular schedule. Be sure to choose a time when the computer will be on but you won't be needing Media Center, because you won't be able to use Media Center for the few minutes it takes to complete those tasks.

TV settings

The TV Settings button on the Settings page lets you configure TV recording and other aspects of using TV in Media Center. The Recorder button takes you to a page where you can view your recording history and set defaults for TV recording. The Recorder Storage button lets you choose where you want to store recorded TV. It has to be a hard drive, but not necessarily your C: drive.

You can't record TV straight to DVD in Media Center. But after you've recorded a show you can burn it to DVD. Verify that you can play the DVD in your TV's DVD player. Then you can delete the copy of the show that's still on your hard disk.

Use the Record on Drive option to choose where you want to store recorded TV. You'll see the option shown in Figure 26.13. Choose the drive on which you want to store recorded TV shows. The maximum number of hours of recorded video that will fit on the selected drive is shown. The slider shows how much live TV can be buffered (stored) during a live TV pause.

FIGURE 26.13

Recording Storage settings.

The TV Locations option allows you to specify folders that contain recorded TV, so Media Center can find them and add them to your library.

The Recording Defaults button takes you to still more options for controlling TV recording. Figure 26.14 shows the first four options. There are nine options in all. To scroll through hidden options, use the Up and Down buttons on a remote control. Or use the arrow buttons on your keyboard, or click the up and down arrows near the lower-right corner with your mouse.

FIGURE 26.14

Recoding defaults.

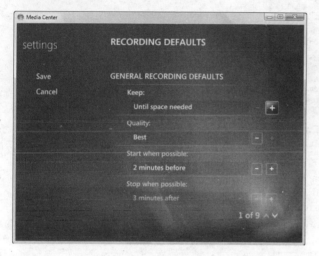

Again, I think the options are self explanatory. You can choose how long you want to keep recorded TV shows, a quality, a little extra leeway at the start and end of every show, and settings that apply only to recorded TV series. Other buttons on the TV page include the following:

- **Guide:** Use this button to configure the program guide, add missing channels, tell it what region you live in (in case the guide is incorrect), and manually update the guide.

- **Set up TV Signal:** Clicking this button takes you through a step-by-step wizard for configuring your incoming TV signal.

- **Configure your TV or Monitor:** This is the same setting as the one under the General options. Use it to get the best picture quality on your TV or monitor.

- **Audio:** Choose Stereo, SAP, or any other audio option provided by your hardware.

- **Closed Captioning:** Turn closed captioning on or off and choose between CC1 and CC2.

Pictures Settings

Clicking Pictures on the Settings tab shows you the options in Figure 26.15. Again, I think they're self-explanatory. You can show pictures in random order (or not), show pictures from subfolders in your Pictures folder (or not), and show captions (the filename and date taken) with each picture (or not).

FIGURE 26.15

Pictures Settings.

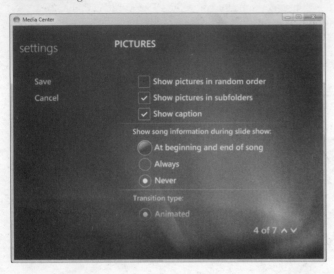

When you launch a slide show from the Music area to play along with the music, the song title usually appears briefly at the start of each song, and then again at the end. You can choose to have the song title shown the whole time that the song is playing, or not at all.

The Animated option causes each picture in the slide show to pan and zoom into view. Clearing the Animated option makes each picture appear more abruptly without any special effects.

Music Settings

The Music button provides options for controlling music visualizations when no slide show is playing. You can choose which visualizations you want to use, and when you want visualizations to begin and end.

DVD Settings

The DVD Settings option lets you choose a default language for multi-language DVDs. You can also control closed captions for DVDs from the page. If you use a remote control to work Media Center, you can configure Program Skip and Replay buttons, and the Channels buttons according to your own preferences.

Extender Settings

Media Center extenders are devices and programs that extend Media Center's capabilities. For example, Microsoft Xbox 360 acts as an extender to share your Media Center library with other players in the house. You need to purchase an extender first. Then follow the instructions that came with that extender to hook it into Media Center on your PC.

Library Setup

Click Library Setup to add folders to, or remove folders from, Media Center's watch list. Pictures, music, videos, and recorded TV from all the folders you specify are added to Media Center automatically, so you can play them whenever you want.

Clicking Tasks on the home page provides more than just the Setting option. You'll find options for burning optical discs (CDs and DVDs), syncing with other devices, shutting down or restarting the computer, and adding extenders.

Burning CDs and DVDs from Media Center

There are many ways to burn CDs and DVDs in Windows Vista. For example, Chapter 23 talks about creating audio CDs with Windows Media Player. Chapter 32 talks about the many other ways you can copy files to CDs and DVDs and create DVD video disks with Windows DVD Maker. The disks you end up with are the same whether you burn them using those techniques or Media Center.

Of course, with Media Center, it's easy to get to all your media files (music, pictures, videos, recorded TV). And you can do it all from a TV screen with a remote control, if that's the way you want to do it. Here's how it works, starting from within Media Center:

1. If you haven't already done so, put a recordable CD or DVD into the CD or DVD burner.
2. After a brief delay you should see Burn a CD or DVD. Click that (not the X that appears to the right of it).

 If the disk was already in the drive before you started Media Center, choose Tools from Media Center's home page and click Burn CD/DVD.

3. Choose which type of disc you want to create. The options available to you depend on the type of disc you inserted:

    ▪ **Audio CD:** Create a music CD for playing in a stereo, CD player, or computer.

    ▪ **Data CD:** Create a CD that contains files for playback on a computer only (and devices that can play audio files).

    ▪ **Data DVD:** Create a DVD that contains files to be played on a computer.

    ▪ **Video DVD:** Create a DVD Video disk that contains video to be watched from a standard DVD player or on a computer.

    ▪ **DVD Slide Show:** Create a picture slide show on a DVD that can be played in a computer or watched on a TV with a DVD player.

4. Click or choose Next.
5. Follow the onscreen instructions.

Exactly what happens next depends on what you choose in step 3. But it's just a matter of reading and following the instructions that appear on the screen.

 You cannot burn protected content to Audio CDs or Video DVDs. However, in some cases you can copy them to data discs.

That's one way to burn CDs and DVDs from Media Center. Another is to navigate to the specific item you want to burn and start the process from there. In some cases you'll see a Burn CD or DVD button right on the screen. In other cases you might have to right-click the item to burn or press the More button on a remote control. For example, you can navigate to a recorded TV program where you see the Play, Delete, Keep Until, and other options for a TV show. Then right-click an empty spot on that page or press the More button to see an option for burning to CD or DVD.

Syncing, Shut Down, and Extenders

The Sync option in Tools makes it easy to sync a compatible device with your Media Center content. Exactly how it works depends on the specific device you're using. If you can't get it to work by guessing, check the manual that came with the device for instructions on syncing with Windows Vista Media Center.

The Shut Down option in Tools offers a way of closing Media Center from a mouse or remote control. You'll also have options to Log Off, Shut Down the computer, Restart the computer, or put the computer into Standby mode.

Wrap Up

Digital media is the future. Windows Media Center is a premiere tool for enjoying all forms of digital media in the current and future forms. To keep up with what's happening, be sure to check out the Media Center Web site. As I write this chapter, it's at

http://www.microsoft.com/windowsvista/features/forhome/mediacenter.mspx. But that could change. If it does, just go to www.live.com or http://search.microsoft.com and search for Vista Media Center.

What you've learned here has gotten you off to a good start on a whole new world. As I've mentioned, Media Center is the kind of program you can learn just by spending a little time exploring your options. Here's a summary of the basics:

- Windows Media Center comes with the Home Premium and Ultimate Editions of Windows Vista.
- You can use Media Center to enjoy all forms of digital media including photos, music, radio, video, movies, games, and TV.
- To start Windows Media Center, click the Start button and choose All Programs ⇨ Media Center.
- Media Center gets pictures from your Windows Photo Gallery and music from your Windows Media Player media library.
- If you have an appropriate graphics card, you can display Media Center on a TV screen and operate it with a remote control.
- If your computer has a TV Tuner or PVR (Personal Video Recorder) card, you can watch and record live TV in Media Center.
- Choosing Tasks ⇨ Settings in Media Center takes you to many options for configuring and personalizing Media Center to your liking.
- Choosing Tasks in Media Center takes you to options for burning CDs and DVDs, syncing with compatible devices, adding extender devices, and shutting down your computer.

Chapter 27

Troubleshooting Multimedia

Troubleshooting Pictures and Photos

Most problems I see in the "pictures and photos" category stem from people who don't know how to work their digital cameras. So, if you fall into that category, remember that the only place to learn about your specific camera is from the instructions that came with that camera. Here we focus on common, everyday problems. Then at the end of the chapter I'll point out other resources for troubleshooting multimedia.

No Copy option when right-clicking a picture in a Web page

Not all Web browsers offer a copy option on the shortcut menu. Try browsing to the same page using Internet Explorer. Optionally, you can right-click a picture and choose Save Picture As to store the picture in your Pictures folder, or any other folder of your choosing.

Cannot copy thumbnail from my Pictures folder to open document

Thumbnails represent closed documents and cannot be copied and pasted into an open document. You'll either need to insert the picture into the open document using whatever commands that program supports, or open (double-click) the picture, right-click the open picture and choose Copy, and then paste the picture into an open document.

Troubleshooting Windows Media Player

Multimedia is a combination of computer hardware (your graphics card, CD or DVD drives, and the like) as well as software (Windows Media Player and the specific song or movie with which you're having a problem). It's not always easy to tease out exactly where a problem lies. The following sections cover solutions to some of the more common Windows Media Player maladies.

When I first start Media Player I get prompted to install URGE

URGE is the result of Microsoft and MTV Networks joining together to offer an online music store. When you first start Media Player, you may be prompted with the screen shown in Figure 27.1.

FIGURE 27.1

Media Player prompting for installation of the URGE utility.

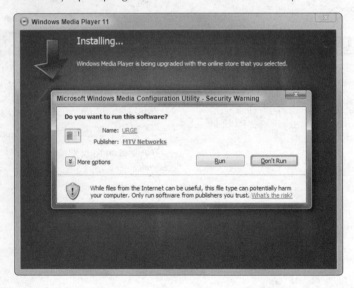

After URGE has been installed, a link will appear in Media Player that will allow you to set up a new account. URGE pulls together MTV, VH1, and CMT channels.

Message "Invalid Function" when trying to burn a CD

Follow these steps to verify that your CD-R or CD-RW is able and ready to burn CDs:

1. Click the Start button and select Computer.
2. Right-click the icon that represents your CD or DVD drive and choose Properties.
3. Click the Recording tab.
4. Under Desktop disc recording, verify that you have selected the correct device under "Select a drive that Windows can use as the default recorder for your system." Also make sure that the correct drive is selected under "Choose a drive that has sufficient free space to burn a disc."
5. Click OK.

Some other program opens when you open an icon or insert a CD

If the problem arises when you double-click the icon for a song or video file, follow these steps:

1. Open the Default Programs applet by clicking Start ⟿ Control Panel ⟿ Default Programs.

2. To change the default action that happens when you open an icon, click the Set your default programs link.

3. Select the Windows Media Player from the Programs column and click the Choose defaults button.

4. In the "Set associations for a program" window, check each file type you want associated with Windows Media Player and click the Save button.

If the problem arises when you insert a CD or DVD, follow these steps:

1. Open the Default Programs applet by clicking Start ⟿ Control Panel ⟿ Default Programs.

2. To change the default action that happens, insert a CD or DVD and click the Change AutoPlay settings link.

3. In the "Choose what happens when you insert each type of media or device" window, choose the default application next to each type of Media.

4. When you have finished making your selections, click the Save button.

 **TIP** Media Player can't play all types of media files. It can play only the file types listed on the "Set associations for a program" window under Set Program Associations.

I'm unable to locate the menus within Media Player

If you're not able to find the menus within the new version of Windows Media Player, follow these steps:

1. Open Windows Media Player normally. Right-click in the empty space to the right of the Forward and Back navigation buttons as shown in Figure 27.2.

FIGURE 27.2

The menu that shows up after right-clicking in Windows Media Player.

2. Optionally, you can select Show Classic Menus from the menu shown in Figure 27.2 to permanently keep the menu available.

Cannot see captions when playing a CD or DVD

Verify that the CD or DVD you're playing offers captions or subtitles (not all do). In Windows Media Player, choose Play ➪ Lyrics, Captions, and Subtitles ➪ On if Available from Media Player's menu. Even if you've already done so, you may need to do so again after the computer goes into Stand By or Hibernate mode.

If the problem persists, choose Tools ➪ Options from Media Player's menu. Then, click the Security tab, select (check) Show local captions when present, and click OK.

Media Player can't find my MP3 player

Verify that the MP3 player is properly connected to the computer and turned on. If the player is brand new, wait a few minutes for Windows Media Player to detect the device. If nothing happens within several minutes, read the instructions that came with the device. You may need to install the original drivers and then update those drivers.

Once you've installed the drivers that came with the device, there may still be several minutes of delay while Media Player checks the Windows Update site for new drivers. Make sure that you go online, and stay online, for several minutes after connecting the device so that Media Player can check for updated drivers.

You might also want to check the player manufacturer's Web site for information on using the device with Windows Media Player 11. Not all devices are 100 percent compatible with Media Player.

Song titles don't appear after inserting a CD

Song titles only appear in the Rip window if (1) you're online when you insert the CD and 2) the CD media information is stored in the online CDDB.

Error message appears with 0xC00 or other number

There are lots of these, more than I could even begin to fit into a single chapter. But the number you see in the message is ideal for online searching, because it's so unique. Microsoft's http://search.microsoft .com page is a good starting point, because it searches only Microsoft's site and includes a lot of technical information. If that fails, you can search the Web at large using Windows Live Search (http://www.live .com), Google (www.google.com), or your search engine of choice.

All other Windows Media Player issues

Windows Media Player has its own Web page at www.microsoft.com/windows/windowsmedia/ player/11. It also has its own troubleshooting page at the site. When you get to that page, click Windows Media Player 11 in the left column and choose Troubleshooting and Support. You can also get to that page from within Windows Media Player. Right-click Media Player's title bar or press the Alt key and click Help ➪ Troubleshooting Online.

Troubleshooting Windows Movie Maker

The most common Movie Maker problems stem from not quite understanding how to use the program. When I look at the questions posted in the message boards, I see that most don't require any troubleshooting. Rather, the problem stems from not knowing how to use Windows Movie Maker.

There's also much confusion between what is a movie project file (.MSWMM) and what is a finished movie (.wmv or .avi) file. As discussed under "Saving your work" in Chapter 25, the .MSWMM file is for storing a movie "work in progress," and never represents a finished movie to watch or copy to a CD or DVD. You need to complete the steps under "Publishing Your Movie" in Chapter 25, and be able to recognize the icons as displayed there, to discriminate between a movie project file and an actual finished movie.

Aside from the common confusions, there are some actual error messages that can arise. Those really do come under the heading of "troubleshooting," and many are covered in the sections that follow.

Message "Your system is currently set to 800x600 . . ."

This isn't an error message — more like a suggestion. Click OK to use Windows Media Player at the current resolution. Optionally, you can increase your screen resolution to 1024 x 768 as described under "Choosing a screen resolution" in Chapter 11.

No audio when capturing content

This is usually a codec problem. The K-Lite Codec Pack, which you can download for free online, often resolves the problem. For more information, see www.k-litecodecpack.com or search the Web for K-Lite codec pack.

More Troubleshooting Resources

Multimedia is a complex topic and there are many things that can go wrong. Troubleshooting multimedia requires some resourcefulness. If it's a problem with a camera or other media device, the manufacturer's Web site is a good first step. At the Microsoft Communities site, Microsoft.public.windows.vista .music_pictures_video is the perfect place to ask questions about Windows Vista and multimedia.

Windows Help and Support also offers several pages of help for troubleshooting multimedia files. As always you can use the Search Help box to search for the word troubleshoot followed by a specific word or phrase to zero in on topics that are most likely to help. Here are some suggestions:

- troubleshoot music
- troubleshoot drm
- troubleshoot photos
- troubleshoot media
- troubleshoot video
- troubleshoot importing
- troubleshoot cd
- troubleshoot dvd
- troubleshoot media center

Part VI

Managing Files and Folders

Long gone are the days when people used floppy disks and small hard drives to manage a few dozen or a few hundred files. Today's enormous capacity hard drives let every user store thousands, even tens of thousands, of personal files in their personal computers. Microsoft was keenly aware that most people were struggling with managing enormous file collections when they designed Vista. And it really shows.

Chapter 28 starts off with the basics of what drives, folders, and files are all about. It's primarily intended for people who are new to all of this, or at least pretty fuzzy on what those terms are all about. Chapter 29 gets into the specifics of managing files and folders, including important skills for moving, copying, renaming, deleting, and recovering files.

Chapters 30 and 31 get into the new Search Index, perhaps the single most important and useful (and least understood) feature of Windows Vista. As you'll discover in those chapters, the new search index is basically a search engine for your own computer's content rather than the Internet's content. It's a real boon to those who have a lot of files stored on their hard drives.

Chapter 32 gets into the confusing world of optical media, a.k.a. CDs and DVDs. Vista has many new features built right into it that makes working with those discs easier than ever. Chapter 33 gets into new features for protecting your files, including the new Backup and Restore Center, previous versions of lost or damaged files, and BitLocker drive encryption for protecting data on portable computers. Chapter 34 covers common file management problems and their solutions.

Chapter 28

Understanding Drives, Folders, and Files

Beginners and casual users are often thrown by terms like *drive, folder, file, icon, kilobyte, megabyte, gigabyte,* and so forth. Virtually every resource you turn to assumes that you already know what these things mean. Nobody ever bothers to explain them. That's because these terms and concepts have remain unchanged for the past 25 years or so.

Of course, just because those terms have been around for a long time doesn't mean they're common knowledge. In fact, for every person who does know what those terms are about, you can be sure many thousands don't. So in this chapter, I'm going to break from the tradition and explain what those terms are all about.

Understanding Disks and Drives

Computers work with information. That information has to be stored on some type of *medium*. These days that medium is most likely to be in the form of a disk or a card. You can also store information on tape. But tape is slow and difficult to work with, so few people use it.

Your computer's hard disk

All the programs and information that's in your computer is actually stored on a disk. You never see that disk because it's sealed inside a case that cannot be opened. That disk goes by many names including *hard disk, hard drive, fixed disk,* and *drive C:.*

Windows Vista, every program you use, every saved e-mail message, and every photo, song, video, and other document that you can open without inserting a disk into a disk drive is on your hard disk. In fact, the only things that aren't on your hard disk are things you can only get to through the Internet, and things you can only get to by inserting some other kind of disk (or a memory card) into your computer.

IN THIS CHAPTER

Disk drives, disks, and memory cards

Navigating through folders with Windows Explorer

Clicking, viewing, and arranging icons your way

Stop losing saved files

Customize file and folder icons

Don't confuse your hard disk with *memory* (also called RAM for *random access memory*). Your hard disk stores everything that's in your computer. Memory stores only *open* stuff — whatever you happen to be using at the moment.

You can also add extra hard drives to your system, either internally or externally. Each shows up as an icon in your Computer folder, as discussed later in this chapter.

Your main hard disk, drive C:, is called *a non-removable* disk because you can't just pop it out of the computer by pressing some button. Other types of disks are called *removable* media because you can pop them in and out of the computer quite easily.

Removable media

Removable media are disks and devices you can pop into, and out of, the computer at will. Most removable media require a specific disk drive, or *drive* for short. The drive is a device into which you can pop the disk. The drive then spins the disk around. A drive head can then read data from, or write data to, the disk as it is spinning. The sections to follow are about removable media.

Floppies and Zip disks

Floppy disks and Zip disks have been around a long time. They're both *magnetic media* (meaning they use magnetism to store data, like your hard disk). There was a time where virtually every PC came with a floppy disk drive built in for using floppy disks. But that's no longer the case. The extremely limited storage capacity of floppy disks has rendered them obsolete in today's storage-hungry world.

Zip disks are still fairly popular, mainly because of their greater capacity. A single Zip disk can store as much information as many floppy disks. How many depends on the capacity of the disk and the drive. But anywhere from 100 to 1,000 floppies per Zip disk is not unusual.

Few computers come with Zip drives built in. So if your computer has neither a floppy drive nor a Zip drive, it's no big deal and no reason to feel cheated. You could easily and inexpensively add either type of drive to your system. But unless you have a good and specific reason for doing so, there's no need to bother.

Zip disks are not the same as Zip files, so don't confuse the two. In fact, the two aren't even related. A Zip disk is an actual piece of hardware you can hold in your hand. A Zip file is a file that can be stored on any type of disk.

Figure 28.1 shows examples of what a floppy disk looks like. A Zip disk looks very similar, it's just slightly larger. If you do have drives for these, make sure you put the disk in correctly. The sliding metal door faces the disk. The label should be facing upward. If there is no label on the disk, make sure the metal wheel in the center of the disk is facing down when you put the disk in the drive.

The write-protect tab in a floppy is used to prevent accidentally erasing or replacing important information on the floppy. When the write-protect tab is closed (you cannot see through the hole), you're free to do whatever you want with the disk. When the slider is open, you can only read the contents of the disk. You can't erase the disk or change its contents.

FIGURE 28.1

Floppy disk.

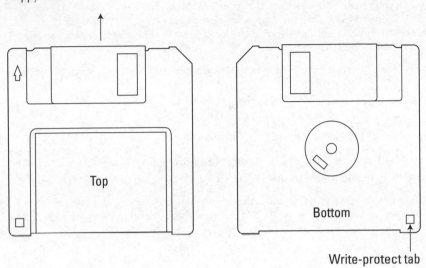

Write-protect tab

CDs and DVDs

CDs and DVDs are very popular storage media. The record companies use CDs to sell albums. The movie industry sells movies on DVDs. The computer industry uses both CDs and DVDs to distribute software. Figure 28.2 shows an example of a CD or DVD. The two look exactly alike, so the figure could be either.

FIGURE 28.2

CD or DVD?

When putting a CD or DVD disk into its drive, make sure to do so with the label facing up. Then push the eject button on the drive, and gently push the drive drawer so the disk and drawer slide in.

To listen to music on a CD, you usually just stick the CD in your CD drive, wait a few seconds, and the CD starts playing, usually in Windows Media. The same is true for most movie DVDs, but only if your computer has the appropriate hardware and software. Here's a quick rundown on where to look for more information on CDs and DVDs (besides this chapter):

- **Listen to, copy from, or create your own music CDs:** Chapter 23, "Making Music with Media Player 11."
- **Watch DVD movies:** Chapter 24, "DVD, Video, and More."

 You can use Windows Media Center (Chapter 26) to play CDs and watch movies. But only if you have a version of Vista that includes Media Center.

- **Make your own DVD movies:** Chapter 25, "Making Movies with Movie Maker."
- **Copy computer files to and from CDs and DVDs:** Chapter 32, "Using CDs and DVDs."

The most common mistake people make with CDs and DVDs is assuming they're the same. After all, they *look* exactly the same. But they're not the same at all. Nor do you treat them like other kinds of disks. That's why I've dedicated a whole chapter (32) just to CDs and DVDs.

Portable devices

Technically, portable devices aren't disks or disk drives. But some can store files. For example, digital cameras store pictures. Portable MP3 players store songs. When you connect such a device to your computer, it looks like a disk drive to Windows Vista, in the sense that it shows up in your Computer folder.

You can copy things to and from portable devices using many different techniques. For example, you can use Windows Photo Gallery (Chapter 22) to get pictures from a digital camera. Use Windows Media Player to copy songs to and from a portable MP3 player. You can also use more general techniques described in Chapter 29 to copy files to and from some portable devices.

Flash cards and memory sticks

Flash cards (also called *memory cards* and *memory sticks*) are a solid state medium, which just means there's no spinning disk or drive head involved in getting information to and from the card. Memory cards come in many shapes and sizes. Figure 28.3 shows some examples.

Most digital cameras and portable MP3 players use memory cards to store songs and pictures. When you connect the device to the computer, you get access to that memory card so you can copy files from it, or to it.

If your card has memory card slots, you also have the option of putting the card right into a slot. Each slot into which you can insert a card shows up as an icon in your Computer folder. When you insert a card into a slot, you can copy files from it (or to it) using techniques described in Chapter 29.

FIGURE 28.3

Memory cards.

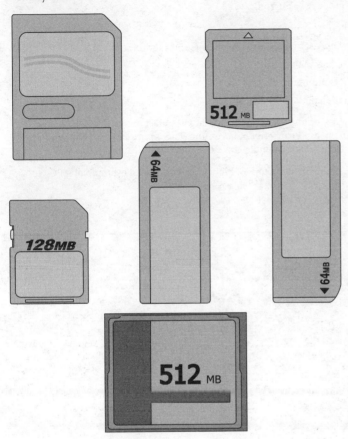

Jump drives

A jump drive (or *flash drive*) isn't a disk at all. It's more like a little gizmo you hang from a keychain, though you can also hide them in pens and pocket knives. Furthermore, you don't need any special kind of drive for this storage medium because it *is* a drive. You just plug it into a USB port on your computer.

 **A jump drive is basically a memory stick with a USB plug connected to it.**

Once the jump drive is plugged in, it looks and acts just like a disk drive to Windows. You can move or copy files to it and from it using any technique described in Chapter 29. Jump drives come in all shapes and sizes. To see examples, go to any online retailer that sells nerd stuff (www.newegg.com, www.cdw.com, www.togerdirect.com, www.amazon.com, or wherever) and search for jump drive.

Viewing your computer's drives

Every disk drive in your computer is represented by an icon in your Computer folder. To open that folder, use whichever of the following techniques works for you:

- Click the Start button and choose Computer.
- Click the Start button, click your user name, and open the Computer folder.
- Double-click the Computer icon on your desktop.
- Tap ⊞, type comp, and click Computer.
- Press ⊞+E (hold down ⊞, tap the E key, release ⊞).

> **NOTE** If you don't have a Computer option on the right side of your Start menu, but want one, right-click the Start button and choose **Properties**. Choose the **Start Menu** option and click the **Customize** button to its right. Choose Display as **Link** under the **Computer** heading and click **OK**.

Exactly what you see depends on what's available in your PC. Figure 28.4 shows an example of a PC with lots of different drives.

FIGURE 28.4

Sample Computer folder.

Don't expect your Computer folder to look like the one in Figure 28.4. All computers are different and have different drives, slots, and portable devices that can connect. But you should see at least two categories of drives.

 Your Computer folder is unique in that it contains an icon for each disk drive in your computer, as well as for devices that can store files. Most other folders contain subfolders and files.

The first category is Hard Disk Drives. Your computer will have at least one of these named C:. That's that drive where everything that's in your computer is stored. The computer in the example shows icons for four hard drives. But one hard drive is sufficient for most folks.

Under the Devices with Removable Storage, you'll see icons for other media. You might have a Floppy Disk drive (A:). You probably have a CD or DVD drive. Its letter could be D: or something else. In the figure, the DVD drive is E:. The computer in that picture also has several memory card slots, showing as drives F: through I:. The Lexar Media icon, drive J:, represents a flash drive manufactured by a company named Lexar.

The last category, Portable Devices, shows icons only for devices that are currently connected to your computer. If you don't have a camera or similar device connected when you open your Computer folder, you might not see a Portable Devices category. In the figure, I have a digital camera connected to the computer and turned on, so it shows up under Portable Devices.

You can leave your Computer folder open as you insert and remove disks. The names of icons that represent removable drives change to reflect the content of the disk that's currently in the drive. When you remove the disk, the name reverts to the generic name for the drive. That's a good thing to know if you're new to all of this and don't know what the icons in your own Computer represent on your system.

Sizes and capacities

Every disk is like a container in which you store things. There's a limit to how much stuff you can put on a disk. This is no different from any other container. For example, you can store water in a drinking glass, bucket, bathtub, or swimming pool. They're all containers for water. But they just vary greatly in their *capacity* (how much water each can hold).

If we liken different computer media to water containers, a floppy disk is like a drinking glass. A CD is like a bucket, a DVD like a bathtub, your hard disk like a swimming pool. Memory cards, jump drives, and Zip disks vary in capacity. So it's tough to liken any one to a water container. But they're basically in the bucket-to-bathtub range.

With water we measure things in ounces, liters, gallons, and such. In the computer world the basic unit of measure is the *byte*. One byte equals roughly the amount of space required to store one character like the letter *a*. For example, the word *cat* requires three bytes.

 The smallest unit of measure is the *bit* (binary digit), which can contain either 0 or 1. A byte is eight bits.

Most disks can hold thousands, millions, or even billions of bytes. We tend to round their capacities to the nearest thousand, million, or billion bytes. That's because disk storage is cheap and plentiful and there's no point in fussing over a few thousand bytes here or there. Also, computer folks don't even use the words "thousand," "million," or "billion." We have shorter terms as follows:

- Kilo — thousand
- Mega — million
- Giga — billion

That's all you really need to know about those terms. For those who like their numbers more exact, Table 28.1 shows the facts in detail.

TABLE 28.1

Buzzwords for Disk Capacities and File Sizes

Word	Abbreviation	Approximate (number)	Approximate (word)	Actual
Kilo	K or KB	1,000	Thousand	2^{10} or 1,024
Mega	M or MB	1,000,000	Million	2^{20} or 1,048,576
Giga	G or GB	1,000,000,000	Billion	2^{30} or 1,073,741,824
Tera	T or TB	1,000,000,000,000	Trillion	2^{40} or 1,099,511,627,776

Getting back to our analogy of water containers, here are approximate capacities of common disk types:

- **Floppy:** 1.44 MB
- **CD:** 650–700 MB
- **DVD:** 4.7 GB
- **Hard disk:** 20+ GB

The reason I have 20+ for hard disk is because hard disks are available in many different capacities from about 20 GB to 500 GB or more. Zip disks, memory cards, jump drives, and portable devices also vary greatly in capacity. The hard disk reigns supreme in its ability to store large amounts of information.

How much room is there?

Everything you store on a disk takes up some space. So once you start putting things on a disk, you have some used space and some free space. It's easy to see how much space you have on a disk.

When you open your Computer folder, each hard disk has a little meter under it that shows how much space is used (blue) and how much free space is still available for storing stuff (white). It also tells you how much under the bar. For example, back in Figure 28.4, Xternal HD (drive X:) has 20.1 GB left of free space. Its total capacity is 111 GB.

TIP If your Computer folder doesn't show the meters, click Views in its toolbar and choose Tiles. If yours aren't grouped, point to the Type column heading, click the arrow that appears and choose Group. If your hard drives aren't listed first, click the Type column heading.

To see how much space is left on a jump drive, floppy disk, or memory card, first insert the disk or card. Right-click the icon for that drive and choose Properties. You see a dialog box like the example shown in Figure 28.5. There you can see how much space is used, how much is still available, and the total capacity of the disk or card.

If you see 0 bytes capacity, that means you right-clicked the icon for a drive or slot that's empty. An empty drive has no capacity because there's no disk in it. The drive or slot doesn't have a capacity. The disk or card in it has a capacity. No disk or card in a drive means no capacity (0 bytes).

If you check the capacity of a CD or DVD that's already been burned, you might see 0 bytes free, even if the used space doesn't match the total capacity of that drive. That's because optical media (CDs and DVDs) don't work quite like other types. We'll get into all of that in Chapter 32.

FIGURE 28.5

Sample used space, free space, capacity.

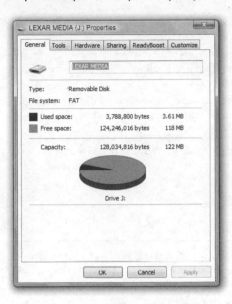

If you right-click the icon for a portable device, you might not see used space, free space, or capacity. Again, that's just because the Properties sheet for a portable device tends to show information about the device as a whole, not just its storage. It's no big deal though because typically you copy files *from* portable devices, not to them. Also you tend to use programs like Photo Gallery and Windows Media Player to work with portable devices, not your Computer folder.

Viewing disk contents

Disks exist for one reason only — to store information. That information is stored in files, often organized into folders. To view the contents of a disk or memory card, insert it into its drive or slot and then open (double-click) its icon in your Computer folder. Make sure you insert the disk or card first, because it makes no sense to open the icon for an empty drive.

For example, if there is no floppy disk in your floppy drive, it makes no sense to open that icon. There has to be a disk in the drive whose contents you want to view. The same goes for CD/DVD drives and memory card slots.

Like your hard disk, external disks store data in folders and files. Each folder and file on the disk is represented by an icon. Double-click a folder's icon to view its contents. Double-click a file's icon to open the file and see its contents. Use the Back button to back out of a folder to wherever you were before.

Formatting disks

It seems just about everyone has heard of the concept of *formatting* a disk. But not many people really understand what that's about. So let's start with some basic rules of thumb:

- Not all disks need to be formatted. Only blank, unformatted floppy disks and a few other types need to be formatted. But only once, not each time you use the disk.

- Never presume that you have to format a disk. If a disk needs to be formatted, you'll see a message telling you so and an option to format it right on the spot. If you don't see such a message, don't format the disk or even think about formatting the disk.

- Formatting a disk permanently erases the contents of that disk. Never format a disk unless you are 100 percent certain you will never need anything on that disk again for the rest of your life.

Don't even *think* about formatting your hard disk. You won't be able to anyway. But formatting your hard disk would erase Windows Vista, all of your installed programs, Contacts, saved e-mails, saved files — everything. You don't want to do that unless you really know what you're doing and are certain that you can easily get back everything you lost in the process.

About Folders

Information stored on a disk is organized into files. For example, a photograph is stored as a file. A song is stored as a file. The files may be organized into *folders*. Folders on a disk play exactly the same role as folders in a filing cabinet — to organize things so they're easier to find when you need them.

If you're confused as to why folders exist at all, look at it this way. Suppose you went to your filing cabinet (the real one with paper in it) and dumped the contents of every single folder onto your desk. You end up with a big messy pile of paper on your desk. Finding anything in that pile would not be easy. That's why we put things into folders in filing cabinets in the first place — to make it easy to find things when we need them.

Disks can store thousands of files. If every time you opened a disk's icon you were faced with thousands of filenames, you'd have the same basic problem as the mountain of papers on your desk. You'd spend all your time looking through icons and filenames rather than getting stuff done.

In short, folders on disks exist for exactly the same reason manila file folders in filing cabinets exist — to organize information. Nothing more, nothing less. When you're looking at a disk's contents, it's fairly easy to tell which icons represent folders:

- The icon for a folder usually looks like a manila file folder.
- Folders are usually listed first.

Figure 28.6 shows some examples of icons that represent folders.

FIGURE 28.6

Icons that represent folders.

Viewing the contents of a folder

To open a folder and see what's inside, you just double-click the folder's icon. The name of the folder whose contents you're currently viewing always appears at the end of the breadcrumb trail near the top of the window. The contents of the folder appear in the main pane at the center of the window. Figure 28.7 shows an example where I'm viewing the contents of a folder named Music in my user account (Alan).

FIGURE 28.7

Viewing the contents of a folder.

It might seem odd that the folder named Music contains icons for still more folders. But that's the way it often works. Any folder can contain still more folders, files, or both. That's different from the way folders in a filing cabinet work. So let's take a look at what's up with that.

Folders in folders (subfolders)

In a filing cabinet, a folder usually contains documents, not other folders. But any computer folder can contain still more folders. We call the folders within a folder *subfolders*. But they're still just folders. For example, Figure 28.7 is showing the contents of a folder named Music. All the folder icons that appear in the main pane are subfolders of that Music folder (but they're still just folders).

Subfolders allow you to organize information hierarchically so things are easier to find when you need them. For example, let's say you copy thousands of songs from your audio CDs into your Music folder with Windows Media Player. If you opened your Music folder and saw an icon for every single song, that could be a pain if you were looking for a specific song. You'd have to read through lots of filenames until you found the one you want.

To better organize things, Media Player organizes your songs by artist and album. So when you open your Music folder you see a folder icon for each artist. When you open an artist's folder, you see an icon for each album by that artist. And when you open the folder for an album, you see all the songs by that artist.

So once again, the important thing to remember about folders and subfolders is that they're really no big technical thing. They're just a means of organizing files into groups — same as folders in a filing cabinet. Of course, you need to know how to *navigate* through folders for any of this to be useful, because all of your files are stored in folders. Before we get to navigation though, let's talk about files.

Parent folders

The folder in which a subfolder is contained is called the *parent* to that folder. For example, if you click the Start button and then click your user name, you open the main document folder for your user account. That folder you opened is the parent to all the subfolders you see in the main pane.

 **When you're navigating through folders, it's easy to get to the current folder's parent. Just click its name in the Address bar. That name is the second-to-last one in the breadcrumb trail.**

About Files

The smallest unit of storage on a disk is the *file*. Every file has a filename and an icon. A file can be just about anything — a photograph, a song, a video clip, a typed report, a spreadsheet, a contact — whatever. In the preceding section, I likened a computer folder to a manila file folder in a filing cabinet. Using the same analogy here, a file is roughly equivalent to one thing you'd put inside a manila file folder. In fact, that's the whole idea. You organize your computer files into folders just as you organize your paper files into manila file folders.

In the preceding section, you also saw how the icon that represents a folder often looks like a manila file folder. Icons that represent files don't have a manila file folder in their icon, because that would just confuse things. Icons that represent files tend to look more like little dog-eared sheets of paper. On top of that sheet of paper you might see the logo of the program that opens or plays the file. More on that topic in a moment.

Figure 28.8 shows examples of some icons that represent files. But you have to bear in mind that there are thousands of different kinds of files, and thousands of different programs. So don't expect to find those exact examples anywhere on your system. The key thing is that the icons for files don't look like manila file folders.

FIGURE 28.8

Sample icons that represent files.

Pictures and videos are also files. But their icons don't always sport the dog-eared sheet of paper look. Instead, their icons usually look like the actual picture that's in the file, or the first frame of the video in the file. Windows Vista shows them that way because it saves you from having to open the file to see what picture it contains. See Figure 28.9.

FIGURE 28.9

Sample icons for pictures (top) and videos (bottom).

Opening and closing files

To see, change, or print what's in a file, you *open* that file. You do that in the same way you open a folder or the icon that represents a disk drive — by double-clicking the file's icon.

 You might be able to open a drive, folder, or file by single-clicking its icon. It all depends on a setting in the Folder and Search Options dialog box described later in this chapter.

Document files never open by themselves. A file has to open within some program. There are thousands of different kinds of files, and thousands of different programs. So I can't tell you off hand what program that will be. But if you can open the file at all, it will open and appear within a program.

 Chapter 2 discusses the basics of using programs and program windows.

Showing/hiding filename extensions

Windows uses a file's *extension* to determine what program to use to open a file. The extension is a short abbreviation, preceded by a period, at the end of the filename as in the example shown in Figure 28.10.

FIGURE 28.10

Filename and extension.

If you want to see the filename extension for a single file, right-click the file's icon and choose Properties. In the Properties dialog box that opens, you'll see the file's type (in words) followed by the extension in parentheses. For example, if you right-click the icon for a video file, you might see something like the following (The `.wmv` in parentheses is the filename extension that's hidden in Explorer's main contents pane.):

`Type of file: Windows Media Audio/Video file (.wmv)`

To see filename extensions for all files in Explorer, click the Organize button and choose Folder and Search Options. In the dialog box that opens, click the View tab and clear the checkmark next to Hide extensions for known file types. Then click OK.

> **NOTE** Folders don't have extensions on their names. So you'll never see an extension in either its Properties sheet or Explorer.

If you opt to make filename extensions visible in Explorer, you have to be careful not to change the extension when renaming a file. Changing a file's extension doesn't change the file's type. It just assigns the wrong type to the file, which could make it impossible to open the file. You'll need to rename the file back to its original extension before you can open the file again.

Choosing a program to open a file

The program that opens automatically when you open a file icon is called the *default program* for that file type. But you're not stuck with that. If you have two or more programs capable of opening a file type, you can right-click the file's icon, choose Open With, and then click the name of the program you want to open the file with (see Figure 28.11). The file will open in the specified program this one time.

FIGURE 28.11

Choosing Open With.

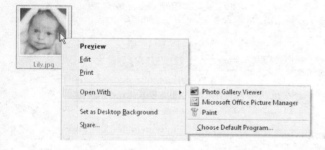

Changing the default program

If you want to permanently change the default program that opens when you open a particular type of file, right-click the file's icon and choose Open With as just described. But don't click a program name. Instead, click Choose Default Program. The Open With dialog box opens. Figure 28.12 shows an example. But the programs that appear in your dialog box depend on the type of file you right-clicked and the programs installed on your computer.

FIGURE 28.12

The Open With dialog box.

You can click any program name to make it the default for opening files of the same type as the one you right-clicked. If the program you want to use doesn't show in the Open With dialog box, you can use the Browse button to choose the program's startup file. But you must know the name and location of that file in advance — the Browse button won't find it for you.

When choosing a program to open the file, make sure you choose a program that *can* open that file type. Otherwise you'll end up with an error message or gobbledygook when the file tries to open in that program.

To make the change permanent, select (check) the Always use the selected program to open this kind of file checkbox. Click OK after making your selections.

To test the change, double-click the icon for which you changed the default program. It should open in the program you specified. If you chose a program that cannot open that file type, you'll end up with an error message or a bunch of meaningless gobbledygook. If that happens, you need to get back to the Open With dialog box and choose a recommended program, or any program that you know for sure can handle that type of file.

Windows cannot open this file

It's possible that Windows won't be able to open a file at all. For example, suppose someone sends you a Microsoft Excel spreadsheet attached to an e-mail message. If you don't have Microsoft Excel installed on your computer, Windows won't be able to open the file. Instead it will display an error message like the example in Figure 28.13.

FIGURE 28.13

When Windows can't open a file.

If you're new to all of this, there's no easy way to guess what program might work to open the file. Like I said, there are thousands of file types and thousands of programs out there. Your best bet might be to ask the person who sent you the file what program you need to open the file. Or, ask them to send you the file in some other format that you can open.

File paths

Every file on your system is in a specific location defined as the *path* to the file. The path starts with the drive letter (for example, C: for your primary hard disk), the folder in which the file is stored, and all the higher-level folders leading up to that folder. Each part of the path is separated by a backslash (\).

For example, let's say I'm in my user account (Alan) and I save a file named `MyMovie.wmv` to my Videos folder. The path to that folder would be:

`C:\Users\Alan\Videos\MyMovie.wmv`

Figure 28.14 shows why this is so. It starts with the fact that your hard disk has, at its highest level, at least three folders. One is named Program Files, and it contains subfolders and files for all of the programs that are installed on your system. A second folder named Users contains a subfolder for each user account. A third folder, named Windows, contains all the folders and files that make up the Windows Vista operating system.

CAUTION   The Program Files and Windows folders contain files used by the system. There is nothing in those folders that's intended for use by people. Your best bet is to stay out of those folders, and try to pretend they don't exist. Never save your own files to those folders. And whatever you do, never delete, move, or rename a file in any of those folders. Doing so could render your computer useless until a professional can figure out how to fix your mistake!

Each user account folder in the Users folder contains the built-in folders people can use to store their documents. These include the Music, Pictures, and Videos folders among others.

The path `C:\Users\Alan\Videos\MyMovie.wmv` tells Windows exactly how to get to the file. It has to start by going to the hard drive (C:), drilling down through the folders named Users and Alan until it gets to the folder named Videos. There it will find the file named `MyMovie.wmv`. Figure 28.14 shows the basic idea, using a few sample folders from the folder hierarchy.

FIGURE 28.14

C:\Users\Alan\Videos\MyMovie.wmv

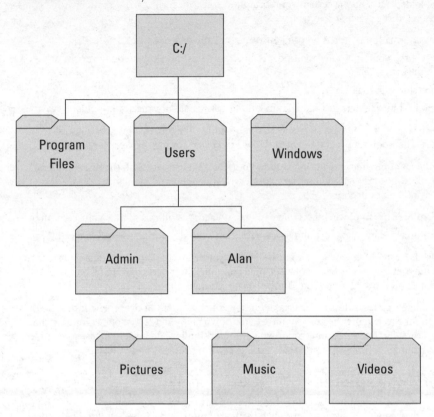

It's unlikely that you would ever need to type — even know — the path to a file. I only mention it because you'll see paths like that from time to time. The program you'll use to navigate through folders, Windows Explorer, makes it very easy to get around without worrying about paths.

TIP   If you ever do need to see the actual path to the folder you're currently viewing, there's an easy way to do it. Just click the folder icon at the left side of the Address bar. The breadcrumb trail in the Address bar changes to the actual path of the folder. The path is also selected so you can press Ctrl+C to copy it to the Clipboard and paste wherever appropriate.

Using Windows Explorer

Knowing about drives, folders, and files is certainly important. In fact, you really can't do much with a computer until you've mastered those concepts. To review:

- All computer information is stored on some medium, usually disks.
- All the stuff that's in your computer right now is stored on a hard disk that you never see or remove from the computer.
- Information is stored in files.
- Files are organized into folders just like files in a filing cabinet are organized into folders.

Once you understand the concepts, the next step is to learn how to use the tool that gives you access to drives, folders, and files. That tool is a program named *Windows Explorer* (or just *Explorer* for short).

Windows Explorer is the main program for getting around your computer to access all the disks, folders, and files available to you. Notice I didn't say Internet Explorer. Despite the name similarity, the two programs serve two entirely different purposes:

- **Windows Explorer** (or **Explorer**): Lets you explore and access stuff that's *inside* your computer.
- **Internet Explorer:** Lets you explore and access stuff that's *outside* your computer on the Internet.

That's a huge difference. For one thing, you have to be online (connected to the Internet) to use Internet Explorer, because the Internet exists outside of your personal computer. You don't have to be online to use Windows Explorer because all the stuff you're exploring is inside your computer.

There's also a big size difference. The Internet consists of millions of computers all over the world. A lifetime isn't nearly enough time to explore the entire Internet. Your own computer is just one computer. It doesn't take anywhere near a lifetime to explore your own computer! But you do have to invest some time in learning how to use Explorer if you want to be able to use everything your computer has to offer.

Opening Windows Explorer

You start most programs on your computer by going through the Start menu or All Programs menu. You *can* start Windows Explorer that way if you want to. Just click the Start button and choose All Programs ⇨ Accessories ⇨ Windows Explorer. But there's no reason to do that because Windows Explorer opens automatically whenever you open *any* folder. For example, if you click the Start button and then click your user name, Documents, Pictures, Music, or Computer, Windows Explorer opens automatically to show you the contents of that folder.

Windows Explorer components

Windows Explorer has many optional panes and other gizmos. Figure 28.15 points out the names of the main ones. Some may not be visible when you first open a folder. But they're easy to show or hide, so don't worry about that.

FIGURE 28.15

Explorer panes and tools.

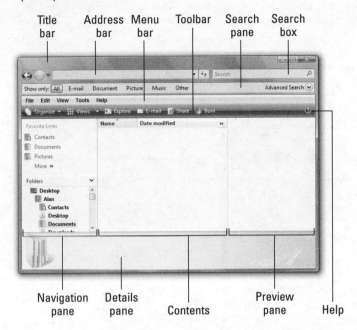

Here's a quick overview of the main components:

- **Title bar:** Use this to move the whole window as convenient. Use the Minimize, Maximize, and Close buttons to size the window as you would in any other program. (See "Sizing program windows" and "Moving a program window" in Chapter 2.)

- **Address bar:** Displays a breadcrumb trail (also called an eyebrow menu) of drives and folders leading up to the folder you're viewing. The name of the folder you're currently viewing appears at the end.

- **Search box:** Lets you search by name for an item within the current folder.

- **Search pane:** Lets you conduct a more thorough and exact search than the Search box. This topic is covered in Chapter 30.

- **Classic menus:** Similar to the menu bar in earlier versions of Windows. When this is hidden, you can tap the Alt key to make it visible.

- **Toolbar:** Buttons in the toolbar let you do things with files and folders in the contents pane. They change depending on the types of icons you select in the folder.

- **Navigation pane:** Makes it easy to get to any drive or folder in your computer.

- **Contents:** The contents of the folder you're currently viewing.

- **Preview pane:** When you select an icon, this pane provides a sneak peek into the file's contents, when possible. Otherwise it just shows an enlarged version of the icon.

- **Details pane:** Shows some detailed information about the icon(s) currently selected in the contents pane.

Show or hide optional panes

To show or hide optional components, click the Organize toolbar button and choose Layout as in Figure 28.16. Items that are currently showing have a light blue highlight. Items that aren't showing have no highlight. To show or hide an item, click its name on the menu.

FIGURE 28.16

Show or hide Explorer panes.

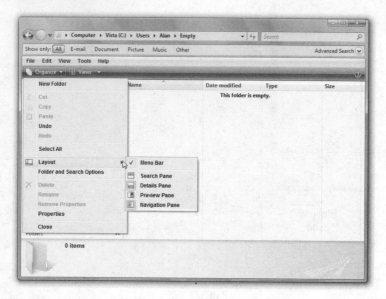

Navigating with the Address bar

No matter how you open Windows Explorer, it's easy to get just about anywhere from the Address bar. Don't assume that only the names in the Address bar matter. You can click the << or >> symbol (if any), or any triangle between names to see nearby places to which you can navigate just by clicking the item's name. So here's how it works:

- If you see the name of the folder you want to open, click that name.

- Otherwise, click the triangle to the right of any name to see its subfolders, as in Figure 28.17, and then click the folder you want to open.

FIGURE 28.17

Show or hide Explorer components.

- Or click the << symbol at the left side of the trail to get to higher-level places.
- Or, click the Previous Locations button (the down-pointing triangle at the right side of the Address bar) or the Recent Pages button (the triangle to the right of the Forward button) to return to any recently visited folder.

NOTE The button with the two curvy arrows is a Refresh button. That one doesn't take you to a different location. Rather, it just ensures that the contents of the folder you're currently viewing are up-to-date.

You can also type the name of the folder to which you want to navigate right into the Address bar. But that only works with certain built-in folders. First, click the icon that appears at the left side of the Address bar. Then type the first few letters of the place you want to go. A drop-down menu will display matching locations as you type. When you see the name of the folder to which you want to navigate, click that name. Or type the entire name and press Enter.

TIP You can type the URL (address) of an Internet location into the Address bar. When you press Enter, Internet Explorer will open to show the page at that URL. To return to Windows Explorer, close Internet Explorer or click the taskbar button on the folder you were in.

Of course, you can also use the Back and Forward buttons to the left of the Address bar to navigate. At first, both buttons may be disabled (dimmed) because there's no place to go back or forward to. But when you go from one folder to another, the Back button is enabled. So you can click that to return to the place you just left. After you click the Back button, the Forward button is enabled. Click that to return to the folder you just backed out of.

Navigating with Navigation pane

You can get anywhere from the Address bar. But at times you may find it more convenient to use the Navigation pane. When open, the Navigation pane offers two ways to get around. The first way is the Favorite Links box at the top of the pane. That one shows links for commonly used folders, or any locations you want. Click any link to open it in the current window. Or right-click a link and choose Open to open it in a new window. This is handy when you want to move or copy files to the new location by dragging.

TIP Choosing Open Folder Location also opens in a new, separate window. But that new window ends up behind, rather than on top of, the current window.

The lower half of the Navigation pane shows the Folders list. If you don't see the Folders list, click the Folders bar at the bottom of the Navigation pane.

To widen or narrow the Navigation pane, get the tip of the mouse pointer on its right border so the mouse pointer turns to a two-headed arrow. Then drag left or right. Similarly, to make the Folders list taller or shorter, drag the upper border up or down.

You can expand and collapse drives and folders in the Folders list to see more, or fewer, details. Click the white triangle next to any name to expand. Click the black triangle next to any name to collapse. Figure 28.18 show where all these things are located.

FIGURE 28.18

Working the Navigation pane.

When you click a folder name or drive in the Folders list, it opens in the current window. If you want to open the folder or drive in a separate window, right-click and choose Open.

Adding places to Favorite Links

The Favorite Links box provides easy one-click access to any drive or folder on your system. Initially, you'll see a few links in there. But you can replace those with any you like. Just drag the icon for any item to which you want easy access into the Favorite Links pane. Figure 28.19 shows an example where I'm in the process of dragging the Contacts icon from my user account folder into the Favorite Links pane. Release the mouse button to create the link.

FIGURE 28.19

Create your own favorite link.

Managing favorite links

Managing favorite links is easy too. Here are the basics:

- To rename a link, right-click the link, choose Rename, type the new name or edit the existing name, and press Enter.

- To alphabetize links, right-click any link and choose Sort by Name.

- To remove a link you don't use, right-click it and choose Remove Link. Then choose Yes when asked for confirmation.

> **NOTE** Removing a favorite link does not delete the associated folder. So don't worry about losing anything when you right-click and choose Remove Link.

Navigating from the contents pane

The main contents pane at the center of Explorer's program window shows you the contents of whatever folder you're viewing at the moment. If the folder you've opened contains subfolders, you can open a subfolder by double-clicking its icon, or by single-clicking, if you've configured Folder and Search Options for single clicking. After you've opened a subfolder, you can click the Back button to return to the parent folder.

If you want to open a subfolder in a separate window, right-click the folder's icon and choose Explore. Then you can size and position the two open folder windows so you can see the contents of both. Then you can move files from one folder to the other just by dragging their icons.

What About E-mail Messages?

Computer files are like files in your filing cabinet. There's a basic assumption that you intend to keep them forever. E-mail messages aren't files, per se. They're *messages*, and they have roughly the same status as messages left on your telephone answering machine. There is a basic assumption that you don't intend to keep them. As such, messages are usually stored in folders that exist only in your e-mail client (the program you use to send and receive e-mail).

Attachments to e-mail messages are files. But they don't automatically go into the kinds of folders we're discussing in this chapter. An attachment stays in your e-mail client unless you specifically save the attachment to a regular folder like Pictures or Documents. Exactly how you save an attachment depends on your e-mail client. But typically you right-click the attachment's icon and choose Save or Save As.

If you happen to use Windows Mail as your e-mail client, I just told a little white lie. Each message in Windows Mail *is* stored as an `.eml` file in a folder. If you use Windows Mail and want to explore that some more, see "Where and How Messages Are Stored" in Chapter 18.

Regardless of how you navigate, you can get to any folder on any drive on your system. Some people will want to use buttons in the Address bar. Others will want to use the more traditional Folders list in the Navigation pane. It doesn't matter which you use or how you get to the folder you need. All that matters is that you be able to get there when you need to.

Navigating to a disk drive

You can get to any disk drive on your system from the Computer folder. You've already seen several ways to get to that folder. If you use it often, you might consider adding a Computer link to your Favorite Links pane (if it doesn't already have one). To do that, type the word Desktop into the Address bar and press Enter. Then drag the Computer icon from the content area into the Favorite Links pane. While you're at it, you might consider dragging any other frequently used folders, like the one for your user account or the Public folder, into Favorite Links.

If you have other disk drives you use often, you can create links for them as well. Just open your Computer folder and drag the drive's icon into Favorite Links.

You can also get to any disk drive right from the Folders list. If you see a white triangle next to Computer in the Folders list, click the triangle to see all of your available drives. Click the name of the drive you want to open. Or right-click the drive and choose Open to open it in a new window. If the drive name shows a white triangle in the Folders list, you can click that triangle to see folders and files on the disk in the drive without opening the drive.

TIP Here are a couple tricks you can use with USB drives in the Folders list. Right-click and choose Open As Portable Device to see how much space is available. Right-click and choose Safely Remove to close the drive before pulling it from the USB slot.

Choosing an icon view

Once you're in a folder, you can view its contents in several different ways. As usual, there's no right or wrong way, or good or bad way. There's just different ways and you should use whichever one is most convenient at the moment. To choose how you want to view icons, click the Views toolbar button to see the slider and options shown in Figure 28.20.

FIGURE 28.20

Choosing a view.

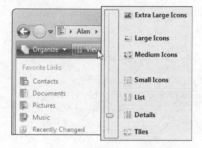

To choose how you want to view icons, click any option along the slider, or drag the box up and down the slider. If your mouse has a wheel, you don't even have to click the Views button. Just hold down the Ctrl key while you spin the mouse wheel as you would to size desktop icons.

Most of the options show each item as an icon and filename. The Tiles view shows the type and size of each file. For folders it just shows File Folder.

Using columns in the Details view

The Details view of a folder shows icons for folders and files in a tabular view like the example in Figure 28.19. You can use this view to show a lot of information about each folder and file. The column headings you see across the top of the display (Name, Date Modified, Type, and so forth) don't tell the whole story. You can choose columns to view as you see fit. Just right-click any column heading to reveal more column names as in Figure 28.21.

FIGURE 28.21

Right-click any column heading.

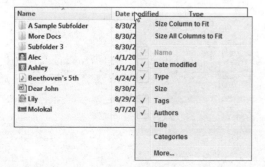

To add a column to the display, click its name on the menu. To remove a column, click its name on the menu to clear its checkmark. To see other columns to display, click More... at the bottom of the menu. Then select (check) the columns you want to see. Clear the checkmarks of columns you don't want to see. Then click OK.

If you choose more columns than can fit within the window, you'll see a horizontal scroll bar at the bottom of the contents pane. Use that to scroll left and right through the columns you've selected.

To size a column, put the tip of the mouse pointer on the right border of the column heading so the mouse pointer turns to a two-headed arrow. Then drag left or right. To move a column left or right, put the tip of the mouse pointer right on the column name, then drag left or right.

 The techniques for moving and sizing columns aren't unique to the Details view. They work in just about any tabular view in any program.

Sorting icons

The View menu let's you choose different ways of viewing icons. The column headings under the toolbar let you choose different ways of *arranging* the icon in a folder. Those column headings aren't only visible in the Details view. They're visible in all views. It might seem weird to have column headings showing when the icons aren't arranged into columns. But they're there for a good reason — you can click any one of them to sort and alphabetize icons on an as-needed basis.

To sort icons, you just click the column heading by which you want to sort. The first click usually puts then in ascending order (A to Z, smallest to largest, or oldest to newest). When icons are sorted into ascending order, the column heading shows an up-pointing triangle.

For example, when you click the Name column heading and see an up-pointing triangle in that column heading, you know the icons are in ascending alphabetical order. Folders are always listed before files. So the folders will be listed first in alphabetical order, followed by files in alphabetical order. Figure 28.22 shows an example.

FIGURE 28.22

Icons in alphabetical order.

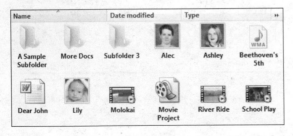

When you click the Date Modified column heading, you sort icons by the date they were last modified. The first click puts them in ascending order (newest to oldest). The second click puts them in descending order (oldest to newest).

You can sort icons by any column heading, in any view. When you see a >> symbol at the right side of the column headings, you can click it to sort by some other column. If the column on which you want to base the sort isn't available, you can add that column heading as described in the previous section.

Grouping and stacking icons

When you point to a column heading, a triangle appears to the right of the column name. Clicking that triangle displays options for sorting, grouping, and filtering icons in the folder. These options work best in folders or search results that contain lots of icons. The exact options you see vary from one column heading to the next, because different columns offer different ways of arranging things. As a general example, Figure 28.23 shows options that appear when you click the arrow next to Date Modified.

FIGURE 28.23

Click the arrow next to a Date Modified.

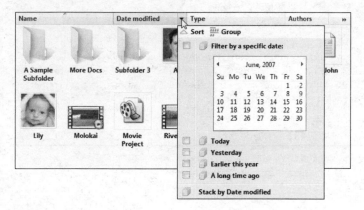

Clicking Group groups icons into categories that appear next to checkboxes. For example, clicking the Group option in Figure 28.23 groups icons into Today, Yesterday, Earlier this Year, and A Long Time Ago categories. If the sort order is ascending, then the groups are from newest to oldest as in Figure 28.24.

FIGURE 28.24

Icons grouped by Date Modified.

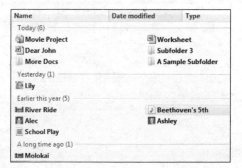

When icons are grouped, you see a title and separator line above each group. You can do the following with that line:

- Click the line to select all icons in the group. To select or unselect icons in additional groups, hold down the Ctrl key as you click their lines.
- Click the arrow at the right side of the line to expand (show) or collapse (hide) the group.
- Right-click the line to expand or collapse all groups.
- Point to the column heading and click that arrow to bring back the Sorting and Group options. Then select (check) the groups you want to see. Leave checkboxes empty for groups that you don't want to see.
- To ungroup, click the arrow on the column heading and click Sort.
- To undo all grouping and filtering, click the folder name in the Address bar.

 To select only files of a certain type in a folder, group by the Type column. Then click the heading of the group whose icons you want to select.

Stacking icons

A stack is similar to a folder in that it can contain multiple icons. But it's a *virtual folder* because it isn't a permanent container like a folder. Instead it's just a logical grouping of icons based on some criterion rather than the actual file location. Figure 28.25 shows the same icons from Figure 28.23 shown stacked (rather than grouped) by Date Modified. To see what's in a stack, double-click the stack icon.

FIGURE 28.25

Icons stacked by Date Modified.

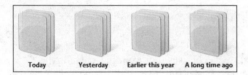

To unstack icons, click the arrow on the column heading again and click Sort.

Filtering icons

Filtering is a means of temporarily hiding things when they're just in the way. For example, let's say you're viewing a folder that contains dozens, or even hundreds of icons. You want to focus on just the files and folders you modified today or yesterday. You don't want to delete the other icons. You just want to put them into hiding temporarily so you can focus on the more recently edited icons.

To view just the icons you modified today and yesterday, you would select (check) the Today and Yesterday checkboxes shown back in Figure 28.23. Then click outside the menu. Icons that were not modified today or yesterday remain visible while all other icons disappear. The Date Modified column heading shows a checkmark to serve as a visual reminder that you're not viewing all icons — only icons that meet certain Date Modified criteria, as in Figure 28.26.

FIGURE 28.26

The checkmark next to Date Modified tells you some icons are hidden.

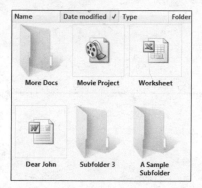

The Search Box in the upper-right corner of a folder also plays a filtering role. As you type in the Search box, only files from the current folder and its subfolders that match those characters remain visible. Icons that don't match what you've typed are temporarily hidden from view. This makes it easy to quickly locate icons in a large folder based on their names. When you search from the Search box, the Address bar shows the words Search Results rather than the folder name. To undo the search and bring all icons from the folder back into view, click the Search box and press Escape (Esc).

 Chapters 30 and 31 discuss searching in detail.

Using the Preview pane

The optional Preview pane at the right side of Explorer tries to show the contents of whatever icon is selected in Explorer. If no icon is selected, the Preview pane shows only the words "Select a file to preview." If the Preview pane isn't open, click the Organize button and choose Layout ➪ Preview Pane to open it. The window has to be wide enough to accommodate the contents pane and whatever else is showing. If the window is too narrow, the Preview pane disappears. You have to widen the window or close the Navigation pane to make room for the Preview pane.

 See "How to Select Icons" in Chapter 29 for the many different ways you can select icons.

What shows in the Preview pane depends on the type of icon you select, as follows:

- If you select a picture's icon, the pane shows that picture.
- If you select a music or video file, the pane shows options for playing that file.
- If you select an icon whose contents can be read directly by Windows Vista, you see a portion of the file's contents in the pane.
- If you select a folder icon or any file that can't be previewed, the pane just shows No preview available.

As with any pane, you can widen and narrow the Preview pane by dragging its inner border. Just make sure you get the tip of the mouse pointer right on the bar, so you see the two-headed arrow before you hold down the left mouse button and start dragging. The wider you make the Preview pane, the larger the pre-view image.

Figure 28.27 shows an example where I've selected a video file icon in a folder. I've also pointed out the two-headed mouse pointer you need to see in order to widen or narrow the pane.

FIGURE 28.27

Preview pane, selected icon, and sizing mouse pointer.

Using the Details pane

The optional Details pane at the bottom of Explorer's window also shows information about the currently selected icon or icons. To show or hide that pane, click the Organize button and choose Layout ⇨ Details Pane. How much information shows depends on the icon(s) you select and how tall you make the pane. Drag the upper border of the pane to make it shorter or taller.

Figure 28.28 shows an example where I've selected three icons that represent files containing pictures. Depending on the type of file(s) selected, you might be able to change the Authors, Tags, Comments, Categories, Status, Content Type, or Subject of the selected items right in the Details pane. That information becomes metadata used by the search index for quickly finding and arranging icons in a way that transcends their physical locations in folders. Chapter 31 gets into the whole business of metadata and searching.

FIGURE 28.28

Detail pane and three icons selected.

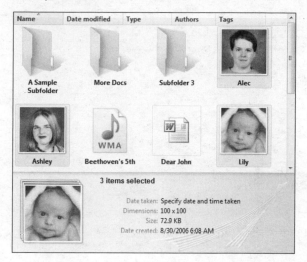

To Click or Double-Click?

As mentioned throughout this book, you may have to double-click icons to open them. Or you may only have to click once on an icon to open it. Whether you have to double-click or single-click is entirely up to you. The default is usually to double-click, because that method allows you to select icons by clicking, which is easier for people who haven't fully mastered the mouse.

You use the Folder and Search Options dialog box to choose between the double-click and single-click methods. Here's how:

1. Open any folder so you're in Windows Explorer.
2. Click the Organize button and choose Folder and Search Options. Or if you're using the Classic Menus, choose Tools ➪ Folder and Search Options. Either way, the Folder and Search Options dialog box opens as in Figure 28.29.

FIGURE 28.29

The General tab of Folder and Search Options.

3. Under click Items as follow choose how you want to handle icons:

    ■ **Single-click to open an item (point to select):** Choose this option if you want to be able to open icons by clicking once. If you choose this option, also choose one of the following:

        ■ **Underline icon titles consistent with my browser:** Choosing this option will usually make all icon names look like hyperlinks (blue and underlined).

        ■ **Underline icon titles only when I point at them:** Choosing this option leaves icon names alone so they look normal. The name only looks like a hyperlink when you touch it with your mouse pointer.

    ■ **Double-click to open an item (single-click to select):** This is the more classical approach where you have to double-click icons to open them. If you're new to computers or have difficulty using a mouse, this might be your best bet.

4. Click **OK**.

TIP Here are a couple of other ways to get to Folder and Search Options: Tap ⊞, type `fol`, and click Folder Options under the Programs heading; or click the Start button and choose Control Panel ➪ Appearance and Personalization ➪ Folder Options.

Personalizing folder behavior

The Folder and Search Options dialog box offers many more options than double-click/single-click. On the General tab, you can choose from the following options:

- **Show preview and filters:** Choosing this option makes your folders look like most of the examples shown in this book, with a toolbar and optional panes.

- **Use Windows classic folders:** Choosing this option hides most of the newer Vista features and makes folders look the way they did in older versions of Windows. Use the menu bar to choose options and get things done.

- **Open each folder in the same window:** This is the default behavior where each time you open a folder, the current instance of Explorer shows the contents of that folder.

- **Open each folder in its own window:** Choosing this option causes each folder to open in a separate instance of Explorer. So you end up with an instance of Explorer for each open folder.

When two or more folders are open, you can right-click the clock and choose a Tile or Cascade option to organize them. Use taskbar buttons, Alt+Tab, or ⊞+Tab to switch among them.

If you open enough separate instances of Explorer, their taskbar buttons will eventually collapse into a single taskbar button titled Windows Explorer. You can close them all in one fell swoop by right-clicking that taskbar button and choosing Close Group.

Options on the View tab

Clicking the View tab in the Folder and Search Options dialog box takes you to a whole bunch of options for controlling folder behavior (see Figure 28.30). Most of the options are self-explanatory. If you open a folder that shows icons for pictures and a Navigation pane, you'll be able to try out many on the fly. Just fill or clear a checkbox and click Apply to see how it affects that open folder.

FIGURE 28.30

The View tab of Folder and Search Options.

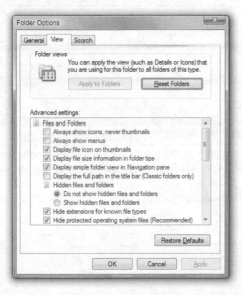

CAUTION The settings you choose in Folder and Search Options apply to all folders, not just the folder you have open at the moment. The one oddball exception is the first one on the tab. See "Personalizing your folder" later in this chapter for ways of customizing a single folder.

Some options aren't quite so obvious. In the interest of being complete, I'll run through them all in the sections to follow.

Always show icons, never thumbnails

If you choose this option, icons for pictures and videos will be generic icons rather than mini-pictures of the file's contents. It might help speed things along on an extremely slow computer. But to see the picture in a file, you'll need to open that picture. You won't be able to see the picture in Explorer.

This option has no effect on Windows Photo Gallery. That's because Windows Photo Gallery is a program, not a folder.

Always show menus

Choose this option if you want the classic menu bar to open automatically with Explorer. If you don't choose this option, the menu bar is hidden when you first open Explorer. To open it, tap the Alt key or click Organize ➪ Layout ➪ Classic Menus.

Display file icon on thumbnails

If you choose this option, thumbnails will show the logo of the default program for opening the file, as at the left of Figure 28.31. The icon represents a video that will play in Windows Media Player. The icon on the thumbnail is Media Player's logo. If you clear the option, thumbnails show without the logo, as on the right side of Figure 28.31.

FIGURE 28.31

Thumbnail with (left) and without (right) icon.

Display file size information in folder tips

This option is about the size of files and folders in terms of how much disk space they use, not the visual size of the icon on the screen. When you choose this option, you're telling Explorer to show a folder's size when you point to (rest the mouse pointer on) a folder's icon. That size is the sum of the sizes of all the files in the folder. For example, all the songs in the Music folder shown in Figure 28.32 are taking up 1.48 GB of disk space. You can see that in the tooltip that appears under the mouse pointer.

FIGURE 28.32

Size of folder (1.48 GB) in folder's tooltip.

If you clear this option, the tooltip shows only the Date Created for the folder.

Display simple folder view in Navigation pane

This option applies to the Folders list that you can open at the bottom of the Navigation pane. If you choose this option, you see lines connecting folders and subfolders in that list. If you clear this option, the lines don't show.

Display the full path in the title bar (Classic folders only)

This option applies only if you select "Use Windows Classic folders" on the General tab to remove Vista features from Explorer. It has no effect if you choose "Show preview and tasks" on that tab.

In Classic folders, the title bar normally displays only the name of the folder you're currently viewing, such as `Music`. If you choose this option, the title bar shows the complete path to the file, like `C:\Users\YourUserAccountName\Music`.

Show hidden files and folders

Hidden files are those that have the Hidden attribute checked on the Properties sheet. If you choose Do not show hidden files and folders, then files and folders that have the Hidden attribute checked won't appear at all in Explorer. If you choose Show hidden files and folders, you'll see those folders and files. But their icons are dimmed to distinguish them from items that aren't marked as hidden.

 **TIP** To get to the Properties sheet for a file or folder, right-click its icon and choose Properties.

Hide extensions for known file types

As mentioned earlier in this chapter, every file has a filename extension that indicates the file type. That extension also determines which program will open when you open the file. A *known file* is one for which you already have a default program installed and defined.

Choosing *Hide extensions for known file types* hides filename extensions for known file types. So you see only the filename without the extension for those kinds of files as at the left side of Figure 28.33. Clearing that option displays filename extensions for all files, as at the right side of Figure 28.33.

FIGURE 28.33

Extensions hidden (left) and not hidden (right).

As always, choosing one option or the other is strictly a matter of personal preference. Sometimes it's convenient to see filename extensions. Other times they might just seem to be adding unnecessary clutter. Of course, it only takes a few mouse clicks to turn them on or off. So you can easily change from one setting to the other as convenient.

There's a slight security risk to hiding filename extensions. Malware files delivered by e-mail sometimes have a dot in the filename, like ILuvYou.txt.exe. If filename extensions are hidden, you only see ILuvYou.txt because the extension is the part that comes after the last dot in the name. Text (.txt) files are harmless, so you might open the file. Executable (.exe) files can contain malware. Of course, there are millions of .exe files that are perfectly safe. But one where someone is trying to hide the .exe extension is certainly suspicious, and probably not safe. Then again, opening e-mail attachments from people you don't know, in general, isn't safe either!

Hide protected operating system files (recommended)

Protected operating system files are files that Windows Vista needs to do its job. These files are not intended for human use, they're for the computer's use. Choosing this option keeps those files hidden so you don't see their icons. This is the recommended choice based on the "out of sight, out of mind" theory. If you can't see files you shouldn't be concerned with, you don't have to wonder what they are. Nor can you do bad things, like delete or rename them, which could cause a lot of problems with your computer.

If you clear this option, those protected operating system files will be visible in Explorer. Do this at your own risk. If you mess with one of those files, you could render your computer inoperable.

Launch folder windows in a separate process

This oddly named option really has nothing to do with processes listed in Task Manager. Normally, Windows Explorer sets aside a little bit of memory to store the contents of the currently selected folder. As you go from one folder to the next, it overwrites that portion of memory with the current folder's contents.

If you choose this option, each folder's contents are stored in a separate area in memory. This won't change how things look on your screen. But if your computer crashes frequently while exploring folders, this setting might solve the problem.

Managing pairs of Web pages and folders

If you use Internet Explorer as your Web browser, you can save a copy of any Web page you're viewing. Just click the Page button in Internet Explorer's toolbar and choose Save As. A Save As dialog box opens so you can specify a folder in which to save the page, as well as a filename and file type.

TIP   Your Downloads folder might be a good place to save Web pages. In the Save As dialog box, choose your User Account name from the Save In drop-down list. Then double-click Downloads in the main pane of the Save As dialog box.

In the Save As Type drop-down list, your best bet is to choose Web Archive, single file (*.mht). Doing so saves the Web page as a single file.

If Web Archive isn't an option, your next best bet is to choose Webpage, complete (*.htm, *.html). That way you're sure to get all the text and pictures. The only problem is that you'll end up with two icons: a document file that represents the text, and a folder that contains the pictures. When you open the document, you see the Web page with the pictures in place. But you can't delete the folder because the page needs that folder to get the pictures to show.

 The other options, Webpages, HTML only (*.htm, *.html) **and** Text File (*.txt) **save only the text, not the pictures.**

The "Managing pairs . . ." option in the Folders Options dialog box gives you three choices for the two separate icons you get when you download a Web page using the Webpage, Complete option:

- **Show and manage the pair as a single file:** Oddly, this option never seems to *show* the pair as a single file (unless you choose the aforementioned .mht format). But it does ensure that anything you do to one icon gets carried out on the other. For example, if you move, copy, or delete one of the icons, the other icon gets moved, copied, or deleted with it.

- **Show both parts and manage them individually:** Choosing this option breaks the bond between the folder and the document, so you can move, copy, and delete them independently.

- **Show both parts but manage them as a single file:** This option is the same as the first. However, it is applied to pages you've downloaded in the past as well as pages you download in the future.

TIP   As an alternative to using Save As to save a Web page, you can use offline browsing. It's a cleaner approach that doesn't require managing files yourself in a folder. See "Avoiding the Wait with Offline Browsing" in Chapter 17 for more information.

Remember each folder's view settings

Every folder you open has a default view that's used when you first open it. To see (or change) that setting, right-click the folder's icon and choose Properties. Then click the Customize tab. The default view is on the button under "Use this folder type as a template." You'll learn more about this under "Personalizing your folder" later in this chapter.

As an alternative to having each folder open in its default view, choose this option. Each folder will open in whatever view you were using when you last accessed the folder.

Restore previous folder windows at logon

In older versions of Windows, when you first logged on, Windows automatically reopened folders that were open when you last logged off. Whether or not that was a good idea is debatable, but now it doesn't matter. If you want folders you left open at shut down to automatically reopen when you log in, just select (check) this option.

Show drive letters

By default, whenever you open your Computer folder, each drive's icon displays both a friendly name and a drive letter (like C:). Choose this option if you want to hide the drive letters and see only the friendly name.

Show encrypted or compressed NTFS files in color

The NTFS file system used in Windows Vista lets you mark folders as encrypted or compressed. Choose this option if you want the names of those folders to appear in color, to distinguish them from regular unencrypted, uncompressed folders. Names of encrypted folders will be green. Names of compressed folders will be blue.

> **NOTE** To compress or encrypt a file, right-click its icon and choose Properties. Then, click the Advanced button in the Properties dialog box that opens. You can compress the folder (to reduce its size) or encrypt it to secure its contents. But you can't do both.

Show pop-up description for folder and desktop items

Selecting this option ensures that when you point to a file, folder, or desktop icon you see a tooltip like the example in Figure 28.34. If you clear this option, pointing to such an icon won't show the tooltip (or anything else).

FIGURE 28.34

Pointing to a desktop icon shows a description in a tooltip.

Show preview handlers in preview pane

When you select a file icon in Explorer, the Preview pane (if open) will attempt to show some content from that file. It doesn't work with all file types, so often you'll just see "No preview available."

If you clear this option, the Preview pane will never attempt to show the contents of any file icon you select. If it takes too long to show the contents of a file, and that's slowing you down, clearing this option will help speed things along. But you won't see the contents of any file you select.

Use check boxes to select items

The section titled "Selecting icons" in Chapter 29 describes different ways you can select icons in a folder. If you find it difficult to use those techniques, choose this option to have each icon show a checkbox. Then you can select multiple icons by clicking their checkboxes. You'll also see a checkbox next to the Name column heading. Select (check) that one if you want to select all icons in the folder.

Figure 28.35 shows an example. The files named Alec, Ashley, and Lily are selected, as indicated by highlighting and their checkmarks. The figure also points out the location of the optional Select All checkbox.

FIGURE 28.35

Use checkboxes to select icons.

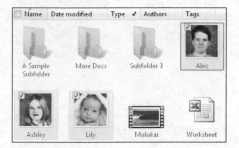

Use Sharing Wizard (recommended)

To share a folder or file with other users, you typically right-click the icon and choose Share, or select icons and click Share in Explorer's toolbar. When you choose this option, the Sharing Wizard opens to help you through the sharing process.

If you clear this option, the Sharing Wizard won't open when you click the Share button. Instead you're taken to the folder's Properties dialog box. There you share the folder by choosing specific options rather than using the simpler wizard.

Restore defaults

Click this button if you've experimented with settings and want to get things back the way they were originally set in Windows Vista.

As always, be sure to click OK after changing options in the Folder and Search Options dialog box.

Saving Things in Folders

The most common complaint among casual computer users is the inability to find things they're certain they've saved. The reason this happens is because they don't choose *where* they want to save an item, or *what* they want to name it. They just click the Save button. This is roughly the same as handing an important paper document to a colleague and saying "stick this in the filing cabinet somewhere, but don't tell me where you put it." Finding that document later isn't going to be easy.

Another common newbie mistake is to save things on external media like floppies, jump drives, CDs, and such. That's a bad idea. You only use external media to save *copies* of files that you've previously saved on your hard disk. The copy might be for backup, or to give to a friend. But either way it should be a copy of the file, not the one-and-only original file.

TIP If the goal of storing a file on an external disk is to conserve hard disk space, ask yourself this: "How much hard disk space do I have available right now, and how much will I have after I save this file to my hard disk?" If the answer is "I don't know," you may be wasting your time, energy, and a ton of available hard disk space!

What folder should I use?

Windows Vista comes with several folders already created for you to store your files in. When you click the Start button and then your user account name, you see those folders. When you're saving a file, first ask yourself "What is this thing I'm saving?" Then based on your answer, use the folder whose name matches the type of thing you're saving:

- If it's a picture or photograph, save it in your Pictures folder.
- If it's a video, save it in your Videos folder.
- If it's a song or sound clip, save it in your Music folder.
- If it's any other kind of typed document or worksheet, save it in your Documents folder.

There's no rule that states you *must* save a file in a specific folder. Remember, folders exist mainly to help you organize files so they're easy to find later when you need them. Also, saving to a folder is no big commitment. You can easily move any file from any folder to another folder whenever you want.

How to save in folders

There are basically two times when you have to choose where to save a folder:

- After you've created a new document from scratch in some program and chosen File ➪ Save from that program's menu, or closed the program and answered Yes when asked if you want to save it
- When you've opted to download a file from the Internet and chosen Save

In either case, a dialog box titled Save... (perhaps Save As, Save Picture, or Save Webpage, or something like that) appears. It's in that dialog box where most people make their big mistake. They click the Save button without first thinking about and specifying where to put the file and what to name it.

Unfortunately, there isn't a Save dialog box that all programs use. Different products may display different Save dialog boxes. So you have to learn to use whichever one you're faced with. However, there are two basic "styles" of Save dialog boxes that I'll call the Vista style and the Classic style (because "classic" sounds better than "old"). Let's start with the Vista style.

Saving in Vista style dialog boxes

The Vista style Save dialog box will likely look something like Figure 28.36 when it first appears. The name at the end of the Address bar is the name of the folder where the file will be saved unless you specify otherwise. In the example shown, you can see that the file will be saved in the Documents folder for the user account named Alan. At the very least, you should look at that name so you know where the file is going, and where you can find it in the future.

FIGURE 28.36

Sample Vista style Save dialog box.

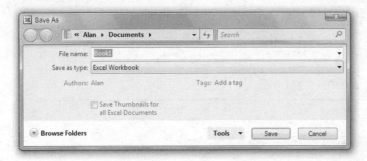

If you don't want to save the file to the folder that's suggested in the Address bar, navigate to the folder in which you want to save the file. A simple way to do this is to click the arrow to the right of your user name so you can see the folders available to you. Then click the folder into which you want to save the document.

If you're an advanced user and want to save to a location that's not easily accessible from the Address bar, click Browse folders to expand the dialog box as shown in Figure 28.37. Then you can use the Favorite Links or Folders list at the left side of the Save As dialog box to navigate to the location to which you want to save the file.

FIGURE 28.37

Save As dialog box with Browse Folders open.

CAUTION   Another common mistake is to save the file in some inappropriate place like the Desktop, or a subfolder under C:\Program Files or C:\Windows. Those places are not for storing documents, so don't save things there.

Depending on the type of document you're saving, you may be given an option to enter *metadata* like an author, tags, or other information. Metadata is information *about* the file that is stored in the file's properties or Vista's search index. At first you might see only a couple of metadata options. If you enlarge the Save As dialog box by dragging any corner or edge, you might see many more. Figure 28.38 shows an example.

FIGURE 28.38

Sample metadata options.

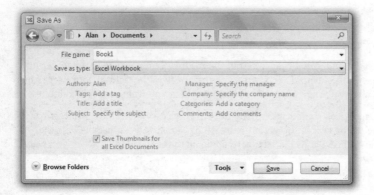

Fill in whatever metadata seems appropriate for your way of organizing and searching for things. If you're not up on Vista style searching yet, don't worry about it. You can still add any information that seems reasonable. But the main thing to keep in mind when filling in the blanks is the question "If I lost this thing, what word(s) might I type into the Search box to find it?" Whatever words come to mind are the words you should put into metadata.

TIP   The Save Thumbnails... option lets you see the file's contents in the Preview pane. That's a handy feature because you can see at least some portion of the file's contents without opening the file. So if a file offers that option, you'd do well to select it.

After you've chosen where you want to save the file (and filled in some metadata, if available), you can name the file. I'll talk about that in a moment. First a slight diversion to the Classic style Save As dialog boxes.

Saving in Classic style dialog boxes

Older style Save dialog boxes don't show the breadcrumb trail leading up to the folder in which the file will be saved. Instead they just show the name of the folder in a box titled Save In. Again, you should at least look at that name so you know where the file will be saved. If you want to save to a different folder, click the drop-down arrow next to that name to see some other common locations for saving files as in Figure 28.39.

FIGURE 28.39

Classic style Save dialog box.

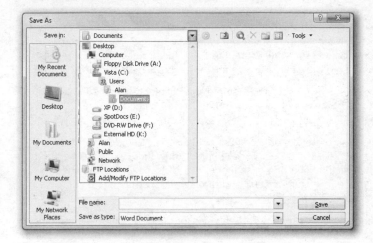

If you find the old-style dialog box confusing, click your user account name in the drop-down list (I would click Alan). The main folders for saving files (Documents, Music, Pictures, Videos) will show in the main pane at the center of the dialog box. Double-click the folder in which you want to save your file. That name will then appear in the Save In box. Remember: Whatever name appears in the Save In box is where the file will be saved, and where you can find it when you need it.

If your user name doesn't appear in the drop-down list, choose My Documents or Documents from the drop-down menu, or click My Documents in the left column to get to the Documents folder for your user account. If that's the folder in which you want to save the file, move on to the next step. Otherwise you can click the Up or Up One Level button at the top of the dialog box (shown at the mouse pointer in Figure 28.40) to go up one level to the main folder for your user account. Then in the main window, double-click the folder in which you do want to save the file (Music, Pictures, Videos, or whatever).

FIGURE 28.40

Up One Level button in classic Save dialog box.

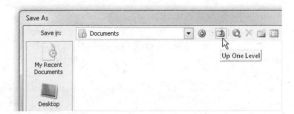

Tips on Naming Things

Whenever you save a file or create a folder, you need to give it a name. Before you do, ask yourself "If I needed this thing a year from now, and forgot its name, what would I look for?" Whatever word pops into your head is probably the best name to give to the item. You're not limited to a single word. But you want to keep the name short. There's not always room to show the entire name of a file or folder. So put the most important word first so that if the name is cut off, you can at least see the most recognizable part of the name.

In some situations, it makes sense to name things by number. For example, this chapter (Chapter 28) was a file on my computer named 28Chap. Each picture was its own, separate file. Those I named 2801fig, 2802fig, 2803fig, each name corresponding to the figure number.

When using numbers to name things, it's best to use the same amount of digits in each number. Otherwise, when you sort by name, they won't be in the order you expect. For example, I know there will never be more than 99 pictures in a chapter. So I use two-digit numbers for each figure. The 28 is the chapter number. The 01, 02, and 03 are the figure number. So the first figure is 2802 and the highest possible figure number is 2899. You can use hyphens.

If you name things by date, consider using *yyyymmdd* format. This provides for the best results when sorting by name. But again, you need to be consistent about it, always using four digits for the year, two for the month, and two for the day, for instance, 19990101 or 20071231. It's okay to use hyphens if you like.

Naming the file

After you've chosen *where* you want to save the file, the next step is to choose *what* to name it. Again, think to yourself "If I were to look for this thing six months from now, what name would I look for?" Then name the file accordingly. Keep the name short and specific. You can use spaces and some basic punctuation like apostrophes. But don't use any of these: \ / ? : * " > < | because those have special meanings and will be rejected.

Choosing a Save As Type

It's usually best to leave alone the Save As Type drop-down at the bottom of a Save dialog box. The suggested type is the "normal" type for the type of file you're saving. If you have a good and specific reason for choosing a different type, then go ahead and choose it. But otherwise you might just create unnecessary headaches for yourself!

Click Save

The last step in the process of saving a file is to click the Save button in the dialog box. Before you do you might want to take a quick look at the last folder name in the Address bar again or the name in the Save In box so you know where you're about to save the file. Take another quick look at the name in the File Name box so you know its name. Then click Save. The file is saved to the folder you specified with the name you specified.

Opening the saved file

To open the file in the future, use Windows Explorer to navigate to the folder in which you placed the file, as described earlier in this chapter. Then double-click the file's icon.

Nothing Happens When I Save!

The *first* time you save a new document, the Save dialog box opens so you can tell Windows where you want to put the file and what you want to name it. When you click Save, the document is saved.

Every time you save after that, the program saves only changes you made since your last save to that same file. It doesn't ask where to put the file or what to name it again. It just brings the currently saved copy up-to-date with what's on your screen. That's important, and not doing that often enough is yet another common beginner mistake.

It's important to save your work often because that's what keeps the permanent copy on your disk up-to-date with the copy you see on the screen. While creating or editing a document, you should save every two minutes or so. That way, if a power outage or other mishap wipes the document off your screen, the most you can lose it two minutes of work!

If the file you saved is a document, you may be able to re-open it by clicking the Start button, Recent Items, and then the filename. Or open the program you used to create the document, open its File menu, and click the filename at the bottom of the File menu. But keep in mind that those things only include recently used files. Your file won't stay in either list forever!

After you open the file, keep in mind that changes you make are not *saved* automatically. Changes you make to an open file are stored in RAM, not on the hard disk. If you want to save changes you've made, you must choose Save from the File menu while the document is open. Or remember to choose Yes when asked about saving your changes when you close the document.

Creating Your Own Folders

You can create your own folders at any time. For example, if you have many files in your Documents folder or some other folder, you might want to start organizing into subfolders within your Documents folder. You can create as many folders as you wish, and name them anything you wish. You can move or save any files you wish into any folder you create.

The main trick to creating your own folders is putting them where they make the most sense. Any folder you create will be a subfolder of some other folder. So the first thing you want to do is get to that *parent folder* — the folder in which your own custom folder will be stored. If you're new to all of this and are not sure what I'm talking about, here are some suggestions:

- If you're creating a subfolder to organize pictures, use your Pictures folder as the parent folder.
- If you're creating a subfolder to organizing songs, use your Music folder as the parent folder.
- If you're creating a subfolder to organize videos, use your Videos folder as the parent folder.
- If you're creating a subfolder to organize some other type of files, use your Documents folder as the parent folder.

Like I said, you can create a folder anywhere you like. The preceding items are just suggestions. For example, you can create a folder on an external magnetic disk (floppy, Zip disk, jump drive, memory card, or external hard disk). In those cases, whatever disk is currently in the drive would be like the parent folder. Make sure you put a disk in the drive before you perform the following steps:

 **CAUTION** You can create folders on CDs and DVDs too, but not necessarily by following the steps here. See Chapter 32 for information on working with those kinds of disks.

1. In Windows Explorer, open the parent folder for the folder you're about to create. Or open your Computer folder and then open the icon for the disk drive on which you want to create a folder.

2. Do whichever of the following is easiest for you:

   ■ Click Organize in the toolbar and click New Folder.

   ■ If you're using Classic menus, choose File ➪ New ➪ Folder.

   ■ Right-click some empty space below or to the right of icons in the current folder and choose New ➪ Folder.

3. Type in a name of your own choosing and press Enter.

The new folder appears with the name you specified. When you double-click its icon to open it, you'll find it's empty. That's because it's brand new and you haven't put anything in it yet. (Click the Back button or press Backspace to leave the folder.)

TIP If you're not happy with the name you gave to a folder, right-click its icon and choose Rename. Then type the new name or edit the existing name and press Enter.

You can move existing files into the folder using techniques described in Chapter 29. You can save new files to the folder just by opening the folder from the Save dialog box.

Creating folders on-the-fly while saving

There may be times when you're in the middle of saving a file and suddenly think "I should have created a new folder for this file and others like it." You don't have to cancel out of the current save operation to create a folder. Instead, navigate to the folder that will act as the parent to the new folder you want to create.

If you're using a Vista style Save dialog box, click Organize ➪ New Folder as at the top of Figure 28.41. If you're using an older style Save dialog box, point to each toolbar button until you find the one that lets you create a new folder as at the bottom of that same figure, and click it. A new empty folder appears in the main pane at the center of the dialog box. Type in a new name of your own choosing and press Enter.

FIGURE 28.41

Create a folder on-the-fly while saving.

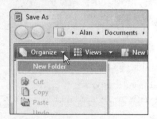

The new folder should open automatically. If it doesn't, double-click its icon in the main pane of the Save dialog box, so that name appears at the end of the Address bar or in the Save In box. Then click the Save button in the dialog box. Your file is saved in that new folder.

Personalizing your folder

You can customize a folder in several ways. Unlike the Folder and Search Options described earlier, which apply to all folders, these settings apply to only one folder — the one whose icon you right-click then specify your settings. To get started on customization, first right-click the icon you want to customize and choose Properties. In the Properties dialog box that opens, click the Customize tab to see the options shown in Figure 28.42.

FIGURE 28.42

Customize tab for a folder's properties.

Specify a folder type

All folders have a default view that defines what tools appear in the toolbar and how icons look when you first open the folder. To define a default view, click the button under "What kind of folder do you want?" and choose from the menu. There isn't any rule that says you must choose a specific kind. But in general, you want to choose an option that reflects the type of items that the folder contains, or will contain:

- **All items:** Use this option if the folder will contain multiple file types and subfolders.
- **Documents:** Use this type if the folder will contain mostly non-media document files (text, spreadsheets, database data, and such).
- **Pictures and video:** Use this if the folder will contain pictures, videos, or both.
- **Music details:** Use this if the folder will contain mostly songs.
- **Music icons:** Use this if the folder will contain mostly albums or other subfolders that contain songs.

If you want your selection to be applied to subfolders within the folder, choose Also apply this template to all subfolders.

 If you chose "Remember each folder's view settings" in the Folder and Search Options dialog box, the view you were using when you left the folder will override the default view.

Folder pictures

Folder icons always look like partially opened manila file folders because like real-world manila file folders, computer folders are containers in which you store files (written documents, pictures, songs, videos, and such). Items in the folder icon represent one or more files that are actually in the folder. For example, folders that contain albums show the covers of albums that are in the folder as in Figure 28.43.

Folder icons showing album covers.

If you don't like the file that a folder icon shows, you can change it to a picture. Just click the Change File button on the Customize tab and click the file you want the folder icon to show.

 If you can't use a file because it's not the right type, you can take a screenshot of the open file you want to use. Save the screenshot as a JPEG file. Then use the JPEG as the folder's picture.

If you ever change your mind and want to go back to the original, click the Restore Default button in Properties sheet.

Changing a folder's icon

You can choose an entirely different icon for a folder. You'll likely lose the open folder effect you normally see in folder icons, so you might consider changing the folder's picture rather than its icon. But if you really want to change the folder's icon to something else, just click the Change Icon button. Click the icon you want to use, or use the Browse button to browse to any location that contains icon (.ico) files and choose an icon there.

If you change the icon and then change your mind, click the Change Icon button again and click Restore Default. Don't forget to click OK or Apply after changing any settings in any dialog boxes. Your changes won't take effect until you do.

If your changes don't take effect immediately, refresh the folder. (Right-click some empty space in the folder and choose Refresh, or press F5, or choose View ⇨ Refresh from the menu bar in the folder.)

Read-Only, Hidden, and Advanced attributes

When you right-click a folder icon (or file icon) and choose Properties, the General tab of the Properties dialog box shows the options shown in Figure 28.44. The Read-Only and Hidden options often confuse folks, so let's take a moment to discuss what those are about.

FIGURE 28.44

General tab of a folder's Properties.

The Read-Only attribute can be empty, checked, or colored. Here's the difference:

- **Empty:** The contents of the folder can be read (viewed and opened) by everyone who has access to the folder.

- **Colored:** The contents can be read and written to (changed) by the owner of the folder (the person who created the folder). Other users with whom the folder is shared can view the contents of the folder, but not change its contents.

- **Checked:** Everyone can view the contents of the folder, but nobody (not even the owner) can change the folder's contents.

The Hidden attribute, if checked, makes the folder's icon invisible in the folder if the "Do not show hidden files and folders" option in Folder and Search Options is selected. The folder's icon is dimmed if "Show hidden files and folders" is selected in Folder and Search Options.

Clicking the Advanced button on the General tab reveals the options shown in Figure 28.45.

FIGURE 28.45

Advanced folder or file attributes.

The Folder is ready for archiving checkbox is handled automatically by Windows Backup. So it's unlikely you'd ever need to change that yourself. The checkbox is checked if you've never backed up the folder (or file), or if its contents have changed since the last backup. That tells Windows Backup to back it up again the next time you do a backup. The checkbox is empty if its contents haven't changed since the last backup. That tells Windows Backup that there's no need to back it up again.

The Index this folder for faster searching checkbox, if selected, tells Windows to maintain the item in the search index. The more items there are in the search index, the more computer resources are required to maintain the index. Searches also take longer when the index is large.

The basic idea is to include only folders that contain documents, e-mail messages, and other user files in the search index. Omit system folders that contain files not intended for humans to open and edit — like programs and files that make up the Windows operating system. That's the way it's handled automatically. So you might never need to mess with this option. There are exceptions though.

For example, let's say you store many files on an external hard drive or a separate partition on your C: drive. When you do a search, you want those files included. In that case, checking the Index this folder for faster searching ensures that those external files are treated like other files in your user account. They're rapidly searched every time you perform a search.

The other two options in the dialog box deserve some special attention and are described next.

Compress contents to conserve disk space

Choosing this option tells Windows to automatically compress everything in the folder to reduce its disks space consumption. (This works only on hard disks that use the NTFS filesystem.) When you open a file from the folder, it's automatically decompressed for you. So the compression is transparent, in the sense that you don't have to constantly compress and decompress files yourself.

CAUTION   This option has nothing to do with Zip files (also called compressed folders). If your goal is to e-mail someone a Zip file, this option won't help at all. See "Zipping and Unzipping Files" in Chapter 15 for information on Zip files and compressed folders.

This might seem like a great idea and a good way to conserve disk space. But before you jump in and start compressing all your folders, there are some costs to consider. For one, there is a time cost. It takes a little time to automatically compress every file you save, and automatically decompress every file you open. Furthermore, many file types already have a degree of compression built into them. Putting such files into a compressed folder may have little or no effect on the amount of disk space they consume.

Keep in mind that hard disk space is dirt cheap and plentiful. People's time is neither. So before you start compressing all your folders to save a little disk space, ask yourself what your time is worth to you. If you compress a folder, then later change your mind, no problem. Just go back to the same dialog box and clear the checkmark next to

Encrypt contents to secure data

This checkbox lets you apply EFS (Encrypting File System) to the folder. This is the most powerful form of securing a folder's contents from prying eyes. The same technique is used in government and corporate settings to protect top-secret data, trade secrets, financial information, and the like. But it's not a toy. It's serious business and must be treated accordingly. If not handled properly, you stand to lose everything you store in that folder. So it's not the kind of thing you want to play around with.

First, understand that anyone who has access to your user account also has access to files in your encrypted folders. Therefore, there is no point in using EFS if your user account isn't password-protected.

If you forget the password to your user account, then you will lose access to all files in the encrypted folders. To play it safe, you must make a backup copy of your encryption key, preferably on a CD-R or other disk where it can't be erased. You need to store that disk in a safe place. The big boys store them in fireproof safes, often in multiple locations throughout the country!

Assuming you understand the risks and responsibilities, the act of encrypting a folder is easy. Just select (check) the Encrypt contents to secure data checkbox. Then follow the steps in the wizard that appears to make a backup copy of your encryption key. If you save that file to your hard disk, copy it to a CD-R or other medium, then delete the copy that's on your hard disk.

> **NOTE** An encryption key applies to all encrypted folders in your user account. So you'll only be prompted to back up your key the first time you encrypt a folder.

Once you've encrypted a folder, you really don't have to do anything else to secure its contents. When you save a file to that folder, or move a file into that folder, its contents are encrypted automatically. When you open a file, the contents are decrypted. So working with the files in the encrypted folder is like working with any other files in any other folder.

If someone tries to open a file in the encrypted folder from another user account, they will be denied access to the file. There is no way they can access anything in the folder unless they can get a copy of your encryption key.

> **NOTE** For more information on encryption and backing up keys, search Windows help for EFS and certificate backup.

After all this talk of creating folders, you may be wondering how to get some of your existing files into one. That's a topic for the next chapter. First, here's a quick recap of the important points from this chapter.

Wrap Up

This chapter has been about some basic facts about how computers store information. It's also covered some basic (and some not-so-basic) skills for navigating through your system to find things. Here's a quick review:

- Everything that's in your computer is stored on your hard disk, typically drive C:.

- The Computer folder shows icons for all the disk drives in your system. To open that folder, click the Start button and choose Computer.

- A folder is a container in which files (and perhaps subfolders) are stored.

- Icons that represent folders usually look like little manila file folders. Double-click a folder's icon to open the folder and see what's inside.

- Windows Explorer (also called Explorer) is the program you use to navigate through and explore the contents of all the drives and folders in your system.

- You don't have to go through the All Programs menu to get to Windows Explorer. Any time you open a folder, Windows Explorer opens automatically.

- Explorer's Address bar, Navigation pane, and main contents window are all tools for navigating through drives and folders in your system.

- When saving a file, always navigate to an appropriate folder and provide a meaningful filename before you click Save. Otherwise, it may be difficult to find the file later when you need it.

- You can create your own folders from the Organize button in Explorer or from the Save dialog box.

- To customize a folder, right-click its icon and choose Customize.

Chapter 29

Managing Files and Folders

Your computer's hard disk has enough space on it to store thousands of pictures, songs, and other files. Having lots of stuff in your computer is a good thing. But only if you can find what you're looking for when you need it. Therefore, keeping things organized so they're easy to find is an important basic skill that every computer user needs to learn.

Chapter 28 talked about drives, folders, and files in terms of what they are and why you need them. There you also learned how to use Explorer to navigate your system and get to things you need. We also talked about how you can save things in such a way that prevents you from losing them.

This chapter picks up where that one left off. Here I assume you've read and understood most of that chapter. Now you're ready to start reorganizing what you already have. That requires knowing how to select, move, and copy files. Here you'll also discover other important techniques, like how to rename, delete, and un-delete files. These basic skills are important to acquire if you ever intend to use your computer for anything beyond basic e-mail and Web browsing.

How to Select Icons

There will be many times where you want to perform some operation on many files. For example, let's say you want to copy a couple dozen files to an external disk. You could do them one at a time, but that would take a lot of time and effort. Better and easier to *select* all the icons you want to copy, and copy them all in one fell swoop.

As you'll see, there are many ways to select icons. As always there is no right way or wrong way, no good way or bad way. There's no advantage or disadvantage to any particular method. It's simply a matter of choosing which method is easiest for you. Or which method is best for whatever you're trying to accomplish.

 How you select icons depends largely on whether you're using the double-click or single-click method to open icons. If you don't know what that's about, see "To Click or Double-click?" in Chapter 28.

Thumbnails for pictures and videos are icons too. So all the techniques described in this chapter apply to thumbnails.

Select one icon

Selecting a single icon is easy. If you're using the double-click method to open icons, then you click (once) on the icon you want to select. If you're using the single-click method to open icons, then you just point to the icon (rest the tip of the mouse pointer right on the icon you want to select). The selected icon will be highlighted to stand out from the others. The toolbar will likely change to reflect things you can do with that selected icon. If the Details pane is open, it will show information about the selected icon, as illustrated in Figure 29.1.

FIGURE 29.1

Sample selected icon.

 If you're new to selecting multiple icons, you might find it easiest with the new checkbox feature in Vista.

If you turned on the option to select icons using checkboxes in Folder and Search Options, then you have to point to the icon first, then click its checkbox. The only thing that's unique about this method is that the selected icon's checkbox has a checkmark, as in Figure 29.2.

FIGURE 29.2

Selected icon shows a checkmark.

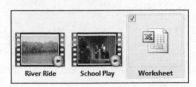

To turn on the option to use checkboxes, click the Organize button and choose Folder and Search Options. Click the View tab in the dialog box that opens. Then scroll down to and check Use check boxes to select items. Click OK. The checkbox won't show on an icon until you point to or click the icon. See Chapter 28 for more information on folder options.

TIP If you unintentionally keep opening files when you only intended to select their icons, consider using the double-click method to open icons.

Selecting all icons

If you want to select all the icons in a folder, use whichever of the following techniques is easiest for you:

- Click the Organize button and click Select All.
- Press Ctrl+A.
- If you're using Classic menus, choose Edit ➪ Select All.

All of the icons are selected.

Select a range of icons

You can easily select a range of icons using the mouse and keyboard. If there are many icons in the folder, you might consider using the View button (or the Ctrl key and your mouse wheel) to make the icons small enough so you can see all the ones you want to select. If the items you want to select have something in common, consider sorting the icons so the ones you want to select are adjacent to one another. To select multiple icons:

1. Select the first one by pointing or clicking.
2. Hold down the Shift key and click the last one.

Both icons and all the icons in between are selected. The toolbar changes to show things you can do with all of those icons. If the Details pane is open, it shows some information about the selected icons. The Size detail tells the combined size of all the selected icons. Figure 29.3 shows an example.

FIGURE 29.3

Range of icons selected.

Selecting and unselecting one at a time

To select a single icon without unselecting others, Ctrl+Click the icons you want to select (or unselect). Ctrl+Click means "hold down the Ctrl key as you click." For example, if you wanted to unselect only the Beethovens 5th icon in Figure 29.3, you'd Ctrl+Click its icon. All the other icons would remain selected.

If you're using the single-click method to open icons, then you can Ctrl+Click or Ctrl+point to select or unselect a single icon. It doesn't matter which, the result is the same.

Here's another way to look at it. When you select an icon by pointing or clicking, only that one icon is selected. Any other selected icons are instantly unselected. But if you hold down the Ctrl key as you go, other selected icons remain unchanged. So you can hold down the Ctrl key to select, or unselect without disturbing other selected icons.

Of course you can use the Ctrl key to select multiple non-adjacent icons, as illustrated in Figure 29.4.

Select multiple icons.

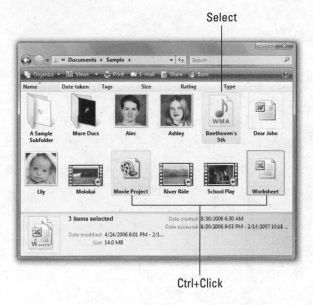

Select

Ctrl+Click

Selecting with the keyboard

You can select icons without using the mouse at all. First you have to make sure the keyboard focus is in Explorer's main contents pane. If you're not sure, press arrow keys on the keyboard until you notice the selection box moving from icon to icon within the main content pane. Then move the focus to the first icon you want to select using the navigation keys (→, ←, ↓, ↑, Home, End, PgUp, PgDn).

To select multiple adjacent icons, hold down the Shift key as you move through icons using the navigation keys. All icons through which you pass are selected. To select multiple non-adjacent icons, hold down the Ctrl key as you move from icon to icon with the navigation keys. When you get to an icon you want to select, tap the Spacebar (but don't let go of the Ctrl key). To unselect all selected icons with the keyboard, press any navigation key alone, without holding down Shift or Ctrl.

Select groups or stacks

NEW FEATURE Vista's grouping and stacking features, discussed in Chapter 28, offer new ways of organizing icons.

If you want to select one or more groups of icons that have something in common, you can group them first. For example, let's say you want to select all the video files in a folder, perhaps to move them elsewhere or copy to an external disk. First point to the Type column heading, click the Arrow that appears, and click Group. The icons are separated into groups by type.

To select all the icons in a group, click the line at the top of the group. To add another group's icons to the selection, Ctrl+Click the line at the top of that other group. Figure 29.5 shows an example where I've selected all of the Video Clip and Windows Media Audio/Video files after grouping icons by type.

FIGURE 29.5

Select groups of icons.

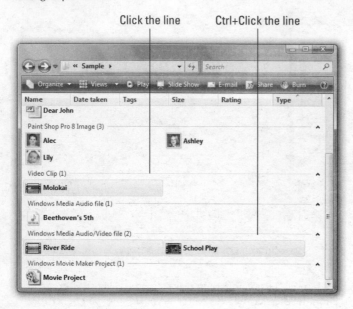

Rather than grouping, you can stack the icons by whatever criteria you like. Then select the stacks that contain the icons of interest. For example, let's say you click the arrow next to Type and click Stack by Type. To select all the Video Clip and Windows Media Audio/Video files, click one stack. Then hold down the Ctrl key and click the other stack, as illustrated in Figure 29.6.

TIP Don't forget that if you don't see a column heading you need, you can click the >> symbol at the end of the column headings to see other open columns. Or right-click any column heading to see other columns you can choose.

FIGURE 29.6

Select stacks.

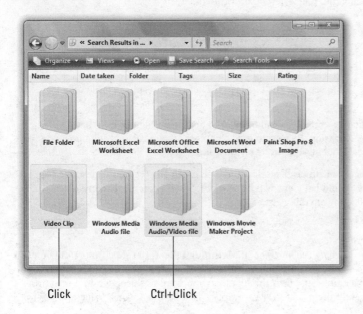

Select by filtering

Yet another way to select icons that have something in common is to filter out (hide) the icons you don't want to select. For example, let's say you want to select only files that were created or edited today. Click the arrow next to the Date Modified column heading and choose the Today option as in Figure 29.7.

FIGURE 29.7

Hide all except files created or edited today.

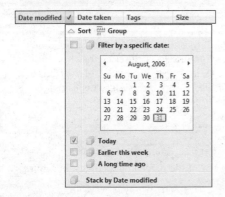

You can also filter by using the Search box at the top of the folder. Just be aware that the search results might include files from subfolders. It all depends on your selection choice in Folder and Search Options, as discussed in Chapter 30. But for the sake of example, let's say you want to select all PNG and GIF images in a folder. You could type the following into the Search box for the folder:

```
type:gif OR type:png
```

or the following:

```
*.gif OR *.png
```

Just make sure you use an uppercase OR to separate the two types. The search results include only files with .gif and .png extensions.

> **CAUTION**   Using AND in the preceding examples wouldn't work because no file can have both a .gif extension AND a .png extension. Be sure to read Chapters 30 and 31 for a full understanding of how index searches work, because it's not always intuitively obvious.

When only the icons you want to select remain visible, select them all using any technique described earlier (for example, press Ctrl+A). None of the hidden icons will be selected. So you can move, copy, delete, or rename the selected icons without affecting anything else.

Selecting by lassoing

You can also select multiple icons by dragging the mouse pointer through them. But this is more difficult to do in Vista than in older versions of Windows. The problem is that if you want to select by lassoing, you have to get the mouse pointer to some empty spot near the first icon you want to select, without selecting any icons. That's difficult in Vista because there is little or no empty space between icons. What appears to be empty space isn't empty at all.

You can see this if you use the single-click method to open icons. Once you get the mouse pointer anywhere near an icon, you select the icon. Once you've selected an icon, if you start dragging, you only move the icon, you don't select multiple icons. The mouse pointer has to be in neutral territory (not on an icon) *before* you start dragging.

To see where the empty space is (if any) in the current view, press Ctrl+A to select icons. If there's any empty space at all it will be white. To select by dragging, you have to get the tip of the mouse pointer into a white area near the first icon you want to select. Then hold down the left mouse button and drag through all the icons you want to select.

Select most icons in a folder

The old "invert selection" technique from previous versions of Windows still works too. But the option is available only from the menu bar. As the name implies, invert selection unselects all selected icons and selects the ones that weren't selected. Say, for example, you want to select most, but not all, of the icons in a folder. You could start by selecting the few icons you *don't* want to select. Then press Alt to display the menu bar (if it's not already visible) and choose Edit ➪ Invert Selection.

Selecting from multiple folders

To select icons from multiple folders, perform a search that finds all the icons you want to select. In the search results, you can select all icons, or just specific icons using any of the preceding methods. For more information on performing searches, see Chapters 30 and 31.

Unselecting all icons

If you have one ore more icons selected and want to unselect them all, click some neutral area to the right of, below, or between icons (if you can find such an area). Or click the Refresh button (the two arrows to the right of the Address bar).

Moving and Copying Files

There are many reasons for moving and copying files. If you've been saving files in a willy-nilly manner, you may want to move them around into folders that make more sense so they're easier to find. Or, if end up with hundreds or thousands of files in a folder and you get sick of looking through all their names, you might want to create some subfolders. Then move some of those files into subfolders.

If you have a bunch of files on external disks, you may want to copy them to your hard disk where they're easier to get to and work with. Or, if you need to send someone some files and they don't have e-mail, you might want to copy some files to an external disk to put in the mail. Then again, you may want to copy some files to an external disk as backups, just in case some mishap damages the copy on your hard disk.

Whatever your reason for moving or copying files, the techniques are the same. First, understand that there is a difference between moving and copying. The words mean the same things they do in English. When you move a file from one place to another, you still have only one copy of the file. It's just in the new location rather than the old location. When you copy a file, you end up with two copies: the original in the original location and an exact copy in the new location.

Moving and copying usually involves two locations. They may be two different folders in the same drive, or two entirely different drives. But that doesn't really matter because one location is always the *source*. The other location is the *target* or *destination*. Here's the difference:

■ **Source:** The drive and/or folder that contains the files you want to move or copy (the *"from"* drive and/or folder).

■ **Destination** or **target:** The drive and/or folder to which you want to move or copy files (the *"to"* drive and/or folder).

The source can be any folder on your hard disk, a floppy disk, a Zip disk, a thumb drive, a memory card, or a CD. The same is true for the destination in most cases, though copying files to CDs and DVDs requires methods that are different from those described in this chapter, as you'll discover in Chapter 32.

Moving files to a subfolder

One of the most common reasons to move files is when you create a new, empty subfolder within some existing folder. Then, you want to move some files into that new subfolder. That's easy to do:

■ Drag any item onto the subfolder's icon, and release the mouse button.

■ Or, select the items you want to move, and drag any one of the selected items to the subfolder's icon, and then release the mouse button.

The main trick is making sure that you get the mouse pointer right on the subfolder's icon. When the mouse pointer is right on the subfolder's icon, you'll see the words Move to foldername at the mouse pointer (where *foldername* is the name of the folder into which you're moving the file). For example, in Figure 29.8 I'm about to drop a selected icon into a subfolder named Kid Pix. To drop the files into the folder, release the mouse button without moving the mouse pointer away from that folder.

FIGURE 29.8

About to drop selected icons onto a subfolder's icon.

If you change your mind partway through the drag-and-drop operation, just tap the Esc key, and then release the mouse button. If it's too late for that because you've already dropped the items, press Ctrl+Z to undo the move.

If you want to copy, rather than move the files to a subfolder, drag with the right mouse button. After you drop, click Copy Here on the menu that appears. Optionally, you can drag with the left mouse button, but you have to press and hold down the Ctrl key before you release the mouse button.

 Make sure you don't select the subfolder into which you want to move or copy the items. It won't work if you do it that way. Select only the items you want to move or copy into the subfolder.

Copying to/from external disks

There are many ways to copy things to external disks. But don't forget that size is limited on those. And also the rules for copying to CDs and DVDs are different from those described here. You'll want to refer to Chapter 32 if you plan on copying files to a CD or DVD.

Anyway, you first have to know how much space you have on the external disk, which means you have to put it into its drive and open your Computer folder. When you view icons in the Computer folder as Tiles, each drive's available space shows with its icon. Or if you can see the drive's icon in the Folders list, right-click that and choose Properties. In the Properties sheet that opens, the Free Space number tells you how much room you have.

Then you need to know how much space the file(s) you're about to copy will require. For that you can select the icons you intend to copy. If the Details pane is open, you'll see their combined size next to the Size: option. But that size isn't entirely accurate because it doesn't take into account the small amount of additional overhead involved in storing files on disk. For a more accurate size, right-click any selected icon and choose Properties. The Size on Disk number in the Properties sheet more accurately describes how much disk space you'll need to store all of the selected files. If there isn't enough space on the external disk, you'll need to select and copy fewer files.

Once you know the files will fit, you can use any of the techniques in the sections to follow to copy to the external disk. Or for that matter, to copy files from an external disk or portable device (camera or music player) to your hard disk.

Moving and copying by dragging

You can move or copy any file (or selected files) to any location whose name you can see in the Navigation pane. As usual, if you want to move or copy multiple items, first select their icons. Then just drag any one of them to the appropriate location in the Navigation pane as illustrated in Figure 29.9. That location can be any folder or any drive.

FIGURE 29.9

Drag icons to any drive/folder in the Navigation pane.

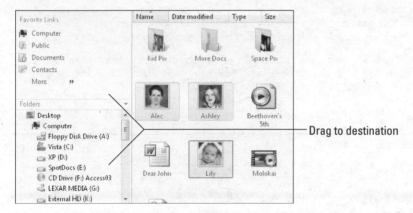

Drag to destination

When dragging, make sure you get the tip of the mouse pointer right on the name of the drive or folder to which you want to copy. If you drag with the left mouse button, you'll see "move to. . ." or "copy to. . ." when the mouse pointer is in position. The rule is:

- If you drag to an external drive, Windows assumes you want to copy.
- If you drag to another folder on the same drive, Windows assumes you want to move.

The reason being that there's rarely any need to move a file to an external disk. External disks are mainly used for copies of files on your hard disk. Likewise, there's rarely any need to have two copies of the same file on your hard drive. But you're not stuck with either move or copy. Just press and hold down Alt or Ctrl before you release the mouse button to drop the files. That rule is:

- **Ctrl:** Files will be copied to the location.
- **Shift:** Files will be copied to the location.

As an alternative to relying on the keys, you can drag with the right mouse button instead of the left. When you release the mouse button to drop, you'll see a menu like the one in Figure 29.10. Click Move or Copy depending on what you want to do. Or click Cancel if you change your mind and decide to do neither.

FIGURE 29.10

Menu when you right-drag and then drop.

Move or copy using two open folders

It's not always easy getting the tip of the mouse pointer right on the destination drive or folder in the Navigation pane. You might find it easier to open both the source and destination locations at the same time. Then just drag from one open window to the other. They make much bigger targets.

The trick here is to open two instances of Explorer, one for the source and one for the destination. Then size and position so you can see at least some portion of both. For example, in Figure 29.11, the left window is a folder on the hard drive. The right window is a jump drive.

FIGURE 29.11

Drag icons from one folder to the other.

1. Open the source folder or drive (from which you want to move/copy files).

2. Click the Start button and open your Computer folder or user account folder.

3. In the new folder window you just opened, navigate to the destination drive or folder.

4. Right-click the clock in the lower-right corner of the screen and choose Cascade Windows.

5. Move the destination folder down and to the right by dragging its title bar.

> **TIP** Windows Explorer is the program that displays all open folders. You can use all the techniques described in Chapter 2 to move and size its program window.

That gets you to the point where you can see both open folders. Now you just have to select the items you want to move or copy. Then drag them into the main center pane of the destination folder and drop them there. Or, right-drag the items so you can choose Move or Copy after you release the mouse button.

> **CAUTION** Don't drag to the Navigation pane in the destination window. Either close the Navigation pane in the destination location's window, or make sure you drag past it into the main center pane of that window.

Using cut-and-paste to move or copy files

You can also copy and paste files to copy them, or cut and paste to move files. The procedure goes like this:

1. Navigate to the drive or folder that contains the items you want to move or copy.

2. To move or copy multiple items, select their icons. Then:

   - To move the item(s), right-click its icon or any selected item and choose Cut or press Ctrl+X.
   - To copy the items(s), right-click its icon or any selected icon and choose Copy or press Ctrl+C.

3. Navigate to the destination drive or folder.

4. Paste using any of the following methods:

   - Click the Organize button and choose Paste.
   - Press Ctrl+V.
   - Right-click some empty space in the main, center pane of the destination window and choose Paste.

Making a copy in the same folder

There may be times when you want to make a copy of a file within the same folder. For example, maybe you have a large photo from your digital camera. You want to make a smaller version for e-mail or for use in documents. Of course, you don't want to shrink down your original because that's the best one to use for editing and printing. Here's the quick and easy way to make copies:

1. Select the icon (or icons) you want to copy.

2. Press Ctrl+C and then press Ctrl+V (to copy, then paste).

The copied files have the same name as the originals followed by – Copy as in Figure 29.12. You can rename the copies if you like, but it isn't necessary. You can make any changes you want to the copies. Those changes will have no effect on the originals.

FIGURE 29.12

Original files and copies.

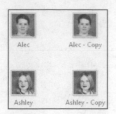

TIP   Click the Name column heading once or twice to get the files back into alphabetical order.

Undoing a move or copy

If you complete a move or copy operation and then change your mind, you can undo the action. But you have to do it soon because you can only undo your most recent action. For example, you can't move or copy, then do a bunch of other things, then come back and undo the move or copy. Use whichever technique is easiest for you to undo a move/copy:

- Press Ctrl+Z.
- Click the Organize button and choose Undo.
- Right-click some empty white space in the main pane of either folder and choose Undo Move or Undo Copy.

This location already contains. . .

A folder cannot contain two files that have the same name. If you move or copy a file into a folder (or onto a drive) and that destination already has a file with the same name as the one you're bringing in, you'll see a message like the one in Figure 29.13. Notice that the message simply explains what's going on and gives you some choices as to what you can do about it.

Before you make a decision, take a look at the source you're copying from and the destination to which you're copying. That appears just under each item's filename (A:\ and G:\ in Figure 29.12). If that isn't where you intended to copy from and to, click Cancel to cancel the whole operation. Then re-think where you want to move/copy from and to, and start over. But this time make sure you get both locations right.

FIGURE 29.13

Destination already has file with that name.

If the source and destination are correct, then think what you want to do about the copy that's already in the destination. Notice that the size and the date you last edited each file are listed next to each icon. Your options are clearly explained right in the message window:

- If you want to replace the file at the destination with the one you're moving or copying, click the first option, Copy this file or Move this file.
- If you want to keep the file that's already at the destination and leave well enough alone, click Keep this original file or Cancel. Either way, the move/copy operation will be cancelled and it will be just as though you never even tried to move or copy.
- If you want to keep the original but proceed with the move or copy, click the third option, Copy using another name or Move using another name. If you choose this option, the file will be moved or copied. Its name will be the same as the original name followed by a number, like Alec (2).

So the bottom line here is that you can move or copy any file anywhere at any time. There are no restrictions. It's simply a matter of first knowing why you want to move or copy, because there is no point in doing such things purely for the heck of it. Then you need to know where the item is now and where you want to move or copy it to. Once all that is squared away, use either a dragging method or a copy-and-paste method described earlier to do the move or copy.

In addition to the techniques already described, you can get stuff into your computer using methods listed here:

- To get pictures from a digital camera into your computer, use Windows Photo Gallery (Chapter 22).

- To get music from a CD or portable music player into your computer, use Windows Media Player (Chapter 23).

- To get video from a DVD into your computer, use Windows Movie Maker (Chapter 25).

- For information on copying *to* CD and DVD, see Chapter 32.

Renaming Files

Renaming a file or folder is simple. Just right-click the item you want to rename and choose Rename. The existing name will turn blue and gain a blinking cursor. You can type a new name, or edit the current name, and then press Enter.

If you've taken filename extensions out of hiding, that part of the name won't be highlighted. For example, the .doc extension on the Word document file shown in Figure 29.14 isn't highlighted. That's because you don't want to change the extension unless you *really* know what you're doing. Guessing is unlikely to work. At the very least, make sure you know the extension you're about to change. That way if you ruin the file, you can rename the file back to the original extension (in case you miss the opportunity to undo the rename).

FIGURE 29.14

Filename extension is not highlighted.

NOTE In case you're wondering why I don't just tell you what is and isn't okay, it's because there are thousands of file types and millions of possible combinations. Changing the extension on a guess will fail about 99.9 percent of the time.

Undoing a rename

You can undo a rename like you can undo just about anything else. But as always, you have to do so fairly soon after the rename. Just press Ctrl+Z or click the Organize button and choose Undo. If it's too late for that, you have to rename the file again, back to its original name and extension.

So How Do I Change a File's Type?

The answer to that question is a resounding "It depends". If you can open the file, and it's not a music or video file, you may be able to just choose File ⇨ Save As from the opening program's menu. Then set the Save As Type option to the file type you want, before you click the Save button.

If it's a music or video file, you'll likely need a conversion program. Search the Web or a download site like www.download.com or www.tucows.com for convert ext1 to ext2 (where *ext1* is the extension of the file type from which you want to copy, and *ext2* is the extension of the file type to which you want to copy) and see what programs you can find. Or check out Digital Media Converter by DeskShare (www.deskshare.com) to see if it can handle the music and video formats you're interested in.

Then there are cases where you simply need the right program or reader to open the file without converting it. Some common examples include .pdf files, which require Adobe Reader (www.adobe.com), QuickTime movies and iTunes (players are available from www.apple.com), and Office documents and snapshots. Viewers for many such files are available from download.microsoft.com.

Renaming multiple files

To rename multiple files, select all of their icons using any methods described near the start of the chapter. Then right-click any one of them and choose Rename. Type the new name (again, don't change the extension if it shows up) and press Enter. The files will all be given the name you specified. All but the first will have numbers. For example, if you renamed to River, then the files will be named River, River (2), River (3), River (4), and so forth.

 If the lack of a number on the first renamed file bugs you, right-click its icon and choose Rename. Then add the (1) to the name yourself.

Deleting Files

In computers, the term *delete* is synonymous with "throw in the trash." That's important to know because you wouldn't want to throw in the trash any important paper documents from your filing cabinet. Likewise, you don't want to delete anything important that's in your computer.

It's easy to delete files and folders. Perhaps too easy, because it's a leading cause of headaches and disasters. Especially among beginners and casual computer users who try to learn by guessing and figuring things out. Deleting and "moving to the Recycle Bin" are basically the same thing. So let's start with a couple of good rules of thumb. Before you delete an item or move it to the Recycle Bin, ask yourself two questions:

- Do I know exactly what this file (or folder) is?
- Am I 100 percent certain neither I nor my computer will need it in the future, ever?

If the answer to both questions is "Yes" then go ahead and delete the file. If the answer to either question is "No," don't delete the file or move it to the Recycle Bin.

> **CAUTION**   When you delete a folder, you delete all of the files and subfolders inside that folder! That means one small delete can lead to many lost files. Never delete a folder unless you're absolutely sure that the folder and its subfolders contain only files that you'll never need again.

Don't delete files and folders just to conserve hard disk space. Never presume that there won't be enough room for other files if you don't start deleting things now. Know exactly how much free space you have on your hard disk, and what the number means, before you start worrying about running out of space.

That said, deleting is a simple process. If you want to delete a single file or folder, first select its icon. Optionally, if you want to delete multiple items in one fell swoop, select their icons. Then, do whichever of the following is most convenient for you:

- Right-click the icon (or any selected icon), and choose Delete.
- Press the Delete (Del) key.
- Choose File ⇨ Delete from Explorer's menu bar.
- Drag the selected item(s) to the Recycle Bin.

Because deleting is serious business, you'll be asked for confirmation before the item(s) are actually deleted. The confirmation appears as a question asking if you're sure, and gives you a choice on whether or not you want to proceed. Figure 29.15 shows examples of a couple such confirmation messages.

FIGURE 29.15

Asking for confirmation before deleting.

The idea is to read the message, then click Yes only if you're sure. If you're not so sure, you should click No. Clicking Yes deletes the files. Clicking No keeps the files right where they are.

Notice that the top message asks if you're sure you want to send the items to the Recycle Bin, while the second message asks if you're sure that you want to permanently delete the items. The difference is as follows.

When you send something to the Recycle Bin, you still get one last chance to change your mind. Kind of like fishing something out of the wastepaper basket before the cleaning crew comes and empties your trash. That doesn't mean you should put things you intend to keep in the Recycle Bin. You wouldn't put important papers in your trash can. Never put important files or folders in your Recycle Bin.

> **CAUTION**   Despite its environmentally friendly name, the Recycle Bin *is* a trash can and should be treated as such. Neither the Recycle Bin nor your trash can are good places to put things you intend to keep!

When you permanently delete a file or folder, there's no turning back. Whatever you permanently deleted is gone for good and there's no changing your mind and getting it back. Think of permanently deleting as being like putting something down the garbage disposal. Or dousing the thing with gasoline and burning it to ashes. There is no "undo" for such actions.

TIP Actually, I just told you a little white lie. It may be possible to use the Previous Versions feature described in Chapter 33 to recover a permanently deleted file. But to play it safe, you should treat all deletions as though they were permanent.

Using the Recycle Bin

The Recycle Bin stores copies of files you've deleted from your hard disk. To open your Recycle Bin, use whichever method is easiest for you:

- Open the Recycle Bin on the desktop.
- Click Recycle Bin in the Folder list in Explorer's Navigation pane.
- Click the leftmost arrow in Explorer's Address bar and choose Recycle Bin.
- Type `Recycle Bin` in Explorer's Address bar and press Enter.

When the Recycle Bin opens, it looks like any other folder. Figure 29.16 shows an example.

FIGURE 29.16

An open Recycle Bin.

Each icon in the Recycle Bin represents an item that's in your computer trash can, so to speak. There are basically two ways to use the Recycle Bin:

- *Restore* files that you've accidentally deleted, so they go back to their original folders. (Same as fishing something out of your real trash can.)
- *Empty* the Recycle Bin, thereby permanently deleting the files within it to reclaim the disk space they were using. (Same as emptying your real trash can into a trash truck or incinerator.)

We'll look at each option in the sections that follow.

Recovering accidentally deleted files

If you accidentally deleted some files or folders from your hard disk, and if they were sent to the Recycle Bin, you can get them back, provided that you don't empty the Recycle Bin first. There are three ways to do that:

- To put all items back where they were, click Restore all items in the toolbar.
- To put a single item back where it was, right-click its icon and choose Restore.
- Optionally, you can select multiple icons, right-click any selected icon, and choose Restore to put all those selected items back where they were.

Each file and folder you restore will be returned to its original location.

Permanently deleting Recycle Bin files

When you feel confident that the Recycle Bin contains only folders and files that you'll never need again, click Empty the Recycle Bin in the toolbar. The icons in the Recycle Bin disappear. The files and folders that those icons represented are permanently deleted from your hard disk. The space they occupied is freed up for anything you might want to save in the future.

> **TIP**   You can empty the Recycle Bin without opening it first. Right-click the Recycle Bin's icon, and choose Empty Recycle Bin. Just keep in mind that in doing so, you're presuming there's nothing in the Recycle Bin you intended to keep.

When you've finished with the Recycle Bin, you can close it as you would any other window — by clicking the Close (X) button in its upper-right corner.

For all intents and purposes, you should consider the files that were in the Recycle Bin as permanently gone. But if you messed up and emptied too early, you *might* be able to get some of the files that were in there back using the Previous Versions feature discussed in Chapter 33.

Creating and Deleting Shortcuts

Shortcuts provide an easy way to get to a file or folder without having to navigate through a bunch of folders. For example, let's say you have an external disk drive X. On that drive you have a folder named My Big Project inside another folder named Xternal Docs. To view the contents of your My Big Project folder, you have to open your Computer folder, open the icon for drive X:, open the Xternal Docs folder, and then open the My Big Project folder. Doing that repeatedly gets tiresome.

If you create a shortcut to My Big Project, you won't have to go through all those steps. You just have to open the My Big Project shortcut icon. That shortcut icon can be any place you like — on the desktop, in your Documents folder, in the Favorite Links pane, on the Start menu — or any combination thereof.

You can create a desktop shortcut to virtually any program, folder, or file just by right-clicking that item's icon and choosing Send To ⇨ Desktop (create shortcut). You can also use any of the following methods to create a shortcut to a file or folder:

- Hold down the Alt key as you drag an icon to the folder in which you want to place the shortcut.
- Drag, using the right mouse button, the selected icon(s) to where you want to put the shortcuts. After you release the right mouse button, click Create shortcuts here.
- Copy the selected icon(s) to the Clipboard (press Ctrl+C or right-click and choose Copy). Then right-click some empty space at the location where you want to place the shortcuts and choose Paste Shortcut.

Once you have a shortcut, you can double-click (or click) its icon to open the item to which the shortcut refers.

It's important to understand that when you delete a shortcut to a resource, you delete only the shortcut. You don't delete the folder or file to which the shortcut refers. That means you can easily create a bunch of shortcuts to a folder you're working with right now.

Later, when you move on to another project in another folder, you can delete all those shortcuts and replace them with new shortcuts to whatever folder you're working in currently. But you have to make sure you delete the shortcuts only, not the real folder. Because when you delete the real folder, you also delete everything that's in that folder. You also render the shortcuts useless, because the location to which they refer no longer exists. When you try to open a shortcut that points to a non-existent file or folder, you see a message like the one in Figure 29.17.

FIGURE 29.17

Opening a shortcut that leads nowhere.

If you deleted the item recently and it's still in the Recycle Bin, click the Restore button. The original item will be taken out of the trash, put back where it belongs, and the shortcut will work. Otherwise, if there's no way to recover the item to which the shortcut refers, all you can do is delete the now-useless shortcut by clicking the Delete It button.

NOTE If the shortcut refers to an item on an external disk, then that disk has to be in its drive for the shortcut to work. You should only use shortcuts for items on local hard drives.

If you're thinking about deleting an icon, but aren't sure if it's a shortcut or the real thing, there are ways to find out. For one thing, all icons on the Start menu, All Programs menu, and their submenus are shortcuts. Likewise, all links in the Favorite Links portion of Explorer's Navigation bar are shortcuts. Desktop icons you control from the Desktop Icon Settings dialog box are also shortcuts. I'm not suggesting you delete any of those unless you have a very good reason. But if you delete one, be aware that you're deleting only the shortcut and not the actual item.

 Chapters 11 and 28 provide more detailed information about the items described in the preceding paragraph.

Shortcut icons of your own making have many characteristics that make it easy to distinguish them from the items to which they refer. The most obvious is the curved arrow that appears right on the icon. The name of the icon usually has - shortcut at the end (if you don't rename the shortcut). The filename extension for a shortcut icon is always .lnk (for link). The size of a shortcut will always be tiny (1 KB or less). When you right-click the icon and choose Properties, the General tab shows the Type of File as Shortcut (.lnk). The Shortcut tab shows information about the icon and its target as in Figure 29.18.

FIGURE 29.18

Anatomy of a custom shortcut icon.

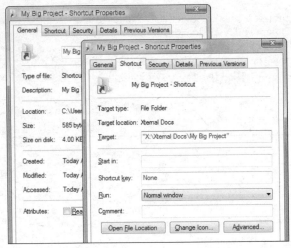

Like I said at the outset of this section, when you delete a shortcut you delete only the shortcut, not the item to which it refers. So you can create and delete shortcuts on-the-fly without losing any important files or folders. But the #1 rule of deleting still applies: Know exactly what you're deleting and why you're deleting it *before* you delete. It's as simple as that.

Managing Files with DOS Commands

This section is for people who were around in the DOS days and remember commands like CD (change directory), Copy (to copy files), and so forth. All those old DOS commands still work, even though there is no DOS in Windows XP. There are some instances where using DOS commands is useful, such as when you want to print a list of filenames or paste them into a file. So, we'll look at how all that works in this section.

Getting to a command prompt

The first step to using DOS commands is to get to the Command Prompt window. To do so, click the Start button and choose All Programs ➪ Accessories ➪ Command Prompt. Or click the Start button, type com, and choose Command Prompt. A window reminiscent of ye olde DOS days opens, complete with the standard prompt that displays the folder (er, I mean, *directory*) that you're currently in (or "on," or whatever the terminology was back then). Figure 29.19 shows an example.

Command Prompt window.

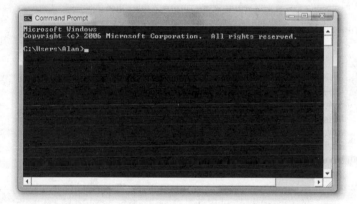

The Command Prompt window has a title bar and taskbar button. You can drag the window around by its title bar. To a limited extent, you can size the Command Prompt window by dragging any corner or edge. But the height is limited to the number of lines currently displayed within the window.

To get full control over the size of the Command Prompt window, you need to use its Properties dialog box. That Properties dialog box also lets you choose a cursor size, a Full Screen View, a font, text and background colors, and so forth.

There are two ways to get to the Command Prompt window's Properties dialog box, If you want to change properties for the current session only, right-click the Command Prompt title bar and choose Properties. If you want to change the defaults for future sessions as well, right-click the title bar and choose Defaults. The dialog box that opens is self-explanatory and is a normal Windows dialog box.

You can scroll up and down through the Command Prompt window using the vertical scroll bar at its right. The navigation keys don't work unless you right-click within the window and choose Scroll. You can't type normal characters in the scroll mode, just navigate up and down. To get out of scroll mode and back to normal typing, press Enter.

To exit a command prompt session, type `exit` and press Enter. Or close the Command Prompt program window by clicking its Close (X) button or by right-clicking its taskbar button and choosing Close.

Using the command prompt

The Command Prompt window works just like the screen did in DOS. You type a command and press Enter (assuming that you're not in the aforementioned "scroll mode," wherein typing normal characters just sounds a beep). After you press Enter, you see the results of the command and another command prompt appears. For example, if you enter `Help` (that is, type the word `Help` and press Enter), you see a list of all the supported DOS commands.

To get help with a command, type its name followed by a slash and question mark. For example, entering the command `dir /?` shows help for the dir command. The Doskey feature is enabled automatically (again assuming that you're not in the bizarre scroll mode). So, you can use the ↑ and ↓ keys to retrieve previous commands from the current session. Press the → and ← keys to bring back and remove the previous command one character at a time.

NOTE If the characters you type result only in a beep, and nothing on the screen, right-click in the Command Prompt window and choose Scroll to get back to normal typing.

The mouse doesn't do much in the Command Prompt window. As mentioned, you can right-click the title bar (or its taskbar button) to get to the Properties sheet. You can right-click and choose Scroll to enter the (disturbing) scroll mode where navigation keys move through the window and normal characters do nothing but beep at you. (Though pressing Enter terminates the disturbing scroll mode.)

Copy and paste in the Command Prompt window

Right-clicking in the Command Prompt window provides some options that allow you to use copy and paste. It's a bit tricky, but handy when you want to copy a lengthy list of filenames into a Word, WordPad, or Notepad document. If you'll be using the keyboard to select only a portion of the text, you first want to use the scroll bar to get up to where you can see where you want to start selecting text. If you'll be using the mouse to select a portion of text, or will be selecting all the text in the window, it's not so important where you start.

To select the entire window, right-click within the window and choose Select All. To select only a portion of the window's contents, right-click within the Command Prompt window and choose Mark. You'll see a square cursor. To select with the keyboard, hold down the Shift key and use the →, ←, ↑, ↓, PgUp, and PgDn keys to extend the selection through the text you want to select. With the mouse, move the mouse pointer to the far-right edge of the window, hold down the left mouse button, and then drag diagonally through the text you want to select.

Once you've selected some text, press Enter to copy the selected text and also clear the selection. From there, you can paste the copied text into any document that accepts pasted text.

You can paste a command into the window, but it has to be a valid DOS command. Just right-click near the command prompt and choose Paste.

Navigating from the command prompt

Navigating to a particular drive at the command prompt is easy. Type the drive letter followed by a colon and press Enter. For example, entering `d:` takes you to drive D:. Entering `c:` takes you to drive C:.

Use the `cd` (Change Directory) command, just as you did in DOS, to go to a folder on the current drive. Two short `cd` commands you can use are

- `cd\`   Takes you to the root folder of the current drive.
- `cd..`   Takes you to the parent of the current folder.

Printing a list of filenames

Perhaps the one thing that the DOS command has that Explorer doesn't is the ability to easily print a list of filenames from any folder, or even a parent folder and all its subfolders. While you can print directly by following any command with a >prn character, I'm sure most people would prefer to get that list into a Word or WordPad document. From there you can edit and sort the filename list to your liking, and then print it.

You'll use the `dir` command to list the filenames. You may find some of the following optional switches useful for controlling how `dir` displays its output:

- **/s** — Include filenames from subfolders
- **/b** — Display filenames in bare format (not headings or summary)
- **/w** — Show in wide format
- **/d** — Same as wide, but sorted by columns
- **/n** — Use long list format with filenames to the far right
- **/l** — Use lowercase letters
- **/o** — Sort output by column as follows: N (by name), S (by size), E (by extension), D (by date), - (prefix for descending sort), G (group folder names first)

As an example of using the /o switch, the command `dir /on` lists filenames in ascending alphabetical order. The command `dir /o-s` lists filenames by size, in descending order.

So, let's look at a practical example. Suppose that you've used Windows Media Player to copy lots of CDs to your Music folder. The songs are organized into folders by artist and album. But you want a list of all song filenames, from all the subfolders.

Step 1 is to get to the parent folder of all the files you want to list. The DOS command would be cd followed by the full path to that folder. For example, `cd C:\ Users\yourUserName\Music` where *yourUserName* is the name of your user account.

Next, you need to enter a `dir` command with the /s switch to list the filenames from all the subfolders. You can use any other switches in combination with /s. For example, here's a `dir` command that lists all the filenames in bare format:

```
dir /b /s
```

Here's one that lists files in the columnar wide format with filenames listed alphabetically by name:

```
dir /d /on /s
```

You can try out various DOS commands to see which presents the most reasonable list of filenames. Then, when you get a decent list, enter that command again, but follow it with >filename.txt where *filename* is any name of your choosing. The file will be stored in whatever folder you're currently in. For this example, I'll use SongList.txt as the filename. So, you might enter a command like this at the command prompt:

```
dir /d /on /s >SongList.txt
```

You won't get any feedback on the screen after you pipe the output to a file. But no matter. You can just exit the Command Prompt window. Then use Windows Explorer to navigate to the folder from which you ran the dir command. You'll find your SongList.txt file there. Right-click it and choose Open With ⇨ Microsoft Word (or whatever program you want to use to edit the file).

The list will look exactly like DOS output, which might not be ideal. But if you know how to use the program, it shouldn't be too tough to select and delete anything you don't want in the document. Then, save it, print it, and keep it for future reference.

> **TIP** If you're a Microsoft Office guru, you could create a macro to clean up the output from a DOS command, maybe even convert it to a list of comma-separated values. Then, you could save *that* file as a text file, and import it into an Access table or Excel spreadsheet.

Whether or not this example of exporting filenames is of any value to you, I couldn't say. But it is just an example. If you know DOS, you may be able to come up with more useful applications of your own. You can do anything at the Command Prompt window that you could do in DOS, even copy and delete files. Remember, for a quick overview of all the DOS commands available in the Command Prompt window, just type help at the command prompt and press Enter.

Wrap Up

Managing files and folders in Windows Vista is a lot like it was in earlier versions of Windows. You just have more ways of doing things. Here's a quick wrap up of the main topics covered in this chapter:

- To select a single icon to work with, click it (if you're using double-click to open files) or point to it (if you're using single-click to open files).
- To select multiple icons, use Ctrl+Click, Shift+Click, or the drag-through method, whichever is appropriate to your goal and easiest for you to use.
- To move or copy selected files and folders, drag them to some new location, or use copy and paste, or use the Copy or Move options under File and Folder tasks in the Explorer bar.
- To rename a file or selected files, right-click and choose Rename.
- To delete a file or selected files, right-click and choose Delete.
- Small items you delete from your hard drive are just moved to the Recycle Bin.
- Large files, and files you delete from removable media, are not sent to the Recycle Bin.
- To recover a file from the Recycle Bin, right-click its icon and choose Restore.
- To permanently delete all the files in the Recycle Bin and reclaim the disk space they're using, empty the Recycle Bin.
- When you delete a shortcut to a resource, you delete only the shortcut — not the resource itself.
- If you're a DOS guru, you can still use DOS commands to manage files. Click Start and choose All Programs ⇨ Accessories ⇨ Command Prompt to get to the Command Prompt window.

Chapter 30

Searching for Files and Messages

Hard disk storage in the twenty-first century is reliable, fast, and cheap. Just about every computer sold in the last few years has lots of it. The result is that people now store many thousands of files on their computers. To organize their folders, people use lots of folders and subfolders. While it's certainly good to have lots of well-organized files on your hard disk, there are a couple of downsides to it. For one, drilling down through a ton of folders to get to a specific file gets tedious. For another, it's easy to forget where you put things and what you named them.

In earlier versions of Windows, you could use shortcuts and searches to help with these problems. But too many shortcuts just add that much more clutter to the screen. The old style of searching for things is slow and tedious. Searching for things in Vista is a lot like searching for things on the Internet. You don't have to search for specific filenames. You can search for things by content and meaning. And in most cases the search results are instantaneous. You don't have to wait for the system to slog through the whole file system looking at every file.

Basics of Searching

Like filing cabinets, computers just store information. The information in your filing cabinet has no "meaning" to your filing cabinet. Likewise, the information in your computer has no meaning to the computer. Searching a computer is much like searching through a filing cabinet or the index at the back of a book.

In the next sections, I'll try to clear up some common misconceptions about searching. Along the way I'll offer some tips and techniques that should make it easier to find what you're looking for.

You're not asking it questions

The most basic thing you need to understand about searching is that you're not asking the computer a question. Computers don't understand human languages the way people do. As mentioned, searching a computer (or the Internet) is much like searching the index at the back of a book. You need to zero-in on a specific word or phrase. The more specific that word or phrase, the more specific the search results.

Let's use the Internet as an example. You certainly can search for something like:

What is the capital of Kansas?

You will likely get your answer from any Internet search engine. However, you'd probably get the same or similar results if you search for:

capital Kansas

The reason for this is because the "keywords" in the search are "capital" and "Kansas." The other words don't help to narrow the search much. That's because you're searching for words, not meaning. Virtually every page on the Internet contains the words "what," "is," "the," and "of," even if the page has nothing to do with Kansas or capital.

I'm not saying you *can't* conduct a search for "What is the capital of Kansas?" You certainly can if you want to, and you will get results. However, the results won't be much different than if you left out the *noise words*. A noise word is any word that appears in virtually all written documents and doesn't help describe what the page is about. Examples of noise words include the following:

a about an are but did how is it me my of should so than that the then there these they this to too want was we were what when where which who will with would you your

Some search programs will actually remove all the noise words before conducting the search. Others will include them. But sometimes that works against you because you find things in your search results that have nothing to do with what you were really searching for.

So the bottom line is this: When you search for something, don't try to word it as a question. Instead, search for an exact word or phrase that has a specific meaning.

Be specific

I remember a college professor announcing to the class that the three rules of good writing are 1) be specific, 2) be specific, and 3) be specific. The same goes for searching. The more specific you are about what you're searching for, the better the results.

I'll use an Internet search as an example. Suppose I'm looking for quotes by H. L. Mencken on truth. If I search Google for *truth*, I get links to about 315 million pages. That doesn't help much because a lifetime isn't enough time to look through all those. If I search Google for *Mencken*, I get links to one million Web pages. Still too many.

If I search Google for *Mencken truth*, I get links to 726,000 pages. If I search for *Mencken truth quotation*, I get links to 466,000 pages. Notice how the more specific words there are in the search, the smaller (and also better targeted) the search results. In fact, one of the first pages listed will probably contain exactly what I'm looking for. The moral of the story being: The more specific the search, the more specific the search results.

TIP After you've clicked a link to a page, you can search that specific page for a word by choosing Edit ➪ **Find on this page** in Microsoft Internet Explorer. If you use some other Web browser, check its Edit menu or help for a similar feature.

Of course, searching the Internet and searching your own computer are two entirely different things, for the simple reason that the Internet exists *outside* your computer, and its searches don't include things that are inside your computer. But the general rule of specificity applies to all searches.

Spelling counts

When you write text for a human to read, you can get away with a ton of spelling errors. For example, the following sentence is loaded with spelling errors. But you can probably still figure out what the sentence says:

Th kwik brwn dogg jmpt ovr teh lzy mune.

You can figure it out because you have a brain, and brains have many strategies for figuring things out based on context, the sounds the letters make when read aloud, and so forth. Computers don't have brains and can't figure things out.

There are plenty of computer programs that can correct your spelling, suggest alternate spellings, and such. But those programs aren't as good as a human brain. I realize that spelling is one of those traits that some people are good at, and some people aren't. But knowing how to spell the words you're searching for is a good thing.

If you're not sure how to spell something, try typing into a word processing system that has spell checking. Or, if that's not an option for you, try an online service like www.spellcheck.net or www.dictionary .com. If it's a tech term, try www.webopedia.com.

Where you start the search matters

You can search in many different places and for many different kinds of things. Where you start your search and what you search for matters a lot. For example, there's the World Wide Web, which consists of several billion pages of text that exist outside your computer. It makes no sense to search the Internet when you're looking for something that's in your own computer.

Inside your own computer there are basically two types of searches to consider. One is a search for *help*. There you're typically looking for instructions on how to perform some task. Chapter 5 provides strategies for getting help with Windows Vista. Chapter 15 offers suggestions for getting help with other programs. This chapter has nothing to do with searching for help.

This chapter is mostly about searching for programs, folders, files, and messages that are inside, or directly connected to, your computer; the kinds of things you can use even when you're offline (not connected to the Internet).

How Searching Works

Understanding how searches work in Vista is critical to performing quick, successful searches. Most searches are performed on an *index*. The index is like the index at the back of this or any other book. It's basically a list of key words. Of course Vista's index doesn't contain page numbers. In place of page numbers it contains filenames and locations. You never see the index with your own eyes. The index is built, maintained, and searched behind the scenes without any intervention on your part.

It's Not a Replacement for Search Companion

Readers who are familiar with XP's Search Companion need to realize that the search features in Vista are a whole different ball game. You *can* use Vista's search features to find lost files. But that's just one tiny capability of the overall strategy. The search boxes are more like an Internet search engine for your own computer. You don't have to look for filenames or wildcard characters. You can look for any word or phrase in any file, as well as file properties.

For instance, if you type `modified:this week` into the Search box at the bottom of the Start menu, you see items modified this week. Try typing the first name of someone in your Contacts folder to see what shows up for that person. If you type `about:word`, where *word* is a word from a file or Windows Mail message, you find all related items. It's all very different from searching for filenames and patterns. And in most cases the results are instantaneous. But you do have to invest a little time in learning how it works to take full advantage of its capabilities.

Some searches you perform will search the entire index. Others will search only for programs, or files, or e-mail messages, or contacts. Still others will ignore the index and search through every single folder on one or more drives. It all depends on where you start the search and how you perform the search. Let's start with common everyday searches that are fast and easy to do.

NEW FEATURE   The Start menu Search box provides a quick and easy way to open programs, folders, files, and messages.

Quickie Start Menu Searches

The quick and easy way to find a program, favorite Web site, document file, contact, or e-mail or newsgroup message is to search right from the Start menu. Press ⊞ or Ctrl+Esc, or click the Start button to open the Start menu. The Search box is at the bottom left of the Start menu (see Figure 30.1). It contains the words *Start search*. The cursor is already in the Search box, so you can just start typing. You don't need to delete the words Start search. They're removed the moment you type a character.

FIGURE 30.1

Search box at the bottom left of the Start menu.

As soon as you type one character, the search results appear on the Start menu. Each character you type reduces the search results to include only items that contain those letters. You get instant feedback as you type. So you can just keep typing as many characters as necessary until you see the item you want. The search results are categorized as in the example shown in Figure 30.2.

FIGURE 30.2

Results of searching for "live".

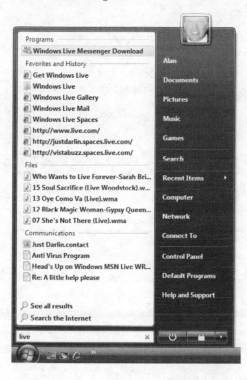

Here's what each category represents:

- **Programs:** Programs that are currently installed on your computer and ready to use.

- **Favorites and History:** Web sites in your Internet Explorer favorites and history. (Some other browser might also support this type of search.)

- **Files:** Documents in your user account files (Documents, Pictures, Music, Videos, and so forth).

- **Communications:** E-mail messages and newsgroup postings from Windows Mail. Some other e-mail clients might also be included. People in your Windows Contacts are also included in this category.

Unlike searches of yesteryear, Start menu searches don't look only at file and folder names. They look at the contents of files, tags, and properties as well. We'll talk about what those things are in Chapter 31. I mention it here in case you're wondering why some of the found Communications files don't show the word "live". It's because the word "live" appears within the message or contact's information.

You can do many things with the search results, as follows:

- To open an item, click it.
- To see other things you can do with an item, right-click it.
- If an item you were expecting to find doesn't show up, or if you want to improve the search, click See all results.
- To convert the local search to an Internet search, click Search the Internet.
- To discard the search results, press Esc or click the Start button again.

You can do wildcard searches from the Start menu, where * stands for any characters and ? stands for a single character. But do keep in mind that when you search from the Start menu, you're only searching the index, not the entire hard disk. So don't be too surprised if some files don't show up.

You can also do AND and OR searches from the Start menu. For example, a search for *.jpg OR *.jpeg finds files that have either a .jpg or .jpeg extension. I'll talk about these kinds of searches in more detail in this chapter and the next.

Customizing Start menu searches

You can customize the Start menu's search box to include or exclude categories. Right-click the Start button and choose Properties. On the Start Menu tab of the dialog box that opens, choose the Start Menu style and click the Customize button to its right. Scroll down to the options shown in Figure 30.3.

FIGURE 30.3

Start menu search options.

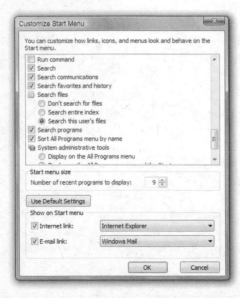

Here's what each option offers:

- **Search:** This one isn't related to the Search box. But if you select (check) it, you'll see a Search option on the right side of the menu, which is handy for other kinds of options.

- **Search Communications:** If selected, searches from the Start menu search Windows Mail e-mail and newsgroup messages as well as Windows Contacts.

- **Search Favorites and History:** If selected, searches from the Start menu search Web pages in your Internet Explorer Favorites and history.

- **Don't search for files:** Choosing this option prevents Start menu searches from finding files.

- **Search entire index:** Choosing this option searches for files beyond those in your own user account. This is required if you add your own folders to the search index and want to be able to search them from the Start menu.

- **Search the user's files:** Searches files in the Documents, Music, Pictures, and other standard folders in your user account.

- **Search programs:** Searches through programs accessible from your Start menu and Control Panel.

Don't forget to click OK after making your selections.

Extending a Start menu search

If the thing you're looking for doesn't show up in your search, first check your spelling. Make sure the word you're searching for matches something on your computer. For example, if you're looking for photos of your dog named Spot, a search for Spot won't find them unless the photos have Spot in the filename, tags, or properties.

There isn't a whole lot of space to show things on the Start menu. Some things might not show up just because there isn't enough room. To see more items, click Show all results at the bottom of the Start menu.

 To convert your Start menu search to an Internet search, click Search the Internet at the bottom of the search results.

Start menu searches are ideal for finding the kinds of things most people use most often — programs, folders, Control Panel dialog boxes, favorite Web sites, messages, and documents (text, worksheets, pictures, music, and videos). If you're a quick typist, using the Search box can save you a lot of time you'd otherwise spend clicking and opening things through the traditional methods. But Start menu searches aren't the end of the story. Not by a long shot. There's much more, as you'll see.

 The Search box in Windows Explorer's upper-right corner provides a quick and easy way to search the current folder and its subfolders.

Searching Folders and Views

By now you may have noticed Windows Explorer has a Search box in its upper-right corner. When you point to that one, its tooltip reads *Type to search the current view* as in Figure 30.4.

FIGURE 30.4

Search box in Explorer (all folders).

Like the Search box on the Start menu, the one in Windows Explorer gives you instant keystroke-by-keystroke search results. But this one doesn't search for programs, messages, and such. Instead, this one searches only the current *view*. The view consists of all files and subfolders you see in the main content pane. The Search box in Explorer doesn't look strictly at file and folder names either. It looks at the contents of files that contain text, tags, and other metadata. So once again you use it in much the same way you use an Internet search engine: Not just to search for a specific filename, but to search for keywords or phrases.

The Search box in Explorer works best when you have some idea where the item you're looking for is located. For example, let's say you have thousands of songs in your Music folder and its subfolders. You want to see all songs in the Jazz genre. Step 1 is to open your Music folder. Step 2 is to type the word `Jazz` into the Search box. Instantly you see all songs in the Jazz genre.

You certainly aren't limited to searching a genre. You can type an artist's name to see all songs by that artist. You can type a few characters from a song title. Basically, you can type anything you want to find whatever it is you're looking for. Just keep in mind that you're searching only the current folder or view.

If you're looking for something that's in one of your user account folders, but don't know which one, start by opening your user account folder (click the Start button and click your user name). That folder contains all the main subfolders for your user account, as in Figure 30.5. Then start typing whatever it is you're looking for into the Search box. Instantly you see all files and folders from your user account that match or contain the text you've typed.

 Searching subfolders is optional. If you're not getting results from subfolders, you need to change a setting in the Folder and Search Options dialog box.

If you don't really want to search all the folders in Figure 30.5, no big deal. Just open (double-click) the folder you *do* want to search, and start your search from that folder's Search box.

FIGURE 30.5

Contents of a user account folder.

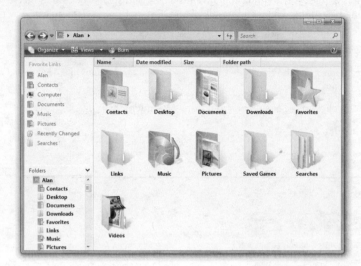

When you're first learning to use the Search box in Explorer, there will be times when you don't find a file you might have been expecting to find. There are several reasons why that might happen:

- The file isn't in the folder you're searching (or one of its subfolders).
- The way you spelled the search term in the Quick Search box doesn't match how it's spelled in the file(s).
- The file you were expecting to find isn't one of the common file types included in file searches launched from Explorer.

If you get more stuff than you were expecting, keep in mind the search isn't looking only at the filenames, or only at the columns you see in the results. It's searching properties that might not even be visible in the Details view and the contents of files that contain text.

Those of you with experience in earlier versions of Windows are probably wondering how you can do the old-style searching where you can look at all files and folders in all drives. For that kind of searching, you use the Advanced Search tools.

Using Advanced Search Tools

The Search box on the Start menu offers a quick way to find programs, messages, and such. The Search box in Explorer provides a means of finding files in that folder and its subfolders. For everything else you can use the Advanced Search tools. You can start from the Search window. There are two ways to get there:

■ Click the Start button and click Search on the right side of the Start menu.

TIP If you don't have a Search option on the right side of your Start menu, and would like one, see "Personalizing the Start Menu" in Chapter 11.

■ Or if you're already in a folder, click in the Search box and press Alt+Enter.

The Search window opens as in Figure 30.6.

FIGURE 30.6

The Search window.

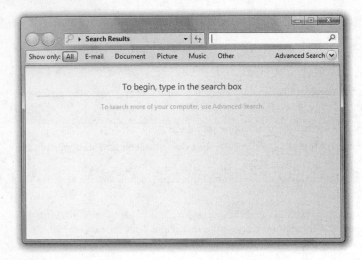

To extend the search beyond the search index, you use the Advanced Search tools shown in Figure 30.7.

FIGURE 30.7

Advanced Search tools.

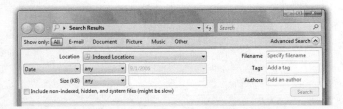

Here are a couple of ways to get to those Advanced Search tools:

- If you're already in the Search window, click the button next to Advanced Search.
- If you're in some other folder and don't see an Advanced Search button, click the Organize button and choose Layout ➪ Search Pane. Then click the Advanced Search button.
- If you just completed a search, click Advanced Search at the bottom of your search results.

Searching your computer

The Location drop-down list in the Advanced Search tools is your key to searching outside the speedy search index. When you click that, as in Figure 30.8, you'll have many locations to choose from. You can choose Computer to search the entire computer. Or you can choose a specific hard drive or all hard drives.

FIGURE 30.8

Choose a search location.

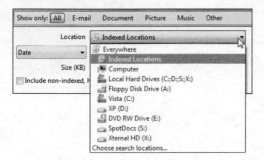

If you want to search for files outside your document folders, choose All next to Show Only. Then check the Include non-indexed, hidden, and system files (might be slow) option. The word "slow" here is relative. It's about the same speed as searches you performed in earlier versions of Windows. It's just a lot slower than the indexed searches in Windows Vista. Basically this set of options tells Vista to do a traditional search where you have to wait for it to slog through the whole file system.

To search for a specific file, use the Filename box to specify the file you want to find. You can use wildcard characters in the Filename box. For example, a search for `*.exe` finds all executable files. A search for `*.dll` finds all dynamic link libraries. After you've filled in the Filename box, click the Search button to perform the search.

Searching your own network

If your computer is part of a private network, you can use the Location box to search other computers in your network. Click the Location box and click Choose other locations. In the dialog box that opens, click the white triangle next to Network to see other computers in your network. Then you can expand any computer in the network to search a shared resource on that computer. Figure 30.9 shows an example where I've opted to search a folder named SharedDocs on a computer named Max within my private network. Choose as many locations as you wish and then click OK.

FIGURE 30.9

Searching another computer in a network.

After you've chosen the location, use the Filename box to enter the name of the file for which you're searching. You can use wildcards, as usual. For example, you could enter `*.tif` to find all files on the remote computer that have a `.tif` extension. Use other boxes in the Advanced Search tool to search by date, size, or whatever is most convenient at the moment.

 **TIP** To stop a lengthy search before it's finished, click the red X at the right side of the Address bar.

So, let's take a breather here and review what you now know:

■ The Start menu Search box provides a quick way to search for files, messages, contacts, Internet favorites, and such in your user account.

■ The Search box in Explorer provides a quick way to search for contacts and document files (pictures, songs, and such) in your user account. But it only searches the current location and its subfolders.

■ To extend the search beyond the locations and items mentioned here, open the Advanced Search tools and choose a location from the Location box.

Specifying search criteria

Anything you type into a Search box is a *search criterion*. Basically the search criterion is telling Vista "show me all items that have these characteristics." The *items* are things like files, folders, messages, contacts, and Internet Explorer favorites.

The search criterion can be as simple as a few characters of text. For example, you can click the Start button, type a person's name, and find whatever files and messages on your computer contain that person's name. Optionally, you can use the boxes you see in the Advanced Search tools to specify your search criterion. You can create complex searches by filling in multiple boxes.

Before you fill in any boxes though, be sure to choose an option next to Show only, because that determines the boxes and options available to you. You can use any combination of search boxes to specify your search criteria. In sections that follow, I'll discuss how you can use them to find files.

Search by Date

Depending on what you choose next to Show Only, you can narrow your search to specific kinds of dates by clicking the Date button. For example, you can search by Date Modified (the last time you opened, changed, and saved the file), Date Accessed (the last time you opened the file), or Date Created. If you click E-mail next to Show Only, you can also search by Date Sent or Date Received. If you click Pictures next to Show Only, you can choose Date Taken. For general searches, you can just choose Date and it will search all possible dates.

After you specify the type of date you're looking for, choose "is" for files that have an exact date, or "is before" or "is after" for dates before or after a date. Then click the Date box and choose a date using the calendar that drops down. If you don't want Date to be a criterion at all, leave the box next to Date set to "any."

So, let's say today is March 31, 2007, and you've just created or downloaded a file. Only you clicked the Save button without choosing where to put the file. And you didn't notice the name of the file. So now you don't know where it is. You could choose Date Created, Is, and 3/31/2007 and then click Search to see all files created today. That might help you find the file.

To search for files within a range of dates, choose one of the date types (like Date Modified) and then choose is. Then click the current date. In the calendar that drops down, click the start or end date. Then hold down the Shift key and click the other date. Both dates, and all the dates in between, are highlighted.

Search by Size

The Size option lets you search for files that are an exact size, or files that are larger or smaller than some size. For example, let's say you bought a second hard drive and want to move some large video files to it. You could search for Size (KB) Is Greater Than 1000000 to find all files that are larger than about 1 GB in size.

 **A megabyte (MB) is about 1,000 KB (exactly 1,024 KB). A gigabyte (GB) is about 1,000,000 KB (exactly 1,048,576 KB).**

Search by Filename or Subject

In the Filename box, you can type a specific filename or part of a filename. For example, a search for sunset finds all files that have the word "sunset" in the filename. You can use wildcard characters as in earlier versions of Windows (and DOS). Use ? to stand for a single character, and * to stand for any group of characters. For example, let's say you have files named Sunset (1), Sunset (2), Sunset (3), and so forth. A search for sunset* will find them all.

You can include filename extensions to narrow down the search. For example, a search for *.jpg finds all files that have a .jpg extension. A search for sunset*.jpg finds all files that start with sunset and end with a .jpg filename extension.

You can use the word OR (in uppercase letters, with a space before and after the word) to extend the search to multiple criteria. For example, consider the following typed into the Filename box:

*.jpg OR *.jpeg

When you click the Search button, you get all files that have either a .jpg extension or a .jpeg extension. Similarly, you could search for

sunset*.jpg OR sunset*.jpeg

to find all files that start with sunset and end with either .jpg or .jpeg.

You're not limited to just one OR. For example, placing the following in the Filename box finds all files that end with .avi, .wmv, .mpg, or .mpeg.

*.avi OR *.wmv OR *.mpg OR *.mpeg

 **Make sure you use OR, not AND. It's a common misunderstanding that I'll discuss under "Power Searches" in Chapter 31.**

If you choose E-mail next to Show Only, the Filename box is replaced by a Subject box. So you can search for e-mail messages that have a certain word or phrase in the Subject line. There's no need to use wildcards or filename extensions because the Subject line is just text, not a filename. So just type a word or phrase, click the Search button, and you'll get all messages with that word or phrase in the Subject line.

Search by Tags, Authors, Title, and Others

Depending on what you choose next to Show Only, you'll see other boxes like Tags, Authors, or Title for specifying search criteria. These correspond to metadata stored in file properties. You can type in any word or phrase to search for files that have that word or phrase in the corresponding property. I'll talk more about those properties in Chapter 31.

If you choose E-mail next to Show Only, then you'll see To Names and From Names boxes. Again, you can fill in either box, or both, to find messages with the name you specify.

Performing the Search

Unlike when you search from a Search box, the Advanced Search options don't provide keystroke-by-keystroke search results. You have to click the Search button to actually perform the search and see the results below the toolbar as in Figure 30.10. In that example I chose Pictures as Show Only, set Date Taken to dates after 4/10/2007, and put Surf in the Filename box. Then I clicked the Search button. Icons in the main pane represent files that meet those search criteria.

You can't tell by looking at the figure that the Date Taken property is a date after 4/10/2007. That's because the files are shown as thumbnails. You would have to switch to Details view to see the Date Taken column. But it's not necessary to do that unless you're looking for verification that the search worked.

FIGURE 30.10

Search results after you click Search.

You can treat the search results like any other Explorer window. For example, choose Details from the Views button to see detailed information about each file. Right-click any column heading to choose which column of information you want to see. Click any column heading to sort items by that column.

Saving a search

Searches can be used in two ways. In some cases you might just be looking for a file you've lost track of. In that case, once you've found the file, there's probably no need to repeat the search in the future. You can just double-click the found file to open it. Then close the Search window.

There may be other times when you put some time into constructing a search to pull together files from multiple folders. For example, a search for *.avi OR *.wmv OR *.mpg OR *.mpeg shows all video files with those extensions. If you think you'll want to check up on your current video files often, it's not necessary to re-create the search from scratch each time. You can save the search. Any time you want to check up on your current video files, open the saved search. It will show you all *current* files that meet those criteria.

Saving a search is easy. After you've clicked the Search button to perform the search, you'll see a Save Search button in the toolbar. Just click that button and a Save As dialog box opens. The name of the search will reflect the search criteria you specified. But you don't need to keep that name. Type in any name that will be easy to recognize in the future. For example, in Figure 30.11 I've named a search I'm about to save Video Files. Vista will suggest putting it in the Search folder for your user account. That's as good a place as any to keep it. So don't change that unless you have some good reason. You can also enter an Author name and Tags if you like. Then click the Save button.

FIGURE 30.11

Saving a search.

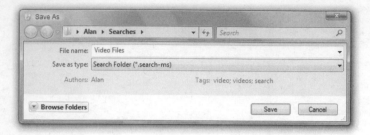

Using saved searches

Unless you specify otherwise, your saved searches are stored in the Searches folder for your user account. You can open that using any of the following techniques:

- Click the Start button, click your user account name, and open the Searches folder.
- If you're in a folder and the Navigation pane is open, click Searches under Favorite Links (if available).
- Press ⊞, type sea, and click the Searches folder under Files.

The Searches folder opens. You'll see some sample searches in there. Those are examples that come with Windows Vista. You'll also see searches you've saved yourself. Figure 30.12 shows an example.

To perform a saved search, just open (double-click) its icon. The search opens looking just like any real folder. In fact, you can treat it just as you would any real folder. The only difference between a saved search and a real folder is that the saved search doesn't actually "contain" files. The saved search is a *virtual folder* that looks and acts like a real folder. But the files you see in the saved search are still in whatever folder you originally saved them. The virtual folder just lets you see all the files that match the search criteria *as though* they were all in one folder. This allows you to work with the files as a unit, regardless of their actual physical location in folders.

A search in Vista is similar to an Internet search. When you search in Vista, or open a saved search, you're really just looking at links to files that match the search criteria. But do be aware that when you do something to a file in the search results, you perform that action on the actual file. For example, when you delete a file from a saved search, you delete it from its actual location. Likewise, if you restore that file from the Recycle Bin, you restore it back to its original location.

FIGURE 30.12

FIGURE 30.12

Saved searches.

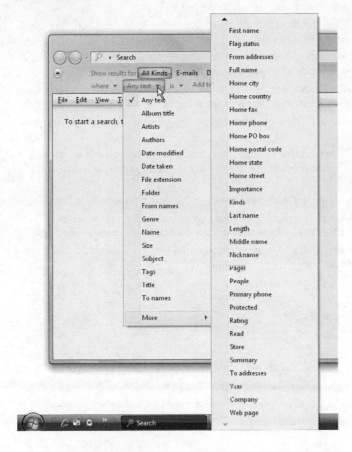

Wrap Up

There are many ways to find things in Windows Vista. For those of you with no prior computer experience, the main thing to know is that you can type a word in the Search box at the bottom of the Start menu to find items that contain that word.

For experienced users, the trick is to realize that the Search boxes are not at all like the Search Companion from Windows XP. Each box is more like a mini search engine for finding documents and messages based on content, properties, tags, or name. By default, only items in your user account are searched. If you want to include more items in those searches, see Chapter 31.

Here's a quick review of the main points covered in this chapter:

- Windows Vista has a built-in index of programs, files, folders, and messages in your user account. When you search the index, you get keystroke-by-keystroke results.

- To search from the Start menu, tap the ⊞ key, or press Ctrl+Esc, or click the Start button to open the Start menu. Then start typing your search text.

- To search for a file when you know its general location, open the folder or a parent folder of the item. Then use the Search box in Explorer's upper-right corner to search.

- To search broadly, use the Search folder. To open it, click the Start button and choose Search. Or click the empty Search box in any folder and press Alt+Enter.

- In the Search folder, use options to the right of Show Only to narrow your search to specific types of items.

- To search outside the index, click Advanced Search. Then click Location and specify what you want to search. Use the "Include non-indexed..." checkbox to extend the search to all files and folders at the selected location.

- To save a successful search for future use, click Save Search in the Search window's toolbar.

- To reuse saved searches, click the Start button, click your user name, then open the Searches folder. Or click Searches under Favorite Links (if available) in the Navigation pane of any folder.

- If you frequently use files that are outside of your user account folders, see Chapter 31 for info on adding those folders to your search index.

Chapter 31

Metadata and Power Searches

Chapter 30 was about different ways you can search your computer. When you search for files, you actually search an index of filenames and properties. The index isn't something you see on the screen. Nor do you have to do anything to create or update the index. Windows Vista takes care of all the details automatically and behind the scenes. The beauty of the index is that it allows Windows Vista to find things much more quickly than it could without the index.

The information about files that's in the index comes from each file's properties. Those properties are sometimes referred to as *metadata* because they're different from the file's content. The file's content is what you see on the screen when you open the file. The file's properties are stored in the file's properties sheet.

Properties provide a way of organizing files that goes beyond their physical location in folders. This is a great boon to people who have many files to manage, because sometimes a simple folder name and filename just aren't enough. Sometimes you want to see all files based on authorship, date created, tags, subject, or even comments you've jotted down about the file. In other words, you want to pull together and work with files in a way that transcends their physical locations in folders. Metadata in Vista's indexed searches allow you to do that quickly and easily.

NEW FEATURE You can view file metadata in Explorer's Details pane.

Working with File Properties

Taking a wild guess, I'd say there's somewhere between 50,000 and 100,000 different types of files you can put on a PC. No one person needs them all or uses them all. Some are so esoteric you might never come across one. Some of those many different file types support the use of *properties*, some don't.

There are many ways to view and edit a file's properties. One way is to open the folder in which the file is contained, then select the file's icon. The Details pane, if open, display's the file's properties. If the Details pane isn't open, click the Organize button and choose Layout ⇨ Details pane. Or get the tip of the mouse pointer just above the window's bottom border and drag up.

Initially, the Details pane might be too short to show all the file's properties. But you can drag its top border upward to see more properties. Figure 31.1 shows an example where I'm viewing the properties for a Microsoft Word 2007 document. Other file types will have other properties.

FIGURE 31.1

A file's properties in the Details pane.

Viewing properties sheets

Here's another way to view a file's properties: Right-click its icon and choose Properties. Or, if the file's icon is already selected and its properties are visible in the Details pane, click Edit in the Details pane. A dialog box opens. If that dialog box has a Details tab, that's where you're most likely to find the kinds of properties you can create and edit. You'll often hear the term *properties sheet* used to describe that set of properties, because it's kind of like a sheet of paper on which properties are written.

Figure 31.2 shows a couple of sample properties sheets. On the left is the properties sheet for the Word document shown in Figure 31.1. On the right is the properties sheet for a JPEG image. When there are more properties than fit in the box, use the scroll bar at the right side of the box to see others.

Every property has a name and a *value*. The value is some text, date, or number that's assigned to the property. In the properties sheets, the property names are listed down the left column. The value assigned to each property (if any) appears to the right of the property name.

FIGURE 31.2

Examples of properties sheets.

Viewing properties in columns

Yet a third way to view properties is through the Details view in Windows Explorer. In any folder (including the results of a search), click the Views button and choose Details. You'll see a few columns across the top of the contents pane. But what you see isn't necessarily all there is. The horizontal scroll bar across the bottom of the pane lets you scroll to other columns. You can also add columns to the view (or remove columns) by right-clicking any column heading, as in Figure 31.3. The menu that appears shows a few other columns from which you can choose. Click More... at the bottom of that menu to see others.

FIGURE 31.3

Choosing columns in Details view.

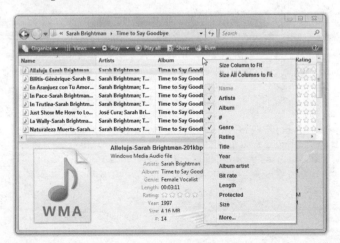

 See "Using columns in the Details view" in Chapter 28 for the goods on choosing, moving, and sizing columns in the Details view.

Editing properties

To change a file's properties, select its icon. Then make your changes in the Details pane. Or right-click the file's icon, choose Properties, click the Details tab, and make your changes there.

You can change properties for multiple files using the same basic method. You just have to select the icons for the files first. But there is a catch. You'll be limited to changing properties that all the selected files have in common. This can be a real pain when you're working with multiple file types. For example, there are many different types of files for storing pictures — JPEG, TIFF, PNG, BMP, and GIF to name a few. The newer file types, JPEG, TIFF, and PNG, offer many properties. The older file types, BMP and GIF, offer relatively few.

Figure 31.4 shows an example of what can happen when you select multiple file types. There I've selected all the icons in the folder, each of which is a picture. Then I right-clicked one of them, chose Properties, and clicked the Details tab. There are hardly any properties showing because all those different file types have few properties in common.

FIGURE 31.4

Properties for multiple files of different types.

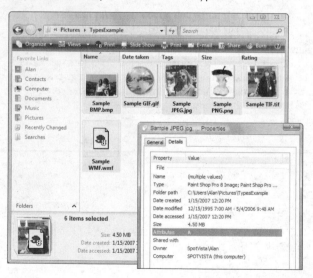

With old file types that support few properties, about the only thing you can do is convert them to newer file types. For example, I had a lot of GIF images on my system when I installed Vista. That file type doesn't offer any really usable properties. So I used the batch conversion feature of my graphics program (Paint Shop Pro) to convert them all to PNG files. I chose PNG because it supports transparency like GIF does.

PNG does not support animation. So you may not want to convert animated GIFs to PNG.

If you have so many files to which you want to assign new properties, your might consider creating a search that brings similar files together all under one roof, so to speak. For example, click the Start button, choose Search, and click Advanced Search. If you need to include files that aren't yet in your search index, choose Computer or an appropriate location from the Location button. Then use the Filename box to specify the types of files you want to work with. In Figure 31.5, I typed the following into the Filename box:

```
*.jpg OR *.jpeg OR *.tif OR *.tiff or *.png NOT *.lnk
```

FIGURE 31.5

Specify the types of files in the Filename box.

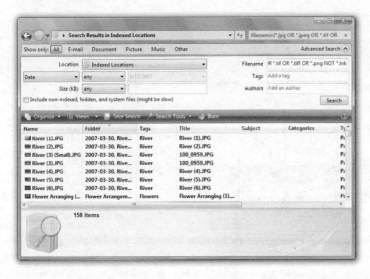

That brings together all my TIFF, JPEG, and PNG files, and omits any shortcuts (.lnk files). (The .lnk files won't have many editable properties either.) Perform the search and then use column headings to sort items based on their current folder location. You can also add columns that allow you to see the properties you intend to work with. Of course that's just an example. You can set up searches to find and organize things as you see fit.

Save the search when you're done so you can open and use it whenever you have time to work with properties. To change properties for any single file, click its name. To assign the same property value to multiple files, select their icons. Then use the Details pane or properties sheet to make your changes. It will take some time if you have many files to work with. But having all the files together in one place, and the properties of interest in plain view, can make the job less daunting.

Vista's Save As dialog box offers new tools for entering metadata when you save a file.

Setting Properties When You Save

Search indexes are nothing new. Database people have been using them for decades. Every time you do an Internet search, you're actually searching an index of Web sites somewhere. Windows XP and other operating systems allow for some limited indexed searching through add-on programs. But Windows Vista is the first Windows version to have indexed searching—its own built-in search engine—built in from the ground up. People in the software business understand the value of that. As the years roll by, new versions of old programs will include the ability to tag files and set properties at the moment you first save the program.

When you save a new file, be sure to look around for any options in the Save As dialog box that allow you to add tags or properties. Figure 31-6 shows an example where I'm in the Save As dialog box for a Microsoft Word 2007 document. As you can see, the dialog box allows me to add tags, a title, subject, categories, and comments right on the spot.

When you're faced with such options, think about words you might want to type into a Search box to find the file in the future. Ask yourself "If I need this thing six months from now and forget its file name, what word might I use to search for it?" or "How should I categorize this file in relation to other similar kinds of documents?" As your collection of files grows, and your searching skills grow, the few moments you spend thinking up keywords for tags and properties will pay off in spades.

FIGURE 31.6

Save As dialog box for Word 2007.

 You have many options for personalizing and configuring Vista's new Search tools.

Personalizing Searches

Getting the most from Vista's searches includes knowing how to tweak its settings to work in ways that support the kinds of things you do. You can tweak some aspects of indexed searches through the Folder and Search Options dialog box. To get to the search options, do any of the following:

- If you're in a folder, click the Organize button and click Folders and Search Options.
- If you're in Search Results, click Search Tools and click Search Options.
- Press ⊞ or click the Start button, type fol, and then click Folder Options.

The Folder and Search Options dialog box opens. Click the Search tab to see the options shown in Figure 31.7.

FIGURE 31.7

Search options.

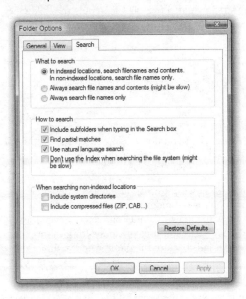

The first set of options under *What to search* dictates how searches are performed:

- **In indexed locations, search filenames and contents. In non-indexed locations, search file names only:** This is the default setting and gives the best performance for searching documents, messages, and such.

TIP If some files aren't showing up in your searches because they're not in your user account folders, these options really won't help. Better to extend the index to include those files. I'll talk about how you do that in the next section.

- **Always search file names and contents (might be slow):** This option forces searches to look at the contents of non-indexed files, which can really slow things down. Better to index the non-indexed document files to get the speedier index searches.

- **Always search file names only:** Choosing this option excludes file contents from the searches, but won't find files based on words inside those files. You'll have to know the name of the file for which you're searching.

The How to search options affect different aspects of Vista searching. The Include subfolders when typing in the Search box only applies to the Search box in Explorer's upper-right corner. If you choose this option, the Search box only filters out files from the current folder that don't match the search criteria. It doesn't dig down into subfolders to find other files that do match the search criteria.

The Find partial matches option, when selected, lets you type a few characters into the Search box and still get a match. For example, let's say you have numerous files with the name Sarah in the filename, Artist name, or whatever. When you type `sar` into the Search box, you see those items that contain Sarah. But if you clear the Find partial matches checkbox, it won't work that way. You wouldn't see items that contain Sarah until you typed all five characters, `sarah`.

The Use natural language search is an interesting option related to typing search criteria directly into the Search box. I'll talk about that under "Power Searches" later in this chapter. But here's the gist of it: If you don't choose that option, you have to type queries following strict syntax. For example, typing the following into the Search box on the Start menu displays all Windows Mail messages from Alan that contain the word "lunch":

`from:alan about:lunch`

The following example would work, but only if Use natural language search is selected in the Search options:

`from alan about lunch`

The advantage is that the natural language option relaxes the rules, so that if you forget the colons the search still works. But sometimes that works against you because when you don't follow stricter syntax rules you can't always be sure exactly how Vista is interpreting the query. How you see the query, and how Vista sees it, might be two different ways. So the results from the search might not be what you were expecting.

The Don't use the Index when searching the file system (might be slow) option applies when you search non-indexed locations. When you select that option, searches outside the index work like non-indexed searches from older Windows versions. The search looks at every file in every folder and doesn't even look at the search option. When you leave that option unselected, the search still uses the index for files in indexed locations. So that part of the search goes quickly. Then it falls back to the old non-indexed method, but only for files that aren't indexed.

The last two options apply only when you're searching non-indexed locations. Choose Include system directories if you want non-indexed searches to include Windows and other program files that are essential to proper functioning of your PC. These are not files you normally open or modify yourself. So it would only make sense to choose this option if you're a programmer or administrator who needs frequent access to files in those locations. Otherwise you're just slowing down your searches for no good reason.

Choosing the Include compressed files (ZIP, CAB...) option extends the search into compressed Zip folders and the like. Typically people only use those for *archived* files that they don't use often, because the compression and decompression add some time overhead to opening and closing the files. Including their contents in searches can also slow down searches. But if you want to include those files' contents in your non-indexed searches, just select the checkbox.

As always, clicking Restore Defaults sets all options back to their original defaults. Those are the options that provide the best performance for indexed searches, and cover the things most people would typically want included in their searches.

Managing the Search Index

To get the best performance and value from the search index, you want to make sure it includes all of the files you regularly use in your work. But you don't want to go overboard and also include files you never, or rarely, use. If you do, you're forcing it to search through thousands of filenames and properties for no good reason. By default, Vista maximizes the search index by including messages and documents from a limited number of folders.

Of course there are many people who use multiple hard disks to store their files. If you want to include files from other drives and folders, you'll need to add them to your search index. But do exercise some discretion. The larger the index, the more overhead involved in maintaining the index and the slower things go. Don't add a folder to the index if it contains a bunch of non-document files or files you don't open and use regularly.

Add a folder to your search index

There are a couple of ways to add folders to your search index. All require administrative privileges. You don't need to log in to an administrative account though, so long as you know the password to an administrative account.

One way to add folders to the search index is to simply search those folders and choose yes when given the opportunity to add those folders. Here are the steps:

1. Click the Start button and choose Search.
2. Click Advanced Search.
3. Click the button next to Location, then click Choose Search Locations.
4. Navigate to the drive that you want to add to the search index.
5. Expand the drive to show folders. Then select (check) the folder you want to add to the index. For example, in Figure 31.8, I'm about to search three folders named Books, etg, and Just Darlin from drive S:.
6. Click OK.
7. Type something into the Search box (like * to find all files) to start searching.
8. Once the search gets started, you see a message stating that searches might be slow followed by "Click to add to index...". Go ahead and click that bar and then click Add to Index.
9. A dialog box asks for confirmation. Click Add to Index, enter the password for an Administrator account, and click OK.

FIGURE 31.8

Choosing folders to search.

If the selected locations contain thousands of files, it might take several hours for Vista to index them all. You won't get any feedback on the screen during that time. Index maintenance is given low priority. So you shouldn't notice any decrease in overall computer performance while the index is being updated. If you can leave the computer running without using it for a while, the index will be updated more quickly. You can view indexing progress in the Indexing Options dialog box, described next.

 **NOTE**   To let the computer run without going to sleep, click the Start button, type `pow` and click Power Options, and then choose High Performance.

Advanced indexing options

Advanced options for tweaking the search index are in the Indexing Options dialog box. There are a couple of different ways to open that dialog box:

- Click the Start button, type `ind`, and click Indexing Options.
- Or click the Start button, open Control Panel, choose System and Maintenance, and click Indexing Options.

The Indexing Options dialog box opens as in Figure 31.9.

What's with the Offline Files?

Offline files are files that primarily exist on some other computer. You use Sync Center, described in Chapter 49, to copy them to and from a portable computer in a way the prevents the copies on your computer from becoming out of sync with copies on the main computer. The files are included in the search index, by default, because they're usually documents. And the search index is all about finding and opening documents quickly.

You can exclude offline files from the search index just by clearing the checkbox in the Indexed Locations dialog box. Any user can do that; administrative privileges aren't required. If you don't use offline files, there's no overhead to leaving that option selected. After all, if you don't use offline files, then the folder is empty. It takes no time at all to index an empty folder.

FIGURE 31.9

Indexing options.

Adding and removing indexed locations

In the previous section you saw how to add new locations to the search index just by searching those locations. As an alternative, you can add locations through the Indexing Options dialog box. Here are the steps:

1. Click Modify.

2. Click the Show all locations button and enter an administrative password if prompted.

3. Expand drives and folders, as necessary, to get to the folder(s) you want to add. Use white triangles to expand, black triangles to collapse.

CAUTION Items with checkmarks are already indexed. Don't clear any checkmarks unless you specifically want to remove that folder from your index. If you goof and lose track, click Cancel to leave the dialog box without saving any changes.

761

4. Select (check) the folder(s) you want to add. For example, in Figure 31.10 I'm adding a folder named Xternal docs from an external hard drive to my index. Choosing a folder automatically chooses all subfolders, so there's no need to select those individually. But you could clear the checkmark on one if you wanted to exclude it from the index. Those excluded folders will show up in the Excluded column in Indexing Options.

5. Click OK.

The folder is added to the index without any fanfare. About the only change you'll see is that the folder name appears in the Indexed Locations list in Indexing Options. Use the scroll bar to the right of that list if the folder name isn't immediately visible. Also, if you look at the text near the top of Indexing Options, you'll see the number of items indexed.

If you're actively using the computer, you see a message indicating that indexing speed is reduced due to user activity. Not to worry, it just means that the index-building process is giving priority to things you want to do. The message is replaced by others when the index is being built at full speed, and when indexing is compete.

You can add as many folders as you wish, from as many drives as you wish, using those same methods. But again, prudence is a virtue. But remember, don't add folders just for the heck of it or because you don't know what's in a given folder. The more you can keep your index focused on files you want to find in searches and access through virtual folders, the better performance you'll get from the index.

FIGURE 31.10

Adding Xternal docs to the index.

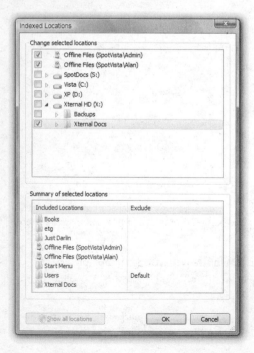

When indexing is complete, you can search for any file in any folder in a couple of ways. If you chose the option to search the entire index from the Start menu, as discussed under "Customizing Start menu searches" in Chapter 30, then you can find any indexed file from the Start menu. Otherwise, you can launch the search from the Start menu and click See all results to extend the search into the newly indexed folders. You can also click Start, choose Search, and start your search from the Search box in the Search folder that opens.

Remove a location from the index

Removing a folder from the index is the opposite of adding one. Repeat the preceding steps to get to the Indexed Locations dialog box shown in Figure 31.10. Expand drives and folders, as necessary, so you can see the items you've selected (checked). If you want to exclude some subfolders from one of your indexed folders, expand that folder first. Then clear the checkmarks from the subfolders you don't want in the index. Those subfolders show up in the Exclude column in the lower pane of the dialog box. Click OK after making your changes.

Choosing file types to index

The index intentionally excludes unknown file types, certain kinds of executable files, and libraries, because they're not normally the kinds of things you want to locate in a quick file search or virtual folder. You can add any file type you wish to your index. And you can remove any file type you don't want to see.

Filenames and properties of selected file types are always indexed. For files that contain text, like word processing documents and spreadsheets, you can choose whether or not to index file contents. The advantage of indexing file contents is that when you search for files, the file shows up even if the search term isn't in the filename or properties. The slight disadvantage is that it adds some size to the index. But in this case I think the advantage of including file contents probably outweighs the cost. Unless you're using older, slower hardware and your searches are very slow.

To change options for file types, starting from the Indexing Options dialog box:

1. Click the Advanced button.
2. In the dialog box that opens, click the File Types tab. You see a list of all file extensions as in Figure 31.11.
    - To include a file type, select its checkbox.
    - To exclude a file type, clear its checkbox.
    - If you opted to include a file type, choose whether you want to index properties only or properties and contents.
3. To add a file extension that isn't in the list, type the extension next to the Add button and click the Add button.
4. Click OK after making your changes.

FIGURE 31.11

Choosing file types to index.

More advanced options

There are some more advanced tweaks you can make to the index to change how it operates. You'll see them when you first click the Advanced button in Indexing Options. Figure 31.12 shows those advanced options.

Choosing Index encrypted files ensures that encrypted files are included in searches and virtual indexes. People encrypt files to keep prying eyes out. Keeping those same files out of the index adds another layer of security by making them invisible to basic file searches. But if that's not a problem for you and you want your encrypted files to show up in searches, just choose the option to index encrypted files.

A *diacritic* (or diacritical mark) is an accent mark added to a letter to change a word's pronunciation. Some examples include the acute accent (á), circumflex (ˆ), and umlaut (ä). When used in filenames and properties, Vista usually treats characters with diacritics as being identical to the character without the mark. Choosing Index similar words with diacritics separately changes that so that the diacritics are no longer lumped together as though they were a single character.

The Index location option lets you specify where you want to store the search index. The default is the `c:\programdata\microsoft\search` folder. If you have a separate hard drive that runs faster than your C: drive, you could relocate the index to that drive for better performance. Just make sure you choose a drive that's always attached to the computer, not a removable drive. Click the Move button and use the Browse dialog box that appears to navigate the drive and folder in which you want to store the index.

FIGURE 31.12

Advanced indexing options.

Rebuilding the index

If you see error messages about a corrupt index, or the system is crashing when you try to perform a search, the problem might be a corrupted index. You can rebuild the index to see if that helps. But the process could take several hours. So if at all possible, you might consider doing this job as an overnighter. The process is simple: Just click the Rebuild button in the Advanced Options shown back in Figure 31.12.

You can continue to use the computer while the index is being rebuilt. Any searches you perform while the index is being rebuilt will likely be incomplete.

Restoring index defaults

The Restore Defaults button sets all indexing back to the original factory settings. If you ever make a mess of things while messing with search index options, you can use that button to get back to square one.

Moving the index

Vista stores the index in the ProgramData/Microsoft folder of its own drive (typically C:). If you have a separate hard drive that's faster than the Vista drive, you can move the index to that drive. Whether or not you actually get quicker indexed search results depends on the size of the index and how fast the alternative drive is. To move the index to a different location, click the Select New button and use the Browse for Folder option to specify a new location for the index. To move the index, click OK and Close in the open dialog boxes. Then restart the computer.

NEW FEATURE Vista's query language goes way beyond filename and wildcard searches.

Power Searches

The ability to click the Start button (or press ⊞), type a few characters, and see all items that contain those characters is really a great thing. For most people it'll save a lot of time otherwise spent opening programs or navigating through folders to open a program, document, contact, or message. It's so useful you might not even need to bother with more complex searches.

When you do need a more complex search, you can just use the Advanced Search options to search for particular types of files, and limit the search by date, filename, size, or whatever. You can create complex searches and save them. When you want to do the same search again in the future, that's handy too. For folks who want still more, there's the query language.

You may have noticed that after you fill in the blanks in an Advanced Search and click the Search button, you see some text in the Search box. Take a look at Figure 31.13 for an example. There I set the date criterion to Date modified is after 12/1/2007, and set Authors to Alan. Clicking the Search button puts the following into the Search box:

```
modified:>12/1/2007 author(alan)
```

FIGURE 31.13

Sample search.

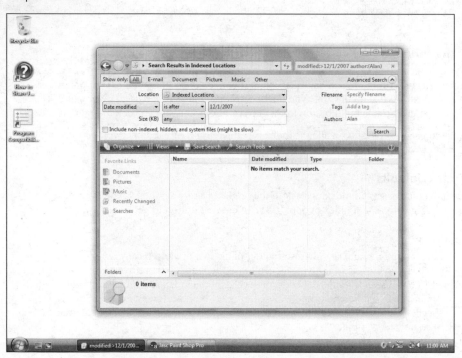

That little line of text, called a *query*, in the Search box is what's actually returning the search results. When you perform the search, Vista actually looks through the whole index. But the query acts as a filter of sorts. Only items that meet the conditions set forth by the query show in the search results. In this example, only files whose Date Modified date is after 12/1/2007 and that have Alan in the Author property show in the search results. Items that don't match the criterion don't appear in the search results. Those items aren't deleted or changed in any way. They're simply "filtered out" so as not to show up in the search results.

You can type your own queries into the Search box to perform complex searches. But, it's not as simple as "asking a question" or typing a bunch of words at random. You have to follow some rules and write the query in such a way that it can be interpreted properly. Otherwise, the search returns the wrong items, or no items at all. We'll look at some ways you can type your own complex queries in the sections to follow.

Searching specific properties

When you type a word into the search box, the results show files that contain that word in their filename, contents, and properties. For example, a search for `jazz` finds songs in the Jazz music genre, any folder or file that has the word jazz in its filename or contents, and any file that has the word jazz in any property. In other words, you could end up with a whole lot of files in the search results.

You can always narrow a search down by specifying a property name followed by a colon and the text for which you're searching. For example, a search for `genre:jazz` only finds music files in the Jazz genre.

Similarly, a search for `susan` finds all files that have Susan somewhere in the file, name, or a property, whereas a search for `from:susan` finds only e-mail messages that have the name Susan in the From address.

You can assign ratings to pictures and music files, and use ratings as a search word. For example, `rating:5 stars` finds files with 5-star ratings.

When you perform a search from the Advanced Search options, you see the property name that you can use in your own queries. For example, back in Figure 31.13, the Search box shows `modified:>12/1/2007 author(Alan)`. That lets you know that `modified:` and `author:` are valid property names you can search. Searches based on other fields show other property names. I'll show you others in the sections to follow.

Greater than and less than

When you're searching a property that contains a date or number, you can use the following comparison operators:

- `=`: Equal to (this is assumed if you don't specify an operator below)
- `>`: Greater than
- `>=`: Greater than or equal to
- `<`: Less than
- `<=`: Less than or equal to
- `<>`: Does not equal

A search for `rating:>=4 stars` finds pictures and music with 4- or 5-star ratings. A search for `width:<600` finds pictures with widths less than 600 pixels. The query `modified:<2007` finds files last modified in 2006 or earlier. A search for `kind:video size:<300KB` finds video files less than 3,000 KB in size.

AND, OR, and NOT searches

You can use the keywords AND, OR, and NOT in searches. You must type the word in uppercase letters. Be sure to include a space before and after the word.

Not using any word is the same as using AND. For example, the query from Figure 31.13 looked like this:

```
modified:>12/1/2007 author(alan)
```

That means the same thing as this:

```
modified:>12/1/2007 AND author(alan)
```

Any time you create an AND query, you *narrow* the search results. Intuitively, you might think it would have the opposite effect. But that's not the way it works. The query is a filter. And in order to show up in the search results, a file must meet *all* criteria posed by the filter. For example, files that don't have *alan* in the Authors property won't show up at all, no matter what's in their Date Modified property. And files that were modified before 12/1/2007 won't show up either, even if they do have *alan* in the Author field.

Here's a common mistake that might help to better illustrate. Take a look at this:

```
filename:(*.jpg AND *.jpeg)
```

Intuitively you might expect the result of this search to be files with .jpg and .jpeg extensions. But it's not. The result of this search is nothing! Why? Because the criterion is a filter, not a question. In order to get through the filter, a file would need to have a .jpg extension *and also* a .jpeg extension. But a file can't have two extensions. Every file has only one filename extension. Therefore no single file could get past this filter.

When you want to *broaden*, not narrow, a search, you use OR. For example, take a look at this:

```
filename:(*.jpg OR *.jpeg)
```

To get past this filter a file needs to have either a .jpg *or* .jpeg extension. So the result of the search is all files that have either a .jpg or .jpeg filename extension.

> **TIP** If you don't see filename extensions in search results, click the Organize button and choose Folder and Search Options. Then click the View tab, clear the checkmark next to Hide extensions for known file types, and click OK.

By the way, you don't have to use the * and dot if you use extension:, ext:, or type: as the property name. For example, this search criterion also shows all files that have .jpg or .jpeg extensions:

```
ext:(jpg OR jpeg)
```

You're not limited to a single OR. Here's a search that shows all files that have .avi, .wmv, .mpg, and .mpeg extensions:

```
ext:(avi OR wmv OR mpg OR mpeg)
```

When you use type: you can use whatever appears in the Type column (in Details view) rather than the extension. For example this search finds Microsoft Word documents:

```
type:word
```

This one finds Word documents that have the word John in the filename or inside the document text:

```
john AND type:word
```

Because the keyword AND is assumed if omitted, the following works the same as the preceding one:

`john type:word`

If you want to look only at the filename and not the contents, use the `name:` property. For example, here's a query that looks for Excel spreadsheets that have the word Festival in the filename:

`name:festival type:excel`

In addition to searching for extensions, you can use `kind:` to find certain kinds of files. For example, `kind:music` finds music files, `kind:picture` finds pictures, `kind:contact` finds contacts, `kind:e-mail` finds e-mail messages, and `kind:communication` finds messages and contacts.

The NOT keyword narrows a search by excluding items that match the criterion that follows. For example, when you use the `kind:` keyword you get both the file type as well as shortcuts that open the file type. To hide the shortcut files, use `NOT shortcut`. For example, here's a search criterion that shows all communications files excluding any shortcuts to those files:

`kind:(communication NOT shortcut)`

A search for `kind:video` shows all video files. This search shows all video files except the ones that have a .mov filename extension.

`kind:video NOT extension:mov`

It's not always necessary to specify the kind or type of file. For example, consider this query:

`homecity:Cucamonga`

That one finds all contacts whose Home City is Cucamonga. Because Contacts are the only type of file that have a Home City property, you'd probably only get contacts in the search results even without specifying `kind:contact`.

You can use `tag:` as a search property too. For example, the query `tag:(alec OR ashley)` finds files and that have either Alec or Ashley in the Tags property. The query `tag:(alec AND Ashley)` finds files that have both the names Alec and Ashley in the Tags property.

If you use the Comments and Categories properties in files, use `comment:` and `category:` to search just those properties. Similarly you can use `title:` to search the Title property and `subject:` to search the Subject property.

Date and number searches

When searching for files based on a date, you can use the following property names for specific dates:

- **modified:** Date the file was last modified.
- **accessed:** Date the file was last opened.
- **created:** Date the file was created.
- **sent:** Date that a message was sent.
- **received:** Date that a message was received
- **taken:** Date that a picture was taken

To search a range of dates, use the keywords followed by a start date, two dots (..), and an end date. For example, to find all pictures taken between June 1, 2007, and September 1, 2007, use the criterion:

`taken:6/1/2007..9/1/2007`

You can also use comparison operators with date searches. For example, to see all files modified on or after January 1, 2007, use:

`modified:>=1/1/2007`

You can also use the following keywords with dates:

`today`

`tomorrow`

`yesterday`

`this week`

`last week`

`this month`

`last month`

`next month`

`this year`

`last year`

`next year`

For example, this search finds all files modified today:

`modified: today`

This search shows all files that were created this week:

`created:this week`

Here's a query that lists all picture files that were taken this month:

`taken:this month`

To see all files modified between some date (say 1/1/2007) and today, use this query:

`modified:>=1/1/2007 AND modified:<=today`

If you're interested in a certain month and year, use the month name and year like this:

`modified:july 2007`

For a day of the week, use the weekday name like this:

`modified:monday`

The comparison operators work with numbers too. When searching sizes, you can use KB, MB, and GB abbreviations. For example, here's a search criterion that finds all files that are 1MB or greater in size:

`size:>=1MB`

Here is one that finds files larger than 2GB in size:

```
size:>2GB
```

Here's one that finds files between 500KB and 1,000KB in size:

```
size:>=500KB AND size:<=1000KB
```

If you save music in various bit rates, here's a query that will find all files with bit rates greater than 300 kbps:

```
bitrate:>=300kbps
```

If you wanted only mp3 files with those large bit rates, use:

```
bitrate:>=300kbps AND type:mp3
```

Here's a query that finds all pictures whose height is 800 pixels or less:

```
kind:picture height:<=800
```

Searching for phrases

When searching for two or more words, you'll likely end up with documents that contain the words you specified, but not necessarily in the order you typed them. To prevent that problem, you can enclose the phrase is quotation marks. For example, typing this into a Search box displays all files that contain the words *dear* and *wanda*:

```
dear wanda
```

But typing the following into a Search box displays files where the words *dear* and *wanda* appear right next to each other in the document:

```
"dear wanda"
```

Message searching

For Windows Mail messages (both e-mail and newsgroup), key properties include to:, from:, about:, subject:, sent:, and received:. Both to: and from: can contain any word that appears in the To: and From: columns in the message. The about: keyword looks at the contents of the messages, not just the subject line. For example, here is a query that you could enter in the Search box on the Start menu that finds all messages from someone named Kay that contain the word *lunch*:

```
from:kay about:lunch
```

Here's a query that shows all messages addressed to Alan that arrived today:

```
to:alan received:today
```

Here's a search that shows all messages addressed to Susan, sent by Alan, that have *contract* in the Subject line:

```
to:susan from:alan subject:contract
```

Here's a query for e-mail messages sent this week from Alan to Wanda that contain the words chow mein:

```
to:wanda about:"chow mein" from:alan sent:this week
```

Natural language queries

Earlier in this chapter you saw an option titled Use natural language search in the Folder and Search Options dialog box. If you choose that, you can omit the colons after property names, and use uppercase or lowercase letters in search queries. This really does make it easier to type most queries. For example, with natural language, the following query finds all messages from Susan that contain the word *dinner*:

```
from susan about dinner
```

This search finds all video files excluding ones with an `.avi` filename extension:

```
kind video not avi
```

Here's the natural language version of the query about chow mein e-mail messages:

```
to wanda about chow mein from alan sent this week
```

Here's a query that finds all files whose size is greater than 5 megabytes:

```
size > 5MB
```

Here's a natural language query that finds all songs by Led Zeppelin:

```
music by zeppelin
```

This natural language query finds all pictures that have the word *flower* in the filename:

```
flower pictures
```

Here's a natural language query that finds all files that contain the word *peas*, the word *carrots*, or both words:

```
peas or carrots
```

Here's a natural language search that finds files that contain the word *peas* and the word *carrots* (though not necessarily together):

```
peas and carrots
```

Here's one that finds files that contain all three words, *peas and carrots*, together:

```
"peas and carrots"
```

Looking for a file you just downloaded or saved today? Try this natural language search in the Search box on the Start menu:

```
created today
```

Here's a natural language search that lists all files modified yesterday:

```
modified yesterday
```

Here are some other natural language searches you can probably figure out without my telling you what they mean:

```
e-mail received today
```

```
e-mail from alec received yesterday
```

```
contact message
```

```
pictures alec

genre rock

artists Santana

rating 5 stars
```

Using natural language syntax doesn't mean you can ignore all of the other things described in this chapter. The folder from which you start the search still matters. And all of the other options in the Folder and Search Options and Indexing Options dialog boxes still apply. But in most cases you can type a useful search query with minimal fuss. If you can't get a search to work, try turning off natural language searches and use the stricter syntax with colons after property names.

Wrap Up

Vista's searching and indexing features are a far cry from the Search Companion and other simple search tools of yesterday. Vista searching isn't really about finding lost files, though you can certainly use it for that. But if you use it only for that, you're missing out on the big picture and some key features of Windows Vista.

Vista searches use an index of filenames, properties, and file contents to make searches quick and nimble. It also looks only at files in the search index, because that's a lot faster than slogging through the entire file system to look at every file in every folder. But it only works right if your index includes all the locations where you keep your frequently used document files.

One thing is for sure. If you've been managing thousands of files in hundred of folders, and are sick of opening programs and folders to get to things, you're sure to love the new search index. Maybe not at first, because you really have to understand what it is and how it works. And you may have to spend some time tweaking settings in a couple of dialog boxes. But once you're past that small bump in the road, you'll spend a lot less time *getting to* things, and a lot more time *doing* things!

Here's a summary of the main points covered in this chapter:

- The search index includes information about files stored in the file's properties sheets.
- When you select a file in a folder, the Details pane shows the properties currently assigned to the file.
- You can also view a file's properties by right-clicking its icon and choosing Properties. Most editable properties are on the Details tab.
- File properties are also visible in any folder's Details view. That includes virtual folders (saved searches).
- The search index generally covers all files in your user account, people in your Contacts folder, and Windows Mail messages.
- The Folder and Search Options dialog box provides some options for personalizing searches.
- The Indexing Options dialog box provides a means of customizing the index to better suit how you organize your files.

Chapter 32

Using CDs and DVDs

C D (compact disc) and DVD (digital versatile disc) are media for storing information. In that regard, they're like any other type of disks like floppies, Zip disks, and hard disks. But unlike those other types of disks, CDs and DVDs are *optical* media, not magnetic media. That means they use a laser rather than a magnet to read and write data to and from the disk.

When you copy information to a CD or DVD, the laser essentially *burns* the data to the disk. That's why copying files to CDs is commonly referred to as *burning* to the disk.

Copying files to CDs and DVDs is much slower and a lot more complicated than copying to magnetic media like jump drives and floppies. If you're new to all of this, brace yourself for the complicated world of CDs, DVDs, ISO format, File System (UDF) format, and other bizarre new concepts.

Understanding CDs and DVDs

Even though CDs and DVDs look exactly alike, there's a big difference in capacity. A CD holds about 650–700 MB of data. A DVD holds about 4.7 GB (or 4,700 MB). In other words, one DVD can hold more information than half a dozen CDs. This is also why albums are sold on CDs and movies on DVDs—there isn't enough room on a CD to store a feature-length movie.

As though to complicate matters, many different kinds of CDs and DVDs are available, including CD-ROM, CD-R, CD-RW, DVD-R, DVD-RW, DVD+R, DVD+RW, and DVD-RAM. So let's untangle that mess, starting with the most common types of disks—the CD-ROM and DVD-ROM.

CD-ROM and DVD-ROM

The ROM in CD-ROM and DVD-ROM stands for *read-only memory*. The term "read only" means you can read (or play) the contents of the disk whenever you want. The disk is not *writeable*. You can't add new files to the disk, remove files from the disk, or change files that are already on the disk.

CD-R, DVD-R, and DVD+R

The R in CD-R, DVD-R, and DVD+R stands for *recordable*. These are often referred to as *distribution media* because they're the blank disks that software companies, record companies, and the movie industry use to stamp out thousands of copies of the programs, albums, and movies they sell. In other words, they buy –R disks to create the –ROM disks that they sell you.

CD-RW, DVD-RW, DVD+RW

The RW in CD-RW, DVD-RW, and DVD+RW stands for *read/write*. The -RW disks are often called *backup media*. You can use a CD-RW, DVD-RW, or DVD+RW disk to back up important files. You can erase the disk and start over if you like. And you can delete individual files. In short, the RW disks are much more like floppies and jump drives. Just not as fast!

Data CD versus audio CD

CDs come in two capacities, commonly referred to as *data CDs* and *audio CDs*. A data CD has a capacity of about 650 MB, or enough space to store about 74 minutes worth of music. Those are best to use when your goal is to use the CD to store backup copies of files on your hard disk, or to distribute copies of files to other people.

An audio CD has a capacity of about 700 MB, or enough space to store about 80 minutes worth of music. Those are best to use when you want to create your own custom music CDs to play in your car stereo or in a CD player. You use Windows Media Player (Chapter 23) to create those custom music CDs.

DVD– versus DVD+

DVD is a relatively new medium, and there are still different factions warring over exactly how they should be used. The differences have little to do with DVDs as used in computers. They're more subtle differences having to do with how DVDs store data for watching movies on TV. So for the average computer user, choosing between a + and – DVD is largely a matter of knowing what works with your DVD player, DVD burner, and whatever other equipment you have.

NOTE   The only way to find out which types of disks your DVD equipment can handle is from the documentation for that specific equipment. As a rule, the DVD+ disks are compatible with more DVD players than the DVD-R disks.

Disc, Disk, What's the Diff?

The only difference between a "disk" and a "disc" is the spelling. Computer people usually spell it "disk." The people who invented CDs and DVDs decided to spell it "disc." But no matter how you spell it, it's a medium on which you can store information. I'll use "disc" in places you're likely to see it spelled that way. Otherwise I'll stick with "disk" only because that's the way you'll see it spelled in other places throughout the book.

DVD Variations

In addition to the types of DVDs described so far, there's DVD-RAM (random access memory), mini-DVD (small DVD disks used in some video cameras), and Double-Layer DVD (which doubles the capacity to 9.4 GB). There are also different modes to which you can store video on DVD. For example, a DVD recorder might use VR (Video Record) mode to record video. To use those disks in a computer, you have to *close* or *finalize* the disk.

Things like the VR mode, closing and finalizing disks, and so forth vary greatly from one product to the next. There are hundreds of products on the market. There is no simple one-rule-fits-all that I can give you here that will tell you exactly how to work your equipment. The only way to learn about the equipment you own is to read the instructions that came with that equipment.

X marks the speed

CDs and DVDs have a basic spin speed referred to as 1x. If you listen to a CD that's spinning at faster than 1x, it sounds like the Chipmunks. If you watch a movie that's spinning faster than 1x, you get fast motion.

You can record a disk at faster than 1x. Doing so means it takes less time to make the CD or DVD. For example, at 1x it would take 80 minutes to fill an 80-minute audio CD with music. At 16x it takes 1/16th that amount of time, about 5 minutes. The resulting disk will still play at 1x so it sounds normal. The 16x speed applies only to how long it takes to create the disk.

Every CD drive and DVD drive has a maximum speed at which it can spin a disk, indicated by the x. For example, a CD burner rated at 48x can spin a CD at 48 times its normal speed. Hence, it can create a disk in 1/48th the amount of time it takes to play the disk.

Blank CDs and DVDs also have a top recommended speed. If you want to take full advantage of your CD or DVD burner's speed, find blank disks that have the same (or better) x rating as the drive.

Disk and drive compatibility

Buying CDs and DVDs that already contain music or a movie is easy. You just go to the store and buy the album or movie of your choice. Of course, you need a stereo or CD player to listen to commercial CDs. And you need a DVD player and a TV to watch DVD movies. But you don't have to worry about all the different types of disks.

When buying blank disks to make your own CDs or DVDs, things are a little more complicated. First, you need to know the capabilities of the CD/DVD drive in your computer. This isn't always easy because most people buy computers without even realizing there's a difference.

What Kind of Drive Do I Have?

Getting information about your CD/DVD drive isn't quite as easy as you might expect. You *might* be able to get some information right from your Computer folder. First make sure there isn't a disk in the drive. Then open your computer and take a look at the icon for the empty drive. The icon and description may provide some clues. You can right-click that icon, choose Properties, and click the Hardware tab for more specific information. For example, in Figure 32.1, drive F: is a DVD-RW drive (you can tell by the icon near the mouse pointer). In the Properties dialog box, you can see it's specifically a Sony drive, model DRU-15A.

FIGURE 32.1

Icon and Properties for a DVD drive.

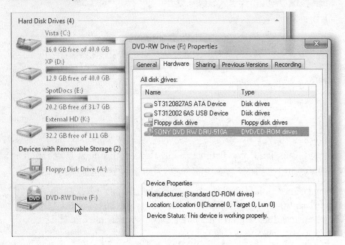

There's also a System Information window you can use to get specs on your system. Click the Start button, type sys, and click System Information on the Start menu. In the window that opens, click the + sign (if any) next to Components and click CD-ROM. The pane to the right shows detailed information about the drive as in the example shown in Figure 32.2.

FIGURE 32.2

System Information about a CD/DVD drive.

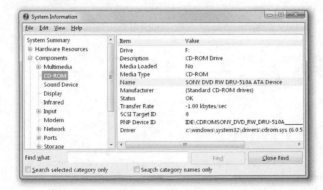

Unfortunately, knowing the make and model of the drive doesn't tell you all the different types of disks it can handle. For instance, the Sony DRU-510A example shown previously can read and write virtually all CD and DVD disk types. But there's no indication of that in either figure. But after you know the make and model of the drive, you can search the manufacturer's Web site for the model number for more detailed specs. Or you can use a general search engine like Google to search for both the make and model name (Sony DRU-510A in my example) and hope you don't get too many irrelevant links.

Of course, there's always the old-fashioned method of calling your computer manufacturer on the phone, or contacting them by e-mail, and asking about the drive. At the very least, you'll need to know the model of your computer. Then ask them what kinds of disks the drive can handle. This route may take some patience — maybe even some money.

Using Disks that Already Contain Data

Using disks that already have information on them isn't too tough. Starting with the basics, if you have a DVD drive, you can read (use) both CD and DVD disks. If you have a CD drive, you can only use CD disks.

Playing the kind of CD that you buy in a music store is usually pretty easy. You stick the CD in your CD drive and, most likely, Windows Media Player will play it for you. To copy songs from that kind of CD, you *rip* the CD in Media Player. See Chapter 23 for the goods on how all that works.

To watch a DVD movie, you stick the DVD in your DVD drive and hope it plays. If you have a CD drive (not a DVD drive), it won't play at all. To copy files from DVDs, you typically have to use DVD ripping software. See "Ripping DVDs" in Chapter 24 for more information.

 If you have Windows Media Center, that program might open rather than Media Player Movie Maker. See Chapter 26 for information on Media Center.

Exactly what happens when you insert a CD or DVD really depends on your AutoPlay options. For example, you might see an AutoPlay dialog box asking what you want to do with the CD. The options in that dialog box depend on the contents of the disk and the programs installed on your computer. Figure 32.3 shows a general example. You just click whichever option describes what you want to do.

FIGURE 32.3

Sample AutoPlay dialog box.

Then again, nothing at all may happen after you insert a CD or DVD. It all depends on the type of drive you have, the type of disk you put in the drive, and how you've configured AutoPlay options. But no matter what happens, you can use your Computer folder to view the disk's contents.

What kind of disk is this?

As discussed in Chapter 28, every disk drive on your system is represented by an icon in your Computer folder. To open your Computer folder, click the Start button and choose Computer.

 **If you want your icons to look like the ones in the examples I'll be showing here, click the Views button in the toolbar and choose Tiles.**

When your CD or DVD drive contains a disk, its icon changes to show some basic information about that disk. If the drive can handle that type of disk, the icon shows the disk type. If there's any empty space on the disk, you'll see just how much space there is. Figure 32.4 shows several examples using a single icon and how it looks with different types of disks in it.

FIGURE 32.4

Examples of a CD/DVD drive icon containing different disks.

 **A CD or DVD drive can contain only one disk at a time. Don't try to put multiple disks into the drive to get multiple icons.**

Each example is showing the same drive with a different disk in the drive. You might notice it's referred to as CD Drive F:. It's actually the kind of drive that can read and write many different kinds of CD and DVD disks. Windows often shows the general title CD Drive for those kinds of multipurpose drives. The look of that icon varies a lot depending on the disk that's in drive at the moment, as follows:

- **CD-ROM:** The disk is a CD that contains a program I purchased. The disk has 0 bytes free because it's a CD-ROM, and you can't add files to a CD-ROM. (In other words, it's not a writeable disk.) The title, PVRMCE_A50_2_4A, was put there by the company that created the disk. It's an acronym for the name and version of the program that's on the CD. A CD-ROM that contains only music might show only a musical note on the icon.

- **CD-R:** The drive contains a blank CD-R disk. All of that disk's space is free (available for saving files). The disk has no title because I haven't given it one yet.

- **CD-RW:** The drive contains a CD-RW disk titled Movie (a title I created myself). The disk has 664 MB of free space available.

- **DVD:** The drive contains a DVD like the kind you rent in a video store. The disk title is also the movie's title. This is not a writeable disk as indicated by the fact that there are 0 bytes free.

- **DVD-R:** The disk in the drive is a DVD-R disk that's empty. It has no title and has 4.37 GB of space available for storing files. It could also be a DVD+R disk because they're functionally the same as DVD-R disks.

- **DVD-RW:** The disk in the drive is a partially filled DVD-RW disk with 2.33 GB of space left. The disk might also be a DVD+RW disk, because they're functionally the same as DVD-RW disks.

> **NOTE** The 4.37 GB capacity is typical, even though the official specs state 4.7 GB. That's because the 4.7 GB rating is based on the decimal binary system. Windows shows capacities using the binary numbering system.

I'll talk about how you copy files to the writeable disks (disks that have more than 0 bytes free) a little later in this chapter.

Viewing a disk's contents

To see what's already on the CD or DVD in a drive, right-click its icon in your Computer folder and choose Explore. You'll see its contents in Explorer. As with folders on your hard disk, any folders on the CD appear as manila file folders. Files are represented by document icons. If the disk is empty, no icons show.

Copying files from a CD or DVD

To copy files or folders from a CD, use any method described in Chapter 29. But first, for those of you who skipped straight here without reading anything else, some quick reminders on when *not* to use the method described here:

- To copy songs from a commercial CD where songs are titled Track1, Track2, and so forth, and have `.cda` extensions, rip the CD using Windows Media Player (Chapter 23).

- To copy a movie from a video DVD that has a folder named Video_TS, use DVD ripping software to copy and convert to a more computer-compatible format like `.avi`, `.mpg`, or `.wmv`. See Chapter 24 for more information.

> **TIP** Often you can copy the `.vob` files to a folder on your hard disk, then change the extension to `.mpg`. Typically the largest `.vob` file is the most important one. Smaller `.vob` files are often just background video scenes.

What's Video_TS and Audio_TS?

DVD Video disks (the kind of DVD disks you rent at video stores or create using Windows DVD Burner) store data in folders with names like Video_TS and Audio_TS. DVD players (the kind you connect to a TV) expect to find folders and files like that. The Audio_TS folder may be empty because it's commonly used for DVDs that contain music rather than video.

For other types of CDs that you or someone else created using a computer, the more traditional file-copying techniques from Chapter 29 will do. For example, you can select any icons and drag them to a folder name in the Navigation pane, as illustrated in Figure 32.5. Or open the destination folder in a separate Explorer instance and drag right into the folder.

FIGURE 32.5

Copy from a CD or DVD by dragging.

Drag to destination

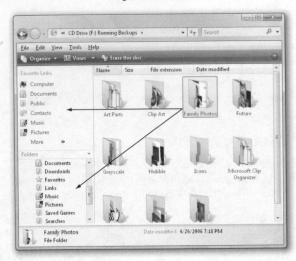

> **NOTE** You must drag to a specific drive or folder name in the Navigation pane. It won't work if you drag to empty space within that pane.

You can also use the copy-and-paste method from Chapter 29 to copy from a CD or DVD. If you specifically want to send the selected items to your Documents folder, right-click any selected icon and choose Send To ➪ Documents.

> **NEW FEATURE** Vista's new AutoPlay page makes it easy to control CD and DVD behavior.

Changing what happens when you insert a CD or DVD

When you insert a CD or DVD into your CD or DVD drive, just about anything can happen. Exactly what happens depends on what kinds of files are on the disk and how Windows is configured to deal with those files. To configure how Windows responds to various types of CDs, use the AutoPlay program. To open AutoPlay, use whichever technique is easiest for you:

- Tap ⊞, type **auto**, and click AutoPlay on the Start menu.
- Click the Start button and choose Control Panel ➪ Programs ➪ Default Programs ➪ Change AutoPlay Settings.
- Right-click your CD or DVD drive's icon in your Computer folder and choose Open AutoPlay. Then click Set AutoPlay defaults in Control Panel.

Regardless of which method you use, AutoPlay opens looking something like Figure 32.6. To ensure that your options play out, first make sure that the Use AutoPlay for all media and devices checkbox is checked. Then you can set options for responses to different types of CD content as summarized here.

FIGURE 32.6

AutoPlay options (use scroll bar to see all options).

- **Audio CD**: A commercial audio CD (the type you buy at a music store and can play in any stereo).
- **Enhanced audio CD**: Similar to above, but contains special visual content that appears only when played in a computer.
- **DVD movie**: A commercial DVD like you buy or rent in a video store.
- **Enhanced DVD**: Similar to above but with advanced features for computers and advanced playback equipment.
- **Software and games**: A CD that contains a program or game you can play.
- **Pictures**: A CD that contains only picture files.
- **Video files**: A CD that contains video files, such as the .wmv movies you create using Windows Movie Maker.
- **Audio files**: A CD that contains compressed non-commercial music files stored in .wma, mp3, or a similar format.
- **Blank CD**: An empty CD-R or CD-RW disk.
- **Blank DVD**: An empty DVD-R, DVD+R, DVD-RW, or DVD+RW disk.

- **Mixed content:** A CD or DVD that contains two or more different kinds of files. For example, worksheets, word processing documents, pictures, and video clips.
- **HD DVD movie:** A High-Definition DVD.
- **Blu-Ray Disc movie:** Similar to high definition video but provides capacities up to 25 GB per disk.
- **DVD-Audio:** A DVD disk that contains music, no video.
- **Video CD:** Also known as a VCD, a CD that contains a movie.
- **Super Video CD:** Also known as SVCD, similar to above with better quality and resolution.

The options available to you for each kind of disk depend on the programs installed on your computer. But there are some options that apply to virtually all types of disks:

- **Ask me every time:** When you insert a disk you'll see the AutoPlay dialog box with options relevant to the type of disk you inserted. That way you can decide what you want to do right on the spot.
- **Open folder to view files using Windows Explorer:** When you insert a CD, Windows Explorer will open automatically to show you the contents of the disk.
- **Take no action:** Absolutely nothing will happen on the screen after you insert the CD.

You're free to pick and choose whatever works for you. If ever you want to get things back to the way they were originally, click the Restore Default button at the bottom of the AutoPlay window. Whatever options you choose, bear in mind that they won't be applied until you click the Save button at the bottom of the AutoPlay window.

Purchasing Blank CDs and DVDs

When you shop for blank disks, you have many types to choose from (CD-R, CD-RW, DVD-R, DVD-RW, and so forth). First and foremost, you have to choose a disk type that your drive can write to. DVD-R or DVD-RW disks won't do you any good if your computer has only a CD burner.

If your drive can handle different kinds of disks, then you make your purchase based on your goals. Two relatively easy decisions are as follows:

- If you want to make custom music CDs to listen to in a stereo or CD player, use Audio CD-R disks and Windows Media Player (Chapter 23).
- If you want to make DVD movies to watch on TV, you'll probably want to use DVD+R or DVD−R disks depending on which type your drive and DVD player support.

If you're not looking to make music CDs or DVD movies, but rather just want to copy files to the disk, then your intentions and compatibility become deciding factors. There are no hard-and-fast rules here. Table 32.1 offers some suggestions that might help you decide.

NEW FEATURE   Copy files to CD and DVD using simple drag-and-drop.

TABLE 32.1

Differences among Optical Media

Disk type	Capacity	Suggested use	Can delete burned files?	Compatibility with other computers
CD-R	650 MB and 700 MB	Sharing files with others when large capacity isn't required.	No	Virtually all computers and many stereos and CD players.
CD-RW	650 MB	Making backups of your files, sharing with other people who can read CD/RW disks.	Yes	Only computers that have drives capable of reading CD-RW disks.
DVD-R, DVD+R	4.7 GB	Sharing larger files like videos, making movies to watch on TV.	No	Only computers that have DVD drives.
DVD-RW, DVD+RW	4.7 GB	Making larger capacity backups. Use File System (UDF) for maximum flexibility.	Yes	Only computers and DVD players that can read DVD+RW and/or DVD-RW disks.
DVD-RAM	2.6, 4.7, 5.2, and 9.4 GB	Use primarily for storing video and backups.	Yes	Only computers with DVD-RAM drives.

Copying Files to Blank CDs and DVDs

When you put a blank CD or DVD in your drive, it'll take a few seconds for the disk to settle in. Then Windows will do whatever action you specified in AutoPlay. For example, if you chose Prompt me each time, you'll see a prompt like the example in Figure 32.7. Your choices are as follows:

FIGURE 32.7

Sample AutoPlay prompts for blank CDs and DVDs.

■ **Burn. . . using Windows Media Player:** Choose this option if you want to copy music, pictures, or video from your Windows Media Player Media Library to the disk. You're taken straight into Windows Media Player. See "Burning DVD Data Disks with Media Player" later in this chapter for more information.

■ **Burn a DVD Video Disc using Windows DVD Maker:** Choose this option to make a DVD you can watch on TV from video files, such as movies you created with Windows Movie Maker. You're taken straight to Windows DVD Maker. See "Burning Your Own DVD Movies" later in this chapter.

■ **Burn files to disc using Windows:** Choose this option if you want to copy any kind of files from any folder to the disk for use in this computer or another computer.

Assuming you opted to burn files using Windows, you see a dialog box like the one in Figure 32.8. The disc title need not be the date. You can replace that with a title of your own choosing, up to 16 characters in length.

FIGURE 32.8

Enter a brief title here.

Now you get to make some more decisions. Basically you get to choose between creating a Live File System disk (also called a UDF disk) or a Mastered disk (also called Mastered ISO). A Live File System disk is preferred if you want to treat the disk like a flash drive or floppy, where you can add and delete files at will. A Mastered disk is preferred only if you intend to use the disk in CD or DVD players, or computers that don't have Windows Vista or Windows XP installed. You cannot delete individual files from a Mastered disk.

Here's how to proceed based on the kind of disk you want to create:

■ If you want to create a Live File System (UDF) disk, and only care about the disc being compatible with Windows Vista and Windows XP, click Next.

■ If you want to create a Live File System (UDF) disk, but need the disk to be compatible with other operating systems, click Show formatting options ⇨ Change Version. Choose your version as discussed under "Formatting CDs and DVDs" later in this chapter and click OK. Then click Next.

■ If you want to create a Mastered disk, choose Mastered.

If you didn't choose the Mastered (ISO) option, it will take a few seconds for Windows to format the disk. An Explorer window opens so you can start adding files to the CD. Because the disk is empty, you won't see any icons. You'll see Drag items to this folder to add them to the disk where the disk's contents would otherwise appear.

CAUTION Don't click a drive or folder name in the Navigation pane that opens. Otherwise you'll navigate away from the empty disc, which can be confusing. To make things less confusing, close the Navigation pane by clicking the Organize button and choosing Layout ➪ Navigation Pane. Then open the source folder in a new window. For example, you can click the Start button and click your User Name to get to the main folder for your user account in a new window. Then navigate to the source folder from that new window.

When you have both the source folder and the disk's contents open in separate windows, size and position both the source and destination windows so you can see at least a portion of each, like in Figure 32.9. Then select and drag folders and files to the destination window (the window that shows the contents of the CD or DVD).

FIGURE 32.9

Drag items from any location (source) to the CD/DVD (destination).

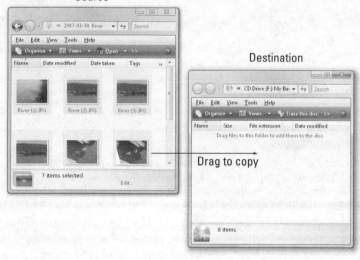

TIP Right-click the current time in the lower-right corner of the screen and choose Cascade Windows to get the windows to a good size. Then drag the destination window down and to the right. See Chapter 2 for the basics on moving and sizing program windows.

You can navigate around through the source window and drag items from multiple locations into the destination window. You can keep doing that until the disk is full. Or until you've copied all the files you want to copy, whichever comes first.

When you've finished copying files to the disk and want to remove it, push the eject button on the drive door. But don't expect the disk to pop out right away. It'll take about 15 to 30 seconds for Vista to close the session so the disk can be read in other computers. Just wait for the disk to pop out on its own. Don't try to force it. Don't worry, you'll still be able to add more files to the disk later, even after the session is closed.

Burning a Mastered (ISO) disk

If you chose the Mastered (ISO) format for the disk, icons for the files you drag into the disk's Explorer window are dimmed and show little arrows. That's because they're *temporary files* waiting to be burned to the CD. You'll also see reminder notifications, like at the bottom of Figure 32.10, telling you that there are files waiting to be written to the disk. You don't need to respond to that immediately. You can wait until all the files you intend to copy to the disk are in the window.

FIGURE 32.10

Files waiting to be burned to Mastered (ISO) disk.

> **TIP** To remove a temporary file, right-click its icon and choose Delete. To remove them all, click the Delete temporary files button on the toolbar. Note that the original files will remain intact in their original locations. You're only removing the temporary file icons so the files aren't burned to the CD.

When you're certain you have temporary files for all the items you intend to copy to the disk, click the Burn to disc toolbar button. You'll be prompted to add or change the disk title and choose a burn speed. Click Next, wait for the disk to be written, and then click Finish. Click the eject button on the drive to remove the disk.

Closing a Live File System (UDF)

When you copy files to a Live File System CD-R, DVD-R, or DVD+R disk and click the eject button, Windows closes the session so that the disk can be read by other computers. If, for whatever reason, the disk doesn't close and its contents don't show up in another computer, don't fret. You can bring the disk back to the computer in which you created it and close it there. Here's how:

1. Put the disk back into the CD or DVD drive on the Windows Vista computer (the same computer you used to create the disk).

2. If the AutoPlay dialog box opens, click the Close (X) button in its upper-right corner to take no action.

3. Open your Computer folder.

4. Right-click the drive's icon and choose Close session.

The closing puts a little information about the disk contents onto the disk, which makes the disk readable to other computers. But it doesn't prevent you from adding more files to the disk later. So you're not making any big commitment when you close a session.

Adding more files later

You can add more files to your CD or DVD at any time in the future. Put the disk back in the drive. If the AutoPlay dialog box opens, click "Open folder to view files." Or, right-click the drive's icon in your Computer folder and choose Open. Either way, the current disk contents will be visible in a standard Explorer window. Add more files by dragging them into that window, just as you did the first time.

When adding files to a Mastered disk, you'll be prompted to format the disk again. Just keep the suggested Mastered format and click Next. Otherwise you'll lose all of the files that are currently on the Mastered disk.

Erasing Discs

Many writeable CDs and DVDs can also be erased. But you have to erase the entire disk. You can't pick-and-choose individual files unless it's a Live File System (UDF) RW disk.

Before you erase a disc, be aware that the act is permanent. There is no Recycle Bin or other safety net. So if the disc contains the files that you value, and you have no other copies, copy the files to a folder on your hard drive *before* you erase the disk!

To erase a disk, first put it in the drive. If AutoPlay opens, choose Open folder to view files. If nothing happens, open your Computer folder to see the disc's icon. Then right-click and choose Open to view the disk's icon. The rest is easy.

- To erase the entire disk, click Erase this disc in the toolbar (visible in Figure 32.11).
- To delete a single file, right-click its icon and choose Delete (also visible in Figure 32.11).
- To delete multiple files, select their icons and press DELETE (Del), or right-click a selected icon and choose Delete.

NEW FEATURE Format CDs and DVDs so you can treat them like magnetic media.

FIGURE 32.11

Erase entire disk from toolbar, or right-click to delete one item.

Formatting CDs and DVDs

There are two basic ways to format CDs and DVDs: Mastered (ISO) and Live File System (UDF). The Mastered (ISO) format is compatible with almost everything. When you create CDs to play in stereos or DVDs to watch on TV, Mastered (ISO) is usually selected for you because they're the only ones that play in such devices. The Mastered (ISO) format is also compatible with virtually all computers.

The Live File System (UDF) format is much more specialized. Its advantage is that you can copy files directly to the CD using drag-and-drop. There's no need to take the extra step of burning temporary files to the CD. The disadvantage to Live File System (UDF) is its incompatibility with CD players, stereos, DVD players, and even other computers. Exactly how compatible a UDF disk is with other computers depends on the UDF version you use as listed here:

- **UDF 1.02:** Can be read by Windows 98 and some Apple computers. Also, the best format to use for DVD-RAM and MO (magneto-optical) disks.

- **UDF 1.5:** Compatible with Windows 2000, XP, and Server 2003. May be unreadable by Windows 98 and Apple computers.

- **UDF 2.01:** Compatible with Windows XP and Windows Server 2003. Earlier Windows versions and Apple computers might not be able to read these disks. This format is used if you don't specify another.

- **UDF 2.5:** Designed specifically for use in Windows Vista. Don't use this format if you intend to copy files from the disk to a computer that doesn't have Windows Vista installed.

There are a couple of ways to format a CD. When you first attempt to use a blank CD, you'll likely be presented with an option to title the CD. If you don't specify otherwise, the CD will be formatted in UDF 2.01 format. To see other options, click Show formatting options. The window will expand as in Figure 32.12.

FIGURE 32.12

Formatting options.

Choose Live File System to use the UDF format. Then click Change version if you don't want to use the default 2.01 version. To create a more widely compatible disk, choose Mastered instead. To review your options, click Which CD or DVD format should I use?

You can also format a CD or DVD straight from the Computer folder. You might need administrative privileges when you take this approach. Right-click the disk's icon and choose Format. The dialog box shown in Figure 32.13 opens.

To choose a UDF version, click the box. You can't, and don't need to, choose Mastered (ISO) here. That's because a Mastered (ISO) disk is really one that isn't formatted at all. If you want that kind of format, just click Close without formatting.

The Volume Label is the title of the CD. The Quick Format option is available only if the disk has already been formatted. The other options don't apply to CD or DVD disks and can't be changed. After choosing your options, click Start to format the disk.

FIGURE 32.13

Format dialog box.

NOTE The 4.37 GB capacity you see for a DVD is normal, even when it says 4.7 GB on the disk. You're not being ripped off for 330 MB. Capacities tend to be rough and vary depending on whether or not you format the disc.

NEW FEATURE Copy files from folders to CD or DVD on-the-fly in Windows Explorer.

Burn as You Go in Explorer

As discussed in Chapter 28, Windows Explorer is the program used to explore stuff *inside* your computer. When you're viewing the contents of a folder, you may notice a Burn toolbar button (see Figure 32.14).

FIGURE 32.14

Burn button in Explorer.

That button lets you burn files to a writeable CD or DVD as convenient. It works best if you use a File System (UDF) formatted –RW or +RW disk in your drive, because those work most like floppies and jump drives. Though it also works with -R and +R disks.

Anyway, the basic idea is to treat the disk as you would a jump drive or floppy. Leave the disk in the drive as you browse from folder to folder on your hard drive. When you come across a file you want to copy to the disk, select its icon. Or select multiple icons that you want to copy to the disk. Then click the Burn toolbar button. You'll get some feedback on the screen as the files are copied.

NEW FEATURE Copy music, videos, and pictures from your Media Player library to DVD.

Burning DVD Data Disks with Media Player

When you insert a blank DVD and AutoPlay opens, one of your options is to Burn a DVD data disc using Windows Media Player. You can use that option to copy songs and other media files from Windows Media player to a DVD disk. Understand that a data disk is one that most likely won't play in a DVD player that's attached to a TV. But you can play songs and videos on the disk on any computer that has a DVD drive. So you can use the disk to back up things in your Media Player Library, as well as to play unprotected items on other computers.

After you choose the option to burn a DVD data disc, you're taken to the Burn area in Windows Media Player. The rest is like making a custom audio CD for a stereo. Except that you're not limited to choosing songs. You can copy music, pictures, video, recorded TV, or any combination thereof. It's just a matter of choosing only as much stuff as will fit on the DVD.

First you'll want to click Select a category at the left side of the toolbar (see Figure 32.15) and choose the kinds of files you want to copy. To add an item to the disk, just drag it from the center pane to the Burn List at the bottom right. When the Burn List contains all the items you want to put on the DVD, click Start Burn to copy the items to the DVD.

FIGURE 32.15

Drag icons to Burn List.

NEW FEATURE Create your own custom DVDs with Vista's built-in DVD Maker.

Using Windows DVD Maker

Windows DVD Maker lets you create DVDs that play in any DVD player. So anyone who has a TV and DVD player can watch the disk you create. They don't need a computer. Some things to consider before you use DVD Maker:

- Your computer must have a DVD burner.

- The type of disk you use must be compatible with your DVD burner and DVD player. For general distribution to family and friends, DVD+R disks may be your best bet.

- If the video you want to put on a DVD is currently on video tape, use Windows Movie Maker to import the tape (see Chapter 25).

- You can add video, still pictures, or both to the DVD. Still pictures will play as a slide show.

- If your computer supports DVD+RW and DVD-RW disks, you can practice burning disks to those. That way if you're not happy with the results, you can erase the disk and start over. The RW disk may not work with your DVD player. But you should be able to watch it on your computer.

If you've ever rented a movie on DVD, you know that the movie typically opens to a main menu with options for viewing different content on the DVD. For example, you can click Scenes to choose specific scenes to watch. The DVDs you create with DVD Maker can also have an opening menu and scenes menu. You can design both menus in DVD Maker. The first step, of course, is to open the DVD Maker program.

Opening Windows DVD Maker

Before you open Windows DVD Maker, make sure you put a writeable DVD into your computer's DVD burner. Then you can use any of the following methods to start DVD Maker:

- If an AutoPlay option appears, click Burn a DVD video disc using Windows DVD Maker.

- Or click the Start button and choose All Programs ⇨ Windows DVD Maker.

- Or tap ⊞, type dvd, and click Windows DVD Maker on the Start menu.

Adding photos and videos

The main page for choosing photos and videos to put on a DVD is (appropriately) titled Add pictures and video to the DVD. Click the Add items button to proceed. An Open dialog box titled Add items to DVD opens, like the example shown in Figure 32.16.

In the Open dialog box, navigate to a folder that contains pictures or videos you want to add. These will likely be in your Pictures and Videos folders (unless you put them somewhere else). When you get to the folder that contains items you want to add to the disk, select their icons and click Open. Optionally, you can double-click a single icon to add it to DVD Maker.

FIGURE 32.16

Open dialog box.

Files stored in incompatible file formats, like .mov videos, won't show up in the Open dialog box. You'll need to convert those to a compatible format before burning to DVD. Use a third-party program like DeskShare's Digital Media Converter (www.deskshare.com) or AVS Video Tools (www.avsmedia.com) to convert the files.

 Use any technique described under "How to Select Icons" in Chapter 29 to select icons in the Open dialog box.

You can click Add Items as many times as necessary to add all the items you want. Photos will be grouped together in a folder titled Slide Show. Each video will appear as its own icon.

Look to the indicator at the bottom-left side of the window to see how you're doing in terms of disk consumption. If you go over the limit, the indicator will show how far over you are. If you need to remove an item, right-click its name in the main pane and choose Remove. Or click the item and click Remove Items in the toolbar. To change an item's position, click it and use the up and down arrows in the toolbar to move it up and down.

To make changes within a slide show, double-click the Slide Show folder and use the same tools to make your changes. Then click the Back to Videos button (to the right of the arrow buttons) to get back to the larger view.

Choosing DVD options

Near the lower-right corner of the window, you'll see an Options link. Click that to see the options shown in Figure 32.17 and described here:

FIGURE 32.17

DVD Video Options.

- **Start with DVD menu:** This is how most commercial DVDs work, by showing a menu of options before playing video.

- **Play video and end with DVD menu:** The DVD starts playing as soon as it's in the DVD player without showing a menu. The menu doesn't appear until all items have played.

- **Play video in a continuous loop:** The DVD never displays a menu. The video on the DVD plays continuously until removed from the DVD player.

- **4:3 aspect ratio:** Choose his option for playback on regular television screens.

- **16:9 aspect ratio:** Choose this option for playback on widescreen TVs.

- **NTSC:** Choose this option if the DVD will be played on DVD players in the United States and other countries that follow National Television Standards Committee standards.

- **PAL:** Choose this option if the DVD will be played in countries that follow PAL specifications.

- **DVD burner speed:** Choose a burn speed. Slower speeds are more reliable than faster speeds.

- **Temporary file location:** Leave this empty unless you're certain your hard disk doesn't have enough free space to hold the temporary file created briefly during the burn process.

Make sure of your selections and click OK.

Optionally, fill in a Disk Title near the bottom of the page. Figure 32.18 shows an example where I've chosen several video files and 22 pictures to burn to DVD. Notice that the Status column shows Ready for each item. The indicator at the bottom left shows there's room for more stuff. It's not necessary to fill the disk to capacity. When finished choosing videos and photos, click Next.

FIGURE 32.18

Ready to burn videos and pictures.

Designing the menus

The next page lets you create a menu for your DVD. Of course this only makes sense if you didn't choose the option to show the DVD as a continuous loop in the Options dialog box. The first step is to scroll through all the options in the right pane to see what looks interesting. Click any one that looks interesting. Click the Preview button to get a preview of how it will look when people play your DVD on their TV.

 If you create your own custom styles, use the button at the top of the right pane to switch between Custom Styles and the built-in menu styles.

After you've chosen a basic menu style, feel free to style other aspects to your liking using the Menu Text, Customize, and Slideshow options described next.

Customize menu text

Clicking Menu text takes you to a page where you can customize the text that shows on your DVD menu. Use items on the top row to choose a font and color. You can also choose to add boldface or italics.

 Be sure to choose a font color that contrasts well with your selected background. Otherwise, the text will be difficult or impossible to see!

You can also change the wording of the Disc title, Play button, Scenes button, and Notes button. Use the Notes box to add your own personal text to the title as in the example shown in Figure 32.19. (The notes show on the screen when the person who is viewing the CD clicks the Notes button on their screen.) To get a better look at how your text selections will look on the DVD, click the Preview button.

FIGURE 32.19

Menu text options.

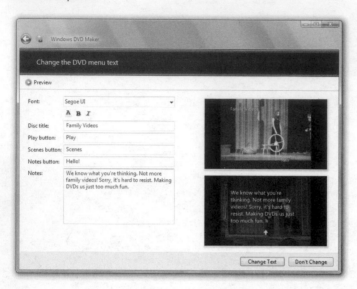

When you're happy with your changes, click the Change Text button.

TIP The small preview screens to the right show how your changes affect the DVD's opening menu (top), and the screen that appears if the viewer clicks the Scenes button (bottom). If they're too small to see, you can enlarge the page to full screen by clicking the Maximize button near the upper-right corner.

Customize the menus

Click the Customize menu button to style the DVD screen menu pages. The menu pages usually show some content from videos on the DVD. But you can use the Browse buttons to choose different videos or a still picture. As you browse through folders that contain pictures and video, only compatible files will show. If a file doesn't show, that means it's not an acceptable format for DVD Maker. Click the Browse button next to the Menu Audio option to choose a song or other sound file to play as background music while the menu is on the screen. You can use any unprotected wav, mp2, or wma song as the background music.

The Scenes button styles button lets you choose a style for buttons on the scenes menu bar. When you choose an option, the bottom preview pane shows how the buttons will look on the screen.

Click the Preview button in the upper-left corner to see how your choices will look on the DVD. At first you'll see the opening menu page. Click the Scenes button there to see the scene selection menu. After viewing the scene selection menu, click Menu near the bottom of the page to return to the DVD's menu. Click OK when you've finished previewing.

If you think you might want to use the same settings you've chosen here in future DVDs, click Save as new style, give the style a name, and click OK. Styles you save appear down the right column of DVD Maker's program window when you choose Custom Styles from the button at the top of that pane.

If you don't want to reuse the same style in future DVDs, just click the Change Style button.

Customize the slide show

Any photos you added to the DVD are displayed as a slide show. Click the Slide show button to customize how your slide show plays. You can choose background music for the slide show, and automatically adjust the duration of the slide show to match the duration of the music. Or, can set how long you want each picture to show.

You can choose from a variety of transitions to play between photos in the slide show. Choose Random to use multiple transitions between pictures. The Pan and Zoom checkbox ensures that still photos show some subtle motion during the slide show. Clear that checkbox to have each photo hold steady during the show.

Click the Preview button to see how your slide show will look with your current selections. When you're happy with your selections and slide show, click the Change Slide Show button. Or, if you want to cancel your choices, click Don't Change.

Make the DVD

To create the DVD, click the Burn button. Then there's nothing left to do but wait. You can use the computer for other tasks while the DVD is being burned. When the disk is complete, remove it from the drive. When you exit DVD Maker, you'll be asked if you want to save your project. Choosing Yes saves all of your selections so you can make more copies of the DVD later, or make changes to it.

If you used a DVD disk that's compatible with your DVD player, put the DVD into the player and you should be able to watch it on TV. You can work its menus with your remote control as you would any other DVD movie.

If you copied to an DVD-RW for practice, you can still play the DVD on your computer using Windows Media Play or Media Center. On the computer screen, use the mouse to work the DVD menu. If you're not happy with the movie and want to try something else, you can erase the RW disk and reuse it to create a different DVD.

When all is said and done, close Windows DVD Maker by clicking its Close (X) button. You'll see a message asking if you want to save your project. The project consists of the items you chose to put on the DVD and all your customization selections. It's a good idea to save the project, because that will allow you to make more copies of the DVD. You can also change the project in case you decide to do something different with future DVDs. So click Yes, then enter a name for your project. By default, the project will be saved to the Videos folder in your user account. That's as good a place as any to store the project. But if you prefer a different location, just click the Browse folders button and choose a different location. Then click Save.

 TIP You need not burn the DVD before saving a project. You can close DVD Maker at any time and save your project. Or click the File button in DVD Maker and choose Save Project.

Opening a saved DVD project

When you want to burn another copy of a DVD, or resume work on a previously saved project, open the folder in which you stored your project. If that's the default Videos folder, click the Start button, click your user account name, and open your Videos folder. The icon for a saved DVD project looks like the example shown in Figure 32.20.

FIGURE 32.20

Icon for a saved DVD project.

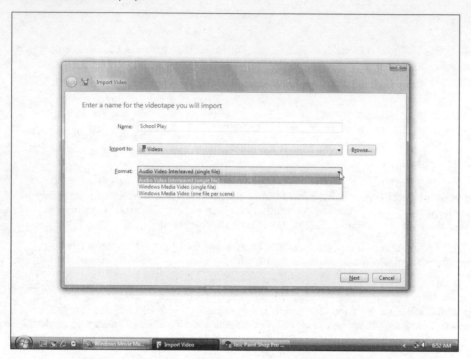

Double-click the icon of the project you want to open. DVD Maker opens with all of the videos and pictures you added. Any customization settings you chose before saving the project are still intact. If you just want to burn another copy of the DVD, click the Next button and then click Burn. If you want to change things before burning a DVD, use the same tools you used when creating the initial project:

- To change the Disc title, use the Disc Title box near the bottom of the program window.
- To change how the video plays, use the Options link near the bottom of the program window.
- Click Add items to add more items to the DVD.
- To remove a video from the DVD, click it and then click Remove Items.
- To reposition an item, click it and use the up and down arrows in the toolbar to move it up or down.
- To delete or rearrange pictures in a slide show, double-click the Slide Show folder and use the Remove Items and arrow buttons to make changes. Then click the Back to Videos button (just to the right of the arrow buttons).

To save your changes, click File in the toolbar and choose Save. You won't be prompted for a new filename. Your changes are saved to the current project. If you want to retain the original project and save the changed version as a new project, click the File button and choose Save As. Then give this new project a different filename. To make a DVD from your new project, click Next and then click Burn.

DVD Maker help and troubleshooting

For more information on DVD Maker, and help with troubleshooting, click the Help button (blue button with question mark) in the DVD Maker program. Or click the Start button, choose Help and Support, and search for DVD Maker.

Burning a Movie to DVD from Movie Maker

If you use Windows Movie Maker (Chapter 25) to create your own movie, you can burn whatever movie is in your Storyboard/Timeline straight to DVD. You can add photos and other movies saved to your Videos folder, providing the current movie doesn't fill up the entire DVD.

So here's how it works in Movie Maker. First you want to make sure the Storyboard/Timeline contains the complete movie project. You won't be able to change the movie you're about to burn to DVD. So make sure you're happy with the whole movie in the Storyboard/Timeline, beginning to end. Put a writeable DVD disk into your DVD burner. If AutoPlay opens, click the Close (X) button in its upper-right corner to close it without taking any action. Then click the Publish Movie button in Movie Maker's toolbar, or choose File ➪ Publish Movie from its menu bar. When asked where you want to publish your movie, click DVD and then click Next.

You'll see a message about Movie Maker closing and DVD Maker opening. Click OK. If you haven't saved your Storyboard/Timeline as a project, you'll be given the opportunity to do so. Type in a filename and click Save. The Movie Maker project is saved as an .mswmm file (Microsoft Windows Movie Maker) in the Videos folder for your user account.

The movie from your Storyboard/Timeline appears in DVD Maker's Add Videos and Pictures page. The rest of the process is as described under the heading "Adding photos and videos" earlier in this chapter. Just follow the same procedure as described there to customize your menus and burn the DVD.

Wrap Up

This chapter has been about the confusing world of CDs and DVDs. These disks use lasers, rather than magnets, to read and write data. And that has a big impact on how you use them. To make matters even more confusing, the record companies use CDs to distribute albums. The motion picture industry uses DVDs to distribute movies. And neither type of disk is like a computer disk. So you can't copy files from those disks as easily as you can from other types of disks. Hopefully this chapter has given you the information and skills you need to use all the different kinds of CDs and DVDs. Here's a summary of the key facts:

- CDs and DVDs look the same, but there's a big difference in capacity. One DVD holds more information the six CDs.

- Virtually all DVD drives can handle CDs. But CD drives can't handle DVDs.

- The –R and +R disks are *recordable*. But once you burn a file to an R disk you can't delete it or update it with a newer version of the file. These are mainly used to create music CDs for stereos and video DVDs for TVs.

- The –RW and +RW disks are reusable, in that you can erase information you've previously burned to the disk. These are preferred for making backup copies of important files.

- Use the AutoPlay program to choose what happens each time you insert a CD or DVD.

- To create CDs and DVDs that work like magnetic disks for storing computer files, use Live File System (UDF) format.

- To create the kind of DVDs you can watch on a TV, use Windows DVD Maker.

Chapter 33

Protecting Your Files

Some things on your hard disk are valuable. Music you purchase online costs money. Pictures and videos from digital cameras are irreplaceable. Documents you spent hours creating required an investment of your time. You wouldn't want to lose those things because of some technical problem or mistake you made. So it's a good idea to keep backups. That way, if you do lose the originals on your hard disk, you can just restore them from your backup copy.

In addition to the files you create and use yourself, there are many *system files* on your hard disk. These are files that Windows Vista needs to function properly. If those files get messed up, your computer may not work correctly. So you need some means of backing up those system files as well.

This chapter explains how to back up both your personal files and your system files. Of course, the backups won't do you any good if you can't use them when you need them. So, of course, we'll talk about how to use those backups should the need ever arise to get your system back in shape. We'll also talk about System Protection, which keeps copies of some files around temporarily, to help you fix minor mishaps on the spot, without having to fumble around with external disks.

Simple File Backups

A simple way to back up items from your user account is to copy them to an external disk. You can use any of the methods described in Chapter 29 for copying files to accomplish this sort of backup. You just need to make sure that the disk to which you're copying has enough space to store what you're copying.

To see how much stuff is in a folder in your user account, click the Start button and then click your user name. Then point to the folder you're considering backing up, or right-click that folder and choose Properties. When you point, the size of the folder shows in a tooltip. When you right-click and choose Properties, the size of the folder shows up next to Size on Disk in the Properties dialog box (see Figure 33.1).

FIGURE 33.1

A folder's size in tooltip (left) and Properties (right).

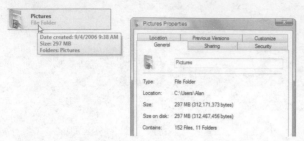

> **NOTE**   Folder sizes show in tooltips only if you selected "Display file size information in folder tips" in the Folder Options dialog box. For more information on that and other terms and concepts used in this chapter, see Chapter 28.

To see how much space is available on a disk, insert that disk into the appropriate drive on your computer. Or if it's a flash drive, connect it to a USB port. Then open your Computer folder. With some kinds of drives you'll see the amount of available space right on the icon. For example, the disk in CD Drive F: in Figure 33.2 has 1.93 GB of space left.

FIGURE 33.2

A disc's available space in the Computer folder.

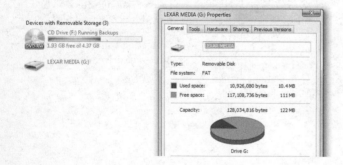

If there is no meter, choose View ⇨ Tiles from the toolbar. Or right-click the drive's icon and choose Properties to see the amount of free space in the Properties dialog box.

> **TIP**   Remember, 1 KB is about 1,000 bytes, 1 MB about a million, 1 GB about a billion. See Chapter 28 for exact numbers.

If there's enough space on the disk for the item you want to copy, just go ahead and copy it using any method described in Chapter 29. Should you ever lose or damage a file on your hard disk, you can get it back from the copy that's on the external disk.

Backing up e-mail messages isn't quite so easy, for a couple of reasons. For one, messages don't get the same status as files do. Files have the same status as items in your filing cabinet. The basic assumption is that you'll keep them forever or at least a long time. E-mail messages have a status akin to telephone answering machine messages. The basic assumption is that you won't keep them forever. Or at least, don't need to make backups of them to protect against loss.

Another reason why it's difficult for me to tell you how to back up your e-mail messages is because there are dozens, if not hundreds, of different e-mail services out there. They don't all work the same. In fact, e-mail really has nothing to do with Windows Vista at all. It's a service provided by your ISP or mail service provider. Your only real resource for information on that is the tech support provided by your ISP or mail service (or someone who happens to use and know that same service).

If you use Windows Mail, there are some simple ways to back up important e-mail messages. One is to use the Backup and Restore Center described in the next section. Another is to simply copy your entire message store folder to another disk. You can find out where that is from the Maintenance button in the Options dialog box for Windows Mail (Chapter 18).

Optionally, you can save just your important messages as files. Create a folder, perhaps named Saved Messages, in your Documents folder. Then save copies of important messages to that folder. You can do so by clicking the message header and choosing Save As. Then specify that folder as the place to save the message. Or, just drag the message header out of Windows Mail and into that Saved Messages folder.

Each saved message will be a file with an .eml extension and an envelope icon. To back up your saved messages, just copy that Saved Messages folder to an external disk.

That's the quick and easy way to make backups of important files. There are more elaborate methods. The next two sections discuss ways of backing up all your files, and even your entire hard disk.

NEW FEATURE The Backup and Restore Center is a big improvement over the Backup programs from earlier Windows versions.

Using the Backup and Restore Center

Windows Backup is an alternative to the simple method for backing up files described earlier. It doesn't allow you to back up individual files and folders on-the-fly. It backs up all files for all user accounts, or even your entire hard disk. Windows Backup works best if you have a second hard disk that you can use for backups. It can be an internal disk or an external hard disk connected through a USB port.

Very few computers sold come with multiple hard disks. So your system most likely has only one. If you want to back up to another hard disk, you'll either need to purchase and install one yourself, have it installed, or use an external hard drive that you can easily connect with a USB cable.

TIP If you're familiar with computer hardware, you'll probably find it much cheaper to create your own external hard disk. Just choose the hard drive you want. Then find a compatible drive enclosure that connects through a USB 2.0 port. It takes about two minutes to stick the drive in the enclosure. Go to any online nerd-o-rama like www.tigerdirect.com or www.newegg.com and search for *hard drive* and *drive enclosure* to scope out some products.

You can also back up to removable media like CDs and DVDs. It's not always easy to know in advance how many disks you'll need. It depends on how many files you back up, and whether or not you back up just your personal files or the entire hard disk. You might want to consider buying CDs or DVDs in spindles of 50 or 100. They're cheaper in those quantities. It won't take that many to make backups. But you'll probably find plenty of uses for the extras.

If you have a DVD burner, your best bet would be to use DVDs because one DVD holds as much information as about six CDs. Backup media (RW disks) are better than distribution media (R) disks for backup, because RW disks are reusable.

Starting the Backup and Restore Center

The Backup and Restore Center is a tool for backing up files in all user accounts. So you need administrative privileges to run it. If you're logged in to a standard account, log off. Then log back in to an administrative account. Use either of the following methods to open the Backup and Restore Center:

- Press ⊞, type back, and click Backup and Restore Center.
- Click the Start button and choose Control Panel ➪ System and Maintenance ➪ Backup and Restore Center.

The Backup and Restore Center opens looking something like Figure 33.3.

FIGURE 33.3

Backup and Restore Center.

Backing up files and settings

The Back up files button in the Backup and Restore Center backs up all user files and personal settings in all user accounts. It does not back up Windows or any installed programs. Its main purpose is to make sure that you can recover documents like pictures, music, videos, and such in case you lose the originals on your hard disk.

The first file backup you perform might take several hours. It will run in the background so you can continue to use your computer during the backup. But the backup will consume some resources, slowing things down. So you may want to run the first backup as an overnighter, starting it at a time when you can leave the computer on and running.

To back up files and settings, click the Back up files button. The Back Up Wizard opens to take you through the process step by step. Just answer the questions on each page and click Next to move on to the next page.

If you're using the Ultimate or Premium version of Windows Vista, you can also opt for automatic backups. Windows Vista will automatically back up files according to whatever schedule you specify. If you use an external hard drive for backups, you'll need to remember to connect that drive before the scheduled time arrives.

When you've finished answering all the questions, the backup starts. As mentioned, the first backup may take a while. But subsequent backups will copy only files that have changed since the last backup. So they'll go more quickly. Also, you won't have to answer all the same questions again. Subsequent backups will assume you want to keep the same settings.

If you back up to an external hard disk, the backup files will be in a folder that has the same name as the computer you backed up. If you delete the folder, you lose the backup. Exploring that folder won't reveal files in their original form. The backed up files are combined and compressed to minimize storage requirements. To restore from backups, use the method described in the next section.

Should you ever want to change the settings you specified for backups, click Change Settings under the Back up Files button. You come to the options shown in Figure 33.4. There, you can run an immediate backup, change settings for backups, and disable automatic backups.

 Here's another way to get to the options shown in Figure 33.4. Press ⊞, type `back`, and click Backup Status and Configuration.

I Lost/Messed Up My Backup Files

If you encounter a problem while trying to do subsequent backups, the reason might be because you inserted the wrong disc to back up to, or you deleted the folder or files that contain the previous backups. (Backups don't do you any good if you lose the backup disk or erase the backed up data.)

If you get in a jam where Windows encounters a problem on subsequent backups, use the Change Settings link or Backup and Restore Center to start a new backup from scratch. When you get toward the end of the wizard, watch for the option to do a complete backup and select (check) its checkbox. That will keep Windows from trying to limit the backup to files that have changed since the last backup and prevent the error message from returning.

FIGURE 33.4

Change settings for file backups.

Restoring files from a backup

If there ever comes a time when you've lost or destroyed some important files, you can restore them from your backup. But understand that this method is only required if the files or folders are not in the Recycle Bin. Before you bother with the method described here, open the Recycle Bin and look for the missing file or folder. If you find what you're looking for, right-click it and choose Restore. The deleted item is right back where it was, and there's no need to proceed with the procedure described here.

Even if the folder or file isn't in the Recycle Bin, you might be able to use the quick and easy method described under "Returning to a previous version of a file or folder" later in this chapter. In fact, you might even be able to recover a file you didn't back up! Be sure to check out that section if you don't intend to restore a whole slew of backed-up files.

If neither of these methods helps you recover the lost items, you can restore from your backup. First, log in to the user account from which you lost the files. If you used a CD or DVD to make the backup, insert the disk into the drive. If you used an external hard disk, make sure that drive is connected and turned on. Then start the Backup and Restore Center as described earlier in this chapter. Click the Restore Files button. The Restore Wizard opens to take you step by step through the process of recovering files from the backup. It's just a matter of answering questions on each page and clicking Next.

When you get to the page shown in Figure 33.5, use the Add Files button to locate specific files to recover. Or click Add Folders if you're trying to recover a folder. Or click Search to locate a specific item to restore. When you find the file or folder you want to restore, click its icon and the Add button. You can repeat the process as necessary to add as many files and folders as needed to the list of files and folders to restore. When the list is complete, click Next to move on to the next steps.

FIGURE 33.5

Choose files and folders to restore.

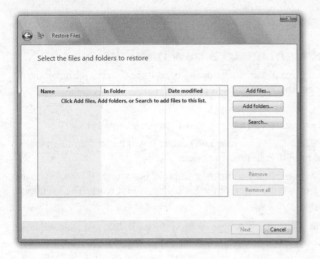

On the last wizard page, you're given the option to restore items to their original location or a new location. Stick with the original location if you're recovering files you've accidentally deleted. If you still have the originals and want to use the restored files as extra copies, specify a different location for the restored files. Then click Start Restore.

Backing up the entire PC with CompletePC

The Back up computer button in the Backup and Restore Center backs up everything on your primary hard disk (drive C:). That includes Windows Vista and all of your installed programs. That backup takes considerably more time and storage space than a file backup. But it offers the advantage of being able to recover everything in the event of a disaster that makes your hard disk inoperable.

A complete PC backup is also different from a file backup in that it doesn't allow you to restore only specific lost files. It's an all-or-none thing. The most common use is to make a brand-new empty replacement hard disk contain exactly the same stuff that was on the old hard disk the last time you made a backup.

You don't need to back up your entire PC often, because the vast majority of files in your Windows and Program Files folders rarely, if ever, change. How often you back up is entirely up to you. The usual recommendation is every six months.

To back up your entire hard disk, click the Back up computer button. A wizard opens to take you through the process step by step. You'll need to choose where you want to place your backup image.

If your primary hard drive is partitioned into multiple logical drives, you can choose in include or exclude those. Just make your selections and click Next on each page. When you've finished, the backup will begin. It will run in the background so you can continue to use your computer during the backup process.

When the backup is complete, the drive to which you backed up has a new folder icon named WindowsImageBackup. The "image" part of the name stems from the fact that the backup is like a "snapshot" of the drive's contents. It's not the kind of image you can see with your own eyes though. And you can't open that folder and navigate through your original folders. The image file is only of value to the Windows Recovery Environment (Windows RE) described next.

Restoring from a CompletePC image to a new hard disk

If you lose your entire hard disk and need to replace it, use the following procedure to restore from your CompletePC backup. It's important to remember this is an all-or-none recovery. You cannot use this method to restore specific folders or files:

1. Leave the computer turned off (it won't start with a brand-new hard drive anyway).
2. If you backed up to DVD, insert the first DVD into your DVD drive. If you backed up to an external hard disk, connect that external hard disk to the computer.
3. Turn on the computer and hold down the F8 key while the computer is starting. If your keyboard has a Function Lock (or F Lock) key, make sure it's on or the F8 key might not work. The Windows Recovery Environment page will appear.

> **NOTE** If you can't use the F8 key to get to the recovery options from the hard disk, put your Windows Vista Installation disk into a CD or DVD drive. Then start the computer and hold down the F8 key as the computer is starting.

4. When the Windows Recovery Environment page appears, click Windows Complete PC Restore.
5. Follow the onscreen instructions to perform the recovery.

When you've completed all the steps, you should be able to start the computer normally without the backup disks. Everything will be exactly as it was at the time you made the backup. If you need to install other files you backed up using Back Up Files, follow the procedure under "Restoring files from a backup" to restore those.

Restore a CompletePC image to a partially damaged disk

If your situation is such that you can still start the computer with Windows Vista, but need to bring back previous programs, settings, and files, you can restore from the image file from the Backup and Recover Center. That will make your hard disk identical to the way it was when you created the CompletePC backup. Just open the Backup and Recovery Center as described earlier in this chapter. Then click Restore Computer and follow the onscreen instructions.

Using System Protection

System Protection is yet another means of backing up important system files. Unlike either of the previous methods, it doesn't require or use any external disks. Nor does it back up any installed programs or all of Windows Vista. Rather it maintains copies of the most important system files needed for Windows Vista to operate properly, as well as hidden *shadow copies* of some of your own personal files.

The idea behind System Protection isn't to protect you from rare catastrophic hard disk disasters. Rather, it's to protect you from smaller and much more common mishaps. For example, you install some program or device that wasn't really designed for Vista, on the grounds that "Heck, it worked fine in XP so it should work fine here," only to discover that it doesn't work as well as you assumed it would (because it wasn't designed for Vista). And even after uninstalling the program, you find that some Vista features don't work like they did before you got the notion to give the old program or device a try.

Another common mishap is when you make some changes to an important file, only they're not particularly good changes. But you save the changes anyway out of habit, thereby losing the original good copy of the file you started with. Sometimes it can even help you recover a file that you deleted and removed from the Recycle Bin.

Turning System Protection on or off

System Protection is turned on by default for the drive on which Windows Vista is installed. That means it's protecting your Windows Vista operating system and also documents you keep in your user account folders like Documents, Pictures, Music, and so forth.

If you have documents on other hard disks, you can extend System Protection to protect documents on those drives, too. However, it would be best not to try to use System Protection to protect a hard drive that has another operating system installed on it, like Windows XP. Windows XP has its own System Restore feature.

System Protection is an optional feature. You can turn it on and off at will (providing you have administrative privileges, because it affects all user accounts). And you can choose for yourself which *volumes* it will monitor. (A volume is any hard disk or hard disk partition that looks like a hard drive in your Computer folder.) To get to the options for controlling System Protection, first open your System folder using any of the following techniques:

- Click the Start button, right-click Computer, and choose Properties.
- Click the Start button, type sys, and click System.
- Click the Start button and choose Control Panel ➪ System and Maintenance ➪ System.

In the left pane of your System folder, click System Protection. The System Properties dialog box opens to the System Protection tab as in Figure 33.6.

To ensure that system protection for Windows Vista and user account files is turned on, select (check) the checkbox next to the *system volume* (the drive on which Vista is installed). That volume will sport a little Windows icon and will be drive C: for most folks. That's the most important one to protect, so it should definitely have a checkmark.

The rest of the volumes are optional and require a knowledgeable judgment call based on what's on the volume and how you use it. If in doubt, leave it out. For example, in Figure 33.6, drive D: contains Windows XP so I wouldn't use System Protection on that one. It's just too risky to mingle different operating systems that way. Drive E: contains only document files, no programs or operating system. It includes the documents I work with most often, so I could (and did) protect that one.

The Xternal HD (X:) drive example is an external drive I often use mostly for backups. That one floats from one computer to the next, so I wouldn't try to protect that one. It's disconnected from my Vista computer too often for System Protection to be of any real value.

After you've made your selections, click OK. You're done. Nothing will happen immediately. But Vista will create *restore points* every 24 hours. Each restore point contains copies of your important system files, and *shadow copies* of files on the volumes you specified.

System Protection will set aside about 300 MB of space on each protected volume for restore points. If necessary it will use more space than that, up to 15 percent of the total drive capacity. It won't grow indefinitely or consume a significant amount of disk space. Instead it will delete old restore points before creating new ones. Old restore points are of dubious value anyway.

FIGURE 33.6

System Protection tab in System Properties.

Creating a restore point

System Restore is the component of System Protection that protects your important system files — the ones Vista needs to work correctly. System Restore automatically creates a restore point daily. It also creates a restore point when it detects that you're about to do something that changes system files. But you can also create your own restore points. This might be a good idea when you're about to install some older hardware or software that wasn't specifically designed for Windows Vista. It's certainly not required, but it's a smart and safe thing to do.

To create a restore point, get to the System Protection tab shown back in Figure 33.6 and click the Create button. When prompted, you can type in a brief description as to why you manually created the restore point. Perhaps "Pre-Acme Widget install" if you're about to install an Acme widget. Then click Create and OK.

Next you install your Acme Widget or whatever. Take it for a spin, make sure it works. If it works fine and you don't notice any adverse effects, great. You can forget about the restore point and go on your merry way.

If it turns out that installing that non-Vista product wasn't such a great idea after all, first you have to uninstall it. That's true whether its hardware or software. Don't even think about the restore point until you've uninstalled the device or program.

After you've uninstalled the bad device or program, then you can make sure no remnants of it lag behind by returning to the restore point you specifically set up for that program or device.

If you install other programs or devices after the bad one, don't skip over other restore points to the one you created for the new item. If you do, you'll also undo the good changes made by the good programs and devices, which will likely make those stop working! You have to be methodical about these things. Set the restore point, install the program or device, and test the program or device. If (and only if) you encounter problems, uninstall the device or program and return to the last restore point you set.

Returning to a previous restore point

So, let's say you installed something that didn't work out, uninstalled it, and now you want to make sure your system files are exactly as they were before. There are two ways to get started on that:

- On the System Protection tab shown back in Figure 33.6, click System Restore.
- Press ⊞, type sys, and click System Restore.

The System Restore Wizard starts. Just read what it says and follow its directions. When you get to the page shown in Figure 33.7, click the restore point you created just before the installation. If you forgot to create a restore point manually, click the most recent restore point in the list.

FIGURE 33.7

Choose the specific or most recent restore point.

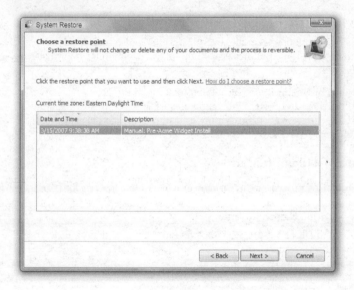

Click Next, then just continue on, reading and following the onscreen instructions. After you click Finish, your computer will restart and you'll see a conformation about restoring your system files.

> **NOTE** For technical readers, I should mention that you can run System Restore from a command prompt. This is good to know if you can only start the computer in Safe Mode with the command prompt. Type rstrui.exe at the command prompt and press Enter.

Undoing a System Restore

If you use System Restore and restore points exactly as described in the preceding sections, things will go smoothly. If you try to use it in other ways, things probably will not go smoothly. In fact, returning your system to an earlier restore point might cause more problems than it solves. When that happens, you can undo that last restore. Here's how:

1. Open System Restore (click the Start button, type sys, and click System Restore).
2. Click Choose a restore point from a list and click Next.
3. Choose the restore point labeled Undo and click Next.
4. Click Finish and follow the onscreen instructions.

Your computer will restart, and you'll see a confirmation message about undoing the restore point.

System Restore and the restore points you've just learned about have absolutely nothing to do with your document files. System Restore does not change, delete, undelete, or affect document files in any way, shape, or form. You should only use System Restore and restore points exactly as described. To take advantage of System Protection's ability to maintain shadow copies of documents, use the *previous versions* feature described next.

> **NEW FEATURE** System Protection makes daily backups of changed document files too. Use them to replace damaged or missing files, even when you don't have a backup.

Using previous versions (shadow copies)

When System Protection makes copies of important system files every 24 hours, it also makes hidden *shadow copies* of every folder and file that was modified in the last 24 hours. The common term for that shadow copy is a *previous version* of the folder or file.

Previous versions of files are available only on volumes you checked on the System Protection tab shown back in Figure 33.6. They're also only available after System Protection creates at least one restore point. Once those criteria are met, you can use the Previous Versions feature to restore corrupted files, previous versions of files you messed up yourself, and even deleted files that aren't in the Recycle Bin.

Returning to a previous version of a file or folder

If you still have the icon for a corrupted or messed up file or folder, follow these steps to restore it to its previous version:

1. Right-click the file or folder's icon and choose Properties.
2. Click the Previous Versions tab. You'll see a list of available previous versions (if any), their source, and date. Figure 33.8 shows an example.
3. Click a previous version and then click Open to review it.
4. Close whatever program opened to show you the previous version.
5. If the version you just viewed is the one you want to recover, proceed to the next step. Otherwise repeat steps 3 and 4 until you find the version you want to restore.
6. Next, decide how you want to restore the file:
   - To replace the copy you have with the previous version, click Restore. Read the warning and follow the instructions.
   - To keep the copy you have and also recover the previous version, click Copy. Navigate to the folder in which you want to put the previous version and click Copy. When prompted about overwriting the existing file, choose Copy using a different name. The previous version of the file will have a (2) at the end of its filename to distinguish it from the copy that was already in the folder.
7. Click OK to close the Properties dialog box.

FIGURE 33.8

Previous versions of a file.

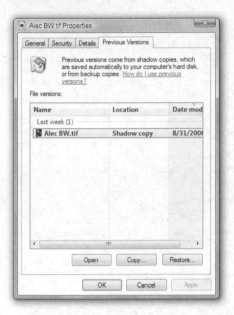

If the location in which the previous version was previously stored no longer exists, the Restore button will be disabled (dimmed). Try using the Copy button to save the file to a new location. Or click the Open button to open the file. Then save the open copy to an existing folder using the Save method of whatever program the file opened in. Pressing Ctrl+S or choosing File ⇨ Save from the program's menu will usually do the trick.

Restoring deleted files from previous versions

As you know, most files that you delete are held in the Recycle Bin, to give you a chance to change your mind. The file stays in the Recycle Bin until you empty the Recycle Bin. You should never empty the Recycle Bin unless you're sure there's nothing in it of value. But we all make mistakes, like emptying the

Why no Previous Versions?

There are several reasons why the Previous Versions tab of a file or folder might be empty. System Protection might not be turned on for the drive in which the file is located. Or System Protection is turned on, but there is no restore point yet that contains the previous version. Automatic restore points are created every 24 hours. Also, restore points and shadow copies aren't kept around forever. Old ones are deleted to make room for new ones. If you accidentally deleted a file long ago, and also emptied the Recycle Bin, there may be no hope of recovering the file through previous versions unless you have a backup of the file on an external disk.

Recycle Bin without first checking its contents. If you make that mistake and can't recover a deleted file from the Recycle Bin, you may be able to recover a previous version of the file instead. You need to know the original location from which you deleted the file. Then follow these steps:

1. Open the folder in which the accidentally deleted file was stored.

2. Get the mouse pointer onto a empty area within the folder. The easiest way is to get the mouse pointer about an inch below the last row of icons in the folder. You'll know the mouse pointer is touching an empty spot when no icon is selected (highlighted).

3. Right-click that empty space and choose Properties. Then click the Previous Versions tab in the dialog box. If there are previous versions of the folder available, they'll be listed on that tab.

NOTE If you see icons for a file rather than for the current folder, you right-clicked an icon rather than empty space within the folder. Click Cancel and try steps 2 and 3 again.

4. Double-click a previous version of the folder to see its contents. Try to choose a folder that's before, but close to, the date of accidental deletion. If the first folder you try doesn't contain the file you want, click its Close (X) button and try an earlier folder.

5. If you find the file you're looking for, right-click that file's icon and choose Copy.

6. Paste a copy of the file to a folder of your choosing or the desktop. For example, click the Start button, click Documents, and press Ctrl+V. A copy of the file is placed in your Documents folder.

7. Click OK to close the Properties dialog box.

That copy you pasted is a normal file that you can use in normal ways. You can move it from wherever you pasted it to whatever folder you like.

If you can't restore the accidentally deleted item from previous versions, but you have a backup on removable disks, use the method described under "Restoring files from a backup" earlier in this chapter to restore a copy.

NEW FEATURE BitLocker drive encryption ensures the confidentiality of data stored in portable computers.

Using BitLocker Drive Encryption

Backup and System Protection ensure the *availability* of your files, in that they allow you to restore lost or damaged files by restoring from a backup copy. BitLocker drive encryption isn't about availability. It's about *confidentiality*. If your notebook computer is lost or stolen, that's certainly a bad thing. But if it contains confidential personal, client, or patient information, that's even worse. BitLocker drive encryption ensures that lost or stolen data can't be read by prying eyes.

BitLocker drive encryption works by encrypting all the data on a hard drive. With BitLocker drive encryption active, you can still use the computer normally. All the necessary encryption and decryption takes place automatically behind the scenes. But a thief would be unable to access data, passwords, or confidential information on the drive.

BitLocker hardware requirements

BitLocker drive encryption uses an encryption key to encrypt and decrypt data. That key must be stored in a TMP Version 1.2 (Trusted Platform Module) microchip and compatible BIOS. Only newer computers come with the appropriate hardware preinstalled. You'll also need a USB flash drive to store a copy of the password.

Caution, Caution, and More Caution

BitLocker drive encryption is primarily designed for organizations that have sensitive data stored on note-books and PCs. Theft of those data could have a negative impact on the organization, its customers, or its shareholders. While transparent to the user, the act of setting up BitLocker would normally be entrusted to IT professionals within the organization.

If you're not an IT professional, you need to be aware of the risks involved. Especially if you plan to set up BitLocker on a hard drive that already contains files. First, always back up your data before re-partitioning a drive. While there are many programs on the market that allow you to repartition a disk without losing data, there's always a risk involved. A backup is your only real insurance. For information on partitioning with Windows, see Chapter 47.

More importantly, understand that BitLocker is not for the technologically faint-of-heart. There is no way to undo any bad guesses or mistakes. If not handled with the utmost care, BitLocker can render your computer useless and your data unrecoverable. If you're not technologically inclined, but have a serious need for drive encryption, consider getting professional support in setting up BitLocker for your system.

NOTE The first time you open the BitLocker task page, you'll see a message indicating whether you do, or don't, have a TPM Version 1.2 chip installed. If you're certain that you have such a chip, but Vista fails to recognize it, check with your computer manufacturer for instructions on making it available to Vista.

In addition to a TPM chip, your hard disk must contain at least two volumes (also called partitions). One volume, called the *system volume*, must be at least 1.5 GB in size. That one contains some startup files and cannot be encrypted. The other volume, called the *operating system volume*, will contain Windows Vista, your installed programs, and user account folders. Both volumes must be formatted with NTFS.

Encrypting the volume

When all the necessary hardware is in place, setting up BitLocker Drive Encryption is a relatively easy task:

1. Click the Start button, choose Control Panel, click Security, and then click BitLocker Drive Encryption.
2. If your hardware setup doesn't support BitLocker, you'll see messages to that effect. You cannot continue without appropriate hardware and disk partitions.
3. If all systems are go, click the option to turn on BitLocker for the operating system volume.
4. If your TMP isn't initialized, a wizard takes you through the steps to initialize it. Follow the onscreen instructions to complete the initialization.
5. When prompted, choose your preferred password storage method, store the password, and click Next.
6. On the encryption page, select (check) the Run BitLocker system check and click Continue.
7. Insert the password recovery USB flash drive (or whatever medium you used for password recovery) and click Restart Now.
8. Follow the onscreen instructions.

The wizard will ensure that all systems are working and it's safe to encrypt the drive. Just follow the instructions to the end to complete the procedure.

Make sure you password-protect all user accounts to prevent unauthorized access to the system. Otherwise a thief can get at the encrypted data just by logging in to a user account that requires no password!

When the computer won't start

Once BitLocker is enabled, you should be able to start and log in to the computer normally. BitLocker will only prevent normal startup if it detects changes that could indicate tampering. For example, putting the drive in a different computer, or even making BIOS changes that look like tampering, will cause BitLocker to prevent bootup. To get past the block, you'll need to supply the appropriate password.

Turning off BitLocker

Should you ever change your mind about using BitLocker, repeat the steps under "Encrypting the volume" and choose the option to turn off BitLocker drive encryption.

More info on BitLocker

The setup wizard for BitLocker drive encryption is designed to simplify the process as much as possible for people using computers with TPM 1.2. Other scenarios are possible, but go beyond the scope of this book. For more information, search Windows Help for `BitLocker`. Or better yet, browse to `www.TechNet.com` and search for `BitLocker`.

Wrap Up

Any way you slice it, having two or more copies of important files is better than having only one copy. The reason is simple and obvious: If you have two or more copies, you can afford to lose one copy. This chapter has been about different ways to make backup copies of important files. Here's a summary:

- To make simple backups of files on-the-fly, copy them to external disks as convenient.
- To back up all the document files in all user accounts, use the Back up files button in Windows Backup and Restore Center.
- To back up your entire hard disk, use the Back up computer button in the Back Up and Restore Center.
- To recover deleted files or an entire hard disk image, use the Restore buttons in Backup and Restore.
- Use System Protection to make automatic daily backups of important system files and documents. These won't protect you from a hard disk disaster because they're on the same disk as the system files and documents. But they provide a relatively easy means of recovering from minor mishaps without messing with external disks.
- To use System Restore properly, create a restore point just before installing new hardware or software. If the new product creates a problem, uninstall it. Then return to your restore point to ensure all traces of the installation are wiped away.

- To restore a previous version of a file or folder, right-click the item's icon and choose Properties. Then click the Previous Versions tab to see what versions are available.

- To restore an accidentally deleted file, first try to restore it from the Recycle Bin.

- If you forget to restore the file before emptying the Recycle Bin, you can try the previous versions. Open the folder in which the file was stored. Right-click some empty space in that folder and choose Properties. Then click Previous Versions to view previous versions of the folder.

- If you can't restore a file using either of the preceding techniques, but you made a backup, use Restore Files in Backup and Restore Center to recover the file.

- For data confidentiality on portable computers, Vista offers BitLocker Drive Encryption.

Chapter 34

Troubleshooting Files and Folders

Troubleshooting Folders, Files, and Shortcuts

Here are some common problems and their solutions for working with files and folders in Windows Explorer. Remember, Windows Explorer is the program that opens whenever you open any folder. You don't need to specifically open Windows Explorer from the All Programs menu.

The Classic Menu bar is missing from Explorer

When re-creating Windows Explorer for Vista, Microsoft moved the most used functions to the different toolbars in the product. Not all of the functionality appears on the toolbars, though. As mentioned in Chapter 28 under "Windows Explorer Components," you can temporarily bring back the Classic Menu by tapping the Alt key.

If you want the menu to show up on a more permanent basis, do so by selecting Organize ➪ Layout ➪ Classic Menus.

Where is the Up button to go to the parent folder?

There is no Up button in Vista's Explorer. To go to the parent of the current folder, click its name in the Address bar. Or click the arrow to the left of the current folder's name and choose a folder from there.

What happened to the Folders list?

The Folders list is in the Navigation pane. Click the word Folders at the bottom of the Navigation pane. If the Navigation pane isn't visible, click Organize and choose Layout ➪ Navigation pane.

Slide Show is not available as an option in the Explorer Toolbar

Based on the contents of the folder, Windows Explorer builds the items that appear on the Toolbar on the fly. If Windows Explorer has determined that the folder you're looking at doesn't require the Slide Show option and you want that option, follow these steps to enable it:

1. Make sure no files are selected within the folder and choose Organize ➪ Properties from the toolbar.

2. In the Properties window for the folder, click the Customize tab.

3. From the "Use this folder type as a template" choose Pictures and Videos.

4. Optionally, you can choose a different template from the drop-down list.

5. Check the box "Also apply this template to all subfolders" if you want folders below this folder to also use the same format.

6. Click the OK button, and the Explorer interface should now contain the Slide Show button in the toolbar.

I don't see the file extensions on files

By default, the file extensions are not shown under Windows Explorer. Sometimes, it is necessary to alter the file extension of a file. To show the file extensions, follow these steps:

1. Select Organize ➪ Folder Options.

2. In the Folder Options window, select the View tab.

3. In the Advanced settings section, scroll down to Hide extensions for known file types, clear the checkmark from its checkbox, and click OK.

For more information on this topic, see the section titled "Options on the View Tab," in Chapter 28.

When I try to select by dragging, the icons move, and nothing is selected

To *move* an item, you put the mouse pointer *on* the item you want to move, and then drag. To *select* items by dragging, start with the mouse pointer *near* the first item you want to select, but not at a point where it's actually touching an icon. It's tricky in Vista because the mouse pointer selects when you get close to an icon. You can tell an icon is selected when the background color changes. The Tiles view is the easiest one to use when you want to select multiple icons by dragging.

Error message "Application is using this file. You must close the file before proceeding."

Whenever you see this message, it means that the file you're trying to delete, rename, or move is currently open. Close the open document on the desktop (or from the taskbar, if it's minimized). Then, try again.

Error message "If you change a file name extension, the file may become unstable."

You've attempted to rename both the filename and the extension. Changing a filename extension can be bad news because the extension will no longer accurately reflect the format of the data in the file. Choose No and then rename the file. This time, don't change the file extension.

Error message "This location already contains a file with the same name"

No two files in a folder can have the same name. Here, you're trying to move or copy a file to a folder that already contains a file with the name of the one you're trying to move or copy. Your best bet would be to choose Keep this original file. Next, rename the file or folder you're trying to move or copy and then move or copy the renamed file.

Optionally, if you choose Copy this file, the file that's already in the folder will be replaced by the one you're trying to move or copy, which means that the original file will be lost forever.

You're also given a third option of Copy using another name that will copy the file to this folder and give the file you're copying a different name. Windows will give the new file the same name as the original but append a number enclosed with parentheses.

"Problem with Shortcut" dialog box opens

When a shortcut stops working, that means the folder, file, or Web page to which the shortcut refers no longer exists. In the case of a file or folder, you've deleted, moved, or renamed the original item since creating the shortcut. If the file or folder has been deleted and still remains in the Recycle Bin, Windows gives you the option of restoring the file or folder. If the file or folder has been deleted and removed from the Recycle Bin, Windows only gives you the options of deleting or keeping the shortcut. In the case of a Web page, either you're not online, or the Web page no longer exists at that location.

Deleting a shortcut from my desktop deletes it from all users' desktops

When you create a desktop shortcut in your own user account by right-clicking an icon and choosing Send To ⇨ Desktop (create shortcut), that icon is unique to your desktop. So, when you delete the icon, it should disappear from your desktop only. That's because the icon is stored in the Desktop folder for your user account only. That folder's name is `C:\Users\Username\Desktop`, where *Username* is the name of your user account.

Sometimes, when you install a new program, that setup procedure automatically creates a new desktop shortcut icon on every user's desktop. That icon is stored in the Public Desktop folder at `C:\Users\Public\Public Desktop`. So, when you delete that icon from your desktop, you actually delete it from the folder and all other users' desktops.

If you just want to get the icon back, so that other users have it again, open the Recycle Bin and restore the icon from there. If you're a patient administrator, you can then copy the shortcut from the Public Desktop folder to every other user's Desktop folder except your own. If you're not that patient, you can just remind other users that they can create any shortcut they want in two seconds flat by right-clicking any icon and choosing Send To ⇨ Desktop (create shortcut) to make any shortcut they want.

Troubleshooting Documents

It's very frustrating trying to save a document that you've spent hours on only to have the system tell you that you can't save it. This section covers some of the common problems when trying to save your hard work.

You cannot save in the folder specified

The folder you've chosen in the drop-down list can't be used to store files. Click OK to close the message box. Choose a different folder, such as Documents, from the drop-down list. Then, click the Save button again.

The file name is invalid

The filename you entered contains an invalid character. Try a different filename; make sure that it doesn't contain any of the following characters:

    \ : / * ? " > < |

Click the Save button to save the document with the new name.

Please insert a disk into drive A:

The error occurs when you attempt to save a document to an empty disk drive. Your best bet would be to click the Cancel button and choose a folder such as Documents. However, if you really want to save the document to a floppy, you'll need to put a floppy disk with sufficient empty space on it into the floppy drive.

My document isn't in the Open dialog box

Make sure that the location at the top of the Open dialog box is showing the name of the folder in which the document is contained. If it doesn't, navigate to the appropriate folder. If the document still isn't visible in the main pane, change the file type option at the bottom-right corner of the dialog box to All Files or the type of file you're trying to open.

Troubleshooting CDs and DVDs

CDs and DVDs pose some unique problems because unlike most computer storage media, they use laser technology rather than magnetism. You can't read from and write to CDs and DVDs as you can other types of disks. And, CDs and DVDs are likely to generate some unique error messages, described and addressed in the sections that follow.

Error message "Invalid function" when attempting to write files to a CD

You can only write files with CD-R and CD-RW drives, not a CD-ROM drive. Also, the recording capabilities of your CD-R or CD-ROM drive must be enabled as follows:

1. Click the Start button and choose My Computer.
2. Right-click the icon for your CD drive and choose Properties.
3. In the Properties dialog box that opens, click the Recording tab.

4. Make sure that your drive shows up under "Select a drive that Windows can use as the default recorder for your system."

5. Click OK.

An invalid or outdated CD driver can also cause the problem. See Chapter 51 for the goods on finding an updated driver.

Finally, a conflict with third-party CD-burning software can generate this message. Try using that third-party program to copy files to a CD. For general information about Roxio CD-burning products, see www.roxio.com. See www.nero.com for general information on Nero Burn products.

I'm unable to read recorded CDs and DVDs on other computers

The most likely cause of this problem is that you did not properly close the session after you were finished copying information to the CD or DVD. To close the session:

1. Put the CD or DVD back into the drive.

2. Navigate to the contents of the disc if they don't come up automatically.

3. Right-click within the window and select Close session.

Even though you have closed the session, you can add more data to the disc later. Closing the session allows you to use the disc on other computers.

Troubleshooting Searches

Searches in Windows Vista are a whole new ballgame, nothing like Search Companion or similar tools from earlier versions of Windows. The kinds of searches that return keystroke-by-keystroke results don't search the entire file system. If they did, the searches wouldn't be nearly as fast. Searches that return keystroke-by-keystroke results are searching only the search index. By default, the search index includes only the kinds of things most users access all the time, like documents, messages, programs, and dialog boxes.

Search didn't find my file

Where you start a search has a big effect. When you search using the Search box in the upper-right corner of a folder, you search only that folder and its subfolders. Limiting the search in that manner is what allows Vista to return keystroke-by-keystroke results. For more traditional file system searches, you have to use the Search window, and extend the search beyond the search index.

When a search fails, click Advanced Search under the search results to expand your search. Use techniques described in Chapters 30 and 31 to master Vista's instant searches.

No Search option on the Start menu

To add the Search option to your Start menu, follow these steps:

1. Right-click the Start button and choose Properties.

2. Click the Customize button next to the Start menu.

3. Scroll down to and select (check) the Search option.

4. Click OK in each open dialog box.

More Troubleshooting Resources

For live help with troubleshooting files, consider the `Microsoft.public.windows.vista`
`.file_management` newsgroup in Microsoft Communities. Whatever problem you're having, chances
are you'll find someone who has had that same problem and solved it.

You can also search Vista's built-in Help and Support for the specific topic with which you're having a
problem. Here are some examples of searches you might enter into the Search Help box:

- `troubleshoot folders`
- `troubleshoot files`
- `troubleshoot search`
- `troubleshoot cd`
- `troubleshoot dvd`
- `troubleshoot backup`
- `troubleshoot previous versions`

Part VII

Printing, Faxing, and Scanning

Despite early predictions to the contrary, the truly paperless office doesn't exist. Sometimes, you just have to get a document onto paper, no two ways about it. Likewise, not everything can be downloaded or copied from disk. Sometimes, you can only get text or pictures from paper. Part VII covers both sides of the story.

Chapter 35 starts with the basics of installing and managing printers. If you already have a working printer, you can skip that one.

Chapter 36 moves onto the actual task of printing. Chapter 37 follows with a discussion of managing print jobs, which includes things like stopping a runaway printer before it wastes all your paper and ink!

When your only copy of a favorite photo is printed on paper, the only way to get it into the computer is by scanning it. Chapter 38 explains how to do that. It also covers faxing, which is sort of like scanning except that the output ends up on someone's fax machine rather than a computer. Chapter 39 covers solutions to problems relating to printing, faxing, and scanning.

Chapter 35

Installing and Managing Printers

Installing a printer is usually an easy job. There's one rule that applies to installing any hardware, and it certainly applies to printers. The rule is: *Read the instructions that came with the printer first.* Trying to save time by ignoring the instructions and winging it is likely to cost you more time in getting the thing to work.

In many cases, you'll have the option to connect the printer to a USB port or a printer port. If your computer is a member of a network, you might want to install a shared printer that's physically connected to some other computer. This chapter looks at different ways of installing printers, as well as techniques for managing installed printers.

Opening the Printers Folder

Aside from actually printing documents, just about everything you do with printers will take place in the Printers folder. As with everything else in Vista, you can get to that folder in several ways. Use whichever works for you and is most convenient at the moment:

- Click the Start button and choose Printers from the right side of the Start menu.
- Tap ⊞, type prin, and click Printers under the Program heading.
- Click the Start button and choose Control Panel ➪ Printers.

When you're in your Printers folder, you'll see an icon for each printer (or similar device) to which you can print. Figure 35.1 shows an example; your folder will, of course, look different.

FIGURE 35.1

Sample Printers folder.

Setting the default printer

If your Printers folder contains more than one icon, only one of them will be the *default* device for printing. By "default," I mean the printer that's used automatically if you don't specify something else. For example, many programs allow you to print a document to the default printer by pressing Ctrl+P. The program may not ask what printer you want to use. Instead, it just sends the document to the default printer.

In the Printers folder, the default printer is indicated by a checkmark. If you want to change the default printer, right-click the printer's icon and choose Set As Default Printer. The printer or device you specified will now sport the green checkmark, and will be used for printing when you don't specify some other printer or device.

Testing a printer

If you've just installed a printer and want to test it out, follow these steps (here, I'm assuming that you're already in the Printers folder):

1. Right-click the printer's icon and choose Properties.
2. At the bottom of the Properties dialog box that opens, click the Print Test Page button.
3. Wait a few seconds (few printers start immediately). The printer should print a sample page.

   ■ If the page prints and doesn't look like gobbledygook, click OK in each open box.

   ■ If nothing prints within 15 or 30 seconds, click Troubleshoot for some tips on solving the problem.

If you had to click Troubleshoot, follow the advice in the Printer Troubleshooter first to resolve the problem. If you still can't get your printer to work, see Chapter 39 for more options. Also, keep in mind that there are hundreds of different makes and models of printers on the market, and no one rule that applies to all. So, don't overlook the documentation that came with your printer, or the printer manufacturer's Web site, which may provide troubleshooting advice.

Adding a Printers Option to Your Start Menu

You don't need to open your Printers folder to print things. When you want to print a document that's currently open on your screen, you can usually do so by pressing Ctrl+P, by clicking the Print button in that program's toolbar, or by choosing File ➪ Print from that program's menu bar.

Nonetheless, if you need to open your Printers folder often and don't have a Printers option on your Start menu, you can easily add that option. Right-click the Start button and choose Properties. Click the Customize button next to the Start menu and scroll down through the list of Start menu options. Select (check) Printers and then click OK. From then on, whenever you click the Start button, you'll see a Printers option on the right side of the Start menu.

Installing a New Printer

Before you can use a new printer, you need to connect it to the computer and install it. Many printers give you the choice of using the "easy" USB port to connect the printer, or a standard printer port. Personally, I think the USB port is a bad idea, because you can run into a lot of problems when you disconnect the printer to plug some other item, such as a digital camera, into the port. In the long run, it's best to use the USB ports for devices you connect and disconnect often. You're better off using other ports, whenever possible, for devices that are connected to the computer all the time.

As mentioned at the top of this chapter, the main rule on installing a printer is to follow the instructions that came with the printer. Sometimes you need to install drivers first, sometimes you don't. There is no "one rule fits all" when it comes to installing printers, or any other hardware device for that matter. But in a pinch, where there are no instructions, the techniques in the following sections will be your best first guess.

Installing printers with parallel and serial port connections

If your printer is a typical plug-and-play printer that connects to the computer via an LPT port or COM port, the best approach is:

1. Save any unsaved work, close all open programs, shut down Windows, and turn off your computer.
2. Plug the printer into the wall, connect the printer to the computer's LPT or serial port, turn on the printer, and turn on the computer.
3. When Windows restarts, look for the *Found new hardware* notification message to appear.

It's tough to say what will happen next. If you see a notification message indicating that the printer is installed and ready to use, you're probably done.

Installing printers with USB and infrared connections

If your only option is to connect the printer through a USB port, or by infrared, the installation procedure should go like this:

1. Close all open programs on your Windows desktop, so that you're at the Windows desktop with nothing else showing.

2. Plug the printer into the wall; connect the printer to the computer with its USB connection, or configure the infrared connection as instructed by the printer manufacturer.

3. Turn on the printer, and wait a few seconds.

You should see a message in the Notification area that tells you the device is connected and ready to use. You're done. The printer is installed and ready to go.

Regardless of which of these methods you used, you'll want to test the printer, and perhaps make it the default printer, as discussed later in this chapter.

Installing a network, wireless, or Bluetooth printer

If your computer is a member of a home or small-business network, and you know of a shared printer on another computer in that network, you can use the technique described here to install that printer on your own computer. The same is true of many wireless and Bluetooth printers. But again, this procedure may not be necessary because Windows Vista often detects network printers and makes them available automatically. Be sure to check the manual that came with a wireless or Bluetooth printer for an alternative procedure before trying the method described here. Also, be sure to turn the printer on before you try to install it.

If you're trying to install a printer that's attached to another computer in your private network, make sure that both the printer and the computer to which the printer is physically connected are turned on. Make sure your network is set up and you've enabled discovery and sharing as discussed in Part X of this book. Then go to the computer that needs to access the network printer and perform the steps to follow on that computer. You install a network, wireless, or Bluetooth printer in much the same way you install a local printer. First open the Printers folder using any technique described at the start of this chapter. Here's a quick reminder:

- Click the Start button and click Printers on the right side of the Start menu.
- Tap ⊞, type `prin`, and click Printers under the Programs heading.
- Click the Start button and choose Control Panel ➪ Printers.

At this point you'll be in the Printers folder. If the printer's name appears in the folder, you need not install it. Though, if you want to make it the default printer, right-click its icon and choose Set as Default Printer. Then, close the Printers folder and Control Panel. You'll be able to use the printer as described in Chapter 36.

If there's no sign of the printer in your Printers folder, follow these steps to install it:

1. Click Add a Printer in the toolbar, or right-click some empty space in the folder and choose Add a printer. The Add a Printer Wizard opens.

2. Choose the second option, A network, wireless, or Bluetooth printer, and then click Next. The wizard searches the network for shared printers.

   - If the search finds the printer you're looking for, click its name and then click Next.

   - Otherwise, if the search doesn't find your printer, click The printer that I want isn't listed. If you know the UNC name or IP address of the printer to which you want to connect, fill in the appropriate information. Otherwise, click Browse for a printer, click Next, and navigate to the computer and printer to which you want to connect. Click the printer's name and click OK. Then click Next.

NOTE If you see a warning about printer drivers potentially containing viruses, don't worry about it. It's extremely unlikely that you'd ever find a virus in a printer driver. You need to click Yes to let Windows Vista install the printer driver if you want to use that shared printer. If you're worried about viruses, you can scan for viruses after you install the shared printer.

3. On the next wizard page you can opt to print a test page and make the shared printer your default printer. Make your choices and click Next.

4. Click Finish on the last wizard page.

An icon for the shared printer will show in your Printers folder. If you made it the default printer, it will also show a checkmark.

Managing Print Drivers

Virtually all hardware devices, including printers, come with a special program called a *device driver*, or just *driver* for short. The driver provides the interface between the device and a specific operating system, such as Windows Vista or Windows XP. You need to have the correct and current print driver installed on your computer to get your printer to work correctly.

Many printers come with the drivers on a CD or floppy disk. How you install a driver from the disk depends on the printer you're using. But an older printer may not even have a Windows Vista driver to offer. In that case, you'll need to look for a current driver online. Try Windows Update first by following these steps:

1. Click the Start button and choose All Programs ⇨ Windows Update.

2. If Vista doesn't start searching for updates immediately, click Check for updates in the left column.

3. When the update search is complete, click View available updates or View optional updates.

4. If the driver for your printer appears, go ahead and install it per the onscreen instructions.

If Windows Update doesn't find an updated driver, it might mean your printer manufacturer hasn't posted the driver on that site yet. Browse to the printer manufacturer's Web site and look around for a Drivers link. Or go to their Support page and send an e-mail asking if there's an updated driver for your printer model.

Setting Default Printer Properties

Like objects on your screen, many devices have properties that you can customize. Most printers have such properties. You can make selections from those properties to define defaults for the printer. Those default settings for properties won't be set in stone. As you'll see in Chapter 36, you can override the defaults any time you print a document. The defaults are just a way of choosing a specific option every time you print a document.

As with other objects, a printer's properties are accessible from its icons. To view the properties for an installed printer, first open the Printers folder if you haven't already done so. Then, right-click the printer's icon and choose Printing Preferences. The options available to you depend on your printer. The options shown in Figure 35.2 are from an HP OfficeJet R80 printer.

FIGURE 35.2

Sample Printers preferences.

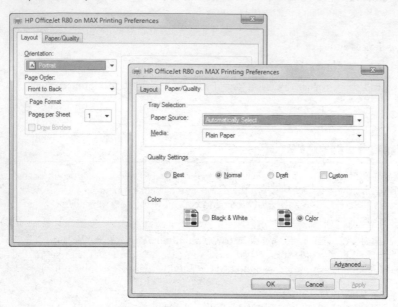

The sections to follow cover options available on most (but not all) printers.

Making pages print in the right order

When you print a multiple-page document, you don't want to have to shuffle the pages around to get them in the correct order. You want the pages to come out of the printer in the right order. The Page Order property, which you can see in Figure 35.2, is the option that determines whether or not the pages are printed in the right order. The rules are as follows:

- If the pages come out of the printer face down, use Front to Back order.
- If the pages come out of the printer face up, use Back to Front order.

Said another way, if you have to reshuffle printed pages, choose whichever of those options currently *isn't* selected.

Normal versus sideways printing

Unless your printing needs are very unusual, you'll probably want to print most of your documents in a portrait orientation. That's the orientation that normal letters and other documents use, so you'll almost always want to choose Portrait as your default Orientation, as in Figure 35.2.

You can always override that default and print the occasional document in Landscape orientation (sideways, so the page is wider than it is tall). Chapter 36 talks about choosing Landscape orientation for a document on-the-fly.

Saving time and money

Printers, as a rule, are just plain slow. That's because they're clunky mechanical devices, and it takes time to move a page through a printer and get the ink or toner onto the paper. If you want a really fast printer, you're going to pay really big bucks for it. But, no matter what the cost or general speed of your printer, one general rule will apply: The higher the print quality of the document you're printing at the moment, the longer it will take to print.

Here's another fact about printers in general. Printers are cheap, but ink cartridges cost an arm and a leg. Sort of like the shaving industry where they give you the razor for free, and then drive you to bankruptcy when you buy blades.

The printer property that most determines how quickly your documents print and how much ink you use per document is called *print quality*. The higher the print quality, the longer it takes to print a document, and the more ink you use in the process. You can save time and money by doing all your day-to-day printing in Draft quality, perhaps even without color if you want to conserve color ink.

On my OfficeJet printer, quality and color settings are on the Paper/Quality tab shown in Figure 35.2. Your printer will likely have similar options.

As with other printer properties, setting the printer defaults to low-quality and black-and-white settings won't prevent you from printing the occasional fancy color document. As you'll learn in Chapter 36, you can override those defaults any time you print a document. When you want to print a professional-looking report or a fine photo, just increase the print quality and activate color for the one print job.

Those three properties that I've just mentioned are the ones that most printers have. Beyond those, the properties vary greatly from one printer to the next. The only resource for learning all the details of your particular make and model of printer is the documentation that came with that printer. Or, the printer manufacturer's Web site.

Wrap Up

That about wraps it up for installing and managing printers. In the next chapter, you learn how to print documents, how to choose color and quality settings on the fly, and so forth. The main points from this chapter are as follows:

- There are many makes and models of printers. Your best resource for your specific printer is the documentation that came with that printer.

- Installed printers, and options for installing printers, are in your Printers folder. You can open that folder from the Start menu, Search box, or Control Panel.

- If you have access to multiple printers, right-click the icon for the printer you want to use on a day-to-day basis and choose Set as Default Printer.

- To test a printer, right-click its icon, and choose Properties. Then, click the Print Test Page button.

- When installing a new printer, if you have a choice between using USB or a printer port to connect your printer, seriously consider using the printer port to keep your USB ports free for other devices.

- The typical scenario for installing a printer that connects to a printer port is to shut down the computer, connect the printer and turn it on, and then restart the computer.

- To connect a printer by USB, don't shut down the computer. Instead, leave the computer on, connect the printer to the computer, and then turn the printer on.

- To ensure that your printer driver is appropriate for your operating system, check the Windows Update site and the printer manufacturer's Web site.

- To set default properties for day-to-day printing, right-click the printer's icon and choose Printing Preferences.

Chapter 36

Printing Documents and Screenshots

Windows Vista, in and of itself, doesn't print documents. The main reason is that Windows Vista can't even open documents. You use programs, not Windows, to print documents. Typically, you open the document first by clicking or double-clicking its icon. Then, you print the document from the program that opens.

This chapter looks at different ways to print documents. As everyone knows, printer ink, toner, and paper are expensive. For that reason, I'll be sure to present some techniques to help you get the most for your printing buck.

Printing a Document

If you have a printer, using it should be easy. First, you want to make sure that the printer is turned on, has paper, and is ready to go. Then if the document you want to print is open and on the screen, do whichever of the following is most convenient:

- Choose File ➪ Print from the program's menu bar.
- Click the Print button in the program's toolbar.
- Press Ctrl+P.
- Right-click any page of the document and choose Print.

In many cases, you can print a document, or several documents, without first opening the document. To print a single document that way, right-click its icon and choose Print. To print multiple documents, select the icons first, using any technique from Chapter 29. Then click the Print button in the toolbar. Or right-click any selected icon and choose Print, as shown in Figure 36.1.

FIGURE 36.1

Printing multiple closed documents.

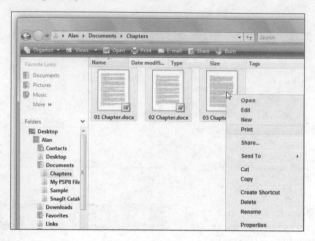

Yet another option for printing closed documents is to open the Printers folder. Select the icons for any documents you want to print, drag them into the Printers folder, and drop them onto the printer's icon.

What happens next depends on what program you're using, and which method you used. Often, right-clicking a closed document or pressing Ctrl+P starts the print job automatically. So, no further input is required.

 **Don't expect the document to start printing immediately. There's always some prep work that needs to be done, and that will take a few seconds.**

In most cases, printing a document will first take you to the Print dialog box. Exactly how the Print dialog box looks varies depending on the program and printer you're using. Figure 36.2 shows a couple of sample Print dialog boxes.

In the Print dialog box, click the Print or OK button to print to whatever printer is currently selected near the top of the dialog box. That's the simple approach, if you want to print the entire document immediately to the default printer. But as you can see in the sample Print dialog boxes, you may also have quite a few options to choose from before you click the Print or OK button.

 **See "Printing Pictures" in Chapter 22 for specifics on printing photos and other pictures.**

FIGURE 36.2

Examples of Print dialog boxes.

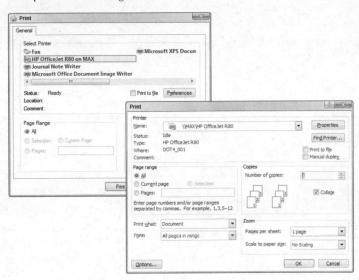

Common printing options

Because different programs offer different Print dialog boxes, I can't really say exactly what you'll see when you print a document. However, the options shown in the sample dialog box are fairly common. Those common options include:

- **Select Printer:** If you have access to multiple printers (for example, when you're connected to a network), choose the printer you want to use.

- **Page Range:** Choose which pages you want to print, ranging from *All* (the entire document), the *current page* (the page visible on your screen), *Selection* (only the text and pictures you selected in the document prior to getting here), or *Pages* (define a specific page, such as 1, or a range of pages, such as 2-5, to print only pages 2, 3, 4, and 5).

- **Manual Duplex:** Print pages back to back on printers that don't have the capability to do that automatically. (*Duplex* is the nerd word for *back to back*.) When you choose this option, odd-numbered pages will be printed first. You'll then be prompted to reinsert those pages, so the remaining pages can be printed on their backs.

- **Number of Copies:** Specify the number of copies to print.

- **Collate:** If this is selected, and you print multiple copies, pages are collated. If you print multiple copies, and clear the Collate option, you'll get multiple page 1s, followed by multiple page 2s, and so forth.

Choosing a print quality and other options

The general options that appear in the Print dialog box are almost universal. Depending on the make and model of your printer, you might have some other options to choose from. For example, you might be able to control the print quality of a document, opting for a quick draft or a time-consuming but better-quality job.

In most cases, you'll click the Properties button in the Print dialog box to get to those options. Figure 36.3 shows an example from an HP R80 OfficeJet printer. The figure shows options on both of the tabs in that dialog box.

FIGURE 36.3

Sample Printer Properties dialog box.

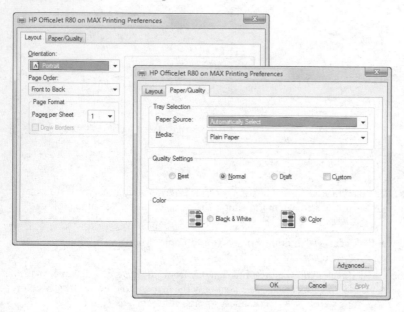

Here's a description of what each option in the sample dialog box offers:

- **Orientation:** Portrait prints in the normal vertical orientation; Landscape prints horizontally across the page.

- **Page Order:** Front to Back prints pages from lowest page number to highest. It keeps printed pages in the correct order if those printed pages come out of the printer face down. Back to Front prints pages from last to first, which keeps them in order if the printed pages come out face up.

- **Pages per Sheet:** If you specify a number greater than one, multiple pages are reduced to fit on the page. For example, choosing 2 prints two document pages on each piece of paper, making each document half its actual size.

- **Paper Source:** If your printer has more than one paper feeder, use this option to choose which one you want to use. For example, if you can keep regular paper in one printer bin and envelopes in a second bin, choose the second bin whenever you want to print envelopes.

- **Media:** Lets you specify the type or quality of paper you're printing on, such as Plain Paper or Premium Photo Paper.

- **Quality Settings:** To conserve ink, consider choosing this option and using a low-quality setting, such as Draft, and perhaps Black and White or Grayscale printing, for day-to-day printing. Use higher-quality settings and color for more professional-looking documents and photos.

- **Color:** Lets you print a color document in black and white, to conserve color ink.

TIP If you have to change print options often, consider setting the printer's default properties to the options you select often. See "Setting Default Printer Properties" in Chapter 35 for details.

After you've made your selections in the Printer Properties dialog box, click OK to return to the Print dialog box. There, you can choose additional options. Or, click the OK or Print button in the Print dialog box to start printing.

If you change your mind after starting the print job, there's no simple "undo" that can stop the print job. You'll have to open the printer's icon in the Printers folder, and then right-click the document job and choose Cancel.

NOTE See Chapter 37 for information on canceling a print job.

Still more print options

Depending on the program and printer you're using, you might also see an Options button in the Print dialog box. Clicking that button takes you to still more options like the ones shown in Figure 36.4. In that example, I'm about to print a document from Microsoft Office Word 2003.

FIGURE 36.4

Still more printing options.

Most of the options in Figure 36.4 apply only to Word documents. For example, fields, forms, hidden text, and such are features of Microsoft Word documents. Perhaps the noteworthy option is the one to print only odd or even pages. You can use this to print back to back with printers that don't offer such options in the Print or Properties dialog box.

Printing the Screen

If you were around in the olden days of computers with text screens, you might remember a time when you could print whatever was on the screen just by pressing the Print Screen key (perhaps abbreviated PrtScn, Prnt Scrn, or something like that). This was a so-called *screen dump*. It doesn't work that way in Windows. You can't print the screen directly to the printer. But you can *capture* the screen, paste it into a program, and print it from there. Here are the steps:

1. Get the screen to look the way you want.
2. To capture the entire screen, press the Print Screen key. To capture only the active window, dialog box, or message, press Alt+Print Screen.

NOTE If your keyboard has a Function Lock (or F Lock) key, it may need to be off for the PrtScn key to work. Some notebook computers require that you hold down an Fn or similar key while pressing PrtScn.

3. Open your favorite graphics program.

TIP If you don't have a favorite graphics program, you can use the simple Paint program that comes with Windows. Click the Start button and choose All Programs ⇨ Accessories ⇨ Paint.

4. Press Ctrl+V or choose Edit ⇨ Paste from the graphics program's menu bar.

A snapshot of the screen or program window opens in your graphics program. If you view it at 100 percent magnification, it might look like a hole through your graphics program or something hovering over it. If your graphics program allows it, zoom out to get a more complete view. For example, Figure 36.5 shows a screenshot in Jasc Paint Shop Pro, a third-party program that I use for most of my graphics and photo editing.

TIP In some graphics programs, you can spin your mouse wheel to change the image's magnification. In others, you have to choose some option from the program's View menu, such as View ⇨ Zoom.

Once the screenshot is in a graphics program, print it as you would any other open document, using any technique described earlier in this chapter. If you plan to use the screenshot as a picture in a Web page, save it as a JPEG or Portable Network Graphics (PNG) file (if possible), using the Save As Type option in the Save As dialog box.

NEW FEATURE As an alternative to using the technique just described, you can use Vista's new Snipping Tool to capture and annotate screenshots. See "Annotating Screenshots with Snipping Tool" in Chapter 15 for the whole story.

FIGURE 36.5

Screenshot in a graphics program.

Using Print Preview

Many programs offer a Print Preview feature that lets you see how a document will look on paper before you actually print it. That way, you'll know what to expect, and avoid unpleasant surprises and wasted paper. Like expecting to print one page and ending up with twenty pages!

To use Print Preview, you'll need to open the document first, or browse to the Web page you want to print. Then, choose File ⇨ Print Preview from the program's menu bar (assuming that the program you're using has a Print Preview feature). Or right-click the page and choose Print Preview.

For example, suppose that you're considering printing a Web page that you're currently viewing. Before you start printing, you'd like to know how many pages will print and how things will look on paper. Click the arrow next to Print in the toolbar and choose Print Preview to see how the page(s) will look printed. Down at the bottom of the window you see a Page x of y indicator, where y tells you how many pages will print. Use the Show Multiple Pages drop down list in the toolbar to display multiple pages, like in the example shown in Figure 36.6.

FIGURE 36.6

Internet Explorer's Print Preview window.

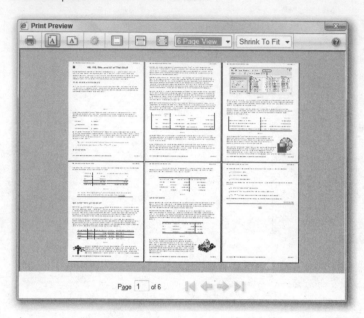

Use the arrows at the bottom of Print Preview to scroll through individual pages. Point to any button in the toolbar to see its name and purpose. To print straight from the Print Preview window, click the Print button at the left side of the toolbar. The Print dialog box will open. From there you should be able to choose specific pages to print. When you're finished with Print Preview, close it to return to the original program.

Wrap Up

Printing should be a simple matter of choosing File ➪ Print from a program's menu bar. Or you can right-click a document and choose Print. Here's a quick recap of the main points of this chapter:

- To print the document you're currently viewing, choose File from that program's menu bar. Or, click the Print button in its toolbar, or press Ctrl+P.

- To print a closed document from its icon, right-click that icon and choose Print.

- When the Print dialog box opens, you can choose a printer, a print quality, and other settings before you print.

- To print the screen, first capture the entire screen by pressing the Print Screen key. Or, press Alt+Print Screen to capture just the current window. Then, open any graphics program and press Ctrl+V. Finally, print the screenshot from that program.

- To see what an open document will look like before you print it, choose File ➪ Print Preview from the program's menu bar.

Chapter 37

Managing Print Jobs

When you print a document, there's more going on than you might expect. The printer doesn't immediately start printing. Instead, the computer needs to convert your document to a set of instructions that tells the printer what to do. Then, those printer instructions have to be sent to the printer in small chunks, because the printer is a slow mechanical device compared to a computer, which is much faster.

When you print multiple documents, each has to wait its turn. Each document you print becomes a *print job* that has to wait its turn in line if there are other documents already printing, or waiting to be printed. Most of this activity takes place in the background, meaning that you don't have to do anything to make it happen. In fact, you can just go about using your computer normally. There's no need to sit there and wait for the document to finish printing.

How Printing Works

When you print a document, quite a bit of work takes place invisibly in the background before the printer even "knows" there's a document to print. First, a program called a *print spooler* (or *spooler* for short) makes a special copy of the document that contains instructions that tell the printer exactly what to do. Those instructions don't look anything like the document you're printing. They're just codes that tell the printer what to do so that the document its spits out ends up looking like the document that you printed.

After the spooler creates the special printer file, it can't just hand the whole thing off to the printer as one giant set of instructions. A printer is a slow mechanical device that can hold only a small amount of information at a time in a *buffer*. The buffer is a small storage area within the printer that contains instructions for printing perhaps a page or two of text. Perhaps even less than a page if the document is a large photograph.

845

Furthermore, when the spooler has finished creating the special printer file, there may be another document already printing. There may even be several documents waiting to be printed. So, the spooler has to put all the print jobs into a *queue* (line). All of this activity takes computer time (not *your* time, per se). And because each document has to be spoon fed to the printer in small chunks, there's often time for you to do things like cancel documents you've told Windows to print but that haven't yet been fully printed.

To manage those print jobs, you use the *print queue*. If a document is already printing, or waiting to print, you'll see a tiny printer icon in the Notification area. When you point to that icon, the number of documents waiting to be printed appears in a tooltip, like the example shown in Figure 37.1. Double-click that small icon to open the print queue.

FIGURE 37.1

Printer icon in the Notification area.

As an alternative to using the Notification area, you can get to the print queue from the Printers folder. As mentioned in Chapter 35, you can use any of these techniques to open your Printers folder:

- Click the Start button and click Printers on the right side of the menu (if that option is available).
- Tap ▦, type `prin`, and click Printers under the Programs heading.
- Or, click the Start button and choose Control Panel ➪ Printers.

Once you're in the Printers folder, double-click the printer's icon to open its print queue.

> **TIP** To make a desktop shortcut to a specific printer, right-click the printer's icon in the Printer's folder and choose Create Shortcut. Choose Yes when prompted. Any time you need to open the printer's queue, just double-click (or click) that shortcut icon on the desktop.

Managing Print Jobs

The print queue for a printer contains all the documents that are currently printing or waiting to print. Figure 37.2 shows an example where I've already told Windows to print four documents. The first document I sent is currently printing. The other three are waiting in line for their turn.

FIGURE 37.2

Sample documents in a print queue.

Managing a single document

To pause or cancel a specific print job, right-click its line in the print queue and choose one of the following options from the shortcut menu that appears:

- **Pause:** Stops printing the document until you restart it.
- **Restart:** Restarts the paused print job.
- **Cancel:** Cancels the print job so that it doesn't print and removes the job from the print queue.
- **Properties:** Provides detailed information about the print job. You can also set the document's priority. The higher the priority, the more likely the print job is to butt in line ahead of other documents waiting to be printed.

Managing several documents

To pause, restart, or cancel several documents in the queue, select their icons. For example, click on the first job you want to change. Then, hold down the Shift key and select the last one. Optionally, you can select (or deselect) icons by holding down the Ctrl key as you click. Then, right-click any selected item, or choose Document from the menu bar, and choose an action. The action will be applied to all selected icons.

Managing all documents

You can use commands on the print queue's Printer menu, shown in Figure 37.3, to manage all the documents in the queue without selecting any items first. The options that apply to all documents are as follows:

- **Pause Printing:** Pauses the current print job and all those waiting in line. See "Printing Offline" later in this chapter for an example of when this would be useful.
- **Cancel All Documents:** You guessed it — this cancels the current print job and all those waiting to be printed.

How Do I Stop This Thing?

Don't expect a paused or canceled print job to stop right away. Several more pages may print, even after you've canceled a print job. That's because the print queue sends chunks of a document to the printer's buffer. That buffer, in turn, holds information waiting to be printed. Canceling a print job prevents any more data from being sent to the buffer. But the printer won't stop printing until its buffer is empty (unless, of course, you just turn the printer off).

FIGURE 37.3

Printer menu in the print queue.

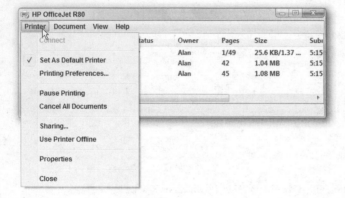

Butting in line

In the print queue, you can change the order in which documents in the queue will print. For example, if you need a printout right now, and there's a long line of documents waiting ahead of yours, you can give your document a higher priority so it prints sooner. In other words, your print job gets to butt in line ahead of others.

To change an item in the print queue's priority, right-click the item in the queue and choose Properties. On the General tab of the dialog box that opens, drag the Priority slider, shown in Figure 37.4, to the right. The farther you drag, the higher your document's priority. Click OK. Your document won't stop the document that's currently printing, but it may well be the next one to print.

FIGURE 37.4

Priority slider in a print queue item's Properties dialog box.

You can close the print queue as you would any other window—by clicking the Close button in its upper-right corner or by choosing Printer ➪ Close from its menu bar. To get help with the print queue while it's open, choose Help from its menu bar.

Solving Common Printer Problems

When Windows can't print a document, it alerts you through a Notification area message like the example shown in Figure 37.5. Before you assume the worst and delve into any major troubleshooting, check for some of the more common problems that cause such errors, as listed next.

FIGURE 37.5

Notification message for a printing problem.

- Is the printer turned on and ready to go?
- Are both ends of the printer cable plugged in securely?
- Is there paper in the printer, and is it inserted properly?
- Does the printer still have ink or toner?

 **TIP** To make Windows show the error message in Figure 37.5, I just loosened the printer cable at the back of my computer slightly. To fix the problem, I pushed the cable back in securely.

More often than not, you'll find that the printer problem is something as simple as the printer being out of paper or out of ink.

Printing Offline

Printing is a means of going through the process of creating the spool file for the printer without actually printing the document. There are times when this is useful, such as when you're working on a notebook computer with no printer attached, but intend to print later when you can attach the computer to a printer or network.

To make this work, right-click the printer's icon and choose Use Printer Offline, as shown in Figure 37.6. The printer's icon will dim and show the word *offline*. You can disconnect the printer from the computer.

FIGURE 37.6

Right-click and choose **Use printer offline**.

You can print any document while the printer is offline. Of course, the document won't actually print because the printer isn't connected to the computer. When you get back to the printer, connect the printer to the computer again. Open the Printers folder, right-click the printer's icon, and choose Use Printer Online. Any documents you "printed" while disconnected from the printer will start printing.

 XPS documents are a great way to share electronic printouts with people who don't have the same program you used to create the document.

Creating XPS Documents

As an alternative to printing on paper, you can print to an XPS document. The XPS document will look exactly like the printed document will look. But it will be a file rather than a sheet of paper. You can then e-mail that XPS document to other people. Or, if you have a Web site, let people download it from your site.

 You can also use this technique to print other people's Web pages to files on your own hard disk. You can view that file at any time; you don't need to be online.

To print to an XPS document, start printing as you normally would. For example, choose File ➪ Print from the program's menu bar. Or if you're in Internet Explorer, click the Print toolbar button. When the Print dialog box opens, choose Microsoft XPS Document Writer instead of your usual printer, as in Figure 37.7. Then click OK or Print.

FIGURE 37.7

Print an XPS document.

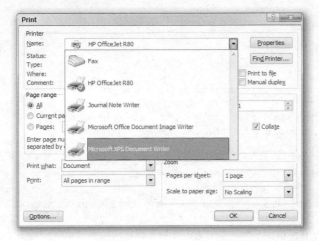

Because you're printing to a file, a Save As dialog box will open. There you can choose the folder in which you want to place the file, and give the file a name. Figure 37.8 shows an example where I'm about to print to a file named SampleXPSDocument.xps in my Documents folder. Click Save.

FIGURE 37.8

Put SampleXPSDocument.xps in Documents folder.

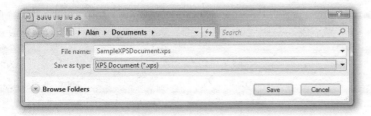

The Save As dialog box closes. To verify that the document was printed to a file, open the folder you printed to. The file is closed so it will look like an icon (see Figure 37.9). But you can treat it as any other document. For example, double-click the icon to open it. Or, if you want to e-mail it to someone using Windows Mail, right-click the icon and choose Send To ➪ Mail Recipient.

FIGURE 37.9

Icon for an XPS document.

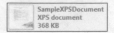

Wrap Up

The typical printing scenario is that you choose File ➪ Print from a program's menu bar, or press Ctrl+P, to print whatever document you're viewing at the moment. But as you've seen in this chapter, there's more going on behind the scenes, and things you can do to manage your print jobs.

- Every document you print is a print job, temporarily stored in a print queue.

- To open the print queue, double-click the printer icon in the Notification area, or the printer's icon in the Printers folder.

- To manage print jobs in the queue, right-click any job and choose an option from the shortcut menu.

- To cancel all documents that are waiting to be printed, choose Printer ➪ Cancel All Documents from the print queue's menu bar.

- To print to an XPS document rather than paper, start printing and get to the Print dialog box as you normally would. But choose Microsoft XPD Document Writer as the printer.

Chapter 38

Faxing and Scanning

ax machines have been around for a long time. The way they work is fairly simple. A fax machine is sort of like a copy machine that's connected to a phone line. To send a fax, you put the item you want to send into the machine and specify the recipient's phone number. When you send the fax, the copy machine part copies your document. But rather than spit out the copy at your end, it sends it through the phone lines to the recipient's fax machine. The recipient's fax machine prints the copy.

There isn't as much reason to use faxes in today's world. If the item you want to send someone is a file, it's much easier to send an e-mail message to the recipient with a copy of the file attached. It doesn't matter what program you use for e-mail. They all allow you to attach files to messages.

On the other hand, if the person to whom you're sending a file doesn't have an e-mail account, or doesn't know how to use e-mail and attachments, then fax might be your best alternative.

NEW FEATURE Though faxing and scanning are nothing new, Windows Fax and Scan provides new and easier ways to use fax equipment and scanners.

What You Need for Fax

To use Fax, your computer must have a fax modem that's connected to an analog phone line. Or your computer needs to have access to a fax server on the same local network. A fax server is a program on a computer that has a faxmodem installed and allows other computers in the network to send and receive faxes through that device. To use a fax server, you need to know the name of that server. If you didn't set up the fax server, ask the person who did for that name.

NOTE   If you have a multi-function printer that includes fax capabilities, you'll likely use the printer, not Windows or your computer, to send and receive faxes. See the manual that came with your printer for instructions. The information presented in this chapter may not apply.

Opening Windows Fax and Scan

Windows Fax and Scan is the program that comes with Windows Vista for faxing and scanning. To open that program, use whichever of the following methods is most convenient for you:

- Click the Start button and choose All Programs ⇨ Windows Fax and Scan.
- Tap ⊞, type fax, and click Windows Fax and Scan.

Figure 38.1 shows how the program looks when you first open it.

FIGURE 38.1

Windows Fax and Scan.

Creating a fax account

To send and receive faxes from your computer, you need a fax account. You need only set up the account once, not each time you want to use faxes. To create a fax account, open Windows Fax and Scan as described in the previous section. Make sure that you're viewing faxes rather than scans (click Fax in the left column if you're unsure). Then follow these steps:

1. In the menu bar, click Tools ⇨ Fax Accounts.
2. Click Add to create a new account.

3. On the first page to open, click the type of account you want to set up, either for a faxmodem in your own computer or a fax server on your local network.

4. Follow the onscreen instructions depending on which type of account you're creating.

NOTE If you're trying to connect to a fax server but don't know its name, ask your network administrator or the person who installed the fax server. Guessing won't work.

When you're finished, the Fax Accounts dialog box shows the name of the fax account you created. Before you send or receive faxes, you'll want to configure the account to best suit your needs. See the next section if you're using a faxmodem. Or see the section after next if you're using a fax server.

Configuring faxmodem options

If you'll be using a faxmodem in your own computer to send and receive faxes, you need to make some decisions about how you want to use it. The options available to you are in the Fax Settings dialog box. In Windows Fax and Scan, first make sure that you're in the Fax view (click Fax in the left column if you're not sure). Then follow these steps:

1. Choose Tools ⇨ Fax Settings from the menu.

2. If you want to send faxes from the faxmodem, select (check) the first option, Enable device to send faxes.

3. If you want the faxmodem to receive faxes, select Enable device to answer the phone and receive faxes. Then choose one of the following options:

   ▪ **Manual answer:** Choose this option if you want to manually answer incoming calls by clicking the Answer Now button in Fax Monitor as described under "Receiving Faxes" later in this chapter.

   ▪ **Automatically answer after X rings:** Choose this option if you want the faxmodem to answer automatically. Then specify a ring delay (the number of times the phone must ring before the faxmodem answers).

4. To configure fax alerts and how Fax Monitor operates, click Tracking. You see the options in Figure 38.2.

5. Select or clear any options on the Tracking tab according to your personal preferences. If you don't have any preferences yet, select them all as in the figure.

6. Optionally, click the Advanced tab to configure options shown in Figure 38.3.

7. Finally, to grant faxing permissions to standard users, click the Security tab. Click the Everyone group and then use checkboxes to Allow permissions as you see fit.

8. Click OK.

Sharing Fax with a Voice Line

Faxing is easiest when you have a dedicated phone line for faxes. If the faxmodem uses the same phone number as your voice phone, your best bet will be to choose Manual Answer. That way if you hear the high-pitched tone of an incoming fax when you answer the phone, you can click the Receive Now button in Fax Monitor to accept the incoming fax.

Also, if you have an answering machine or service that automatically answers after x rings, you don't want Fax Monitor beating it to the punch every time. Otherwise nobody will be able to leave you a voice message!

FIGURE 38.2

Faxmodem tracking options.

FIGURE 38.3

Advanced faxmodem options.

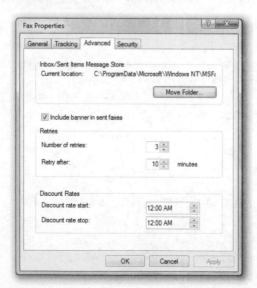

If you send and receive faxes through a fax server, there is no need to configure options for receiving faxes. Any faxes you receive will automatically be sent to your Inbox.

Defining Dialing Rules

If this will be the first time you're using your modem, you may need to take a moment to configure your dialing rules. For example, most locations in the United States require dialing a 1 before you dial a number outside your own area code. When dialing within your own area code, you might only need to dial seven digits. Or, if your area uses ten-digit dialing, you have to dial your area code plus the seven-digit phone number.

To configure dialing rules, click the Start button and choose Control Panel. Click Hardware and Sound, then click Setup dialing rules under the Phone and Modem Options heading. The Phone and Modem Options dialog box opens.

If you're using a modem with a desktop computer, you can set up one set of dialog rules for your location. If you use the modem in a portable computer and travel around, you can set up dialing rules for multiple locations.

The default location (the main location from which you dial) is referred to as My Location by default. Chances are you'll see that location in the Phone and Modem Locations as soon as the dialog box opens. If not, click the New button to create it. Use the New button to set up dialing rules for multiple locations, too.

To create or change dialing rules for any location listed in the Phone and Modem Options dialog box, click the location name and then click the Edit button. The first set of options, shown in Figure 38.4, are self-explanatory.

Edit Locations dialog box.

Keep in mind that all the options refer to where you're dialing *from*, not to. So you want to choose the country and specify the area code you're in when using the modem. If you need to dial a number carrier code for an outside line, choose the appropriate options and specify the number you dial.

Call waiting can interfere with modems. So if there's a way to turn that off, choose the Disable call waiting option and specify the number you dial to disable that. Leave the Tone option selected unless you're in an area that still uses the old dial phones rather than buttons.

To create a rule for dialing area codes, click the Area Code Rules tab. Then click New to get to the options shown in Figure 38.5. The instructions on the tab explain how to define a rule. Remember that these rules apply to phone numbers you dial. For example, if you need to include the area code (but not a 1 prefix) when dialing within the 215 area code, enter that area code up top and choose Include the area code near the bottom of the dialog box, as in the figure. Then click OK.

If you need to define a rule for an area code and prefix combination (which is rare), you can specify the area code in the top box and then specify one or more prefixes under the Prefixes heading.

If you want all your phone charges to be put on a calling card, click the Calling Card tab. Choose the calling card company you use and click New. Then fill in the blanks to ensure that the calls are billed to your account. Click OK in all open dialog boxes after defining rules and accounts.

FIGURE 38.5

Defining an area code rule.

If you later discover that you're having a problem reaching a certain phone number, open the Phone and Modem Options dialog box again and choose the location from which you're dialing. Then click the Edit button to fix any rules or account information that might be causing incorrect dialing.

Setting Up Your Cover Sheets

It's generally a good idea to send cover sheets with faxes. You can define some general information to appear on cover sheets in advance, so you don't have to re-type that information every time you send a fax. If you've closed the Windows Fax and Scan program, re-open it using any of the methods described earlier in this chapter. Then choose Tools ⇨ Sender Information from the menu bar. You'll see the dialog box shown in Figure 38.6.

FIGURE 38.6

Defining sender information.

Fill in only as much information as you want to appear on each fax cover sheet. Then click OK.

Sending Faxes

There are two ways to send faxes to people: right from the Windows Fax and Scan program, or from the program you used to create the document you want to scan. The end result is the same either way. So just use whichever method is easiest for you.

Faxing from Windows Fax and Scan

To create and send a fax from the Windows Fax and Scan program, open that program as described earlier in this chapter. Click Fax in the left column to ensure you're in the faxing mode. Then follow these steps:

1. Click the New Fax toolbar button and choose File ⇨ New ⇨ Fax from the menu.

2. If you want to include a cover sheet, click Cover Page and choose the style you want.

> **TIP**
>
> To create and manage your own fax cover sheets, choose Tools ⇨ Cover Pages from the Windows Fax and Scan menu bar.

3. To specify recipients, do any of the following:

   - Type the recipient's fax number directly into the box to the right of the To: button.

   - Or, if the recipients are already in your Contacts, click To:, use the To ⇨ button to add each recipient's name to the Message Recipient's list, and then click OK.

   - Or, to add recipients to your Contacts, click To:, click New Contact, and fill in the recipient's name and fax number (plus any other information you have). Click OK and then click To ⇨ to add the recipient to the Message Recipients list. Click OK.

> **CAUTION**
>
> If a recipient's name is red in the To: box, that means there is no fax number for that recipient. Edit the recipient's Contact information to include a fax number.

4. Fill in the Subject line with a brief description of the fax. If you send the fax to another computer, the Subject text will appear in the fax header, like the Subject line in an e-mail message.

5. Type the body of your fax in the main program window. You can use standard text selection techniques and options in the toolbar to format the text. (See "Basic text editing" in Chapter 15 for more information.)

6. Optionally, to insert a picture or file to send with your fax, click Insert on the menu bar to see the options shown in Figure 38.7. Then choose whichever option best describes what you want to insert as listed next.

FIGURE 38.7

Insert options.

■ **File Attachment:** Choose this option to attach any printable document to your fax. The file you choose will be converted to a TIF image and sent as part of the fax.

■ **Picture:** Choose this option to insert a picture into the body of your fax message. When the picture is in the message, you can size it using the dragging handles. To wrap text around a small picture, right-click the picture and choose Properties, then set the Alignment property to Left or Right.

■ **Text from file:** Choose this option to add text from any `.txt`, `.htm`, or `.html` file to your message. You can edit the inserted text using the same techniques used to edit text you typed yourself.

■ **Pages from scanner:** If you have one or more pages in your scanner to send, choose this option to scan the printed page(s) and add them immediately.

7. Optionally, to preview how your fax will look to the recipient, choose View ➪ Preview from the menu. Close the preview window when done.

8. Finally, to send the fax immediately, click Send. Or, to schedule when the fax is sent, choose Tools ➪ Fax Options to see the options shown in Figure 38.8. Choose to send the fax when discount rates apply, or at a specific time of day. Then click OK.

FIGURE 38.8

Sending options.

The fax message will go to the Outbox until it is sent to the recipient. Once sent, a copy of the fax will be added to your Sent Items folder.

Sending faxes from programs

As an alternative to going through Fax and Scan, you can often fax a file using the same procedure you use to print. Open the document you want to fax using whatever program you typically use for that type of document. For example, open a document in Word, or a Web page in Internet Explorer.

CAUTION When you fax a document, you send the recipient a non-editable photo of the document. If you want to send an editable copy of the document, you should attach it to an e-mail message. Don't use fax at all.

Next, choose File ⇨ Print from the program's menu bar as though you were going to print the document yourself. When the Print dialog box opens, choose Fax from the list of available printers, as in Figure 38-9. Then click Print.

FIGURE 38.9

Choose Fax as the printer.

A copy of the document is converted to a TIFF picture and attached to a fax message. If sent to a standard fax machine, the recipient sees the document printed on paper only. If the recipient is using software like Windows Fax and Scan, the document will be a TIFF image in their Inbox.

Receiving Faxes

If you've configured Windows Fax and Scan to receive faxes, you can receive incoming faxes in your Inbox. You might want to keep the Fax Monitor open at all times to make it easier to detect incoming faxes. This is especially important if you did not configure Fax and Scan to answer all calls automatically. To open Fax Monitor:

1. Open Windows Fax and Scan using any technique described near the start of this chapter.
2. Choose Tools ⇨ Fax Status Monitor from the menu bar. The monitor opens as in Figure 38.10.
3. Optionally, close Windows Fax and Scan leaving only the monitor on the screen.
4. Optionally, choose Keep on top to make sure the monitor is always visible on your screen.

FIGURE 38.10

FIGURE 38.10

Fax monitor.

When the phone rings, you can pick up the handset on your phone to see who is calling. If you hear the high-pitched sound of an incoming fax, click Receive Now to accept the fax and add it to your Windows Fax and Scan Inbox.

 Here's another way to get to your fax Inbox: Click the Start button and choose Documents. Then open the Fax icon in your Documents folder.

If you use a fax server rather than a faxmodem in your own computer, you don't need to do anything to receive a fax. The fax server will add the fax to your Inbox automatically. Just check your Inbox occasionally to see what's available.

 You can also get to faxes by opening your Documents folder, then opening the Fax folder.

Working with Faxes

Windows Fax and Scan handles faxes in much the same way Windows Mail handles e-mail. New faxes you receive are placed in your Inbox. To see all the faxes in your Inbox:

1. Open Windows Fax and Scan using any method described near the start of this chapter.
2. In the left column, click Inbox under the Fax heading.

The top half of the main pane shows a header for each received fax. The header includes the sender's name, subject, time, pages, and other useful information. Click any header to see the contents of the fax message in the lower pane. Or double-click any header to open the fax in a separate larger window. The rest is easy.

To reply to the fax, click the Reply toolbar button.

- To forward the fax to another fax recipient, click Forward as Fax in the toolbar.
- To forward the fax as an e-mail message, click Forward as E-mail.
- To close the fax, click the Close (X) button.

You can also work directly with fax headers in the top pane of your Inbox. For example:

- To print a fax, right-click its header and choose Print.
- To delete a fax, click its header and click the Delete (red X) toolbar button. Or right-click the header and choose Delete.

For more information on faxing with Windows Vista and basic troubleshooting techniques, search Vista's help for fax.

Scanning Documents

A scanner is a device similar to a copy machine. You put a piece of paper in the scanner according to the instructions that came with your scanner. Then you scan the document. But unlike a copier, a scanner doesn't give a copy of the document on paper. Instead it stores a copy of the printed document as a file in your computer.

You use a scanner to get copies of things that exist only on paper into your computer. The scanned image is like a photocopy of the original. In fact, it will be a "photograph" of the original document. This means that even if the scanned document contains words, you won't be able to edit it in a program like WordPad, WordPerfect, or Microsoft Word.

If you want to edit a scanned document, you first need to use OCR (Optical Character Recognition) software to convert the scanned document to an editable form. Windows Vista doesn't come with OCR software built in. However, many programs that work with Windows do have built-in OCR capabilities. Chances are, when you bought your scanner, you got OCR software with it. To find out, check the documentation that came with your scanner.

If you have a scanner, there are three ways you can use it to scan:

■ You can use the scanning software that came with the scanner to scan any document. Use that method if neither of the following methods work with your scanner.

■ If the item you want to scan is a picture or photograph, and Windows Vista recognizes your scanner, use Windows Photo Gallery described in Chapter 22 to scan.

■ If the item you want to scan is not a picture or photo, and Windows Vista recognizes your scanner, you can use the techniques described in this section to scan the document.

Scanning with Windows Fax and Scan

To scan a document using Windows Fax and Scan, first open that program as described earlier in this chapter. At the bottom of the left pane, click Scan. Clicking Documents in the left pane lists all documents you've scanned with that program. If you haven't scanned yet, the list will be empty as in Figure 38.11.

To scan a document, load it into your scanner according to the scanner manufacturer's instructions. For example, if it's a flatbed scanner, place the document face down on the glass and close the cover. If it's the kind of scanner where you load pages into a document feeder, load them accordingly. On a scanner where sheets feed from the top, this usually means putting the sheets into the feeder with the printed side facing away from you. Then follow these steps:

1. In Windows Fax and Scan, click New Scan in the toolbar or choose File ➪ New ➪ Scan from the menu bar.

2. In the first dialog box to open, click your scanner's icon and click OK.

3. In the next window (see Figure 38.12), choose a scan profile you created earlier (if any).

4. Optionally, click the Preview button to see how the scanned image will look.

5. Optionally, use sizing handles in the preview area to crop out the portion of the document you want to scan.

FIGURE 38.11

Windows Fax and Scan in scan mode.

FIGURE 38.12

Choose a scan profile.

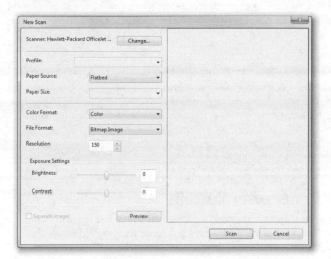

6. If there's anything you don't like about the preview image, use any combination of the following options to make adjustments:

   ▪ **Paper Source:** If your scanner offers multiple paper sources, choose the one that contains the document you're about to scan.

   ▪ **Paper Size:** If you're using a non-standard paper size with an automatic document feeder, use this option to specify that size.

   ▪ **Color Format:** Choose Color, Grayscale, or Black & White according to your preferences.

 Use Black & White for text documents and forms that contain no shades of gray. Use grayscale for photos and documents that do contain some shades of gray.

   ▪ **File format:** Choose your preferred file format. Bitmap Image is fine if you don't have a preference.

   ▪ **Resolution:** Set this to 150 for clean standard printing. You can set it higher for more detailed scans. For example, if the preview of a scan looks like it's missing some text, try using a higher resolution.

   ▪ **Exposure settings:** Use these options to adjust brightness and contrast if the preview image looks too dark or too flat.

7. If you changed any of these options, you can click Preview again to see how things will look. You can keep changing settings and clicking Preview until the scan looks the way you want.

 When you get the optional settings just right, you can click Save Profile to make it easy to reuse those same settings when scanning similar documents in the future.

8. Click Scan to scan the document. Wait for the scanner to scan the document.

If you don't see the scanned document right away, click Documents in the left pane. You'll see a header for every document you've scanned. To change the name of a scanned document, click its current name and type in a new name.

Using scanned documents

Each document you scan is saved in the Scanned Documents folder in your Documents folder. Clicking Documents at the left side of Windows Fax and Scan shows the names of those same documents. To print, e-mail, fax, delete, or do something else with a scanned document, right-click its header in the top main pane, like in Figure 38.13.

You'll find the same scanned documents in the Scanned Documents folder of you user account. Click the Start button and choose Documents ⇨ Scanned Documents ⇨ Documents.

Forwarding scanned documents automatically

If you use a scanner in a local network, you can automatically send a copy of all scanned documents to another computer on the network. Choose Tools ⇨ Automatically Forward Scans from the Windows Fax and Scan menu (while you're in the scan mode).

To forward all scans to an e-mail address, choose the first option and specify the e-mail address. Or, choose the second option and specify the folder or UNC name of the folder to which you want to forward scanned documents.

Right-click a scanned document header.

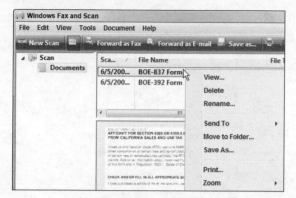

Wrap Up

Faxing and scanning are like two sides of the same coin. When you fax a document, you essentially send a photocopy of the document to a fax machine, or to a fax program on another computer. When you scan a document, you send a photocopy of the document to a file on your own computer's hard disk. You can use Windows Fax and Scan for both operations. Here's a quick wrap up of the main points covered in this chapter:

- To open Windows Fax and Scan, click the Start button and choose All Programs ⇨ Windows Fax and Scan.

- To work with faxes, click Faxes in the left column. To work with scans, click Scans in the left column.

- To create a new fax, click the New Fax toolbar button or choose File ⇨ New Fax from the menu.

- To scan a document, load the document into the scanner and click the New Scan toolbar button. Or choose File ⇨ New ⇨ Scan from the menu bar.

- To work with a received fax or scanned document, right-click its header in the main pane in Windows Fax and Scan.

Chapter 39

Troubleshooting Printing and Faxing

Troubleshooting Printing

Because no two printers are exactly alike, printing is more a matter of knowing your printer rather than knowing your computer or Windows. The best I can do here is provide some general pointers that apply to most printers. But for specifics on your printer, the manual that came with the printer, or the main Web page for the product, will be your best bet.

First aid for printing problems

Before you start digging around the computer for solutions to a printing problem, check the most common physical problems:

- Make sure that the printer is plugged in and turned on.
- If the printer has an Online/Offline switch, make sure that it's online.
- Make sure that the printer cable is connected snugly at both the printer and computer ends.
- Make sure that the printer has paper.
- Make sure that the printer has ink or toner.
- Check for, and clear, a paper jam.

If none of the preceding help, take a look at the Help topics for printing, as described next.

Document appears to print, but nothing comes out of the printer

You may have selected a printer that produces files (like the Microsoft XPS Document Writer). After you choose File ⇨ Print to print a document, make sure you choose an appropriate printer from the Print dialog box. To avoid making the mistake in the printer, make the printer you use most often the default printer, as discussed in Chapter 35.

Problem with a network printer

If your computer is a member of a network and your printing problems start right after installing or upgrading to Vista, the most likely problem is that the firewall has blocked communication with the printer. You'll need administrative privileges to unblock the firewall port. Follow these steps on each computer involved:

1. Open the Windows Firewall Control Panel applet by selecting Start ➪ Control Panel ➪ Allow a program through Windows Firewall.

2. On the Exceptions tab, make sure that File and Printer Sharing is selected (checked) as shown in Figure 39.1.

FIGURE 39.1

File and Printer Sharing enabled in Windows Firewall.

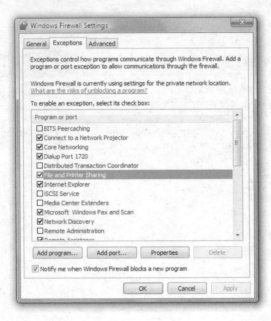

3. Click OK and close Control Panel.

Printer prints garbage

If the printer used to print properly, turn off the printer. Then, close all open program windows and turn off the computer (click Start ➪ Shut Down). Make sure that there is no paper jam in the printer, turn the printer back on, and wait a few seconds. Then, restart the computer normally.

If the trouble persists, delete all documents in the print queue and repeat the preceding procedure. If it still persists, consider updating the printer driver as discussed later in this chapter.

Advanced printing features are disabled

To use all the capabilities of a printer, you need to make sure that you have the most current printer drivers installed. Also, make sure that the printer's advanced features are enabled by following these steps:

1. Click Start ➪ Control Panel ➪ Printer to open the printer window.
2. Right-click the icon for the printer, and choose Properties.
3. On the General tab, click the Printing Preferences button.
4. Click the Advanced tab.
5. If you see Disabled next to Advanced Printing Features under Document Options, click that word and choose Enabled, as shown in Figure 39.2.

FIGURE 39.2

Advanced Options dialog box for a sample printer.

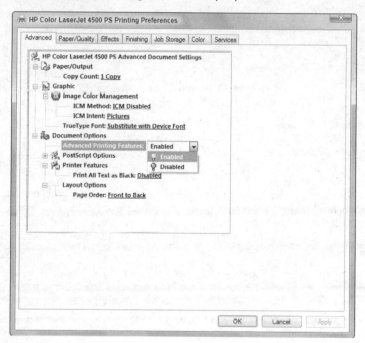

6. Click OK in all open dialog boxes.

Printed colors don't match screen colors

On some Hewlett Packard and Cannon BubbleJet printers, ICM (Image Color Management) may incorrectly color the printed page. To fix the problem, go to the Advanced Options shown in Figure 39.2, and choose Disable ICM.

Error message "Problem communicating with printer"

This error occurs on some Lexmark printers that connect through a USB port. Getting the latest driver for the printer should resolve the problem. Optionally, you can turn off the USB hub's ability to turn off the device as follows:

1. Right-click the Computer link from the Start menu and choose Properties.
2. In the System window, click the Device Manager link in the Tasks column on the left side of the window.
3. Click the + sign next to Universal Serial Bus controllers.
4. Right-click USB Root Hub and choose Properties.
5. Click the Power Management tab.
6. Clear the Allow the computer to turn off this device to save power checkbox.
7. Click OK in the Properties dialog box.

> **NOTE**   If you have multiple USB root hubs, you'll need to repeat steps 4 through 7 for each one.

8. Close Device Manager.
9. Close the System window.

Updating your printer driver

A printer driver that's not specifically designed for Windows Vista can cause problems ranging from the printer not printing at all to garbled printer output. Most printer manufacturers submit updated drivers to Microsoft, so you may be able the update your printer driver right from Microsoft's Update Web site. You'll need to sign into a user account that has administrative privileges. Also, make sure your computer is online. Then follow these steps:

1. Tap ⊞, type dev, and click Device Manager. Or click the Start button, right-click the Computer option, choose Properties, and click Device Manager in the left column of the System window that opens.
2. Look for the printer name under the Printers heading (if you have such a heading) or under one of the IEEE 1284.4 headings.
3. When you find the printer's name, right-click it and choose Update Driver Software as in Figure 39.3.
4. Follow the onscreen instructions to search for an updated printer online.

If you can't download a printer driver automatically using the preceding steps, browse to the printer manufacturer's Web site using your Web browser. Then search for an updated Windows Vista driver there.

FIGURE 39.3

Update a printer driver.

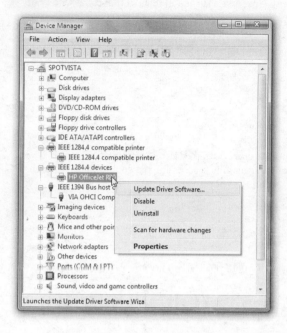

Troubleshooting Faxing

Like printing and scanning, faxing is more a matter of knowing your specific faxing hardware than it is about knowing your computer or Windows. Your best bet is to learn to use your fax hardware as described in the manual that came with the hardware device before you try to fax directly from Windows or a program. Again, the best I can do here is provide some general troubleshooting tips.

First aid for faxing problems

Windows Vista only provides access to your faxing hardware. To learn to use the fax that's part of an all-in-one printer, refer to the manual that came with the printer, or the manual that came with your faxmodem or computer. If the fax device came with its own software, you may be better off using that software as opposed to Windows Fax and Scan.

Also, make sure that the fax phone port on your computer or printer is attached to a phone jack on the wall.

> **TIP** Remember, if you're trying to send a document that's already on your hard disk (as opposed to on paper only), you'll get better results by e-mailing the document as an attachment.

Printing and Faxing Troubleshooting Resources

Not all printers or faxmodems are the same. Be sure to check the instruction manual that came with your printer or fax device for their troubleshooting suggestions.

You can also check Vista's built-in help and support for troubleshooting tips. Click the Start button and choose Help and Support. Then type any of the following phrases to get help with troubleshooting your printer or faxing:

`troubleshoot printer`

`troubleshoot fax`

`troubleshoot scan`

For live help, post a question in the `Microsoft.public.windows.vista.print_fax_scan` newsgroup at Windows Communities. See Chapter 18 for information on accessing the communities through Windows Mail.

Part VIII

Installing and Removing Programs

I n a sense, a computer is a simple machine that does only one thing—run programs. And that's the real beauty of it. It can be a stereo, TV, e-mail machine, Web browser, appointment book, a place to hang out online, a way to keep in touch with people, whatever you want it to be. Because it is whatever program you have running at the moment.

The main reason why Windows is so popular and successful is because literally thousands of programs are available for it. Part VIII is all about finding and using programs that make your computer do what you want it to do.

Chapter 40 starts off with the ever-popular task of downloading programs. That's followed by Chapter 41, which covers installing programs from disks.

Chapter 42 covers getting older programs to run on Vista (which can be a real challenge, given Vista's insistence on security!).

Chapter 43 covers important skills for repairing and removing programs. Chapter 44 covers different ways of configuring programs' default actions and processes. Chapter 45 gets into some of the more technical aspects of managing programs and processes. Chapter 46 wraps it all up with solutions to common software problems.

Chapter 40

Downloading Programs

T here are several ways to acquire new programs for your computer. One is to go to the store and buy the program. Another is to order a program online and have it sent to you by mail. The third option, downloading and installing the program on the spot, is what this chapter is all about.

Before you read any further, let me remind you that you should never believe anything you get in junk e-mail messages or pop-up ads. Especially if they're offering programs to fix some imaginary problem with your computer.

Try to stick with reputable software companies (like Microsoft, Adobe, Corel, and so forth). Also, consider going to download sites like www.download.com and www.tucows.com and read what others are saying about a program before you download and install it.

Before You Install a Program

When you install new hardware or software, there's always a slight risk that the product won't be 100 percent compatible with everything else that's in your computer. Unfortunately, you won't know if there's a problem until after you install the program. By then, the installation procedure has already made some sweeping changes to your system.

TIP Windows Vista does a good job of keeping track of changes to your system and giving you a fallback position. But to play it extra safe, consider manually creating a restore point before you install new software. For more information, see "Using System Protection" in Chapter 33.

If the new program causes any problems, you can uninstall (remove) the program. Then go back into System Protection and return your computer to the restore point that you created just before installing the program. That will erase all changes made by the new program, and things will be just as they were before you installed the new program.

To Run or to Save?

Programs are different from documents in several ways. A document is just *data* that a program can use. Examples of documents include typed text, pictures, music, and video.

Programs, on the other hand, contain *executable code*, instructions that tell the computer what to do. Unlike documents, programs need to be *installed* before you can use them. Among other things, the installation process adds an icon to your All Programs menu, which you can click to run the installed program.

When you download a program, you'll usually be given the option to Save the program, or to Run (or Open) the program. The difference is as follows:

- **Save:** Choosing Save copies the program's installation file to a folder on your hard disk, but doesn't install the program. You must install the program yourself before you can use it.
- **Run** (or **Open**): Choosing Run or Open downloads and installs the program in one fell swoop. You don't need to go through an extra installation step.

Whether you choose Save or Run is entirely up to you. Obviously, Run offers the convenience of not having to go through the extra installation step. After the download is completed, you should be able to start the program from your All Programs menu.

On the other hand, choosing Save puts a copy of the installation program into a folder on your hard disk. If you ever need to re-install the program due to some mishap, you can do so right from the downloaded installation program.

Read the instructions

The procedures in this chapter are general and apply to most programs. But "most programs" isn't the same as "every program ever created." Before you download and install a program, you should check the site from which you're downloading the program for specific instructions. Better to spend five minutes reviewing those instructions before you download than to spend five hours figuring out why the download didn't work after the fact.

Only administrators can install programs

Finally, keep in mind installing programs requires administrative privileges in Windows Vista. You'll need to know the password for an administrative account on your system in order to install any program.

Downloading Programs

Here I'll go through the typical procedure for downloading and installing a program. I'll use Microsoft's Calculator Plus as an example. It's a great little program that everyone can use, and is 100 percent safe. But do keep in mind that this is an *example*. There are many thousands of programs you can download and install. And you should always refer to the download instructions for any program you install for information that's specific to that program.

Download and install a program

The next step is to get to the link that launches the program download. Obviously, where you find that link depends on the program you're downloading. For this example I went to `http://download.microsoft.com` and searched for Calculator Plus. Then I clicked the Microsoft Calculator Plus link, which took me to the page shown in Figure 40.1. (The page might look different when you try this.)

FIGURE 40.1

Sample Web page for downloading a program.

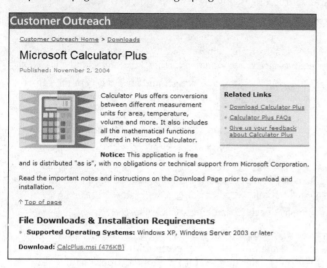

Moving right along, here are the steps to perform the download from the Web page shown in the example:

1. Click the Download Calculator Plus link. You're taken to another page with still more information about the program.

2. Click Continue and then click Download on the next page that opens.

3. You see the standard Security Warning shown in Figure 40.2. If that box gets covered by your browser, click the taskbar button that shows 0% of CalcPlus.

FIGURE 40.2

Standard security warning for downloading a program.

4. Now you have to decide for yourself if you just want to install the program, or save it and install it later. Because this program would be easy to find in the future, click Run for this example.

5. You see another security warning about running the program. Click Run to proceed.

6. Next you're taken to some setup instructions. Normally you'd read those. But for this example you can just click Next.

7. Typically you'll need to accept the license agreement, which basically says you can use the program, but you can't sell it to other people, give it away, and so forth. Click I agree and click Next.

8. The next page asks where you want to install the program. You should always accept the suggested path unless you really know what you're doing and have some good reason for choosing some other folder.

9. This program also asks if you want to install the program so that it's accessible only from your user account, or everyone's user account. For this example you can choose Everyone.

10. Click Next.

11. If you're not logged in to an administrative user account, you'll be prompted for an administrative password. Type that password and click Submit.

12. The program installs and you get some feedback to that effect. Click Close.

Installing a program is not the same as running it. So you may not see the program at this point. To run a program, you use the Start menu. In the case of Calculator Plus, click the Start button, choose All Programs, and then click the Microsoft Calculator Plus folder. The startup icon for the program appears under the folder as in Figure 40.3. Click that icon, and the program will start.

FIGURE 40.3

Start Calculator Plus.

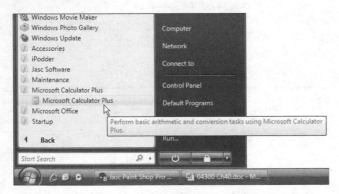

Much as we all crave, demand, and expect immediate gratification, few programs are simple enough to deliver that. More often than not, you have to invest some time in learning to use the program. Like most programs, Calculator Plus has its own built-in help for that. Click the Help button as in Figure 40.4 and choose Help Topics for info on using Calculator Plus.

FIGURE 40.4

Calculator Plus Help button.

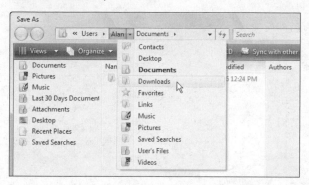

Download, but don't install

In the preceding section, you were able to run Calculator Plus right after installing it because you chose Run from the options shown in Figure 40.2. Had you chosen Save, you wouldn't be able to run the program right away. You'd need to open the folder in which you saved the program, and then open the icon that represents the file you downloaded and perform the installation at that point.

To better illustrate, I'll go through the procedure using the Calculator Plus program as an example again. Of course in real life, there'd be no reason to download the same program twice. This is just an example to illustrate the difference between choosing Save or Run when prompted. I'll start at the same step 1 as in the preceding example:

1. Click the Download Calculator Plus link. You're taken to another page with still more information about the program.

2. Click Continue and then click Download on the next page that opens.

3. You see the standard Security Warning shown previously in Figure 40.2. For this example let's assume you choose Save.

4. The Save As window opens. Navigate to the folder in which you want to store the file. There is no mandatory folder. Feel free to use the Downloads folder for your user account if you don't have a preference. (Click the arrow next to your user name in the eyebrow menu and then click the Downloads folder name as in Figure 40.5.)

5. Take a look at the filename so you know what to look for later.

TIP You can create a subfolder within your Documents folder that has the exact name of the program you're downloading. Then put the file in that subfolder. The subfolder's name will make it easier to recognize the programs you have in your Downloads folder.

6. Click the Save button.

FIGURE 40.5

Choose a folder for the download.

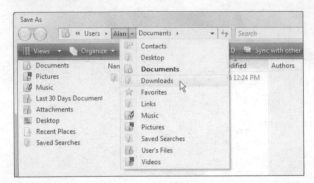

When the download is finished, the Download Complete box opens (see Figure 40.6). There are no installation steps with this approach because you only saved the file, you didn't run it. Your Start menu won't have an icon for running the downloaded program until after you've installed the program.

FIGURE 40.6

The Download Complete dialog box.

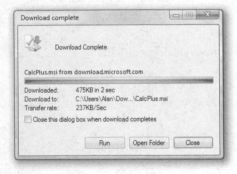

You can decide for yourself when you want to install the program. From the Download Complete dialog box, you have the following options:

- **Run:** Choose this option if you want to install the program right now.

- **Open Folder:** Choose this option if you just want to open the folder into which you put the downloaded file. From there you can double-click the icon that represents the downloaded program if you want to install immediately.

- **Close:** Choose this option if you don't want to do anything right now.

The most important thing to realize here is that you cannot use the downloaded program until you install it. You'll know the program is installed when you can find its icon on the All Programs menu and click its icon to run the program.

If you don't install it from the Download Complete dialog box, you'll need to install it at some point. To do so, open the folder in which you put the downloaded file. Then open (click or double-click) the icon that represents the downloaded file.

In the case of Calculator Plus, that icon will look like one of the examples in Figure 40.7 when viewing icons as Tiles. Whether or not the filename extension (.msi) is visible depends on whether or not the "Hide extensions for known file types" option is selected in the Folder Options dialog box.

FIGURE 40.7

Icon for downloaded Calculator Plus program.

You don't need to use the downloaded file to run the program. In fact, you could delete that file if you wanted. But the whole idea behind using Save rather than Run when downloading a program is to have a copy of the installation program on your system as a backup, in case some mishap causes you to lose the installed copy.

Windows Marketplace and Digital Locker

NEW FEATURE This one is so new, it's still under construction as I write this chapter. But it should be ready by the time you read this.

As I write this chapter, I can see that Microsoft has some big plans for Windows Marketplace. This is an online service, not a part of Vista per se. But there are links to the service within Vista, which you'll find in the Programs and Features window. Use either of these techniques to get there:

- Click the Start button and choose Control Panel ➪ Programs ➪ Programs and Features.
- Tap ⊞, type fea, and choose Programs and Features on the Start menu.

Once you're in Programs and Features you'll see two links in the left column: Get new programs online at Windows Marketplace and View purchased software (digital locker). Click either one to learn more.

Wrap Up

Downloading and installing programs is fairly easy. The main thing to realize is that every program needs to be installed (once) before you can use it. Whether or not a program you download from the Internet is installed automatically depends on whether you choose Run or Save when asked what you want to do with the file you're downloading. Here are the key points from this chapter:

- It's always a good idea to create a restore point before installing any new hardware or software. See "Using System Protection" in Chapter 33 for the goods on creating restore points.

- Only users who know the administrative password for the computer can install programs.

- When downloading a program, you'll have to decide whether you want to Run or Save the file you're downloading.

  - If you choose Run, the program will install immediately. So you can start it from the Start menu as soon as you've completed the download and installation.

  - If you choose Save, the program will be downloaded but not installed. You'll need to open the downloaded file to install the program. Once installed, you'll start the program from the Start menu.

- Use the Start button and All Programs menu to open any installed program.

Chapter 41

Installing and Upgrading Programs

Unlike documents, which you can freely copy to your hard disk and use on the spot, any new program you acquire needs to be installed before you can use it. The installation process configures the software to work with your particular hardware and software. The process also creates an icon or program group on your All Programs menu so that you can start the new program as you would any other.

You need to install a program only once, not each time you intend to use it. Once you've installed a program from a disk, you can put the disk from which you installed away for safe keeping. You'll need the original installation disk to reinstall the program only if you accidentally delete it from your hard disk or if some sort of hard disk crash damages the program on your hard disk.

IN THIS CHAPTER

Playing it safe with program installations

Updates versus upgrades

Installing programs from disks

Playing It Safe with Program Installations

Programs you buy in a store aren't likely to contain any malicious code such as viruses, worms, or spyware. Those things tend to be spread by e-mail attachments and freebie downloads from the Web. However, there's always an outside chance that the new program is incompatible with Windows Vista or a hardware device on your computer. So there may be times when you need to uninstall a program and then get all your system files back into shape to undo any changes made to your system by the new program.

Windows Vista's System Protection greatly simplifies the task of getting things back in shape should a program installation or upgrade cause problems. But it only helps if it's turned on and you know how to use it. For details see "Using System Protection" in Chapter 33.

Updates versus Upgrades

Normal (non-nerd) people often assume that updates and upgrades are the same thing. They aren't. An *update* is usually something you do online. There is nothing to buy at a store, no disk to insert in a disk drive. Updates are generally free, and automatic. So you don't have to make an effort to seek those out and install them.

Updates for some programs may not be quite so automatic. But you can often find out if any updates are available right from the program's Help menu. For example, in many Microsoft Office programs, you can choose Help ➪ Check for Updates from the program's menu bar to see what free updates are available for that program.

Unlike updates, upgrades are usually not free. You have to purchase them and install them. For example, let's say you have Microsoft Office XP or 2003 installed on a computer. You want to get Office 2007 on that computer. In that case, you'd seek out an Office 2007 *Upgrade Edition* (which is cheaper than the regular edition). Then you'd install that upgrade edition right over your existing version. In other words, you wouldn't uninstall (remove) your existing version first.

Installing and Upgrading from a Disk

Before we get started here, know that you must have administrative privileges to install a program. In other words, you need to know the password for an administrative account on your computer. If you have a limited user account and don't know the administrative password, you'll need to get an administrator to install the program for you.

Most programs that you purchase will be delivered on a CD or DVD disk. You should always follow the installation instructions that come with such a program. But just so you know what to expect, here's how the process usually works, once you have the CD (or DVD) in hand:

1. Close all open program windows on your desktop by clicking their Close buttons or by right-clicking their taskbar buttons and choosing Close. You want to start from a clean Windows desktop.

 You don't need to close programs whose icons are in the Notification area, unless specifically instructed to by the installation instructions for the program you're installing.

2. Insert the CD or DVD into your computer's CD or DVD drive and wait a few seconds.

3. Wait for the installation program to appear on your screen. If it doesn't appear within 30 seconds, see "Using the installed program" later in this chapter.

4. Follow the onscreen instructions to perform the installation.

That really is all there is to it. You will be presented with some questions and options along the way. Exactly what you see varies from one program to the next. But some common items include the End User License Agreement (EULA), and choosing a folder in which to store the program, which I'll discuss in a moment.

If nothing happens within half a minute or so after inserting a program's installation CD into your computer's CD drive, you may need to start the installation program manually. Here's how:

1. Open your Computer folder (click the Start button and choose Computer).

2. Open the icon that represents the drive into which you placed the disk.

3. If the installation program doesn't start automatically in a few seconds, open the icon named Setup or Setup.exe. (Click or double-click that icon.)

That should be enough to get the installation program started. From there you can follow the onscreen instructions to complete the installation.

The onscreen instructions and prompts you see during the installation will vary from one program to the next. In the next section I'll discuss some common things you're likely to come across when installing just about any program.

 You need not install a program every time you want to use it. You need only install the program once. From then on you can run it from the Start menu without the installation disk.

Common Installation Prompts

Even though every program is unique in some ways, there are some elements you're likely to come across during a program installation. When you install a program, you probably won't see all the prompts described in the sections to follow. So don't be alarmed if your installation procedure is much simpler. (Be thankful instead.)

The initial CD or DVD prompt

Shortly after you insert the installation disk for a program, you may see a prompt like the one in Figure 41.1. Your choice there is easy—click the Run SETUP.EXE option.

First prompt after inserting an installation CD.

Prove you have the right

Only people with administrative privileges can install programs in Windows Vista. If you're signed into a limited account, you'll see a dialog box similar to the one shown in Figure 41.2. To install the program, you'll need to enter an administrative password. Then click Submit.

The product key or serial number

Some programs (especially Microsoft's) require that you enter a product key or serial number to install the program. That number is usually on a sticker on the case or sleeve in which the program was delivered.

FIGURE 41.2

Prove you're an administrator.

> **TIP**   You may want to write down all your product keys on a sheet of paper in case you ever need to re-install everything. Belarc (`www.belarc.com`) offers a free program that will list the product keys for all your installed programs, as well as a good deal more useful information about your systems. One of those free program's that's worth its proverbial weight in gold!

If you do need to enter a product key or serial number, you'll see a prompt like the example shown in Figure 41.3. Type in the product key very carefully, because if you get it wrong, you'll be prompted to enter it again. Click Next after you type in the product key.

FIGURE 41.3

Enter a product key.

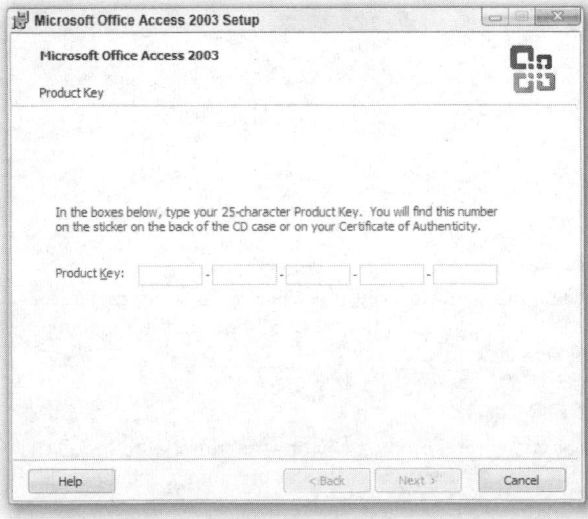

Compliance check

If you are installing the Upgrade edition of a new program, and don't already have a previous edition of the program installed, you'll see a prompt like the one in Figure 41.4. This part can be tricky and confusing. So let's take it slow and easy.

FIGURE 41.4

Enter a previous version's CD.

First you need to choose the drive into which you'll be inserting the previous version's CD. This, of course, will be the CD or DVD drive (or one of your CD drives). If you only have one drive, it will be the same one that currently contains the new program's CD. So you'll need to press the eject button on the drive, remove that CD, replace it with the older version's CD, and close the drive door.

You might see a message asking what you want to do with the CD you just inserted. You do *not* want to install the program on the CD. The goal here is to simply prove you have the older version, not to install the older version. So if you do see a dialog box asking what you want to do with the CD, click the Close (X) button in the upper-right corner of that dialog box. Then click OK in the box shown in Figure 41.4.

Assuming you entered a qualifying CD, you'll probably be taken to the next page of the current program's installation procedure. But, you can't forge ahead until you get the old CD out of the drive and the new program's back in. After you make the switch, you might again see the prompt asking what you want to do with the CD you just inserted. Again, you should just close that message box (if it appears) without running its setup program.

User information prompt

Some programs will offer prompts like the ones in Figure 41.5. These are optional, but useful. The User Name will automatically be entered as the Author name in any documents you create with the program. The initials will be used in settings where multiple people edit documents to identify changes you made to the document.

Click Next after filling in the blanks.

FIGURE 41.5

User information page.

The End User License Agreement (EULA)

Just about every commercial program requires that you accept the End User License Agreement (EULA) as part of the installation process. Figure 41.6 shows an example. The agreement is a bunch of legalese that basically says you have the right to install and use the program on one computer. You do not have the right to sell or give away copies. You can't install the program if you don't accept the terms of the agreement, so choose (check) the "I accept..." option and click Next.

Type of installation

Sometimes you'll be given some choices as to how and where you want to install the program. I suggest you choose Complete Installation, as in Figure 41.7. Otherwise, months later you may go to use some advanced or esoteric feature of the program only to get an error message saying it's not installed. Of course by then you will have long since forgotten that you didn't do a complete install, leaving you wondering what the heck is wrong and where you can go to find the missing component.

As to the "where" to install the program, there is rarely any reason to change the suggested location. That will typically be some folder in C:\Program Files. Don't change that unless you really know what you're doing and have some good reason for doing it. Whatever you do, don't make the common newbie mistake of installing it in your Documents folder or someplace like that. You're not installing a document. You're installing a program. And it's best to keep all your programs in subfolders under C:\Program Files.

Click Next to move onto the next page of the installation process.

FIGURE 41.6

Sample End User License Agreement.

FIGURE 41.7

Type of installation.

Installation summary

The next page of the procedure may just give you a summary of what you chose along the way. This includes a Back button so you can back up and correct any goof ups. Figure 41.8 shows an example.

FIGURE 41.8

Installation summary.

You're almost finished at this point. Just click the Install button and wait for the program to install.

Setup completed

The last page of the installation options might offer a couple of final options, like in the example shown in Figure 41.9. Whether or not you choose these options is relatively unimportant. You can check the Web for updates and additional downloads at any time, usually by choosing Help ➪ Check for Updates from the installed program's menu bar.

Keeping the installation files can make it easier to change program settings or install missing components in the future. They don't take up any significant amount of disk space. Click Finish, remove the CD from the drive, and put it someplace safe in case you ever need to re-install in the future.

 **Most insurance policies don't cover computer software. So if at all possible, consider keeping your original program CDs in a fireproof safe.**

Using the installed program

Once the program is installed, you can run it from the Start menu. In the preceding steps, I installed Microsoft Office Access 2003. So to run it, I'd click the Start button, choose All Programs ➪ Microsoft Office, then click Microsoft Office Access 2003, as shown in Figure 41.10.

FIGURE 41.9

Setup complete.

FIGURE 41.10

Running the program.

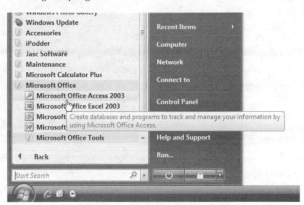

Wrap Up

Installing programs from CDs is easy to do. It's basically a matter of putting the program installation CD into your CD drive and following the onscreen instructions. Here's a quick summary of the main points presented in this chapter:

- Consider creating a protection point before installing any program. That way, if the new program creates problems, you can uninstall and return to the protection point to undo every change made during the program installation.

- You need only install a program once, not each time you want to use it. Once installed, you run the program from the Start menu, without the program CD in the drive.

- If you're upgrading a program that's already installed, do not remove the existing version.

- Standard operating procedure for installing a new program is to insert the program's installation CD and follow the onscreen instructions.

- If nothing happens within a minute of inserting the installation CD, open your Computer folder, open the icon for the CD drive, and double-click the Setup or Setup.exe icon on the CD.

- When the installation is complete, store the installation CD in a safe place. You won't need it to run the program. But you may need it to re-install the program should some mishap cause you to lose the program.

Chapter 42

Getting Older Programs to Run

You can run just about any program that's installed on your computer just by clicking its startup icon on the All Programs menu. But, there are always exceptions to the rule. Chief among the list of exceptions are old programs that were originally written to work with earlier versions of Windows. Or, even worse, programs that were written to run on DOS.

That's not to say Windows *can't* run old programs. Most of the time, it can run an older program as is, without any messing about or tweaking things at all on your part. Especially if the program was written for Windows XP. So, before you assume that you have to do something to try to get an older program to run, try running the program normally. If it runs, you're done. If it won't run, then this is the chapter you need to (hopefully) get the program to run.

What Makes a Program "Old"

In the software world, there's *old* and there's *really old* (as in ancient). Those aren't official buzzwords. But ancient would be 16-bit and old would be pre-Windows XP 32-bit. Let's take a minute to discuss what the 16-bit/32-bit business is about.

The smallest unit of information that the computer works with is called a *bit*, short for binary digit. A bit can have one of two possible values, 0 or 1. We could say the bit can be "on" or "off," or "True" or "False," or whatever. But anyway you slice it, a bit can only have one of two possible values.

The workhorse inside any computer is the *microprocessor*, or *processor* for short. It's a chip about the size of your thumbnail in which electrons, representing bits, zoom around at the speed of light (186,000 miles per second). The amount of work a processor can do in any given time depends heavily on how many bits it can work with at a time.

The earliest PCs were built around Intel's 16-bit 8086 and 80286 processors. Microsoft's operating system of the day was called DOS (pronounced *DAW-sss*), which stood for Disk Operating System. In the 1980s, Intel released the 32-bit 80386 processor, which in turn was followed by the 80486 and the Pentium and Celeron processors used in most computers today.

Despite the fact that processors had evolved to 32-bit processing power, the 16-bit DOS operating system hung around for years. DOS largely became "hidden" behind products like Windows 3.1, Windows 95, Windows 98, and Windows ME. But hidden or not, its 16-bit heritage never really allowed it to take full advantage of modern 32-bit processors.

Microsoft did, eventually, develop a 32-bit operating system. Initially it was marketed as Windows NT (for New Technology), and eventually it became Windows 2000. But those programs were marketed primarily to corporations. Casual computers tended to slog on through one 16-bit version of Windows to the next.

The year 2001 changed all that when Microsoft released Windows XP. Windows XP is a true 32-bit operating system that's marketed to both individuals and corporations. The release of Windows XP was the death knell for 16-bit computing. Microsoft has not created any 16-bit software since the release of Windows XP, nor will it ever create any 16-bit software in the future. I'm sure that the same can be said of virtually every software company in business today.

Despite its radically different look, Windows Vista is still a 32-bit operating system like Windows XP. (Unless, of course, you're using a 64-bit version of Vista on a 64-bit computer.) Most application programs that ran in Windows XP should run fine in Vista without any tweaking. Programs that run a little close to the metal, like antivirus programs and utility programs, may not be as easy to run as basic productivity applications.

Ancient history, today, and the future

These days, 16-bit computing is ancient history, 32-bit is mainstream, and 64-bit computing is available but not quite mainstream. You might look at the numbers 16, 32, and 64 and think "Big deal, how much difference could a few bits make?" You'd be mistaken there, however, because each number is an exponent to the number 2 and the differences are enormous.

The number of bits that the processor can handle at once defines the number of unique addresses that the processor can address directly (referred to as *addressable memory*). Simply stated, the more addressable memory, the more the computer can do within a given time frame. When you realize that the numbers involved are exponents of 2, and you do the math, you can see that the differences between 16-, 32-, and 64-bit computing, in terms of addressable memory, are truly astronomical, as summarized in Table 42.1.

TABLE 42.1

Processor Technology and Directly Addressable Memory

Technology	Meaning	Memory Addresses
16-bit	2^{16}	65,536
32-bit	2^{32}	4,294,967,296
64-bit	2^{64}	18,446,744,073,709,600,000

NOTE A 64-bit processor can directly address about 18,000,000,000 GB of RAM. Yes, that's 18 billion gigabytes, and a lot more than the 4-GB maximum of today's 32-bit processors! Current processors get over their limitations by indirectly addressing memory beyond their limitations. But that indirect addressing adds some processing overhead that slows things down a little.

So what does any of this have to do with getting older programs to run in Windows Vista? Basically an "old program" is a 16-bit program, or a program that was written to run on Windows 95, 98, or ME. An *ancient* program would be some little game you run right from a floppy disk (though "ancient" isn't an official buzzword). Many such programs were written before there were such things as program windows occupying only a portion of the screen, even before there was any need to install a program to a hard disk!

Old programs to avoid altogether

Windows Vista is much more than Windows XP with a facelift. What you see on the screen is only a snowflake on the tip of the proverbial iceberg. Well over 99 percent of what really is Windows Vista is hidden from view and never appears on your screen. That hidden stuff is *really* new in Vista, and many XP and other programs simply will not work. As mentioned, many of your basic XP application programs will work. But there are other kinds of programs you should seriously consider staying away from. These include:

- **Old disk utility programs:** Older disk utility programs such as Norton Utilities and various disk compression and partitioning tools should never be run on Windows Vista. Many older CD-burning programs are likely to cause problems too. If you have such a program, you should really upgrade to the Vista version of that program, or find a similar product that's designed to work with Windows Vista.

- **Old backup programs:** If you have an older backup program, using it in compatibility mode could prove disastrous. Even if you're able to perform the backup, there's an outside chance you won't be able to restore from the backup if and when you need to. Consider using Windows Backup, which came with your copy of Vista.

- **Old cleanup programs:** Older programs that purport to keep your computer running in tip-top shape, clean up your registry, and so forth should not be used at all in Vista. If you like the program, look into getting a version that's specifically written for Windows Vista.

- **Old optimizing programs:** Programs designed to make your XP or other computer run at maximum performance won't necessarily make Vista run that way. In fact, they may do a lot more harm than good. If you use such programs, check to see if there's a Vista version available before you install the old XP version.

- **Old antivirus programs:** Virus detection and removal is dicey business, and needs to be handled with great care. Antivirus programs written for pre-Vista versions of Windows should never be installed or run on a Windows Vista computer. The same goes for anti-spyware and other anti-malware programs. Better to seek out a Vista version of the program than to presume the XP version will work.

Installing Incompatible Programs

To install an older program, first try installing it normally. For example, if it's on a CD, insert the CD and wait for the installation program to appear automatically. If nothing starts automatically, open your Computer folder (click Start and choose Computer). Then open the icon for the drive that contains the installation disk. Then double-click the setup launcher program (typically setup.exe, setup, install.exe, or install). If Windows Vista determines that the program is older, you'll see the Program Compatibility Advisor shown in Figure 42.1.

FIGURE 42.1

Program Compatibility Advisor.

If the program installed normally, just click the second option. Otherwise, click the first option. Windows Vista will assign some compatibility mode attributes to the program and try the installation again. Hopefully, the second try will do the trick.

If you still have problems, here are some things to consider:

- If you're installing from a standard user account, log out and log in to an administrative account, then try to install from that account.
- If you have to create any file or folder names, use old 8.3 conventions (keep filenames to eight characters maximum with no blank spaces).
- If you get stuck in an installation program, use the Applications tab in Task Manager to end the stuck program. See Chapter 45 for details on Task Manager.

If all else fails, contact the program publisher (if they're still in business). They're the only ones who really know if the program will even run in Vista, and what's required to get it to run.

Using the Program Compatibility Wizard

Installing a program is one thing; getting it to run after it's installed is another. If an installed program won't start or isn't working right, try using the Program Compatibility Wizard on it.

The Program Compatibility Wizard provides a step-by-step means of configuring and testing an older program so that it will run in Windows Vista. Before you bother to use it, try running the installed program without it. I mention this because I've seen people spend much time messing with this on the assumption that it's needed. When in fact, the assumption was wrong and they could have just run the program as-is!

If you're sure an installed program isn't running, or is not running correctly, follow these steps to start the Program Compatibility Wizard:

1. Click the Start button and choose All Programs ⇨ Accessories ⇨ Program Compatibility Wizard.
2. Read the first wizard page and click Next>.
3. On the second wizard page, shown in Figure 42.2, choose whichever option best describes what you want to do:

FIGURE 42.2

First selections in the Program Compatibility Wizard.

- **I want to choose from a list of programs:** If the program is already installed and has an icon on the All Programs menu, choose this option.
- **I want to use the program in the CD-ROM drive:** If the program isn't installed and needs to be installed or run from a CD, choose this option.
- **I want to locate the program manually:** If the program isn't on the All Programs menu, but you know the path and filename of the program, choose this option.

4. Follow the instructions on the next wizard page. For example, if you chose the first option, scroll through the list of program names and click the program you want to run in compatibility mode. Then click Next>.
5. On the next page, choose the operating system that the program was written for, or the last operating system on which you were able to run the program. Then click Next>
6. The next wizard page will ask about display settings, such as 256 colors, 640 x 480 screen resolution, and visual themes. If the program is an old game or educational program that fills the entire screen with simple graphics, choose all three options. If the program runs in a program window, you probably don't need to choose any of those options. Click Next>.
7. The next page asks about running the program with full administrative privileges. Choose that option only if you're an administrator and the program doesn't run at all. Click Next>.
8. You're taken to a summary of your selected options. Click Next> again to test your choices.

The rest is trial-and-error. If the program runs, great. You can answer accordingly in the wizard and be done with it. Otherwise you can try some different settings until you can get the program to work right.

There's no guarantee that the Program Compatibility Wizard will make the program run. Some programs are so old, and so far removed from modern computing capabilities, that there's just no way to force them to run. In those cases, the only hope is to contact the program publisher to see if they have any solutions or a compatible version of the program.

Quick-and-Dirty Program Compatibility

The Program Compatibility Wizard provides an easy way to choose and test settings for program compatibility. Those settings are stored on the Compatibility tab of the program file's Properties sheet. You can change settings right in the Properties sheet by following these steps:

1. Click the Start button, choose All Programs, and get to the startup icon that you'd normally click to run the program.
2. Right-click the program's startup icon and choose Properties.
3. In the Properties dialog box that opens, click the Compatibility tab. You'll see the options shown in Figure 42.3.

FIGURE 42.3

Compatibly settings.

4. Choose the operating system for which the program was written.
5. If the program is an old game or educational program, choose appropriate Display settings.

6. To turn off advanced text services such as speech recognition (which probably wouldn't work anyway), choose the option to turn off those features for the program.

7. Click OK.

The compatibility settings will stick to the program. So you can just start the program normally, from the All Programs menu, at any time. Though again, there's no guarantee that you'll be able to force all programs to run in Windows Vista.

Doing DOS Commands in Windows Vista

Readers who have been in this game since the DOS days might still wish to enter the occasional DOS command. DOS commands will let you do things you can't really do in Windows. For example, in those rare instances where you can't delete a file in Windows, using a DOS erase or del command with the /F switch will often do the trick. You can use the DOS dir command to print filenames from a folder to paper or a text file.

There is one big catch to use commands in Vista. UAC may prevent you from doing things you'd otherwise take for granted. You can get around many of those by using the Run As Administrator option to get to the command prompt. Here are two different ways to get to the Command Prompt window:

- Click the Start button and choose All Programs ⇨ Accessories ⇨ Command Prompt. Or right-click Command Prompt and choose Run As Administrator.

- Press ⊞, type cmd, and choose cmd.exe or right-click cmd.exe and choose Run as Administrator.

The Command Prompt window that opens is much like DOS. By default you're taken to the home directory for your user account. But you can navigate around using the DOS cd command. For example, enter cd .. to go to the parent directory, or cd \program files to go to the Program Files folders.

To see a list of all supported commands, enter help at the command prompt. For the syntax of a command, type the command followed by /?. For example, entering dir /? displays the help for the dir command.

> **NOTE** You can make the Command Prompt window as tall as you like. But its maximum width is about 640 pixels.

You can copy-and-paste a lengthy path name from a file's Properties sheet to a cd command. In Windows, right-click any icon within the folder of interest and choose Properties. Drag the mouse pointer through the path name next to Location to select it, as in Figure 42.4, and press Ctrl+C to copy it.

> **TIP** To see the name you need to type in order to launch any program, right-click the program's icon on the All Programs menu and choose Properties. The filename at the end of the Target path is the name you type in the Search or Run box.

In the Command Prompt window, type cd and a space. Then right-click the Command Prompt window and choose Paste. Press Enter, and you'll be in that folder.

FIGURE 42.4

Select a directory path.

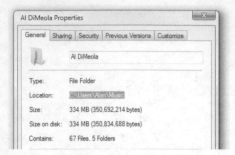

Use the `dir` command with various switches to view, or optionally print, all the filenames in a folder and also its subfolders if you like. For example, let's say you navigate to the Music folder for your account (`C:\Users\yourUserName\Music`). From that folder, entering

`dir /s`

lists all file and folder names for all artists, albums, and songs in your Music folder.

You can use the `/b`, `/n/`, and `/w` switches to choose how you want the information displayed. For example, entering

`dir /s /w`

shows filenames in the wide format.

To send `dir` output directly to the printer, try

`dir /s /w > prn`

You're probably better off sending the output to a text file rather than straight to the printer. That way you can open and edit the text file before you print. Or even import it into Excel or Access to make it more like tabular data. To send output to a file, end the command with a filename (or path and filename). For example, entering this command from the Music folder

`dir /s /w >MyMusic.txt`

puts the output listing in a file named `MyMusic.txt` in the Music folder. You can then open that file with any text editor or word processor to clean it up. If you have database management skills, you can import the data to Access or a similar program and treat it like any other tabular data.

> **CAUTION** This section is just a side topic for people who are already familiar with DOS. Don't experiment with DOS commands carelessly. You could lose a lot of files and have no means of getting them back!

To exit the Command Prompt window, enter the `exit` command or just close its window.

Wrap Up

This chapter has focused on techniques for getting older programs to work in Windows Vista. Windows Vista offers several tools to help with compatibility issues. Whether or not you have any luck with them depends on how old and how incompatible the program is. Windows Vista is a big change. As big a change as the one from DOS to Windows in 1990. Don't expect all your old programs to work. Many won't, until you upgrade to the Vista version. The main points are as follows:

- Programs written for Windows XP and later are already compatible with Vista and require no special handling.

- When you attempt to install an older program, the Program Compatibility Advisor kicks in automatically to help out.

- The Program Compatibility Wizard helps you with installed programs that won't start or run correctly.

- Compatibility settings are stored in the program file's Properties sheet, on the Compatibility tab.

- To use DOS commands in Vista with minimal flack from UAC, choose Run as Administrator to open the Command Prompt window.

Chapter 43

Repairing and Removing Programs

Many thousands of programs run on Windows Vista. Nobody owns them all or needs them all. In fact, a lifetime isn't enough time to even learn to use them all. Finding programs you like and can use is often a trial-and-error process.

In this chapter, you learn techniques for managing installed programs. You learn how to change or repair programs, as well as to remove programs you no longer need or want. You'll do most of these tasks on Control Panel's Programs and Features page.

Changing and Repairing Programs

Some large programs let you choose how you want to install the program. For example, you may be given options to do a Minimum Install, Typical Install, or Complete Install. You might do a Minimum or Typical installation to conserve disk space. Then later discover you need a feature that only the Complete install would have provided.

Sometimes a large program might become *corrupted* and not work properly anymore. That can happen when you inadvertently delete a file that the program needed. Or it might be caused by some minor glitch that compromised a file that the program uses.

The first step to changing or repairing a program is to get to the Programs and Features page in Control Panel. Here's how:

1. Click the Start button and choose Control Panel.
2. In the category view, click Programs.
3. Click Programs and Features.

You can also get to Programs and Features from the keyboard. Press ▦, type fea, and choose Programs and Features from the Start menu.

The page that opens lists all of your installed application programs. (It doesn't include programs that come with Windows Vista.)

Not all programs offer change or repair options. Typically only large programs that you purchase and install from CD offer those features. To see what options an installed program offers, right-click the program name. Or, click the program name and take a look at the buttons above the list of program names. Things you can do with that program will be listed in a toolbar above the list. For example, in Figure 43.1, I clicked Microsoft Office, which offers options to Uninstall, Change, or Repair.

FIGURE 43.1

List of installed programs.

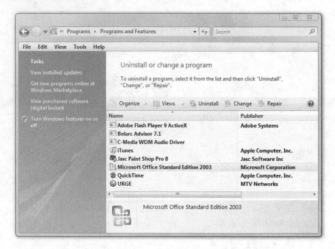

In most cases, you'll need the CD from which you originally installed the program to change or repair the program. If you have the CD handy, go ahead and put it in the CD drive. If AutoPlay asks what you want to do with the disk, choose Take no Action. Or if the program to install opens automatically, just cancel or close that program.

> **NOTE**   Changes you make to a program affect all users. Therefore you must know the password for an Administrator account on your computer to change or repair programs.

Exactly how things play out from here will vary from one program to the next, so I can only provide some general guidelines and examples. But all you really have to do is make your selections and follow the instructions on the screen. For example, to repair a corrupted program, click the Repair button and do whatever the next page to open tells you to do.

The Change option for a program is about adding components you didn't install the first time around, though you can also remove any components you don't need. The exact process will vary from one program to the next. But a typical approach is to list all program features in a hierarchical tree, like the example in Figure 43.2.

> **NOTE**   Don't use Programs and Features to change settings within a program. Instead, use the program's Options or Preferences dialog box. Open the program as you normally would and look through its menus for a Tools or Preferences option. Or search that program's help for the word *preferences* or *options*.

FIGURE 43.2

Click an optional component.

In the tree, click a program feature to choose an action. For example, choose Run From My Computer to install a feature. To remove an optional feature, choose Not Available. That feature will be removed and its icon will display a red X. When you're finished making your selections, click OK or Next and follow the onscreen instructions.

Removing (Uninstalling) Programs

Unlike documents and other files, copying a program to your hard disk isn't enough to make it usable. You have to *install* programs before you can use them. Likewise, simply deleting the startup icon for a program isn't enough to remove the program from your system. You have to *uninstall* the program. All of this is because a program often consists of many files. For example, Microsoft Office contains more than 600 files! Furthermore, installing a program makes other changes to the system. Uninstalling is necessary to undo those changes.

NOTE You must be logged in to an administrative account, or know the administrator password for your PC, to remove a program.

Before you remove (uninstall) any program, make sure you know what you're removing and why. Just because you don't know what a program is or what purpose it serves, that doesn't mean you should remove it. Removing programs isn't likely to solve any computer programs. So you shouldn't remove a program as a means of solving some problem through sheer guesswork. The following caution provides a second reason why you should never remove programs in a willy-nilly manner.

CAUTION There is no Undo or Recycle Bin for reinstating removed programs. The only way to get a removed program back is to reinstall it from its original installation CD or download it again from the original Web site.

With all those cautions out of the way, removing a program is quite simple. Assuming you're already on the Programs and Features page, right-click the name of the program you want to remove and choose Remove. Or, select that program's icon or name and click the Remove button in the toolbar. If prompted, enter an administrative password. Follow any additional instructions that appear on the screen.

Uninstalling from the All Programs menu

If you don't find a program that you want to remove in Programs and Features, you might still be able to remove it right from the All Programs menu. Click the Start button, choose All Programs, and then look for an Uninstall or Remove option like the example in Figure 43.3. If you find such an option, you can click it to remove the program from your system.

FIGURE 43.3

Uninstall from the All Programs menu.

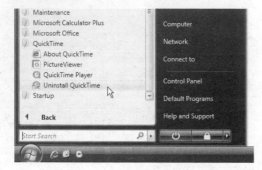

Dealing with stuck programs

Occasionally you might come across a situation where removing a program generates an error message before the program is completely removed. The first thing to do, of course, is to read the error message and see what options it offers. You may be able to finish the removal just by choosing options that the error message provides.

If you can't get rid of a program through the normal means or error message, your next best bet would be to install the program again. That might seem counterproductive. But the problem might be that the program only partially installed in the first place. A partially installed program may not have enough stuff installed to do a thorough removal. Once you've completed the initial installation, you should be able to remove the program without any problems.

Returning to a Previous Version

NEW FEATURE Returning to the previous version of a program is a quick and easy way to deal with program updates that cause more problems than they solve.

It seems computer programs are never done. Every program evolves through versions, each version a little bigger and better than its predecessor. But sometimes the latest and greatest version of a program won't quite work correctly on your computer. When that happens, you may be able to return to the previous version of the program with minimal fuss. Get to the program's startup icon on the All Programs menu and right-click it. If you see a Restore Previous Versions option like in Figure 43.4, click it. Then follow the onscreen instructions to return to the previous version.

FIGURE 43.4

Restore the previous version of a program.

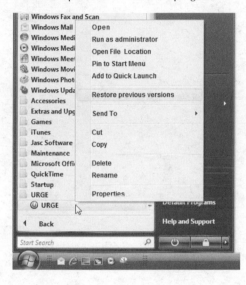

Updates to programs are a little different than upgrades and can't always be removed using the Restore Previous Versions option. But should an update cause problems on your system, you can remove it. Click View installed updates in the left column of the Programs and Features window. The list of installed programs changes to a list of installed updates. As with programs, you can click an installed update to remove or change it.

Turning Windows Features On and Off

NEW FEATURE   Unlike Add/Remove Windows Programs in Windows XP, Program Features in Vista allows you to turn features on and off without the hassles of installing and uninstalling.

Windows Vista comes with many programs and features built right in. How many depends on which edition of Windows Vista you purchased. Regardless of the version you bought, there may be some features you do want to use and some you don't.

To turn Windows Features on or off, get to the Programs and Features dialog box discussed earlier in this chapter. (Press ⊞, type fea, and choose Programs and Features.) A list of available Windows Features opens as in Figure 43.5. Items that are checked are currently installed and working. Unchecked features are not active. A filled checkbox represents a feature that's active, but also has additional subfeatures. Click the + sign next to a feature to see what subfeatures it offers.

FIGURE 43.5

Windows Features.

Only turn off program features that you know and are certain you don't need. If you don't know what a feature is or does, better to err in favor of keeping it active than to find out, the hard way, that you shouldn't have disabled it!

The rest is easy. To disable a feature or subfeature, clear its checkbox. To enable a disabled feature, click its empty checkbox to select it. Click OK after making your changes.

Wrap Up

Managing installed programs in Windows Vista is easy enough. It all takes place through the Programs and Features page. Here's a quick review of what's involved:

- You need administrative privileges to change, repair, or remove programs.

- Use Programs and Features to change, repair, or remove installed programs (click the Start button and choose Control Panel ➪ Programs ➪ Programs and Features).

- To see what options an installed program offers, click its name in Programs and Features and look at the buttons in the toolbar.

- Repairing a program generally involves reinstalling it from the original CD.

- Changing a program refers to installing features you didn't choose initially or removing features you don't use.

- Uninstalling a program removes it from your computer and from all user accounts.

- If a program upgrade creates problems on your system, use Restore to Previous Version on the startup icon's shortcut menu to revert to the previous working version.

- The Programs and Features window also provides an option to turn Windows features on and off.

Chapter 44

Setting Default Programs

A s everyone knows, there are many different brands of toothpaste, shampoo, cars, and just about every other kind of product you can buy. The same is true of software. Everyone uses a Web browser to browse the Internet. And there are many different brands of Web browsers to choose from. There's Internet Explorer, which comes with Windows Vista. There's also AOL Explorer, Firefox, and Netscape to name a few.

For media players, Windows Vista comes with Media Player, Media Center, or both depending on which version of Vista you have. In addition to those, there's QuickTime, Musicmatch, and many others. When you have two or more programs capable of handling the same type of document, you might want to make one the *default program* that opens automatically when you open a document. Setting such defaults is what this chapter is all about.

IN THIS CHAPTER

Setting default programs for documents

Setting defaults for your user account

Setting default actions for disks and devices

Setting defaults for all users

Setting Default Programs for Documents

Documents are files that you create (or download) yourself. Typed text, pictures, music files, and video clips are all examples of documents. There are thousands of different types of documents. Each document is a particular *type* as indicated by its filename extension. For example, a picture might be a JPEG (.jpeg or .jpg), bitmap (.bmp), GIF (.gif), TIFF (.tif or .TIFF), Portable Network Graphics (.PNG), or any of a couple dozen other formats.

When you click (or double-click) a document icon, the document opens in whatever is the *default program* for its type. If you have more than one program that can open the document type, you can override the default and open the document with some other program. Right-click the document icon and choose Open With as in Figure 44.1. The Open With option will be available only if you have two or more programs installed that can open that type of document.

FIGURE 44.1

Sample Open With options for a JPEG picture.

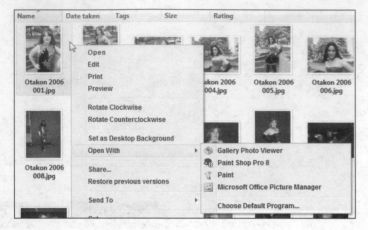

If you want to keep the current default program for this type of document, and override that just this time, click the name of the program you want to use to open the document.

If you want to change the default program that Windows always uses to open that type of document, click Change Default Program at the bottom of the Open With menu. The Open With dialog box shown in Figure 44.2 opens.

FIGURE 44.2

The Open With dialog box.

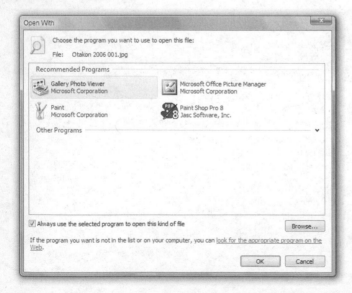

I Don't See Any Filename Extensions

If Windows is configured to hide filename extensions, you won't see them in your Pictures folder or other document folders. But you can point to a document icon and see the filename extension in the tooltip that appears at the mouse pointer. Optionally, you can make filename extensions visible by clearing the checkmark next to Hide extensions for known file types in Folder Options. You can open the Folder Options dialog box from the Organize button in any folder. Or open Control Panel, choose Appearance and Personalization, and then choose Folder Options. In the Folder Options dialog box, click the View tab and scroll down to the "Hide extensions. . ." option.

Click whatever program you want to use for opening that type of document. Also, make sure the Always use the selected program to open this kind of file option is selected (checked). Otherwise your new choice won't be saved.

If you can't find the program you want to use as the default, you can click the Browse button to look for it. Just make sure that the program you want to use is capable of opening that type of document.

Setting default programs using the Open With dialog box is just one way to do it. Many programs have options within them that let you choose which file types you want to associate with the program. The settings within the program might even override the settings you specify in Windows. So sometimes you have to go into the program that's acting as the default for a file type, and make a change there.

Unfortunately there's no one-rule-fits-all for the hundreds of programs that allow you to change associations within a program. Typically you start by opening the program and choosing Tools ⇨ Options or Edit ⇨ Preferences or something like that, to get to the program's main options. To illustrate, I'll use QuickTime (Version 7) as an example, because many people have that program.

In QuickTime, you first open the QuickTime player from the All Programs menu, or by double-clicking its Notification area icon. Then choose Edit ⇨ Preferences ⇨ QuickTime Preferences from its menu bar. Click the File Types tab, and you're taken to a dialog box where you can specify file types that should open automatically in QuickTime. Select (check) the file types you do want to open in QuickTime automatically. Clear the checkmarks for those file types for which QuickTime should not act as the default program. Figure 44.3 shows an example.

Of course, there's no right or wrong program to associate with a given file type. The choice is up to you. You just have to make sure to always specify a program that *can* open files of a given type. For example, it wouldn't make sense to associate video or audio files with Microsoft Word or Excel, because those programs don't play multimedia files.

File Types preferences for QuickTime 7.

Using the Default Programs Page

Right-clicking a document's icon and choosing Open With is the quick-and-easy way to set a default program on the fly. But it's not the only method. And you're not limited to setting defaults based on file types either. You can also set defaults for *protocols*. A protocol is a standardized way of doing things. Different Internet services use different protocols. For example, the Web uses HTTP, which stands for Hypertext Transfer Protocol.

You can also set default actions for CDs, DVDs, and devices you connect to you computer. Use the Default Programs page in Control Panel to set all of these different kinds of defaults. To get there use whichever method is easiest for you:

- Click the Start button and choose Control Panel ➪ Programs ➪ Default Programs.
- Press ⊞, type def, and choose Default Programs.

You'll see the options shown in Figure 44.4 and summarized here.

- **Set your default programs:** Use this option to choose default programs for your user account only.
- **Associate a file type or protocol with a program:** Like the preceding item, except you start by choosing a file type or protocol rather than a program.
- **Change AutoPlay settings:** Use this option to change what happens when you insert a CD or DVD, or connect a camera to your computer.
- **Set program access and computer defaults:** This one is strictly for administrators. It sets defaults for Internet access and media players for all user accounts.

The sections that follow describe each option.

FIGURE 44.4

Default Programs page.

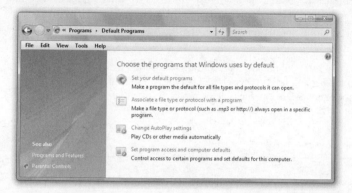

Set your Default Programs

The first item in Default Programs lets you pick and choose which file types and protocols you want to associate with programs. When you click that option, you're taken to a page like the one in Figure 44.5.

FIGURE 44.5

Choose a program in the left column.

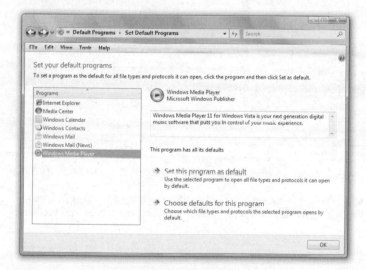

Click a program name in the left column to see a description of that program in the right column. Then you can choose one of the following options below that description:

- **Set this program as the default:** Choose this option to make the selected program the default for all file types and protocols it can handle.
- **Choose defaults for this program:** Limit the program to act as the default for only certain file types and protocols.

Choosing the second option takes you to a list of all the file types and protocols that program supports, as in Figure 44.6. You can scroll through the list and select (check) the file types and protocols for which the program should act as default. Clear the checkbox of any file type or protocol for which you want some other program to act as the default. Then click Save to return to the previous page.

FIGURE 44.6

Choose file types and protocols for a program.

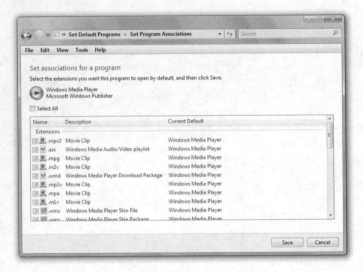

When you've finished choosing defaults for programs, click OK to return to the main Default Programs page.

Associate a file type or protocol with a program

The second option in Default Programs is similar to the first. But rather than starting with a program, you start with a file type or protocol. When you click "Associate a file type or protocol with a program" you see options similar to those in Figure 44.7.

File types are listed first, in alphabetical order. Protocols are separate at the bottom of the list. Use the scroll bar to scroll through the list. To assign a default program to a file type or protocol, first click the item you want to change. Then click the Change Program button. Then use the Open With dialog box that opens to choose a program.

FIGURE 44.7

File types and protocols.

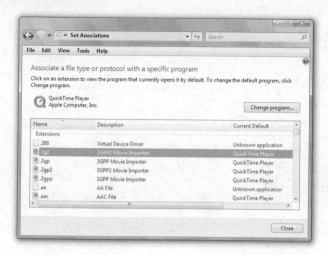

NOTE Don't worry about items marked as Unknown Application. Most of those aren't documents anyway and don't need to have a default program. You don't have to assign a default program to every item in the list!

Change AutoPlay settings

AutoPlay is a Windows Vista feature that lets you choose what program you want to use to play content on CDs, DVDs, and devices. Chances are you've already seen the AutoPlay dialog box at least once, after you inserted a CD or DVD, or connected a camera or disk drive. Figure 44.8 shows an example.

FIGURE 44.8

AutoPlay dialog box for a DVD.

Notice the first option in the dialog box, "Always do this for. . . ." When that option is selected, and you click a program name from the options beneath it, you automatically set the default program for that type of disk. Meaning that the next time you insert a disk of the same type as the one you just inserted, you don't get the dialog box anymore. Instead, the program you chose the first time around opens to play the disk's contents.

When you click Change AutoPlay settings in Program Defaults, you get to see all of your current AutoPlay default settings, as in Figure 44.9. Scroll to the bottom of the list to find icons for devices you connect to your computer, such as digital cameras.

FIGURE 44.9

Change AutoPlay settings.

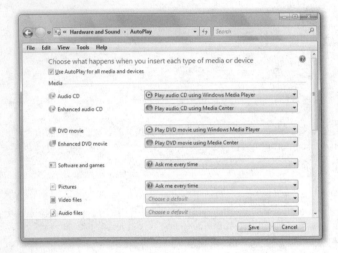

> **NOTE**   Chapter 32 describes all the different types of CDs and DVDs and provides some suggestions for choosing AutoPlay defaults.

To change the default action for any item, click the current action and choose the action you want from the menu that drops down. Click Save after making your changes to return to Program Defaults.

The Shift Key Doesn't Work Like It Used To

In previous versions of Windows, you could hold down the Shift key while inserting a disk or connecting a device to override the default action for the device. You can still do that in Windows Vista. But the AutoPlay dialog box still opens. (The default program doesn't open.) To prevent the AutoPlay dialog box from opening when using the Shift key, you need to clear the **Use AutoPlay for all media and devices** checkbox at the top of the AutoPlay page shown in Figure 44.9.

Set program access and computer defaults

Anybody that has a user account can choose defaults using any of the methods described in this chapter. The Set program access and computer defaults option is strictly for computer administrators. It sets defaults that apply to all user accounts, and can even be used to limit programs that they can use. This is most often used in corporate settings when administrators want very tight control over how staff members use their computers. But anyone with an administrative user account on a home computer can use it to control family members' program use as well.

Because the Set program access and computer defaults option can so severely limit what all users can do, you need administrative privileges just to start it. If you're in a standard user account, you'll need to log out. Then log in to an administrative account to open that option. When you first open it, you'll see three options:

- **Microsoft Windows Vista:** Choose this option if you want to set the Internet programs that came with Windows Vista as the default programs.
- **Non-Microsoft:** Choose this option if you don't want to use any Microsoft Internet programs.
- **Custom:** Choose this option if you want to use a combination of Microsoft and non-Microsoft Internet programs.

After you choose one of these options, you'll see more options under that category. The exact options vary depending on what you choose. But they work in a similar manner. I'll use the Custom category, shown in Figure 44.10, as an example, because it offers the most options.

FIGURE 44.10

Default Internet Programs page.

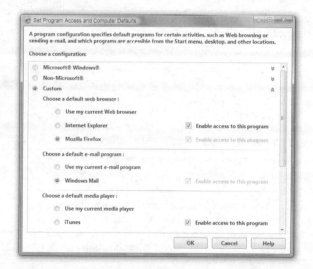

What's a Java Virtual Machine?

Well, it's not a coffee maker, if that's what you were thinking. Java is a programming language often used with Internet programs and applets (small programs embedded in Web pages). The virtual machine (also called a runtime environment) allows those programs to run on your computer. It's not a mandatory item, unless you use programs that require it or visit Web sites that require it.

Typically, if you needed the Java virtual machine, you'd be prompted to download it automatically when it's required. You can also download and install it at any time from www.java.com/download. Or if that link doesn't work, try http://sun.java.com.

As you can see in Figure 44.10, the first options let you choose the default Web browser, e-mail client, and media player for online music and video. Scrolling down lets you choose a default instant messaging program and Java virtual machine. The options available to you depend on what programs you have installed on your computer at the moment. For each program, you have the following options:

- **Use my current. . .:** Choose this option to keep whatever program you're currently using as the default program. This will be the only option when you don't have multiple programs to choose from.

- **<program name>:** To specify a program as the default, click the option button to the left of its name.

- **Enable access to this program:** Choosing this option allows users to run the program. Clearing the checkbox hides the program's icon on the Start menu and elsewhere, preventing users from running the program.

There will be times when you can't choose exactly the option you want. Or when you choose an option, the selected program doesn't comply. That's because the programmers who create these programs aren't required to make them work with the Program Defaults selections. If that's a problem, your only recourse is to contact the program publisher. They may have a newer version that's compatible with setting program defaults in Vista.

Click OK when you've finished making your selections. You might see a message stating that your choices might not work because of current file associations. If you click Yes, Vista will try to change the File Associations to go with the new default program automatically. If it doesn't work, you can change file associations manually.

Wrap Up

Default programs are programs that start automatically when you open a document or use an Internet protocol like e-mail or the Web. When you have two or more programs that can open a document or use an Internet protocol, you can choose which one acts as the default. Choosing a default doesn't preclude you from using other programs. The default just determines which program is used when you don't specify otherwise. Windows Vista offers several methods of choosing default programs:

- To set the default for a file type on the fly, right-click a file's icon and choose Open With ➪ Choose Default Program.

- To use some program other than the default for a document, right-click the icon, choose Open With and the name of the program you want to use.

- The Program Defaults page in Control Panel provides ways of setting multiple default programs from a single page.

- The Set your default programs option lets you choose a program and specify the documents and protocols for which it should act as the default.

- The Associate a file type or protocol with a program option lets you first choose a filename extension or protocol, and then choose the program that will be the default.

- Change AutoPlay Setting lets you choose what happens when you insert a disc or connect a device.

- Set program access and computer defaults allows an administrator to control defaults and programs for all user accounts.

Chapter 45

Managing Programs and Processes

T he term *application program* refers to most programs you start from the Start menu. These programs all tend to run within a program window and show a button in the taskbar when open. In addition to application programs, many *processes* are running in the background. Processes don't have program windows or taskbar buttons.

Task Manager is a program built into Windows Vista for viewing and managing running application programs and processes. You can use it to seek out performance bottlenecks, close hung programs without restarting the system, and more.

Getting to Know Task Manager

Every running program and process is generally referred to as a *task*. As its name implies, Task Manager is a program that lets you view and manage those running programs. There are two ways to start Task Manager:

- Press Ctrl+Alt+Del and then click Start Task Manager.
- Right-click the clock or an empty spot on the taskbar and choose Task Manager.

> **TIP** If a program is hung (frozen), right-clicking the taskbar might not work. But pressing Ctrl+Alt+Del might still work. It's worth a try.

Task Manager opens looking like Figure 45.1. It behaves much like any program window. It has a taskbar button when open. You can drag it around by its title bar. Size it by dragging any corner or edge. About the only thing that's different is that it stays on the top of the stack of open windows so you can always see it. But you can change that by choosing Options ➪ Always On Top from its menu.

IN THIS CHAPTER

Starting and using Task Manager

What to do when your system hangs (freezes up)

Viewing running processes

Monitoring performance and resource use

FIGURE 45.1

Task Manager in its normal view.

Task Manager also has a mini-mode where the title bar, menu bar, and tabs are hidden, as in Figure 45.2. When you're in that mode, double-click the empty space inside the window border to go to the normal mode. Double-click that same area, or to the right of the tabs, in the normal mode to go to mini-mode.

FIGURE 45.2

Task Manager mini-mode.

Choosing Task Manager Views

There are several ways to view and use Task Manager. On the Options menu in the menu bar, you have the following options:

- **Always On Top:** Choosing this option ensures that Task Manager is always on the top of the stack when it's open, so no other program windows can cover it.

- **Minimize On Use:** If selected, this option just minimizes Task Manager whenever you choose the Switch To option to switch to another running program.

- **Hide When Minimized:** Normally when you minimize Task Manager, only its taskbar button remains visible. Choosing this option will also hide the taskbar button when you minimize Task Manager.

Whenever Task Manager is open, you'll see a small green square in the Notification area. Pointing to that icon displays the current CPU (processor) usage, as shown in Figure 45.3. When Task Manager is minimized, you can double-click that little square to bring Task Manager back onto the desktop.

FIGURE 45.3

Task Manager notification icon.

On the View menu in Task Manager, you have the following choices:

- **Refresh Now:** Causes Task Manager to refresh all of its data immediately, regardless of the Update Speed setting.

- **Update Speed:** Task Manager needs to use some computer resources to keep itself up to date with what's happening in the system at the moment. The Update Speed option lets you choose how often Task Manager updates itself as follows:

  - **High:** Updates Task Manager twice per second.

  - **Normal:** Updates Task Manager every two seconds.

  - **Low:** Updates Task Manager every four seconds.

  - **Paused:** Updates Task Manager only when you choose View ⇨ Refresh Now.

Not Responding? Task Manager to the Rescue

One of Task Manager's most useful roles is that of dealing with problems that cause programs, or your whole computer, to *hang* (to "freeze up," so that the mouse and keyboard don't work normally). Even when you can't get the mouse or keyboard to work, pressing Ctrl+Alt+Del and choosing Open Task Manager may get Task Manager open for you.

Closing frozen programs

Once Task Manager is open, click the Applications tab. If a particular program is hung, its Status column will read Not Responding rather than Running. To close the hung program, click its name in the Task column, and then click the End Task button. Task Manager will try to close the program normally, so that if you were working on a document at the time, you may be able to save any changes. (So, don't expect the program to close immediately.)

If the program won't close, you'll see a warning that moving ahead will close the program leaving unsaved work behind. To forge ahead, click End Now. Most likely, a process of reporting the problem and finding a solution will start. The program may even try to restart itself. That's all fine if you have time to wait. But don't expect someone to call on the phone or appear on your screen to fix things for you. It doesn't work that way.

Basically you're sending information to a database of problems, and searching that database for known problems and their solutions. The program might also try to restart. If you didn't leave any unsaved work behind and don't have time to wait through that whole process, you can cancel out of each dialog box by clicking its Cancel button.

Switching and starting tasks

If the system is hung in such a way that you can't use the Start menu or taskbar normally, and you want to work with open program windows individually, Task Manager provides some ways to accomplish that.

To bring a running program to the top of the stack of windows on the screen, and make it the active window, click its name in the list of running tasks, and then click the Switch To button. If you were working on a document in that program, you can save your work, and then exit the program normally.

If you need to bring up some diagnostic program or debugger, and you know the startup command for that program, click the New Task button. The Create New Task dialog box, shown in Figure 45.4, opens. Type the startup command for the program (or the complete path to the program, if necessary), and then click OK.

FIGURE 45.4

Create New Task dialog box.

The Windows menu shown in Figure 45.5 offers many of the same window-arranging options you see when you right-click the clock. You can click any program name in the Tasks column (on the Applications tab) and choose Bring to Front to bring a buried program window to the top of the stack. This is handy when a hung program is hogging up the entire screen, and you need to see something, perhaps to save some work in progress, behind that hung program window.

FIGURE 45.5

Window options in Task Manager.

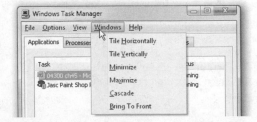

Restarting a hung computer

If your computer is so locked up that you can't get to Task Manager, or stop the offending program, there are other things you can try. If pressing Ctrl+Alt+Del works, taking you to the options in Figure 45.6, you can try any of the options shown. Logging off or restarting will likely be your best bet. If at all possible, Windows will attempt to give you a chance to save any unsaved work.

FIGURE 45.6

Options when you first press Ctrl+Alt+Del.

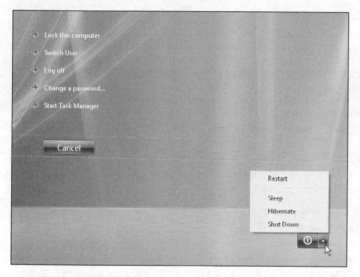

If the program that's hung is also the one that contains the unsaved work, there may be no way to save that work. You might just have to restart without saving. Hopefully you save your work often so you don't lose too much work.

Peeking at Resource Usage

In addition to helping you deal with hung programs, Task Manager lets you see which activities in your system are using computer resources. In this context, resource usage is about things that are currently open (which is all Task Manager ever shows). When you're talking about things that are open (or running), you're talking about two pieces of computer hardware, the CPU and memory.

Your computer's CPU (central processing unit) is the workhorse of your computer. In fact, the CPU *is* the computer. Just about everything else is just a peripheral device that feeds data to the processor. Also called the microprocessor or processor, it's a chip that's smaller than your thumbnail in which electrons travel at about 670 million miles per hour to perform billions of instructions per second. (Those numbers are accurate, not exaggerations.)

Most PC microprocessors are manufactured by two companies, Intel and AMD. The speed of a CPU is the number of instructions it can perform per second, usually expressed in gigahertz (GHz). For example, a 3-GHz computer can process three billion instructions per second.

Memory (also called random access memory, or RAM) is a group of chips that store information that the CPU operates on. Memory stores only what's currently open (and therefore visible in Task Manager).

TIP Your hard disk has nothing to do with memory. Memory contains only what you're using right now. Your hard disk is more like a filing cabinet — a place to store programs and documents you want to open and use in the future. To see examples of CPUs, RAM chips, and hard drives, go to `www.tigerdirect.com` and click on `CPUs(Processors)`, `Memory`, or `Hard Drives` in the left column.

The CPU and memory combined are the real workhorses of your PC. The faster the CPU, and the more memory available, the faster your PC runs. The reason why the *amount*, rather than *speed*, of RAM counts so much is because when RAM is full, Windows has to use a special area of the hard disk, called a *paging file*, to handle the overflow. The hard disk has moving parts, and therefore can't get data to and from the CPU as quickly as RAM can.

Exactly how fast your computer runs at any given moment depends on the resources available to it at that moment. For example, if you have half a dozen programs running, all doing very busy things, they are eating up CPU resources. If you start another program, that program may run slower than usual, because the other running programs are consuming CPU resources.

Likewise, everything you open stores something in RAM. If RAM is nearly full, and you start another program that needs more memory than what's currently left in RAM, Windows has to start sloughing some of what's currently in RAM off to the hard disk to make room. It takes time to do that, so everything slows down.

The status bar along the bottom of Task Manager's program window gives you a bird's-eye view of how much stuff is going on in your system, and how much of your available resources are being used by all that stuff. Going from left to right along the status bar you see:

- **Processes:** Shows the total number of processes currently running on the system.
- **CPU Usage:** Shows what percentage of CPU capability is currently being used by the above processes.
- **Commit Charge:** Shows *total commit charge/total available memory*, where *total commit charge* is the amount of memory currently taken up by (committed to) all the currently running processes, and *total available memory* is the total amount of physical and virtual memory available in your system.

Physical Memory versus Virtual Memory

The term *physical memory* refers to the actual amount of RAM, on computer chips, installed in your computer. When you right-click My Computer and choose Properties, the number to the left of the words ". . . of RAM" indicate the amount of physical memory installed on the motherboard inside your computer.

When things are busy in RAM, Windows moves some lesser-used items out to a special section of the hard disk called a *paging file*. The paging file looks and acts like RAM (to the CPU), even though it's actually space on your hard disk. Every computer has some hard disk space set aside for this paging file. (More on that topic in Chapter 50.)

A *page fault* is when the CPU "expects" to find something in RAM, but has to fetch it from virtual memory instead. The term *fault* is a bit harsh here, because a certain amount of memory paging is normal and to be expected. Other terms used in this context include *Nonpaged memory* for physical memory and *Paged memory* for virtual memory.

Managing Processes with Task Manager

Whereas application programs run in program windows and are listed on the Applications tab in Task Manager, processes have no program window. We say that processes run in the background, because they don't show anything in particular on the screen. Furthermore, processes tend to have a lower priority than application programs. This means that when you're actively using some program, a process won't take away resources and slow you down.

Your running application programs are actually processes. You can see which process correlates with a given program by right-clicking that program's name on the Applications tab and choosing Go To Process. To see all currently running processes, click the Processes tab in Task Manager. Each process is referred to by *its image name* (in most cases, the name of the program's main executable file), as in the example shown in Figure 45.7.

FIGURE 45.7

Processes tab in Task Manager.

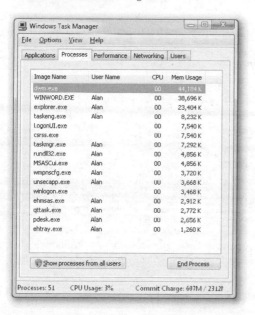

The Processes tab shows its information in columns. You can size columns in the usual manner (by dragging the bar at the right side of the column heading). You can sort items by clicking any column heading. For example, you can click the Mem Usage column to sort processes by the amount of memory each one takes up, in ascending order (smallest to largest) or descending order (largest to smallest). Seeing those in largest-to-smallest order lets you know which processes are using up the most memory.

Here's what each column shows:

- **Image Name:** The name of the process. In most cases, this matches the name of the file in which the process is stored when not open.
- **User Name:** The user account in which the process is running. System, Local, and Network services are available to all users and are necessary just to keep the computer running.
- **CPU:** The percent of CPU resources that the process is currently using.
- **Mem Usage:** The amount of memory the process needs to do its job.

Memory usage is probably the main cause of slow-running computers. The more stuff you cram into RAM, the more Windows has to use the paging file, and hence the slower everything goes. You can see which processes are hogging up the most RAM just by clicking the Mem Usage column heading until the largest numbers are at the top of the list.

Amazingly, if you just minimize (not close) a program that's open on the desktop, its Mem Usage number will drop significantly. Even though the program is still in RAM, getting the visible doodads off the desktop will reduce the amount of memory it consumes. That's a good thing to know if your computer is light on RAM and you need to conserve memory!

Hidden processes

Normally, the Processes tab only shows processes running in the user account into which you're currently logged. Clicking *Show processes from all users* shows the true number of running processes (but requires administrative privileges).

Multiple users not logging out of their accounts is one of the most common reasons for computer sluggishness. If users are using Switch User to leave their accounts, you'll see why when you view processes for all users. There's just a lot of unnecessary stuff going on when people don't log out of their user accounts when they've finished using the computer.

Task Manager might not show old 16-bit processes. To show or hide those processes, choose Options ⇨ Show 16-bit Tasks from Task Manager's menu bar. That menu option is available only when you're viewing the Processes tab.

Common processes

You can end any running process by right-clicking its name and choosing End Process (or by clicking its name and clicking the End Process button). But doing so isn't a good idea unless you know exactly what service you're terminating. If a process represents a running program with unsaved work, ending the process will close the program without saving the work.

Some processes are required for normal operation of the computer. For example, dwm.exe (Windows Desktop Manager) and explorer.exe are important parts of Windows Vista. So you definitely don't want to mess with those.

NOTE Just because a process is near the top of the list when you sort things in largest-to-smallest order doesn't mean the biggest items are hogs or outrageously large. Even seemingly large numbers like 50,000 K and 60,000 K are trivial when you consider how much RAM most systems have, and how cheap it is to add more.

If you're unsure about a process, you can search for it by name on Google or any other search engine. Just be sure to check out multiple sources. And read carefully. Virtually ever resource you find will tell you that perfectly legitimate and necessary processes like dwm.exe and explorer.exe could be Trojan, spyware, or other malicious item. But *could* is not synonymous with *is*. So read carefully and don't assume the worst.

Choosing columns in processes

The four column names that appear in Task Manager by default don't tell the whole story. When you're viewing the Processes tab in Task Manager, you can choose View ⇨ Select Columns to choose other columns to view. Each column shows some detail of the process, mostly related to resource consumption. A programmer might use this information to fine-tune a program she's writing. Beyond that it's hard to think of anything terribly practical to be gained from this information. But here's a quick summary of what the other, optional columns show:

- **Base Priority:** The priority assigned to the process. When the CPU is busy, low-priority processes have to wait for normal and high-priority processes to be completed. To change a process's priority, right-click its name and choose Set Priority.

> **CAUTION** Don't experiment with priorities, and never set a process's priority to Realtime without good reason. Doing so can really foul up your PC's performance.

- **CPU Time:** Total number of seconds of CPU time this process has used since starting. The number will be doubled for dual-processor systems, quadrupled for systems with four processors.

- **CPU Usage:** The amount of processor time, as a percent of the whole, this process has used since first started (the CPU column).

- **GDI Objects:** The number of Graphics Device Interface objects used by this process, since starting, to display content on the screen.

- **Handle Count:** The number of objects to which the process currently has handles.

- **I/O Other:** Non-disk input/output calls made by the object since it started. Excludes file, network, and device operations.

- **I/O Other Bytes:** The number of bytes transferred to devices since the process started. Excludes file, network, and device operations.

- **I/O Reads:** The number of file, network, and device Read input/output operations since the process started.

- **I/O Read Bytes:** The number of bytes transferred by Read file, network, and device input/output operations.

- **I/O Writes:** The number of file, network, and device Write input/output operations since the process started.

- **I/O Write Bytes:** The number of bytes transferred by Write file, network, and device input/output operations.

- **Memory Usage:** The amount of memory blocks used by the process (also called the process's *working set*) since starting.

- **Memory Usage Delta:** The change in memory usage since the last Task Manager update.

- **Non-paged Pool:** The amount of physical RAM used by the process since starting.

- **Page Faults:** The number of times the process has read data from virtual memory since starting.

- **Page Faults Delta:** The change in the number of page faults since the last Task Manager update.

- **Paged Pool:** The amount of system-allocated virtual memory that's been committed to the process by the operating system.

- **Peak Memory Usage:** The largest amount of physical memory used by the process since it started.

- **PID (Process Identifier):** A number assigned to the process at startup. The operating system accesses all processes by their numbers, not their names.

- **Session ID:** The Terminal Session ID that owns the process. Always zero unless Terminal Services are in use on the network.

- **Thread Count:** The number of threads running in a process.

 A thread is a tiny sequence of instructions that the CPU must carry out to perform some task. Some programs divide tasks into separate threads that can be executed in parallel (simultaneously), to speed execution.

- **User Name:** The user, user account, or service that started the process.
- **User Objects:** The number of objects from Window Manager used by the object, including program windows, cursors, icons, and other objects.
- **Virtual Memory Size:** The amount of virtual memory currently committed to the process.

Much of the information available from the extra columns on the Processes tab is summarized on the Performance tab.

Monitoring Performance with Task Manager

The Performance tab in Task Manager, shown in Figure 45.8, provides both graphical and numeric summaries of CPU and memory resource usage. To watch resource usage, leave Task Manager open and "always on top" as you run programs and use your computer in the usual ways. If you have multiple processors, or a multi-core processor, each may be represented in a separate pane in the SPU history as at the top of the figure. Choose View ➪ CPU History to decide whether you want to see a single pane or multiple panes.

 Double-click any chart to expand it to a larger size or to restore it to its previous size.

FIGURE 45.8

Performance tab in Task Manager.

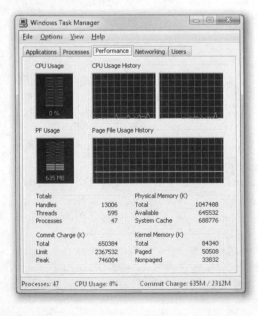

Here's what all the things you see on the Performance tab represent:

- **CPU Usage:** Indicates how much of the CPU's capability you're using at the moment.
- **CPU Usage History:** Shows CPU usage over time. Choosing View ➪ Show Kernel Times adds a second red line to the chart, which shows the amount of CPU resources used by kernel operations (core operating system processes).
- **PF Usage:** Paging file usage; the amount of data being paged to virtual memory.
- **Page File Usage History:** The amount of virtual memory usage over time.
- **Totals:** The number of handles, threads, and processes running at the time.
- **Physical Memory (K):** The total amount of physical memory in the system, the amount that's currently Available, and the amount used by the System Cache, which maps to data stored in files. Each measurement is expressed in kilobytes.
- **Commit Charge (K):** The total amount of physical and virtual memory committed to programs and the operating system. The Limit is the sum of physical and virtual memory allocated to the system. The Peak is the largest amount of total memory used in the current session.
- **Kernel Memory (K):** The total memory used by the operating system kernel and device drivers; also shown as the amount of Paged (virtual) and Non-paged (physical) memory.

The Performance charts are useful for identifying major *performance bottlenecks*. For example, if the CPU Usage and History charts run high, your CPU is working very hard. Unfortunately, the only real solution to that is to install a faster CPU, which generally means a whole new motherboard.

> **NOTE** The performance statistics in Figure 45.8 are from a PC with a 3.0-GHz Pentium 4 CPU and 1 GB (1,024 MB) of RAM. To make the CPU Usage History line reach the heights shown, I simultaneously saved a movie file in Movie Maker, played a song in Media Player, checked my e-mail, and just did whatever I else could think of to keep the machine as busy as possible for a few seconds.

The most common performance bottleneck is limited physical memory. For example, 128 MB of RAM is "light" for Windows Vista and modern programs. Running lots of programs with limited memory forces the system to use lots of virtual memory, which in turn slows things down. Increasing the amount of virtual memory (as discussed in Chapter 50) can help. The best solution is to add more RAM (physical memory) to the system, or have it installed professionally.

Networking and Users Tabs

The Networking and Users tabs in Task Manager display information about your network and user accounts. The Networking tab, shown in Figure 45.9, shows network traffic, or the amount of network bandwidth used. If you have multiple network interface cards installed on the computer, each is displayed in its own chart.

The Users tab shows the names of people currently logged in to the computer. Most users will see only themselves, even if other users are logged in. If you're an administrator and click Show processors from all users on the Processes tab, the Users tab will show all current users. Users who are logged in but have used Switch User to exit their accounts will show as Disconnected.

If people not logging out of their accounts is causing your system to run as slow as molasses in Alaska, here's your chance to give them a wake-up call. You can be nice about it. Click a user name and then click Send Message. Then write a friendly little reminder to log out when done. The user will see the message next time they go into their account.

FIGURE 45.9

Networking tab in Task Manager.

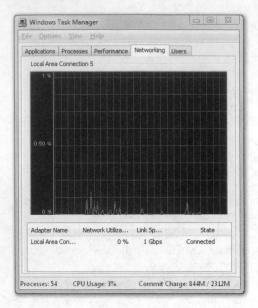

If you want to be nasty about it, you can click the user's name and click Log Off. That will log them out of their account without saving their work. (Heh heh heh.)

Wrap Up

Task Manager is a handy tool for terminating hung programs (programs that are not responding), and for monitoring computer resource usage. Task Manager also provides detailed information that's of interest only to programmers and network administrators. The main things to know about Task Manager are as follows:

- To open Task Manager, press Ctrl+Alt+Del and click Open Task Manager or right-click the time and choose Task Manager.
- The Applications tab shows the names of all running application programs. To end a program that's not responding, right-click its name and choose End Task.
- To see which process an application relates to, right-click the application name and choose Go To Process.
- The Processes tab shows all running processes, including application programs, background programs like antivirus software, and operating system processes.
- The Performance tab presents a bird's-eye view of overall CPU and memory usage.
- The Networking tab shows network bandwidth usage.
- The Users tab shows who is currently logged in.

Chapter 46

Troubleshooting Software Problems

Troubleshooting Installation

Not all programs that were designed for Windows XP (or earlier versions of Windows) will work with Windows Vista. In fact, you should avoid installing utility and security programs that are specifically written for Windows Vista altogether. (Most basic application programs will run fine.)

If you can't get an older program to install, or it doesn't work after you install it, check the program manufacturer's Web site to see if they have a Vista version available.

Troubleshooting Programs

Because there are so many programs available for Windows, there are no troubleshooting magic bullets that will solve all problems. Every program is unique and every problem is unique.

One of the most common mistakes people make is to not learn to use a program. They guess and hack their way through it, and when things don't work the way they guessed they would work, they think there's something wrong with the program, when in fact, the problem is that the person using the program has no clue how to use the program correctly. Troubleshooting can't fix ignorance; only learning can fix that.

You must eventually understand that every program has its own built-in Help for a reason — it's because every program is unique. The only way to get information about a specific program is from the Help that came with that program, or from the support Web site for that program. The Help menu, which is always the last item on the menu bar, provides all the help options available to you.

The whole concept of troubleshooting only applies when you *do* know how to do something, but things don't work the way the documentation from which you

935

learned said they should work. (I realize that this is obvious to most readers. But you should see some of the e-mail I get.)

Anyway, the big trick is to not just try one resource and then give up. There is no book, Web page, person, place, or thing that has all the answers to all questions, nor the solutions to all problems. Sometimes you really have to dig around for a solution. Start with the narrowest, most simple solution and work your way out from there, as follows.

Try the Help that's available from the program's menu bar.

Then try the program manufacturer's Web site. With Microsoft products, you may want to try searching `http://search.microsoft.com`, `http://support.microsoft.com`, or `http://office. microsoft.com` for Office products. At the program manufacturer's Web site, look around for other support options such as FAQs (Frequently Asked Questions), Troubleshooting, and Discussion Groups or Newsgroups.

For Microsoft products, you'll also want to go to `http://support.microsoft.com` and click the Select a Product link for links to support for specific products. The Microsoft Public Newsgroups link on that same page will take you to areas for specific products where you can post questions and get answers.

Don't forget, too, that you can search the entire planet using a search engine like Google. Though, when you're searching the entire planet, you want to use as many exact, descriptive words as possible in your search. Otherwise you'll get links to more pages than you could visit in a lifetime. Include the product name, version number, and specific words that describe what you're looking for.

 To find out what version of a program you're using, choose Help ➪ About . . . from that program's menu bar.

Don't bother trying to form a question like "What is . . . ?" or "How do I . . . ?" because there are no human beings at the other side of the search — just 30 million or so computers. For example, if you're looking for help with Windows Mail version 7 backups, get all of the appropriate words into your search as in `Backup Windows Mail 7`. Be as specific as you can possibly be. The more specific you are when typing your search words, the better your results will be.

Researching Application Errors

Many software errors will provide hexadecimal memory locations in their error messages. Sometimes searching for the number won't do any good. The title bar may provide some clues as to exactly what caused the problem. Look through the error messages for some unique keywords that you can enter into different support search engines.

Searching for a combination of the program name and keywords from the error message text can sometimes provide clues. You may want to start with a narrow search, such as `http://support.microsoft.com` to avoid getting too many hits. If that doesn't work, you can broaden the search to all of Microsoft.com (`http://search.microsoft.com`). If all else fails, you can search all five billion (or so) pages in Google's index at `www.google.com`.

But the key thing, in all searches, is to get the most unique words from the message into your search string. For example, if searching for the hexadecimal memory addresses from the error message don't pan out, you could try a combination of other words. Getting rid of some of these things can take some doing. If the thing keeps coming back, scouring the registry for the item's name can help you find where the item is located. Deleting all references to the item from the registry, performing a clean boot, and then deleting the folder in which the item is contained could work, but this is risky business unless you *really* know what you're doing. See the following "Editing the Registry" section for registry editing information.

Ideally, you'll want to try to dig up as much information about the error as you can via the Web. Search the company's Web site; because they are the ones who created that application, they may be able to provide additional information.

Editing the Registry

After researching a software problem, you might find that the solution involves a "registry hack," also known as *editing the registry*. This is serious business with no margin for error. Never attempt to fix a problem by guessing at a registry hack. When you do get specific instructions on making a registry change, make sure you make *exactly* the change indicated in the message. Even the slightest typographical error can cause a world of problems. If you're not a technical person and don't want to risk creating a really big mess you can't rectify, consider hiring a professional to resolve the problem.

Before you launch into registry hacking, you need to understand what you're doing. First, be aware that the registry is a database where Windows and other programs store data that they need to operate properly on your computer. The average computer user can go through life without ever even knowing that the registry exists. In fact, I'm sure most do. There is absolutely nothing that's "user friendly" about the registry. In fact, it's probably just about as "user hostile" as you can get. Microsoft provides the Registry Editor described in this chapter because programmers and other IT professionals occasionally need to get in there and fix something manually.

 The registry is not a safe place to mess around. Pay attention to all cautions in this chapter!

How registry data is organized

Windows and all your programs need to get information from the registry often. To keep things running at top speed, it's important that every request for information placed on the registry be handled quickly and efficiently. As with organizing your own files into folders, a hierarchical arrangement that organizes information from the general to the specific provides the best means of ensuring quick access to data.

But all the registry data is stored in one large file, so the concept of folders and files doesn't apply to the registry directly. Only the hierarchical arrangement is similar. Rather than folders, the registry uses *keys* and *subkeys* to organize data. Just as a folder can contain subfolders, a key can contain subkeys.

The registry doesn't store files or documents. Rather, it stores simple *values* — some number or code that has "meaning" to the software. The meaning of a particular value isn't at all obvious to a human being. Rather, the software that uses those values is just written in such as way as to do different things, depending on the value that happens to be stored in a subkey.

Standard root keys and subkeys

We'll get into the specifics of editing the registry in a moment. But first, Figure 46.1 shows an example of the Registry Editor as it might look when you first open it. The names listed down the left column are keys. Specifically, we refer to them as the *standard root keys*, because they're at the top (root) of the hierarchy, and each contains subkeys. Each standard root key stores a particular type of information, as summarized in Table 46.1. Note that most keys have a standard abbreviation, like HKCU for HKEY_CURRENT_USER.

FIGURE 46.1

Standard root keys at left in the Registry Editor.

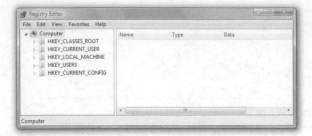

TABLE 46.1

Standard Root Keys

Key Name	Abbreviation	Description
HKEY_CLASSES_ROOT	HKCR	Stores information about document types and extensions, registered programs that can open each file type, the default program for each file type, and options that appear when you right-click an icon.
HKEY_CURRENT_USER	HKCU	Stores information about the person who is currently using the computer, based on which user account that person is logged in to, and settings that particular user chose within his or her account.
HKEY_LOCAL_MACHINE	HKLM	Stores information about all the hardware that's available to the computer, including devices that might not be plugged in at the moment.
HKEY_USERS	HKU	Stores information about all users, based on user accounts you've defined via Control Panel.
HKEY_CURRENT_CONFIG	<none>	Similar to HKEY_LOCAL_MACHINE, this key stores information about hardware available to the computer. However, this key limits its storage to hardware that's connected and functioning currently.

When you click the white triangle next to a standard root key, it expands to display its subkeys. Some of the subkeys may have subkeys of their own. In that case, the subkey itself will have a white triangle too, which you can click to see another level of subkeys. For example, in Figure 46.2, I've expanded the HKEY_ CLASSES_ROOT key to reveal its subkeys. Each subkey represents a particular file type in that case. I've also expanded a few subkeys in that example.

FIGURE 46.2

The HKEY_CLASSES_ROOT and some subkeys expanded.

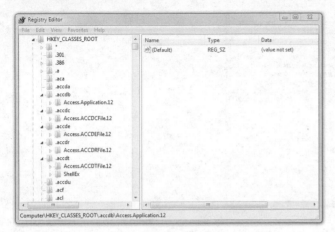

You'll often see a reference to a specific subkey expressed as a path, in much the way that you might see a file's location and name expressed as a path. For example, the path to a file might be expressed as `C:\Users\Alan\Pictures\Summit01.jpg`. The path tells Windows exactly where to find the file: "Go to drive C:, drill down through the folders named Users, Alan, Pictures, and there you'll find a file named Summit01.jpg."

A registry path is the same idea, and even uses backslashes to separate the key and subkey names. For example, the highlighted subkey in Figure 46.2 is at `Computer\HKEY_CLASSES_ROOT\..accdb\Access.Application.12`.

Sometimes you'll see instructions telling you the path to a key or subkey, like `HKEY_CURRENT_USER\Control Panel\Appearance\Schemes`. You have to manually expand each folder down the path to get to the subkey. Figure 46.3 shows the result of following that sample path. The values in the Data column for that key are mostly binary numbers. A good example of just how user *un*friendly the registry can be!

Key values

The data stored in a subkey is called a *value*. The value is a specific piece of information that can be stored as a string (text) or a number. However, the terms "string" and "number" don't tell the whole story, because those types can be further broken down into the specific *data type*s listed in Table 46.2.

FIGURE 46.3

The HKEY_CURRENT_USER\Control Panel\Appearance\Schemes subkey selected.

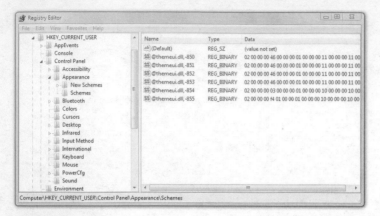

TABLE 46.2

Registry Value Data Types

Name	Data type	Description
Binary Value	REG_BINARY	Raw binary data used mostly by hardware components. Often displayed in hexadecimal format.
DWORD Value	REG_DWORD	An integer often used to store parameters for device drivers and services. Subtypes include related types such as DWORD_LITTLE_ENDIAN and REG_DWORD_BIG_ENDIAN with the least significant bit at the lowest/highest address, respectively.
Expandable String Value	REG_EXPAND_SZ	A variable-length string often used to store data for application programs and services.
Multi-String Value	REG_MULTI_SZ	A string that actually consists of multiple substrings separated by spaces, commas, or other special characters.
String Value	REG_SZ	A simple fixed-length text string.
Binary Value	REG_RESOURCE_LIST	A series of nested arrays (lists) often used by hardware and device drivers. Usually displayed in hexadecimal.

Name	Data type	Description
Binary Value	REG_RESOURCE_REQUIREMENTS_LIST	A series of nested arrays (lists) containing a device driver's hardware resources, displayed in hexadecimal.
Binary Value	REG_FULL_RESOURCE_DESCRIPTOR	A series of nested lists of actual hardware device capabilities, usually displayed in hexadecimal.
None	REG_NONE	Data with no particular type that's displayed as a Binary Value in hexadecimal.
Link	REG_LINK	A string naming a symbolic link.
QWORD	Value REG_QWORD	A 64-bit number displayed as a binary value.

Numbering Systems

Admittedly, I've already given you much more information about the registry than you'd probably ever need to know. About the only time you want to mess with the registry is when you've found the solution to some problem, and that solution requires a *registry hack* (a manual modification to the registry). In that case, the solution will always tell exactly what value to put in what key. So, you don't have to figure out how to convert some decimal value, such as 16, to a hexadecimal value (10) or binary (10000). But, for the techno-curious, here's a quick overview of how the numbering systems work.

In our day-to-day work, we use decimal *base ten* numbers. The "base ten" part tells us that there are 10 unique characters for expressing all numbers, 0 to 9. After you go from 0 to 9, you run out of characters and have to start using two characters to express numbers, 10, 11, 12, and so forth. Eventually, you get to 99, at which point you've exhausted all possible unique pairs of the characters 0 to 9, so you have to go to three digits, 100, 101, 102, and so forth, up to 999.

Other numbering systems use a different number of characters for expressing numbers. For example, hexadecimal is base 16, meaning that it has 16 unique characters, 0 through 9 plus A, B, C, D, E, and F. Counting from 0 to 20 in hexadecimal goes like this: 0, 1, 2, 3, 4, 5, 6, 7, 8, 9, A, B, C, D, E, F, 10, 11, 12, 13, 14. The binary system is base 2 because it offers only two unique characters, 0 and 1. Counting from 0 to 5 in binary goes 0, 1, 10, 11, 100, 101. The octal base 8 system uses the unique characters 0 to 7 to express numbers.

I think it's safe to say that the alternative numbering systems aren't terribly important in day-to-day life. And it's a good thing, because if everybody didn't agree to use decimal, numbers would be a very confusing thing. For example, Table 46.3 shows the numbers 1 to 16, and some higher numbers, in decimal, hexadecimal, octal, binary, and exponential formats.

TABLE 46.3

Examples of Numbering Systems

Decimal	Hex	Octal	Binary	Exponent
0	0	0	0	
1	1	1	1	
2	2	2	10	2^1
3	3	3	11	
4	4	4	100	2^2
5	5	5	101	
6	6	6	110	
7	7	7	111	
8	8	10	1000	2^3
9	9	11	1001	
10	A	12	1010	
11	B	13	1011	
12	C	14	1100	
13	D	15	1101	
14	E	16	1110	
15	F	17	1111	
16	10	20	10000	2^4
32	20	40	100000	2^5
64	40	100	1000000	2^6
128	80	200	10000000	2^7
256	100	400	100000000	2^8
512	200	1000	1000000000	2^9
1024	400	2000	10000000000	2^{10}

After you get to 16 and start doubling each number, you encounter numbers that appear often in the computer world, 32, 64, 128, 256, 512, and 1,024. Those numbers appear frequently because they're powers of two, and everything a computer does centers around two digits, 0 and 1. That's because every little switch in the processor, and every little tiny dot of data on a disk can have only one of two possible values, "on" (1) or "off" (0). As a human being, you work with text, pictures, sound, and video. But the computer itself doesn't "see" or "know" anything about text, pictures, human beings, or anything else. It's just a machine that juggles "on" (1) and "off" (0) values.

Even the abbreviations K (kilo), M (mega), and G (giga) are powers of two. We say that K equals about a thousand, M about a million, and G about a trillion. But in truth, K is 210 or 1,024, M is 220 or 1,048,576, and G is 230 or 1,073,741,824.

Unless you get into some serious programming or writing device drivers, it's very unlikely that you'll ever need to mess with hex or binary numbers directly. But just so you know, there is an easy way to convert numbers in Windows. Click the Start button and choose All Programs ⇨ Accessories ⇨ Calculator. From Calculator's menu bar, choose View ⇨ Scientific to see the larger scientific calculator shown in Figure 46.4.

FIGURE 46.4

Windows Calculator in Scientific View.

With Calculator in Scientific View, you first need to tell it which system you'll be converting the number *from*. For example, if you want to convert decimal 255 to some other numbering system, click Dec.

Next, enter your number by typing it, or by clicking the appropriate calculator buttons. Finally, click the option that represents the numbering system you want to convert *to*. For example, to convert that decimal 255 to hexadecimal, click Hex. You'll see FF because FF is the value 255 expressed in hexadecimal.

When you start by clicking Hex, Oct, or Bin to convert a value *from* one of those numbering systems, you'll see the options Qword (64 bits), Dword (32 bits), Word (16 bits), and Byte (8 bits) to the right. Choosing one of those options puts an upper limit on how large a number you can enter, as summarized in Table 46.4. The limitation is caused by the number of bits (binary digits, or "ones and zeros" in simple terms) that each data type stores.

TABLE 46.4

Maximum Values for Types of Data

Type	Bits	Max number (Hex)	Max number (Decimal)
Byte	8	FF	255
Word	16	FFFF	65,535
Dword	32	FFFFFFFF	4,294,967,295
Qword	64	FFFFFFFFFFFFFFFF	18,446,744,073,709,551,615

> **TIP** Microsoft Excel can convert values among the decimal, octal, hexadecimal, and binary systems. You first need to load the Analysis ToolPak by choosing Tools ➪ Add-Ins from Excel's menu bar. Then, you can search Excel's help for conversion functions such as DEC2HEX(), HEX2DEC(), DEC2BIN(), BIN2DEC(), and so forth.

Well, I think that's about enough "theory" in terms of how things work. From a practical standpoint, most people only need to know how to make an occasional change to the registry to fix some problem. One important rule, though, is that before you do *anything* to the registry, you should make a quick backup copy of its current contents.

> **TIP** Modern computers are based upon a 32-bit processing model, which basically provides for 4,294,967,295 bits of directly addressable memory. As 64-bit processors enter the mainstream, you'll see much more powerful computing capabilities just because of the walloping 18,446,744,073,709,551,615 bits of addressable memory the 64-bit model provides.

Backing up the registry

Every time you start your computer, Windows automatically creates the registry based on the hardware and software available to it. Then, it makes a backup copy of that registry. When you plan to manually change the registry, you should also make a backup copy of the registry just before you make your change. Because when it comes to editing the registry, there is no margin for error and even a tiny typographical error can have far-reaching, unpleasant consequences.

> **TIP** The System Restore feature described in Chapter 33 also makes periodic backup copies of the registry.

You need administrative privileges to edit the registry. The program you use is named regedit. You can start it using either of these methods:

- Tap ⊞, type `regedit`, and click regedit.exe on the Start menu.
- Click the Start button, choose Run, type `regedit`, and press Enter.

> **NOTE** If you don't have a Run option on your Start menu, you can add it. Right-click the Start button and choose Properties. Then click Customize, check Run Command in the list of programs, and click OK in each open dialog box.

The Registry Editor opens. You *always* want to make a backup of the registry before you change anything. It's easy to do:

1. Choose File ➪ Export from the menu bar in the Registry Editor.
2. Choose a folder and enter a filename of your own choosing.
3. To export the entire registry, choose All under the Export range heading.
4. Click the Save button.

That's it. In the event of a disaster, you can choose File ➪ Import from the Registry Editor's menu bar to restore all the entries you copied in the preceding steps.

Making the registry change

You can change any value in the registry. First you need to get to the appropriate subkey. For example, let's say that you've found the solution to some problem via Microsoft's Web site. Part of that solution involves changing the following subkey:

```
HKEY_LOCAL_MACHINE\SOFTWARE\Microsoft\Windows\CurrentVersion\Run
```

The first step is to get to the subkey by expanding the HKEY_LOCAL_MACHINE, SOFTWARE, Microsoft, Windows, and CurrentVersion node. Then click Run. The pane to the right shows values in the subkey. The status bar shows the complete path name as in Figure 46.5.

FIGURE 46.5

HKEY_LOCAL_MACHINE\SOFTWARE\Microsoft\Windows\CurrentVersion\Run selected.

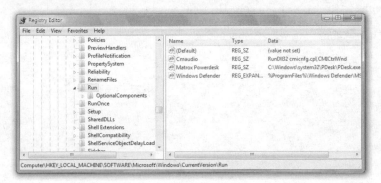

To change the subkey's value, double-click that value. A dialog box will open allowing you to make a change. The appearance of the dialog box depends on the type of value you're editing. Figure 46.6 shows a general example.

FIGURE 46.6

Dialog box to edit a Dword value.

CAUTION Make sure you get to the correct key, and make *exactly* the change your instructions tell you to. Even the slightest mistake here could cause big problems down the road.

The Value data box contains the value you can edit. Make your change there and click OK. Then close the Registry Editor. The change is made, and you have finished making your registry change.

Whether or not you see any change on the screen depends on the subkey you changed. Many registry hacks will have no effect until you close the Registry Editor, close all open program windows, and restart the computer.

If it turns out you created more problems than you solved, you can restore your registry from the backup you make. Open the Registry Editor and choose File ⇨ Import to import the backed-up file. Otherwise, if all seems well, you can delete the backed-up registry file.

Help with Troubleshooting Software

For more help with troubleshooting programs, open Windows Help and Support and search for `trouble-shoot program` or `troubleshoot software`. Or post a question in the `Microsoft.public .windows.vista.general` newsgroup at Microsoft Communities.

Part IX

Hardware and Performance Tuning

Computer hardware is the physical stuff you can touch or hold in your hand. This includes the many gadgets you can connect to your computer, like cameras and disk drives. Part IX is all about the hardware and gadgets.

Chapter 47 starts off with the general tools and techniques for installing hardware, getting it to work, and removing hardware that you no longer use.

Chapter 48 focuses on working with Bluetooth devices. Plenty of Bluetooth devices are on the market already. We're likely to see many more in the years ahead.

Chapter 49 covers the new Sync Center, a single point of entry for syncing your computer with many different kinds of devices.

Chapter 50 looks at hardware from the standpoint of performance—getting the most from the hardware you already have.

As always, we end the part with a discussion of common hardware and performance problems and solutions to make those problems go away.

Chapter 47

Installing and Removing Hardware

Computers are all about hardware and software. Software is the stuff you see on your screen. It works in conjunction with hardware to get things done. Basically, software is instructions written in a computer language that tell hardware what to do and when to do it. You can't see or touch software, because it's just information stored on a disk and transmitted across wires.

Hardware is any gadget that you can hold in your hand and connect to your computer. A single hardware gadget is referred to as a hardware device or just *device* for short. You can buy and use thousands of hardware devices with a computer. Printers, scanners, mice, keyboards, monitors, disk drives, digital cameras, MP3 players, modems, and routers are all examples of hardware devices. This chapter is about installing and using hardware devices.

IN THIS CHAPTER

Using hot-pluggable devices

Disconnecting hot-pluggable devices

Installing not-so-hot-pluggable devices

Removing hardware devices

Before You Install Anything

Before we get started, first a few words that will mainly be of interest to readers who have experience with earlier versions of Windows. In 1990, the PC world went through a major transition from DOS to Windows. It wasn't an easy transition. Many were bitter and angry, swearing never to defect from DOS. That's all long forgotten now. And since 1990, the transitions have been relatively minor going from one version of Windows to the next, Windows 3.0, 3.1, 95, 98, and so forth.

Every now and then the industry has to change course like we did in 1990. It has to stop building things that focus on compatibility and the past. We have to turn the other direction and build things that look to the future. Windows Vista is really that kind of transition. Simply stated, Vista isn't XP with transparent window borders and a cute Flip 3D thing. Under the covers, it's really a whole new operating system and a whole new way of doing things. And the change isn't based on incompetence or a desire to irritate people and make them spend money. It's about overcoming limitations and problems from the past to open the way to a brighter future.

The downside to such a change is that a lot of old stuff won't work. At least, not without drivers specifically written for Vista. Microsoft doesn't create the drivers. The people who create the products that work with Vista create the drivers for their own products. However, product manufacturers can post their drivers to Microsoft's Windows Update site. This is a good thing because it means you can download drivers easily and automatically on an as-needed basis. I'll talk about drivers in some more detail later in this chapter. But here are a couple of good things to know:

- If you don't have an "always on" Internet connection, connect to the Internet before you install any device. That way Windows can search for current drivers automatically after you install the device.

- If you see a prompt asking if it's OK to search online for updated drivers, always choose Yes. Product manufacturers don't taint their own products with viruses or other malware. So there's no security risk involved in downloading drivers.

With those two thoughts in mind, let's take it from the top and begin with a discussion of the most common types of hardware installations.

Using Hot-Pluggable Devices

Many modern hardware devices are *hot-pluggable*, which means you just connect them to your computer and start using them. There's no need to shut down the computer before connecting the device. Nor is there any need to go through a formal installation process after you connect the device. However, you should always read the instructions that came with a device before you connect it for the first time because sometimes you do need to install some software before you connect the device. When that's the case, the software is usually on a CD that comes with the device.

Hot-pluggable devices generally connect to the computer through one of three main ports: USB, IEEE 1392, or PC Card (also called PCMCIA or Cardbus). We'll look at those in the sections to follow.

Connecting USB devices

USB (Universal Serial Bus) is the most common type of hot-pluggable device. USB is used by digital cameras, microphones, external disk drives, and many other types of devices. Like most technologies, USB has evolved over the years, and there are currently three versions of USB on the market.

The main differences among USB standard versions have to do with speed. USB 1.0 and 1.1 have two speeds: Low Speed (1.5 Mbps) used by mice and keyboards, and Full Speed (12 Mbps), more often used by digital cameras and disk drives. USB 2.0 added a third, High Speed, data rate, which can transfer data at the much faster rate of 480 Mbps.

USB 2.0 is downwardly compatible with USB 1.1 and 1.0, which means that you can use a USB 2.0 device in a computer with USB 1.x ports. However, the device will transfer at the 12 Mbps speed rather than the 480 Mbps speed available only in USB 2.0. So you don't really need to know exactly which type of USB your computer has. If you plug a USB 2.0 device into a USB 1.0 or 1.1 port, Windows will display a message telling you that you'd get better performance from a USB 2.0 port. But the device will still work. It'll just be a little slower than if you'd plugged it into a USB 2.0 port.

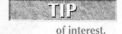 **If you ever want to learn more about a technology mentioned in this chapter, like USB, IEEE 1394, IDE, SATA, or whatever, browse to** www.wikipedia.org **and search for the acronym of interest.**

There are three different USB plug shapes, named Type A, Type B, and Mini-USB or On-the-Go (OTG). The computer has female Type A ports, into which you plug the male Type A plug on the cable. The device might have Type A, B, or a mini-port. Figure 47.1 shows the symbol for USB and the general shape of USB ports on the computer. Examples of Type A, B, and mini-ports are shown to the right of those. The plugs are all keyed so that they only fit one way. Try pushing the plug gently into the port, and it if won't fit, flip the plug over and try again.

FIGURE 47.1

USB symbol, ports, and plug types.

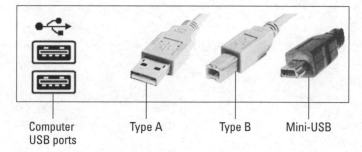

Computer USB ports   Type A   Type B   Mini-USB

Connecting a USB device should be easy, providing you've done any preliminary installations required by your specific device. The steps are as follows:

1. If the device has an on/off switch, turn it off.
2. Connect the device to the computer using the appropriate USB cable.
3. If the device has an on/off switch, turn it on.

The very first time you connect a device, you might get some feedback on the screen indicating that Windows is loading drivers for the device. That message will be followed by one indicating that the device is ready for use.

In many cases, you'll get an AutoPlay dialog box after you've connected the device. Figure 47.2 shows an example. From the AutoPlay dialog box, click whichever option best describes what you want to do with the device. In the case of a hard drive, that would most likely be the Open Folder to View Files option, unless you were using that hard drive to store one specific type of file.

What's "Speed up my system" and ReadyBoost?

Some USB devices can be used to speed up your system with ReadyBoost. When you plug a flash drive into a USB port, AutoPlay options might include an option to speed up your system using ReadyBoost. ReadyBoost is a Vista feature designed to speed up some operations by using flash memory as intermediary storage between the processor and the hard drive. It only works with USB devices that actually can play that role. Flash memory has fast random I/O capabilities, and therefore isn't supported by all USB devices. See Chapter 50 for more information on ReadyBoost.

FIGURE 47.2

Sample AutoPlay dialog box for an external hard drive.

Connecting IEEE 1394 devices

IEEE 1394 (often called 1394 for short) is a high-speed (400-Mbps) standard typically used to connect digital video cameras and high-speed disk drives to computers. The symbol and plug shape for an IEEE 1394 port is shown in Figure 47.3. IEEE 1394 also goes by the names FireWire and iLink.

FIGURE 47.3

FireWire symbol and plug shape.

Connecting a 1394 device is much the same as connecting a USB device:

1. Leave the computer running, and turn the device off (if it has an on/off switch).
2. Connect one end of the 1394 cable to the computer and the other end to the device.
3. Turn on the device and wait.

As always, what happens next depends on the device. If it's a digital video camera, you'll see the dialog box shown in Figure 47.4.

FIGURE 47.4

AutoPlay dialog box for a digital video camera.

PC Cards and Cardbus

PC Cards and Cardbus cards (also called PCMCIA devices) are commonly used on notebook computers. The device is usually a little larger and thicker than a credit card. Figure 47.5 shows an example of a PC Card wireless network adapter.

FIGURE 47.5

PC Card.

Connecting a PC Card to a notebook computer is simple. Just slide the card into the slot, right side up, and push until it's firmly seated. As with USB and FireWire devices, you should get some feedback on the screen indicating when the device is connected and ready for use. How you use the device depends on the type of device you inserted.

Using memory cards

Memory cards are hot-pluggable storage devices. Figure 47.6 shows examples of some memory cards. Most memory cards are used in digital cameras and jump drives. You just connect the camera or jump drive to a USB port to access the content on the memory card. However, if your computer has slots for memory cards, you can also insert the card directly into the appropriate slot.

Examples of memory cards.

After you insert a memory card into a slot, you should get some feedback on the screen indicating that the card is ready for use. That may be in the form of an AutoPlay dialog box. Or an Explorer window may open to show you the contents of the card. Either way, the card will be treated as a USB Mass Storage device, as discussed next.

Memory cards and USB mass storage

Memory cards and USB devices that store data act like disk drives when you connect them to a computer. As such, each will have an icon in your Computer folder when it's connected. Figure 47.7 shows an example where I have an external hard drive connected through a USB port, and a memory card in one of four memory card slots on a computer.

Using such a device is no different from using any other disk drive. To see the contents of the device, open its icon. Use the standard techniques to navigate through folders, to delete files and folders, and to move and copy files and folders. See Chapters 28 and 29 for the necessary buzzwords and basic skills.

Disconnecting hot-pluggable devices

Before you disconnect a hot-pluggable device from a computer, you might want to make sure it's not in the middle of a file transfer, or holding a file that you have open in some program. To do that, point to each of the icons in your Notification area and see if there's one named Safely Remove Hardware. (That icon shows only when you have a storage device attached.) Figure 47.8 shows what the icon looks like when the tip of the mouse pointer touches it.

FIGURE 47.7

External drive and memory card in Computer folder.

FIGURE 47.8

Safely remove hardware icon.

To safely remove a device, click that icon and then click the device you want to disconnect. Or double-click the tiny Safely Remove Hardware icon. The dialog box shown in Figure 47.9 opens listing each connected mass storage device.

> **TIP** If it's difficult to reach around to the back of the computer to connect a USB or FireWire device, just leave that end of the cable plugged into the computer. Disconnect the cable from the device, and leave that end of the cable within easy reach for future connections.

If only one device is listed, click its name, click the Stop button, and click OK. You then can safely remove or disconnect the device.

If two or more devices are listed, double-click any one to see what it is. Then:

■ If it's the device you want to disconnect, click OK.

■ If it's not the device you want to disconnect, click Cancel and double-click the next device.

Not all devices are hot-pluggable. Some require a more elaborate connection and installation procedures. We'll talk about those kinds of devices in the next section.

Safely Remove Hardware dialog box.

Not-so-Hot-Pluggable Devices

Hardware devices that aren't hot-pluggable require a bit more effort than hot-pluggable devices. Most require that you turn off the computer, connect the device, turn the device on, and then turn the computer back on. You might also need to install some software to get the device to work. It all depends on the device you're connecting. As always, you have to read the instructions that came with the device for specifics. I can only provide general guidelines and examples here that give you an idea of what to expect.

Most computers have the ports pointed out in Figure 47.10. Your computer may have more or fewer such ports. Your ports probably won't be arranged exactly like that. On a notebook computer, the ports will likely be on the side of the computer, perhaps hidden under a sliding door. But the basic shape of each port will be as shown in the figure.

There are also devices you can install inside the computer case. These connect to ports inside the computer case on the *motherboard* (also called the *mainboard*). Some of those ports are referred to as *expansion slots*, or just *slots* because of their rectangular shape. The motherboard is a circuit board that provides the wiring between all the hardware devices that make up the system, including the CPU, memory (RAM), internal disk drives, and everything else.

Figure 47.11 provides a general idea of what different types of internal slots and ports look like. If you're not the technical type and just looking at that figure gives you the willies, you should consider having an expert install any internal hardware.

FIGURE 47.10

Ports on the back of a computer.

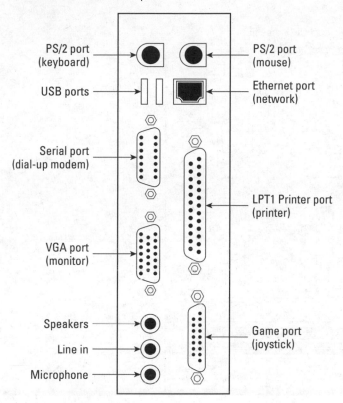

PS/2 port (keyboard)

PS/2 port (mouse)

USB ports

Ethernet port (network)

Serial port (dial-up modem)

LPT1 Printer port (printer)

VGA port (monitor)

Speakers

Line in

Microphone

Game port (joystick)

Installing expansion cards

Many internal hardware devices are PCI Cards, which slide into a PCI slot. The slots are positioned so that one end of the card lines up perfectly with the back of the computer, exposing an external plug. Figure 47.12 shows a general example of what such a card looks like.

Newer motherboards may have PCI Express (PCIe) and PCI Express 16. These provide faster communication between the motherboard, which in turn allows for more powerful expansion cards. The PCI Express 16 slot is ideal for high-powered graphics cards designed to work with advanced graphics and large High Definition TV screens. The AGP (Accelerated Graphics Port) port is strictly for a graphics card. The newer, faster PCIe 16 slot will likely put the AGP slot out of business eventually.

Before you buy an expansion card, you need to know what slots are available on your motherboard. Before you install a card, you need to read the instructions that came with the card. There is no one-rule-fits-all fact that applies to all of the thousands of hardware devices you can add to a PC. You should install the device exactly as told to in the instructions provided by the manufacturer of the device. Winging it is likely to lead to many hours of hair-pulling frustration.

FIGURE 47.11

Slots on a computer motherboard.

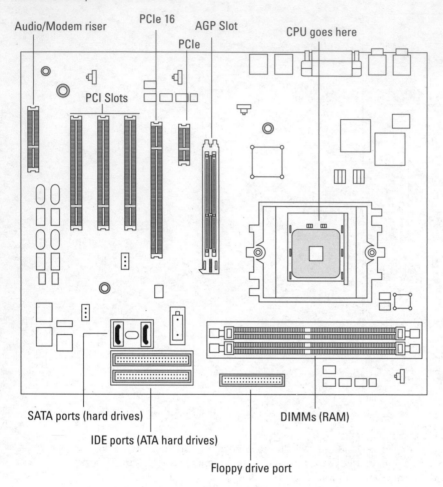

Audio/Modem riser

PCIe 16

AGP Slot

PCIe

CPU goes here

PCI Slots

SATA ports (hard drives)

IDE ports (ATA hard drives)

DIMMs (RAM)

Floppy drive port

It's also very important that you turn off the computer before opening the case to install a card. Remove the power cord too. Ideally, you should wear an antistatic wrist strap so that you don't generate any static electricity sparks. One little spark like that could turn the motherboard to trash, and void the warranty to boot. Then you have a real mess on your hands.

TIP   You can buy an antistatic wrist strap at computer hardware stores, including online stores such as TigerDirect (www.tigerdirect.com), CompUSA (www.compusa.com), CDW (www.cdw.com), and Cyberguys (www.cyberguys.com).

Many AGP and PCIe 16 slots have a locking mechanism to hold the card steady in the slot. You have to make sure that it's in the unlocked position before you try to insert the card into the slot. When installing the card, push firmly on the card to make sure you really get it in there. Don't force it and break it. But push it in well enough to ensure that it's firmly and evenly seated within its slot. If the slot has a locking mechanism, push it into the locked position. Put the case cover back together again, plug in the power cord, and then turn on the PC.

FIGURE 47.12
_____

A sample expansion card.

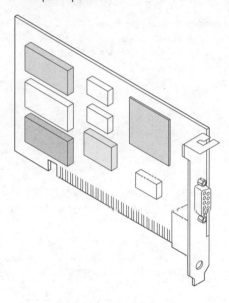

> **CAUTION** When removing a card that has a locking device, don't forget to slide it into the unlocked position. Trying to force the card out of the locked slot would likely cause a lot of damage!

If the device is plug-and-play (as virtually all modern devices are), the rest should be easy. The computer should boot up normally, but you won't necessarily get to the desktop right away. Instead, Windows should detect the new device, and go through an installation procedure to get the device working. You'll get some feedback on the screen as that's happening, in the form of Notification area messages. When the notification messages stop and the desktop looks normal, the device should be ready to use.

Installing more memory (RAM)

Installing more RAM isn't exactly like installing other devices, because you're not likely to get any feedback at all on the Windows desktop when you're done. RAM is such an integral part of the computer that it doesn't really get "installed." The processor just detects it as soon as you turn on the power. The only place you'd even see that you have more RAM is on the General tab of the System Properties dialog box.

The big trick to adding more RAM is finding the right type of memory. You need to match the type and speed of your existing RAM chip, and you need an available DIMM slot on the motherboard. Also, every motherboard has a limit as to the maximum speed and type of memory it can handle. When you build a PC, you know exactly what's involved. But when you buy a prebuilt PC, it's not always easy to find out what you need to know.

Upgrading the CPU

Every motherboard has a certain maximum CPU speed it can handle. You won't know what that is unless you can get the specs on your exact motherboard. Rather than try to upgrade just the CPU, you'd probably be better off upgrading the motherboard, CPU, and RAM while you're at it. That way you can speed up everything, but still use your existing hard drive, CD/DVD drive, mouse, keyboard, monitor, and everything else.

A barebones kit might be the best way to go. With a barebones kit you can get a motherboard, CPU, RAM, and power supply already assembled in a new case. You then transfer your existing hard drive, CD drive, mouse, keyboard, monitor, and everything else to that new case. So you get the benefits of a newer, faster computer without the expense of buying an entirely new PC.

Your best bet is to go to the computer manufacturer's Web site and find the main Web page for your exact model of computer. You can often find out exactly what type and speed of RAM chip is currently installed using that method. PNY (a company that sells RAM chips) has a Memory Configurator link on its home page (www.pny.com). When you click that link, it asks some basic questions about your system and then tells you which RAM chips will work with that system.

TIP   The PNY site also has a How To Install link, which might help you get the feel for what you'll be doing when you purchase more RAM. Remember, you have to look inside the computer and see if you even have an available slot for adding more RAM first.

Even so, installing more RAM isn't really something for the technologically timid to undertake. Even the slightest mistake could prevent the computer from starting at all. If the speed of the new chip doesn't exactly match the speed of the existing chip, the computer will start but you're likely to end up with endless error messages when you try to do just about anything.

CAUTION   People will tell you that you can mix RAM chip speeds. Rather than argue the issue, let me just give you some general advice. If you want your computer to work right, don't mix RAM speeds.

Installing a second hard drive

If you need more hard disk space, installing a second hard drive is the only way to go. Hard disk space is cheap, and it's a lot easier to just toss another 100-GB or 200-GB drive in there than it is to try to pinch a few more bytes out of a single drive by compressing files and moving things out to removable disks.

However, internal hard drive installations can be very difficult. Personally I think that sort of thing is best left to the pros. You need to know how to get to and change settings in your computer's BIOS. You need to know what kind of drives the motherboard can handle, and a whole lot more. These are topics that go well beyond the scope of a Windows book like this. I offer this information mainly for IT pros who are already familiar with hardware topics, and just need to know how to configure things in Vista.

External hard drives are relatively simple to install. Basically you just connect the drive to a USB or FireWire port. If you already bought an internal hard drive but haven't connected it yet, you can convert it to an external drive just by putting it in an external drive enclosure. Just make sure you get an enclosure that has the right internal connectors (IDE or SATA) for your drive.

TIP    To see examples of hard drive enclosures, search an online retailer like www.newegg.com, www.tigerdirect.com, or even froogle.google.com for external drive enclosure. Drives that connect via USB 2.0 can move data at 480 Mbps, which is plenty fast for a hard drive and won't be a performance bottleneck.

Hard drives fall into two main categories, SATA (Serial ATA) and PATA (Parallel ATA), more commonly referred to as IDE (Integrated Drive Electronics) drives. (The ATA stands for Advanced Technology Attachment.) SATA is the newer, faster, and easier technology.

The original SATA drives moved data at a good 150 Mbps (150 million bits per second). The newer SATA II drives move data at a walloping 300 Mbps. Before adding a second SATA drive, you'll need to make sure your motherboard has SATA connectors, and whether they're regular SATA or SATA II connectors.

IDE drives come in multiple speeds too, ranging from 33 Mbps to 133 Mbps. The maximum speed your PC can use depends on the speed of the IDE connectors on the motherboard.

IDE drives have an unusual configuration where you can connect two drives to a single IDE port. One drive is called the master drive, the other the slave drive. You have to physically set a jumper on the drive to make the drive either master or slave. Then you have to connect the drive to the right place on the cable. The master goes at the end of the cable. The slave goes on the plug in the center of the cable, as illustrated in Figure 47.13.

FIGURE 47.13

Internal IDE drives.

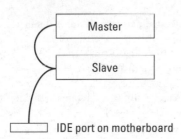

Again, your best bet before installing any hardware device is to follow the instructions that came with the device — to a tee — before you even turn the computer back on and use Windows to configure the device. If in doubt, have a pro install the hardware for you. But, assuming you've installed the drive, either internally or externally, you can then use Windows Vista to partition and format the drive.

Primary and extended partitions

You can divide a basic disk into multiple *partitions*. Each partition looks like a separate item in your Computer folder. The drive can be divided into a maximum of four *primary* partitions, or three primary partitions and one *extended* partition. The difference is that a primary partition can be used as a *system partition*, meaning you can install an operating system on it and boot the computer from it.

An extended partition can't be a boot disk and can't contain an operating system. However, you can divide an extended partition into multiple logical drives, where each logical drive has its own drive letter and icon in My Computer, and looks like a separate drive.

Partitioning and formatting the disk

CAUTION Repartitioning and/or reformatting a disk that already contains files will result in the *permanent* loss of all files on that disk. You should not attempt to repartition or reformat an existing disk unless you fully understand the consequences, and are fully prepared to recover any lost files. Again, if you don't have any formal training and experience in technical matters, it's best to leave this sort of thing to the pros. An in-depth treatment of these more technical hardware matters is beyond the scope of this book.

After you have a new hard drive installed, you can restart Windows Vista and use the Disk Management tool to partition and format the drive. You might as well log in to an account with administrative privileges for this task. If the Computer Management tool doesn't start automatically after you've logged in, you can get to it by following these steps:

1. Click the Start button and choose Control Panel.
2. Click System and Maintenance ⇨ Administrative Tools.
3. Click Computer Management and then click Disk Management in the left column.

 Optionally, press ⊞, type comp, and click Computer Management. Then choose Disk Management in the Computer Management tool that opens.

The new drive appears at the bottom of the display, most likely as Disk 1 (assuming the system has one other disk drive, which will show as Disk 0). The drive's space is indicated by a striped bar showing Unallocated in the lower-left corner. To partition the drive:

1. Right-click within the unallocated space of the new drive and choose New Partition.
2. On the first page of the New Partition Wizard that opens, click Next>.
3. The next page asks whether you want to create a Primary or Extended partition. If this is the first partition, choose Primary, and then click Next. (If you choose Extended, the wizard will end and you'll need to create logical drives before you can proceed with formatting the disk.)
4. The next wizard page asks what size you want to make the partition, and suggests the full capacity of the disk. In my case, where this is a second drive, I would just click Next> to use the suggested size, equal to the capacity of the disk. You can choose a smaller size if you intend to divide the disk into multiple partitions.
5. The next wizard page asks you to assign a drive letter to the drive. It suggests the next available drive letter, which is a good choice. Click Next>.
6. The next wizard page asks how you want to format and label the disk. Your options are as follows:

   ▪ **Do not format this partition:** If you choose this option, you'll have to format the partition later. I suggest that you not choose this option.

   ▪ **File system:** Your choices here are NTFS or FAT32. In Windows Vista, **NTFS** is the only way to go.

   ▪ **Allocation unit size:** This defines the cluster size. Larger clusters mean faster performance but more wasted space. The Default option automatically chooses the best allocation unit size given the type and capacity of the disk, so that would be your best choice.

   ▪ **Volume label:** This is the name that appears with the drive's icon in My Computer. You can enter any name you want up to 12 characters in length (including spaces). You can also change that name at any time in the future.

   ▪ **Perform a quick format:** If you choose this option, formatting will go quickly, but the drive won't be checked for errors. Better to leave this option unselected.

   ▪ **Enable file and folder compression:** Only available if you chose NTFS as the file system, this option automatically compresses all files and folders on the drive. This conserves disk space, but you pay for it in time, because it takes longer to open and save files when they're always compressed. You can still compress individual files and folders if you leave this option unselected. So, I suggest you leave this unselected.

7. Click Next> after making your selections.

8. The last wizard page summarizes your selections. Click Finish.

Now you get to wait for the disk to be formatted. This could take a long, long time. You can continue to use your computer while that's going on. Or you can just let the computer run and go out to lunch or something. It's up to you. But you'll have to be patient.

If you set up the drive as one large partition, you're done when the Formatting . . . indicator reaches 100%. You can close the Computer Management tool and Control Panel, and go to the section titled "Viewing the new drive's icon."

If you are partitioning the disk into smaller units, you can repeat steps 1 to 8 for each partition. Just make sure that you right-click an unpartitioned portion of the disk in step 1. If you create an extended partition, the wizard will end as soon as you do. You'll then need to right-click the extended partition, choose New Logical Drive, and follow the instructions presented by the wizard.

Figure 47.14 shows an example where my original drive (Disk 0) contains three partitions, drives C, D, and E. Their volumes' labels are Vista, XP, and SpotDocs, respectively. Disk 1 is an external drive partitioned and formatted as a single drive labeled External HD with G: as its drive letter.

FIGURE 47.14

Two hard drives in the Computer Management tool.

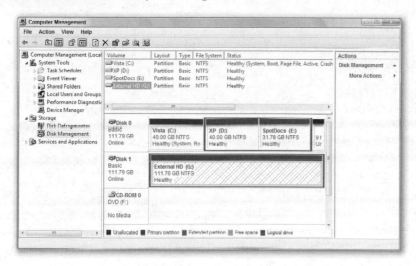

When all the partitioning and formatting is complete, exit the Computer Management tool. Access the drive as you would any other — through the Computer folder. Figure 47.15 shows an example. Notice how each Hard Disk Drive icon represents a drive (or partition) defined in the Disk Management tool.

By the way, I set up all these drives and partitions long before writing this chapter. So that's why most of them already contain a considerable amount of data. The important point to glean from all of this is the fact that each formatted partition on a physical hard drive appears as a single drive icon in your Computer folder.

FIGURE 47.15

Drives and partitions as viewed through the Computer folder.

Other hard drive operations

In this section, I'll cover some general issues concerning hard disks. All of these operations pose some risk of data loss, and should only be attempted by people who understand the risks and are confident they have backups of all important data.

Converting a FAT disk to NTFS

Windows offers three different file systems for formatting a hard drive. The earliest file system, FAT (File Allocation Table), was used in DOS, and the earliest versions of Windows. FAT32 was introduced with Windows 95. NTFS (New Technology File System) was introduced in Windows NT 4.0, largely to support user access control required in domain networking.

When you divide a hard drive into multiple volumes, you can format each independently of the other. (A volume is any partition or logical drive that has its own drive letter and icon in My Computer.) NTFS is the preferred file system for Windows Vista. There's no reason to use FAT32 or FAT unless you have multiple operating systems installed and can choose one or the other at startup. For example, if you can boot to Windows Vista, XP, and 98, the Windows 98 operating system will not be able to access files on a local NTFS volume.

 On a network, a Windows 98 computer can access files on an NTFS volume from a remote computer in the network.

Each file system imposes minimum and maximum volume sizes, and a maximum file size. Keep in mind that these file systems apply only to the hard drives, not to floppies or laser media like CDs or DVDs. Table 47.1 summarizes the differences among the file systems.

TABLE 47.1

Differences among NTFS, FAT32, and FAT File Systems for Hard Drives

	NTFS	FAT32	FAT
Locally accessible to	Windows Vista, 2003, XP, and 2000	Windows 95 and later	DOS and all Windows versions
Minimum volume size	10 MB	512 MB	1 MB
Maximum volume size	> 2 TB*	32 GB	4 GB
Maximum file size	Entire volume	4 GB	2 GB
Supports domain networks	Yes	No	No

* Terabyte, a trillion bytes or 1,024 GB.

 Changing the file system on a drive poses some risk of data loss, and should only be attempted by people who understand the risks and are prepared to recover from any loss of data.

You can convert a FAT or FAT32 file system to NTFS, but it's not possible to go in the other direction. That is, you can always upgrade to NTFS, but you cannot downgrade. Be sure to close all open documents and program windows prior to starting the conversion. To convert a FAT or FAT32 volume to NTFS, use the following syntax with the convert command:

```
convert drive: /fs:ntfs
```

where *drive* is the letter of the hard drive you want to convert. Advanced users can enter convert /? at the command prompt, or search Windows Help and Support, for more advanced options such as /cvtarea, which places all NTFS metadata in a contiguous placeholder file. To enter the command:

1. Close all open documents and program windows.
2. Click the Start button and choose All Programs ⇨ Accessories ⇨ Command Prompt.
3. Type the command using the syntax shown. For example, to convert hard disk drive D: from FAT or FAT32 to NTFS, type convert d: /fs:ntfs.
4. Press Enter, and follow the instructions on the screen.

If you're converting your system drive (C:), you'll need to restart the computer to start the conversion. Don't use the computer during the conversion process.

Shrinking and extending partitions

NEW FEATURE You can shrink and extend partitions without reformatting, either from the Disk Management tool or by using the DISKPART command.

You can shrink existing partitions to free up unallocated space. And if you have any unallocated space, you can extend existing partitions into that space. As always, there is some risk in doing this. Therefore you should back up everything before even attempting to shrink or extend a partition.

CAUTION The techniques described in this section will *not* increase the amount of hard disk space you have. The techniques described in this section are best left to professionals and highly knowledgeable computer users. The slightest error could cost you everything on your hard drive! Not recommended for casual computer users.

You can shrink a basic volume that's either raw (unformatted) or formatted with NTFS quite easily right in the Disk Management tool. You can shrink to the current used space size or to the first unmovable files (such as a paging file) on the volume. To shrink a volume, just right-click it at the bottom of the Disk Management screen and choose Shrink Volume. A dialog box opens to show how far you can shrink the selected volume. Just make your selection and click OK.

Likewise, if you have some unallocated space on the drive, you can extend an existing partition into that space. A wizard opens to take you step-by-step through the process.

For more information on extending and shrinking volumes, including spanned volumes, search the Help in the Disk Management tool.

Changing a volume label

A *volume label* is the name of a volume as it appears in your Computer folder. By default, each volume is labeled Local Disk. To change a drive's Volume Label, right-click its icon in your Computer folder and choose Properties. On the General tab of the Properties sheet, type the new name into the first textbox, where you see External HD in Figure 47.16.

FIGURE 47.16

Changing a volume label.

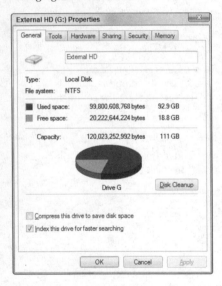

Changing a drive letter

Drive letters A, B, and C are reserved for floppy disk drives and your hard drive, and cannot be changed. Beyond those first three letters, you can assign drive letters as you see fit. Just be aware that when you do, Windows will *not* update your settings and programs to the change. All settings you've made concerning locations of files in all programs will be fouled up. Virtual folders and items in Media Player, Movie Maker, and Photo Gallery will need to be updated to reflect the new drive locations. If you're not sure how to deal with these things, better not to change any drive letters.

CAUTION Changing drive letters is an operation that's best left to experienced users who understand the consequences and can solve, on their own, the problems that are likely to follow. Asking people for help after the fact won't help unless that person can sit at your computer and figure out what's going on.

No two drives can have the same drive letter. If you need to swap two drive letters (for example, change drive E: to drive F: and change drive F: to drive E:), you'll need to temporarily leave one of the drives without a letter. The Disk Management tool, which you need to make this change, will allow you to do that though. Here's how it works:

1. Get back to the Disk Management tool described at the start of this section.
2. Right-click the graphical representation of the drive whose letter you want to change. Or, to change a removable drive, right-click its drive letter like in Figure 47.17. Choose Change Drive Letter and Paths.

FIGURE 47.17

Changing a drive letter.

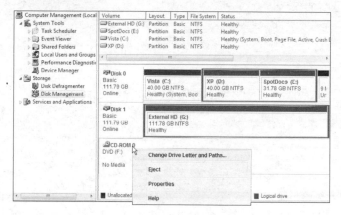

3. If the new letter to which you want to assign the drive is available, click Change, choose the new drive letter, and click OK. Otherwise, if you want to assign the current drive's letter to a different drive, click Remove and click Yes.
4. Repeat steps 2 and 3 until all drives have the letters you want them to have. Then close the Disk Management tool.

The new drive letters will show up the next time you open your Computer folder.

Removing Hardware

Hot-pluggable devices don't follow the type of removal discussed in this section. To remove a USB or FireWire Device, or a PC card or memory card, see the section titled "Disconnecting hot-pluggable devices" earlier in this chapter. This section is about removing more complex devices like internal components. Before you follow the procedures described in this section, make sure you understand what you're removing and why you're removing it. Do not attempt to fix some problem by removing devices through sheer guesswork.

You'll need administrative privileges to perform the tasks described here. It might be best to sign into a user account before you get started so you don't have to rely on privilege escalation along the way.

Before you physically remove a device from the system, first uninstall it through Device Manager by following these steps:

1. Click the Start button, right-click the Computer option, and choose Properties.

2. In the left side of the System page that opens, click Advanced System Settings. Click Allow if prompted.

3. In the System Properties dialog box that opens, click the Hardware tab, then click the Device Manager button.

4. Expand the category in which the device is listed. Then right-click the name of the device you intend to remove and choose Uninstall, like in Figure 47.18.

FIGURE 47.18

Uninstall a hardware device.

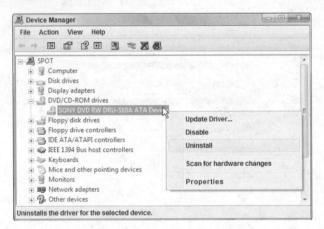

5. Click OK.

Now you need to shut down the computer, unplug the power cord, and physically remove the device from the system. Then plug the machine back in, start it up, and everything should be back to the way it was before you ever installed the device. If you set a protection point just before installing the hardware, you can return to that protection point just to make sure.

Updating Drivers

At the start of this chapter I discussed the importance of using Windows Vista drivers with your hardware. The quickest and easiest way to get an updated driver for a device is usually to search for it online by following these steps:

1. Open Device Manager (tap ⊞, type dev, and choose Device Manager).

2. Right-click the device that needs an updated driver and choose Update Driver Software as in Figure 47.19.

FIGURE 47.19

Update a device driver.

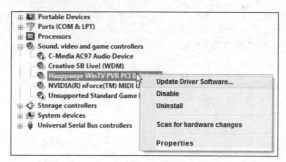

3. Click Search automatically for updated driver software, and then follow the onscreen instructions.

Often, that's all it takes. You might need to restart the computer after the driver installation is complete.

If that method doesn't work, you may have to go to the product manufacturer's Web site and search for a Vista driver there. If you find the driver, make sure to follow the manufacturer's instructions carefully to download and install the updated driver.

Dealing with Devices that Prevent Vista from Starting

There may be times when a newly installed hardware device prevents Windows from starting properly. In most cases, such devices will be disabled automatically so that Windows can start. If it works that way, then you can typically do the steps described in the preceding section to try and get the updated driver online.

If Vista cannot disable or get around the new device, you may be able to start in Safe Mode and either get updated drivers there, or disable the device manually. Here are the steps:

1. Close all open programs and documents and save any work in progress.
2. Restart the computer (click the Start button, click the arrow next to the lock, and choose Restart).
3. As the computer is restarting, press the F8 key a few times. The window of opportunity is after the POST (Power on Self Test) and before Vista is too far into loading.

CAUTION If your keyboard has a Function Lock (F Lock) key, keep an eye on it during the reboot process. If it turns off at any time, be sure to turn it back on before pressing F8.

4. When the Advanced Boot Options appear, choose Safe Mode with Networking.
5. Log in to the Administrator account.

When you're at the desktop, follow the procedure described under "Updating Drivers" to search for updated drivers. If you cannot find updated drivers, your best bet might be to disable the device by right-clicking its name and choosing Disable from the shortcut menu. Close Device Manager and restart the computer again normally.

If you had to disable the device, it won't work. But at least you can get Vista started and try to find an updated driver through the product manufacturer's Web site.

Wrap Up

This chapter has been about connecting, installing, and removing hardware. Some of this material is intended for more advanced users who are familiar with computer hardware. If some of the content was over your head and you need to install or remove some hardware, consider having the job done professionally. The main points of this chapter are summarized here:

- Most modern devices are hot-pluggable, which means you just connect them to the computer as needed.

- Always read and follow the instructions that came with a device before connecting it to your computer. Winging it will likely result in frustration.

- Hot-pluggable devices that act as storage devices have icons in your Computer folder while connected. You can transfer files to and from such a device using basic techniques described in Chapter 29.

- More advanced hardware devices generally require shutting down the computer, connecting the device, turning the device on, and then starting the computer again.

- Hard drive installations are best left to professionals. Use the Disk Management tool to partition and format a new drive.

- To remove a hot-pluggable storage device, click the Safely Remove Hardware icon in the Notification area and stop the device before physically removing it.

- To remove other devices, first uninstall it in Device Manager. Then shut down the computer and physically remove the device from the system.

Chapter 48

Using Wireless Bluetooth Devices

The World of Bluetooth

In a nutshell, Bluetooth is a wireless technology that provides wireless communications among computers, printers, mobile phones, PDAs, digital cameras, and other electronic devices. You can connect as many as eight devices together with Bluetooth, with one device acting as the master device and up to seven slave devices. For example, you could have a desktop PC, a notebook, PDA, digital camera, MP3 player, digital video camera, headphones, and mobile phone all linked together wirelessly. They could all share a high-speed Internet connection, shared data, and use a single printer.

As I write this chapter late in 2006, the current Bluetooth version is 2.0. Bluetooth transfers data at up to 3 Mbps, which is slower than 802.11b (11 Mbps) and 802.11g (54 Mbps). So, if you're thinking of setting up a permanent wireless network between computers, you may want to stick with the 802.11 standards described in Chapter 52 of this book. But when it comes to connecting noncomputer Bluetooth devices, or wirelessly connecting a printer, or occasionally transferring files between computers, Bluetooth can't be beat.

There are three types of Bluetooth devices, classified by the range across which devices can communicate:

- **Class 1:** Transmit and receive data up to 330 feet (100m)
- **Class 2:** Transmit and receive data up to 32 feet (10m).
- **Class 3:** Transmit and receive data up to 3 feet (1m).

Some Bluetooth buzzwords and concepts that you'll encounter in this section as well as in the instructions that come with Bluetooth devices are as follows:

- **Discovery:** A Bluetooth device finds other Bluetooth devices to which it can connect through a process called discovery. To prevent Bluetooth devices from connecting at random, discovery is usually turned off on a Bluetooth device. After a device has been discovered, you can turn discovery off.

IN THIS CHAPTER

What Bluetooth is all about

Connecting and configuring a Bluetooth adapter

Associating with different Bluetooth devices

Connecting to a Bluetooth-enabled personal area network

Transferring files between two systems using the personal area network

- **Discoverable:** A discoverable (or *visible*) Bluetooth device is one that has discovery turned on, so other Bluetooth devices within range can "see" and connect to the device.

- **Pairing:** Once two or more Bluetooth devices have discovered one another and have been paired (connected), you can turn off their discovery features. The devices will forever be able to connect to one another, and unauthorized foreign devices will not be able to discover and hack into the paired devices.

- **Encryption:** A process by which data transferred is encoded to make it unreadable to any unauthorized device that picks up a signal from the device. Bluetooth offers powerful 128-bit data encryption to secure the content of all transferred data.

- **Passkey:** Similar to a password, only devices that share a passkey can communicate with one another. This is yet another means of preventing unauthorized access to data transmitted across Bluetooth radio waves.

A noncomputer gadget like a phone or PDA that supports Bluetooth is called a *Bluetooth device*. A standard desktop PC or laptop computer usually isn't a Bluetooth device. But as a rule, it's easy to turn your PC or laptop into a Bluetooth device. You just plug a Bluetooth USB adapter — a tiny device about the size of your thumb — into any available USB port, and presto, your computer is a Bluetooth device. Making your computer into a Bluetooth device doesn't limit it in any way. It just extends the capabilities of your computer so that you can do things like:

- Connect a Bluetooth mouse or keyboard
- Use the Add Printer Wizard to use a Bluetooth printer wirelessly
- Use a Bluetooth-enabled phone or dial-up device as a modem
- Transfer files between Bluetooth-ready computers or devices by using Bluetooth
- Join an ad hoc personal area network (PAN) of Bluetooth-connected devices (an ad hoc network is an "informal" network, where devices connect and disconnect on an as-needed basis, without the need for a central hub or base station)

Bluetooth devices use radio signals to communicate wirelessly. When you install a Bluetooth adapter on your PC or laptop, you also install *radio drivers*. Windows Vista comes with many radio drivers preinstalled.

 If a built-in radio driver doesn't work with your device, install the drivers that came with the device per the device manufacturer's instructions.

Configuring Your Bluetooth Adapter

If you plan to share a single Internet account among several computers or Bluetooth devices, you should install your first Bluetooth USB adapter in the computer that connects directly to the modem or router. That will give other Bluetooth devices that you add later easy access to the Internet through that computer's Internet connection.

After you've installed a Bluetooth adapter, you'll find a new icon named BlueTooth Devices in Control Panel. To get to it, click the Start button, choose Control Panel, and click Network and Internet. Or, after you open Control Panel, click Classic View in the left column to see individual icons. The BlueTooth icon looks like a large letter B as in Figure 48.1. You might also notice a Bluetooth icon in the Notification area, as is also shown in Figure 48.1.

FIGURE 48.1

New icon on a PC that's configured as a Bluetooth device.

Bluetooth
Devices

TIP To return to the Category view in Control Panel, click Control Panel Home in the left column. If you don't see that option, you're probably not in Control Panel's home page. Click the Back button until you get there, or click Control Panel in the Address bar.

The Bluetooth Devices dialog box will be your central point for installing Bluetooth. To open that dialog box, double-click the Bluetooth Devices Notification area icon, or open the icon in Control Panel. Initially, the Devices tab in the dialog box will be empty. But as you install devices and join devices to a Bluetooth PAN, you'll see the names of those devices listed on that tab.

The Options tab in the Bluetooth Devices dialog box, shown in Figure 48.2, provides general options for controlling discovery and the ability to install Bluetooth devices. If you don't see a Bluetooth Devices icon in your Notification area, make sure to choose the Show the Bluetooth icon in the notification area checkbox.

The shortcut icon that appears when you right-click the Notification area, also shown in Figure 48.2, provides options for adding a Bluetooth device, sending and receiving files, and joining a PAN.

FIGURE 48.2

Options tab of the Bluetooth Devices dialog box and Notification area shortcut menu.

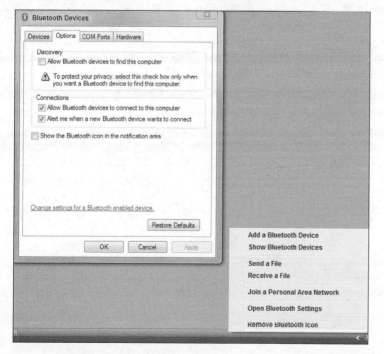

Adding Bluetooth-Enabled Devices

There are many different types of Bluetooth devices on the market. Most have some means of making the device discoverable (visible) to other devices. Whether or not you have to make your PC discoverable to install a device depends on the type of installation you're about to perform. As always, you need to read the documentation that came with your device for specifics. But if you do need to make your computer discoverable, it's simply a matter of choosing the "Turn discovery on" option, visible in Figure 48.2.

On the shortcut menu for the Bluetooth Devices notification icon, the Add a Bluetooth Device option opens the Add Bluetooth Device Wizard, which takes you step by step through the process of adding a device. The sections that follow discuss general techniques for adding Bluetooth devices, many of which will involve the Add Bluetooth Device Wizard.

Installing a Bluetooth printer

To install a Bluetooth printer, follow the printer manufacturer's instructions for turning on the printer and enabling its ability to connect to a computer. Then, on your PC:

1. Click the Start button and choose Printers. Or, click Start and choose Control Panel. If Control Panel opens in Category view, click Hardware and Sound. Select the Printers link to continue.

2. In the Explorer bar, click on Add a printer.

3. On the first wizard page, select the *Add a network, wireless or Bluetooth printer* option.

4. Click Next, and Windows will start searching for your Bluetooth-compatible printer. If Windows is unable to locate the printer, it probably means that either the printer is not powered up or there is a problem with the Bluetooth device connected to your computer. Try clicking the link *The printer that I want isn't listed* and then select *Add a Bluetooth printer*.

5. After your printer has been found, follow the remaining wizard instructions until you can click the Finish button to complete the job.

When it is installed, you should be able to print from any Bluetooth device according to the instructions that came with that device. To print a document from your computer, follow the usual procedure (choose File ⇨ Print from the program's menu bar), and choose the Bluetooth printer from the Printer Name options in the Print dialog box.

Install a Bluetooth keyboard or mouse

To install a Bluetooth keyboard or mouse, you must first connect the device by cable, or use a cable-connected mouse or keyboard to provide the initial connectivity. Also, you must know how to make your mouse or keyboard discoverable (visible). If you're not sure how to get started, refer to the instructions that came with the mouse or keyboard.

If you're installing a keyboard, check its documentation to see if the keyboard supports the use of a passkey. And if so, find out if it already has a pre-assigned passkey, or if you can use a passkey of your own choosing. Then, to perform the installation, follow these steps:

1. Right-click the Bluetooth Device Notification area icon and choose Add a Bluetooth Device. Or open the Bluetooth Devices applet from Control Panel or its notification icon, and click the Add button at the bottom of the Devices tab.

2. Choose My device is set up and ready to be found and click Next.

3. Click the discovered device's name, and then click Next.

4. If you're adding a keyboard, do one of the following as appropriate for your device:

  ■ To have Windows create a safe, random passkey, click Choose a passkey for me.

  ■ If your device has a predefined passkey, choose Use the passkey found in the documentation, and then type the passkey.

  ■ If you want to create your own custom passkey, click Let me choose my own passkey, and then type a passkey.

  ■ If the device doesn't support the use of passkeys, choose Don't use a passkey.

5. Click Next and follow the remaining instructions presented by the wizard.

Install a Bluetooth mobile phone

Some Bluetooth mobile phones can connect to a computer to synchronize phone books and transfer files. Some (but not all) mobile phones can also act as modems to connect to the Internet. Make sure that you read the documentation that came with the phone so that you understand how to make the phone discoverable, how to name the phone (if necessary), basic information on setting up a passkey, and whether or not you can use the phone as a modem.

If your mobile phone can act as a modem, you'll need a dial-up Internet account to connect to the Internet. Most likely this will be a mobile service provider. You'll need to know your user name, password, carrier code or phone number, and other basic account information prior to setting up your Internet account. Only your Internet service provider (or mobile service provider) can give you that information.

The exact procedure for installing a Bluetooth phone will vary from one phone to the next. But to get started, make sure that discovery and the ability to add new devices is enabled on your PC. Then, follow these steps:

1. Right-click the Bluetooth Device Notification area icon and choose Add a Bluetooth Device. Or, open the Bluetooth Devices dialog box from Control Panel or its notification icon, and click the Add button at the bottom of the Devices tab.

2. Follow the instructions presented by the wizard, and as specified by the mobile phone manufacturer.

If the phone you installed in the preceding steps can act as a modem, you can then proceed with the following steps to set up a Bluetooth connection to the Internet:

1. Open the Network and Sharing Center folder by clicking the Start button and choose Control Panel. If Control Panel opens in Category view, click Network and Internet. Open the Network and Sharing Center icon.

2. Click Set up a connection or network from the left column.

3. Select the option Set up a dial-up connection and then click Next.

4. If your computer sees the mobile phone connected via Bluetooth, it will prompt you for the information shown in Figure 48.3. When the information is filled out, click the Connect button to continue.

5. When you have successfully dialed your ISP, either click the link Browse the Internet now or click the Close button.

When your connection is configured, you should be able to get online by opening Network and Sharing Center from the Control Panel. Click Connect to a network link on the left side of the window. The

Connect to a network dialog box will list all of the available connections that have been set up on your system. Select the connection and click the Connect button. The mobile phone should dial based on the information you included. When you're finished using the Internet connection, click the Disconnect link within Network and Sharing Center next to the mobile connection.

FIGURE 48.3

The settings necessary for configuring the dial-up connection.

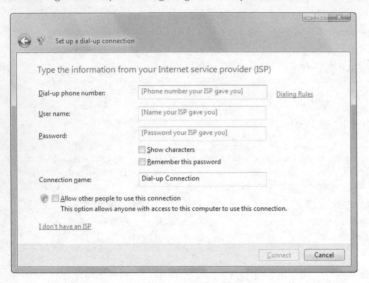

Connect a Bluetooth Blackberry

To connect a Bluetooth Blackberry device to your computer, make sure that you first make the Blackberry discoverable (visible) and (if necessary) give the Blackberry a name. Complete the following steps:

1. Right-click the Bluetooth Device Notification area icon and choose Add a Bluetooth Device. Or open the Bluetooth Devices dialog box from the Control Panel or its notification icon and click the Add button at the bottom of the Devices tab.

2. Make sure that the Blackberry option for Discoverable is set to Yes under the Bluetooth settings.

3. From within Vista, check the box My Device is set up and ready to be found and then click the Next button.

4. Follow the remaining steps in the wizard including setting the passkey so that your computer and Blackberry can communicate.

After the wizard completes, Windows may prompt for additional software to be installed. You can tell Windows to look locally and on the Internet or to load the software for the device from a CD provided by the vendor.

Connect a Bluetooth Windows Mobile device

To connect a Bluetooth Windows Mobile device to your computer, make sure that you know the handheld PC well enough to make it discoverable (visible), and (if necessary) to give the handheld a name. Complete the necessary steps, and then follow these steps on your PC:

1. Right-click the Bluetooth Device Notification area icon, and choose Add a Bluetooth Device. Or, open the Bluetooth Devices dialog box from Control Panel or its notification icon, and click the Add button at the bottom of the Devices tab.

2. Follow the instructions in the Add Bluetooth Device Wizard to install your Pocket PC. Enter the passphrase when prompted, and then click Finish when the wizard completes.

After you've completed the wizard, the Windows Mobile Device Center application should start.

> **NOTE** Prior to Windows Vista, Microsoft provided the ActiveSync software that you installed on your computer to communicate and synch your handheld device. With Windows Vista, however, the functionality has been incorporated into the operating system in the Windows Mobile Device Center application.

From this point on, the Windows Mobile device is paired with your computer. You should be able to follow the instructions that came with your Windows Mobile device to synchronize that device with your PC.

Install a Bluetooth Palm PC

To connect a Bluetooth Palm PC to your computer, make sure that you know the handheld PC well enough to make it discoverable (visible) and (if necessary) to give the handheld a name. Complete the necessary steps, and then follow these steps on your PC:

1. Right-click the Bluetooth Device Notification area icon and choose Add a Bluetooth Device. Or open the Bluetooth Devices dialog box from Control Panel or its notification icon and click the Add button at the bottom of the Devices tab.

2. Follow the instructions presented by the Add Bluetooth Device Wizard.

3. If you see COM (serial) port numbers on the Finish page of the wizard, write them down, because you'll need those numbers later.

> **NOTE** If the Finish page in the wizard doesn't list COM ports (or serial ports), don't worry about it. That just means your Palm PC doesn't use, or require, a COM port.

Now you can install, on your PC, the HotSync software, and any other software that came with your Palm PC (unless, of course, you've already installed that software). But whether or not you've already installed the software, at some point you'll be asked to provide COM port, or serial port, numbers. Be sure to use the numbers provided on the Finish page of the Add Bluetooth Device Wizard as described in step 3. To use your synchronization software, follow the instructions that came with your Palm PC.

Joining a Bluetooth personal area network

A Bluetooth personal area network (PAN) is a short-range wireless network used to connect devices together wirelessly. It's commonly used to connect a laptop to a desktop PC, though it can be used to connect other types of Bluetooth devices. As a rule, there's not much to joining Bluetooth devices to a Bluetooth network. Most of the action takes place automatically behind the scenes.

To understand the basic procedure, let's assume you already have a desktop computer with a functional Internet connection. You've already installed a Bluetooth USB adapter on that computer, so it's now a

Bluetooth device. On that desktop computer, you can open the Bluetooth Settings dialog box, click the Options tab, and make sure that the *Turn discovery on* and *Allow Bluetooth devices to connect to this computer* options are selected.

On a laptop computer, plug in a second Bluetooth USB adapter. You want to connect the laptop to the desktop in a personal area network. To do so, starting from the laptop computer, follow these steps:

1. Right-click the Bluetooth Devices Notification area icon and choose Join a Personal Area Network. A list of Bluetooth devices should appear. If at least one device does not appear, click the Add button and follow the steps to locate a Bluetooth-enabled computer. When the search is complete, you should see a list of all of the available devices as shown in Figure 48.4.

FIGURE 48.4

Bluetooth devices you can join in a PAN.

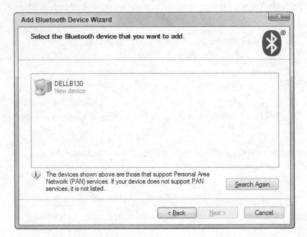

2. Click the name of the computer to which you want to connect, and click the Connect or Next button.

3. Choose a passkey method from the next wizard screen (the Choose a passkey for me option is sufficient), and then click Next.

4. You'll be given a passkey as in the upper-left corner of Figure 48.5. On the other computer, you'll be asked to type in that same passkey, as in the lower-right corner of that same figure. Type in the passkey exactly as shown in the first computer and click Next.

5. Follow any remaining instructions in the wizards on both computers until you get to the Finish page and then click the Finish button in each wizard.

Once the connection is established, you should have Internet access on both computers. You can share printers and folders, and move and copy files between computers using the techniques described in Chapters 29 and 35.

Note, however, that if you made the Bluetooth connection to only one computer in an existing LAN, you'll have access only to the shared resources on the Bluetooth-enabled computer, not all the computers in the LAN.

FIGURE 48.5

Assigning a passkey to two computers in a Bluetooth network.

Troubleshooting a Bluetooth Network Connection

If you can't get any connectivity at all using Bluetooth, try the following remedy:

1. Go to the computer that's having trouble connecting to the PAN.

2. Open Network and Sharing Center. Tap ⊞, type net, and click Network and Sharing Center. Or click the Start button and choose Control Panel ⇨ Network and Internet ⇨ Network and Sharing Center.

3. Scroll down to the Bluetooth Network Connection group. If you're unable to locate the Bluetooth Network Connection group, you'll need to follow the steps outlined earlier including entering a passkey from the other system in the PAN.

By the time you complete the wizards on both screens, you should have a connection. The Network and Sharing Center folders on each PC should have similar Bluetooth network entries, as in the example shown in Figure 48.6.

Sharing an Internet connection

If you're unable to get Internet connectivity from the laptop computer, go to the computer that's connected to the modem or router. Open Network and Sharing Center and choose Manage network connections from the left side of the screen. Right-click that Internet connection icon and choose Properties.

In the Properties dialog box for the Internet connection, click the Sharing tab and choose *Allow other network users to connect through this computer's Internet connection* as in Figure 48.7.

FIGURE 48.6

Bluetooth network in Network and Sharing Center folder.

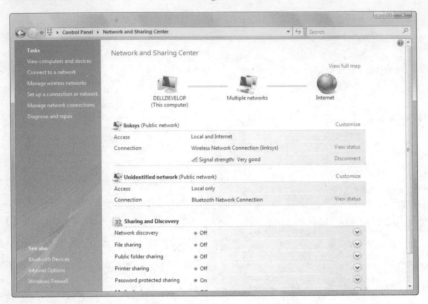

FIGURE 48.7

Internet connection sharing enabled.

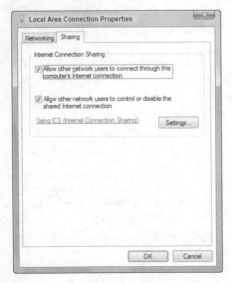

Also, check the settings for the Windows Firewall:

1. Press ⊞, type `fire`, and click Windows Firewall. Or click the Start button and choose Control Panel ➪ Security ➪ Windows Firewall.

2. Click the Change settings link and then the Advanced tab.

3. Make sure that Bluetooth Network Connection is checked to enable that type of network connection.

With these settings you should now be able to connect to the Internet from the other computers in the PAN.

Transferring files between Bluetooth devices

When you connect two computers in a Bluetooth network, you can move and copy multiple files between computers using the techniques described under "Transferring Files between Computers" in Chapter 54.

You can also use the Send a File and Receive a File options on the Bluetooth Devices shortcut menu as an alternative. However, you can't move files that way, and you can only copy one file at a time. So, this method usually is best for transferring files to a noncomputer Bluetooth device. But still, if you want to transfer one file between computers using this method, here are the steps:

1. On the computer to which you plan to send a file, right-click the Bluetooth Devices icon in the Notification area and choose Receive a File. The Bluetooth File Transfer Wizard opens and waits for you to send a file from the other computer.

2. On the computer that contains the file you want to copy, right-click the Bluetooth Devices notification icon and choose Send a File.

3. In the wizard that opens, click the Browse button, choose the computer (or device) to which you want to send the file, and then click OK.

4. If the two devices are already paired using a passkey, the passkey options will be disabled, and you can ignore those options. Just click Next.

5. Click the Browse button on the next wizard page, and navigate to the folder that contains the file on the local system that you want to send. Then, click the icon of the file you want to send, and click the Open button. Then click Next.

6. On the receiving computer, the wizard asks what you want to name the file and where you want to put it. Type a filename for the file you're about to receive, and use the Browse button to choose the folder in which you want to put the file. Then click Next.

7. When the transfer is complete, click the Finish button in the last wizard page on both computers.

Remember, there are many different Bluetooth devices on the market. If none of the techniques described here help you make the connection between two computers in a personal area network, be sure to refer to the instructions that came with your Bluetooth device.

Wrap Up

This chapter has been about installing and configuring Bluetooth devices and Bluetooth networks. Bluetooth devices provide an excellent alternative to many commonly wired devices. Also, they usually are fast and easy to set up and can provide a great way to communicate between computers without having to rely on more complex networking. Here's a recap of the technologies covered in this chapter:

- Bluetooth is currently at version 2.0 and allows you to connect cell phones, PDAs, mice, keyboards, and other Bluetooth devices.

- To turn a computer into a Bluetooth device, simply connect a Bluetooth USB adapter to a USB port on the computer.

- To connect a Bluetooth device to a computer, activate discovery on the device, bring it within range of the computer, right-click the Bluetooth Devices icon in the Notification area, and choose Add a Bluetooth Device.

- To create a personal area network between two or more computers, add a Bluetooth USB adapter to each computer. Then, right-click the Bluetooth Devices Notification area icon and choose Join a Personal Area Network.

- Regardless of what type of device you intend to connect to your computer, always read the instructions that came with the device first.

Chapter 49

Syncing Devices

I f you've ever had files on a remote device that you wish you could easily take with you and keep in sync, Windows Sync Center and Offline Files provide the solutions that fit your need. The two solutions work together to remove the time-consuming chore of always copying data between a remote system and your local computer. There are many options discussed throughout this chapter for scheduling and conflict resolution that Sync Center provides.

Sync Center works with many devices, including PDAs and portable music players. I'll briefly discuss these topics, but the majority of functionality regarding synchronizing these devices is included with the software included with the device.

Syncing with Network Files

One of the most common uses for Windows synchronization is for offline files. This is most frequently used for laptop computers but can also be used with desktop systems. To do this, you'll need to have a Network Location set up on your local computer that connects to a server (see Chapter 53). You are able to set up offline files to synchronize the data on the server down to your local system. This makes the content available when you are away from that server.

You can edit the data while disconnected from the network, and Sync Center will make sure that the changes you have made while disconnected will be sent back to the server when you're connected back to the network. In the event someone has edited or changed the files on the server, Sync Center will ask for your assistance. There are several steps to setting up offline files; the first of which starts with making the files and folders available offline.

NOTE Not all versions of Windows Vista support synchronizing files with another system. Vista Home Basic and Vista Home Premium do not support synchronizing with Network Locations.

Using Sync Center for offline files

The first step to setting up offline files is to add a Network Location to your system if you don't already have one. This is covered in more detail in Chapter 53. When you have a Network Location configured, clicking your Computer link should look similar to Figure 49.1.

FIGURE 49.1

A list of Network Locations on my computer.

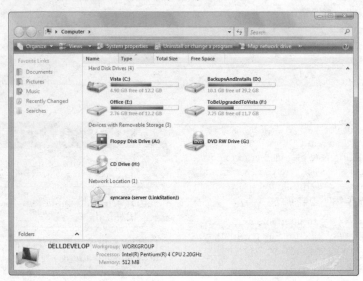

When you have at least one Network Location configured, you need to right-click the location and select Always Available Offline. A dialog box will appear showing the progress of the synchronization. At this point, the content has synchronized to your local system, and you can disconnect from the network and still use the files that once only existed on the server. At this point, you're able to right-click the Network Location again and this time select Sync. This will make sure that the two locations, the server and your local computer, are synchronized. This process could be a little tedious if you always needed to remember to sync your files before disconnecting. To automate this process, you can schedule the task of synchronizing the files and folder.

NOTE Synchronizing with Network Locations only works on Network Locations local to your network. You are not able to use File Transfer Protocol (FTP) Network Locations to synchronize content. The Always Available Offline option is not available for Network Locations not connected to the local network.

Using Sync Center

To configure offline files to run on a scheduled basis, you'll need to configure Sync Center using the following steps:

1. Click the Start button and choose Control Panel ⇨ Network and Internet ⇨ Sync Center. Or press ⊞, type sync, and click Sync Center.

2. When Sync Center is open, click the link View sync partnerships under the Tasks heading on the left side of the window as shown in Figure 49.2.

FIGURE 49.2

Sync Center with the default appearance for offline files.

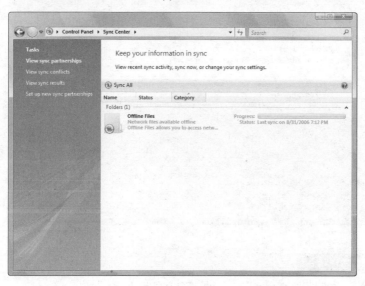

3. Right-click the Offline Folders entry and choose Schedule for Offline Files, which will start the Offline Files Sync Schedule dialog box.

4. Select the Network Location that you want to synchronize and click the Next button.

5. You're now able to determine what starts the file synchronization. As shown in Figure 49.3, you can choose a recurring date and time or have the synchronization start as a result of an event that takes place on your computer.

6. Based on the selection, you'll initially see two different screens. If you choose the first option, At a scheduled time, you'll see the screen shown in Figure 49.4, which allows you to set when the schedule should start and how often it should occur. The drop-down box allows you to select a range of units from minutes up to months. This means you could schedule the synchronization to happen every minute.

7. If you choose the second option, On an event or action, you'll see the screen shown in Figure 49.5, which allows you to choose an action that will cause a synchronization. You can trigger the synchronization based on when you log on, when you lock Windows, when you unlock Windows, or when the system is idle for a given amount of time.

8. Regardless of what option you choose to trigger the file synchronization, there is a More Options button in both of the windows shown in Figures 49.4 and 49.5. Clicking this button will provide you the opportunity to tell Windows when to start and stop synchronization. After you've made any changes to the More scheduling dialog box shown in Figure 49.6, click the OK button.

FIGURE 49.3

Offline Folders gives you the option for setting the schedule for synchronization.

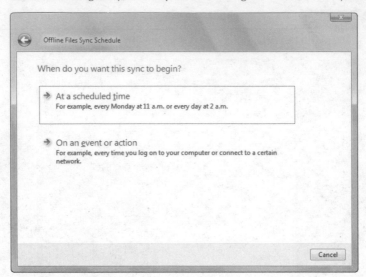

FIGURE 49.4

Set a schedule based on time for file synchronization.

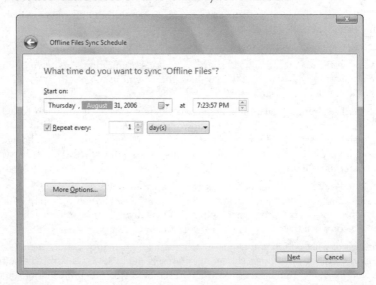

FIGURE 49.5

Setting the options to trigger the synchronization based on an event.

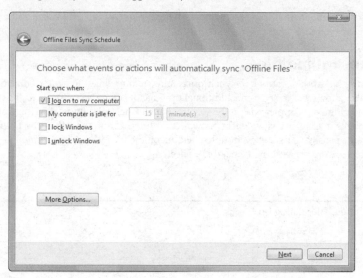

FIGURE 49.6

Additional options for scheduling your synchronization.

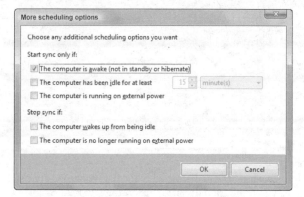

9. Next, you'll need to name your synchronization schedule. Enter a descriptive name in the Name textbox and then click the Save schedule button.

When your schedule is configured, it will run either based on the time schedule you set or based on the events on the computer. You're able to view, edit, or delete your schedule by opening Sync Center, right-clicking the Offline Folder entry, and choosing Schedule for Offline Folders as before in previous steps. This time, you're prompted with a dialog box that allows you to create a new schedule, view or edit an

987

existing schedule, or delete an existing sync schedule. Clicking the View or edit existing schedule option will run you through the steps similar to the ones you used to create the original schedule. You're also able to click the Schedule button in the toolbar to bring up the scheduling functions for offline files.

There are still some additional settings to configure offline files including disk usage and encryption settings, which are covered next.

Settings for offline files

Beyond setting the Network Locations to synchronize and deciding when to synchronize the files and folders, Windows also allows you to set some additional options for offline files. To get to these settings, you'll need to open the offline files applet within the Control Panel. Click Start and select the Control Panel. If the Control Panel opens in Category view, select Network and Internet and then click the Offline Files icon. If the Control Panel opens in Classic view, double-click the offline files icon. The Offline Files dialog box, shown in Figure 49.7, opens with the General tab selected.

FIGURE 49.7

The General tab for the Offline Files dialog box.

- **Disable Offline Files:** This button will disable all of the file synchronizations you have set up. If you currently have file synchronization disabled, the button will read Enable Offline Files. If you disable Offline Files, you'll need to restart your system for the changes to take effect.
- **Open Sync Center:** This button will open Sync Center just as you have earlier in the chapter.
- **View your offline files:** Clicking this button will bring up a window that shows all of your synchronizations. I first clicked Computers, then server, and finally syncarea, the folder on the server. This path to the files is shown in the navigation bar in Figure 49.8. You'll notice that each of the icons has a green wave circle in the bottom-left corner of the icons indicating that this is synched content.

FIGURE 49.8

A listing of the synchronized files.

It's necessary to keep track of the amount of space your offline files are using and put limits on the amount of disk space used. To do this, you'll need to click the Disk Usage tab in the Offline Files dialog box. To make adjustments to the default values, click the Change Limits button, which will bring up the dialog box shown in Figure 49.9.

FIGURE 49.9

The dialog box used to set limits on the amount of space used by offline files.

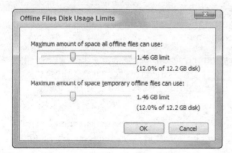

Make changes to the values using the slide bars; after you've set your limits, click the OK button to continue.

It is fairly common today that you hear of some institution that has had a laptop stolen with confidential information. Knowing this, Microsoft has included an option to encrypt any data with offline files synchronized with your local computer. Microsoft has also made it very easy to set up security. By clicking the Encryption tab within the Offline File dialog box, you're able to click the Encrypt button to encrypt the data that resides on your local system. When you do encrypt the data, only the data that resides on your local system is encrypted, not the data that resides on the server with which you are synchronizing. There is also no need for you to attempt to decrypt the files before using them. The decryption takes place when you attempt to use the synchronized file.

The final tab within the Offline Files dialog box is for working with a slow network connection. Clicking the Network tab will allow you to determine how your system works after it determines you have a slow network connection. If you open up the Network Location that is currently being synchronized with your local system and double-click a file, Windows will use a cached version if Windows determines the network connection is too slow. With the settings on the Network tab, you're able to determine whether you would rather wait for the real version of the file. If the On slow connections, automatically work offline option is checked, Windows will use the local version of the file. Additionally, Windows will check to see whether you still have a slow connection every five minutes by default. You're able to change this setting by setting the Check for a slow connection every value in minutes option.

With all of the settings for Offline Folders and Sync Center, you're well on your way to using offline files. If you've set up the schedule, then you'll have the latest versions of the files on your system based on your schedule. You've also determined how much disk space to dedicate to offline files and set up encryption if the data you are storing is sensitive. On occasion, you may hit a conflict in your synchronizations. This happens when the file on the remote computer changes and you also make changes to the file using your local offline version.

Dealing with conflict

Sync Center really comes in useful when you have a conflict with synchronization. The most common scenario is outlined in the following steps:

1. You have set up a synchronization using offline files to a folder named ImportantDocuments located on a remote server.

2. You disconnect from the network and edit some of the files within the folder.

3. While you are away and disconnected from the network, a coworker makes copies to the same files up on the server.

4. When you connect back to the network, Sync Center resumes the schedule you defined and realizes that there's a conflict and asks you to resolve the issue.

The likelihood of this scenario goes up with the number of users you have sharing the same data. Files that don't frequently change won't run into this scenario very often. To introduce this scenario, follow these steps but first make sure that you have a Network Location set up and offline files working as outlined earlier in the chapter:

1. Verify that your synchronization schedule is working by opening Sync Center within the Control Panel. Make sure that you verify that the status of your synchronization is fairly recent by clicking View sync partnerships as shown in Figure 49.10.

2. Disconnect from the network either by disconnecting your network cable or using the Disconnect link shown in Figure 49.11. You can get to this window by selecting Networking and Sharing Center in the Control Panel in Classic view. Or you can select Network and Internet in the Control Panel if you are using Category view and then click the Network and Sharing Center link. Click Disconnect next to your network connection.

FIGURE 49.10

The status of the synchronization is fairly recent.

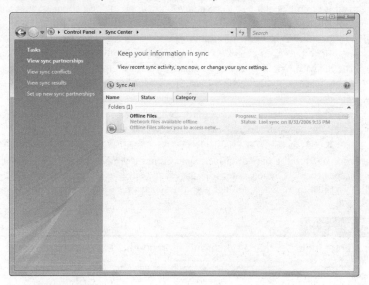

FIGURE 49.11

Disconnect from your network connection.

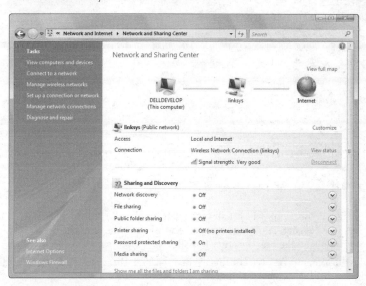

3. With your network connection disabled, navigate to the Offline Files. To do this, open your Computer folder, and the files will be located under the Network Locations group. Select a file you can edit. This can be any type of file including a text document, an image, or any other file you can afford to make changes to. When you are done making changes, save the file. The contents of the file will be stored locally on your system, and your system will attempt to synchronize the next time you connect to the network.

4. From another system on the network, connect to the original location of the file (this is the location of the file with which you were originally syncing). Open the file and make some changes to the same file that you made changes to in the previous step. Save your changes to the Network Location.

5. Go back to the computer that was recently disconnected from the network and reconnect. To reconnect to the network, open the Network and Sharing Center again and click the Connect to a network link. Select your original network connection and click the Connect button.

6. When connected to the network, open Sync Center if you've closed it. The status will change from Disconnected as Sync Center tries to resync your files. This time, however, the system notifies you that there was a conflict with the synchronization as shown in Figure 49.12.

FIGURE 49.12

Sync Center indicates that a synchronization conflict has occurred.

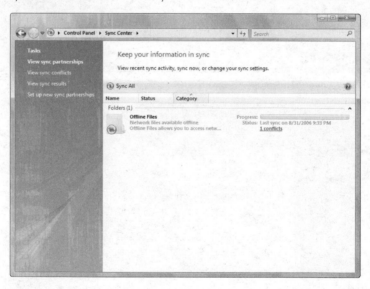

7. Clicking the conflict link will list all of the files that had a synchronization conflict. The Details column indicates that "A file was changed on this computer and the server while this computer was offline." Right-clicking the entry provides three options:

   ■ **View options to resolve conflict:** When selected, this option shows the dialog box shown in Figure 49.13. You have the option to keep the local version on your system and overwrite the changes on the server. You have the option to use the version on the server and overwrite your local copy. Finally, you have the option to keep both of them. As shown in Figure 49.13, the file on your local system will be given a different name.

- **Ignore:** Selecting Ignore removes the conflict from the list. Both of the files remain in their original states — the one on your local system and the one on the remote system. However, the next time a synchronization occurs, the same synchronization conflict will occur.

- **Properties:** The Properties dialog box shows the details regarding the type of partnership along with the date and details regarding the synchronization conflict.

FIGURE 49.13

The available options for resolving synchronization conflicts.

Microsoft has provided quite a few options for dealing with the synchronization conflicts that arise with offline folders. In addition to the conflicts showing up in Sync Center, there is also a notification from the Notification area on the taskbar, which will notify you when a conflict has occurred. In the previous examples, the Offline Files entry within Sync Center is referred to as a sync partnership. Besides synchronizing with Network Locations, Microsoft also provides functionality for synchronizing with other types of devices including PDAs and portable music devices.

NOTE   Microsoft also provides a different mechanism for keeping files in sync between two client computers. If you have a server and client, the best route for syncing files is still using Offline Files and Sync Center, but between two client computers, you can use Briefcase. To find out more about Briefcase, search for Briefcase under Help and Support.

Synchronizing with Other Devices

Synchronizing with devices other than files and folders within a Network Location provides you with the ability to keep devices other than just your computer synchronized. One of the biggest differences is that most devices that provide synchronization capability do so using the software that comes with the device. The software will usually set up a partnership within Sync Center, but the majority of the configuration and maintenance is done within the software applications that come with the device. Because each device that provides syncing options is different, I've included some general guidelines for working with different devices:

- The first step is to follow the instructions provided by the manufacturer. They will provide details specific to the product and the steps necessary for installing the software and configuring the device.

- It is necessary to connect the device in some way to the computer. This may include connecting the device via USB, or you may be required to connect the device via a Bluetooth connection.

- Not all devices are designed to work with Sync Center. If you open Sync Center and your device does not show up as an available partner after clicking Set up new sync partnerships, your device manufacturer may address synchronization in their own software.

The most important guideline is to follow the documentation provided by the manufacturer of the device. Also, if the device appears to have problems communicating with your computer, you should update to the latest available drivers found online at the product's Web site.

Wrap Up

This chapter has gone into the details of Sync Center and also how to synchronize offline folders. Specifically, we've covered:

- The basics of setting up synchronization for a Network Location.

- Using Sync Center to view partnerships. Specifically, we used Sync Center to view the Offline Files partnership.

- Setting schedules and different events for starting synchronizations.

- Configuring the details regarding Offline Files for Disk Usage, Encryption, and what to do when synchronizing over a slow network connection.

- How to deal with conflicts that occur when synchronization determines a file has changed in two locations while your system has been disconnected from the network. The details for available options were also discussed to resolve the synchronization failure.

- The available options for connecting and synchronizing other types of devices to keep content on the devices in sync with your computer.

Chapter 50

Performance Tuning Your System

Compared to most machines, a computer requires virtually no maintenance. That's because there are fewer moving parts compared to other machines. The vast majority of the components in the computer are lots of little electrons whizzing around at the speed of light through microscopically small wires. The real workhorse of your computer is its central processing unit (CPU). It's a tiny chip that's smaller than your thumbnail, and there are several brands and models of them on the market, including Intel's Core Duo, Pentium and Celeron processors, and AMD's Dual Core, Athlon, and Sempron processors, among others.

The information on which the CPU does its work is stored in random access memory (RAM), often referred to as *memory*. The memory in your computer is just a few thumbnail-sized chips, and again there are no moving parts.

The hard disk determines how long it takes to open and save files. As you'll learn in this chapter, there are ways to control how Windows uses the CPU and memory. And there are things you can do to keep your hard disk running at tip-top speed.

Getting to Know Your System

A computer system is made up of many different components. The two main components that make up the actual "computer" are the CPU and RAM. The overall speed of your system is largely determined by the speed of your CPU, and the amount of RAM in your system. The speed of a CPU is measured in gigahertz (GHz), billions of instructions per second, or for slower systems in megahertz (MHz), millions of instructions per second.

The amount of RAM determines how much data the CPU can work with at any one time without accessing the much slower hard disk. RAM chips do come in various speeds. But the amount of RAM you have, more so than its speed, really determines the overall speed of your system. We generally measure RAM in megabytes

(MB), and a megabyte is roughly a million bytes. A gigabyte (GB) is 1,024 megabytes. A byte, in turn, is the amount of space it takes to store a single character such as the letter "A." In short, the faster your CPU and the more RAM you have, the faster your computer can get things done, and the less time you have to wait.

Knowing your CPU and RAM

To see the brand name and speed of your processor and the amount of RAM you have, right-click your Computer icon from the Start menu and choose Properties. Or click Show More Details in the Information Center. Or, tap ⊞, type sys, and click System. The System window that opens shows that basic computer information as well as information about the version of Windows you're using, as in the example shown in Figure 50.1.

FIGURE 50.1

The System page.

NEW FEATURE   The Windows Experience Index provides a quick snapshot of the major components that determine how you experience Windows Vista on your computer.

Windows Experience Index

The first thing most people will notice is the Windows Experience Index. It is not a measure of your computer's overall speed or ability. Rather, it's an indicator of the weakest component in the system, the one that's most likely to give you a less than optimal experience. That experience includes things like 3D gaming and 3D modeling, things that many people don't even do with their computers. So don't interpret the value as being a general measure of your computer's overall performance. For a better understanding of what the number means, click the Windows Experience Index link next to the number. You're taken to a page like the one in Figure 50.2.

FIGURE 50.2

The Performance Information and Tools window.

The second page shows that the 2.0 rating on that computer comes from the Graphics category. Notice that the index isn't an average. It's strictly the lowest score. That particular computer actually runs Windows Vista and all of my programs quite nicely. And I get the full Aero Glass effect everywhere. It's just that the graphics card in that system is old and has limited memory. Programs that require intense 3D graphics calculations would probably run slowly on that computer. But that's not important to me, personally, because I don't really use those kinds of programs.

The items that have the most impact on overall computer speed are the processor, Memory (RAM), and primary hard disk. Those scores are higher, which explains why, overall, I get good performance from Vista on that computer.

NOTE None of the numbers in the index relate to Internet speed. Only one thing determines how long it takes you to download stuff from the Internet: the bandwidth (speed) of your Internet connection. The faster your Internet connection, the less time it takes to download things, regardless of the numbers on the Performance Information and Tools page.

The Performance and Information Tools page shown in Figure 50.2 provides links to more information about the meanings of the numbers, ways to improve your computer's performance. The Update my score link performs all the tests needed to calculate those numbers. If you changed some hardware in your system, but still got the same performance rating, you could use that link to re-run the tests against your new hardware.

The View and print details link shows all the information from the page, and additional details, and includes a button to print the page. The other blue links provide general information.

Getting more detailed information about your PC

You can get more detailed information about all the components that make up your computer system from the System Information program. To open System Information, click the Start button and choose All Programs ➪ Accessories ➪ System Tools ➪ System Information. Or press ⌨, type sys, and click System Information. The System Information window shown in Figure 50.3 opens.

FIGURE 50.3

The System Information program window.

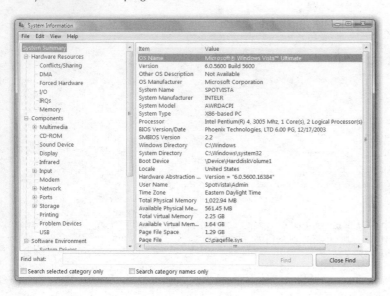

The left column of System Information organizes your system information into expandable and collapsible categories. For example, clicking the + sign next to the Components category expands that category to display subcategories and the names of specific device types. When you click a specific type, such as Drives under the Storage category, the pane on the right shows information about the components installed in your computer system.

You don't actually do any work in the System Information program. Its job is to just present the facts about your particular computer's installed hardware and software. However, you can export a copy of the System Information data to a text file, which in turn you can open, format, or print using any word processing program or text editor. To export a copy of your system information to a file, just choose File ➪ Export from System Information's menu bar.

You can also print your system information, either in whole or in part. To print all of your system information, first click System Summary at the top of the left column. To print just a category, first click a category name, such as Components. Then, choose File ➪ Print from System Information's menu bar. In the Print dialog box that opens, choose All if you want to print everything, choose Selection to print just the text you may have selected, or choose Current Page to print the page you are viewing. To close System Information, click its Close (X) button or choose File ➪ Exit.

Maximizing CPU and Memory Resources

Your operating system (Windows Vista) takes care of managing the CPU and memory for you. It does this behind the scenes in such a way that a person could use a computer productively for his or her entire life without ever knowing that CPU and RAM exist. When you use an *application program* (which is basically any program you start from the Start menu), you control the action by choosing menu commands and so on.

In addition to the application programs you choose, RAM needs to maintain copies of certain *processes* that perform various day-to-day chores behind the scenes. Open application programs and processes both take up some space in RAM, and both require some CPU resources to do their jobs.

Priorities, foreground, and background

Your computer's CPU and RAM are very busy places. To keep the computer running at tip-top speed, and to ensure that the computer responds immediately to everything you do at your mouse and keyboard, Windows prioritizes tasks that need to be done. Your application programs always run in the *foreground*, which means that when you click an item with your mouse or do something at the keyboard, fulfilling that request gets top priority in terms of being sent to the CPU for execution.

Most processes, by comparison, run in the *background*. This means that they get a lower priority and have to momentarily step aside when you tell Windows or an application to do something. For example, printing a document is treated as a low-priority background process, and for a good reason. All printers are basically slow, mechanical devices anyway. So, by making printing a low-priority process, you can continue to use your computer at near normal speeds while the printer is slowly churning out its printed pages.

Controlling CPU priorities

By default, programs that you're using are given a higher priority than background processes. It's possible to reverse that by giving processes a higher priority than applications. Offhand, I can't think of any reason why a normal person would want to reverse the order. If you want to make sure that your applications are getting top priority, as they should be, follow these steps:

1. Right-click your Computer icon from the Start menu, and choose Properties to open the System window for your system.

TIP The System icon in Control Panel also opens the System window. If Control Panel opens in Category view, click System and Maintenance to get to the System icon. If the Control Panel opens in Classic view, double-click the System icon.

2. Click the Advanced system settings link on the left side of the screen to bring up the System Properties dialog box. Click the Advanced tab in the System Properties dialog box.
3. Under the Performance heading, click the Settings button. The Performance Options dialog box opens.
4. In the Performance Options dialog box, click the Advanced tab shown in Figure 50.4.

FIGURE 50.4

The Performance Options dialog box.

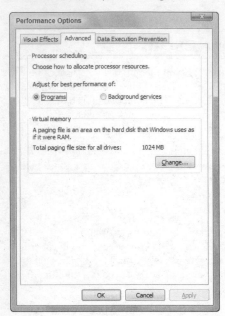

The Processor Scheduling options determine whether your actions, or processes, get top priority when vying for CPU resources to do their jobs. If you choose Background Services, your computer may not be as responsive as you'd like. So, you always want to choose Programs under Processor Scheduling.

> **NOTE**   Choosing Background Services won't make your printer print any faster. There's really nothing you can do to speed printing, other than use the printer's Draft mode (if it has one). But even so, printers are just inherently slow mechanical devices. Not even a supercomputer can make a printer run any faster than the printer's mechanics allow.

Reliability and Performance Monitor

> **NEW FEATURE**   Reliability and Performance Monitor provides a centralized interface for watching detailed performance metrics of your system.

The Windows Reliability and Performance Monitor is a tool for monitoring your computer's performance. You can get to it in a couple ways. From the keyboard, press ⊞, type reli, and click Reliability and Performance Monitor. Optionally, you can take the more traditional route through the Start menu:

1. Click the Start button, right-click the Computer icon, and choose Properties.
2. Click the Windows Experience Index link in the middle of the System window.
3. Click Advanced tools in the left column.
4. Click the Open Reliability and Performance Monitor link.

You may need to escalate your privileges by clicking Continue or by entering the password for an administrative account. When the monitor opens, it will look something like Figure 50.5. The lines that appear in the charts are measures of resource usage.

Reliability and Performance Monitor.

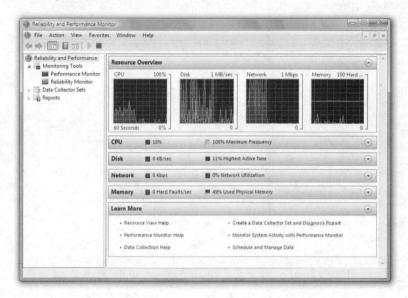

The default page for the Diagnostic Console shows four graphs, CPU, Disk, Network, and Memory, and is known as the Resource Overview screen. These are the core hardware components for your system and usually dictate the overall performance of your system. Below the four graphs are expandable areas that provide additional details about each of the graphs. By clicking the arrow on the right side of the screen, you'll expand more detail about each resource. Each section provides additional columns of information specific to that resource.

The Diagnostic Console provides you with several methods for finding bottlenecks in your system. It first includes ways to monitor the health of both hardware and software of your system. The console also provides a way to store the information gathered by the monitors. Finally, the interface provides an advanced reporting interface for analyzing the data gathered by the application. Each of the different areas are covered in the following sections.

Monitoring tools

The monitoring tools included in the Diagnostic Console provide you with methods to analyze the system performance at a deeper depth than what Task Manager provides.

Performance Monitor

Performance Monitor, included in Vista, has also been available under previous versions of Windows. It provides an interface for viewing performance counters on your system. To view Performance Monitor within Reliability and Performance Monitor, click the Performance Monitor icon under Monitoring Tools, as shown in Figure 50.6.

FIGURE 50.6

Performance Monitor being accessed within the Diagnostic Console.

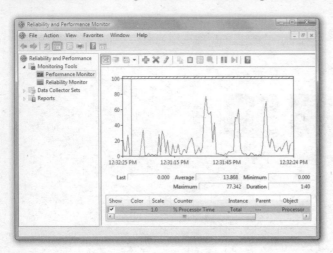

NOTE   Performance Monitor is a very complex application and could easily cover several chapters of detail. For this reason, I'm only covering some of the basic functions of the application. To get more information, search for Performance Monitor under Windows Help and Support.

The line crossing the screen as you watch the performance monitor plots your system's CPU activity. The graph has a timeline along the bottom and a percentage on the side. Only tracking the CPU doesn't provide much more information than what Task Manager provides. By adding counters to the grid, you can track your system's performance. To add more counters to the graph, follow these steps:

1. Start by clicking the plus (+) sign in the toolbar located just above the graph.

2. The Add Counters dialog box, shown in Figure 50.7, shows all of the available performance objects for your system. In the left column, click the arrow to the right of the performance objects to expand and display the available counters for that object. I've selected Network Interface in Figure 50.7.

3. Depending on the counter you select, you may also have the option of selecting an instance of that counter. In the case of the Network Interface object, there are multiple network interfaces on my computer, as shown in the Instance of selected objects list box. I selected the Bytes Total/sec as the counter and then chose the wireless adapter on my system for the instance.

4. Optionally, you can check the Show description checkbox so you can view additional information about the counter.

5. Click the Add button to move the selection over to the Added counters section of the window.

6. When you've selected all of the counters you want to monitor, click the OK button to return to the graph.

FIGURE 50.7

The Add Counters window that allows you to add counters to Performance Monitor.

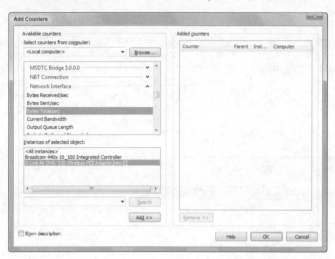

7. As shown in Figure 50.8, the counter is added to the bottom of the window. If you select the counter in the list and click the highlighter icon in the toolbar, it will highlight that specific counter. In this case, it has changed the color to a bold black. This is very helpful when you have several counters on the screen at the same time.

FIGURE 50.8

The Network Interface is in the middle of a download.

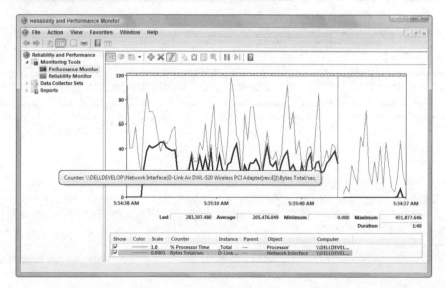

You may have noticed that the scale is also set by default. In the case of the previous example, if the network utilization went off the screen, you're able to adjust the scale for that specific counter so you have more meaningful information instead of a line running off the top of the graph.

Reliability Monitor

Reliability Monitor provides information regarding your system's overall stability. In Figure 50.9, my stability index is shown to the right of the graph, under the date drop-down box, and is a number ranging from 1 to 10. I've selected a single day in Figure 50.9, and the data for all of the events on that day are displayed in the grid below the timeline. Reliability Monitor uses five groups of information to determine the index, including software installs, application failures, hardware failures, Windows failures, and miscellaneous failures.

FIGURE 50.9

Reliability Monitor watching for overall system stability.

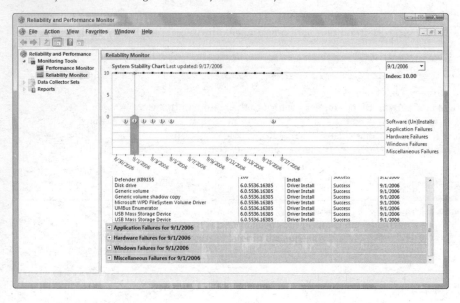

Reliability Monitor starts monitoring your system right after the operating system is installed, and will keep one year's worth of data for analysis. Reliability Monitor requires 28 days of information before it will accurately determine a stability index. The line in the graph will also be dashed until Reliability Monitor has 28 days of information.

Data Collector Sets and Reports

The Reliability and Performance Monitor interface provides a mechanism to log the information and events that occur on your system. Besides just logging the information, it also provides a way for you to use reports to look at the information.

 Data Collector Sets and Reports are very involved topics. For this reason, I cover the basics in this section and suggest searching Help and Support for Data Collector Sets to get more details.

Within the Reliability and Performance Monitor interface, you're able to create User Defined Data Collector Sets, but that's beyond the scope of this book. I'll show you how to utilize the predefined Data Collector Sets. To get started, follow these steps:

1. Click the arrow to the left of Data Collector Sets to expand the tree beneath it. Then expand the System icon beneath Data Collector Sets.

2. Right-click LAN Diagnostics and choose Start. The system will start collecting data for the different components of the collector.

3. Let the system run for a while, and when you're ready, right-click LAN Diagnostics again and choose Stop this time. Stopping the collector may take a little while. On my system it took almost 30 seconds.

4. Next, navigate to the Reports section within Reliability and Performance Monitor as shown in Figure 50.10.

FIGURE 50.10

Reliability and Performance Monitor Reports interface.

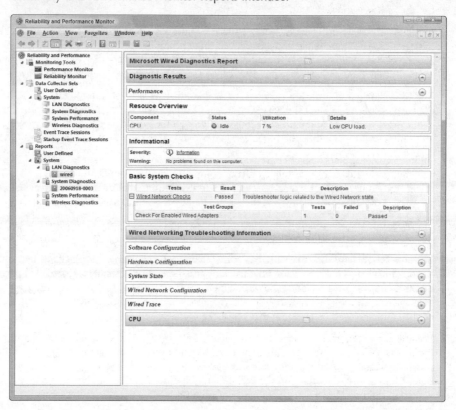

5. Navigate your way through the tree by clicking the arrow next to System, then LAN Diagnostics, and finally Wired. This will pull up a report from the Data Collector Set you have just run. You're able to expand different areas by clicking the down arrows next to each group.

Data Collectors are made up of three types of data, event trace, configuration, and performance data, each described here:

- **Event Trace data:** This data is gathered when different system events occur on your system.
- **Configuration data:** This data is gathered from changes that occur to the registry of your system.
- **Performance data:** This information is the same information that you're able to gather from Performance Monitor, discussed earlier in the chapter.

You're able to create your own user-defined Data Collector Sets, which involves adding data from one of the three categories. From the properties window of the collector, you're able to set a schedule if you'd like the collection to fire off on a regular basis, and you're also able to set stop conditions based on the duration of the collection or amount of data that it's collected.

Managing virtual memory

In the olden days of DOS, a computer could only run one program at a time. Programs had to be written to fit in the available 64 K (or whatever) of memory. Otherwise, the program wouldn't fit, wouldn't run, and would just end up displaying the message Not Enuf Memory on the screen (yes, I know it's spelled "enough," but the message showed "enuf").

In the Windows world, you can load up and run almost as many programs as you want. But, if you tried to start a new program when you already had some running, and RAM was already full, or near full, you'd get a "Not Enuf Memory" error. Computer scientists realized you could avoid that error by using a small portion of the hard disk as extra memory, called *virtual memory*, to handle the overflow.

The CPU can't get information to and from the hard disk as fast as it can to and from RAM. That's because the hard disk is a mechanical device with moving parts. The disk spins around, and the drive head moves about the disk to read and write data. But even though the hard disk isn't quite as speedy as RAM, better to let things slow down a little than to just stop dead and announce "Not Enuf Memory."

All modern computers actually have two types of memory. There's the speedy *physical memory* (RAM) that's actually on the RAM chips installed on your computer's motherboard. And there's the slower virtual memory, stored on hard disk, used as a backup to handle anything that goes beyond the capacity of the physical memory. A system's total memory is the sum of its physical and virtual memory.

> **TIP** The amount of RAM shown on the General tab of the System Properties dialog box (see Figure 50.1) is the amount of physical RAM in your system.

The area on the hard disk that's used as virtual memory is often called a *paging file*, because information is swapped back and forth between physical and virtual memory in small chunks called pages. When you fill up both your physical memory and virtual memory, the computer doesn't just stop dead in its tracks and display "Not Enuf Memory." Rather, it displays a message in advance, warning that you're about to run out of virtual memory and suggesting that you make room for more.

Because the virtual memory is just a tiny paging file on the hard disk, you can easily add more just by increasing the size of the paging file. You don't have to buy or install anything. To the contrary, the only way to increase physical memory is to buy and install more RAM. As you may have guessed, the Change button under Virtual memory in the Performance Options dialog box (shown in Figure 50.4) is the place you go to do that. When you click the Change button, you'll see the options shown in Figure 50.11.

In almost all cases, it makes sense to choose the top checkbox labeled "Automatically manage paging file size for all drives" to allow Windows to adjust the page file.

FIGURE 50.11

The Virtual Memory dialog box.

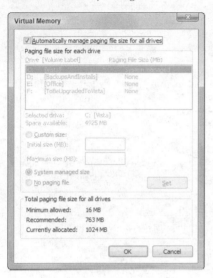

If you don't want Windows to manage the page file for you, your main options in the "Paging file size for each drive" area of the Virtual Memory dialog box are

- **Custom size:** You choose where you want to put your paging file(s), their initial size, and maximum size.

- **System managed size:** Tells Windows to create and size the paging file automatically for you.

- **No paging file:** Eliminates the paging file from a drive. Not recommended unless you're moving the paging file from one drive to another.

If you have multiple hard drives, you can get the best performance by using the least busy drive for virtual memory. For example, if you have a D: drive on which you store documents, it may be better to use that, rather than the C: drive, because the C: drive is pretty busy with Windows and your installed programs.

If you have multiple *physical drives*, you can get a little performance boost by splitting the paging file across the two drives. A single drive that's partitioned into two or more partitions, to look like multiple drives, doesn't count. You don't want to divide the paging file across multiple partitions on a single drive, because that will have the reverse effect of slowing things down.

If you do opt for a custom size, you can work with any one hard drive at a time. The drives are listed by letter and label at the top of the dialog box. In the example shown, all of the partitions actually reside on a single disk.

TIP The Disk Management tool discussed in Chapter 47 lists hard drives by number. If you have a single physical hard drive, it will be Disk 0. If you have two physical hard drives, they'll be listed as Drive 0 and Drive 1, and so forth.

If you don't choose the checkbox at the top of the Virtual Memory dialog box, you'll need to set the paging file sizes individually. For example, to move the paging from drive C: to D:, first click Drive C: at the top of the dialog box, choose No Paging File, and then click the Set button. Then, click Drive D:, choose Custom Size, set your sizes, and click Set.

The Total Paging File Size for All Drives section at the bottom of the dialog box shows the minimum allowable size, a recommended size, and the currently allocated size (the last measurement being the sum of all the Initial Size settings). The recommended size is usually about 1.5 times the amount of physical memory. The idea is to prevent you from loading up *way* more stuff than you have physical RAM to handle, which would definitely make your computer run in slow motion.

If your computer keeps showing messages about running out of virtual memory, you'll definitely want to increase the initial and maximum size of the paging file. A gigabyte (1,024 MB) is a nice round number. But if the computer runs slowly after you increase the amount of virtual memory, the best solution would be to add more physical RAM.

If you do change the Virtual Memory settings and click OK, you'll be asked if you want to restart your computer. If you have programs or documents open, you can choose No and close everything up first. But because the paging file is only created when you first start your computer, you'll eventually need to restart the computer to take advantage of your new settings.

NEW FEATURE Windows ReadyBoost uses flash memory, rather than your hard disk, for the paging file. This allows programs to get disk data more quickly, providing a faster, more fluid computing experience.

Using Windows ReadyBoost

Historically, PCs had two ways to store data: memory and the hard disk. Memory (RAM) is very fast. But it's *volatile*, meaning everything in it gets erased the moment you shut down the computer. The hard disk isn't nearly as fast. But it has *persistence*, meaning that it retains information even when the computer is turned off.

RAM is also more expensive, and therefore scarcer than hard disk storage. For example, a computer might have less than 1 gigabyte of RAM, or maybe up to 4 gigabytes or a little more. The hard disk, on the other hand, usually holds tens or even hundreds of gigabytes of data.

When you try to do things for which you don't have enough RAM, Vista automatically uses the paging file (discussed in the previous section) to store the data that won't fit in RAM. Many programmers also use the paging file intentionally to conserve RAM. So the paging file can be a busy file no matter how much actual RAM you have.

The downside to using the paging file is that the processor cannot move data to and from it as quickly as it can with RAM. The paging file becomes a little performance bottleneck. Prior to Windows Vista, there was no real solution to the problem. Vista is the first version of Windows to offer a real solution. It's called ReadyBoost, and it lets you use flash memory for the paging file. For paging file operations, flash memory is about 10 times faster than a hard disk, which means ReadyBoost can get rid of many little short delays and offer a faster, smoother overall computing experience.

NOTE Contrary to some popular belief, ReadyBoost doesn't add more RAM to your computer. It improves performance by using flash memory, rather than the hard disk, to store and access frequently used disk data.

Windows Vista takes care of all the potential problems that using flash memory for disk data might impose. For example, it keeps the actual paging file on the disk in sync with the copy on the flash drive. So if the flash memory suddenly disappears (as when you pull a flash drive out of its USB slot), there's no loss of data. Vista even compresses and encrypts the data on the flash drive using government-strength AES encryption. If someone steals a ReadyBoost flash drive from your computer, they will not be able to read data from it to steal sensitive information.

There are basically three ways to get ReadyBoost capabilities in your system. One is to use a *hybrid* hard disk drive, which puts the flash memory right on the drive. Another is to have ReadyBoost capability on the computer's motherboard. If you have neither of those, the third approach is to use a USB flash drive for ReadyBoost. This is a small device, usually small enough to fit on a keychain, that you just plug into a USB 2.0 port on your computer.

Not all flash drives are ReadyBoost capable. They vary greatly in their capacity and speed. Vista will only use a flash drive for ReadyBoost if it makes sense to do so. A flash drive that wouldn't help with performance can't be used for ReadyBoost. When it's ReadyBoost performance you're after, a 4 GB flash drive with fast random I/O capability is your best ally.

NOTE Four gigabytes is the maximum size for ReadyBoost. But because of compression, you actually get about double the drive's capacity. So a 4 GB flash drive really gives you about 8 GB of ReadyBoost storage.

If you already have a USB flash drive, and want to see if it's ReadyBoost capable, just plug the drive into a USB slot. After Vista recognizes and analyzes the drive, you'll get some feedback on the screen like the example shown in Figure 50.12.

FIGURE 50.12

Windows recognizes a new USB device and allows me to speed up my system using it.

NOTE ReadyBoost requires that you use a USB 2.0-compliant thumb drive. Anything preceding USB 2.0 is too slow to work as a ReadyBoost device.

If you want to use the device as virtual memory, select the Speed up my system option. After you've selected that option, the properties for the removable disk will pop up as shown in Figure 50.13. You can also bring up that dialog box by opening your Computer folder, right-clicking the drive's icon, and choosing Properties.

Select the Use this device option and then you are able to set the amount of space for ReadyBoost. By default, Windows sets the value to the recommended amount and also lets you know that the space you allocate won't be available for general use. When you've set your value, click the OK button.

ReadyBoost works by copying as much of the information as possible from virtual memory to the USB thumb drive. There is still a copy of all of the information within virtual memory; the system now knows to look at the ReadyBoost device first. If the system can't find the information there, it will look to the real virtual memory located on your hard drive. By keeping the original copy on your hard drive, you're able to remove your USB thumb drive without disrupting the computer.

FIGURE 50.13

Select the option for enabling ReadyBoost on your system.

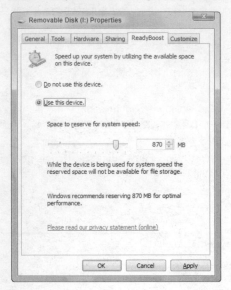

Don't expect to see everything suddenly run faster with ReadyBoost. Its benefits might not be immediate. Remember, the main purpose of ReadyBoost is to eliminate the short delays you might experience when loading certain programs, switching among open programs, and other activities that usually involve a paging file. With time, you should experience quicker response times in those areas. You might even find your computer starts more quickly because it takes less time to load programs at startup.

Trading pretty for performance

All the fancy stuff you see on your screen while using Windows comes with a price. It takes CPU resources to show drop-shadows beneath 3D objects, make objects fade into and out of view, and so forth. On an old system that has minimal CPU capabilities and memory, those little visual extras can bog the system down.

The Visual Effects tab of the Performance Options dialog box lets you choose how much performance you're willing to part with for a "pretty" interface. As you can see in Figure 50.14, the Visual Effects tab gives you four main options:

- **Let Windows choose what's best for my computer:** Choosing this option automatically chooses visual effects based on the capabilities of your computer.
- **Adjust for best appearance:** If selected, all "pretty" effects are used, even at the cost of slowing you down.
- **Adjust for best performance:** Choosing this option minimizes "pretty" effects to preserve overall speed and responsiveness.
- **Custom:** If you choose this option, you can then pick and choose any or all of the visual effects listed beneath the Custom option.

FIGURE 50.14

The Visual Effects tab of the Performance Options dialog box.

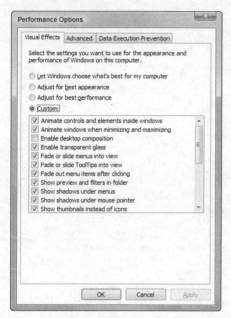

NOTE   To get to Visual Effects Performance Options from the desktop, click Start, type `perf`, and click Performance Information and Tools. Then click Adjust visual effects in the left column.

How you choose options is entirely up to you. If you have a powerful system, then the visual effects won't amount to a hill of beans. So, there's no need to back off on the visual effects. But if your computer isn't immediately responsive to operations that involve opening and closing menus, dragging, and other things you do on the screen, eliminating some visual effects should help make your computer more responsive.

Maintaining Your Hard Disk

Your hard drive plays an important role in determining the overall speed of your computer. That's because the hard drive comes into play when you're opening programs or documents, when you're saving documents, or when you're moving and copying files. It also comes into play when you are running low on RAM by moving less used applications to your hard drive from RAM.

Determining disk capacity and free space

Icons for all your disk drives are in your Computer folder. When you open your Computer folder, you'll see hard drives listed under the Hard Disk Drives group heading, as in Figure 50.15. Though, any icon could represent a partition on a single drive. For example, drives C:, D:, E:, and F: in the figure are each a partition in a single physical hard drive.

FIGURE 50.15

Icons for drives C:, D:, E:, and F: all represent partitions on a single internal hard drive.

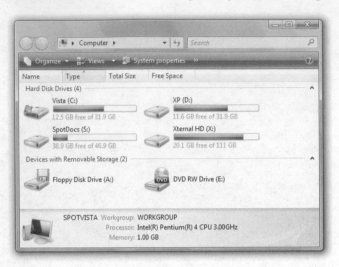

To see the total storage capacity of a drive, the amount of space you're currently using, and how much free space you have on that drive, right-click the drive's icon and choose Properties. The Used Space and Free Space are shown both in bytes and gigabytes (GB). The total capacity of the drive (or partition) is shown just above the pie chart that compares used space to free space. Figure 50.16 shows an example.

> **NOTE** For "exact number" lovers, the GB (gigabytes) number to the right of the bytes number is the number of bytes divided by (roughly) a billion. Though, if you do the math, it's 1,073,741,824, which is the true number of bytes (2^{30}) in a gigabyte.

One gigabyte is roughly enough space to store 500,000 (half a million) typed, double-spaced pages of text. Or put another way, 1 GB equals about 1,000 floppy disks. If the amount of free space on your hard drive ever dips much below 1 GB, you'll start seeing a notification icon that reads "You are running low on disk space."

> **NOTE** For you "exact number" folks, the "You are running low . . ." notification message kicks in when the free space drops below 800 MB, which is 8/10 of a gigabyte.

Recovering wasted hard disk space

At any given time, some of the space on your hard drive is being eaten up by *temporary files*. As the name implies, temporary files are not like the programs you install or documents you save. Programs and documents are "forever," in the sense that Windows never deletes them at random. The only time a program is deleted is when you use Programs in Control Panel to remove the program. Likewise, documents aren't deleted unless you intentionally delete them and also empty the Recycle Bin.

The files in your *Internet cache*, also called your *Temporary Internet Files* folder, are a good example of temporary files. Every time you visit a Web page, all the text and pictures that make up that page are stored in your Internet cache. When you use the Back or Forward button to revisit a page you've viewed recently, your browser just pulls a copy of the page out of the Internet cache. That saves a lot of time when compared to how long it would take to re-download a page each time you clicked the Back or Forward button to revisit a recently viewed page.

 Before you click the Disk Cleanup tool, be forewarned that the process could take several minutes, maybe longer. It's never *necessary* to use Disk Cleanup to get rid of temporary files.

To recover some wasted disk space, click the Disk Cleanup button on the Properties sheet. You'll see a prompt asking if you want to clean up only your own temporary files, or temporary files for all users. If you choose the option to clean up for all users, you'll need to elevate to administrative privileges. You'll also get some extra options for deeper cleaning, which I'll discuss in a moment.

Next you get to wait while Disk Cleanup analyzes the disk for expendable files. Eventually you'll get to the Disk Cleanup dialog box shown in Figure 50.17. The list of the Files to delete shows categories of temporary files. When you click a category name, the Description below the names explains the types of files in that category. Don't worry, all the categories represent temporary files that you can definitely live without. There won't ever be any important programs or documents you saved on your own in the list of temporary files.

The number to the right of each category name indicates how much disk space the files in that category are using, and how much space you'll gain if you delete them. Choose which categories of files you want to delete by selecting (checking) their checkboxes. If you don't want to delete a category of files, clear the checkmark for that category. The amount of disk space you'll recover by deleting all the selected categories appears under the list. After you've selected the categories of files you want to delete, click OK. The files are deleted and the dialog box closes.

FIGURE 50.16

The General tab of a hard drive's Properties dialog box.

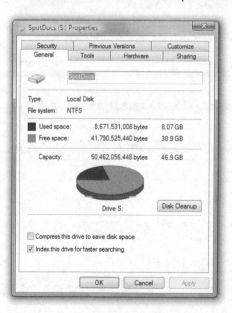

FIGURE 50.17

The Disk Cleanup dialog box.

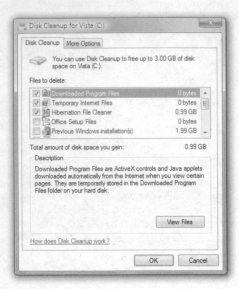

Deleting System Restore files and unwanted features

If you chose the option to delete files for all users after clicking Disk Cleanup, you'll see the More Options tab, visible near the top of Figure 50.17. Clicking that tab provides two more options for freeing up disk space:

- **Programs and Features:** Takes you to the Programs and Features window, where you can uninstall programs and Windows Features you don't use.

- **System Restore:** Deletes all restore points except the most recent one. This can be significant because system protection files are allowed to consume up to 15 percent of your available disk space.

For more information on removing programs, see Chapter 43. For more information on restore points, see "Using System Protection" in Chapter 33.

Scanning the disk for errors

Your hard disk spins at a walloping 5,400 to 15,000 RPM, and all the while the head that reads and writes data to the drive is zipping across its surface not more than a few molecules' distance away from its surface. With so much activity, it's not unusual for an occasional little hiccup to occur. These usually go by unnoticed. But they, too, can accumulate in the form of bad links and bad sectors. If enough of them accumulate, the speed at which you're able to move data to and from the disk can diminish.

If you scan your hard disk for errors two to four times a year (or whenever your hard disk seems to be running slowly), you can clean up the little blemishes and get the disk back to running at peak performance. Scanning can take a long time, and you can't use the computer while scanning. So, it's the kind of job you might want to do as an overnighter, or at least when you'll be away from the computer for an hour or two. Doing the scan is easy.

1. Open your Computer folder, if it isn't already open.
2. Right-click the icon for your hard drive, and choose Properties.
3. In the Properties dialog box that opens, click the Tools tab.
4. Under Error-checking, click Check Now.
5. For maximum cleanup, select (check) both checkboxes.
6. Click the Start button.
7. If you see a message indicating that the disk check couldn't be performed because Windows can't check the disk while it's in use, choose Schedule disk check to proceed.
8. Click OK in the dialog box.
9. Close all open programs, and save any unsaved work.
10. Click the Start button, choose the arrow to the right of the lock, and choose Restart.

Your computer will be busy for a while; this is going to take some time (maybe an hour or more). The screen will initially be gray when the computer restarts and will display the progress of the scan. When the scan is complete, Windows will boot up normally, and everything will be normal.

Defragmenting your hard drive

Whenever you delete a file, Windows makes the space it was using available to new files you save. If a file you're about to save is too big for one of the empty spaces available, Windows might divide up the file into several different deleted files' old space. Though this is not problem, it can get to a point where you have a lot of little chunks of files spread all over the disk.

When that happens, the drive head has to move around a lot to read and write files. You might even be able to hear the drive chattering when things get really *fragmented* (spread out). This puts some extra stress on the mechanics of the drive and also slows things down a bit.

To really get things back together and running smoothly, you can *defragment* (or *defrag* for short) the drive. When you do, Windows takes all the files that are split up into little chunks and brings them all together into single files again. It also moves most files to the beginning of the drive, where they're easiest to get to. The result is a drive that's no longer fragmented, doesn't chatter, and runs faster.

Defragmenting is one of those things you don't really have to do too often. Four or five times a year is probably sufficient. The process could take a few minutes up to several hours. So, it's another one of those "overnighter" jobs. Or at least one you'd want to start just prior to leaving for lunch.

> **TIP** For the ultimate in hard-drive performance tuning, do the maintenance tasks in the order described in this section. First, clean up the hard disk to get rid of any unnecessary temporary files. Next, do your error checking to fix any little blemishes. Then defragment what's left so that everything is perfectly arranged for quick and easy access by your computer.

To defragment a hard drive, starting at the desktop:

1. Open your Computer folder by clicking the Start button.
2. Right-click the icon for your hard drive (c:), and choose Properties.
3. In the Properties dialog box that opens, click the Tools tab.
4. Click the Defragment Now button. The Disk Defragmenter program opens, as shown in Figure 50.18.

FIGURE 50.18

The Disk Defragmenter default settings.

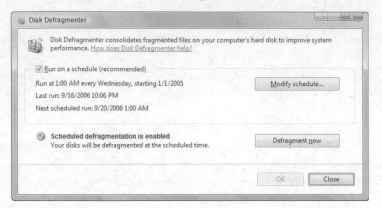

TIP   When it says you don't *need to* defragment, that doesn't mean that you can't or shouldn't. It just means the drive's not badly fragmented. But you can still defragment it.

5. In the Disk Defragmenter dialog box, you're able to set up a schedule to run the defragmenter or click the Defragment now button. The program will start analyzing your disk and may take as long as a few minutes or up to a few hours.

6. When the defragmentation is complete, the icon on the left side of the screen should turn to a green circle with a checkmark.

Defrag defragments all the fragmented files and moves some frequently used files to the beginning of the disk, where they can be accessed in the least time with the least effort. Some files won't be moved. That's normal. If Windows decides to leave them where they are, it's for good reason. You may hear a lot of disk chatter as defrag is doing its thing. That's because the drive head is moving things around to get everything into a better position.

Not all files can be defragmented, so don't expect everything to be perfect when you've finished. But things will be better than they were. When defrag is finished, you can just close any open dialog boxes and the Disk Defragmenter program window.

The Power Settings

The power settings under Power Options in the Control Panel provide features that enable you to adjust the performance of your system while conserving energy. To get to the power options for your system, click the Start button and select Control Panel. If the Control Panel opens in Category view, click the System and Maintenance link. Then click the Power Options icon. The Power Options window will open, shown in Figure 50.19.

The Power Options page provides the basic configuration for the power options on your system. The three plans listed, Balanced, Power saver, and High performance, are the default power plans for the system. You're able to alter the settings for the three default plans by either clicking the Change plan settings link below the plan or, for the selected plan, clicking either Choose when to turn off display or Change when computer sleeps from the left column. Clicking Change plan settings brings up Figure 50.20.

FIGURE 50.19

The different options for conserving the power of your system.

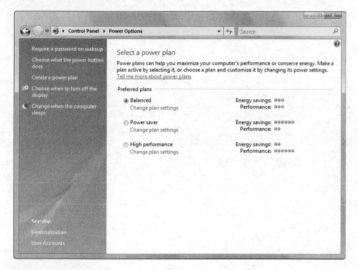

FIGURE 50.20

The basic options for setting the power conservation features of Vista.

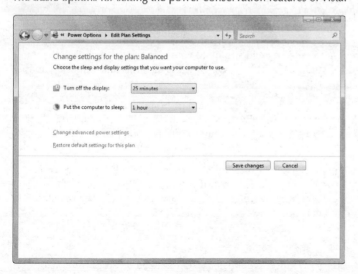

Adjusting either of these options will alter the default plan you have selected. Clicking the Change advanced power settings link will bring up the Power Options dialog box, which includes the Advanced settings tab shown in Figure 50.21.

FIGURE 50.21

The Advanced power settings.

With these options, you're able to drill down on individual options at a more granular level. If you change something that you think you shouldn't have, you can click the Restore plan defaults button to get back to where you were.

Create a power plan

If none of the default options meet your needs and you'd like to build your own power plan, click the third link on the left side of the Power Options window, Create a power plan. Clicking this link will bring up the window shown in Figure 50.22.

To make it easier, Windows lets you create your power plan from one of the three defaults. You're also able to name the plan on this page. After you've set the name of your plan, click Next. The next window allows you to set when you want to turn off the display and when you want to put the computer to sleep, as shown in Figure 50.23.

After you've configured these last two options, click the Create button. When you are back at the Power Options window, your plan should be first on the list and selected. If you want to change some of the advanced options in your plans, click the Change plan settings link and then click the Change advanced power settings as mentioned earlier in the chapter.

System settings

Clicking the first two links on the left side of the Power Options page, either Require a password on wakeup or Choose what the power button does, takes you to the System Settings page shown in Figure 50.24.

The first step to creating your own power plan.

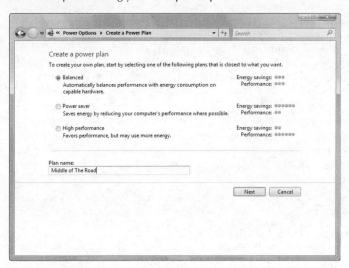

The last step of the process allows you to set two power options.

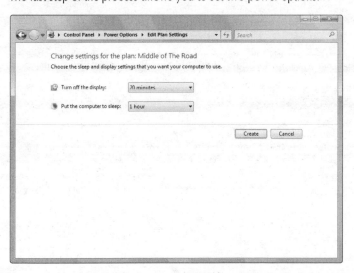

In the old days of computers, when you pressed the power button, the system would power off. With current computers, the power buttons take on a different role. Under the first heading in this window, Power button, you determine what happens when the power button is pushed. You're given three options, discussed here:

- **Sleep:** On a desktop computer, if you select this option, the data you are working on will be stored in memory and to the hard disk. The system will run using very little power until you press the keyboard or move the mouse. If you're using a laptop and have this option selected, pressing the power button will store the information in memory. When Windows notices that the system is running low on battery power, Windows will start writing the information to the hard drive. Upon restarting, the system will move all of the information from the hard disk to memory, just as the system was left originally. Usually, it takes 2 to 3 seconds to bring the computer back from Sleep.

- **Hibernate:** Using this option will take all of the information you have in memory and write it to the hard disk. Upon resuming, your system understands that there is a file on the hard disk that contains the picture of what was on memory, and the system copies the information from the hard disk to memory. This is an instant snapshot of what you had running before you hibernated the system last.

- **Shut down:** This selection will shut down the computer without saving any of the data you have in memory. Windows might attempt to prompt you to save your work before you shut down. This method does a graceful shutdown of Windows.

After you've determined which option you want, click the Save changes button.

On the System Settings window, you're also able to set the password option for what happens when the computer wakes up. As indicated by the text next to each of the options, when your system wakes from Sleep, the user may be prompted for a password. Obviously, the more secure option is to use a password. However, if this is your home system and you are the only one with physical access to the system, it's okay to pick the second option.

FIGURE 50.24

The System Settings window allows you to assign what the power button does and the option to set a password when the system wakes up.

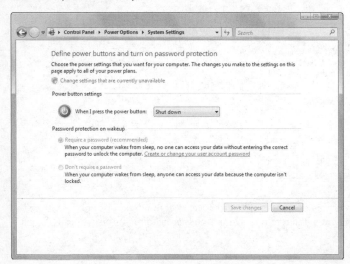

NEW FEATURE Windows Vista includes a new technology called ReadyDrive. As I'm writing this, the ReadyDrive technology is very new. The overall goal of the technology is to combine hard drives with flash memory to help with performance and power consumption. When the hard drive spins down to conserve battery life, some of the information can still be accessed from the flash memory on the hard drive. The flash memory consumes a fraction of the power compared to that of a typical hard drive. This technology looks like it will definitely benefit laptop users first.

NOTE The settings described in this section are the most common settings based on the hardware. For instance, if you're using a laptop, you may have two additional or different options on the left side of the Power Options window: Choose what closing the lid does and Choose what power buttons do. These options are specific to the system and offer additional options for power management.

With all of the power options available in Vista, you should be able to conserve resources on your system while still making your system very responsive. The power options will probably benefit a portable user more so than a desktop user.

Wrap Up

The components of your computer system that most determine how quickly things move along are its CPU and memory. (Internet access speed is determined solely by the bandwidth of your Internet connection, and isn't related to any of the topics discussed in this chapter.) As an alternative to buying a faster computer, there are things you can do to make your current computer run faster, and keep it running at top speed. The main points in this chapter are as follows:

- The System Information program provides detailed information about all the components that make up your computer system.

- To ensure that your computer is responsive to your every mouse click and keyboard tap, Windows automatically prioritizes programs as foreground (high-priority) and background (low-priority) tasks.

- When your system runs out of physical memory (RAM), Windows automatically uses a portion of the hard disk as virtual memory to handle the overflow.

- ReadyBoost uses flash memory to store frequently accessed disk files to provide a faster, more fluid computing experience.

- If your computer is usually sluggish and unresponsive, consider turning off some of Vista's visual effects.

- The speed of your hard disk determines how long it takes to open and save files.

- To keep your hard disk running at top speed, consider deleting temporary files, scanning for and fixing bad sectors, and defragmenting the drive a couple of times a year.

- Power settings play a role in your system's overall performance and can also be adjusted to conserver power, especially when using a laptop.

Chapter 51

Troubleshooting Hardware and Performance

H ere are some common problems and their solutions for hardware on your system including the normal components of a computer. Additionally, information for troubleshooting Bluetooth connectivity is included. Finally, some information for troubleshooting general performance issues is addressed.

First Aid for Troubleshooting Hardware

Whenever you have a hardware problem that's causing a device to misbehave or just not work at all, finding an updated driver will usually be your best bet. But even before you do that, you might want to try Windows's built-in Help and Support to see if it can determine what's up. (Help and Support may just tell you to get a newer driver, but it's worth a try.)

To get help on hardware and drivers:

1. Click the Start button and choose Help and Support.
2. Click the Troubleshooting link.
3. Under "Hardware and drivers" near the bottom of the page (see Figure 51.1), click whichever option best describes the type of problem you're trying to resolve.

FIGURE 51.1

Windows Help and Support provides options for troubleshooting hardware and driver issues.

After you've reached an appropriate page in Help and Support, just click links to the scenarios that best describe your problem.

A second alternative is to get support right from the hardware device's Properties dialog box in Device Manager. To open Device Manager, tap ▦, type dev, and click Device Manager. Or click the Start button, right-click Computer, and choose Properties. Then click the Device Manager link on the left side of the screen. In Device Manager:

1. Right-click the name of the device that's causing problems and choose Properties.
2. If the General tab of the device Properties dialog box offers a Check for solutions button, like the example in Figure 51.2, click that button to see what solutions Windows can find.

FIGURE 51.2

Use Device Manager to help troubleshoot hardware problems.

Dealing with Error Messages

Error messages come in all forms, from simple warnings to the *stop errors* and "the blue screen of death," which causes the computer to stop dead in its tracks. The more serious errors are often accompanied by one or more of the following pieces of information:

- **An error number:** An error number will often be a hexadecimal number in the format 0x00000*xxx* where the italicized numbers could be any numbers in the message.

- **Symbolic error name:** Symbolic error names are usually shown in all uppercase with underlines between words, like PAGE_FAULT_IN_NONPAGED_AREA.

- **Driver Details:** If a device driver caused the problem, you might see a filename with a .sys extension in the error message.

- **Troubleshooting info:** Some errors will have their own built-in troubleshooting advice, or a Help button. Use that information to learn more about what went wrong.

Whenever you get an error message that you can't solve just by reading the advice presented on the screen, go to http://support.microsoft.com and search for the error number, or the symbolic error name, the driver name, or some combination of words in the text or troubleshooting of the error message.

If searching Microsoft's support site doesn't do the trick, consider searching the entire Internet using Google. You never know, someone out there in the world may have had the same problem, and posted the solution somewhere on the Internet. When using a search engine, provide as much detail as possible to get the best results for your problem.

Performing a Clean Boot

The biggest problem with hardware errors is that even a tiny error can have seemingly catastrophic results, like suddenly shutting down the system and making it difficult to get the system started again. Clean booting can also help with software problems that prevent the computer from starting normally or cause frequent errors.

Not for the technologically challenged, this procedure is best left to more experienced users who can use it to diagnose the source of a problem that's preventing the computer from starting normally. The procedure for performing a clean boot is as follows:

NOTE A clean boot is not the same as a clean install. During a clean boot, you may temporarily lose some normal functionality. But once you perform a normal startup, you should regain access to all your programs and documents, and full functionality.

1. Close all open programs and save any work in progress.
2. At the Window desktop, click Start ⇨ All Programs ⇨ Accessories ⇨ Run, or press ⊞+R.
3. Type msconfig and press Enter or click OK. The System Configuration Utility opens.
4. On the General tab, choose Selective startup and make sure the Load startup checkbox is cleared.
5. Click the Services tab.
6. Select Hide all Microsoft services and click the Disable all button.
7. Click OK and click Restart to reboot.

To return to normal startup after diagnosis, open the System Configuration Utility. On the General tab, choose Normal startup and click the OK button.

Using the System Recovery Options

For more severe problems that require repairing an existing Windows Vista installation, troubleshooting startup issues, system and complete PC restoration, using Windows Memory Diagnostic Tool, or getting to a command prompt, you'll need to use the System Recovery Options. This method should only be used by hardware experts who can perform such tasks from a command prompt.

To boot from the Windows disc, first make sure that the disc is enabled as a boot device in the BIOS with a higher priority than any hard drives. Insert the Windows disc into the drive. Restart the computer and follow these steps:

1. During the POST, watch for the Press any key to boot from CD or DVD prompt, and tap a key.
2. After all files load from the disc, click the Next button on the page that is prompting for language, currency, and keyboard type.
3. On the next page, click the Repair your computer link near the bottom of the page.
4. Windows will bring up the System Recovery Options dialog box, which looks for an existing installation of Vista. If your system requires special hard drive controller drivers, you can click the Load Drivers button so your installation of Vista can be located. If you see your version of Vista in the list box, select it and click the Next button.
5. The next window shows all of your options for recovery.

The System Recovery Options window provides different troubleshooting tools based on your set of circumstances:

- **Startup Repair:** Use this option if your system won't start up. This could be for any number of reasons including a bad or misconfigured driver, an application that attempts to start at startup but causes the system to hang, or a faulty piece of hardware.

- **System Restore:** System Restore restores back to a designated restore point. By default, Windows is making restore points of your computer that store the state of your system. You'll be able to choose a restore point for your system from a previous day when you knew your system was performing correctly. The System Restore option will not alter any of your personal data or documents.

- **Windows Complete PC Restore:** For this feature to work, you would have needed to have done a backup in the past. Windows will search hard disks and DVDs for valid backups to restore from. See Chapter 33 for information on backing up your system.

- **Windows Memory Diagnostic Tool:** Some of the issues you may be experiencing may be the result of memory problems. Windows Memory Diagnostic Tool will perform tests against the RAM in your system to see if there are any problems. For this tool to run, click the link, which will prompt you to restart your computer now and check for problems or to check for problems the next time you restart.

- **Command Prompt:** The Command Prompt option is for experienced users who need to access the file system and run commands specific to Vista. Only choose this option if you're sure you need it, and be careful when using the Command Prompt.

When you're finished using the System Recovery Options, you can click either Shut Down or Restart to exit. For additional information on System Recovery Options, use Help and Support and search on System Recovery Options.

Trouble Setting a Passkey in the Add Bluetooth Device Wizard

Adding a Bluetooth device can be difficult at times when trying to enter your passkey generated by the host computer. The most common cause of the problem is the time allowed to enter a passkey. For security purposes, the wizard only allows a very limited amount of time to enter the information on the Bluetooth-enabled device. A passkey can be difficult to enter especially on devices that require special key sequences to enter numeric or character-based passkeys. Also, passkeys can be up to 16 characters, further complicating entry in the limited amount of time. You have a couple of options when dealing with the limited time-out. As shown in Figure 51.3, you could:

- **Let me choose my own passkey:** This will allow you to enter something a little simpler than the one generated by the system.

- **Don't use a passkey:** While not recommended for security reasons, if you're sure no one will step in and attempt to associate with your computer, use this option to configure the Bluetooth device.

If you're using a Bluetooth-enabled device in public, it is best to use some form of a passkey. The system-generated passkey is best to use if possible.

FIGURE 51.3

Available options for entering your passkey for the Bluetooth device.

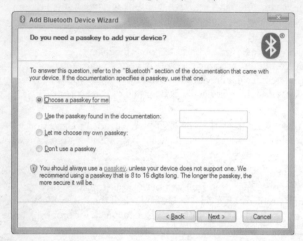

Troubleshooting Performance Problems

This section covers basic troubleshooting in terms of using Task Manager and Reliability and Performance Monitor to monitor performance. You need to remember, though, that the speed of the hardware dictates the speed of the software, not vice versa. If you suddenly find your computer running much more slowly than usual, your best resource for help is likely to be your computer manufacturer. After all, they're the ones who built the computer. So, they should know best what kinds of things might cause that hardware to slow down unexpectedly.

If your CPU Usage chart consistently runs at a high percentage in Task Manager, you may be running two or more firewalls. Most likely, you'll need to disable and remove any third-party firewalls. Or disable the built-in Windows Firewall.

Also, scan your system for viruses, adware, and other malware, and remove all that you can find to eliminate their resource consumption.

If neither of the previous suggestions fix your problem, you may need to see if an individual process is keeping your system overly busy. To do this, follow these steps:

1. Click the Start button, right-click Computer, and select Properties.
2. Click the Windows Experience Index link, which shows the Performance Information and Tools window.
3. Click the Advanced tools in the left column.
4. Click the Open Task Manager link to launch Task Manager.
5. Optionally, right-click the taskbar and click Task Manager.

Once you're in Task Manager, click the Processes tab and then click Show processes from all users. This will list all of the processes running on the system. Next, sort the information in the grid based on CPU, as shown in Figure 51.4.

FIGURE 51.4

Task Manager sorting the processes based on CPU percentage.

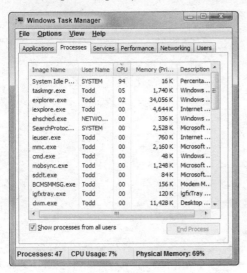

You should be able to identify the process that is using the majority of your CPU. You have a couple of options at this point:

- Use the name of the process under the Image Name column to search the Internet to see if the process is a valid file or a potential virus. If it is a virus of some form, you'll need to update your virus definitions and rerun your virus scan. If it does not appear to be a virus, you'll need to contact the vendor who provided the software to see if they can help troubleshoot the problem.

- Short term, you can right-click the process and choose End Process. Sometimes applications run into problems or situations the developer never imagined and the process gets stuck in a loop, which taxes the CPU. Restarting the application will reset the process, hopefully avoiding the circumstances that put the application in a loop. In addition to using Task Manager, Vista includes several other utilities located in Advanced Tools under (see Chapter 50).

More Hardware Troubleshooting Support

There are many thousands of hardware devices that you can use with Windows, and no one rule that applies to troubleshooting all of them. So you'll likely have to consider all of your resources. Be sure to check the manual that came with the hardware device first. If that doesn't work, the device manufacturer's Web site will likely be your next best bet.

When you need to ask a question, consider the `Microsoft.public.windows.vista.hardware_ devices` newsgroup in Microsoft Communities.

And, as mentioned at the start of this chapter, search Vista's built-in Help and Support for the word `troubleshoot` followed by the type of device that's giving you the problem.

Part X

Networking and Sharing

Networking is all about getting two or more computers to talk to each other. Not over the Internet, but within a private network in your home or office. Networked computers can share resources, like an Internet account, printer, and files. Networking and sharing is what Part X is all about.

Chapter 52 starts off with a discussion of network hardware, the physical components you need to get computers connected. It covers both traditional wired networks and the newer Wireless WiFi variety.

Chapter 53 covers the ways in which you share resources on a network. After you've shared a resource, other computers on the network can access it through the network. Chapter 54 describes how that works.

Then there's the *ad-hoc*, occasional, temporary network where people come together, connect their computers for a brief time to have an online meeting, and then disband. Windows Meeting Space makes that job easy and even has built-in tools to keep such meetings secure.

Chapter 56 covers the kinds of problems many people encounter when trying to set up their own networks and offers solutions to overcome those problems.

Chapter 52

Creating a Home Network

I f you have two or more computers, you may already be using what's known as a *sneaker network*. For example, to get files from one computer to another, you copy files to a floppy or CD. Then, you walk over to the other computer and copy the files from the disk to that computer. Wouldn't it be nice if you could just drag icons from one computer to the other without having to use a floppy or CD?

What if you have several computers, but only one printer, one Internet connection, or one DVD burner? Wouldn't it be nice if all the computers could use that one printer, that one Internet connection, and that one burner? All of these things are possible if you connect the computers to one another in a *local area network* (LAN).

After you've purchased and installed networking hardware, you're ready to set up your network. Windows Vista includes features that remove the complexities commonly associated with network configurations.

This chapter describes how to configure Windows for different types of hardware setups. Remember, you should always follow the instructions that came with your networking hardware first. After all, those instructions are written for the exact products you've purchased.

What Is a LAN?

A *local area network* (sometimes referred to as a *LAN*, a *workgroup*, a *private network*, or just a *network*) is a small group of computers within a single building or household that can communicate with one another and share *resources*. A resource is anything useful to the computer. For example:

- All computers in the LAN can use a single printer.
- All computers in the LAN can connect to the Internet through a single modem and Internet account.
- All computers in the LAN can access shared files and folders on any other computer in the LAN.

In addition, you can move and copy files and folders among computers using exactly the same techniques you use to move and copy files among folders on a single computer. Though, it's not entirely necessary to move or copy a document that you want to work on, because if a document is in a shared folder, you can open and edit it from any computer in the network. This is good, because you only have one copy of the document, and you don't have to worry about having multiple, slightly different copies of the same document all over the place to confuse matters.

Planning a LAN

To create a LAN, you need a plan and special hardware to make that plan work. For one thing, each computer will need a device known as a *network interface card* (NIC) or *Ethernet card*. Those you can purchase and install yourself. However, many PCs come with an Ethernet card already installed for connecting to a wired network. In that case, you'll have an RJ-45 port on the back of the computer. It looks a lot like the plug for a telephone, just a little bigger. You just plug one side of an Ethernet cable into that port, and plug the other side of the cable into a network hub or cable. You can also connect computers without any cables at all by using wireless networking hardware. Exactly what you need, in terms of hardware, depends on what you want to do. The rest of this chapter describes your options.

Creating a Wired LAN

If you have two or more computers to connect, and they're all in the same room and close to one another, you can use a traditional Ethernet hub and Ethernet cables to connect the computers with cables. You'll need exactly one NIC and one traditional Ethernet cable for each computer in the LAN. Figure 52.1 shows an example of four computers connected in a traditional LAN. Notice how each computer connects to the hub only — there are no cables that run directly from one computer to another computer.

By the way, even though the printer in Figure 52.1 is connected to the same computer as the modem, that's just an example. The printer can be connected to any computer. In fact, you could have several printers connected to several computers. All computers will be able to use all printers, no matter which computer that printer is (or those printers are) connected to.

Traditional Ethernet speeds

When it comes time to purchase network interface cards, cables, and a hub, you'll need to decide on the speed you want. As with everything else in the computer industry, network speed costs money. However, in the case of networks, the cost differences are minor, while the speed differences are huge. The three possible speeds for Ethernet LANs are listed in Table 52.1.

FIGURE 52.1

Example of four computers connected in a traditional Ethernet LAN.

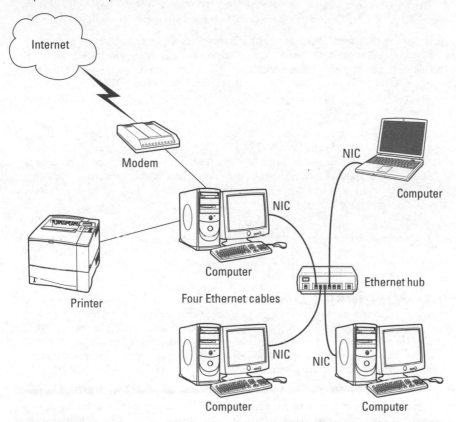

TABLE 52.1

Common Ethernet Network Component Speeds

Name	Transfer Rate (speed)	Bits per second	Cable
10Base-T	10 Mbps	10 million	Category 3 or better
100Base-T	100 Mbps	100 million	Category 5 or better
Gigabit Ethernet	1 Gbps	1,000 million (billion)	Category 6 or better

If it's difficult to relate the numbers to actual transfer rates, consider a dial-up modem, which tops out at 50 Kbps. That's 50,000 bits per second. A 100Base-T network moves 100,000,000 bits per second. That's 2,000 times faster or, in other words, you only have to wait 1/2,000 as long for the same file to transfer across a 100Base-T connection. So, a file that takes 33 minutes (2,000 seconds) to transfer over a dial-up modem takes 1 second to transfer over a 100Base-T network.

The slowest component rules

When purchasing hardware, it's important to understand that the slowest component always rules. For example, if you get Gigabit Ethernet cards, but connect them to a 100Base-T hub, the LAN will run at 100 Mbps. The faster Gigabit NICs can't force the slower hub to move any faster.

It makes sense if you envision the electrons going through the wire as cars on a freeway. Let's say lots of cars are zooming down a 10-lane freeway. But there's some road construction where the freeway narrows to one lane. Cars are going to pile up behind that point, because the one-lane portion is slowing things down. Where the one lane reopens back to 10 lanes, cars will still be trickling out of the *bottleneck* — the single lane — one at a time. The 10 lanes at the other side of the bottleneck can't "suck the cars through" the bottleneck any faster than one car at a time.

Likewise, if your computers are connected together with a Gigabit LAN, but all share a single broadband connection to the Internet, your Internet connection is still 512 Kbps. Your fast LAN can't force the data from your ISP to get to your computer any faster than 512 Kbps. Furthermore, if two people are using the 512-KBps broadband connection at the same time, they have to share the available bandwidth, meaning that each user gets only 256 Kbps. But, if only one person is online, she gets the full 512 Kbps because she's not sharing any bandwidth when nobody else is online.

 If you have only two computers to connect, and each has an Ethernet card, you don't really need a hub. Instead you can connect the two computers directly using an Ethernet *crossover cable.*

Creating a Wireless LAN

Wireless networking reigns supreme when it comes to convenience and ease of use. As the name implies, with wireless networks you don't have to run any cables. Plus, no computer is tied down to any one cable. For example, you can use your notebook computer in any room in the house, or even out on the patio, and still have Internet access without being tied to a cable.

To set up a wireless LAN, you need a wireless NIC for each computer. To set up an *ad-hoc* wireless network, that's all you need. The computers can communicate with each other, so long as they're within range of one another. Windows Meeting Space, discussed in Chapter 55, lets you conduct meetings with just such an ad-hoc wireless LAN.

If you want Internet connectivity for all of the computers in a wireless LAN, you'll need some kind of access point that acts as a central location for all the computers and also provides an Internet connection. Typically that device would be a Wireless Broadband Router, as illustrated in Figure 52.2.

Wireless Broadband Router

The big advantage of wireless networking is, of course, the lack of cables. This is especially handy on a notebook computer, because the computer isn't tethered to one location by a cable. Granted, you can't stray too far from the wireless access point. Maybe 100 or 150 feet from the wireless access point, indoors. Not quite as far outdoors. But that's probably enough that you can access the Internet from your bed and patio.

Also, many universities and other locations offer public Internet access from any computer that has an 802.11b or 802.11g wireless network interface card installed. So, if you create your home wireless network using either of those standards, you'll also be able to use public Wi-Fi Internet access where it's available.

FIGURE 52.2

Example of four computers connected in a wireless LAN.

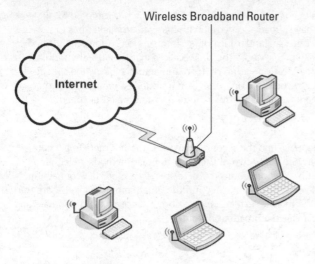

TIP What Intel calls their Centrino technology is the same as the 802.11g specification described in this chapter. In other words, "Centrino" is just another name for 802.11g. The Centrino/802.11g standards are rapidly gaining ground as *the* wireless network standard to use.

The only disadvantages to wireless networking, as compared to wired networks, are speed and reliability. As I write this chapter, the fastest standards-based wireless networks run at about 54 Mbps. That's still pretty darn fast. It's just not as fast as the 100 Mbps or 1 Gbps speeds of traditional Ethernet cables. The reliability problem isn't a problem with the technology, per se. Rather, it has to do with the rare little "blind spot" here and there where the computer just won't connect to the network.

Wireless networks are built around three different standards. The 802.11g standard is the newest and most popular. Table 52.2 summarizes the main differences between the three standards. The Public Access column refers to Internet Wi-Fi hotspots such as those found at some airports, hotels, and other places. 802.11g is the preferred standard for Wi-Fi hotspots.

TABLE 52.2

Wireless Networking Standards and Speeds

Standard	Speed	Range	Public Access
802.11b	11 Mbps	100–150 feet	Yes
802.11a	54 Mbps	25–75 feet	No
802.11g	54 Mbps	100–150 feet	Yes

In most cases, when setting up your network you're really setting up two networks. The first network involves the computer-to-computer communication. This includes the 802.11b or 802.11g wireless setup

The 802.11n Standard

As I write this, there is a new specification that is becoming a standard, 802.11n, which is rumored to offer speeds of 200 Mbps or more. Many companies have already come out with hardware that attempts to support what will become the standard, but until it becomes a standard it's difficult to support. Additionally, you may find companies that offer speeds much greater than 54 Mbps. The drawback is that they usually require hardware specific to that manufacturer to get that speed. As long as all of the manufacturers follow the specification for 54 Mbps, any manufacturer could connect to your network. After you introduce a manufacturer that offers speeds higher than 54 Mbps, you need that manufacturer's hardware to connect at the faster speed.

or a wired setup talked about earlier in the chapter. Then the second network is the Internet. To get connected to the Internet involves some form of an ISP. Today two of the most popular methods are either a standard dial-up modem connection or a broadband connection. If you're sharing an Internet connection, one device in your network will have physical access to the Internet and the other computers will share the connection. The one device that actually sees the Internet can either be a computer or you can purchase an inexpensive device that connects to the Internet called a Broadband Router.

Other useful wireless goodies

If you already have a wired network with Internet connectivity, and just want to add some wireless computers to that network, you don't need a Wireless Broadband Router. Instead you need a *Wireless Access Point* (WAP). First you'll need to configure the hub, as per the manufacturer's instructions, by connecting it directly to one of the computers in your wired network. Then you can disconnect the WAP from the computer and connect it directly to the hub for your wireless network. The wireless computer can use the same shared Internet connection that the wired network uses.

Getting a wireless network to cover a whole house can be a challenge, especially if you have two or more floors. If you want to Wi-Fi the entire house, you may need to use one or more *wireless range expanders* to extend the reach of the network. Putting one near the staircase is a good idea when you need to reach upstairs or downstairs.

A Wi-Fi finder can also be helpful. It's a device that's small enough to fit on a keychain and it measures the strength of a wireless network signal at wherever you're standing. It can help you determine where the edge of a signal is, which is a good place to put a range expander to get more coverage.

Acquiring and Installing Network Hardware

Now that you know what you need to network two or more computers, you need to purchase and install networking hardware. There's little I can do to help you with that, except give you a couple quick pointers:

- If you're not too keen on opening the computer case and installing things inside the computer, consider getting hardware that connects to the computer via USB ports. Typically you just plug the devices in, and you're done.

- If you'll be adding a notebook to the network, you'll probably want a PC Card NIC (not to be confused with a PCI card, which goes in a motherboard slot inside the computer).

If you're new to all of this and just want to see what some of this stuff looks like, here are some Web sites you can visit. They're all network hardware manufacturers, not retailers:

- D-Link: www.d-link.com
- Gigafast: www.gigafast.com
- LinkSys: www.linksys.com
- Netgear: www.netgear.com
- SMC Networks: www.smc.com
- TrendNET: www.trendnet.com
- U.S. Robotics: www.usr.com

In terms of actually purchasing the products, you can find these products at any store that sells computer supplies, including many of the large office supply chains such as Staples and OfficeMax. Of course, you can buy the devices online at any Web site that sells computer stuff. Shopping jaunts include Web sites such as www.amazon.com, www.cdw.com, www.cyberguys.com, www.officemax.com, www.staples.com, www.tigerdirect.com, and www.walmart.com, just to name a few.

After you've acquired the hardware, you need to install it. I can't help you much there either. You'll have to follow the manufacturer's instructions on that one, because there is no one-rule-fits-all when it comes to installing hardware. As a general rule of thumb, you'll probably want to:

- Get the hub or router (if any) set up first.
- Install the network interface cards second.
- Connect all the cables last.

Once all the hardware is connected and installed, you're ready to set up the network. That part isn't so complicated because Windows does a great job of searching out networks. We'll work through that next.

After the Hardware Setup

There are a couple of steps involved in actually setting up the networking hardware. First, make sure that the hardware you purchased is installed based on the manufacturer's instructions. This may include plugging in the device, then connecting the device to the Internet, and finally plugging in the other computers to the device. When this is complete, you can run the Set Up a Network Wizard to let Windows finish the process.

CAUTION Read and follow the network hardware manufacturer's instructions to a tee before you configure your network. If there's any conflict between what they say and what's stated in this chapter, do as the manufacturer's instructions say. Failure to do so will lead to many hours of hair-pulling frustration!

Close any open programs and documents before you start configuring your network. The type of network hardware you have set up will determine what configuration you'll need to use. Here's where to look, depending on your network configuration:

- If you have an Ethernet network, and your modem is inside of, or connected to, one computer in the network, you'll use Internet Connection Sharing (ICS) to share a single Internet account. See the section titled "Setting Up a Wired Network with an ICS Host."

- If you have a router or residential gateway that all computers in your network connect to, you will *not* use Internet Connection Sharing. Each computer will have its own direct access to your Internet account via the router. See the section titled "Setting Up a Wired Network with a Router."

- If you have a wireless network, see the section titled "Setting Up a Wireless Network" later in this chapter.

- If you want to set up a Bluetooth personal area network, see Chapter 48, "Using Wireless Bluetooth Devices."

Be sure to turn off all computers before you install the networking hardware. Then install all of the networking hardware and turn on all of the computers. Chances are Vista will detect the hardware and start setting things up automatically. If you see any prompts asking what type of network you're installing, make sure you specify that it's a *private* network (not a public network). When asked about file sharing, make sure you make choices that allow for file and printer sharing among computers in the private network.

With those buzzwords and tips in mind, let's move on to the specifics of things to do after you get all the network hardware in place and all the computers turned on.

Setting Up a Wired Network with an ICS Host

The method for setting up a network described here applies only for a network that's connected by cables (not a wireless network). If you're using a router, see the section titled "Setting Up a Wired Network with a Router." If you're setting up a wireless network, see the sections on setting up a wireless network.

The scenario where these instructions do apply is illustrated in Figure 52.3. Only one computer in the network is connected to the Internet. That computer might have an internal modem that connects directly to a phone or cable jack on the wall. Or, it might have an external modem that connects to that one computer and a wall jack. That same computer uses a separate plug and cable to connect to the network hub.

In such a network, the computer that connects to the wall jack (or modem and wall jack) is the only computer that can access the Internet on its own. We call that computer the *Internet Connection Sharing Host*, or ICS Host for short. You must know, beforehand, which computer has that Internet connection. If you don't, and try to guess your way through it, your network won't work. To play it safe, you should sit down at the computer, and make sure you can get online. Leave that computer online as you configure the ICS host.

Setting up the ICS host

With all your hardware in place, and your ICS host online, you're ready to start setting up the ICS host. Go to the computer to which the modem is directly connected and log in to a user account that has administrative privileges. Then open the Network and Sharing Center using either of the following methods:

- Click the Start button and choose Control Panel ⇨ Network and Internet ⇨ Network and Sharing Center.

- Tap ⊞, type net, and click Network and Sharing Center.

From the Network and Sharing Center follow these steps:

1. In the left column, choose the Manage network connections link to view all of the available network connections on your computer.

2. Right-click the icon that represents the Internet connection and choose Properties.

3. In the Properties window for that connection, click the Sharing tab as shown in Figure 52.4.

4. Check Allow other network users to connect through this computer's Internet connection and click OK.

That's it for the computer that's connected directly to the Internet. You'll need to configure the network connection for every computer in your network, as discussed next.

FIGURE 52.3

Example of networks with an ICS host.

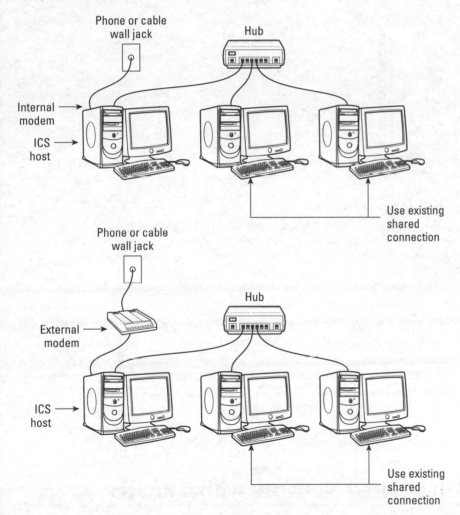

FIGURE 52.4

The Sharing property sheet for the ICS host connection.

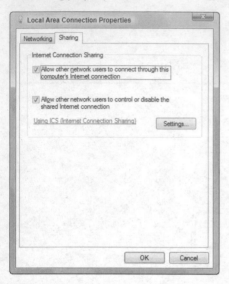

Setting up other computers

You need to configure the rest of the computers on your network to use the ICS host connection to the Internet. But first, make sure that you are still online, or can get online, from the ICS host. You want a live Internet connection as you set up other computers in the network. To connect the next system to the Internet, follow these steps:

1. You will use Internet Explorer to configure the ICS client computer. Click Start ➪ Internet Explorer.
2. Click Tools ➪ Internet Options to bring up the Internet Options window.
3. Click the Connections tab and click the LAN settings button.
4. Make sure that each of the checkboxes that appear on this tab are unchecked as shown in Figure 52.5.
5. Click OK on all of the open windows.

Remember, you need to follow the preceding steps for every computer you want connected to the Internet. When you've finished, you should be able to get online from every computer in the network. You should now be able to go straight to Chapter 53 to view shared resources on your network.

Setting Up a Wired Network with a Router

If your computer connects to the Internet through a residential gateway or router, there won't be an Internet Connection Sharing host. With a residential gateway, you'll likely have an Ethernet hub to which all computers, and the gateway, attach. The gateway, in turn, connects to a cable or DSL modem, which in turn connects to a phone jack or cable jack on the wall, as shown in Figure 52.6.

FIGURE 52.5

The LAN settings within Internet Explorer.

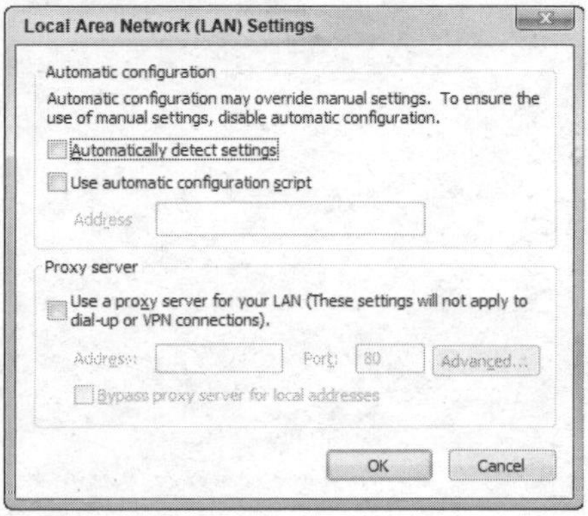

Local Area Network (LAN) Settings
Automatic configuration
Automatic configuration may override manual settings. To ensure the use of manual settings, disable automatic configuration.
Automatically detect settings
Use automatic configuration script
Address
Proxy server
Use a proxy server for your LAN (These settings will not apply to dial-up or VPN connections).
Address:
Port:
80
Advanced...
Bypass proxy server for local addresses
OK
Cancel

FIGURE 52.6

Sample residential gateway network.

Phone or cable wall jack
Cable or DSL modem
Residential Gateway
Ethernet Hub

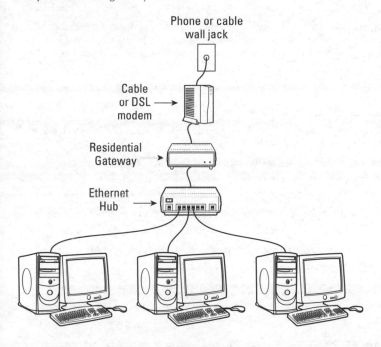

A router behaves in much the same way as a residential gateway, but everything is combined in a single unit. In fact, the router will look like a modem. But the big difference is that you can connect several computers — not just one computer — to the router. Figure 52.7 shows an example.

FIGURE 52.7

Sample router connection to the Internet.

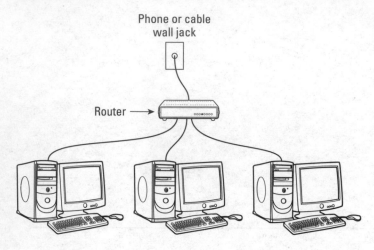

With a router or residential gateway, your first step will usually be to get online from one computer. You'll need to refer to instructions that came with your router, as well as your ISP's instructions, to do that. Windows will attempt to find the network for you. To see where you stand, follow these steps:

1. Click the Start button and choose Control Panel.

2. If Control Panel opens in Category view, click the Network and Internet icon.

3. Open the View network status and tasks link below Network and Sharing Center.

4. As shown in Figure 52.8, the system is connected to a local network, but the local network does not have a connection to the Internet.

5. After reconfiguring the wiring connecting the network hardware and opening Network and Sharing Center, the network now looks like Figure 52.9.

In Figure 52.9, Windows sees the local network and also sees the Internet connection from the local network. If your networking hardware is configured correctly, Windows sees the network and will set it up for you appropriately.

If your network is configured correctly for the first computer, try configuring your next system on the network using the steps outlined earlier.

If you have wireless devices that you want to connect to the network, follow the instructions in the next section.

FIGURE 52.8

A computer connected to the network but no Internet connection.

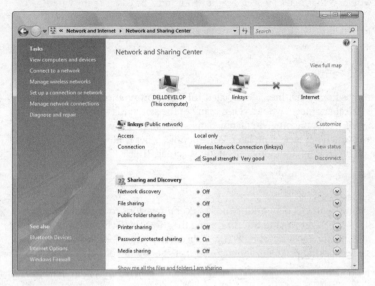

FIGURE 52.9

A computer connected to the network and also connected to the Internet.

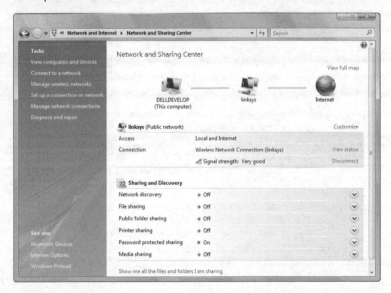

Setting Up a Wireless Network

There's something about the term "wireless" that makes it seem as though it must be easier than "wired." In truth, wireless networking is quite a bit more complicated terminology-wise. There are lots of buzzwords and acronyms everyone assumes that you already know. So, before we get into this topic, let's get all of that out of the way.

The 802.11 standard

The Institute of Electrical and Electronics Engineers, Inc., abbreviated IEEE and pronounced *EYE-triple-E*, is an organization of some 360,000 electrical engineers who develop many of the standards that PC products use to interact with one another. The IEEE isn't big on giving fancy names to things. They prefer numbers (which somehow seems fitting). Names often get tacked on later. For example, what is now called Ethernet is actually IEEE 802.3. What Apple calls FireWire and Sony calls iLink is actually IEEE 1394.

 **The home page for IEEE is at** www.ieee.net.

IEEE created the 802.11 standard for most wireless networking today. Several revisions to the original specification have been proposed, with 802.11a, 802.11b, and 802.11g being the three that actually have made it to market as I write this chapter. Most likely you'll be using 802.11g, because it's the standard to which most of the recently released wireless networking products adhere. And that's about all you really need to know about 802.11 right now.

Access point, SSID, WEP, and WPA

Wireless networking requires some kind of *wireless access point*, also called a *base station*. The base station is the central unit with which all computers in the network communicate. It's the same idea as a hub in Ethernet networking. It's just that there are no wires connecting computers to the access point. Instead, each computer has a wireless network interface card (NIC), as illustrated in Figure 52.10.

The access point in a wireless network plays the same role as the hub in a wired network, in that all traffic goes to the access point first, and is passed on to the appropriate destination from there. The problem is, with wireless networks, you have radio waves, which aren't confined to the inside of a wire. Radio waves go all over the place, just like when you throw a rock in the water and make waves that spread out in a circle.

The radio waves can be a problem when you have multiple wireless networks that are close to each other. For example, let's say that a company has several departments, and each department has its own, separate wireless network. If the departments are fairly close to each other in the same building, then it's possible that network messages from one department might get picked up by another department's wireless access point, which in turn might send the message off to a computer in its own network rather than to the correct recipient.

To avoid that problem, you need some means of discriminating among multiple wireless access points. For example, you need some means of setting rules like "these six computers in the marketing department communicate only with each other through access point *X*, while these 12 computers in Accounting communicate with each other, only, through access point *Z*." The way you do that in today's wireless networking is through things like network names, SSID, WEP, and WPA.

About SSIDs

Every wireless network has a unique name called a *service set identifier* (SSID) or just a *wireless network name* for simplicity. The access point in the network holds the SSID, and broadcasts it out at regular intervals. When you start a wireless network computer, it scans the airwaves for SSID. When you set up a wireless network access point (by reading the manufacturer's instructions, of course), you assign an SSID to your access point.

The name you assign doesn't have to be anything fancy. But it should be unique enough to avoid conflict with any close neighbors who also have wireless networks. The SSID doesn't provide any real network security. After all, the access point broadcasts the SSID out some distance from the access point. So if some hackers happened to be driving by with a notebook computer, they might be able to pick up the name of your wireless LAN from the car. Then they could join your network and receive data being sent by computers in your network. WEP and WPA are encryption tools designed to avoid such intrusions.

About WEP and WPA

Open System Wired Equivalent Protocol (WEP) is a wireless security protocol that protects wireless network data from falling into the wrong hands. Before any information leaves your computer, it's encrypted using a WEP key. The key is a simple string of characters that you can generate automatically, or have Windows generate for you.

Wi-Fi Protected Access (WPA) is a newer and stronger encryption system that supports modern EAP security devices such as smart cards, certificates, token cards, one-time passwords, and biometric devices. Eventually, IEEE will release a new 802.11i standard, which will offer the type of security currently found only in WPA. If your wireless networking hardware supports both WEP and WPA, you should go with WPA because that's the wave of the future.

FIGURE 52.10

Wireless communications all go through an access point or base station.

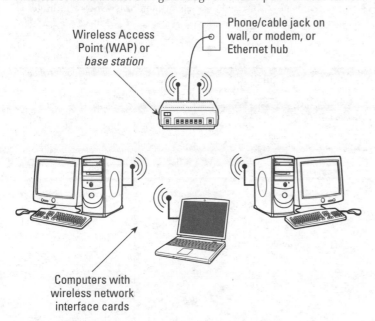

Installing the wireless networking hardware

The most critical step in setting up a wireless network is installing the hardware devices. It's imperative that you follow the instructions that came with the device to a tee, because guessing almost never works. In particular, it's important to note that even devices that plug into a hot-pluggable port like USB devices or a PC Card need you to install drives *before* you install the hardware device. That's unusual for hot-pluggable devices, and most people just assume that they can plug in the device and go. But it just doesn't work that way with wireless networking devices.

Connecting to available networks

The main trick to wireless networking is setting up the base station (access point). Typically, you do this by choosing one computer to operate the access point, and you configure the access point from that computer. There you give the network its name (SSID) and choose your encryption method. The access point then begins transmitting that name at regular intervals.

On any computer that's to join the LAN, you install a wireless network adapter. On a notebook computer, it's likely that a card resides internal to the system. On a desktop computer, you can install an internal wireless network adapter, connect one to a USB port, or even slide one into a Compact Flash slot.

Once you've installed the network adapter, you can check and configure one of the available networks by following these steps. If you have enabled security on your access point, move on to the next set of steps. To connect to an unsecured access point, follow these steps:

1. Click the Start button and choose Control Panel.
2. If Control Panel opens in Category view, click the Network and Internet icon.
3. Open the View network status and tasks link below Network and Sharing Center.
4. As shown in Figure 52.11, the system is not connected to a network, but this window indicates that wireless networks are available.

FIGURE 52.11

Windows sees that there are networks available.

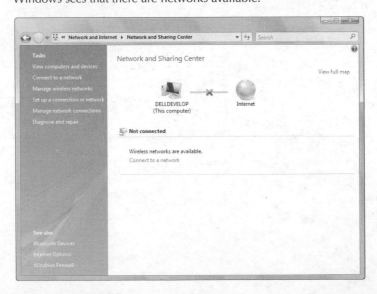

5. After clicking the Connect to a network link, you will see what networks Windows says are available in screens similar to Figure 52.12.

FIGURE 52.12

Windows sees two networks.

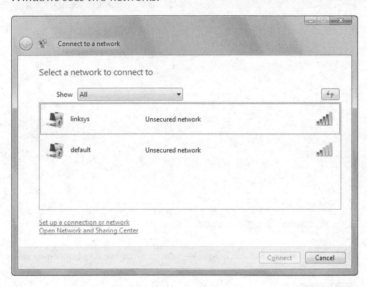

6. If you choose an unsecured network and click the Connect button, Windows may prompt you with a window confirming that you want to connect to an unsecured network. Click to connect to the unsecured network.

7. After you are successfully connected, you will see a window similar to the one shown in Figure 52.13.

8. After Windows has successfully connected to the network, a dialog box may pop up asking what type of network you just connected to. To learn more about the different types of network categories, search for Network Categories under Windows Help and select "What are network categories?"

If you have enabled either WEP or WPA encryption at your access point, you can follow these steps to get connected to your wireless network.

1. Click the Start button and choose Control Panel.

2. If Control Panel opens in Category view, click the Network and Internet icon.

3. Open the View network status and tasks link below Network and Sharing Center.

4. As shown in Figure 52.11, the system is not connected to a network, but this window indicates that wireless networks are available.

5. After clicking the Connect to a Network link, you will see what networks Windows says are available in a screen similar to Figure 52.12.

6. I have chosen the linksys network, which is the secured network in my environment. Windows has indicated that the network adapter in my system does not meet the requirements of the network. To fix this, right-click your secured network connection and choose Diagnose.

FIGURE 52.13

Windows has successfully connected to the wireless network.

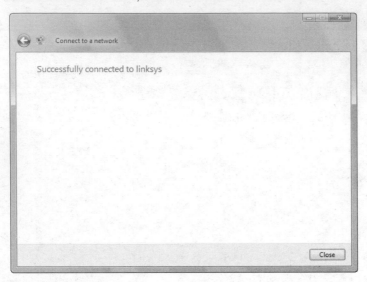

7. After a moment, a Windows Network Diagnostics window will pop up as shown in Figure 52.14.

FIGURE 52.14

Windows indicates that it was unable to connect.

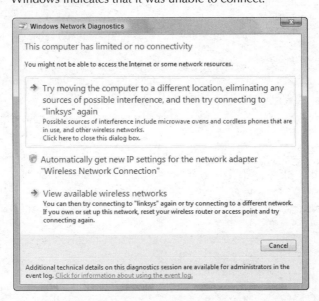

8. Click the View available wireless networks link to close the Windows Diagnostics window and return to the Connect to a network dialog box. Right-click the secured network icon and choose Properties. This will bring up the Wireless Network properties window for your network adapter.

9. Check the box labeled Connect automatically when this network is in range shown in Figure 52.15, which will prevent you from having to take these steps each time you restart your computer.

FIGURE 52.15

Wireless Network properties allow you to connect to this network automatically.

10. Switch to the Security tab shown in Figure 52.16.

11. Fill in the appropriate setting based on the manufacturer's configuration of your access point. After filling in the settings based on the type of network security, click the OK button.

12. Your system should now be connected to your local network and also the Internet if you have configured your router. To test this, use Internet Explorer and try browsing to a Web site.

The notification icon

Windows Vista can include your network connectivity information within the Notification area. It includes it as a network icon, which includes two computers. If you don't see an icon resembling two computers, check to make sure that it's not just hidden by clicking the < button at the left side of the Notification area. If you still don't see the icon, right-click an empty space on the taskbar and select Properties. Click the Notification tab and make sure that Network is checked under the System icons section. Click the OK button.

When you've finished, you're ready to move on to Chapter 53 where you'll learn to share resources and use those shared resources from any computer in the network.

FIGURE 52.16

Available options for different security levels within Windows.

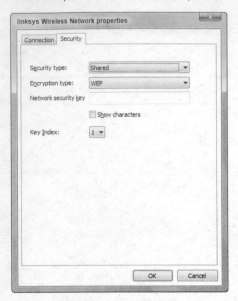

Wrap Up

A local area network (LAN) consists of two or more computers that can communicate with one another through networking hardware. Multiple computers in a network can share a single Internet account, share printers, and share files and folders. Moving and copying files between networked computers is a simple matter of dragging and dropping. No fumbling around with floppies, CDs, or other removable disks is required. The main points to remember when it comes to buying network hardware are as follows:

- The first step to creating a LAN is to purchase the computer networking hardware.
- Each computer in the network needs a network interface card (NIC) installed.
- Ethernet LANs provide the fastest speeds, but require running special Ethernet cables.
- Wireless networking provides complete freedom from cables and wires.
- USB networking devices are easy to install and don't require opening the computer case.
- On a notebook computer, you can use a PC Card NIC (not to be confused with PCI card) to connect to the network or an integrated wireless network card.
- After you acquire your network hardware, you have to set it all up per the manufacturer's instructions. When you've finished that step, you can use the Network and Sharing Center to help configure the hardware.

Chapter 53

Sharing Resources on a Network

A local area network (LAN) consists of two or more computers connected through some sort of networking hardware. In a local area network, you can use *shared resources* from other computers in much the same way as you use local resources on your own computer. In fact, the way you do things in a LAN is almost identical to the way you do things on a single computer.

For example, everything you learned about printing documents on your own computer earlier in this book works just as well for printing on a network printer. Opening a document on some other computer in a network is no different from opening a document on your own computer.

In this chapter, I'll briefly discuss options for using shared resources on a network, mainly to help you ensure that your shared resources are, indeed, shared.

Some Networking Buzzwords

Like everything else computerish, networking has its own set of buzzwords. All the buzzwords you learned in earlier chapters still apply. But there are some new words to learn, as defined here:

- **Resource:** Anything useful, including a folder, a printer, or other device.
- **Shared:** A resource accessible to all users on a computer and to all computers within a network. A shared folder is often referred to as a *share* or *network share*.
- **Local computer:** The computer at which you're currently sitting.
- **Local resource:** A folder, printer, or other useful thing on the local computer or directly connected to the local computer by a cable. For example, if there's a printer connected to your computer by a cable, it's a local resource (or more specifically, a *local printer*).
- **Remote computer:** Any computer in the network other than the one at which you're currently sitting.
- **Remote resource:** A folder, printer, or other useful thing on some computer other than the local computer. For example, a printer connected to someone else's computer on the network is a remote resource (or more specifically, a *remote printer*).

Figure 53.1 shows an example of how the terms *local* and *remote* are always used in reference to the computer at which you're currently sitting.

FIGURE 53.1

Examples of local and remote resources, from your perspective.

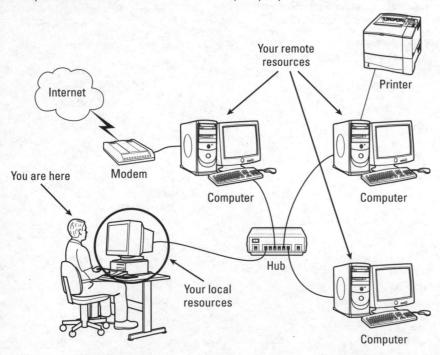

Windows Firewall and Shared Network Resources

Before you share a folder or printer, File and Print Sharing is disabled in the exceptions list for the Windows Firewall. If you have any trouble at all sharing printers, files, or folders, make sure you understand how Windows Firewall works. See Chapter 7, "Blocking Hackers with Windows Firewall," for the full scoop on configuring Windows Firewall. The key to firewall success is making sure the File and Printer Sharing and Network Discovery exceptions, shown in Figure 53.2, are selected (checked) on all of the Vista computers in your local network.

FIGURE 53.2

The Exceptions tab under Windows Firewall provides a way to enable only specific protocols.

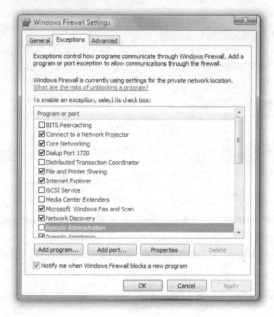

NEW FEATURE Network Sharing and Discovery provides a single point of administration for controlling network sharing and the discovery of shared resources.

Turn on Sharing and Discovery

By default, Windows does not make network resources available to everyone. Microsoft has tightened the security of Vista, and by doing so, it requires users to explicitly share resources. A first step on each computer is to make sure sharing and discovery is enabled, and all computers belong to the same workgroup. You need administrative privileges to makes these kinds of changes. So log in to an account that has those privileges before you get started. Then get to the Network and Sharing Center using either of these methods:

- Click the Start button and choose Control Panel ⇨ Network and Internet ⇨ Network and Sharing Center.
- Press ⊞, type net, and click Network and Sharing Center.

The center opens as in Figure 53.3. Your goal is to set things up with all the Sharing and Discovery settings turned on as in the figure.

> **TIP** If you see any messages about connecting to your network for the first time and questions about the network type, choose Private. Your local network is a private network. The Internet is a public network.

FIGURE 53.3

Network and Sharing Center.

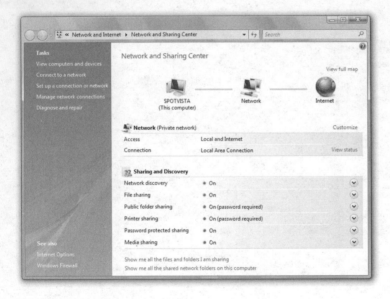

If you see Unidentified Network or Public Network where the figure shows a private network, click the Customize link. Change the setting from Public to Private as in Figure 53.4, and then click Next and Close.

Making the network private makes it discoverable to other computers within the same private network. However, it's important that all computers belong to the same workgroup. So on each computer you also want to make sure Network Discovery is turned on and all computers have the same workgroup name. Click the arrow to the right of Discovery and choose Turn on network discovery. The workgroup name is set to WORKGROUP by default as in Figure 53.5. Vista seems to work best if you stick with that name. If you have any non-Vista computers with a different workgroup name, better to change their names to WORKGROUP.

FIGURE 53.4

Make your local network private.

If you had to make any changes under Network Discovery, click Apply. Otherwise just click the button next to Network Discovery again. Remember, you'll want to follow the same procedure on all Vista computers in your network.

FIGURE 53.5

Setting the workgroup name.

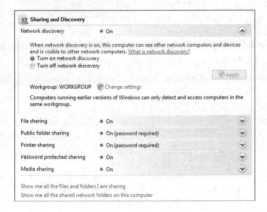

Changing the Workgroup Name on an XP Computer

To change the workgroup name on a Windows XP computer, right-click the My Computer icon in XP and choose Properties. Then click the Computer Name tab. The current workgroup name appears next to the Workgroup heading. If you need to change it, click the Change button next to "To rename this computer or join a workgroup, click change." Change the name under the Workgroup heading and click OK. Click OK in each open dialog box and restart the computer.

Unless you have some compelling reason to limit what's shared on your private network, your best bet is to turn on all the other forms of sharing. If any are turned off, you can just click the word Off (or the button to the right) and turn the option on. Each time you do so you'll see a description of what the option shares. Here's a quick summary (Note that the Apply button for each option is enabled only if you make a change. If you don't make a change, use the arrow button to shrink the option back down to a single line.):

- Clicking the down arrow to the right of either File sharing or Printer sharing will enable file and printer sharing on your local computer. Turning on File sharing will also turn on Printer sharing and vice versa.

- Under Public folder sharing, the default is not to allow network access. You can change to allow users to have read access, meaning that they can only read but not change content, by selecting Turn on sharing so anyone with network access can open files. Or you can grant users access to update information within the Public folder by selecting the Turn on sharing so anyone with network access can open, change, and create files option.

- If you enable the Password protected sharing option, you will require any user who wants to access resources on your system to have a user account. When this option is enabled and a user attempts to connect to your system, they will be prompted for authentication. Leaving this option off will allow any user on the network access to your resources.

- Turn on Media Sharing to allow sharing of your Windows Media Player library files across the network. Each user account on the current computer can change media sharing independently. Expand the Media Sharing option and click the Change button. If you see a checkbox titled Share my media, select it and click OK. Click **Other users of this PC** and click **Allow**. Then click OK. The actual sharing you can do from Media Player is discussed in the next section.

 The *Learn more about sharing* and *How does sharing change firewall settings?* links provide more detailed information on sharing media files.

When you've turned on all the Sharing and Discovery options, you're ready to move to the next Vista computer in the network and repeat the process. Once all of the computers have sharing and discovery enabled and belong to the same workgroup, they'll be able to find each others' shared resources automatically. But it's still up to each user to decide what they want to share. We'll look at techniques for sharing resources in the sections to follow.

NEW FEATURE You can share media files from Windows Media Library, rather than from the folders in which those files are contained.

Sharing Media

Each user that has an account on the computer also has a Windows Media Center media library. Any user can choose media to share and how to share it by following these steps:

1. In your own user account, start Windows Media Player.
2. Click the button under Library and click Media Sharing.
3. Select (check) Share my media and click OK to extend the Media Sharing dialog box as in Figure 53.6.

FIGURE 53.6

Media Sharing.

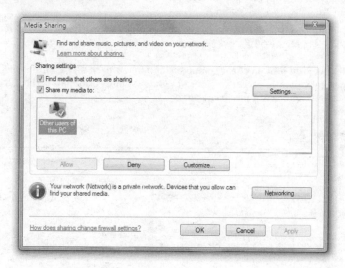

4. Optionally, to limit sharing to certain types of media, star ratings, and parental ratings, or to allow new media devices to be shared automatically, click Settings. Then choose sharing options and click OK.

 The Learn more about sharing link in the Media Sharing dialog box provides detailed information.

5. Click OK to close the Media Sharing dialog box.

Other users will be able to view and play media files from their own Windows Media Player libraries. Chapter 54 explains how.

Sharing a Printer

Printers in a local area network will usually be connected to one of the computers in that network. To ensure that the printer is shared, so everybody in the network can use it, follow these steps:

 With the right hardware, you can connect a printer directly to a LAN without going through a computer. With that type of arrangement, you need only to make sure that the printer is turned on.

1. Go to the computer to which the printer is connected by cable. If either is turned off, turn on the printer first and the computer second.

2. Click Start ➪ Control Panel ➪ Printer. Or press ⊞, type prin, and choose Printers.

3. Right-click the printer icon that you want to share and select Sharing.

4. If the Sharing tab contains a message "In order to share this printer, an administrator must configure Windows Firewall to permit the sharing of printers," then the Windows Firewall has not been configured correctly.

5. Click Change Sharing options. If prompted, elevate your privileges by clicking Continue or by entering an administrative password.

6. Choose the option to share the printer, give the printer a name, and choose to render print jobs on the client as in Figure 53.7.

NEW FEATURE   The Render print jobs on client computers option lets each user control print jobs from his or her own computer. In earlier versions of Windows, most print jobs had to be managed from the printer to which the computer was physically attached.

FIGURE 53.7

Sharing a printer.

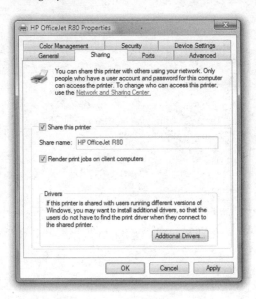

7. Click OK.

The printer's icon will show two small people in front of it. The printer should show up automatically in all network computers' Print dialog boxes. If it doesn't show up on a particular computer, see Chapter 35 for information on installing a shared network printer.

What about Sharing Programs?

Though you can share folders and documents freely on a LAN, there's no way to share programs. You can only run programs currently installed on your computer and accessible from your All Programs menu. If you try to open a document on another computer, but don't have the appropriate program for that document type, you can't open the document.

Don't bother trying to copy an installed program from one computer to another—it won't work. Only programs that you specifically install on your own computer will run on your computer.

The only solution will be to install the necessary program on your own computer. If the program you need is a freebie, like Adobe Acrobat Reader, you can download and install the program in the usual manner. (For Acrobat Reader, go to www.adobe.com and click Get Adobe Reader.)

Sharing Folders

Windows Vista includes a Public folder from which files are shared automatically. For those of you with XP experience, this is the same idea as Shared Documents. You can simply move any files that you intend to share across all user accounts or computers in a private network to that folder. To get to that folder:

1. Open any folder (for example, click the Start button and choose Computer or your user name).
2. Click Folders at the bottom of the Navigation pane.
3. Expand the icons for the Computer folder, Vista drive, and Users folder as necessary.
4. Click Public under the Users folder as in Figure 53.8.

The Public folder is organized like your Documents folders. It contains icons for storing Documents, Downloads, Music, Pictures, and Videos. If you have the Premium or Ultimate Edition of Vista, it also contains a Recorded TV folder, in which Media Center recorded TV files are stored.

> **TIP** Clicking the leftmost button in the Address bar of any folder also provides a quick link to the Public folder.

Perhaps the easiest way to move files into a public folder would be to open one of its subfolders, like Public Documents or Public Pictures. Then open the folder that contains the files you want to share. Size and position the two windows so you can see both. Then drag files from one folder to the other. See Chapter 29 for more information on moving and copying files.

The Public folder is shared in a way where every user on the computer (and in the network) has free reign over its contents. In other words, every user has equal rights to the Public folder. If you have files you want to share more selectively, such as only with certain people or only with certain permissions, use the method described next rather than the Public folder.

> **NEW FEATURE** When you share a folder from your account, you have the option of sharing with only certain people. You can also control each person's permissions.

Sharing selectively

As an alternative to using the built-in Public folder, you can share any folder within your user account. Open the parent folder to the folder you want to share so that you can see the folder's icon. Then right-click the icon of the folder you want to share and click Share.... You'll see a File Sharing Wizard as in Figure 53.9. (It doesn't look like a typical wizard, but it is.)

FIGURE 53.8

The Public folder.

FIGURE 53.9

File Sharing Wizard.

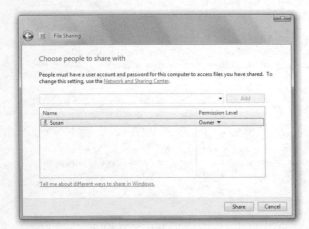

NOTE The File Sharing Wizard only appears if "Use Sharing Wizard (recommended)" is selected in Folder and Search Options. To get to that option, click Start, type `fol`, and choose Folder Options. Then click the View tab and scroll down to the bottom of the list.

Next, click the drop-down list button and click the name of the person with whom you want to share the folder, or Everyone to share with everybody who has a user account on the computer and network. Then click Add. Then use the Permission Level column to choose how much permission you want to grant to that user, as follows:

- **Reader:** The person can view any file in the folder, but cannot add files to the folder or change or delete the files in the folder.
- **Contributor:** The person can view files in the folder and add files to the folder. However, that person can change or delete only files that the person added to the folder personally.
- **Co-Owner:** The person has the same rights as the person who shared the folder. They can add, change, or delete any file in the folder.

Figure 53.10 shows an example where the owner of the folder Susan has granted Alan Contributor permissions to the folder. User Alec is allowed to open and view files in the folder, but not make any changes to the files or add/delete files.

FIGURE 53.10

Permission levels for shared folder.

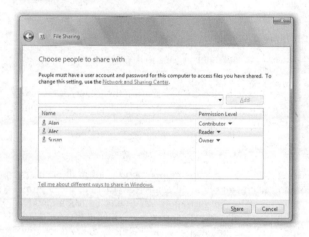

Click the Share button after making your selections. A second page opens to verify that you're sharing the folder. From that page you can e-mail links to the other users to let them know where the folder is located. Or copy the links and paste them into any program of your choosing so you can print them out. Click Done to close the wizard page.

NEW FEATURE Vista makes it easy to keep track of what you've shared and change permissions.

Make the Public Folder More Accessible

To make the Public folder easier to get to, create shortcuts to it wherever appropriate. First click Users in the Address bar so you can see the Public folder. It should already show the sharing icon with two people. To add a shortcut to the Favorite Links pane in the Navigation bar, just drag the Public folder's icon into the Favorite Links area. To put a shortcut on the desktop, right-click that icon and choose Send To ➪ Desktop (create shortcut). To add one to the Quick Launch toolbar, drag the desktop shortcut onto the Quick Launch toolbar.

To add shortcuts to other folders, right-click the desktop shortcut icon and choose Copy. Then open any folder in which you want to place a shortcut and paste (press Ctrl+V or right-click some empty space in the folder and choose Paste). Your user account folder and Documents folders might be good candidates for shortcuts, because both are readily accessible from other folders as well as the Open and Save As dialog boxes. You can use similar methods to create shortcuts to Public Pictures, Recorded TV, or any other public folder you use frequently.

Reviewing shared folders

You can review your shared folders at any time just by opening the Shared By Me saved search. Here are three ways to get to your saved searches:

- If you're already in a folder and see your user name in the Address bar, click the arrow to the right of your user name and click Searches.
- Tap , type sea, and click Searches on the Start menu.
- Click the Start button, click your user name, and open the Searches folder.

> **TIP** Of course, if Searches is in your Favorite Links, you can just click that as well.

Once you're in the Search folders, just open the Shared By Me folder. To stop sharing the folder, or change permissions, right-click the folder's icon and choose Search. Then choose the option to change permissions or stop sharing, depending on which you want to do.

Advanced Sharing

Advanced Sharing allows a user with administrative privileges to set custom permissions for multiple users, control the number of simultaneous connections and caching for offline files, and set other advanced properties. Some of these topics require formal training in network administration. Personally, I'd recommend you stay away from them if you have no formal training in such matters. They can be difficult to work with and the mess you create could be very difficult (and expensive) to untangle. The Public folder and selective sharing methods described in the preceding sections should be adequate for a home network, and much easier and safer to work with.

For people who understand the concepts (and potential problems) involved, I'll just quickly run through the process, but if you're that advanced, you can probably figure it out on your own. The basic process is to get to the folder you want to share, right-click that folder's icon, and choose Properties. Click the Sharing tab and click Advanced Sharing. Elevate your privileges and choose Share this folder. Then click the Apply button. Set the number of simultaneous users up to a maximum of 10 and (optionally) add a comment.

To configure permissions, click the Permissions button. You're taken to traditional access control tools. For example, to set share permissions for users or groups, click the Add button and enter the object names separated by semicolons. To set permissions for standard user accounts, use the name Users. Use Administrators to enter permissions for the administrators group. Or, enter individual user account names separated by semicolons. Click Check Names to add locations to the account names and then click OK. Set Allow and Deny permissions for the group or users. Repeat the process to define share permissions for other users and groups. Click OK and Close as appropriate after setting permissions.

To review or change permissions, use the Security tab in the folder's Properties dialog box. Right-click the folder's icon and choose Properties. Then click the Security tab. Click a user or group name in the top half of the dialog box. Permissions for that user or group appear in the lower half of the dialog box as in the example shown in Figure 53.11. Click the Edit button to change permissions. Click Advanced for special permissions, auditing, and such. Click *Learn about access control and permissions* for details.

FIGURE 53.11

Security tab for a shared folder.

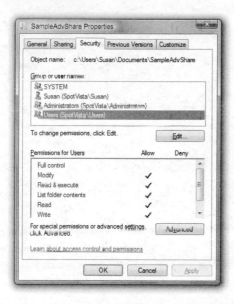

There are entire books, courses, and certifications devoted to the access control methods I've breezed through in the preceding paragraphs. I think the average user will do just fine sticking with the two methods described at the start of this chapter. I only mention them here to professionals in the general direction of the dialog boxes. In the next chapter you'll discover how to access those shared resources.

Wrap Up

People create computer networks to share resources among computers. Resources include things like an Internet connection, media files, folders, and printers. Windows Vista's sharing and discovery makes it relatively easy to share resources and discover them. This chapter has focused on the "sharing" part. In summary:

- To turn on sharing and discovery, open the Network and Sharing Center. Make sure you are connected to your private network and that all computers in the network share a common workgroup name.
- For maximum ease-of-use, turn on all the options under Sharing and Discovery.
- To share your media library, open Windows Media Player, click the button under Library, and choose Media Sharing.
- To share a printer, right-click its icon and choose Sharing.
- One way to share files is to move them to the Public folder or one of its subfolders.
- To share a folder more selectively, right-click its icon and click Share....
- To review your shared folder, open the Searches folder, and then open the Shared By Me saved search.

Chapter 54

Using Shared Resources

Chapters 52 and 53 covered all the basics of setting up and sharing resources on a private home or small business network. This chapter assumes that you've already done all of that. Nothing in this chapter will work until the network is set up, you've turned on network sharing and discovery on each Windows Vista computer, and shared some things on the network.

This chapter looks at how you get to and use shared resources from computers within the network. It looks at opening documents from remote resources, moving and copying files between networked computers, using remote printers, and ways of using shared media.

Accessing Remote Resources

Every Windows Vista computer on which you've enabled network sharing and discovery should show up in every computer's Network folder. The same is true of any Windows XP computers in the network that have at least one shared resource (such as the built-in Shared Documents folder). To open the Network folder on a Windows Vista computer, use whichever technique is most convenient:

- Click the Start button and choose Network.
- Or press ⊞, type net, click Network and Sharing Center, and then click View computers and devices in the left column.
- Or if you're already in a folder, click Network in the Folders list.

The first time you open the Network folder on a computer, it might take a few seconds for it to discover other computers in the network. But within a few seconds you should see an icon for each computer in the network as in the example shown in Figure 54.1. In that example the first two icons aren't computers. The Residential Gateway Device is a shared cable modem. The SPOTVISTA:Alan is a shared Media Player library. But each of the other icons is a computer on my private network. Notice how each computer is also accessible from the Folders list after expanding the Network category in that list.

FIGURE 54.1

Sample Network folder.

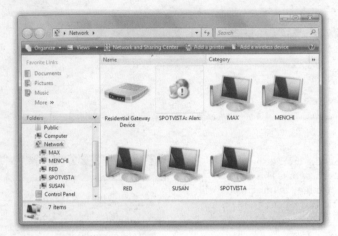

Each computer's icon is like a folder in that when you open it, you see shared resources from that computer. That includes a folder icon for each shared folder and printer icons for any shared printers connected to that computer.

If you use the Network folder often, you'll want to make sure it's easy to find its icon. To put a Network icon on your desktop, right-click the desktop and choose Personalize. In the left column, click Change desktop icons. Select the Network checkbox (and the checkboxes of any other icons you want) and click OK.

If you don't have a Network option on the right side of your Start menu, you can add one using methods for customizing the Start menu discussed in Chapter 11.

To add Network to you Favorite Links in Windows Explorer, open a folder and make sure you can see the Navigation pane. Open the Folders list, and then drag the Network icon in the Folders list into the Favorite Links pane.

 Any time you're in Windows Explorer, clicking the leftmost arrow in the Address bar will usu-
ally provide a quick link to the Network folder.

Opening Remote Documents

One of the advantages to having a network is that you can put documents in shared folders and open them from any computer in the network. For example, you might put all your important work documents in a shared folder on your main work computer. If you also have a portable computer you can use outside on sunny days (or in bed on lazy days), you can work directly with those documents from the remote computer.

The process is really no different from opening a document on a local computer. You could, for instance, just navigate to the folder, via the Network folder, in which the document is stored. Double-click (or click) the document you want to edit, and the document will open from the remote computer (providing that the local computer has the appropriate program installed for working with that type of document).

Optionally, you can go through the program's Open dialog box to get to the document. Here's how:

1. Open the program you want to use and choose File ⇨ Open from its menu bar.

2. In the Open dialog box, click Network (if available) at the left side of the dialog box. Or, choose Network from the Look In drop-down list in the Open dialog box.

3. First select the computer on the network where the document resides. Then navigate to the folder for (or a parent folder to) the document. If you have to open a parent folder, just navigate down through the subfolders until you get to the document's icon.

4. Click or double-click the document's icon.

Once the document is open, you can edit it or print it however you like. When you save the document, your changes will be saved at the original location. If you want to save a local copy of the document to work with, choose File ⇨ Save As from the program's menu bar, navigate to a local folder such as your Documents folder, and save your copy there.

Opening a read-only copy

If you try to open a document that someone already has open on another computer, you'll see a message telling you what your options are. Those options will vary from one program to the next. In Microsoft Word 2003, I got the message shown in Figure 54.2.

FIGURE 54.2

Someone else already has this document open.

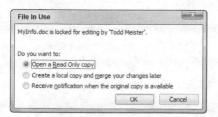

You can always open a read-only copy of the document on the local computer. Then, you can choose File ⇨ Save As from the program's menu bar to save a new, separate copy of the document. Once you've done that, your copy of the document will no longer be read-only, so you can edit it all you want. The only problem is, your changes won't be made to the original copy of the document.

Using merge features of Office programs

Some programs, like Microsoft Word, provide the second option, *Create a local copy and merge your documents later*, to handle the situation where another user on the network already has the document open. If you choose that second option, Word will open an editable copy of the document. If the other user closes her copy of the document while you still have yours open, you'll see the message shown in Figure 54.3. At that point, you can click Merge to merge your changes to the original copy of the document and continue work on the document.

FIGURE 54.3

Using the Create a local copy and merge your documents later option.

If the other person doesn't close his or her copy of the document before you save your copy, you'll be taken to the Save As dialog box. Word will suggest saving the file to the original folder with the original filename followed by the words *--for merge*. Later, when both copies of the document are closed, you can go to the computer on which the original copy of the document is stored and open the original document from there. Then, in Word, choose Tools ⇨ Merge Documents from the menu bar, and follow the instructions to merge in changes from the *--for merge* copy of the document.

The third alternative, *Receive notification when the original copy is available*, will also allow you to edit a copy of the document. You'd choose this option if you were reasonably sure that the other person was going to close her copy of the document before you're done. (For example, if you are the "other person" who left the document open, you can just walk over to the other computer and close the document.)

When you choose this option, and the other user closes her open copy of the document, you'll see the message shown in Figure 54.4. At that point, you can just click the Read-Write button to make your open copy of the document the only open copy, so that all your changes are made to the original document when you save the document.

FIGURE 54.4

Using the Receive notification when the original copy is available option.

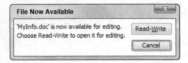

Admittedly, I've digressed from "pure Windows" here by getting into Word options for simultaneously opening documents. Different programs will handle the situation differently. For example, I did the same little experiment with a digital photo in Paint Shop Pro. Paint Shop Pro just opened the second copy of the document as a Read-Write file with no warning whatsoever. I was able to edit, and save, both open copies of the document. Paint Shop Pro used a very simple technique to handle the situation. The most recently saved changes to the document are the ones that "stick."

In Microsoft Access, you can create a *project* and save it to a shared folder. You can also create *pages*, which are basically Access forms written in Hypertext Markup Language (HTML). Up to five people on five separate computers can then simultaneously edit data in the database through Internet Explorer and the pages.

In summary, when it comes to dealing with multiple copies of the same document open on multiple computers in a network, it's really up to the program you're using at the moment, not Windows, as to how this gets handled. Your best bet would be to check the Help or documentation that came with that program. Or, just experiment with it for a while until you get the hang of how the program is going to handle the situation. You can always choose File ⇨ Save As to save your open copy of the document with a new filename. Then decide what you want to do later, when all open copies of the document are closed.

Creating Network Locations

If you have your own Web site, or permission to upload to an FTP site, or really anything on the Internet to which you can upload files, you can add an icon for that location to your Computer folder. Doing so will allow you to upload files to that location using the same techniques you use to save a file to your own computer.

You'll need to know the URL (address) to which you can download. Chances are you'll need a user name and password as well. The people who own the site to which you'll be uploading will provide that information when you set up your account. They might also provide upload instructions. But as long as you know the URL and your user name and password, you should be able to use the technique described here in addition to whatever method they provide.

To create a link to the Internet location, follow these steps:

1. Open your Computer folder.
2. Right-click any unused space in the window and choose Add a Network Location.
3. Click Next> on the first wizard page.
4. Click the Choose a custom network location and then click Next>.
5. Type the complete URL of the remote site. For example, if it's a Web site you own, include the `http://`. For instance, in Figure 54.5 I'm about to create a shortcut to the `www.sycamore solutions.com` site. If the shortcut is to an FTP site for which you have upload permissions, use the `ftp://` prefix on the URL. Click Next>. To see a list of examples, click the View examples link in the middle of the window.

FIGURE 54.5

Providing the URL of an Internet resource.

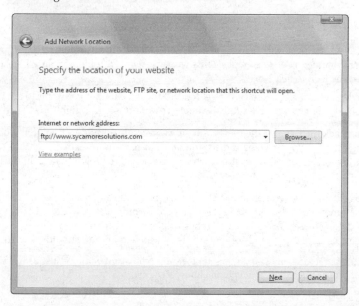

6. In the next dialog box that opens, you'll probably need to uncheck the Log on anonymously box and enter your user name as provided by the service, as in Figure 54.6. In some cases you are able to connect to resources anonymously, but this is probably not the case if you're connecting to a protected resource on the Internet. Once you've entered your user name, click the Next button.

FIGURE 54.6

Enter your user name.

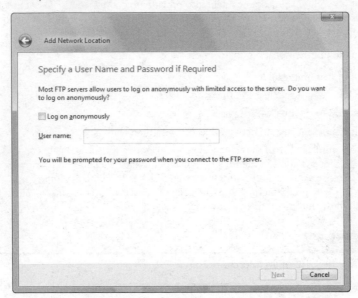

7. The next wizard page will suggest the URL (without the `http://` or `ftp://` prefix) as the name of the shortcut icon. You can replace that with any name you like, because it's used only as the label for the icon. Click Next.

8. On the last wizard page, you can select (check) the checkbox if you want to see the remote folder immediately. Or clear the checkbox if you don't want to see that right now. Then click Finish.

When you double-click the icon for the remote site, it will open in Windows Explorer, looking much the same as any local folder on your own hard disk. You may not have quite as many options to choose from in the Explorer bar. Figure 54.7 show an example where I've opened the folder where all the files for my `www.sycamoresolutions.com` site are stored.

You can treat the folder as you would any other. For example, you can create a new folder, or rename or delete existing files and folders by right-clicking, just as you would in any folder on your C: drive. You can also move and copy files to/from the site. Things will be slower than on your own computer, because the remote resource could be thousands of miles away, but the techniques should all be the same.

 You can rename any icon, at any time, under Network Locations just as you would any other icon. Just right-click the icon and choose Rename.

FIGURE 54.7

www.sycamoresolutions.com site as a folder in Windows Explorer.

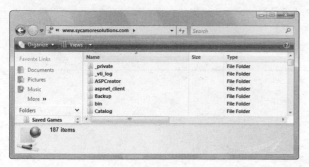

If things don't work as described here, your best resource for getting answers would be the people who provided the site. They're the only ones who know the details of that site.

Saving to a Remote Computer

Any time you save a new document—whether it's one you've created yourself, or something you're downloading—you'll get some kind of Save As dialog box. It may be titled File Download or something like that. But it will have a Folders list so that you can choose where you want to save the document.

As with the Open dialog box, you can choose the Network folder from the Folders list to get to all of the locations in your Network folder, and then navigate to wherever you want to save the file from there.

Downloading Programs to a Network

If you regularly download programs to install on multiple computers, consider using the folder named Public Downloads within your Public folder. After you save a downloaded program file to that folder, you'll be able to install it on all the computers in the network. You have to install it on each computer individually still. But it beats downloading it on every computer, especially if you're sharing a not-so-speedy Internet connection.

I'll go through the procedure here using an example of a file I'm downloading from Tucows.com. In this example, I'm using the folder named Public Downloads in the Public folder on a network computer. Start the download as you normally would. When you get to the Save/Run options, as shown at the bottom of Figure 54.8 (or Save/Open options), choose Save. (If you choose Open or Run, the program will install to the local computer only.)

When the Save As (or File Download) dialog box opens, choose the Public Downloads folder from the Folders list as shown in Figure 54.9. If the filename of the downloaded program doesn't adequately describe the file, click the New Folder button, give the folder a more descriptive name, and choose that folder in the Folders list. Then, click the Save button to download the file.

In most cases, you should be able to install the program right from that Public Downloads folder to any computer in your network. Go to any computer and open the Network folder. Navigate to the Public Downloads folder and the subfolder (if any) in which you placed the downloaded program file. For example, in Figure 54.10 I've navigated to the folder in which I downloaded the program I chose in Figures 54.8 and 54.9. You can see the path to the file in the Navigation bar at the top of the window.

FIGURE 54.8

About to download and save a program.

FIGURE 54.9

Saving the downloaded file to the Public Downloads folder.

When you see the icon for the downloaded program file, double-click it. The installation process should begin, so you can just follow the onscreen instructions to complete the installation. In the unlikely event that it doesn't work, you can try copying the downloaded program file to the local computer first, then open the icon from there. Or, if all else fails, go back to the original Web site from the local computer, start the download, and then choose Run or Open, when prompted, to install the program on the local computer.

FIGURE 54.10

Icon for downloaded program file on remote computer.

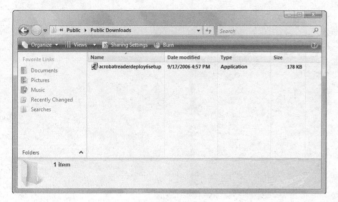

Transferring Files between Computers

Moving and copying files on a LAN is virtually identical to doing so on a single computer. You can use any of the techniques described in Chapter 29 to select, move, or copy files from any folder on your own computer to any shared folder or from any shared folder to any folder on your own computer. You can also use those same techniques to move and copy files between shared folders on any two remote computers on the network.

For example, let's say you're sitting at a computer named Spot, and you have a bunch of files in a subfolder named Common Downloads in a folder named Shared Docs on a computer named Max. You want to copy one or more files to the Downloads folder of your own user account on Spot. Just open the Network folder. Then open the Max, SharedDocs, and Common Downloads folders. Then, click the Start button and open the Documents folder for your user account. It might be easiest if you size and position the windows as in Figure 54.11.

With both folders open, as in the figure, you can select the files you want to copy in the top window using any technique you like, as discussed in Chapter 29. To copy (rather than move) the items to the remote folder, right-drag any selected icon to the remote folder, and then choose Copy Here after you release the mouse button. (If you drag using the left mouse button, the files will be moved, rather than copied.) That's all there is to it. As I said, it's no different from moving and copying files between folders and drives on your own computer, except that you have to use the Network folder to open the remote folder.

FIGURE 54.11

Remote shared folder (top) and local folder (bottom).

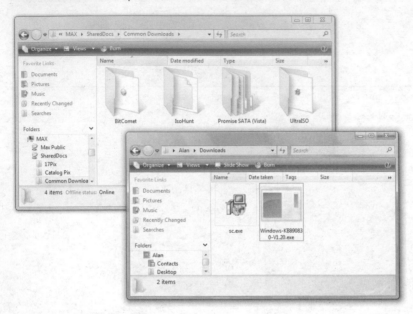

Universal Naming Convention (UNC)

In the Windows Explorer Address bar, you may see the path to the remote resource expressed in Universal Naming Convention (UNC) format. That format uses the syntax

`\\machineName\folderpath`

where *machineName* is the name of the remote computer, and *folderpath* is the name of shared folder on that computer, followed by any subfolders within that folder. For example, the following figure shows a normal view of the Address bar where the breadcrumb trail shows the computer name (Max) followed by the name of the shared folder and a subfolder.

The normal appearance of the Address bar within Windows Explorer.

If you click the folder icon to the left of the Network, the path will change to a UNC-formatted path as shown in the following figure.

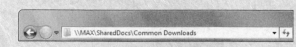

The UNC-formatted path to the Copied Fonts folder within Windows Explorer.

Mapping Drive Letters to Shared Folders

Some programs and networks require that you assign a drive letter to remote resources. You can assign any unused drive letter to a resource. For example, if you already have drives A: through F: in use, then you can assign drive letters G: through Z: to any shared resource. To map a drive letter to a shared folder:

1. Go to the computer on which you need to assign a drive letter and open its Network folder.
2. Click the computer that contains the Shared folder; right-click the folder and choose Map Network Drive. Or press the Alt key to view the Classic menu and choose Tools ➪ Map Network Drive from Explorer's menu bar. Either way, the Map Network Drive dialog box opens.
3. Click the Browse button if the Folder entry is not filled in already to open the Browse for Folder dialog box.
4. In the Browse for Folder dialog box, click the name of the shared resource to which you want to map a drive letter, so its name is selected (highlighted). For example, in Figure 54.12 I'm about to map the drive letter Y: to the shared ClipArt folder on a computer named DellDevelop.

FIGURE 54.12

Map a Drive Letter dialog box.

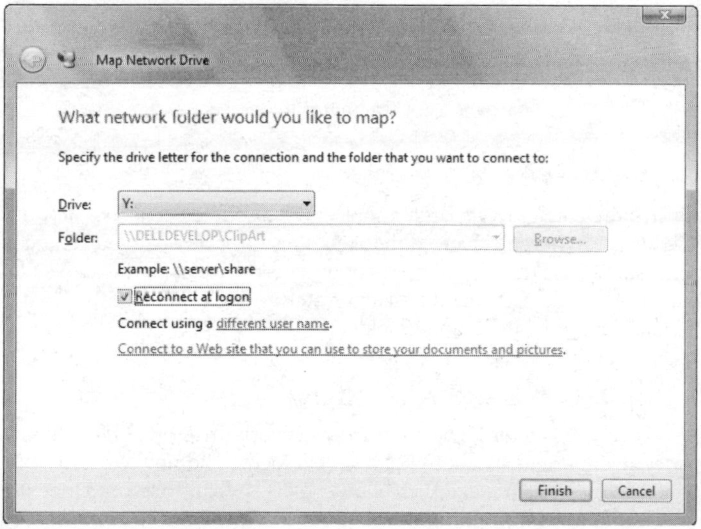

5. Click the Finish button.

The remote resource will open. You can close that folder, and also close the Network folder. Because you've mapped a drive letter to the remote resource, it will appear in your Computer folder under the Network Location heading. Figure 54.13 shows an example where I've mapped two resources, where Y: refers to the ClipArt folder on the computer named DellDevelop, and Z: refers to the folder named filebackups on the computer named Server.

 The network used for the examples in Figures 54.12 and 54.13 is different from the network shown earlier in this chapter. So don't let those names confuse you.

FIGURE 54.13

Drives Y: and Z: are actually folders.

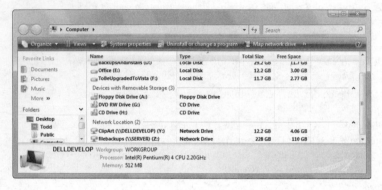

From that point on, you can access the folder either by going through the Network folder as usual, or you can just open your Computer and open the resource's icon under Network Location.

TIP   If the folders in your Computer folder aren't arranged like the example in Figure 54.12, use the menu bar in your Computer folder by pressing the Alt key to choose View and then choose either Sort By, Group By, or Stack By to alter the order and grouping of the folders. You can also access these options by right-clicking an empty area in your Computer folder.

About network drives

Once you've mapped a drive letter to a shared resource, the resource becomes a *network drive*. But that's just a terminology thing. You haven't changed the shared resource or what you can do with the resource, in any way, shape, or form. And the "drive" need not be a disk drive at all. It can be a folder. The term "network drive" just refers to the fact that the shared resource "looks like" a drive, by virtue of the fact that it has a drive letter and icon in your Computer folder.

Disconnecting from a network drive

In your Computer folder, you can disconnect from any network drive by right-clicking the drive's icon and choosing Disconnect. If you originally chose Reconnect at logon, and now want to stop doing that, press the Alt key to show the Classic menu, and then choose Tools ⇨ Map Network Drive from the menu bar in your Computer folder. From the Drive drop-down list, choose the existing drive letter name. Then, choose a different shared folder from the Folder drop-down list or Browse button. Clear the Reconnect at logon checkbox if its checked, and then click Finish.

A message will ask if you want to replace the existing drive letter assignment with the new one. Choose Yes. You can then disconnect from the drive by right-clicking its icon and choosing Disconnect. The network drive icon won't appear in your Computer folder automatically in the future either.

Using a Shared Printer

You use a shared printer from a remote computer exactly as you use a local printer. Choose File ⇨ Print from the program's menu bar. In many cases you can just right-click the text you want to print and choose Print. Or right-click the icon for a document you want to print and choose Print. Or select items to print in a folder or Photo Gallery and click Print in the toolbar. When the Print dialog box opens, look for the shared printer, click it, and click the Print button.

If the shared printer doesn't show up in the Print dialog box, exit the program. Then install the printer using the method described under "Installing a network, wireless, or Bluetooth printer" in Chapter 35. If that's the printer you'll use most often, make it the default printer as described in Chapter 35.

 You can play shared media from a Vista computer on any other Vista computer in the network, and on compatible networked digital media players.

Using Shared Media

Shared media are different from shared files because they're *streamed* to the local computer when played. This allows you to play the media files on non-computer network devices such as the Xbox 360 or a networked digital media player. Exactly how you work such a device depends on the device. You'll need to refer to the instructions that came with the device for specifics.

You can also play the shared media files from Windows Media Player. There are a couple of ways to do this. The first step is to go to the computer where you want to play the music. Log in to the user account from which you'll be playing the music. Then open the Network folder (click the Start button and choose Network). You should see a shared media icon with the name of the computer on which the media files are stored, the name of the user who is sharing the media, and an exclamation point. If you right-click that icon, you'll notice that one of the options on the menu is Open Media Player. That's the default action. You can choose that option, or just double-click the icon to open Media Player.

If you've never used Media Player in that user account, you'll need to go through the short setup process. You can just choose Express Setup and click Finish. A Media Sharing dialog box opens with Windows Media Player. Make sure "Find media that others are sharing" is selected (checked) and click OK.

You can also access the shared media by opening Windows Media Player normally. Click the arrow under the Library button and choose Add to Library. Then choose My folders and those of others I can access and click OK.

Either way, you should end up with a folder in Media Player's Navigation pane. That folder shows the name of the user who shared the media files and the computer from which they shared it. Use the Select a Category button, shown near the mouse pointer in Figure 54.14, to select the type of media you want to view. Then expand the shared media folder (Alan on spotvista in the figure) and click a category (Artist, Album, Genre, Playlists, or whatever). The pane to the right shows icons for the shared media. Double-click any icon in that main pane to play the shared item.

FIGURE 54.14

Alan on spotvista is a remote shared library.

For more information on using Windows Media Player, see Chapter 23.

Wrap Up

In this chapter, we've looked at ways to access shared network resources from computers in the same private network.

- To get to shared folders on other computers in the network, first open the Network folder on the computer at which you're sitting.

- To open a remote document from within a program, choose File ⇨ Open from the program's menu bar, as usual. Then, choose the Network folder from the Folders drop-down list in the Open dialog box.

- To save a document to a remote computer, choose File ⇨ Save (or File ⇨ Save As), and choose your Network folder from the Folders drop-down list.

- To create a Network Location link to an Internet site, right-click within your Computer folder and choose Add a Network Location.

- To move or copy files between computers in a network, use your Network folder to open the source and/or destination folders. Then, use the standard techniques described in Chapter 29 to select, move, or copy the files.

- To use a shared printer, print normally but select the shared printer's name in the Print dialog box.

- If you don't see a shared printer in the Print dialog box, install the printer on the local computer using techniques described in Chapter 35.

- To play shared media using Windows Media Player, open the Network folder and double-click the shared media's icon.

Chapter 55

Using Windows Meeting Space

W indows Meeting Space is a cool new tool for setting up quick meetings with up to 10 people. The most common use would be to set up a meeting in a conference room, on a private network, a WiFi hotspot, or even among a group of computers that have wireless networking cards with ad-hoc networking capabilities.

Meeting Space gives you the ability to share your desktop, programs, and documents with other participants in a meeting. You can also distribute handouts, which any meeting member can view and edit. You can also use Meeting Space to give a presentation over a network projector.

Setting Up Meeting Space

NEW FEATURE Meeting Space is the Vista alternative to programs like NetMeeting. It's easier to use, and you can set up a secure meeting over an ad-hoc wireless network with minimal fuss.

Meeting Space works only with Windows Vista computers on the same private network or in a single WiFi hotspot. In a business setting, someone with administrative privileges should first go to each PC that will participate in meetings and get some basic settings squared away. This is simply a matter of sitting at any one computer and starting Windows Meeting Space using either of the following techniques:

- Press ⊞, type me, and choose Windows Meeting Space.
- Or click the Start button and choose All Programs ➪ Windows Meeting Space.

You'll first see a description of what needs to be configured to enable Meeting Spaces. Click Yes, continue setting up Windows Meeting Space to continue. Assuming that this is the first time you've run Meeting Space, you're prompted to set up account information for People Near Me. As its name implies, this is a service that makes it easy for people who participate in meetings to locate one another. Figure 55.1 shows the dialog box.

FIGURE 55.1

People Near Me.

I trust that the options in the dialog box are self-explanatory. Under "Your display name," type your name as you want it to appear to other people with whom you meet. If you've already identified yourself in Windows Contacts, your name appears automatically. Choose the checkbox to be signed in automatically each time you start Windows so other people know when you're available. If you're willing to accept invitations from anyone, leave the option unchanged. Otherwise you can choose Trusted Contacts or No One. If you choose Trusted Contacts, only contacts for whom you've received a digital certificate will be able to send you invitations. Most likely you would use this feature when using Meeting Space to conduct a meeting over the Internet to prevent imposters from sending you meeting invitations. Each person must acquire a digital certificate and send it to you by e-mail or on disk.

NOTE   See "Securing E-mail with Digital IDs" in Chapter 18 for more information on digital certificates.

Click OK after filling in the blanks. You'll see a new icon in the Notification area (see Figure 55.2). You can use that icon to sign in or out of People Near Me at any time or to change your settings.

FIGURE 55.2

People Near Me Notification area icon.

You're taken to the main Meeting Space window described in the next section. If you're just getting things set up and are not ready to launch or join a meeting, just close that program window.

If you need to change the information you entered into People Near Me, right-click the People Near Me notification icon and choose Properties. Or click the Start button, type me, and click People Near Me. In the dialog box that opens, you can add your picture to your contact information, and change any contact information. You can also use the People Near Me dialog box that opens to manually sign in and out of People Near Me.

 **You can distribute handouts in your meeting. Create the files in advance so they're ready to go when people join the meeting.**

Starting a Meeting

To start a meeting, open Windows Meeting Space using either method described in the previous section. Click Start a new meeting to see the options shown in Figure 55.3.

FIGURE 55.3

Start a new meeting.

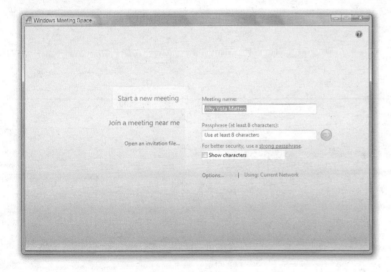

Enter a name and password for the meeting you're about to create. The passphrase must be at least eight characters long but can be much longer and can contain multiple words. A passphrase of at least 20 characters is recommended.

If you need to change visibility settings or the network for a meeting, click Options to get to the options shown in Figure 55.4. If the computers in the network have WiFi cards with ad-hoc networking capabilities and are within range of one another, you can set up an ad-hoc wireless network right on the spot just by choosing Create a private ad-hoc wireless network.

NOTE **All communications within a Meeting Space are encrypted to prevent eavesdropping.**

After making your selections, click the arrow next to the passphrase. You're taken to the page shown in Figure 55.5. From that page you can invite people to your meeting and conduct the meeting.

FIGURE 55.4

Network options.

FIGURE 55.5

The meeting page.

NOTE   If you're unable to get to the page shown in Figure 55.4, some required services might not be running. Restart the computer and try again.

Inviting people to a meeting

To invite people to your meeting, click Invite People. You can invite others who are currently in People Near Me just by selecting the checkboxes next to their names. Then click Send Invitations.

To invite outsiders who aren't in People Near Me, click Invite Others. Keep in mind that only people who are using Windows Vista will be able to attend the meeting. To send e-mail invitations, click Invite Others. Optionally, you can create an invitation file. This is the same file that's automatically attached to e-mail invitations. You then can distribute copies of the invitation file through any means you like, such as in a shared folder or on removable disks.

Conducting the meeting

When all members are in a meeting, conducting the meeting is easy. You can show your entire desktop or just a single running program. If you want to share a single program only, open it. Then click Share a program or your desktop. Click the program to share or Desktop. Then you can minimize Meeting Space and work directly with your desktop.

Near the top-right corner of your screen, you'll see options and buttons shown in Figure 55.6. The first three let you stop sharing, pause sharing (so others can't see what you're doing on your screen), or see how your program or desktop looks to other meeting members.

FIGURE 55.6

Buttons atop a shared desktop.

Use the Give Control option to hand control of your desktop or shared program over to another meeting member. To take back control, click that same button and choose Take Control. Or press ⊞+ESC.

To share handouts, click the Share Handouts button and then click the file you want to share. To add more handouts at any time, click Add a handout in that same part of the meeting space. All members can view the handout by double-clicking its icon. Only one member at a time can edit the handout. The changes are reflected in other members' copies automatically.

Changes to a handout are not saved to the original handout automatically. To save a changed handout, drag it to a folder. Or right-click the handout icon and choose Save As.

Leaving or Ending a Meeting

You (or any member) can leave the meeting by clicking the arrow on the Meeting button and choosing Leave Meeting. Optionally, you can stay in the meeting but change your status to Busy or Be Right Back by clicking your name in the list of attendees. To terminate a meeting, click the arrow on the Meeting button and choose Exit.

Using a Network Projector

NEW FEATURE   A network projector lets you project from your desktop, notebook, or mobile PC screen through a wired or wireless LAN.

Although not the same thing as a meeting, network projectors deserve some mention here. A network projector is a device that projects what's on your computer screen onto a wall or movie screen. If you've ever been to a meeting where you can see the speaker's computer screen projected onto the wall, then you know what a projector is. A network projector is the same thing. The only difference is that you don't have to physically connect your computer to a network projector. You can connect to it through a wired or wireless LAN instead.

If you work in an environment that has just projectors, you can connect to one or more network projectors simultaneously using either method here:

- Press ⊞, type `proj`, and choose Connect to a Network Projector.
- Click the Start button and choose All Programs ➪ Accessories ➪ Connect to a Network Projector.

You see the options shown in Figure 55.7. If the network projector is a shared device on your network, choose the first option. If you find the project to which you want to connect, click its name. If the projector is password-protected, you'll need to enter the appropriate password.

FIGURE 55.7

Connect to a network projector.

If you can't find the projector using that method, you'll need to know the projector's URL (network address) to connect. The name might be expressed like a Web URL (address) in http://*servername/projectorname* format. Or it might be in UNC (Universal Naming Convention) format. If you don't know the correct name, check with your network administrator. Then click the second option, enter the projector address, and type the address. If the projector is password-protected, you'll need to enter the password as well.

If you want to use multiple projectors, repeat the process for each projector to which you want to connect.

 **Data sent over the network to the projector is encrypted to prevent eavesdropping.**

After you've connected to the projector, a Network Presentation dialog box appears in the taskbar. People in the same room as the projector can see everything you do on your computer screen. To pause, resume, or end a network projection, open that dialog box and choose whichever option describes what you want to do.

Wrap Up

Windows Meeting Space is an easy way to set up meetings with multiple Windows Vista users. An ideal use would be to have meeting members bring in their notebook computers equipped with wireless network cards that support *ad-hoc* networking. Then set up a quick ad-hoc network right on the spot.

Windows Vista also supports modern network projectors, which allow you to project your computer screen onto a wall or movie screen without physically connecting your computer to the projector. In summary:

- Open Windows Meeting Space to set up a meeting.
- Use People Near Me to make it easy to find and send invitations to people who regularly attend meetings.
- Create meeting handouts before a meeting and share them with meeting members from Meeting Space.
- You can project your desktop or any open program onto other meeting members' screens.
- You can turn control of your computer over to any meeting member. Take back control at any time.
- Use Connect to a Network Projector to connect your computer to one or more network projectors.

Chapter 56

Troubleshooting Networks

Troubleshooting a Wired Network

Whenever you have a problem with a wired network, you always want to check your network hardware first. Even experts have been known to spend much time trying to troubleshoot a network problem from mouse and keyboard, when the problem turned out to be a loose cable.

Make sure the computer is firmly connected to the hub using an appropriate cable. For example, if you're using gigabit Ethernet, use Cat 6 straight through cables (not crossover cables) to connect all computers to the hub. Make sure each cable is firmly plugged in. If the hub and cards have indicator lights, they should be lit green when the computer is properly connected. The amber light only flashes when there's data crossing the cable.

Always refer to the installation and troubleshooting documentation that came with your networking hardware. Remember, not all products are exactly alike. You have to understand and properly install whatever network hardware you've purchased. Windows Vista can only use that hardware for networking if that hardware is properly installed and working correctly.

If you're confident that the hardware is working properly, then you can use Windows Vista techniques to help with troubleshooting. Here are the steps for troubleshooting your local connection:

1. Click Start ➪ Control Panel. If the Control Panel is in Category view, select Network and Internet and then Network and Sharing Center. If the Control Panel is in Classic view, click Network and Sharing Center.

2. Next click Manage network connections from the left column, which lists all of the available connections on your computer. Right-click the connection that does not appear to be functioning and choose Diagnose from the menu as shown in Figure 56.1.

FIGURE 56.1

The context menu for a network connection.

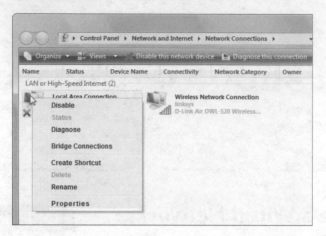

3. After selecting Diagnose for the connection, Windows will start troubleshooting the connection. On my system, the network cable was disconnected, and Windows returned the information shown in Figure 56.2. Windows provides a suggestion to fix the problem and also the option to click the link after I think the problem has been resolved.

FIGURE 56.2

Windows has tried to determine the cause of the problem.

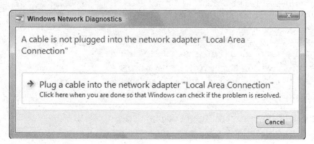

Hopefully, the diagnostics will solve the problem for you. If your local network connection appears to be working correctly, but the Internet connection is not working as expected, follow these steps to diagnose your Internet connection:

1. Click Start ➪ Control Panel. If the Control Panel is in Category view, select Network and Internet and then Network and Sharing Center. If the Control Panel is in Classic view, click Network and Sharing Center.

2. Next, click Diagnose and repair from the left column. This will start the diagnosis of your network connection. If Windows finds a problem with your Internet connection, it might return a dialog box as shown in Figure 56.3.

FIGURE 56.3

Windows has attempted to determine the issue with the Internet connection.

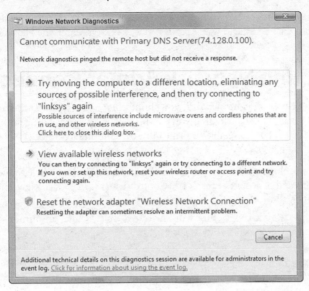

3. With this information, it would be best to attempt to check the information provided by the hardware manufacturer. You should also make sure that a single computer can connect to the Internet before including additional systems. If you're unable to get your connection working with a single computer, try contacting your Internet service provider.

Troubleshooting a Wireless Network

The two most common problems with wireless networking are

- The computer from which you're working is too far away from the router or access point.
- The hardware isn't properly configured, as per the manufacturer's instructions.

The Most Common Network Problem

The most common problem connecting to another system on your network is the Windows Firewall. By default, Windows does not allow sharing between two computers. This is something that you need to do within the Windows Firewall.

To enable file sharing, click Start ⇨ Control Panel to bring up the Control Panel. If the Control Panel is in Category view, you'll need to click Security and then click Windows Firewall. If the Control Panel is in Classic view, you'll need to double-click Windows Firewall. Leave the firewall On and click the Change settings link. Click the Exceptions tab, select (check) File and Printer Sharing, and click OK in each open dialog box.

Always check the troubleshooting material in the hardware manufacturer's documentation first. When you're confident that the computer is in range and the hardware is set up properly, use the wireless network troubleshooting in Vista's Help and Support to explore other possibilities.

Click Start ➪ Help and Support. In the Search box in the Windows Help and Support window, type `Troubleshooting problems finding wireless networks`. Or search the Help for `wireless`.

Troubleshooting Network Printer Connections

If you're unable to locate a printer on your network, you should first make sure that the printer is shared correctly off of the remote system. First verify that you can print when you are sitting at the computer connected directly to the printer. When you're able to print from the computer connected to the printer, you need to verify that print sharing is enabled. To do this, follow these steps:

1. Click Start ➪ Control Panel. If the Control Panel is in Category view, click Network and Internet and then Network and Sharing Center. If the Control Panel is in Classic view, choose Network and Sharing Center.

2. When the Network and Sharing Center window opens, select "Turn on printer sharing" under the Printer sharing group as shown in Figure 56.4.

FIGURE 56.4

Configuration for sharing a printer.

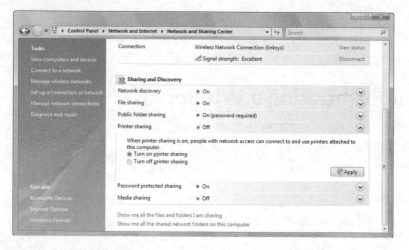

3. Click Apply to continue.

After you have verified that the printer has been shared correctly, sit down at the other computer, the one from which you are trying to connect. Click the Start button and then Network. Double-click the remote computer and then the printer to which you are trying to connect. You can double-click the printer to install it on your system.

Troubleshooting Windows Meeting Space

Windows Vista comes with built-in troubleshooting support for Windows Meeting Space. That's your best resource for solving problems. To get to it, click the Help button in Meeting Space, then click the Troubleshooting link on the Help page. Or search Windows Help and Support for appropriate terms like `meeting space` or `collaboration`.

 During the beta testing phase of Windows Vista, Meeting Space was named Windows Collaboration. That name might still appear in some Help pages, so it's worth including in a search.

Use All Available Resources

Network troubleshooting can be difficult. There are people with lots of formal training and certifications who spend a lot of time designing and building networks. And even they often have to spend many hours diagnosing and fixing network problems. And they rely on many resources for help.

As mentioned, you always want to check the most obvious things first (network cables, or making sure you're within range on a wireless network). Links in the left pane of the Network and Sharing Center can provide First Aid help after you've eliminated the more obvious suspects as the source of the problem.

Windows Vista offers general Troubleshooting help. To get to it click the Start button and choose Help and Support. Then click Troubleshooting. If you don't find appropriate links on the first page that opens, search help for a relevant keyword such as `network`, `networking`, `wireless`, `share`, or `sharing`.

Finally, don't forget Windows Communities. Chances are, someone in Communities has already experienced and resolved the very problem you're experiencing. The `Microsoft.public.windows.networking_sharing` community is the perfect location to ask questions about Windows Vista networking. You can get to the newsgroups from the Windows Communities link in Help and Support. Or set up Windows Mail as a newsgroup reader for Communities. See Chapter 19 for more information on that topic.

Part XI

Appendixes

Appendix A

Upgrading to
Windows Vista

If you purchased your PC with Windows Vista already installed and have no interest in dual-booting, you need to hang a U-turn. There's nothing in this appendix for you. Go straight to the Introduction, or Chapter 1, at the beginning of this book, and forget all about this appendix.

If you purchased an upgrade version of Windows Vista to replace your current version of Windows, and you haven't yet installed that upgrade, this is the place to be. To tell you the truth, you really don't have to read this entire appendix to install your upgrade. You really just have to do this:

1. Insert the disc that came with your Windows Vista upgrade into your computer's disc drive and wait a few seconds.
2. Follow the instructions that appear on the screen to install Vista by upgrading your current version of Windows.

When the installation is complete, remove the new disc from your disc drive, put it someplace safe, and ignore the rest of this appendix. If these two steps don't quite get the job done, please read on.

IN THIS APPENDIX

Windows Vista System Requirements

Pre-installation Housekeeping

Installing Windows Vista

Dual-booting with Windows Vista

Windows Vista System Requirements

Windows Vista requires a bit more hardware horsepower than the previous versions of Windows. The more hardware capability you have, the better Vista will run. The absolute minimum hardware requirements are as follows:

- 512 MB of RAM (although 1 GB is more like it)
- An 800 megahertz (MHz) 32-bit (x86) or 64-bit (x64) processor
- A 20 GB or larger hard disk with at least 15 GB free space available
- An SVGA (800 x 600) or better monitor
- A keyboard
- A mouse or similar pointing device
- A CD-ROM or DVD drive

Before upgrading your installation of Windows XP, it would be a good idea to run the Windows Upgrade Advisor available at http://www.microsoft.com/windowsvista/getready/upgradeadvisor as a free download. The tool generates a report that will indicate any shortcomings of your system and what you need to do to upgrade your computer if necessary.

Pre-installation Housekeeping

If you've been using your PC for a while with an earlier version of Windows, you'll want to do some things before you begin your upgrade:

- If your computer has any time-out features, such as the power-down features found on some portable PCs, disable those features now.

- If you have an antivirus program handy, run it now to check for, and delete, dormant viruses that may still be lurking on your hard disk.

- Disable your antivirus software after you've run the check. Leave it disabled until after you've completed the upgrade.

- Make sure that any external devices (printers, modems, external disk drives, and so on) are connected and turned on so that Windows Vista can detect them during installation.

- If at all possible, back up the entire hard disk at this point. At the very least, jot down all the information you need to connect to your Internet account. Back up all your documents, e-mail messages, names and addresses, and anything else you'll need after you complete the upgrade.

I realize that few people outside the corporate world have a means of backing up their entire hard disk. But you should be able to at least back up documents, e-mail messages, names and addresses, and so forth. Windows Vista now includes Windows Easy Transfer. See Chapter 13, "Transferring Files from Another Computer," for information on Easy Transfer.

 See Chapter 33 for some general pointers on backing up documents.

Installing Windows Vista

To upgrade an existing version of Windows, start your computer normally. You'd do well to restart the computer and get to a clean desktop with no open program windows or dialog boxes. Then put the Windows Vista disc in your disc drive and wait for the Welcome screen to open. If nothing appears on the screen within a minute or so, follow these steps:

1. Open My Computer.
2. Open the icon for your disc drive. If the Welcome screen opens, skip the next step.
3. Click (or double-click) the setup (or setup.exe) file on the disc.

By now, you should definitely see on your screen some options for installing Windows Vista. To get things rolling:

1. Choose the Install now option.
2. When the Get important updates for installation window appears, you're able to go online to get the latest updates for your installation of Vista. If you choose this option, your system needs to stay connected throughout the installation.

NOTE
Before clicking Install, you can use the Windows Easy Transfer, an application included with Windows Vista for copying your files and settings to a different computer. See Chapter 13 for more information on Easy Transfer.

The installation procedure will begin. You might notice that the screen goes blank once in a while during the installation. Don't be alarmed; that's normal. If the screen goes blank for a long time, try moving the mouse around a bit to bring it back. From here on out, you can just follow the instructions on the screen.

Installation options

The exact procedure from this point on will vary a bit, depending on what version of Vista you're installing. Also, the specific hardware that's connected to your computer will affect the information that the setup procedure requests. Each request is largely self-explanatory, but here's a summary of the items you're likely to encounter along the way.

- **Regional, Currency, and Language Options:** Choose your preferred location, currency, and keyboard layout.
- **Product Key:** Type the product key. You should be able to find it on the sleeve in which the Windows Vista disc was delivered.
- **License Terms:** If you agree with the terms and conditions of the license, click the I accept the license terms checkbox.
- **Upgrade or Custom Installation:** If you decide that you want to do a fresh installation, choose the Custom option. This will not keep your personal files and programs. The Upgrade option will.
- **Compatibility Report:** The installation application will look at your existing configuration and indicate whether it finds devices that are incompatible with Vista.
- **Security Settings:** These settings let you determine how you want to protect your system.
- **Date and Time Settings:** Set the date and current time, choose your time zone, and decide whether or not you want Windows to automatically adjust the time for daylight savings changes.

The Welcome Center

When the installation is complete, the Welcome Center application will start. The Welcome Center offers many options; some of the more popular ones (under the Get started with Windows section) are listed here:

- **View computer details:** Double-clicking this icon will bring up information about your computer system. This includes your Windows Experience Index, the amount of RAM in your system, and the System type. You're also able to easily activate Windows from this window if you haven't already done so.
- **Connect to the Internet:** This utility will allow you to set up and configure your network connection. If your Windows XP installation already had a connection, Vista should have used what was already there and allow you to connect to the Internet the same way.
- **Transfer files and settings:** Selecting this icon will start Windows Easy Transfer, discussed in Chapter 13.
- **Windows Vista Demos:** This icon will bring up Windows Help and Support to the topic, which includes several starter videos. These include information on files and folders, using the Internet and e-mail, security and maintenance, and many more.
- **Add new users:** If you're not going to be the only user on this system, then you'll want to add more users to the system. In addition to just creating accounts, clicking this link will allow you to change your account picture and update your password.

 If you don't see all of the preceding items, you can click the link near the bottom of the Get started with Windows section, Show all items.

Re-enabling old startup programs

You may discover that some of the programs that used to start automatically on your computer don't do so after you've installed Windows Vista. You can follow these steps to get those programs to start automatically again in the future:

1. Click Start ⇨ All Programs ⇨ Accessories, and then choose Run, type msconfig, and then click OK.

2. In the System Configuration Utility that opens, click the Startup tab.

3. To enable all previous auto-start programs, click the Enable all button. Optionally, select (check) only those programs you want to auto-start.

4. Click OK.

5. Click the Start button, click the arrow to the right of the lock icon, and select Restart.

Windows Vista should restart with the programs from your previous version of Windows open and running.

Dual-booting with Windows Vista

If you'd rather try Windows Vista before making it your primary operating system, you may want to try running both operating systems at the same time. This is commonly called *dual-booting*. This means that you can still run your existing version of Windows XP with all of your applications and settings but also use Windows Vista. In a dual-boot environment, you run only one version at a time, and when you want to run the other version you need to restart your system.

WARNING Installing Windows Vista and Windows XP in a dual-boot environment means that you will need to install applications on each installation of the operating system. This would mean that if you had Microsoft Office installed on Windows XP, you would have to reinstall it in your new version of Windows Vista. Additionally, it is best to keep your personal documents in a single location preferably on a separate partition. This is discussed later in the appendix.

Drive partitions

To set up your computer to a dual-boot environment, you will need multiple partitions on your hard disk. A partition is usually a logical separation of the hard disk. Your first physical hard disk in your computer could have two partitions, drive C: and drive D:. There may only be one physical disk but two logical partitions. Unless you specified otherwise, your system probably has one large partition, which is your primary boot drive. To set up a dual-boot environment, you will need a separate partition for each operating system; in this case you would need two partitions.

CAUTION Working with partitions is pretty low level, and this means you can do a lot of damage very fast. Be very careful when working with partitions and formatting. Changes made to existing partitions means your data could be lost for good with just a few clicks of the keyboard. It's very important that you know what partitions contain your personal files and data and which one needs to be formatted.

If your system does contain a single hard disk and one large partition that occupies that hard disk, the easiest and safest solution is to purchase an additional hard disk. In this scenario, your first hard disk would not be changed. You could partition your second hard disk into two partitions, one for Windows Vista and one for the files you want to share between the two operating systems.

Microsoft Virtual PC

Microsoft offers a free product that does not require you to create a second partition on your system. The software is called Microsoft Virtual PC. As I'm writing this, the current version is Virtual PC 2004 with a Virtual PC 2007 in the works. The details of Virtual PC deserve several chapters of their own, and for this reason I'll just mention the basics. If you have Windows XP installed, you can create a Virtual PC for other operating systems such as Vista. You will still boot your computer to Windows XP as you have done in the past, but after booting you would start Virtual PC. You're able to install additional operating systems in their own environment. When you're done experimenting with the additional operating system, you can remove it. Virtual PC runs as an application just like Microsoft Office does. For more information on Virtual PC, visit http://www.microsoft.com/windows/virtualpc.

If you do have a single hard disk and one large partition, purchase a second hard disk. Before installing the second hard disk, follow these steps to minimize your chances of data loss:

1. Start up your system and boot to Windows XP.

2. After Windows XP has started, click the Start button and click My Computer. Double-click the drive that you think is your system drive with all of your files and folders. Verify that you can locate your files and folders.

3. After you have verified and located the system drive, right-click the drive image and choose Rename. Rename the drive to something meaningful and something that you can identify later.

> **TIP** In addition to renaming your Windows XP partition, you can also record the used and free space. You can use these numbers to also help identify your installation of Windows XP later in the appendix. To get the used and free space of the partition, click Start ⇨ My Computer. Right-click the partition that you have identified as your Windows XP installation and choose Properties. You'll see the Used space and Free space numbers in the middle of the screen. Write both of them down for later use.

4. After you have renamed the drive, shut down Windows XP.

When your system has been shut down, you need to install the second hard drive in your system. Follow the instructions provided by the manufacturer. Different vendors have different requirements for installation. After you have successfully installed your hard drive, you'll need to find your Windows Vista disc and follow these steps:

1. Power up your computer and place the Vista disc in the drive. Also make sure that your system is set up in the BIOS to boot from that drive.

2. When you see the *Press any key to boot from CD or DVD* message, press any key to boot from your Vista disc. If you do not see this message, your system may not be configured to boot from that disc. Check your BIOS and try booting again from your Windows Vista disc.

3. The system will start to load files as discussed in Appendix B. Continue through the installation including clicking the Install now link.

4. When you get to the Which type of installation do you want? dialog box, choose the Custom (advance) option.

5. You're now presented with a window asking where you would like Windows to be installed. You should see Disk 0, which is your installation of Windows XP and a second disk, Disk 1. In the Disk 0 row, you should see the name of the partition you renamed earlier in the chapter.

Additionally, you can match up the size of the partition if you saved those numbers from earlier in the appendix. If you can't identify the partition, restart the computer rebooting to Windows XP and name the drive so you can identify it once you come back to this step.

> **CAUTION** You need to be certain that you have selected the correct partition before continuing. If you're uncertain, don't continue. Make sure that you've selected the empty disk. Formatting the wrong disk will result in losing your data.

6. Select Disk 1 so it's highlighted, and click the Drive options in the lower-right corner of the window. Click the New link and set the size of the partition by changing the value in the Size text box. You won't want to use the entire drive for your Vista installation because you'll want to save some space for your files and folders.

7. After you've set the size of the partition, click the Apply button. The installation application will create the partition to the size you have specified. After the partition has been allocated, you should see three separate partitions with the new one highlighted. Click the Next button and the installation will continue installing Vista to the newly created partition.

The installation will continue just as if it was a new installation of Windows Vista outlined in Appendix B. After the installation of Windows Vista has completed, your system should reboot. This time you will see a different screen after the system starts. Before the system boots to an operating system, you'll see Windows Boot Manager. The system now has two operating systems, and it wants to know which operating system you want to use. You'll see two options:

- **Earlier Version of Windows:** Use this option if you want to boot your previous edition of Windows, Windows XP in your case.

- **Microsoft Windows Vista:** Use this option if you want to boot to the new installation of Windows, Windows Vista.

After you select to boot to Windows Vista, you'll be asked to complete some of the installation steps that are outlined in Appendix B. The last step for setting your system up to dual-boot is to configure the common partition between Windows Vista and Windows XP for sharing documents between the two operating systems. To configure the partition, follow these steps:

1. Boot your system to Windows Vista.

2. Click the Start button, right-click your Computer icon, and select Manage.

3. When the Computer Management window opens, expand the Storage item and click the Disk Management icon.

4. In the bottom half of the window, right-click the partition that is Unallocated on Disk 1. Select New Simple Volume from the menu, which will start the New Simple Volume Wizard.

> **CAUTION** Make sure to select the correct partition. Make sure that the text indicates that the space is unallocated. Any other choice will lead to losing your data.

5. Click the Next button on the first screen.

6. On the second screen, you can specify the size of the partition, and then click the Next button.

7. Select a drive letter for your partition in the next step of the wizard. Once assigned, click the Next button.

8. Choose to format the partition in the next step. NTFS is the best selection. You can also name the partition. Click the Next button to continue.

9. The last step of the wizard summarizes your choices up to this point. Click the Finish button, and Windows Vista will start formatting the drive.

After the system has formatted the partition, you can start storing files and folders on it. You'll be able to access the partition from both your Windows XP installation and your Windows Vista installation.

Remember that you'll still need to install applications to the Windows Vista installation because applications are not shared between the two operating systems.

Appendix B

Installing Vista on a New System

If you've just built a new computer from scratch, or if you've replaced your old drive C: with a new hard drive, you won't be able to upgrade to Windows Vista. In fact, you probably won't be able to boot the computer at all, because the hard drive won't contain an operating system from which you can boot the system. You'll have to do a *clean install*.

You can also opt to do a clean install even if you already have a version of Windows installed on the hard drive. However, you must realize that doing so is *very* serious business. When you do a clean install, you wipe out everything on your hard disk. And I do mean *everything*—all programs, documents, settings, Internet account information—everything. And there's no getting *any* of that stuff back. Just to make sure nobody misses this important fact, let me say it with a big caution icon:

Gearing Up for a Clean Install

Most experts prefer to do a clean install when they upgrade to a new version of Windows, largely because it gets everything off to a clean start. Besides, it's a great excuse for upgrading to a bigger and faster hard drive. You can use your original hard drive as a second hard disk, and easily transfer documents from that drive to the new drive after you've installed Windows Vista on the new drive. However, you'll still need to reinstall all of your programs and redo all your settings after you complete the installation.

IN THIS APPENDIX

Gearing Up for a Clean Install

Doing the Clean Install

The Rest of the Installation

> **CAUTION**   If you upgrade a significant amount of hardware, especially the motherboard and processor, Windows Activation may prevent you from reinstalling programs that you activated on the old hardware. Contact Microsoft about reactivating Windows via http://support.microsoft.com before you upgrade your hardware.

Back up all your data

If you intend to keep your existing C: as the C: drive after the clean install, it's important that you understand that you will permanently lose everything on that drive during the clean install. Therefore you should:

- Write down all of your Internet connection data so you can reestablish your account after the clean install.

- Back up or export all your e-mail messages, names and addresses, Favorites, and anything else you'll want after the clean install, so that you can recover them after the clean install. Remember, whatever you don't save will be lost forever. No ifs, ands, or buts about it.

- Back up all of your documents, because each and every one of them will be wiped out along with Windows and all your programs.

> **CAUTION**   A clean install permanently erases everything on your hard drive, which is basically everything that's "in your computer." Users who do not fully understand the ramifications of this should not attempt to do a clean install of Windows Vista or any other operating system. Nobody on the planet can help you get back that which you've lost if you fail to heed this advice.

If Windows Vista is currently installed on the C: drive you intend to reuse, you can use the Windows Easy Transfer to back up all your documents and settings as covered in Chapter 13. Ideally, you want to back up the data to another computer in the network. Windows Easy Transfer allows you to transfer files and folders, e-mail settings, and many other personal items from your existing computer to the new computer or hard drive. You can do this by using a USB Easy Transfer cable, the network, DVDs or CDs, or other external USB devices.

Given that hard drives are so inexpensive these days, it almost seems a shame *not* to start the clean install from a new hard drive. You don't have to worry about losing any data from the old drive if you clean-install Vista to a new drive.

Make sure that you can boot from your CD or DVD

By far the easiest way to do a clean install on a new drive is to boot from the Windows Vista disc. You'll want to make sure that you *can* do this before you do anything inside the computer. Most discs aren't bootable, so you'll need to insert the Windows disc into the drive and restart the computer. Watch for the *Press any key to boot from CD or DVD* countdown, and tap the Spacebar before the countdown runs out.

If you see the message *Windows is loading files*, then you know you can boot from a disc. Press Ctrl+Alt+Del to reboot before setup actually starts, and remove the disc from the drive while the system is rebooting. Then, shut down the PC altogether.

If you can't boot the system from the Windows disc, you'll need to adjust your BIOS settings. Again, this isn't something I can tell you how to do specifically, because it depends on your system's BIOS. But the usual scenario is to press F2 or Del as the computer is starting up to get to your BIOS setup. Once you get into the BIOS settings, make sure that booting from the disc drive is enabled, and that the disc drive has a higher priority than the hard drive.

After you change the BIOS settings, put the Windows disc back in the disc drive, save your BIOS settings, and exit so that the computer reboots again. If you got it right, you should see the *Windows is loading files* message again on restart, indicating that you've successfully booted from the disc. Cancel that startup as well, by pressing Ctrl+Alt+Del, and remove the disc from the drive before the computer gets another chance to boot from the disc.

Installing a new C: drive

If you're upgrading your C: drive along with your version of Windows, step 1 is to hide existing hard drives from the system altogether so that the new drive appears, to the BIOS, to be the only hard drive in the system. Simply disconnecting the power and interface plugs from the backs of the drives will do the trick.

CAUTION Never do anything inside your system case while the computer is turned on, or even plugged into a power outlet. Wear an antistatic wrist strap to prevent static discharge from wiping out components and the warranties that go with them!

The next step involves getting the new drive installed to the point where it's at least recognized by the BIOS. I can't tell you how to do that because the procedure varies from one drive manufacturer to the next. You must follow the instructions that came with the drive, or the instructions on the drive manufacturer's Web site, to get to the point where the system recognizes that drive at startup.

Chances are the drive manufacturer's instructions will include steps to partition and format the drive. You should probably do so, even if you intend to repartition and reformat the drive during the Windows Vista clean installation. You still won't be able to boot from the drive. But at least the drive will be recognized as C: during the Windows installation.

Doing the Clean Install

When you feel confident that you'll be able to get back everything you want from your hard drive, you're ready to start the clean install. Put the Windows disc in the disc drive and shut down the computer. Then, restart the computer, and boot from the disc. Your system's screen will go blank with a progress bar across the bottom of the screen while it copies some setup files. After the copy, the screen will change to a blue and green background, and you'll be given a mouse pointer. Follow these steps to continue the installation:

1. At the Install Windows dialog box, select the Language, Time, and Currency format and the type of keyboard, and click the Next button.

2. Click the Install now link, and you'll be prompted for the product key. After entering the product key, click the Next button.

3. If you accept the license terms, check the box I accept the license terms and click the Next button.

4. Select the Custom option to continue.

5. The next dialog box lists all of the drives and partitions that the installation application sees on your system. Select the partition on which you would like to install Windows Vista. If you don't see your drive, it may be that the controller your hard drive is connected to requires a special driver that the installation application doesn't know about. You can click the Load Driver link to load the driver provided by the controller's manufacturer. Clicking the Drive Options link will enable the option to format the drive before installing Vista.

6. Select the partition on which Vista will be installed and click the Format link. The installation application will prompt that the data on the drive will be erased and permanently deleted. Click the OK button as long as you are sure that your database has been saved elsewhere.

7. Once formatted, the Total Size and Free Space columns will be almost identical. Click the Next button to continue. At this point, the installation application will start copying files.

The Rest of the Installation

Copying the files and installing them to your system takes some time. When the installation continues, follow these steps to continue:

1. You'll be prompted to create a user name and password and to choose a picture for your account.

2. Next you'll need to create a name for your computer or use the name that the installation application has chosen for you. You can also choose a background image for your desktop.

3. In the Help protect Windows automatically dialog box, it's usually best to choose Use recommended settings.

4. Choose your time zone and set the date and time in the Review your time and date settings dialog box, and then click the Next button.

5. Finally, click the Start button, and the Windows Vista installation is complete.

The installation will check your system's performance for a short time and then ask you to log in. At this point, Windows Vista has been installed, and you're ready to start using it.

Appendix C

Universal Shortcut Keys

Here is a quick reference to shortcut keys used throughout Windows Vista. Many application programs use the same shortcut keys. That's why I've titled this appendix *Universal Shortcut Keys*. Of course, any program can have additional shortcuts to its own unique features. Those are visible in pull-down menus, as in the example shown in the Edit menu for Microsoft Word 2003 in Figure C.1. The *key+key* combination to the right of each menu command is the shortcut key for using that command from the keyboard without the menu.

Many programs show shortcut keys in the tooltip that appears when you point to a button or icon. For example, in Figure C.2 I'm pointing to the B (Boldface) button in Microsoft Excel 2007. Below the mouse pointer, you can see that Ctrl+B is the shortcut key for boldfacing text.

Virtually every program also comes with its own help. Typically, you get to that by pressing Help (F1) while the program is in the active window. Or choose Help from that program's menu bar. Use the Help feature of that program to search for the term `shortcut` or `shortcut keys` to see whether you can find a summary of that program's shortcut keys.

Of course, Windows Vista has its own Help, too, which you can learn about in Chapter 5 of this book. For help with shortcut keys, click the Start button and choose Help and Support. Type `shortcuts keys` as your search text and press Enter. The search results will include shortcut keys for Windows Vista and many programs that are built into Vista.

IN THIS APPENDIX

General, dialog box, and Explorer shortcut keys

Ease of Access shortcut keys

Text editing shortcut keys

Photo Gallery and Movie Maker shortcut keys

Microsoft Internet Explorer shortcut keys

FIGURE C.1

Shortcut keys on menus and toolbar buttons.

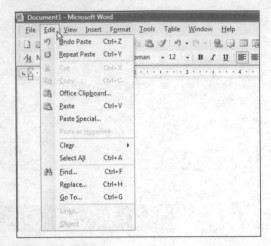

FIGURE C.2

Microsoft Office 2007 shortcut key hints.

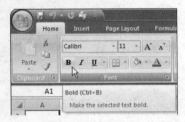

General Shortcut Keys

To do this	Press this key
Copy selected icon(s)	CTRL+C
Cut selected icons(s)	CTRL+X
Paste cut or copied text or item(s) to current folder	CTRL+V
Undo your most recent action	CTRL+Z
Delete selected icon(s) to Recycle Bin	DELETE or DEL
Delete selected icons(s) without moving to Recycle Bin	SHIFT+DELETE
Rename selected icon(s)	F2
Extend selection through additional icons	SHIFT+*any arrow key*
Select all items in a document or window	CTRL+A
Search for a file or folder	F3
Display properties for selected icon	ALT+ENTER
Close program in the active window	ALT+F4
Open the shortcut menu for the active window	ALT+SPACEBAR
Close the active document in multiple document program	CTRL+F4
Show Flip 3D	⊞+TAB
Switch between open programs	ALT+TAB
Cycle through open programs in the order they were opened	ALT+ESC
Cycle through screen elements on the desktop or in a window	F6
Display the shortcut menu for the selected item	SHIFT+F10
Open/close the Start menu	CTRL+ESC or ⊞
Open menu or perform menu command	ALT+underlined letter
View menu bar in active program	F10 or Alt
Move left or right in menu bar	← and →
Move up or down in menu	↑ and ↓
Select highlighted menu command	ENTER
Refresh the active window	F5
View the folder one level up Windows Explorer	BACKSPACE
Cancel the current task	ESC
Open Task Manager	CTRL+SHIFT+ESC
Prevent the CD from automatically playing	SHIFT when you insert a CD
Copy dragged item to destination	CTRL+*drag*
Move dragged item to destination	CTRL+SHIFT+*drag*

Dialog Box Keyboard Shortcuts

Description	Key
Choose option with underlined *letter*	ALT+*letter*
Select a button if the active option is a group of option buttons	Arrow keys
Open a folder one level up if a folder is selected in the Save As or Open dialog box	BACKSPACE
Go to previous tab	CTRL+SHIFT+TAB
Go to next tab	CTRL+TAB
Same as clicking OK	ENTER
Same as clicking Cancel	ESC
Help	F1 key
Display the items in the active list	F4 key
Move to previous option	SHIFT+TAB
Select or clear the checkbox	SPACEBAR
Move to next option	TAB

Windows Explorer Keyboard Shortcuts

Description	Key
Collapse the selected folder	– on numeric keypad
Display all of the subfolders under selected folder	* on numeric keypad
Select or collapse parent folder	←
Expand current folder or move to next subfolder	→
Display the contents of the selected folder	+ on numeric keypad
Display the bottom of the active window	END
Display the top of the active window	HOME
Open selected folder in new instance	SHIFT+Double-Click

Ease of Access Keyboard Shortcuts

Description	Key
Open Ease of Access Center	⊞+U
Switch the MouseKeys either on or off	LEFT ALT+LEFT SHIFT+NUM LOCK
Switch High Contrast either on or off	LEFT ALT+LEFT SHIFT+PRINT SCREEN
Switch the ToggleKeys either on or off	NUM LOCK for five seconds
Switch FilterKeys either on or off	RIGHT SHIFT for eight seconds
Switch the StickyKeys either on or off	SHIFT five times

Windows Help Shortcut Keys

To do this	Press this key
Open Windows Help and Support	F1 or ⊞+F1
Display the Table of Contents	ALT+C
Display the Connection Settings menu	ALT+N
Display the Options menu	F10
Move back to the previously viewed topic	ALT+←
Move forward to the next (previously viewed) topic	ALT+→
Display the customer support page	ALT+A
Display the Help home page	ALT+HOME
Move to the beginning of a topic	HOME
Move to the end of a topic	END
Search the current topic	CTRL+F
Print a topic	CTRL+P
Move to the Search box	F3

Microsoft Natural Keyboard Shortcuts

Description	Key
Display or hide the Start menu	⊞
Lock the computer	⊞+L
Display the System Properties dialog box	⊞+BREAK
Show the desktop	⊞+D
Open Computer folder	⊞+E
Search for file or folder	⊞+F
Search for computers	CTRL+⊞+F
Display Windows Help	⊞+F1
Minimize all of the windows	⊞+M
Restore all minimized window	⊞+Shift+M
Open the Run dialog box	⊞+R
Restore the minimized windows	⊞+SHIFT+M
Show Flip 3D	⊞+Tab
Open Ease of Access Center	⊞+U
Open Windows Mobility Center	⊞+X

Text Navigation and Editing Shortcuts

Description	Key
Move cursor down one line	↓
Move cursor left one character	←
Move cursor right one character	→
Move cursor up one line	↑
Delete character to left of cursor	BACKSPACE
Move cursor to start of next paragraph	CTRL+↓
Move cursor to start of previous paragraph	CTRL+↑
Move cursor to start of previous word	CTRL+←
Move cursor to start of next word	CTRL+→
Select all	CTRL+A
Copy to Clipboard	CTRL+C
Copy the selected text to destination	CTRL+*drag*
Select to end of paragraph	CTRL+SHIFT+↓
Select to end of word	CTRL+SHIFT+→
Select to beginning of word	CTRL+SHIFT+←
Select to beginning of paragraph	CTRL+SHIFT+↑
Select to end of document	CTRL+SHIFT+END
Select to top of document	CTRL+SHIFT+HOME
Paste clipboard contents to cursor position	CTRL+V
Cut to clipboard	CTRL+X
Undo last action	CTRL+Z
Delete selected text or character at cursor	DEL
Cancel the current task	ESC
Select to character in line above	SHIFT+↑
Select to character in line below	SHIFT+↓
Select character to left	SHIFT+←
Select character to right	SHIFT+→
Select from cursor to here	SHIFT+Click
Select to end of line	SHIFT+END
Select to beginning of line	SHIFT+HOME
Select text down one screen	SHIFT+PAGE DOWN
Select text up one screen	SHIFT+PAGE UP

Windows Character Map Shortcut Keys

Key	Description
↑	Move up one row
↓	Move down one row
←	Move to the left or to the end of the previous line
→	Move to the right or to the beginning of the next line
CTRL+END	Move to the last character
CTRL+HOME	Move to the first character
END	Move to the end of the line
HOME	Move to the beginning of the line
PAGE DOWN	Move down one screen at a time
PAGE UP	Move up one screen at a time
SPACEBAR	Switch between Enlarged and Normal modes

Windows Photo Gallery Shortcut Keys

To do this	Press this key
Back to Gallery	Backspace
Best fit	CTRL+B
Duplicate selected photo(s)	CTRL+D
Forward	ALT+→
Next screen	PAGE DOWN
Open or close the Preview pane	CTRL+I
Open the Fix pane	CTRL+F
Permanently delete the selected item	SHIFT+DELETE
Previous item (Easel) or previous row (Thumbnail)	↑
Previous screen	PAGE UP
Print the selected picture	CTRL+P
Rename the selected item	F2
Rotate the picture clockwise	CTRL+PERIOD (.)
Rotate the picture counter-clockwise	CTRL+COMMA (,)
Search for an item	CTRL+E
Select the first item	HOME
Select the last item	END
Select the next item or row	↓

continued

Windows Photo Gallery Shortcut Keys *(continued)*

To do this	Press this key
Select the previous item	←
Send the selected item to the Recycle Bin	DELETE
View the selected picture at a larger size	ENTER
Zoom-in or resize the picture thumbnail	PLUS SIGN (+)
Zoom-out or resize the picture thumbnail	MINUS SIGN (–)

Movie Maker and Video Preview Shortcut Keys

To do this	Press this
Advance to the next frame	ALT+→ or L
Back to the previous frame	ALT+← or J
Move to the start trim point	HOME
Move to the end trim point	END
Pause the playback	K
Play from the current location	CTRL+P
Seek to nearest split point after the current location	PAGE DOWN
Seek to nearest split point before the current location	PAGE UP
Set the end trim point	O
Set the start trim point	I
Split a clip	M
Stop and rewind all the way back to the start trim point	HOME
Stop and rewind playback	CTRL+K

Microsoft Internet Explorer Shortcuts

To do this	Press this
Add "www." to the beginning and ".com" to the end of text in Address bar	CTRL+ENTER
Add the current page to favorites	CTRL+D
Click the Information bar	SPACEBAR
Close current tab (or the current window if tabbed browsing is disabled)	CTRL+W
Close other tabs	CTRL+ALT+F4
Close Print Preview	ALT+C
Close the current window (if you only have one tab open)	CTRL+W
Copy selection to Clipboard	CTRL+C

To do this	Press this
Display a list of addresses you've typed	F4
Display a shortcut menu for a link	SHIFT+F10
Display first page to be printed	ALT+HOME
Display last page to be printed	ALT+END
Display next page to be printed	ALT+→
Display previous page to be printed	ALT+←
Display zoom percentages	ALT+Z
Find on this page	CTRL+F
Go to home page	ALT+HOME
Go to selected link	ENTER
Go to the next page	ALT+→
Go to the previous page	ALT+← or BACKSPACE
Go to the Toolbar Search box	CTRL+E
Help	F1
Move back through the items on a Web page, the Address bar, or the Links bar	SHIFT+TAB
Move back through the list of AutoComplete matches	↓
Move backward between frames (if tabbed browsing is disabled)	CTRL+SHIFT+TAB
Move focus to the Information bar	ALT+N
Move forward through frames and browser elements (if tabbed browsing is disabled)	CTRL+TAB or F6
Move forward through the items on a Web page, the Address bar, or the Links bar	TAB
Move forward through the list of AutoComplete matches	↑
Move selected item down in the Favorites list in the Organize Favorites dialog box	ALT+↓
Move selected item up in the Favorites list in the Organize Favorites dialog box	ALT+↑
Move the cursor left to the next punctuation in the Address bar	CTRL+←
Move the cursor right to the next punctuation in the Address bar	CTRL+→
Move to the beginning of page	HOME
Move to the end of page	END
Open a new tab in the foreground	CTRL+T
Open a new tab in the foreground from the Address bar	ALT+ENTER
Open a new Web site or page	CTRL+O
Open a new window	CTRL+N
Open Favorites	CTRL+I
Open Favorites Center to display favorites	CTRL+I
Open Favorites Center to display feeds	CTRL+J

continued

1117

Microsoft Internet Explorer Shortcuts *(continued)*

To do this	Press this
Open Favorites Center to display history	CTRL+H
Open Feeds	CTRL+J
Open History	CTRL+H
Open links in a new background tab	CTRL+click
Open links in a new foreground tab	CTRL+SHIFT+click
Open search query in a new tab	ALT+ENTER
Open the Organize Favorites	CTRL+B
Open the search provider menu	CTRL+↓
Page Setup	ALT+U
Paste Clipboard contents	CTRL+V
Print the current page or active frame	CTRL+P
Refresh the current Web page	F5
Refresh the current Web page regardless of timestamp	CTRL+F5
Save the current page	CTRL+S
Scroll down a line	↓
Scroll down a page	PAGE DOWN
Scroll up a line	↑
Scroll up a page	PAGE UP
Select all items on the current Web page	CTRL+A
Select frames to print in framed Web site	ALT+F
Select the text in the Address bar	ALT+D
Set printing options and print the page	ALT+P
Stop downloading a page	ESC
Switch between tabs	CTRL+TAB or CTRL+SHIFT+TAB
Switch to a specific tab number	CTRL+n (where n is a number between 1 and 8)
Switch to the last tab	CTRL+9
Toggle between full-screen and regular views	F11
Toggle Quick Tabs on or off	CTRL+Q
Type the number of the page you want displayed	ALT+A
Zoom in	ALT+PLUS SIGN
Zoom in 10%	CTRL+PLUS SIGN
Zoom out	ALT+MINUS SIGN
Zoom out 10%	CTRL+MINUS SIGN
Zoom to 100%	CTRL+0

Index

M

X

Y

Office heaven.

Get the first and last word on Microsoft® Office 2007 with our comprehensive Bibles and expert authors. These are the books you need to succeed!

978-0-470-04691-3

978-0-470-04403-2

978-0-470-04689-0

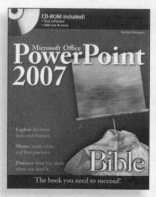

978-0-470-04368-4

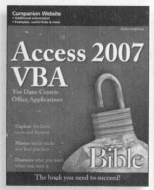

978-0-470-04702-6

978-0-470-04645-6

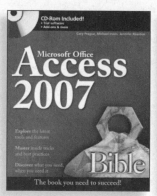

978-0-470-04673-9

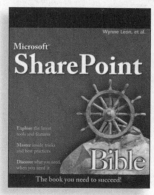

978-0-470-00861-4

WILEY
Now you know.

Available wherever books are sold